THE WORL[...]

LIFE OF [...]

D0445839

JAMES BOSWELL was born in 1740, the son of an Edinburgh lawyer. His ambitions lay in politics or literature, but he followed his father's wishes in studying law at Edinburgh and Glasgow. He went to London in 1762, then on a tour of Europe which included the visit to Corsica that inspired his successful *Account of Corsica* (1768). In 1763 he met Samuel Johnson, over thirty years older than himself and famous as the author of the *Rambler*, the *Dictionary*, and *Rasselas*. The two men became friends, and Boswell started to record the details of Johnson's life and conversation which formed the basis of the *Life*. Having married his cousin in 1769, Boswell practised at the bar in Edinburgh, making several visits to London. In 1773 he and Johnson toured Scotland and the Hebrides together, described in Boswell's *Journal of a Tour to the Hebrides* (1785). After Johnson's death in 1784 Boswell began the painful process of piecing together his biography. It appeared triumphantly in 1791, a testimony as much to Boswell's superlative biographical talents as to Johnson himself. Thereafter Boswell's mental and physical health deteriorated steadily, and he died in 1795.

PAT ROGERS, Professor of English at Bristol University, is the author of *The Augustan Vision* and *An Introduction to Pope*. He has also edited several of Defoe's writings and written a biography of Fielding.

THE WORLD'S CLASSICS

JAMES BOSWELL

Life of Johnson

Edited by
R. W. CHAPMAN

Revised by
J. D. FLEEMAN

With a new Introduction by
PAT ROGERS

Oxford New York Toronto Melbourne
OXFORD UNIVERSITY PRESS
1980

Oxford University Press, Walton Street, Oxford OX2 6DP

Oxford London Glasgow
New York Toronto Melbourne Wellington
Kuala Lumpur Singapore Jakarta Hong Kong Tokyo
Delhi Bombay Calcutta Madras Karachi
Nairobi Dar Es Salaam Cape Town

British Library Cataloguing in Publication Data
Boswell, James, b. 1740
Life of Samuel Johnson. Life of Johnson.—New ed.
1. Johnson, Samuel – Biography
2. Authors, English – 18th century – Biography
I. Title   II. Life of Johnson   III. Chapman, Robert William, b. 1881
IV. Fleeman, John David
828'.6'09   PR3533   80-40175
ISBN 0-19-281537-7

Printed in Great Britain by
Hazell Watson & Viney Limited
Aylesbury, Bucks

INTRODUCTION

For a century and more, Boswell's *Life of Johnson* stood in lonely eminence. All other English biographies seemed mere foothills; the great massif of the *Life* towered over lesser works, including Boswell's own *Tour* of the Hebrides with Johnson and his account of General Paoli. Lives and letters abounded in the Victorian era, but scarcely anyone doubted that it was Boswell who dominated the skyline. 'Homer is not more decidedly the first of heroic poets, Shakespeare is not more decidedly the first of dramatists, Demosthenes is not more decidedly the first of orators, than Boswell is the first of biographers. He has no second.' Thus Macaulay in 1831, reviewing one of the many nineteenth-century editions of the book. Not even Lockhart's famous life of Scott, published in 1838, caused this opinion to be revised: Lockhart, intriguingly, had himself reviewed the new Boswell along with Macaulay and Carlyle. One might go further. The appearance of *Eminent Victorians*, as late as 1918, though it greatly affected the practice of biography, hardly altered the history and theory of the form. Little else was known about Boswell, whilst Johnson's own popular reputation derived from his presence in the *Life* – above all from his conversation reported there. Carlyle had predicted this in 1832: 'All Johnson's own Writings . . . stand on a quite inferior level to [the *Life*]; already, indeed, they are becoming obsolete for this generation; and for some future generation may be valuable chiefly as Prolegomena and expository Scholia to this *Johnsoniad* of Boswell.' By 1920 that 'future generation' had seemingly arrived.

Now we have changed all that. There has been an astonishing era of rediscovery and revaluation, to the extent that a great range of lesser peaks have appeared around the *Life*, as though by some vast seismic shift. A whole breed of guides have emerged to conduct readers through this unfamiliar terrain, and some of them spend little time on the central massif itself. There are new routes to the summit, and vistas unsuspected by the

v

Victorians. Johnson's greatness as a writer has happily been reaffirmed; a huge amount concerning Boswell has come to light, most of it in one way or another bearing on the creation of his masterpiece, but possessing its own independent interest; and apart from all this, literary history has been in large measure rewritten. We know, for instance, much more about the earlier development of biography, and whilst it would be wrong to say that Plutarch or Isaak Walton are direct ancestors of Boswell, the strong innovative element in the *Life* can be more accurately defined in the light of this new awareness.

Much of the credit for this revival must go to a distinguished line of collectors and scholars, the Johnsonians of the 1920s (the term in general implies Boswellians). They include C. B. Tinker, L. F. Powell and R. W. Chapman. But it was the dramatic discovery of two separate caches of Boswell manuscripts, the first at the end of the decade, which (after much delicate negotiation and legal argument) fixed Yale University as the centre of Boswell studies, and brought Professor F. A. Pottle to special authority in this field. A limited edition of the *Private Papers*, that is, the first cache discovered, was published between 1928 and 1934. Subsequent finds have prepared the way for two series, now in progress, intended for the general reader as well as the scholar: indeed, the first volume to appear (the *London Journal*, published in 1950) proved an unexpected best-seller. It is no longer possible for anyone remotely in touch with events to see Boswell as Macaulay had done, the chance creator of a single brilliant book.

Some people, understandably, think that this process has gone too far. The wealth of Boswelliana, for such readers, hides the fact that the *Life* is after all only 'an edited diary', not truly a biography at all. Without accepting this view in its entirety, one can certainly agree that the more extreme claims for the 'art' of Boswell in recent years have been strained and unconvincing. Nevertheless, most of those who have looked carefully at the complex body of materials Boswell used to construct his book have reached the view that he showed astonishing literary powers of a very rare kind. I do not mean that the twentieth-century finds dispose of all the charges which have ever been laid against Boswell. They do, however, reinforce our sense of his industry, his constructive power, his unlikely tact and discrimination, his resilience. The *Life* came out when he was just fifty; he had recently lost his wife, his long-established drinking habits had started to catch up with him, and he was undergoing bitter failure at the bar and in politics. These facts do not augment the merits of the book, either in terms of artistry or documentary value. They serve rather to emphasize the human achievement involved in creating the *Life*, and that is important because it is above all a record of human vitality. Although Boswell was so unlike Johnson in most ways, the making of his masterpiece enlisted some authentically Johnsonian qualities: courage, will, imagination, independence, and pure obstinacy.

I

It is a paradox (some would say a grim irony) that we know today more about the early life of the biographer than about that of his subject. Boswell was born in 1740, in an Edinburgh close, over which lowered both kirk and law: St Giles's, Parliament House and the grim Tolbooth gaol ('Heart of Midlothian'). By this date Samuel Johnson was thirty-one, but he had done little to make himself known in the world. His youth had been troubled by illness and family upheavals: his father, a neurotic and unsuccessful bookseller in sleepy Lichfield, had died a few years earlier, and although his mother continued to run the bookshop she was forced to mortgage it in the same year Boswell was born. Meanwhile Samuel had acquired a wife twenty years his senior, and was going through a period of considerable strain: his poverty, his wife's declining sexual interest, and long periods of separation meant that he led an irregular quasi-bachelor existence much of the time.

Johnson was an almost exact contemporary of Boswell's father, a lawyer who was raised to the position of a judge in 1754. Alexander Boswell thus became Lord Auchinleck, a title which did not carry any hereditary honours which he might pass on to his eldest son James. He was a stern Presbyterian and a Whig, as decisive in mind as Johnson. The two men met once, when the younger Boswell brought his friend to Auchinleck at the end of their Highland jaunt in 1773. There was a violent quarrel, as might have been foretold: Boswell drew a discreet veil over the affair in his *Journal* of the tour, observing that 'it would certainly be very unbecoming in me to exhibit my honoured father and my respected friend as intellectual gladiators, for the entertainment of the public.' Auchinleck was an estate in Ayrshire which had been in the family since 1504. When James was growing up, chiefly in Edinburgh, his father spent a considerable sum building a neoclassic mansion at Auchinleck. It is a gesture not immediately compatible with the character of a shrewd, folksy, wry, and austere man. James and he never got on very well, but it was not until the son reached his later teens that serious trouble broke out.

Boswell attended Edinburgh University between the ages of thirteen and nineteen. During this period he went through several stages, all of them self-regarding and more or less consciously experimental. Interest had dawned in sex and in metaphysics, in poetry and in social life. For a time he thought of himself as a Methodist, that is a member of a new radical sect (or at least an adherent of its ideology). He had his first affair with an actress, and characteristically made it the occasion for highly coloured journalism, in the shape of some laudatory notices of her theatrical performances. He also pursued an heiress with his lifelong mixture of bluster and self-doubt. As he approached his nineteenth birthday, this course of life prompted Lord Auchinleck to remove him from Edinburgh and send him instead to Glasgow University: there was, for one thing, no playhouse in Glasgow. That Adam Smith happened to be Professor of Moral Philosophy there would have been a secondary consideration, for Smith was not yet famous for his pioneering work in economics, and his lectures to Boswell centred rather on rhetoric and *belles lettres*. Seeking an outlet for his growing independence of spirit, Boswell began to take instruction from a Jesuit father. He soon decided that he must not only join the Roman Catholic church, but must take up the vocation of a monk. When his father heard, he ordered the young man home. Boswell instead ran off to London. There he spent three months early in 1760, and altered his sense of vocation to that of a libertine. His father hauled him back home after some ineffectual attempts on Boswell's part to get a commission in the Guards. For the next two years he glumly pursued his study of the law back in Edinburgh, writing occasional poems and pamphlets to console himself. In return for an allowance of £100 a year, he signed away most of his rights over the estate after his father's death. One of his cherished self-images, the ancestral laird, was already threatened. But he managed to pass his examination in law; it was taken, orally, on 30 July 1762, and even his pawky father had to admit that – given application – he showed high talent for the law. Now he could exact more generous terms from Lord Auchinleck, and the result was that he set off for an extended stay in London on 15 November 1762, with his allowance now fixed at £200 a year.

The period of establishing himself in the capital is well known, as it forms the background to the *London Journal*. This is the first sustained portion of Boswell's diary, though some abortive attempts a little earlier have been preserved. The varied and convivial life he spent over the next nine months has caught the attention of thousands of readers, some of whom no doubt consider Johnson a bore. But it was on Johnson, above all, that Boswell's ambitions came to fix. He had only been in London a matter of a month when the actor and bookseller Tom Davies told him it would be easy enough to arrange a meeting on Christmas Day, when Johnson would be dining with Davies. This was not the first promise of an introduction Boswell had received, and he must have been all the more eager for the great day to dawn. In the event Johnson decided to spend Christmas in Oxford, and Boswell was forced to make do with lesser luminaries: the publisher Dodsley and Oliver Goldsmith, 'a curious, odd pedantic fellow with some genius', as the *Journal* complacently notes.

Introduction

It was five months before the long-awaited meeting took place, and then in an apparently inconsequential way. The force of that imperishable scene, recorded in the *Life* on 16 May 1763 (p. 277 below) is all the greater when one looks at it alongside the *Journal* entry for that date. The drama is more personal in the original account, the comedy less close to the surface, and surprisingly perhaps the anguish less marked: Boswell has imported a more immediate quality of feeling into the narrative in his revision for the *Life*. A number of stray hints are taken in from marginal notes in the *Journal*. The whole scene is animated by Boswell's typical stage directions, not present in the original ('cried Davies roguishly'; 'with a stern look'). There is a sustained vigour of presentation which has nothing to do with total recall, or literal accuracy in description: it is a matter of fidelity of impression, and that is where the *Life* excels.

Johnson, of course, was by this date middle-aged and famous: known to his contemporaries principally as the author of the *Rambler*, the *Dictionary* and *Rasselas*, and now the recipient of a well-publicised government pension of £300 a year. He quickly warmed to the young man, sensing perhaps a little of Boswell's emotional warmth behind the coxcombry, some of the existential yearnings behind the extrovert facade. Within three months he was taking the stage-coach to Harwich with Boswell, ready to see his young friend off on a journey to Holland. The plan was for Boswell to study law in Utrecht. As it turned out, the sojourn abroad was to last two and a half years: it included a kind of intellectual Grand Tour, with visits to Voltaire and Rousseau amongst others, a pilgrimage to Rome, and an affair with a liberated and intelligent woman named Belle de Zuylen. Boswell also made his way to Corsica, and established contact with another of his great heroes, the independence leader Pasquale Paoli, a high-minded patriot full of stoic virtues. It was this visit which laid the foundations for Boswell's first great success as a writer, his *Account of Corsica*, published in 1768. By the time he returned to England in February 1766 (having somehow acquired the duty of escorting Rousseau's mistress to London and – according to one story – having made rather unsuccessful love to her) he was more worldly and self-confident, though still subject to fits of sudden depression. He immediately headed for Johnson's house just off Fleet Street and, in his own phrasing, was greeted 'with open arms'. The great man had further enhanced his standing with the edition of Shakespeare and had helped to found the famous Club, to which Boswell was later to be admitted with such pride (see p. 529 below).

There could be only a short stay, however, and Boswell had to return to Scotland: to take his final law examination, to gain admittance as an advocate, and to begin the hard grind of earning a living at the bar. For the next decade he could make only short visits to London, during the Edinburgh law vacation; it is important to remember that Boswell and Johnson rarely spent more than a month or so in company each year, and some years there was no meeting at all. During this period Boswell, after a number of trial sorties, fixed on a wife: in November 1769 he married his cousin Margaret Montgomerie, douce, frail in health (she was consumptive, though this was not yet known), and endlessly patient with her husband's infidelities and irresolutions. Boswell at the same time had achieved considerable fame as the author of his book on Corsica: it included a journal of Boswell's tour there in 1765, preceded by a subjective account of Corsican history, and 'memoirs' of the independence fighter Paoli. The author had been heavily influenced by Rousseau, who had actually been invited by the rebels to draft his own constitution for a free Corsica (a task never to be completed). Boswell's *Account* enjoyed immediate success: the first edition was quickly sold out, and a second edition within another year – 3500 copies in all. There were translations into all the major European languages: Belle de Zuylen began a French version, probably unfinished. A large number of reviews appeared, mostly couched in strongly favourable terms: the pretensions of Boswell's pseudo-Plutarchian method were overlooked, and his naive ardour emphasized instead.

Cheered by this publicity, Boswell attempted to cultivate a new role in society. He became 'Corsican Boswell'. One expression of this was a volume he edited called *British Essays in Favour of the Brave Corsicans*. A sillier gesture, less than three months before his wedding, was his appearance at the Shakespeare Jubilee at Stratford 'in the dress of an armed Corsican chief'. This unlucky festival had been organized by David Garrick, and was to have featured some worthwhile activities including an oratorio by Thomas Arne, but heavy rain turned it into a muddy farce, and Boswell was one of the few people attending impervious to its futility. Back in London he had time to welcome Paoli to England, introduce him to Johnson, and show the General the sights of the town – all with the aim of increasing his own public visibility. His return to Ayrshire for his marriage seems to have presented itself as an anticlimax.

The fifteen years intervening between these events and the death of Johnson in 1784 cover the best known period of Boswell's life, at least as far as his London experiences go. This is because the *Life* devotes so much space to the last period of Johnson's career, with Boswell almost always on the fringes of the story. What the biography does not reveal is that Boswell led another life in Scotland, and it was for the most part a less cheerful train of events. He had only fitful success at the bar; his relations with his father showed no improvement, particularly as Lord Auchinleck took a second wife (his first having died whilst James was on the Continent), on the very same day that his son married. The younger Boswell loved his wife in his way, but too much of his nervous and emotional life went into disparate projects for marriage and family life ever to be fully satisfactory. Mrs Boswell's health began to give grounds for concern: there were miscarriages, one son died in his infancy, and from 1778 the ominous became actual when Margaret began spitting blood. Boswell was drinking more and more heavily; he had bouts of gambling, and his sexual irregularities continued despite frequent remorse and self-laceration.

By the time of Johnson's death, he was unmistakably on the

descent. His final decade was made gloomier by his injudicious move to London and efforts to achieve renown at the English bar. So unsuccessful were these attempts that for months on end he did not get a single brief. He courted the favour of an influential nobleman, the Earl of Lonsdale, but three years of toadying brought him little tangible reward: the Earl treated him with brutal contempt, and in the end Boswell abandoned yet another hopeless quest. He offered to stand for parliament for his home constituency, Ayrshire, but could not raise sufficient support. His wife died in 1789 when he was away on a trivial errand for Lonsdale. His own health was steadily undermined by his drinking, by venereal disease and by morbid hypochondria. He would sit in his rented house in London, lonely, idle and depressed. Everything seemed to have gone sour: his whole fantasy of fame, wealth, and distinction had turned to a bitter sense of failure. Only one thing kept him alive until 1795. It was on the *Life of Johnson* that all his hopes now centred: nothing else mattered.

II

Boswell had begun keeping a journal before he met Johnson, but it was this meeting which transformed the activity from a habit into a ritual of self-expression. As early as 1768 he was asking Johnson whether he might publish the great man's letters after his death (see p. 396 below). The characteristically blunt reply was, 'Nay, Sir, when I am dead, you may do as you will.' Plans were hardening for a formal biographic treatment by 1772, when the *Journal* records, 'I have a constant plan to write the *Life* of Mr Johnson. I have not told him of it yet; nor do I know if I should tell him.' When Boswell asked Johnson to supply 'the little circumstances of his life', the response was quite favourable: 'He did not disapprove of my curiosity as to these particulars; but said "They'll come out by degrees".' (This section of the *Journal* was later edited to form part of the *Life*: see p. 474 below.) This answer seems to indicate that Johnson had a shrewd idea of what was going on, and was happy to allow Boswell to go ahead. The picture was confirmed a year later:

I again solicited him to communicate to me the particulars of his early life. He said, 'You shall have them all for twopence. I hope you shall know a great deal more of me before you write my Life. He mentioned to me this day many circumstances, which I wrote down when I went home, and have interwoven in the former part of this narrative. (p. 513 below)

Then, on the Scottish tour that autumn, the intention became still more explicit:

The Sunday evening that we sat by ourselves at Aberdeen, I asked him several particulars of his life from his early years, which he readily told me, and I marked down before him. This day I proceeded in my inquiries, also marking up before him. I have them on separate leaves of paper. I shall lay up authentic materials for The Life of Samuel Johnson, ll.d., and if I survive him, I shall be one who shall most faithfully do honour to his memory. I have now a vast treasure of his conversation at different times since the year 1762 [*recte* 1763] when I first obtained his acquaintance; and by assiduous inquiry I can make up for not knowing him sooner.

When Boswell published this entry in his *Tour to the Hebrides*, he added a note: 'It is no small satisfaction to me to reflect that Dr Johnson read this, and, after being apprised of my intention, communicated to me, at subsequent periods, many particulars of his life, which probably could not otherwise have been preserved.' When the note appeared in 1785, the motive was clearly to puff the promised but still unwritten *Life*.

It is true that a different story emerges from the *Anecdotes* of Mrs Thrale, about whom I shall say more in a moment. She records a conversation under 18 July 1773, in which Johnson waggishly asks who will be his biographer. A number of names are canvassed, starting with Goldsmith, and including Johnson's old friend Dr John Taylor and the miscellaneous writer John Hawkesworth. The conclusion is interesting: 'I intend, however, to disappoint the rogues, and either make you [Mrs Thrale] write the life, with Taylor's intelligence; or, which is better, do it myself, after outliving you all. I am now (added he), keeping a diary, in hopes of using it for that purpose some time.' Some portions of Johnson's diary have been preserved, but he did not attempt a formal autobiography – or if he did, it must have been among the papers destroyed in the last week of his life (see pp. 1381–4 below). The mood of the exchange with Mrs Thrale is jocular, and we cannot rely on her not to suppress Boswell's name in such a context, any more than we could rely on Boswell not to suppress hers.

Signs of increasing commitment to the project appear in Boswell's correspondence with a fellow member of the Literary Club, Bennet Langton. On 31 December 1774 Boswell was promising Langton titbits from the Hebridean journey that would find no place in Johnson's published account. In the same letter Boswell gave Langton a discreet warning to keep off his patch: 'Why do you not become an Author as well as many of your friends have done? . . . You once I think mentioned to me that you had thoughts of Biography. Mr Johnson told me that he was for you writing the History of Lincolnshire. That would be an excellent Work for you.' Then on 24 October 1775: 'You promised to me or at least resolved to put down in writing all the sayings of Dr Johnson that you remember. Pray favour me with them, that the crown of his own jewels which I am preparing may be more brilliant.' By such means Boswell was already seeking to make up for not knowing Johnson sooner.

At this stage, of course, his main source was his own journal. His working methods are clear: he jotted down first short notes of the day's events, whenever possible late the same evening or first thing next day. These were usually nothing more than a rapid series of headings, to be discarded when the journal proper was written up, at intervals of time that varied between a few days after the event to several weeks. A few of the rough notes escaped destruction and survive to show us how Boswell first set down his impressions. It is important to scotch the idea that Boswell used some mysterious shorthand to record everything on the spot. Some credence has been given to this notion by a passage in the *Life* under 10 April 1778 (see

p. 929 below), but in fact Boswell is referring to his ways of summarizing conversation *after* it has taken place. It must be admitted that Mrs Thrale speaks pointedly of the 'ill-bred' habit of nameless persons who sat down at the far end of the room to write down Johnson's sayings. And even Burke took the view that Boswell's 'habit of recording' threw a restraint 'on convivial ease and negligence'. But the evidence as a whole lies the other way: Boswell normally took away in his head from company the materials he was later to use.

Steadily the foundations of the *Life* were laid. Not everyone approved of Boswell's plan. In 1777 he was advised against pursuing it by Lord Monboddo, the prominent Scottish lawyer and philosopher:

Dr Johnson is a man of good natural parts and a good Latin scholar, but in that, as well as in his manners, he is still what he was originally [a provincial schoolmaster]. For he has no fine taste nor correct taste of writing; and even as to his learning, he is no Greek scholar, and he confessed in my house that he was not well acquainted with the fountain of all good learning and fine writing: I mean Homer.

Doubtless Monboddo's opinion was affected by a mild contretemps when Johnson visited his home, not far from Aberdeen, on the Highland trip. But there were others in polite society who would have given similar advice. Nevertheless Boswell stuck to his plan. By 1780 he had decided to compose his great work 'in Scenes'. He was collecting more and more documents, which he labelled 'Papers Apart' and planned to use as a central feature of his book. He had increasing confidence, too, in his ability to reproduce Johnson's manner on paper when writing up the journal: in a famous phrase he speaks of his mind as having been '*strongly impregnated with the Johnsonian æther*' (see p. 297 below). The long preparation was bearing fruit.

Now and then, Boswell being Boswell, there were moments of irresolution: 'I am now writing on the same day between one or two, to catch half an hour before dinner. I am fallen sadly behind in my journal. I should live no more than I can record, as one should not have more corn growing than one can get in. There is a waste of good if it be not preserved.' Mostly, however, the recording went on happily enough, even when the living was at a low ebb. Johnson from time to time provided further details of his earlier life, and there were other useful informants, such as the important printer and publisher William Strahan. Boswell continued to struggle on in Edinburgh, with limited opportunities for first-hand communication with Johnson; he was never able to get the great man away by himself, as had happened during the Highland jaunt. Still he persevered with his task. Already it was coming to have more meaning than anything else in his muddled existence.

Johnson died at the age of seventy-five on 13 December 1784. Boswell received the news in Edinburgh; even before the funeral took place in Westminster Abbey, a week later, he had been asked by the publisher Charles Dilly if he could have an octavo volume of 400 pages of Johnson's conversations ready by the February following. Boswell replied that he had a large collection of materials for a life, but would write it deliberately. His familiar doubts arose: 'I was now uneasy to think that there would be considerable expectations from me of Memoirs of my illustrious Friend; but that habits of indolence and dejection of spirit would probably hinder me from laudable exertion.'

Others were less diffident. By the end of the year William Cooke had already got out a memoir, and he was shortly followed by Thomas Tyers. William Shaw's biography also came out in 1785; the year after saw Joseph Towers's more critical *Essay* on Johnson. However, Boswell's main area of concern lay in a different direction, or rather two different directions. There were two serious rivals known to be in the field, who might possibly rob him of his long-anticipated triumph. Both writers duly produced their biographies, and in the event they were to be much quicker about it than was Boswell. Both were well-known figures with whom Boswell had been acquainted for several years. The first was Sir John Hawkins; the second was the former Mrs Thrale, recently married to Gabriel Piozzi – an event that cast its shadow over Johnson's last days.

III

Hawkins was a man of sixty-five, best known for an ambitious history of music, published in 1776, which had been somewhat eclipsed by Dr Burney's parallel venture. He had met Johnson early in the latter's career as a professional writer, possibly as early as 1740. By 1749 they had helped to form the Ivy Lane Club; and Hawkins was a founder member of the Literary Club in 1764, until a tiff with Burke provoked both his resignation and the imperishable Johnsonian phrase for his character — 'unclubbable' (the source for this is not Boswell but Fanny Burney's diary). In the meantime Hawkins had built up a solid reputation: as Chairman of the Middlesex Quarter Sessions from 1765, with a knighthood in 1772, and as a literary scholar, with a successful edition of Isaak Walton in 1760. Boswell was introduced to him in 1773: the two men were not close, but there was no great enmity at this stage.

When Johnson died, it was Hawkins who was named as the 'authentic' biographer by the influential group of booksellers who presided over the publishing world. (Unlike Boswell, he was named as one of Johnson's executors; the former was inconveniently remote in Edinburgh.) Within days of Johnson's death, the press began to fan the flames of a possible rivalry between the two biographers; the exchange went on for years, more often provoked by partisans of Boswell than by those of Hawkins. The older man had considerable advantages, many of them deriving from his longer period of acquaintance with Johnson. He has actually been termed by a modern Johnsonian scholar 'better qualified for the task than Boswell'. I do not think this is true, either in respect of the collections they had each made or in respect of the human insights they could bring. But there are many good things in Hawkins's life amply to justify its republication in later years and to warrant the statement of Bertram H. Davis that without Boswell 'our most important source for Johnsonian biography would unquestionably be Hawkins' *Life.*' From the start it had distinguished admirers: the poet Cowper remarked that in fifty years the world would come to set a true value on the book. But there was a well-orchestrated campaign in the press denouncing Hawkins. The antipathy of members of the Club lay behind this opposition to the book; it was spearheaded by the Shakespearian scholar George Steevens, a vitriolic writer and a good hater, who inserted in the newspapers several paragraphs exalting Boswell above his rival. This he did out of dislike for Hawkins, rather than any great liking for Boswell. At the same time, the Club was rallying round Boswell, particularly the more distinguished members: 'They sided, as was natural, with their own, and to James Boswell one after another – Sir Joshua Reynolds, Bishop Percy, Bennet Langton, Edmond Malone – turned over his memorabilia of Johnson and left Hawkins to rummage where he might' (B. H. Davis). The life, when it appeared, was condemned on every kind of ground: critics accused Hawkins of plagiarism, inaccuracy, digressive habits, hostility to Johnson, stylistic barbarism, and much else. There is a little in some of these charges, but again the influence of the Club can be discerned in the reviews.

This is the background to Boswell's onslaught on Hawkins at the start of his own *Life* (see pp. 20–1 below). After the earlier biography appeared, Boswell attempted to get some Johnsonian papers which he thought were in Hawkins's custody. Hawkins responded with gruff dignity, and turned over what little he had: the two men had a meeting of embarrassing cordiality in April 1788, when Hawkins spoke 'with such a courteous formality' that Boswell sat back in his armchair and grew almost to like him.

The opposite process is evident in the case of Mrs Thrale. When Boswell fires off his opening salvo against Hawkins, he permits himself only a bare half-sentence concerning 'the slighter aspersions of a lady who once lived in great intimacy with [Johnson].' Yet in many ways he had more to fear from Mrs Piozzi, as she now was. She was an observant woman of high intelligence, with more literary gifts than Hawkins. Her relations with Boswell are the subject of an entertaining study by Mary Hyde, *The Impossible Friendship* (1973), and no one reading this book could underestimate the threat she posed to Boswell as the most personal and intimate chronicler of Johnson's daily life. It was not the official biographer but the unofficial anecdotalist who presented the greater challenge.

In Boswell's very first letter to Mrs Thrale, written back in 1769, he had observed that they were 'rivals for that great man', and so it was to prove. Their first meeting took place the year before: Boswell leapt into Mrs Thrale's coach when she came to fetch Johnson to her home at Streatham Park. They were almost the same age, and had known Johnson for about the same length of time. Mrs Thrale had been introduced to the great man early in 1765, through the good offices of Arthur Murphy, who was himself to write a much-reprinted life of Johnson. At the time Boswell was away on his travels, sampling the delights of Turin. Coincidentally Mrs Piozzi would be living in Italy when her quarrel with Boswell came to a head. Throughout the 1770s, while Boswell ploughed his unrewarding furrow in Edinburgh, Mrs Thrale had Johnson to herself much of the time. He got on well with her husband, the hale and hearty brewer, and was enchanted by her own spirited company. She was bright, sympathetic, strong-minded, and very well-read; she exerted the peculiar sexual power commanded by intellectual women; and Johnson confided to her secrets he had withheld from all others, including (we may plausibly surmise) his masochistic fantasies.

But the worst thing about Mrs Thrale, from Boswell's point of view, was not her attractive character — not even the fact that she was always *there*. It lay in the fact that she was herself collecting anecdotes concerning Johnson. Boswell found out about this 'Thralian Miscellany' in 1776, and he was naturally beside himself to get a sight of it. In May of that year he had a long conversation with Mrs Thrale on their object of common devotion, and Boswell did an uncharacteristic thing. He handed over to her a portion of his Hebridean *Tour*. There had been a measure of rivalry even in connection with the jaunts, for the year after Johnson's Scottish trip he was carried off to North Wales with the Thrales, and the year after that he went to Paris in the same company. There were plans for an Italian visit, never to be realized. Mrs Hyde has speculated that Boswell left his manuscript at Streatham 'with the hope of further convincing his hostess that he was "as Johnsonian" as she was, and to let her sample his style.' Very likely: but I suspect he may also have been angling for a return gesture, unable to contain his eagerness to peep into the 'Book of Johnsoniana' he knew to be kept in the family.

If so, his hopes were not fulfilled. Up to 1783 he remained on terms of outward cordiality with Mrs Thrale. He earned some variable marks in her celebrated ranking table of her friends in 1778: his scores out of twenty included 19 for good humour, 5 for religion and morality, and 10 for 'person and voice'. (In the latter category Johnson was awarded nil.) As Johnson's failing health made his imminent death a likelihood, the improbability of the friendship emerged, and cracks began to appear. In 1782, when Boswell's father died and he succeeded to Auchinleck, Mrs Thrale fell in love with the Italian musician Gabriel Piozzi. She had lost her husband in April 1781, and since that time her relations with Johnson had grown less easy. Whilst Thrale lived, Johnson was an agreeable person to have around the house at Streatham; but now that she was a widow she became more aware of his oddities, his inconvenient habits, and his strange dependence on her. Matters came to a head with her marriage to Piozzi in July 1784 and subsequent departure for Italy. All Johnson's friends took his disparaging view of the marriage, and Boswell was among them. He never saw Mrs Piozzi in the flesh after 1783.

The rivalry now converted itself into a battle of the books. Mrs Piozzi naturally proved the quicker off the mark; she was resolute and sure of her inner resources, where Boswell was self-analytic and depressive. She managed to obtain £300 for the copyright of her *Anecdotes* from a leading figure in the book trade, Thomas Cadell. They were published in March 1786, with an audience made expectant by much gossip in the press. The first edition of a thousand copies was sold out on the very day of publication, and three more editions were required that year. Boswell occurs only twice in the narrative, once as

'Mr B——', an unfortunate *Shamela*-like condition to endure. It was almost better when Hawkins referred to 'Mr James Boswell, a native of Scotland' (for which Boswell got in the riposte, 'Mr John Hawkins, an attorney' – see p. 137 below). The *Anecdotes* are bitty and ill organized, it is true, but they give many insights into Johnson's domestic living which were denied to Boswell. It is to this book that we owe many splendid touches that are often attributed to Boswell: a phrase which I have already used, 'good hater', comes from Mrs Piozzi, with reference to Johnson's commendation of his friend Dr Bathurst. So does the sturdy comment, 'I would advise no man to marry, Sir, who is not likely to propagate understanding.' And so does the splendid story concerning the young man who lamented that he had lost all his Greek: 'I believe it happened at the same time, Sir (said Johnson), that I lost all my large estate in Yorkshire.'

Two years later Mrs Piozzi produced two volumes of letters to and from Johnson. She and Boswell were the only two people to recover the letters they had written to Johnson; she had hoarded those sent to her, and managed to get a few of the Doctor's correspondents to pass on his letters. Most, however, had a prior commitment to Boswell. This time she received £500 from Cadell. She had some three hundred letters, not including thirty to her estranged daughter which were withheld. Naturally Boswell read the letters with great attention. The letters would have augmented his own haul of about 340 items; but, quite apart from copyright difficulties, he did not want to give Mrs Piozzi the prominence in his biography which the letters would have yielded her. He himself figured very little in Johnson's correspondence with Mrs Piozzi: in an ill-tempered mood he wrote in his journal that he had been wasting his time collecting materials about a man who could write such trifling letters. It was one of the many crises of confidence that interrupted the making of the *Life*.

IV

Two such rivals in the wings, and public expectations high: it was a daunting task Boswell faced when he contemplated his 'deliberate' undertaking. It should therefore occasion no surprise that he made a slow start. In 1784 he had a variety of materials to hand. First of all, there was his *Journal* as written up from 1763, together with a few loose notes that had happened to survive. Secondly, there were the 'Papers Apart', that is, documents and records to be reproduced more or less verbatim. Thirdly, there were Johnson's letters to him. Assorted miscellaneous materials filled out the collection, but it remained notably weak on the first fifty-four years of Johnson's life, and suffered from certain gaps elsewhere.

For the next few years Boswell set about repairing these omissions. The efforts he made can be followed in a splendid edition by Professor Marshall Waingrow of his papers as they bear on the making of the *Life*. Thanks to this edition, we can now pick up Boswell's traces, in the very act of composition, in a way that was previously impossible. We see him consulting and cajoling, begging and threatening, copying and collating, editing and paraphrasing. He went to Johnson's boyhood friends in Lichfield, men and women like the surgeon Edmund Hector, the clergyman John Taylor, the informative widow Mary Cobb, and the dignified Elizabeth Aston: all were to predecease Boswell and it is thus highly important that he exploited such sources. He obtained local information, too, from the 'Swan of Lichfield', the poet Anna Seward; but their relations broke down and an acrimonious exchange in the press ensued. Boswell kept on better terms with most of his informants, though he was to disturb Bishop Percy, the ballad collector and scholar, with some of his revelations in the *Life*. Other scholars to aid Boswell were Isaac Reed and Samuel Parr; but there were also clergymen, soldiers, poets, actors, philosophers, men about town, and members of parliament. Boswell wrote to Warren Hastings and arranged a characteristic meeting: he views Hastings as Alexander and himself as Diogenes. The Club rallied round, and the *Life* owes something to the contributions of men like Burke and Reynolds.

The biggest single debt Boswell incurred, however, was to Edmond Malone. Malone (1741–1812), an Irish lawyer, achieved fame as the editor of Shakespeare, Dryden, and others. He had been prominent in the Club, and led the opposition to Hawkins's *Life*. He was a considerable scholar, orderly and single-minded where Boswell was impulsive and moody. For years he encouraged his friend to go on with the *Life*, nudging him along through periods of gloom and literary impotence. The two men had long been acquaintances, though their friendship did not ripen until just before Johnson's death. Without Malone, it has been truly said, the *Life* would never have come into being. His offices extended to proof-reading the first edition, and later to preparing the third, fourth, fifth, and sixth editions. It is the mark of a great scholar to have taken this self-effacing role in the production of a masterpiece, the kind of work Malone would have liked to write, though he knew himself incapable of it.

Boswell decided to publish first of all his *Tour* of the Hebrides. This would serve to herald the greater work, and would allow him to try out certain techniques. The manuscript journal needed comparatively little editing: there were few 'Papers Apart' to be incorporated. Even here, however, there were decisions to be taken, about what could and could not be included. Indiscretions and indelicacies had to be removed; Boswell's own observations of the Highlands, where they did not illuminate the central figure of Johnson, were also cut. In this task of revision he was helped by Malone, with whom he passed much of the summer of 1785. On 1 October of that year the *Tour* came before the public; there were two more editions in Boswell's lifetime. One or two passages that were too candid in their treatment of individuals had to be softened in the second edition; there was a vague threat of a duel over one of these. Most readers gave the *Tour* a warm welcome, although sharp old Horace Walpole could find in it only 'the story of a mountebank and his zany'. It was Boswell's first real success as a writer since the heady Corsican triumphs, seventeen years before. Then he had been a promising young man. Now he was middle-aged and not very far short of manic-depressive.

For the next few months he persevered with his collecting,

but could not get down to writing the *Life*. Even the appearance of Mrs Piozzi's *Anecdotes* in March 1786 failed to stir him into action. But early in June, Malone gave him a valuable piece of advice – 'to make a Skeleton, with references to the materials, in order of time'. This enabled him to sort the materials more effectively, and on 9 July he eventually made a start. To achieve as much he had to shut himself up all day and live on a frugal diet of toast and boiled milk: but the discipline served. From this point on there is a regular pattern in the *Journal*, with bursts of energy and relapses into torpor. He was making slow headway, and meanwhile continued to solicit information from persons of every description. He had even told the King of his project: 'There will be many lives of Dr Johnson,' was the response, 'do you give the best.'

At the start of 1786 Boswell heard that Hawkins's *Life* would soon be out. He wrote to a friend, 'I have waited till I should first see Hawkin's compilation. But my friends urge me to dispatch, that the ardour of curiosity may not be allowed to cool.' He inserted an anonymous note in the press on 9 February regarding 'the etiquette of precedency' between Hawkins and Boswell: 'the truth is, that the competition between them is not who shall be *first*, but who shall be *last*; in short which shall *see the other's back*, so as to hold the lash of animadversion.' This unconvincing excuse was repeated in a letter: 'I have solid reasons for delay ... from the motive of having Sir John Hawkins to precede me that I might profit by his gross faults.' The real reason, of course, was Boswell's inability to cope speedily with his huge mass of materials, alone with his refusal to give up the quest for new information.

The Hawkins *Life* came out on 1 March 1787, with a second edition in June. Boswell was provoked into issuing a famous advertisement, assuring the public that his own *Life* was in a state of 'great Forwardness', and promising that he would deliver something more worthwhile than 'the light Effusions of Carelessness and Pique, or the ponderous Labours of solemn Inaccuracy and dark uncharitable Conjecture.' It needed no percipience to identify the works of Mrs Piozzi and Hawkins in this description. It must again be emphasized that Boswell was contributing to an ongoing controversy, as well as constructing a funeral tribute. People who had not been specially interested in Samuel Johnson during his lifetime were now fully aware of the wrangles between Boswell, Hawkins, and Piozzi. None of the Club had a good word for Hawkins, and Malone suggested that a solemn protest be drawn up, damning it as 'a false and injurious account'. Only the temporizing Reynolds blocked the move.

The appearance of Mrs Piozzi's volumes of letters the next year prompted less of a response from Boswell. This time he did not rush into print with 'Piozzian rhymes', as he had when the *Anecdotes* appeared: he grumbled about the volumes in his correspondence, but could find no such neat phrase to dismiss them as he had two years earlier: 'She puts cherries in the brandy.' 1788 was a bad, unproductive year. There was a long hiatus in the summer, about which he wrote shamefacedly to Malone: 'You will be very angry when I confess to you that I have not yet advanced a single page in Johnson's *Life*.' And again: 'Done nothing to Dr Johnson's *Life* – literally nothing – not a single line of the remaining part of the first draught which I hoped and trusted should be completely finished here.' By November he had taken his narrative as far as the year 1783, but much remained to be done. Malone gave him quiet support, and a draft was completed in March 1789. Revision occupied the next few months. Boswell was still surprisingly unsure about the ultimate form his book would take: in January 1790 he was abandoning his plan of publishing in two quarto volumes, and thinking in terms of a folio instead. 'Malone said I might as well throw it into the Thames, for a folio would not now be read.' Even this did not finally settle the issue; in September he was discovering anew that it would have to be two volumes after all. In February the manuscript had finally gone to press and the elaborate business of printing had begun.

The compositors must have had a fearsome task on their hands. The greater part of the manuscript has turned up among the Malahide Castle finds and is preserved at Yale. It shows that Boswell expected the printer to take in the 'Papers Apart' (letters, quotations from printed sources, etc.), and had to decipher an elaborate semaphoring system to know which insertion to make. Extensive rewriting went on all through the text, and the verso of the manuscript, originally left blank, was generally filled with alterations and additions. The method has prompted the great Johnsonian scholar James L. Clifford to observe, 'If anyone still has the mistaken notion that Boswell was artistically lazy, that he merely joined together a mass of fragments and called it a biography, let him examine the minute revisions and major rearrangements made during the revision of his first draft.' The first and second set of proofs also survive, and so we can see that this editing process went on right up to the last minute.

Boswell was planning to produce the work at his own expense. A bookseller named Robinson had offered '*A Cool Thousand*' for the copyright – or Boswell thought he had. After a good deal of indecision he resolved to hold on to the rights. However, he did accept an advance from the distributor Dilly and the printer Baldwin, each loaning him a sum of £200. The trouble was that Boswell was badly in need of money, having unwisely negotiated for the purchase of some land formerly belonging to the Auchinleck estate. It is sad to think that the success of such a great book was mortgaged in advance on a scheme of so little moment. Boswell had heard that Arthur Murphy was receiving £200 for his short life of Johnson, and this increased his determination to reap a good financial reward.

As late as February 1791 Boswell was still making changes, still asking Malone, 'Pray how shall I wind up. Shall I give the Character [of Johnson] in my *Tour*, somewhat enlarged?' But the time for rewriting was running out; the book was advertised in March and at long last it appeared on 16 May 1791, one of the great days in English letters. 1750 copies were printed; the set of two quarto volumes cost two guineas. Within two years the edition was exhausted, and Boswell had made £600 even after paying production expenses, his loans, and all. The second edition was to follow in July 1793, this time in three octavo volumes. Even with Malone's help Boswell, in his declining state, had not been up to the task of adroitly revising a text which was already in print; the result was a confused jumble. The third edition, published in May 1799, was the responsibility of Malone, and has come to be regarded as the standard edition; it forms the basis for the present text.

When the *Life* first appeared, Boswell received letters of congratulation from a wide range of people. Along with men such as Joseph Warton, Warren Hastings, Vicesimus Knox, Dr Burney, Sir William Forbes, Samuel Parr, and others, he was addressed by the obscure and unknown. An Eton schoolboy's comments were sent on by Boswell's son, who was also at Eton. An apostle of reformed spelling sent a freakish letter in the new orthography: 'Az for Garrics vaporing on dhe subject, no won hoo knows me wil believ . . .' (Why 'know' remains intact does not emerge.) Understandably Boswell displayed a certain vainglory: he wrote to Wilkes and Burke, asking them to confirm in writing the splendid things that had been said about the *Life*. In Burke's case it was the King himself who had, so Boswell understood, pronounced it 'the most entertaining book he had ever read'. Burke, with some embarrassment, agreed this was more or less the case. By now Boswell's high royalist sentiments were conjuring up some pleasing visions of future grandeur. For the second edition he drafted a preface drawing attention to the King's approbation, and wanted to style himself, 'By appointment to his Majesty, Biographer of Samuel Johnson, Ll.D.' Malone could not take this, probably on grounds of taste as much as those of politics. The printed leaf was cancelled, and the boast disappeared until its resurrection, with so much else, among the Yale papers.

That was one late flourish of the old Boswell: there were few more such. In June 1793 Boswell was the victim of a mugging as he returned in an alcoholic stupor to his home in Great Portland Street. He was robbed and left lying in the gutter with a bad cut to his head. The city watchmen, proverbially senile, made a belated arrival and took him off home, where he spent weeks in bed. Such events were but a prelude to the final indignity of death, brought on before its time by his unregulated habits. Boswell was fifty-four when he died, just a few months older than Johnson had been when the famous meeting took place at Tom Davies' shop. There was not much to live for, once the *Life* had been completed. In 1790 he had seen in it ' the most important, perhaps *now* the only concern of any consequence that I ever shall have in this world.'

V

The overwhelming verdict of posterity has been that the *Life of Johnson* is one of the supreme examples of the art of biography, combining entertainment with instruction in the most natural manner. However, from the start, a number of criticisms have been levelled at the work. For convenience these may be divided into criticisms of Boswell's technique and approach, and criticisms of the documentary value of his book. Naturally there is a degree of overlap.

What might be called the artistic reservations tend to concentrate on the alleged disproportion of the narrative. It will be pointed out that half of the book is devoted to the last eight years of seventy-five which Johnson spent on earth. In the most literal sense, this charge is unanswerable. There is a good deal that can be said by way of supplementary comment, nevertheless. First, Boswell catches Johnson at his moment of greatest public visibility, and since his biography is public rather than private (stressing Johnson's role as moralist, arbiter of taste, and professional author) that emphasis is appropriate. Second, Boswell does fit in many hints concerning the younger Johnson, which suggest how he developed into his later self. For example, Boswell has a far more inward sense than any of his rivals concerning the place of Lichfield in Johnson's affections. Hawkins, it is true, briefly mentions the ' enthusiastic ' love Johnson preserved for his home-town; but there is none of the detailed evidence which Boswell provides. An important factor here was Boswell's presence in Lichfield together with Johnson, which prompted so many revealing stories (see, for example, p. 708

below). Third, the truth is that Boswell's ignorance of the first half of Johnson's life is one we continue to share in very large measure. The middle years are still notoriously obscure. This point can be enforced by examining the schedule of letters in the standard edition by R. W. Chapman (the relatively few items to have turned up subsequently do not affect the picture in any material way). Out of some 1500 datable letters from Johnson, only about 2½ per cent date from before 1750; only about 10 per cent date from before 1760; and only about 20 per cent date from before 1770. Granted that devoted enquiries by A. L. Reade and others have turned up a few odd facts regarding the early years, it is still a grey area. There is a discomforting resemblance to studies of Shakespeare's boyhood, with the same vague use of Midlands folklore and the same betraying impulse to wander off into the lawsuits of second cousins. The main difference is that we are now readier to speculate than Boswell was.

Another charge uttered by hostile voices is that the year-by-year scheme of the narrative produces stiffness. I am inclined to think that chronological order is generally the most revealing way of disclosing a life-history; and there is nothing in principle wrong with the arrangement by years – it is used to great effect by Mary Hyde in the study of Boswell and Mrs Thrale mentioned earlier. And there is a more particular justification with an eighteenth-century narrative. Boswell's annual absences and returns reflect a major fact of life then, the *seasonal* pattern of events. Business and pleasure alike were geared to the calendar far more directly than is the case today. The agricultural rhythms had not been drowned in most people's consciousness by an industrial continuum. Even in London, the law vacations and parliamentary sessions had a major impact on daily living. When great men left town, so did a whole army of retainers and providers. You could have easily guessed the season, without references to clothes or weather, from the activities going on in the street. Newspapers suffered a huge drop in sales during the summer after their peak period in mid-winter. Horace Walpole could predict the entire round of social events twelve months in advance (see his letter to Lord Hertford, 29 December 1763). Boswell's method emphasizes this sense of life starting up anew each year, and is faithful to Hanoverian experience for that very reason.

The other group of charges relates to Boswell's alleged bias or incomprehension. Some amount of distortion must be conceded: the deliberate relegation of Mrs Thrale, the haziness with regard to Burke (compared to Goldsmith, say), the lack of curiosity in areas remote from Boswell's experience. However, more serious accusations have been made recently. It is argued that Boswell distorted Johnson's political opinions, turning him into a romantic Tory in his own image. The matter is too complex to dispose of briefly: we might just note that when William Strahan wanted to put Johnson up for parliament, the first and most insistent emphasis was on Johnson's 'perfect good affection to his Majesty, and his government, which . . . he wishes to support by every means in his power' (see p. 451 below).

A further contention is that Boswell put too much stress on Johnson as a talker, and thus helped to found the tradition of the Great Clubman, as opposed to the 'real', intellectual being, the writer and thinker. This line of reasoning copes awkwardly with the large amount of space Boswell devotes to the writings, from the opening catalogue onwards. More seriously, it fails to recognize that the performing bear is a genuine expression of Johnson's humanity and moral identity. It perversely downgrades the conversations, long acknowledged as a salient virtue of the book and as an intensely revelatory focus on Johnson. Ian Jack has written of Boswell 'waiting – like a photographer of exotic animals or birds – for the moment of greatest display on the part of his subject.' This is exactly right, and it works so well because Boswell is prepared to seize on the slightest hint or *obiter dictum*. Finally, this objection pays far too little attention to one of the glories of the *Life*, its comedy. One of the prime attributes Boswell had for the job was a sense of humour he shared with Johnson. It was doubtless one of the things which drew the older man so quickly to him in the summer of 1763.

This quality was not so much in evidence with Hawkins, and that is one of many reasons (along with Boswell's acceptance of oddity) for believing Boswell rather than Hawkins on crucial points.

This last consideration does not apply in one of the most hotly debated points of comparison. Hawkins gives a much more unfavourable picture of Johnson's marriage, and most Johnsonian scholars today are inclined to accept his version. There is the added factor here that Boswell knew of Johnson's plan at one stage to take a second wife. Boswell copied down the relevant entries from Johnson's diary for 1753 (he actually did this as early as May 1776, during the period described on p. 753 below). In the end he felt unable to make use of this material in his *Life*. This is one of a number of omissions Boswell conceived himself as obliged to make on grounds of delicacy and propriety. In 1785 Boswell had a conversation with Hawkins when they met at dinner at the home of Bennet Langton: their talk veered towards Johnson's 'strong amorous passions'. Hawkins had read diary entries which related to this subject. Boswell was naturally intrigued, but could get no further, though he pursued it with Hawkins the following year. The episodes Hawkins had in mind may be similar to one Boswell had heard of from Mrs Desmoulins, one of the strange menagerie of misfits who shared Johnson's house for many years. She reported in 1783 that Johnson's wife had refused him sexual favours, with the result that she herself had been regularly called into Johnson's bedroom and had been petted in a rather chaste manner. This story went into some notes Boswell labelled 'Tacenda', and of course was not to figure in the *Life*.

But then there was a great deal Boswell collected which ended up, as one might say, on the cutting-room floor. He pruned assiduously, and often propriety was not remotely in question. An entertaining book could be compiled from the materials printed by Marshall Waingrow, which came to Boswell from his correspondents but found no place in the book. There is Edmund Hector's tale of a drunken evening at the Swan Inn in Lichfield, perhaps around 1730. There is Johnson glutting himself on a haunch of venison at Dr Taylor's house. There are graphic descriptions such as this passage on the theatre: 'That it would afford him more entertainment to sit up to the chin in water for an hour than be obliged to listen to the whining, daggle-tail Cibber, during the tedious representation of a fulsome tragedy without the possibility of receiving from it either pleasure or instruction.' There are more harrowing touches: Johnson's admission to Percy that he 'had lived twenty years in London but *not very happily*' is one. Other matters censored were Johnson's dependence on opium in his final illness, and a passage in which Boswell had accused Mrs Thrale of turning 'a wolf dog into a lap dog.'

Some of these criticisms may appear convincing to some readers. But to others they will appear unconscious endorsements. For instance, the alleged defect sometimes noted – that Boswell makes a hero of Johnson – is, from a different perspective, one of the major interests of the work. The *Life* has been called 'the almost involuntary tribute of a great human weakness to a great human strength' (B. H. Bronson), and that precisely states one facet of its appeal. Boswell knew he could not be Johnson, in the way that he might once have vaguely aspired to be a philosopher like Rousseau, a man of action like Paoli, or a great lawyer like Lord Mansfield. This recognition permits that William C. Dowling terms 'the commodiousness of Boswellian narrative, which allows the hero so much room for direct and personal expression.' Egocentric and intrusive as he was, James Boswell somehow possessed the gift of standing aside when necessary. The greatness of his book lies in the plenitude of its observation, the richness of its concrete detail, the comprehensiveness of its human portraiture. These things will survive when the infights over his 'Tacenda' have long died down.

A striking comment on the *Life* was once made by the learned lady Mrs Barbauld, who gets a brief and disguised mention in the text (see p. 662 below). She wrote that reading the book was 'like going to Ranelagh; you meet all your acquaintance.' This is true in a deeper and more permanent sense than the

Introduction

writer intended. The *Life of Johnson* reveals a whole age to us: it arrives at social truth through human truth. It is the story of a great life, told by one whose own life was otherwise shabby and disconsolate.

July 1979

PAT ROGERS

SELECT BIBLIOGRAPHY

EDITIONS

The *Life of Johnson* first appeared in 2 vols. (1791); after an unsatisfactory Dublin edition (1792) came the second edition in 3 vols. (1793). Edmond Malone edited the versions appearing in 1799, 1804, 1807, and 1811: his notes are designated 'M.' in the text which follows.

Important subsequent editions are by J. W. Croker (1831) and R. Ingpen (1907). The standard edition is that of G. B. Hill, revised by L. F. Powell, 6 vols. (1934–50; with corrections, 1964). These editors are referred to in the notes by their surnames.

BOSWELL'S PAPERS

Private Papers from Malahide Castle were edited by G. Scott and F. A. Pottle in 18 vols. (1928–34). See especially Vol. 6, on the making of the *Life*. References in the notes take the form '*Boswell Papers*'.

The Yale edition of the papers has been in progress since 1950, edited by F. A. Pottle *et al*. Eleven vols. of the trade edition have so far appeared; three of the research edition. See especially *The Correspondence of Boswell relating to the Making of the Life of Johnson*, edited by M. Waingrow (1969).

OTHER BIOGRAPHIC AIDS

Mrs Piozzi's *Anecdotes* (1786) are indicated in the notes by '*Mrs. Piozzi*'. See also *Thraliana*, ed. K. C. Balderston, 2 vols. (1942; rev. 1951), and Mary Hyde, *The Impossible Friendship: Boswell and Mrs Thrale* (1973).

Sir John Hawkins's *Life* (1787) has been abridged by B. H. Davis (1961); see also Davis's study of this work, *Johnson before Boswell* (1960; reprinted 1973).

Select Bibliography

Extensive biographic collections are found in A. L. Reade, *Johnsonian Gleanings*, 11 vols. (1909–52), cited as ' *Reade*'.

Boswelliana, ed. C. Rogers (1874).

Boswell's Notebook, ed. R. W. Chapman (1923).

See also *The Letters of Samuel Johnson*, ed. R. W. Chapman, 3 vols. (1952).

BOSWELL STUDIES

For bibliographical matters see F. A. Pottle, *The Literary Career of James Boswell esq.* (1929).

Biographic works include C. B. Tinker, *Young Boswell* (1922) and F. A. Pottle, *James Boswell: The Earlier Years* 1840–1769 (1966).

Letters of Boswell, ed. C. B. Tinker, 2 vols. (1924) has not yet been entirely superseded by the Yale edition of private papers.

For the discovery of Boswell's manuscripts at Malahide and Fettercairn, see D. Buchanan, *The Treasure of Auchinleck* (1975).

The most valuable study of Boswell's literary skill to date is that of W. C. Dowling, *The Boswellian Hero* (1979).

P. R.

DEDICATION TO SIR JOSHUA REYNOLDS

My Dear Sir,—Every liberal motive that can actuate an Authour in the dedication of his labours, concurs in directing me to you, as the person to whom the following Work should be inscribed.

If there be a pleasure in celebrating the distinguished merit of a contemporary, mixed with a certain degree of vanity not altogether inexcusable, in appearing fully sensible of it, where can I find one, in complimenting whom I can with more general approbation gratify those feelings? Your excellence not only in the Art over which you have long presided with unrivalled fame, but also in Philosophy and elegant Literature, is well known to the present, and will continue to be the admiration of future ages. Your equal and placid temper, your variety of conversation, your true politeness, by which you are so amiable in private society, and that enlarged hospitality which has long made your house a common centre of union for the great, the accomplished, the learned, and the ingenious; all these qualities I can, in perfect confidence of not being accused of flattery, ascribe to you.

If a man may indulge an honest pride, in having it known to the world, that he has been thought worthy of particular attention by a person of the first eminence in the age in which he lived, whose company has been universally courted, I am justified in availing myself of the usual privilege of a Dedication, when I mention that there has been a long and uninterrupted friendship between us.

If gratitude should be acknowledged for favours received, I have this opportunity, my dear Sir, most sincerely to thank you for the many happy hours which I owe to your kindness,—for the cordiality with which you have at all times been pleased to welcome me,—for the number of valuable acquaintances to whom you have introduced me,—for the *noctes cœnæque Deûm*,[1] which I have enjoyed under your roof.

If a work should be inscribed to one who is master of the subject

[1] [nights and suppers of gods. Horace, *Sat.* II. vii. 85.]

1

of it, and whose approbation, therefore, must ensure it credit and success, the *Life of Dr. Johnson* is, with the greatest propriety, dedicated to Sir Joshua Reynolds, who was the intimate and beloved friend of that great man; the friend, whom he declared to be 'the most invulnerable man he knew; whom, if he should quarrel with him, he should find the most difficulty how to abuse.' You, my dear Sir, studied him, and knew him well: you venerated and admired him. Yet, luminous as he was upon the whole, you perceived all the shades which mingled in the grand composition; all the little peculiarities and slight blemishes which marked the literary Colossus. Your very warm commendation of the specimen which I gave in my *Journal of a Tour to the Hebrides*, of my being able to preserve his conversation in an authentick and lively manner, which opinion the Publick has confirmed, was the best encouragement for me to persevere in my purpose of producing the whole of my stores.

In one respect, this Work will, in some passages, be different from the former. In my *Tour*, I was almost unboundedly open in my communications, and from my eagerness to display the wonderful fertility and readiness of Johnson's wit, freely shewed to the world its dexterity, even when I was myself the object of it. I trusted that I should be liberally understood, as knowing very well what I was about, and by no means as simply unconscious of the pointed effects of the satire. I own, indeed, that I was arrogant enough to suppose that the tenour of the rest of the book would sufficiently guard me against such a strange imputation. But it seems I judged too well of the world; for, though I could scarcely believe it, I have been undoubtedly informed, that many persons, especially in distant quarters, not penetrating enough into Johnson's character, so as to understand his mode of treating his friends, have arraigned my judgement, instead of seeing that I was sensible of all that they could observe.

It is related of the great Dr. Clarke, that when in one of his leisure hours he was unbending himself with a few friends in the most playful and frolicksome manner, he observed Beau Nash approaching; upon which he suddenly stopped:—'My boys, (said he,) let us be grave: here comes a fool.' The world, my

Dedication

friend, I have found to be a great fool, as to that particular, on which it has become necessary to speak very plainly. I have, therefore, in this Work been more reserved; and though I tell nothing but the truth, I have still kept in my mind that the whole truth is not always to be exposed. This, however, I have managed so as to occasion no diminution of the pleasure which my book should afford; though malignity may sometimes be disappointed of its gratifications.

I am, my dear Sir,

Your much obliged friend,

And faithful humble servant,

JAMES BOSWELL.

London,

April 20, 1791.

ADVERTISEMENT TO THE FIRST EDITION

I AT last deliver to the world a Work which I have long promised, and of which, I am afraid, too high expectations have been raised. The delay of its publication must be imputed, in a considerable degree, to the extraordinary zeal which has been shewn by distinguished persons in all quarters to supply me with additional information concerning its illustrious subject; resembling in this the grateful tribes of ancient nations, of which every individual was eager to throw a stone upon the grave of a departed Hero, and thus to share in the pious office of erecting an honourable monument to his memory.

The labour and anxious attention with which I have collected and arranged the materials of which these volumes are composed, will hardly be conceived by those who read them with careless facility. The stretch of mind and prompt assiduity by which so many conversations were preserved, I myself, at some distance of time, contemplate with wonder; and I must be allowed to suggest, that the nature of the work, in other respects, as it consists of innumerable detached particulars, all which, even the most minute, I have spared no pains to ascertain with a scrupulous authenticity, has occasioned a degree of trouble far beyond that of any other species of composition. Were I to detail the books which I have consulted, and the inquiries which I have found it necessary to make by various channels, I should probably be thought ridiculously ostentatious. Let me only observe, as a specimen of my trouble, that I have sometimes been obliged to run half over London, in order to fix a date correctly; which, when I had accomplished, I well knew would obtain me no praise, though a failure would have been to my discredit. And after all, perhaps, hard as it may be, I shall not be surprized if omissions or mistakes be pointed out with invidious severity. I have also been extremely careful as to the exactness of my quotations; holding that there is a respect due to the publick which should oblige every Authour to attend to this, and never to presume to introduce them with,—'I think I have read;'—*or,—*'If I remember right;'—*when the originals may be examined.*

I beg leave to express my warmest thanks to those who have been pleased to favour me with communications and advice in the conduct of my Work. But I cannot sufficiently acknowledge my obligations to my friend Mr. Malone, who was so good as to allow me to read to him almost the whole of my manuscript, and make such remarks as were greatly for the advantage of the Work; though it is but fair to him to mention, that upon many occasions I differed from him, and followed my own judgement. I regret exceedingly that I was deprived of the benefit of his revision, when not more than one half of the book had passed through the press; but after having completed his very laborious and admirable edition of Shakspeare, for which he generously would accept of no other reward but that fame which he has so deservedly obtained, he fulfilled his promise of a long-wished-for visit to his relations in Ireland; from whence his safe return finibus Atticis[1] *is desired by his friends here, with all the classical ardour of* Sic te Diva potens Cypri[2]; *for there is no man in whom more elegant and worthy qualities are united; and whose society, therefore, is more valued by those who know him.*

It is painful to me to think, that while I was carrying on this Work, several of those to whom it would have been most interesting have died. Such melancholy disappointments we know to be incident to humanity; but we do not feel them the less. Let me particularly lament the Reverend Thomas Warton, and the Reverend Dr. Adams. Mr. Warton, amidst his variety of genius and learning, was an excellent Biographer. His contributions to my Collection are highly estimable; and as he had a true relish of my Tour to the Hebrides, I trust I should now have been gratified with a larger share of his kind approbation. Dr. Adams, eminent as the Head of a College, as a writer, and as a most amiable man, had known Johnson from his early years, and was his friend through life. What reason I had to hope for the countenance of that venerable Gentleman to this Work, will appear from what he wrote to me upon a former occasion from Oxford, November 17, 1785:—'Dear Sir, I hazard this letter, not knowing where it will find you, to thank you for your very agreeable *Tour*, which I found here on my return from the country, and in which you have depicted our friend so perfectly to my fancy, in every attitude, every scene and situation, that

[1, 2] ['To the Attic shore' . . . 'So guide thee the goddess queen of Cyprus'. Horace, *Odes* i. iii. 5, 1. (Wickham.)]

I have thought myself in the company, and of the party almost throughout. It has given very general satisfaction; and those who have found most fault with a passage here and there, have agreed that they could not help going through, and being entertained with the whole. I wish, indeed, some few gross expressions had been softened, and a few of our hero's foibles had been a little more shaded; but it is useful to see the weaknesses incident to great minds; and you have given us Dr. Johnson's authority that in history all ought to be told.'

Such a sanction to my faculty of giving a just representation of Dr. Johnson I could not conceal. Nor will I suppress my satisfaction in the consciousness, that by recording so considerable a portion of the wisdom and wit of 'the brightest ornament of the eighteenth century,'[1] *I have largely provided for the instruction and entertainment of mankind.—*London, April 20, 1791.

ADVERTISEMENT TO THE SECOND EDITION

That I was anxious for the success of a Work which had employed much of my time and labour, I do not wish to conceal: but whatever doubts I at any time entertained, have been entirely removed by the very favourable reception with which it has been honoured. That reception has excited my best exertions to render my Book more perfect; and in this endeavour I have had the assistance not only of some of my particular friends, but of many other learned and ingenious men, by which I have been enabled to rectify some mistakes, and to enrich the Work with many valuable additions. These I have ordered to be printed separately in quarto, for the accommodation of the purchasers of the first edition. May I be permitted to say that the typography of both editions does honour to the press of Mr. Henry Baldwin, *now Master of the Worshipful Company of Stationers, whom I have long known as a worthy man and an obliging friend.*

In the strangely mixed scenes of human existence, our feelings are often at once pleasing and painful. Of this truth, the progress of the present Work furnishes a striking instance. It was highly gratifying to me that my friend, Sir Joshua Reynolds, *to whom it is inscribed,*

[1] See Mr. Malone's Preface to his edition of Shakspeare.

lived to peruse it, and to give the strongest testimony to its fidelity; but before a second edition, which he contributed to improve, could be finished, the world has been deprived of that most valuable man; a loss of which the regret will be deep, and lasting, and extensive, proportionate to the felicity which he diffused through a wide circle of admirers and friends.

In reflecting that the illustrious subject of this Work, by being more extensively and intimately known, however elevated before, has risen in the veneration and love of mankind, I feel a satisfaction beyond what fame can afford. We cannot, indeed, too much or too often admire his wonderful powers of mind, when we consider that the principal store of wit and wisdom which this Work contains, was not a particular selection from his general conversation, but was merely his occasional talk at such times as I had the good fortune to be in his company; and, without doubt, if his discourse at other periods had been collected with the same attention, the whole tenor of what he uttered would have been found equally excellent.

His strong, clear, and animated enforcement of religion, morality, loyalty, and subordination, while it delights and improves the wise and the good, will, I trust, prove an effectual antidote to that detestable sophistry which has been lately imported from France, under the false name of Philosophy, and with a malignant industry has been employed against the peace, good order, and happiness of society, in our free and prosperous country; but thanks be to GOD, without producing the pernicious effects which were hoped for by its propagators.

It seems to me, in my moments of self-complacency, that this extensive biographical work, however inferior in its nature, may in one respect be assimilated to the ODYSSEY. Amidst a thousand entertaining and instructive episodes the HERO is never long out of sight; for they are all in some degree connected with him; and HE, in the whole course of the History, is exhibited by the Author for the best advantage of his readers.

'— Quid virtus et quid sapientia possit,
Utile proposuit nobis exemplar Ulyssen.'[1]
Should there be any cold-blooded and morose mortals who really

---

[1] ['Of the power of virtue and of wisdom he has given us a profitable example in Ulysses.' Horace, *Ep*. i. ii. 17. (Wickham.)]

7

dislike this Book, I will give them a story to apply. When the great
Duke of Marlborough, *accompanied by* Lord Cadogan, *was one
day reconnoitering the army in Flanders, a heavy rain came on, and
they both called for their cloaks.* Lord Cadogan's *servant, a good
humoured alert lad, brought his Lordship's in a minute. The Duke's
servant, a lazy sulky dog, was so sluggish, that his Grace being wet
to the skin, reproved him, and had for answer with a grunt, 'I came
as fast as I could,' upon which the Duke calmly said,* 'Cadogan, I
would not for a thousand pounds have that fellow's temper.'

*There are some men, I believe, who have, or think they have, a very
small share of vanity. Such may speak of their literary fame in a
decorous style of diffidence. But I confess, that I am so formed by
nature and by habit, that to restrain the effusion of delight, on having
obtained such fame, to me would be truly painful. Why then should
I suppress it? Why 'out of the abundance of the heart' should I not
speak? Let me then mention with a warm, but no insolent exultation,
that I have been regaled with spontaneous praise of my work by
many and various persons eminent for their rank, learning, talents
and accomplishments; much of which praise I have under their hands
to be reposited in my archives at* Auchinleck. *An honourable and
reverend friend*[1] *speaking of the favourable reception of my volumes,
even in the circles of fashion and elegance, said to me, 'you have made
them all talk Johnson,'—Yes, I may add, I have* Johnsonised *the
land; and I trust they will not only* talk, *but* think, *Johnson.*

*To enumerate those to whom I have been thus indebted, would be
tediously ostentatious. I cannot however but name one whose praise
is truly valuable, not only on account of his knowledge and abilities,
but on account of the magnificent, yet dangerous embassy, in which
he is now employed, which makes every thing that relates to him
peculiarly interesting.* Lord MACARTNEY *favoured me with his own
copy of my book, with a number of notes, of which I have availed
myself. On the first leaf I found in his Lordship's hand-writing, an
inscription of such high commendation, that even I, vain as I am,
cannot prevail on myself to publish it.* [*July* 1, 1793.]

---

[1] [Probably the Hon. and Rev. William Stuart. *Hill.*]

8

ADVERTISEMENT TO THE THIRD EDITION

Several valuable letters, and other curious matter, having been communicated to the Author too late to be arranged in that chronological order which he had endeavoured uniformly to observe in his work, he was obliged to introduce them in his Second Edition, by way of ADDENDA, as commodiously as he could. In the present edition these have been distributed in their proper places. In revising his volumes for a new edition, he had pointed out where some of these materials should be inserted; but unfortunately in the midst of his labours, he was seized with a fever, of which, to the great regret of all his friends, he died on the 19th of May, 1795. All the Notes that he had written in the margin of the copy which he had in part revised, are here faithfully preserved; and a few new Notes have been added, principally by some of those friends to whom the Author in the former editions acknowledged his obligations. Those subscribed with the letter B, were communicated by Dr. Burney: those to which the letters J B are annexed, by the Rev. J. Blakeway, of Shrewsbury, to whom Mr. Boswell acknowledged himself indebted for some judicious remarks on the first edition of his work: and the letters J B—O. are annexed to some remarks furnished by the Author's second son, a Student of Brazen-Nose College in Oxford. Some valuable observations were communicated by James Bindley, Esq. First Commissioner in the Stamp-Office, which have been acknowledged in their proper places. For all those without any signature, Mr. Malone is answerable.— Every new remark, not written by the Author, for the sake of distinction has been enclosed within crotchets: in one instance, however, the printer by mistake has affixed this mark to a note relative to the Rev. Thomas Fysche Palmer, which was written by Mr. Boswell, and therefore ought not to have been thus distinguished.

I have only to add, that the proof-sheets of the present edition not having passed through my hands, I am not answerable for any typographical errours that may be found in it. Having, however, been printed at the very accurate press of Mr. Baldwin, I make no doubt it will be found not less perfect than the former edition; the greatest care having been taken, by correctness and elegance to do justice to one of the most instructive and entertaining works in the English language.—*April* 8, 1799.   EDMOND MALONE.

9

A CHRONOLOGICAL CATALOGUE OF THE
PROSE WORKS[1] OF SAMUEL JOHNSON, LL.D.

[N.B. To those which he himself acknowledged is added *acknowl*. To those which may be fully believed to be his from internal evidence, is added *intern. evid.*]

1735. ABRIDGEMENT and translation of Lobo's Voyage to Abyssinia. *acknowl.*

1738. Part of a translation of Father Paul Sarpi's History of the Council of Trent. *acknowl.*

[N.B. As this work after some sheets were printed, suddenly stopped, I know not whether any part of it is now to be found.]

For the Gentleman's Magazine.

Preface. *intern. evid.*

Life of Father Paul. *acknowl.*

1739. A complete vindication of the Licenser of the Stage from the malicious and scandalous aspersions of Mr. Brooke, authour of Gustavus Vasa. *acknowl.*

Marmor Norfolciense: or, an Essay on an ancient prophetical inscription in monkish rhyme, lately discovered near Lynne in Norfolk; by PROBUS BRITANNICUS. *acknowl.*

For the Gentleman's Magazine.

Life of Boerhaave. *acknowl.*

Address to the Reader. *intern. evid.*

Appeal to the Publick in behalf of the Editor. *intern. evid.*

Considerations on the case of Dr. Trapp's Sermons; · a plausible attempt to prove that an authour's work may be abridged without injuring his property. *acknowl.*

1740. *For the Gentleman's Magazine.*

Preface. *intern. evid.*

Life of Admiral Drake. *acknowl.*

Life of Admiral Blake. *acknowl.*

Life of Philip Barretier. *acknowl.*

Essay on Epitaphs. *acknowl.*

[1] I do not here include his Poetical Works; for, excepting his Latin Translation of Pope's *Messiah*, his *London*, and his *Vanity of Human Wishes* imitated from *Juvenal;* his Prologue on the opening of Drury-Lane Theatre by Mr. Garrick, and his *Irene*, a Tragedy, they are very numerous, and in general short; and I have promised a complete edition of them, in which I shall with the utmost care ascertain their authenticity, and illustrate them with notes and various readings.

1741.   *For the Gentleman's Magazine.*

Preface. *intern. evid.*

A free translation of the Jests of Hierocles, with an introduction. *intern. evid.*

Debate on the *Humble Petition and Advice* of the Rump Parliament to Cromwell in 1657, to assume the Title of King; abridged, methodized and digested. *intern. evid.*

Translation of Abbé Guyon's Dissertation on the Amazons. *intern. evid.*

Translation of Fontenelle's Panegyrick on Dr. Morin. *intern. evid.*

1742.   *For the Gentleman's Magazine.*

Preface. *intern. evid.*

Essay on the Account of the Conduct of the Duchess of Marlborough. *acknowl.*

An Account of the Life of Peter Burman. *acknowl.*

The Life of Sydenham, afterwards prefixed to Dr. Swan's Edition of his Works. *acknowl.*

Proposals for printing Bibliotheca Harleiana, or a Catalogue of the Library of the Earl of Oxford, afterwards prefixed to the first Volume of that Catalogue, in which the Latin Accounts of the Books were written by him. *acknowl.*

Abridgement intitled, Foreign History, *intern. evid.*

Essay on the Description of China, from the French of Du Halde. *intern. evid.*

1743. Dedication to Dr. Mead of Dr. James's Medicinal Dictionary. *intern. evid.*

                    For the Gentleman's Magazine.

Preface. *intern. evid.*

Parliamentary Debates under the Name of Debates in the Senate of Lilliput, from Nov. 19, 1740, to Feb. 23, 1742–3, inclusive. *acknowl.*

Considerations on the Dispute between Crousaz and Warburton on Pope's Essay on Man. *intern. evid.*

A Letter announcing that the Life of Mr. Savage was speedily to be published by a person who was favoured with his Confidence. *intern. evid.*

Advertisement for Osborne concerning the Harleian Catalogue. *intern. evid.*

1744. Life of Richard Savage. *acknowl.*

Preface to the Harleian Miscellany, *acknowl.*

                    For the Gentleman's Magazine.

Preface. *intern. evid.*

1745. Miscellaneous Observations on the Tragedy of Macbeth, with

1745.   remarks on Sir T. H.'s (Sir Thomas Hanmer's) Edition of Shak-speare, and proposals for a new Edition of that Poet. *acknowl.*

1747.   Plan for a Dictionary of the ENGLISH LANGUAGE, addressed to Philip Dormer, Earl of Chesterfield. *acknowl.*

1748.   *For the Gentleman's Magazine.*
        Life of Roscommon. *acknowl.*
        Foreign History, November. *intern. evid.*

                    For Dodsley's PRECEPTOR.
        Preface. *acknowl.*
        Vision of Theodore the Hermit. *acknowl.*

1750.   The RAMBLER, the first Paper of which was published 20th of March this year, and the last 17th of March 1752, the day on which Mrs. Johnson died. *acknowl.*

        Letter in the General Advertiser to excite the attention of the Publick to the Performance of Comus, which was next day to be acted at Drury-Lane Playhouse for the Benefit of Milton's Granddaughter. *acknowl.*

        Preface and Postscript to Lauder's Pamphlet intitled, 'An Essay on Milton's Use and Imitation of the Moderns in his Paradise Lost.' *acknowl.*

1751.   Life of Cheynel in the Miscellany called 'The Student.' *acknowl.*

        Letter for Lauder, addressed to the Reverend Dr. John Douglas, acknowledging his Fraud concerning Milton in Terms of suitable Contrition. *acknowl.*

        Dedication to the Earl of Middlesex of Mrs. Charlotte Lennox's 'Female Quixote.' *intern. evid.*

1753.   Dedication to John Earl of Orrery, of Shakspeare Illustrated, by Mrs. Charlotte Lennox. *acknowl.*

        During this and the following year he wrote and gave to his much loved friend Dr. Bathurst the Papers in the Adventurer, signed T. *acknowl.*

1754.   Life of Edw. Cave in the Gentleman's Magazine. *acknowl.*

1755.   A DICTIONARY, with a Grammar and History, of the ENGLISH LANGUAGE. *acknowl.*

        An Account of an Attempt to ascertain the Longitude at Sea, by an exact Theory of the Variations of the Magnetical Needle, with a Table of the Variations at the most remarkable Cities in Europe from the year 1660 to 1680. *acknowl.* This he wrote for Mr. Zachariah Williams, an ingenious ancient Welch Gentleman, father of Mrs. Anna Williams whom he for many years kindly lodged in his House. It was published with a Translation into Italian by Signor Baretti. In a Copy of it which he presented to the Bodleian Library at Oxford, is pasted a Character of the late Mr. Zachariah Williams, plainly written by Johnson. *intern. evid.*

1756. An Abridgement of his Dictionary. *acknowl.*

Several Essays in the Universal Visitor, which there is some difficulty in ascertaining. All that are marked with two Asterisks have been ascribed to him, although I am confident from internal Evidence, that we should except from these 'The Life of Chaucer,' 'Reflections on the State of Portugal,' and 'An Essay on Architecture:' And from the same Evidence I am confident that he wrote 'Further Thoughts on Agriculture,' and 'A Dissertation on the State of Literature and Authours.' The Dissertation on the Epitaphs written by Pope he afterwards acknowledged, and added to his 'Idler.'

Life of Sir Thomas Browne prefixed to a new Edition of his Christian Morals. *acknowl.*

In the Literary Magazine; or, Universal Review, which began in January 1756.

His *Original Essays* are

Preliminary Address. *intern. evid.*

An introduction to the Political State of Great Britain. *intern. evid.*

Remarks on the Militia Bill. *intern. evid.*

Observations on his Britannick Majesty's Treaties with the Empress of Russia and the Landgrave of Hesse Cassel. *intern. evid.*

Observations on the Present State of Affairs. *intern. evid.*

Memoirs of Frederick III. King of Prussia. *intern. evid.*

In the same Magazine his Reviews are of the following Books:

'Birch's History of the Royal Society.'—'Browne's Christian Morals.'—'Warton's Essay on the Writings and Genius of Pope, Vol. I.'—'Hampton's Translation of Polybius.'—'Sir Isaac Newton's Arguments in Proof of a Deity.'—'Borlase's History of the Isles of Scilly.'—'Home's Experiments on Bleaching.'—'Browne's History of Jamaica.'—'Hales on Distilling Sea Water, Ventilators in Ships, and curing an ill Taste in Milk.'—'Lucas's Essay on Waters.'—'Keith's Catalogue of the Scottish Bishops.'—'Philosophical Transactions, Vol. XLIX.'—'Miscellanies by Elizabeth Harrison.'—'Evans's Map and Account of the Middle Colonies in America.'—'The Cadet, a Military Treatise.'—'The Conduct of the Ministry relating to the present War impartially examined.' *intern. evid.*

'Mrs. Lennox's Translation of Sully's Memoirs.'—'Letter on the Case of Admiral Byng.'—'Appeal to the People concerning Admiral Byng.'—'Hanway's Eight Days' Journey, and Essay on Tea.'—'Some further Particulars in Relation to the Case of Admiral Byng, by a Gentleman of Oxford.' *acknowl.*

Mr. Jonas Hanway having written an angry Answer to the Review

1756. of his Essay on Tea, Johnson in the same Collection made a Reply to it. *acknowl.* This is the only Instance, it is believed, when he condescended to take Notice of any Thing that had been written against him; and here his chief Intention seems to have been to make Sport.

Dedication to the Earl of Rochford of, and Preface to, Mr. Payne's Introduction to the Game of Draughts. *acknowl.*

Introduction to the London Chronicle, an Evening Paper which still subsists with deserved credit. *acknowl.*

1757. Speech on the Subject of an Address to the Throne after the Expedition to Rochefort; delivered by one of his Friends in some publick Meeting: it is printed in the Gentleman's Magazine for October 1785. *intern. evid.*

The first two Paragraphs of the Preface to Sir William Chambers's Designs of Chinese Buildings, &c. *acknowl.*

1758. THE IDLER, which began April 5, in this year, and was continued till April 5, 1760. *acknowl.*

An Essay on the Bravery of the English Common Soldiers was added to it when published in Volumes. *acknowl.*

1759. Rasselas Prince of Abyssinia, a Tale. *acknowl.*

Advertisement for the Proprietors of the Idler against certain Persons who pirated those Papers as they came out singly in a Newspaper called the Universal Chronicle or Weekly Gazette. *intern. evid.*

For Mrs. Charlotte Lennox's English Version of Brumoy,—'A Dissertation on the Greek Comedy,' and the General Conclusion of the Book. *intern. evid.*

Introduction to the World Displayed, a Collection of Voyages and Travels. *acknowl.*

Three Letters in the Gazetteer, concerning the best plan for Blackfriars Bridge. *acknowl.*

1760. Address of the Painters to George III. on his Accession to the Throne. *intern. evid.*

Dedication of Baretti's Italian and English Dictionary to the Marquis of Abreu, then Envoy-Extraordinary from Spain at the Court of Great-Britain. *intern. evid.*

Review in the Gentleman's Magazine of Mr. Tytler's acute and able Vindication of Mary Queen of Scots. *acknowl.*

Introduction to the Proceedings of the Committee for Cloathing the French Prisoners. *acknowl.*

1761. Preface to Rolt's Dictionary of Trade and Commerce. *acknowl.*

Corrections and Improvements for Mr. Gwyn the Architect's Pamphlet, intitled 'Thoughts on the Coronation of George III.' *acknowl.*

1762. Dedication to the King of the Reverend Dr. Kennedy's Complete System of Astronomical Chronology, unfolding the Scriptures, Quarto Edition. *acknowl.*

1762. Concluding Paragraph of that Work. *intern. evid.*
Preface to the Catalogue of the Artists' Exhibition. *intern. evid.*
1763. Character of Collins in the Poetical Calendar, published by Fawkes and Woty. *acknowl.*
Dedication to the Earl of Shaftesbury of the Edition of Roger Ascham's English Works, published by the Reverend Mr. Bennet. *acknowl.*
The Life of Ascham, also prefixed to that edition. *acknowl.*
Review of Telemachus, a Masque, by the Reverend George Graham of Eton College, in the Critical Review. *acknowl.*
Dedication to the Queen of Mr. Hoole's Translation of Tasso. *acknowl.*
Account of the Detection of the Imposture of the Cock-Lane Ghost, published in the Newspapers and Gentleman's Magazine. *acknowl.*
1764. Part of a Review of Grainger's 'Sugar Cane, a Poem,' in the London Chronicle. *acknowl.*
Review of Goldsmith's Traveller, a Poem, in the Critical Review.
1765. The Plays of William Shakspeare, in eight volumes, 8vo. with Notes. *acknowl.*
1766. The Fountains, a Fairy Tale, in Mrs. Williams's Miscellanies. *acknowl.*
1767. Dedication to the King of Mr. Adam's Treatise on the Globes. *acknowl.*
1769. Character of the Reverend Mr. Zachariah Mudge, in the London Chronicle. *acknowl.*
1770. The False Alarm. *acknowl.*
1771. Thoughts on the late Transactions respecting Falkland's Islands. *acknowl.*
1772. Defence of a Schoolmaster; dictated to me for the House of Lords. *acknowl.*
Argument in Support of the Law of *Vicious Intromission;* dictated to me for the Court of Session in Scotland. *acknowl.*
1773. Preface to Macbean's 'Dictionary of Ancient Geography.' *acknowl.*
Argument in Favour of the Rights of Lay Patrons; dictated to me for the General Assembly of the Church of Scotland. *acknowl.*
1774. The Patriot. *acknowl.*
1775. A Journey to the Western Islands of Scotland. *acknowl.*
Proposals for publishing the Works of Mrs. Charlotte Lennox, in Three Volumes Quarto. *acknowl.*
Preface to Baretti's Easy Lessons in Italian and English. *intern. evid.*
Taxation no Tyranny; an Answer to the Resolutions and Address of the American Congress. *acknowl.*
Argument on the Case of Dr. Memis; dictated to me for the Court of Session in Scotland. *acknowl.*

15

1775. Argument to prove that the Corporation of Stirling was corrupt; dictated to me for the House of Lords. *acknowl.*

1776. Argument in Support of the Right of immediate, and personal reprehension from the Pulpit; dictated to me. *acknowl.*

Proposals for publishing an Analysis of the Scotch Celtick Language, by the Reverend William Shaw. *acknowl*

1777. Dedication to the King of the Posthumous Works of Dr. Pearce, Bishop of Rochester. *acknowl.*

Additions to the Life and Character of that Prelate; prefixed to those Works. *acknowl.*

Various Papers and Letters in Favour of the Reverend Dr. Dodd. *acknowl.*

1780. Advertisement for his Friend Mr. Thrale to the Worthy Electors of the Borough of Southwark. *acknowl.*

The first Paragraph of Mr. Thomas Davies's Life of Garrick, *acknowl.*

1781. Prefaces Biographical and Critical to the Works of the most eminent English Poets; afterwards published with the Title of Lives of the English Poets. *acknowl.*

Argument on the Importance of the Registration of Deeds; dictated to me for an Election Committee of the House of Commons. *acknowl.*

On the Distinction between TORY and WHIG; dictated to me. *acknowl.*

On Vicarious Punishments, and the great Propitiation for the Sins of the World, by JESUS CHRIST; dictated to me. *acknowl.*

Argument in favour of Joseph Knight, an African Negro, who claimed his Liberty in the Court of Session in Scotland, and obtained it; dictated to me. *acknowl.*

Defence of Mr. Robertson, Printer of the Caledonian Mercury, against the Society of Procurators in Edinburgh, for having inserted in his Paper a ludicrous Paragraph against them; demonstrating that it was not an injurious Libel; dictated to me. *acknowl.*

1782. The greatest part, if not the whole, of a Reply, by the Reverend Mr. Shaw, to a Person at Edinburgh, of the Name of Clark, refuting his arguments for the authenticity of the Poems published by Mr. James Macpherson as Translations from Ossian. *intern. evid.*

1784. List of the Authours of the Universal History, deposited in the British Museum, and printed in the Gentleman's Magazine for December, this year. *acknowl.*

Various Years.

Letters to Mrs. Thrale. *acknowl.*

Prayers and Meditations, which he delivered to the Rev. Mr. Strahan, enjoining him to publish them. *acknowl.*

Sermons *left for Publication* by John Taylor, LL.D., Prebendary of Westminster, and given to the World by the Reverend Samuel Hayes, A.M. *intern. evid.*

16

Such was the number and variety of the Prose Works of this extraordinary man, which I have been able to discover, and am at liberty to mention; but we ought to keep in mind, that there must undoubtedly have been many more which are yet concealed; and we may add to the account, the numerous Letters which he wrote, of which a considerable part are yet unpublished. It is hoped that those persons in whose possession they are, will favour the world with them.

JAMES BOSWELL.

> 'After my death I wish no other herald,
> 'No other speaker of my living actions,
> 'To keep mine honour from corruption,
> 'But such an honest chronicler as Griffith.'[1]
>
> SHAKSPEARE, *Henry VIII. [Act IV. Sc. 2.]*

[1] See Dr. Johnson's letter to Mrs. Thrale, dated Ostick in Skie, September 30, 1773:—'Boswell writes a regular Journal of our travels, which I think contains as much of what I say and do, as of all other occurrences together; "*for such a faithful chronicler* is *Griffith.*" '

THE LIFE OF
SAMUEL JOHNSON, LL.D.

To write the Life of him who excelled all mankind in writing the lives of others, and who, whether we consider his extraordinary endowments, or his various works, has been equalled by few in any age, is an arduous, and may be reckoned in me a presumptuous task.

Had Dr. Johnson written his own life, in conformity with the opinion which he has given,[1] that every man's life may be best written by himself; had he employed in the preservation of his own history, that clearness of narration and elegance of language in which he has embalmed so many eminent persons, the world would probably have had the most perfect example of biography that was ever exhibited. But although he at different times, in a desultory manner, committed to writing many particulars of the progress of his mind and fortunes, he never had persevering diligence enough to form them into a regular composition. Of these memorials a few have been preserved; but the greater part was consigned by him to the flames, a few days before his death.

As I had the honour and happiness of enjoying his friendship for upwards of twenty years; as I had the scheme of writing his life constantly in view; as he was well apprised of this circumstance, and from time to time obligingly satisfied my inquiries, by communicating to me the incidents of his early years; as I acquired a facility in recollecting, and was very assiduous in recording, his conversation, of which the extraordinary vigour and vivacity constituted one of the first features of his character; and as I have spared no pains in obtaining materials concerning him, from every quarter where I could discover that they were to be found, and have been favoured with the most liberal communications by his friends; I flatter myself that few biographers have entered upon such a work as this, with more advantages; independent of literary abilities, in which I am not

[1] *Idler*, No. 84.

vain enough to compare myself with some great names who have gone before me in this kind of writing.

Since my work was announced, several Lives and Memoirs of Dr. Johnson have been published, the most voluminous of which is one compiled for the booksellers of London, by Sir John Hawkins, Knight,[1] a man, whom, during my long intimacy with Dr. Johnson, I never saw in his company, I think but once, and I am sure not above twice. Johnson might have esteemed him for his decent, religious demeanour, and his knowledge of books and literary history; but from the rigid formality of his manners, it is evident that they never could have lived together with companionable ease and familiarity; nor had Sir John Hawkins that nice perception which was necessary to mark the finer and less obvious parts of Johnson's character. His being appointed one of his executors, gave him an opportunity of taking possession of such fragments of a diary and other papers as were left; of which, before delivering them up to the residuary legatee, whose property they were, he endeavoured to extract the substance. In this he has not been very successful, as I have found upon a perusal of those papers, which have been since transferred to me. Sir John Hawkins's ponderous labours, I must acknowledge, exhibit a *farrago*, of which a considerable portion is not devoid of entertainment to the lovers of literary gossiping; but besides its being swelled out with long unnecessary extracts from various works (even one of several leaves from Osborne's Harleian Catalogue, and those not compiled by Johnson, but by Oldys), a very small part of it relates to the person who is

[1] The greatest part of this book was written while Sir John Hawkins was alive; and I avow, that one object of my strictures was to make him feel some compunction for his illiberal treatment of Dr. Johnson. Since his decease, I have suppressed several of my remarks upon his work. But though I would not 'war with the dead' *offensively*, I think it necessary to be strenuous in *defence* of my illustrious friend, which I cannot be without strong animadversions upon a writer who has greatly injured him. Let me add, that though I doubt I should not have been very prompt to gratify Sir John Hawkins with any compliment in his life-time, I do now frankly acknowledge, that, in my opinion, his volume, however inadequate and improper as a life of Dr. Johnson, and however discredited by unpardonable inaccuracies in other respects, contains a collection of curious anecdotes and observations, which few men but its author could have brought together.

the subject of the book; and, in that, there is such an inaccuracy in the statement of facts, as in so solemn an authour is hardly excusable, and certainly makes his narrative very unsatisfactory. But what is still worse, there is throughout the whole of it a dark uncharitable cast, by which the most unfavourable construction is put upon almost every circumstance in the character and conduct of my illustrious friend; who, I trust, will, by a true and fair delineation, be vindicated both from the injurious misrepresentations of this authour, and from the slighter aspersions of a lady who once lived in great intimacy with him.[1]

There is, in the British Museum, a letter from Bishop Warburton to Dr. Birch, on the subject of biography; which, though I am aware it may expose me to a charge of artfully raising the value of my own work, by contrasting it with that of which I have spoken, is so well conceived and expressed, that I cannot refrain from here inserting it:—

'I shall endeavour, (says Dr. Warburton,) to give you what satisfaction I can in any thing you want to be satisfied in on ye subject of Milton, and am extremely glad you intend to write his life. Almost all the life-writers we have had before Toland and Desmaiseaux, are indeed strange insipid creatures; and yet I had rather read the worst of them, than be obliged to go through with this of Milton's, or the other's life of Boileau, where there is such a dull, heavy succession of long quotations of disinteresting passages, that it makes their method quite nauseous. But the verbose, tasteless Frenchman seems to lay it down as a principle, that every life must be a book, and what's worse, it proves a book without a life; for what do we know of Boileau, after all his tedious stuff? You are the only one, (and I speak it without a compliment) that by the vigour of your stile and sentiments, and the real importance of your materials, have the art, (which one would imagine no one could have missed,) of adding agreements to the most agreeable subject in the world, which is literary history.'[2]

'Nov. 24, 1737.'

[1] [Mrs. Thrale.]
[2] Brit. Mus. 4320, Ayscough's Catal., Sloane MSS.

21

Instead of melting down my materials into one mass, and constantly speaking in my own person, by which I might have appeared to have more merit in the execution of the work, I have resolved to adopt and enlarge upon the excellent plan of Mr. Mason, in his Memoirs of Gray. Wherever narrative is necessary to explain, connect, and supply, I furnish it to the best of my abilities; but in the chronological series of Johnson's life, which I trace as distinctly as I can, year by year, I produce, wherever it is in my power, his own minutes, letters or conversation, being convinced that this mode is more lively, and will make my readers better acquainted with him, than even most of those were who actually knew him, but could know him only partially; whereas there is here an accumulation of intelligence from various points, by which his character is more fully understood and illustrated.

Indeed I cannot conceive a more perfect mode of writing any man's life, than not only relating all the most important events of it in their order, but interweaving what he privately wrote, and said, and thought; by which mankind are enabled as it were to see him live, and to 'live o'er each scene' with him, as he actually advanced through the several stages of his life. Had his other friends been as diligent and ardent as I was, he might have been almost entirely preserved. As it is, I will venture to say that he will be seen in this work more completely than any man who has ever yet lived.

And he will be seen as he really was; for I profess to write, not his panegyrick, which must be all praise, but his Life; which, great and good as he was, must not be supposed to be entirely perfect. To be as he was, is indeed subject of panegyrick enough to any man in this state of being; but in every picture there should be shade as well as light, and when I delineate him without reserve, I do what he himself recommended, both by his precept and his example.

'If the biographer writes from personal knowledge, and makes haste to gratify the publick curiosity, there is danger lest his interest, his fear, his gratitude, or his tenderness overpower his fidelity, and tempt him to conceal, if not to invent. There are many who think it an act of piety to hide the faults or failings of their friends, even when they can no longer suffer by their detection; we therefore see whole ranks of characters adorned with uniform panegyrick, and not to be known from one another but by extrinsick and casual circumstances. "Let me remember, (says Hale,) when I find myself inclined to pity a criminal, that there is likewise a pity due to the country." If we owe regard to the memory of the dead, there is yet more respect to be paid to knowledge, to virtue and to truth.'[1]

What I consider as the peculiar value of the following work, is, the quantity that it contains of Johnson's conversation; which is universally acknowledged to have been eminently instructive and entertaining; and of which the specimens that I have given upon a former occasion, have been received with so much approbation, that I have good grounds for supposing that the world will not be indifferent to more ample communications of a similar nature.

That the conversation of a celebrated man, if his talents have been exerted in conversation, will best display his character, is, I trust, too well established in the judgment of mankind, to be at all shaken by a sneering observation of Mr. Mason, in his *Memoirs of Mr. William Whitehead*, in which there is literally no *Life*, but a mere dry narrative of facts. I do not think it was quite necessary to attempt a depreciation of what is universally esteemed, because it was not to be found in the immediate object of the ingenious writer's pen; for in truth, from a man so still and so tame, as to be contented to pass many years as the domestick companion of a superannuated lord and lady,[2] conversation worth recording could no more be expected, than from a Chinese mandarin on a chimney-piece, or the fantastick figures on a gilt leather skreen.

If authority be required, let us appeal to Plutarch, the prince of ancient biographers. Οὔτε ταῖς ἐπιφανεστάταις πράξεσι πάντως ἔνεστι δήλωσις ἀρετῆς ἢ κακίας, ἀλλὰ πρᾶγμα βραχὺ πολλάκις, καὶ ῥῆμα, καὶ παιδιά τις ἔμφασιν ἤθους ἐποίησεν μᾶλλον ἢ μάχαι

[1] *Rambler*, No. 60.
[2] [William, 3rd Earl of Jersey and his wife. *Croker.*[2]]

23

μυριόνεκροι, καὶ παρατάξεις αἱ μέγισται, καὶ πολιορκίαι πόλεων. 'Nor is it always in the most distinguished atchievements that men's virtues or vices may be best discerned; but very often an action of small note, a short saying, or a jest, shall distinguish a person's real character more than the greatest sieges, or the most important battles.'[1]

To this may be added the sentiments of the very man whose life I am about to exhibit.

'The business of the biographer is often to pass slightly over those performances and incidents which produce vulgar greatness, to lead the thoughts into domestick privacies, and display the minute details of daily life, where exteriour appendages are cast aside, and men excel each other only by prudence and by virtue. The account of Thuanus is with great propriety said by its authour to have been written, that it might lay open to posterity the private and familiar character of that man, *cujus ingenium et candorem ex ipsius scriptis sunt olim semper miraturi*, whose candour and genius will to the end of time be by his writings preserved in admiration.

'There are many invisible circumstances, which whether we read as enquirers after natural or moral knowledge, whether we intend to enlarge our science, or increase our virtue, are more important than publick occurrences. Thus Sallust, the great master of nature, has not forgot in his account of Catiline to remark, that his walk was now quick, and again slow, as an indication of a mind revolving with violent commotion. Thus the story of Melancthon affords a striking lecture on the value of time, by informing us, that when he had made an appointment, he expected not only the hour, but the minute to be fixed, that the day might not run out in the idleness of suspence; and all the plans and enterprises of De Wit are now of less importance to the world than that part of his personal character, which represents him as careful of his health, and negligent of his life.

'But biography has often been allotted to writers, who seem very little acquainted with the nature of their task, or very negligent about the performance. They rarely afford any other account

[1] Plutarch's *Life of Alexander*, Langhorne's Translation.

than might be collected from publick papers, but imagine themselves writing a life, when they exhibit a chronological series of actions or preferments; and have so little regard to the manners or behaviour of their heroes, that more knowledge may be gained of a man's real character, by a short conversation with one of his servants, than from a formal and studied narrative, begun with his pedigree, and ended with his funeral.

'There are, indeed, some natural reasons why these narratives are often written by such as were not likely to give much instruction or delight, and why most accounts of particular persons are barren and useless. If a life be delayed till interest and envy are at an end, we may hope for impartiality, but must expect little intelligence; for the incidents which give excellence to biography are of a volatile and evanescent kind, such as soon escape the memory, and are transmitted by tradition. We know how few can pourtray a living acquaintance, except by his most prominent and observable particularities, and the grosser features of his mind; and it may be easily imagined how much of this little knowledge may be lost in imparting it, and how soon a succession of copies will lose all resemblance of the original.'[1]

I am fully aware of the objections which may be made to the minuteness on some occasions of my detail of Johnson's conversation, and how happily it is adapted for the petty exercise of ridicule, by men of superficial understanding and ludicrous fancy; but I remain firm and confident in my opinion, that minute particulars are frequently characteristick, and always amusing, when they relate to a distinguished man. I am therefore exceedingly unwilling that any thing, however slight, which my illustrious friend thought it worth his while to express, with any degree of point, should perish. For this almost superstitious reverence, I have found very old and venerable authority, quoted by our great modern prelate, Secker, in whose tenth sermon there is the following passage:

'*Rabbi David Kimchi*, a noted Jewish Commentator, who lived above five hundred years ago, explains that passage in the first Psalm, *His leaf also shall not wither*, from Rabbins yet older than

[1] *Rambler*, No. 60.

25

himself, thus: That *even the idle talk*, so he expresses it, *of a good man ought to be regarded;* the most superfluous things he saith are always of some value. And other ancient authours have the same phrase, nearly in the same sense.'

Of one thing I am certain, that considering how highly the small portion which we have of the table-talk and other anecdotes of our celebrated writers is valued, and how earnestly it is regretted that we have not more, I am justified in preserving rather too many of Johnson's sayings, than too few; especially as from the diversity of dispositions it cannot be known with certainty beforehand, whether what may seem trifling to some, and perhaps to the collector himself, may not be most agreeable to many; and the greater number that an authour can please in any degree, the more pleasure does there arise to a benevolent mind.

To those who are weak enough to think this a degrading task, and the time and labour which have been devoted to it misemployed, I shall content myself with opposing the authority of the greatest man of any age, JULIUS CÆSAR, of whom Bacon observes, that 'in his book of Apothegms which he collected, we see that he esteemed it more honour to make himself but a pair of tables, to take the wise and pithy words of others, than to have every word of his own to be made an apothegm or an oracle.'[1]

Having said thus much by way of introduction, I commit the following pages to the candour of the Publick.

SAMUEL JOHNSON was born at Lichfield, in Staffordshire, on the 18th of September, N.S., 1709; and his initiation into the Christian Church was not delayed; for his baptism is recorded, in the register of St. Mary's parish in that city, to have been performed on the day of his birth. His father is there stiled *Gentleman*, a circumstance of which an ignorant panegyrist has praised him for not being proud; when the truth is, that the appellation of Gentleman, though now lost in the indiscriminate assumption of *Esquire*, was commonly taken by those who could not boast of gentility. His father was Michael Johnson, a native

[1] Bacon's *Advancement of Learning*, Book I.

of Derbyshire, of obscure extraction, who settled in Lichfield as a bookseller and stationer. His mother was Sarah Ford, descended of an ancient race of substantial yeomanry in Warwickshire. They were well advanced in years when they married, and never had more than two children, both sons; Samuel, their first born, who lived to be the illustrious character whose various excellence I am to endeavour to record, and Nathanael, who died in his twenty-fifth year.

Mr. Michael Johnson was a man of a large and robust body, and of a strong and active mind; yet, as in the most solid rocks veins of unsound substance are often discovered, there was in him a mixture of that disease, the nature of which eludes the most minute enquiry, though the effects are well known to be a weariness of life, an unconcern about those things which agitate the greater part of mankind, and a general sensation of gloomy wretchedness. From him then his son inherited, with some other qualities, 'a vile melancholy,' which in his too strong expression of any disturbance of the mind, 'made him mad all his life, at least not sober.'[1] Michael was, however, forced by the narrowness of his circumstances to be very diligent in business, not only in his shop, but by occasionally resorting to several towns in the neighbourhood,[2] some of which were at a considerable distance from Lichfield. At that time booksellers' shops in the provincial towns of England were very rare, so that there was not one even in Birmingham, in which town old Mr. Johnson used to open a shop every market-day. He was a pretty good Latin scholar, and a citizen so creditable as to be made one of the magistrates of Lichfield; and, being a man of good sense, and skill in his trade, he acquired a reasonable share of wealth, of

---

[1] *Journal of a Tour to the Hebrides*, 3rd edit. p. 213 [Sept. 16].

[2] Extract of a letter, dated 'Trentham, St. Peter's day, 1716,' written by the Rev. George Plaxton, Chaplain at that time to Lord Gower, which may serve to show the high estimation in which the Father of our great Moralist was held: 'Johnson, the Litchfield Librarian, is now here; he propagates learning all over this diocese, and advanceth knowledge to its just height; all the Clergy here are his Pupils, and suck all they have from him; Allen cannot make a warrant without his precedent, nor our quondam John Evans draw a recognizance *sine directione Michaelis.' Gentleman's Magazine,* October, 1791.

which however he afterwards lost the greatest part, by engaging unsuccessfully in a manufacture of parchment. He was a zealous high-churchman and royalist, and retained his attachment to the unfortunate house of Stuart, though he reconciled himself, by casuistical arguments of expediency and necessity, to take the oaths imposed by the prevailing power.

There is a circumstance in his life somewhat romantick, but so well authenticated, that I shall not omit it. A young woman of Leek, in Staffordshire, while he served his apprenticeship there, conceived a violent passion for him; and though it met with no favourable return, followed him to Lichfield, where she took lodgings opposite to the house in which he lived, and indulged her hopeless flame. When he was informed that it so preyed upon her mind that her life was in danger, he with a generous humanity went to her and offered to marry her, but it was then too late: her vital power was exhausted; and she actually exhibited one of the very rare instances of dying for love. She was buried in the cathedral of Lichfield; and he, with a tender regard, placed a stone over her grave with this inscription:

Here lies the body of
Mrs. ELIZABETH BLANEY, a stranger.
She departed this life
20 of September, 1694.

Johnson's mother was a woman of distinguished under-standing. I asked his old school-fellow, Mr. Hector, surgeon, of Birmingham, if she was not vain of her son. He said, 'she had too much good sense to be vain, but she knew her son's value.' Her piety was not inferiour to her understanding; and to her must be ascribed those early impressions of religion upon the mind of her son, from which the world afterwards derived so much benefit. He told me, that he remembered distinctly having had the first notice of Heaven, 'a place to which good people went,' and hell, 'a place to which bad people went,' communicated to him by her, when a little child in bed with her; and that it might be the better fixed in his memory, she sent him to repeat it to Thomas Jackson, their man-servant; he not being in the way, this was not done; but there was no occasion for any artificial aid for its preservation.

In following so very eminent a man from his cradle to his grave, every minute particular, which can throw light on the progress of his mind, is interesting. That he was remarkable, even in his earliest years, may easily be supposed; for to use his own words in his Life of Sydenham,

'That the strength of his understanding, the accuracy of his discernment, and ardour of his curiosity, might have been remarked from his infancy, by a diligent observer, there is no reason to doubt. For, there is no instance of any man, whose history has been minutely related, that did not in every part of life discover the same proportion of intellectual vigour.'

In all such investigations it is certainly unwise to pay too much attention to incidents which the credulous relate with eager satisfaction, and the more scrupulous or witty enquirer considers only as topicks of ridicule: Yet there is a traditional story of the infant Hercules of toryism, so curiously characteristick, that I shall not withhold it. It was communicated to me in a letter from Miss Mary Adye, of Lichfield.

'When Dr. Sacheverel was at Lichfield, Johnson was not quite three years old. My grandfather Hammond observed him at the cathedral perched upon his father's shoulders, listening and gaping at the much celebrated preacher. Mr. Hammond asked Mr. Johnson how he could possibly think of bringing such an infant to church, and in the midst of so great a croud. He answered, because it was impossible to keep him at home; for, young as he was, he believed he had caught the publick spirit and zeal for Sacheverel, and would have staid for ever in the church, satisfied with beholding him.'

Nor can I omit a little instance of that jealous independence of spirit, and impetuosity of temper, which never forsook him. The fact was acknowledged to me by himself, upon the authority of his mother. One day, when the servant who used to be sent to school to conduct him home, had not come in time, he set out by himself, though he was then so near-sighted, that he was obliged to stoop down on his hands and knees to take a view of the kennel before he ventured to step over it. His school-mistress, afraid that he might miss his way, or fall into the kennel, or be run over by a cart, followed him at some distance. He happened to turn about and perceive her. Feeling her careful attention as an insult to his manliness, he ran back to her in a rage, and beat her, as well as his strength would permit.

Of the power of his memory, for which he was all his life eminent to a degree almost incredible, the following early instance was told me in his presence at Lichfield, in 1776, by his step-daughter, Mrs. Lucy Porter, as related to her by his mother. When he was a child in petticoats, and had learnt to read, Mrs. Johnson one morning put the common prayer-book into his hands, pointed to the collect for the day, and said, 'Sam, you must get this by heart.' She went up stairs, leaving him to study it: But by the time she had reached the second floor, she heard him following her. 'What's the matter?' said she. 'I can say it,' he replied; and repeated it distinctly, though he could not have read it over more than twice.

But there has been another story of his infant precocity generally circulated, and generally believed, the truth of which I am to refute upon his own authority. It is told,[1] that, when a child of three years old, he chanced to tread upon a duckling, the eleventh of a brood, and killed it; upon which, it is said, he dictated to his mother the following epitaph:

> 'Here lies good master duck,
>   Whom Samuel Johnson trod on;
> If it had liv'd, it had been *good luck*,
>   For then we'd had an *odd one*.'

There is surely internal evidence that this little composition combines in it, what no child of three years old could produce, without an extension of its faculties by immediate inspiration; yet Mrs. Lucy Porter, Dr. Johnson's step-daughter, positively maintained to me, in his presence, that there could be no doubt of the truth of this anecdote, for she had heard it from his mother. So difficult is it to obtain an authentick relation of facts, and such

[1] *Anecdotes of Dr. Johnson*, by Hester Lynch Piozzi, p. 11. *Life of Dr. Johnson*, by Sir John Hawkins, p. 6.

authority may there be for errour; for he assured me, that his father made the verses, and wished to pass them for his child's. He added, 'my father was a foolish old man; that is to say, foolish in talking of his children.'[1]

Young Johnson had the misfortune to be much afflicted with the scrophula, or king's evil, which disfigured a countenance naturally well formed, and hurt his visual nerves so much, that he did not see at all with one of his eyes, though its appearance was little different from that of the other. There is amongst his prayers, one inscribed *'When my* EYE *was restored to its use,'*[2] which ascertains a defect that many of his friends knew he had, though I never perceived it.[3] I supposed him to be only near-sighted; and indeed I must observe, that in no other respect could I discern any defect in his vision; on the contrary, the force of his attention and perceptive quickness made him see and distinguish all manner of objects, whether of nature or of art, with a nicety that is rarely to be found. When he and I were travelling in the Highlands of Scotland, and I pointed out to him a mountain which I observed resembled a cone, he corrected my

---

[1] This anecdote of the duck, though disproved by internal and external evidence, has nevertheless, upon supposition of its truth, been made the foundation of the following ingenious and fanciful reflections of Miss Seward, amongst the communications concerning Dr. Johnson with which she has been pleased to favour me: 'These infant numbers contain the seeds of those propensities which through his life so strongly marked his character, of that poetick talent which afterwards bore such rich and plentiful fruits; for, excepting his orthographick works, every thing which Dr. Johnson wrote was Poetry, whose essence consists not in numbers, or in jingle, but in the strength and glow of a fancy, to which all the stores of nature and of art stand in prompt administration; and in an eloquence which conveys their blended illustrations in a language "more tuneable than needs or rhyme or verse to add more harmony."

'The above little verses also shew that superstitious bias which "grew with his growth, and strengthened with his strength," and, of late years particularly, injured his happiness, by presenting to him the gloomy side of religion, rather than that bright and cheering one which gilds the period of closing life with the light of pious hope.'

This is so beautifully imagined, that I would not suppress it. But like many other theories, it is deduced from a supposed fact, which is, indeed, a fiction.

[2] *Prayers and Meditations*, p. 27.

[3] Speaking himself of the imperfection of one of his eyes, he said to Dr. Burney, 'the dog was never good for much.' [M.]

inaccuracy, by shewing me, that it was indeed pointed at the top, but that one side of it was larger than the other. And the ladies with whom he was acquainted agree, that no man was more nicely and minutely critical in the elegance of female dress. When I found that he saw the romantick beauties of Islam, in Derbyshire, much better than I did, I told him that he resembled an able performer upon a bad instrument. How false and contemptible then are all the remarks which have been made to the prejudice either of his candour or of his philosophy, founded upon a supposition that he was almost blind. It has been said, that he contracted this grievous malady from his nurse. His mother yielding to the superstitious notion, which, it is wonderful to think, prevailed so long in this country, as to the virtue of the regal touch; a notion, which our kings encouraged, and to which a man of such inquiry and such judgement as Carte could give credit; carried him to London, where he was actually touched by Queen Anne. Mrs Johnson indeed, as Mr. Hector informed me, acted by the advice of the celebrated Sir John Floyer, then a physician in Lichfield. Johnson used to talk of this very frankly; and Mrs. Piozzi has preserved his very picturesque description of the scene, as it remained upon his fancy. Being asked if he could remember Queen Anne, 'He had (he said) a confused, but somehow a sort of solemn recollection of a lady in diamonds, and a long black hood.'[1] This touch, however, was without any effect. I ventured to say to him, in allusion to the political principles in which he was educated, and of which he ever retained some odour, that 'his mother had not carried him far enough; she should have taken him to Rome.'

He was first taught to read English by Dame Oliver, a widow, who kept a school for young children in Lichfield. He told me she could read the black letter, and asked him to borrow for her, from his father, a bible in that character. When he was going to Oxford, she came to take leave of him, brought him, in the simplicity of her kindness, a present of gingerbread, and said, he was the best scholar she had ever had. He delighted in mentioning this early compliment: adding, with a smile, that 'this was as

[1] *Anecdotes*, p. 10.

high a proof of his merit as he could conceive.' His next instructor
in English was a master, whom, when he spoke of him to me, he
familiarly called Tom Brown, who, said he, 'published a spelling-
book, and dedicated it to the UNIVERSE; but, I fear, no copy of it
can now be had.'

He began to learn Latin with Mr. Hawkins, usher, or under-
master of Lichfield school, 'a man (said he) very skilful in his
little way.' With him he continued two years, and then rose to
be under the care of Mr. Hunter, the head-master, who, according to his account, 'was very severe, and wrong-headedly
severe. He used (said he) to beat us unmercifully; and he did
not distinguish between ignorance and negligence; for he would
beat a boy equally for not knowing a thing, as for neglecting to
know it. He would ask a boy a question; and if he did not answer
it, he would beat him, without considering whether he had an
opportunity of knowing how to answer it. For instance, he
would call up a boy and ask him Latin for a candlestick, which the
boy could not expect to be asked. Now, Sir, if a boy could answer
every question, there would be no need of a master to teach him.'

It is, however, but justice to the memory of Mr. Hunter to
mention, that though he might err in being too severe, the
school of Lichfield was very respectable in his time. The late
Dr. Taylor, Prebendary of Westminster, who was educated
under him, told me, that 'he was an excellent master, and that
his ushers were most of them men of eminence; that Holbrook,
one of the most ingenious men, best scholars, and best preachers
of his age, was usher during the greatest part of the time that
Johnson was at school. Then came Hague, of whom as much
might be said, with the addition that he was an elegant poet.
Hague was succeeded by Green, afterwards Bishop of Lincoln,
whose character in the learned world is well known. In the same
form with Johnson was Congreve, who afterwards became
chaplain to Archbishop Boulter, and by that connection obtained
good preferment in Ireland. He was a younger son of the ancient
family of Congreve, in Staffordshire, of which the poet was a
branch. His brother sold the estate. There was also Lowe, afterwards Canon of Windsor.'

Indeed Johnson was very sensible how much he owed to Mr. Hunter. Mr. Langton one day asked him how he had acquired so accurate a knowledge of Latin, in which, I believe, he was exceeded by no man of his time; he said, 'My master whipt me very well. Without that, Sir, I should have done nothing.' He told Mr. Langton, that while Hunter was flogging his boys unmercifully, he used to say, 'And this I do to save you from the gallows.' Johnson, upon all occasions, expressed his approbation of enforcing instruction by means of the rod. 'I would rather (said he) have the rod to be the general terrour to all, to make them learn, than tell a child, if you do thus, or thus, you will be more esteemed than your brothers or sisters. The rod produces an effect which terminates in itself. A child is afraid of being whipped, and gets his task, and there's an end on't; whereas, by exciting emulation and comparisons of superiority, you lay the foundation of lasting mischief; you make brothers and sisters hate each other.'

When Johnson saw some young ladies in Lincolnshire who were remarkably well behaved, owing to their mother's strict discipline and severe correction, he exclaimed, in one of Shakspeare's lines a little varied,

'*Rod*, I will honour thee for this thy duty.'

That superiority over his fellows, which he maintained with so much dignity in his march through life, was not assumed from vanity and ostentation, but was the natural and constant effect of those extraordinary powers of mind, of which he could not but be conscious by comparison; the intellectual difference, which in other cases of comparison of characters is often a matter of undecided contest, being as clear in his case as the superiority of stature in some men above others. Johnson did not strut or stand on tiptoe: He only did not stoop. From his earliest years his superiority was perceived and acknowledged. He was from the beginning *Ἄναξ ἀνδρῶν*, a king of men. His school-fellow, Mr. Hector, has obligingly furnished me with many particulars of his boyish days: and assured me that he never knew him corrected at school, but for talking and diverting other boys from their business. He seemed to learn by intuition; for though indolence and procrastination were inherent in his constitution, whenever he made an exertion he did more than any one else. In short, he is a memorable instance of what has been often observed, that the boy is the man in miniature: and that the distinguishing characteristicks of each individual are the same, through the whole course of life. His favourites used to receive very liberal assistance from him; and such was the submission and deference with which he was treated, such the desire to obtain his regard, that three of the boys, of whom Mr. Hector was sometimes one, used to come in the morning as his humble attendants, and carry him to school. One in the middle stooped, while he sat upon his back, and one on each side supported him; and thus he was borne triumphant. Such a proof of the early predominance of intellectual vigour is very remarkable, and does honour to human nature. Talking to me once himself of his being much distinguished at school, he told me, 'they never thought to raise me by comparing me to any one; they never said, Johnson is as good a scholar as such a one; but such a one is as good a scholar as Johnson; and this was said but of one, but of Lowe; and I do not think he was as good a scholar.'

He discovered a great ambition to excel, which roused him to counteract his indolence. He was uncommonly inquisitive; and his memory was so tenacious, that he never forgot any thing that he either heard or read. Mr. Hector remembers having recited to him eighteen verses, which, after a little pause, he repeated *verbatim*, varying only one epithet, by which he improved the line.

He never joined with the other boys in their ordinary diversions: his only amusement was in winter, when he took a pleasure in being drawn upon the ice by a boy barefooted, who pulled him along by a garter fixed round him; no very easy operation, as his size was remarkably large. His defective sight, indeed, prevented him from enjoying the common sports; and he once pleasantly remarked to me, 'how wonderfully well he had contrived to be idle without them.' Lord Chesterfield, however, has justly observed in one of his letters, when earnestly cautioning

a friend against the pernicious effects of idleness, that active
sports are not to be reckoned idleness in young people; and that
the listless torpor of doing nothing, alone deserves that name.
Of this dismal inertness of disposition, Johnson had all his life
too great a share. Mr. Hector relates, that 'he could not oblige
him more than by sauntering away the hours of vacation in the
fields, during which he was more engaged in talking to himself
than to his companion.'

Dr. Percy, the Bishop of Dromore, who was long intimately
acquainted with him, and has preserved a few anecdotes concerning him, regretting that he was not a more diligent collector,
informs me, that 'when a boy he was immoderately fond of
reading romances of chivalry, and he retained his fondness for
them through life; so that (adds his Lordship) spending part of
a summer at my parsonage-house in the country, he chose for
his regular reading the old Spanish romance of *Felixmarte of
Hircania*, in folio, which he read quite through. Yet I have heard
him attribute to these extravagant fictions that unsettled turn of
mind which prevented his ever fixing in any profession.'

1725: ÆTAT. 16.—AFTER having resided for some time at the
house of his uncle, Cornelius Ford, Johnson was, at the age of
fifteen, removed to the school of Stourbridge, in Worcestershire,
of which Mr. Wentworth was then master. This step was taken
by the advice of his cousin, the Reverend Mr. Ford, a man in
whom both talents and good dispositions were disgraced by
licentiousness,[1] but who was a very able judge of what was right.
At this school he did not receive so much benefit as was expected.
It has been said, that he acted in the capacity of an assistant to
Mr. Wentworth, in teaching the younger boys. 'Mr. Wentworth (he told me) was a very able man, but an idle man, and to
me very severe; but I cannot blame him much. I was then a big
boy; he saw I did not reverence him; and that he should get no
honour by me. I had brought enough with me, to carry me
through; and all I should get at his school would be ascribed to

[1] He is said to be original of the parson in Hogarth's *Modern Midnight
Conversation.*

my own labour, or to my former master. Yet he taught me a great deal.'

He thus discriminated, to Dr. Percy, Bishop of Dromore, his progress at his two grammar-schools. 'At one, I learnt much in the school, but little from the master; in the other, I learnt much from the master, but little in the school.'

The Bishop also informs me, that 'Dr. Johnson's father, before he was received at Stourbridge, applied to have him admitted as a scholar and assistant to the Reverend Samuel Lea, M.A., head master of Newport school, in Shropshire' (a very diligent, good teacher, at that time in high reputation, under whom Mr. Hollis is said, in the Memoirs of his Life, to have been also educated[1]). This application to Mr. Lea was not successful; but Johnson had afterwards the gratification to hear that the old gentleman, who lived to a very advanced age, mentioned it as one of the most memorable events of his life, that 'he was *very near* having that great man for his scholar.'

He remained at Stourbridge little more than a year, and then returned home, where he may be said to have loitered, for two years, in a state very unworthy his uncommon abilities. He had already given several proofs of his poetical genius, both in his school-exercises and in other occasional compositions. Of these I have obtained a considerable collection, by the favour of Mr. Wentworth, son of one of his masters, and of Mr. Hector, his school-fellow and friend; from which I select the following specimens:

Translation of VIRGIL. Pastoral I.

MELIBŒUS.

Now, Tityrus, you, supine and careless laid,
Play on your pipe beneath this beechen shade;
While wretched we about the world must roam,
And leave our pleasing fields and native home,
Here at your ease you sing your amorous flame,
And the wood rings with Amarillis' name.

[1] As was likewise the Bishop of Dromore many years afterwards.

TITYRUS.

Those blessings, friend, a deity bestow'd,
For I shall never think him less than God;
Oft on his altar shall my firstlings lie,
Their blood the consecrated stones shall dye:
He gave my flocks to graze the flowery meads,
And me to tune at ease th' unequal reeds.

MELIBŒUS.

My admiration only I exprest,
(No spark of envy harbours in my breast)
That, when confusion o'er the country reigns,
To you alone this happy state remains.
Here I, though faint myself, must drive my goats,
Far from their antient fields and humble cots.
This scarce I lead, who left on yonder rock
Two tender kids, the hopes of all the flock.
Had we not been perverse and careless grown,
This dire event by omens was foreshown;
Our trees were blasted by the thunder stroke,
And left-hand crows, from an old hollow oak,
Foretold the coming evil by their dismal croak.

Translation of HORACE. Book I. Ode xxii.

THE man, my friend, whose conscious heart
    With virtue's sacred ardour glows,
Nor taints with death the envenom'd dart,
    Nor needs the guard of Moorish bows:

Though Scythia's icy cliffs he treads,
    Or horrid Africk's faithless sands;
Or where the fam'd Hydaspes spreads
    His liquid wealth o'er barbarous lands.

For while by Chloe's image charm'd,
    Too far in Sabine woods I stray'd;
Me singing, careless and unarm'd,
    A grizly wolf surprised, and fled.

No savage more portentous stain'd
    Apulia's spacious wilds with gore;

38

None fiercer Juba's thirsty land,
    Dire nurse of raging lions, bore.

Place me where no soft summer gale
    Among the quivering branches sighs;
Where clouds condens'd for ever veil
    With horrid gloom the frowning skies:

Place me beneath the burning line,
    A clime deny'd to human race;
I'll sing of Chloe's charms divine,
    Her heav'nly voice, and beauteous face.

Translation of HORACE. Book II. Ode ix.

CLOUDS do not always veil the skies,
    Nor showers immerse the verdant plain
Nor do the billows always rise,
    Or storms afflict the ruffled main.

Nor, Valgius, on th' Armenian shores
    Do the chain'd waters always freeze;
Not always furious Boreas roars,
    Or bends with violent force the trees.

But you are ever drown'd in tears,
    For Mystes dead you ever mourn;
No setting Sol can ease your cares,
    But finds you sad at his return.

The wise experienc'd Grecian sage
    Mourn'd not Antilochus so long;
Nor did King Priam's hoary age
    So much lament his slaughter'd son.

Leave off, at length, these woman's sighs,
    Augustus' numerous trophies sing;
Repeat that prince's victories,
    To whom all nations tribute bring.

Niphates rolls an humbler wave,
    At length the undaunted Scythian yields,
Content to live the Roman's slave,
    And scarce forsakes his native fields.

39

Translation of part of the Dialogue between HECTOR *and* ANDROMACHE;
from the Sixth Book of HOMER'S ILIAD.

SHE ceas'd: then godlike Hector answer'd kind,
(His various plumage sporting in the wind)
That post, and all the rest, shall be my care;
But shall I, then, forsake the unfinished war?
How would the Trojans brand great Hector's name!
And one base action sully all my fame,
Acquired by wounds and battles bravely fought!
Oh! how my soul abhors so mean a thought.
Long since I learn'd to slight this fleeting breath,
And view with cheerful eyes approaching death
The inexorable sisters have decreed
That Priam's house, and Priam's self shall bleed:
The day will come, in which proud Troy shall yield,
And spread its smoking ruins o'er the field.
Yet Hecuba's, nor Priam's hoary age,
Whose blood shall quench some Grecian's thirsty rage,
Nor my brave brothers, that have bit the ground,
Their souls dismiss'd through many a ghastly wound,
Can in my bosom half that grief create,
As the sad thought of your impending fate:
When some proud Grecian dame shall tasks impose,
Mimick your tears, and ridicule your woes;
Beneath Hyperia's waters shall you sweat,
And, fainting, scarce support the liquid weight:
Then shall some Argive loud insulting cry,
Behold the wife of Hector, guard of Troy!
Tears, at my name, shall drown those beauteous eyes,
And that fair bosom heave with rising sighs!
Before that day, by some brave hero's hand
May I lie slain, and spurn the bloody sand.

To a YOUNG LADY *on her* BIRTH-DAY.[1]

THIS tributary verse receive my fair,
Warm with an ardent lover's fondest pray'r.
May this returning day for ever find
Thy form more lovely, more adorn'd thy mind;

[1] Mr. Hector informs me, that this was made almost *impromptu*, in his presence.

All pains, all cares, may favouring heav'n remove,
All but the sweet solicitudes of love!
May powerful nature join with grateful art,
To point each glance, and force it to the heart!
O then, when conquered crouds confess thy sway,
When ev'n proud wealth and prouder wit obey,
My fair, be mindful of the mighty trust,
Alas! 'tis hard for beauty to be just.
Those sovereign charms with strictest care employ;
Nor give the generous pain, the worthless joy:
With his own form acquaint the forward fool,
Shewn in the faithful glass of ridicule;
Teach mimick censure her own faults to find, ⎫
No more let coquettes to themselves be blind, ⎬
So shall Belinda's charms improve mankind. ⎭

THE YOUNG AUTHOUR.[1]

WHEN first the peasant, long inclin'd to roam,
Forsakes his rural sports and peaceful home,
Pleas'd with the scene the smiling ocean yields,
He scorns the verdant meads and flow'ry fields;
Then dances jocund o'er the watery way,
While the breeze whispers, and the streamers play:
Unbounded prospects in his bosom roll,
And future millions lift his rising soul;
In blissful dreams he digs the golden mine,
And raptur'd sees the new-found ruby shine.
Joys insincere! thick clouds invade the skies,
Loud roar the billows, high the waves arise;
Sick'ning with fear, he longs to view the shore,
And vows to trust the faithless deep no more.
So the young Authour, panting after fame,
And the long honours of a lasting name,
Entrusts his happiness to human kind,
More false, more cruel, than the seas or wind.
'Toil on, dull croud, in extacies he cries,
For wealth or title, perishable prize;
While I those transitory blessings scorn,

[1] This he inserted, with many alterations, in the *Gentleman's Magazine*,
1743 [p. 378].

41

Secure of praise from ages yet unborn.'
This thought once form'd, all counsel comes too late,
He flies to press, and hurries on his fate;
Swiftly he sees the imagin'd laurels spread,
And feels the unfading wreath surround his head.
Warn'd by another's fate, vain youth be wise,
Those dreams were Settle's once, and Ogilby's:
The pamphlet spreads, incessant hisses rise,
To some retreat the baffled writer flies;
Where no sour criticks snarl, no sneers molest,
Safe from the tart lampoon, and stinging jest;
There begs of heaven a less distinguish'd lot,
Glad to be hid, and proud to be forgot.

EPILOGUE, *intended to have been spoken by a* LADY *who was to personate
the Ghost of* HERMIONE.[1]

YE blooming train, who give despair or joy,
Bless with a smile, or with a frown destroy;
In whose fair cheeks destructive Cupids wait,
And with unerring shafts distribute fate;
Whose snowy breasts, whose animated eyes,
Each youth admires, though each admirer dies;
Whilst you deride their pangs in barb'rous play, ⎫
Unpitying see them weep, and hear them pray, ⎬
And unrelenting sport ten thousand lives away; ⎭
For you, ye fair, I quit the gloomy plains;
Where sable night in all her horrour reigns;
No fragrant bowers, no delightful glades,
Receive the unhappy ghosts of scornful maids.
For kind, for tender nymphs the myrtle blooms,
And weaves her bending boughs in pleasing glooms:
Perennial roses deck each purple vale,
And scents ambrosial breathe in every gale:
Far hence are banish'd vapours, spleen, and tears,
Tea, scandal, ivory teeth, and languid airs:
No pug, nor favourite Cupid there enjoys
The balmy kiss, for which poor Thyrsis dies;

---

[1] Some young ladies at Lichfield having proposed to act *The Distressed
Mother*, Johnson wrote this, and gave it to Mr. Hector to convey it privately
to them.

> Form'd to delight, they use no foreign arms,
> Nor torturing whalebones pinch them into charms;
> No conscious blushes there their cheeks inflame,
> For those who feel no guilt can know no shame;
> Unfaded still their former charms they shew,
> Around them pleasures wait, and joys for ever new.
> But cruel virgins meet severer fates;
> Expell'd and exil'd from the blissful seats,
> To dismal realms, and regions void of peace,
> Where furies ever howl, and serpents hiss.
> O'er the sad plains perpetual tempests sigh,
> And pois'nous vapours, black'ning all the sky,
> With livid hue the fairest face o'ercast,
> And every beauty withers at the blast:
> Where e'er they fly their lover's ghosts pursue,
> Inflicting all those ills which once they knew;
> Vexation, Fury, Jealousy, Despair,
> Vex ev'ry eye, and every bosom tear;
> Their foul deformities by all descry'd,
> No maid to flatter, and no paint to hide.
> Then melt, ye fair, while crouds around you sigh,
> Nor let disdain sit lowring in your eye;
> With pity soften every awful grace,
> And beauty smile auspicious in each face;
> To ease their pains exert your milder power,
> So shall you guiltless reign, and all mankind adore.'

The two years which he spent at home, after his return from Stourbridge, he passed in what he thought idleness, and was scolded by his father for his want of steady application. He had no settled plan of life, nor looked forward at all, but merely lived from day to day. Yet he read a great deal in a desultory manner, without any scheme of study, as chance threw books in his way, and inclination directed him through them. He used to mention one curious instance of his casual reading, when but a boy. Having imagined that his brother had hid some apples behind a large folio upon an upper shelf in his father's shop, he climbed up to search for them. There were no apples; but the large folio proved to be Petrarch, whom he had seen mentioned in some preface, as one of the restorers of learning. His curiosity having been thus excited, he sat down with avidity, and read a great part of the book. What he read during these two years he told me, was not works of mere amusement, 'not voyages and travels, but all literature, Sir, all ancient writers, all manly: though but little Greek, only some of Anacreon and Hesiod; but in this irregular manner (added he) I had looked into a great many books, which were not commonly known at the Universities, where they seldom read any books but what are put into their hands by their tutors; so that when I came to Oxford, Dr. Adams, now master of Pembroke College, told me I was the best qualified for the University that he had ever known come there.'

In estimating the progress of his mind during these two years, as well as in future periods of his life, we must not regard his own hasty confession of idleness; for we see, when he explains himself, that he was acquiring various stores; and, indeed, he himself concluded the account with saying, 'I would not have you think I was doing nothing then.' He might, perhaps, have studied more assiduously; but it may be doubted whether such a mind as his was not more enriched by roaming at large in the fields of literature than if it had been confined to any single spot. The analogy between body and mind is very general, and the parallel will hold as to their food, as well as any other particular. The flesh of animals who feed excursively, is allowed to have a higher flavour than that of those who are cooped up. May there not be the same difference between men who read as their taste prompts and men who are confined in cells and colleges to stated tasks?

That a man in Mr. Michael Johnson's circumstances should think of sending his son to the expensive University of Oxford, at his own charge, seems very improbable. The subject was too delicate to question Johnson upon. But I have been assured by Dr. Taylor that the scheme never would have taken place had not a gentleman of Shropshire, one of his schoolfellows, spontaneously undertaken to support him at Oxford, in the character of his companion; though, in fact, he never received any assistance whatever from that gentleman.[1]

[1] [Probably Andrew Corbet. *Hawkins.*]

He, however, went to Oxford, and was entered a Commoner of Pembroke College on the 31st of October, 1728, being then in his nineteenth year.

The Reverend Dr. Adams, who afterwards presided over Pembroke College with universal esteem, told me he was present, and gave me some account of what passed on the night of Johnson's arrival at Oxford. On that evening, his father, who had anxiously accompanied him, found means to have him introduced to Mr. Jorden, who was to be his tutor. His being put under any tutor reminds us of what Wood says of Robert Burton, authour of the 'Anatomy of Melancholy,' when elected student of Christ Church: 'for form sake, *though he wanted not a tutor*, he was put under the tuition of Dr. John Bancroft, afterwards Bishop of Oxon.'[1]

His father seemed very full of the merits of his son, and told the company he was a good scholar, and a poet, and wrote latin verses. His figure and manner appeared strange to them; but he behaved modestly, and sat silent, till upon something which occurred in the course of conversation, he suddenly struck in and quoted Macrobius; and thus he gave the first impression of that more extensive reading in which he had indulged himself.

His tutor, Mr. Jorden, fellow of Pembroke, was not, it seems, a man of such abilities as we should conceive requisite for the instructor of Samuel Johnson, who gave me the following account of him. 'He was a very worthy man, but a heavy man, and I did not profit much by his instructions. Indeed, I did not attend him much. The first day after I came to college I waited upon him, and then staid away four. On the sixth, Mr. Jorden asked me why I had not attended. I answered I had been sliding in Christ-Church meadow. And this I said with as much *nonchalance* as I am now[2] talking to you. I had no notion that I was wrong or irreverent to my tutor. Boswell: 'That, Sir, was great fortitude of mind.' Johnson: 'No, Sir; stark insensibility.'[3]

---

[1] *Athen. Oxon.* edit. 1721, i. 627.   [2] Oxford, 20th March, 1776.
[3] It ought to be remembered that Dr. Johnson was apt, in his literary as well as moral exercises, to overcharge his defects. Dr. Adams informed me, that he attended his tutor's lectures, and also the lectures in the College Hall, very regularly.

The fifth of November was at that time kept with great solemnity at Pembroke College, and exercises upon the subject of the day were required. Johnson neglected to perform his, which is much to be regretted; for his vivacity of imagination, and force of language, would probably have produced something sublime upon the gunpowder plot. To apologise for his neglect, he gave in a short copy of verses, entitled *Somnium*, containing a common thought; 'that the Muse had come to him in his sleep, and whispered, that it did not become him to write on such subjects as politicks; he should confine himself to humbler themes:' but the versification was truly Virgilian.

He had a love and respect for Jorden, not for his literature, but for his worth. 'Whenever (said he) a young man becomes Jorden's pupil, he becomes his son.'

Having given such a specimen of his poetical powers, he was asked by Mr. Jorden to translate Pope's Messiah into Latin verse, as a Christmas exercise. He performed it with uncommon rapidity, and in so masterly a manner, that he obtained great applause from it, which ever after kept him high in the estimation of his College, and, indeed, of all the University.

It is said, that Mr. Pope expressed himself concerning it in terms of strong approbation. Dr. Taylor told me, that it was first printed for old Mr. Johnson, without the knowledge of his son, who was very angry when he heard of it. A Miscellany of Poems, collected by a person of the name of Husbands, was published at Oxford in 1731. In that Miscellany Johnson's Translation of the Messiah appeared, with this modest motto from Scaliger's Poeticks. *Ex alieno ingenio Poeta, ex suo tantum versificator.*[1]

I am not ignorant that critical objections have been made to this and other specimens of Johnson's Latin Poetry. I acknowledge myself not competent to decide on a question of such extreme nicety. But I am satisfied with the just and discriminative eulogy pronounced upon it by my friend Mr. Courtenay.

'And with like ease his vivid lines assume
    The garb and dignity of ancient Rome.—

[1] ['A poet by another's genius, merely a versifier by his own.']

> Let college *verse-men* trite conceits express,
> Trick'd out in splendid shreds of Virgil's dress;
> From playful Ovid cull the tinsel phrase,
> And vapid notions hitch in pilfer'd lays:
> Then with mosaick art the piece combine,
> And boast the glitter of each dulcet line:
> Johnson adventur'd boldly to transfuse
> His vigorous sense into the Latian muse;
> Aspir'd to shine by unreflected light,
> And with a Roman's ardour *think* and write.
> He felt the tuneful Nine his breast inspire,
> And, like a master, wak'd the soothing lyre:
> Horatian strains a grateful heart proclaim,
> While Sky's wild rocks resound his Thralia's name.
> Hesperia's plant, in some less skilful hands,
> To bloom a while, factitious heat demands:
> Though glowing Maro a faint warmth supplies,
> The sickly blossom in the hot-house dies:
> By Johnson's genial culture, art, and toil,
> Its root strikes deep, and owns the fost'ring soil;
> Imbibes our sun through all its swelling veins,
> And grows a native of Britannia's plains.'[1]

The 'morbid melancholy,' which was lurking in his constitution, and to which we may ascribe those particularities, and that aversion to regular life, which, at a very early period, marked his character, gathered such strength in his twentieth year, as to afflict him in a dreadful manner. While he was at Lichfield, in the college vacation of the year 1729, he felt himself overwhelmed with an horrible hypochondria, with perpetual irritation, fretfulness, and impatience; and with a dejection, gloom, and despair, which made existence misery. From this dismal malady he never afterwards was perfectly relieved; and all his labours, and all his enjoyments, were but temporary interruptions of its baleful influence. How wonderful, how unsearchable are the ways of Gon! Johnson, who was blest with all the powers of genius and understanding in a degree far above the ordinary

---

[1] *Poetical Review of the Literary and Moral Character of Dr. Johnson*, by John Courtenay, Esq., M.P.

state of human nature, was at the same time visited with a disorder so afflictive, that they who know it by dire experience, will not envy his exalted endowments. That it was, in some degree, occasioned by a defect in his nervous system, that inexplicable part of our frame, appears highly probable. He told Mr. Paradise that he was sometimes so languid and inefficient, that he could not distinguish the hour upon the town-clock.

Johnson, upon the first violent attack of this disorder, strove to overcome it by forcible exertions. He frequently walked to Birmingham and back again, and tried many other expedients, but all in vain. His expression concerning it to me was, 'I did not then know how to manage it.' His distress became so intolerable, that he applied to Dr. Swinfen, physician in Lichfield, his god-father, and put into his hands a state of his case, written in Latin. Dr. Swinfen was so much struck with the extraordinary acuteness, research, and eloquence of this paper, that in his zeal for his godson he shewed it to several people. His daughter, Mrs. Desmoulins, who was many years humanely supported in Dr. Johnson's house in London, told me, that upon his discovering that Dr. Swinfen had communicated his case, he was so much offended, that he was never afterwards fully reconciled to him. He indeed had good reason to be offended; for though Dr. Swinfen's motive was good, he inconsiderately betrayed a matter deeply interesting and of great delicacy, which had been entrusted to him in confidence; and exposed a complaint of his young friend and patient, which, in the superficial opinion of the generality of mankind, is attended with contempt and disgrace.

But let not little men triumph upon knowing that Johnson was an HYPOCHONDRIACK, was subject to what the learned, philosophical, and pious Dr. Cheyne has so well treated under the title of 'The English Malady.' Though he suffered severely from it, he was not therefore degraded. The powers of his great mind might be troubled, and their full exercise suspended at times; but the mind itself was ever entire. As a proof of this, it is only necessary to consider, that, when he was at the very worst, he composed that state of his own case, which shewed an uncommon vigour, not only of fancy and taste, but of judgement. I am aware that he himself was too ready to call such a complaint by the name of *madness*; in conformity with which notion, he has traced its gradations, with exquisite nicety, in one of the chapters of his RASSELAS. But there is surely a clear distinction between a disorder which affects only the imagination and spirits, while the judgement is sound, and a disorder by which the judgement itself is impaired. This distinction was made to me by the late Professor Gaubius of Leyden, physician to the Prince of Orange, in a conversation which I had with him several years ago, and he expanded it thus: 'If (said he) a man tells me that he is grievously disturbed, for that he *imagines* he sees a ruffian coming against him with a drawn sword, though at the same time he is *conscious* it is a delusion, I pronounce him to have a disordered imagination; but if a man tells me that he *sees* this, and in consternation calls to me to look at it, I pronounce him to be *mad*.'

It is a common effect of low spirits or melancholy, to make those who are afflicted with it imagine that they are actually suffering those evils which happen to be most strongly presented to their minds. Some have fancied themselves to be deprived of the use of their limbs, some to labour under acute diseases, others to be in extreme poverty; when, in truth, there was not the least reality in any of the suppositions; so that when the vapours were dispelled, they were convinced of the delusion. To Johnson, whose supreme enjoyment was the exercise of his reason, the disturbance or obscuration of that faculty was the evil most to be dreaded. Insanity, therefore, was the object of his most dismal apprehension; and he fancied himself seized by it, or approaching to it, at the very time when he was giving proofs of a more than ordinary soundness and vigour of judgement. That his own diseased imagination should have so far deceived him, is strange; but it is stranger still that some of his friends should have given credit to his groundless opinion, when they had such undoubted proofs that it was totally fallacious; though it is by no means surprising that those who wish to depreciate him, should, since his death, have laid hold of this circumstance, and insisted upon it with very unfair aggravation.

Amidst the oppression and distraction of a disease which very few have felt in its full extent, but many have experienced in a slighter degree, Johnson, in his writings, and in his conversation, never failed to display all the varieties of intellectual excellence. In his march through this world to a better, his mind still appeared grand and brilliant, and impressed all around him with the truth of Virgil's noble sentiment—

'*Igneus est ollis vigor et cœlestis origo.*'[1]

The history of his mind as to religion is an important article. I have mentioned the early impressions made upon his tender imagination by his mother, who continued her pious care with assiduity, but, in his opinion, not with judgement. 'Sunday (said he) was a heavy day to me when I was a boy. My mother confined me on that day, and made me read "The Whole Duty of Man," from a great part of which I could derive no instruction. When, for instance, I had read the chapter on theft, which from my infancy I had been taught was wrong, I was no more convinced that theft was wrong than before; so there was no accession of knowledge. A boy should be introduced to such books, by having his attention directed to the arrangement, to the style, and other excellencies of composition; that the mind being thus engaged by an amusing variety of objects, may not grow weary.'

He communicated to me the following particulars upon the subject of his religious progress. 'I fell into an inattention to religion, or an indifference about it, in my ninth year. The church at Lichfield, in which we had a seat, wanted reparation, so I was to go and find a seat in other churches; and having bad eyes, and being awkward about this, I used to go and read in the fields on Sunday. This habit continued till my fourteenth year; and still I find a great reluctance to go to church. I then became a sort of lax *talker* against religion, for I did not much *think* against it; and this lasted till I went to Oxford, where it would not be *suffered.* When at Oxford, I took up Law's *Serious Call to a Holy Life,*' expecting to find it a dull book (as such books generally are), and perhaps to laugh at it. But I found Law quite an over-

[1] ['To these seeds a flame-like vigour pertains, and an origin celestial.' *Æneid* vi. 730. (Jackson.)]

match for me; and this was the first occasion of my thinking in earnest of religion, after I became capable of rational inquiry.'[1] From this time forward religion was the predominant object of his thoughts; though, with the just sentiments of a conscientious Christian, he lamented that his practice of its duties fell far short of what it ought to be.

This instance of a mind such as that of Johnson being first disposed, by an unexpected incident, to think with anxiety of the momentous concerns of eternity, and of 'what he should do to be saved,' may for ever be produced in opposition to the superficial and sometimes profane contempt that has been thrown upon those occasional impressions which it is certain many Christians have experienced; though it must be acknowledged that weak minds, from an erroneous supposition that no man is in a state of grace who has not felt a particular conversion, have, in some

[1] Mrs. Piozzi has given a strange fantastical account of the original of Dr. Johnson's belief in our most holy religion. 'At the age of *ten* years his mind was disturbed by scruples of infidelity, which preyed upon his spirits, and made him very uneasy, the more so, as he revealed his uneasiness to none, being naturally (as he said) of a sullen temper, and reserved disposition. He searched, however, diligently, but fruitlessly, for evidences of the truth of revelation; and, at length, *recollecting* a book he had *once* seen [*I suppose at five years old*] in his father's shop, intitled *De veritate Religionis*, etc., he began to think himself *highly culpable* for neglecting such a means of information, and took himself severely to task for this *sin*, adding many acts of voluntary, and, to others, unknown *penance*. The first opportunity which offered, of course, he seized the book with avidity; but, on examination, *not finding himself scholar enough to peruse its contents*, set his heart at rest; and not thinking to enquire whether there were any English books written on the subject, followed his usual amusements and *considered his conscience as lightened of a crime*. He redoubled his diligence to learn the language that contained the information he most wished for; but from the pain which guilt [*namely having omitted to read what he did not understand*] had given him, he now began to deduce the soul's immortality [*a sensation of pain in this world being an unquestionable proof of existence in another*], which was the point that belief first stopped at; *and from that moment resolving to be a Christian*, became one of the most zealous and pious ones our nation ever produced.' *Anecdotes*, p. 17.

This is one of the numerous misrepresentations of this lively lady, which it is worth while to correct; for if credit should be given to such a childish, irrational, and ridiculous statement of the foundation of Dr. Johnson's faith in Christianity, how little credit would be due to it. Mrs. Piozzi seems to wish, that the world should think Dr. Johnson also under the influence of that easy logick, *Stet pro ratione voluntas*. ['Let my wishes be reason enough'. Juvenal, *Sat.* vi, 223.]

cases, brought a degree of ridicule upon them; a ridicule of which it is inconsiderate or unfair to make a general application.

How seriously Johnson was impressed with a sense of religion, even in the vigour of his youth, appears from the following passage in his minutes kept by way of diary: Sept. 7, 1736. I have this day entered upon my twenty-eighth year. 'Mayest thou, O God, enable me, for JESUS CHRIST's sake, to spend this in such a manner that I may receive comfort from it at the hour of death, and in the day of judgement! Amen.'

The particular course of his reading while at Oxford, and during the time of vacation which he passed at home, cannot be traced. Enough has been said of his irregular mode of study. He told me that from his earliest years he loved to read poetry, but hardly ever read any poem to an end; that he read Shakspeare at a period so early, that the speech of the ghost in Hamlet terrified him when he was alone; that Horace's Odes were the compositions in which he took most delight, and it was long before he liked his Epistles and Satires. He told me what he read *solidly* at Oxford was Greek; not the Grecian historians, but Homer and Euripides, and now and then a little Epigram; that the study of which he was the most fond was Metaphysicks, but he had not read much, even in that way. I always thought that he did himself injustice in his account of what he had read, and that he must have been speaking with reference to the vast portion of study which is possible, and to which a few scholars in the whole history of literature have attained; for when I once asked him whether a person, whose name I have now forgotten, studied hard, he answered 'No, Sir; I do not believe he studied hard. I never knew a man who studied hard. I conclude, indeed, from the effects, that some men have studied hard, as Bentley and Clarke.' Trying him by that criterion upon which he formed his judgement of others, we may be absolutely certain, both from his writings and his conversation, that his reading was very extensive. Dr. Adam Smith, than whom few were better judges on this subject, once observed to me that 'Johnson knew more books than any man alive.' He had a peculiar facility in seizing at once what was valuable in any book, without submitting to

the labour of perusing it from beginning to end. He had, from
the irritability of his constitution, at all times, an impatience and
hurry when he either read or wrote. A certain apprehension,
arising from novelty, made him write his first exercise at College
twice over; but he never took that trouble with any other composition; and we shall see that his most excellent works were
struck off at a heat, with rapid exertion.[1]

Yet he appears, from his early notes or memorandums in my
possession, to have at various times attempted, or at least
planned, a methodical course of study, according to computation,
of which he was all his life fond, as it fixed his attention steadily
upon something without, and prevented his mind from preying
upon itself. Thus I find in his handwriting the number of lines in
each of two of Euripides' Tragedies, of the Georgicks of Virgil,
of the first six books of the Æneid, of Horace's Art of Poetry, of
three of the books of Ovid's Metamorphosis, of some parts of
Theocritus, and of the tenth Satire of Juvenal; and a table, shewing at the rate of various numbers a day (I suppose verses to be
read), what would be, in each case, the total amount in a week,
month, and year.

No man had a more ardent love of literature, or a higher
respect for it than Johnson. His apartment in Pembroke College
was that upon the second floor, over the gateway. The enthusiasts of learning will ever contemplate it with veneration. One
day, while he was sitting in it quite alone, Dr. Panting, then
master of the College, whom he called 'a fine Jacobite fellow,'
overheard him uttering this soliloquy in his strong, emphatick
voice: 'Well, I have a mind to see what is done in other places
of learning. I'll go and visit the Universities abroad. I'll go to
France and Italy. I'll go to Padua.—And I'll mind my business.
For an *Athenian* blockhead is the worst of all blockheads.'[2]

---

[1] He told Dr. Burney that he never wrote any of his works that were
printed, twice over. Dr. Burney's wonder at seeing several pages of his
Lives of the Poets, in Manuscript, with scarce a blot or erasure, drew this
observation from him. [M.]

[2] I had this anecdote from Dr. Adams, and Dr. Johnson confirmed it.
Bramston, in his *Man of Taste*, has the same thought:
'Sure, of all blockheads, scholars are the worst.'

Dr. Adams told me that Johnson, while he was at Pembroke College, 'was caressed and loved by all about him, was a gay and frolicksome fellow, and passed there the happiest part of his life.' But this is a striking proof of the fallacy of appearances, and how little any of us know of the real internal state even of those whom we see most frequently; for the truth is, that he was then depressed by poverty, and irritated by disease. When I mentioned to him this account as given me by Dr. Adams, he said, 'Ah, Sir, I was mad and violent. It was bitterness which they mistook for frolick. I was miserably poor, and I thought to fight my way by my literature and my wit; so I disregarded all power and all authority.'

The Bishop of Dromore observes in a letter to me,

'The pleasure he took in vexing the tutors and fellows has been often mentioned. But I have heard him say, what ought to be recorded to the honour of the present venerable master of that College, the Reverend William Adams, D.D., who was then very young, and one of the junior fellows; that the mild but judicious expostulations of this worthy man, whose virtue awed him, and whose learning he revered, made him really ashamed of himself, "though I fear (said he) I was too proud to own it."

'I have heard from some of his contemporaries that he was generally seen lounging at the College gate, with a circle of young students round him, whom he was entertaining with wit, and keeping from their studies, if not spiriting them up to rebellion against the College discipline, which in his maturer years he so much extolled.'

He very early began to attempt keeping notes or memorandums, by way of a diary of his life. I find, in a parcel of loose leaves, the following spirited resolution to contend against his natural indolence:

'*Oct.* 1729. *Desidiæ valedixi; syrenis istius cantibus surdam posthac aurem obversurus.*—I bid farewell to Sloth, being resolved henceforth not to listen to her syren strains.' I have also in my possession a few leaves of another *Libellus*, or little book, entitled ANNALES, in which some of the early particulars of his history are registered in Latin.

I do not find that he formed any close intimacies with his fellow-collegians. But Dr. Adams told me that he contracted a love and regard for Pembroke College, which he retained to the last. A short time before his death he sent to that College a present of all his works, to be deposited in their library; and he had thoughts of leaving to it his house at Lichfield; but his friends who were about him very properly dissuaded him from it, and he bequeathed it to some poor relations. He took a pleasure in boasting of the many eminent men who had been educated at Pembroke. In this list are found the names of Mr. Hawkins the Poetry Professor, Mr. Shenstone, Sir William Blackstone, and others;[1] not forgetting the celebrated popular preacher, Mr. George Whitefield, of whom, though Dr. Johnson did not think very highly, it must be acknowledged that his eloquence was powerful, his views pious and charitable, his assiduity almost incredible; and, that since his death, the integrity of his character has been fully vindicated. Being himself a poet, Johnson was peculiarly happy in mentioning how many of the sons of Pembroke were poets; adding, with a smile of sportive triumph, 'Sir, we are a nest of singing birds.'

He was not, however, blind to what he thought the defects of his own College; and I have, from the information of Dr. Taylor, a very strong instance of that rigid honesty which he ever inflexibly preserved. Taylor had obtained his father's consent to be entered of Pembroke, that he might be with his schoolfellow Johnson, with whom, though some years older than himself, he was very intimate. This would have been a great comfort to Johnson. But he fairly told Taylor that he could not, in conscience, suffer him to enter where he knew he could not have an able tutor. He then made inquiry all round the University, and having found that Mr. Bateman, of Christ Church, was the tutor of highest reputation, Taylor was entered of that College. Mr. Bateman's lectures were so excellent, that Johnson used to come and get them at second-hand from Taylor, till his poverty being so extreme that his shoes were worn out, and his feet appeared through them, he saw that this humiliating circumstance was

[1] See Nash's *History of Worcestershire*, vol. i. p. 529.

perceived by the Christ Church men, and he came no more. He was too proud to accept of money, and somebody[1] having set a pair of new shoes at his door, he threw them away with indignation. How must we feel when we read such an anecdote of Samuel Johnson!

His spirited refusal of an eleemosynary supply of shoes, arose, no doubt, from a proper pride. But, considering his ascetick disposition at times, as acknowledged by himself in his 'Meditations,' and the exaggeration with which some have treated the peculiarities of his character, I should not wonder to hear it ascribed to a principle of superstitious mortification; as we are told by Tursellinus, in his Life of St. Ignatius Loyola, that this intrepid founder of the order of Jesuits, when he arrived at Goa, after having made a severe pilgrimage through the Eastern desarts persisted in wearing his miserable shattered shoes, and when new ones were offered him rejected them as an unsuitable indulgence.

The *res angusta domi*[2] prevented him from having the advantage of a complete academical education. The friend to whom he had trusted for support had deceived him. His debts in College, though not great, were increasing; and his scanty remittances from Lichfield, which had all along been made with great difficulty, could be supplied no longer, his father having fallen into a state of insolvency. Compelled, therefore, by irresistible necessity, he left the College in autumn, 1731, without a degree, having been a member of it little more than three years.

Dr. Adams, the worthy and respectable master of Pembroke College, has generally had the reputation of being Johnson's tutor. The fact, however, is, that in 1731 Mr. Jorden quitted the College, and his pupils were transferred to Dr. Adams; so that had Johnson returned, Dr. Adams *would have been his tutor*. It is to be wished, that this connection had taken place. His equal temper, mild disposition, and politeness of manners, might have insensibly softened the harshness of Johnson, and infused into him those more delicate charities, those *petites morales*, in which,

[1] Perhaps the Rev. William Vyse. *Reade*.
[2] ['narrow means at home.' Juvenal, *Sat*. iii. 164.]

it must be confessed, our great moralist was more deficient than his best friends could fully justify. Dr. Adams paid Johnson this high compliment. He said to me at Oxford, in 1776, 'I was his nominal tutor; but he was above my mark.' When I repeated it to Johnson, his eyes flashed with grateful satisfaction, and he exclaimed, 'That was liberal and noble.'

And now (I had almost said *poor*) Samuel Johnson returned to his native city, destitute, and not knowing how he should gain even a decent livelihood. His father's misfortunes in trade rendered him unable to support his son; and for some time there appeared no means by which he could maintain himself. In the December of this year his father died.

The state of poverty in which he died, appears from a note in one of Johnson's little diaries of the following year, which strongly displays his spirit and virtuous dignity of mind.

'1732, *Julii* 15. *Undecim aureos deposui, quo die quicquid ante matris funus (quod serum sit precor) de paternis bonis sperari licet, viginti scilicet libras accepi. Usque adeo mihi fortuna fingenda est. Interea, ne paupertate vires animi languescant, nec in flagitia egestas abigat, cavendum.*—I layed by eleven guineas on this day, when I received twenty pounds, being all that I have reason to hope for out of my father's effects, previous to the death of my mother; an event which I pray GOD may be very remote. I now therefore see that I must make my own fortune. Meanwhile, let me take care that the powers of my mind may not be debilitated by poverty, and that indigence do not force me into any criminal act.'

Johnson was so far fortunate, that the respectable character of his parents, and his own merit, had, from his earliest years, secured him a kind reception in the best families at Lichfield. Among these I can mention Mr. Howard, Dr. Swinfen, Mr. Simpson, Mr. Levett, Captain Garrick, father of the great ornament of the British stage; but above all, Mr. Gilbert Walmsley,[1]

---

[1] Mr. Warton informs me, 'that this early friend of Johnson was entered a Commoner of Trinity College, Oxford, aged seventeen, in 1698; and is the authour of many Latin verse translations in the *Gent. Mag.* (vol. xv. 102). One of them is a translation of
'My time, O ye Muses, was happily spent,' &c.
He died Aug. 3, 1751, and a monument to his memory has been erected in

Register of the Prerogative Court of Lichfield, whose character, long after his decease, Dr. Johnson has, in his Life of Edmund Smith, thus drawn in the glowing colours of gratitude:

'Of Gilbert Walmsley, thus presented to my mind, let me indulge myself in the remembrance. I knew him very early; he was one of the first friends that literature procured me, and I hope that, at least, my gratitude made me worthy of his notice.

'He was of an advanced age, and I was only not a boy, yet he never received my notions with contempt. He was a whig, with all the virulence and malevolence of his party; yet difference of opinion did not keep us apart. I honoured him, and he endured me.

'He had mingled with the gay world without exemption from its vices or its follies; but had never neglected the cultivation of his mind. His belief of revelation was unshaken; his learning preserved his principles; he grew first regular, and then pious.

'His studies had been so various, that I am not able to name a man of equal knowledge. His acquaintance with books was great, and what he did not immediately know, he could, at least, tell where to find. Such was his amplitude of learning, and such his copiousness of communication, that it may be doubted whether a day now passes, in which I have not some advantage from his friendship.

'At this man's table I enjoyed many cheerful and instructive hours, with companions, such as are not often found—with one who has lengthened, and one who has gladdened life; with Dr. James, whose skill in physick will be long remembered; and with David Garrick, whom I hoped to have gratified with this character of our common friend. But what are the hopes of man! I am disappointed by that stroke of death, which has eclipsed the gaiety of nations, and impoverished the publick stock of harmless pleasure.'

In these families he passed much time in his early years. In most of them, he was in the company of ladies, particularly at Mr. Walmsley's, whose wife and sisters-in-law, of the name of Aston, and daughters of a Baronet, were remarkable for good breeding; so that the notion which has been industriously cir-

the Cathedral of Lichfield, with an inscription written by Mr. Seward, one of the Prebendaries.

culated and believed, that he never was in good company till late in life, and, consequently had been confirmed in coarse and ferocious manners by long habits, is wholly without foundation. Some of the ladies have assured me, they recollected him well when a young man, as distinguished for his complaisance.

And that this politeness was not merely occasional and temporary, or confined to the circles of Lichfield, is ascertained by the testimony of a lady, who, in a paper with which I have been favoured by a daughter of his intimate friend and physician, Dr. Lawrence, thus describes Dr. Johnson some years afterwards:

'As the particulars of the former part of Dr. Johnson's life do not seem to be very accurately known, a lady hopes that the following information may not be unacceptable.

'She remembers Dr. Johnson on a visit to Dr. Taylor, at Ashbourn, some time between the end of the year 37, and the middle of the year 40; she rather thinks it to have been after he and his wife were removed to London. During his stay at Ashbourn, he made frequent visits to Mr. Meynell, at Bradley, where his company was much desired by the ladies of the family, who were, perhaps, in point of elegance and accomplishments, inferiour to few of those with whom he was afterwards acquainted. Mr. Meynell's eldest daughter was afterwards married to Mr. Fitzherbert, father to Mr. Alleyne Fitzherbert, lately minister to the court of Russia. Of her, Dr. Johnson said, in Dr. Lawrence's study, that she had the best understanding he ever met with in any human being. At Mr. Meynell's he also commenced that friendship with Mrs. Hill Boothby, sister to the present Sir Brook Boothby, which continued till her death. *The young woman whom he used to call Molly Aston,*[1] was sister to Sir Thomas Aston, and daughter to a Baronet; she was also sister to the wife of his friend Mr. Gilbert Walmsley.[2] Besides his intimacy with the

---

[1] The words of Sir John Hawkins, p. 316.

[2] Sir Thomas Aston, Bart., who died in January, 1724–5, left one son, named Thomas also, and eight daughters. Of the daughters, Catherine married Johnson's friend, the Hon. Henry Hervey; Margaret, Gilbert Walmsley. Another of these ladies married the Rev. Mr. Gastrell; Mary, or *Molly* Aston, as she was usually called, became the wife of Captain Brodie of the navy.

above-mentioned persons, who were surely people of rank and education, while he was yet at Lichfield he used to be frequently at the house of Dr. Swinfen, a gentleman of a very ancient family in Staffordshire, from which, after the death of his elder brother, he inherited a good estate. He was, besides, a physician of very extensive practice; but for want of due attention to the management of his domestick concerns, left a very large family in indigence. One of his daughters, Mrs. Desmoulins, afterwards found an asylum in the house of her old friend, whose doors were always open to the unfortunate, and who well observed the precept of the Gospel, for he "was kind to the unthankful and to the evil." '

In the forlorn state of his circumstances, he accepted of an offer to be employed as usher in the school of Market-Bosworth, in Leicestershire, to which it appears, from one of his little fragments of a diary, that he went on foot, on the 16th of July.— '*Julii* 16. *Bosvortiam pedes petii.*'[1] But it is not true, as has been erroneously related, that he was assistant to the famous Anthony Blackwall, whose merit has been honoured by the testimony of Bishop Hurd,[2] who was his scholar; for Mr. Blackwall died on the 8th of April, 1730,[3] more than a year before Johnson left the University.

This employment was very irksome to him in every respect, and he complained grievously of it in his letters to his friend Mr. Hector, who was now settled as a surgeon at Birmingham. The letters are lost; but Mr. Hector recollects his writing 'that the poet had described the dull sameness of his existence in these words, "*Vitam continet una dies*" (one day contains the whole of my life); that it was unvaried as the note of the cuckow; and that he did not know whether it was more disagreeable for him to teach, or the boys to learn, the grammar rules.' His general aversion to this painful drudgery was greatly enhanced by a disagreement between him and Sir Wolstan Dixey, the patron of

---

[1] ['I betook myself to Bosworth on foot.']

[2] Bishop Hurd does not praise Blackwall, but the Rev. Mr. Budworth, headmaster of the grammar school at Brewood, who had himself been bred under Blackwall. [M.]

[3] See *Gent. Mag.* Dec. 1784, p. 957.

the school, in whose house, I have been told, he officiated as a kind of domestick chaplain, so far, at least, as to say grace at table, but was treated with what he represented as intolerable harshness; and, after suffering for a few months such complicated misery,[1] he relinquished a situation which all his life afterwards he recollected with the strongest aversion, and even a degree of horrour. But it is probable that at this period, whatever uneasiness he may have endured, he laid the foundation of much future eminence by application to his studies.

Being now again totally unoccupied, he was invited by Mr. Hector to pass some time with him at Birmingham, as his guest, at the house of Mr. Warren, with whom Mr. Hector lodged and boarded. Mr. Warren was the first established bookseller in Birmingham, and was very attentive to Johnson, who he soon found could be of much service to him in his trade, by his knowledge of literature; and he even obtained the assistance of his pen in furnishing some numbers of a periodical Essay printed in the news-paper, of which Warren was proprietor. After very diligent inquiry, I have not been able to recover those early specimens of that particular mode of writing by which Johnson afterwards so greatly distinguished himself.

He continued to live as Mr. Hector's guest for about six months, and then hired lodgings in another part of the town, finding himself as well situated at Birmingham as he supposed he could be anywhere, while he had no settled plan of life, and very scanty means of subsistence. He made some valuable acquaintances there, amongst whom were Mr. Porter, a mercer, whose widow he afterwards married, and Mr. Taylor, who by his ingenuity in mechanical inventions, and his success in trade, acquired an immense fortune. But the comfort of being near Mr. Hector, his old schoolfellow and intimate friend, was Johnson's chief inducement to continue here.

In what manner he employed his pen at this period, or whether he derived from it any pecuniary advantage, I have not been able

---

[1] It appears from a letter of Johnson's to a friend, dated Lichfield, July 27, 1732, that he had left Sir Wolstan Dixie's house recently, before that letter was written. [M.]

to ascertain. He probably got a little money from Mr. Warren; and we are certain, that he executed here one piece of literary labour, of which Mr. Hector has favoured me with a minute account. Having mentioned that he had read at Pembroke College a Voyage to Abyssinia, by Lobo, a Portuguese Jesuit, and that he thought an abridgement and translation of it from the French into English might be an useful and profitable publication, Mr. Warren and Mr. Hector joined in urging him to undertake it. He accordingly agreed; and the book not being to be found in Birmingham, he borrowed it of Pembroke College. A part of the work being very soon done, one Osborn, who was Mr. Warren's printer, was set to work with what was ready, and Johnson engaged to supply the press with copy as it should be wanted; but his constitutional indolence soon prevailed, and the work was at a stand. Mr. Hector, who knew that a motive of humanity would be the most prevailing argument with his friend, went to Johnson, and represented to him, that the printer could have no other employment till this undertaking was finished, and that the poor man and his family were suffering. Johnson upon this exerted the powers of his mind, though his body was relaxed. He lay in bed with the book, which was a quarto, before him, and dictated while Hector wrote. Mr. Hector carried the sheets to the press, and corrected almost all the proof sheets, very few of which were even seen by Johnson. In this manner, with the aid of Mr. Hector's active friendship, the book was completed, and was published in 1735, with LONDON upon the title-page, though it was in reality printed in Birmingham, a device too common with provincial publishers. For this work he had from Mr. Warren only the sum of five guineas.

This being the first prose work of Johnson, it is a curious object of inquiry how much may be traced in it of that style which marks his subsequent writings with such peculiar excellence; with so happy an union of force, vivacity, and perspicuity. I have perused the book with this view, and have found that here, as I believe in every other translation, there is in the work itself no vestige of the translator's own style; for the language of translation being adapted to the thoughts of another person, insensibly follows their cast, and, as it were, runs into a mould that is ready prepared.

Thus, for instance, taking the first sentence that occurs at the opening of the book, p. 4.

'I lived here above a year, and completed my studies in divinity; in which time some letters were received from the fathers in Ethiopia, with an account that Sultan Segned, Emperour of Abyssinia, was converted to the church of Rome; that many of his subjects had followed his example, and that there was a great want of missionaries to improve these prosperous beginnings. Every body was very desirous of seconding the zeal of our fathers, and of sending them the assistance they requested; to which we were the more encouraged, because the Emperour's letter informed our Provincial, that we might easily enter his dominions by the way of Dancala; but, unhappily, the secretary wrote Geila for Dancala, which cost two of our fathers their lives.'

Every one acquainted with Johnson's manner will be sensible that there is nothing of it here; but that this sentence might have been composed by any other man.

But, in the Preface, the Johnsonian style begins to appear; and though use had not yet taught his wing a permanent and equable flight, there are parts of it which exhibit his best manner in full vigour. I had once the pleasure of examining it with Mr. Edmund Burke, who confirmed me in this opinion, by his superiour critical sagacity, and was, I remember, much delighted with the following specimen:

'The Portuguese traveller, contrary to the general vein of his countrymen, has amused his reader with no romantick absurdity, or incredible fictions; whatever he relates, whether true or not, is at least probable; and he who tells nothing exceeding the bounds of probability, has a right to demand that they should believe him who cannot contradict him.

'He appears, by his modest and unaffected narration, to have described things as he saw them, to have copied nature from the life, and to have consulted his senses, not his imagination. He meets with no basilisks that destroy with their eyes, his crocodiles devour their prey without tears, and his cataracts fall from the rocks without deafening the neighbouring inhabitants.

'The reader will here find no regions cursed with irremediable barrenness, or blessed with spontaneous fecundity; no perpetual gloom, or unceasing sunshine; nor are the nations here described either devoid of all sense of humanity, or consummate in all private or social virtues. Here are no Hottentots without religious polity or articulate language; no Chinese perfectly polite, and completely skilled in all sciences; he will discover, what will always be discovered by a diligent and impartial enquirer, that wherever human nature is to be found, there is a mixture of vice and virtue, a contest of passion and reason; and that the Creator doth not appear partial in his distributions, but has balanced, in most countries, their particular inconveniences by particular favours.'

Here we have an early example of that brilliant and energetick expression, which, upon innumerable occasions in his subsequent life, justly impressed the world with the highest admiration.

Nor can any one, conversant with the writings of Johnson, fail to discern his hand in this passage of the Dedication to John Warren, Esq. of Pembrokeshire, though it is ascribed to Warren the bookseller:

'A generous and elevated mind is distinguished by nothing more certainly than an eminent degree of curiosity;[1] nor is that curiosity ever more agreeably or usefully employed, than in examining the laws and customs of foreign nations. I hope, therefore, the present I now presume to make, will not be thought improper; which, however, it is not my business as a dedicator to commend, nor as a bookseller to depreciate.'

It is reasonable to suppose, that his having been thus accidentally led to a particular study of the history and manners of Abyssinia, was the remote occasion of his writing, many years afterwards, his admirable philosophical tale, the principal scene of which is laid in that country.

Johnson returned to Lichfield early in 1734, and in August that year he made an attempt to procure some little subsistence

---

[1] See *Rambler*, No. 103.

by his pen; for he published proposals for printing by subscription the Latin Poems of Politian:[1] *'Angeli Politiani Poemata Latina, quibus, Notas cum historiâ Latinæ poeseos, a Petrarchæ ævo ad Politiani tempora deductâ, et vitâ Politiani fusius quam antehac enarratâ, addidit* SAM. JOHNSON.*'*[2]

It appears that his brother Nathanael had taken up his father's trade; for it is mentioned that 'subscriptions are taken in by the Editor, or N. Johnson, bookseller, of Lichfield.' Notwithstanding the merit of Johnson, and the cheap price at which this book was offered, there were not subscribers enough to insure a sufficient sale; so the work never appeared, and probably, never was executed.

We find him again this year at Birmingham, and there is preserved the following letter from him to Mr. Edward Cave,[3] the original compiler and editor of the *Gentleman's Magazine:*

To MR. CAVE

'SIR,   *Nov.* 25, 1734.

    'As you appear no less sensible than your readers of the defects of your poetical article, you will not be displeased, if, in order to the improvement of it, I communicate to you the sentiments of a person, who will undertake, on reasonable terms, sometimes to fill a column.

'His opinion is, that the publick would not give you a bad reception, if, beside the current wit of the month, which a critical

[1] May we not trace a fanciful similarity between Politian and Johnson? Huetius, speaking of Paulus Pelissonius Fontanerius, says, '. . . in quo Natura, ut olim in Angelo Politiano, deformitatem oris excellentis ingenii præstantia compensavit.' ['in whom, as formerly in A.P., nature compensated bodily ugliness with great intellectual eminence'.] *Comment. de reb. ad eum pertin.* Edit. Amstel. 1718, p. 200.

[2] 'The Latin Poems of Angelus Politianus, edited by Samuel Johnson with notes, a history of Latin poetry from Petrarch to Politian, and a fuller life of Politian than has hitherto been written.' The book was to contain more than thirty sheets, the price to be two shillings and sixpence at the time of subscribing, and two shillings and sixpence at the delivery of a perfect book in quires.

[3] Miss Cave, the grand-niece of Mr. Edward Cave, has obligingly shewn me the originals of this and the other letters of Dr. Johnson, to him, which were first published in the *Gent. Mag.* [lv. 3], with notes by Mr. John Nichols, the worthy and indefatigable editor of that valuable miscellany, signed N.; some of which I shall occasionally transcribe in the course of this work.

examination would generally reduce to a narrow compass, you admitted not only poems, inscriptions, &c. never printed before, which he will sometimes supply you with; but likewise short literary dissertations in Latin or English, critical remarks on authours ancient or modern, forgotten poems that deserve revival, or loose pieces, like Floyer's,[1] worth preserving. By this method, your literary article, for so it might be called, will, he thinks, be better recommended to the publick than by low jests, aukward buffoonery, or the dull scurrilities of either party.

'If such a correspondence will be agreeable to you, be pleased to inform me in two posts, what the conditions are on which you shall expect it. Your late offer[2] gives me no reason to distrust your generosity. If you engage in any literary projects besides this paper, I have other designs to impart, if I could be secure from having others reap the advantage of what I should hint.

'Your letter by being directed to *S. Smith*, to be left at the Castle in Birmingham, Warwickshire, will reach

'Your humble servant.'

Mr. Cave has put a note on this letter, 'Answered Dec. 2.' But whether any thing was done in consequence of it we are not informed.

Johnson had, from his early youth, been sensible to the influence of female charms. When at Stourbridge school, he was much enamoured of Olivia Lloyd, a young quaker, to whom he wrote a copy of verses, which I have not been able to recover; but with what facility and elegance he could warble the amorous lay, will appear from the following lines which he wrote for his friend Mr. Edmund Hector.

VERSES *to a* LADY, *on receiving from her a* SPRIG *of* MYRTLE.

'WHAT hopes, what terrours does thy gift create,
Ambiguous emblem of uncertain fate:
The myrtle, ensign of supreme command,
Consign'd by Venus to Melissa's hand;

[1] Sir John Floyer's Treatise on Cold Baths. *Gent. Mag.* 1734, p. 197.
[2] A prize of fifty pounds for the best poem on 'Life, Death, Judgement, Heaven, and Hell.' See *Gent. Mag.* vol. iv. p. 560. N.

> Not less capricious than a reigning fair,
> Now grants, and now rejects a lover's prayer.
> In myrtle shades oft sings the happy swain,
> In myrtle shades despairing ghosts complain;
> The myrtle crowns the happy lovers' heads,
> The unhappy lovers' grave the myrtle spreads:
> O then the meaning of thy gift impart,
> And ease the throbbings of an anxious heart!
> Soon must this bough, as you shall fix his doom,
> Adorn Philander's head, or grace his tomb.'[1]

[1] Mrs. Piozzi gives the following account of this little composition from Dr. Johnson's own relation to her, on her inquiring whether it was rightly attributed to him:—'I think it is now just forty years ago, that a young fellow had a sprig of myrtle given him by a girl he courted, and asked me to write him some verses that he might present her in return. I promised, but forgot; and when he called for his lines at the time agreed on—Sit still a moment, (says I) dear Mund, and I'll fetch them thee—So stepped aside for five minutes, and wrote the nonsense you now keep such a stir about.' *Anec.* p. 34.

In my first edition I was induced to doubt the authenticity of this account, by the following circumstantial statement in a letter to me from Miss Seward, of Lichfield:—'*I know* those verses were addressed to Lucy Porter, when he was enamoured of her in his boyish days, two or three years before he had seen her mother, his future wife. He wrote them at my grandfather's, and gave them to Lucy in the presence of my mother, to whom he showed them on the instant. She used to repeat them to me, when I asked her for *the Verses Dr. Johnson gave her on a Sprig of Myrtle, which he had stolen or begged from her bosom.* We all know honest Lucy Porter to have been incapable of the mean vanity of applying to herself a compliment not *intended* for her.' Such was this lady's statement, which I make no doubt she supposed to be correct; but it shows how dangerous it is to trust too implicitly to traditional testimony and ingenious inference; for Mr. Hector has lately assured me that Mrs. Piozzi's account is in this instance accurate, and that he was the person for whom Johnson wrote those verses, which have been erroneously ascribed to Mr. Hammond.

I am obliged in so many instances to notice Mrs. Piozzi's incorrectness of relation, that I gladly seize this opportunity of acknowledging, that however often, she is not always inaccurate.

The author having been drawn into a controversy with Miss Anna Seward, in consequence of the preceding statement, (which may be found in the *Gent. Mag.* vol. liii. and liv.) received the following letter from Mr. Edmund Hector, on the subject:—

'DEAR SIR,—I am sorry to see you are engaged in altercation with a Lady, who seems unwilling to be convinced of her errors. Surely it would be more ingenuous to acknowledge, than to persevere.

'Lately, in looking over some papers I meant to burn, I found the original manuscript of the *Myrtle,* with the date on it, 1731, which I have inclosed.

'The true history (which I could swear to) is as follows: Mr. Morgan

His juvenile attachments to the fair sex were, however, very transient; and it is certain that he formed no criminal connection whatsoever. Mr. Hector, who lived with him in his younger days in the utmost intimacy and social freedom, has assured me, that even at that ardent season his conduct was strictly virtuous in that respect; and that though he loved to exhilarate himself with wine, he never knew him intoxicated but once.

In a man whom religious education has secured from licentious indulgences, the passion of love, when once it has seized him, is exceedingly strong; being unimpaired by dissipation, and totally concentrated in one object. This was experienced by Johnson, when he became the fervent admirer of Mrs. Porter, after her first husband's death. Miss Porter told me, that when he was first introduced to her mother, his appearance was very forbidding: he was then lean and lank, so that his immense structure of bones was hideously striking to the eye, and the scars of the scrophula were deeply visible. He also wore his hair, which was straight and stiff, and separated behind: and he often had, seemingly, convulsive starts and odd gesticulations, which tended to excite at once surprize and ridicule. Mrs. Porter was so much engaged by his conversation that she overlooked all these external disadvantages, and said to her daughter, 'this is the most sensible man that I ever saw in my life.'

Though Mrs. Porter was double the age of Johnson,[1] and her

Graves, the elder brother of a worthy Clergyman near Bath, with whom I was acquainted, waited upon a lady in this neighbourhood, who at parting presented him the branch. He shewed it me, and wished much to return the compliment in verse. I applied to Johnson, who was with me, and in about half an hour dictated the verses which I sent to my friend.

'I most solemnly declare, at that time Johnson was an entire stranger to the Porter family; and it was almost two years after that I introduced him to the acquaintance of Porter, whom I bought my cloaths of.

'If you intend to convince this obstinate woman, and to exhibit to the publick the truth of your narrative, you are at liberty to make what use you please of this statement.

'I hope you will pardon me for taking up so much of your time. Wishing you *multos et felices annos* [many years and happy ones], I shall subscribe myself,   'Your obliged humble servant,
                                                                              'E. HECTOR.'
'*Birmingham*, Jan. 9th, 1794.'
    [1] Mrs. Johnson was born on Feb. 4, 1688–9. [M.]

person and manner, as described to me by the late Mr. Garrick, were by no means pleasing to others, she must have had a superiority of understanding and talents, as she certainly inspired him with a more than ordinary passion; and she having signified her willingness to accept of his hand, he went to Lichfield to ask his mother's consent to the marriage, which he could not but be conscious was a very imprudent scheme, both on account of their disparity of years, and her want of fortune. But Mrs. Johnson knew too well the ardour of her son's temper, and was too tender a parent to oppose his inclinations.

I know not for what reason the marriage ceremony was not performed at Birmingham; but a resolution was taken that it should be at Derby, for which place the bride and bridegroom set out on horseback, I suppose in very good humour. But though Mr. Topham Beauclerk used archly to mention Johnson's having told him, with much gravity, 'Sir, it was a love-marriage upon both sides,' I have had from my illustrious friend the following curious account of their journey to church upon the nuptial morn:

9*th* JULY:—'Sir, she had read the old romances, and had got into her head the fantastical notion that a woman of spirit should use her lover like a dog. So, Sir, at first she told me that I rode too fast, and she could not keep up with me; and, when I rode a little slower, she passed me, and complained that I lagged behind. I was not to be made the slave of caprice; and I resolved to begin as I meant to end. I therefore pushed on briskly, till I was fairly out of her sight. The road lay between two hedges, so I was sure she could not miss it; and I contrived that she should soon come up with me. When she did, I observed her to be in tears.'

This, it must be allowed, was a singular beginning of connubial felicity; but there is no doubt that Johnson, though he thus shewed a manly firmness, proved a most affectionate and indulgent husband to the last moment of Mrs. Johnson's life: and in his *Prayers and Meditations* we find very remarkable evidence that his regard and fondness for her never ceased, even after her death.

He now set up a private academy, for which purpose he hired

a large house, well situated near his native city. In the *Gentleman's Magazine* for 1736, there is the following advertisement:

'At Edial, near Lichfield, in Staffordshire, young gentlemen
are boarded and taught the Latin and Greek languages, by
SAMUEL JOHNSON.'

But the only pupils that were put under his care were the
celebrated David Garrick and his brother George, and a Mr.
Offely, a young gentleman of good fortune who died early. As
yet, his name had nothing of that celebrity which afterwards commanded the highest attention and respect of mankind. Had such
an advertisement appeared after the publication of his *London*,
or his *Rambler*, or his *Dictionary*, how would it have burst upon
the world! with what eagerness would the great and the wealthy
have embraced an opportunity of putting their sons under the
learned tuition of SAMUEL JOHNSON. The truth, however, is, that
he was not so well qualified for being a teacher of elements, and
a conductor in learning by regular gradations, as men of inferiour
powers of mind. His own acquisitions had been made by fits and
starts, by violent irruptions into the regions of knowledge; and
it could not be expected that his impatience would be subdued,
and his impetuosity restrained, so as to fit him for a quiet guide
to novices. The art of communicating instruction, of whatever
kind, is much to be valued; and I have ever thought that those
who devote themselves to this employment, and do their duty
with diligence and success, are entitled to very high respect from
the community, as Johnson himself often maintained. Yet I am
of opinion that the greatest abilities are not only not required
for this office, but render a man less fit for it.

While we acknowledge the justness of Thomson's beautiful
remark,

> 'Delightful task! to rear the tender thought,
> And teach the young idea how to shoot!'

we must consider that this delight is perceptible only by 'a mind at
ease,' a mind at once calm and clear; but that a mind gloomy and
impetuous like that of Johnson, cannot be fixed for any length
of time in minute attention, and must be so frequently irritated
by unavoidable slowness and errour in the advances of scholars,

as to perform the duty, with little pleasure to the teacher, and no great advantage to the pupils. Good temper is a most essential requisite in a Preceptor. Horace paints the character as *bland:*

> '. . . . *Ut pueris olim dant crustula* blandi
> *Doctores, elementa velint ut discere prima.*'[1]

Johnson was not more satisfied with his situation as the master of an academy, than with that of the usher of a school; we need not wonder, therefore, that he did not keep his academy above a year and a half. From Mr. Garrick's account he did not appear to have been profoundly reverenced by his pupils. His odditics of manner, and uncouth gesticulations, could not but be the subject of merriment to them; and, in particular, the young rogues used to listen at the door of his bed-chamber, and peep through the key-hole, that they might turn into ridicule his tumultuous and awkward fondness for Mrs. Johnson, whom he used to name by the familiar appellation of *Tetty* or *Tetsey,* which, like *Betty* or *Betsey,* is provincially used as a contraction for *Elisabeth,* her christian name, but which to us seems ludicrous, when applied to a woman of her age and appearance. Mr. Garrick described her to me as very fat, with a bosom of more than ordinary protuberance, with swelled cheeks of a florid red, produced by thick painting, and increased by the liberal use of cordials; flaring and fantastick in her dress, and affected both in her speech and her general behaviour. I have seen Garrick exhibit her, by his exquisite talent for mimickry, so as to excite the heartiest bursts of laughter; but he, probably, as is the case in all such representation, considerably aggravated the picture.

That Johnson well knew the most proper course to be pursued in the instruction of youth, is authentically ascertained by the following paper in his own hand-writing, given about this period to a relation,[2] and now in the possession of Mr. John Nichols:

'SCHEME *for the* CLASSES *of a* GRAMMAR SCHOOL.

'When the introduction, or formation of nouns and verbs, is perfectly mastered, let them learn

---

[1] ['as teachers sometimes give little boys cakes to coax them into learning their letters.' Hor. 1 *Sat.* 1. 25. (Wickham.)]
[2] The Rev. Samuel Ford. *Reade.*

'Corderius by Mr. Clarke, beginning at the same time to translate out of the introduction, that by this means they may learn the syntax. Then let them proceed to

'Erasmus, with an English translation, by the same authour.

'Class II. Learns Eutropius and Cornelius Nepos, or Justin, with the translation.

'N.B. The first class gets for their part every morning the rules which they have learned before, and in the afternoon learns the Latin rules of the nouns and verbs.

'They are examined in the rules which they have learned every Thursday and Saturday.

'The second class doth the same whilst they are in Eutropius; afterwards their part is in the irregular nouns and verbs, and in the rules for making and scanning verses. They are examined as the first.

'Class III. Ovid's Metamorphoses in the morning, and Cæsar's Commentaries in the afternoon.

'Practise in the Latin rules till they are perfect in them; afterwards in Mr. Leeds's Greek Grammar. Examined as before.

'Afterwards they proceed to Virgil, beginning at the same time to write themes and verses, and to learn Greek; from thence passing on to Horace, &c. as shall seem most proper.

'I know not well what books to direct you to, because you have not informed me what study you will apply yourself to. I believe it will be most for your advantage to apply yourself wholly to the languages, till you go to the University. The Greek authours I think it best for you to read are these: Cebes; Ælian, Lucian by Leeds, Xenophon (Attick); Homer (Ionick); Theocritus (Dorick); Euripides (Attick and Dorick).

'Thus you will be tolerably skilled in all the dialects, beginning with the Attick, to which the rest must be referred.

'In the study of Latin, it is proper not to read the latter authours, till you are well versed in those of the purest ages; as Terence, Tully, Cæsar, Sallust, Nepos, Velleius Paterculus, Virgil, Horace, Phædrus.

'The greatest and most necessary task still remains, to attain a habit of expression, without which knowledge is of little use.

This is necessary in Latin, and more necessary in English; and can only be acquired by a daily imitation of the best and correctest authours.

'SAM. JOHNSON.'

While Johnson kept his academy, there can be no doubt that he was insensibly furnishing his mind with various knowledge; but I have not discovered that he wrote any thing except a great part of his tragedy of *Irene.* Mr. Peter Garrick, the elder brother of David, told me that he remembered Johnson's borrowing the *Turkish History* of him, in order to form his play from it. When he had finished some part of it, he read what he had done to Mr. Walmsley, who objected to his having already brought his heroine into great distress, and asked him, 'How can you possibly contrive to plunge her into deeper calamity?' Johnson, in sly allusion to the supposed oppressive proceedings of the court of which Mr. Walmsley was register, replied, 'Sir, I can put her into the Spiritual Court!'

Mr. Walmsley, however, was well pleased with this proof of Johnson's abilities as a dramatick writer, and advised him to finish the tragedy, and produce it on the stage.

Johnson now thought of trying his fortune in London, the great field of genius and exertion, where talents of every kind have the fullest scope, and the highest encouragement. It is a memorable circumstance that his pupil David Garrick went thither at the same time,[1] with intention to complete his education, and follow the profession of the law, from which he was soon diverted by his decided preference for the stage.

This joint expedition of those two eminent men to the metropolis, was many years afterwards noticed in an allegorical poem

[1] Both of them used to talk pleasantly of this their first journey to London. Garrick, evidently meaning to embellish a little, said one day in my hearing, 'we rode and tied.' And the Bishop of Killaloe informed me, that at another time, when Johnson and Garrick were dining together in a pretty large company, Johnson humorously ascertaining the chronology of something, expressed himself thus: 'that was the year when I came to London with two-pence half-penny in my pocket.' Garrick over-hearing him, exclaimed, 'Eh? what do you say? with two-pence half-penny in your pocket?' —JOHNSON, 'Why yes; when I came with two-pence half-penny in *my* pocket, and thou, Davy, with three half-pence in thine.'

on Shakspeare's Mulberry Tree, by Mr. Lovibond, the ingenious authour of *The Tears of Old-Mayday*.

They were recommended to Mr. Colson,[1] an eminent mathematician and master of an academy, by the following letter from Mr. Walmsley:

'*To* The Reverend Mr. Colson

'Dear Sir,   'Lichfield, March 2, 1737.

'I had the favour of yours, and am extremely obliged to you; but I cannot say I had a greater affection for you upon it than I had before, being long since so much endeared to you, as well by an early friendship, as by your many excellent and valuable qualifications; and, had I a son of my own, it would be my ambition, instead of sending him to the University, to dispose of him as this young gentleman is.

'He, and another neighbour of mine, one Mr. Samuel Johnson, set out this morning for London together. Davy Garrick is to be with you early the next week, and Mr. Johnson to try his fate with a tragedy, and to see to get himself employed in some translation, either from the Latin or the French. Johnson is a very good scholar and poet, and I have great hopes will turn out a fine tragedy-writer. If it should any way lie in your way, doubt not but you would be ready to recommend and assist your countryman.

'G. Walmsley.'

How he employed himself upon his first coming to London is not particularly known.[2] I never heard that he found any protection or encouragement by the means of Mr. Colson, to whose academy David Garrick went. Mrs. Lucy Porter told me, that Mr. Walmsley gave him a letter of introduction to Lintot his bookseller, and that Johnson wrote some things for him; but I

[1] Mr. Colson was First Master of the Free School at Rochester. In 1739 he was appointed Lucasian Professor of Mathematics at Cambridge. [M.]

[2] One curious anecdote was communicated by himself to Mr. John Nichols. Mr. Wilcox, the bookseller, on being informed by him that his intention was to get his livelihood as an authour, eyed his robust frame attentively, and with a significant look, said, 'You had better buy a porter's knot.' He however added, 'Wilcox was one of my best friends.'

imagine this to be a mistake, for I have discovered no trace of it, and I am pretty sure he told me that Mr. Cave was the first publisher by whom his pen was engaged in London.

He had a little money when he came to town, and he knew how he could live in the cheapest manner. His first lodgings were at the house of Mr. Norris, a staymaker, in Exeter-street, adjoining Catherine-street, in the Strand. 'I dined (said he) very well for eight-pence, with very good company, at the Pine Apple in New-street, just by. Several of them had travelled. They expected to meet every day; but did not know one another's names. It used to cost the rest a shilling, for they drank wine; but I had a cut of meat for six-pence, and bread for a penny, and gave the waiter a penny; so that I was quite well served, nay, better than the rest, for they gave the waiter nothing.' He at this time, I believe, abstained entirely from fermented liquors: a practice to which he rigidly conformed for many years together, at different periods of his life.

His Ofellus in the *Art of Living in London*, I have heard him relate, was an Irish painter,[1] whom he knew at Birmingham, and who had practised his own precepts of œconomy for several years in the British capital. He assured Johnson, who, I suppose, was then meditating to try his fortune in London, but was apprehensive of the expence, 'that thirty pounds a year was enough to enable a man to live there without being contemptible. He allowed ten pounds for clothes and linen. He said a man might live in a garret at eighteen-pence a week; few people would inquire where he lodged; and if they did, it was easy to say, 'Sir, I am to be found at such a place.' By spending three-pence in a coffee-house, he might be for some hours every day in very good company; he might dine for six-pence, breakfast on bread and milk for a penny, and do without supper. On *clean-shirt-day* he went abroad, and paid visits.' I have heard him more than once talk of this frugal friend, whom he recollected with esteem and kindness, and did not like to have any one smile at the recital. 'This man (said he, gravely) was a very sensible man, who perfectly understood common affairs: a man of a great deal of

[1] Possibly Michael Ford (d. *c.* 1759) as suggested by Prof. J. B. Kirby.

knowledge of the world, fresh from life, not strained through books. He borrowed a horse and ten pounds at Birmingham. Finding himself master of so much money, he set off for West Chester, in order to get to Ireland. He returned the horse, and probably the ten pounds too, after he got home.'

Considering Johnson's narrow circumstances in the early part of his life, and particularly at the interesting æra of his launching into the ocean of London, it is not be wondered at, that at an actual instance, proved by experience, of the possibility of enjoying the intellectual luxury of social life, upon a very small income, should deeply engage his attention, and be ever recollected by him as a circumstance of much importance. He amused himself, I remember, by computing how much more expence was absolutely necessary to live upon the same scale with that which his friend described, when the value of money was diminished by the progress of commerce. It may be estimated that double the money might now with difficulty be sufficient.

Amidst this cold obscurity, there was one brilliant circumstance to cheer him; he was well acquainted with Mr. Henry Hervey,[1] one of the branches of the noble family of that name, who had been quartered at Lichfield as an officer of the army, and had at this time a house in London, where Johnson was frequently entertained, and had an opportunity of meeting genteel company. Not very long before his death, he mentioned this, among other particulars of his life, which he was kindly communicating to me; and he described this early friend, 'Harry Hervey,' thus: 'He was a vicious man, but very kind to me. If you call a dog HERVEY, I shall love him.'

He told me he had now written only three acts of his *Irene*, and that he retired for some time to lodgings at Greenwich, where he proceeded in it somewhat further, and used to compose, walking in the Park; but did not stay long enough at that place to finish it.

---

[1] The honourable Henry Hervey, third son of the first Earl of Bristol, quitted the army and took orders. He married a sister of Sir Thomas Aston, by whom he got the Aston Estate, and assumed the name and arms of that family. Vide Collins's *Peerage*.

At this period we find the following letter from him to Mr. Edward Cave, which, as a link in the chain of his literary history, it is proper to insert:

'*To* Mr. Cave

'Greenwich, next door to the Golden Heart, Church-street, July 12, 1737.

'Sir,

'Having observed in your papers very uncommon offers of encouragement to men of letters, I have chosen, being a stranger in London, to communicate to you the following design, which, I hope, if you join in it, will be of advantage to both of us.

'The History of the Council of Trent having been lately translated into French, and published with large Notes by Dr. Le Courayer, the reputation of that book is so much revived in England, that, it is presumed, a new translation of it from the Italian, together with Le Courayer's Notes from the French, could not fail of a favourable reception.

'If it be answered, that the History is already in English, it must be remembered, that there was the same objection against Le Courayer's undertaking, with this disadvantage, that the French had a version by one of their best translators, whereas you cannot read three pages of the English History without discovering that the style is capable of great improvements; but whether those improvements are to be expected from the attempt, you must judge from the specimen, which, if you approve the proposal, I shall submit to your examination.

'Suppose the merit of the versions equal, we may hope that the addition of the Notes will turn the balance in our favour, considering the reputation of the Annotator.

'Be pleased to favour me with a speedy answer, if you are not willing to engage in this scheme; and appoint me a day to wait upon you, if you are. I am, Sir, your humble servant,

'Sam. Johnson.'

It should seem from this letter, though subscribed with his own name, that he had not yet been introduced to Mr. Cave.

We shall presently see what was done in consequence of the proposal which it contains.

In the course of the summer he returned to Lichfield, where he had left Mrs. Johnson, and there he at last finished his tragedy, which was not executed with his rapidity of composition upon other occasions, but was slowly and painfully elaborated. A few days before his death, while burning a great mass of papers, he picked out from among them the original unformed sketch of this tragedy, in his own hand-writing, and gave it to Mr. Langton, by whose favour a copy of it is now in my possession. It contains fragments of the intended plot, and speeches for the different persons of the drama, partly in the raw materials of prose, partly worked up into verse; as also a variety of hints for illustration, borrowed from the Greek, Roman, and modern writers. The hand-writing is very difficult to read, even by those who were best acquainted with Johnson's mode of penmanship, which at all times was very particular. The King having graciously accepted of this manuscript as a literary curiosity, Mr. Langton made a fair and distinct copy of it, which he ordered to be bound up with the original and the printed tragedy; and the volume is deposited in the King's library. His Majesty was pleased to permit Mr. Langton to take a copy of it for himself.

The whole of it is rich in thought and imagery, and happy expressions; and of the *disjecta membra*[1] scattered throughout, and as yet unarranged, a good dramatick poet might avail himself with considerable advantage. I shall give my readers some specimens of different kinds, distinguishing them by the Italick character.

> '*Nor think to say, here will I stop,*
> *Here will I fix the limits of transgression,*
> *Nor farther tempt the avenging rage of heaven.*
> *When guilt like this once harbours in the breast,*
> *Those holy beings, whose unseen direction*
> *Guides through the maze of life the steps of man,*
> *Fly the detested mansions of impiety,*
> *And quit their charge to horrour and to ruin.*'

[1] ['dismembered limbs']. Horace, *Sat.* I. iv. 62.

A small part only of this interesting admonition is preserved in the play, and is varied, I think, not to advantage:

> 'The soul once tainted with so foul a crime,
> No more shall glow with friendship's hallow'd ardour,
> Those holy beings whose superior care
> Guides erring mortals to the paths of virtue,
> Affrighted at impiety like thine,
> Resign their charge to baseness and to ruin.'

> *'I feel the soft infection*
> *Flush in my cheek, and wander in my veins.*
> *Teach me the Grecian arts of soft persuasion.'*

'Sure this is love, which heretofore I conceived the dream of idle maids, and wanton poets.'

'Though no comets or prodigies foretold the ruin of Greece, signs which heaven must by another miracle enable us to understand, yet might it be foreshewn, by tokens no less certain, by the vices which always bring it on.'

This last passage is worked up in the tragedy itself, as follows:

LEONTIUS.

> '———That power that kindly spreads
> The clouds, a signal of impending showers,
> To warn the wand'ring linnet to the shade,
> Beheld, without concern, expiring Greece,
> And not one prodigy foretold our fate.

DEMETRIUS.

> 'A thousand horrid prodigies foretold it;
> A feeble government, eluded laws,
> A factious populace, luxurious nobles,
> And all the maladies of sinking States.
> When publick villainy, too strong for justice,
> Shows his bold front, the harbinger of ruin,
> Can brave Leontius call for airy wonders,
> Which cheats interpret, and which fools regard?
> When some neglected fabrick nods beneath
> The weight of years, and totters to the tempest
> Must heaven despatch the messengers of light,
> Or wake the dead, to warn us of its fall?'

MAHOMET (to IRENE). '*I have tried thee, and joy to find that thou deservest to be loved by Mahomet,—with a mind great as his own. Sure, thou art an errour of nature, and an exception to the rest of thy sex, and art immortal; for sentiments like thine were never to sink into nothing. I thought all the thoughts of the fair had been to select the graces of the day, dispose the colours of the flaunting (flowing) robe, tune the voice and roll the eye, place the gem, choose the dress, and add new roses to the failing cheek, but—sparkling.*'

Thus in the tragedy:

> 'Illustrious maid, new wonders fix me thine;
> Thy soul completes the triumphs of thy face:
> I thought, forgive my fair, the noblest aim,
> The strongest effort of a female soul
> Was but to choose the graces of the day,
> To tune the tongue, to teach the eyes to roll,
> Dispose the colours of the flowing robe,
> And add new roses to the faded cheek.'

I shall select one other passage, on account of the doctrine which it illustrates. IRENE observes,

'*That the Supreme Being will accept of virtue, whatever outward circumstances it may be accompanied with, and may be delighted with varieties of worship:* but is answered, *That variety cannot affect that Being, who, infinitely happy is his own perfections, wants no external gratifications; nor can infinite truth be delighted with falshood; that though he may guide or pity those he leaves in darkness, he abandons those who shut their eyes against the beams of day.*'

Johnson's residence at Lichfield, on his return to it at this time, was only for three months; and as he had as yet seen but a small part of the wonders of the Metropolis, he had little to tell his townsmen. He related to me the following minute anecdote of this period: 'In the last age, when my mother lived in London, there were two sets of people, those who gave the wall, and those who took it; the peaceable and the quarrelsome. When I returned to Lichfield, after having been in London, my mother asked me, whether I was one of those who gave the wall, or those who took it. *Now* it is fixed that every man keeps to the right; or, if one is taking the wall, another yields it; and it is never a dispute.'[1]

He now removed to London with Mrs. Johnson; but her daughter, who had lived with them at Edial, was left with her relations in the country. His lodgings were for some time in Woodstock-street, near Hanover-square, and afterwards in Castle-street, near Cavendish-square. As there is something pleasingly interesting, to many, in tracing so great a man through all his different habitations, I shall, before this work is concluded, present my readers with an exact list of his lodgings and houses, in order of time, which, in placid condescension to my respectful curiosity, he one evening dictated to me, but without specifying how long he lived at each. In the progress of his life I shall have occasion to mention some of them as connected with particular incidents, or with the writing of particular parts of his works. To some, this minute attention may appear trifling; but when we consider the punctilious exactness with which the different houses in which Milton resided have been traced by the writers of his life, a similar enthusiasm may be pardoned in the biographer of Johnson.

His tragedy being by this time, as he thought, completely finished and fit for the stage, he was very desirous that it should be brought forward. Mr. Peter Garrick told me, that Johnson and he went together to the Fountain tavern, and read it over, and that he afterwards solicited Mr. Fleetwood, the patentee of Drury-lane theatre, to have it acted at his house; but Mr. Fleetwood would not accept it, probably because it was not patronized by some man of high rank; and it was not acted till 1749, when his friend David Garrick was manager of that theatre.

The Gentleman's Magazine, begun and carried on by Mr. Edward Cave, under the name of Sylvanus Urban, had attracted the notice and esteem of Johnson, in an eminent degree, before he came to London as an adventurer in literature. He told me, that when he first saw St. John's Gate, the place where that deservedly popular miscellany was originally printed, he 'beheld

[1] *Journal of a Tour to the Hebrides,* 3rd edit. p. 232 [Sept. 20, 1773].

it with reverence.' I suppose, indeed, that every young authour
has had the same kind of feeling for the magazine or periodical
publication which has first entertained him, and in which he has
first had an opportunity to see himself in print, without the risk
of exposing his name. I myself recollect such impressions from
The Scots Magazine, which was begun at Edinburgh in the year
1739, and has been ever conducted with judgement, accuracy,
and propriety. I yet cannot help thinking of it with an affectionate
regard. Johnson has dignified the *Gentleman's Magazine*, by the
importance with which he invests the life of Cave; but he has
given it still greater lustre by the various admirable Essays
which he wrote for it.

Though Johnson was often solicited by his friends to make a
complete list of his writings, and talked of doing it, I believe
with a serious intention that they should all be collected on his
own account, he put it off from year to year, and at last died
without having done it perfectly. I have one in his own hand-
writing, which contains a certain number; I indeed doubt if he
could have remembered every one of them, as they were so
numerous, so various, and scattered in such a multiplicity of
unconnected publications; nay, several of them published under
the names of other persons, to whom he liberally contributed
from the abundance of his mind. We must, therefore, be content
to discover them, partly from occasional information given by
him to his friends, and partly from internal evidence.[1]

His first performance in the *Gentleman's Magazine*, which for
many years was his principal resource for employment and support, was a copy of Latin verses, in March 1738, addressed to
the editor in so happy a style of compliment, that Cave must
have been destitute both of taste and sensibility had he not felt
himself highly gratified.

---

[1] While in the course of my narrative I enumerate his writings, I shall
take care that my readers shall not be left to waver in doubt, between certainty and conjecture, with regard to their authenticity; and, for that purpose, shall mark with an *asterisk* (*) those which he acknowledged to his
friends, and with a *dagger* (†) those which are ascertained to be his by
internal evidence. When any other pieces are ascribed to him, I shall give
my reasons.

'*Ad* URBANUM.*

'URBANE, *nullis fesse laboribus,*
URBANE, *nullis victe calumniis,*
    Cui fronte sertum in eruditâ
        Perpetuò viret et virebit;

Quid moliatur gens imitantium,
Quid et minetur, solicitus parùm,
    Vacare solis perge Musis,
        Juxta animo studiisque felix.

Linguæ procacis plumbea spicula,
Fidens, superbo frange silentio;
    Victrix per obstantes catervas
        Sedulitas animosa tendet.

Intende nervos, fortis, inanibus
Risurus olim nisibus æmuli;
    Intende jam nervos, habebis
        Participes operæ Camænas.

Non ulla Musis pagina gratior,
Quam quæ severis ludicra jungere
    Novit, fatigatamque nugis
        Utilibus recreare mentem.

Texente Nymphis serta Lycoride,
Rosæ ruborem sic viola adjuvat
    Immista, sic Iris refulget
        Æthereis variata fucis.'[1]   S. J.

---

[1] A translation of this Ode, by an unknown correspondent, appeared in
the *Magazine* for the month of May following:

'Hail, URBAN! indefatigable man,
Unwearied yet by all thy useful toil!
    Whom num'rous slanderers assault in vain;
Whom no base calumny can put to foil.
    But still the laurel on thy learned brow
    Flourishes fair, and shall for ever grow.

'What mean the servile imitating crew,
What their vain blust'ring, and their empty noise,
    Ne'er seek: but still thy noble ends pursue,
Unconquer'd by the rabble's venal voice.
    Still to the Muse thy studious mind apply,
    Happy in temper as in industry.

It appears that he was now enlisted by Mr. Cave as a regular coadjutor in his magazine, by which he probably obtained a tolerable livelihood. At what time, or by what means, he had acquired a competent knowledge both of French and Italian, I do not know; but he was so well skilled in them, as to be sufficiently qualified for a translator. That part of his labour which consisted in emendation and improvement of the productions of other contributors, like that employed in levelling ground, can be perceived only by those who had an opportunity of comparing the original with the altered copy. What we certainly know to have been done by him in this way, was the Debates in both houses of Parliament, under the name of 'The Senate of Lilliput,' sometimes with feigned denominations of the several speakers, sometimes with denominations formed of the letters of their real names, in the manner of what is called anagram, so that they might easily be decyphered. Parliament then kept the press in a kind of mysterious awe, which made it necessary to have recourse to such devices. In our time it has acquired an

'The senseless sneerings of an haughty tongue,
Unworthy thy attention to engage,
    Unheeded pass: and tho' they mean thee wrong,
By manly silence disappoint their rage.
    Assiduous diligence confounds its foes,
    Resistless, tho' malicious crouds oppose.

'Exert thy powers, nor slacken in the course,
Thy spotless fame shall quash all false reports:
    Exert thy powers, nor fear a rival's force,
But thou shalt smile at all his vain efforts:
    Thy labours shall be crown'd with large success;
    The Muse's aid thy Magazine shall bless.

'No page more grateful to th' harmonious nine
Than that wherein thy labours we survey;
    Where solemn themes in fuller splendour shine,
(Delightful mixture,) blended with the gay,
    Where in improving, various joys we find,
    A welcome respite to the wearied mind.

'Thus when the nymphs in some fair verdant mead,
Of various flow'rs a beauteous wreath compose,
    The lovely violet's azure-painted head
Adds lustre to the crimson-blushing rose.
    Thus splendid Iris, with her varied dye,
    Shines in the æther, and adorns the sky.   BRITON.'

84

unrestrained freedom, so that the people in all parts of the kingdom have a fair, open, and exact report of the actual proceedings of their representatives and legislators, which in our constitution is highly to be valued; though, unquestionably, there has of late been too much reason to complain of the petulance with which obscure scribblers have presumed to treat men of the most respectable character and situation.

This important article of the *Gentleman's Magazine* was, for several years, executed by Mr. William Guthrie, a man who deserves to be respectably recorded in the literary annals of this country. He was descended of an ancient family in Scotland; but having a small patrimony, and being an adherent of the unfortunate house of Stuart, he could not accept of any office in the state; he therefore came to London, and employed his talents and learning as an 'Authour by profession.' His writings in history, criticism, and politicks, had considerable merit.[1] He was the first English historian who had recourse to that authentick source of information, the Parliamentary Journals; and such was the power of his political pen, that, at an early period, Government thought it worth their while to keep it quiet by a pension, which he enjoyed till his death. Johnson esteemed him enough to wish that his life should be written. The debates in Parliament, which were brought home and digested by Guthrie, whose memory, though surpassed by others who have since followed him in the same department, was yet very quick and tenacious, were sent by Cave to Johnson for his revision; and, after some time, when Guthrie had attained to greater variety of employment, and the speeches were more and more enriched by the accession of Johnson's genius, it was resolved that he should do the whole himself, from the scanty notes furnished by persons employed to attend in both houses of Parliament. Sometimes, however, as he himself told me, he had nothing more communicated to him than the names of the several speakers, and the part which they had taken in the debate.

[1] How much poetry he wrote, I know not: but he informed me, that he was the authour of the beautiful little piece, *The Eagle and Robin Redbreast*, in the collection of poems entitled *The Union*, though it is there said to be written by Archibald Scott, before the year 1600. It is by Allan Ramsay.

Thus was Johnson employed, during some of the best years of his life, as a mere literary labourer 'for gain not glory,' solely to obtain an honest support. He however indulged himself in occasional little sallies, which the French so happily express by the term *jeux d'esprit*, and which will be noticed in their order, in the progress of this work.

But what first displayed his transcendent powers, and 'gave the world assurance of the MAN,' was his *London, a Poem, in Imitation of the Third Satire of Juvenal:* which came out in May this year, and burst forth with a splendour, the rays of which will for ever encircle his name. Boileau had imitated the same satire with great success, applying it to Paris; but an attentive comparison will satisfy every reader, that he is much excelled by the English Juvenal. Oldham had also imitated it, and applied it to London; all which performances concur to prove, that great cities, in every age, and in every country, will furnish similar topicks of satire. Whether Johnson had previously read Oldham's imitation, I do not know; but it is not a little remarkable, that there is scarcely any coincidence found between the two performances, though upon the very same subject. The only instances are, in describing London as the *sink* of foreign worthlessness:

'———— the *common shore*,
Where France does all her filth and ordure pour.' OLDHAM.
'The *common shore* of Paris and of Rome.' JOHNSON.

and,

'No calling or profession comes amiss,
A *needy monsieur* can be what he please.' OLDHAM.
'All sciences a *fasting monsieur* knows.' JOHNSON.

The particulars which Oldham has collected, both as exhibiting the horrours of London, and of the times, contrasted with better days, are different from those of Johnson, and in general well chosen, and well exprest.[1]

[1] I own it pleased me to find amongst them one trait of the manners of the age in London, in the last century, to shield from the sneer of English ridicule, which was some time ago too common a practice in my native city of Edinburgh:—

There are, in Oldham's imitation, many prosaick verses and bad rhymes, and his poem sets out with a strange inadvertent blunder:

> 'Tho' much concern'd to *leave* my dear old friend,
> I must, however, *his* design commend
> Of fixing in the country——.'

It is plain he was not going to leave his *friend*; his friend was going to leave *him*. A young lady at once corrected this with good critical sagacity, to

> 'Tho' much concern'd to *lose* my dear old friend.'

There is one passage in the original, better transfused by Oldham than by Johnson:

> '*Nil habet infelix paupertas durius in se,*
> *Quàm quod ridiculos homines facit.*'

which is an exquisite remark on the galling meanness and contempt annexed to poverty: JOHNSON's imitation is:

> 'Of all the griefs that harass the distrest,
> Sure the most bitter is a scornful jest.'

OLDHAM's, though less elegant, is more just:

> 'Nothing in poverty so ill is borne,
> As its exposing men to grinning scorn.'

Where, or in what manner this poem was composed, I am sorry that I neglected to ascertain with precision, from Johnson's own authority. He has marked upon his corrected copy of the first edition of it, 'Written in 1738;' and, as it was published in the month of May in that year, it is evident that much time was not employed in preparing it for the press. The history of its publication I am enabled to give in a very satisfactory manner; and judging from myself, and many of my friends, I trust that it will not be uninteresting to my readers.

> 'If what I've said can't from the town affright,
> Consider other *dangers of the night*;
> When brickbats are from upper stories thrown,
> And *emptied chamberpots come pouring down*
> *From garret windows*.'

We may be certain, though it is not expressly named in the following letters to Mr. Cave, in 1738, that they all relate to it:
'*To* Mr. Cave

'Castle-street, Wednesday Morning.
'Sir,   [*No date.* 1738.]
    'When I took the liberty of writing to you a few days ago, I did not expect a repetition of the same pleasure so soon; for a pleasure I shall always think it, to converse in any manner with an ingenious and candid man; but having the inclosed poem in my hands to dispose of for the benefit of the authour, (of whose abilities I shall say nothing, since I send you his performance,) I believed I could not procure more advantageous terms from any person than from you, who have so much distinguished yourself by your generous encouragement of poetry; and whose judgement of that art nothing but your commendation of my trifle[1] can give me any occasion to call in question. I do not doubt but you will look over this poem with another eye, and reward it in a different manner, from a mercenary bookseller, who counts the lines he is to purchase, and considers nothing but the bulk. I cannot help taking notice, that, besides what the author may hope for on account of his abilities, he has likewise another claim to your regard, as he lies at present under very disadvantageous circumstances of fortune. I beg, therefore, that you will favour me with a letter to-morrow, that I may know what you can afford to allow him, that he may either part with it to you, or find out, (which I do not expect,) some other way more to his satisfaction.
    'I have only to add, that as I am sensible I have transcribed it very coarsely, which, after having altered it, I was obliged to do, I will, if you please to transmit the sheets from the press, correct it for you; and take the trouble of altering any stroke of satire which you may dislike.
    'By exerting on this occasion your usual generosity, you will not only encourage learning, and relieve distress, but (though it be in comparison of the other motives of very small account) oblige in a very sensible manner, Sir, your very humble servant,
                                                    'Sam. Johnson.'

[1] His Ode *Ad Urbanum* probably. Nichols.

'*To* Mr. Cave

    'Sir,   'Monday, No. 6, Castle-street.

    'I am to return you thanks for the present you were so kind as to send by me, and to intreat that you will be pleased to inform me by the penny-post, whether you resolve to print the poem. If you please to send it me by the post, with a note to Dodsley, I will go and read the lines to him, that we may have his consent to put his name in the title-page. As to the printing, if it can be set immediately about, I will be so much the authour's friend, as not to content myself with mere solicitations in his favour. I propose, if my calculation be near the truth, to engage for the reimbursement of all that you shall lose by an impression of 500; provided, as you very generously propose, that the profit, if any, be set aside for the authour's use, excepting the present you made, which, if he be a gainer, it is fit he should repay. I beg that you will let one of your servants write an exact account of the expense of such an impression, and send it with the poem, that I may know what I engage for. I am very sensible, from your generosity on this occasion, of your regard to learning, even in its unhappiest state; and cannot but think such a temper deserving of the gratitude of those who suffer so often from a contrary disposition. I am, Sir, your most humble servant,

                                           'Sam. Johnson.'

'*To* Mr. Cave

    'Sir,   [*No date.*]

    'I waited on you to take the copy to Dodsley's: as I remember the number of lines which it contains, it will be longer than *Eugenio*,[1] with the quotations, which must be subjoined at the bottom of the page; part of the beauty of the performance (if any beauty be allowed it) consisting in adapting Juvenal's sentiments to modern facts and persons. It will, with those additions, very conveniently make five sheets. And since the expense will be no more, I shall contentedly insure it, as I mentioned in my last. If it be not therefore gone to Dodsley's, I beg

    [1] A poem, published in 1737, of which see an account under April 30, 1773.

it may be sent me by the penny-post, that I may have it in the evening. I have composed a Greek epigram to Eliza,[1] and think she ought to be celebrated in as many different languages as Lewis le Grand. Pray send me word when you will begin upon the poem, for it is a long way to walk. I would leave my Epigram, but have not daylight to transcribe it. I am, Sir, your's, &c.,

'SAM. JOHNSON.'

'*To* MR. CAVE
  'SIR,   [*No date.*]
     'I am extremely obliged by your kind letter, and will not fail to attend you to-morrow with *Irene*, who looks upon you as one of her best friends.

'I was to-day with Mr. Dodsley, who declares very warmly in favour of the paper you sent him, which he desires to have a share in, it being, as he says, *a creditable thing to be concerned in*. I knew not what answer to make till I had consulted you, nor what to demand on the authour's part, but am very willing that, if you please, he should have a part in it, as he will undoubtedly be more diligent to disperse and promote it. If you can send me word to-morrow what I shall say to him, I will settle matters, and bring the poem with me for the press, which, as the town empties, we cannot be too quick with. I am, Sir, your's, &c.,

'SAM. JOHNSON.'

To us who have long known the manly force, bold spirit, and masterly versification of this poem, it is a matter of curiosity to observe the diffidence with which its authour brought it forward into publick notice, while he is so cautious as not to avow it to be his own production; and with what humility he offers to allow the printer to 'alter any stroke of satire which he might dislike.' That any such alteration was made, we do not know. If we did, we could not but feel an indignant regret; but how painful is it to see that a writer of such vigorous powers of mind was actually in such distress, that the small profit which so short a poem, however excellent, could yield, was courted as a 'relief.'

---

[1] The learned Mrs. Elizabeth Carter.

It has been generally said, I know not with what truth, that Johnson offered his *London* to several booksellers, none of whom would purchase it. To this circumstance Mr. Derrick alludes in the following lines of his *Fortune, a Rhapsody*:

> 'Will no kind patron JOHNSON own?
> Shall JOHNSON friendless range the town?
> And every publisher refuse
> The offspring of his happy Muse?'

But we have seen that the worthy, modest, and ingenious Mr. Robert Dodsley had taste enough to perceive its uncommon merit, and thought it creditable to have a share in it. The fact is, that, at a future conference, he bargained for the whole property of it, for which he gave Johnson ten guineas; who told me, 'I might, perhaps, have accepted of less; but that Paul Whitehead had a little before got ten guineas for a poem and I would not take less than Paul Whitehead.'

I may here observe, that Johnson appeared to me to under-value Paul Whitehead upon every occasion when he was men-tioned, and, in my opinion, did not do him justice; but when it is considered that Paul Whitehead was a member of a riotous and profane club, we may account for Johnson's having a pre-judice against him. Paul Whitehead was, indeed, unfortunate in being not only slighted by Johnson, but violently attacked by Churchill, who utters the following imprecation:

> 'May I (can worse disgrace on manhood fall?)
> Be born a Whitehead, and baptiz'd a Paul!'

yet I shall never be persuaded to think meanly of the authour of so brilliant and pointed a satire as *Manners*.

Johnson's *London* was published in May, 1738;[1] and it is

---

[1] Sir John Hawkins, p. 86, tells us 'The event is *antedated*, in the poem of *London*; but in every particular, except the difference of a year, what is there said of the departure of Thales, must be understood of Savage, and looked upon as *true history*.' This conjecture is, I believe, entirely groundless. I have been assured, that Johnson said he was not so much as acquainted with Savage when he wrote his *London*. If the departure mentioned in it was the departure of Savage, the event was not *antedated* but *foreseen*; for *London* was published in May, 1738, and Savage did not set out for Wales

remarkable, that it came out on the same morning with Pope's satire, entitled '1738;' so that England had at once its Juvenal and Horace as poetical monitors. The Reverend Dr. Douglas, now Bishop of Salisbury, to whom I am indebted for some obliging communications, was then a student at Oxford, and remembers well the effect which *London* produced. Every body was delighted with it; and there being no name to it, the first buz of the literary circles was 'here is an unknown poet, greater even than Pope.' And it is recorded in the *Gentleman's Magazine* of that year,[1] that it 'got to the second edition in the course of a week.'

One of the warmest patrons of this poem on its first appearance was General Oglethorpe, whose 'strong benevolence of soul' was unabated during the course of a very long life; though it is painful to think, that he had but too much reason to become cold and callous, and discontented with the world, from the neglect which he experienced of his publick and private worth, by those in whose power it was to gratify so gallant a veteran with marks of distinction. This extraordinary person was as remarkable for his learning and taste, as for his other eminent qualities; and no man was more prompt, active, and generous, in encouraging merit. I have heard Johnson gratefully acknowledge, in his presence, the kind and effectual support which he gave to his *London*, though unacquainted with its authour.

Pope, who then filled the poetical throne without a rival, it may reasonably be presumed, must have been particularly struck by the sudden appearance of such a poet; and, to his credit, let it be remembered, that his feelings and conduct on the occasion were candid and liberal. He requested Mr. Richardson, son of the painter, to endeavour to find out who this new authour was. Mr. Richardson, after some inquiry, having informed him that he had discovered only that his name was Johnson, and that he was some obscure man, Pope said, 'he will soon be *déterré*.'[2] We

till July, 1739. However well Johnson could defend the credibility of *second sight*, he did not pretend that he himself was possessed of that faculty. BOSWELL.

[1] P. 269.

[2] Sir Joshua Reynolds, from the information of the younger Richardson.

shall presently see, from a note written by Pope, that he was
himself afterwards more successful in his inquiries than his friend.

That in this justly-celebrated poem may be found a few rhymes
which the critical precision of English prosody at this day would
disallow, cannot be denied; but with this small imperfection,
which in the general blaze of its excellence is not perceived, till
the mind has subsided into cool attention, it is, undoubtedly, one
of the noblest productions in our language, both for sentiment
and expression. The nation was then in that ferment against the
court and the ministry, which some years after ended in the
downfall of Sir Robert Walpole; and as it has been said, that
Tories are Whigs when out of place, and Whigs, Tories when
in place; so, as a Whig administration ruled with what force it
could, a Tory opposition had all the animation and all the eloquence of resistance to power, aided by the common topicks of
patriotism, liberty, and independence! Accordingly, we find in
Johnson's *London* the most spirited invectives against tyranny
and oppression, the warmest predilection for his own country,
and the purest love of virtue; interspersed with traits of his own
particular character and situation, not omitting his prejudices as
a 'true-born Englishman,'[1] not only against foreign countries,
but against Ireland and Scotland. On some of these topicks I
shall quote a few passages:

'The cheated nation's happy fav'rites see;
Mark whom the great caress, who frown on me.'

'Has heaven reserv'd in pity to the poor,
No pathless waste, or undiscover'd shore?
No secret island in the boundless main?
No peaceful desart yet unclaim'd by Spain?
Quick let us rise, the happy seats explore,
And bear Oppression's insolence no more.'

'How, when competitors like these contend,
Can *surly Virtue* hope to fix a friend?'

[1] It is, however, remarkable, that he uses the epithet, which undoubtedly,
since the union between England and Scotland, ought to denominate the
natives of both parts of our island:—
       'Was early taught a Briton's rights to prize.'

'This mournful truth is every where confess'd,
SLOW RISES WORTH, BY POVERTY DEPRESS'D!'

We may easily conceive with what feeling a great mind like
his, cramped and galled by narrow circumstances, uttered this
last line, which he marked by capitals. The whole of the poem
is eminently excellent, and there are in it such proofs of a knowledge of the world, and of a mature acquaintance with life, as
cannot be contemplated without wonder, when we consider that
he was then only in his twenty-ninth year, and had yet been so
little in the 'busy haunts of men.'

Yet, while we admire the poetical excellence of this poem,
candour obliges us to allow, that the flame of patriotism and zeal
for popular resistance with which it is fraught, had no just cause.
There was, in truth, no 'oppression;' the 'nation' was *not*
'cheated.' Sir Robert Walpole was a wise and a benevolent
minister, who thought that the happiness and prosperity of a
commercial country like ours, would be best promoted by peace,
which he accordingly maintained, with credit, during a very long
period. Johnson himself afterwards honestly acknowledged the
merit of Walpole, whom he called 'a fixed star;' while he characterised his opponent, Pitt, as 'a meteor.' But Johnson's juvenile
poem was naturally impregnated with the fire of opposition, and
upon every account was universally admired.

Though thus elevated into fame, and conscious of uncommon
powers, he had not that bustling confidence, or, I may rather
say, that animated ambition, which one might have supposed
would have urged him to endeavour at rising in life. But such
was his inflexible dignity of character, that he could not stoop
to court the great; without which, hardly any man has made his
way to high station. He could not expect to produce many such
works as his *London*, and he felt the hardship of writing for
bread; he was, therefore, willing to resume the office of a schoolmaster, so as to have a sure, though moderate income for his life;
and an offer being made to him of the mastership of a school,[1]

---

[1] In a billet written by Mr. Pope in the following year, this school is said
to have been in *Shropshire*; but as it appears from a letter from Earl Gower,
that the trustees of it were 'some worthy gentlemen in Johnson's neighbour-

provided he could obtain the degree of Master of Arts, Dr.
Adams was applied to, by a common friend, to know whether
that could be granted him as a favour from the University of
Oxford. But though he had made such a figure in the literary
world, it was then thought too great a favour to be asked.

Pope, without any knowledge of him but from his *London*,
recommended him to Earl Gower, who endeavoured to procure

hood,' I in my first edition suggested that Pope must have, by mistake,
written Shropshire, instead of Staffordshire. But I have since been obliged
to Mr. Spearing, attorney-at-law, for the following information:—'William
Adams, formerly citizen and haberdasher of London, founded a school at
Newport, in the county of Salop, by deed dated 27th November, 1656, by
which he granted "the yearly sum of *sixty pounds* to such able and learned
schoolmaster, from time to time, being of godly life and conversation, who
should have been educated at one of the Universities of Oxford or Cambridge, and had taken the degree of *Master of Arts*, and was well read in the
Greek and Latin tongues, as should be nominated from time to time by the
said William Adams, during his life, and after the decease of the said
William Adams, by the Governours (namely, the Master and Wardens of
the Haberdashers' Company of the City of London) and their successors."
The manour and lands out of which the revenues for the maintenance of the
school were to issue are situate *at Knighton and Adbaston in the county of
Stafford.*' From the foregoing account of this foundation, particularly the
circumstances of the salary being sixty pounds, and the degree of Master
of Arts being a requisite qualification in the teacher, it seemed probable that
this was the school in contemplation; and that Lord Gower erroneously
supposed that the gentlemen who possessed the lands, out of which the
revenues issued, were trustees of the charity.

Such was probable conjecture. But in the *Gent. Mag.* for May, 1793,
there is a letter from Mr. Henn, one of the masters of the school of Appleby,
in Leicestershire, in which he writes as follows:—

'I compared time and circumstance together, in order to discover whether
the school in question might not be this of Appleby. Some of the trustees at
that period were "worthy gentlemen of the neighbourhood of Litchfield."
Appleby itself is not far from the neighbourhood of Litchfield. The salary,
the degree requisite, together with the *time of election*, all agreeing with the
statutes of Appleby. The election, as said in the letter, "could not be delayed
longer than the 11th of next month," which was the 11th of September, just
three months after the annual audit-day of Appleby school, which is always
on the 11th of June; and the statutes enjoin *ne ullius praeceptorum electio
diutius tribus mensibus moraretur, etc.* ["that no election of a teacher be delayed more than three months.']

'These I thought to be convincing proofs that my conjecture was not ill-
founded, and that, in a future edition of that book, the circumstance might
be recorded as fact. But what banishes every shadow of doubt is the *Minute-
book* of the school, which declares the headmastership to be *at that time* VACANT.'

I cannot omit returning thanks to this learned gentleman for the very handsome manner in which he has in that letter been so good as to speak of this work.

for him a degree from Dublin, by the following letter to a friend of Dean Swift:

'Sir,—Mr. Samuel Johnson (authour of *London*, a satire, and some other poetical pieces) is a native of this country, and much respected by some worthy gentlemen in his neighbourhood, who are trustees of a charity school now vacant; the certain salary is sixty pounds a year, of which they are desirous to make him master; but, unfortunately, he is not capable of receiving their bounty, which *would make him happy for life*, by not being a *Master of Arts*; which, by the statutes of this school, the master of it must be.

'Now these gentlemen do me the honour to think that I have interest enough in you, to prevail upon you to write to Dean Swift, to persuade the University of Dublin to send a diploma to me, constituting this poor man Master of Arts in their University. They highly extol the man's learning and probity; and will not be persuaded, that the University will make any difficulty of conferring such a favour upon a stranger, if he is recommended by the Dean. They say he is not afraid of the strictest examination, though he is of so long a journey; and will venture it, if the Dean thinks it necessary; choosing rather to die upon the road, *than be starved to death in translating for booksellers*; which has been his only subsistence for some time past.

'I fear there is more difficulty in this affair, than those good-natured gentlemen apprehend; especially as their election cannot be delayed longer than the 11th of next month. If you see this matter in the same light that it appears to me, I hope you will burn this, and pardon me for giving you so much trouble about an impracticable thing; but, if you think there is a probability of obtaining the favour asked, I am sure your humanity, and propensity to relieve merit in distress, will incline you to serve the poor man, without my adding any more to the trouble I have already given you, than assuring you that I am, with great truth, Sir, your faithful humble servant,

'Trentham, Aug. 1, 1739.'   'Gower.'

It was, perhaps, no small disappointment to Johnson that this respectable application had not the desired effect; yet how much reason has there been, both for himself and his country, to rejoice that it did not succeed, as he might probably have wasted in obscurity those hours in which he afterwards produced his incomparable works.

About this time he made one other effort to emancipate himself from the drudgery of authorship. He applied to Dr. Adams, to consult Dr. Smalbroke of the Commons, whether a person might be permitted to practice as an advocate there, without a doctor's degree in Civil Law. 'I am (said he) a total stranger to these studies; but whatever is a profession, and maintains numbers, must be within the reach of common abilities, and some degree of industry.' Dr. Adams was much pleased with Johnson's design to employ his talents in that manner, being confident he would have attained to great eminence. And, indeed, I cannot conceive a man better qualified to make a distinguished figure as a lawyer; for, he would have brought to his profession a rich store of various knowledge, an uncommon acuteness, and a command of language, in which few could have equalled, and none have surpassed him. He who could display eloquence and wit in defence of the decision of the House of Commons upon Mr. Wilkes's election for Middlesex, and of the unconstitutional taxation of our fellow-subjects in America, must have been a powerful advocate in any cause. But here, also, the want of a degree was an insurmountable bar.

He was, therefore, under the necessity of persevering in that course, into which he had been forced; and we find that his proposal from Greenwich to Mr. Cave, for a translation of Father Paul Sarpi's History, was accepted.[1]

---

[1] In the *Weekly Miscellany*, October 21, 1738, there appeared the following advertisement:—'Just published, Proposals for printing the *History of the Council of Trent*, translated from the Italian of Father Paul Sarpi; with the Authour's Life, and Notes theological, historical, and critical, from the French edition of Dr. Le Courayer. To which are added, Observations on the History, and Notes and Illustrations from various Authours, both printed and manuscript. By S. Johnson. 1. The work will consist of two hundred sheets, and be two volumes in quarto, printed on good paper and letter. 2. The price will be 18*s.* each volume, to be paid, half-a-guinea at the time of subscribing, half-a-guinea at the delivery of the first volume, and the

Some sheets of this translation were printed off, but the design was dropt; for it happened, oddly enough, that another person of the name of Samuel Johnson, Librarian of St. Martin's in the Fields, and Curate of that parish, engaged in the same undertaking, and was patronised by the Clergy, particularly by Dr. Pearce, afterwards Bishop of Rochester. Several light skirmishes passed between the rival translators, in the newspapers of the day; and the consequence was, that they destroyed each other, for neither of them went on with the work. It is much to be regretted, that the able performance of that celebrated genius. Fra Paolo lost the advantage of being incorporated into British literature by the masterly hand of Johnson.

I have in my possession, by the favour of Mr. John Nichols, a paper in Johnson's hand-writing, entitled 'Account between Mr. Edward Cave and Sam. Johnson, in relation to a version of Father Paul, &c. begun August the 2d, 1738;' by which it appears, that from that day to the 21st of April, 1739, Johnson received for this work £49 7s. in sums of one, two, three, and sometimes four guineas at a time, most frequently two. And it is curious to observe the minute and scrupulous accuracy with which Johnson has pasted upon it a slip of paper, which he has entitled 'Small Account,' and which contains one article, 'Sept. 9th, Mr. Cave laid down 2s. 6d.' There is subjoined to this account, a list of some subscribers to the work, partly in Johnson's hand-writing, partly in that of another person; and there follows a leaf or two on which are written a number of characters which have the appearance of a short hand, which, perhaps, Johnson was then trying to learn.

'To Mr. Cave

   'Sir,   'Wednesday.

   'I did not care to detain your servant while I wrote an answer

rest at the delivery of the second volume in sheets. 3. Two-pence to be abated for every sheet less than two hundred. It may be had on a large paper, in three volumes, at the price of three guineas; one to be paid at the time of subscribing, another at the delivery of the first, and the rest at the delivery of the other volumes. The work is now in the press, and will be diligently prosecuted. Subscriptions are taken in by Mr. Dodsley in Pall-Mall, Mr. Rivington in St. Paul's Church-yard, by E. Cave at St. John's Gate, and the Translator, at No. 6, in Castle-street, by Cavendish-square.'

to your letter, in which you seem to insinuate that I had promised more than I am ready to perform. If I have raised your expectations by any thing that may have escaped my memory, I am sorry; and if you remind me of it, shall thank you for the favour. If I made fewer alterations than usual in the Debates, it was only because there appeared, and still appears to be, less need of alteration. The verses to Lady Firebrace[1] may be had when you please, for you know that such a subject neither deserves much thought, nor requires it.

'The Chinese Stories[2] may be had folded down when you please to send, in which I do not recollect that you desired any alterations to be made.

'An answer to another query I am very willing to write, and had consulted with you about it last night if there had been time; for I think it the most proper way of inviting such a correspondence as may be an advantage to the paper, not a load upon it.

'As to the Prize Verses, a backwardness to determine their degrees of merit is not peculiar to me. You may, if you please, still have what I can say; but I shall engage with little spirit in an affair, which I shall *hardly* end to my own satisfaction, and *certainly* not to the satisfaction of the parties concerned.[3]

'As to Father Paul, I have not yet been just to my proposal, but have met with impediments, which, I hope, are now at an end; and if you find the progress hereafter not such as you have a right to expect, you can easily stimulate a negligent translator.

'If any or all of these have contributed to your discontent, I will endeavour to remove it; and desire you to propose the question to which you wish for an answer. I am, Sir, your humble servant,   'SAM. JOHNSON.'

[1] They afterwards appeared in the *Gent. Mag.* 1738 [viii. 486] with this title—*Verses to Lady Firebrace, at Bury Assizes.*

[2] Du Halde's Description of China was then publishing by Mr. Cave in weekly numbers, whence Johnson was to select pieces for the embellishment of the *Magazine*. NICHOLS.

[3] The premium of forty pounds proposed for the best poem on the Divine Attributes is here alluded to. NICHOLS.

'*To* Mr. Cave

'Sir,   [*No date.*]

'I am pretty much of your opinion, that the Commentary cannot be prosecuted with any appearance of success; for as the names of the authours concerned are of more weight in the performance than its own intrinsick merit, the publick will be soon satisfied with it. And I think the Examen should be pushed forward with the utmost expedition. Thus, "This day, &c., An Examen of Mr. Pope's Essay, &c., containing a succinct Account of the Philosophy of Mr. Leibnitz on[1] the System of the Fatalists, with a Confutation of their Opinions, and an Illustration of the Doctrine of Free-will;" [with what else you think proper.]

'It will, above all, be necessary to take notice, that it is a thing distinct from the Commentary.

'I was so far from imagining they stood still,[2] that I conceived them to have a good deal before-hand, and therefore was less anxious in providing them more. But if ever they stand still on my account, it must doubtless be charged to me; and whatever else shall be reasonable, I shall not oppose; but beg a suspense of judgement till morning, when I must entreat you to send me a dozen proposals, and you shall then have copy to spare. I am, Sir, your's, *impransus*,[3]   'Sam. Johnson.'

'Pray muster up the Proposals if you can, or let the boy recall them from the[4] booksellers.'

But although he corresponded with Mr. Cave concerning a translation of Crousaz's *Examen* of Pope's *Essay on Man*, and gave advice as one anxious for its success, I was long ago convinced by a perusal of the Preface, that this translation was erroneously ascribed to him; and I have found this point ascertained, beyond all doubt, by the following article in Dr. Birch's Manuscripts in the British Museum:

---

[1] [or *orig*.]
[2] The Compositors in Mr. Cave's printing-office, who appear by this letter to have then waited for copy. Nichols.
[3] ['not having dined'.]
[4] [the *not* in *orig*.]

'ELISÆ CARTERÆ. S. P. D. THOMAS BIRCH.
'*Versionem tuam Examinis Crousaziani jam perlegi. Summam styli et elegantiam, et in re difficillimâ proprietatem, admiratus.*

'*Dabam Novemb.* 27° 1738.'[1]

Indeed Mrs. Carter has lately acknowledged to Mr. Seward, that she was the translator of the *Examen*.

It is remarkable, that Johnson's last quoted letter to Mr. Cave concludes with a fair confession that he had not a dinner; and it is no less remarkable, that, though in this state of want himself, his benevolent heart was not insensible to the necessities of an humble labourer in literature, as appears from the very next letter:

'*To* MR. CAVE

'DEAR SIR,   [*No date.*]
'You may remember I have formerly talked with you about a Military Dictionary. The eldest Mr. Macbean, who was with Mr. Chambers, has very good materials for such a work, which I have seen, and will do it at a very low rate.[2] I think the terms of War and Navigation might be comprised, with good explanations, in one 8vo. Pica, which he is willing to do for twelve shillings a sheet, to be made up a guinea at the second impression. If you think on it, I will wait on you with him. I am, Sir, your humble servant,

'SAM. JOHNSON.'
'Pray lend me Topsel on Animals.'
I must not omit to mention, that this Mr. Macbean was a native of Scotland.

In the *Gentleman's Magazine* of this year, Johnson gave a Life of Father Paul;* and he wrote the Preface to the Volume,† which, though prefixed to it when bound, is always published with the Appendix, and is therefore the last composition belonging to it. The ability and nice adaptation with which he could draw up a prefatory address, was one of his peculiar excellencies.

[1] ['I have now read your translation of Crousaz' *Examen*, with admiration of the consummate elegance of your style and of its fitness to a very difficult subject.'] Birch MSS. Brit. Mus. 4323.
[2] This book was published. [It has not been found.]

101

It appears too, that he paid a friendly attention to Mrs. Elizabeth Carter; for in a letter from Mr. Cave to Dr. Birch, November 28, this year, I find 'Mr. Johnson advises Miss C. to undertake a translation of *Boethius de Cons.* because there is prose and verse, and to put her name to it when published.' This advice was not followed; probably from an apprehension that the work was not sufficiently popular for an extensive sale. How well Johnson himself could have executed a translation of this philosophical poet, we may judge from the following specimen which he has given in the *Rambler*: (*Motto to No.* 7.)

'O qui perpetuâ mundum ratione gubernas,
Terrarum cælique sator!————
Disjice terrenæ nebulas et pondera molis,
Atque tuo splendore mica! Tu namque serenum,
Tu requies tranquilla piis. Te cernere finis,
Principium, vector, dux, semita, terminus, idem.'

'O thou whose power o'er moving worlds presides,
Whose voice created, and whose wisdom guides,
On darkling man in pure effulgence shine,
And cheer the clouded mind with light divine.
'Tis thine alone to calm the pious breast,
With silent confidence and holy rest;
From thee, great God! we spring, to thee we tend,
Path, motive, guide, original, and end!'

In 1739, beside the assistance which he gave to the Parliamentary Debates, his writings in the *Gentleman's Magazine* were, 'The Life of Boerhaave,'* in which it is to be observed, that he discovers that love of chymistry which never forsook him; 'An Appeal to the publick in behalf of the Editor;'† 'An Address to the Reader;'† 'An Epigram both in Greek and Latin to Eliza,'* and also English verses to her;* and, 'A Greek Epigram to Dr. Birch.'* It has been erroneously supposed, that an Essay published in that Magazine this year, entitled 'The Apotheosis of Milton,' was written by Johnson; and on that supposition it has been improperly inserted in the edition of his works by the Booksellers, after his decease. Were there no positive testimony as to this point, the style of the performance, and

the name of Shakspeare not being mentioned in an Essay professedly reviewing the principal English poets, would ascertain
it not to be the production of Johnson. But there is here no
occasion to resort to internal evidence; for my Lord Bishop of
Salisbury (Dr. Douglas) has assured me, that it was written by
Guthrie. His separate publications were, 'A Complete Vindication of the Licensers of the Stage, from the malicious and scandalous Aspersions of Mr. Brooke, Authour of Gustavus Vasa,'*
being an ironical Attack upon them for their Suppression of that
Tragedy; and, 'Marmor Norfolciense; or an Essay on an ancient
prophetical Inscription in monkish Rhyme, lately discovered
near Lynne in Norfolk, by Probus Britannicus.'* In this performance, he, in a feigned inscription, supposed to have been
found in Norfolk, the county of Sir Robert Walpole, then the
obnoxious prime minister of this country, inveighs against the
Brunswick succession, and the measures of government con-
sequent upon it.[1] To this supposed prophecy he added a Commentary, making each expression apply to the times, with warm
Anti-Hanoverian zeal.

This anonymous pamphlet, I believe, did not make so much
noise as was expected, and, therefore, had not a very extensive
circulation. Sir John Hawkins relates, that, 'warrants were issued,
and messengers employed to apprehend the authour; who, though
he had forborne to subscribe his name to the pamphlet, the
vigilance of those in pursuit of him had discovered;' and we are
informed, that he lay concealed in Lambeth-marsh till the scent
after him grew cold. This, however, is altogether without foundation; for Mr. Steele, one of the Secretaries of the Treasury, who
amidst a variety of important business, politely obliged me with
his attention to my inquiry, informs me, that 'he directed every
possible search to be made in the records of the Treasury and
Secretary of State's Office, but could find no trace whatever of
any warrant having been issued to apprehend the authour of this
pamphlet.'

Marmor Norfolciense became exceedingly scarce, so that I, for

[1] The Inscription and the Translation of it are preserved in the *London Magazine* for the year 1739, p. 244.

many years, endeavoured in vain to procure a copy of it. At last I was indebted to the malice of one of Johnson's numerous petty adversaries, who, in 1775, published a new edition of it, 'with Notes and a Dedication to SAMUEL JOHNSON, LL.D. by TRIBUNUS;' in which some puny scribbler invidiously attempted to found upon it a charge of inconsistency against its authour, because he had accepted of a pension from his present Majesty, and had written in support of the measures of government. As a mortification to such impotent malice, of which there are so many instances towards men of eminence, I am happy to relate, that this *telum imbelle*[1] did not reach its exalted object, till about a year after it thus appeared, when I mentioned it to him, supposing that he knew of the re-publication. To my surprize, he had not yet heard of it. He requested me to go directly and get it for him, which I did. He looked at it and laughed, and seemed to be much diverted with the feeble efforts of his unknown adversary, who, I hope, is alive to read this account. 'Now (said he) here is somebody who thinks he has vexed me sadly; yet, if it had not been for you, you rogue, I should probably never have seen it.'

As Mr. Pope's note concerning Johnson, alluded to in a former page, refers both to his *London*, and his *Marmor Norfolciense*, I have deferred inserting it till now. I am indebted for it to Dr. Percy, the Bishop of Dromore, who permitted me to copy it from the original in his possession. It was presented to his Lordship by Sir Joshua Reynolds, to whom it was given by the son of Mr. Richardson the painter, the person to whom it is addressed. I have transcribed it with minute exactness, that the peculiar mode of writing, and imperfect spelling of that celebrated poet, may be exhibited to the curious in literature. It justifies Swift's epithet of 'paper-sparing Pope,' for it is written on a slip no larger than a common message-card, and was sent to Mr. Richardson, along with the *Imitation of Juvenal*.

'This is imitated by one Johnson who put in for a Publick-

[1] [*Sic fatus senior telumque imbelle sine ictu Conjecit.* 'Thus spake the old king, and cast forth his warless spear, and wounded not.' *Æneid.* ii. 544. (Jackson.)]

school in Shropshire,[1] but was disappointed. He has an infirmity
of the convulsive kind, that attacks him sometimes, so as to make
him a sad Spectacle. Mr. P. from the Merit of this Work which
was all the knowledge he had of him endeavour'd to serve him
without his own application; & wrote to my L^d gore, but he did
not succeed. Mr. Johnson published afterw^{ds} another Poem in
Latin with Notes the whole very Humerous call'd the Norfolk
Prophecy. P.'

Johnson had been told of this note; and Sir Joshua Reynolds
informed him of the compliment which it contained, but, from
delicacy, avoided shewing him the paper itself. When Sir Joshua
observed to Johnson that he seemed very desirous to see Pope's
note, he answered, 'Who would not be proud to have such a
man as Pope so solicitous in inquiring about him?'

The infirmity to which Mr. Pope alludes, appeared to me also,
as I have elsewhere[2] observed, to be of the convulsive kind, and
of the nature of that distemper called St. Vitus's dance; and in
this opinion I am confirmed by the description which Sydenham
gives of that disease. 'This disorder is a kind of convulsion. It
manifests itself by halting or unsteadiness of one of the legs,
which the patient draws after him like an ideot. If the hand of
the same side be applied to the breast, or any other part of the
body, he cannot keep it a moment in the same posture, but it will
be drawn into a different one by a convulsion, notwithstanding
all his efforts to the contrary.' Sir Joshua Reynolds, however,
was of a different opinion, and favoured me with the following
paper.

'Those motions or tricks of Dr. Johnson are improperly called
convulsions. He could sit motionless, when he was told so to do,
as well as any other man; my opinion is that it proceeded from
a habit which he had indulged himself in, of accompanying his
thoughts with certain untoward actions, and those actions always
appeared to me as if they were meant to reprobate some part of
his past conduct. Whenever he was not engaged in conversation,
such thoughts were sure to rush into his mind; and, for this

[1] See note, p. 94.
[2] *Journal of a Tour to the Hebrides*, 3rd edit. p. 8.

reason, any company, any employment whatever, he preferred to being alone. The great business of his life (he said) was to escape from himself; this disposition he considered as the disease of his mind, which nothing cured but company.

'One instance of his absence and particularity, as it is characteristick of the man, may be worth relating. When he and I took a journey together into the West, we visited the late Mr. Banks, of Dorsetshire; the conversation turning upon pictures, which Johnson could not well see, he retired to a corner of the room, stretching out his right leg as far as he could reach before him, then bringing up his left leg, and stretching his right still further on. The old gentleman observing him, went up to him, and in a very courteous manner assured him, that though it was not a new house, the flooring was perfectly safe. The Doctor started from his reverie, like a person waked out of his sleep, but spoke not a word.'

While we are on this subject, my readers may not be displeased with another anecdote, communicated to me by the same friend, from the relation of Mr. Hogarth.

Johnson used to be a pretty frequent visitor at the house of Mr. Richardson, authour of *Clarissa*, and other novels of extensive reputation. Mr. Hogarth came one day to see Richardson, soon after the execution of Dr. Cameron, for having taken arms for the house of Stuart in 1745–6; and being a warm partisan of George the Second, he observed to Richardson, that certainly there must have been some very unfavourable circumstances lately discovered in this particular case, which had induced the King to approve of an execution for rebellion so long after the time when it was committed, as this had the appearance of putting a man to death in cold blood,[1] and was very unlike his

[1] Impartial posterity may, perhaps, be as little inclined as Dr. Johnson was to justify the uncommon rigour exercised in the case of Dr. Archibald Cameron. He was an amiable and truly honest man; and his offence was owing to a generous, though mistaken principle of duty. Being obliged, after 1746, to give up his profession as a physician, and to go into foreign parts, he was honoured with the rank of Colonel, both in the French and Spanish service. He was a son of the ancient and respectable family of Cameron, of Lochiel; and his brother, who was the Chief of that brave clan, distinguished himself by moderation and humanity, while the Highland

Majesty's usual clemency. While he was talking, he perceived a person standing at a window in the room, shaking his head, and rolling himself about in a strange ridiculous manner. He concluded that he was an ideot, whom his relations had put under the care of Mr. Richardson, as a very good man. To his great surprize, however, this figure stalked forwards to where he and Mr. Richardson were sitting, and all at once took up the argument, and burst out into an invective against George the Second, as one, who, upon all occasions, was unrelenting and barbarous; mentioning many instances, particularly, that when an officer of high rank had been acquitted by a Court Martial, George the Second had, with his own hand, struck his name off the list. In short, he displayed such a power of eloquence, that Hogarth looked at him with astonishment, and actually imagined that this ideot had been at the moment inspired. Neither Hogarth nor Johnson were made known to each other at this interview.

1740: ÆTAT. 31.]—In 1740 he wrote for the *Gentleman's Magazine* the 'Preface,'† 'Life of Sir Francis Drake,'* and the first parts of those of 'Admiral Blake,'* and of 'Philip Baretier,'* both which he finished the following year. He also wrote an 'Essay on Epitaphs,'† and an 'Epitaph on Philips, a Musician,'* which was afterwards published with some other pieces of his, in Mrs. Williams's *Miscellanies.* This Epitaph is so exquisitely beautiful, that I remember even Lord Kames, strangely prejudiced as he was against Dr. Johnson, was compelled to allow it very high praise. It has been ascribed to Mr. Garrick, from its appearing at first with the signature G; but I have heard Mr. Garrick declare, that it was written by Dr. Johnson, and give the following account of the manner in which it was composed. Johnson and he were sitting together; when, amongst other things, Garrick repeated an Epitaph upon this Philips by a Dr. Wilkes, in these words:

> 'Exalted soul! whose harmony could please
> The love-sick virgin, and the gouty ease;

army marched victorious through Scotland. It is remarkable of this Chief, that though he had earnestly remonstrated against the attempt as hopeless, he was of too heroick a spirit not to venture his life and fortune in the cause, when personally asked by him whom he thought his prince.

> Could jarring discord, like Amphion, move
> To beauteous order and harmonious love;
> Rest here in peace, till angels bid thee rise,
> And meet thy blessed Saviour in the skies.'

Johnson shook his head at these common-place funereal lines, and said to Garrick, 'I think, Davy, I can make a better.' Then, stirring about his tea for a little while, in a state of meditation, he almost extempore produced the following verses:

> 'Philips, whose touch harmonious could remove
> The pangs of guilty power or hapless love;
> Rest here, distress'd by poverty no more,
> Here find that calm thou gav'st so oft before;
> Sleep, undisturb'd, within this peaceful shrine,
> Till angels wake thee with a note like thine!'

At the same time that Mr. Garrick favoured me with this anecdote, he repeated a very pointed Epigram by Johnson, on George the Second and Colley Cibber, which has never yet appeared, and of which I know not the exact date. Dr. Johnson afterwards gave it to me himself:

> 'Augustus still survives in Maro's strain,
> And Spenser's verse prolongs Eliza's reign;
> Great George's acts let tuneful Cibber sing;
> For Nature form'd the Poet for the King.'

In 1741 he wrote for the *Gentleman's Magazine* 'the Preface,'* 'Conclusion of his lives of Drake and Baretier,'† 'A free translation of the Jests of Hierocles, with an Introduction;'† and, I think, the following pieces: 'Debate on the Proposal of Parliament to Cromwell, to assume the Title of King, abridged, methodised, and digested;'† 'Translation of Abbé Guyon's Dissertation on the Amazons;'† 'Translation of Fontenelle's Panegyrick on Dr. Morin.'† Two notes upon this appear to me undoubtedly his. He this year, and the two following, wrote the *Parliamentary Debates.* He told me himself, that he was the sole composer of them for those three years only. He was not, however, precisely exact in his statement, which he mentioned from hasty recollection; for it is sufficiently evident, that his composition of them began November 19, 1740, and ended February 23, 1742–3.

It appears from some of Cave's letters to Dr. Birch, that Cave had better assistance for that branch of his Magazine, than has been generally supposed; and that he was indefatigable in getting it made as perfect as he could.

Thus, 21st July, 1735.[1] 'I trouble you with the inclosed, because you said you could easily correct what is herein given for Lord C——ld's speech. I beg you will do so as soon as you can for me, because the month is far advanced.'

And 15th July, 1737. 'As you remember the debates so far as to perceive the speeches already printed are not exact, I beg the favour that you will peruse the inclosed, and, in the best manner your memory will serve, correct the mistaken passages, or add any thing that is omitted. I should be very glad to have something of the Duke of N——le's speech, which would be particularly of service.

'A gentleman has Lord Bathurst's speech to add something to.'

And July 3, 1744. 'You will see what stupid, low, abominable stuff is put[2] upon your noble and learned friend's[3] character, such as I should quite reject, and endeavour to do something better towards doing justice to the character. But as I cannot expect to attain my desires in that respect, it would be a great satisfaction to me, as well as an honour to our work to have the favour of the genuine speech. It is a method that several have been pleased to take, as I could show, but I think myself under a restraint. I shall say so far, that I have had some by a third hand, which I understood well enough to come from the first; others by penny-post, and others by the speakers themselves, who have been pleased to visit St. John's Gate, and show particular marks of their being pleased.'[4]

There is no reason, I believe, to doubt the veracity of Cave. It is, however, remarkable, that none of these letters are in the

---

[1] [1737 *orig.*]
[2] I suppose in another compilation of the same kind.
[3] Doubtless, Lord Hardwick.
[4] Birch's *MSS. in the British Museum,* 4302.

years during which Johnson alone furnished the Debates, and
one of them is in the very year after he ceased from that labour.
Johnson told me that as soon as he found that the speeches were
thought genuine, he determined that he would write no more of
them; for 'he would not be accessary to the propagation of falsehood.' And such was the tenderness of his conscience, that a
short time before his death he expressed a regret for his having
been the authour of fictions, which had passed for realities.

He nevertheless agreed with me in thinking, that the debates
which he had framed were to be valued as orations upon questions of publick importance. They have accordingly been collected in volumes, properly arranged, and recommended to the
notice of parliamentary speakers by a preface, written by no
inferior hand.[1] I must, however, observe, that although there is
in those debates a wonderful store of political information, and
very powerful eloquence, I cannot agree that they exhibit the
manner of each particular speaker, as Sir John Hawkins seems to
think. But, indeed, what opinion can we have of his judgement,
and taste in publick speaking, who presumes to give, as the
characteristicks of two celebrated orators, 'the deep-mouthed
rancour of Pulteney, and the yelping pertinacity of Pitt.'[2]

This year I find that his tragedy of *Irene* had been for some
time ready for the stage, and that his necessities made him
desirous of getting as much as he could for it, without delay; for
there is the following letter from Mr. Cave to Dr. Birch, in the
same volume of manuscripts in the British Museum, from which
I copied those above quoted. They were most obligingly pointed
out to me by Sir William Musgrave, one of the Curators of that
noble respository.

'Sept. 9, 1741.

'I have put Mr. Johnson's play into Mr. Gray's[3] hands, in
order to sell it to him, if he is inclined to buy it; but I doubt
whether he will or not. He would dispose of the copy, and what-

---

[1] I am assured that the editor is Mr. George Chalmers, whose commercial works are well known and esteemed.
[2] Hawkins's *Life of Johnson*, p. 100.
[3] A bookseller of London.

ever advantage may be made by acting it. Would your society,[1] or any gentleman, or body of men that you know, take such a bargain? He and I are very unfit to deal with theatrical persons. Fleetwood was to have acted it last season, but Johnson's diffidence or   [2] prevented it.'

I have already mentioned that *Irene* was not brought into publick notice till Garrick was manager of Drury-lane theatre.

1742: ÆTAT. 33.]—In 1742 he wrote for the *Gentleman's Magazine* the 'Preface,'† the 'Parliamentary Debates,'* 'Essay on the Account of the conduct of the Duchess of Marlborough,'* then the popular topick of conversation. This 'Essay' is a short but masterly performance. We find him, in No. 13 of his *Rambler*, censuring a profligate sentiment in that 'Account;' and again insisting upon it strenuously in conversation.[3] 'An account of the Life of Peter Burman,'* I believe chiefly taken from a foreign publication; as, indeed, he could not himself know much about Burman; 'Additions to his Life of Baretier;'* 'The Life of Sydenham,'* afterwards prefixed to Dr. Swan's edition of his works; 'Proposals for Printing Bibliotheca Harleiana, or a Catalogue of the Library of the Earl of Oxford.'* His account of that celebrated collection of books, in which he displays the importance to literature of what the French call a *catalogue raisonné*, when the subjects of it are extensive and various, and it is executed with ability, cannot fail to impress all his readers with admiration of his philological attainments. It was afterwards prefixed to the first volume of the Catalogue, in which the Latin accounts of books were written by him. He was employed in this business by Mr. Thomas Osborne the bookseller, who purchased the library for 13,000*l.*, a sum which Mr. Oldys says, in one of his manuscripts, was not more than the binding of the books had cost; yet, as Dr. Johnson assured me, the slowness of the sale

---

[1] Not the Royal Society; but the Society for the encouragement of learning, of which Dr. Birch was a leading member. Their object was to assist authors in printing expensive works. It existed from about 1735 to 1746, when having incurred a considerable debt, it was dissolved.

[2] There is no erasure here, but a mere blank; to fill up which may be an exercise for ingenious conjecture.

[3] *Journal of a Tour to the Hebrides*, 3rd edit. p. 167. [Sept. 10, 1773.]

was such, that there was not much gained by it. It has been confidently related, with many embellishments, that Johnson one day knocked Osborne down in his shop, with a folio, and put his foot upon his neck. The simple truth I had from Johnson himself. 'Sir, he was impertinent to me, and I beat him. But it was not in his shop: it was in my own chamber.'

A very diligent observer may trace him where we should not easily suppose him to be found. I have no doubt that he wrote the little abridgement entitled 'Foreign History,' in the *Magazine* for December. To prove it, I shall quote the Introduction. 'As this is that season of the year in which Nature may be said to command a suspension of hostilities, and which seems intended, by putting a short stop to violence and slaughter, to afford time for malice to relent, and animosity to subside; we can scarce expect any other accounts than of plans, negotiations and treaties, of proposals for peace, and preparations for war.' As also this passage: 'Let those who despise the capacity of the Swiss, tell us by what wonderful policy, or by what happy conciliation of interests, it is brought to pass, that in a body made up of different communities and different religions, there should be no civil commotions, though the people are so warlike, that to nominate and raise an army is the same.'

I am obliged to Mr. Astle for his ready permission to copy the two following letters, of which the originals are in his possession. Their contents shew that they were written about this time, and that Johnson was now engaged in preparing an historical account of the British Parliament.

'*To* Mr. Cave

'Sir, [*No date.*]

'I believe I am going to write a long letter, and have therefore taken a whole sheet of paper. The first thing to be written about is our historical design.

'You mentioned the proposal of printing in numbers, as an alteration in the scheme, but I believe you mistook, some way or other, my meaning; I had no other view than that you might rather print too many of five sheets, than of five and thirty.

'With regard to what I shall say on the manner of proceeding, I would have it understood as wholly indifferent to me, and my opinion only, not my resolution. *Emptoris sit eligere.*[1]

'I think the insertion of the exact dates of the most important events in the margin, or of so many events as may enable the reader to regulate the order of facts with sufficient exactness, the proper medium between a journal, which has regard only to time, and a history which ranges facts according to their dependence on each other, and postpones or anticipates according to the convenience of narration. I think the work ought to partake of the spirit of history, which is contrary to minute exactness, and of the regularity of a journal, which is inconsistent with spirit. For this reason, I neither admit numbers or dates, nor reject them.

'I am of your opinion with regard to placing most of the resolutions &c., in the margin, and think we shall give the most complete account of Parliamentary proceedings that can be contrived. The naked papers, without an historical treatise interwoven, require some other book to make them understood. I will date the succeeding facts with some exactness, but I think in the margin. You told me on Saturday that I had received money on this work, and found set down 13*l.* 2*s.* 6*d.*, reckoning the half guinea of last Saturday. As you hinted to me that you had many calls for money, I would not press you too hard, and therefore shall desire only, as I send it in, two guineas for a sheet of copy; the rest you may pay me when it may be more convenient; and even by this sheet-payment I shall, for some time, be very expensive.

'The *Life of Savage* I am ready to go upon; and in Great Primer, and Pica notes, I reckon on sending in half a sheet a day; but the money for that shall likewise lye by in your hands till it is done. With the debates, shall not I have business enough? if I had but good pens.

'Towards Mr. Savage's *Life* what more have you got? I would willingly have his trial, &c., and know whether his defence be at Bristol, and would have his collection of poems, on account

[1] ['The purchaser has the right of choice.']

of the Preface.—*The Plain Dealer*,[1]—all the magazines that have anything of his, or relating to him.

'I thought my letter would be long, but it is now ended; and I am, Sir, yours, &c.

'SAM. JOHNSON.'

'The boy found me writing this almost in the dark, when I could not quite easily read yours.

'I have read the Italian[2]—nothing in it is well.

'I had no notion of having any thing for the Inscription. I hope you don't think I kept it to extort a price. I could think of nothing, till to day. If you could spare me another guinea for the history, I should take it very kindly, to night; but if you do not I shall not think it an injury.—I am almost well again.'

'*To* MR. CAVE

'SIR,—You did not tell me your determination about the "Soldier's Letter,"[3] which I am confident was never printed. I think it will not do by itself, or in any other place, so well as the *Mag. Extraordinary*. If you will have it at all, I believe you do not think I set it high, and I will be glad if what you give, you will give quickly.

'You need not be in care about something to print, for I have got the State Trials, and shall extract Layer, Atterbury, and Macclesfield from them, and shall bring them to you in a fortnight; after which I will try to get the South Sea Report.'[4]

[*No date, nor signature.*].

I would also ascribe to him an 'Essay on the Description of China, from the French of Du Halde.'†

His writings in the *Gentleman's Magazine* in 1743, are, the 'Preface,'† the 'Parliamentary Debates,'† 'Considerations on the Dispute between Crousaz and Warburton, on Pope's Essay on Man;'† in which, while he defends Crousaz, he shews an ad-

[1] *The Plain Dealer* was published in 1724, and contained some account of Savage. [2] [Latin *orig.*] [3] I have not discovered what this was. [4] [*The letter continues* 'and then I hope to proceed regularly'. Boswell failed to turn the page, or he would have found the missing words and the signature.]

mirable metaphysical acuteness and temperance in controversy; 'Ad Lauram parituram Epigramma;'*[1] and, 'A Latin Translation of Pope's Verses on his Grotto;'* and, as he could employ his pen with equal success upon a small matter as a great, I suppose him to be the authour of an advertisement for Osborne, concerning the great Harleian Catalogue.

But I should think myself much wanting, both to my illustrious friend and my readers, did I not introduce here, with more than ordinary respect, an exquisitely beautiful Ode, which has not been inserted in any of the collections of Johnson's poetry, written by him at a very early period, as Mr. Hector informs me, and inserted in the *Gentleman's Magazine* of this year.

FRIENDSHIP, *an* ODE.*

'Friendship, peculiar boon of heav'n,
    The noble mind's delight and pride,
To men and angels only giv'n,
    To all the lower world deny'd.

While love, unknown among the blest,
    Parent of thousand wild desires,
The savage and the human breast
    Torments alike with raging fires;

With bright, but oft destructive, gleam,
    Alike o'er all his lightnings fly;
Thy lambent glories only beam
    Around the fav'rites of the sky.

Thy gentle flows of guiltless joys
    On fools and villains ne'er descend;
In vain for thee the tyrant sighs,
    And hugs a flatterer for a friend.

---

[1] *Angliacas inter pulcherrima Laura puellas,*/*Mox uteri pondus depositura grave,*/*Adsit, Laura, tibi facilis Lucina dolenti,*/*Neve tibi noceat prænituisse Deæ.*

['Laura, prettiest girl in England, you will soon be rid of your grievous burden. May Lucina be kind to you in your pains; may you not suffer for having excelled a goddess.']

Mr. Hector was present when this Epigram was made *impromptu*. The first line was proposed by Dr. James, and Johnson was called upon by the company to finish it, which he instantly did.

Directress of the brave and just,
    O guide us through life's darksome way!
And let the tortures of mistrust,
    On selfish bosoms only prey.

Nor shall thine ardours cease to glow,
    When souls to blissful climes remove;
What rais'd our virtue here below,
    Shall aid our happiness above.'

Johnson had now an opportunity of obliging his schoolfellow
Dr. James, of whom he once observed, 'no man brings more mind
to his profession.' James published this year his *Medicinal Dictionary*, in three volumes folio. Johnson, as I understood from
him, had written, or assisted in writing, the proposals for this
work; and being very fond of the study of physick, in which
James was his master, he furnished some of the articles. He,
however, certainly wrote for it the Dedication to Dr. Mead,†
which is conceived with great address, to conciliate the patronage
of that very eminent man.[1]

It has been circulated, I know not with what authenticity, that
Johnson considered Dr. Birch as a dull writer, and said of him,
'Tom Birch is as brisk as a bee in conversation; but no sooner
does he take a pen in his hand, than it becomes a torpedo to him,
and benumbs all his faculties.' That the literature of this country
is much indebted to Birch's activity and diligence must certainly
be acknowledged. We have seen that Johnson honoured him
with a Greek Epigram; and his correspondence with him, during
many years, proves that he had no mean opinion of him.

---

[1] 'To Dr. Mead.

'Sir,—That the *Medicinal Dictionary* is dedicated to you, is to be imputed
only to your reputation for superior skill in those sciences which I have
endeavoured to explain and facilitate: and you are, therefore, to consider
this address, if it be agreeable to you, as one of the rewards of merit; and
if otherwise, as one of the inconveniences of eminence.

'However you shall receive it, my design cannot be disappointed; because
this publick appeal to your judgement will shew that I do not found my
hopes of approbation upon the ignorance of my readers, and that I fear his
censure least, whose knowledge is most extensive. I am, Sir, your most
obedient humble servant,

                                                        'R. James.

'*To* Dr. Birch

'Sir,   'Thursday, Sept. 29, 1743.

'I hope you will excuse me for troubling you on an occasion on which I know not whom else I can apply to; I am at a loss for the Lives and Characters of Earl Stanhope, the two Craggs, and the minister Sunderland; and beg that you will inform [me] where I may find them, and send any pamphlets, &c. relating to them to Mr. Cave, to be perused for a few days by, Sir, your most humble servant,   'Sam. Johnson.'

His circumstances were at this time much embarrassed; yet his affection for his mother was so warm, and so liberal, that he took upon himself a debt of her's, which, though small in itself, was then considerable to him. This appears from the following letter which he wrote to Mr. Levett, of Lichfield, the original of which lies now before me.

'*To* Mr. Levett; *in Lichfield.*

'Sir,   'December 1, 1743.

'I am extremely sorry that we have encroached so much upon your forbearance with respect to the interest, which a great perplexity of affairs hindered me from thinking of with that attention that I ought, and which I am not immediately able to remit to you, but will pay it (I think twelve pounds,) in two months. I look upon this, and on the future interest of that mortgage, as my own debt; and beg that you will be pleased to give me directions how to pay it, and not mention it to my dear mother. If it be necessary to pay this in less time, I believe I can do it; but I take two months for certainty, and beg an answer whether you can allow me so much time. I think myself very much obliged to your forbearance, and shall esteem it a great happiness to be able to serve you. I have great opportunities of dispersing any thing that you may think it proper to make publick. I will give a note for the money, payable at the time mentioned, to any one here that you shall appoint. I am, Sir, your most obedient, and most humble servant,

'Sam. Johnson.
'At Mr. Osborne's, bookseller, in Gray's Inn.'

1744: ÆTAT. 35.]—IT does not appear that he wrote any
thing in 1744 for the *Gentleman's Magazine*, but the Preface.†
His *Life of Baretier* was now re-published in a pamphlet by itself.
But he produced one work this year, fully sufficient to maintain
the high reputation which he had acquired. This was *The Life of
Richard Savage*;* a man, of whom it is difficult to speak impartially, without wondering that he was for some time the
intimate companion of Johnson; for his character was marked by
profligacy, insolence, and ingratitude:[1] yet, as he undoubtedly
had a warm and vigorous, though unregulated mind, had seen
life in all its varieties, and been much in the company of the
statesmen and wits of his time, he could communicate to Johnson
an abundant supply of such materials as his philosophical curiosity
most eagerly desired; and as Savage's misfortunes and misconduct had reduced him to the lowest state of wretchedness as a
writer for bread, his visits to St. John's Gate naturally brought
Johnson and him together.[2]

---

[1] As a specimen of his temper, I insert the following letter from him to
a noble Lord [Lord Tyrconnel. *Croker*[1].] to whom he was under great
obligations, but who, on account of his bad conduct, was obliged to discard
him. The original was in the hands of the late Francis Cockayne Cust, Esq.,
one of His Majesty's Counsel learned in the law:
'*Right Honourable* BRUTE, *and* BOOBY,
'I FIND you want (as Mr. ——— is pleased to hint,) to swear away my
life, that is, the life of your creditor, because he asks you for a debt.—The
publick shall soon be acquainted with this, to judge whether you are not
fitter to be an Irish Evidence, than to be an Irish Peer.—I defy and despise
you. I am, your determined adversary,   R. S.'
[2] Sir John Hawkins gives the world to understand, that Johnson, 'being
an admirer of genteel manners, was captivated by the address and demeanour
of Savage, who, as to his exterior, was, to a remarkable degree, accomplished.' Hawkins's *Life*, p. 52. But Sir John's notions of gentility must
appear somewhat ludicrous, from his stating the following circumstance as
presumptive evidence that Savage was a good swordsman: 'That he understood the exercise of a gentleman's weapon, may be inferred from the use
made of it in that rash encounter which is related in his life.' The dexterity
here alluded to was, that Savage, in a nocturnal fit of drunkenness, stabbed
a man at a coffee-house, and killed him; for which he was tried at the Old-
Bailey, and found guilty of murder.
Johnson, indeed, describes him as having 'a grave and manly deportment,
a solemn dignity of mien; but which, upon a nearer acquaintance, softened
into an engaging easiness of manners.' How highly Johnson admired him
for that knowledge which he himself so much cultivated, and what kindness

It is melancholy to reflect, that Johnson and Savage were sometimes in such extreme indigence,[1] that they could not pay for a lodging; so that they have wandered together whole nights in the streets. Yet in these almost incredible scenes of distress, we may suppose that Savage mentioned many of the anecdotes with which Johnson afterwards enriched the life of his unhappy companion, and those of other Poets.

He told Sir Joshua Reynolds, that one night in particular, when Savage and he walked round St. James's-square for want of a lodging, they were not at all depressed by their situation; but in high spirits and brimful of patriotism, traversed the square for several hours, inveighed against the minister, and 'resolved they would *stand by their country.*'

I am afraid, however, that by associating with Savage, who was habituated to the dissipation and licentiousness of the town, Johnson, though his good principles remained steady, did not entirely preserve that conduct, for which, in days of greater simplicity, he was remarked by his friend Mr. Hector; but was imperceptibly led into some indulgencies which occasioned much distress to his virtuous mind.

That Johnson was anxious that an authentick and favourable account of his extraordinary friend should first get possession of the publick attention, is evident from a letter which he wrote in

he entertained for him, appears from the following lines in the *Gentleman's Magazine* for April, 1738, which I am assured were written by Johnson:

'*Ad* RICARDUM SAVAGE.
'*Humani studium generis cui pectore fervet
O colat humanum te foveatque genus.*' *

[1] The following striking proof of Johnson's extreme indigence, when he published the *Life of Savage*, was communicated to the author, by Mr. Richard Stow, of Apsley, in Bedfordshire, from the information of Mr. Walter Harte, author of the *Life of Gustavus Adolphus*:
Soon after Savage's *Life* was published, Mr. Harte dined with Edward Cave, and occasionally praised it. Soon after, meeting him, Cave said, 'You made a man very happy t'other day.'—'How could that be,' says Harte; 'nobody was there but ourselves.' Cave answered, by reminding him that a plate of victuals was sent behind a screen, which was to Johnson, dressed so shabbily, that he did not choose to appear; but on hearing the conversation, was highly delighted with the encomiums on his book. [M.]

* ['May the human race cherish him, in whose breast burns the love of human kind.']

the *Gentleman's Magazine* for August of the year preceding its publication.

'MR. URBAN,—As your collections show how often you have owed the ornaments of your poetical pages to the correspondence of the unfortunate and ingenious Mr. Savage, I doubt not but you have so much regard to his memory as to encourage any design that may have a tendency to the preservation of it from insults or calumnies; and therefore, with some degree of assurance, intreat you to inform the publick, that his life will speedily be published by a person who was favoured with his confidence, and received from himself an account of most of the transactions which he proposes to mention, to the time of his retirement to Swansea in Wales.

'From that period, to his death in the prison of Bristol, the account will be continued from materials still less liable to objection; his own letters, and those of his friends, some of which will be inserted in the work, and abstracts of others subjoined in the margin.

'It may be reasonably imagined, that others may have the same design; but as it is not credible that they can obtain the same materials, it must be expected they will supply from invention the want of intelligence; and that under the title of "The Life of Savage," they will publish only a novel, filled with romantick adventures, and imaginary amours. You may therefore, perhaps, gratify the lovers of truth and wit, by giving me leave to inform them in your Magazine, that my account will be published in 8vo. by Mr. Roberts, in Warwick-lane.'

[No signature.]

In February, 1744, it accordingly came forth from the shop of Roberts, between whom and Johnson I have not traced any connection, except the casual one of this publication. In Johnson's *Life of Savage*, although it must be allowed that its moral is the reverse of—'*Respicere exemplar vitæ morumque jubebo,*'[1] a very useful lesson is inculcated, to guard men of warm passions from a too free indulgence of them; and the various incidents are

---

[1] ['I advise him to take as his model real life and manners'. Horace *Ars Poetica*, l. 317. (Wickham.)]

related in so clear and animated a manner, and illuminated throughout with so much philosophy, that it is one of the most interesting narratives in the English language. Sir Joshua Reynolds told me, that upon his return from Italy he met with it in Devonshire, knowing nothing of its authour, and began to read it while he was standing with his arm leaning against a chimney-piece. It seized his attention so strongly, that, not being able to lay down the book till he had finished it, when he attempted to move, he found his arm totally benumbed. The rapidity with which this work was composed, is a wonderful circumstance. Johnson has been heard to say, 'I wrote forty-eight of the printed octavo pages of the *Life of Savage* at a sitting; but then I sat up all night.'[1]

He exhibits the genius of Savage to the best advantage in the specimens of his poetry which he has selected, some of which are of uncommon merit. We, indeed, occasionally find such vigour and such point, as might make us suppose that the generous aid of Johnson had been imparted to his friend. Mr. Thomas Warton made this remark to me; and, in support of it, quoted from the poem entitled *The Bastard*, a line, in which the fancied superiority of one 'stamped in Nature's mint with extasy,' is contrasted with a regular lawful descendant of some great and ancient family:

           'No tenth transmitter of a foolish face.'

But the fact is, that this poem was published some years before Johnson and Savage were acquainted.

It is remarkable, that in this biographical disquisition there appears a very strong symptom of Johnson's prejudice against players; a prejudice which may be attributed to the following causes: first, the imperfection of his organs, which were so defective that he was not susceptible of the fine impressions which theatrical excellence produces upon the generality of mankind; secondly, the cold rejection of his tragedy; and, lastly, the brilliant success of Garrick, who had been his pupil, who had come to London at the same time with him, not in a much more prosperous state than himself, and whose talents he undoubtedly rated low, compared with his own. His being outstripped by his

---

[1] *Journal of a Tour to the Hebrides*, 3rd edit. p. 35 [p. 55 Aug. 19, 1773].

pupil in the race of immediate fame, as well as of fortune, probably made him feel some indignation, as thinking that whatever
might be Garrick's merits in his art, the reward was too great
when compared with what the most successful efforts of literary
labour could attain. At all periods of his life Johnson used to talk
contemptuously of players; but in this work he speaks of them
with peculiar acrimony; for which, perhaps, there was formerly
too much reason from the licentious and dissolute manners of
those engaged in that profession. It is but justice to add, that in
our own time such a change has taken place, that there is no
longer room for such an unfavourable distinction.

His schoolfellow and friend, Dr. Taylor, told me a pleasant
anecdote of Johnson's triumphing over his pupil David Garrick.
When that great actor had played some little time at Goodman's-
fields, Johnson and Taylor went to see him perform, and afterwards passed the evening at a tavern with him and old Giffard.
Johnson, who was ever depreciating stage-players, after censuring some mistakes in emphasis which Garrick had committed in
the course of that night's acting, said, 'The players, Sir, have
got a kind of rant, with which they run on, without any regard
either to accent or emphasis.' Both Garrick and Giffard were
offended at this sarcasm, and endeavoured to refute it; upon
which Johnson rejoined, 'Well now, I'll give you something to
speak, with which you are little acquainted, and then we shall
see how just my observation is. That shall be the criterion. Let
me hear you repeat the ninth Commandment, "Thou shalt not
bear false witness against thy neighbour." ' Both tried at it, said
Dr. Taylor, and both mistook the emphasis, which should be
upon *not* and *false witness*.[1] Johnson put them right, and enjoyed
his victory with great glee.

His *Life of Savage* was no sooner published, than the following
liberal praise was given to it, in *The Champion*, a periodical paper:
'This pamphlet is, without flattery to its authour, as just and

---

[1] I suspect Dr. Taylor was inaccurate in this statement. The emphasis
should be equally upon *shalt* and *not*, as both concur to form the negative
injunction; and *false witness*, like the other acts prohibited in the Decalogue,
should not be marked by any peculiar emphasis, but only be distinctly
enunciated.

well written a piece as of its kind I ever saw; so that at the same
time that it highly deserves, it certainly stands very little in
need of this recommendation. As to the history of the unfortunate
person, whose memoirs compose this work, it is certainly penned
with equal accuracy and spirit, of which I am so much the better
judge, as I know many of the facts mentioned to be strictly true,
and very fairly related. Besides, it is not only the story of Mr.
Savage, but innumerable incidents relating to other persons, and
other affairs, which renders this a very amusing, and, withal, a
very instructive and valuable performance. The author's observations are short, significant, and just, as his narrative is remarkably smooth, and well disposed. His reflections open to all the
recesses of the human heart; and, in a word, a more just or
pleasant, a more engaging or a more improving treatise, on all
the excellencies and defects of human nature, is scarce to be
found in our own, or, perhaps, any other language.'[1]

Johnson's partiality for Savage made him entertain no doubt
of his story, however extraordinary and improbable. It never
occurred to him to question his being the son of the Countess of
Macclesfield, of whose unrelenting barbarity he so loudly complained, and the particulars of which are related in so strong and
affecting a manner in Johnson's life of him. Johnson was certainly
well warranted in publishing his narrative, however offensive
it might be to the lady and her relations, because her alledged
unnatural and cruel conduct to her son, and shameful avowal of
guilt, were stated in a *Life of Savage* now lying before me, which
came out so early as 1727, and no attempt had been made to
confute it, or to punish the authour or printer as a libeller: but
for the honour of human nature, we should be glad to find the
shocking tale not true; and, from a respectable gentleman[2] connected with the lady's family, I have received such information
and remarks, as joined to my own inquiries, will, I think, render

---

[1] This character of the *Life of Savage* was not written by Fielding as has
been supposed, but most probably by Ralph, who, as appears from the
minutes of the partners of *The Champion*, in the possession of Mr. Reed of
Staple Inn, succeeded Fielding in his share of the paper, before the date of
that eulogium.

[2] The late Francis Cockayne Cust, Esq., one of his Majesty's Counsel.

it at least somewhat doubtful, especially when we consider that it must have originated from the person himself who went by the name of Richard Savage.

If the maxim *falsum in uno, falsum in omnibus*,[1] were to be received without qualification, the credit of Savage's narrative, as conveyed to us, would be annihilated; for it contains some assertions which, beyond a question, are not true.

1. In order to induce a belief that Earl Rivers, on account of a criminal connection with whom, Lady Macclesfield is said to have been divorced from her husband, by Act of Parliament,[2] had a peculiar anxiety about the child which she bore to him, it is alledged, that his Lordship gave him his own name, and had it duly recorded in the register of St. Andrew's, Holborn. I have carefully inspected that register, but no such entry is to be found.[3]

2. It is stated, that 'Lady Macclesfield having lived for some time upon very uneasy terms with her husband, thought a publick confession of adultery the most obvious and expeditious method of obtaining her liberty;' and Johnson, assuming this to be true, stigmatises her with indignation, as 'the wretch who had, without scruple, proclaimed herself an adulteress.' But I have perused the Journals of both houses of Parliament at the period of her divorce, and there find it authentically ascertained, that so far from voluntarily submitting to the ignominious charge of adultery, she made a strenuous defence by her Counsel; the bill having been first moved 15th January, 1697, in the House of Lords, and proceeded on, (with various applications for time to bring up witnesses at a distance, &c.) at intervals, till the 3d of March, when it passed. It was brought to the Commons, by a message from the Lords, the 5th of March, proceeded on the 7th, 10th, 11th, 14th, and 15th, on which day, after a full examina-

---

[1] ['False in one point, false in all.'] [2] 1697.

[3] The story on which Mr. Cust so much relies, that Savage was a supposititious child, not the son of Lord Rivers and Lady Macclesfield, but the offspring of a shoemaker, introduced in consequence of her real son's death, was, without doubt, grounded on the circumstance of Lady Macclesfield having, in 1696, previously to the birth of Savage, had a daughter by the Earl Rivers, who died in her infancy; a fact which was proved in the course of the proceedings on Lord Macclesfield's Bill of Divorce. Most fictions of this kind have some admixture of truth in them. [M.]

tion of witnesses on both sides, and hearing of Counsel, it was reported without amendments, passed, and carried to the Lords.

That Lady Macclesfield was convicted of the crime of which she was accused, cannot be denied; but the question now is, whether the person calling himself Richard Savage was her son.

It has been said, that when Earl Rivers was dying, and anxious to provide for all his natural children, he was informed by Lady Macclesfield that her son by him was dead. Whether, then, shall we believe that this was a malignant lie, invented by a mother to prevent her own child from receiving the bounty of his father, which was accordingly the consequence, if the person whose life Johnson wrote, was her son; or shall we not rather believe that the person who then assumed the name of Richard Savage was an impostor, being in reality the son of the shoemaker, under whose wife's care Lady Macclesfield's child was placed; that after the death of the real Richard Savage, he attempted to personate him; and that the fraud being known to Lady Macclesfield, he was therefore repulsed by her with just resentment?

There is a strong circumstance in support of the last supposition, though it has been mentioned as an aggravation of Lady Macclesfield's unnatural conduct, and that is, her having prevented him from obtaining the benefit of a legacy left to him by Mrs. Lloyd his god-mother. For if there was such a legacy left, his not being able to obtain payment of it, must be imputed to his consciousness that he was not the real person. The just inference should be, that by the death of Lady Macclesfield's child before its god-mother, the legacy became lapsed, and therefore that Johnson's Richard Savage was an impostor. If he had a title to the legacy, he could not have found any difficulty in recovering it; for had the executors resisted his claim, the whole costs, as well as the legacy, must have been paid by them, if he had been the child to whom it was given.

The talents of Savage, and the mingled fire, rudeness, pride, meanness, and ferocity of his character,[1] concur in making it

[1] Johnson's companion appears to have persuaded that lofty-minded man, that he resembled him in having a noble pride; for Johnson, after painting in strong colours the quarrel between Lord Tyrconnel and Savage, asserts

credible that he was fit to plan and carry on an ambitious and daring scheme of imposture, similar instances of which have not been wanting in higher spheres, in the history of different countries, and have had a considerable degree of success.

Yet, on the other hand, to the companion of Johnson, (who through whatever medium he was conveyed into this world,— be it ever so doubtful 'To whom related, or by whom begot,' was, unquestionably, a man of no common endowments,) we must allow the weight of general repute as to his *Status* or parentage, though illicit; and supposing him to be an impostor, it seems strange that Lord Tyrconnel, the nephew of Lady Macclesfield, should patronise him, and even admit him as a guest in his family.[1] Lastly, it must ever appear very suspicious, that three different accounts of the Life of Richard Savage, one published in *The Plain Dealer*, in 1724, another in 1727, and another by the powerful pen of Johnson, in 1744, and all of them while Lady Macclesfield was alive, should, notwithstanding the severe attacks upon her, have been suffered to pass without any publick and effectual contradiction.

that 'the spirit of Mr. Savage, indeed, never suffered him to solicit a reconciliation: he returned reproach for reproach, and insult for insult.' But the respectable gentleman to whom I have alluded, has in his possession a letter from Savage, after Lord Tyrconnel had discarded him, addressed to the Reverend Mr. Gilbert, his Lordship's Chaplain, in which he requests him, in the humblest manner, to represent his case to the Viscount.

[1] Trusting to Savage's information, Johnson represents this unhappy man's being received as a companion by Lord Tyrconnel, and pensioned by his Lordship, as if posteriour to Savage's conviction and pardon. But I am assured, that Savage had received the voluntary bounty of Lord Tyrconnel, and had been dismissed by him, long before the murder was committed, and that his Lordship was very instrumental in procuring Savage's pardon, by his intercession with the Queen, through Lady Hertford. If, therefore, he had been desirous of preventing the publication by Savage, he would have left him to his fate. Indeed I must observe, that although Johnson mentions that Lord Tyrconnel's patronage of Savage was 'upon his promise to lay aside his design of exposing the cruelty of his mother,' the great biographer has forgotten that he himself has mentioned, that Savage's story had been told several years before in *The Plain Dealer*; from which he quotes this strong saying of the generous Sir Richard Steele, that 'the inhumanity of his mother had given him a right to find every good man his father.' At the same time it must be acknowledged, that Lady Macclesfield and her relations might still wish that her story should not be brought into more conspicuous notice by the satirical pen of Savage.

I have thus endeavoured to sum up the evidence upon the case, as fairly as I can; and the result seems to be, that the world must vibrate in a state of uncertainty as to what was the truth.

This digression, I trust, will not be censured, as it relates to a matter exceedingly curious, and very intimately connected with Johnson, both as a man and an authour.[1]

He this year wrote the *Preface to the Harleian Miscellany.** The selection of the pamphlets of which it was composed was made by Mr. Oldys, a man of eager curiosity and indefatigable diligence, who first exerted that spirit of inquiry into the literature of the old English writers, by which the works of our great dramatick poet have of late been so signally illustrated.

In 1745 he published a pamphlet entitled *Miscellaneous Observations on the Tragedy of Macbeth, with remarks on Sir T. H.'s (Sir Thomas Hanmer's) Edition of Shakspeare.** To which he affixed, proposals for a new edition of that poet.

As we do not trace any thing else published by him during the course of this year, we may conjecture that he was occupied entirely with that work. But the little encouragement which was given by the publick to his anonymous proposals for the execution of a task which Warburton was known to have undertaken, probably damped his ardour. His pamphlet, however, was highly esteemed, and was fortunate enough to obtain the approbation even of the supercilious Warburton himself, who, in the Preface to his *Shakspeare* published two years afterwards, thus mentioned it: 'As to all those things which have been published under the titles of *Essays, Remarks, Observations,* &c. on Shakspeare, if you except some critical notes on *Macbeth,* given as a specimen

---

[1] Miss Mason, after having forfeited the title of Lady Macclesfield by divorce, was married to Colonel Brett, and, it is said, was well known in all the polite circles. Colley Cibber, I am informed, had so high an opinion of her taste and judgement as to genteel life, and manners, that he submitted every scene of his *Careless Husband* to Mrs. Brett's revisal and correction. Colonel Brett was reported to be too free in his gallantry with his Lady's maid. Mrs. Brett came into a room one day in her own house, and found the Colonel and her maid both fast asleep in two chairs. She tied a white handkerchief round her husband's neck, which was a sufficient proof that she had discovered his intrigue; but she never at any time took notice of it to him. This incident, as I am told, gave occasion to the well-wrought scene of Sir Charles and Lady Easy and Edging.

of a projected edition, and written, as appears, by a man of parts and genius, the rest are absolutely below a serious notice.'

Of this flattering distinction shewn to him by Warburton, a very grateful remembrance was ever entertained by Johnson, who said, 'He praised me at a time when praise was of value to me.'

1746: ÆTAT. 37.]—IN 1746 it is probable that he was still employed upon his *Shakspeare,* which perhaps he laid aside for a time, upon account of the high expectations which were formed of Warburton's edition of that great poet. It is somewhat curious, that his literary career appears to have been almost totally suspended in the years 1745 and 1746, those years which were marked by a civil war in Great-Britain, when a rash attempt was made to restore the House of Stuart to the throne. That he had a tenderness for that unfortunate House, is well known; and some may fancifully imagine, that a sympathetick anxiety impeded the exertion of his intellectual powers: but I am inclined to think, that he was, during this time, sketching the outlines of his great philological work.

None of his letters during those years are extant, so far as I can discover. This is much to be regretted. It might afford some entertainment to see how he then expressed himself to his private friends, concerning State affairs. Dr. Adams informs me, that 'at this time a favourite object which he had in contemplation was *The Life of Alfred*; in which, from the warmth with which he spoke about it, he would, I believe, had he been master of his own will, have engaged himself, rather than on any other subject.'

1747: ÆTAT. 38.]—IN 1747 it is supposed that the *Gentleman's Magazine* for May was enriched by him with five short poetical pieces, distinguished by three asterisks. The first is a translation, or rather a paraphrase, of a Latin Epitaph on Sir Thomas Hanmer. Whether the Latin was his, or not, I have never heard, though I should think it probably was, if it be certain that he wrote the English; as to which my only cause of doubt is, that his slighting character of Hanmer as an editor, in his *Observations on Macbeth*, is very different from that in the 'Epitaph.' It may be said, that there is the same contrariety between the character in the *Observations*, and that in his own Preface to Shakspeare; but a considerable time elapsed between the one publication and the other, whereas the *Observations* and the 'Epitaph' came close together. The others are 'To Miss ——, on her giving the Authour a gold and silk net-work Purse of her own weaving;' 'Stella in Mourning;' 'The Winter's Walk;' 'An Ode;' and, 'To Lyce, an elderly Lady.' I am not positive that all these were his productions;[1] but as 'The Winter's Walk' has never been controverted to be his, and all of them have the same mark, it is reasonable to conclude that they are all written by the same hand. Yet to the Ode, in which we find a passage very characteristick of him, being a learned description of the gout,

> 'Unhappy, whom to beds of pain
>   *Arthritick* tyranny consigns;'

there is the following note: 'The authour being ill of the gout:' but Johnson was not attacked with that distemper till at a very late period of his life. May not this, however, be a poetical fiction? Why may not a poet suppose himself to have the gout, as well as suppose himself to be in love, of which we have innumerable instances, and which has been admirably ridiculed by Johnson in his *Life of Cowley*? I have also some difficulty to believe that he could produce such a group of *conceits* as appear in the verses to Lyce, in which he claims for this ancient personage as good a right to be assimilated to *heaven*, as nymphs whom other poets have flattered; he therefore ironically ascribes to her the attributes of the *sky*, in such stanzas as this:

> 'Her teeth the *night* with *darkness* dies,
>   She's *starr'd* with pimples o'er;
> Her tongue like nimble *lightning* plies,
>   And can with *thunder* roar.'

But as at a very advanced age he could condescend to trifle in

[1] In the *Universal Visiter*, to which Johnson contributed, the mark which is affixed to some pieces unquestionably his, is also found subjoined to others, of which he certainly was not the author. The mark therefore will not ascertain the poems in question to have been written by him. They were probably the productions of Hawkesworth, who, it is believed, was afflicted with the gout. [M.]

namby-pamby rhymes, to please Mrs. Thrale and her daughter, he may have, in his earlier years, composed such a piece as this.

It is remarkable, that in this first edition of *The Winter's Walk*, the concluding line is much more Johnsonian than it was afterwards printed; for in subsequent editions, after praying Stella to 'snatch him to her arms,' he says,

> 'And *shield* me from the *ills* of life.'

Whereas in the first edition it is

> 'And *hide* me from the *sight* of life.'

A horrour at life in general is more consonant with Johnson's habitual gloomy cast of thought.

I have heard him repeat with great energy the following verses, which appeared in the *Gentleman's Magazine* for April this year; but I have no authority to say they were his own. Indeed one of the best criticks of our age[1] suggests to me, that 'the word *indifferently* being used in the sense of *without concern*,' and being also very unpoetical, renders it improbable that they should have been his composition.

> *'On Lord* LOVAT's *Execution.*
>
> 'Pity'd by *gentle minds* KILMARNOCK died;
> The *brave*, BALMERINO, were on thy side;
> RADCLIFFE, unhappy in his crimes of youth,
> Steady in what he still mistook for truth,
> Beheld his death so decently unmov'd,
> The *soft* lamented, and the *brave* approv'd.
> But LOVAT's fate indifferently we view,
> True to no *King*, to no *religion* true:
> No *fair* forgets the *ruin* he has done;
> No *child* laments the *tyrant* of his *son*;
> No *tory* pities, thinking what he was;
> No *whig* compassions, *for he left the cause*;
> The *brave* regret not, for he was not brave;
> The *honest* mourn not, knowing him a knave!'[2]

---

[1] [Probably Malone. *Hill.*]

[2] These verses are somewhat too severe on the extraordinary person who is the chief figure in them, for he was undoubtedly brave. His pleasantry during his solemn trial (in which, by the way, I have heard Mr. David

This year his old pupil and friend, David Garrick, having become joint patentee and manager of Drury-lane theatre, Johnson honoured his opening of it with a Prologue, * which for just and manly dramatick criticism, on the whole range of the English stage, as well as for poetical excellence,[1] is unrivalled. Like the celebrated Epilogue to the *Distressed Mother*, it was, during the season, often called for by the audience. The most striking and brilliant passages of it have been so often repeated, and are so well recollected by all the lovers of the drama and of poetry, that it would be superfluous to point them out. In the *Gentleman's Magazine* for December this year, he inserted an 'Ode on Winter,' which is, I think, an admirable specimen of his genius for lyrick poetry.

But the year 1747 is distinguished as the epoch, when Johnson's arduous and important work, his DICTIONARY OF THE ENGLISH LANGUAGE, was announced to the world, by the publication of its Plan or *Prospectus*.

How long this immense undertaking had been the object of his contemplation, I do not know. I once asked him by what means he had attained to that astonishing knowledge of our language, by which he was enabled to realise a design of such extent, and accumulated difficulty. He told me, that 'it was not

Hume observe, that we have one of the very few speeches of Mr. Murray, now Earl of Mansfield, authentically given) was very remarkable. When asked if he had any questions to put to Sir Everard Fawkener, who was one of the strongest witnesses against him, he answered, 'I only wish him joy of his young wife.' And after sentence of death, in the horrible terms in cases of treason, was pronounced upon him, and he was retiring from the bar, he said, 'Fare you well, my Lords, we shall not all meet again in one place.' He behaved with perfect composure at his execution, and called out *'Dulce et decorum est pro patriâ mori.'* ['To die for fatherland is a sweet thing and becoming.' Horace, *Odes* III. ii. 13. (Wickham.)]

[1] My friend, Mr. Courtenay, whose eulogy on Johnson's Latin Poetry has been inserted in this Work, is no less happy in praising his English Poetry.

> But hark, he sings! the strain ev'n Pope admires;
> Indignant virtue her own bard inspires.
> Sublime as Juvenal he pours his lays,
> And with the Roman shares congenial praise;—
> In glowing numbers now he fires the age,
> And Shakspeare's sun relumes the clouded stage.

the effect of particular study; but that it had grown up in his mind insensibly.' I have been informed by Mr. James Dodsley, that several years before this period, when Johnson was one day sitting in his brother Robert's shop, he heard his brother suggest to him, that a Dictionary of the English Language would be a work that would be well received by the publick; that Johnson seemed at first to catch at the proposition, but, after a pause, said, in his abrupt decisive manner, 'I believe I shall not undertake it.' That he, however, had bestowed much thought upon the subject, before he published his *Plan*, is evident from the enlarged, clear, and accurate views which it exhibits; and we find him mentioning in that tract, that many of the writers whose testimonies were to be produced as authorities, were selected by Pope; which proves that he had been furnished, probably by Mr. Robert Dodsley, with whatever hints that eminent poet had contributed towards a great literary project, that had been the subject of important consideration in a former reign.

The booksellers who contracted with Johnson, single and unaided, for the execution of a work, which in other countries has not been effected but by the co-operating exertions of many, were Mr. Robert Dodsley, Mr. Charles Hitch, Mr. Andrew Millar, the two Messieurs Longman, and the two Messieurs Knapton. The price stipulated was fifteen hundred and seventy-five pounds.

The *Plan* was addressed to Philip Dormer, Earl of Chesterfield, then one of his Majesty's Principal Secretaries of State; a nobleman who was very ambitious of literary distinction, and who, upon being informed of the design, had expressed himself in terms very favourable to its success. There is, perhaps in every thing of any consequence, a secret history which it would be amusing to know, could we have it authentically communicated. Johnson told me,[1] 'Sir, the way in which the *Plan* of my *Dictionary* came to be inscribed to Lord Chesterfield, was this: I had neglected to write it by the time appointed. Dodsley suggested a desire to have it addressed to Lord Chesterfield.

[1] September 22, 1777, going from Ashbourne in Derbyshire, to see Islam.

I laid hold of this as a pretext for delay, that it might be better
done, and let Dodsley have his desire. I said to my friend, Dr.
Bathurst, "Now if any good comes of my addressing to Lord
Chesterfield, it will be ascribed to deep policy, when, in fact, it
was only a casual excuse for laziness." '

It is worthy of observation, that the *Plan* has not only the
substantial merit of comprehension, perspicuity, and precision,
but that the language of it is unexceptionably excellent; it being
altogether free from that inflation of style, and those uncommon
but apt and energetick words, which in some of his writings have
been censured, with more petulance than justice; and never was
there a more dignified strain of compliment than that in which
he courts the attention of one who, he had been persuaded to
believe, would be a respectable patron.

'With regard to questions of purity or propriety, (says he) I
was once in doubt whether I should not attribute to myself too
much in attempting to decide them, and whether my province
was to extend beyond the proposition of the question, and the
display of the suffrages on each side; but I have been since
determined by your Lordship's opinion, to interpose my own
judgement, and shall therefore endeavour to support what appears to me most consonant to grammar and reason. Ausonius
thought that modesty forbade him to plead inability for a task
to which Cæsar had judged him equal:

> *Cur me posse negem posse quod ille putat?*[1]

And I may hope, my Lord, that since you, whose authority in
our language is so generally acknowledged, have commissioned
me to declare my own opinion, I shall be considered as exercising
a kind of vicarious jurisdiction; and that the power which might
have been denied to my own claim, will be readily allowed me
as the delegate of your Lordship.'

This passage proves, that Johnson's addressing his *Plan* to
Lord Chesterfield was not merely in consequence of the result of
a report by means of Dodsley, that the Earl favoured the design;
but that there had been a particular communication with his

[1] ['Why should I say that I cannot do what he reckons that I can?'
Ausonius, *Epigrams* i. 12.]

Lordship concerning it. Dr. Taylor told me, that Johnson sent his *Plan* to him in manuscript, for his perusal; and that when it was lying upon his table, Mr. William Whitehead happened to pay him a visit, and being shewn it, was highly pleased with such parts of it as he had time to read, and begged to take it home with him, which he was allowed to do; that from him it got into the hands of a noble Lord,[1] who carried it to Lord Chesterfield. When Taylor observed this might be an advantage, Johnson replied, 'No, Sir; it would have come out with more bloom, if it had not been seen before by any body.'

The opinion conceived of it by another noble authour, appears from the following extract of a letter from the Earl of Orrery to Dr. Birch:

'Caledon, Dec. 30, 1747.
'I have just now seen the specimen of Mr. Johnson's Dictionary, addressed to Lord Chesterfield. I am much pleased with the plan, and I think the specimen is one of the best that I have ever read. Most specimens disgust, rather than prejudice us in favour of the work to follow; but the language of Mr. Johnson's is good, and the arguments are properly and modestly expressed. However, some expressions may be cavilled at, but they are trifles. I'll mention one. The *barren* Laurel. The laurel is not barren, in any sense whatever; it bears fruits and flowers. *Sed hæ sunt nugæ*,[2] and I have great expectation from the performance.'[3]

That he was fully aware of the arduous nature of the undertaking, he acknowledges; and shews himself perfectly sensible of it in the conclusion of his *Plan*; but he had a noble consciousness of his own abilities, which enabled him to go on with undaunted spirit.

Dr. Adams found him one day busy at his *Dictionary*, when the following dialogue ensued. 'ADAMS. This is a great work, Sir. How are you to get all the etymologies? JOHNSON. Why, Sir, here is a shelf with Junius, and Skinner, and others; and there is

---

[1] [Perhaps William, 3rd Earl of Jersey. *Powell*.]
[2] ['But they are trifles.']
[3] Birch, *MSS. Brit. Mus.* 4303.

a Welch gentleman who has published a collection of Welch proverbs, who will help me with the Welch. ADAMS. But, Sir, how can you do this in three years? JOHNSON. Sir, I have no doubt that I can do it in three years. ADAMS. But the French Academy, which consists of forty members, took forty years to compile their Dictionary. JOHNSON. Sir, thus it is. This is the proportion. Let me see; forty times forty is sixteen hundred. As three to sixteen hundred, so is the proportion of an Englishman to a Frenchman.' With so much ease and pleasantry could he talk of that prodigious labour which he had undertaken to execute.

The publick has had, from another pen,[1] a long detail of what had been done in this country by prior Lexicographers; and no doubt Johnson was wise to avail himself of them, so far as they went: but the learned, yet judicious research of etymology, the various, yet accurate display of definition, and the rich collection of authorities, were reserved for the superior mind of our great philologist. For the mechanical part he employed, as he told me, six amanuenses; and let it be remembered by the natives of North-Britain, to whom he is supposed to have been so hostile, that five of them were of that country. There were two Messieurs Macbean; Mr. Shiels, who we shall hereafter see partly wrote the *Lives of the Poets* to which the name of Cibber is affixed;[2] Mr. Stewart, son of Mr. George Stewart, bookseller at Edinburgh; and a Mr. Maitland. The sixth of these humble assistants was Mr. Peyton, who, I believe, taught French, and published some elementary tracts.

To all these painful labourers, Johnson shewed a never-ceasing kindness, so far as they stood in need of it. The elder Mr. Macbean had afterwards the honour of being Librarian to Archibald, Duke of Argyle, for many years, but was left without a shilling. Johnson wrote for him a Preface to *A System of Ancient Geography*; and, by the favour of Lord Thurlow, got him admitted a poor brother of the Charterhouse. For Shiels, who died of a consumption, he had much tenderness; and it has been thought

---

[1] See Sir John Hawkins's *Life of Johnson.*
[2] See *post*, under April 10, 1776.

that some choice sentences in the *Lives of the Poets* were supplied by him. Peyton, when reduced to penury, had frequent aid from the bounty of Johnson, who at last was at the expense of burying both him and his wife.

While the *Dictionary* was going forward, Johnson lived part of the time in Holborn, part in Gough-square, Fleet-street; and he had an upper room fitted up like a counting-house for the purpose, in which he gave to the copyists their several tasks. The words, partly taken from other dictionaries, and partly supplied by himself, having been first written down with spaces left between them, he delivered in writing their etymologies, definitions, and various significations. The authorities were copied from the books themselves, in which he had marked the passages with a black-lead pencil, the traces of which could easily be effaced. I have seen several of them, in which that trouble had not been taken; so that they were just as when used by the copyists. It is remarkable, that he was so attentive in the choice of the passages in which words were authorised, that one may read page after page of his *Dictionary* with improvement and pleasure; and it should not pass unobserved, that he has quoted no authour whose writings had a tendency to hurt sound religion and morality.

The necessary expence of preparing a work of such magnitude for the press, must have been a considerable deduction from the price stipulated to be paid for the copy-right. I understand that nothing was allowed by the booksellers on that account; and I remember his telling me, that a large portion of it having by mistake been written upon both sides of the paper, so as to be inconvenient for the compositor, it cost him twenty pounds to have it transcribed upon one side only.

He is now to be considered as 'tugging at his oar,' as engaged in a steady continued course of occupation, sufficient to employ all his time for some years; and which was the best preventive of that constitutional melancholy which was ever lurking about him, ready to trouble his quiet. But his enlarged and lively mind could not be satisfied without more diversity of employment, and the pleasure of animated relaxation. He therefore not only exerted his talents in occasional composition very different from

Lexicography, but formed a club in Ivy-lane, Paternoster-row, with a view to enjoy literary discussion, and amuse his evening hours. The members associated with him in this little society were his beloved friend Dr. Richard Bathurst, Mr. Hawkesworth, afterwards well known by his writings, Mr. John Hawkins, an attorney,[1] and a few others of different professions.

In the *Gentleman's Magazine* for May of this year he wrote a 'Life of Roscommon,'* with Notes, which he afterwards much improved, indented the notes into text, and inserted it amongst his *Lives of the English Poets.*

Mr. Dodsley this year brought out his *Preceptor,* one of the most valuable books for the improvement of young minds that has appeared in any language; and to this meritorious work Johnson furnished 'The Preface,'* containing a general sketch of the book, with a short and perspicuous recommendation of each article; as also, 'The Vision of Theodore the Hermit, found in his Cell,'* a most beautiful allegory of human life, under the figure of ascending the mountain of Existence. The Bishop of Dromore heard Dr. Johnson say, that he thought this was the best thing he ever wrote.

1749: ÆTAT. 40.]—In January, 1749, he published *The Vanity of Human Wishes, being the Tenth Satire of Juvenal imitated.* He, I believe, composed it the preceding year.[2] Mrs. Johnson, for the sake of country air, had lodgings at Hampstead, to which he resorted occasionally, and there the greatest part, if not the whole, of this *Imitation* was written. The fervid rapidity with which it was produced, is scarcely credible. I have heard him say, that he composed seventy lines of it in one day, without putting one of them upon paper till they were finished. I

---

[1] He was afterwards for several years Chairman of the Middlesex Justices, and upon occasion of presenting an address to the King, accepted the usual offer of Knighthood. He is authour of 'A History of Musick,' in five volumes in quarto. By assiduous attendance on Johnson in his last illness, he obtained the office of one of his executors; in consequence of which, the booksellers of London employed him to publish an edition of Dr. Johnson's works, and to write his Life.

[2] Sir John Hawkins, with solemn inaccuracy, represents this poem as a consequence of the indifferent reception of his tragedy. But the fact is, that the poem was published on the 9th of January, and the tragedy was not acted till the 6th of the February following.

remember when I once regretted to him that he had not given us more of Juvenal's *Satires*, he said he probably should give more, for he had them all in his head; by which I understood that he had the originals and correspondent allusions floating in his mind, which he could, when he pleased, embody and render permanent without much labour. Some of them, however, he observed were too gross for imitation.

The profits of a single poem, however excellent, appear to have been very small in the last reign, compared with what a publication of the same size has since been known to yield. I have mentioned, upon Johnson's own authority, that for his *London* he had only ten guineas; and now, after his fame was established, he got for his *Vanity of Human Wishes* but five guineas more, as is proved by an authentick document in my possession.[1]

It will be observed, that he reserves to himself the right of printing one edition of this satire, which was his practice upon occasion of the sale of all his writings; it being his fixed intention to publish at some period, for his own profit, a complete collection of his works.

His *Vanity of Human Wishes* has less of common life, but more of a philosophick dignity than his *London*. More readers, therefore, will be delighted with the pointed spirit of *London*, than with the profound reflection of *The Vanity of Human Wishes*. Garrick, for instance, observed in his sprightly manner, with more vivacity than regard to just discrimination, as is usual with wits, 'When Johnson lived much with the Herveys, and saw a good deal of what was passing in life, he wrote his *London*, which is lively and easy. When he became more retired, he gave us his *Vanity of Human Wishes*, which is as hard as Greek. Had he gone on to imitate another satire, it would have been as hard as Hebrew.'[2]

---

[1] 'Nov. 25, 1748. I received of Mr. Dodsley fifteen guineas, for which I assign to him the right of copy of an imitation of the *Tenth Satire of Juvenal*, written by me; reserving to myself the right of printing one edition.
'SAM. JOHNSON.'
'London, 29 June, 1786. A true copy, from the original in Dr. Johnson's handwriting.
'JAS. DODSLEY.'
[2] From Mr. Langton.

But *The Vanity of Human Wishes* is, in the opinion of the best judges, as high an effort of ethick poetry as any language can shew. The instances of variety of disappointment are chosen so judiciously and painted so strongly, that, the moment they are read, they bring conviction to every thinking mind. That of the scholar must have depressed the too sanguine expectations of many an ambitious student.[1] That of the warrior, Charles of Sweden, is, I think, as highly finished a picture as can possibly be conceived.

Were all the other excellencies of this poem annihilated, it must ever have our grateful reverence from its noble conclusion; in which we are consoled with the assurance that happiness may be attained, if we 'apply our hearts' to piety:

> 'Where then shall hope and fear their objects find?
> Shall dull suspense corrupt the stagnant mind?
> Must helpless man, in ignorance sedate,
> Roll darkling down the torrent of his fate?
> Shall no dislike alarm, no wishes rise,
> No cries attempt the mercy of the skies?
> Inquirer, cease; petitions yet remain,
> Which Heav'n may hear, nor deem Religion vain.

[1] In this poem one of the instances mentioned of unfortunate learned men is *Lydiat*:
'Hear Lydiat's life, and Galileo's end.'
The history of Lydiat being little known, the following account of him may be acceptable to many of my readers. It appeared as a note in the Supplement to the *Gent. Mag.* for 1748, in which some passages extracted from Johnson's poem were inserted, and it should have been added in the subsequent editions.—A very learned divine and mathematician, fellow of New College, Oxon, and Rector of Okerton, near Banbury. He wrote, among many others, a Latin treatise *De Natura cœli*, etc., in which he attacked the sentiments of Scaliger and Aristotle, not bearing to hear it urged, *that some things are true in philosophy and false in divinity*. He made above 600 Sermons on the harmony of the Evangelists. Being unsuccessful in publishing his works, he lay in the prison of Bocardo at Oxford, and in the King's Bench, till Bishop Usher, Dr. Laud, Sir William Boswell, and Dr. Pink, released him by paying his debts. He petitioned King Charles I. to be sent into Ethiopia, etc., to procure MSS. Having spoken in favour of monarchy and bishops, he was plundered by the parliament forces, and twice carried away prisoner from his rectory; and afterwards had not a shirt to shift him in three months, without he borrowed it, and died very poor in 1646.

> Still raise for good the supplicating voice,
> But leave to Heaven the measure and the choice.
> Safe in his hand, whose eye discerns afar
> The secret ambush of a specious pray'r;
> Implore his aid, in his decisions rest,
> Secure whate'er he gives he gives the best.
> Yet when the sense of sacred presence fires,
> And strong devotion to the skies aspires,
> Pour forth thy fervours for a healthful mind,
> Obedient passions, and a will resign'd;
> For love, which scarce collective man can fill,
> For patience, sovereign o'er transmuted ill;
> For faith, which panting for a happier seat,
> Counts death kind Nature's signal for retreat.
> These goods for man the laws of Heaven ordain,
> These goods he grants, who grants the power to gain;
> With these celestial wisdom calms the mind,
> And makes the happiness she does not find.'

Garrick being now vested with theatrical power by being manager of Drury-lane theatre, he kindly and generously made use of it to bring out Johnson's tragedy, which had been long kept back for want of encouragement. But in this benevolent purpose he met with no small difficulty from the temper of Johnson, which could not brook that a drama which he had formed with much study, and had been obliged to keep more than the nine years of Horace, should be revised and altered at the pleasure of an actor. Yet Garrick knew well, that without some alterations it would not be fit for the stage. A violent dispute having ensued between them, Garrick applied to the Reverend Dr. Taylor to interpose. Johnson was at first very obstinate. 'Sir, (said he) the fellow wants me to make Mahomet run mad, that he may have an opportunity of tossing his hands and kicking his heels.'[1] He was, however, at last, with difficulty, prevailed on to comply with Garrick's wishes, so as to allow of some changes; but still there were not enough.

Dr. Adams was present the first night of the representation

---

[1] Mahomet was, in fact, played by Mr. Barry, and Demetrius by Mr. Garrick: but probably at this time the parts were not yet cast.

of *Irene*, and gave me the following account: 'Before the curtain drew up, there were catcalls whistling, which alarmed Johnson's friends. The Prologue, which was written by himself in a manly strain, soothed the audience,[1] and the play went off tolerably, till it came to the conclusion, when Mrs. Pritchard, the heroine of the piece, was to be strangled upon the stage, and was to speak two lines with the bow-string round her neck. The audience cried out *"Murder! Murder!"* She several times attempted to speak; but in vain. At last she was obliged to go off the stage alive.' This passage was afterwards struck out, and she was carried off to be put to death behind the scenes, as the play now has it. The Epilogue, as Johnson informed me, was written by Sir William Yonge. I know not how his play came to be thus graced by the pen of a person then so eminent in the political world.

Notwithstanding all the support of such performers as Garrick, Barry, Mrs. Cibber, Mrs. Pritchard, and every advantage of dress and decoration, the tragedy of *Irene* did not please the publick. Mr. Garrick's zeal carried it through for nine nights, so that the authour had his three nights' profits; and from a receipt signed by him, now in the hands of Mr. James Dodsley, it appears that his friend Mr. Robert Dodsley gave him one hundred pounds for the copy, with his usual reservation of the right of one edition.

[1] The expression used by Dr. Adams was 'soothed.' I should rather think the audience was *awed* by the extraordinary spirit and dignity of the following lines:

> 'Be this at least his praise, be this his pride,
> To force applause no modern arts are tried:
> Should partial catcalls all his hopes confound,
> He bids no trumpet quell the fatal sound;
> Should welcome sleep relieve the weary wit,
> He rolls no thunders o'er the drowsy pit;
> No snares to captivate the judgement spreads,
> Nor bribes your eyes to prejudice your heads.
> Unmov'd, though witlings sneer and rivals rail,
> Studious to please, yet not asham'd to fail,
> He scorns the meek address, the suppliant strain,
> With merit needless, and without it vain;
> In Reason, Nature, Truth, he dares to trust;
> Ye fops be silent, and ye wits be just!'

Irene, considered as a poem, is intitled to the praise of superiour excellence. Analysed into parts, it will furnish a rich store of noble sentiments, fine imagery, and beautiful language; but it is deficient in pathos, in that delicate power of touching the human feelings, which is the principal end of the drama.[1] Indeed Garrick has complained to me, that Johnson not only had not the faculty of producing the impressions of tragedy, but that he had not the sensibility to perceive them. His great friend Mr. Walmsley's prediction, that he would 'turn out a fine tragedy-writer,' was, therefore, ill-founded. Johnson was wise enough to be convinced that he had not the talents necessary to write successfully for the stage, and never made another attempt in that species of composition.

When asked how he felt upon the ill success of his tragedy, he replied, 'Like the Monument;' meaning that he continued firm and unmoved as that column. And let it be remembered, as an admonition to the *genus irritabile*[2] of dramatick writers, that this great man, instead of peevishly complaining of the bad taste of the town, submitted to its decision without a murmur. He had, indeed, upon all occasions, a great deference for the general opinion: 'A man (said he) who writes a book, thinks himself wiser or wittier than the rest of mankind; he supposes that he can instruct or amuse them, and the publick to whom he appeals, must, after all, be the judges of his pretensions.'

On occasion of his play being brought upon the stage, Johnson had a fancy that as a dramatick authour his dress should be more gay than what he ordinarily wore; he therefore appeared behind the scenes, and even in one of the side boxes, in a scarlet waist-coat, with rich gold lace, and a gold-laced hat. He humourously observed to Mr. Langton, 'that when in that dress he could not treat people with the same ease as when in his usual plain clothes.' Dress indeed, we must allow, has more effect even upon strong

[1] Aaron Hill (vol. ii. p. 355), in a letter to Mr. Mallett, gives the following account of *Irene* after having seen it: 'I was at the anomalous Mr. Johnson's benefit, and found the play his proper representative; strong sense ungraced by sweetness or decorum.'
[2] [*Genus irritabile vatum*, Horace, *Ep.* ii. 2. 102. 'The fretful tribe of poets.']

minds than one should suppose, without having had the experience of it. His necessary attendance while his play was in
rehearsal, and during its performance, brought him acquainted
with many of the performers of both sexes, which produced a
more favourable opinion of their profession than he had harshly
expressed in his *Life of Savage*. With some of them he kept up
an acquaintance as long as he and they lived, and was ever ready
to shew them acts of kindness. He for a considerable time used
to frequent the *Green Room*, and seemed to take delight in dissipating his gloom, by mixing in the sprightly chit-chat of the
motley circle then to be found there. Mr. David Hume related
to me from Mr. Garrick, that Johnson at last denied himself
this amusement, from considerations of rigid virtue; saying, 'I'll
come no more behind your scenes, David; for the silk stockings
and white bosoms of your actresses excite my amorous propensities.'

1750: ÆTAT. 41.]—IN 1750 he came forth in the character
for which he was eminently qualified, a majestick teacher of
moral and religious wisdom. The vehicle which he chose was
that of a periodical paper, which he knew had been, upon former
occasions, employed with great success. *The Tatler*, *Spectator*,
and *Guardian*, were the last of the kind published in England,
which had stood the test of a long trial; and such an interval had
now elapsed since their publication, as made him justly think
that, to many of his readers, this form of instruction would, in
some degree, have the advantage of novelty. A few days before
the first of his *Essays* came out, there started another competitor
for fame in the same form, under the title of *The Tatler Revived*,
which I believe was 'born but to die.' Johnson was, I think, not
very happy in the choice of his title, *The Rambler*, which certainly is not suited to a series of grave and moral discourses;
which the Italians have literally, but ludicrously, translated by
Il Vagabondo; and which has been lately assumed as the denomination of a vehicle of licentious tales, *The Rambler's Magazine*. He
gave Sir Joshua Reynolds the following account of its getting
this name: 'What *must* be done, Sir, *will* be done. When I was
to begin publishing that paper, I was at a loss how to name it.

I sat down at night upon my bedside, and resolved that I would not go to sleep till I had fixed its title. *The Rambler* seemed the best that occurred, and I took it.'[1]

With what devout and conscientious sentiments this paper was undertaken, is evidenced by the following prayer, which he composed and offered up on the occasion: 'Almighty GOD, the giver of all good things, without whose help all labour is ineffectual, and without whose grace all wisdom is folly; grant, I beseech Thee, that in this undertaking thy Holy Spirit may not be withheld from me, but that I may promote thy glory, and the salvation of myself and others: grant this, O LORD, for the sake of thy son JESUS CHRIST. Amen.'[2]

The first paper of *The Rambler* was published on Tuesday the 20th of March, 1750; and its authour was enabled to continue it, without interruption, every Tuesday and Friday, till Saturday the 17th of March, 1752,[3] on which day it closed. This is a strong confirmation of the truth of a remark of his, which I have had occasion to quote elsewhere,[4] that 'a man may write at any time, if he will set himself doggedly to it;' for, notwithstanding his constitutional indolence, his depression of spirits, and his labour in carrying on his *Dictionary*, he answered the stated calls of the press twice a week from the stores of his mind, during all that time; having received no assistance, except four billets in No. 10, by Miss Mulso, now Mrs. Chapone; No. 30, by Mrs. Catharine Talbot; No. 97, by Mr. Samuel Richardson, whom he describes in an introductory note as 'An author who has enlarged the

---

[1] I have heard Dr. Warton mention, that he was at Mr. Robert Dodsley's with the late Mr. Moore, and several of his friends, considering what should be the name of the periodical paper which Moore had undertaken. Garrick proposed *The Sallad*, which, by a curious coincidence, was afterwards applied to himself by Goldsmith:

'Our Garrick's a sallad, for in him we see
Oil, vinegar, sugar, and saltness agree!'

At last, the company having separated, without any thing of which they approved having been offered, Dodsley himself thought of *The World*.

[2] *Prayers and Meditations*, p. 9.

[3] In the original folio edition of *The Rambler* the concluding paper is dated Saturday, March 17. But Saturday was in fact March 14. This circumstance is worth notice, for Mrs. Johnson died on the 17th. [M.]

[4] *Journal of a Tour to the Hebrides*, 3rd edit. p. 28. [Aug. 16, 1773.]

knowledge of human nature, and taught the passions to move at the command of virtue;' and Nos. 44 and 100 by Mrs. Elizabeth Carter.

Posterity will be astonished when they are told, upon the authority of Johnson himself, that many of these discourses, which we should suppose had been laboured with all the slow attention of literary leisure, were written in haste as the moment pressed, without even being read over by him before they were printed. It can be accounted for only in this way; that by reading and meditation, and a very close inspection of life, he had accumulated a great fund of miscellaneous knowledge, which, by a peculiar promptitude of mind, was ever ready at his call, and which he had constantly accustomed himself to clothe in the most apt and energetick expression. Sir Joshua Reynolds once asked him by what means he had attained his extraordinary accuracy and flow of language. He told him, that he had early laid it down as a fixed rule to do his best on every occasion, and in every company; to impart whatever he knew in the most forcible language he could put it in; and that by constant practice, and never suffering any careless expressions to escape him, or attempting to deliver his thoughts without arranging them in the clearest manner, it became habitual to him.

Yet he was not altogether unprepared as a periodical writer; for I have in my possession a small duodecimo volume, in which he has written, in the form of Mr. Locke's *Common-Place Book*, a variety of hints for essays on different subjects. He has marked upon the first blank leaf of it, 'To the 128th page, collections for *The Rambler*;' and in another place, 'In fifty-two there were seventeen provided; in 97—21; in 190—25.' At a subsequent period (probably after the work was finished) he added, 'In all, taken of provided materials, 30.'

Sir John Hawkins, who is unlucky upon all occasions, tells us, that 'this method of accumulating intelligence had been practised by Mr. Addison, and is humourously described in one of the *Spectators*, wherein he feigns to have dropped his paper of *notanda*, consisting of a diverting medley of broken sentences and loose hints, which he tells us he had collected, and meant to

make use of. Much of the same kind is Johnson's *Adversaria.*[1]
But the truth is, that there is no resemblance at all between them.
Addison's note was a fiction, in which unconnected fragments of
his lucubrations were purposely jumbled together, in as odd a
manner as he could, in order to produce a laughable effect.
Whereas Johnson's abbreviations are all distinct, and applicable
to each subject of which the head is mentioned.

For instance, there is the following specimen:

Youth's Entry, &c.

'Baxter's account of things in which he had changed his mind
as he grew up. Voluminous.—No wonder.—If every man was to
tell, or mark, on how many subjects he has changed, it would make
vols. but the changes not always observed by man's self.—From
pleasure to bus. [*business*] to quiet; from thoughtfulness to reflect.
to piety; from dissipation to domestic. by impercept. gradat. but
the change is certain. Dial *non progredi, progress. esse conspicimus.*[2]
Look back, consider what was thought at some dist. period.

'*Hope predom. in youth. Mind not willingly indulges unpleasing
thoughts.* The world lies all enameled before him, as a distant
prospect sun-gilt;[3] inequalities only found by coming to it. *Love
is to be all joy—children excellent*—Fame to be constant—caresses
of the great—applauses of the learned—smiles of Beauty.

'*Fear of disgrace—bashfulness*—Finds things of less importance.
Miscarriages forgot like excellencies;—if remembered, of no
import. Danger of sinking into negligence of reputation. Lest
the fear of disgrace destroy activity.

'*Confidence in himself.* Long tract of life before him.—No
thought of sickness.—Embarrassment of affairs.—Distraction
of family. Publick calamities.—No sense of the prevalence of
bad habits.—Negligent of time—ready to undertake—careless
to pursue—all changed by time.

'*Confident of others*—unsuspecting as unexperienced—imagin-

[1] Hawkins's *Life of Johnson*, p. 268 [p. 265].
[2] ['The sly shadow steals away upon the dial, and the quickest eye can
discover no more than that it is gone.' Glanvill, *Scepsis Sci.* xi. 60.]
[3] This most beautiful image of the enchanting delusion of youthful prospect
has not been used in any of Johnson's essays.

ing himself secure against neglect, never imagines they will
venture to treat him ill. Ready to trust; expecting to be trusted.
Convinced by time of the selfishness, the meanness, the cowardice,
the treachery of men.

'Youth ambitious, as thinking honours easy to be had.

'Different kinds of praise pursued at different periods. Of the
gay in youth. dang. hurt, &c. despised.

'Of the fancy in manhood. Ambit.—stocks—bargains.—Of the
wise and sober in old age—seriousness—formality—maxims,
but general—only of the rich, otherwise age is happy—but at
last every thing referred to riches—no having fame, honour,
influence, without subjection to caprice.

'Horace.

'Hard it would be if men entered life with the same views with
which they leave it, or left as they enter it.—No hope—no
undertaking—no regard to benevolence—no fear of disgrace, &c.

'Youth to be taught the piety of age—age to retain the honour
of youth.'

This, it will be observed, is the sketch of Number 196 of *The
Rambler*. I shall gratify my readers with another specimen:

'Confederacies difficult; why.

'Seldom in war a match for single persons—nor in peace;
therefore kings make themselves absolute. Confederacies in
learning—every great work the work of one. *Bruy.* Scholars'
friendship like ladies. Scribebamus, &c. Mart.[1] the apple of discord—the laurel of discord—the poverty of criticism. Swift's
opinion of the power of six geniuses united. That union scarce
possible. His remarks just; man a social, not steady nature.
Drawn to man by words, repelled by passions. Orb drawn by
attraction rep. [*repelled*] by centrifugal.

'Common danger unites by crushing other passions—but they
return. Equality hinders compliance. Superiority produces insolence and envy. Too much regard in each to private interest—
too little.

[1] Lib. xii. 96 [*95*]. 'In Tuccam æmulum omnium suorum studiorum.'
[M.] ['Epigram on Tucca, his rival in all his learning.']

'The mischiefs of private and exclusive societies—the fitness of social attraction diffused through the whole. The mischiefs of too partial love of our country. Contraction of moral duties—οἱ φίλοι οὐ φίλος.[1]

'Every man moves upon his own center, and therefore repels others from too near a contact, though he may comply with some general laws.

'Of confederacy with superiours, every one knows the inconvenience. With equals, no authority;—every man his own opinion—his own interest.

'Man and wife hardly united;—scarce ever without children. Computation, if two to one against two, how many against five? If confederacies were easy—useless;—many oppresses many.— If possible only to some, dangerous. *Principum amicitias.*'[2]

Here we see the embryo of Number 45 of *The Adventurer*; and it is a confirmation of what I shall presently have occasion to mention, that the papers in that collection marked T. were written by Johnson.

This scanty preparation of materials will not, however, much diminish our wonder at the extraordinary fertility of his mind; for the proportion which they bear to the number of essays which he wrote, is very small; and it is remarkable, that those for which he had made no preparation, are as rich and as highly finished as those for which the hints were lying by him. It is also to be observed, that the papers formed from his hints are worked up with such strength and elegance, that we almost lose sight of the hints, which become like 'drops in the bucket.' Indeed, in several instances, he has made a very slender use of them, so that many of them remain still unapplied.[3]

---

[1] ['He had friends, but no friend.' Diogenes Laertius, bk. v, ch. i.]

[2] [*gravesque Principum amicitias*, 'leagues, deadly in issue, of chief leaders.' Horace, *Odes* ii. i. 4. (Wickham.)]

[3] Sir John Hawkins has selected from this little collection of materials, what he calls the 'Rudiments of two of the papers of *The Rambler.*' But he has not been able to read the manuscript distinctly. Thus he writes, p. 266, 'Sailor's fate any mansion;' whereas the original is 'Sailor's life my aversion.' He has also transcribed the unappropriated hints on *Writers for bread*, in which he decyphers these notable passages, one in Latin, *fatui non famæ*, instead of *fami non famæ*; Johnson having in his mind what Thuanus says of

As *The Rambler* was entirely the work of one man, there was, of course, such a uniformity in its texture, as very much to exclude the charm of variety; and the grave and often solemn cast of thinking, which distinguished it from other periodical papers, made it, for some time, not generally liked. So slowly did this excellent work, of which twelve editions have now issued from the press, gain upon the world at large, that even in the closing number the authour says, 'I have never been much a favourite of the publick.'

Yet, very soon after its commencement, there were who felt and acknowledged its uncommon excellence. Verses in its praise appeared in the newspapers; and the editor of the *Gentleman's Magazine* mentions, in October, his having received several letters to the same purpose from the learned. *The Student, or Oxford and Cambridge Miscellany*, in which Mr. Bonnell Thornton and Mr. Colman were the principal writers, describes it as 'a work that exceeds anything of the kind ever published in this kingdom, some of the *Spectators* excepted—if indeed they may be excepted.' And afterwards, 'May the publick favours crown his merits, and may not the English, under the auspicious reign of GEORGE the Second, neglect a man, who, had he lived in the first century, would have been one of the greatest favourites of Augustus.' This flattery of the monarch had no effect. It is too well known, that the second George never was an Augustus to learning or genius.

Johnson told me, with an amiable fondness, a little pleasing circumstance relative to this work. Mrs. Johnson, in whose judgement and taste he had great confidence, said to him, after a few numbers of *The Rambler* had come out, 'I thought very well of you before; but I did not imagine you could have written any thing equal to this.' Distant praise, from whatever quarter, is not so delightful as that of a wife whom a man loves and

the learned German antiquary and linguist, Xylander, who, he tells us, lived in such poverty, that he was supposed *fami non famæ scribere*; [to write—for bread not fame] and another in French, *Degentede fate* [fatu] *et affaméd'argent*, instead of *Dégouté de fame*, (an old word for *renommée*) *et affamé d'argent*. The manuscript being written in an exceedingly small hand, is indeed very hard to read; but it would have been better to have left blanks than to write nonsense.

esteems. Her approbation may be said to 'come home to his *bosom*;' and being so near, its effect is most sensible and permanent.

Mr. James Elphinston, who has since published various works, and who was ever esteemed by Johnson as a worthy man, happened to be in Scotland while *The Rambler* was coming out in single papers at London. With a laudable zeal at once for the improvement of his countrymen, and the reputation of his friend, he suggested and took the charge of an edition of those Essays at Edinburgh, which followed progressively the London publication.[1]

The following letter written at this time, though not dated, will show how much pleased Johnson was with this publication, and what kindness and regard he had for Mr. Elphinston.

'*To* Mr. James Elphinston

  '*Dear Sir*,   [*No date.*[2]]

  'I cannot but confess the failures of my correspondence, but hope the same regard which you express for me on every other occasion, will incline you to forgive me. I am often, very often, ill; and, when I am well, am obliged to work: and, indeed, have never much used myself to punctuality. You are, however, not to make unkind inferences, when I forbear to reply to your kindness; for be assured, I never receive a letter from you without great pleasure, and a very warm sense of your generosity and friendship, which I heartily blame myself for not cultivating with more care. In this, as in many other cases, I go wrong, in opposition to conviction; for I think scarce any temporal good equally to be desired with the regard and familiarity of worthy men. I hope we shall be some time nearer to each other, and have a more ready way of pouring out our hearts.

  [1] It was executed in the printing-office of Sands, Murray, and Cochran, with uncommon elegance, upon writing-paper, of a duodecimo size, and with the greatest correctness; and Mr. Elphinston enriched it with translations of the mottos. When completed, it made eight handsome volumes. It is, unquestionably, the most accurate and beautiful edition of this work; and there being but a small impression, it is now become scarce, and sells at a very high price.

  [2] [The letter is misplaced; it belongs to 1751 or 1752.]

'I am glad that you still find encouragement to proceed in your publication, and shall beg the favour of six more volumes to add to my former six, when you can, with any convenience, send them me. Please to present a set, in my name, to Mr. Ruddiman,[1] of whom, I hear, that his learning is not his highest excellence. I have transcribed the mottos, and returned them, I hope not too late, of which I think many very happily performed. Mr. Cave has put the last in the magazine, in which I think he did well. I beg of you to write soon, and to write often, and to write long letters, which I hope in time to repay you; but you must be a patient creditor. I have, however, this of gratitude, that I think of you with regard, when I do not, perhaps, give the proofs which I ought, of being, Sir, your most obliged and most humble servant,

'SAM. JOHNSON.'

This year he wrote to the same gentleman another letter, upon a mournful occasion.

'*To* MR. JAMES ELPHINSTON

'DEAR SIR,   September 25, 1750.

'You have, as I find by every kind of evidence, lost an excellent mother; and I hope you will not think me incapable of partaking of your grief. I have a mother, now eighty-two years of age, whom, therefore, I must soon lose, unless it please GOD that she rather should mourn for me. I read the letters in which you relate your mother's death to Mrs. Strahan, and think I do myself honour, when I tell you that I read them with tears; but tears are neither to *you* nor to *me* of any further use, when once the tribute of nature has been paid. The business of life summons us away from useless grief, and calls us to the exercise of those virtues of which we are lamenting our deprivation. The greatest benefit which one friend can confer upon another, is to guard, and excite, and elevate his virtues. This your mother will still

---

[1] Mr. Thomas Ruddiman, the learned grammarian of Scotland, well known for his various excellent works, and for his accurate editions of several authours. He was also a man of a most worthy private character. His zeal for the Royal House of Stuart did not render him less estimable in Dr. Johnson's eye.

perform, if you diligently preserve the memory of her life, and of her death: a life, so far as I can learn, useful, wise, and innocent; and a death resigned, peaceful, and holy. I cannot forbear to mention, that neither reason nor revelation denies you to hope, that you may increase her happiness by obeying her precepts; and that she may, in her present state, look with pleasure upon every act of virtue to which her instructions or example have contributed. Whether this be more than a pleasing dream, or a just opinion of separate spirits, is, indeed, of no great importance to us, when we consider ourselves as acting under the eye of God: yet, surely, there is something pleasing in the belief, that our separation from those whom we love is merely corporeal; and it may be a great incitement to virtuous friendship, if it can be made probable, that that union that has received the divine approbation shall continue to eternity.

'There is one expedient by which you may, in some degree, continue her presence. If you write down minutely what you remember of her from your earliest years, you will read it with great pleasure, and receive from it many hints of soothing recollection, when time shall remove her yet farther from you, and your grief shall be matured to veneration. To this, however painful for the present, I cannot but advise you, as to a source of comfort and satisfaction in the time to come; for all comfort and all satisfaction is sincerely wished you by, dear Sir, your most obliged, most obedient, and most humble servant,

'Sam. Johnson.'

The Rambler has increased in fame as in age. Soon after its first folio edition was concluded, it was published in six duodecimo volumes; and its authour lived to see ten numerous editions of it in London, beside those of Ireland and Scotland.

I profess myself to have ever entertained a profound veneration for the astonishing force and vivacity of mind which *The Rambler* exhibits. That Johnson had penetration enough to see, and seeing would not disguise the general misery of man in this state of being, may have given rise to the superficial notion of his being too stern a philosopher. But men of reflection will be

sensible that he has given a true representation of human existence, and that he has, at the same time, with a generous benevolence, displayed every consolation which our state affords us;
not only those arising from the hopes of futurity, but such as may
be attained in the immediate progress through life. He has not
depressed the soul to despondency and indifference. He has
every where inculcated study, labour, and exertion. Nay, he has
shewn, in a very odious light, a man whose practice is to go
about darkening the views of others, by perpetual complaints of
evil, and awakening those considerations of danger and distress,
which are, for the most part, lulled into a quiet oblivion. This he
has done very strongly in his character of Suspirius,[1] from which
Goldsmith took that of Croaker, in his comedy of *The Good-
Natured Man*, as Johnson told me he acknowledged to him, and
which is, indeed, very obvious.

To point out the numerous subjects which *The Rambler* treats,
with a dignity and perspicuity which are there united in a manner
which we shall in vain look for any where else, would take up
too large a portion of my book, and would, I trust, be superfluous, considering how universally those volumes are now dis-
seminated. Even the most condensed and brilliant sentences
which they contain, and which have very properly been selected
under the name of *Beauties*,[2] are of considerable bulk. But I may
shortly observe, that *The Rambler* furnishes such an assemblage
of discourses on practical religion and moral duty, of critical
investigations, and allegorical and oriental tales, that no mind
can be thought very deficient that has, by constant study and
meditation, assimilated to itself all that may be found there.
No. 7, written in Passion-week on abstraction and self-examination, and No. 110, on penitence and the placability of the Divine
Nature, cannot be too often read. No. 54, on the effect which the

[1] No. 55 [59].
[2] Dr. Johnson was gratified by seeing this selection, and wrote to Mr.
Kearsley, bookseller in Fleet-Street, the following note:—
'Mr. Johnson sends compliments to Mr. Kearsley, and begs the favour
of seeing him as soon as he can. Mr. Kearsley is desired to bring with him
the last edition of what he has honoured with the name of BEAUTIES. May 20,
1782.'

death of a friend should have upon us, though rather too dispiriting, may be occasionally very medicinal to the mind. Every one must suppose the writer to have been deeply impressed by a real scene; but he told me that was not the case; which shows how well his fancy could conduct him to the 'house of mourning.' Some of these more solemn papers, I doubt not, particularly attracted the notice of Dr. Young, the authour of *The Night Thoughts,* of whom my estimation is such, as to reckon his applause an honour even to Johnson. I have seen some volumes of Dr. Young's copy of *The Rambler,* in which he has marked the passages which he thought particularly excellent, by folding down a corner of the page; and such as he rated in a supereminent degree, are marked by double folds. I am sorry that some of the volumes are lost. Johnson was pleased when told of the minute attention with which Young had signified his approbation of his Essays.

I will venture to say, that in no writings whatever can be found *more bark and steel for the mind,* if I may use the expression; more that can brace and invigorate every manly and noble sentiment. No. 32 on patience, even under extreme misery, is wonderfully lofty, and as much above the rant of stoicism, as the Sun of Revelation is brighter than the twilight of Pagan philosophy. I never read the following sentence without feeling my frame thrill: 'I think there is some reason for questioning whether the body and mind are not so proportioned, that the one can bear all which can be inflicted on the other; whether virtue cannot stand its ground as long as life, and whether a soul well principled, will not be sooner separated than subdued.'

Though instruction be the predominant purpose of *The Rambler,* yet it is enlivened with a considerable portion of amusement. Nothing can be more erroneous than the notion which some persons have entertained, that Johnson was then a retired authour, ignorant of the world; and, of consequence, that he wrote only from his imagination when he described characters and manners. He said to me, that before he wrote that work, he had been 'running about the world,' as he expressed it, more than almost any body; and I have heard him relate, with much satisfaction, that several of the characters in *The Rambler* were drawn so naturally, that when it first circulated in numbers, a club in one of the towns in Essex imagined themselves to be severally exhibited in it, and were much incensed against a person who, they suspected, had thus made them objects of publick notice; nor were they quieted till authentick assurance was given them, that *The Rambler* was written by a person who had never heard of any one of them. Some of the characters are believed to have been actually drawn from the life, particularly that of Prospero from Garrick, who never entirely forgave its pointed satire. For instances of fertility of fancy, and accurate description of real life, I appeal to No. 19, a man who wanders from one profession to another, with most plausible reasons for every change. No. 34, female fastidiousness and timorous refinement. No. 82, a Virtuoso who has collected curiosities. No. 88,[1] petty modes of entertaining a company, and conciliating kindness. No. 182, fortune-hunting. No. 194–195, a tutor's account of the follies of his pupil. No. 197–198, legacy-hunting. He has given a specimen of his nice observation of the mere external appearances of life, in the following passage in No. 179, against affectation, that frequent and most disgusting quality: 'He that stands to contemplate the crouds that fill the streets of a populous city, will see many passengers whose air and motion it will be difficult to behold without contempt and laughter; but if he examine what are the appearances that thus powerfully excite his risibility, he will find among them neither poverty nor disease, nor any involuntary or painful defect. The disposition to derision and insult, is awakened by the softness of foppery, the swell of insolence, the liveliness of levity, or the solemnity of grandeur; by the sprightly trip, the stately stalk, the formal strut, and the lofty mien; by gestures intended to catch the eye, and by looks elaborately formed as evidences of importance.'

Every page of *The Rambler* shews a mind teeming with classical allusion and poetical imagery: illustrations from other writers are, upon all occasions, so ready, and mingle so easily in his periods, that the whole appears of one uniform vivid texture.

[1] [No. 98.]

The style of this work has been censured by some shallow criticks as involved and turgid, and abounding with antiquated and hard words. So ill-founded is the first part of this objection, that I will challenge all who may honour this book with a perusal, to point out any English writer whose language conveys his meaning with equal force and perspicuity. It must, indeed, be allowed, that the structure of his sentences is expanded, and often has somewhat of the inversion of Latin; and that he delighted to express familiar thoughts in philosophical language; being in this the reverse of Socrates, who, it was said, reduced philosophy to the simplicity of common life. But let us attend to what he himself says in his concluding paper: 'When common words were less pleasing to the ear, or less distinct in their signification, I have familiarised the terms of philosophy, by applying them to popular ideas.'[1] And, as to the second part of this objection, upon a late careful revision of the work, I can with confidence say, that it is amazing how few of those words, for which it has been unjustly characterised, are actually to be found in it; I am sure, not the proportion of one to each paper. This idle charge has been echoed from one babbler to another, who have confounded Johnson's Essays with Johnson's *Dictionary*; and because he thought it right in a Lexicon of our language to collect many words which had fallen into disuse, but were supported by great authorities, it has been imagined that all of these have been interwoven into his own compositions. That some of them have been adopted by him unnecessarily, may, perhaps, be allowed; but, in general they are evidently an advantage, for without them his stately ideas would be confined and cramped. 'He that thinks with more extent than another, will want words of larger meaning.'[2] He once told me, that he had formed his style upon that of Sir William Temple, and upon Chambers's Proposal for his *Dictionary*. He certainly was mistaken; or if he imagined at first that he was imitating Temple,

---

[1] Yet his style did not escape the harmless shafts of pleasant humour; for the ingenious Bonnell Thornton published a mock *Rambler* in the *Drury-lane Journal*.

[2] *Idler*, No. 70.

he was very unsuccessful; for nothing can be more unlike than the simplicity of Temple, and the richness of Johnson. Their styles differ as plain cloth and brocade. Temple, indeed, seems equally erroneous in supposing that he himself had formed his style upon Sandys's *View of the State of Religion in the Western parts of the World.*

The style of Johnson was, undoubtedly, much formed upon that of the great writers in the last century, Hooker, Bacon, Sanderson, Hakewell, and others; those 'Giants,' as they were well characterised by A GREAT PERSONAGE,[1] whose authority, were I to name him, would stamp a reverence on the opinion.

We may, with the utmost propriety, apply to his learned style that passage of Horace, a part of which he has taken as the motto to his *Dictionary*:

> '*Cum tabulis animum censoris sumet honesti;*
> *Audebit quæcumque parùm splendoris habebunt*
> *Et sine pondere erunt, et honore indigna ferentur,*
> *Verba movere loco, quamvis invita recedant,*
> *Et versentur adhuc intra penetralia Vestæ.*
> *Obscurata diu populo bonus eruet, atque*
> *Proferet in lucem speciosa vocabula rerum,*
> *Quæ priscis memorata Catonibus atque Cethegis,*
> *Nunc situs informis premit et deserta vetustas:*
> *Adsciscet nova, quæ genitor produxerit usus:*
> *Vehemens, et liquidus, puroque simillimus amni,*
> *Fundet opes Latiumque beabit divite linguâ.*'[2]

To so great a master of thinking, to one of such vast and

---

[1] [George III. *Croker.*[1]]
[2] Horat. *Epist.* Lib. ii. Epist. ii. [l. 110]. ['When he takes his tablets to write he will take also the spirit of an honest censor. Any words that he shall find lacking in dignity, or without proper weight, or that are held unworthy of the rank, he will have heart of courage to degrade from their position, however unwilling they may be to retire, and bent still on haunting Vesta's precincts. Phrases of beauty that have been lost to popular view he will kindly disinter and bring into the light, phrases which, though they were on the lips of a Cato and a Cethegus of old time, now lie uncouth because out of fashion and disused because old. He will admit to the franchise new phrases which use has fathered and given to the world. In strength and clearness, like a crystal stream, he will pour his wealth along, and bless Latium with a richer tongue.' (Wickham.)]

various knowledge as Johnson, might have been allowed a liberal indulgence of that licence which Horace claims in another place:

'————*Si fortè necesse est*
Indiciis monstrare recentibus abdita rerum,
Fingere cinctutis non exaudita Cethegis
Continget, dabiturque licentia sumpta pudenter;
Et nova fictaque nuper habebunt verba fidem si
Græco fonte cadant, parce detorta. Quid autem
Cæcilio Plautoque dabit Romanus, ademptum
Virgilio Varioque? Ego cur, acquirere pauca
Si possum, invideor; cum lingua Catonis et Enni
Sermonem patrium ditaverit, et nova rerum
Nomina protulerit? Licuit semperque licebit
Signatum præsente notâ producere nomen.'[1]

Yet Johnson assured me, that he had not taken upon him to add more than four or five words to the English language, of his own formation; and he was very much offended at the general licence, by no means 'modestly taken' in his time, not only to coin new words, but to use many words in senses quite different from their established meaning, and those frequently very fantastical.

Sir Thomas Brown, whose life Johnson wrote, was remarkably fond of Anglo-Latian diction; and to his example we are to ascribe Johnson's sometimes indulging himself in this kind of phraseology.[2] Johnson's comprehension of mind was the mould

[1] ['If so be there are abstruse things which absolutely require new terms to make them clear, it will be in your power to frame words which never sounded in the ears of a cinctured Cethegus, and free pardon will be granted if the licence be used modestly. New words and words of yesterday's framing will find acceptance if the source from which they flow be Greek, and if the stream be turned on sparingly. Think you that there is any licence which the Romans will grant to Caecilius and Plautus, and then refuse to Virgil and Varius? Why should you grudge even such an one as myself the right of adding, if I can, something to the store, when the tongue of Cato and of Ennius has been permitted to enrich our mother-speech by giving to the world new names for things? Each generation has been allowed, and will be allowed still to issue words that bear the mint-mark of the day.' Horace, *Ars Poet.* 48 (Wickham).]
[2] The observation of his having imitated Sir Thomas Brown has been made by many people; and lately it has been insisted on, and illustrated by a variety of quotations from Brown, in one of the popular Essays written by

for his language. Had his conceptions been narrower, his expression would have been easier. His sentences have a dignified march; and, it is certain, that his example has given a general elevation to the language of his country, for many of our best writers have approached very near to him; and, from the influence which he has had upon our composition, scarcely any thing is written now that is not better expressed than was usual before he appeared to lead the national taste.

This circumstance, the truth of which must strike every critical reader, has been so happily enforced by Mr. Courtenay, in his *Moral and Literary Character of Dr. Johnson*, that I cannot prevail on myself to withhold it, notwithstanding his, perhaps, too great partiality for one of his friends:

> 'By nature's gifts ordain'd mankind to rule,
> He, like a Titian, form'd his brilliant school;
> And taught congenial spirits to excel,
> While from his lips impressive wisdom fell.
> Our boasted GOLDSMITH felt the sovereign sway;
> From him deriv'd the sweet, yet nervous lay.
> To Fame's proud cliff he bade our Raphael rise;
> Hence REYNOLDS' pen with REYNOLDS' pencil vies.
> With Johnson's flame melodious BURNEY glows,
> While the grand strain in smoother cadence flows.
> And you, MALONE, to critick learning dear,
> Correct and elegant, refin'd, though clear,
> By studying him, acquir'd that classick taste,
> Which high in Shakspeare's fane thy statue plac'd.
> Near Johnson STEEVENS stands, on scenick ground,
> Acute, laborious, fertile, and profound.
> Ingenious HAWKESWORTH to this school we owe,
> And scarce the pupil from the tutor know.
> Here early parts accomplish'd JONES sublimes,
> And science blends with Asia's lofty rhymes:
> Harmonious JONES! who in his spendid strains
> Sings Camdeo's sports, on Agra's flowery plains:
> In Hindu fictions while we fondly trace

the Reverend Mr. Knox, master of Tunbridge school, whom I have set down in my list of those who have sometimes not unsuccessfully imitated Dr. Johnson's style.

Love and the Muses, deck'd with Attick grace.
Amid these names can BOSWELL be forgot,
Scarce by North Britons now esteem'd a Scot?[1]
Who to the sage devoted from his youth,
Imbib'd from him the sacred love of truth;
The keen research, the exercise of mind,
And that best art, the art to know mankind.—
Nor was his energy confin'd alone
To friends around his philosophick throne;
Its influence wide improv'd our letter'd isle,
And lucid vigour marked the general style:
As Nile's proud waves, swoln from their oozy bed,
First o'er the neighbouring meads majestick spread;
Till gathering force, they more and more expand,
And with new virtue fertilise the land.'

Johnson's language, however, must be allowed to be too masculine for the delicate gentleness of female writing. His ladies, therefore, seem strangely formal, even to ridicule; and are well denominated by the names which he has given them, as Misella, Zozima, Properantia, Rhodoclia.

It has of late been the fashion to compare the style of Addison and Johnson, and to depreciate, I think very unjustly, the style of Addison as nerveless and feeble, because it has not the strength and energy of that of Johnson. Their prose may be balanced like the poetry of Dryden and Pope. Both are excellent, though in different ways. Addison writes with the ease of a gentleman. His readers fancy that a wise and accomplished companion is talking to them; so that he insinuates his sentiments and taste into their minds by an imperceptible influence. Johnson writes

---

[1] The following observation in Mr. Boswell's *Journal of a Tour to the Hebrides* may sufficiently account for that Gentleman's being 'now scarcely esteem'd a Scot' by many of his countrymen:—'If he [Dr. Johnson] was particularly prejudiced against the Scots, it was because they were more in his way; because he thought their success in England rather exceeded the due proportion of their real merit; and because he could not but see in them that nationality which, I believe, no liberal-minded Scotchman will deny.' Mr. Boswell, indeed, is so free from national prejudices, that he might with equal propriety have been described as—
'Scarce by *South* Britons now esteem'd a Scot.'
                                                            COURTENAY.

like a teacher. He dictates to his readers as if from an academical chair. They attend with awe and admiration; and his precepts are impressed upon them by his commanding eloquence. Addison's style, like a light wine, pleases everybody from the first. Johnson's, like a liquor of more body, seems too strong at first, but, by degrees, is highly relished; and such is the melody of his periods, so much do they captivate the ear, and seize upon the attention, that there is scarcely any writer, however inconsiderable, who does not aim, in some degree, at the same species of excellence. But let us not ungratefully undervalue that beautiful style, which has pleasingly conveyed to us much instruction and entertainment. Though comparatively weak, when opposed to Johnson's Herculean vigour, let us not call it positively feeble. Let us remember the character of his style, as given by Johnson himself: 'What he attempted, he performed; he is *never feeble*, and he did not wish to be energetick; he is never rapid, and he never stagnates. His sentences have neither studied amplitude, nor affected brevity: his periods, though not diligently rounded, are voluble and easy. Whoever wishes to attain an English style, familiar but not coarse, and elegant but not ostentatious, must give his days and nights to the volumes of Addison.'[1]

Though *The Rambler* was not concluded till the year 1752, I shall, under this year, say all that I have to observe upon it. Some of the translations of the mottos by himself are admirably done. He acknowledges to have received 'elegant translations' of many of them from Mr. James Elphinston; and some are very happily translated by a Mr. *F. Lewis*, of whom I never heard more, except that Johnson thus described him to Mr. Malone: 'Sir, he lived in London, and hung loose upon society.' The concluding paper of his *Rambler* is at once dignified and pathetick. I cannot, however, but wish that he had not ended it with an unnecessary Greek verse, translated also into an English couplet. It is too much like the conceit of those dramatick poets, who used to conclude each act with a rhyme; and the expression in the first line of his couplet, *'Celestial powers,'* though proper in Pagan

---

[1] I shall probably, in another work, maintain the merit of Addison's poetry, which has been very unjustly depreciated.

poetry, is ill suited to Christianity, with 'a conformity' to which he consoles himself. How much better would it have been, to have ended with the prose sentence 'I shall never envy the honours which wit and learning obtain in any other cause, if I can be numbered among the writers who have given ardour to virtue, and confidence to truth.'

His friend, Dr. Birch, being now engaged in preparing an edition of Ralegh's smaller pieces, Dr. Johnson wrote the following letter to that gentleman:

'*To* DR. BIRCH.

'SIR,   Gough-square, May 12, 1750.

'Knowing that you are now preparing to favour the publick with a new edition of Ralegh's miscellaneous pieces, I have taken the liberty to send you a Manuscript, which fell by chance within my notice. I perceive no proofs of forgery in my examination of it; and the owner tells me, that as *he* has heard, the handwriting is Sir Walter's. If you should find reason to conclude it genuine, it will be a kindness to the owner, a blind person,[1] to recommend it to the booksellers. I am, Sir, your most humble servant,
                                        'SAM. JOHNSON.'

His just abhorrence of Milton's political notions was ever strong. But this did not prevent his warm admiration of Milton's great poetical merit, to which he has done illustrious justice, beyond all who have written upon the subject. And this year he not only wrote a Prologue, which was spoken by Mr. Garrick before the acting of *Comus* at Drury-lane theatre, for the benefit of Milton's grand-daughter, but took a very zealous interest in the success of the charity. On the day preceding the performance, he published the following letter in the 'General Advertiser,' addressed to the printer of that paper;

'SIR,—That a certain degree of reputation is acquired merely by approving the works of genius, and testifying a regard to the memory of authours, is a truth too evident to be denied; and therefore to ensure a participation of fame with a celebrated

---

[1] Mrs. Williams is probably the person meant.

poet, many who would, perhaps, have contributed to starve him when alive, have heaped expensive pageants upon his grave.

'It must, indeed, be confessed, that this method of becoming known to posterity with honour, is peculiar to the great, or at least to the wealthy; but an opportunity now offers for almost every individual to secure the praise of paying a just regard to the illustrious dead, united with the pleasure of doing good to the living. To assist industrious indigence, struggling with distress and debilitated by age, is a display of virtue, and an acquisition of happiness and honour.

'Whoever, then, would be thought capable of pleasure in reading the works of our incomparable Milton, and not so destitute of gratitude as to refuse to lay out a trifle in rational and elegant entertainment, for the benefit of his living remains, for the exercise of their own virtue, the increase of their reputation, and the pleasing consciousness of doing good, should appear at Drury-lane theatre to-morrow, April 5, when *Comus* will be performed for the benefit of Mrs. Elizabeth Foster, grand-daughter to the author, and the only surviving branch of his family.

'N.B. There will be a new prologue on the occasion, written by the authour of *Irene*, and spoken by Mr. Garrick; and, by particular desire, there will be added to the Masque a dramatick satire, called *Lethe*, in which Mr. Garrick will perform.'

1751: ÆTAT. 42.]—IN 1751 we are to consider him as carrying on both his *Dictionary* and *Rambler*. But he also wrote *The Life of Cheynel*,* in the miscellany called *The Student*; and the Reverend Dr. Douglas having, with uncommon acuteness, clearly detected a gross forgery and imposition upon the publick by William Lauder, a Scotch schoolmaster, who had, with equal impudence and ingenuity, represented Milton as a plagiary from certain modern Latin poets, Johnson, who had been so far imposed upon as to furnish a Preface and Postscript to his work, now dictated a letter for Lauder, addressed to Dr. Douglas, acknowledging his fraud in terms of suitable contrition.[1]

[1] Lest there should be any person, at any future period, absurd enough to suspect that Johnson was a partaker in Lauder's fraud, or had any know-

This extraordinary attempt of Lauder was no sudden effort. He had brooded over it for many years: and to this hour it is uncertain what his principal motive was, unless it were a vain notion of his superiority, in being able, by whatever means, to deceive mankind. To effect this, he produced certain passages from Grotius, Masenius, and others, which had a faint resemblance to some parts of the *Paradise Lost.* In these he interpolated some fragments of Hog's Latin translation of that poem, alledging that the mass thus fabricated was the archetype from which Milton copied. These fabrications he published from time to time in the *Gentleman's Magazine*; and, exulting in his fancied success, he in 1750 ventured to collect them into a pamphlet, entitled *An Essay on Milton's Use and Imitation of the Moderns in his Paradise Lost.* To this pamphlet Johnson wrote a Preface, in full persuasion of Lauder's honesty, and a Postscript recommending, in the most persuasive terms, a subscription for the relief of a grand-daughter of Milton, of whom he thus speaks:

'It is yet in the power of a great people to reward the poet whose name they boast, and from their alliance to whose genius, they claim some kind of superiority to every other nation of the earth; that poet, whose works may possibly be read when every other monument of British greatness shall be obliterated; to reward him, not with pictures or with medals, which, if he sees, he sees with contempt, but with tokens of gratitude, which he, perhaps, may even now consider as not unworthy of an immortal spirit.'

Surely this is inconsistent with 'enmity towards Milton,'

ledge of it, when he assisted him with his masterly pen, it is proper here to quote the words of Dr. Douglas, now Bishop of Salisbury, at the time when he detected the imposition. 'It is to be hoped, nay it is *expected*, that the elegant and nervous writer, whose judicious sentiments and inimitable style point out the authour of Lauder's Preface and Postscript, will no longer allow one to *plume himself with his feathers*, who appeareth so little to deserve [his] assistance: an assistance which I am persuaded would never have been communicated, had there been the least suspicion of those facts which I have been the instrument of conveying to the world in these sheets.' *Milton no Plagiary*, 2nd edit. p. 78. And his Lordship has been pleased now to authorise me to say, in the strongest manner, that there is no ground whatever for any unfavourable reflection against Dr. Johnson, who expressed the strongest indignation against Lauder.

which Sir John Hawkins imputes to Johnson upon this occasion, adding,

'I could all along observe that Johnson seemed to approve not only of the design, but of the argument; and seemed to exult in a persuasion, that the reputation of Milton was likely to suffer by this discovery. That he was not privy to the imposture, I am well persuaded; but that he wished well to the argument, may be inferred from the Preface, which indubitably was written by Johnson.'

Is it possible for any man of clear judgement to suppose that Johnson, who so nobly praised the poetical excellence of Milton in a Postscript to this very 'discovery,' as he then supposed it, could, at the same time, exult in a persuasion that the great poet's reputation was likely to suffer by it? This is an inconsistency of which Johnson was incapable; nor can any thing more be fairly inferred from the Preface, than that Johnson, who was alike distinguished for ardent curiosity and love of truth, was pleased with an investigation by which both were gratified. That he was actuated by these motives, and certainly by no unworthy desire to depreciate our great epick poet, is evident from his own words; for, after mentioning the general zeal of men of genius and literature 'to advance the honour, and distinguish the beauties of *Paradise Lost,*' he says,

'Among the inquiries to which this ardour of criticism has naturally given occasion, none is more obscure in itself, or more worthy of rational curiosity, than a retrospection of the progress of this mighty genius in the construction of his work; a view of the fabrick gradually rising, perhaps, from small beginnings, till its foundation rests in the centre, and its turrets sparkle in the skies; to trace back the structure through all its varieties, to the simplicity of its first plan; to find what was first projected, whence the scheme was taken, how it was improved, by what assistance it was executed, and from what stores the materials were collected; whether its founder dug them from the quarries of Nature, or demolished other buildings to embellish his own.'

Is this the language of one who wished to blast the laurels of Milton?

Though Johnson's circumstances were at this time far from being easy, his humane and charitable disposition was constantly exerting itself. Mrs. Anna Williams, daughter of a very ingenious Welsh physician, and a woman of more than ordinary talents and literature, having come to London in hopes of being cured of a cataract in both her eyes, which afterwards ended in total blindness, was kindly received as a constant visitor at his house while Mrs. Johnson lived; and after her death, having come under his roof in order to have an operation upon her eyes performed with more comfort to her than in lodgings, she had an apartment from him during the rest of her life, at all times when he had a house.

1752: ÆTAT. 43.]—IN 1752 he was almost entirely occupied with his *Dictionary*. The last paper of his *Rambler* was published March 2, this year; after which, there was a cessation for some time of any exertion of his talents as an essayist. But, in the same year, Dr. Hawkesworth, who was his warm admirer, and a studious imitator of his style, and then lived in great intimacy with him, began a periodical paper, entitled *The Adventurer*, in connection with other gentlemen, one of whom was Johnson's much-loved friend, Dr. Bathurst; and, without doubt, they received many valuable hints from his conversation, most of his friends having been so assisted in the course of their works.

That there should be a suspension of his literary labours during a part of the year 1752, will not seem strange, when it is considered that soon after closing his *Rambler*, he suffered a loss which, there can be no doubt, affected him with the deepest distress. For on the 17th of March, O.S., his wife died. Why Sir John Hawkins should unwarrantably take upon him even to *suppose* that Johnson's fondness for her was *dissembled* (meaning simulated or assumed,) and to assert, that if it was not the case, 'it was a lesson he had learned by rote,' I cannot conceive; unless it proceeded from a want of similar feelings in his own breast. To argue from her being much older than Johnson, or any other circumstances, that he could not really love her, is absurd; for love is not a subject of reasoning, but of feeling, and therefore there are no common principles upon which one can persuade another concerning it. Every man feels for himself, and knows how he is affected by particular qualities in the person he admires, the impressions of which are too minute and delicate to be substantiated in language.

The following very solemn and affecting prayer was found after Dr. Johnson's decease, by his faithful servant, Mr. Francis Barber, who delivered it to my worthy friend the Reverend Mr. Strahan, Vicar of Islington, who at my earnest request has obligingly favoured me with a copy of it, which he and I compared with the original. I present it to the world as an undoubted proof of a circumstance in the character of my illustrious friend, which though some whose hard minds I never shall envy, may attack as superstitious, will I am sure endear him more to numbers of good men. I have an additional, and that a personal motive for presenting it, because it sanctions what I myself have always maintained and am fond to indulge.

'April 26, 1752, being after 12 at Night of the 25th.
'O Lord! Governour of heaven and earth, in whose hands are embodied and departed Spirits, if thou hast ordained the Souls of the Dead to minister to the Living, and appointed my departed Wife to have care of me, grant that I may enjoy the good effects of her attention and ministration, whether exercised by appearance, impulses, dreams or in any other manner agreeable to thy Government. Forgive my presumption, enlighten my ignorance, and however meaner agents are employed, grant me the blessed influences of thy holy Spirit, through Jesus Christ our Lord. Amen.'

What actually followed upon this most interesting piece of devotion by Johnson, we are not informed; but I, whom it has pleased GOD to afflict in a similar manner to that which occasioned it, have certain experience of benignant communication by dreams.

That his love for his wife was of the most ardent kind, and, during the long period of fifty years, was unimpaired by the lapse of time, is evident from various passages in the series of his *Prayers and Meditations*, published by the Reverend Mr.

Strahan, as well as from other memorials, two of which I select, as strongly marking the tenderness and sensibility of his mind.

'March 28, 1753. I kept this day as the anniversary of my Tetty's death, with prayer and tears in the morning. In the evening I prayed for her conditionally, if it were lawful.'

'April 23, 1753. I know not whether I do not too much indulge the vain longings of affection; but I hope they intenerate my heart, and that when I die like my Tetty, this affection will be acknowledged in a happy interview, and that in the mean time I am incited by it to piety. I will, however, not deviate too much from common and received methods of devotion.'

Her wedding-ring, when she became his wife, was, after her death, preserved by him, as long as he lived, with an affectionate care, in a little round wooden box, in the inside of which he pasted a slip of paper, thus inscribed by him in fair characters, as follows:

> '*Eheu!*
> *Eliz. Johnson,*
> *Nupta Jul.* 9° 1736,
> *Mortua, eheu!*
> *Mart.* 17° 1752.'

After his death, Mr. Francis Barber, his faithful servant and residuary legatee, offered this memorial of tenderness to Mrs. Lucy Porter, Mrs. Johnson's daughter; but she having declined to accept of it, he had it enamelled as a mourning ring for his old master, and presented it to his wife, Mrs. Barber, who now has it.

The state of mind in which a man must be upon the death of a woman whom he sincerely loves, had been in his contemplation many years before. In his *Irene*, we find the following fervent and tender speech of Demetrius, addressed to his Aspasia:

> 'From those bright regions of eternal day,
> Where now thou shin'st amongst thy fellow saints,
> Array'd in purer light, look down on me!
> In pleasing visions and delusive dreams,
> O! sooth my soul, and teach me how to lose thee.'

I have, indeed, been told by Mrs. Desmoulins, who, before her marriage, lived for some time with Mrs. Johnson at Hampstead, that she indulged herself in country air and nice living, at an unsuitable expense, while her husband was drudging in the smoke of London, and that she by no means treated him with that complacency which is the most engaging quality in a wife. But all this is perfectly compatible with his fondness for her, especially when it is remembered that he had a high opinion of her understanding, and that the impressions which her beauty, real or imaginary, had originally made upon his fancy, being continued by habit, had not been effaced, though she herself was doubtless much altered for the worse. The dreadful shock of separation took place in the night; and he immediately dispatched a letter to his friend, the Reverend Dr. Taylor, which, as Taylor told me, expressed grief in the strongest manner he had ever read; so that it is much to be regretted it has not been preserved.[1] The letter was brought to Dr. Taylor, at his house in the Cloisters, Westminster, about three in the morning; and as it signified an earnest desire to see him, he got up, and went to Johnson as soon as he was dressed, and found him in tears and in extreme agitation. After being a little while together, Johnson requested him to join with him in prayer. He then prayed extempore, as did Dr. Taylor; and thus, by means of that piety which was ever his primary object, his troubled mind was, in some degree, soothed and composed.

The next day he wrote as follows:

'To THE REVEREND DR. TAYLOR

'DEAR SIR,—Let me have your company and instruction. Do not live away from me. My distress is great.

'Pray desire Mrs. Taylor to inform me what mourning I should buy for my mother and Miss Porter, and bring a note in writing with you.

[1] In the *Gent. Mag.* for February, 1794 (p. 100) was printed a letter pretending to be that written by Johnson on the death of his wife. But it is merely a transcript of the 41st number of *The Idler*. A fictitious date (March 17, 1751, O.S.) was added by some person previous to this paper being sent to the publisher of that miscellany, to give a colour to this deception. [M.]

'Remember me in your prayers, for vain is the help of man. I am, dear Sir, &c.

'March 18, 1752.'   'SAM. JOHNSON.'

That his sufferings upon the death of his wife were severe, beyond what are commonly endured, I have no doubt, from the information of many who were then about him, to none of whom I give more credit than to Mr. Francis Barber, his faithful negro servant,[1] who came into his family about a fortnight after the dismal event. These sufferings were aggravated by the melancholy inherent in his constitution; and although he probably was not oftener in the wrong than she was, in the little disagreements which sometimes troubled his married state, during which, he owned to me, that the gloomy irritability of his existence was more painful to him than ever, he might very naturally, after her death, be tenderly disposed to charge himself with slight omissions and offences, the sense of which would give him much uneasiness. Accordingly we find, about a year after her decease, that he thus addressed the Supreme Being: 'O LORD, who givest the grace of repentance, and hearest the prayers of the penitent, grant that by true contrition I may obtain forgiveness of all the sins committed, and of all duties neglected in my union with the wife whom thou hast taken from me; for the neglect of joint devotion, patient exhortation, and mild instruction.'[2] The kindness of his heart, notwithstanding the impetuosity of his temper, is well known to his friends; and I cannot trace the smallest foundation for the following dark and uncharitable assertion by

[1] Francis Barber was born in Jamaica, and was brought to England in 1750 by Colonel Bathurst, father of Johnson's very intimate friend, Dr. Bathurst. He was sent, for some time, to the Reverend Mr. Jackson's school, at Barton, in Yorkshire. The Colonel by his will left him his freedom, and Dr. Bathurst was willing that he should enter into Johnson's service, in which he continued from 1752 till Johnson's death, with the exception of two intervals; in one of which, upon some difference with his master, he went and served an apothecary in Cheapside, but still visited Dr. Johnson occasionally; in another, he took a fancy to go to sea. Part of the time, indeed, he was, by the kindness of his master, at a school in Northamptonshire [Bishop's Stortford, Hertfordshire], that he might have the advantage of some learning. So early and so lasting a connection was there between Dr. Johnson and this humble friend.   [2] *Pr. and Med.* p. 19.

Sir John Hawkins: 'The apparition of his departed wife was altogether of the terrifick kind, and hardly afforded him a hope that
she was in a state of happiness.'[1] That he, in conformity with the
opinion of many of the most able, learned, and pious Christians
in all ages, supposed that there was a middle state after death,
previous to the time at which departed souls are finally received
to eternal felicity, appears, I think, unquestionably from his
devotions: 'And, O LORD, so far as it may be lawful in me, I
commend to thy fatherly goodness *the soul of my departed wife*;
beseeching thee to *grant* her whatever is best in her *present state*,
and *finally to receive her to eternal happiness*.'[2] But this state has
not been looked upon with horrour, but only as less gracious.

He deposited the remains of Mrs. Johnson in the church of
Bromley, in Kent, to which he was probably led by the residence
of his friend Hawkesworth at that place. The funeral sermon
which he composed for her, which was never preached, but having
been given to Dr. Taylor, has been published since his death, is
a performance of uncommon excellence, and full of rational and
pious comfort to such as are depressed by that severe affliction
which Johnson felt when he wrote it. When it is considered that
it was written in such an agitation of mind, and in the short
interval between her death and burial, it cannot be read without
wonder.

From Mr. Francis Barber I have had the following authentick
and artless account of the situation in which he found him recently
after his wife's death:

'He was in great affliction. Mrs. Williams was then living in
his house, which was in Gough-square. He was busy with the
Dictionary. Mr. Shiels, and some others of the gentlemen who had
formerly written for him, used to come about him. He had then
little for himself, but frequently sent money to Mr. Shiels when in
distress. The friends who visited him at that time, were chiefly
Dr. Bathurst,[3] and Mr. Diamond, an apothecary in Cork-street,

---

[1] Hawkins's *Life of Johnson*, p. 316.
[2] *Pr. and Med.* p. 20.
[3] Dr. Bathurst, though a Physician of no inconsiderable merit, had not
the good fortune to get much practice in London. He was, therefore, willing

Burlington-gardens, with whom he and Mrs. Williams generally dined every Sunday. There was a talk of his going to Iceland with him, which would probably have happened had he lived. There were also Mr. Cave, Dr. Hawkesworth, Mr. Ryland, merchant on Tower Hill, Mrs. Masters, the poetess, who lived with Mr. Cave, Mrs. Carter, and sometimes Mrs. Macaulay, also Mrs. Gardiner, wife of a tallow-chandler on Snow-hill, not in the learned way, but a worthy good woman; Mr. (now Sir Joshua) Reynolds; Mr. Millar, Mr. Dodsley, Mr. Bouquet, Mr. Payne of Paternoster-row, booksellers; Mr. Strahan, the printer; the Earl of Orrery, Lord Southwell, Mr. Garrick.'

Many are, no doubt, omitted in this catalogue of his friends, and, in particular, his humble friend Mr. Robert Levet, an obscure practiser in physick amongst the lower people, his fees being sometimes very small sums, sometimes whatever provisions his patients could afford him; but of such extensive practice in that way, that Mrs. Williams has told me, his walk was from Houndsditch to Marybone. It appears from Johnson's diary that their acquaintance commenced about the year 1746; and such was Johnson's predilection for him, and fanciful estimation of his moderate abilities, that I have heard him say he should not be satisfied, though attended by all the College of Physicians, unless he had Mr. Levet with him. Ever since I was acquainted with Dr. Johnson, and many years before, as I have been assured by those who knew him earlier, Mr. Levet had an apartment in his house, or his chambers, and waited upon him every morning, through the whole course of his late and tedious breakfast. He was of a strange grotesque appearance, stiff and formal in his manner, and seldom said a word while any company was present.

The circle of his friends, indeed, at this time was extensive and various, far beyond what has been generally imagined. To trace

to accept of employment abroad, and, to the regret of all who knew him, fell a sacrifice to the destructive climate, in the expedition against the Havannah. Mr. Langton recollects the following passage in a letter from Dr. Johnson to Mr. Beauclerk: 'The Havannah is taken;—a conquest too dearly obtained; for, Bathurst died before it. "*Vix Priamus tanti totaque Troja fuit.*" ['The death of Priam and the capture of Troy were hardly worth the cost.' Ovid, *Heroides* i. 4.]

his acquaintance with each particular person, if it could be done, would be a task, of which the labour would not be repaid by the advantage. But exceptions are to be made; one of which must be a friend so eminent as Sir Joshua Reynolds, who was truly his *dulce decus*,[1] and with whom he maintained an uninterrupted intimacy to the last hour of his life. When Johnson lived in Castle-street, Cavendish-square, he used frequently to visit two ladies, who lived opposite to him, Miss Cotterells, daughters of Admiral Cotterell. Reynolds used also to visit there, and thus they met. Mr. Reynolds, as I have observed above, had, from the first reading of his *Life of Savage*, conceived a very high admiration of Johnson's powers of writing. His conversation no less delighted him; and he cultivated his acquaintance with the laudable zeal of one who was ambitious of general improvement. Sir Joshua, indeed, was lucky enough at their very first meeting to make a remark, which was so much above the common-place style of conversation, that Johnson at once perceived that Reynolds had the habit of thinking for himself. The ladies were regretting the death of a friend, to whom they owed great obligations; upon which Reynolds observed, 'You have, however, the comfort of being relieved from a burthen of gratitude.' They were shocked a little at this alleviating suggestion, as too selfish; but Johnson defended it in his clear and forcible manner, and was much pleased with the *mind*, the fair view of human nature, which it exhibited, like some of the reflections of Roche-faucault. The consequence was, that he went home with Reynolds, and supped with him.

Sir Joshua told me a pleasant characteristical anecdote of Johnson about the time of their first acquaintance. When they were one evening together at the Miss Cotterells', the then Duchess of Argyle and another lady of high rank came in. Johnson thinking that the Miss Cotterells were too much engrossed by them, and that he and his friend were neglected, as low company of whom they were somewhat ashamed, grew angry; and resolving to shock their supposed pride, by making their great visitors imagine that his friend and he were low indeed, he addressed

[1] ['dear dignity'. Horace, *Odes* I. i. 2.]

himself in a loud tone to Mr. Reynolds, saying, 'How much do you think you and I could get in a week, if we were to *work as hard* as we could?'—as if they had been common mechanicks.

His acquaintance with Bennet Langton, Esq. of Langton, in Lincolnshire, another much valued friend, commenced soon after the conclusion of his *Rambler*; which that gentleman, then a youth, had read with so much admiration, that he came to London chiefly with the view of endeavouring to be introduced to its authour. By a fortunate chance he happened to take lodgings in a house where Mr. Levet frequently visited; and having mentioned his wish to his landlady, she introduced him to Mr. Levet, who readily obtained Johnson's permission to bring Mr. Langton to him; as, indeed, Johnson, during the whole course of his life, had no shyness, real or affected, but was easy of access to all who were properly recommended, and even wished to see numbers at his *levee*, as his morning circle of company might, with strict propriety, be called. Mr. Langton was exceedingly surprised when the sage first appeared. He had not received the smallest intimation of his figure, dress, or manner. From perusing his writings, he fancied he should see a decent, well-drest, in short, a remarkably decorous philosopher. Instead of which, down from his bed-chamber, about noon, came, as newly risen, a huge uncouth figure, with a little dark wig which scarcely covered his head, and his clothes hanging loose about him. But his conversation was so rich, so animated, and so forcible, and his religious and political notions so congenial with those in which Mr. Langton had been educated, that he conceived for him that veneration and attachment which he ever preserved. Johnson was not the less ready to love Mr. Langton, for his being of a very ancient family; for I have heard him say, with pleasure, 'Langton, Sir, has a grant of free warren from Henry the Second; and Cardinal Stephen Langton, in King John's reign, was of this family.'

Mr. Langton afterwards went to pursue his studies at Trinity College, Oxford, where he formed an acquaintance with his fellow student, Mr. Topham Beauclerk; who, though their opinions and modes of life were so different, that it seemed utterly improbable that they should at all agree, had so ardent a love of literature, so acute an understanding, such elegance of manners, and so well discerned the excellent qualities of Mr. Langton, a gentleman eminent not only for worth and learning, but for an inexhaustible fund of entertaining conversation, that they became intimate friends.

Johnson, soon after this acquaintance began, passed a considerable time at Oxford. He at first thought it strange that Langton should associate so much with one who had the character of being loose, both in his principles and practice; but, by degrees, he himself was fascinated. Mr. Beauclerk's being of the St. Alban's family, and having, in some particulars, a resemblance to Charles the Second, contributed, in Johnson's imagination, to throw a lustre upon his other qualities; and, in a short time, the moral, pious Johnson, and the gay, dissipated Beauclerk, were companions. 'What a coalition! (said Garrick, when he heard of this;) I shall have my old friend to bail out of the Round-house.' But I can bear testimony that it was a very agreeable association. Beauclerk was too polite, and valued learning and wit too much, to offend Johnson by sallies of infidelity or licentiousness; and Johnson delighted in the good qualities of Beauclerk, and hoped to correct the evil. Innumerable were the scenes in which Johnson was amused by these young men. Beauclerk could take more liberty with him, than any body with whom I ever saw him; but, on the other hand, Beauclerk was not spared by his respectable companion, when reproof was proper. Beauclerk had such a propensity to satire, that at one time Johnson said to him, 'You never open your mouth but with intention to give pain; and you have often given me pain, not from the power of what you said, but from seeing your intention.' At another time applying to him, with a slight alteration, a line of Pope, he said,

'Thy love of folly, and thy scorn of fools—[1]
Every thing thou dost shews the one, and every thing thou say'st the other.' At another time he said to him, 'Thy body is all vice, and thy mind all virtue.' Beauclerk not seeming to relish the compliment, Johnson said, 'Nay, Sir, Alexander the Great,

[1] ['Your Taste of Follies, with our Scorn of Fools.' *Moral Essays*, ii. 275.]

175

marching in triumph into Babylon, could not have desired to have had more said to him.'

Johnson was some time with Beauclerk at his house at Windsor, where he was entertained with experiments in natural philosophy. One Sunday, when the weather was very fine, Beauclerk enticed him, insensibly, to saunter about all the morning. They went into a church-yard, in the time of divine service, and Johnson laid himself down at his ease upon one of the tombstones. 'Now, Sir, (said Beauclerk) you are like Hogarth's Idle Apprentice.' When Johnson got his pension, Beauclerk said to him, in the humorous phrase of Falstaff, 'I hope you'll now purge and live cleanly like a gentleman.'

One night when Beauclerk and Langton had supped at a tavern in London, and sat till about three in the morning, it came into their heads to go and knock up Johnson, and see if they could prevail on him to join them in a ramble. They rapped violently at the door of his chambers in the Temple, till at last he appeared in his shirt, with his little black wig on the top of his head, instead of a nightcap, and a poker in his hand, imagining, probably, that some ruffians were coming to attack him. When he discovered who they were, and was told their errand, he smiled, and with great good humour agreed to their proposal: 'What, is it you, you dogs! I'll have a frisk with you.' He was soon drest, and they sallied forth together into Covent-Garden, where the greengrocers and fruiterers were beginning to arrange their hampers, just come in from the country. Johnson made some attempts to help them; but the honest gardeners stared so at his figure and manner, and odd interference, that he soon saw his services were not relished. They then repaired to one of the neighbouring taverns, and made a bowl of that liquor called *Bishop*, which Johnson had always liked; while in joyous contempt of sleep, from which he had been roused, he repeated the festive lines,

> 'Short, O short then be thy reign,
> And give us to the world again!'[1]

[1] Mr. Langton has recollected, or Dr. Johnson repeated, the passage

They did not stay long, but walked down to the Thames, took a boat, and rowed to Billingsgate. Beauclerk and Johnson were so well pleased with their amusement, that they resolved to persevere in dissipation for the rest of the day: but Langton deserted them, being engaged to breakfast with some young Ladies. Johnson scolded him for 'leaving his social friends, to go and sit with a set of wretched *un-idea'd* girls.' Garrick being told of this ramble, said to him smartly, 'I heard of your frolick t'other night. You'll be in the Chronicle.' Upon which Johnson afterwards observed, '*He* durst not do such a thing. His *wife* would not *let* him!'

1753: ÆTAT. 44.]—HE entered upon this year 1753 with his usual piety, as appears from the following prayer, which I transcribed from that part of his diary which he burnt a few days before his death:

'Jan. 1, 1753, N.S. which I shall use for the future.

'Almighty GOD, who hast continued my life to this day, grant that, by the assistance of thy Holy Spirit, I may improve the time which thou shalt grant me, to my eternal salvation. Make me to remember, to thy glory, thy judgements and thy mercies. Make me so to consider the loss of my wife, whom thou hast taken from me, that it may dispose me, by thy grace, to lead the residue of my life in thy fear. Grant this, O LORD, for JESUS CHRIST's sake. Amen.'

He now relieved the drudgery of his *Dictionary*, and the melancholy of his grief, by taking an active part in the composition of *The Adventurer*, in which he began to write April 10, marking his essays with the signature T, by which most of his papers in that collection are distinguished: those, however, which have that signature and also that of *Mysargyrus*, were not written by him, but, as I suppose, by Dr. Bathurst. Indeed Johnson's energy of thought and richness of language, are still more decisive marks than any signature. As a proof of this, my

wrong. The lines are in Lord Lansdowne's Drinking Song to Sleep, and run thus:—

> 'Short, very short be then thy reign,
> For I'm in haste to laugh and drink again.'

readers, I imagine, will not doubt that Number 39, on sleep, is
his; for it not only has the general texture and colour of his style,
but the authours with whom he was peculiarly conversant are
readily introduced in it in cursory allusion. The translation of a
passage in Statius quoted in that paper, and marked C. B. has
been erroneously ascribed to Dr. Bathurst, whose Christian
name was Richard. How much this amiable man actually contributed to *The Adventurer*, cannot be known. Let me add, that
Hawkesworth's imitations of Johnson are sometimes so happy,
that it is extremely difficult to distinguish them, with certainty,
from the compositions of his great archetype. Hawkesworth was
his closest imitator, a circumstance of which that writer would
once have been proud to be told; though, when he had become
elated by having risen into some degree of consequence, he, in
a conversation with me, had the provoking effrontery to say he
was not sensible of it.

Johnson was truly zealous for the success of *The Adventurer*;
and very soon after his engaging in it, he wrote the following
letter:

'*To* THE REVEREND DR. JOSEPH WARTON

'DEAR SIR,—I ought to have written to you before now, but
I ought to do many things which I do not; nor can I, indeed,
claim any merit from this letter; for being desired by the
authours and proprietor of *The Adventurer* to look out for another
hand, my thoughts necessarily fixed upon you, whose fund of
literature will enable you to assist them, with very little interruption of your studies.

'They desire you to engage to furnish one paper a month, at
two guineas a paper, which you may very readily perform. We
have considered that a paper should consist of pieces of imagination, pictures of life, and disquisitions of literature. The part
which depends on the imagination is very well supplied, as you
will find when you read the paper; for descriptions of life, there
is now a treaty almost made with an authour and an authouress;[1]

---

[1] [Perhaps Mrs. Chapone. Chapman, *Johnson's Letters*, No. 46.]

and the province of criticism and literature they are very desirous to assign to the commentator on Virgil.

'I hope this proposal will not be rejected, and that the next post will bring us your compliance. I speak as one of the fraternity, though I have no part in the paper, beyond now and then a motto; but two of the writers are my particular friends,[1] and I hope the pleasure of seeing a third united to them, will not be denied to, dear Sir, your most obedient, and most humble servant,

'March 8, 1753.'   'SAM. JOHNSON.'

The consequence of this letter was, Dr. Warton's enriching the collection with several admirable essays.

Johnson's saying 'I have no part in the paper beyond now and then a motto,' may seem inconsistent with his being the authour of the papers marked T. But he had, at this time, written only one number; and besides, even at any after period, he might have used the same expression, considering it as a point of honour not to own them; for Mrs. Williams told me that, 'as he had *given* those Essays to Dr. Bathurst, who sold them at two guineas each, he never would own them; nay, he used to say he did not *write* them: but the fact was, that he *dictated* them, while Bathurst wrote.' I read to him Mrs. Williams's account; he smiled, and said nothing.

I am not quite satisfied with the casuistry by which the productions of one person are thus passed upon the world for the productions of another. I allow that not only knowledge, but powers and qualities of mind may be communicated; but the actual effect of individual exertion never can be transferred, with truth, to any other than its own original cause. One person's child may be made the child of another person by adoption, as among the Romans, or by the ancient Jewish mode of a wife having children born to her upon her knees, by her handmaid. But these were children in a different sense from that of nature. It was clearly understood that they were not of the blood of their nominal parents. So in literary children, an authour may give the profits and fame of his composition to another man, but

[1] [Hawkesworth and (probably) Bathurst. *Chapman.*]

cannot make that other the real authour. A Highland gentleman, a younger branch of a family, once consulted me if he could not validly purchase the Chieftainship of his family, from the Chief who was willing to sell it. I told him it was impossible for him to acquire, by purchase, a right to be a different person from what he really was; for that the right of Chieftainship attached to the blood of primogeniture, and, therefore, was incapable of being transferred. I added, that though Esau sold his birth-right, or the advantages belonging to it, he still remained the first-born of his parents; and that whatever agreement a Chief might make with any of the clan, the Herald's Office could not admit of the metamorphosis, or with any decency attest that the younger was the elder; but I did not convince the worthy gentleman.

Johnson's papers in *The Adventurer* are very similar to those of *The Rambler*; but being rather more varied in their subjects, and being mixed with essays by other writers, upon topicks more generally attractive than even the most elegant ethical discourses, the sale of the work, at first, was more extensive. Without meaning, however, to depreciate *The Adventurer*, I must observe that as the value of *The Rambler* came, in the progress of time, to be better known, it grew upon the publick estimation, and that its sale has far exceeded that of any other periodical papers since the reign of Queen Anne.

In one of the books of his diary I find the following entry:

'Apr. 3, 1753. I began the second vol. of my Dictionary, room being left in the first for Preface, Grammar, and History, none of them yet begun.

'O GOD, who hast hitherto supported me, enable me to proceed in this labour, and in the whole task of my present state; that when I shall render up, at the last day, an account of the talent committed to me, I may receive pardon, for the sake of JESUS CHRIST. Amen.'

He this year favoured Mrs. Lennox with a Dedication* to the Earl of Orrery, of her *Shakspeare Illustrated*.

1754: ÆTAT. 45.]—IN 1754 I can trace nothing published by him, except his numbers of *The Adventurer*, and 'The Life of Edward Cave,'* in the *Gentleman's Magazine* for February. In biography there can be no question that he excelled, beyond all who have attempted that species of composition; upon which, indeed, he set the highest value. To the minute selection of characteristical circumstances, for which the ancients were re- markable, he added a philosophical research, and the most per- spicuous and energetick language. Cave was certainly a man of estimable qualities, and was eminently diligent and successful in his own business, which, doubtless, entitled him to respect. But he was peculiarly fortunate in being recorded by Johnson, who, of the narrow life of a printer and publisher, without any digressions or adventitious circumstances, has made an interest- ing and agreeable narrative.

The *Dictionary*, we may believe, afforded Johnson full occupa- tion this year. As it approached to its conclusion, he probably worked with redoubled vigour, as seamen increase their exertion and alacrity when they have a near prospect of their haven.

Lord Chesterfield, to whom Johnson had paid the high com- pliment of addressing to his Lordship the *Plan* of his *Dictionary*, had behaved to him in such a manner as to excite his contempt and indignation. The world has been for many years amused with a story confidently told, and as confidently repeated with additional circumstances, that a sudden disgust was taken by Johnson upon occasion of his having been one day kept long in waiting in his Lordship's antechamber, for which the reason assigned was, that he had company with him; and that at last, when the door opened, out walked Colley Cibber; and that John- son was so violently provoked when he found for whom he had been so long excluded, that he went away in a passion, and never would return. I remember having mentioned this story to George Lord Lyttelton, who told me, he was very intimate with Lord Chesterfield; and holding it as a well-known truth, defended Lord Chesterfield, by saying, that 'Cibber, who had been intro- duced familiarly by the back-stairs, had probably not been there above ten minutes.' It may seem strange even to entertain a doubt concerning a story so long and so widely current, and thus implicitly adopted, if not sanctioned, by the authority which I have mentioned; but Johnson himself assured me, that there was not the least foundation for it. He told me, that there never was any particular incident which produced a quarrel between Lord Chesterfield and him; but that his Lordship's continued neglect was the reason why he resolved to have no connection with him. When the *Dictionary* was upon the eve of publication, Lord Chesterfield, who, it is said, had flattered himself with expectations that Johnson would dedicate the work to him, attempted, in a courtly manner, to sooth, and insinuate himself with the Sage, conscious, as it should seem, of the cold indifference with which he had treated its learned authour; and further attempted to conciliate him, by writing two papers in *The World*, in recommendation of the work; and it must be confessed, that they contain some studied compliments, so finely turned, that if there had been no previous offence, it is probable that Johnson would have been highly delighted. Praise, in general, was pleasing to him; but by praise from a man of rank and elegant accomplishments, he was peculiarly gratified.

His Lordship says,

'I think the publick in general, and the republick of letters in particular, are greatly obliged to Mr. Johnson, for having undertaken, and executed, so great and desirable a work. Perfection is not to be expected from man; but if we are to judge by the various works of Johnson already published, we have good reason to believe, that he will bring this as near to perfection as any one man could do. The *Plan* of it, which he published some years ago, seems to me to be a proof of it. Nothing can be more rationally imagined, or more accurately and elegantly expressed. I therefore recommend the previous perusal of it to all those who intend to buy the *Dictionary*, and who, I suppose, are all those who can afford it.' . . .

'It must be owned, that our language is, at present, in a state of anarchy, and hitherto, perhaps, it may not have been the worse for it. During our free and open trade, many words and expressions have been imported, adopted, and naturalized from other languages, which have greatly enriched our own. Let it still preserve what real strength and beauty it may have borrowed from others; but let it not, like the Tarpeian maid, be overwhelmed and crushed by unnecessary ornaments. The time for discrimination seems to be now come. Toleration, adoption, and naturalization have run their lengths. Good order and authority are now necessary. But where shall we find them, and, at the same time, the obedience due to them? We must have recourse to the old Roman expedient in times of confusion, and chuse a dictator. Upon this principle, I give my vote for Mr. Johnson to fill that great and arduous post. And I hereby declare, that I make a total surrender of all my rights and privileges in the English language, as a free-born British subject, to the said Mr. Johnson, during the term of his dictatorship. Nay more, I will not only obey him, like an old Roman, as my dictator, but, like a modern Roman, I will implicitly believe in him as my Pope, and hold him to be infallible while in the chair, but no longer. More than this he cannot well require; for, I presume, that obedience can never be expected, when there is neither terrour to enforce, nor interest to invite it.' . . .

'But a Grammar, a Dictionary, and a History of our Language through its several stages, were still wanting at home, and importunately called for from abroad. Mr. Johnson's labours will now, I dare say, very fully supply that want, and greatly contribute to the farther spreading of our language in other countries. Learners were discouraged, by finding no standard to resort to; and, consequently, thought it incapable of any. They will now be undeceived and encouraged.'

This courtly device failed of its effect. Johnson, who thought that 'all was false and hollow,' despised the honeyed words, and was even indignant that Lord Chesterfield should, for a moment, imagine that he could be the dupe of such an artifice. His expression to me concerning Lord Chesterfield, upon this occasion, was, 'Sir, after making great professions, he had, for many years, taken no notice of me; but when my *Dictionary* was coming out, he fell a scribbling in *The World* about it. Upon which, I wrote him a letter expressed in civil terms, but such as might shew him that I did not mind what he said or wrote, and that I had done with him.'

This is that celebrated letter of which so much has been said, and about which curiosity has been so long excited, without being gratified. I for many years solicited Johnson to favour me with a copy of it, that so excellent a composition might not be lost to posterity. He delayed from time to time to give it me;[1] till at last in 1781, when we were on a visit at Mr. Dilly's, at Southill in Bedfordshire, he was pleased to dictate it to me from memory. He afterwards found among his papers a copy of it, which he had dictated to Mr. Baretti, with its title and corrections, in his own handwriting. This he gave to Mr. Langton; adding that if it were to come into print, he wished it to be from that copy. By Mr. Langton's kindness, I am enabled to enrich my work with a perfect transcript of what the world has so eagerly desired to see.

'*To* THE RIGHT HONOURABLE THE EARL OF CHESTERFIELD

'MY LORD,   February 1755.

'I have been lately informed, by the proprietor of *The World*, that two papers, in which my Dictionary is recommended to the publick, were written by your Lordship. To be so distinguished, is an honour, which, being very little accustomed to favours from the great, I know not well how to receive, or in what terms to acknowledge.

'When, upon some slight encouragement, I first visited your Lordship, I was overpowered, like the rest of mankind, by the enchantment of your address; and could not forbear to wish that I might boast myself *Le vainqueur du vainqueur de la terre*;—that I might obtain that regard for which I saw the world contending; but I found my attendance so little encouraged, that neither pride nor modesty would suffer me to continue it. When I had once

---

[1] Dr. Johnson appeared to have had a remarkable delicacy with respect to the circulation of this letter; for Dr. Douglas, Bishop of Salisbury, informs me that, having many years ago pressed him to be allowed to read it to the second Lord Hardwicke, who was very desirous to hear it (promising at the same time, that no copy of it should be taken), Johnson seemed much pleased that it had attracted the attention of a nobleman of such a respectable character; but after pausing some time, declined to comply with the request, saying, with a smile, 'No, Sir; I have hurt the dog too much already;' or words to that purpose.

addressed your Lordship in publick, I had exhausted all the art of pleasing which a retired and uncourtly scholar can possess. I had done all that I could; and no man is well pleased to have his all neglected, be it ever so little.

'Seven years, my Lord, have now past, since I waited in your outward rooms, or was repulsed from your door; during which time I have been pushing on my work through difficulties, of which it is useless to complain, and have brought it, at last, to the verge of publication, without one act of assistance,[1] one word of encouragement, or one smile of favour. Such treatment I did not expect, for I never had a Patron before.

'The shepherd in Virgil grew at last acquainted with Love, and found him a native of the rocks.[2]

'Is not a Patron, my Lord, one who looks with unconcern on a man struggling for life in the water, and, when he has reached ground, encumbers him with help? The notice which you have been pleased to take of my labours, had it been early, had been kind; but it has been delayed till I am indifferent, and cannot enjoy it; till I am solitary, and cannot impart it;[3] till I am known, and do not want it. I hope it is no very cynical asperity not to confess obligations where no benefit has been received, or to be unwilling that the Publick should consider me as owing that to a Patron, which Providence has enabled me to do for myself.

'Having carried on my work thus far with so little obligation to any favourer of learning, I shall not be disappointed though

[1] The following note is subjoined by Mr. Langton:—'Dr. Johnson, when he gave me this copy of his letter, desired that I would annex to it his information to me, that whereas it is said in the letter that "no assistance has been received," he did once receive from Lord Chesterfield the sum of ten pounds; but as that was so inconsiderable a sum, he thought the mention of it could not properly find place in a letter of the kind that this was.'

[2] ['I know thee, Love; in Desarts thou wast bred.' *Eclogue* viii. 43. (Dryden.)]

[3] In this passage Dr. Johnson evidently alludes to the loss of his wife. We find the same tender recollection recurring to his mind upon innumerable occasions: and, perhaps no man ever more forcibly felt the truth of the sentiment so elegantly expressed by my friend Mr. Malone, in his Prologue to Mr. Jephson's tragedy of Julia:—'Vain—wealth, and fame, and fortune's fostering care, / If no fond breast the splendid blessings share; / And, each day's bustling pageantry once past, / There, only there, our bliss is found at last.'

I should conclude it, if less be possible, with less; for I have been long wakened from that dream of hope, in which I once boasted myself with so much exultation, my Lord, your Lordship's most humble, most obedient servant,

'SAM. JOHNSON.'[1]

'While this was the talk of the town, (says Dr. Adams, in a letter to me) I happened to visit Dr. Warburton, who finding that I was acquainted with Johnson, desired me earnestly to carry his compliments to him, and to tell him, that he honoured him for his manly behaviour in rejecting these condescensions of Lord Chesterfield, and for resenting the treatment he had received from him, with a proper spirit. Johnson was visibly pleased with this compliment, for he had always a high opinion of Warburton.[2] Indeed, the force of mind which appeared in this letter, was congenial with that which Warburton himself amply possessed.'

There is a curious minute circumstance which struck me, in comparing the various editions of Johnson's imitations of Juvenal. In the tenth Satire, one of the couplets upon the vanity of wishes even for literary distinction stood thus:

'Yet think what ills the scholar's life assail,
Pride, envy, want, the *garret*, and the jail.'

But after experiencing the uneasiness which Lord Chesterfield's fallacious patronage made him feel, he dismissed the word *garret*

---

[1] Upon comparing this copy with that which Dr. Johnson dictated to me from recollection, the variations are found to be so slight, that this must be added to the many other proofs which he gave of the wonderful extent and accuracy of his memory. To gratify the curious in composition, I have deposited both the copies in the British Museum. [Only one is there.]

[2] Soon after Edwards's *Canons of Criticism* came out, Johnson was dining at Tonson the Bookseller's, with Hayman the Painter and some more company. Hayman related to Sir Joshua Reynolds, that the conversation having turned upon Edwards's book, the gentleman praised it much, and Johnson allowed its merit. But when they went farther, and appeared to put that authour upon a level with Warburton, 'Nay, (said Johnson,) he has given him some smart hits to be sure; but there is no proportion between the two men; they must not be named together. A fly, Sir, may sting a stately horse and make him wince; but one is but an insect, and the other is a horse still.'

from the sad group, and in all the subsequent editions the line stands

'Toil, envy, want, the *Patron*, and the jail.'

That Lord Chesterfield must have been mortified by the lofty contempt, and polite, yet keen satire with which Johnson exhibited him to himself in this letter, it is impossible to doubt. He, however, with that glossy duplicity which was his constant study, affected to be quite unconcerned. Dr. Adams mentioned to Mr. Robert Dodsley that he was sorry Johnson had written his letter to Lord Chesterfield. Dodsley, with the true feelings of trade, said 'he was very sorry too; for that he had a property in the *Dictionary*, to which his Lordship's patronage might have been of consequence.' He then told Dr. Adams, that Lord Chesterfield had shewn him the letter. 'I should have imagined (replied Dr. Adams) that Lord Chesterfield would have concealed it.' 'Poh! (said Dodsley) do you think a letter from Johnson could hurt Lord Chesterfield? Not at all, Sir. It lay upon his table, where any body might see it. He read it to me; said, "this man has great powers," pointed out the severest passages, and observed how well they were expressed.' This air of indifference, which imposed upon the worthy Dodsley, was certainly nothing but a specimen of that dissimulation which Lord Chesterfield inculcated as one of the most essential lessons for the conduct of life. His Lordship endeavoured to justify himself to Dodsley from the charges brought against him by Johnson; but we may judge of the flimsiness of his defence, from his having excused his neglect of Johnson, by saying that 'he had heard he had changed his lodgings, and did not know where he lived;' as if there could have been the smallest difficulty to inform himself of that circumstance, by inquiring in the literary circle with which his Lordship was well acquainted, and was, indeed, himself one of its ornaments.

Dr. Adams expostulated with Johnson, and suggested, that his not being admitted when he called on him, was, probably, not to be imputed to Lord Chesterfield; for his Lordship had declared to Dodsley, that 'he would have turned off the best servant he ever had, if he had known that he denied him to a man who would have been always more than welcome;' and, in confirmation of this, he insisted on Lord Chesterfield's general affability and easiness of access, especially to literary men. 'Sir, (said Johnson) that is not Lord Chesterfield; he is the proudest man this day existing.' 'No, (said Dr. Adams) there is one person, at least, as proud; I think, by your own account, you are the prouder man of the two.' 'But mine (replied Johnson, instantly) was *defensive* pride.' This, as Dr. Adams well observed, was one of those happy turns for which he was so remarkably ready.

Johnson having now explicitly avowed his opinion of Lord Chesterfield, did not refrain from expressing himself concerning that nobleman with pointed freedom: 'This man (said he) I thought had been a Lord among wits; but, I find, he is only a wit among Lords!' And when his *Letters* to his natural son were published, he observed, that 'they teach the morals of a whore, and the manners of a dancing master.'[1]

The character of 'a respectable Hottentot,' in Lord Chesterfield's letters, has been generally understood to be meant for Johnson, and I have no doubt that it was. But I remember when the *Literary Property* of those letters was contested in the Court of Session in Scotland, and Mr. Henry Dundas,[2] one of the

---

[1] That collection of letters cannot be vindicated from the serious charge of encouraging, in some passages, one of the vices most destructive to the good order and comfort of society, which his Lordship represents as mere fashionable gallantry; and, in others, of inculcating the base practice of dissimulation, and recommending, with disproportionate anxiety, a perpetual attention to external elegance of manners. But it must, at the same time, be allowed, that they contain many good precepts of conduct, and much genuine information upon life and manners, very happily expressed; and that there was considerable merit in paying so much attention to the improvement of one who was dependent upon his Lordship's protection; it has probably been exceeded in no instance by the most exemplary parent; and though I can by no means approve of confounding the distinction between lawful and illicit offspring, which is, in effect, insulting the civil establishment of our country, to look no higher; I cannot help thinking it laudable to be kindly attentive to those, of whose existence we have, in any way, been the cause. Mr. Stanhope's character has been unjustly represented as diametrically opposite to what Lord Chesterfield wished him to be. He has been called dull, gross, and aukward: but I knew him at Dresden, when he was envoy to that court; and though he could not boast of the *graces*, he was, in truth, a sensible, civil, well-behaved man. BOSWELL.
[2] Now one of his Majesty's principal Secretaries of State.

counsel for the proprietors, read this character as an exhibition of Johnson, Sir David Dalrymple, Lord Hailes, one of the Judges, maintained, with some warmth, that it was not intended as a portrait of Johnson, but of a late noble Lord,[1] distinguished for abstruse science. I have heard Johnson himself talk of the character, and say that it was meant for George Lord Lyttelton, in which I could by no means agree; for his Lordship had nothing of that violence which is a conspicuous feature in the composition. Finding that my illustrious friend could bear to have it supposed that it might be meant for him, I said, laughingly, that there was one trait which unquestionably did not belong to him; 'he throws his meat any where but down his throat.' 'Sir, (said he,) Lord Chesterfield never saw me eat in his life.'

On the 6th of March came out Lord Bolingbroke's works, published by Mr. David Mallet. The wild and pernicious ravings, under the name of *Philosophy*, which were thus ushered into the world, gave great offence to all well-principled men. Johnson, hearing of their tendency, which nobody disputed, was roused with a just indignation, and pronounced this memorable sentence upon the noble authour and his editor. 'Sir, he was a scoundrel, and a coward: a scoundrel, for charging a blunderbuss against religion and morality; a coward, because he had not resolution to fire it off himself, but left half a crown to a beggarly Scotchman, to draw the trigger after his death!' Garrick, who I can attest from my own knowledge, had his mind seasoned with pious reverence, and sincerely disapproved of the infidel writings of several, whom, in the course of his almost universal gay intercourse with men of eminence, he treated with external civility, distinguished himself upon this occasion. Mr. Pelham having died on the very day on which Lord Bolingbroke's works came out, he wrote an elegant Ode on his death, beginning

> 'Let others hail the rising sun,
>   I bow to that whose course is run;'

in which is the following stanza:

> 'The same sad morn, to Church and State
>   (So for our sins 'twas fix'd by fate,)

---

[1] [Probably George, 2nd Earl of Macclesfield. *Croker*[1].]

189

> A double stroke was given;
> Black as the whirlwinds of the North,
> St. John's fell genius issued forth,
> And Pelham fled to heaven.'

Johnson this year found an interval of leisure to make an excursion to Oxford, for the purpose of consulting the libraries there. Of this, and of many interesting circumstances concerning him, during a part of his life when he conversed but little with the world, I am enabled to give a particular account, by the liberal communications of the Reverend Mr. Thomas Warton, who obligingly furnished me with several of our common friend's letters, which he illustrated with notes. These I shall insert in their proper places.

'*To* THE REVEREND MR. THOMAS WARTON

'SIR,—It is but an ill return for the book with which you were pleased to favour me, to have delayed my thanks for it till now. I am too apt to be negligent; but I can never deliberately shew my[1] disrespect to a man of your character: and I now pay you a very honest acknowledgement, for the advancement of the litera-ture of our native country. You have shewn to all, who shall hereafter attempt the study of our ancient authours, the way to success; by directing them to the perusal of the books which those authours had read. Of this method, Hughes and men much greater than Hughes, seem never to have thought. The reason why the authours, which are yet read, of the sixteenth century, are so little understood, is, that they are read alone; and no help is borrowed from those who lived with them, or before them. Some part of this ignorance I hope to remove by my book, which now draws towards its end; but which I cannot finish to my mind, without visiting the libraries at Oxford, which I, there-fore, hope to see in[2] a fortnight. I know not how long I shall stay, or where I shall lodge: but shall be sure to look for you at my arrival, and we shall easily settle the rest. I am, dear Sir, your most obedient, &c.

'[London,] July 16, 1754.'   'SAM. JOHNSON.'

[1] [any *orig.*]   [2] [in about *orig.*]

Of his conversation while at Oxford at this time, Mr. Warton preserved and communicated to me the following memorial, which, though not written with all the care and attention which that learned and elegant writer bestowed on those compositions which he intended for the publick eye, is so happily expressed in an easy style, that I should injure it by any alteration:

'When Johnson came to Oxford in 1754, the long vacation was beginning, and most people were leaving the place. This was the first time of his being there, after quitting the University. The next morning after his arrival, he wished to see his old College, *Pembroke*. I went with him. He was highly pleased to find all the College-servants which he had left there still remaining, particularly a very old butler; and expressed great satisfaction at being recognised by them, and conversed with them familiarly. He waited on the master, Dr. Radcliffe, who received him very coldly. Johnson at least expected, that the master would order a copy of his Dictionary, now near publication: but the master did not choose to talk on the subject, never asked Johnson to dine, nor even to visit him, while he stayed at Oxford. After we had left the lodgings, Johnson said to me, "*There* lives a man, who lives by the revenues of literature, and will not move a finger to support it. If I come to live at Oxford, I shall take up my abode at Trinity." We then called on the Reverend Mr. Meeke, one of the fellows, and of Johnson's standing. Here was a most cordial greeting on both sides. On leaving him, Johnson said, "I used to think Meeke had excellent parts, when we were boys together at the College: but, alas!

'Lost in a convent's solitary gloom!'

I remember, at the classical lecture in the Hall, I could not bear Meeke's superiority, and I tried to sit as far from him as I could, that I might not hear him construe."

'As we were leaving the College, he said, "Here I translated Pope's Messiah. Which do you think is the best line in it?—My own favourite is,

'*Vallis aromaticas fundit Saronica nubes*.' "[1]

[1] ['See spicy clouds from lowly Saron rise.' (Pope, l. 27.)]

191

I told him, I thought it a very sonorous hexameter. I did not tell
him, it was not in the Virgilian style. He much regretted that
his *first* tutor was dead; for whom he seemed to retain the
greatest regard. He said, "I once had been a whole morning
sliding in Christ-Church Meadow, and missed his lecture in
logick. After dinner, he sent for me to his room. I expected a
sharp rebuke for my idleness, and went with a beating heart.
When we were seated, he told me he had sent for me to drink a
glass of wine with him, and to tell me, he was *not* angry with me
for missing his lecture. This was, in fact, a most severe reprimand.
Some more of the boys were then sent for, and we spent a
very pleasant afternoon." Besides Mr. Meeke, there was only
one other Fellow of Pembroke[1] now resident: from both of
whom Johnson received the greatest civilities during this
visit, and they pressed him very much to have a room in the
College.

'In the course of this visit (1754,) Johnson and I walked,
three or four times, to Ellsfield, a village beautifully situated
about three miles from Oxford, to see Mr. Wise, Radclivian
librarian, with whom Johnson was much pleased. At this place,
Mr. Wise had fitted up a house and gardens, in a singular
manner, but with great taste. Here was an excellent library;
particularly, a valuable collection of books in Northern literature, with which Johnson was often very busy. One day Mr.
Wise read to us a dissertation which he was preparing for the
press, intitled, "A History and Chronology of the fabulous
Ages." Some old divinities of Thrace, related to the Titans, and
called the CABIRI, made a very important part of the theory of
this piece; and in conversation afterwards, Mr. Wise talked
much of his CABIRI. As we returned to Oxford in the evening,
I out-walked Johnson, and he cried out *Sufflamina*, a Latin word
which came from his mouth with peculiar grace, and was as
much as to say, *Put on your drag chain.* Before we got home, I
again walked too fast for him; and he now cried out, "Why, you
walk as if you were pursued by all the CABIRI in a body." In an
evening, we frequently took long walks from Oxford into the

[1] [The Rev. John Collins. *Powell.*]

country, returning to supper. Once, in our way home, we viewed the ruins of the abbies of Oseney and Rewley, near Oxford. After at least half an hour's silence, Johnson said, "I viewed them with indignation!" We had then a long conversation on Gothick buildings; and in talking of the form of old halls, he said, "In these halls, the fire place was anciently always in the middle of the room, till the Whigs removed it on one side."—About this time there had been an execution of two or three criminals at Oxford on a Monday. Soon afterwards, one day at dinner, I was saying that Mr. Swinton the chaplain of the gaol, and also a frequent preacher before the University, a learned man, but often thoughtless and absent, preached the condemnation-sermon on repentance, before the convicts, on the preceding day, Sunday; and that in the close he told his audience, that he should give them the remainder of what he had to say on the subject, the next Lord's Day. Upon which, one of our company, a Doctor of Divinity, and a plain matter-of-fact man, by way of offering an apology for Mr. Swinton, gravely remarked, that he had probably preached the same sermon before the University: "Yes, Sir, (says Johnson) but the University were not to be hanged the next morning."

'I forgot to observe before, that when he left Mr. Meeke, (as I have told above) he added, "About the same time of life, Meeke was left behind at Oxford to feed on a Fellowship, and I went to London to get my living: now, Sir, see the difference of our literary characters!"'

The following letter was written by Dr. Johnson to Mr. Chambers, of Lincoln College, afterwards Sir Robert Chambers, one of the judges in India:[1]

'To Mr. Chambers of Lincoln College

'Dear Sir,—The commission which I delayed to trouble you with at your departure, I am now obliged to send you; and beg that you will be so kind as to carry it to Mr. Warton, of Trinity,

---

[1] Communicated by the Reverend Mr. Thomas Warton, who had the original.

to whom I should have written immediately, but that I know not if he be yet come back to Oxford.

'In the Catalogue of MSS. of Gr. Brit. see vol. I. pag. 18. MSS. Bodl. MARTYRIUM XV. *martyrum sub Juliano, auctore Theophylacto*.

'It is desired that Mr. Warton will inquire, and send word, what will be the cost of transcribing this manuscript.

'VOL. II. pag. 32. Num. 1022. 58. COLL. NOV.—*Commentaria in Acta Apostol.*—*Comment. in Septem Epistolas Catholicas*.

'He is desired to tell what is the age of each of these manuscripts: and what it will cost to have a transcript of the two first pages of each.

'If Mr. Warton be not in Oxford, you may try if you can get it done by any body else; or stay till he comes, according to your own convenience. It is for an Italian *literato*.

'The answer is to be directed to his Excellency Mr. Zon, Venetian Resident, Soho-Square.

'I hope, dear Sir, that you do not regret the change of London for Oxford. Mr. Baretti is well, and Miss Williams;[1] and we shall all be glad to hear from you, whenever you shall be so kind as to write to, Sir, your most humble servant,

'Nov. 21, 1754.'   'SAM. JOHNSON.'

The degree of Master of Arts, which, it has been observed, could not be obtained for him at an early period of his life, was

[1] 'I presume she was a relation of Mr. Zachariah Williams, who died in his eighty-third year, July 12, 1755. When Dr. Johnson was with me at Oxford, in 1775, he gave to the Bodleian Library a thin quarto of twenty-one pages, a work in Italian, with an English translation on the opposite page. The English title-page is this: "An Account of an Attempt to ascertain the Longitude at Sea, by an exact Variation of the Magnetical Needle, &c. By Zachariah Williams. London, printed for Dodsley, 1755." The English translation, from the strongest internal marks, is unquestionably the work of Johnson. In a blank leaf, Johnson has written the age, and time of death, of the authour Z. Williams, as I have said above. On another blank leaf, is pasted a paragraph from a newspaper, of the death and character of Williams, which is plainly written by Johnson. He was very anxious about placing this book in the Bodleian: and, for fear of any omission or mistake, he entered, in the great Catalogue, the title-page of it with his own hand.' WARTON. In this statement there is a slight mistake. The English account, which was written by Johnson, was the *original*; the Italian was a *translation*, done by Baretti. See *post*, end of 1755. [M.]

now considered as an honour of considerable importance, in order to grace the title-page of his *Dictionary*; and his character in the literary world being by this time deservedly high, his friends thought that, if proper exertions were made, the University of Oxford would pay him the compliment.

'*To* THE REVEREND MR. THOMAS WARTON

'DEAR SIR,—I am extremely obliged to you and to Mr. Wise, for the uncommon care which you have taken of my interest:[1] if you can accomplish your kind design, I shall certainly take me a little habitation among you.

'The books which I promised to Mr. Wise,[2] I have not been able to procure: but I shall send him a *Finnick Dictionary*, the only copy, perhaps, in England, which was presented me by a learned Swede:[3] but I keep it back, that it may make a set of my own books of the new edition, with which I shall accompany it, more welcome. You will assure him of my gratitude.

'Poor dear Collins![4]—Would a letter give him any pleasure? I have a mind to write.

'I am glad of your hindrance in your Spenserian design,[5] yet I would not have it delayed. Three hours a day stolen from sleep and amusement will produce it. Let a Servitour[6] transcribe the quotations, and interleave them with references, to save time. This will shorten the work, and lessen the fatigue.

'Can I do any thing to promoting the diploma? I would not be wanting to co-operate with your kindness; of which, whatever be the effect, I shall be, dear Sir, your most obliged, &c.

'[London,] Nov. 28, 1754.'　　　　　　　'SAM. JOHNSON.'

[1] 'In procuring him the degree of Master of Arts by diploma at Oxford.' WARTON.

[2] 'Lately fellow of Trinity College, and at this time Radclivian librarian, at Oxford. He was a man of very considerable learning, and eminently skilled in Roman and Anglo-Saxon antiquities. He died in 1767.' WARTON.

[3] [Perhaps Peter Chriström. *Mod. Lang. Rev.* 1932, pp. 210–12. *See* Index, s.v. Kristrom.]

[4] 'Collins (the poet) was at this time at Oxford, on a visit to Mr. Warton; but labouring under the most deplorable languor of body, and dejection of mind.' WARTON.

[5] 'Of publishing a volume of observations on the rest of Spenser's works. It was hindered by my taking pupils in this College.' WARTON.

[6] 'Young students of the lowest rank at Oxford are so called.' WARTON.

To THE SAME

'Dear SIR,—I am extremely sensible of the favour done me, both by Mr. Wise and yourself. The book[1] cannot, I think, be printed in less than six weeks, nor probably so soon; and I will keep back the title-page, for such an insertion as you seem to promise me. Be pleased to let me know what money I shall send you, for bearing the expence of the affair; and I will take care that you may have it ready at your hand.

'I had lately the favour of a letter from your brother, with some account of poor Collins, for whom I am much concerned. I have a notion, that by very great temperance, or more properly abstinence, he may yet recover.

'There is an old English and Latin book of poems by Barclay, called "The Ship of Fools;" at the end of which are a number of *Eglogues*; so he writes it, from *Egloga*,[2] which are probably the first in our language. If you cannot find the book I will get Mr. Dodsley to send it you.

'I shall be extremely glad to hear from you again, to know, if the affair proceeds.[3] I have mentioned it to none of my friends for fear of being laughed at for my disappointment.

'You know poor Mr. Dodsley has lost his wife; I believe he is much affected. I hope he will not suffer so much as I yet suffer for the loss of mine.

$$Ο\ddot{ι}μι. \ \ τί \ δ' \ ο\ddot{ι}μι; \ θνητὰ \ γὰρ \ πεπόνθαμεν.[4]$$

I have ever since seemed to myself broken off from mankind; a kind of solitary wanderer in the wild of life, without any direction, or fixed point of view: a gloomy gazer on a world to which I have little relation. Yet I would endeavour, by the help of you and your brother, to supply the want of closer union, by friendship: and hope to have long the pleasure of being, dear Sir, most affectionately your's,

'[London,] Dec. 21, 1754.'   'SAM. JOHNSON.'

---

[1] 'His Dictionary.' WARTON.
[2] [*Ægloga orig.*]
[3] 'Of the degree at Oxford.' WARTON.
[4] ['Alas, but wherefore alas? We have suffered the lot of men.' Euripides, *Fragment* 300N².]

1755: ÆTAT. 46.]—IN 1755 we behold him to great advantage; his degree of Master of Arts conferred upon him, his
Dictionary published, his correspondence animated, his benevolence exercised.

'To THE REVEREND MR. THOMAS WARTON

'DEAR SIR,—I wrote to you some weeks ago, but believe did
not direct accurately, and therefore know not whether you had
my letter. I would, likewise, write to your brother, but know
not where to find him. I now begin to see land, after having
wandered, according to Mr. Warburton's phrase, in this vast
sea of words. What reception I shall meet with on the shore, I
know not; whether the sound of bells, and acclamations of the
people, which Ariosto talks of in his last Canto, or a general
murmur of dislike, I know not: whether I shall find upon the
coast a Calypso that will court, or a Polypheme that will resist.[1]
But if Polypheme comes, have at his eyes [sic *orig.*] I hope,
however, the criticks will let me be at peace; for though I do
not much fear their skill and strength, I am a little afraid of myself, and would not willingly feel so much ill-will in my bosom
as literary quarrels are apt to excite.

'Mr. Baretti is about a work for which he is in great want of
Crescimbeni, which you may have again when you please.

'There is nothing considerable done or doing among us here.
We are not, perhaps, as innocent as villagers, but most of us
seem to be as idle. I hope, however, you are busy; and should
be glad to know what you are doing. I am, dearest Sir, your
humble servant,

'[London,] Feb. 1, 1755.'　　　　　　'SAM. JOHNSON.'

To THE SAME

'DEAR SIR,—I received your letter this day, with great sense
of the favour that has been done me;[2] for which I return my

---

[1] [eat me *orig.*]
[2] 'His degree had now past, according to the usual form, the suffrages of
the heads of Colleges; but was not yet finally granted by the University. It
was carried without a single dissentient voice.' WARTON.

most sincere thanks: and entreat you to pay to Mr. Wise such returns as I ought to make for so much kindness so little deserved.

'I sent Mr. Wise the *Lexicon*, and afterwards wrote to him; but know not whether he had either the book or letter. Be so good as to contrive to enquire.

'But why does my dear Mr. Warton tell me nothing of himself? Where hangs the new volume?[1] Can I help? Let not the past labour be lost, for want of a little more: but snatch what time you can from the Hall, and the pupils, and the coffee-house, and the parks, and complete your design. I am, dear Sir, &c.

'[London,] Feb. 4, 1755.'   'SAM. JOHNSON.'

To THE SAME

'DEAR SIR,—I had a letter last week from Mr. Wise, but have yet heard nothing from you, nor know in what state my affair stands;[2] of which I beg you to inform me, if you can, to-morrow, by the return of the post.

'Mr. Wise sends me word, that he has not had the *Finnick Lexicon* yet, which I sent some time ago; and if he has it not, you must enquire after it. However, do not let your letter stay for that.

'Your brother, who is a better correspondent than you, and not much better, sends me word, that your pupils keep you in College: but do they keep you from writing too? Let them, at least, give you time to write to, dear Sir, your most affectionate, &c.

'[London,] Feb. 13, 1755.'   'SAM. JOHNSON.'

To THE SAME

'DEAR SIR,—Dr. King[3] was with me a few minutes before your letter; this, however, is the first instance in which your kind intentions to me have ever been frustrated.[4] I have now the

---

[1] 'On Spenser.' WARTON.   [2] 'Of the degree.' WARTON.
[3] 'Principal of St. Mary Hall at Oxford. He brought with him the diploma from Oxford.' WARTON.
[4] 'I suppose Johnson means that my *kind intention* of being the *first* to

full effect of your care and benevolence; and am far from thinking it a slight honour, or a small advantage; since it will put the enjoyment of your conversation more frequently in the power of, dear Sir, your most obliged and affectionate

'SAM. JOHNSON.'

'P.S. I have enclosed a letter to the Vice-Chancellor,[1] which you will read; and, if you like it, seal and give him.

'[London,] Feb. 1755.'

As the Publick will doubtless be pleased to see the whole progress of this well-earned academical honour, I shall insert the Chancellor of Oxford's letter to the University,[2] the diploma, and Johnson's letter of thanks to the Vice-Chancellor.

'*To the Reverend Dr.* HUDDESFORD, Vice-Chancellor *of the* University *of* Oxford; *to be communicated to the Heads of Houses, and proposed in Convocation.*

'MR. VICE-CHANCELLOR, AND GENTLEMEN,—Mr. Samuel Johnson, who was formerly of Pembroke College, having very eminently distinguished himself by the publication of a series of essays, excellently calculated to form the manners of the people, and in which the cause of religion and morality is every where maintained by the strongest powers of argument and language; and who shortly intends to publish a *Dictionary of the English Tongue,* formed on a new plan, and executed with the greatest labour and judgement; I persuade myself that I shall act agreeably to the sentiments of the whole University, in desiring that it may be proposed in convocation to confer on him the degree of Master of Arts by diploma, to which I readily give my consent; and am, Mr. Vice-Chancellor, and Gentlemen, your affectionate friend and servant,

'Grosvenor-street, Feb. 4, 1755.'   'ARRAN.'

give him the good news of the degree being granted was *frustrated*, because Dr. King brought it before my intelligence arrived.' WARTON.
[1] 'Dr. Huddesford, President of Trinity College.' WARTON.
[2] Extracted from the Convocation-Register, Oxford.

Term. S^{cti}.

Hilarii.   'Diploma Magistri Johnson.[1]

1755.

'*CANCELLARIUS, Magistri et Scholares Universitatis Oxoniensis omnibus ad quos hoc presens scriptum pervenerit, salutem in Domino sempiternam.*

'*Cùm eum in finem gradus academici à majoribus nostris instituti fuerint, ut viri ingenio et doctrinâ præstantes titulis quoque præter cæteros insignirentur; cùmque vir doctissimus* Samuel Johnson *è Collegio Pembrochiensi, scriptis suis popularium mores informantibus dudum literato orbi innotuerit; quin et linguæ patriæ tum ornandæ tum stabiliendæ (Lexicon scilicet Anglicanum summo studio, summo à se judicio congestum propediem editurus) etiam nunc utilissimam impendat operam; Nos igitur Cancellarius, Magistri, et Scholares antedicti, nè virum de literis humanioribus optimè meritum diutius inhonoratum prætereamus, in solenni Convocatione Doctorum, Magistrorum, Regentium, et non Regentium, decimo die Mensis Februarii Anno Domini Millesimo Septingentesimo Quinquagesimo quinto habitâ, præfatum virum* Samuelem Johnson (*conspirantibus omnium suffragiis) Magistrum in Artibus renunciavimus et constituimus; eumque, virtute præsentis diplomatis, singulis juribus privilegiis et honoribus ad istum gradum quàquà pertinentibus frui et gaudere jussimus.*

'*In cujus rei testimonium sigillum Universitatis Oxoniensis præsentibus apponi fecimus.*

'*Datum in Domo nostra Convocationis die* 20° *Mensis Feb.*

Anno Dom. prædicto.

'*Diploma supra scriptum per Registrarium lectum erat, et ex decreto venerabilis Domus communi Universitatis sigillo munitum.*'[2]

---

[1] ⌐The non-formal part of this document is to this purport:
Whereas our ancestors instituted academic degrees to the end that men of outstanding genius and learning might be distinguished by titles also; and whereas the learned S. J. of Pem. Coll. has long been known to the world of letters by writings that have shaped the manners of his countrymen and is even now labouring at a work of the greatest usefulness in adorning and fixing our native tongue (he is about to publish an English Dictionary, compiled with the greatest diligence and judgement); therefore we, the Chancellor, Masters, and Scholars, have unanimously made the said S. J. a Master of Arts, and we wish him joy of all the rights and privileges that belong to that degree.⌐

[2] The original is in my possession. ⌐'Both you and I would think me

'DOM. DOCTORI HUDDESFORD, OXONIENSIS ACADEMIÆ VICE-CANCELLARIO.

'*INGRATUS planè et tibi et mihi videar, nisi quanto me gaudio affecerint, quos nuper mihi honores (te credo auctore) decrevit Senatus Academicus, literarum, quo tamen nihil levius, officio, significem: ingratus etiam, nisi comitatem, quâ vir eximius*[1] *mihi vestri testimonium amoris in manus tradidit, agnoscam et laudem. Si quid est undè rei tam gratæ accedat gratia, hoc ipso magis mihi placet, quod eo tempore in ordines Academicos denuo cooptatus sim, quo tuam imminuere auctoritatem, famamque Oxonii lædere, omnibus modis conantur homines vafri, nec tamen acuti: quibus ego, prout viro umbratico licuit, semper restiti, semper restiturus. Qui enim, inter has rerum procellas, vel Tibi vel Academiæ defuerit, illum virtuti et literis, sibique et posteris, defuturum existimo.*

'S. JOHNSON.'

'*To* THE REVEREND MR. THOMAS WARTON

'DEAR SIR,—After I received my diploma, I wrote you a letter of thanks, with a letter to the Vice-Chancellor, and sent another to Mr. Wise; but have heard from nobody since, and begin to think myself forgotten. It is true, I sent you a double letter, and you may fear an expensive correspondent; but I would have taken it kindly, if you had returned it treble: and what is a double letter to a *petty king*, that having *fellowship and fines*, can sleep without a *Modus in his head?*[2]

ungrateful if I failed to express in a letter (the most trifling form of acknowledgement) the pleasure I feel in the honour which (I imagine at your instigation) the Senatus Academicus has done me. I should be equally ungrateful if I did not acknowledge the kindness of the excellent man who has put into my hands the proof of your regard. My pleasure is enhanced by this, that I am enrolled in your ranks at a time when cunning but foolish men are straining every nerve to lessen your authority and to injure the good name of Oxford. I have always opposed them, in so far as an obscure scholar can, and always shall. Whoever, in these days of trouble, fails in his duty to you and the University, I regard as failing in his duty to virtue and learning, to himself and posterity.']

[1] We may conceive what a high gratification it must have been to Johnson to receive his diploma from the hands of the great Dr. KING, whose principles were so congenial with his own.

[2] 'The words in Italicks are allusions to passages in Mr. Warton's poem, called *The Progress of Discontent*, now lately published.' WARTON.

'Dear Mr. Warton, let me hear from you, and tell me something, I care not what, so I hear it but from you. Something I will tell you:—I hope to see my *Dictionary* bound and lettered, next week;—*vastâ mole superbus.*[1] And I have a great mind to come to Oxford at Easter; but you will not invite me. Shall I come uninvited, or stay here where nobody perhaps would miss me if I went? A hard choice! But such is the world to, dear Sir, your, &c.

'[London,] March 20, 1755.'   'SAM. JOHNSON.'

To THE SAME

'DEAR SIR,—Though not to write, when a man can write so well, is an offence sufficiently heinous, yet I shall pass it by. I am very glad that the Vice-Chancellor was pleased with my note. I shall impatiently expect you at London, that we may consider what to do next. I intend in the winter to open a *Bibliothèque,* and remember, that you are to subscribe a sheet a year; let us try, likewise, if we cannot persuade your brother to subscribe another. My book is now coming *in luminis oras.*[2] What will be its fate I know not, nor think much, because thinking is to no purpose. It must stand the censure of the *great vulgar and the small;* of those that understand it, and that understand it not. But in all this, I suffer not alone: every writer has the same difficulties, and, perhaps, every writer talks of them more than he thinks.

'You will be pleased to make my compliments to all my friends: and be so kind, at every idle hour, as to remember, dear Sir, your, &c.

'[London,] March 25, 1755.'   'SAM. JOHNSON.'

Dr. Adams told me, that this scheme of a *Bibliothèque* was a serious one: for upon his visiting him one day, he found his parlour floor covered with parcels of foreign and English literary journals, and he told Dr. Adams he meant to undertake a Review. 'How, Sir, (said Dr. Adams,) can you think of doing it alone?

---

[1] ['proud in its vast bulk'—source not traced.]
[2] ['into the bright coasts of light'. Lucretius, i. 23. (C. Bailey.)]

All branches of knowledge must be considered in it. Do you know Mathematics? Do you know Natural History?' Johnson answered, 'Why, Sir, I must do as well as I can. My chief purpose is to give my countrymen a view of what is doing in literature upon the continent; and I shall have, in a good measure, the choice of my subject, for I shall select such books as I best understand.' Dr. Adams suggested, that as Dr. Maty had just then finished his *Bibliothèque Britannique,* which was a well-executed work, giving foreigners an account of British publications, he might, with great advantage, assume him as an assistant. '*He,* (said Johnson) the little black dog! I'd throw him into the Thames.' The scheme, however, was dropped.

In one of his little memorandum-books I find the following hints for his intended *Review or Literary Journal:*

'*The Annals of Literature, foreign as well as domestick.* Imitate Le Clerk—Bayle—Barbeyrac. Infelicity of Journals in England. Works of the learned. We cannot take in all. Sometimes copy from foreign Journalists. Always tell.'

'*To* DR. BIRCH

'SIR,   'March 29, 1755.

'I have sent some parts of my *Dictionary,* such as were at hand, for your inspection. The favour which I beg is, that if you do not like them, you will say nothing. I am, Sir, your most affectionate humble servant,   'SAM. JOHNSON.'

'*To* MR. SAMUEL JOHNSON

'SIR,   'Norfolk-street, April 3, 1755.

'The part of your *Dictionary* which you have favoured me with the sight of has given me such an idea of the whole, that I most sincerely congratulate the publick upon the acquisition of a work long wanted, and now executed with an industry, accuracy, and judgement, equal to the importance of the subject. You might, perhaps, have chosen one in which your genius would have appeared to more advantage; but you could not have fixed upon any other in which your labours would have done such substantial service to the present age and to posterity.

I am glad that your health has supported the application necessary to the performance of so vast a task; and can undertake to
promise you as one (though perhaps the only) reward of it, the
approbation and thanks of every well-wisher to the honour of
the English language. I am, with the greatest regard, Sir, your
most faithful and most affectionate humble servant,

'Tho. Birch.'

Mr. Charles Burney, who has since distinguished himself so
much in the science of Musick, and obtained a Doctor's degree
from the University of Oxford, had been driven from the capital
by bad health, and was now residing at Lynne Regis, in Norfolk.
He had been so much delighted with Johnson's *Rambler* and the
Plan of his *Dictionary*, that when the great work was announced
in the news-papers as nearly finished, he wrote to Dr. Johnson,
begging to be informed when and in what manner his *Dictionary*
would be published; intreating, if it should be by subscription,
or he should have any books at his own disposal, to be favoured
with six copies for himself and friends.

In answer to this application, Dr. Johnson wrote the following
letter, of which (to use Dr. Burney's own words) 'if it be remembered that it was written to an obscure young man, who at this
time had not much distinguished himself even in his own profession, but whose name could never have reached the authour of
The Rambler, the politeness and urbanity may be opposed to some
of the stories which have been lately circulated of Dr. Johnson's
natural rudeness and ferocity.'

'*To* Mr. Burney, *in Lynne Regis, Norfolk*

'Sir,—If you imagine that by delaying my answer I intended
to shew any neglect of the notice with which you have favoured
me, you will neither think justly of yourself nor of me. Your
civilities were offered with too much elegance not to engage
attention; and I have too much pleasure in pleasing men like
you, not to feel very sensibly the distinction which you have
bestowed upon me.

'Few consequences of my endeavours to please or to benefit

mankind have delighted me more than your friendship thus voluntarily offered, which now I have it I hope to keep, because I hope to continue to deserve it.

'I have no *Dictionaries* to dispose of for myself, but shall be glad to have you direct your friends to Mr. Dodsley, because it was by his recommendation that I was employed in the work.

'When you have leisure to think again upon me, let me be favoured with another letter; and another yet, when you have looked into my *Dictionary*. If you find faults, I shall endeavour to mend them; if you find none, I shall think you blinded by kind partiality: but to have made you partial in his favour, will very much gratify the ambition of, Sir, your most obliged and most humble servant,   'SAM. JOHNSON.'

'Gough-square, Fleet-street, April 8, 1775.'

Mr. Andrew Millar, bookseller in the Strand, took the principal charge of conducting the publication of Johnson's *Dictionary*; and as the patience of the proprietors was repeatedly tried and almost exhausted, by their expecting that the work would be completed within the time which Johnson had sanguinely supposed, the learned authour was often goaded to dispatch, more especially as he had received all the copy-money, by different drafts, a considerable time before he had finished his task. When the messenger who carried the last sheet to Millar returned, Johnson asked him, 'Well, what did he say?'—'Sir, (answered the messenger) he said, thank GOD I have done with him.' 'I am glad (replied Johnson, with a smile) that he thanks GOD for any thing.'[1] It is remarkable that those with whom Johnson chiefly contracted for his literary labours were Scotchmen, Mr. Millar and Mr. Strahan. Millar, though himself no great judge of literature, had good sense enough to have for his friends very able men to give him their opinion and advice in the purchase of copy-right; the consequence of which was his acquiring a very

---

[1] Sir John Hawkins, p. 341, inserts two notes as having passed formally between Andrew Millar and Johnson, to the above effect. I am assured this was not the case. In the way of incidental remark it was a pleasant play of raillery. To have deliberately written notes in such terms would have been morose.

large fortune, with great liberality. Johnson said of him, 'I respect Millar, Sir; he has raised the price of literature.' The same praise may be justly given to Panckoucke, the eminent bookseller of Paris. Mr. Strahan's liberality, judgement, and success, are well known.

'*To* Bennet Langton, Esq., *at Langton near Spilsby, Lincolnshire*

'Sir,—It has been long observed, that men do not suspect faults which they do not commit; your own elegance of manners, and punctuality of complaisance, did not suffer you to impute to me that negligence of which I was guilty, and which I have not since atoned. I received both your letters and received them with pleasure proportionate to the esteem which so short an acquaintance strongly impressed, and which I hope to confirm by nearer knowledge, though I am afraid that gratification will be for a time withheld.

'I have, indeed, published my Book,[1] of which I beg to know your father's judgement, and yours; and I have now staid long enough to watch its progress into the world. It has, you see, no patrons, and, I think, has yet had no opponents, except the criticks of the coffee-house, whose outcries are soon dispersed into the air, and are thought on no more: from this, therefore, I am at liberty, and think of taking the opportunity of this interval to make an excursion; and why not then into Lincolnshire? or, to mention a stronger attraction, why not to dear Mr. Langton? I will give the true reason, which I know you will approve:—I have a mother more than eighty years old, who has counted the days to the publication of my book, in hopes of seeing me; and to her, if I can disengage myself here, I resolve to go.

'As I know, dear Sir, that to delay my visit for a reason like this, will not deprive me of your esteem, I beg it may not lessen your kindness. I have very seldom received an offer of friendship which I so earnestly desire to cultivate and mature. I shall rejoice to hear from you, till I can see you, and will see you as soon as I can; for when the duty that calls me to Lichfield is discharged,

[1] His *Dictionary*.

my inclination will carry[1] me to Langton. I shall delight to hear the ocean roar, or see the stars twinkle, in the company of men to whom Nature does not spread her volumes or utter her voice in vain.

'Do not, dear Sir, make the slowness of this letter a precedent for delay, or imagine that I approved the incivility that I have committed; for I have known you enough to love you, and sincerely to wish a further knowledge; and I assure you, once more, that to live in a house that contains such a father and such a son, will be accounted a very uncommon degree of pleasure, by, dear Sir, your most obliged, and most humble servant,

    'May 6, 1755.'   'Sam. Johnson.'

'*To* The Reverend Mr. Thomas Warton

'Dear Sir,—I am grieved that you should think me capable of neglecting your letters; and beg you will never admit any such suspicion again. I purpose to come down next week, if you shall be there; or any other week, that shall be more agreeable to you. Therefore let me know. I can stay this visit but a week, but intend to make preparations for a longer stay next time; being resolved not to lose sight of the University. How goes Apollonius?[2] Don't let him be forgotten. Some things of this kind must be done, to keep us up. Pay my compliments to Mr. Wise, and all my other friends. I think to come to Kettel-Hall.[3] I am, Sir, your most affectionate, &c.

    '[London,] May 13, 1755.'   'Sam. Johnson.'

To The Same

'Dear Sir,—It is strange how many things will happen to intercept every pleasure, though it [be] only that of two friends meeting together. I have promised myself every day to inform you when you might expect me at Oxford, and have not been

---

[1] [*The MS. has* hurry. *R.W.C.*]   [2] 'A translation of Apollonius Rhodius was now intended by Mr. Warton.' Warton.

[3] Kettel Hall is an ancient tenement built about the year 1615 by Dr. Ralph Kettel, President of Trinity College, for the accommodation of commoners of that Society. It adjoins the College; and was a few years ago converted into a private house. [M.]

able to fix a time. The time, however, is, I think, at last come; and I promise myself to repose in Kettel-Hall, one of the first nights of the next week. I am afraid my stay with you cannot be long; but what is the inference? We must endeavour to make it chearful. I wish your brother could meet us, that we might go and drink tea with Mr. Wise in a body. I hope he will be at Oxford, or at his nest of British and Saxon antiquities.[1] I shall expect to see *Spenser* finished, and many other things begun. Dodsley is gone to visit the Dutch. The *Dictionary* sells well. The rest of the world goes on as it did. Dear Sir, your most affectionate, &c.

    '[London,] June 10, 1755.'   'SAM. JOHNSON.'

To THE SAME

    'DEAR SIR,—To talk of coming to you, and not yet to come, has an air of trifling which I would not willingly have among you; and which, I believe, you will not impute to me, when I have told you, that since my promise, two of our partners[2] are dead, and that I was solicited to suspend my excursion till we could recover from our confusion.

    'I have not laid aside my purpose; for every day makes me more impatient of staying from you. But death, you know, hears not supplications, nor pays any regard to the convenience of mortals. I hope now to see you next week; but next week is but another name for to-morrow, which has been noted for promising and deceiving. I am, &c.

    '[London,] June 24, 1755.'   'SAM. JOHNSON.'

To THE SAME

    'DEAR SIR,—I told you, that among the manuscripts are some things of Sir Thomas More. I beg you to pass an hour in looking on them, and procure a transcript of the ten or twenty first lines of each, to be compared with what I have; that I may know whether they are yet unpublished. The manuscripts are these:

    'Catalogue of Bodl. MS. pag. 122. F. 3. Sir Thomas More.

---

[1] 'At Ellsfield, a village three miles from Oxford.' WARTON.
[2] 'Booksellers concerned in his *Dictionary*.' WARTON.

'1. Fall of angels. 2. Creation and fall of mankind. 3. Deter-mination of the Trinity for the rescue[1] of mankind. 4. Five lectures of our Saviour's passion. 5. Of the institution of the sacrament, three lectures. 6. How to receive the blessed body of our Lord sacramentally. 7. Neomenia, the new moon. 8. *De tristitia, tædio, pavore, et oratione Christi, ante captionem ejus.*[2]

'Catalogue, pag. 154. Life of Sir Thomas More. *Qu.* Whether Roper's? Pag. 363. *De resignatione Magni Sigilli in manus Regis per D. Thomam Morum.*[3] Pag. 364. *Mori Defensio Moriæ.*[4]

'If you procure the young gentleman in the library to write out what you think fit to be written, I will send to Mr. Prince the bookseller to pay him what you shall think proper.

'Be pleased to make my compliments to Mr. Wise, and all my friends. I am, Sir, your affectionate, &c.

'[London,] Aug. 7, 1755.'   'SAM. JOHNSON.'

The *Dictionary*, with a *Grammar and History of the English Language*, being now at length published, in two volumes folio, the world contemplated with wonder so stupendous a work atchieved by one man, while other countries had thought such undertakings fit only for whole academies. Vast as his powers were, I cannot but think that his imagination deceived him, when he supposed that by constant application he might have performed the task in three years. Let the Preface be attentively perused, in which is given, in a clear, strong, and glowing style, a comprehensive, yet particular view of what he had done; and it will be evident, that the time he employed upon it was comparatively short. I am unwilling to swell my book with long quotations from what is in every body's hands, and I believe there are few prose compositions in the English language that are read with more delight, or are more impressed upon the memory, than that preliminary discourse. One of its excellencies has always struck me with peculiar admiration: I mean the perspicuity with which he has expressed abstract scientifick notions.

---

[1] restauration *in an earlier edition.*
[2] ['Of the passion, weariness, fear, and prayer of Christ before his arrest.']
[3] ['Of Sir Thomas More's resignation of the Great Seal into the King's hands.']   [4] ['More's Defence of Folly.']

As an instance of this, I shall quote the following sentence: 'When the radical idea branches out into parallel ramifications, how can a consecutive series be formed of senses in their own nature collateral?' We have here an example of what has been often said, and I believe with justice, that there is for every thought a certain nice adaptation of words which none other could equal, and which, when a man has been so fortunate as to hit, he has attained, in that particular case, the perfection of language.

The extensive reading which was absolutely necessary for the accumulation of authorities, and which alone may account for Johnson's retentive mind being enriched with a very large and various store of knowledge and imagery, must have occupied several years. The Preface furnishes an eminent instance of a double talent, of which Johnson was fully conscious. Sir Joshua Reynolds heard him say, 'There are two things which I am confident I can do very well: one is an introduction to any literary work, stating what it is to contain, and how it should be executed in the most perfect manner; the other is a conclusion, shewing from various causes why the execution has not been equal to what the authour promised to himself and to the publick.'

How should puny scribblers be abashed and disappointed, when they find him displaying a perfect theory of lexicographical excellence, yet at the same time candidly and modestly allowing that he 'had not satisfied his own expectations.' Here was a fair occasion for the exercise of Johnson's modesty, when he was called upon to compare his own arduous performance, not with those of other individuals, (in which case his inflexible regard to truth would have been violated, had he affected diffidence,) but with speculative perfection; as he, who can outstrip all his competitors in the race, may yet be sensible of his deficiency when he runs against time. Well might he say, that 'the *English Dictionary* was written with little assistance of the learned,' for he told me, that the only aid which he received was a paper containing twenty etymologies, sent to him by a person then unknown, who he was afterwards informed was Dr. Pearce, Bishop of Rochester. The etymologies, though they exhibit learning and judgement, are not, I think, entitled to the first praise amongst the various parts of this immense work. The definitions have always appeared to me such astonishing proofs of acuteness of intellect and precision of language, as indicate a genius of the highest rank. This it is which marks the superiour excellence of Johnson's *Dictionary* over others equally or even more voluminous, and must have made it a work of much greater mental labour than mere Lexicons, or *Word-books*, as the Dutch call them. They, who will make the experiment of trying how they can define a few words of whatever nature, will soon be satisfied of an unquestionable justice of this observation, which I can assure my readers is founded upon much study, and upon communication with more minds than my own.

A few of his definitions must be admitted to be erroneous. Thus, *Windward* and *Leeward*, though directly of opposite meaning, are defined identically the same way; as to which inconsiderable specks it is enough to observe, that his Preface announces that he was aware there might be many such in so immense a work; nor was he at all disconcerted when an instance was pointed out to him. A lady once asked him how he came to define *Pastern* the *knee* of a horse: instead of making an elaborate defence, as she expected, he at once answered, 'Ignorance, Madam, pure ignorance.' His definition of *Network* has been often quoted with sportive malignity, as obscuring a thing in itself very plain. But to these frivolous censures no other answer is necessary than that with which we are furnished by his own Preface.

'To explain, requires the use of terms less abstruse than that which is to be explained, and such terms cannot always be found. For as nothing can be proved but by supposing something intuitively known, and evident without proof, so nothing can be defined but by the use of words too plain to admit of definition. Sometimes easier words are changed into harder; as, *burial*, into *sepulture* or *interment*; *dry*, into *desiccative*; *dryness*, into *siccity or aridity*; *fit*, into *paroxysm*; for the *easiest* word, whatever it be, can never be translated into one more easy.'

His introducing his own opinions, and even prejudices, under

general definitions of words, while at the same time the original
meaning of the words is not explained, as his *Tory*, *Whig*, *Pension*, *Oats*, *Excise*, and a few more, cannot be fully defended, and
must be placed to the account of capricious and humourous indulgence.[1] Talking to me upon this subject when we were at Ashbourne in 1777, he mentioned a still stronger instance of the
predominance of his private feelings in the composition of this
work, than any now to be found in it. 'You know, Sir, Lord
Gower forsook the old Jacobite interest. When I came to the
word *Renegado*, after telling that it meant "one who deserts to
the enemy, a revolter," I added, *Sometimes we say a* GOWER.
Thus it went to the press; but the printer had more wit than I,
and struck it out.'

Let it, however, be remembered, that this indulgence does not
display itself only in sarcasm towards others, but sometimes in
playful allusion to the notions commonly entertained of his own
laborious task. Thus: '*Grub-street*, the name of a street in London,
much inhabited by writers of small histories, *dictionaries*, and
temporary poems; whence any mean production is called *Grub-
street*.'—'*Lexicographer*, a writer of dictionaries, a *harmless
drudge*.'

At the time when he was concluding his very eloquent Preface,
Johnson's mind appears to have been in such a state of depression,

[1] He thus defines Excise: 'A hateful tax levied upon commodities, and
adjudged not by the common judges of property, but wretches hired by
those to whom Excise is paid.' The Commissioners of Excise being offended
by this severe reflection, consulted Mr. Murray, then Attorney General, to
know whether redress could be legally obtained. I wished to have procured
for my readers a copy of the opinion which he gave, and which may now be
justly considered as history; but the mysterious secrecy of office, it seems,
would not permit it. I am, however, informed, by very good authority, that
its import was, that the passage might be considered as actionable; but that
it would be more prudent in the board not to prosecute. Johnson never made
the smallest alteration in this passage. We find he still retained his early
prejudice against Excise; for in *The Idler*, No. 65, there is the following
very extraordinary paragraph: 'The authenticity of *Clarendon's* history,
though printed with the sanction of one of the first Universities of the world,
had not an unexpected manuscript been happily discovered, would, with the
help of factious credulity, have been brought into question by the two lowest
of all human beings, a Scribbler for a party, and a Commissioner of Excise.'
—The persons to whom he alludes were Mr. John Oldmixon, and George
Ducket, Esq.

that we cannot contemplate without wonder the vigorous and splendid thoughts which so highly distinguish that performance. 'I (says he) may surely be contented without the praise of perfection, which if I could obtain in this gloom of solitude, what would it avail me? I have protracted my work till most of those whom I wished to please have sunk into the grave; and success and miscarriage are empty sounds. I therefore dismiss it with frigid tranquillity, having little to fear or hope from censure or from praise.' That this indifference was rather a temporary than an habitual feeling, appears, I think, from his letters to Mr. Warton; and however he may have been affected for the moment, certain it is that the honours which his great work procured him, both at home and abroad, were very grateful to him. His friend the Earl of Corke and Orrery, being at Florence, presented it to the *Academia della Crusca*. That Academy sent Johnson their *Vocabulario*, and the French Academy sent him their *Dictionnaire*, which Mr. Langton had the pleasure to convey to him.

It must undoubtedly seem strange, that the conclusion of his Preface should be expressed in terms so desponding, when it is considered that the authour was then only in his forty-sixth year. But we must ascribe its gloom to that miserable dejection of spirits to which he was constitutionally subject, and which was aggravated by the death of his wife two years before. I have heard it ingeniously observed by a lady of rank and elegance, that 'his melancholy was then at its meridian.' It pleased God to grant him almost thirty years of life after this time; and once, when he was in a placid frame of mind, he was obliged to own to me that he had enjoyed happier days, and had had many more friends, since that gloomy hour than before.

It is a sad saying, that 'most of those whom he wished to please had sunk into the grave;' and his case at forty-five was singularly unhappy, unless the circle of his friends was very narrow. I have often thought, that as longevity is generally desired, and, I believe, generally expected, it would be wise to be continually adding to the number of our friends, that the loss of some may be supplied by others. Friendship, 'the wine of life,' should, like a well-stocked cellar, be thus continually renewed;

and it is consolatory to think, that although we can seldom add what will equal the generous *first-growths* of our youth, yet friendship becomes insensibly old in much less time than is commonly imagined, and not many years are required to make it very mellow and pleasant. *Warmth* will, no doubt, make a considerable difference. Men of affectionate temper and bright fancy will coalesce a great deal sooner than those who are cold and dull.

The proposition which I have now endeavoured to illustrate was, at a subsequent period of his life, the opinion of Johnson himself. He said to Sir Joshua Reynolds, 'If a man does not make new acquaintance as he advances through life, he will soon find himself left alone. A man, Sir, should keep his friendship *in constant repair.*'

The celebrated Mr. Wilkes, whose notions and habits of life were very opposite to his, but who was ever eminent for literature and vivacity, sallied forth with a little *Jeu d'Esprit* upon the following passage in his Grammar of the English Tongue, prefixed to the *Dictionary*: '*H* seldom, perhaps never, begins any but the first syllable.' In an Essay printed in *The Publick Advertiser*, this lively writer enumerated many instances in opposition to this remark; for example, 'The authour of this observation must be a man of a quick *appre-hension*, and of a most *comprehensive* genius.' The position is undoubtedly expressed with too much latitude.

This light sally, we may suppose, made no great impression on our Lexicographer; for we find that he did not alter the passage till many years afterwards.[1]

He had the pleasure of being treated in a very different manner by his old pupil Mr. Garrick, in the following complimentary Epigram:

'*On* JOHNSON'S DICTIONARY.

'Talk of war with a Briton, he'll boldly advance,
That one English soldier will beat ten of France;
Would we alter the boast from the sword to the pen,

[1] In the third [fourth] edition, published in 1773, he left out the words *perhaps never*, and added the following paragraph:—

'It sometimes begins middle or final syllables in words compounded, as *block-head*, or derived from the Latin, as *compre-hended*.'

Our odds are still greater, still greater our men:
In the deep mines of science though Frenchmen may toil,
Can their strength be compar'd to Locke, Newton, and Boyle?
Let them rally their heroes, send forth all their pow'rs,
Their verse-men and prose-men, then match them with ours!
First Shakspeare and Milton, like gods in the fight,
Have put their whole drama and epick to flight;
In satires, epistles, and odes, would they cope,
Their numbers retreat before Dryden and Pope;
And Johnson, well arm'd like a hero of yore,
Has beat forty French,[1] and will beat forty more!'

Johnson this year gave at once a proof of his benevolence, quickness of apprehension, and admirable art of composition, in the assistance which he gave to Mr. Zachariah Williams, father of the blind lady whom he had humanely received under his roof. Mr. Williams had followed the profession of physick in Wales; but having a very strong propensity to the study of natural philosophy, had made many ingenious advances towards a discovery of the longitude, and repaired to London in hopes of obtaining the great parliamentary reward. He failed of success; but Johnson having made himself master of his principles and experiments, wrote for him a pamphlet, published in quarto, with the following title: *An Account of an Attempt to ascertain the Longitude at Sea, by an exact Theory of the Variation of the Magnetical Needle; with a Table of the Variations at the most remarkable Cities in Europe, from the year* 1660 *to* 1680.† To diffuse it more extensively, it was accompanied with an Italian translation on the opposite page, which it is supposed was the work of Signor Baretti, an Italian of considerable literature, who having come to England a few years before, had been employed in the capacity both of a language-master and an authour, and formed an intimacy with Dr. Johnson. This pamphlet Johnson presented to the Bodleian Library.[2] On a blank leaf of it is pasted a paragraph cut out of a news-paper, containing an account of the death and character of Williams, plainly written by Johnson.[3]

---

[1] The number of the French Academy employed in settling their language.
[2] See note by Mr. Warton, *ante*, p. 194.
[3] 'On Saturday the 12th, about twelve at night, died Mr. Zachariah

In July this year he had formed some scheme of mental improvement, the particular purpose of which does not appear. But we find in his *Prayers and Meditations*, p. 25, a prayer entitled 'On the Study of Philosophy, as an Instrument of living;' and after it follows a note, 'This study was not pursued.'

On the 13th of the same month he wrote in his *Journal* the following scheme of life, for Sunday:

'Having lived' (as he with tenderness of conscience expresses himself) 'not without an habitual reverence for the Sabbath, yet without that attention to its religious duties which Christianity requires;

'1. To rise early, and in order to do it, to go to sleep early on Saturday.

'2. To use some extraordinary devotion in the morning.

'3. To examine the tenour of my life, and particularly the last week; and to mark my advances in religion, or recession from it.

'4. To read the Scripture methodically with such helps as are at hand.

'5. To go to church twice.

'6. To read books of Divinity, either speculative or practical.

'7. To instruct my family.

'8. To wear off by meditation any worldly soil contracted in the week.'

1756: ÆTAT. 47.]—IN 1756 Johnson found that the great fame of his *Dictionary* had not set him above the necessity of 'making provision for the day that was passing over him.' No royal or noble patron extended a munificent hand to give independence to the man who had conferred stability on the language of his country. We may feel indignant that there should have been such unworthy neglect; but we must, at the same time,

Williams, in his eighty-third year, after an illness of eight months, in full possession of his mental faculties. He has been long known to philosophers and seamen for his skill in magnetism, and his proposal to ascertain the longitude by a peculiar system of the variation of the compass. He was a man of industry indefatigable, of conversation inoffensive, patient of adversity and disease, eminently sober, temperate, and pious; and worthy to have ended life with better fortune.'

congratulate ourselves, when we consider, that to this very
neglect, operating to rouse the natural indolence of his constitution, we owe many valuable productions, which otherwise, perhaps, might never have appeared.

He had spent, during the progress of the work, the money for
which he had contracted to write his *Dictionary*. We have seen
that the reward of his labour was only fifteen hundred and
seventy-five pounds; and when the expence of amanuenses and
paper, and other articles are deducted, his clear profit was very
inconsiderable. I once said to him, 'I am sorry, Sir, you did not
get more for your *Dictionary*.' His answer was, 'I am sorry, too.
But it was very well. The booksellers are generous, liberal-
minded men.' He, upon all occasions, did ample justice to their
character in this respect. He considered them as the patrons of
literature; and, indeed, although they have eventually been considerable gainers by his *Dictionary*, it is to them that we owe
its having been undertaken and carried through at the risk of
great expence, for they were not absolutely sure of being in-
demnified.

On the first day of this year we find from his private devotions,
that he had then recovered from sickness;[1] and in February that
his eye was restored to its use.[2] The pious gratitude with which
he acknowledges mercies upon every occasion is very edifying;
as is the humble submission which he breathes, when it is the
will of his heavenly Father to try him with afflictions. As such
dispositions become the state of man here, and are the true effects
of religious discipline, we cannot but venerate in Johnson one of
the most exercised minds that our holy religion hath ever formed.
If there be any thoughtless enough to suppose such exercise the
weakness of a great understanding, let them look up to Johnson
and be convinced that what he so earnestly practised must have
a rational foundation.

His works this year were, an abstract or epitome, in octavo,
of his folio *Dictionary*, and a few essays in a monthly publication,
entitled, *The Universal Visiter*. Christopher Smart, with whose
unhappy vacillation of mind he sincerely sympathised, was one

[1] *Prayers and Meditations* p. 40 [25].   [2] *Ib.*, p. 27.

of the stated undertakers of this miscellany; and it was to assist
him that Johnson sometimes employed his pen. All the essays
marked with two *asterisks* have been ascribed to him; but I am
confident, from internal evidence, that of these, neither 'The
Life of Chaucer,' 'Reflections on the State of Portugal,' nor an
'Essay on Architecture,' were written by him. I am equally confident, upon the same evidence, that he wrote 'Further Thoughts
on Agriculture;'† being the sequel of a very inferiour essay on
the same subject, and which, though carried on as if by the same
hand, is both in thinking and expression so far above it, and so
strikingly peculiar, as to leave no doubt of its true parent; and
that he also wrote 'A Dissertation on the State of Literature and
Authours,'† and 'A Dissertation on the Epitaphs written by
Pope.'† The last of these, indeed, he afterwards added to his
Idler. Why the essays truly written by him are marked in the
same manner with some which he did not write, I cannot explain;
but with deference to those who have ascribed to him the three
essays which I have rejected, they want all the characteristical
marks of Johnsonian composition.

He engaged also to superintend and contribute largely to
another monthly publication, entitled *The Literary Magazine, or
Universal Review*;* the first number of which came out in May
this year. What were his emoluments from this undertaking,
and what other writers were employed in it, I have not discovered. He continued to write in it, with intermissions, till the
fifteenth number; and I think that he never gave better proofs
of the force, acuteness, and vivacity of his mind, than in this
miscellany, whether we consider his original essays, or his reviews of the works of others. The 'Preliminary Address'† to the
Publick is a proof how this great man could embellish, with
the graces of superiour composition, even so trite a thing as
the plan of a magazine.

His original essays are, 'An Introduction to the Political State
of Great Britain;'† 'Remarks on the Militia Bill;'† 'Observations on his Britannick Majesty's Treaties with the Empress of
Russia and the Landgrave of Hesse Cassel;'† 'Observations on
the Present State of Affairs;'† and 'Memoirs of Frederick III,

King of Prussia.'† In all these he displays extensive political knowledge and sagacity, expressed with uncommon energy and perspicuity, without any of those words which he sometimes took a pleasure in adopting in imitation of Sir Thomas Browne; of whose *Christian Morals* he this year gave an edition, with his 'Life'† prefixed to it, which is one of Johnson's best biographical performances. In one instance only in these essays has he indulged his *Brownism*. Dr. Robertson, the historian, mentioned it to me, as having at once convinced him that Johnson was the author of the 'Memoirs of the King of Prussia.' Speaking of the pride which the old King, the father of his hero, took in being master of the tallest regiment in Europe, he says, 'To review this *towering* regiment was his daily pleasure; and to perpetuate it was so much his care, that when he met a tall woman he immediately commanded one of his *Titanian* retinue to marry her, that they might *propagate procerity*.' For this Anglo-Latian word *procerity*, Johnson had, however, the authority of Addison.

His reviews are of the following books: 'Birch's History of the Royal Society;'† 'Murphy's Gray's Inn Journal;'†'Warton's Essay on the Writings and Genius of Pope, Vol. I;'† 'Hampton's Translation of Polybius;'† 'Blackwell's Memoirs of the Court of Augustus;'† 'Russel's Natural History of Aleppo;'† 'Sir Isaac Newton's Arguments in Proof of a Deity;'† 'Borlase's History of the Isles of Scilly;'† 'Home's Experiments on Bleaching;'† 'Browne's Christian Morals;'† 'Hales on Distilling Sea-Water, Ventilators in Ships, and curing an ill Taste in Milk;'† 'Lucas's Essay on Waters;'† 'Keith's Catalogue of the Scottish Bishops;† 'Browne's History of Jamaica;'† 'Philosophical Transactions, Vol. XLIX.'† 'Mrs. Lennox's Translation of Sully's Memoirs;'* 'Miscellanies by Elizabeth Harrison;'† 'Evans's Map and Account of the Middle Colonies in America;'† 'Letter on the Case of Admiral Byng;'* 'Appeal to the People concerning Admiral Byng;'* 'Hanway's Eight Days' Journey, and Essay on Tea;'* 'The Cadet, a Military Treatise;'† 'Some further Particulars in Relation to the Case of Admiral Byng, by a Gentleman of Oxford;'* 'The Conduct of the Ministry relating to the present War impartially examined;'† 'A Free Inquiry into the Nature and Origin of Evil.'* All these, from internal evidence, were written by Johnson; some of them I know he avowed, and have marked them with an *asterisk* accordingly. Mr. Thomas Davies indeed, ascribed to him the Review of Mr. Burke's 'Inquiry into the Origin of our Ideas of the Sublime and Beautiful;' and Sir John Hawkins, with equal discernment, has inserted it in his collection of Johnson's works: whereas it has no resemblance to Johnson's composition, and is well known to have been written by Mr. Murphy, who has acknowledged it to me and many others.

It is worthy of remark, in justice to Johnson's political character, which has been misrepresented as abjectly submissive to power, that his 'Observations on the present State of Affairs' glow with as animated a spirit of constitutional liberty as can be found any where. Thus he begins:

'The time is now come, in which every Englishman expects to be informed of the national affairs; and in which he has a right to have that expectation gratified. For, whatever may be urged by Ministers, or those whom vanity or interest make the followers of ministers, concerning the necessity of confidence in our governours, and the presumption of prying with profane eyes into the recesses of policy, it is evident that this reverence can be claimed only by counsels yet unexecuted, and projects suspended in deliberation. But when a design has ended in miscarriage or success, when every eye and every ear is witness to general discontent, or general satisfaction, it is then a proper time to disentangle confusion and illustrate obscurity; to shew by what causes every event was produced, and in what effects it is likely to terminate; to lay down with distinct particularity what rumour always huddles in general exclamation, or perplexes by indigested narratives; to shew whence happiness or calamity is derived, and whence it may be expected; and honestly to lay before the people what inquiry can gather of the past, and conjecture can estimate of the future.'

Here we have it assumed as an incontrovertible principle, that in this country the people are the superintendants of the conduct and measures of those by whom government is administered; of the beneficial effect of which the present reign afforded an illustrious example, when addresses from all parts of the kingdom controuled an audacious attempt to introduce a new power subversive of the crown.

A still stronger proof of his patriotick spirit appears in his review of an 'Essay on Waters, by Dr. Lucas;' of whom, after describing him as a man well known to the world for his daring defiance of power, when he thought it exerted on the side of wrong, he thus speaks:

'The Irish ministers drove him from his native country by a proclamation, in which they charged him with crimes of which they never intended to be called to the proof, and oppressed him by methods equally irresistible by guilt and innocence.

'Let the man thus driven into exile, for having been the friend of his country, be received in every other place as confessor of liberty; and let the tools of power be taught in time, that they may rob, but cannot impoverish.'

Some of his reviews in this *Magazine* are very short accounts of the pieces noticed, and I mention them only that Dr. Johnson's opinion of the works may be known; but many of them are examples of elaborate criticism, in the most masterly style. In his review of the 'Memoirs of the Court of Augustus,' he has the resolution to think and speak from his own mind, regardless of the cant transmitted from age to age, in praise of the ancient Romans. Thus,

'I know not why any one but a school-boy in his declamation should whine over the Common-wealth of Rome, which grew great only by the misery of the rest of mankind. The Romans, like others, as soon as they grew rich, grew corrupt; and in their corruption sold the lives and freedoms of themselves, and of one another.'

Again,—'A people, who, while they were poor, robbed mankind; and as soon as they became rich, robbed one another.'

In his review of the *Miscellanies* in prose and verse, published by Elizabeth Harrison, but written by many hands, he gives an eminent proof at once of his orthodoxy and candour:

'The authours of the essays in prose seem generally to have

221

imitated, or tried to imitate, the copiousness and luxuriance of Mrs. *Rowe*. This, however, is not all their praise; they have laboured to add to her brightness of imagery, her purity of sentiments. The poets have had Dr. *Watts* before their eyes; a writer, who, if he stood not in the first class of genius, compensated that defect by a ready application of his powers to the promotion of piety. The attempt to employ the ornaments of romance in the decoration of religion, was, I think, first made by Mr. *Boyle's Martyrdom of Theodora*; but *Boyle's* philosophical studies did not allow him time for the cultivation of style; and the completion of the great design was reserved for Mrs. *Rowe*. Dr. *Watts* was one of the first who taught the Dissenters to write and speak like other men, by shewing them that elegance might consist with piety. They would have both done honour to a better society, for they had that charity which might well make their failings be forgotten, and with which the whole Christian world might wish for communion. They were pure from all the heresies of an age, to which every opinion is become a favourite that the universal church has hitherto detested!

'This praise, the general interest of mankind requires to be given to writers who please and do not corrupt, who instruct and do not weary. But to them all human eulogies are vain, whom I believe applauded by angels, and numbered with the just.'

His defence of tea against Mr. Jonas Hanway's violent attack upon that elegant and popular beverage, shews how very well a man of genius can write upon the slightest subject, when he writes, as the Italians say, *con amore*: I suppose no person ever enjoyed with more relish the infusion of that fragrant leaf than Johnson. The quantities which he drank of it at all hours were so great, that his nerves must have been uncommonly strong, not to have been extremely relaxed by such an intemperate use of it. He assured me, that he never felt the least inconvenience from it; which is a proof that the fault of his constitution was rather a too great tension of fibres, than the contrary. Mr. Hanway wrote an angry answer to Johnson's review of his *Essay on Tea*, and Johnson, after a full and deliberate pause, made a reply to it;

the only instance, I believe, in the whole course of his life, when he condescended to oppose any thing that was written against him. I suppose when he thought of any of his little antagonists, he was ever justly aware of the high sentiment of Ajax in *Ovid*:

> '*Iste tulit pretium jam nunc certaminis hujus,*
> *Qui, cùm victus erit, mecum certasse feretur.*'[1]

But, indeed, the good Mr. Hanway laid himself so open to ridicule, that Johnson's animadversions upon his attack were chiefly to make sport.

The generosity with which he pleads the cause of Admiral Byng is highly to the honour of his heart and spirit. Though *Voltaire* affects to be witty upon the fate of that unfortunate officer, observing that he was shot '*pour encourager les autres,*' the nation has long been satisfied that his life was sacrificed to the political fervour of the times. In the vault belonging to the Torrington family, in the church of Southill, in Bedfordshire, there is the following Epitaph upon his monument, which I have transcribed:

> 'To the perpetual Disgrace
> of public Justice,
> The Honourable John Byng, Esq.
> Admiral of the Blue,
> Fell a Martyr to political
> Persecution,
> March 14, in the Year, 1757;
> when Bravery and Loyalty
> were insufficient Securities
> for the Life and Honour of
> a Naval Officer.'

Johnson's most exquisite critical essay in the *Literary Magazine*, and indeed any where, is his review of Soame Jenyns's *Inquiry into the Origin of Evil*. Jenyns was possessed of lively talents, and a style eminently pure and easy, and could very happily play with a light subject, either in prose or verse; but when he speculated on that most difficult and excruciating

[1] ['Losing, he wins, because his name will be/Ennobled by defeat who durst contend with me.' *Metam.* xiii. 19. (Dryden.)]

question, the Origin of Evil, he 'ventured far beyond his depth,'
and, accordingly, was exposed by Johnson, both with acute argument and brilliant wit. I remember when the late Mr. Bicknell's
humourous performance, entitled *The Musical Travels of Joel
Collyer*, in which a slight attempt is made to ridicule Johnson,
was ascribed to Soame Jenyns, 'Ha! (said Johnson) I thought I
had given *him* enough of it.'

His triumph over Jenyns is thus described by my friend Mr.
Courtenay in his *Poetical Review of the literary and moral Character of Dr. Johnson*; a performance of such merit, that had I not
been honoured with a very kind and partial notice in it, I should
echo the sentiments of men of the first taste loudly in its praise:

> 'When specious sophists with presumption scan
> The source of evil hidden still from man;
> Revive Arabian tales, and vainly hope
> To rival St. John, and his scholar Pope:
> Though metaphysicks spread the gloom of night,
> By reason's star he guides our aching sight;
> The bounds of knowledge marks, and points the way
> To pathless wastes, where wilder'd sages stray;
> Where, like a farthing link-boy, Jenyns stands,
> And the dim torch drops from his feeble hands.'[1]

[1] Some time after Dr. Johnson's death there appeared in the newspapers
and magazines an illiberal and petulant attack upon him, in the form of
an Epitaph, under the name of Mr. Soame Jenyns, very unworthy of that
gentleman, who had quietly submitted to the critical lash while Johnson
lived. It assumed, as characteristicks of him, all the vulgar circumstances of
abuse which had circulated amongst the ignorant. It was an unbecoming
indulgence of puny resentment, at a time when he himself was at a very
advanced age, and had a near prospect of descending to the grave. I was
truly sorry for it; for he was then become an avowed, and (as my Lord
Bishop of London, who had a serious conversation with him on the subject,
assures me) a sincere Christian. He could not expect that Johnson's numerous friends would patiently bear to have the memory of their master stig-
matized by no mean pen, but that, at least, one would be found to retort.
Accordingly, this unjust and sarcastick Epitaph was met in the same publick
field by an answer, in terms by no means soft, and such as wanton provocation only could justify:

'EPITAPH,

'*Prepared for a creature* not quite dead *yet*.
'HERE lies a little ugly nauseous elf,
Who judging only from its wretched self,

This year Mr. William Payne, brother of the respectable Bookseller of that name, published *An Introduction to the Game of Draughts*, to which Johnson contributed a Dedication to the Earl of Rochford,* and a Preface,* both of which are admirably adapted to the treatise to which they are prefixed. Johnson, I believe, did not play at draughts after leaving College, by which he suffered; for it would have afforded him an innocent soothing relief from the melancholy which distressed him so often. I have heard him regret that he had not learnt to play at cards; and the game of draughts we know is peculiarly calculated to fix the attention without straining it. There is a composure and gravity in draughts which insensibly tranquillises the mind; and, accordingly, the Dutch are fond of it, as they are of smoaking, of the sedative influence of which, though he himself never smoaked, he had a high opinion.[1] Besides, there is in draughts some exercise of the faculties; and, accordingly, Johnson wishing to dignify the subject in his Dedication with what is most estimable in it, observes,

'Triflers may find or make any thing a trifle; but since it is the great characteristick of a wise man to see events in their causes, to obviate consequences, and ascertain contingencies, your Lordship will think nothing a trifle by which the mind is inured to caution, foresight, and circumspection.'

As one of the little occasional advantages which he did not disdain to take by his pen, as a man whose profession was literature, he this year accepted of a guinea from Mr. Robert Dodsley, for writing the introduction to *The London Chronicle*, an evening news-paper; and even in so slight a performance exhibited peculiar talents. This *Chronicle* still subsists, and from what I observed, when I was abroad, has a more extensive circulation

> Feebly attempted, petulant and vain,
> The "Origin of Evil" to explain.
> A mighty Genius at this elf displeas'd,
> With a strong critick grasp the urchin squeez'd.
> For thirty years its coward spleen it kept,
> Till in the dust the mighty Genius slept;
> Then stunk and fretted in expiring snuff,
> And blink'd at JOHNSON with its last poor puff.'

[1] *Journal of a Tour to the Hebrides*, 3rd edit. p. 48. [Aug. 19.]

upon the Continent than any of the English news-papers. It was constantly read by Johnson himself; and it is but just to observe, that it has all along been distinguished for good sense, accuracy, moderation, and delicacy.

Another instance of the same nature has been communicated to me by the Reverend Dr. Thomas Campbell, who has done himself considerable credit by his own writings.

'Sitting with Dr. Johnson one morning alone, he asked me if I had known Dr. Madden, who was authour of the premium-scheme in Ireland. On my answering in the affirmative, and also that I had for some years lived in his neighbourhood, &c., he begged of me that when I returned to Ireland, I would endeavour to procure for him a poem of Dr. Madden's called *Boulter's Monument*. The reason (said he) why I wish for it, is this: when Dr. Madden came to London, he submitted that work to my castigation; and I remember I blotted a great many lines, and might have blotted many more, without making the poem worse. However, the Doctor was very thankful, and very generous, for he gave me ten guineas, *which was to me at that time a great sum.*'

He this year resumed his scheme of giving an edition of *Shakspeare* with notes. He issued Proposals of considerable length, *[1] in which he shewed that he perfectly well knew what a variety of research such an undertaking required; but his indolence prevented him from pursuing it with that diligence which alone can collect those scattered facts that genius, however acute, penetrating, and luminous, cannot discover by its own force. It is remarkable, that at this time his fancied activity was for the moment so vigorous, that he promised his work should be published before Christmas, 1757. Yet nine years elapsed before it saw the light. His throes in bringing it forth had been severe and remittent; and at last we may almost conclude that the Cæsarian operation was performed by the knife of Churchill, whose upbraiding satire, I dare say, made Johnson's friends urge him to dispatch.

[1] They have been reprinted by Mr. Malone, in the Preface to his edition of *Shakspeare*.

'He for subscribers bates his hook,
And takes your cash; but where's the book?
No matter where; wise fear, you know,
Forbids the robbing of a foe;
But what, to serve our private ends,
Forbids the cheating of our friends?'

About this period he was offered a living of considerable value
in Lincolnshire, if he were inclined to enter into holy orders. It
was a rectory in the gift of Mr. Langton, the father of his much
valued friend. But he did not accept of it; partly I believe from
a conscientious motive, being persuaded that his temper and
habits rendered him unfit for that assiduous and familiar instruction of the vulgar and ignorant which he held to be an essential
duty in a clergyman; and partly because his love of a London
life was so strong, that he would have thought himself an exile
in any other place, particularly if residing in the country. Whoever would wish to see his thoughts upon that subject displayed
in their full force, may peruse *The Adventurer*, Number 126.

1757: ÆTAT. 48.]—IN 1757 it does not appear that he published any thing, except some of those articles in *The Literary
Magazine*, which have been mentioned. That magazine, after
Johnson ceased to write in it, gradually declined, though the
popular epithet of *Antigallican* was added to it; and in July 1758
it expired. He probably prepared a part of his *Shakspeare* this
year, and he dictated a speech on the subject of an Address to
the Throne, after the expedition to Rochfort, which was delivered
by one of his friends, I know not in what publick meeting. It is
printed in *The Gentleman's Magazine* for October 1785 as his,
and bears sufficient marks of authenticity.

By the favour of Mr. Joseph Cooper Walker, of the Treasury,
Dublin, I have obtained a copy of the following letter from John-
son to the venerable authour of *Dissertations on the History of
Ireland*.

'*To* CHARLES O'CONNOR, ESQ.

'SIR,—I have lately, by the favour of Mr. Faulkner, seen your
account of Ireland, and cannot forbear to solicit a prosecution of

your design. Sir William Temple complains that Ireland is less
known than any other country, as to its ancient state. The natives
have had little leisure, and little encouragement for enquiry; and
strangers, not knowing the language, have had no ability.

'I have long wished that the Irish literature were cultivated.[1]
Ireland is known by tradition to have been once the seat of piety
and learning; and surely it would be very acceptable to all those
who are curious either in the original of nations, or the affinities
of languages, to be further informed of the revolutions of a
people so ancient, and once so illustrious.

'What relation there is between the Welch and Irish languages, or between the language of Ireland and that of Biscay,
deserves enquiry. Of these provincial and unextended tongues,
it seldom happens that more than one are understood by any one
man; and, therefore, it seldom happens that a fair comparison
can be made. I hope you will continue to cultivate this kind of
learning, which has lain too long neglected, and which, if it be
suffered to remain in oblivion for another century, may, perhaps,
never be retrieved. As I wish well to all useful undertakings, I
would not forbear to let you know how much you deserve in my
opinion, from all lovers of study, and how much pleasure your
work has given to, Sir, your most obliged, and most humble
servant,

'London, April 9, 1757.'   'SAM. JOHNSON.'

'*To* THE REVEREND MR. THOMAS WARTON

'DEAR SIR,—Dr. Marsili of Padua, a learned gentleman, and
good Latin poet, has a mind to see Oxford. I have given him a

---

[1] The celebrated oratour, Mr. Flood, has shown himself to be of Dr.
Johnson's opinion; having by his will bequeathed his estate, after the death
of his wife Lady Frances, to the University of Dublin; 'desiring that immediately after the said estate shall come into their possession, they shall
appoint two professors, one for the study of the native Erse or Irish language, and the other for the study of Irish antiquities and Irish history, and
for the study of any other European language illustrative of, or auxiliary to,
the study of Irish antiquities or Irish history; and that they shall give yearly
two liberal premiums for two compositions, one in verse, and the other in
prose, in the Irish language.'

letter to Dr. Huddesford,[1] and shall be glad if you will introduce
him, and shew him any thing in Oxford.

'I am printing my new edition of *Shakspeare.*

'I long to see you all, but cannot conveniently come yet. You
might write to me now and then, if you were good for any thing.
But *honores mutant mores.*[2] Professors forget their friends.[3] I shall
certainly complain to Miss Jones.[4] I am, your, &c.

'[London,] June 21, 1757.'   'SAM. JOHNSON.'

'Please to make my compliments to Mr. Wise.'

Mr. Burney having enclosed to him an extract from the review
of his *Dictionary* in the *Bibliothèque des Savans,*[5] and a list of
subscribers to his *Shakspeare,* which Mr. Burney had procured
in Norfolk, he wrote the following answer:

'*To* MR. BURNEY. *in Lynne, Norfolk*

'SIR,—That I may show myself sensible of your favours, and
not commit the same fault a second time, I make haste to answer
the letter which I received this morning. The truth is, the other
likewise was received, and I wrote an answer; but being desirous
to transmit you some proposals and receipts, I waited till I could
find a convenient conveyance, and day was passed after day, till
other things drove it from my thoughts; yet not so, but that I
remember with great pleasure your commendation of my *Dictionary.* Your praise was welcome, not only because I believe it
was sincere, but because praise has been very scarce. A man of
your candour will be surprised when I tell you, that among all

[1] 'Now, or late, Vice-Chancellor.' WARTON.
[2] ['Honours change manners.']
[3] 'Mr. Warton was elected Professor of Poetry at Oxford in the preceding year.' WARTON.
[4] 'Miss Jones lived at Oxford, and was often of our parties. She was a
very ingenious poetess, and published a volume of poems; and, on the
whole, was a most sensible, agreeable, and amiable woman. She was a sister
to the Reverend River Jones, Chanter of Christ Church Cathedral at Oxford,
and Johnson used to call her the *Chantress.* I have heard him often address
her in this passage from *Il Penseroso*:
                "Thee, Chantress, oft the woods among
        I woo," etc.
She died unmarried.' WARTON.   [5] Tom. iii, p. 482.

my acquaintance there were only two, who upon the publication of my book did not endeavour to depress me with threats of censure from the publick, or with objections learned from those who had learned them from my own Preface. Your's is the only letter of goodwill that I have received; though, indeed, I am promised something of that sort from Sweden.

'How my new edition[1] will be received I know not; the sub-scription has not been very successful. I shall publish about March.

'If you can direct me how to send proposals, I should wish that they were in such hands.

'I remember, Sir, in some of the first letters with which you favoured me, you mentioned your lady. May I enquire after her? In return for the favours which you have shewn me, it is not much to tell you, that I wish you and her all that can conduce to your happiness. I am, Sir, you most obliged, and most humble servant,

'Gough-square, Dec. 24, 1757.'   'SAM. JOHNSON.'

In 1758 we find him, it should seem, in as easy and pleasant a state of existence, as constitutional unhappiness ever permitted him to enjoy.

'*To* BENNET LANGTON, ESQ., *at Langton, Lincolnshire*[2]

'DEAREST SIR,—I must indeed have slept very fast, not to have been awakened by your letter. None of your suspicions are true; I am not much richer than when you left me; and, what is worse, my omission of an answer to your first letter, will prove that I am not much wiser. But I go on as I formerly did, designing to be some time or other both rich and wise; and yet cultivate neither mind nor fortune. Do you take notice of my example, and learn the danger of delay. When I was as you are now, towering in the confidence of twenty-one, little did I suspect that I should be at forty-nine, what I now am.

'But you do not seem to need my admonition. You are busy

---

[1] Of *Shakspeare*.
[2] [The date 'Jan. 1758' means 1759—a mistake common when the change from 25 March to 1 Jan. for the beginning of the year was still recent.]

in acquiring and in communicating knowledge, and while you are studying, enjoy the end of study, by making others wiser and happier. I was much pleased with the tale that you told me of being tutour to your sisters. I, who have no sisters nor brothers, look with some degree of innocent envy on those who may be said to be born to friends; and cannot see, without wonder, how rarely that native union is afterwards regarded. It sometimes, indeed, happens, that some supervenient cause of discord may overpower this original amity; but it seems to me more frequently thrown away with levity; or lost by negligence, than destroyed by injury or violence. We tell the ladies that good wives make good husbands; I believe it is a more certain position that good brothers make good sisters.

'I am satisfied with your stay at home, as Juvenal with his friend's retirement to Cumæ: I know that your absence is best, though it be not best for me.

> '*Quamvis digressu veteris confusus amici,*
> *Laudo tamen vacuis quod sedem figere Cumis*
> *Destinet, atque unum civem donare Sibyllæ.*'[1]

'*Langton* is a good Cumæ, but who must be Sibylla? Mrs. Langton is as wise as Sibyl, and as good; and will live, if my wishes can prolong life, till she shall in time be as old. But she differs in this, that she has not scattered her precepts in the wind, at least not those which she bestowed upon you.

'The two Wartons just looked into the town, and were taken to see *Cleone*, where, David[2] says, they were starved for want of company to keep them warm. David and Doddy[3] have had a new quarrel, and, I think, cannot conveniently quarrel any more. *Cleone* was well acted by all the characters, but Bellamy left nothing to be desired. I went the first night, and supported it, as well[4] as I might; for Doddy, you know, is my patron, and I would not desert him. The play was very well received. Doddy, after

---

[1] ['Griev'd tho I am, an Ancient Friend to lose, I like the Solitary Seat he chose: In quiet *Cumæ* fixing his Repose: Where, far from noisy Rome secure he lives, And one more Citizen to *Sybil* gives.' Juvenal, *Satires* iii. 7. (Dryden.)]

[2] Mr. Garrick.   [3] Mr. Dodsley, the Authour of *Cleone*.

[4] [*The MS. has* publickly]

the danger was over, went every night to the stage-side, and cried at the distress of poor Cleone.

'I have left off housekeeping, and therefore made presents of the game which you were pleased to send me. The pheasant I gave to Mr. Richardson,[1] the bustard to Dr. Lawrence, and the pot I placed with Miss Williams, to be eaten by myself. She desires that her compliments and good wishes may be accepted by the family; and I make the same request for myself.

'Mr. Reynolds has within these few days raised his price to twenty guineas a head, and Miss is much employed in miniatures. I know not any body [else] whose prosperity has encreased since you left them.

'Murphy is to have his *Orphan of China* acted next month; and is therefore, I suppose, happy. I wish I could tell you of any great good to which I was approaching, but at present my prospects do not much delight me; however, I am always pleased when I find that you, dear Sir, remember, your affectionate, humble servant,

'Jan. 9, 1758.'   'Sam. Johnson.'

'*To* Mr. Burney, *at Lynne, Norfolk*

'Sir,—Your kindness is so great, and my claim to any particular regard from you so little, that I am at a loss how to express my sense of your favours;[2] but I am, indeed, much pleased to be thus distinguished by you.

'I am ashamed to tell you that my *Shakspeare* will not be out so soon as I promised my subscribers; but I did not promise them more than I promised myself. It will, however, be published before summer.

'I have sent you a bundle of proposals, which, I think, do not profess more than I have hitherto performed. I have printed many of the plays, and have hitherto left very few passages unexplained; where I am quite at a loss, I confess my ignorance, which is seldom done by commentators.

'I have, likewise, enclosed twelve receipts; not that I mean

[1] Mr. Samuel Richardson, authour of *Clarissa*.
[2] This letter was an answer to one in which was enclosed a draft for the payment of some subscriptions to his *Shakspeare*.

to impose upon you the trouble of pushing them, with more importunity than may seem proper, but that you may rather have more than fewer than you shall want. The proposals you will disseminate as there shall be opportunity. I once printed them at length in the *Chronicle*, and some of my friends (I believe Mr. Murphy, who formerly wrote the *Gray's-Inn Journal*) introduced them with a splendid encomium.

'Since the *Life of Browne*, I have been a little engaged, from time to time, in the *Literary Magazine*, but not very lately. I have not the collection by me, and therefore cannot draw out a catalogue of my own parts, but will do it, and send it. Do not buy them, for I will gather all those that have anything of mine in them, and send them to Mrs. Burney, as a small token of gratitude for the regard which she is pleased to bestow upon me. I am, Sir, your most obliged and most humble servant,

'London, March 8, 1758.'   'SAM. JOHNSON.'

Dr. Burney has kindly favoured me with the following memorandum, which I take the liberty to insert in his own genuine easy style. I love to exhibit sketches of my illustrious friend by various eminent hands.

'Soon after this, Mr. Burney, during a visit to the capital, had an interview with him in Gough-square, where he dined and drank tea with him, and was introduced to the acquaintance of Mrs. Williams. After dinner, Mr. Johnson proposed to Mr. Burney to go up with him into his garret, which being accepted, he there found about five or six Greek folios, a deal writing-desk, and a chair and a half. Johnson giving to his guest the entire seat, tottered himself on one with only three legs and one arm. Here he gave Mr. Burney Mrs. Williams's history, and shewed him some volumes of his *Shakspeare* already printed, to prove that he was in earnest. Upon Mr. Burney's opening the first volume, at the *Merchant of Venice*, he observed to him, that he seemed to be more severe on Warburton than Theobald. "O poor Tib.! (said Johnson) he was ready knocked down to my hands; Warburton stands between me and him." "But, Sir, (said Mr. Burney,) you'll have Warburton upon your bones, won't

you?" "No, Sir; he'll not come out: he'll only growl in his den."
"But you think, Sir, that Warburton is a superiour critick to
Theobald?" "O, Sir, he'd make two-and-fifty Theobalds, cut
into slices! The worst of Warburton is, that he has a rage for
saying something, when there's nothing to be said." Mr. Burney
then asked him whether he had seen the letter which Warburton
had written in answer to a pamphlet addressed "To the most
impudent Man alive." He answered in the negative. Mr. Burney
told him it was supposed to be written by Mallet. The controversy now raged between the friends of Pope and Bolingbroke;
and Warburton and Mallet were the leaders of the several
parties. Mr. Burney asked him then if he had seen Warburton's
book against Bolingbroke's *Philosophy*? "No, Sir, I have never
read Bolingbroke's impiety, and therefore am not interested
about its confutation."

On the fifteenth of April he began a new periodical paper,
entitled *The Idler*,* which came out every Saturday in a weekly
news-paper, called *The Universal Chronicle, or Weekly Gazette*,
published by Newbery. These essays were continued till April 5,
1760. Of one hundred and three, their total number, twelve were
contributed by his friends; of which, Numbers 33, 93, and 96,
were written by Mr. Thomas Warton; No. 67 by Mr. Langton;
and Nos. 76, 79, and 82, by Sir Joshua Reynolds; the concluding
words of No. 82, 'and pollute his canvas with deformity,' being
added by Johnson, as Sir Joshua informed me.

The Idler is evidently the work of the same mind which produced *The Rambler*, but has less body and more spirit. It has
more variety of real life, and greater facility of language. He
describes the miseries of idleness, with the lively sensations of
one who has felt them; and in his private memorandums while
engaged in it, we find 'This year I hope to learn diligence.'[1]
Many of these excellent essays were written as hastily as an
ordinary letter. Mr. Langton remembers Johnson, when on a
visit at Oxford, asking him one evening how long it was till the
post went out; and on being told about half an hour, he exclaimed,
'then we shall do very well.' He upon this instantly sat down and

[1] *Prayers and Meditations*, p. 30 [36].

finished an *Idler*, which it was necessary should be in London the next day. Mr. Langton having signified a wish to read it, 'Sir, (said he) you shall not do more than I have done myself.' He then folded it up and sent it off.

Yet there are in *The Idler* several papers which shew as much profundity of thought, and labour of language, as any of this great man's writings. No. 14, 'Robbery of Time;' No. 24, 'Thinking;' No. 41, 'Death of a Friend;' No. 43, 'Flight of Time;' No. 51, 'Domestick greatness unattainable;' No. 52, 'Self-denial;' No. 58, 'Actual, how short of fancied, excellence;' No. 89, 'Physical evil moral good;' and his concluding paper on 'The horrour of the last;' will prove this assertion. I know not why a motto, the usual trapping of periodical papers, is prefixed to very few of the *Idlers*, as I have heard Johnson commend the custom: and he never could be at a loss for one, his memory being stored with innumerable passages of the classicks. In this series of essays he exhibits admirable instances of grave humour, of which he had an uncommon share. Nor on some occasions has he repressed that power of sophistry which he possessed in so eminent a degree. In No. 11, he treats with the utmost contempt the opinion that our mental faculties depend, in some degree, upon the weather; an opinion, which they who have never experi-enced its truth are not to be envied, and of which he himself could not but be sensible, as the effects of weather upon him were very visible. Yet thus he declaims:—

'Surely, nothing is more reproachful to a being endowed with reason, than to resign its powers to the influence of the air, and live in dependence on the weather and the wind for the only blessings which nature has put into our power, tranquillity and benevolence. This distinction of seasons is produced only by imagination operating on luxury. To temperance, every day is bright; and every hour is propitious to diligence. He that shall resolutely excite his faculties, or exert his virtues, will soon make himself superiour to the seasons; and may set at defiance the morning mist and the evening damp, the blasts of the east, and the clouds of the south.'

Alas! it is too certain, that where the frame has delicate fibres, and there is a fine sensibility, such influences of the air are irresistible. He might as well have bid defiance to the ague, the palsy, and all other bodily disorders. Such boasting of the mind is false elevation.

'I think the Romans call it Stoicism.'

But in this number of his *Idler* his spirits seem to run riot; for in the wantonness of his disquisition he forgets, for a moment, even the reverence for that which he held in high respect; and describes 'the attendant on a *Court*,' as one 'whose business is to watch the looks of a being, weak and foolish as himself.'

His unqualified ridicule of rhetorical gesture or action is not, surely, a test of truth; yet we cannot help admiring how well it is adapted to produce the effect which he wished. 'Neither the judges of our laws, nor the representatives of our people, would be much affected by laboured gesticulation, or believe any man the more because he rolled his eyes, or puffed his cheeks, or spread abroad his arms, or stamped the ground, or thumped his breast; or turned his eyes sometimes to the ceiling, and sometimes to the floor.'

A casual coincidence with other writers, or an adoption of a sentiment or image which has been found in the writings of another, and afterwards appears in the mind as one's own, is not unfrequent. The richness of Johnson's fancy, which could supply his page abundantly on all occasions, and the strength of his memory, which at once detected the real owner of any thought, made him less liable to the imputation of plagiarism than, perhaps, any of our writers. In *The Idler*, however, there is a paper, in which conversation is assimilated to a bowl of punch, where there is the same train of comparison as in a poem by Blacklock, in his collection published in 1756, in which a parallel is ingeniously drawn between human life and that liquor. It ends,—

> 'Say, then, physicians of each kind,
> Who cure the body or the mind,
> What harm in drinking can there be,
> Since punch and life so well agree?'

To *The Idler*, when collected in volumes, he added, beside the

Essay on Epitaphs and the Dissertation on those of Pope, an Essay on the Bravery of the English common Soldiers. He, however, omitted one of the original papers, which in the folio copy is No. 22.[1]

'*To* The Reverend Mr. Thomas Warton

'Dear Sir,—Your notes upon my poet were very acceptable. I beg that you will be so kind as to continue your searches. It will be reputable to my work, and suitable to your professorship, to have something of yours in the notes. As you have given no directions about your name, I shall therefore put it. I wish your brother would take the same trouble. A commentary must arise from the fortuitous discoveries of many men in devious walks of literature. Some of your remarks are on plays already printed: but I purpose to add an Appendix of Notes, so that nothing comes too late.

'You give yourself too much uneasiness, dear Sir, about the loss of the papers.[2] The loss is nothing, if nobody has found them; nor even then, perhaps, if the numbers be known. You are not the only friend that has had the same mischance. You may repair your want out of a stock, which is deposited with Mr. Allen, of Magdalen-Hall; or out of a parcel which I have just sent to Mr. Chambers[3] for the use of any body that will be so kind as to want them. Mr. Langtons are well; and Miss Roberts, whom I have at last brought to speak, upon the information which you gave me, that she had something to say. I am, &c.

'[London,] April 14, 1758.'   'Sam. Johnson.'

To The Same

'Dear Sir,—You will receive this by Mr. Baretti, a gentleman particularly intitled to the notice and kindness of the Professor of poesy. He has time but for a short stay, and will be glad to have it filled up with as much as he can hear and see.

[1] This paper may be found in Stockdale's supplemental volume of Johnson's *Miscellaneous Pieces*.
[2] 'Receipts for *Shakspeare*.' Warton.
[3] 'Then of Lincoln College. Now Sir Robert Chambers, one of the Judges in India.' Warton.

'In recommending another to your favour, I ought not to omit thanks for the kindness which you have shewn to myself. Have you any more notes on Shakspeare? I shall be glad of them.

'I see your pupil sometimes:[1] his mind is as exalted as his stature. I am half afraid of him; but he is no less amiable than formidable. He will, if the forwardness of his spring be not blasted, be a credit to you, and to the University. He brings some of my plays[2] with him, which he has my permission to shew you, on condition you will hide them from every body else. I am, dear Sir, &c.

'[London,] June 1, 1758.'   'SAM. JOHNSON.'

'*To* BENNET LANGTON, ESQ., *of Trinity College, Oxford*

'DEAR SIR,—Though I might have expected to hear from you, upon your entrance into a new state of life at a new place, yet recollecting, (not without some degree of shame,) that I owe you a letter upon an old account, I think it my part to write first. This, indeed, I do not only from complaisance but from interest; for living on in the old way I am very glad of a correspondent so capable as yourself, to diversify the hours. You have, at present, too many novelties about you to need any help from me to drive along your time.

'I know not any thing more pleasant, or more instructive, than to compare experience with expectation, or to register from time to time the difference between idea and reality. It is by this kind of observation that we grow daily less liable to be disappointed. You, who are very capable of anticipating futurity, and raising phantoms before your own eyes, must often have imagined[3] to yourself an academical life, and have conceived what would be the manners, the views, and the conversation, of men devoted to letters; how they would choose their companions, how they would direct their studies, and how they would regulate their lives. Let me know what you expected, and what you have found. At least record it to yourself before custom has reconciled

[1] 'Mr. Langton.' WARTON.
[2] 'Part of the impression of the *Shakespeare*, which Dr. Johnson conducted alone, and published by subscription. This edition came out in 1765.' WARTON.   [3] [The MS. has *imaged.*]

you to the scenes before you, and the disparity of your discoveries to your hopes has vanished from your mind. It is rule never to be forgotten, that whatever strikes strongly, should be described while the first impression remains fresh upon the mind.

'I love, dear Sir, to think on you, and therefore, should willingly write more to you, but that the post will not now give me leave to do more than send my compliments to Mr. Warton, and tell you that I am, dear Sir, most affectionately, your very humble servant,

'June 27, 1758.'[1]   'SAM. JOHNSON.'

'*To* BENNET LANGTON, ESQ., *at Langton, near Spilsby, Lincolnshire*

'DEAR SIR,—I should be sorry to think that what engrosses the attention of my friend, should have no part of mine. Your mind is now full of the fate of Dury;[2] but his fate is past, and nothing remains but to try what reflection will suggest to mitigate the terrours of a violent death, which is more formidable at the first glance, than on a nearer and more steady view. A violent death is never very painful; the only danger is lest it should be unprovided. But if a man can be supposed to make no provision for death in war, what can be the state that would have awakened him to the care of futurity? When would that man have prepared himself to die, who went to seek death without preparation? What then can be the reason why we lament more him that dies of a wound, than him that dies of a fever? A man that languishes with disease, ends his life with more pain, but with less virtue; he leaves no example to his friends, nor bequeaths any honour to his descendants. The only reason why we lament a soldier's death, is, that we think he might have lived longer; yet this cause of grief is common to many other kinds of death which are not so passionately bewailed. The truth is, that every death is

---

[1] [1799 misprint *June* 28, 1757.]

[2] Major-General Alexander Dury, of the first regiment of foot-guards, who fell in the gallant discharge of his duty, near St. Cas, in the well-known unfortunate expedition against France, in 1758. His lady and Mr. Langton's mother were sisters. He left an only son, Lieutenant-Colonel Dury, who has a company in the same regiment.

violent which is the effect of accident; every death, which is not gradually brought on by the miseries of age, or when life is extinguished for any other reason than that it is burnt out. He that dies before sixty, of a cold or consumption, dies, in reality, by a violent death; yet his death is borne with patience only because the cause of his untimely end is silent and invisible. Let us endeavour to see things as they are, and then enquire whether we ought to complain. Whether to see life as it is, will give us much consolation, I know not; but the consolation which is drawn from truth, if any there be, is solid and durable; that which may be derived from errour must be, like its original, fallacious and fugitive. I am, dear, dear Sir, your most humble servant,

'Sept. 21, 1758.'   'SAM. JOHNSON.'

1759: ÆTAT. 50.]—IN 1759, in the month of January, his mother died at the great age of ninety, an event which deeply affected him; not that 'his mind had acquired no firmness by the contemplation of mortality;'[1] but that his reverential affection for her was not abated by years, as indeed he retained all his tender feelings even to the latest period of his life. I have been told that he regretted much his not having gone to visit his mother for several years, previous to her death. But he was constantly engaged in literary labours which confined him to London; and though he had not the comfort of seeing his aged parent, he contributed liberally to her support.

Soon after this event, he wrote his *Rasselas, Prince of Abyssinia*;* concerning the publication of which Sir John Hawkins guesses vaguely and idly, instead of having taken the trouble to inform himself with authentick precision. Not to trouble my readers with a repetition of the Knight's reveries, I have to mention, that the late Mr. Strahan the printer told me, that Johnson wrote it, that with the profits he might defray the expence of his mother's funeral, and pay some little debts which she had left. He told Sir Joshua Reynolds that he composed it in the evenings of one week, sent it to the press in portions as it was

[1] Hawkins's *Life of Johnson*, p. 365.

written, and had never since read it over.[1] Mr. Strahan, Mr.
Johnston, and Mr. Dodsley purchased it for a hundred pounds,
but afterwards paid him twenty-five pounds more, when it came
to a second edition.

Considering the large sums which have been received for
compilations, and works requiring not much more genius than
compilations, we cannot but wonder at the very low price which
he was content to receive for this admirable performance; which,
though he had written nothing else, would have rendered his
name immortal in the world of literature. None of his writings
has been so extensively diffused over Europe; for it has been
translated into most, if not all, of the modern languages. This
Tale, with all the charms of oriental imagery, and all the force
and beauty of which the English language is capable, leads us
through the most important scenes of human life, and shews us
that this stage of our being is full of 'vanity and vexation of
spirit.'[2] To those who look no further than the present life, or
who maintain that human nature has not fallen from the state in
which it was created, the instruction of this sublime story will be
of no avail. But they who think justly, and feel with strong sensibility, will listen with eagerness and admiration to its truth
and wisdom. Voltaire's *Candide*, written to refute the system of
Optimism, which it has accomplished with brilliant success, is
wonderfully similar in its plan and conduct to Johnson's *Rasselas*;
insomuch, that I have heard Johnson say, that if they had not
been published so closely one after the other that there was not
time for imitation, it would have been in vain to deny that the
scheme of that which came latest was taken from the other.
Though the proposition illustrated by both these works was the
same, namely, that in our present state there is more evil than
good, the intention of the writers was very different. Voltaire,
I am afraid, meant only by wanton profaneness to obtain a
sportive victory over religion, and to discredit the belief of a

---

[1] See *post*, June 2, 1781. Finding it then accidentally in a chaise with
Mr. Boswell, he read it eagerly. This was doubtless long after his declaration to Sir Joshua Reynolds. [M.]
[2] *Ecclesiastes*, i. 14.

superintending Providence: Johnson meant, by shewing the unsatisfactory nature of things temporal, to direct the hopes of man
to things eternal. *Rasselas,* as was observed to me by a very
accomplished lady,[1] may be considered as a more enlarged and
more deeply philosophical discourse in prose, upon the interesting truth, which in his *Vanity of Human Wishes* he had so successfully enforced in verse.

The fund of thinking which this work contains is such, that
almost every sentence of it may furnish a subject of long meditation. I am not satisfied if a year passes without my having read
it through; and at every perusal, my admiration of the mind
which produced it is so highly raised, that I can scarcely believe
that I had the honour of enjoying the intimacy of such a man.

I restrain myself from quoting passages from this excellent
work, or even referring to them, because I should not know
what to select, or rather, what to omit. I shall, however, transcribe one, as it shews how well he could state the arguments
of those who believe in the appearance of departed spirits; a
doctrine which it is a mistake to suppose that he himself ever
positively held:[2]

'If all your fear be of apparitions, (said the Prince,) I will
promise you safety: there is no danger from the dead; he that
is once buried will be seen no more.

'That the dead are seen no more, (said Imlac,) I will not
undertake to maintain, against the concurrent and unvaried testimony of all ages, and of all nations. There is no people, rude or
learned, among whom apparitions of the dead are not related and
believed. This opinion, which prevails as far as human nature is
diffused, could become universal only by its truth; those that
never heard of one another, would not have agreed in a tale
which nothing but experience can make credible. That it is
doubted by single cavillers, can very little weaken the general
evidence; and some who deny it with their tongues, confess it by
their fears.'

Notwithstanding my high admiration of *Rasselas,* I will not
maintain that the 'morbid melancholy' in Johnson's constitution

_____
[1] [*Mrs. Piozzi suggests* (1807) Mrs. Boswell.]   [2] See *ante,* p. 167 and
                                                             post, p. 287.

may not, perhaps, have made life appear to him more insipid and unhappy than it generally is; for I am sure that he had less enjoyment from it than I have. Yet, whatever additional shade his own particular sensations may have thrown on his representation of life, attentive observation and close inquiry have convinced me, that there is too much of reality in the gloomy picture. The truth, however, is, that we judge of the happiness and misery of life differently at different times, according to the state of our changeable frame. I always remember a remark made to me by a Turkish lady,[1] educated in France, '*Ma foi, Monsieur, notre bonheur dépend de la façon que notre sang circule.*' This have I learnt from a pretty hard course of experience, and would, from sincere benevolence, impress upon all who honour this book with a perusal, that until a steady conviction is obtained, that the present life is an imperfect state, and only a passage to a better, if we comply with the divine scheme of progressive improvement; and also that it is a part of the mysterious plan of Providence, that intellectual beings must 'be made perfect through suffering;' there will be a continual recurrence of disappointment and uneasiness. But if we walk with hope in 'the mid-day sun' of revelation, our temper and disposition will be such, that the comforts and enjoyments in our way will be relished, while we patiently support the inconveniences and pains. After much speculation and various reasonings, I acknowledge myself convinced of the truth of Voltaire's conclusion, '*Après tout c'est un monde passable.*' But we must not think too deeply;

'Where ignorance is bliss, 'tis folly to be wise,'

is, in many respects, more than poetically just. Let us cultivate, under the command of good principles, '*la théorie des sensations agréables;*' and, as Mr. Burke once admirably counselled a grave and anxious gentleman, 'live pleasant.'

The effect of *Rasselas*, and of Johnson's other moral tales, is thus beautifully illustrated by Mr. Courtenay:

'Impressive truth, in splendid fiction drest,
Checks the vain wish, and calms the troubled breast;

[1] [Mlle Emetulla, *Boswell's Letters*, i. 51.]

> O'er the dark mind a light celestial throws,
> And sooths the angry passions to repose;
> As oil effus'd illumes and smooths the deep,
> When round the bark the swelling surges sweep.'[1]

It will be recollected, that during all this year he carried on his *Idler*,[2] and, no doubt, was proceeding, though slowly, in his edition of *Shakspeare*. He, however, from that liberality which never failed, when called upon to assist other labourers in literature, found time to translate for Mrs. Lennox's English version of Brumoy, 'A Dissertation on the Greek Comedy,'† and 'The General Conclusion of the book.'†

An inquiry into the state of foreign countries was an object

---

[1] *Literary and Moral Character of Dr. Johnson.* 1786

[2] This paper was in such high estimation before it was collected into volumes, that it was seized on with avidity by various publishers of newspapers and magazines, to enrich their publications. Johnson, to put a stop to this unfair proceeding, wrote for the *Universal Chronicle* the following advertisement; in which there is, perhaps, more pomp of words than the occasion demanded:

'London, January 5, 1759. ADVERTISEMENT. The proprietors of the paper intitled *The Idler*, having found that those essays are inserted in the newspapers and magazines with so little regard to justice or decency, that the *Universal Chronicle*, in which they first appear, is not always mentioned, think it necessary to declare to the publishers of those collections, that however patiently they have hitherto endured these injuries, made yet more injurious by contempt, they have now determined to endure them no longer. They have already seen essays, for which a very large price is paid, transferred, with the most shameless rapacity, into the weekly or monthly compilations, and their right, at least for the present, alienated from them, before they could themselves be said to enjoy it. But they would not willingly be thought to want tenderness, even for men by whom no tenderness hath been shewn. The past is without remedy, and shall be without resentment. But those who have been thus busy with their sickles in the fields of their neighbours, are henceforward to take notice, that the time of impunity is at an end. Whoever shall, without our leave, lay the hand of rapine upon our papers, is to expect that we shall vindicate our due, by the means which justice prescribes, and which are warranted by the immemorial prescriptions of honourable trade. We shall lay hold, in our turn, on their copies, degrade them from the pomp of wide margin and diffuse typography, contract them into a narrow space, and sell them at an humble price; yet not with a view of growing rich by confiscations, for we think not much better of money got by punishment than by crimes. We shall, therefore, when our losses are repaid, give what profit shall remain to the *Magdalens*; for we know not who can be more properly taxed for the support of penitent prostitutes, than prostitutes in whom there yet appears neither penitence nor shame.'

that seems at all times to have interested Johnson. Hence Mr.
Newbery found no great difficulty in persuading him to write the
Introduction* to a collection of voyages and travels published
by him under the title of *The World Displayed*; the first volume
of which appeared this year, and the remaining volumes in subsequent years.

I would ascribe to this year the following letter to a son of one
of his early friends at Lichfield, Mr. Joseph Simpson, Barrister,
and authour of a tract entitled *Reflections on the Study of the Law*.

'*To* JOSEPH SIMPSON, ESQ.

'DEAR SIR,—Your father's inexorability not only grieves but
amazes me: he is your father; he was always accounted a wise
man; nor do I remember any thing to the disadvantage of his
good-nature; but in his refusal to assist you there is neither
good-nature, fatherhood, nor wisdom. It is the practice of good-
nature to overlook faults which have already, by the consequences, punished the delinquent. It is natural for a father to
think more favourably than others of his children; and it is
always wise to give assistance while a little help will prevent the
necessity of greater.

'If you married imprudently, you miscarried[1] at your own
hazard, at an age when you had a right of choice. It would be
hard if the man might not choose his own wife, who has a right
to plead before the Judges of his country.

'If your imprudence has ended in difficulties and inconveniences, you are yourself to support them; and, with the help
of a little better health, you would support them and conquer
them. Surely, that want which accident and sickness produces, is
to be supported in every region of humanity, though there were
neither friends nor fathers in the world. You have certainly from
your father the highest claim of charity, though none of right;
and therefore I would counsel you to omit no decent nor manly
degree of importunity. Your debts in the whole are not large,
and of the whole but a small part is troublesome. Small debts are
like small shot; they are rattling on every side, and can scarcely

[1] [*married* 1788.]

be escaped without a wound: great debts are like cannon; of
loud noise, but little danger. You must, therefore, be enabled
to discharge petty debts, that you may have leisure, with security,
to struggle with the rest. Neither the great nor little debts
disgrace you. I am sure you have my esteem for the courage
with which you contracted them, and the spirit with which you
endure them. I wish my esteem could be of more use. I have
been invited, or have invited myself, to several parts of the kingdom; and will not incommode my dear Lucy by coming to Lichfield, while her present lodging is of any use to her. I hope, in a
few days, to be at leisure, and to make visits. Whither I shall
fly is matter of no importance. A man unconnected is at home
every where; unless he may be said to be at home no where. I
am sorry, dear Sir, that where you have parents, a man of your
merits should not have an home. I wish I could give it you.
I am, my dear Sir, affectionately yours,

                                        'SAM. JOHNSON.'

He now refreshed himself by an excursion to Oxford, of which
the following short characteristical notice, in his own words, is
preserved:—

'* * *[1] is now making tea for me. I have been in my gown
ever since I came here. It was, at my first coming, quite new and
handsome. I have swum thrice, which I had disused for many
years. I have proposed to Vansittart,[2] climbing over the wall,
but he has refused me. And I have clapped my hands till they are
sore, at Dr. King's speech.'[3]

His negro servant, Francis Barber, having left him, and been
some time at sea, not pressed as has been supposed, but with his
own consent, it appears from a letter to John Wilkes, Esq., from
Dr. Smollet, that his master kindly interested himself in procuring his release from a state of life of which Johnson always
expressed the utmost abhorrence. He said, 'No man will be a
sailor who has contrivance enough to get himself into a jail; for

---

[1] [Perhaps 'Van', i.e. Robert Vansittart. *Hill.*]
[2] Dr. Robert Vansittart, of the ancient and respectable family of that
name in Berkshire. He was eminent for learning and worth, and much
esteemed by Dr. Johnson.   [3] *Gentleman's Magazine*, April, 1785.

being in a ship is being in a jail, with the chance of being drowned.'[1] And at another time, 'A man in a jail has more room, better food, and commonly better company.'[2] The letter was as follows:—

'DEAR SIR,   'Chelsea, March 16, 1759.

'I am again your petitioner, in behalf of that great CHAM[3] of literature, Samuel Johnson. His black servant, whose name is Francis Barber, has been pressed on board the Stag Frigate, Captain Angel, and our lexicographer is in great distress. He says the boy is a sickly lad, of a delicate frame, and particularly subject to a malady in his throat, which renders him very unfit for his Majesty's service. You know what manner of animosity the said Johnson has against you; and I dare say you desire no other opportunity of resenting it than that of laying him under an obligation. He was humble enough to desire my assistance on this occasion, though he and I were never cater-cousins; and I gave him to understand that I would make application to my friend Mr. Wilkes, who, perhaps, by his interest with Dr. Hay and Mr. Elliot, might be able to procure the discharge of his lacquey. It would be superfluous to say more on the subject, which I leave to your own consideration; but I cannot let slip this opportunity of declaring that I am, with the most inviolable esteem and attachment, dear Sir, your affectionate, obliged, humble servant,   'T. SMOLLET.'

[1] *Journal of a Tour to the Hebrides*, 3d edit. p. 126 [Aug. 31, 1773].
[2] *Ibid.* p. 251 [Sept. 23].
[3] In my first edition this word was printed *Chum*, as it appears in one of Mr. Wilkes's *Miscellanies*, and I animadverted on Dr. Smollet's ignorance; for which let me propitiate the *manes* of that ingenious and benevolent gentleman. CHUM was certainly a mistaken reading for *Cham*, the title of the Sovereign of Tartary, which is well applied to Johnson, the Monarch of Literature; and was an epithet familiar to Smollet. See *Roderick Random*, chap. 56. For this correction I am indebted to Lord Palmerston, whose talents and literary acquirements accord well with his respectable pedigree of TEMPLE. BOSWELL.—After the publication of the second edition of this work, the authour was furnished by Mr. Abercrombie, of Philadelphia, with the copy of a letter written by Dr. John Armstrong, the poet, to Dr. Smollet at Leghorne, containing the following paragraph:—'As to the K. Bench patriot, it is hard to say from what motive he published a letter of yours asking some trifling favour of him in behalf of somebody, for whom the great CHAM of literature, Mr. Johnson, had interested himself.' [M.]

Mr. Wilkes, who upon all occasions has acted, as a private gentleman, with most polite liberality, applied to his friend Sir George Hay, then one of the Lords Commissioners of the Admiralty; and Francis Barber was discharged, as he has told me, without any wish of his own. He found his old master in Chambers in the Inner Temple, and returned to his service.

What particular new scheme of life Johnson had in view this year, I have not discovered; but that he meditated one of some sort, is clear from his private devotions, in which we find,[1] 'the change of outward things which I am now to make;' and, 'Grant me the grace of thy Holy Spirit, that the course which I am now beginning may proceed according to thy laws, and end in the enjoyment of thy favour.' But he did not, in fact, make any external or visible change.

At this time, there being a competition among the architects of London to be employed in the building of Blackfriars-bridge, a question was very warmly agitated whether semicircular or elliptical arches were preferable. In the design offered by Mr. Mylne the elliptical form was adopted, and therefore it was the great object of his rivals to attack it. Johnson's regard for his friend Mr. Gwyn induced him to engage in this controversy against Mr. Mylne;[2] and after being at considerable pains to

[1] *Prayers and Meditations*, pp. 30 [39] and 40.

[2] Sir John Hawkins (*Life*, p. 373) has given a long detail of it, in that manner vulgarly, but significantly, called *rigmarole*; in which, amidst an ostentatious exhibition of arts and artists, he talks of 'proportions of a column being taken from that of the human figure, and *adjusted by Nature*—masculine and feminine—in a man, *sesquioctave* of the head, and in a woman *sesquinonal*;' nor has he failed to introduce a jargon of musical terms, which do not seem much to correspond with the subject, but serve to make up the heterogeneous mass. To follow the Knight through all this, would be an useless fatigue to myself, and not a little disgusting to my readers. I shall, therefore, only make a few remarks upon his statement.—He seems to exult in having detected Johnson in procuring 'from a person eminently skilled in Mathematicks and the principles of architecture, answers to a string of questions drawn up by himself, touching the comparative strength of semicircular and elliptical arches.' Now I cannot conceive how Johnson could have acted more wisely. Sir John complains that the opinion of that excellent mathematician, Mr. Thomas Simpson, did not preponderate in favour of the semicircular arch. But he should have known, that however eminent Mr. Simpson was in the higher parts of abstract mathematical science, he was little versed in mixed and practical mechanicks. Mr. Muller, of Woolwich

study the subject, he wrote three several letters in the *Gazetteer*, in opposition to his plan.

If it should be remarked that this was a controversy which lay quite out of Johnson's way, let it be remembered, that after all, his employing his powers of reasoning and eloquence upon a subject which he had studied on the moment, is not more strange than what we often observe in lawyers, who, as *Quicquid agunt homines* is the matter of law-suits, are sometimes obliged to pick up a temporary knowledge of an art or science, of which they understood nothing till their brief was delivered, and appear to be much masters of it. In like manner, members of the legislature frequently introduce and expatiate upon subjects of which they have informed themselves for the occasion.

1760: ÆTAT. 51.]—IN 1760 he wrote *An Address of the Painters to George III. on his Accession to the Throne of these Kingdoms,*† which no monarch ever ascended with more sincere

Academy, the scholastick father of all the great engineers which this country has employed for forty years, decided the question by declaring clearly in favour of the elliptical arch.

It is ungraciously suggested, that Johnson's motive for opposing Mr. Mylne's scheme may have been his prejudice against him as a native of North Britain; when, in truth, as has been stated, he gave the aid of his able pen to a friend, who was one of the candidates; and so far was he from having any illiberal antipathy to Mr. Mylne, that he afterwards lived with that gentleman upon very agreeable terms of acquaintance, and dined with him at his house. Sir John Hawkins, indeed, gives full vent to his own prejudice in abusing Blackfriars-bridge, calling it 'an edifice, in which beauty and symmetry are in vain sought for; by which the citizens of London have perpetuated their own disgrace, and subjected a whole nation to the reproach of foreigners.' Whoever has contemplated, *placido lumine* [Hor. *Odes* iv. 3. 2], this stately, elegant, and airy structure, which has so fine an effect, especially on approaching the capital on that quarter, must wonder at such unjust and ill-tempered censure; and I appeal to all foreigners of good taste, whether this bridge be not one of the most distinguished ornaments of London. As to the stability of the fabrick, it is certain that the City of London took every precaution to have the best Portland stone for it; but as this is to be found in the quarries belonging to the publick, under the direction of the Lords of the Treasury, it so happened that parliamentary interest, which is often the bane of fair pursuits, thwarted their endeavours. Notwithstanding this disadvantage, it is well known that not only has Blackfriars-bridge never sunk either in its foundation or in its arches, which were so much the subject of contest, but any injuries which it has suffered from the effects of severe frosts have been already, in some measure, repaired with sounder stone, and every necessary renewal can be completed at a moderate expence.

congratulations from his people. Two generations of foreign princes had prepared their minds to rejoice in having again a King, who gloried in being 'born a Briton.' He also wrote for Mr. Baretti the Dedication † of his *Italian and English Dictionary*, to the Marquis of Abreu, then Envoy-Extraordinary from Spain at the Court of Great Britain.

Johnson was now either very idle, or very busy with his *Shakspeare*; for I can find no other publick composition by him except an Introduction to the proceedings of the Committee for cloathing the French Prisoners;* one of the many proofs that he was ever awake to the calls of humanity; and an account which he gave in the *Gentleman's Magazine* of Mr. Tytler's acute and able vindication of Mary Queen of Scots.* The generosity of Johnson's feelings shines forth in the following sentence:—

'It has now been fashionable, for near half a century, to defame and vilify the house of Stuart, and to exalt and magnify the reign of Elizabeth. The Stuarts have found few apologists, for the dead cannot pay for praise; and who will, without reward, oppose the tide of popularity? Yet there remains still among us, not wholly extinguished, a zeal for truth, a desire of establishing right in opposition to fashion.'

In this year I have not discovered a single private letter written by him to any of his friends. It should seem, however, that he had at this period a floating intention of writing a history of the recent and wonderful successes of the British arms in all quarters of the globe; for among his resolutions or memorandums, September 18, there is, 'Send for books for Hist. of War.'[1] How much is it to be regretted that this intention was not fulfilled. His majestick expression would have carried down to the latest posterity the glorious achievements of his country with the same fervent glow which they produced on the mind at the time. He would have been under no temptation to deviate in any degree from truth, which he held very sacred, or to take a licence, which a learned divine[2] told me he once seemed, in a conversation, jocularly to allow to historians.

---

[1] *Prayers and Meditations*, p. 42.
[2] [Dr. Archibald Maclaine. *Isham Coll.* No. 4; *Boswell's proofs.*]

'There are (said he) inexcusable lies, and consecrated lies. For instance, we are told that on the arrival of the news of the unfortunate battle of Fontenoy, every heart beat, and every eye was in tears. Now we know that no man eat his dinner the worse, but there *should* have been all this concern; and to say there *was*, (smiling) may be reckoned a consecrated lie.'

This year Mr. Murphy, having thought himself ill-treated by the Reverend Dr. Francklin, who was one of the writers of *The Critical Review*, published an indignant vindication in *A Poetical Epistle to Samuel Johnson, A.M.* in which he compliments Johnson in a just and elegant manner:

> 'Transcendant Genius! whose prolifick vein
> Ne'er knew the frigid poet's toil and pain;
> To whom APOLLO opens all his store,
> And every Muse presents her sacred lore;
> Say, pow'rful JOHNSON, whence thy verse is fraught
> With so much grace, such energy of thought;
> Whether thy JUVENAL instructs the age
> In chaster numbers, and new-points his rage;
> Or fair IRENE sees, alas! too late
> Her innocence exchang'd for guilty state;
> Whate'er you write, in every golden line
> Sublimity and elegance combine;
> Thy nervous phrase impresses every soul,
> While harmony gives rapture to the whole.'

Again, towards the conclusion:

> 'Thou then, my friend, who see'st the dang'rous strife
> In which some demon bids me plunge my life,
> To the Aonian fount direct my feet,
> Say where the Nine thy lonely musings meet?
> Where warbles to thy ear the sacred throng,
> Thy moral sense, thy dignity of song?
> Tell, for you can, by what unerring art
> You wake to finer feelings every heart;
> In each bright page some truth important give,
> And bid to future times thy RAMBLER live.'

I take this opportunity to relate the manner in which an acquaintance first commenced between Dr. Johnson and Mr.

Murphy. During the publication of *The Gray's-Inn Journal*, a
periodical paper which was successfully carried on by Mr.
Murphy alone, when a very young man, he happened to be in
the country with Mr. Foote; and having mentioned that he was
obliged to go to London in order to get ready for the press one
of the numbers of that *Journal*, Foote said to him, 'You need not
go on that account. Here is a French magazine, in which you will
find a very pretty oriental tale; translate that, and send it to
your printer.' Mr. Murphy having read the tale, was highly
pleased with it, and followed Foote's advice. When he returned
to town, this tale was pointed out to him in *The Rambler*, from
whence it had been translated into the French magazine. Mr.
Murphy then waited upon Johnson, to explain this curious
incident. His talents, literature, and gentleman-like manners,
were soon perceived by Johnson, and a friendship was formed
which was never broken.[1]

'*To* BENNET LANGTON, Esq., *at Langton, near Spilsby, Lincolnshire*

'DEAR SIR,—You that travel about the world, have more
materials for letters, than I who stay at home; and should, therefore, write with frequency equal to your opportunities. I should
be glad to have all England surveyed by you, if you would
impart your observations in narratives as agreeable as your last.
Knowledge is always to be wished to those who can communicate
it well. While you have been riding and running, and seeing the
tombs of the learned, and the camps of the valiant, I have only
staid at home, and intended to do great things, which I have not
done. Beau[2] went away to Cheshire, and has not yet found his
way back. Chambers passed the vacation at Oxford.

'I am very sincerely solicitous for the preservation or curing[3]
of Mr. Langton's sight, and am glad that the chirurgeon at
Coventry gives him so much hope. Mr. Sharpe is of opinion that

[1] The paper mentioned in the text is No. 38 of the second series of the
Gray's-Inn Journal, published on June 15, 1754; which is a translation from
the French version of Johnson's *Rambler*, No. 190. [M.]
[2] Topham Beauclerk, Esq.
[3] [The original has *recovery*.]

the tedious maturation of the cataract is a vulgar errour, and that it may be removed as soon as it is formed. This notion deserves to be considered; I doubt whether it be universally true; but if it be true in some cases, and those cases can be distinguished, it may save a long and uncomfortable delay.

'Of dear Mrs. Langton you give me no account; which is the less friendly, as you know how highly I think of her, and how much I interest myself in her health. I suppose you told her of my opinion, and likewise suppose it was not followed; however, I still believe it to be right.

'Let me hear from you again, wherever you are, or whatever you are doing; whether you wander or sit still, plant trees or make *Rusticks*,[1] play with your sisters or muse alone; and in return I will tell you the success of Sheridan, who at this instant is playing Cato, and has already played Richard twice. He had more company the second than the first night, and will make, I believe, a good figure in the whole, though his faults seem to be very many; some of natural deficience, and some of laborious affectation. He has, I think, no power of assuming either that dignity or elegance which some men, who have little of either in common life, can exhibit on the stage. His voice when strained is unpleasing, and when low is not always heard. He seems to think too much on the audience, and turns his face too often to the galleries.

'However, I wish him well; and among other reasons, because I like his wife.[2] Make haste to write to, dear Sir, your most affectionate servant,

'Oct. 18, 1760.'   'SAM. JOHNSON.'

1761: ÆTAT. 52.]—IN 1761 Johnson appears to have done little. He was still, no doubt, proceeding in his edition of *Shakspeare*; but what advances he made in it cannot be ascertained. He certainly was at this time not active; for in his scrupulous

[1] Essays with that title, written about this time by Mr. Langton, but not published.
[2] Mrs. Sheridan was authour of *Memoirs of Miss Sydney Biddulph*, a novel of great merit, and of some other pieces.—See her character, *post*, beginning of 1763, pp. 275–6.

examination of himself on Easter eve, he laments, in his too rigorous mode of censuring his own conduct, that his life, since the communion of the preceding Easter, had been 'dissipated and useless.'[1] He, however, contributed this year the Preface* to Rolt's *Dictionary of Trade and Commerce*, in which he displays such a clear and comprehensive knowledge of the subject, as might lead the reader to think that its authour had devoted all his life to it. I asked him whether he knew much of Rolt, and of his work. 'Sir, (said he) I never saw the man, and never read the book. The booksellers wanted a Preface to a *Dictionary of Trade and Commerce.* I knew very well what such a Dictionary should be, and I wrote a Preface accordingly.' Rolt, who wrote a great deal for the booksellers, was, as Johnson told me, a singular character. Though not in the least acquainted with him, he used to say, 'I am just come from Sam. Johnson.' This was a sufficient specimen of his vanity and impudence. But he gave a more eminent proof of it in our sister kingdom, as Dr. Johnson informed me. When Akenside's *Pleasures of the Imagination* first came out, he did not put his name to the poem. Rolt went over to Dublin, published an edition of it, and put his own name to it. Upon the fame of this he lived for several months, being entertained at the best tables as 'the ingenious Mr. Rolt.'[2] His conversation, indeed, did not discover much of the fire of a poet; but it was recollected, that both Addison and Thomson were equally dull till excited by wine. Akenside having been informed of this imposition, vindicated his right by publishing the poem with its real authour's name. Several instances of such literary fraud have been detected. The Reverend Dr. Campbell, of St. Andrew's, wrote *An Enquiry into the original of Moral Virtue*, the manuscript of which he sent to Mr. Innes, a clergyman in England, who was his countryman and acquaintance. Innes pub-

[1] *Prayers and Meditations*, p. 44.

[2] I have had inquiry made in Ireland as to this story, but do not find it recollected there. I give it on the authority of Dr. Johnson, to which may be added that of the *Biographical Dictionary*, and *Biographia Dramatica*; in both of which it has stood many years. Mr. Malone observes, that the truth probably is, not that an edition was published with Rolt's name in the title-page, but, that the poem being then anonymous, Rolt acquiesced in its being attributed to him in conversation.

lished it with his own name to it; and before the imposition was
discovered, obtained considerable promotion, as a reward of his
merit.[1] The celebrated Dr. Hugh Blair, and his cousin Mr.
George Bannatine, when students in divinity, wrote a poem,
entitled, *The Resurrection*, copies of which were handed about in
manuscript. They were, at length, very much surprised to see a
pompous edition of it in folio, dedicated to the Princess Dowager
of Wales, by a Dr. Douglas, as his own. Some years ago a little
novel, entitled *The Man of Feeling*, was assumed by Mr. Eccles,
a young Irish clergyman, who was afterwards drowned near
Bath. He had been at the pains to transcribe the whole book,
with blottings, interlineations, and corrections, that it might be
shewn to several people as an original. It was, in truth, the production of Mr. Henry Mackenzie, an Attorney in the Exchequer
at Edinburgh, who is the authour of several other ingenious
pieces; but the belief with regard to Mr. Eccles became so
general, that it was thought necessary for Messieurs Strahan
and Cadell to publish an advertisement in the news-papers, contradicting the report, and mentioning that they purchased the
copyright of Mr. Mackenzie. I can conceive this kind of fraud
to be very easily practised with successful effrontery. The *Filiation* of a literary performance is difficult of proof; seldom is there
any witness present at its birth. A man, either in confidence or by
improper means, obtains possession of a copy of it in manuscript,
and boldly publishes it as his own. The true authour, in many
cases, may not be able to make his title clear. Johnson, indeed,
from the peculiar features of his literary offspring, might bid
defiance to any attempt to appropriate them to others.

> 'But Shakspeare's magick could not copied be,
> Within that circle none durst walk but he!'

He this year lent his friendly assistance to correct and improve
a pamphlet written by Mr. Gwyn, the architect, entitled, *Thoughts
on the Coronation of George III.**

Johnson had now for some years admitted Mr. Baretti to his

---

[1] I have both the books. Innes was the clergyman who brought Psalmanazar to England, and was an accomplice in his extraordinary fiction.

intimacy; nor did their friendship cease upon their being separated by Baretti's revisiting his native country, as appears from Johnson's letters to him.

'To MR. JOSEPH BARETTI, *at Milan*[1]

'You reproach me very often with parsimony of writing: but you may discover by the extent of my paper, that I design to recompence rarity by length. A short letter to a distant friend is, in my opinion, an insult like that of a slight bow or cursory salutation;—a proof of unwillingness to do much, even where there is a necessity of doing something. Yet it must be remembered, that he who continues the same course of life in the same place, will have little to tell. One week and one year are very like another. The silent changes made by time are not always perceived; and if they are not perceived, cannot be recounted. I have risen and lain down, talked and mused, while you have roved over a considerable part of Europe; yet I have not envied my Baretti any of his pleasures, though, perhaps, I have envied others his company: and I am glad to have other nations made acquainted with the character of the English, by a traveller who has so nicely inspected our manners, and so successfully studied our literature. I received your kind letter from Falmouth, in which you gave me notice of your departure for Lisbon, and another from Lisbon, in which you told me, that you were to leave Portugal in a few days. To either of these how could any answer be returned? I have had a third from Turin, complaining that I have not answered the former. Your English style still continues in its purity and vigour. With vigour your genius will supply it; but its purity must be continued by close attention. To use two languages familiarly, and without contaminating one by the other, is very difficult: and to use more than two is hardly to be hoped. The praises which some have received for their multiplicity of languages, may be sufficient to excite industry, but can hardly generate confidence.

[1] The originals of Dr. Johnson's three letters to Mr. Baretti, which are among the very best he ever wrote, were communicated to the proprietors of that instructive and elegant monthly miscellany, *The European Magazine*, in which they first appeared.

'I know not whether I can heartily rejoice at the kind reception which you have found, or at the popularity to which you are exalted. I am willing that your merit should be distinguished; but cannot wish that your affections may be gained. I would have you happy wherever you are: yet I would have you wish to return to England. If ever you visit us again, you will find the kindness of your friends undiminished. To tell you how many enquiries are made after you, would be tedious, or if not tedious, would be vain; because you may be told in a very few words, that all who knew you wish you well; and all that you embraced at your departure, will caress you at your return: therefore do not let Italian academicians nor Italian ladies drive us from your thoughts. You may find among us what you will leave behind, soft smiles and easy sonnets. Yet I shall not wonder if all our invitations should be rejected: for there is a pleasure in being considerable at home, which is not easily resisted.

'By conducting Mr. Southwell to Venice, you fulfilled, I know, the original contract: yet I would wish you not wholly to lose him from your notice, but to recommend him to such acquaintance as may best secure him from suffering by his own follies, and to take such general care both of his safety and his interest as may come within your power. His relations will thank you for any such gratuitous attention: at least they will not blame you for any evil that may happen, whether they thank you or not for any good.

'You know that we have a new King and a new Parliament. Of the new Parliament Fitzherbert is a member. We were so weary of our old King, that we are much pleased with his successor; of whom we are so much inclined to hope great things, that most of us begin already to believe them. The young man is hitherto blameless; but it would be unreasonable to expect much from the immaturity of juvenile years, and the ignorance of princely education. He has been long in the hands of the Scots, and has already favoured them more than the English will contentedly endure. But, perhaps, he scarcely knows whom he has distinguished, or whom he has disgusted.

'The Artists have instituted a yearly Exhibition of pictures and statues, in imitation, as I am told, of foreign academies. This year was the second Exhibition. They please themselves much with the multitude of spectators, and imagine that the English School will rise in reputation. Reynolds is without a rival, and continues to add thousands to thousands, which he deserves, among other excellencies, by retaining his kindness for Baretti. This Exhibition has filled the heads of the Artists and lovers of art. Surely life, if it be not long, is tedious, since we are forced to call in the assistance of so many trifles to rid us of our time, of that time which never can return.

'I know my Baretti will not be satisfied with a letter in which I give him no account of myself: yet what account shall I give him? I have not, since the day of our separation, suffered or done any thing considerable. The only change in my way of life is, that I have frequented the theatre more than in former seasons. But I have gone thither only to escape from myself. We have had many new farces, and the comedy called *The Jealous Wife*, which, though not written with much genius, was yet so well adapted to the stage, and so well exhibited by the actors, that it was crowded for near twenty nights. I am digressing from myself to the play-house; but a barren plan must be filled with episodes. Of myself I have nothing to say, but that I have hitherto lived without the concurrence of my own judgment; yet I continue to flatter myself, that, when you return, you will find me mended. I do not wonder that, where the monastick life is permitted, every order finds votaries, and every monastery inhabitants. Men will submit to any rule, by which they may be exempted from the tyranny of caprice and of chance. They are glad to supply by external authority their own want of constancy and resolution, and court the government of others, when long experience has convinced them of their own inability to govern themselves. If I were to visit Italy, my curiosity would be more attracted by convents than by palaces: though I am afraid that I should find expectation in both places equally disappointed, and life in both places supported with impatience and quitted with reluctance. That it must be so soon quitted, is a powerful remedy against impatience; but what shall free us from reluctance? Those who have endeavoured to teach us to die well, have taught few to die willingly: yet I cannot but hope that a good life might end at last in a contented death.

'You see to what a train of thought I am drawn by the mention of myself. Let me now turn my attention upon you. I hope you take care to keep an exact journal, and to register all occurrences and observations; for your friends here expect such a book of travels as has not been often seen. You have given us good specimens in your letters from Lisbon. I wish you had staid longer in Spain, for no country is less known to the rest of Europe; but the quickness of your discernment must make amends for the celerity of your motions. He that knows which way to direct his view, sees much in a little time.

'Write to me very often, and I will not neglect to write to you; and I may, perhaps, in time, get something to write: at least, you will know by my letters, whatever else they may have or want, that I continue to be your most affectionate friend,

'London, June 10, 1761.'   'SAM. JOHNSON.'

1762: ÆTAT. 53.]—IN 1762 he wrote for the Reverend Dr. Kennedy, Rector of Bradley in Derbyshire, in a strain of very courtly elegance, a Dedication to the King * of that gentleman's work, entitled, *A complete System of Astronomical Chronology, unfolding the Scriptures.* He had certainly looked at this work before it was printed; for the concluding paragraph is undoubtedly of his composition, of which let my readers judge:

'Thus have I endeavoured to free Religion and History from the darkness of a disputed and uncertain chronology; from difficulties which have hitherto appeared insuperable, and darkness which no luminary of learning has hitherto been able to dissipate. I have established the truth of the Mosaical account, by evidence which no transcription can corrupt, no negligence can lose, and no interest can pervert. I have shewn that the universe bears witness to the inspiration of its historian, by the revolution of its orbs and the succession of its seasons; *that the stars in their courses fight against* incredulity, that the works of GOD give hourly confirmation to the *law*, the *prophets*, and the *gospel*, of which *one day telleth another, and one night certifieth another*; and that the validity of the sacred writings can never be denied, while the moon shall increase and wane, and the sun shall know his going down.'

He this year wrote also the Dedication † to the Earl of Middle-sex of Mrs. Lennox's *Female Quixote*, and the Preface to the *Catalogue of the Artists' Exhibition*.†

The following letter, which, on account of its intrinsick merit, it would have been unjust both to Johnson and the publick to have with-held, was obtained for me by the solicitation of my friend Mr. Seward:

'*To* DR. STAUNTON, (*now Sir George Staunton, Baronet.*)

'DEAR SIR,—I make haste to answer your kind letter, in hope of hearing again from you before you leave us. I cannot but regret that a man of your qualifications should find it necessary to seek an establishment in Guadaloupe, which if a peace should restore to the French, I shall think it some alleviation of the loss, that it must restore likewise Dr. Staunton to the English.

'It is a melancholy consideration, that so much of our time is necessarily to be spent upon the care of living, and that we can seldom obtain ease in one respect but by resigning it in another; yet I suppose we are by this dispensation not less happy in the whole, than if the spontaneous bounty of Nature poured all that we want into our hands. A few, if they were thus left to themselves, would, perhaps, spend their time in laudable pursuits; but the greater part would prey upon the quiet of each other, or, in the want of other objects, would prey upon themselves.

'This, however, is our condition, which we must improve and solace as we can: and though we cannot choose always our place of residence, we may in every place find rational amusements, and possess in every place the comforts of piety and a pure conscience.

'In America there is little to be observed except natural curiosities. The new world must have many vegetables and animals with which philosophers are but little acquainted. I hope you will furnish yourself with some books of natural history, and some glasses and other instruments of observation. Trust as little as you can to report; examine all you can by your own senses. I do not doubt but you will be able to add much to knowledge, and, perhaps, to medicine. Wild nations trust to simples; and, perhaps, the Peruvian bark is not the only specifick which those extensive regions may afford us.

'Wherever you are, and whatever be your fortune, be certain, dear Sir, that you carry with you my kind wishes; and that whether you return hither, or stay in the other hemisphere, to hear that you are happy will give pleasure to, Sir, your most affectionate humble servant,

'June 1, 1762.'   'SAM. JOHNSON.'

A lady having at this time solicited him to obtain the Archbishop of Canterbury's patronage to have her son sent to the University, one of those solicitations which are too frequent, where people, anxious for a particular object, do not consider propriety, or the opportunity which the persons whom they solicit have to assist them, he wrote to her the following answer, with a copy of which I am favoured by the Reverend Dr. Farmer, Master of Emanuel College, Cambridge.

'MADAM,—I hope you will believe that my delay in answering your letter could proceed only from my unwillingness to destroy any hope that you had formed. Hope is itself a species of happiness, and, perhaps, the chief happiness which this world affords: but, like all other pleasures immoderately enjoyed, the excesses of hope must be expiated by pain; and expectations improperly indulged, must end in disappointment. If it be asked, what is the improper expectation which it is dangerous to indulge, experience will quickly answer, that it is such expectation as is dictated not by reason, but by desire; expectation raised, not by the common occurrences of life, but by the wants of the expectant; an expectation that requires the common course of things to be changed, and the general rules of action to be broken.

'When you made your request to me, you should have considered, Madam, what you were asking. You ask me to solicit a great man, to whom I never spoke, for a young person whom I had never seen, upon a supposition which I had no means of knowing to be true. There is no reason why, amongst all the great, I should chuse to supplicate the Archbishop, nor why, among all the possible objects of his bounty, the Archbishop should chuse your son. I know, Madam, how unwillingly conviction is admitted, when interest opposes it; but surely, Madam, you must allow, that there is no reason why that should be done by me, which every other man may do with equal reason, and which, indeed no man can do properly, without some very particular relation both to the Archbishop and to you. If I could help you in this exigence by any proper means, it would give me pleasure; but this proposal is so very remote from all usual methods, that I cannot comply with it, but at the risk of such answer and suspicions as I believe you do not wish me to undergo.

'I have seen your son this morning; he seems a pretty youth, and will, perhaps, find some better friend than I can procure him; but, though he should at last miss the University, he may still be wise, useful, and happy. I am, Madam, your most humble servant,

'June 8, 1762.'   'SAM. JOHNSON.'

'*To* MR. JOSEPH BARETTI, *at Milan*

'SIR,   'London, July 20, 1762.

'However justly you may accuse me for want of punctuality in correspondence, I am not so far lost in negligence as to omit the opportunity of writing to you, which Mr. Beauclerk's passage through Milan affords me.

'I suppose you received the *Idlers*, and I intend that you shall soon receive *Shakspeare*, that you may explain his works to the ladies of Italy, and tell them the story of the editor, among the other strange narratives with which your long residence in this unknown region has supplied you.

'As you have now been long away, I suppose your curiosity may pant for some news of your old friends. Miss Williams and I live much as we did. Miss Cotterel still continues to cling to Mrs. Porter, and Charlotte is now big of the fourth child. Mr.

Reynolds gets six thousands a year. Levet is lately married, not
without much suspicion that he has been wretchedly cheated in
his match. Mr. Chambers is gone this day, for the first time, the
circuit with the Judges. Mr. Richardson is dead of an apoplexy,
and his second daughter has married a merchant.

'My vanity, or my kindness, makes me flatter myself, that you
would rather hear of me than of those whom I have mentioned;
but of myself I have very little which I care to tell. Last winter
I went down to my native town, where I found the streets much
narrower and shorter than I thought I had left them, inhabited
by a new race of people, to whom I was very little known. My
play-fellows were grown old, and forced me to suspect that I was
no longer young. My only remaining friend has changed his
principles, and was become the tool of the predominant faction.
My daughter-in-law, from whom I expected most, and whom I
met with sincere benevolence, has lost the beauty and gaiety
of youth, without having gained much of the wisdom of age.
I wandered about for five days, and took the first convenient
opportunity of returning to a place, where, if there is not much
happiness, there is, at least, such a diversity of good and evil,
that slight vexations do not fix upon the heart.[1]

'I think in a few weeks to try another excursion; though to
what end? Let me know, my Baretti, what has been the result of
your return to your own country: whether time has made any
alteration for the better, and whether, when the first raptures of
salutation were over, you did not find your thoughts confessed
their disappointment.

'Moral sentences appear ostentatious and tumid, when they
have no greater occasions than the journey of a wit to his own
town: yet such pleasures and such pains make up the general
mass of life; and as nothing is little to him that feels it with
great sensibility, a mind able to see common incidents in their
real state, is disposed by very common incidents to very serious
contemplations. Let us trust that a time will come, when the
present moment shall be no longer irksome; when we shall not

[1] This is a very just account of the relief which London affords to
melancholy minds.

borrow all our happiness from hope, which at last is to end in disappointment.

'I beg that you will shew Mr. Beauclerk all the civilities which you have in your power; for he has always been kind to me.

'I have lately seen Mr. Stratico, Professor of Padua, who has told me of your quarrel with an Abbot of the Celestine order; but had not the particulars very ready in his memory. When you write to Mr. Marsili, let him know that I remember him with kindness.

'May you, my Baretti, be very happy at Milan, or some other place nearer to, Sir, your most affectionate humble servant,

'SAM. JOHNSON.'

The accession of George the Third to the throne of these kingdoms, opened a new and brighter prospect to men of literary merit, who had been honoured with no mark of royal favour in the preceding reign. His present Majesty's education in this country, as well as his taste and beneficence, prompted him to be the patron of science and the arts; and early this year Johnson, having been represented to him as a very learned and good man, without any certain provision, his Majesty was pleased to grant him a pension of three hundred pounds a year. The Earl of Bute, who was then Prime Minister, had the honour to announce this instance of his Sovereign's bounty, concerning which many and various stories, all equally erroneous, have been propagated: maliciously representing it as a political bribe to Johnson, to desert his avowed principles, and become the tool of a government which he held to be founded in usurpation. I have taken care to have it in my power to refute them from the most authentick information. Lord Bute told me, that Mr. Wedderburne, now Lord Loughborough, was the person who first mentioned this subject to him. Lord Loughborough told me, that the pension was granted to Johnson solely as the reward of his literary merit, without any stipulation whatever, or even tacit understanding that he should write for administration. His Lordship added, that he was confident the political tracts which Johnson afterwards did write, as they were entirely consonant with his own opinions, would have been written by him though no pension had been granted to him.

Mr. Thomas Sheridan and Mr. Murphy, who then lived a good deal both with him and Mr. Wedderburne, told me, that they previously talked with Johnson upon this matter, and that it was perfectly understood by all parties that the pension was merely honorary. Sir Joshua Reynolds told me, that Johnson called on him after his Majesty's intention had been notified to him, and said he wished to consult his friends as to the propriety of his accepting this mark of the royal favour, after the definitions which he had given in his *Dictionary* of *pension* and *pensioners*. He said he would not have Sir Joshua's answer till next day, when he would call again, and desired he might think of it. Sir Joshua answered that he was clear to give his opinion then, that there could be no objection to his receiving from the King a reward for literary merit; and that certainly the definitions in his *Dictionary* were not applicable to him. Johnson, it should seem, was satisfied, for he did not call again till he had accepted the pension, and had waited on Lord Bute to thank him. He then told Sir Joshua that Lord Bute said to him expressly, 'It is not given you for anything you are to do, but for what you have done.' His Lordship, he said, behaved in the handsomest manner. He repeated the words twice, that he might be sure Johnson heard them, and thus set his mind perfectly at ease. This nobleman, who has been so virulently abused, acted with great honour in this instance, and displayed a mind truly liberal. A minister of a more narrow and selfish disposition would have availed himself of such an opportunity to fix an implied obligation on a man of Johnson's powerful talents to give him his support.

Mr. Murphy and the late Mr. Sheridan severally contended for the distinction of having been the first who mentioned to Mr. Wedderburne that Johnson ought to have a pension. When I spoke of this to Lord Loughborough, wishing to know if he recollected the prime mover in the business, he said, 'All his friends assisted:' and when I told him that Mr. Sheridan strenuously asserted his claim to it, his Lordship said, 'He rang the bell.' And it is but just to add, that Mr. Sheridan told me, that

when he communicated to Dr. Johnson that a pension was to be
granted him, he replied, in a fervour of gratitude, 'The English
language does not afford me terms adequate to my feelings on
this occasion. I must have recourse to the French. I am *pénétré*
with his Majesty's goodness.' When I repeated this to Dr. Johnson, he did not contradict it.

His definitions of *pension* and *pensioner*, partly founded on the
satirical verses of Pope, which he quotes, may be generally true;
and yet every body must allow, that there may be, and have
been, instances of pensions given and received upon liberal and
honourable terms. Thus, then, it is clear, that there was nothing
inconsistent or humiliating in Johnson's accepting of a pension
so unconditionally and so honourably offered to him.

But I shall not detain my readers longer by any words of my
own, on a subject on which I am happily enabled, by the favour
of the Earl of Bute, to present them with what Johnson himself
wrote; his lordship having been pleased to communicate to me
a copy of the following letter to his late father, which does great
honour both to the writer, and to the noble person to whom it is
addressed:

'*To* THE RIGHT HONOURABLE THE EARL OF BUTE

'MY LORD,—When the bills were yesterday delivered to me
by Mr. Wedderburne, I was informed by him of the future
favours which his Majesty has, by your Lordship's recommendation, been induced to intend for me.

'Bounty always receives part of its value from the manner in
which it is bestowed; your Lordship's kindness includes every
circumstance that can gratify delicacy, or enforce obligation. You
have conferred your favours on a man who has neither alliance
nor interest, who has not merited them by services, nor courted
them by officiousness; you have spared him the shame of solicitation, and the anxiety of suspense.

'What has been thus elegantly given, will, I hope, not be
reproachfully enjoyed; I shall endeavour to give your Lordship
the only recompense which generosity desires,—the gratification of finding that your benefits are not improperly bestowed.

I am, my Lord, your Lordship's most obliged, most obedient,
and most humble servant,
   'July 20, 1762.'   'SAM. JOHNSON.'

This year his friend Sir Joshua Reynolds paid a visit of some
weeks to his native county, Devonshire, in which he was accompanied by Johnson, who was much pleased with this jaunt, and
declared he had derived from it a great accession of new ideas.
He was entertained at the seats of several noblemen and gentlemen in the West of England;[1] but the greatest part of the time
was passed at Plymouth, where the magnificence of the navy,
the ship-building and all its circumstances, afforded him a grand
subject of contemplation. The Commissioner of the Dock-yard[2]
paid him the compliment of ordering the yacht to convey him
and his friend to the Eddystone, to which they accordingly sailed.
But the weather was so tempestuous that they could not land.

Reynolds and he were at this time the guests of Dr. Mudge,
the celebrated surgeon, and now physician of that place, not more
distinguished for quickness of parts and variety of knowledge,
than loved and esteemed for his amiable manners; and here
Johnson formed an acquaintance with Dr. Mudge's father, that
very eminent divine, the Reverend Zachariah Mudge, Prebendary of Exeter, who was idolised in the west, both for his excellence as a preacher and the uniform perfect propriety of his private
conduct. He preached a sermon purposely that Johnson might
hear him; and we shall see afterwards that Johnson honoured
his memory by drawing his character. While Johnson was at
Plymouth, he saw a great many of its inhabitants, and was
not sparing of his very entertaining conversation. It was here
that he made that frank and truly original confession, that
'ignorance, pure ignorance,' was the cause of a wrong definition

---

[1] At one of these seats Dr. Amyat, Physician in London, told me he
happened to meet him. In order to amuse him till dinner should be ready,
he was taken out to walk in the garden. The master of the house, thinking
it proper to introduce something scientific into the conversation, addressed
him thus: 'Are you a botanist, Dr. Johnson?' 'No, Sir, (answered Johnson,)
I am not a botanist; and, (alluding, no doubt, to his near sightedness)
should I wish to become a botanist, I must first turn myself into a reptile.'

[2] [Sir Frederick Rogers. *Dr. John Edgcombe*.]

in his *Dictionary* of the word *pastern*,[1] to the no small surprise of the Lady who put the question to him; who having the most profound reverence for his character, so as almost to suppose him endowed with infallibility, expected to hear an explanation (of what, to be sure, seemed strange to a common reader,) drawn from some deep-learned source with which she was unacquainted.

Sir Joshua Reynolds, to whom I was obliged for my information concerning this excursion, mentions a very characteristical anecdote of Johnson while at Plymouth. Having observed that in consequence of the Dock-yard a new town had arisen about two miles off as a rival to the old; and knowing from his sagacity, and just observation of human nature, that it is certain if a man hates at all, he will hate his next neighbour; he concluded that this new and rising town could not but excite the envy and jealousy of the old, in which conjecture he was very soon confirmed; he therefore set himself resolutely on the side of the old town, the *established* town, in which his lot was cast, considering it as a kind of duty to *stand by* it. He accordingly entered warmly into its interests, and upon every occasion talked of the *dockers*, as the inhabitants of the new town were called, as upstarts and aliens. Plymouth is very plentifully supplied with water by a river brought into it from a great distance, which is so abundant that it runs to waste in the town. The Dock, or New-town, being totally destitute of water, petitioned Plymouth that a small portion of the conduit might be permitted to go to them, and this was now under consideration. Johnson, affecting to entertain the passions of the place, was violent in opposition; and, half-laughing at himself for his pretended zeal where he had no concern, exclaimed, 'No, no! I am against the *dockers*; I am a Plymouth man. Rogues! let them die of thirst. They shall not have a drop!'

Lord Macartney obligingly favoured me with a copy of the following letter, in his own hand-writing, from the original, which was found, by the present Earl of Bute, among his father's papers.

[1] See *ante*, p. 211.

'*To* THE RIGHT HONOURABLE THE EARL OF BUTE

'MY LORD,—That generosity, by which I was recommended to the favour of his Majesty, will not be offended at a solicitation necessary to make that favour permanent and effectual.

'The pension appointed to be paid me at Michaelmas I have not received, and know not where or from whom I am to ask it. I beg, therefore, that your Lordship will be pleased to supply Mr. Wedderburne with such directions as may be necessary, which, I believe, his friendship will make him think it no trouble to convey to me.

'To interrupt your Lordship, at a time like this, with such petty difficulties, is improper and unseasonable; but your knowledge of the world has long since taught you, that every man's affairs, however little, are important to himself. Every man hopes that he shall escape neglect; and, with reason, may every man, whose vices do not preclude his claim, expect favour from that beneficence which has been extended to, my Lord, your Lordship's most obliged and most humble servant,

'Temple Lane, Nov. 3, 1762.'   'SAM. JOHNSON.'

'*To* MR. JOSEPH BARETTI, *at Milan*

'SIR,   'London, Dec. 21, 1762.

'You are not to suppose, with all your conviction of my idleness, that I have passed all this time without writing to my Baretti. I gave a letter to Mr. Beauclerk, who, in my opinion, and in his own, was hastening to Naples for the recovery of his health; but he has stopped at Paris, and I know not when he will proceed. Langton is with him.

'I will not trouble you with speculations about peace and war. The good or ill success of battles and embassies extends itself to a very small part of domestick life: we all have good and evil, which we feel more sensibly than our petty part of publick miscarriage or prosperity. I am sorry for your disappointment, with which you seem more touched than I should expect a man of your resolution and experience to have been, did I not know that general truths are seldom applied to particular occasions; and that the fallacy of our self-love extends itself as wide as our interest or affections. Every man believes that mistresses are unfaithful, and patrons capricious; but he excepts his own mistress, and his own patron. We have all learned that greatness is negligent and contemptuous, and that in Courts life is often languished away in ungratified expectation; but he that approaches greatness, or glitters in a Court, imagines that destiny has at last exempted him from the common lot.

'Do not let such evils overwhelm you as thousands have suffered, and thousands have surmounted; but turn your thoughts with vigour to some other plan of life, and keep always in your mind, that, with due submission to Providence, a man of genius has been seldom ruined but by himself. Your Patron's weakness or insensibility will finally do you little hurt, if he is not assisted by your own passions. Of your love I know not the propriety, nor can estimate the power; but in love, as in every other passion, of which hope is the essence, we ought always to remember the uncertainty of events. There is, indeed, nothing that so much seduces reason from vigilance, as the thought of passing life with an amiable woman; and if all would happen that a lover fancies, I know not what other terrestrial happiness would deserve pursuit. But love and marriage are different states. Those who are to suffer the evils together, and to suffer often for the sake of one another, soon lose that tenderness of look, and that benevolence of mind, which arose from the participation of unmingled pleasure and successive amusement. A woman, we are sure, will not be always fair; we are not sure she will always be virtuous: and man cannot retain through life that respect and assiduity by which he pleases for a day or for a month. I do not, however, pretend to have discovered that life has any thing more to be desired than a prudent and virtuous marriage; therefore know not what counsel to give you.

'If you can quit your imagination of love and greatness, and leave your hopes of preferment and bridal raptures to try once more the fortune of literature and industry, the way through France is now open. We flatter ourselves that we shall cultivate, with great diligence, the arts of peace; and every man will be welcome among us who can teach us any thing we do not know.

For your part, you will find all your old friends willing to receive you.

'Reynolds still continues to increase in reputation and in riches. Miss Williams, who very much loves you, goes on in the old way. Miss Cotterel is still with Mrs. Porter. Miss Charlotte is married to Dean Lewis, and has three children. Mr. Levet has married a street-walker. But the gazette of my narration must now arrive to tell you, that Bathurst went physician to the army, and died at the Havannah.

'I know not whether I have not sent you word that Huggins and Richardson are both dead. When we see our enemies and friends gliding away before us, let us not forget that we are subject to the general law of mortality, and shall soon be where our doom will be fixed for ever. I pray GOD to bless you, and am, Sir, your most affectionate humble servant,

'Write soon.'   'SAM. JOHNSON.'

1763: ÆTAT. 54.]—IN 1763 he furnished to *The Poetical Calendar*, published by Fawkes and Woty, a character of Collins*, which he afterwards ingrafted into his entire life of that admirable poet, in the collection of lives which he wrote for the body of English poetry, formed and published by the booksellers of London. His account of the melancholy depression with which Collins was severely afflicted, and which brought him to his grave, is, I think, one of the most tender and interesting passages in the whole series of his writings. He also favoured Mr. Hoole with the Dedication of his translation of *Tasso* to the Queen*, which is so happily conceived and elegantly expressed, that I cannot but point it out to the peculiar notice of my readers.[1]

[1] 'MADAM,—To approach the high and the illustrious has been in all ages the privilege of Poets; and though translators cannot justly claim the same honour, yet they naturally follow their authours as attendants; and I hope that in return for having enabled TASSO to diffuse his fame through the British dominions, I may be introduced by him to the presence of YOUR MAJESTY.
'TASSO has a peculiar claim to YOUR MAJESTY'S favour, as follower and panegyrist of the House of *Este*, which has one common ancestor with the House of HANOVER; and in reviewing his life it is not easy to forbear a wish that he had lived in a happier time, when he might, among the descendants

This is to me a memorable year; for in it I had the happiness
to obtain the acquaintance of that extraordinary man whose
memoirs I am now writing; an acquaintance which I shall ever
esteem as one of the most fortunate circumstances in my life.
Though then but two-and-twenty, I had for several years read
his works with delight and instruction, and had the highest
reverence for their authour, which had grown up in my fancy
into a kind of mysterious veneration, by figuring to myself a
state of solemn elevated abstraction, in which I supposed him to
live in the immense metropolis of London. Mr. Gentleman, a
native of Ireland, who passed some years in Scotland as a player,
and as an instructor in the English language, a man whose
talents and worth were depressed by misfortunes, had given me
a representation of the figure and manner of DICTIONARY JOHN-
SON! as he was then generally called;[1] and during my first visit
to London, which was for three months in 1760, Mr. Derrick
the poet, who was Gentleman's friend and countryman, flattered
me with hopes that he would introduce me to Johnson, an honour
of which I was very ambitious. But he never found an opportunity;
which made me doubt that he had promised to do what was not
in his power; till Johnson some years afterwards told me, 'Derrick, Sir, might very well have introduced you. I had a kindness
for Derrick, and am sorry he is dead.'

of that illustrious family, have found a more liberal and potent patronage.
    'I cannot but observe, MADAM, how unequally reward is proportioned to
merit, when I reflect that the happiness which was withheld from TASSO is
reserved for me; and that the poem which once hardly procured to its authour
the countenance of the Princes of Ferrara, has attracted to its translator the
favourable notice of a BRITISH QUEEN.
    'Had this been the fate of TASSO, he would have been able to have
celebrated the condescension of YOUR MAJESTY in nobler language, but
could not have felt it with more ardent gratitude, than MADAM, Your
MAJESTY's most faithful and devoted servant.'
    [1] As great men of antiquity such as Scipio *Africanus* had an epithet added
to their names, in consequence of some celebrated action, so my illustrious
friend was often called DICTIONARY JOHNSON, from that wonderful atchieve-
ment of genius and labour, his *Dictionary of the English Language*; the merit
of which I contemplate with more and more admiration. BOSWELL. In like
manner we have 'Hermes Harris,' 'Pliny Melmoth,' 'Demosthenes Taylor,'
'Persian Jones,' 'Abyssinian Bruce,' 'Microscope Baker,' 'Leonidas Glover,'
'Hesiod Cooke,' and 'Corsica Boswell.'

In the summer of 1761 Mr. Thomas Sheridan was at Edinburgh, and delivered lectures upon the English Language and
Publick Speaking to large and respectable audiences. I was often
in his company, and heard him frequently expatiate upon Johnson's extraordinary knowledge, talents, and virtues, repeat his
pointed sayings, describe his particularities, and boast of his
being his guest sometimes till two or three in the morning. At
his house I hoped to have many opportunities of seeing the sage,
as Mr. Sheridan obligingly assured me I should not be disappointed.

When I returned to London in the end of 1762, to my surprise
and regret I found an irreconcileable difference had taken place
between Johnson and Sheridan. A pension of two hundred pounds
a year had been given to Sheridan, Johnson, who, as has been
already mentioned, thought slightingly of Sheridan's art, upon
hearing that he was also pensioned, exclaimed, 'What! have they
given *him* a pension? Then it is time for me to give up mine.'
Whether this proceeded from a momentary indignation, as if it
were an affront to his exalted merit that a player should be
rewarded in the same manner with him, or was the sudden effect
of a fit of peevishness, it was unluckily said, and, indeed, cannot
be justified. Mr. Sheridan's pension was granted to him not as a
player, but as a sufferer in the cause of government, when he was
manager of the Theatre Royal in Ireland, when parties ran high
in 1753. And it must also be allowed that he was a man of literature, and had considerably improved the arts of reading and
speaking with distinctness and propriety.

Besides, Johnson should have recollected that Mr. Sheridan
taught pronunciation to Mr. Alexander Wedderburne, whose
sister was married to Sir Harry Erskine, an intimate friend of
Lord Bute, who was the favourite of the King; and surely the
most outrageous Whig will not maintain, that, whatever ought
to be the principle in the disposal of *offices*, a *pension* ought never
to be granted from any bias of court connection. Mr. Macklin,
indeed, shared with Mr. Sheridan the honour of instructing Mr.
Wedderburne; and though it was too late in life for a Caledonian
to acquire the genuine English cadence, yet so successful were

Mr. Wedderburne's instructors, and his own unabating endeavours, that he got rid of the coarse part of his Scotch accent,
retaining only as much of the 'native wood-note wild,' as to
mark his country; which, if any Scotchman should affect to forget,
I should heartily despise him. Notwithstanding the difficulties
which are to be encountered by those who have not had the advantage of an English education, he by degrees formed a mode of
speaking to which Englishmen do not deny the praise of elegance.
Hence his distinguished oratory, which he exerted in his own
country as an advocate in the Court of Session, and a ruling
elder of the *Kirk*, has had its fame and ample reward, in much
higher spheres. When I look back on this noble person at Edinburgh, in situations so unworthy of his brilliant powers, and
behold Lord Loughborough at London, the change seems almost
like one of the metamorphoses in *Ovid*; and as his two preceptors,
by refining his utterance, gave currency to his talents, we may
say in the words of that poet, *'Nam vos mutastis.'*[1]

I have dwelt the longer upon this remarkable instance of successful parts and assiduity, because it affords animating encouragement to other gentlemen of North-Britain to try their
fortunes in the southern part of the Island, where they may hope
to gratify their utmost ambition; and now that we are one people
by the Union, it would surely be illiberal to maintain, that they
have not an equal title with the natives of any other part of his
Majesty's dominions.

Johnson complained that a man[2] who disliked him repeated
his sarcasm to Mr. Sheridan, without telling him what followed,
which was, that after a pause he added, 'However, I am glad that
Mr. Sheridan has a pension, for he is a very good man.' Sheridan
could never forgive this hasty contemptuous expression. It
rankled in his mind; and though I informed him of all that Johnson said, and that he would be very glad to meet him amicably,
he positively declined repeated offers which I made, and once
went off abruptly from a house where he and I were engaged to
dine, because he was told that Dr. Johnson was to be there. I

[1] ['You transformed him.' *Metam*. i. 2.]
[2] [James Macpherson. *Boswell Papers*, xi. 206, xiii. 218.]

have no sympathetick feeling with such persevering resentment. It is painful when there is a breach between those who have lived together socially and cordially; and I wonder that there is not, in all such cases, a mutual wish that it should be healed. I could perceive that Mr. Sheridan was by no means satisfied with Johnson's acknowledging him to be a good man. That could not sooth his injured vanity. I could not but smile, at the same time that I was offended, to observe Sheridan in *The Life of Swift*,[1] which he afterwards published, attempting, in the writhings of his resentment, to depreciate Johnson, by characterising him as 'A writer of gigantick fame in these days of little men;' that very Johnson whom he once so highly admired and venerated.

This rupture with Sheridan deprived Johnson of one of his most agreeable resources for amusement in his lonely evenings; for Sheridan's well-informed, animated, and bustling mind never suffered conversation to stagnate; and Mrs. Sheridan was a most agreeable companion to an intellectual man. She was sensible, ingenious, unassuming, yet communicative. I recollect, with satisfaction, many pleasing hours which I passed with her under the hospitable roof of her husband, who was to me a very kind friend. Her novel, entitled *Memoirs of Miss Sydney Biddulph*, contains an excellent moral, while it inculcates a future state of retribution;[2] and what it teaches is impressed upon the mind by

[1] P. 447.

[2] My position has been very well illustrated by Mr. Belsham of Bedford, in his *Essay on Dramatic Poetry*. 'The fashionable doctrine (says he) both of moralists and criticks in these times is, that virtue and happiness are constant concomitants; and it is regarded as a kind of dramatick impiety to maintain that virtue should not be rewarded, nor vice punished in the last scene of the last act of every tragedy. This conduct in our modern poets is, however, in my opinion, extremely injudicious; for, it labours in vain to inculcate a doctrine in theory, which every one knows to be false in fact, *viz.* that virtue in real life is always productive of happiness; and vice of misery. Thus Congreve concludes the Tragedy of *The Mourning Bride* with the following foolish couplet:—

'For blessings ever wait on virtuous deeds,
And though a late, a sure reward succeeds.'

'When a man eminently virtuous, a Brutus, a Cato, or a Socrates, finally sinks under the pressure of accumulated misfortune, we are not only led to entertain a more indignant hatred of vice than if he rose from his distress, but we are inevitably induced to cherish the sublime idea that a day of future retribution will arrive when he shall receive not merely poetical, but real and a series of as deep distress as can affect humanity, in the amiable and pious heroine who goes to her grave unrelieved, but resigned, and full of hope of 'heaven's mercy.' Johnson paid her this high compliment upon it: 'I know not, Madam, that you have a right, upon moral principles, to make your readers suffer so much.'

Mr. Thomas Davies the actor, who then kept a bookseller's shop in Russel-street, Covent-garden,[1] told me that Johnson was very much his friend, and came frequently to his house, where he more than once invited me to meet him; but by some unlucky accident or other he was prevented from coming to us.

Mr. Thomas Davies was a man of good understanding and talents, with the advantage of a liberal education. Though somewhat pompous, he was an entertaining companion; and his literary performances have no inconsiderable share of merit. He was a friendly and very hospitable man. Both he and his wife, (who has been celebrated for her beauty,) though upon the stage for many years, maintained an uniform decency of character; and Johnson esteemed them, and lived in as easy an intimacy with them as with any family which he used to visit. Mr. Davies recollected several of Johnson's remarkable sayings, and was one of the best of the many imitators of his voice and manner, while relating them. He increased my impatience more and more to see the extraordinary man whose works I highly valued, and whose conversation was reported to be so peculiarly excellent.

At last, on Monday the 16th of May, when I was sitting in

substantial justice.' *Essays Philosophical, Historical, and Literary*, London, 1791, vol. II. 8vo. p. 317.

This is well reasoned and well expressed. I wish, indeed, that the ingenious authour had not thought it necessary to introduce any *instance* of 'a man eminently virtuous;' as he would then have avoided mentioning such a ruffian as Brutus under that description. Mr. Belsham discovers in his *Essays* so much reading and thinking, and good composition, that I regret his not having been fortunate enough to be educated a member of our excellent national establishment. Had he not been nursed in nonconformity, he probably would not have been tainted with those heresies (as I sincerely, and on no slight investigation, think them) both in religion and politicks, which, while I read, I am sure, with candour, I cannot read without offence.

[1] No. 8.—The very place where I was fortunate enough to be introduced to the illustrious subject of this work, deserves to be particularly marked. I never pass by it without feeling reverence and regret.

Mr. Davies's back-parlour, after having drunk tea with him and Mrs. Davies, Johnson unexpectedly came into the shop;[1] and Mr. Davies having perceived him through the glass-door in the room in which we were sitting, advancing towards us,—he announced his aweful approach to me, somewhat in the manner of an actor in the part of Horatio, when he addresses Hamlet on the appearance of his father's ghost, 'Look, my Lord, it comes.' I found that I had a very perfect idea of Johnson's figure, from the portrait of him painted by Sir Joshua Reynolds soon after he had published his *Dictionary*, in the attitude of sitting in his easy chair in deep meditation, which was the first picture his friend did for him, which Sir Joshua very kindly presented to me, and from which an engraving has been made for this work. Mr. Davies mentioned my name, and respectfully introduced me to him. I was much agitated; and recollecting his prejudice against the Scotch, of which I had heard much, I said to Davies, 'Don't tell where I come from.'—'From Scotland,' cried Davies roguishly. 'Mr. Johnson, (said I) I do indeed come from Scotland, but I cannot help it.' I am willing to flatter myself that I meant this as light pleasantry to sooth and conciliate him, and not as an humiliating abasement at the expence of my country. But however that might be, this speech was somewhat unlucky; for with that quickness of wit for which he was so remarkable, he seized the expression 'come from Scotland,' which I used in the sense of being of that country, and, as if I had said that I had come away from it, or left it, retorted, 'That, Sir, I find, is what a very great many of your countrymen cannot help.' This stroke stunned me a good deal; and when we had sat down, I felt myself

---

[1] Mr. Murphy, in his *Essay on the Life and Genius of Dr. Johnson*, [p. 106], has given an account of this meeting considerably different from mine, I am persuaded without any consciousness of errour. His memory, at the end of near thirty years, has undoubtedly deceived him, and he supposes himself to have been present at a scene, which he has probably heard inaccurately described by others. In my note *taken on the very day*, in which I am confident I marked every thing material that passed, no mention is made of this gentleman; and I am sure, that I should not have omitted one so well known in the literary world. It may easily be imagined that this, my first interview with Dr. Johnson, with all its circumstances, made a strong impression on my mind, and would be registered with peculiar attention.

not a little embarrassed, and apprehensive of what might come next. He then addressed himself to Davies: 'What do you think of Garrick? He has refused me an order for the play for Miss Williams, because he knows the house will be full, and that an order would be worth three shillings.' Eager to take any opening to get into conversation with him, I ventured to say, 'O, Sir, I cannot think Mr. Garrick would grudge such a trifle to you.' 'Sir, (said he, with a stern look,) I have known David Garrick longer than you have done: and I know no right you have to talk to me on the subject.' Perhaps I deserved this check; for it was rather presumptuous in me, an entire stranger, to express any doubt of the justice of his animadversion upon his old acquaintance and pupil.[1] I now felt myself much mortified, and began to think that the hope which I had long indulged of obtaining his acquaintance was blasted. And, in truth, had not my ardour been uncommonly strong, and my resolution uncommonly persevering, so rough a reception might have deterred me for ever from making any further attempts. Fortunately, however, I remained upon the field not wholly discomfited; and was soon rewarded by hearing some of his conversation, of which I preserved the following short minute, without marking the questions and observations by which it was produced.

'People (he remarked) may be taken in once, who imagine that an authour is greater in private life than other men. Uncommon parts require uncommon opportunities for their exertion.'

'In barbarous society, superiority of parts is of real consequence. Great strength or great wisdom is of much value to an individual. But in more polished times there are people to do every thing for money; and then there are a number of other superiorities, such as those of birth and fortune, and rank, that

[1] That this was a momentary sally against Garrick there can be no doubt; for at Johnson's desire he had, some years before, given a benefit-night at his theatre to this very person, by which she had got two hundred pounds. Johnson, indeed, upon all other occasions, when I was in his company, praised the very liberal charity of Garrick. I once mentioned to him, 'It is observed, Sir, that you attack Garrick yourself, but will suffer nobody else to do it.' JOHNSON, (smiling) 'Why, Sir, that is true.'

dissipate men's attention, and leave no extraordinary share of respect for personal and intellectual superiority. This is wisely ordered by Providence, to preserve some equality among mankind.'

'Sir, this book (*The Elements of Criticism*, which he had taken up,) is a pretty essay, and deserves to be held in some estimation, though much of it is chimerical.'

Speaking of one[1] who with more than ordinary boldness attacked publick measures and the royal family, he said,

'I think he is safe from the law, but he is an abusive scoundrel; and instead of applying to my Lord Chief Justice to punish him, I would send half a dozen footmen and have him well ducked.'

'The notion of liberty amuses the people of England, and helps to keep off the *tædium vitæ*. When a butcher tells you that *his heart bleeds for his country*, he has, in fact, no uneasy feeling.'

'Sheridan will not succeed at Bath with his oratory. Ridicule has gone down before him, and, I doubt, Derrick is his enemy.'[2]

'Derrick may do very well, as long as he can outrun his character; but the moment his character gets up with him, it is all over.'

It is, however, but just to record, that some years afterwards, when I reminded him of this sarcasm, he said, 'Well, but Derrick has now got a character that he need not run away from.'

I was highly pleased with the extraordinary vigour of his conversation, and regretted that I was drawn away from it by an engagement at another place. I had, for a part of the evening, been left alone with him, and had ventured to make an observation now and then, which he received very civilly; so that I was satisfied that though there was a roughness in his manner, there was no ill-nature in his disposition. Davies followed me to the door, and when I complained to him a little of the hard blows which the great man had given me, he kindly took upon him to console me by saying, 'Don't be uneasy. I can see he likes you very well.'

[1] [Wilkes. *Boswell's 1763 Journal*.]
[2] Mr. Sheridan was then reading lectures upon Oratory at Bath, where Derrick was Master of the Ceremonies; or, as the phrase is, KING.

A few days afterwards I called on Davies, and asked him if he thought I might take the liberty of waiting on Mr. Johnson at his Chambers in the Temple. He said I certainly might, and that Mr. Johnson would take it as a compliment. So upon Tuesday the 24th of May, after having been enlivened by the witty sallies of Messieurs Thornton, Wilkes, Churchill and Lloyd, with whom I had passed the morning, I boldly repaired to Johnson. His Chambers were on the first floor of No. 1, Inner-Temple-lane, and I entered them with an impression given me by the Reverend Dr. Blair, of Edinburgh, who had been introduced to him not long before, and described his having 'found the Giant in his den;' an expression, which, when I came to be pretty well acquainted with Johnson, I repeated to him, and he was diverted at this picturesque account of himself. Dr. Blair had been presented to him by Dr. James Fordyce. At this time the controversy concerning the pieces published by Mr. James Macpherson, as translations of *Ossian*, was at its height. Johnson had all along denied their authenticity; and, what was still more provoking to their admirers, maintained that they had no merit. The subject having been introduced by Dr. Fordyce, Dr. Blair, relying on the internal evidence of their antiquity, asked Dr. Johnson whether he thought any man of a modern age could have written such poems? Johnson replied, 'Yes, Sir, many men, many women, and many children.' Johnson, at this time, did not know that Dr. Blair had just published a *Dissertation*, not only defending their authenticity, but seriously ranking them with the poems of *Homer* and *Virgil*; and when he was afterwards informed of this circumstance, he expressed some displeasure at Dr. Fordyce's having suggested the topick, and said, 'I am not sorry that they got thus much for their pains. Sir, it was like leading one to talk of a book when the authour is concealed behind the door.'

He received me very courteously; but, it must be confessed, that his apartment, and furniture, and morning dress, were sufficiently uncouth. His brown suit of cloaths looked very rusty; he had on a little old shrivelled unpowdered wig, which was too small for his head; his shirt-neck and knees of his breeches were

loose; his black worsted stockings ill drawn up; and he had a
pair of unbuckled shoes by way of slippers. But all these slovenly
particularities were forgotten the moment that he began to talk.
Some gentlemen, whom I do not recollect, were sitting with
him; and when they went away, I also rose; but he said to me,
'Nay, don't go.' 'Sir, (said I,) I am afraid that I intrude upon
you. It is benevolent to allow me to sit and hear you.' He
seemed pleased with this compliment, which I sincerely paid
him, and answered, 'Sir, I am obliged to any man who visits me.'
I have preserved the following short minute of what passed
this day:—

'Madness frequently discovers itself merely by unnecessary
deviation from the usual modes of the world. My poor friend
Smart shewed the disturbance of his mind, by falling upon his
knees, and saying his prayers in the street, or in any other
unusual place. Now although, rationally speaking, it is greater
madness not to pray at all, than to pray as Smart did, I am afraid
there are so many who do not pray, that their understanding is
not called in question.'

Concerning this unfortunate poet, Christopher Smart, who
was confined in a mad-house, he had, at another time, the following conversation with Dr. Burney:—BURNEY. 'How does poor
Smart do, Sir; is he likely to recover?' JOHNSON. 'It seems as if
his mind had ceased to struggle with the disease; for he grows
fat upon it.' BURNEY. 'Perhaps, Sir, that may be from want of
exercise.' JOHNSON. 'No, Sir; he has partly as much exercise as
he used to have, for he digs in the garden. Indeed, before his
confinement, he used for exercise to walk to the ale-house; but
he was *carried* back again. I did not think he ought to be shut up.
His infirmities were not noxious to society. He insisted on
people praying with him; and I'd as lief pray with Kit Smart as
any one else. Another charge was, that he did not love clean
linen; and I have no passion for it.'—Johnson continued. 'Mankind have a great aversion to intellectual labour; but even supposing knowledge to be easily attainable, more people would be
content to be ignorant than would take even a little trouble to
acquire it.'

'The morality of an action depends on the motive from which we act. If I fling half a crown to a beggar with intention to break his head, and he picks it up and buys victuals with it, the physical effect is good; but, with respect to me, the action is very wrong. So, religious exercises, if not performed with an intention to please GOD, avail us nothing. As our Saviour says of those who perform them from other motives, "Verily they have their reward." '

'The Christian religion has very strong evidences. It, indeed, appears in some degree strange to reason; but in History we have undoubted facts, against which, reasoning *à priori*, we have more arguments than we have for them; but then, testimony has great weight, and casts the balance. I would recommend to every man whose faith is yet unsettled, Grotius,—Dr. Pearson [Pearce],—and Dr. Clarke.'

Talking of Garrick, he said, 'He is the first man in the world for sprightly conversation.'

When I rose a second time he again pressed me to stay, which I did.

He told me, that he generally went abroad at four in the afternoon, and seldom came home till two in the morning. I took the liberty to ask if he did not think it wrong to live thus, and not make more use of his great talents. He owned it was a bad habit. On reviewing, at the distance of many years, my journal of this period, I wonder how, at my first visit, I ventured to talk to him so freely, and that he bore it with so much indulgence.

Before we parted, he was so good as to promise to favour me with his company one evening at my lodgings; and, as I took my leave, shook me cordially by the hand. It is almost needless to add, that I felt no little elation at having now so happily established an acquaintance of which I had been so long ambitious.

My readers will, I trust, excuse me for being thus minutely circumstantial, when it is considered that the acquaintance of Dr. Johnson was to me a most valuable acquisition, and laid the foundation of whatever instruction and entertainment they may receive from my collections concerning the great subject of the work which they are now perusing.

I did not visit him again till Monday, June 13, at which time I recollect no part of his conversation, except that when I told him I had been to see Johnson ride upon three horses, he said, 'Such a man, Sir, should be encouraged; for his performances shew the extent of the human powers in one instance, and thus tend to raise our opinion of the faculties of man. He shews what may be attained by persevering application; so that every man may hope, that by giving as much application, although perhaps he may never ride three horses at a time, or dance upon a wire, yet he may be equally expert in whatever profession he has chosen to pursue.'

He again shook me by the hand at parting, and asked me why I did not come oftener to him. Trusting that I was now in his good graces, I answered, that he had not given me much encouragement, and reminded him of the check I had received from him at our first interview. 'Poh, poh! (said he, with a complacent smile,) never mind these things. Come to me as often as you can. I shall be glad to see you.'

I had learnt that his place of frequent resort was the Mitre tavern in Fleet-street, where he loved to sit up late, and I begged I might be allowed to pass an evening with him there soon, which he promised I should. A few days afterwards I met him near Temple-bar, about one o'clock in the morning, and asked if he would then go to the Mitre. 'Sir, (said he) it is too late; they won't let us in. But I'll go with you another night with all my heart.'

A revolution of some importance in my plan of life had just taken place; for instead of procuring a commission in the foot-guards, which was my own inclination, I had, in compliance with my father's wishes, agreed to study the law; and was soon to set out for Utrecht, to hear the lectures of an excellent Civilian in that University, and then to proceed on my travels. Though very desirous of obtaining Dr. Johnson's advice and instructions on the mode of pursuing my studies, I was at this time so occupied, shall I call it? or so dissipated, by the amusements of London, that our next meeting was not till Saturday, June 25, when happening to dine at Clifton's eating-house, in Butcher-row, I

was surprized to perceive Johnson come in and take his seat at
another table. The mode of dining, or rather being fed, at such
houses in London, is well known to many to be particularly unsocial, as there is no Ordinary, or united company, but each
person has his own mess, and is under no obligation to hold any
intercourse with any one. A liberal and full-minded man, however, who loves to talk, will break through this churlish and
unsocial restraint. Johnson and an Irish gentleman got into a
dispute concerning the cause of some part of mankind being
black. 'Why, Sir, (said Johnson,) it has been accounted for in
three ways: either by supposing that they are the posterity of
Ham, who was cursed; or that GOD at first created two kinds of
men, one black and another white; or that by the heat of the sun
the skin is scorched, and so acquires a sooty hue. This matter
has been much canvassed among naturalists, but has never been
brought to any certain issue.' What the Irishman said is totally
obliterated from my mind; but I remember that he became very
warm and intemperate in his expressions; upon which Johnson
rose, and quietly walked away. When he had retired, his
antagonist took his revenge, as he thought, by saying, 'He has a
most ungainly figure, and an affectation of pomposity, unworthy
of a man of genius.'

Johnson had not observed that I was in the room. I followed
him, however, and he agreed to meet me in the evening at the
Mitre. I called on him, and we went thither at nine. We had
a good supper, and port wine, of which he then sometimes
drank a bottle. The orthodox high-church sound of the MITRE,—
the figure and manner of the celebrated SAMUEL JOHNSON,—the
extraordinary power and precision of his conversation, and the
pride arising from finding myself admitted as his companion,
produced a variety of sensations, and a pleasing elevation of
mind beyond what I had ever before experienced. I find in my
journal the following minute of our conversation, which, though
it will give but a very faint notion of what passed, is in some
degree a valuable record; and it will be curious in this view, as
shewing how habitual to his mind were some opinions which
appear in his works.

'Colley Cibber, Sir, was by no means a blockhead; but by arrogating to himself too much, he was in danger of losing that degree of estimation to which he was entitled. His friends gave out that he *intended* his birth-day *Odes* should be bad: but that was not the case, Sir; for he kept them many months by him, and a few years before he died he shewed me one of them, with great solicitude to render it as perfect as might be, and I made some corrections, to which he was not very willing to submit. I remember the following couplet in allusion to the King and himself:

> "Perch'd on the eagle's soaring wing,
> The lowly linnet loves to sing."

Sir, he had heard something of the fabulous tale of the wren sitting upon the eagle's wing, and he had applied it to a linnet. Cibber's familiar style, however, was better than that which Whitehead has assumed. *Grand* nonsense is insupportable. Whitehead is but a little man to inscribe verses to players.'

I did not presume to controvert this censure, which was tinctured with his prejudice against players; but I could not help thinking that a dramatick poet might with propriety pay a compliment to an eminent performer, as Whitehead has very happily done in his verses to Mr. Garrick.

'Sir, I do not think Gray a first-rate poet. He has not a bold imagination, nor much command of words. The obscurity in which he has involved himself will not persuade us that he is sublime. His *Elegy in a Church-yard* has a happy selection of images, but I don't like what are called his great things. His *Ode* which begins

> "Ruin seize thee, ruthless King,
> Confusion on thy banners wait!"

has been celebrated for its abruptness, and plunging into the subject all at once. But such arts as these have no merit, unless when they are original. We admire them only once; and this abruptness has nothing new in it. We have had it often before. Nay, we have it in the old song of Johnny Armstrong:

> "Is there ever a man in all Scotland
> From the highest estate to the lowest degree," &c.

And then, Sir,

> "Yes, there is a man in Westmoreland,
> And Johnny Armstrong they do him call."

There, now, you plunge at once into the subject. You have no previous narration to lead you to it. The two next lines in that *Ode* are, I think, very good:

> "Though fanned by conquest's crimson wing,
> They mock the air with idle state." [1]

Here let it be observed, that although his opinion of Gray's poetry was widely different from mine, and I believe from that of most men of taste, by whom it is with justice highly admired, there is certainly much absurdity in the clamour which has been raised, as if he had been culpably injurious to the merit of that bard, and had been actuated by envy. Alas! ye little short-sighted criticks, could JOHNSON be envious of the talents of any of his contemporaries? That his opinion on this subject was what in private and in publick he uniformly expressed, regardless of what others might think, we may wonder, and perhaps regret; but it is shallow and unjust to charge him with expressing what he did not think.

Finding him in a placid humour, and wishing to avail myself of the opportunity which I fortunately had of consulting a sage, to hear whose wisdom, I conceived in the ardour of youthful imagination, that men filled with a noble enthusiasm for intellectual improvement would gladly have resorted from distant lands; —I opened my mind to him ingenuously, and gave him a little sketch of my life, to which he was pleased to listen with great attention.

I acknowledged, that though educated very strictly in the principles of religion, I had for some time been misled into a certain degree of infidelity; but that I was come now to a better

---

[1] My friend Mr. Malone, in his valuable comments on Shakspeare, has traced in that great poet the *disjecta membra* [see p. 78] of these lines.

way of thinking, and was fully satisfied of the truth of the Christian revelation, though I was not clear as to every point considered to be orthodox. Being at all times a curious examiner of the human mind, and pleased with an undisguised display of what had passed in it, he called to me with warmth, 'Give me your hand; I have taken a liking to you.' He then began to descant upon the force of testimony, and the little we could know of final causes; so that the objections of, why was it so? or why was it not so? ought not to disturb us: adding, that he himself had at one period been guilty of a temporary neglect of religion, but that it was not the result of argument, but mere absence of thought.

After having given credit to reports of his bigotry, I was agreeably surprized when he expressed the following very liberal sentiment, which has the additional value of obviating an objection to our holy religion, founded upon the discordant tenets of Christians themselves: 'For my part, Sir, I think all Christians, whether Papists or Protestants, agree in the essential articles, and that their differences are trivial, and rather political than religious.'

We talked of belief in ghosts. He said, 'Sir, I make a distinction between what a man may experience by the mere strength of his imagination, and what imagination cannot possibly produce. Thus, suppose I should think that I saw a form, and heard a voice cry "Johnson, you are a very wicked fellow, and unless you repent you will certainly be punished;" my own unworthiness is so deeply impressed upon my mind, that I might *imagine* I thus saw and heard, and therefore I should not believe that an external communication had been made to me. But if a form should appear, and a voice should tell me that a particular man had died at a particular place, and a particular hour, a fact which I had no apprehension of, nor any means of knowing, and this fact, with all its circumstances, should afterwards be unquestionably proved, I should, in that case, be persuaded that I had supernatural intelligence imparted to me.'

Here it is proper, once for all, to give a true and fair statement of Johnson's way of thinking upon the question, whether departed spirits are ever permitted to appear in this world, or in any way to operate upon human life. He has been ignorantly misrepresented as weakly credulous upon that subject; and, therefore, though I feel an inclination to disdain and treat with silent contempt so foolish a notion concerning my illustrious friend, yet as I find it has gained ground, it is necessary to refute it. The real fact then is, that Johnson had a very philosophical mind, and such a rational respect for testimony, as to make him submit his understanding to what was authentically proved, though he could not comprehend why it was so. Being thus disposed, he was willing to inquire into the truth of any relation of supernatural agency, a general belief of which has prevailed in all nations and ages. But so far was he from being the dupe of implicit faith, that he examined the matter with a jealous attention, and no man was more ready to refute its falsehood when he had discovered it. Churchill, in his poem entitled *The Ghost,* availed himself of the absurd credulity imputed to Johnson, and drew a caricature of him under the name of 'Pomposo,' representing him as one of the believers of the story of a Ghost in Cock-lane, which, in the year 1762, had gained very general credit in London. Many of my readers, I am convinced, are to this hour under an impression that Johnson was thus foolishly deceived. It will therefore surprize them a good deal when they are informed upon undoubted authority, that Johnson was one of those by whom the imposture was detected. The story had become so popular, that he thought it should be investigated; and in this research he was assisted by the Reverend Dr. Douglas, now Bishop of Salisbury, the great detector of impostures; who informs me, that after the gentlemen who went and examined into the evidence were satisfied of its falsity, Johnson wrote in their presence an account of it, which was published in the newspapers and *Gentleman's Magazine,* and undeceived the world.[1]

[1] The account was as follows:—'On the night of the 1st of February [1762] many gentlemen eminent for their rank and character were, by the invitation of the Reverend Mr. Aldrich, of Clerkenwell, assembled at his house, for the examination of the noises supposed to be made by a departed spirit, for the detection of some enormous crime.

'About ten at night the gentlemen met in the chamber in which the girl, supposed to be disturbed by a spirit, had, with proper caution, been put to bed by several ladies. They sat rather more than an hour, and hearing

Our conversation proceeded. 'Sir, (said he) I am a friend to subordination, as most conducive to the happiness of society. There is a reciprocal pleasure in governing and being governed.'

'Dr. Goldsmith is one of the first men we now have as an authour, and he is a very worthy man too. He has been loose in his principles, but he is coming right.'

I mentioned Mallet's tragedy of *Elvira,* which had been acted the preceding winter at Drury-lane, and that the Honourable Andrew Erskine, Mr. Dempster, and myself, had joined in writing a pamphlet, entitled, *Critical Strictures,* against it.[1] That the mildness of Dempster's disposition had, however, relented; and he had candidly said, 'We have hardly a right to abuse this

nothing, went down stairs, when they interrogated the father of the girl, who denied, in the strongest terms, any knowledge or belief of fraud.

'The supposed spirit had before publickly promised, by an affirmative knock, that it would attend one of the gentlemen into the vault under the Church of St. John, Clerkenwell, where the body is deposited, and give a token of her presence there, by a knock upon her coffin; it was therefore determined to make this trial of the existence or veracity of the supposed spirit.

'While they were enquiring and deliberating, they were summoned into the girl's chamber by some ladies who were near her bed, and who had heard knocks and scratches. When the gentlemen entered, the girl declared that she felt the spirit like a mouse upon her back, and was required to hold her hands out of bed. From that time, though the spirit was very solemnly required to manifest its existence by appearance, by impression on the hand or body of any present, by scratches, knocks, or any other agency, no evidence of any preter-natural power was exhibited.

'The spirit was then very seriously advertised that the person to whom the promise was made of striking the coffin, was then about to visit the vault, and that the performance of the promise was then claimed. The company at one o'clock went into the church, and the gentleman to whom the promise was made, went with another into the vault. The spirit was solemnly required to perform its promise, but nothing more than silence ensued: the person supposed to be accused by the spirit, then went down with several others, but no effect was perceived. Upon their return they examined the girl, but could draw no confession from her. Between two and three she desired and was permitted to go home with her father.

'It is, therefore, the opinion of the whole assembly, that the child has some art of making or counterfeiting a particular noise, and that there is no agency of any higher cause.'

[1] *The Critical Review,* in which Mallet himself sometimes wrote, characterised this pamphlet as 'the crude efforts of envy, petulance and self-conceit.' There being thus three epithets, we, the three authours, had a humourous contention how each should be appropriated.

tragedy: for bad as it is, how vain should either of us be to write one not near so good.' JOHNSON. 'Why no, Sir; this is not just reasoning. You *may* abuse a tragedy, though you cannot write one. You may scold a carpenter who has made you a bad table, though you cannot make a table. It is not your trade to make tables.'

When I talked to him of the paternal estate to which I was heir, he said, 'Sir, let me tell you, that to be a Scotch landlord, where you have a number of families dependent upon you, and attached to you, is, perhaps, as high a situation as humanity can arrive at. A merchant upon the 'Change of London, with a hundred thousand pounds, is nothing: an English Duke, with an immense fortune, is nothing; he has no tenants who consider themselves as under his patriarchal care, and who will follow him to the field upon any emergency.'

His notion of the dignity of a Scotch landlord had been formed upon what he had heard of the Highland Chiefs; for it is long since a lowland landlord has been so curtailed in his feudal authority, that he has little more influence over his tenants than an English landlord; and of late years most of the Highland Chiefs have destroyed, by means too well known, the princely power which they once enjoyed.

He proceeded: 'Your going abroad, Sir, and breaking off idle habits, may be of great importance to you. I would go where there are courts and learned men. There is a good deal of Spain that has not been perambulated. I would have you go thither. A man of inferiour talents to yours may furnish us with useful observations upon that country.' His supposing me, at that period of life, capable of writing an account of my travels that would deserve to be read, elated me not a little.

I appeal to every impartial reader whether this faithful detail of his frankness, complacency, and kindness to a young man, a stranger and a Scotchman, does not refute the unjust opinion of the harshness of his general demeanour. His occasional reproofs of folly, impudence, or impiety, and even the sudden sallies of his constitutional irritability of temper, which have been preserved for the poignancy of their wit, have produced that opinion among those who have not considered that such instances, though collected by Mrs. Piozzi into a small volume, and read over in a few hours, were, in fact, scattered through a long series of years; years, in which his time was chiefly spent in instructing and delighting mankind by his writings and conversation, in acts of piety to GOD, and good-will to men.

I complained to him that I had not yet acquired much knowledge, and asked his advice as to my studies. He said, 'Don't talk of study now. I will give you a plan; but it will require some time to consider of it.' 'It is very good in you (I replied,) to allow me to be with you thus. Had it been foretold to me some years ago that I should pass an evening with the authour of *The Rambler*, how should I have exulted!' What I then expressed, was sincerely from the heart. He was satisfied that it was, and cordially answered, 'Sir, I am glad we have met. I hope we shall pass many evenings and mornings too, together.' We finished a couple of bottles of port, and sat till between one and two in the morning.

He wrote this year in the *Critical Review* the account of 'Telemachus, a Mask,' by the Reverend George Graham, of Eton College. The subject of this beautiful poem was particularly interesting to Johnson, who had much experience of 'the conflict of opposite principles,' which he describes as 'The contention between pleasure and virtue, a struggle which will always be continued while the present system of nature shall subsist: nor can history or poetry exhibit more than pleasure triumphing over virtue, and virtue subjugating pleasure.'

As Dr. Oliver Goldsmith will frequently appear in this narrative, I shall endeavour to make my readers in some degree acquainted with his singular character. He was a native of Ireland, and a contemporary with Mr. Burke at Trinity College, Dublin, but did not then give much promise of future celebrity. He, however, observed to Mr. Malone, that 'though he made no great figure in mathematicks, which was a study in much repute there, he could turn an Ode of Horace into English better than any of them.' He afterwards studied physick at Edinburgh, and upon the Continent; and I have been informed, was enabled to pursue

his travels on foot, partly by demanding at Universities to enter
the list as a disputant, by which, according to the custom of many
of them, he was entitled to the premium of a crown, when luckily
for him his challenge was not accepted; so that, as I once observed to Dr. Johnson, he *disputed* his passage through Europe.
He then came to England, and was employed successively in the
capacities of an usher to an academy, a corrector of the press, a
reviewer, and a writer for a news-paper. He had sagacity enough
to cultivate assiduously the acquaintance of Johnson, and his
faculties were gradually enlarged by the contemplation of such a
model. To me and many others it appeared that he studiously
copied the manner of Johnson, though, indeed, upon a smaller
scale.

At this time I think he had published nothing with his name,
though it was pretty generally known that *one Dr. Goldsmith*
was the authour of *An Enquiry into the present State of polite
Learning in Europe*, and of *The Citizen of the World*, a series of
letters supposed to be written from London by a Chinese. No
man had the art of displaying with more advantage as a writer,
whatever literary acquisitions he made. '*Nihil quod tetigit non
ornavit.*'[1] His mind resembled a fertile, but thin soil. There was
a quick, but not a strong vegetation, of whatever chanced to be
thrown upon it. No deep root could be struck. The oak of the
forest did not grow there; but the elegant shrubbery and the
fragrant parterre appeared in gay succession. It has been generally circulated and believed that he was a mere fool in conversation;[2] but, in truth, this has been greatly exaggerated. He had,

[1] ['He touched nothing that he did not adorn.'] See his Epitaph in Westminster Abbey, written by Dr. Johnson.
[2] In allusion to this, Mr. Horace Walpole, who admired his writings,
said he was 'an inspired ideot;' and Garrick described him as one
'———— for shortness call'd Noll,
Who wrote like an angel, and talk'd like poor Poll.'
Sir Joshua Reynolds mentioned to me that he frequently heard Goldsmith
talk warmly of the pleasure of being liked, and observe how hard it would
be if literary excellence should preclude a man from that satisfaction, which
he perceived it often did, from the envy which attended it; and therefore Sir
Joshua was convinced that he was intentionally more absurd, in order to
lessen himself in social intercourse, trusting that his character would be
sufficiently supported by his works. If it indeed was his intention to appear

no doubt, a more than common share of that hurry of ideas which we often find in his countrymen, and which sometimes produces a laughable confusion in expressing them. He was very much what the French call *un étourdi*, and from vanity and an eager desire of being conspicuous wherever he was, he frequently talked carelessly without knowledge of the subject, or even without thought. His person was short, his countenance coarse and vulgar, his deportment that of a scholar aukwardly affecting the easy gentleman. Those who were in any way distinguished, excited envy in him to so ridiculous an excess, that the instances of it are hardly credible. When accompanying two beautiful young ladies[1] with their mother on a tour in France, he was seriously angry that more attention was paid to them than to him; and once at the exhibition of the *Fantoccini* in London, when those who sat next him observed with what dexterity a puppet was made to toss a pike, he could not bear that it should have such praise, and exclaimed with some warmth, 'Pshaw! I can do it better myself.'[2]

He, I am afraid, had no settled system of any sort, so that his conduct must not be strictly scrutinised; but his affections were social and generous, and when he had money he gave it away very liberally. His desire of imaginary consequence predominated over his attention to truth. When he began to rise into notice, he said he had a brother who was Dean of Durham,[3] a fiction so easily detected, that it is wonderful how he should have been so inconsiderate as to hazard it. He boasted to me at this time of the power of his pen in commanding money, which I believe was true in a certain degree, though in the instance he gave he was

absurd in company, he was often very successful. But with due deference to Sir Joshua's ingenuity, I think the conjecture too refined.

[1] Miss Hornecks, one of whom is now married to Henry Bunbury, Esq., and the other to Colonel Gwyn.

[2] He went home with Mr. Burke to supper; and broke his shin by attempting to exhibit to the company how much better he could jump over a stick than the puppets.

[3] I am willing to hope that there may have been some mistake as to this anecdote though I had it from a Dignitary of the Church [probably Bishop Percy. *Powell.*] Dr. Isaac Goldsmith, his near relation, was Dean of Cloyne, in 1747.

by no means correct. He told me that he had sold a novel for four hundred pounds. This was his *Vicar of Wakefield*. But Johnson informed me, that he had made the bargain for Goldsmith, and the price was sixty pounds. 'And, Sir, (said he,) a sufficient price too, when it was sold; for then the fame of Goldsmith had not been elevated, as it afterwards was, by his *Traveller*; and the bookseller had such faint hopes of profit by his bargain, that he kept the manuscript by him a long time, and did not publish it till after *The Traveller* had appeared. Then, to be sure, it was accidentally worth more money.'

Mrs. Piozzi[1] and Sir John Hawkins[2] have strangely mis-stated the history of Goldsmith's situation and Johnson's friendly interference, when this novel was sold. I shall give it authentically from Johnson's own exact narration:—'I received one morning a message from poor Goldsmith that he was in great distress, and, as it was not in his power to come to me, begging that I would come to him as soon as possible. I sent him a guinea, and promised to come to him directly. I accordingly went as soon as I was drest, and found that his landlady had arrested him for his rent, at which he was in a violent passion. I perceived that he had already changed my guinea, and had got a bottle of Madeira and a glass before him. I put the cork into the bottle, desired he would be calm, and began to talk to him of the means by which he might be extricated. He then told me that he had a novel ready for the press, which he produced to me. I looked into it, and saw its merit; told the landlady I should soon return, and having gone to a bookseller, sold it for sixty pounds. I brought Goldsmith the money, and he discharged his rent, not without rating his landlady in a high tone for having used him so ill.'[3]

---

[1] *Anecdotes of Johnson*, p. 119.

[2] *Life of Johnson*, p. 420.

[3] It may not be improper to annex here Mrs. Piozzi's account of this transaction, in her own words, as a specimen of the extreme inaccuracy with which all her anecdotes of Dr. Johnson are related, or rather discoloured and distorted:—'I have forgotten the year, but it could scarcely, I think, be later than 1765 or 1766, that he was *called abruptly from our house after dinner*, and returning *in about three hours*, said he had been with an enraged authour, whose landlady pressed him for payment within doors, while the bailiffs beset him without; that he was *drinking himself drunk* with Madeira, to drown

My next meeting with Johnson was on Friday the 1st of July, when he and I and Dr. Goldsmith supped together at the Mitre. I was before this time pretty well acquainted with Goldsmith, who was one of the brightest ornaments of the Johnsonian school. Goldsmith's respectful attachment to Johnson was then at its height; for his own literary reputation had not yet distinguished him so much as to excite a vain desire of competition with his great Master. He had increased my admiration of the goodness of Johnson's heart, by incidental remarks in the course of conversation, such as, when I mentioned Mr. Levet, whom he entertained under his roof, 'He is poor and honest, which is recommendation enough to Johnson;' and when I wondered that he was very kind to a man of whom I had heard a very bad character, 'He is now become miserable, and that insures the protection of Johnson.'

Goldsmith attempted this evening to maintain, I suppose from an affectation of paradox, 'that knowledge was not desirable on its own account, for it often was a source of unhappiness.' JOHNSON. 'Why, Sir, that knowledge may in some cases produce unhappiness, I allow. But, upon the whole, knowledge, *per se*, is certainly an object which every man would wish to attain, although, perhaps, he may not take the trouble necessary for attaining it.'

Dr. John Campbell, the celebrated political and biographical writer, being mentioned, Johnson said, 'Campbell is a man of much knowledge, and has a good share of imagination. His *Hermippus Redivivus* is very entertaining, as an account of the Hermetick philosophy, and as furnishing a curious history of the extravagancies of the human mind. If it were merely imaginary it would be nothing at all. Campbell is not always rigidly careful of truth in his conversation; but I do not believe there is any

care, and fretting over a novel, which, when *finished*, was to be his *whole fortune*, but *he could not get it done for distraction*, nor could he step out of doors to offer it for sale. Mr. Johnson, therefore, sent away the bottle, and went to the bookseller, recommending the performance, and *desiring some immediate relief*; which when he brought back to the writer, *he called the woman of the house directly to partake of punch, and pass their time in merriment*. *Anecdotes of Dr. Johnson*, p. 119.

thing of this carelessness in his books. Campbell is a good man, a pious man. I am afraid he has not been in the inside of a church for many years;[1] but he never passes a church without pulling off his hat. This shews that he has good principles. I used to go pretty often to Campbell's on a Sunday evening till I began to consider that the shoals of Scotchmen who flocked about him might probably say, when any thing of mine was well done, 'Ay, ay, he has learnt this of CAWMELL!'

He talked very contemptuously of Churchill's poetry, observing, that 'it had a temporary currency, only from its audacity of abuse, and being filled with living names, and that it would sink into oblivion.' I ventured to hint that he was not quite a fair judge, as Churchill had attacked him violently. JOHNSON. 'Nay, Sir, I am a very fair judge. He did not attack me violently till he found I did not like his poetry; and his attack on me shall not prevent me from continuing to say what I think of him, from an apprehension that it may be ascribed to resentment. No, Sir, I called the fellow a blockhead at first, and I will call him a blockhead still. However, I will acknowledge that I have a better opinion of him now, than I once had; for he has shewn more fertility than I expected. To be sure, he is a tree that cannot produce good fruit: he only bears crabs. But, Sir, a tree that produces a great many crabs is better than a tree which produces only a few.'

In this depreciation of Churchill's poetry I could not agree with him. It is very true that the greatest part of it is upon the

---

[1] I am inclined to think that he was misinformed as to this circumstance. I own I am jealous for my worthy friend Dr. John Campbell. For though Milton could without remorse absent himself from publick worship I cannot. On the contrary, I have the same habitual impressions upon my mind, with those of a truly venerable Judge, who said to Mr. Langton, 'Friend Langton, If I have not been at church on Sunday, I do not feel myself easy.' Dr. Campbell was a sincerely religious man. Lord Macartney, who is eminent for his variety of knowledge, and attention to men of talents, and knew him well, told me, that when he called on him in a morning, he found him reading a chapter in the Greek New Testament, which he informed his Lordship was his constant practice. The quantity of Dr. Campbell's composition is almost incredible, and his labours brought him large profits. Dr. Joseph Warton told me that Johnson said of him, 'He is the richest authour that ever grazed the common of literature.'

topicks of the day, on which account, as it brought him great
fame and profit at the time, it must proportionally slide out of
the publick attention as other occasional objects succeed. But
Churchill had extraordinary vigour both of thought and expression. His portraits of the players will ever be valuable to the
true lovers of the drama; and his strong caricatures of several
eminent men of his age, will not be forgotten by the curious.
Let me add, that there are in his works many passages which are
of a general nature; and his *Prophecy of Famine* is a poem of no
ordinary merit. It is, indeed, falsely injurious to Scotland, but
therefore may be allowed a greater share of invention.

Bonnell Thornton had just published a burlesque *Ode on St.
Cecilia's day, adapted to the ancient British musick, viz. the salt-
box, the jew's-harp, the marrow-bones and cleaver, the hum-strum or
hurdy-gurdy, &c.* Johnson praised its humour, and seemed much
diverted with it. He repeated the following passage:—

> 'In strains more exalted the salt-box shall join,
>   And clattering and battering and clapping combine;
> With a rap and a tap while the hollow side sounds,
> Up and down leaps the flap, and with rattling rebounds.'

I mentioned the periodical paper called *The Connoisseur.* He
said it wanted matter.—No doubt it has not the deep thinking
of Johnson's writings. But surely it has just views of the surface
of life, and a very sprightly manner. His opinion of *The World*
was not much higher than of the *Connoisseur.*

Let me here apologize for the imperfect manner in which I am
obliged to exhibit Johnson's conversation at this period. In the
early part of my acquaintance with him, I was so wrapt in admiration of his extraordinary colloquial talents, and so little accustomed to his peculiar mode of expression, that I found it
extremely difficult to recollect and record his conversation with
its genuine vigour and vivacity. In progress of time, when my
mind was, as it were, *strongly impregnated with the Johnsonian
æther*, I could, with much more facility and exactness, carry in
my memory and commit to paper the exuberant variety of his
wisdom and wit.

At this time *Miss* Williams, as she was then called, though she did not reside with him in the Temple under his roof, but had lodgings in Bolt-court, Fleet-street, had so much of his attention, that he every night drank tea with her before he went home, however late it might be, and she always sat up for him. This, it may be fairly conjectured, was not alone a proof of his regard for *her*, but of his own unwillingness to go into solitude, before that unseasonable hour at which he had habituated himself to expect the oblivion of repose. Dr. Goldsmith, being a privileged man, went with him this night, strutting away, and calling to me with an air of superiority, like that of an esoterick over an exoterick disciple of a sage of antiquity, 'I go to Miss Williams.' I confess, I then envied him this mighty privilege, of which he seemed so proud; but it was not long before I obtained the same mark of distinction.

On Tuesday the 5th of July, I again visited Johnson. He told me he had looked into the poems of a pretty voluminous writer, Mr. (now Dr.) John Ogilvie, one of the Presbyterian ministers of Scotland, which had lately come out, but could find no thinking in them. BOSWELL. 'Is there not imagination in them, Sir?' JOHNSON. 'Why, Sir, there is in them what *was* imagination, but it is no more imagination in *him*, than sound is sound in the echo. And his diction too is not his own. We have long ago seen *white-robed innocence*, and *flower-bespangled meads.*'

Talking of London, he observed, 'Sir, if you wish to have a just notion of the magnitude of this city, you must not be satisfied with seeing its great streets and squares, but must survey the innumerable little lanes and courts. It is not in the showy evolutions of buildings, but in the multiplicity of human habitations which are crouded together, that the wonderful immensity of London consists.'—I have often amused myself with thinking how different a place London is to different people. They, whose narrow minds are contracted to the consideration of some one particular pursuit, view it only through that medium. A politician thinks of it merely as the seat of government in its different departments; a grazier, as a vast market for cattle; a mercantile man, as a place where a prodigious deal of business is done upon

'Change; a dramatick enthusiast, as the grand scene of theatrical entertainments; a man of pleasure, as an assemblage of taverns, and the great emporium for ladies of easy virtue. But the intellectual man is struck with it, as comprehending the whole of human life in all its variety, the contemplation of which is inexhaustible.

On Wednesday, July 6, he was engaged to sup with me at my lodgings in Downing-street, Westminster. But on the preceding night my landlord having behaved very rudely to me and some company who were with me, I had resolved not to remain another night in his house. I was exceedingly uneasy at the aukward appearance I supposed I should make to Johnson and the other gentlemen whom I had invited, not being able to receive them at home, and being obliged to order supper at the Mitre. I went to Johnson in the morning, and talked of it as a serious distress. He laughed, and said, 'Consider, Sir, how insignificant this will appear a twelvemonth hence.'—Were this consideration to be applied to most of the little vexatious incidents of life, by which our quiet is too often disturbed, it would prevent many painful sensations. I have tried it frequently, with good effect. 'There is nothing (continued he) in this mighty misfortune; nay, we shall be better at the Mitre.' I told him that I had been at Sir John Fielding's office, complaining of my landlord, and had been informed, that though I had taken my lodgings for a year, I might, upon proof of his bad behaviour, quit them when I pleased, without being under an obligation to pay rent for any longer time than while I possessed them. The fertility of Johnson's mind could shew itself even upon so small a matter as this. 'Why, Sir, (said he,) I suppose this must be the law, since you have been told so in Bow-street. But, if your landlord could hold you to your bargain, and the lodgings should be yours for a year, you may certainly use them as you think fit. So, Sir, you may quarter two life-guardsmen upon him; or you may send the greatest scoundrel you can find into your apartments; or you may say that you want to make some experiments in natural philosophy, and may burn a large quantity of assafœtida in his house.'

I had as my guests this evening at the Mitre tavern, Dr.

Johnson, Dr. Goldsmith, Mr. Thomas Davies, Mr. Eccles, an
Irish gentleman, for whose agreeable company I was obliged to
Mr. Davies, and the Reverend Mr. John Ogilvie,[1] who was
desirous of being in company with my illustrious friend, while
I, in my turn, was proud to have the honour of shewing one of
my countrymen upon what easy terms Johnson permitted me to
live with him.

Goldsmith, as usual, endeavoured, with too much eagerness,
to *shine*, and disputed very warmly with Johnson against the
well-known maxim of the British constitution, 'the King can do
no wrong;' affirming, that 'what was morally false could not be
politically true; and as the King might, in the exercise of his
regal power, command and cause the doing of what was wrong,
it certainly might be said, in sense and in reason, that he could
do wrong.' JOHNSON. 'Sir, you are to consider, that in our constitution, according to its true principles, the King is the head;
he is supreme; he is above every thing, and there is no power by
which he can be tried. Therefore it is, Sir, that we hold the King
can do no wrong; that whatever may happen to be wrong in
government may not be above our reach, by being ascribed to
Majesty. Redress is always to be had against oppression, by
punishing the immediate agents. The King, though he should
command, cannot force a Judge to condemn a man unjustly;
therefore it is the Judge whom we prosecute and punish. Political
institutions are formed upon the consideration of what will most
frequently tend to the good of the whole, although now and then
exceptions may occur. Thus it is better in general that a nation
should have a supreme legislative power, although it may at
times be abused. And then, Sir, there is this consideration, that
*if the abuse be enormous, Nature will rise up, and claiming her
original rights, overturn a corrupt political system.*' I mark this

---

[1] The northern bard mentioned page 298. When I asked Dr. Johnson's
permission to introduce him, he obligingly agreed; adding, however, with
a sly pleasantry, 'but he must give us none of his poetry.' It is remarkable
that Johnson and Churchill, however much they differed in other points,
agreed on this subject. See Churchill's *Journey.* It is, however, but justice
to Dr. Ogilvie to observe, that his *Day of Judgement* has no inconsiderable
share of merit.

animated sentence with peculiar pleasure, as a noble instance of that truly dignified spirit of freedom which ever glowed in his heart, though he was charged with slavish tenets by superficial observers; because he was at all times indignant against that false patriotism, that pretended love of freedom, that unruly restlessness, which is inconsistent with the stable authority of any good government.

This generous sentiment, which he uttered with great fervour, struck me exceedingly, and stirred my blood to that pitch of fancied resistance, the possibility of which I am glad to keep in mind, but to which I trust I never shall be forced.

'Great abilities (said he) are not requisite for an Historian; for in historical composition, all the greatest powers of the human mind are quiescent. He has facts ready to his hand; so there is no exercise of invention. Imagination is not required in any high degree; only about as much as is used in the lower kinds of poetry. Some penetration, accuracy, and colouring will fit a man for the task, if he can give the application which is necessary.'

'Bayle's *Dictionary* is a very useful work for those to consult who love the biographical part of literature, which is what I love most.'

Talking of the eminent writers in Queen Anne's reign, he observed, 'I think Dr. Arbuthnot the first man among them. He was the most universal genius, being an excellent physician, a man of deep learning, and a man of much humour. Mr. Addison was, to be sure, a great man; his learning was not profound; but his morality, his humour, and his elegance of writing, set him very high.'

Mr. Ogilvie was unlucky enough to choose for the topick of his conversation the praises of his native country. He began with saying, that there was very rich land round Edinburgh. Goldsmith, who had studied physick there, contradicted this, very untruly, with a sneering laugh. Disconcerted a little by this, Mr. Ogilvie then took new ground, where, I suppose, he thought himself perfectly safe; for he observed, that Scotland had a great many noble wild prospects. JOHNSON. 'I believe, Sir, you have a great many. Norway, too, has noble wild prospects; and Lapland is remarkable for prodigious noble wild prospects. But, Sir, let me tell you, the noblest prospect which a Scotchman ever sees, is the high road that leads him to England!' This unexpected and pointed sally produced a roar of applause. After all, however, those, who admire the rude grandeur of Nature, cannot deny it to Caledonia.

On Saturday, July 9, I found Johnson surrounded with a numerous levee, but have not preserved any part of his conversation. On the 14th we had another evening by ourselves at the Mitre. It happening to be a very rainy night, I made some common-place observations on the relaxation of nerves and depression of spirits which such weather occasioned; adding, however, that it was good for the vegetable creation. Johnson, who, as we have already seen, denied that the temperature of the air had any influence on the human frame, answered, with a smile of ridicule, 'Why yes, Sir, it is good for vegetables, and for the animals who eat those vegetables, and for the animals who eat those animals.' This observation of his aptly enough introduced a good supper; and I soon forgot, in Johnson's company, the influence of a moist atmosphere.

Feeling myself now quite at ease as his companion, though I had all possible reverence for him, I expressed a regret that I could not be so easy with my father, though he was not much older than Johnson, and certainly however respectable had not more learning and greater abilities to depress me. I asked him the reason of this. JOHNSON. 'Why, Sir, I am a man of the world. I live in the world, and I take, in some degree, the colour of the world as it moves along. Your father is a Judge in a remote part of the island, and all his notions are taken from the old world. Besides, Sir, there must always be a struggle between a father and son, while one aims at power and the other at independence.' I said, I was afraid my father would force me to be a lawyer. JOHNSON. 'Sir, you need not be afraid of his forcing you to be a laborious practising lawyer; that is not in his power. For as the proverb says, "One man may lead a horse to the water, but twenty cannot make him drink." He may be displeased that you are not what he wishes you to be; but that displeasure will not go far. If he insists only on your having as much law as is necessary for a man of property, and then endeavours to get you into Parliament, he is quite in the right.'

He enlarged very convincingly upon the excellence of rhyme over blank verse in English poetry. I mentioned to him that Dr. Adam Smith, in his lectures upon composition, when I studied under him in the College of Glasgow, had maintained the same opinion strenuously, and I repeated some of his arguments. JOHNSON. 'Sir, I was once in company with Smith, and we did not take to each other; but had I known that he loved rhyme as much as you tell me he does, I should have HUGGED him.'

Talking of those who denied the truth of Christianity, he said, 'It is always easy to be on the negative side. If a man were now to deny that there is salt upon the table, you could not reduce him to an absurdity. Come, let us try this a little further. I deny that Canada is taken, and I can support my denial by pretty good arguments. The French are a much more numerous people than we; and it is not likely that they would allow us to take it. "But the ministry have assured us, in all the formality of *The Gazette*, that it is taken."—Very true. But the ministry have put us to an enormous expence by the war in America, and it is their interest to persuade us that we have got something for our money.— "But the fact is confirmed by thousands of men who were at the taking of it."—Ay, but these men have still more interest in deceiving us. They don't want that you should think the French have beat them, but that they have beat the French. Now suppose you should go over and find that it is really taken, that would only satisfy yourself; for when you come home we will not believe you. We will say, you have been bribed.—Yet, Sir, notwithstanding all these plausible objections, we have no doubt that Canada is really ours. Such is the weight of common testimony. How much stronger are the evidences of the Christian religion!'

'Idleness is a disease which must be combated; but I would not advise a rigid adherence to a particular plan of study. I myself have never persisted in any plan for two days together. A man ought to read just as inclination leads him; for what he reads as a task will do him little good. A young man should read five hours in a day, and so may acquire a great deal of knowledge.'

To a man of vigorous intellect and ardent curiosity like his own, reading without a regular plan may be beneficial; though even such a man must submit to it, if he would attain a full understanding of any of the sciences.

To such a degree of unrestrained frankness had he now accustomed me, that in the course of this evening I talked of the numerous reflections which had been thrown out against him on account of his having accepted a pension from his present Majesty. 'Why, Sir, (said he, with a hearty laugh,) it is a mighty foolish noise that they make.[1] I have accepted of a pension as a reward which has been thought due to my literary merit; and now that I have this pension, I am the same man in every respect that I have ever been; I retain the same principles. It is true, that I cannot now curse (smiling) the House of Hanover; nor would it be decent for me to drink King James's health in the wine that King George gives me money to pay for. But, Sir, I think that the pleasure of cursing the House of Hanover, and drinking King James's health, are amply overbalanced by three hundred pounds a year.'

There was here, most certainly, an affectation of more Jacobitism than he really had; and indeed an intention of admitting, for the moment, in a much greater extent than it really existed, the charge of disaffection imputed to him by the world, merely for the purpose of shewing how dexterously he could repel an attack, even though he were placed in the most disadvantageous position; for I have heard him declare, that if holding up his right hand would have secured victory at Culloden to Prince Charles's army, he was not sure he would have held it up; so little confidence had he in the right claimed by the house of Stuart, and so fearful was he of the consequences of another revolution on the throne of Great-Britain; and Mr. Topham Beauclerk assured

---

[1] When I mentioned the same idle clamour to him several years afterwards, he said, with a smile, 'I wish my pension were twice as large, that they might make twice as much noise.'

me, he had heard him say this before he had his pension. At another time he said to Mr. Langton, 'Nothing has ever offered, that has made it worth my while to consider the question fully.' He, however, also said to the same gentleman, talking of King James the Second, 'It was become impossible for him to reign any longer in this country.' He no doubt had an early attachment to the House of Stuart; but his zeal had cooled as his reason strengthened. Indeed I heard him once say, that 'after the death of a violent Whig, with whom he used to contend with great eagerness, he felt his Toryism much abated.'[1] I suppose he meant Mr. Walmsley.

Yet there is no doubt that at earlier periods he was wont often to exercise both his pleasantry and ingenuity in talking Jacobitism. My much respected friend, Dr. Douglas, now Bishop of Salisbury, has favoured me with the following admirable instance from his Lordship's own recollection. One day when dining at old Mr. Langton's, where Miss Roberts, his niece, was one of the company, Johnson, with his usual complacent attention to the fair sex, took her by the hand and said, 'My dear, I hope you are a Jacobite.' Old Mr. Langton, who, though a high and steady Tory, was attached to the present Royal Family, seemed offended, and asked Johnson, with great warmth, what he could mean by putting such a question to his niece? 'Why, Sir, (said Johnson) I meant no offence to your niece, I meant her a great compliment. A Jacobite, Sir, believes in the divine right of Kings. He that believes in the divine right of Kings believes in a Divinity. A Jacobite believes in the divine right of Bishops. He that believes in the divine right of Bishops believes in the divine authority of the Christian religion. Therefore, Sir, a Jacobite is neither an Atheist nor a Deist. That cannot be said of a Whig; for *Whiggism is a negation of all principle.*'[2]

---

[1] *Journal of a Tour to the Hebrides*, 3rd edit. p. 402 [Nov. 10].

[2] He used to tell, with great humour, from my relation to him, the following little story of my early years, which was literally true: 'Boswell, in the year 1745, was a fine boy, wore a white cockade, and prayed for King James, till one of his uncles (General Cochran) gave him a shilling on condition that he should pray for King George, which he accordingly did. So you see (says Boswell) that *Whigs of all ages are made the same way.*'

He advised me, when abroad, to be as much as I could with the Professors in the Universities, and with the Clergy; for from their conversation I might expect the best accounts of every thing in whatever country I should be, with the additional advantage of keeping my learning alive.

It will be observed, that when giving me advice as to my travels, Dr. Johnson did not dwell upon cities, and palaces, and pictures, and shows, and Arcadian scenes. He was of Lord Essex's opinion, who advises his kinsman Roger Earl of Rutland, 'rather to go an hundred miles to speak with one wise man, than five miles to see a fair town.'[1]

I described to him an impudent fellow[2] from Scotland, who affected to be a savage, and railed at all established systems. JOHNSON. 'There is nothing surprizing in this, Sir. He wants to make himself conspicuous. He would tumble in a hogstye, as long as you looked at him and called to him to come out. But let him alone, never mind him, and he'll soon give it over.'

I added, that the same person maintained that there was no distinction between virtue and vice. JOHNSON. 'Why, Sir, if the fellow does not think as he speaks, he is lying; and I see not what honour he can propose to himself from having the character of a lyar. But if he does really think that there is no distinction between virtue and vice, why, Sir, when he leaves our houses, let us count our spoons.'

Sir David Dalrymple, now one of the Judges of Scotland by the title of Lord Hailes, had contributed much to increase my high opinion of Johnson, on account of his writings, long before I attained to a personal acquaintance with him; I, in return, had informed Johnson of Sir David's eminent character for learning and religion; and Johnson was so much pleased, that at one of our evening meetings he gave him for his toast. I at this time kept up a very frequent correspondence with Sir David; and I read to Dr. Johnson to-night the following passage from the letter which I had last received from him:—

'It gives me pleasure to think that you have obtained the

---

[1] *Letter to Rutland on Travel*, 16mo. 1569.
[2] [James Macpherson. *Boswelliana*, 210.]

friendship of Mr. Samuel Johnson. He is one of the best moral
writers which England has produced. At the same time, I envy
you the free and undisguised converse with such a man. May I
beg you to present my best respects to him, and to assure him
of the veneration which I entertain for the authour of the *Rambler*
and of *Rasselas*? Let me recommend this last work to you; with
the *Rambler* you certainly are acquainted. In *Rasselas* you will see
a tender-hearted operator, who probes the wound only to heal
it. Swift, on the contrary, mangles human nature. He cuts and
slashes, as if he took pleasure in the operation, like the tyrant
who said, *Ita feri ut se sentiat emori.*'[1]

Johnson seemed to be much gratified by this just and well-
turned compliment.

He recommended to me to keep a journal of my life, full and
unreserved. He said it would be a very good exercise, and would
yield me great satisfaction when the particulars were faded from
my remembrance. I was uncommonly fortunate in having had a
previous coincidence of opinion with him upon this subject, for
I had kept such a journal for some time; and it was no small
pleasure to me to have this to tell him, and to receive his approbation. He counselled me to keep it private, and said I might surely
have a friend who would burn it in case of my death. From this
habit I have been enabled to give the world so many anecdotes,
which would otherwise have been lost to posterity. I mentioned
that I was afraid I put into my journal too many little incidents.
JOHNSON. 'There is nothing, Sir, too little for so little a creature
as man. It is by studying little things that we attain the great art
of having as little misery and as much happiness as possible.'

Next morning Mr. Dempster happened to call on me, and was
so much struck even with the imperfect account which I gave him
of Dr. Johnson's conversation, that to his honour be it recorded,
when I complained that drinking port and sitting up late with
him affected my nerves for some time after, he said, 'One had
better be palsied at eighteen, than not keep company with such
a man.'

[1] ['Strike so that he may feel himself dying.' Suetonius, *Caligula*, chap.
xxx.]

On Tuesday, July 18,[1] I found tall Sir Thomas Robinson sitting with Johnson. Sir Thomas said, that the king of Prussia valued himself upon three things;—upon being a hero, a musician, and an authour. JOHNSON. 'Pretty well, Sir, for one man. As to his being an authour, I have not looked at his poetry; but his prose is poor stuff. He writes just as you might suppose Voltaire's footboy to do, who has been his amanuensis. He has such parts as the valet might have, and about as much of the colouring of the style as might be got by transcribing his works.' When I was at Ferney, I repeated this to Voltaire, in order to reconcile him somewhat to Johnson, whom he, in affecting the English mode of expression, had previously characterised as 'a superstitious dog;' but after hearing such a criticism on Frederick the Great, with whom he was then on bad terms, he exclaimed, 'An honest fellow!'

But I think the criticism much too severe; for the *Memoirs of the House of Brandenburgh* are written as well as many works of that kind. His poetry, for the style of which he himself makes a frank apology, '*Jargonnant un François barbare*,' though fraught with pernicious ravings of infidelity, has, in many places, great animation, and in some a pathetick tenderness.

Upon this contemptuous animadversion on the King of Prussia, I observed to Johnson, 'It would seem then, Sir, that much less parts are necessary to make a King, than to make an Authour; for the King of Prussia is confessedly the greatest King now in Europe, yet you think he makes a very poor figure as an Authour.'

Mr. Levet this day shewed me Dr. Johnson's library, which was contained in two garrets over his Chambers, where Lintot, son of the celebrated bookseller of that name, had formerly his warehouse. I found a number of good books, but very dusty and in great confusion. The floor was strewed with manuscript leaves, in Johnson's own handwriting, which I beheld with a degree of veneration, supposing they perhaps might contain portions of *The Rambler* or of *Rasselas*. I observed an apparatus for chymical experiments, of which Johnson was all his life very fond. The place seemed to be very favourable for retirement and medita-

[1] [Tuesday was the 19th.]

tion. Johnson told me, that he went up thither without mentioning it to his servant, when he wanted to study, secure from
interruption; for he would not allow his servant to say he was
not at home when he really was. 'A servant's strict regard for
truth, (said he) must be weakened by such a practice. A philosopher may know that it is merely a form of denial; but few servants are such nice distinguishers. If I accustom a servant to tell
a lie for *me*, have I not reason to apprehend that he will tell many
lies for *himself*?' I am, however, satisfied that every servant, of
any degree of intelligence, understands saying his master is not
at home, not at all as the affirmation of a fact, but as customary
words, intimating that his master wishes not to be seen; so that
there can be no bad effect from it.

Mr. Temple, now vicar of St. Gluvias, Cornwall, who had
been my intimate friend for many years, had at this time chambers
in Farrar's-buildings, at the bottom of Inner Temple-lane, which
he kindly lent me upon my quitting my lodgings, he being to
return to Trinity Hall, Cambridge. I found them particularly
convenient for me, as they were so near Dr. Johnson's.

On Wednesday, July 20, Dr. Johnson, Mr. Dempster, and
my uncle Dr. Boswell, who happened to be now in London,
supped with me at these Chambers. JOHNSON. 'Pity is not
natural to man. Children are always cruel. Savages are always
cruel. Pity is acquired and improved by the cultivation of reason.
We may have uneasy sensations from seeing a creature in
distress, without pity; for we have not pity unless we wish to
relieve them. When I am on my way to dine with a friend, and
finding it late, have bid the coachman make haste, if I happen to
attend when he whips his horses, I may feel unpleasantly that the
animals are put to pain, but I do not wish him to desist. No, Sir,
I wish him to drive on.'

Mr. Alexander Donaldson, bookseller of Edinburgh, had for
some time opened a shop in London, and sold his cheap editions
of the most popular English books, in defiance of the supposed
common-law right of *Literary Property*. Johnson, though he concurred in the opinion which was afterwards sanctioned by a
judgement of the House of Lords, that there was no such right,

was at this time very angry that the Booksellers of London, for whom he uniformly professed much regard, should suffer from an invasion of what they had ever considered to be secure: and he was loud and violent against Mr. Donaldson. 'He is a fellow who takes advantage of the law to injure his brethren; for, notwithstanding that the statute secures only fourteen years of exclusive right, it has always been understood by *the trade*, that he, who buys the copy-right of a book from the authour, obtains a perpetual property; and upon that belief, numberless bargains are made to transfer that property after the expiration of the statutory term. Now Donaldson, I say, takes advantage here, of people who have really an equitable title from usage; and if we consider how few of the books, of which they buy the property, succeed so well as to bring profit, we should be of opinion that the term of fourteen years is too short; it should be sixty years.' DEMPSTER. 'Donaldson, Sir, is anxious for the encouragement of literature. He reduces the price of books, so that poor students may buy them.' JOHNSON, (laughing) 'Well, Sir, allowing that to be his motive, he is no better than Robin Hood, who robbed the rich in order to give to the poor.'

It is remarkable, that when the great question concerning Literary Property came to be ultimately tried before the supreme tribunal of this country, in consequence of the very spirited exertions of Mr. Donaldson, Dr. Johnson was zealous against a perpetuity; but he thought that the term of the exclusive right of authours should be considerably enlarged. He was then for granting a hundred years.

The conversation now turned upon Mr. David Hume's style. JOHNSON. 'Why, Sir, his style is not English; the structure of his sentences is French. Now the French structure and the English structure may, in the nature of things, be equally good. But if you allow that the English language is established, he is wrong. My name might originally have been Nicholson, as well as Johnson; but were you to call me Nicholson now, you would call me very absurdly.'

Rousseau's treatise on the inequality of mankind was at this time a fashionable topick. It gave rise to an observation by Mr.

Dempster, that the advantages of fortune and rank were nothing to a wise man, who ought to value only merit. JOHNSON. 'If man were a savage, living in the woods by himself, this might be true; but in civilized society we all depend upon each other, and our happiness is very much owing to the good opinion of mankind. Now, Sir, in civilized society, external advantages make us more respected. A man with a good coat upon his back meets with a better reception than he who has a bad one. Sir, you may analyse this, and say what is there in it? But that will avail you nothing, for it is a part of a general system. Pound St. Paul's Church into atoms, and consider any single atom; it is, to be sure, good for nothing: but, put all these atoms together, and you have St. Paul's Church. So it is with human felicity, which is made up of many ingredients, each of which may be shewn to be very insignificant. In civilized society, personal merit will not serve you so much as money will. Sir, you may make the experiment. Go into the street, and give one man a lecture on morality, and another a shilling, and see which will respect you most. If you wish only to support nature, Sir William Petty fixes your allowance at three pounds a year; but as times are much altered, let us call it six pounds. This sum will fill your belly, shelter you from the weather, and even get you a strong lasting coat, supposing it to be made of good bull's hide. Now, Sir, all beyond this is artificial, and is desired in order to obtain a greater degree of respect from our fellow-creatures. And, Sir, if six hundred pounds a year procure a man more consequence, and, of course, more happiness than six pounds a year, the same proportion will hold as to six thousand, and so on as far as opulence can be carried. Perhaps he who has a large fortune may not be so happy as he who has a small one; but that must proceed from other causes than from his having the large fortune: for, *cæteris paribus*, he who is rich in a civilized society, must be happier than he who is poor; as riches, if properly used, (and it is a man's own fault if they are not,) must be productive of the highest advantages. Money, to be sure, of itself is of no use; for its only use is to part with it. Rousseau, and all those who deal in paradoxes, are led away by a childish desire of novelty. When I was a boy, I used always to choose the wrong side of a debate, because most ingenious things, that is to say, most new things, could be said upon it. Sir, there is nothing for which you may not muster up more plausible arguments, than those which are urged against wealth and other external advantages. Why, now, there is stealing; why should it be thought a crime? When we consider by what unjust methods property has been often acquired, and that what was unjustly got it must be unjust to keep, where is the harm in one man's taking the property of another from him? Besides, Sir, when we consider the bad use that many people make of their property, and how much better use the thief may make of it, it may be defended as a very allowable practice. Yet, Sir, the experience of mankind has discovered stealing to be so very bad a thing, that they make no scruple to hang a man for it. When I was running about this town a very poor fellow, I was a great arguer for the advantages of poverty; but I was, at the same time, very sorry to be poor. Sir, all the arguments which are brought to represent poverty as no evil, shew it to be evidently a great evil. You never find people labouring to convince you that you may live very happily upon a plentiful fortune.—So you hear people talking how miserable a King must be; and yet they all wish to be in his place.'

It was suggested that Kings must be unhappy, because they are deprived of the greatest of all satisfactions, easy and unreserved society. JOHNSON. 'That is an ill-founded notion. Being a King does not exclude a man from such society. Great Kings have always been social. The King of Prussia, the only great King at present, is very social. Charles the Second, the last King of England who was a man of parts, was social; and our Henrys and Edwards were all social.'

Mr. Dempster having endeavoured to maintain that intrinsick merit *ought* to make the only distinction amongst mankind. JOHNSON. 'Why, Sir, mankind have found that this cannot be. How shall we determine the proportion of intrinsick merit? Were that to be the only distinction amongst mankind, we should soon quarrel about the degrees of it. Were all distinctions abolished, the strongest would not long acquiesce, but would endeavour to obtain a superiority by their bodily strength. But, Sir, as subordination is very necessary for society, and contentions for superiority very dangerous, mankind, that is to say, all civilized nations, have settled it upon a plain invariable principle. A man is born to hereditary rank; or his being appointed to certain offices, gives him a certain rank. Subordination tends greatly to human happiness. Were we all upon an equality, we should have no other enjoyment than mere animal pleasure.'

I said, I considered distinction of rank to be of so much importance in civilized society, that if I were asked on the same day to dine with the first Duke in England, and with the first man in Britain for genius, I should hesitate which to prefer. JOHNSON. 'To be sure, Sir, if you were to dine only once, and it were never to be known where you dined, you would choose rather to dine with the first man for genius; but to gain most respect, you should dine with the first Duke in England. For nine people in ten that you meet with, would have a higher opinion of you for having dined with a Duke; and the great genius himself would receive you better, because you had been with the great Duke.'

He took care to guard himself against any possible suspicion that his settled principles of reverence for rank and respect for wealth were at all owing to mean or interested motives; for he asserted his own independence as a literary man. 'No man (said he) who ever lived by literature, has lived more independently than I have done.' He said he had taken longer time than he needed to have done in composing his *Dictionary*. He received our compliments upon that great work with complacency, and told us that the *Academia della Crusca* could scarcely believe that it was done by one man.

Next morning I found him alone, and have preserved the following fragments of his conversation. Of a gentleman[1] who was mentioned, he said, 'I have not met with any man for a long time who has given me such general displeasure. He is totally unfixed in his principles, and wants to puzzle other people.'

[1] [George Dempster. *Boswell's Letters*, i. 27.]

I said his principles had been poisoned by a noted infidel writer,[1] but that he was, nevertheless, a benevolent good man. JOHN-SON. 'We can have no dependence upon that instinctive, that constitutional goodness which is not founded upon principle. I grant you that such a man may be a very amiable member of society. I can conceive him placed in such a situation that he is not much tempted to deviate from what is right; and as every man prefers virtue, when there is not some strong incitement to transgress its precepts, I can conceive him doing nothing wrong. But if such a man stood in need of money, I should not like to trust him; and I should certainly not trust him with young ladies, for *there* there is always temptation. Hume, and other sceptical innovators, are vain men, and will gratify themselves at any expence. Truth will not afford sufficient food to their vanity; so they have betaken themselves to errour. Truth, Sir, is a cow which will yield such people no more milk, and so they are gone to milk the bull. If I could have allowed myself to gratify my vanity at the expence of truth, what fame might I have acquired. Every thing which Hume has advanced against Christianity had passed through my mind long before he wrote. Always remember this, that after a system is well settled upon positive evidence, a few partial objections ought not to shake it. The human mind is so limited, that it cannot take in all the parts of a subject, so that there may be objections raised against any thing. There are objections against a *plenum*, and objections against a *vacuum*; yet one of them must certainly be true.'

I mentioned Hume's argument against the belief of miracles, that it is more probable that the witnesses to the truth of them are mistaken, or speak falsely, than that the miracles should be true. JOHNSON. 'Why, Sir, the great difficulty of proving miracles should make us very cautious in believing them. But let us consider; although GOD has made Nature to operate by certain fixed laws, yet it is not unreasonable to think that he may suspend those laws, in order to establish a system highly advantageous to mankind. Now the Christian religion is a most beneficial system, as it gives us light and certainty where we were

---

[1] [Hume. *Boswell's Letters*, i. 27.]

before in darkness and doubt. The miracles which prove it are attested by men who had no interest in deceiving us; but who, on the contrary, were told that they should suffer persecution, and did actually lay down their lives in confirmation of the truth of the facts which they asserted. Indeed, for some centuries the heathens did not pretend to deny the miracles; but said they were performed by the aid of evil spirits. This is a circumstance of great weight. Then, Sir, when we take the proofs derived from prophecies which have been so exactly fulfilled, we have most satisfactory evidence. Supposing a miracle possible, as to which, in my opinion, there can be no doubt, we have as strong evidence for the miracles in support of Christianity, as the nature of the thing admits.'

At night Mr. Johnson and I supped in a private room at the Turk's Head coffee-house, in the Strand. 'I encourage this house (said he;) for the mistress of it is a good civil woman, and has not much business.'

'Sir, I love the acquaintance of young people; because, in the first place, I don't like to think myself growing old. In the next place, young acquaintances must last longest, if they do last; and then, Sir, young men have more virtue than old men; they have more generous sentiments in every respect. I love the young dogs of this age: they have more wit and humour and knowledge of life than we had; but then the dogs are not so good scholars. Sir, in my early years I read very hard. It is a sad reflection, but a true one, that I knew almost as much at eighteen as I do now. My judgement, to be sure, was not so good; but I had all the facts. I remember very well, when I was at Oxford, an old gentleman said to me, "Young man, ply your book diligently now, and acquire a stock of knowledge; for when years come upon you, you will find that poring upon books will be but an irksome task." '

This account of his reading, given by himself in plain words, sufficiently confirms what I have already advanced upon the disputed question as to his application. It reconciles any seeming inconsistency in his way of talking upon it at different times; and shews that idleness and reading hard were with him relative terms, the import of which, as used by him, must be gathered from a comparison with what scholars of different degrees of ardour and assiduity have been known to do. And let it be remembered, that he was now talking spontaneously, and expressing his genuine sentiments; whereas at other times he might be induced from his spirit of contradiction, or more properly from his love of argumentative contest, to speak lightly of his own application to study. It is pleasing to consider that the old gentleman's gloomy prophecy as to the irksomeness of books to men of an advanced age, which is too often fulfilled, was so far from being verified in Johnson, that his ardour for literature never failed, and his last writings had more ease and vivacity than any of his earlier productions.

He mentioned to me now, for the first time, that he had been distrest by melancholy, and for that reason had been obliged to fly from study and meditation, to the dissipating variety of life. Against melancholy he recommended constant occupation of mind, a great deal of exercise, moderation in eating and drinking, and especially to shun drinking at night. He said melancholy people were apt to fly to intemperance for relief, but that it sunk them much deeper in misery. He observed, that labouring men who work hard, and live sparingly, are seldom or never troubled with low spirits.

He again insisted on the duty of maintaining subordination of rank. 'Sir, I would no more deprive a nobleman of his respect, than of his money. I consider myself as acting a part in the great system of society, and I do to others as I would have them to do to me. I would behave to a nobleman as I should expect he would behave to me, were I a nobleman and he Sam. Johnson. Sir, there is one Mrs. Macaulay[1] in this town, a great republican. One day when I was at her house, I put on a very grave countenance, and said to her, "Madam, I am now become a convert to your way of thinking. I am convinced that all mankind are upon an equal footing; and to give you an unquestionable proof, Madam, that I am in earnest, here is a very sensible, civil, well-behaved

[1] This *one* Mrs. Macaulay was the same personage who afterwards made herself so much known as 'the celebrated female historian.'

fellow-citizen, your footman; I desire that he may be allowed to sit down and dine with us." I thus, Sir, shewed her the absurdity of the levelling doctrine. She has never liked me since. Sir, your levellers wish to level *down* as far as themselves; but they cannot bear levelling *up* to themselves. They would all have some people under them; why not then have some people above them?' I mentioned a certain authour[1] who disgusted me by his forwardness, and by shewing no deference to noblemen into whose company he was admitted. JOHNSON. 'Suppose a shoemaker should claim an equality with him, as he does with a Lord; how he would stare. "Why, Sir, do you stare? (says the shoemaker,) I do great service to society. 'Tis true I am paid for doing it; but so are you, Sir: and I am sorry to say it, paid better than I am, for doing something not so necessary. For mankind could do better without your books, than without my shoes." Thus, Sir, there would be a perpetual struggle for precedence, were there no fixed invariable rules for the distinction of rank, which creates no jealousy, as it is allowed to be accidental.'

He said, Dr. Joseph Warton was a very agreeable man, and his *Essay on the Genius and Writings of Pope*, a very pleasing book. I wondered that he delayed so long to give us the continuation of it. JOHNSON. 'Why, Sir, I suppose he finds himself a little disappointed, in not having been able to persuade the world to be of his opinion as to Pope.'

We have now been favoured with the concluding volume, in which, to use a parliamentary expression, he has *explained*, so as not to appear quite so adverse to the opinion of the world, concerning Pope, as was at first thought; and we must all agree that his work is a most valuable accession to English literature.

A writer of deserved eminence[2] being mentioned, Johnson said, 'Why, Sir, he is a man of good parts, but being originally poor, he has got a love of mean company and low jocularity; a very bad thing, Sir. To laugh is good, as to talk is good. But

---

[1] [Dr. Robertson. *Boswell's 1763 Journal.*]
[2] [Tom Warton. *Boswell's 1763 Journal.* See *Boswell Papers*, xi. 173, 174–5.]

you ought no more to think it enough if you laugh, than you are to think it enough if you talk. You may laugh in as many ways as you talk; and surely *every* way of talking that is practised cannot be esteemed.'

I spoke of Sir James Macdonald as a young man of most distinguished merit, who united the highest reputation at Eton and Oxford, with the patriarchal spirit of a great Highland Chieftain. I mentioned that Sir James had said to me, that he had never seen Mr. Johnson, but he had a great respect for him, though at the same time it was mixed with some degree of terrour. JOHNSON. 'Sir, if he were to be acquainted with me, it might lessen both.'

The mention of this gentleman led us to talk of the Western Islands of Scotland, to visit which he expressed a wish that then appeared to me a very romantick fancy, which I little thought would be afterwards realized. He told me, that his father had put Martin's account of those islands into his hands when he was very young, and that he was highly pleased with it; that he was particularly struck with the St. Kilda man's notion that the high church of Glasgow had been hollowed out of a rock; a circumstance to which old Mr. Johnson had directed his attention. He said he would go to the Hebrides with me, when I returned from my travels, unless some very good companion should offer when I was absent, which he did not think probable; adding, 'There are few people to whom I take so much to as you.' And when I talked of my leaving England, he said, with a very affectionate air, 'My dear Boswell, I should be very unhappy at parting, did I think we were not to meet again.' I cannot too often remind my readers, that although such instances of his kindness are doubtless very flattering to me, yet I hope my recording them will be ascribed to a better motive than to vanity; for they afford unquestionable evidence of his tenderness and complacency, which some, while they were forced to acknowledge his great powers, have been so strenuous to deny.

He maintained that a boy at school was the happiest of human beings. I supported a different opinion, from which I have never yet varied, that a man is happier; and I enlarged upon the anxiety and sufferings which are endured at school. JOHNSON. 'Ah! Sir, a boy's being flogged is not so severe as a man's having the hiss of the world against him. Men have a solicitude about fame; and the greater share they have of it, the more afraid they are of losing it.' I silently asked myself, 'Is it possible that the great SAMUEL JOHNSON really entertains any such apprehension, and is not confident that his exalted fame is established upon a foundation never to be shaken?'

He this evening drank a bumper to Sir David Dalrymple, 'as a man of worth, a scholar, and a wit.' 'I have (said he) never heard of him except from you; but let him know my opinion of him: for as he does not shew himself much in the world, he should have the praise of the few who hear of him.'

On Tuesday, July 26, I found Mr. Johnson alone. It was a very wet day, and I again complained of the disagreeable effects of such weather. JOHNSON. 'Sir, this is all imagination, which physicians encourage; for man lives in air, as a fish lives in water; so that if the atmosphere press heavy from above, there is an equal resistance from below. To be sure, bad weather is hard upon people who are obliged to be abroad; and men cannot labour so well in the open air in bad weather, as in good: but, Sir, a smith or a taylor, whose work is within doors, will surely do as much in rainy weather, as in fair. Some very delicate frames, indeed, may be affected by wet weather; but not common constitutions.'

We talked of the education of children; and I asked him what he thought was best to teach them first. JOHNSON. 'Sir, it is no matter what you teach them first, any more than what leg you shall put into your breeches first. Sir, you may stand disputing which is best to put in first, but in the mean time your breech is bare. Sir, while you are considering which of two things you should teach your child first, another boy has learnt them both.'

On Thursday, July 28, we again supped in private at the Turk's Head coffee-house. JOHNSON. 'Swift has a higher reputation than he deserves. His excellence is strong sense; for his humour, though very well, is not remarkably good. I doubt whether *The Tale of a Tub* be his; for he never owned it, and it is much above his usual manner.'[1]

'Thomson, I think, had as much of the poet about him as most writers. Every thing appeared to him through the medium of his favourite pursuit. He could not have viewed those two candles burning but with a poetical eye.'

'Has not ——[2] a great deal of wit, Sir?' JOHNSON. 'I do not think so, Sir. He is, indeed, continually attempting wit, but he fails. And I have no more pleasure in hearing a man attempting wit and failing, than in seeing a man trying to leap over a ditch and tumbling into it.'

He laughed heartily, when I mentioned to him a saying of his concerning Mr. Thomas Sheridan, which Foote took a wicked pleasure to circulate. 'Why, Sir, Sherry is dull, naturally dull; but it must have taken him a great deal of pains to become what we now see him. Such an excess of stupidity, Sir, is not in Nature.' 'So (said he,) I allowed him all his own merit.'

He now added, 'Sheridan cannot bear me. I bring his declamation to a point. I ask him a plain question, "What do you mean to teach?" Besides, Sir, what influence can Mr. Sheridan have upon the language of this great country, by his narrow exertions? Sir, it is burning a farthing candle at Dover, to shew light at Calais.'

Talking of a young man[3] who was uneasy from thinking that he was very deficient in learning and knowledge, he said, 'A man has no reason to complain who holds a middle place, and has many below him; and perhaps he has not six of his years above him;—perhaps not one. Though he may not know any thing perfectly, the general mass of knowledge that he has acquired is considerable. Time will do for him all that is wanting.'

The conversation then took a philosophical turn. JOHNSON. 'Human experience, which is constantly contradicting theory, is

[1] This opinion was given by him more at large at a subsequent period. See *Journal of a Tour to the Hebrides*, 3rd edit. p. 32 [Aug. 16].
[2] [Burke. *Mrs. Thrale.*]
[3] [Boswell. *Boswell's 1763 Journal.*]

the great test of truth. A system, built upon the discoveries of a great many minds, is always of more strength, than what is produced by the mere workings of any one mind, which, of itself, can do little. There is not so poor a book in the world that would not be a prodigious effort were it wrought out entirely by a single mind, without the aid of prior investigators. The French writers are superficial, because they are not scholars, and so proceed upon the mere power of their own minds; and we see how very little power they have.'

'As to the Christian religion, Sir, besides the strong evidence which we have for it, there is a balance in its favour from the number of great men who have been convinced of its truth, after a serious consideration of the question. Grotius was an acute man, a lawyer, a man accustomed to examine evidence, and he was convinced. Grotius was not a recluse, but a man of the world, who certainly had no bias to the side of religion. Sir Isaac Newton set out an infidel, and came to be a very firm believer.'

He this evening again recommended to me to perambulate Spain.[1] I said it would amuse him to get a letter from me dated at Salamancha. JOHNSON. 'I love the University of Salamancha; for when the Spaniards were in doubt as to the lawfulness of their conquering America, the University of Salamancha gave it as their opinion that it was not lawful.' He spoke this with great emotion, and with that generous warmth which dictated the lines in his *London*, against Spanish encroachment.

I expressed my opinion of my friend Derrick as but a poor writer. JOHNSON. 'To be sure, Sir, he is; but you are to consider that his being a literary man has got for him all that he has. It has made him King of Bath. Sir, he has nothing to say for himself but that he is a writer. Had he not been a writer, he must have been sweeping the crossings in the streets, and asking halfpence from every body that past.'

---

[1] I fully intended to have followed advice of such weight; but having staid much longer both in Germany and Italy than I proposed to do, and having also visited Corsica, I found that I had exceeded the time allowed me by my father, and hastened to France in my way homewards.

In justice, however, to the memory of Mr. Derrick, who was my first tutor in the ways of London, and shewed me the town in all its variety of departments, both literary and sportive, the particulars of which Dr. Johnson advised me to put in writing, it is proper to mention what Johnson, at a subsequent period, said of him both as a writer and an editor: 'Sir, I have often said, that if Derrick's letters had been written by one of a more established name, they would have been thought very pretty letters.'[1] And, 'I sent Derrick to Dryden's relations to gather materials for his life; and I believe he got all that I myself should have got.'[2]

Poor Derrick! I remember him with kindness. Yet I cannot with-hold from my readers a pleasant humourous sally which could not have hurt him had he been alive, and now is perfectly harmless. In his collection of poems, there is one upon entering the harbour of Dublin, his native city, after a long absence. It begins thus:

> 'Eblana! much lov'd city, hail!
> Where first I saw the light of day.'

And after a solemn reflection on his being 'numbered with forgotten dead,' there is the following stanza:

> 'Unless my lines protract my fame,
>   And those, who chance to read them, cry,
> I knew him! Derrick was his name,
>   In yonder tomb his ashes lie.'

Which was thus happily parodied by Mr. John Home, to whom we owe the beautiful and pathetick tragedy of *Douglas*:

> 'Unless my *deeds* protract my fame,
>   *And he who passes sadly sings*,
> I knew him! Derrick was his name,
>   *On yonder tree his carcase swings!*'

I doubt much whether the amiable and ingenious authour of these burlesque lines will recollect them, for they were produced extempore one evening while he and I were walking together in

---

[1] *Journal of a Tour to the Hebrides*, 3rd edit. p. 104 [Aug. 27, 1773].
[2] *Ibid.* p. 142 [242, Sept. 22, 1773].

the dining-room at Eglintoune Castle, in 1760, and I have never mentioned them to him since.

Johnson said once to me, 'Sir, I honour Derrick for his presence of mind. One night, when Floyd,[1] another poor authour, was wandering about the streets in the night, he found Derrick fast asleep upon a bulk; upon being suddenly waked, Derrick started up, "My dear Floyd, I am sorry to see you in this destitute state; will you go home with me to *my lodgings*?"'

I again begged his advice as to my method of study at Utrecht. 'Come, (said he) let us make a day of it. Let us go down to Greenwich and dine, and talk of it there.' The following Saturday was fixed for this excursion.

As we walked along the Strand to-night, arm in arm, a woman of the town accosted us, in the usual enticing manner. 'No, no, my girl, (said Johnson) it won't do.' He, however, did not treat her with harshness, and we talked of the wretched life of such women; and agreed, that much more misery than happiness, upon the whole, is produced by illicit commerce between the sexes.

On Saturday, July 30, Dr. Johnson and I took a sculler at the Temple-stairs, and set out for Greenwich. I asked him if he really thought a knowledge of the Greek and Latin languages an essential requisite to a good education. JOHNSON. 'Most certainly, Sir; for those who know them have a very great advantage over those who do not. Nay, Sir, it is wonderful what a difference learning makes upon people even in the common intercourse of life, which does not appear to be much connected with it.' 'And yet, (said I) people go through the world very well, and carry on the business of life to good advantage, without learning.' JOHNSON. 'Why, Sir, that may be true in cases where learning cannot possibly be of any use; for instance, this boy rows us as well without learning, as if he could sing the song of Orpheus to the Argonauts, who were the first sailors.' He then called to the boy, 'What would you give, my lad, to know about the Argonauts?' 'Sir, (said the boy,) I would give what I have.' Johnson was much pleased with his answer, and we gave

---

[1] He published a biographical work, containing an account of eminent writers, in three vols. 8vo.

him a double fare. Dr. Johnson then turning to me, 'Sir, (said he) a desire of knowledge is the natural feeling of mankind; and every human being, whose mind is not debauched, will be willing to give all that he has to get knowledge.'

We landed at the Old Swan, and walked to Billingsgate, where we took oars, and moved smoothly along the silver Thames. It was a very fine day. We were entertained with the immense number and variety of ships that were lying at anchor, and with the beautiful country on each side of the river.

I talked of preaching, and of the great success which those called Methodists[1] have. JOHNSON. 'Sir, it is owing to their expressing themselves in a plain and familiar manner, which is the only way to do good to the common people, and which clergymen of genius and learning ought to do from a principle

[1] All who are acquainted with the history of religion, (the most important, surely, that concerns the human mind,) know that the appellation of *Methodists* was first given to a society of students in the University of Oxford, who about the year 1730 were distinguished by an earnest and *methodical* attention to devout exercises. This disposition of mind is not a novelty, or peculiar to any sect, but has been, and still may be found, in many Christians of every denomination. Johnson himself was, in a dignified manner, a Methodist. In his *Rambler*, No. 110, he mentions with respect 'the whole discipline of regulated piety;' and in his *Prayers and Meditations*, many instances occur of his anxious examination into his spiritual state. That this religious earnestness, and in particular an observation of the influence of the Holy Spirit, has sometimes degenerated into folly, and sometimes been counterfeited for base purposes, cannot be denied. But it is not, therefore, fair to decry it when genuine. The principal argument in reason and good sense against methodism is, that it tends to debase human nature, and prevent the generous exertions of goodness, by an unworthy supposition that GOD will pay no regard to them; although it is positively said in the Scriptures that He 'will reward every man according to his works.' But I am happy to have it [in] my power to do justice to those whom it is the fashion to ridicule, without any knowledge of their tenets; and this I can do by quoting a passage from one of their best apologists, Mr. Milner, who thus expresses their doctrine upon this subject. 'Justified by faith, renewed in his faculties, and constrained by the love of Christ, their believer moves in the sphere of love and gratitude, and all his *duties* flow more or less from this principle. And though *they are accumulating for him in heaven a treasure of bliss proportioned to his faithfulness and activity, and it is by no means inconsistent with his principles to feel the force of this consideration*, yet love itself sweetens every duty to his mind; and he thinks there is no absurdity in his feeling the love of GOD as the grand commanding principle of his life.' *Essays on several Religious Subjects, &c.*, by Joseph Milner, A.M., Master of the Grammar School of Kingston-upon-Hull, 1789, p. 11.

of duty, when it is suited to their congregations; a practice, for which they will be praised by men of sense. To insist against drunkenness as a crime, because it debases reason, the noblest faculty of man, would be of no service to the common people: but to tell them that they may die in a fit of drunkenness, and shew them how dreadful that would be, cannot fail to make a deep impression. Sir, when your Scotch clergy give up their homely manner, religion will soon decay in that country.' Let this observation, as Johnson meant it, be ever remembered.

I was much pleased to find myself with Johnson at Greenwich, which he celebrates in his *London* as a favourite scene. I had the poem in my pocket, and read the lines aloud with enthusiasm:

> 'On Thames's banks in silent thought we stood:
> Where Greenwich smiles upon the silver flood:
> Pleas'd with the seat which gave ELIZA birth,
> We kneel, and kiss the consecrated earth.'

He remarked that the structure of Greenwich hospital was too magnificent for a place of charity, and that its parts were too much detached to make one great whole.

Buchanan, he said, was a very fine poet; and observed, that he was the first who complimented a lady, by ascribing to her the different perfections of the heathen goddesses;[1] but that Johnston improved upon this, by making his lady, at the same time, free from their defects.

He dwelt upon Buchanan's elegant verses to Mary Queen of Scots, *Nympha Caledoniæ*, &c., and spoke with enthusiasm of the beauty of Latin verse. 'All the modern languages (said he) cannot furnish so melodious a line as

> *'Formosam resonare doces Amarillida silvas.'*[2]

Afterwards he entered upon the business of the day, which was to give me his advice as to a course of study. And here I am to mention with much regret, that my record of what he said is miserably scanty. I recollect with admiration an animating blaze of eloquence, which rouzed every intellectual power in me to

[1] *Epigram*, Lib. ii. 'In Elizabeth. Angliæ Reg.' [M.]
[2] ['And the woods ring with Amarillis' name' (see *ante*, p. 37).]

the highest pitch, but must have dazzled me so much, that my memory could not preserve the substance of his discourse; for the note which I find of it is no more than this:—'He ran over the grand scale of human knowledge; advised me to select some particular branch to excel in, but to acquire a little of every kind.' The defect of my minutes will be fully supplied by a long letter upon the subject which he favoured me with, after I had been some time at Utrecht, and which my readers will have the pleasure to peruse in its proper place.

We walked in the evening in Greenwich Park. He asked me, I suppose, by way of trying my disposition, 'Is not this very fine?' Having no exquisite relish of the beauties of Nature, and being more delighted with 'the busy hum of men,' I answered, 'Yes, Sir; but not equal to Fleet-street.' JOHNSON. 'You are right, Sir.'

I am aware that many of my readers may censure my want of taste. Let me, however, shelter myself under the authority of a very fashionable Baronet[1] in the brilliant world, who, on his attention being called to the fragrance of a May evening in the country, observed, 'This may be very well; but, for my part, I prefer the smell of a flambeau at the playhouse.'

We staid so long at Greenwich, that our sail up the river, in our return to London, was by no means so pleasant as in the morning; for the night air was so cold that it made me shiver. I was the more sensible of it from having sat up all the night before, recollecting and writing in my journal what I thought worthy of preservation; an exertion, which, during the first part of my acquaintance with Johnson, I frequently made. I remember having sat up four nights in one week, without being much incommoded in the day time.

Johnson, whose robust frame was not in the least affected by the cold, scolded me, as if my shivering had been a paltry

---

[1] My friend Sir Michael Le Fleming. This gentleman, with all his experience of sprightly and elegant life, inherits, with the beautiful family Domain, no inconsiderable share of that love of literature, which distinguished his venerable grandfather, the Bishop of Carlisle. He one day observed to me, of Dr. Johnson, in a felicity of phrase, 'There is a blunt dignity about him on every occasion.'

effeminacy, saying, 'Why do you shiver?' Sir William Scott, of
the Commons, told me, that when he complained of a head-ache
in the post-chaise, as they were travelling together to Scotland,
Johnson treated him in the same manner: 'At your age, Sir, I
had no head-ache.' It is not easy to make allowance for sensations
in others, which we ourselves have not at the time. We must all
have experienced how very differently we are affected by the
complaints of our neighbours, when we are well and when we
are ill. In full health, we can scarcely believe that they suffer
much; so faint is the image of pain upon our imagination: when
softened by sickness, we readily sympathize with the sufferings
of others.

We concluded the day at the Turk's Head coffee-house very
socially. He was pleased to listen to a particular account which
I gave him of my family, and of its hereditary estate, as to the
extent and population of which he asked questions, and made
calculations; recommending, at the same time, a liberal kindness
to the tenantry, as people over whom the proprietor was placed
by Providence. He took delight in hearing my description of the
romantick seat of my ancestors. 'I must be there, Sir, (said he)
and we will live in the old castle; and if there is not a room in
it remaining, we will build one.' I was highly flattered, but could
scarcely indulge a hope that Auchinleck would indeed be honoured
by his presence, and celebrated by a description, as it afterwards
was, in his *Journey to the Western Islands*.

After we had again talked of my setting out for Holland, he
said, 'I must see thee out of England; I will accompany you to
Harwich.' I could not find words to express what I felt upon
this unexpected and very great mark of his affectionate regard.

Next day, Sunday, July 31, I told him I had been that morning
at a meeting of the people called Quakers, where I had heard a
woman preach. JOHNSON. 'Sir, a woman's preaching is like a
dog's walking on his hinder legs. It is not done well; but you
are surprized to find it done at all.'

On Tuesday, August 2 (the day of my departure from London
having been fixed for the 5th,) Dr. Johnson did me the honour
to pass a part of the morning with me at my Chambers. He said,

that 'he always felt an inclination to do nothing.' I observed, that it was strange to think that the most indolent man in Britain had written the most laborious work, *The English Dictionary*.

I mentioned an imprudent publication, by a certain friend[1] of his, at an early period of life, and asked him if he thought it would hurt him. JOHNSON. 'No, Sir; not much. It may, perhaps, be mentioned at an election.'

I had now made good my title to be a privileged man, and was carried by him in the evening to drink tea with Miss Williams, whom, though under the misfortune of having lost her sight, I found to be agreeable in conversation; for she had a variety of literature, and expressed herself well; but her peculiar value was the intimacy in which she had long lived with Johnson, by which she was well acquainted with his habits, and knew how to lead him on to talk.

After tea he carried me to what he called his walk, which was a long narrow paved court in the neighbourhood, overshadowed by some trees. There we sauntered a considerable time; and I complained to him that my love of London and of his company was such, that I shrunk almost from the thought of going away, even to travel, which is generally so much desired by young men. He roused me by manly and spirited conversation. He advised me, when settled in any place abroad, to study with an eagerness after knowledge, and to apply to Greek an hour every day; and when I was moving about, to read diligently the great book of mankind.

On Wednesday, August 3, we had our last social evening at the Turk's Head coffee-house, before my setting out for foreign parts. I had the misfortune, before we parted, to irritate him unintentionally. I mentioned to him how common it was in the world to tell absurd stories of him, and to ascribe to him very strange sayings. JOHNSON. 'What do they make me say, Sir?' BOSWELL. 'Why, Sir, as an instance very strange indeed, (laughing heartily as I spoke,) David Hume told me, you said that you would stand before a battery of cannon, to restore the Convocation to its full powers.' Little did I apprehend that he

[1] [Perhaps Burke. *Croker.*]

had actually said this: but I was soon convinced of my errour; for, with a determined look, he thundered out 'And would I not, Sir? Shall the Presbyterian *Kirk* of Scotland have its General Assembly, and the Church of England be denied its Convocation?' He was walking up and down the room while I told him the anecdote; but when he uttered this explosion of high-church zeal, he had come close to my chair, and his eyes flashed with indignation. I bowed to the storm, and diverted the force of it, by leading him to expatiate on the influence which religion derived from maintaining the church with great external respectability.

I must not omit to mention that he this year wrote *The Life of Ascham* †, and the Dedication to the Earl of Shaftesbury †, prefixed to the edition of that writer's English works, published by Mr. Bennet.

On Friday, August 5, we set out early in the morning in the Harwich stage coach. A fat elderly gentlewoman, and a young Dutchman, seemed the most inclined among us to conversation. At the inn where we dined, the gentlewoman said that she had done her best to educate her children; and particularly, that she had never suffered them to be a moment idle. JOHNSON. 'I wish, madam, you would educate me too; for I have been an idle fellow all my life.' 'I am sure, Sir, (said she) you have not been idle.' JOHNSON. 'Nay, Madam, it is very true; and that gentleman there (pointing to me,) has been idle. He was idle at Edinburgh. His father sent him to Glasgow, where he continued to be idle. He then came to London, where he has been very idle; and now he is going to Utrecht, where he will be as idle as ever.' I asked him privately how he could expose me so. JOHNSON. 'Poh, poh! (said he) they knew nothing about you, and will think of it no more.' In the afternoon the gentlewoman talked violently against the Roman Catholicks, and of the horrours of the Inquisition. To the utter astonishment of all the passengers but myself, who knew that he could talk upon any side of a question, he defended the Inquisition, and maintained, that 'false doctrine should be checked on its first appearance; that the civil power should unite with the church in punishing those who dared to attack the

established religion, and that such only were punished by the
Inquisition.' He had in his pocket *Pomponius Mela de situ Orbis*, in
which he read occasionally, and seemed very intent upon ancient
geography. Though by no means niggardly, his attention to what
was generally right was so minute, that having observed at one
of the stages that I ostentatiously gave a shilling to the coachman, when the custom was for each passenger to give only six-
pence, he took me aside and scolded me, saying that what I had
done would make the coachman dissatisfied with all the rest of
the passengers, who gave him no more than his due. This was
a just reprimand; for in whatever way a man may indulge his
generosity or his vanity in spending his money, for the sake of
others he ought not to raise the price of any article for which
there is a constant demand.

He talked of Mr. Blacklock's poetry, so far as it was descrip-
tive of visible objects; and observed, that 'as its authour had the
misfortune to be blind, we may be absolutely sure that such passages are combinations of what he has remembered of the works
of other writers who could see. That foolish fellow, Spence, has
laboured to explain philosophically how Blacklock may have
done, by means of his own faculties, what it is impossible he
should do. The solution, as I have given it, is plain. Suppose, I
know a man to be so lame that he is absolutely incapable to move
himself, and I find him in a different room from that in which
I left him; shall I puzzle myself with idle conjectures, that,
perhaps, his nerves have by some unknown change all at once
become effective? No, Sir; it is clear how he got into a different
room: he was *carried*.'

Having stopped a night at Colchester, Johnson talked of that
town with veneration, for having stood a siege for Charles the
First. The Dutchman alone now remained with us. He spoke
English tolerably well; and thinking to recommend himself to
us by expatiating on the superiority of the criminal jurisprudence
of this country over that of Holland, he inveighed against the
barbarity of putting an accused person to the torture, in order
to force a confession. But Johnson was as ready for this, as for the
Inquisition. 'Why, Sir, you do not, I find, understand the law of

your own country. The torture in Holland is considered as a favour to an accused person; for no man is put to the torture there, unless there is as much evidence against him as would amount to conviction in England. An accused person among you, therefore, has one chance more to escape punishment, than those who are tried among us.'

At supper this night he talked of good eating with uncommon satisfaction. 'Some people (said he,) have a foolish way of not minding, or pretending not to mind, what they eat. For my part, I mind my belly very studiously, and very carefully; for I look upon it, that he who does not mind his belly will hardly mind anything else.' He now appeared to me *Jean Bull philosophe*, and he was, for the moment, not only serious but vehement. Yet I have heard him, upon other occasions, talk with great contempt of people who were anxious to gratify their palates; and the 206th number of his *Rambler* is a masterly essay against gulosity. His practice, indeed, I must acknowledge, may be considered as casting the balance of his different opinions upon this subject; for I never new knew any man who relished good eating more than he did. When at table, he was totally absorbed in the business of the moment; his looks seemed rivetted to his plate; nor would he, unless when in very high company, say one word, or even pay the least attention to what was said by others, till he had satisfied his appetite, which was so fierce, and indulged with such intenseness, that while in the act of eating, the veins of his forehead swelled, and generally a strong perspiration was visible. To those whose sensations were delicate, this could not but be disgusting; and it was doubtless not very suitable to the character of a philosopher, who should be distinguished by self-command. But it must be owned, that Johnson, though he could be rigidly *abstemious*, was not a *temperate* man either in eating or drinking. He could refrain, but he could not use moderately. He told me, that he had fasted two days without inconvenience, and that he had never been hungry but once. They who beheld with wonder how much he eat upon all occasions when his dinner was to his taste, could not easily conceive what he must have meant by hunger; and not only was he remarkable for the extraordinary quantity which he eat, but he was, or affected to be, a man of very nice discernment in the science of cookery. He used to descant critically on the dishes which had been at table where he had dined or supped, and to recollect very minutely what he had liked. I remember, when he was in Scotland, his praising '*Gordon's palates*,' (a dish of palates at the Honourable Alexander Gordon's) with a warmth of expression which might have done honour to more important subjects. 'As for Maclaurin's imitation of a *made dish*, it was a wretched attempt.' He about the same time was so much displeased with the performances of a nobleman's[1] French cook, that he exclaimed with vehemence, 'I'd throw such a rascal into the river;' and he then proceeded to alarm a lady[2] at whose house he was to sup, by the following manifesto of his skill: 'I, Madam, who live at a variety of good tables, am a much better judge of cookery, than any person who has a very tolerable cook, but lives much at home; for his palate is gradually adapted to the taste of his cook; whereas, Madam, in trying by a wider range, I can more exquisitely judge.' When invited to dine, even with an intimate friend, he was not pleased if something better than a plain dinner was not prepared for him. I have heard him say on such an occasion, 'This was a good dinner enough, to be sure; but it was not a dinner to *ask* a man to.' On the other hand, he was wont to express, with great glee, his satisfaction when he had been entertained quite to his mind. One day when we had dined with his neighbour and landlord in Bolt-court, Mr. Allen, the printer, whose old housekeeper had studied his taste in every thing, he pronounced this eulogy: 'Sir, we could not have had a better dinner had there been a *Synod of Cooks*.'

While we were left by ourselves, after the Dutchman had gone to bed, Dr. Johnson talked of that studied behaviour which many have recommended and practised. He disapproved of it; and said, 'I never considered whether I should be a grave man, or a merry man, but just let inclination, for the time, have its course.'

He flattered me with some hopes that he would, in the course

---

[1] [Perhaps Lord Elibank. *Powell.*]
[2] [Probably Mrs. Boswell. *Powell.*]

of the following summer, come over to Holland, and accompany me in a tour through the Netherlands.

I teized him with fanciful apprehensions of unhappiness. A moth having fluttered round the candle, and burnt itself, he laid hold of this little incident to admonish me; saying, with a sly look, and in a solemn but quiet tone, 'That creature was its own tormentor, and I believe its name was BOSWELL.'

Next day we got to Harwich to dinner; and my passage in the packet-boat to Helvoetsluys being secured, and my baggage put on board, we dined at our inn by ourselves. I happened to say it would be terrible if he should not find a speedy opportunity of returning to London, and be confined to so dull a place. JOHN-SON. 'Don't, Sir, accustom yourself to use big words for little matters. It would *not* be *terrible*, though I *were* to be detained some time here.' The practice of using words of disproportionate magnitude, is, no doubt, too frequent every where; but I think, most remarkable among the French, of which, all who have travelled in France must have been struck with innumerable instances.

We went and looked at the church, and having gone into it and walked up to the altar, Johnson, whose piety was constant and fervent, sent me to my knees, saying, 'Now that you are going to leave your native country, recommend yourself to the protection of your CREATOR and REDEEMER.'

After we came out of the church, we stood talking for some time together of Bishop Berkeley's ingenious sophistry to prove the non-existence of matter, and that every thing in the universe is merely ideal. I observed, that though we are satisfied his doctrine is not true, it is impossible to refute it. I never shall forget the alacrity with which Johnson answered, striking his foot with mighty force against a large stone, till he rebounded from it, 'I refute it *thus*.' This was a stout exemplification of the *first truths* of *Père Bouffier*, or the *original principles* of Reid and of Beattie; without admitting which, we can no more argue in metaphysicks, than we can argue in mathematicks without axioms. To me it is not conceivable how Berkeley can be answered by pure reasoning; but I know that the nice and difficult task was to have been undertaken by one of the most luminous minds of the present age, had not politicks 'turned him from calm philosophy aside.'[1] What an admirable display of subtilty, united with brilliance, might his contending with Berkeley have afforded us! How must we, when we reflect on the loss of such an intellectual feast, regret that he should be characterised as the man,

> 'Who born for the universe narrow'd his mind,
> And to party gave up what was meant for mankind?'

My revered friend walked down with me to the beach, where we embraced and parted with tenderness, and engaged to correspond by letters. I said, 'I hope, Sir, you will not forget me in my absence.' JOHNSON. 'Nay, Sir, it is more likely you should forget me, than that I should forget you.' As the vessel put out to sea, I kept my eyes upon him for a considerable time, while he remained rolling his majestick frame in his usual manner: and at last I perceived him walk back into the town, and he disappeared.

Utrecht seeming at first very dull to me, after the animated scenes of London, my spirits were grievously affected; and I wrote to Johnson a plaintive and desponding letter, to which he paid no regard. Afterwards, when I had acquired a firmer tone of mind, I wrote him a second letter, expressing much anxiety to hear from him. At length I received the following epistle, which was of important service to me, and I trust, will be so to many others.

'*A* MR. MR. BOSWELL, *à la Cour de l'Empereur*, *Utrecht*

'DEAR SIR,—You are not to think yourself forgotten, or criminally neglected, that you have had yet no letter from me. I love to see my friends, to hear from them, to talk to them, and to talk of them; but it is not without a considerable effort of resolution that I prevail upon myself to write. I would not, however, gratify my own indolence by the omission of any important duty, or any office of real kindness.

'To tell you that I am or am not well, that I have or have not

---

[1] [Goldsmith, *Retaliation*. Burke being meant.]

been in the country, that I drank your health in the room in
which we sat last together, and that your acquaintance continue
to speak of you with their former kindness, topicks with which
those letters are commonly filled which are written only for the
sake of writing, I seldom shall think worth communicating; but
if I can have it in my power to calm any harrassing disquiet, to
excite any virtuous desire, to rectify any important opinion, or
fortify any generous resolution, you need not doubt but I shall
at least wish to prefer the pleasure of gratifying a friend much
less esteemed than yourself, before the gloomy calm of idle
vacancy. Whether I shall easily arrive at an exact punctuality of
correspondence, I cannot tell. I shall, at present, expect that you
will receive this in return for two which I have had from you.
The first, indeed, gave me an account so hopeless of the state of
your mind, that it hardly admitted or deserved an answer; by
the second I was much better pleased: and the pleasure will still
be increased by such a narrative of the progress of your studies,
as may evince the continuance of an equal and rational application
of your mind to some useful enquiry.

'You will, perhaps, wish to ask, what study I would recommend. I shall not speak of theology, because it ought not to be
considered as a question whether you shall endeavour to know
the will of GOD.

'I shall therefore, consider only such studies as we are at
liberty to pursue or to neglect; and of these I know not how you
will make a better choice, than by studying the civil law, as your
father advises, and the ancient languages, as you had determined
for yourself; at least resolve, while you remain in any settled
residence, to spend a certain number of hours every day amongst
your books. The dissipation of thought, of which you complain,
is nothing more than the vacillation of a mind suspended between
different motives, and changing its direction as any motive gains
or loses strength. If you can but kindle in your mind any strong
desire, if you can but keep predominant any wish for some particular excellence or attainment, the gusts of imagination will
break away, without any effect upon your conduct, and commonly
without any traces left upon the memory.

'There lurks, perhaps, in every human heart a desire of distinction, which inclines every man first to hope, and then to believe, that Nature has given him something peculiar to himself. This vanity makes one mind nurse aversion, and another actuate desires, till they rise by art much above their original state of power; and as affectation, in time, improves to habit, they at last tyrannise over him who at first encouraged them only for show. Every desire is a viper in the bosom, who, while he was chill, was harmless; but when warmth gave him strength, exerted it in poison. You know a gentleman, who, when first he set his foot in the gay world, as he prepared himself to whirl in the vortex of pleasure, imagined a total indifference and universal negligence to be the most agreeable concomitants of youth, and the strongest indication of an airy temper and a quick apprehension. Vacant to every object, and sensible of every impulse, he thought that all appearance of diligence would deduct something from the reputation of genius; and hoped that he should appear to attain, amidst all the ease of carelessness, and all the tumult of diversion, that knowledge and those accomplishments which mortals of the common fabrick obtain only by mute abstraction and solitary drudgery. He tried this scheme of life awhile, was made weary of it by his sense and his virtue; he then wished to return to his studies; and finding long habits of idleness and pleasure harder to be cured than he expected, still willing to retain his claim to some extraordinary prerogatives, resolved the common consequences of irregularity into an unalterable decree of destiny, and concluded that Nature had originally formed him incapable of rational employment.

'Let all such fancies, illusive and destructive, be banished henceforward from your thoughts for ever. Resolve, and keep your resolution; choose, and pursue your choice. If you spend this day in study, you will find yourself still more able to study to-morrow; not that you are to expect that you shall at once obtain a complete victory. Depravity is not very easily overcome. Resolution will sometimes relax, and diligence will sometimes be interrupted; but let no accidental surprise or deviation, whether short or long, dispose you to despondency. Consider these failings as incident to all mankind. Begin again where you left off, and endeavour to avoid the seducements that prevailed over you before.

'This, my dear Boswell, is advice which, perhaps, has been often given you, and given you without effect. But this advice, if you will not take from others, you must take from your own reflections, if you purpose to do the duties of the station to which the bounty of Providence has called you.

'Let me have a long letter from you as soon as you can. I hope you continue your journal, and enrich it with many observations upon the country in which you reside. It will be a favour if you can get me any books in the Frisick language, and can enquire how the poor are maintained in the Seven Provinces. I am, dear Sir, you most affectionate servant,

'London, Dec. 8, 1763.'   'SAM. JOHNSON.'

I am sorry to observe, that neither in my own minutes, nor in my letters to Johnson, which have been preserved by him, can I find any information how the poor are maintained in the Seven Provinces. But I shall extract from one of my letters what I learnt concerning the other subject of his curiosity.

'I have made all possible enquiry with respect to the Frisick language, and find that it has been less cultivated than any other of the northern dialects; a certain proof of which is their deficiency of books. Of the old Frisick there are no remains, except some ancient laws preserved by *Schotanus* in his *Beschryvinge van die Heerlykheid van Friesland*; and his *Historia Frisica*. I have not yet been able to find these books. Professor Trotz, who formerly was of the University of Vranyker in Friesland, and is at present preparing an edition of all the Frisick laws, gave me this information. Of the modern Frisick, or what is spoken by the boors at this day, I have procured a specimen. It is *Gisbert Japix's Ryme-lerie*, which is the only book that they have. It is amazing, that they have no translation of the bible, no treatises of devotion, nor even any of the ballads and story-books which are so agreeable to country people. You shall have *Japix* by the first convenient opportunity. I doubt not to pick up *Schotanus*. Mynheer Trotz has promised me his assistance.'

1764: ÆTAT. 55.]—EARLY in 1764 Johnson paid a visit to the Langton family, at their seat of Langton, in Lincolnshire, where he passed some time, much to his satisfaction. His friend Bennet Langton, it will not be doubted, did every thing in his power to make the place agreeable to so illustrious a guest; and the elder Mr. Langton and his lady, being fully capable of understanding his value, were not wanting in attention. He, however, told me, that old Mr. Langton, though a man of considerable learning, had so little allowance to make for his occasional 'laxity of talk,' that because in the course of discussion he sometimes mentioned what might be said in favour of the peculiar tenets of the Romish church, he went to his grave believing him to be of that communion.

Johnson, during his stay at Langton, had the advantage of a good library, and saw several gentlemen of the neighbourhood. I have obtained from Mr. Langton the following particulars of this period.

He was now fully convinced that he could not have been satisfied with a country living; for, talking of a respectable clergyman in Lincolnshire, he observed, 'This man, Sir, fills up the duties of his life well. I approve of him, but could not imitate him.'

To a lady who endeavoured to vindicate herself from blame for neglecting social attention to worthy neighbours, by saying, 'I would go to them if it would do them any good,' he said, 'What good, Madam, do you expect to have in your power to do them? It is shewing them respect, and that is doing them good.'

So socially accommodating was he, that once when Mr. Langton and he were driving together in a coach, and Mr. Langton complained of being sick, he insisted that they should go out and sit on the back of it in the open air, which they did. And being sensible how strange the appearance must be, observed, that a countryman whom they saw in a field, would probably be thinking, 'If these two madmen should come down, what would become of me?'

Soon after his return to London, which was in February, was founded that CLUB which existed long without a name, but at

Mr. Garrick's funeral became distinguished by the title of THE LITERARY CLUB. Sir Joshua Reynolds had the merit of being the first proposer of it, to which Johnson acceded, and the original members were, Sir Joshua Reynolds, Dr. Johnson, Mr. Edmund Burke, Dr. Nugent, Mr. Beauclerk, Mr. Langton, Dr. Goldsmith, Mr. Chamier, and Sir John Hawkins. They met at the Turk's Head, in Gerrard-street, Soho, one evening in every week, at seven, and generally continued their conversation till a pretty late hour. This club has been gradually increased to its present number, thirty-five. After about ten years, instead of supping weekly, it was resolved to dine together once a fortnight during the meeting of Parliament. Their original tavern having been converted into a private house, they moved first to Prince's in Sackville-street, then to Le Telier's in Dover-street, and now meet at Parsloe's, St. James's-street. Between the time of its formation, and the time at which this work is passing through the press, (June 1792,)[1] the following persons, now dead, were members of it: Mr. Dunning, (afterwards Lord Ashburton,) Mr. Samuel Dyer, Mr. Garrick, Dr. Shipley Bishop of St. Asaph, Mr. Vesey, Mr. Thomas Warton and Dr. Adam Smith. The present members are,—Mr. Burke, Mr. Langton, Lord Charlemont, Sir Robert Chambers, Dr. Percy Bishop of Dromore, Dr. Barnard Bishop of Killaloe, Dr. Marlay Bishop of Clonfert, Mr. Fox, Dr. George Fordyce, Sir William Scott, Sir Joseph Banks, Sir Charles Bunbury, Mr. Windham of Norfolk, Mr. Sheridan, Mr. Gibbon, Sir William Jones, Mr. Colman, Mr. Steevens, Dr. Burney, Dr. Joseph Warton, Mr. Malone, Lord Ossory, Lord Spencer, Lord Lucan, Lord Palmerston, Lord Eliot, Lord Macartney, Mr. Richard Burke junior, Sir William Hamilton, Dr. Warren, Mr. Courtenay, Dr. Hinchcliffe Bishop of Peterborough, the Duke of Leeds, Dr. Douglas Bishop of Salisbury, and the writer of this account.

Sir John Hawkins[2] represents himself as a '*seceder*' from this society, and assigns as the reason of his '*withdrawing*' himself from it, that its late hours were inconsistent with his domestick

---

[1] The second edition is here spoken of. [M.]
[2] *Life of Johnson*, p. 425.

arrangements. In this he is not accurate; for the fact was, that he one evening attacked Mr. Burke, in so rude a manner, that all the company testified their displeasure; and at their next meeting his reception was such, that he never came again.[1]

He is equally inaccurate with respect to Mr. Garrick, of whom he says, 'he trusted that the least intimation of a desire to come among us, would procure him a ready admission; but in this he was mistaken. Johnson consulted me upon it; and when I could find no objection to receiving him, exclaimed,—"He will disturb us by his buffoonery;"—and afterwards so managed matters that he was never formally proposed, and, by consequence, never admitted.'[2]

In justice both to Mr. Garrick and Dr. Johnson, I think it necessary to rectify this mis-statement. The truth is, that not very long after the institution of our club, Sir Joshua Reynolds was speaking of it to Garrick. 'I like it much, (said he,) I think I shall be of you.' When Sir Joshua mentioned this to Dr. Johnson, he was much displeased with the actor's conceit. '*He'll be of us*, (said Johnson) how does he know we will *permit* him? The first Duke in England has no right to hold such language.' However, when Garrick was regularly proposed some time afterwards, Johnson, though he had taken a momentary offence at his arrogance, warmly and kindly supported him, and he was accordingly elected, was a most agreeable member, and continued to attend our meetings to the time of his death.

Mrs. Piozzi[3] has also given a similar misrepresentation of Johnson's treatment of Garrick in this particular, as if he had used these contemptuous expressions: 'If Garrick *does* apply, I'll black-ball him. Surely, one ought to sit in a society like ours,

"Unelbow'd by a gamester, pimp, or player." '

I am happy to be enabled by such unquestionable authority as that of Sir Joshua Reynolds, as well as from my own knowledge, to vindicate at once the heart of Johnson and the social merit of Garrick.

In this year, except what he may have done in revising *Shak-*

---

[1] From Sir Joshua Reynolds.   [2] *Life of Johnson*, p. 425.
[3] *Letters to and from Dr. Johnson.* Vol. ii. p. 278 [387].

speare, we do not find that he laboured much in literature. He wrote a review of Grainger's *Sugar Cane, a Poem*, in the *London Chronicle*. He told me, that Dr. Percy wrote the greatest part of this review; but, I imagine, he did not recollect it distinctly, for it appears to be mostly, if not altogether, his own. He also wrote in *The Critical Review*, an account † of Goldsmith's excellent poem, *The Traveller*.

The ease and independence to which he had at last attained by royal munificence, increased his natural indolence. In his *Meditations* he thus accuses himself:—'GOOD FRIDAY, April 20, 1764.— I have made no reformation; I have lived totally useless, more sensual in thought, and more addicted to wine and meat.'[1] And next morning he thus feelingly complains:—'My indolence, since my last reception of the sacrament, has sunk into grosser sluggishness, and my dissipation spread into wilder negligence. My thoughts have been clouded with sensuality; and, except that from the beginning of this year I have, in some measure, forborne excess of strong drink, my appetites have predominated over my reason. A kind of strange oblivion has overspread me, so that I know not what has become of the last year; and perceive that incidents and intelligence pass over me, without leaving any impression.' He then solemnly says, 'This is not the life to which heaven is promised;'[2] and he earnestly resolves on amendment.

It was his custom to observe certain days with a pious abstraction; viz. New-year's-day, the day of his wife's death, Good Friday, Easter-day, and his own birth-day. He this year says:— 'I have now spent fifty-five years in resolving; having, from the earliest time almost that I can remember, been forming schemes of a better life. I have done nothing. The need of doing, therefore, is pressing, since the time of doing is short. O GOD, grant me to resolve aright, and to keep my resolutions, for JESUS CHRIST's sake. Amen.'[3]

Such a tenderness of conscience, such a fervent desire of improvement, will rarely be found. It is, surely, not decent in those who are hardened in indifference to spiritual improvement, to treat this pious anxiety of Johnson with contempt.

[1] *Pr. and Med.* p. 50.   [2] *Ibid.* p. 51.   [3] *Ibid.* p. 58.

About this time he was afflicted with a very severe return of the hypochondriack disorder, which was ever lurking about him. He was so ill, as, notwithstanding his remarkable love of company, to be entirely averse to society, the most fatal symptom of that malady. Dr. Adams told me, that, as an old friend, he was admitted to visit him, and that he found him in a deplorable state, sighing, groaning, talking to himself, and restlessly walking from room to room. He then used this emphatical expression of the misery which he felt: 'I would consent to have a limb amputated to recover my spirits.'

Talking to himself was, indeed, one of his singularities ever since I knew him. I was certain that he was frequently uttering pious ejaculations; for fragments of the Lord's Prayer have been distinctly overheard. His friend Mr. Thomas Davies, of whom Churchill says,

'That Davies hath a very pretty wife,'

when Dr. Johnson muttered 'lead us not into temptation,' used with waggish and gallant humour to whisper Mrs. Davies, 'You my dear, are the cause of this.'

He had another particularity, of which none of his friends ever ventured to ask an explanation. It appeared to me some superstitious habit, which he had contracted early, and from which he had never called upon his reason to disentangle him. This was his anxious care to go out or in at a door or passage by a certain number of steps from a certain point, or at least so as that either his right or his left foot, (I am not certain which,) should constantly make the first actual movement when he came close to the door or passage. Thus I conjecture: for I have, upon innumerable occasions, observed him suddenly stop, and then seem to count his steps with a deep earnestness; and when he had neglected or gone wrong in this sort of magical movement, I have seen him go back again, put himself in a proper posture to begin the ceremony, and, having gone through it, break from his abstraction, walk briskly on, and join his companion. A strange instance of something of this nature, even when on horseback, happened when he was in the isle of Sky.[1] Sir Joshua

[1] *Journal of a Tour to the Hebrides*, 3rd edit. p. 316.

Reynolds has observed him to go a good way about rather than cross a particular alley in Leicester-fields; but this Sir Joshua imputed to his having had some disagreeable recollection associated with it.

That the most minute singularities which belonged to him, and made very observable parts of his appearance and manner, may not be omitted, it is requisite to mention, that while talking or even musing as he sat in his chair, he commonly held his head to one side towards his right shoulder, and shook it in a tremulous manner, moving his body backwards and forwards, and rubbing his left knee in the same direction, with the palm of his hand. In the intervals of articulating he made various sounds with his mouth, sometimes as if ruminating, or what is called chewing the cud, sometimes giving a half whistle, sometimes making his tongue play backwards from the roof of his mouth, as if clucking like a hen, and sometimes protruding it against his upper gums in front, as if pronouncing quickly under his breath, *too, too, too*: all this accompanied sometimes with a thoughtful look, but more frequently with a smile. Generally when he had concluded a period, in the course of a dispute, by which time he was a good deal exhausted by violence and vociferation, he used to blow out his breath like a Whale. This I supposed was a relief to his lungs; and seemed in him to be a contemptuous mode of expression, as if he had made the arguments of his opponent fly like chaff before the wind.

I am fully aware how very obvious an occasion I here give for the sneering jocularity of such as have no relish of an exact likeness; which to render complete, he who draws it must not disdain the slightest strokes. But if witlings should be inclined to attack this account, let them have the candour to quote what I have offered in my defence.

He was for some time in the summer at Easton Maudit, Northamptonshire, on a visit to the Reverend Dr. Percy, now Bishop of Dromore. Whatever dissatisfaction he felt at what he considered as a slow progress in intellectual improvement, we find that his heart was tender, and his affections warm, as appears from the following very kind letter:

'*To* JOSHUA REYNOLDS, ESQ., *in Leicester-fields, London*

'DEAR SIR,—I did not hear of your sickness till I heard likewise of your recovery, and therefore escaped that part of your pain, which every man must feel, to whom you are known as you are known to me.

'Having had no particular account of your disorder, I know not in what state it has left you. If the amusement of my company can exhilarate the languor of a slow recovery, I will not delay a day to come to you; for I know not how I can so effectually promote my own pleasure as by pleasing you, or my own interest as by preserving you, in whom, if I should lose you, I should lose almost the only man whom I call a friend.

'Pray let me hear of you from yourself, or from dear Miss Reynolds.[1] Make my compliments to Mr. Mudge. I am, dear Sir, your most affectionate and most humble servant,

'At the Rev. Mr. Percy's, at Easton   'SAM. JOHNSON.'
  Maudit, Northamptonshire, (by
  Castle Ashby,) Aug. 19, 1764.'

1765: ÆTAT. 56.]—EARLY in the year 1765 he paid a short visit to the University of Cambridge, with his friend Mr. Beauclerk. There is a lively picturesque account of his behaviour on this visit, in *The Gentleman's Magazine* for March 1785, being an extract of a letter from the late Dr. John Sharp. The two following sentences are very characteristical:—

'He drank his large potations of tea with me, interrupted by many an indignant contradiction, and many a noble sentiment.'
——'Several persons got into his company the last evening at Trinity, where, about twelve, he began to be very great; stripped poor Mrs. Macaulay to the very skin, then gave her for his toast, and drank her in two bumpers.'

The strictness of his self-examination and scrupulous Christian humility appear in his pious meditation on Easter-day this year.

---

[1] Sir Joshua's sister, for whom Johnson had a particular affection, and to whom he wrote many letters which I have seen, and which I am sorry her too nice delicacy will not permit to be published. [A number of these have since been published. R.W.C.]

'I purpose again to partake of the blessed sacrament; yet when I consider how vainly I have hitherto resolved at this annual commemoration of my Saviour's death, to regulate my life by his laws, I am almost afraid to renew my resolutions.'

The concluding words are very remarkable, and shew that he laboured under a severe depression of spirits.

'Since the last Easter I have reformed no evil habit, my time has been unprofitably spent, and seems as a dream that has left nothing behind. *My memory grows confused, and I know not how the days pass over me.* Good Lord deliver me!'[1]

No man was more gratefully sensible of any kindness done to him than Johnson. There is a little circumstance in his diary this year, which shews him in a very amiable light.

'July 2.—I paid Mr. Simpson ten guineas, which he had formerly lent me in my necessity and for which Tetty expressed her gratitude.'

'July 8.—I lent Mr. Simpson ten guineas more.'

Here he had a pleasing opportunity of doing the same kindness to an old friend, which he had formerly received from him. Indeed his liberality as to money was very remarkable. The next article in his diary is,

'July 16.—I received seventy-five pounds. Lent Mr. Davis twenty-five.'

Trinity College, Dublin, at this time surprised Johnson with a spontaneous compliment of the highest academical honours, by creating him Doctor of Laws. The diploma, which is in my possession, is as follows:—

'*OMNIBUS ad quos præsentes literæ pervenerint, salutem. Nos Præpositus et Socii seniores Collegi sacrosanctæ et individuæ Trinitatis Reginæ Elizabethæ juxta Dublin, testamur,* Samueli Johnson, *Armigero, ob egregiam scriptorum elegantiam et utilitatem,*[2] *gratiam concessam fuisse pro gradu Doctoratûs ın utroque Jure, octavo die Julii, Anno Domini millesimo septingentesimo sexagesimo-quinto. In cujus rei testimonium singulorum manus et sigillum quo in hisce*

---

[1] *Pr. and Med.* p. 61.
[2] ['in recognition of the outstanding elegance and usefulness of his writings.']

utimur apposuimus; vicesimo tertio die Julii, Anno Domini millesimo septingentesimo sexagesimo-quinto.

'Gul. Clement.	Fran. Andrews.	R. Murray.
'Tho. Wilson.	*Præps.*	Rob^{tus} Law.
'Tho. Leland		Mich. Kearney.'

This unsolicited mark of distinction, conferred on so great a literary character, did much honour to the judgement and liberal spirit of that learned body. Johnson acknowledged the favour in a letter to Dr. Leland, one of their number; but I have not been able to obtain a copy of it.

He appears this year to have been seized with a temporary fit of ambition, for he had thoughts both of studying law and of engaging in politics. His 'Prayer before the Study of Law' is truly admirable:—

'Sept. 26, 1765.

'Almighty God, the giver of wisdom, without whose help resolutions are vain, without whose blessing study is ineffectual; enable me, if it be thy will, to attain such knowledge as may qualify me to direct the doubtful, and instruct the ignorant; to prevent wrongs and terminate contentions; and grant that I may use that knowledge which I shall attain, to thy glory and my own salvation, for Jesus Christ's sake. Amen.'[1]

His prayer in the view of becoming a politician is entitled, 'Engaging in Politicks with H———n,' no doubt his friend, the Right Honourable William Gerard Hamilton, for whom, during a long acquaintance, he had a great esteem, and to whose conversation he once paid this high compliment: 'I am very unwilling to be left alone, Sir, and therefore I go with my company down the first pair of stairs, in some hopes that they may, perhaps, return again. I go with you, Sir, as far as the street-door.' In what particular department he intended to engage does not appear, nor can Mr. Hamilton explain. His prayer is in general terms:—

'Enlighten my understanding with knowledge of right, and

[1] *Pr. and Med.* p. 66.

govern my will by thy laws, that no deceit may mislead me, nor temptation corrupt me; that I may always endeavour to do good, and hinder evil.'[1] There is nothing upon the subject in his diary.

This year was distinguished by his being introduced into the family of Mr. Thrale, one of the most eminent brewers in England, and Member of Parliament for the borough of Southwark. Foreigners are not a little amazed when they hear of brewers, distillers, and men in similar departments of trade, held forth as persons of considerable consequence. In this great commercial country it is natural that a situation which produces much wealth should be considered as very respectable; and, no doubt, honest industry is entitled to esteem. But, perhaps, the too rapid advance of men of low extraction tends to lessen the value of that distinction by birth and gentility, which has ever been found beneficial to the grand scheme of subordination. Johnson used to give this account of the rise of Mr. Thrale's father: 'He worked at six shillings a week for twenty years in the great brewery, which afterwards was his own. The proprietor of it had an only daughter, who was married to a nobleman. It was not fit that a peer should continue the business. On the old man's death, therefore, the brewery was to be sold. To find a purchaser for so large a property was a difficult matter; and, after some time, it was suggested, that it would be adviseable to treat with Thrale, a sensible, active, honest man, who had been long employed in the house, and to transfer the whole to him for thirty thousand pounds, security being taken upon the property. This was accordingly settled. In eleven years Thrale paid the purchase-money. He acquired a large fortune, and lived to be Member of Parliament for Southwark. But what was most remarkable was the liberality with which he used his riches. He gave his son and daughters the best education. The esteem which his good conduct procured him from the nobleman who had married his master's daughter, made him be treated with much attention; and his son, both at school and at the University of Oxford, associated with young men of the first rank. His allowance from his father, after he left college, was splendid; no less than a

[1] *Pr. and Med.* p. 67.

thousand a year. This, in a man who had risen as old Thrale did, was a very extraordinary instance of generosity. He used to say, "If this young dog does not find so much after I am gone as he expects, let him remember that he has had a great deal in my own time." '

The son, though in affluent circumstances, had good sense enough to carry on his father's trade, which was of such extent, that I remember he once told me, he would not quit it for an annuity of ten thousand a year; 'Not (said he,) that I get ten thousand a year by it, but it is an estate to a family.' Having left daughters only, the property was sold for the immense sum of one hundred and thirty-five thousand pounds; a magnificent proof of what may be done by fair trade in no long period of time.

There may be some who think that a new system of gentility[1] might be established, upon principles totally different from what have hitherto prevailed. Our present heraldry, it may be said, is suited to the barbarous times in which it had its origin. It is chiefly founded upon ferocious merit, upon military excellence. Why, in civilised times, we may be asked, should there not be rank and honours, upon principles, which, independent of long custom, are certainly not less worthy, and which, when once allowed to be connected with elevation and precedency, would obtain the same dignity in our imagination? Why should not the knowledge, the skill, the expertness, the assiduity, and the spirited hazards of trade and commerce, when crowned with success, be entitled to give those flattering distinctions by which mankind are so universally captivated?

Such are the specious, but false arguments for a proposition

---

[1] Mrs. Burney informs me that she heard Dr. Johnson say, 'An English Merchant is a new species of Gentleman.' He, perhaps, had in his mind the following ingenious passage in *The Conscious Lovers*, act iv. scene ii, where Mr. Sealand thus addresses Sir John Bevil: 'Give me leave to say, that we merchants are a species of gentry that have grown into the world this last century, and are as honourable, and almost as useful as you landed-folks, that have always thought yourselves so much above us; for your trading forsooth is extended no farther than a load of hay, or a fat ox.—You are pleasant people indeed! because you are generally bred up to be lazy, therefore, I warrant you, industry is dishonourable.'

which always will find numerous advocates, in a nation where men are every day starting up from obscurity to wealth. To refute them is needless. The general sense of mankind cries out, with irresistible force, '*Un gentilhomme est toujours gentilhomme.*'

Mr. Thrale had married Miss Hesther Lynch Salusbury, of good Welch extraction, a lady of lively talents, improved by education. That Johnson's introduction into Mr. Thrale's family, which contributed so much to the happiness of his life, was owing to her desire for his conversation, is very probable and a general supposition: but it is not the truth. Mr. Murphy, who was intimate with Mr. Thrale, having spoken very highly of Dr. Johnson, he was requested to make them acquainted. This being mentioned to Johnson, he accepted of an invitation to dinner at Thrale's, and was so much pleased with his reception, both by Mr. and Mrs. Thrale, and they so much pleased with him, that his invitations to their house were more and more frequent, till at last he became one of the family, and an apartment was appropriated to him, both in their house in Southwark, and in their villa at Streatham.

Johnson had a very sincere esteem for Mr. Thrale, as a man of excellent principles, a good scholar, well skilled in trade, of a sound understanding, and of manners such as presented the character of a plain independent English 'Squire. As this family will frequently be mentioned in the course of the following pages, and as a false notion has prevailed that Mr. Thrale was inferiour, and in some degree insignificant, compared with Mrs. Thrale, it may be proper to give a true state of the case from the authority of Johnson himself, in his own words.

'I know no man, (said he,) who is more master of his wife and family than Thrale. If he but holds up a finger, he is obeyed. It is a great mistake to suppose that she is above him in literary attainments. She is more flippant; but he has ten times her learning: he is a regular scholar; but her learning is that of a school-boy in one of the lower forms.' My readers may naturally wish for some representation of the figures of this couple. Mr. Thrale was tall, well proportioned, and stately. As for *Madam*, or *my Mistress*, by which epithets Johnson used to mention Mrs. Thrale, she was short, plump, and brisk. She has herself given us a lively view of the idea which Johnson had of her person, on her appearing before him in a dark-coloured gown; 'You little creatures should never wear those sort of clothes, however; they are unsuitable in every way. What! have not all insects gay colours?'[1] Mr. Thrale gave his wife a liberal indulgence, both in the choice of their company, and in the mode of entertaining them. He understood and valued Johnson, without remission, from their first acquaintance to the day of his death. Mrs. Thrale was enchanted with Johnson's conversation, for its own sake, and had also a very allowable vanity in appearing to be honoured with the attention of so celebrated a man.

Nothing could be more fortunate for Johnson than this connection. He had at Mr. Thrale's all the comforts and even luxuries of life; his melancholy was diverted, and his irregular habits lessened by association with an agreeable and well-ordered family. He was treated with the utmost respect, and even affection. The vivacity of Mrs. Thrale's literary talk roused him to cheerfulness and exertion, even when they were alone. But this was not often the case; for he found here a constant succession of what gave him the highest enjoyment: the society of the learned, the witty, and the eminent in every way, who were assembled in numerous companies, called forth his wonderful powers, and gratified him with admiration, to which no man could be insensible.

In the October of this year he at length gave to the world his edition of *Shakspeare*, which, if it had no other merit but that of producing his Preface, in which the excellencies and defects of that immortal bard are displayed with a masterly hand, the nation would have had no reason to complain. A blind indiscriminate admiration of Shakspeare had exposed the British nation to the ridicule of foreigners. Johnson, by candidly admitting the faults of his poet, had the more credit in bestowing on him deserved and indisputable praise; and doubtless none of all his panegyrists have done him half so much honour. Their praise was, like that of a counsel, upon his own side of the cause: John-

[1] *Mrs. Piozzi's Anecdotes*, p. 279.

son's was like the grave, well-considered, and impartial opinion of the judge, which falls from his lips with weight, and is received with reverence. What he did as a commentator has no small share of merit, though his researches were not so ample, and his investigations so acute as they might have been, which we now certainly know from the labours of other able and ingenious criticks who have followed him. He has enriched his edition with a concise account of each play, and of its characteristick excellence. Many of his notes have illustrated obscurities in the text, and placed passages eminent for beauty in a more conspicuous light; and he has, in general, exhibited such a mode of annotation, as may be beneficial to all subsequent editors.

His *Shakspeare* was virulently attacked by Mr. William Kenrick, who obtained the degree of LL.D. from a Scotch University, and wrote for the booksellers in a great variety of branches. Though he certainly was not without considerable merit, he wrote with so little regard to decency and principles, and decorum, and in so hasty a manner, that his reputation was neither extensive nor lasting. I remember one evening, when some of his works were mentioned, Dr. Goldsmith said, he had never heard of them; upon which Dr. Johnson observed, 'Sir, he is one of the many who have made themselves *publick*, without making themselves *known*.'

A young student of Oxford, of the name of Barclay, wrote an answer to Kenrick's review of Johnson's *Shakspeare*. Johnson was at first angry that Kenrick's attack should have the credit of an answer. But afterwards, considering the young man's good intention, he kindly noticed him, and probably would have done more, had not the young man died.

In his Preface to *Shakspeare*, Johnson treated Voltaire very contemptuously, observing, upon some of his remarks, 'These are the petty criticisms of petty wits.' Voltaire, in revenge, made an attack upon Johnson, in one of his numerous literary sallies, which I remember to have read; but there being no general index to his voluminous works, have searched for it in vain, and therefore cannot quote it.

Voltaire was an antagonist with whom I thought Johnson

should not disdain to contend. I pressed him to answer. He said, he perhaps might; but he never did.

Mr. Burney having occasion to write to Johnson for some receipts for subscriptions to his *Shakspeare*, which Johnson had omitted to deliver when the money was paid, he availed himself of that opportunity of thanking Johnson for the great pleasure which he had received from the perusal of his Preface to *Shakspeare*; which, although it excited much clamour against him at first, is now just ranked among the most excellent of his writings. To this letter Johnson returned the following answer:—

'*To* Charles Burney, Esq., *in Poland-street*

'Sir,—I am sorry that your kindness to me has brought upon you so much trouble, though you have taken care to abate that sorrow, by the pleasure which I receive from your approbation. I defend my criticism in the same manner with you. We must confess the faults of our favourite, to gain credit to our praise of his excellencies. He that claims, either in himself or for another, the honours of perfection, will surely injure the reputation which he designs to assist.

'Be pleased to make my compliments to your family. I am, Sir, your most obliged and most humble servant,

'Oct. 16, 1765.'   'Sam. Johnson.'

From one of his journals I transcribed what follows:—
'At church, Oct.—65.
'To avoid all singularity; *Bonaventura*.[1]
'To come in before service, and compose my mind by meditation, or by reading some portions of scriptures. *Tetty*.
'If I can hear the sermon, to attend it, unless attention be more troublesome than useful.
'To consider the act of prayer as a reposal of myself upon God, and a resignation of all into his holy hand.'

In 1764 and 1765 it should seem that Dr. Johnson was so

---

[1] He was probably proposing to himself the model of this excellent person, who for his piety was named *the Seraphic Doctor*.

busily employed with his edition of Shakspeare, as to have had little leisure for any other literary exertion, or, indeed, even for private correspondence. He did not favour me with a single letter for more than two years, for which it will appear that he afterwards apologised.

He was, however, at all times ready to give assistance to his friends, and others, in revising their works, and in writing for them, or greatly improving their Dedications. In that courtly species of composition no man excelled Dr. Johnson. Though the loftiness of his mind prevented him from ever dedicating in his own person, he wrote a very great number of Dedications for others. Some of these, the persons who were favoured with them are unwilling should be mentioned, from a too anxious apprehension, as I think, that they might be suspected of having received larger assistance; and some, after all the diligence I have bestowed, have escaped my enquiries. He told me, a great many years ago, 'he believed he had dedicated to all the Royal Family round;' and it was indifferent to him what was the subject of the work dedicated, provided it were innocent. He once dedicated some Musick for the German Flute to Edward, Duke of York. In writing Dedications for others, he considered himself as by no means speaking his own sentiments.

Notwithstanding his long silence, I never omitted to write to him when I had any thing worthy of communicating. I generally kept copies of my letters to him, that I might have a full view of our correspondence, and never be at a loss to understand any reference in his letters. He kept the greater part of mine very carefully; and a short time before his death was attentive enough to seal them up in bundles, and order them to be delivered to me, which was accordingly done. Amongst them I found one, of which I had not made a copy, and which I own I read with pleasure at the distance of almost twenty years. It is dated November, 1765, at the palace of Pascal Paoli, in Corte, the capital of Corsica, and is full of generous enthusiasm. After giving a sketch of what I had seen and heard in that island, it proceeded thus: 'I dare to call this a spirited tour. I dare to challenge your approbation.'

This letter produced the following answer, which I found on my arrival at Paris.

'*A Mr. Mr.* BOSWELL, *chez Mr.* WATERS, *Banquier, à Paris*

'DEAR SIR,—Apologies are seldom of any use. We will delay till your arrival the reasons, good or bad, which have made me such a sparing and ungrateful correspondent. Be assured, for the present, that nothing has lessened either the esteem or love with which I dismissed you at Harwich. Both have been increased by all that I have been told of you by yourself or others; and when you return, you will return to an unaltered, and, I hope, unalterable friend.

'All that you have to fear from me is the vexation of disappointing me. No man loves to frustrate expectations which have been formed in his favour; and the pleasure which I promise myself from your journals and remarks is so great, that perhaps no degree of attention or discernment will be sufficient to afford it.

'Come home, however, and take your chance. I long to see you, and to hear you; and hope that we shall not be so long separated again. Come home, and expect such a welcome as is due to him whom a wise and noble curiosity has led, where perhaps no native of this country ever was before.

'I have no news to tell you that can deserve your notice; nor would I willingly lessen the pleasure that any novelty may give you at your return. I am afraid we shall find it difficult to keep among us a mind which has been so long feasted with variety. But let us try what esteem and kindness can effect.

'As your father's liberality has indulged you with so long a ramble, I doubt not but you will think his sickness, or even his desire to see you, a sufficient reason for hastening your return. The longer we live, and the more we think, the higher value we learn to put on the friendship and tenderness of parents and of friends. Parents we can have but once; and he promises himself too much, who enters life with the expectation of finding many friends. Upon some motive, I hope, that you will be here soon; and am willing to think that it will be an inducement to your return, that it is sincerely desired by, dear Sir, your affectionate humble servant,   'SAM. JOHNSON.'

'Johnson's Court, Fleet-street, January 14, 1766.'

I returned to London in February, and found Dr. Johnson in a good house in Johnson's Court, Fleet-street, in which he had accommodated Miss Williams with an apartment on the ground floor, while Mr. Levett occupied his post in the garret: his faithful Francis was still attending upon him. He received me with much kindness. The fragments of our conversation, which I have preserved, are these: I told him that Voltaire, in a conversation with me, had distinguished Pope and Dryden thus:—'Pope drives a handsome chariot, with a couple of neat trim nags; Dryden a coach, and six stately horses.' JOHNSON. 'Why, Sir, the truth is, they both drive coaches and six; but Dryden's horses are either galloping or stumbling: Pope's go at a steady even trot.'[1] He said of Goldsmith's *Traveller*, which had been published in my absence, 'There has not been so fine a poem since Pope's time.'

And here it is proper to settle, with authentick precision, what has long floated in publick report, as to Johnson's being himself the authour of a considerable part of that poem. Much, no doubt, both of the sentiments and expression, were derived from conversation with him; and it was certainly submitted to his friendly revision: but in the year 1783, he, at my request, marked with a pencil the lines which he had furnished, which are only line 420th,

'To stop too fearful, and too faint to go;'

and the concluding ten lines, except the last couplet but one, which I distinguish by the Italick character:

'How small of all that human hearts endure,
That part which kings or laws can cause or cure.

[1] It is remarkable, that Mr. Gray has employed somewhat the same image to characterise Dryden. He, indeed, furnishes his car with but two horses, but they are of 'ethereal race':
    'Behold where Dryden's less presumptuous car,
    Wide o'er the fields of glory bear
    Two coursers of ethereal race,
    With necks in thunder cloath'd, and long resounding pace'.
                    Ode on the Progress of Poesy.

> Still to ourselves in every place consign'd,
> Our own felicity we make or find;
> With secret course, which no loud storms annoy,
> Glides the smooth current of domestick joy.
> *The lifted axe, the agonizing wheel,*
> *Luke's iron crown, and Damien's bed of steel,*
> To men remote from power, but rarely known,
> Leave reason, faith, and conscience, all our own.'

He added, 'These are all of which I can be sure.' They bear a small proportion to the whole, which consists of four hundred and thirty-eight verses. Goldsmith, in the couplet which he inserted, mentions *Luke* as a person well known, and superficial readers have passed it over quite smoothly; while those of more attention have been as much perplexed by *Luke*, as by *Lydiat*, in *The Vanity of Human Wishes*. The truth is, that Goldsmith himself was in a mistake. In the *Respublica Hungarica*, there is an account of a desperate rebellion in the year 1514, headed by two brothers, of the name of *Zeck*, George and Luke. When it was quelled, *George*, not *Luke*, was punished by his head being encircled with a red-hot iron crown: '*coronâ candescente ferreâ coronatur.*' The same severity of torture was exercised on the Earl of Athol, one of the murderers of King James I. of Scotland.

Dr. Johnson at the same time favoured me by marking the lines which he furnished to Goldsmith's *Deserted Village*, which are only the last four:

> 'That trade's proud empire hastes to swift decay,
> As ocean sweeps the labour'd mole away:
> While self-dependent power can time defy,
> As rocks resist the billows and the sky.'

Talking of education, 'People have now a-days, (said he,) got a strange opinion that every thing should be taught by lectures. Now, I cannot see that lectures can do so much good as reading the books from which the lectures are taken. I know nothing that can be best taught by lectures, except where experiments are to be shewn. You may teach chymistry by lectures.—You might teach making of shoes by lectures!'

At night I supped with him at the Mitre tavern, that we might renew our social intimacy at the original place of meeting. But there was now a considerable difference in his way of living. Having had an illness, in which he was advised to leave off wine, he had, from that period, continued to abstain from it, and drank only water, or lemonade.

I told him that a foreign friend[1] of his, whom I had met with abroad, was so wretchedly perverted to infidelity, that he treated the hopes of immortality with brutal levity; and said, 'As man dies like a dog, let him lie like a dog.' JOHNSON. '*If* he dies like a dog, *let* him lie like a dog.' I added, that this man said to me, 'I hate mankind, for I think myself one of the best of them, and I know how bad I am.' JOHNSON. 'Sir, he must be very singular in his opinion, if he thinks himself one of the best of men; for none of his friends think him so.'—He said, 'no honest man could be a Deist; for no man could be so after a fair examination of the proofs of Christianity.' I named Hume. JOHNSON. 'No, Sir; Hume owned to a clergyman in the bishoprick of Durham, that he had never read the New Testament with attention.' I mentioned Hume's notion, that all who are happy are equally happy; a little miss with a new gown at a dancing school ball, a general at the head of a victorious army, and an orator, after having made an eloquent speech in a great assembly. JOHNSON. 'Sir, that all who are happy, are equally happy, is not true. A peasant and a philosopher may be equally *satisfied*, but not equally *happy*. Happiness consists in the multiplicity of agreeable consciousness. A peasant has not capacity for having equal happiness with a philosopher.' I remember this very question very happily illustrated in opposition to Hume, by the Reverend Mr. Robert Brown, at Utrecht. 'A small drinking-glass and a large one, (said he,) may be equally full; but the large one holds more than the small.'

Dr. Johnson was very kind this evening, and said to me, 'You have now lived five-and-twenty years, and you have employed them well.' 'Alas, Sir, (said I,) I fear not. Do I know history? Do I know mathematicks? Do I know law?' JOHNSON. 'Why, Sir, though you may know no science so well as to be able to

---

[1] [Baretti. *Boswell Papers,* vii. 68.]

teach it, and no profession so well as to be able to follow it, your general mass of knowledge of books and men renders you very capable to make yourself master of any science, or fit yourself for any profession.' I mentioned that a gay friend[1] had advised me against being a lawyer, because I should be excelled by plodding block-heads. JOHNSON. 'Why, Sir, in the formulary and statutory part of law, a plodding block-head may excel; but in the ingenious and rational part of it a plodding block-head can never excel.'

I talked of the mode adopted by some to rise in the world, by courting great men, and asked him whether he had ever submitted to it. JOHNSON. 'Why, Sir, I never was near enough to great men, to court them. You may be prudently attached to great men and yet independent. You are not to do what you think wrong; and, Sir, you are to calculate, and not pay too dear for what you get. You must not give a shilling's worth of court for six-pence worth of good. But if you can get a shilling's worth of good for six-pence worth of court, you are a fool if you do not pay court.'

He said, 'If convents should be allowed at all, they should only be retreats for persons unable to serve the publick, or who have served it. It is our first duty to serve society, and, after we have done that, we may attend wholly to the salvation of our own souls. A youthful passion for abstracted devotion should not be encouraged.'

I introduced the subject of second sight, and other mysterious manifestations; the fulfilment of which, I suggested, might happen by chance. JOHNSON. 'Yes, Sir; but they have happened so often, that mankind have agreed to think them not fortuitous.'

I talked to him a great deal of what I had seen in Corsica, and of my intention to publish an account of it. He encouraged me by saying, 'You cannot go to the bottom of the subject; but all that you tell us will be new to us. Give us as many anecdotes as you can.'

Our next meeting at the Mitre was on Saturday the 15th of February, when I presented to him my old and most intimate

[1] [Wilkes. *Boswell Papers*, vii. 70.]

friend, the Reverend Mr. Temple, then of Cambridge. I having mentioned that I had passed some time with Rousseau in his wild retreat, and having quoted some remark made by Mr. Wilkes, with whom I had spent many pleasant hours in Italy, Johnson said (sarcastically,) 'It seems, Sir, you have kept very good company abroad, Rousseau and Wilkes!' Thinking it enough to defend one at a time, I said nothing as to my gay friend, but answered with a smile, 'My dear Sir, you don't call Rousseau bad company. Do you really think *him* a bad man?' JOHNSON. 'Sir, if you are talking jestingly of this, I don't talk with you. If you mean to be serious, I think him one of the worst of men; a rascal who ought to be hunted out of society, as he has been. Three or four nations have expelled him; and it is a shame that he is protected in this country.' BOSWELL. 'I don't deny, Sir, but that his novel may, perhaps, do harm; but I cannot think his intention was bad.' JOHNSON. 'Sir, that will not do. We cannot prove any man's intention to be bad. You may shoot a man through the head, and say you intended to miss him; but the Judge will order you to be hanged. An alleged want of intention, when evil is committed, will not be allowed in a court of justice. Rousseau, Sir, is a very bad man. I would sooner sign a sentence for his transportation, than that of any felon who has gone from the Old Bailey these many years. Yes, I should like to have him work in the plantations.' BOSWELL. 'Sir, do you think him as bad a man as Voltaire?' JOHNSON. 'Why, Sir, it is difficult to settle the proportion of iniquity between them.'

This violence seemed very strange to me, who had read many of Rousseau's animated writings with great pleasure, and even edification; had been much pleased with his society, and was just come from the Continent, where he was very generally admired. Nor can I yet allow that he deserves the very severe censure which Johnson pronounced upon him. His absurd preference of savage to civilised life, and other singularities, are proofs rather of a defect in his understanding, than of any depravity in his heart. And notwithstanding the unfortunate opinion which many worthy men have expressed of his '*Profession de Foi du*

Vicaire Savoyard', I cannot help admiring it as the performance of a man full of sincere reverential submission to Divine Mystery, though beset with perplexing doubts; a state of mind to be viewed with pity rather than with anger.

On his favourite subject of subordination, Johnson said, 'So far is it from being true that men are naturally equal, that no two people can be half an hour together, but one shall acquire an evident superiority over the other.'

I mentioned the advice given us by philosophers, to console ourselves, when distressed or embarrassed, by thinking of those who are in a worse situation than ourselves. This, I observed, could not apply to all, for there must be some who have nobody worse than they are. JOHNSON. 'Why, to be sure, Sir, there are; but they don't know it. There is no being so poor and so contemptible, who does not think there is somebody still poorer, and still more contemptible.'

As my stay in London at this time was very short, I had not many opportunities of being with Dr. Johnson; but I felt my veneration for him in no degree lessened, by my having seen *multorum hominum mores et urbes*.[1] On the contrary, by having it in my power to compare him with many of the most celebrated persons of other countries, my admiration of his extraordinary mind was increased and confirmed.

The roughness, indeed, which sometimes appeared in his manners, was more striking to me now, and from my having been accustomed to the studied smooth complying habits of the Continent; and I clearly recognised in him, not without respect for his honest conscientious zeal, the same indignant and sarcastical mode of treating every attempt to unhinge or weaken good principles.

One evening when a young gentleman[2] teized him with an account of the infidelity of his servant, who, he said, would not believe the scriptures, because he could not read them in the original tongues, and be sure that they were not invented, 'Why, foolish fellow, (said Johnson,) has he any better authority for

---

[1] ['Many cities and many men's manners.' Horace, *Ars Poetica*, l. 142.]
[2] [Boswell. *Boswell Papers*, vii. 74.]

almost every thing that he believes?' BOSWELL. 'Then the vulgar, Sir, never can know they are right, but must submit themselves to the learned.' JOHNSON. 'To be sure, Sir. The vulgar are the children of the State, and must be taught like children.' BOSWELL. 'Then, Sir, a poor Turk must be a Mahometan, just as a poor Englishman must be a Christian?' JOHNSON. 'Why, yes, Sir; and what then? This now is such stuff as I used to talk to my mother, when I first began to think myself a clever fellow; and she ought to have whipt me for it.'

Another evening Dr. Goldsmith and I called on him, with the hope of prevailing on him to sup with us at the Mitre. We found him indisposed, and resolved not to go abroad. 'Come then, (said Goldsmith,) we will not go to the Mitre to-night, since we cannot have the big man with us.' Johnson then called for a bottle of port, of which Goldsmith and I partook, while our friend, now a water-drinker, sat by us. GOLDSMITH. 'I think, Mr. Johnson, you don't go near the theatres now. You give yourself no more concern about a new play, than if you had never had any thing to do with the stage.' JOHNSON. 'Why, Sir, our tastes greatly alter. The lad does not care for the child's rattle, and the old man does not care for the young man's whore.' GOLDSMITH. 'Nay, Sir, but your Muse was not a whore.' JOHNSON. 'Sir, I do not think she was. But as we advance in the journey of life, we drop some of the things which have pleased us; whether it be that we are fatigued and don't choose to carry so many things any farther, or that we find other things which we like better.' BOSWELL. 'But, Sir, why don't you give us something in some other way?' GOLDSMITH. 'Ay, Sir, we have a claim upon you.' JOHNSON. 'No, Sir, I am not obliged to do any more. No man is obliged to do as much as he can do. A man is to have part of his life to himself. If a soldier has fought a good many campaigns, he is not to be blamed if he retires to ease and tranquillity. A physician, who has practised long in a great city, may be excused if he retires to a small town, and takes less practice. Now, Sir, the good I can do by my conversation bears the same proportion to the good I can do by my writings, that the practice of a physician, retired to a small town, does to his practice in a great city.' BOSWELL. 'But I wonder, Sir, you have not more pleasure in writing than in not writing.' JOHNSON. 'Sir, you *may* wonder.'

He talked of making verses, and observed. 'The great difficulty is to know when you have made good ones. When composing, I have generally had them in my mind, perhaps fifty at a time, walking up and down in my room; and then I have written them down, and often, from laziness, have written only half lines. I have written a hundred lines in a day. I remember I wrote a hundred lines of *The Vanity of Human Wishes* in a day. Doctor, (turning to Goldsmith,) I am not quite idle; I made one line t'other day; but I made no more.' GOLDSMITH. 'Let us hear it; we'll put a bad one to it.' JOHNSON. 'No, Sir, I have forgot it.'

Such specimens of the easy and playful conversation of the great Dr. Samuel Johnson are, I think, to be prized; as exhibiting the little varieties of a mind so enlarged and so powerful when objects of consequence required its exertions, and as giving us a minute knowledge of his character and modes of thinking.

'*To* BENNET LANGTON, ESQ., *at Langton, near Spilsby, Lincolnshire*

'DEAR SIR,—What your friends have done, that from your departure till now nothing has been heard of you, none of us are able to inform the rest; but as we are all neglected alike, no one thinks himself entitled to the privilege of complaint.

'I should have known nothing of you or of Langton, from the time that dear Miss Langton left us, had not I met Mr. Simpson, of Lincoln, one day in the street, by whom I was informed that Mr. Langton, your Mamma, and yourself, had been all ill, but that you were all recovered.

'That sickness should suspend your correspondence, I did not wonder; but hoped that it would be renewed at your recovery.

'Since you will not inform us where you are, or how you live, I know not whether you desire to know any thing of us. However, I will tell you that THE CLUB subsists; but we have the loss[1] of Burke's company since he has been engaged in publick busi-

---

[1] [*the loss*; Johnson wrote *less*.]

ness, in which he has gained more reputation than perhaps any man at his [first] appearance ever gained before. He made two speeches in the House for repealing the Stamp-act, which were publickly commended by Mr. Pitt, and have filled the town with wonder.

'Burke is a great man by nature, and is expected soon to attain civil greatness. I am grown greater too, for I have maintained the news-papers these many weeks; and what is greater still, I have risen every morning since New-year's day, at about eight; when I was up, I have indeed done but little; yet it is no slight advancement to obtain for so many hours more, the consciousness of being.

'I wish you were in my new study; I am now writing the first letter in it. I think it looks very pretty about me.

'Dyer is constant at THE CLUB; Hawkins is remiss; I am not over diligent. Dr. Nugent, Dr. Goldsmith, and Mr. Reynolds, are very constant. Mr. Lye is printing his Saxon and Gothick Dictionary; all THE CLUB subscribes.

'You will pay my respects to all my Lincolnshire friends. I am, dear Sir, most affectionately yours,

'March 9, 1766.   'SAM. JOHNSON.'
Johnson's-court, Fleet-street.'

'*To* BENNET LANGTON, ESQ., *at Langton, near Spilsby, Lincolnshire*

'DEAR SIR,—In supposing that I should be more than commonly affected by the death of Peregrine Langton,[1] you were not mistaken; he was one of those whom I loved at once by instinct and by reason. I have seldom indulged more hope of any thing than of being able to improve our acquaintance to friendship. Many a time have I placed myself again at Langton, and imagined the pleasure with which I should walk to Partney[2] in a summer morning; but this is no longer possible. We must now endeavour to preserve what is left us,—his example of piety and œconomy. I hope you make what enquiries you can, and write

[1] Mr. Langton's uncle.
[2] The place of residence of Mr. Peregrine Langton.

down what is told you. The little things which distinguish domestick characters are soon forgotten: if you delay to enquire, you will have no information; if you neglect to write, information will be vain.[1]

'His art of life certainly deserves to be known and studied. He

[1] Mr. Langton did not disregard this counsel, but wrote the following account, which he has been pleased to communicate to me:

'The circumstances of Mr. Peregrine Langton were these. He had an annuity for life of two hundred pounds *per annum*. He resided in a village in Lincolnshire; the rent of his house, with two or three small fields, was twenty-eight pounds; the county he lived in was not more than moderately cheap; his family consisted of a sister, who paid him eighteen pounds annually for her board, and a niece. The servants were two maids, and two men in livery. His common way of living, at his table, was three or four dishes; the appurtenances to his table were neat and handsome; he frequently entertained company at dinner, and then his table was well served with as many dishes as were usual at the tables of the other gentlemen in the neighbourhood. His own appearance, as to clothes, was genteelly neat and plain. He had always a postchaise, and kept three horses.

'Such, with the resources I have mentioned, was his way of living, which he did not suffer to employ his whole income: for he had always a sum of money lying by him for any extraordinary expences that might arise. Some money he put into the stocks; at his death, the sum he had there amounted to one hundred and fifty pounds. He purchased out of his income his household furniture and linen, of which latter he had a very ample store; and, as I am assured by those that had very good means of knowing, not less than the tenth part of his income was set apart for charity: at the time of his death, the sum of twenty-five pounds was found, with a direction to be employed in such uses.

'He had laid down a plan of living proportioned to his income, and did not practise any extraordinary degree of parsimony, but endeavoured that in his family there should be plenty without waste; as an instance that this was his endeavour, it may be worth while to mention a method he took in regulating a proper allowance of malt liquor to be drunk in his family, that there might not be a deficiency, or any intemperate profusion: On a complaint made that his allowance of a hogshead in a month, was not enough for his own family, he ordered the quantity of a hogshead to be put into bottles, had it locked up from the servants, and distributed out, every day, eight quarts, which is the quantity each day at one hogshead in a month; and told his servants, that if that did not suffice, he would allow them more; but, by this method, it appeared at once that the allowance was much more than sufficient for his small family; and this proved a clear conviction, that could not be answered, and saved all future dispute. He was, in general, very diligently and punctually attended and obeyed by his servants; he was very considerate as to the injunctions he gave, and explained them distinctly; and, at their first coming to his service, steadily exacted a close compliance with them, without any remission; and the servants finding this to be the case, soon grew habitually accustomed to the practice of their business, and then very little further attention was necessary. On extraordinary instances lived in plenty and elegance upon an income which, to many would appear indigent, and to most, scanty. How he lived, therefore, every man has an interest in knowing. His death, I hope, was peaceful; it was surely happy.

'I wish I had written sooner, lest, writing now, I should renew your grief; but I would not forbear saying what I have now said.

'This loss is, I hope, the only misfortune of a family to whom

of good behaviour, or diligent service, he was not wanting in particular encouragements and presents above their wages; it is remarkable that he would permit their relations to visit them, and stay at his house two or three days at a time.

'The wonder, with most that hear an account of his œconomy, will be, how he was able, with such an income, to do so much, especially when it is considered that he paid for everything he had; he had no land, except the two or three small fields which I have said he rented; and, instead of gaining any thing by their produce, I have reason to think he lost by them; however, they furnished him with no further assistance towards his housekeeping, than grass for his horses, (not hay, for that I know he bought,) and for two cows. Every Monday morning he settled his family accounts, and so kept up a constant attention to the confining his expences within his income; and to do it more exactly, compared those expences with a computation he had made, how much that income would afford him every week and day of the year. One of his œconomical practices was, as soon as any repair was wanting in or about his house, to have it immediately performed. When he had money to spare, he chose to lay in a provision of linen or clothes, or any other necessaries; as then, he said, he could afford it, which he might not be so well able to do when the actual want came; in consequence of which method, he had a considerable supply of necessary articles lying by him, beside what was in use.

'But the main particular that seems to have enabled him to do so much with his income, was, that he paid for every thing as soon as he had it, except, alone, what were current accounts, such as rent for his house and servants' wages; and these he paid at the stated times with the utmost exactness. He gave notice to the tradesmen of the neighbouring market-towns that they should no longer have his custom, if they let any of his servants have anything without their paying for it. Thus he put it out of his power to commit those imprudences to which those are liable that defer their payments by using their money some other way than where it ought to go. And whatever money he had by him, he knew that it was not demanded elsewhere, but that he might safely employ it as he pleased.

'His example was confined, by the sequestered place of his abode, to the observation of few, though his prudence and virtue would have made it valuable to all who could have known it.—These few particulars, which I knew myself, or have obtained from those who lived with him, may afford instruction, and be an incentive to that wise art of living, which he so successfully practised.'

no misfortune at all should happen, if my wishes could avert it. Let me know how you all go on. Has Mr. Langton got him the little horse that I recommended? It would do him good to ride about his estate in fine weather.

'Be pleased to make my compliments to Mrs. Langton, and to dear Miss Langton, and Miss Di, and Miss Juliet, and to every body else.

'THE CLUB holds very well together. Monday is my night.[1] I continue to rise tolerably well, and read more than I did. I hope something will yet come on it. I am, Sir, your most affectionate servant,

'May 10, 1766.   'SAM. JOHNSON.'
    Johnson's-court, Fleet-street.'

After I had been some time in Scotland, I mentioned to him in a letter that 'On my first return to my native country, after some years of absence, I was told of a vast number of my acquaintance who were all gone to the land of forgetfulness, and I found myself like a man stalking over a field of battle, who every moment perceives some one lying dead.' I complained of irresolution, and mentioned my having made a vow as a security for good conduct. I wrote to him again, without being able to move his indolence; nor did I hear from him till he had received a copy of my inaugural Exercise, or Thesis in Civil Law, which I published at my admission as an Advocate, as is the custom in Scotland. He then wrote to me as follows:

'*To* JAMES BOSWELL, ESQ.

'DEAR SIR,—The reception of your Thesis put me in mind of my debt to you. Why did you * * * * * * * * * * * * *[2] I will punish you for it, by telling you that your Latin wants correction.[3] In the beginning, *Spei alteræ*, not to urge that it

¹ Of his being in the chair of THE LITERARY CLUB, which at this time met once a week in the evening.

² The passage omitted alluded to a private transaction. [Boswell's copy at Yale supplies the lacuna; why had he dedicated to Lord Mountstuart, a man he did not like?]

³ This censure of my Latin relates to the Dedication, which was as follows:

should be *primæ*, is not grammatical: *alteræ* should be *alteri*. In the next line you seem to use *genus* absolutely, for what we call *family*, that is, for *illustrious extraction*, I doubt without authority. *Homines nullius originis*, for *Nullis orti majoribus*, or, *Nullo loco nati*, is, I am afraid, barbarous.—Ruddiman is dead.

'I have now vexed you enough, and will try to please you. Your resolution to obey your father I sincerely approve; but do

---

VIRO NOBILISSIMO, ORNATISSIMO,

JOANNI,

VICECOMITI MOUNTSTUART,

ATAVIS EDITO REGIBUS

EXCELSÆ FAMILIÆ DE BUTE SPEI ALTERÆ;

LABENTE SECULO,

QUUM HOMINES NULLIUS ORIGINIS

GENUS ÆQUARE OPIBUS AGGREDIUNTUR,

SANGUINIS ANTIQUI ET ILLUSTRIS

SEMPER MEMORI,

NATALIUM SPLENDOREM VIRTUTIBUS AUGENTI:

AD PUBLICA POPULI COMITIA

JAM LEGATO;

IN OPTIMATIUM VERO MAGNÆ BRITANNIÆ SENATU,

JURE HÆREDITARIO,

OLIM CONSESSURO:

VIM INSITAM VARIA DOCTRINA PROMOVENTE,

NEC TAMEN SE VENDITANTE,

PRÆDITO:

PRISCA FIDE, ANIMO LIBERRIMO,

ET MORUM ELEGANTIA

INSIGNI:

IN ITALIÆ VISITANDÆ ITINERE,

SOCIO SUO HONORATISSIMO,

HASCE JURISPRUDENTIÆ PRIMITIAS

DEVINCTISSIMÆ AMICITIÆ ET OBSERVANTIÆ

MONUMENTUM,

D. D. C Q.

JACOBUS BOSWELL.

['James Boswell dedicates this the first fruits of his legal study, as a token of devoted friendship and respect, to the honoured companion of his Italian travels, to the most noble John, Viscount Mountstuart, of kingly line, the second hope of the noble family of Bute: a man ever mindful of his ancient and illustrious blood in a degenerate age, when men of no origin strive to equal birth with riches; who by his virtues enhances the splendour of his birthright; already a member of the House of Commons, but destined by hereditary right to the House of Lords; with an education that advances native talent [cf. Horace, *Odes* IV. iv. 33: *doctrina sed vim promovet insitam*], but does not display itself; of ancient faith, liberal understanding, and elegance of manners.']

367

not accustom yourself to enchain your volatility by vows: they will sometimes leave a thorn in your mind, which you will, perhaps, never be able to extract or eject. Take this warning, it is of great importance.

'The study of the law is what you very justly term it, copious and generous;[1] and in adding your name to its professors, you have done exactly what I always wished, when I wished you best. I hope that you will continue to pursue it vigorously and constantly. You gain, at least, what is no small advantage, security from those troublesome and wearisome discontents, which are always obtruding themselves upon a mind vacant, unemployed, and undetermined.

'You ought to think it no small inducement to diligence and perseverance, that they will please your father. We all live upon the hope of pleasing somebody; and the pleasure of pleasing ought to be greatest, and at last always will be greatest, when our endeavours are exerted in consequence of our duty.

'Life is not long, and too much of it must not pass in idle deliberation how it shall be spent; deliberation, which those who begin it by prudence, and continue it with subtilty, must, after long expence of thought, conclude by chance. To prefer one future mode of life to another, upon just reasons, requires faculties which it has not pleased our Creator to give us.

'If, therefore, the profession you have chosen has some unexpected inconveniences, console yourself by reflecting that no profession is without them; and that all the importunities and perplexities of business are softness and luxury, compared with the incessant cravings of vacancy, and the unsatisfactory expedients of idleness.

> *"Hæc sunt quæ nostrâ potui te voce monere;*
> *Vade, age."*[2]

[1] This alludes to the first sentence of the *Procemium* of my Thesis: 'JURISPRUDENTIÆ *studio nullum uberius, nullum generosius: in legibus enim agitandis, populorum mores, variasque fortunæ vices ex quibus leges oriuntur, contemplari simul solemus.*' ['No study is more copious or more generous than jurisprudence; for in discussing laws we pay regard both to the manners of peoples and to the vicissitudes from which laws take their rise.']

[2] [Such the warnings that this voice of mine may give thee. Go then'. *Aeneid*, iii. 461. (Jackson.) But Virgil wrote: 'liceat te voce moneri'.]

'As to your *History of Corsica*, you have no materials which others have not, or may not have. You have, somehow or other, warmed your imagination. I wish there were some cure, like the lover's leap, for all heads of which some single idea has obtained an unreasonable and irregular possession. Mind your own affairs, and leave the Corsicans to theirs. I am, dear Sir, your most humble servant,

'London, Aug. 21, 1766.'   'SAM. JOHNSON.'

'*To* DR. SAMUEL JOHNSON

'Auchinleck, Nov. 6, 1766.

'MUCH ESTEEMED AND DEAR SIR,—I plead not guilty to[1] * *
* *.

'Having thus, I hope, cleared myself of the charge brought against me, I presume you will not be displeased if I escape the punishment which you have decreed for me unheard. If you have discharged the arrows of criticism against an innocent man, you must rejoice to find they have missed him, or have not been pointed so as to wound him.

'To talk no longer in allegory, I am, with all deference, going to offer a few observations in defence of my Latin, which you have found fault with.

'You think I should have used *spei primæ*, instead of *spei alteræ. Spes* is, indeed, often used to express something on which we have a future dependence, as in Virg. Eclog. i. l. 14,

"———————— *modo namque gemellos*
      Spem *gregis ah silice in nuda connixa reliquit.*"[2]

and in Georg. iii. l. 473,

"Spemque *gregemque simul*,"[3]

for the lambs and the sheep. Yet it is also used to express any thing on which we have a present dependence, and is well applied to a man of distinguished influence, our support, our refuge, our

[1] The passage omitted explained the transaction to which the preceding letter had alluded.
[2] ['Her twin kids, hope of my flock, on the naked flint.' (Jackson, and so the following.)]
[3] ['at once the hope and the flock.']

præsidium, as Horace calls Mæcenas. So, Æneid xii. 1. 57, Queen Amata addresses her son-in-law Turnus:—"Spes *tu nunc una:*" and he was then no future hope, for she adds,

> "——— *decus imperiumque Latini*
>   Te penes;"[1]

which might have been said of my Lord Bute some years ago. Now I consider the present Earl of Bute to be '*Excelsæ familiæ de Bute* spes prima;' and my Lord Mountstuart, as his eldest son, to be '*spes altera.*' So in Æneid xii. 1. 168, after having mentioned Pater Æneas, who was the *present* spes, the *reigning* spes, as my German friends would say, the *spes prima,* the poet adds,

> "*Et juxta Ascanius, magnæ* spes altera *Romæ.*"[2]

'You think *alteræ* ungrammatical, and you tell me it should have been *alteri.* You must recollect, that in old times *alter* was declined regularly; and when the ancient fragments preserved in the *Juris Civilis Fontes* were written, it was certainly declined in the way that I use it. This, I should think, may protect a lawyer who writes *alteræ* in a dissertation upon part of his own science. But as I could hardly venture to quote fragments of old law to so classical a man as Mr. Johnson, I have not made an accurate search into these remains, to find examples of what I am able to produce in poetical composition. We find in Plaut. Rudens, act iii. scene 4,

> "*Nam huic* alteræ *patria quæ sit profecto nescio.*"[3]

Plautus is, to be sure, an old comick writer; but in the days of Scipio and Lelius, we find, Terent. Heautontim. act ii. scene 3,

> "——————— *hoc ipsa in itinere* alteræ
>   Dum narrat, forte audivi.*"[4]

'You doubt my having authority for using *genus* absolutely, for what we call *family,* that is, for *illustrious extraction.* Now I take *genus* in Latin, to have much the same signification with

---

[1] ['Thou art now our only hope . . . the honour and sovereignty of Latinus are in thy hands.']
[2] ['At his side Ascanius, second hope of queenly Rome.']
[3] ['I don't know where this other girl comes from.']
[4] ['I chanced to hear Antiphila tell that on the way to the other girl.' (W. Ritchie.)]

birth in English; both in their primary meaning expressing simply descent, but both made to stand κατ' ἐξοχήν,[1] for noble descent. *Genus* is thus used in Hor. lib. ii. Sat. v. l. 8,

"*Et* genus *et virtus, nisi cum re, vilior alga est.*"[2]

And in lib. i. Epist. vi. l. 37,

"*Et* genus *et formam Regina pecunia donat.*"[3]

And in the celebrated contest between Ajax and Ulysses, Ovid's Metamorph. lib. xiii. l. 140,

"*Nam* genus *et proavos, et quæ non fecimus ipsi,*
Vix ea nostra voco."[4]

'*Homines nullius originis,* for *nullis orti majoribus,* or *nullo loco nati,* is, you are "afraid, barbarous."

'*Origo* is used to signify extraction, as in Virg. Æneid i. l. 286,

"*Nascetur pulchrâ Trojanus* origine *Cæsar.*"[5]

And in Æneid x. l. 618.

"*Ille tamen nostrâ deducit* origine *nomen.*"[6]

And as *nullus* is used for obscure, is it not in the genius of the Latin language to write *nullius originis,* for obscure extraction?

'I have defended myself as well as I could.

'Might I venture to differ from you with regard to the utility of vows? I am sensible that it would be very dangerous to make vows rashly, and without a due consideration. But I cannot help thinking that they may often be of great advantage to one of a variable judgement and irregular inclinations. I always remember a passage in one of your letters to our Italian friend Baretti; where talking of the monastick life, you say you do not wonder that serious men should put themselves under the protection of

---

[1] ['par excellence.']
[2] ['Without substance, blood and valour are more valueless than sea-weed.' (Wickham.)]
[3] ['Even birth and beauty are in the gift of Queen Money.' (Wickham.)]
[4] ['For birth and lineage and all such renown, Bequeathed, not made, can scarce be called our own.' (W. F. H. King.)]
[5] ['A prince shall be born of the fair stock of Troy.' (Jackson.)]
[6] ['And yet his name is drawn from our lineage.' (Jackson.)]

a religious order, when they have found how unable they are to take care of themselves. For my own part, without affecting to be a Socrates, I am sure I have a more than ordinary struggle to maintain with *the Evil Principle*; and all the methods I can devise are little enough to keep me tolerably steady in the paths of rectitude. . . . I am ever, with the highest veneration, your affectionate humble servant,

'JAMES BOSWELL.'

It appears from Johnson's diary, that he was this year at Mr. Thrale's, from before Midsummer till after Michaelmas, and that he afterwards passed a month at Oxford. He had then contracted a great intimacy with Mr. Chambers of that University, afterwards Sir Robert Chambers, one of the Judges in India.

He published nothing this year in his own name; but the noble dedication* to the King, of Gwyn's *London and Westminster Improved*, was written by him; and he furnished the Preface,† and several of the pieces, which compose a volume of *Miscellanies* by Mrs. Anna Williams, the blind lady who had an asylum in his house. Of these, there are his 'Epitaph on Philips,'* 'Translation of a Latin Epitaph on Sir Thomas Hanmer,'† 'Friendship, an Ode,'* and, 'The Ant,'* a paraphrase from the Proverbs, of which I have a copy in his own hand-writing; and, from internal evidence, I ascribe to him, 'To Miss ——, on her giving the Authour a gold and silk net-work Purse of her own weaving;'† and, 'The happy Life.'†

Most of the pieces in this volume have evidently received additions from his superiour pen, particularly 'Verses to Mr. Richardson, on his Sir Charles Grandison;' 'The Excursion;' 'Reflections on a Grave digging in Westminster Abbey.' There is in this collection a poem 'On the Death of Stephen Grey, the Electrician;'* which, on reading it, appeared to me to be undoubtedly Johnson's. I asked Mrs. Williams whether it was not his. 'Sir, (said she, with some warmth,) I wrote that poem before I had the honour of Dr. Johnson's acquaintance.' I, however, was so much impressed with my first notion, that I mentioned it to Johnson, repeating, at the same time, what Mrs.

Williams had said. His answer was, 'It is true, Sir, that she wrote it before she was acquainted with me; but she has not told you that I wrote it all over again, except two lines.' 'The Fountains,'† a beautiful little Fairy tale in prose, written with exquisite simplicity, is one of Johnson's productions; and I cannot with-hold from Mrs. Thrale the praise of being the authour of that admirable poem, 'The Three Warnings.'

He wrote this year a letter, not intended for publication, which has, perhaps, as strong marks of his sentiment and style, as any of his compositions. The original is in my possession. It is addressed to the late Mr. William Drummond, bookseller in Edinburgh, a gentleman of good family, but small estate, who took arms for the house of Stuart in 1745; and during his concealment in London till the act of general pardon came out obtained the acquaintance of Dr. Johnson, who justly esteemed him as a very worthy man. It seems, some of the members of the society in Scotland for propagating Christian knowledge, had opposed the scheme of translating the holy scriptures into the Erse or Gaelick language, from political considerations of the disadvantage of keeping up the distinction between the Highlanders and the other inhabitants of North-Britain. Dr. Johnson being informed of this, I suppose by Mr. Drummond, wrote with a generous indignation as follows:

'*To* MR. WILLIAM DRUMMOND

'SIR,—I did not expect to hear that it could be, in an assembly convened for the propagation of Christian knowledge, a question whether any nation uninstructed in religion should receive instruction; or whether that instruction should be imparted to them by a translation of the holy books into their own language. If obedience to the will of GOD be necessary to happiness, and knowledge of his will be necessary to obedience, I know not how he that with-holds this knowledge, or delays it, can be said to love his neighbour as himself. He that voluntarily continues ignorance, is guilty of all the crimes which ignorance produces; as to him that should extinguish the tapers of a light-house, might justly be imputed the calamities of shipwrecks. Christianity is the highest perfection of humanity; and as no man is good but as he wishes the good of others, no man can be good in the highest degree who wishes not to others the largest measures of the greatest good. To omit for a year, or for a day, the most efficacious method of advancing Christianity, in compliance with any purposes that terminate on this side of the grave, is a crime of which I know not that the world has yet had an example, except in the practice of the planters of America, a race of mortals whom, I suppose, no other man wishes to resemble.

'The Papists have, indeed, denied to the laity the use of the bible; but this prohibition, in few places now very rigorously enforced, is defended by arguments, which have for their foundation the care of souls. To obscure, upon motives merely political, the light of revelation, is a practice reserved for the reformed; and, surely, the blackest midnight of popery is meridian sunshine to such a reformation. I am not very willing that any language should be totally extinguished. The similitude and derivation of languages afford the most indubitable proof of the traduction of nations, and the genealogy of mankind. They add often physical certainty to historical evidence; and often supply the only evidence of ancient migrations, and of the revolutions of ages which left no written monuments behind them.

'Every man's opinions, at least his desires, are a little influenced by his favourite studies. My zeal for languages may seem, perhaps, rather over-heated, even to those by whom I desire to be well-esteemed. To those who have nothing in their thoughts but trade or policy, present power, or present money, I should not think it necessary to defend my opinions; but with men of letters I would not unwillingly compound, by wishing the continuance of every language, however narrow in its extent, or however incommodious for common purposes, till it is reposited in some version of a known book, that it may be always hereafter examined and compared with other languages, and then permitting its disuse. For this purpose, the translation of the bible is most to be desired. It is not certain that the same method will not preserve the Highland language, for the purposes of learning, and abolish it from daily use. When the Highlanders read the Bible, they will naturally wish to have its obscurities cleared, and to know the history, collateral or appendant. Knowledge always desires increase: it is like fire, which must first be kindled by some external agent, but which will afterwards propagate itself. When they once desire to learn, they will naturally have recourse to the nearest language by which that desire can be gratified; and one will tell another that if he would attain knowledge, he must learn English.

'This speculation may, perhaps, be thought more subtle than the grossness of real life will easily admit. Let it, however, be remembered, that the efficacy of ignorance has been long tried, and has not produced the consequence expected. Let knowledge, therefore, take its turn; and let the patrons of privation stand awhile aside, and admit the operation of positive principles.

'You will be pleased, Sir, to assure the worthy man who is employed in the new translation,[1] that he has my wishes for his success; and if here or at Oxford I can be of any use, that I shall think it more than honour to promote his undertaking.

'I am sorry that I delayed so long to write. I am, Sir, your most humble servant,

'Johnson's-court, Fleet-street,   'SAM. JOHNSON.'
     Aug. 13, 1766.'

The opponents of this pious scheme being made ashamed of their conduct, the benevolent undertaking was allowed to go on.

The following letters, though not written till the year after, being chiefly upon the same subject, are here inserted.

---

[1] The Rev. Mr. John Campbell, Minister of the Parish of Kippen, near Stirling, who has lately favoured me with a long, intelligent, and very obliging letter upon this work, makes the following remark:—'Dr. Johnson has alluded to the worthy man employed in the translation of the New Testament. Might not this have afforded you an opportunity of paying a proper tribute of respect to the memory of the Rev. Mr. James Stuart, late Minister of Killin, distinguished by his eminent Piety, Learning and Taste? The amiable simplicity of his life, his warm benevolence, his indefatigable and successful exertions for civilizing and improving the Parish of which he was Minister for upwards of fifty years, entitle him to the gratitude of his country, and the veneration of all good men. It certainly would be a pity, if such a character should be permitted to sink into oblivion.'

'*To* Mr. William Drummond

'Dear Sir,—That my letter should have had such effects as
you mention, gives me great pleasure. I hope you do not flatter
me by imputing to me more good than I have really done. Those
whom my arguments have persuaded to change their opinion,
shew such modesty and candour as deserve great praise.

'I hope the worthy translator goes diligently forward. He has
a higher reward in prospect than any honours which this world
can bestow. I wish I could be useful to him.

'The publication of my letter, if it could be of use in a cause
to which all other causes are nothing, I should not prohibit.
But first, I would have you consider whether the publication
will really do any good; next, whether by printing and distributing a very small number, you may not attain all that you
propose; and, what perhaps I should have said first, whether
the letter, which I do not now perfectly remember, be fit to be
printed.

'If you can consult Dr. Robertson, to whom I am a little
known, I shall be satisfied about the propriety of whatever he
shall direct. If he thinks that it should be printed, I entreat him
to revise it; there may, perhaps, be some negligent lines written,
and whatever is amiss, he knows very well how to rectify.[1]

'Be pleased to let me know, from time to time, how this
excellent design goes forward.

'Make my compliments to young Mr. Drummond, whom I
hope you will live to see such as you desire him.

'I have not lately seen Mr. Elphinston, but believe him to be
prosperous. I shall be glad to hear the same of you, for I am,
Sir, your affectionate humble servant,

'Johnson's-court, Fleet-street,   'Sam. Johnson.'
    April 21, 1767.'

To The Same

'Sir,—I returned this week from the country, after an absence

---

[1] This paragraph shews Johnson's real estimation of the character and
abilities of the celebrated Scottish Historian, however lightly, in a moment
of caprice, he may have spoken of his works.

of near six months, and found your letter with many others, which I should have answered sooner, if I had sooner seen them.

'Dr. Robertson's opinion was surely right. Men should not be told of the faults which they have mended. I am glad the old language is taught, and honour the translator as a man whom GOD has distinguished by the high office of propagating his word.

'I must take the liberty of engaging you in an office of charity. Mrs. Heely, the wife of Mr. Heely, who had lately some office in your theatre, is my near relation, and now in great distress. They wrote me word of their situation some time ago, to which I returned them an answer which raised hopes of more than it is proper for me to give them. Their representation of their affairs I have discovered to be such as cannot be trusted; and at this distance, though their case requires haste, I know not how to act. She, or her daughters, may be heard of at Canongate Head. I must beg, Sir, that you will enquire after them, and let me know what is to be done. I am willing to go to ten pounds, and will transmit you such a sum, if upon examination you find it likely to be of use. If they are in immediate want, advance them what you think proper. What I could do, I would do for the women, having no great reason to pay much regard to Heely himself.[1]

'I believe you may receive some intelligence from Mrs. Baker, of the theatre, whose letter I received at the same time with yours; and to whom, if you see her, you will make my excuse for the seeming neglect of answering her.

'Whatever you advance within ten pounds shall be immediately returned to you, or paid as you shall order. I trust wholly to your judgement. I am, Sir, &c.

'London, Johnson's-court, Fleet-   'SAM. JOHNSON.'
    street, Oct. 24, 1767.'

Mr. Cuthbert Shaw,[2] alike distinguished by his genius, misfortunes, and misconduct, published this year a poem, called

---

[1] This is the person concerning whom Sir John Hawkins has thrown out very unwarrantable reflections both against Dr. Johnson and Mr. Francis Barber.

[2] See an account of him in the *European Magazine*, Jan. 1786.

'*The Race*, by Mercurius Spur, Esq.,' in which he whimsically made the living poets of England contend for pre-eminence of fame by running:

> 'Prove by their heels the prowess of the head.'

In this poem there was the following portrait of Johnson:

> 'Here Johnson comes,—unblest with outward grace,
> His rigid morals stamp'd upon his face.
> While strong conceptions struggle in his brain;
> (For even wit is brought to-bed with pain:)
> To view him, porters with their loads would rest,
> And babes cling frighted to the nurse's breast.
> With looks convuls'd he roars in pompous strain,
> And, like an angry lion, shakes his mane.
> The Nine, with terrour struck, who ne'er had seen,
> Aught human with so horrible a mien,
> Debating whether they should stay or run,
> Virtue steps forth, and claims him for her son:
> With gentle speech she warns him now to yield,
> Nor stain his glories in the doubtful field;
> But wrapt in conscious worth, content sit down,
> Since Fame, resolv'd his various pleas to crown,
> Though forc'd his present claim to disavow,
> Had long reserv'd a chaplet for his brow.
> He bows, obeys; for time shall first expire,
> Ere Johnson stay, when Virtue bids retire.'

The Honourable Thomas Hervey[1] and his lady having un-happily disagreed, and being about to separate, Johnson inter-fered as their friend, and wrote him a letter of expostulation, which I have not been able to find; but the substance of it is ascertained by a letter to Johnson, in answer to it, which Mr. Hervey printed. The occasion of this correspondence between Dr. Johnson and Mr. Hervey, was thus related to me by Mr. Beauclerk. 'Tom Hervey had a great liking for Johnson, and in his will had left him a legacy of fifty pounds. One day he said to

---

[1] The Hon. Thomas Hervey, whose *Letter to Sir Thomas Hanmer* in 1742 was much read at that time. He was the second son of John, first Earl of Bristol, and one of the brothers of Johnson's early friend, Henry Hervey. He died Jan. 20, 1775. [M.]

me, "Johnson may want this money now, more than afterwards.
I have a mind to give it him directly. Will you be so good as to
carry a fifty pound note from me to him?' This I positively
refused to do, as he might, perhaps, have knocked me down for
insulting him, and have afterwards put the note in his pocket.
But I said, if Hervey would write him a letter, and enclose a
fifty pound note, I should take care to deliver it. He accordingly
did write him a letter, mentioning that he was only paying a
legacy a little sooner. To his letter he added, "*P.S. I am going
to part with my wife.*" Johnson then wrote to him, saying nothing
of the note, but remonstrating with him against parting with his
wife.'

When I mentioned to Johnson this story, in as delicate terms
as I could, he told me that the fifty pound note was given to him
by Mr. Hervey in consideration of his having written for him
a pamphlet against Sir Charles Hanbury Williams, who, Mr.
Hervey imagined, was the authour of an attack upon him; but
that it was afterwards discovered to be the work of a garreteer[1]
who wrote *The Fool*: the pamphlet therefore against Sir Charles
was not printed.

In February, 1767, there happened one of the most remarkable
incidents of Johnson's life, which gratified his monarchical enthusiasm, and which he loved to relate with all its circumstances,
when requested by his friends. This was his being honoured by
a private conversation with his Majesty, in the library at the
Queen's house. He had frequently visited those splendid rooms
and noble collection of books,[2] which he used to say was more
numerous and curious than he supposed any person could have
made in the time which the King had employed. Mr. Barnard,
the librarian, took care that he should have every accommodation that could contribute to his ease and convenience, while

---

[1] [William Horsley. *Croker.*[1]]

[2] Dr. Johnson had the honour of contributing his assistance towards the
formation of this library; for I have read a long letter from him to Mr.
Barnard, giving the most masterly instructions on the subject. I wished
much to have gratified my readers with the perusal of this letter, and have
reason to think that his Majesty would have been graciously pleased to
permit its publication; but Mr. Barnard, to whom I applied, declined it 'on
his own account.' [No. 206 in Chapman's edition.]

indulging his literary taste in that place; so that he had here a very agreeable resource at leisure hours.

His Majesty having been informed of his occasional visits, was pleased to signify a desire that he should be told when Dr. Johnson came next to the library. Accordingly, the next time that Johnson did come, as soon as he was fairly engaged with a book, on which, while he sat by the fire, he seemed quite intent, Mr. Barnard stole round to the apartment where the King was, and, in obedience to his Majesty's commands, mentioned that Dr. Johnson was then in the library. His Majesty said he was at leisure, and would go to him; upon which Mr. Barnard took one of the candles that stood on the King's table, and lighted his Majesty through a suite of rooms, till they came to a private door into the library, of which his Majesty had the key. Being entered, Mr. Barnard stepped forward hastily to Dr. Johnson, who was still in a profound study, and whispered him, 'Sir, here is the King.' Johnson started up, and stood still. His Majesty approached him, and at once was courteously easy.[1]

His Majesty began by observing, that he understood he came sometimes to the library; and then mentioning his having heard that the Doctor had been lately at Oxford, asked him if he was not fond of going thither. To which Johnson answered, that he was indeed fond of going to Oxford sometimes, but was likewise

[1] The particulars of this conversation I have been at great pains to collect with the utmost authenticity from Dr. Johnson's own detail to myself; from Mr. Langton who was present when he gave an account of it to Dr. Joseph Warton, and several other friends, at Sir Joshua Reynolds's; from Mr. Barnard; from the copy of a letter written by the late Mr. Strahan the printer, to Bishop Warburton; and from a minute, the original of which is among the papers of the late Sir James Caldwell, and a copy of which was most obligingly obtained for me from his son Sir John Caldwell, by Sir Francis Lumm. To all these gentlemen I beg leave to make my grateful acknowledgements, and particularly to Sir Francis Lumm, who was pleased to take a great deal of trouble, and even had the minute laid before the King by Lord Caermarthen, now Duke of Leeds, then one of his Majesty's Principal Secretaries of State, who announced to Sir Francis the Royal pleasure concerning it by a letter, in these words: 'I have the King's commands to assure you, Sir, how sensible his Majesty is of your attention in communicating the minute of the conversation previous to its publication. As there appears no objection to your complying with Mr. Boswell's wishes on the subject, you are at full liberty to deliver it to that gentleman, to make such use of in his *Life of Dr. Johnson*, as he may think proper.'

glad to come back again. The King then asked him what they were doing at Oxford. Johnson answered, he could not much commend their diligence, but that in some respects they were mended, for they had put their press under better regulations, and were at that time printing Polybius. He was then asked whether there were better libraries at Oxford or Cambridge. He answered, he believed the Bodleian was larger than any they had at Cambridge; at the same time adding, 'I hope, whether we have more books or not than they have at Cambridge, we shall make as good use of them as they do.' Being asked whether All-Souls or Christ-Church library was the largest, he answered, 'All-Souls library is the largest we have, except the Bodleian.' 'Aye, (said the King,) that is the publick library.'

His Majesty enquired if he was then writing any thing. He answered, he was not, for he had pretty well told the world what he knew, and must now read to acquire more knowledge. The King, as it should seem with a view to urge him to rely on his own stores as an original writer, and to continue his labours, then said, 'I do not think you borrow much from any body.' Johnson said, he thought he had already done his part as a writer. 'I should have thought so too, (said the King,) if you had not written so well.'—Johnson observed to me, upon this, that 'No man could have paid a handsomer compliment; and it was fit for a King to pay. It was decisive.' When asked by another friend, at Sir Joshua Reynolds's, whether he made any reply to this high compliment, he answered, 'No, Sir. When the King had said it, it was to be so. It was not for me to bandy civilities with my Sovereign.' Perhaps no man who had spent his whole life in courts could have shewn a more nice and dignified sense of true politeness, than Johnson did in this instance.

His Majesty having observed to him that he supposed he must have read a great deal; Johnson answered, that he thought more than he read; that he had read a great deal in the early part of his life, but having fallen into ill health, he had not been able to read much, compared with others: for instance, he said he had not read much, compared with Dr. Warburton. Upon which the King said, that he heard Dr. Warburton was a man of such general knowledge, that you could scarce talk with him on any subject on which he was not qualified to speak; and that his learning resembled Garrick's acting, in its universality.[1] His Majesty then talked of the controversy between Warburton and Lowth, which he seemed to have read, and asked Johnson what he thought of it. Johnson answered, 'Warburton has most general, most scholastick learning; Lowth is the more correct scholar. I do not know which of them calls names best.' The King was pleased to say he was of the same opinion; adding, 'You do not think, then, Dr. Johnson, that there was much argument in the case.' Johnson said, he did not think there was. 'Why truly, (said the King,) when once it comes to calling names, argument is pretty well at an end.'

His Majesty then asked him what he thought of Lord Lyttelton's *History*, which was then just published. Johnson said, he thought his style pretty good, but that he had blamed Henry the Second rather too much. 'Why, (said the King), they seldom do these things by halves.' 'No, Sir, (answered Johnson,) not to Kings.' But fearing to be misunderstood, he proceeded to explain himself; and immediately subjoined, 'That for those who spoke worse of Kings than they deserved, he could find no excuse; but that he could more easily conceive how some might speak better of them than they deserved, without any ill intention; for, as Kings had much in their power to give, those who were favoured by them would frequently, from gratitude, exaggerate their praises; and as this proceeded from a good motive, it was certainly excusable, as far as errour could be excusable.'

The King then asked him what he thought of Dr. Hill. Johnson answered, that he was an ingenious man, but had no veracity; and immediately mentioned, as an instance of it, an assertion of that writer, that he had seen objects magnified to a much greater degree by using three or four microscopes at a time, than by using one. 'Now, (added Johnson,) every one acquainted with

---

[1] The Rev. Mr. Strahan clearly recollects having been told by Johnson, that the King observed that Pope made Warburton a Bishop. 'True, Sir, (said Johnson,) but Warburton did more for Pope; he made him a Christian:' alluding, no doubt, to his ingenious Comments on the *Essay on Man*.

microscopes knows, that the more of them he looks through, the less the object will appear.' 'Why, (replied the King,) this is not only telling an untruth, but telling it clumsily; for, if that be the case, every one who can look through a microscope will be able to detect him.'

'I now, (said Johnson to his friends, when relating what had passed) began to consider that I was depreciating this man in the estimation of his Sovereign, and thought it was time for me to say something that might be more favourable.' He added, therefore, that Dr. Hill was, notwithstanding, a very curious observer; and if he would have been contented to tell the world no more than he knew, he might have been a very considerable man, and needed not to have recourse to such mean expedients to raise his reputation.

The King then talked of literary journals, mentioned particularly the *Journal des Savans*, and asked Johnson if it was well done. Johnson said, it was formerly very well done, and gave some account of the persons who began it, and carried it on for some years; enlarging, at the same time, on the nature and use of such works. The King asked him if it was well done now. Johnson answered, he had no reason to think that it was. The King then asked him if there were any other literary journals published in this kingdom, except the *Monthly* and *Critical Reviews*; and on being answered there were no other, his Majesty asked which of them was the best: Johnson answered, that the *Monthly Review* was done with most care, the *Critical* upon the best principles; adding that the authours of the *Monthly Review* were enemies to the Church. This the King said he was sorry to hear.

The conversation next turned on the Philosophical Transactions, when Johnson observed, that they had now a better method of arranging their materials than formerly. 'Aye, (said the King,) they are obliged to Dr. Johnson for that;' for his Majesty had heard and remembered the circumstance, which Johnson himself had forgot.

His Majesty expressed a desire to have the literary biography of this country ably executed, and proposed to Dr. Johnson to undertake it. Johnson signified his readiness to comply with his Majesty's wishes.

During the whole of this interview, Johnson talked to his Majesty with profound respect, but still in his firm manly manner, with a sonorous voice, and never in that subdued tone which is commonly used at the levee and in the drawing-room. After the King withdrew, Johnson shewed himself highly pleased with his Majesty's conversation and gracious behaviour. He said to Mr. Barnard, 'Sir, they may talk of the King as they will; but he is the finest gentleman I have ever seen.' And he afterwards observed to Mr. Langton, 'Sir, his manners are those of as fine a gentleman as we may suppose Lewis the Fourteenth or Charles the Second.'

At Sir Joshua Reynolds's, where a circle of Johnson's friends was collected round him to hear his account of this memorable conversation, Dr. Joseph Warton, in his frank and lively manner, was very active in pressing him to mention the particulars. 'Come now, Sir, this is an interesting matter; do favour us with it.' Johnson, with great good humour, complied.

He told them, 'I found his Majesty wished I should talk, and I made it my business to talk. I find it does a man good to be talked to by his Sovereign. In the first place, a man cannot be in a passion—.' Here some question interrupted him, which is to be regretted, as he certainly would have pointed out and illustrated many circumstances of advantage, from being in a situation, where the powers of the mind are at once excited to vigorous exertion, and tempered by reverential awe.

During all the time in which Dr. Johnson was employed in relating to the circle at Sir Joshua Reynolds's the particulars of what passed between the King and him, Dr. Goldsmith remained unmoved upon a sopha at some distance, affecting not join in the least in the eager curiosity of the company. He assigned as a reason for his gloom and seeming inattention, that he apprehended Johnson had relinquished his purpose of furnishing him with a Prologue to his play, with the hopes of which he had been flattered; but it was strongly suspected that he was fretting with chagrin and envy at the singular honour Dr. Johnson had lately enjoyed. At length, the frankness and simplicity of his natural character prevailed. He sprung from the sopha, advanced to Johnson, and in a kind of flutter, from imagining himself in the situation which he had just been hearing described, exclaimed, 'Well, you acquitted yourself in this conversation better than I should have done; for I should have bowed and stammered through the whole of it.'

I received no letter from Johnson this year; nor have I discovered any of the correspondence[1] he had, except the two letters to Mr. Drummond, which have been inserted, for the sake of connection with that to the same gentleman in 1766. His diary affords no light as to his employment at this time. He passed three months at Lichfield; and I cannot omit an affecting and solemn scene there, as related by himself:—

'Sunday, Oct. 18, 1767. Yesterday, Oct. 17, at about ten in the morning, I took my leave for ever of my dear old friend, Catharine Chambers, who came to live with my mother about 1724, and has been but little parted from us since. She buried my father, my brother, and my mother. She is now fifty-eight years old.

'I desired all to withdraw, then told her that we were to part for ever; that as Christians, we should part with prayer; and that I would, if she was willing, say a short prayer beside her. She expressed great desire to hear me; and held up her poor hands, as she lay in bed, with great fervour, while I prayed, kneeling by her, nearly in the following words:

'Almighty and most merciful Father, whose loving kindness is over all thy works, behold, visit, and relieve this thy servant, who is grieved with sickness. Grant that the sense of her weakness may add strength to her faith, and seriousness to her repentance. And grant that by the help of thy Holy Spirit, after the pains and labours of this short life, we may all obtain everlasting happiness, through JESUS CHRIST our Lord; for whose sake hear our prayers. Amen. Our Father, &c.

---

[1] It is proper here to mention, that when I speak of his correspondence, I consider it independent of the voluminous collection of letters which, in the course of many years, he wrote to Mrs. Thrale, which forms a separate part of his works; and as a proof of the high estimation set on any thing which came from his pen, was sold by that lady for the sum of five hundred pounds.

'I then kissed her. She told me, that to part was the greatest pain that she had ever felt, and that she hoped we should meet again in a better place. I expressed, with swelled eyes, and great emotion of tenderness, the same hopes. We kissed, and parted. I humbly hope to meet again, and to part no more.'[1]

By those who have been taught to look upon Johnson as a man of a harsh and stern character, let this tender and affectionate scene be candidly read; and let them then judge whether more warmth of heart, and grateful kindness, is often found in human nature.

We have the following notice in his devotional record:— 'August 2, 1767. I have been disturbed and unsettled for a long time, and have been without resolution to apply to study or to business, being hindered by sudden snatches.'[2]

He, however, furnished Mr. Adams with a Dedication* to the King of that ingenious gentleman's *Treatise on the Globes*, conceived and expressed in such a manner as could not fail to be very grateful to a Monarch, distinguished for his love of the sciences.

This year was published a ridicule of his style, under the title of *Lexiphanes*. Sir John Hawkins ascribes it to Dr. Kenrick; but its authour was one Campbell, a Scotch purser in the navy. The ridicule consisted in applying Johnson's 'words of large meaning' to insignificant matters, as if one should put the armour of Goliath upon a dwarf. The contrast might be laughable; but the dignity of the armour must remain the same in all considerate minds. This malicious drollery, therefore, it may easily be supposed, could do no harm to its illustrious object.

'To BENNET LANGTON, ESQ., *at Mr. Rothwell's, perfumer, in New Bond-street, London*

'DEAR SIR,—That you have been all summer in London, is one more reason for which I regret my long stay in the country. I hope that you will not leave the town before my return.

---

[1] *Pr. and Med.*, pp. 77 and 78.
[2] *Ib.*, p. 73. On Aug. 17, he recorded:—'By abstinence from wine and suppers I obtained sudden and great relief, and had freedom of mind restored to me, which I have wanted for all this year, without being able to find any means of obtaining it.' *Ib.* p. 74.

We have here only the chance of vacancies in the passing carriages, and I have bespoken one that may, if it happens, bring
me to town on the fourteenth of this month; but this is not
certain.

'It will be a favour if you communicate this to Mrs. Williams:
I long to see all my friends. I am, dear Sir, your most humble
servant,

'Lichfield, Oct. 10, 1767.'   'SAM. JOHNSON.'

1768: ÆTAT. 59.]—IT appears from his notes of the state of
his mind,[1] that he suffered great perturbation and distraction in
1768. Nothing of his writing was given to the publick this year,
except the Prologue* to his friend Goldsmith's comedy of *The
Good-natured Man*. The first lines of this Prologue are strongly
characteristical of the dismal gloom of his mind; which in his
case, as in the case of all who are distressed with the same
malady of imagination, transfers to others its own feelings. Who
could suppose it was to introduce a comedy, when Mr. Bensley
solemnly began,

> 'Press'd with the load of life, the weary mind
> Surveys the general toil of human kind.'

But this dark ground might make Goldsmith's humour shine
the more.

In the spring of this year, having published my *Account of
Corsica*, with the *Journal of a Tour to that Island*, I returned to
London, very desirous to see Dr. Johnson, and hear him upon
the subject. I found he was at Oxford, with his friend Mr. Chambers, who was now Vinerian Professor, and lived in New Inn
Hall. Having had no letter from him since that in which he
criticised the Latinity of my Thesis, and having been told by
somebody that he was offended at my having put into my Book
an extract of his letter to me at Paris, I was impatient to be with
him, and therefore followed him to Oxford, where I was entertained by Mr. Chambers, with a civility which I shall ever gratefully remember. I found that Dr. Johnson had sent a letter to me

[1] *Ib.*, p. 81.

to Scotland, and that I had nothing to complain of but his being more indifferent to my anxiety than I wished him to be. Instead of giving, with the circumstances of time and place, such fragments of his conversation as I preserved during this visit to Oxford, I shall throw them together in continuation.

I asked him whether, as a moralist, he did not think that the practice of the law, in some degree, hurt the nice feeling of honesty. Johnson. 'Why no, Sir, if you act properly. You are not to deceive your clients with false representations of your opinion: you are not to tell lies to a judge.' Boswell. 'But what do you think of supporting a cause which you know to be bad?' Johnson. 'Sir, you do not know it to be good or bad till the Judge determines it. I have said that you are to state facts fairly; so that your thinking, or what you call knowing, a cause to be bad, must be from reasoning, must be from your supposing your arguments to be weak and inconclusive. But, Sir, that is not enough. An argument which does not convince yourself, may convince the Judge to whom you urge it; and if it does convince him, why, then, Sir, you are wrong, and he is right. It is his business to judge; and you are not to be confident in your own opinion that a cause is bad, but to say all you can for your client, and then hear the Judge's opinion.' Boswell. 'But, Sir, does not affecting a warmth when you have no warmth, and appearing to be clearly of one opinion when you are in reality of another opinion, does not such dissimulation impair one's honesty? Is there not some danger that a lawyer may put on the same mask in common life, in the intercourse with his friends?' Johnson. 'Why no, Sir. Everybody knows you are paid for affecting warmth for your client; and it is, therefore, properly no dissimulation: the moment you come from the bar you resume your usual behaviour. Sir, a man will no more carry the artifice of the bar into the common intercourse of society, than a man who is paid for tumbling upon his hands will continue to tumble upon his hands when he should walk on his feet.'

Talking of some of the modern plays, he said *False Delicacy* was totally void of character. He praised Goldsmith's *Good-natured Man*; said, it was the best comedy that has appeared

since *The Provoked Husband,* and that there had not been of late
any such character exhibited on the stage as that of Croaker.
I observed it was the Suspirius of his Rambler. He said, Goldsmith had owned he had borrowed it from thence. 'Sir, (continued he,) there is all the difference in the world between
characters of nature and characters of manners; and *there* is the
difference between the characters of Fielding and those of
Richardson. Characters of manners are very entertaining; but
they are to be understood by a more superficial observer than
characters of nature, where a man must dive into the recesses of
the human heart.'

It always appeared to me that he estimated the compositions
of Richardson too highly, and that he had an unreasonable prejudice against Fielding. In comparing those two writers, he used
this expression: 'that there was as great a difference between
them as between a man who knew how a watch was made, and
a man who could tell the hour by looking on the dial-plate.'
This was a short and figurative state of his distinction between
drawing characters of nature and characters only of manners.
But I cannot help being of opinion, that the neat watches of
Fielding are as well constructed as the large clocks of Richardson, and that his dial-plates are brighter. Fielding's characters,
though they do not expand themselves so widely in dissertation,
are as just pictures of human nature, and I will venture to say,
have more striking features, and nicer touches of the pencil; and
though Johnson used to quote with approbation a saying of
Richardson's, 'that the virtues of Fielding's heroes were the vices
of a truly good man,' I will venture to add, that the moral tendency of Fielding's writings, though it does not encourage a
strained and rarely possible virtue, is ever favourable to honour
and honesty, and cherishes the benevolent and generous affections.
He who is as good as Fielding would make him, is an amiable
member of society, and may be led on by more regulated instructors, to a higher state of ethical perfection.

Johnson proceeded: 'Even Sir Francis Wronghead is a character of manners, though drawn with great humour.' He then
repeated, very happily, all Sir Francis's credulous account to

Manly of his being with 'the great man,' and securing a place. I asked him, if *The Suspicious Husband* did not furnish a well-drawn character, that of Ranger. JOHNSON. 'No, Sir; Ranger is just a rake, a mere rake, and a lively young fellow, but no *character*.'

The great Douglas Cause was at this time a very general subject of discussion. I found he had not studied it with much attention, but had only heard parts of it occasionally. He, however, talked of it, and said, 'I am of opinion that positive proof of fraud should not be required of the plaintiff, but that the Judges should decide according as probability shall appear to preponderate, granting to the defendant the presumption of filiation to be strong in his favour. And I think too, that a good deal of weight should be allowed to the dying declarations, because they were spontaneous. There is a great difference between what is said without our being urged to it, and what is said from a kind of compulsion. If I praise a man's book without being asked my opinion of it, that is honest praise, to which one may trust. But if an authour asks me if I like his book, and I give him something like praise, it must not be taken as my real opinion.'

'I have not been troubled for a long time with authours desiring my opinion of their works. I used once to be sadly plagued with a man who wrote verses, but who literally had no other notion of a verse, but that it consisted of ten syllables. *Lay your knife and your fork, across your plate*, was to him a verse:

Lay yŏur knife ānd your fŏrk, acrŏss your plāte.

As he wrote a great number of verses, he sometimes by chance made good ones, though he did not know it.'

He renewed his promise of coming to Scotland, and going with me to the Hebrides, but said he would now content himself with seeing one or two of the most curious of them. He said, 'Macaulay, who writes the account of St. Kilda, set out with a prejudice against prejudices, and wanted to be a smart modern thinker; and yet he affirms for a truth, that when a ship arrives there, all the inhabitants are seized with a cold.'

Dr. John Campbell, the celebrated writer, took a great deal of pains to ascertain this fact, and attempted to account for it on physical principles, from the effect of effluvia from human bodies. Johnson, at another time, praised Macaulay for his '*magnanimity*,' in asserting this wonderful story, because it was well attested. A Lady of Norfolk, by a letter[1] to my friend Dr. Burney, has favoured me with the following solution: 'Now for the explica- tion of this seeming mystery, which is so very obvious as, for that reason, to have escaped the penetration of Dr. Johnson and his friend, as well as that of the authour. Reading the book with my ingenious friend, the late Reverend Mr. Christian, of Dock- ing—after ruminating a little, "The cause, (says he,) is a natural one. The situation of St. Kilda renders a North-East Wind in- dispensably necessary before a stranger can land. The wind, not the stranger, causes an epidemic cold." If I am not mistaken, Mr. Macaulay is dead; if living, this solution might please him, as I hope it will Mr. Boswell, in return for the many agreeable hours his works have afforded us.'

Johnson expatiated on the advantages of Oxford for learning. 'There is here, Sir, (said he,) such a progressive emulation. The students are anxious to appear well to their tutors; the tutors are anxious to have their pupils appear well in the college; the colleges are anxious to have their students appear well in the University; and there are excellent rules of discipline in every college. That the rules are sometimes ill observed, may be true; but is nothing against the system. The members of an Univer- sity may, for a season, be unmindful of their duty. I am arguing for the excellency of the institution.'

Of Guthrie, he said, 'Sir, he is a man of parts. He has no great regular fund of knowledge; but by reading so long, and writing so long, he no doubt has picked up a good deal.'

He said he had lately been a long while at Lichfield, but had grown very weary before he left it. BOSWELL. 'I wonder at that, Sir; it is your native place.' JOHNSON. 'Why, so is Scot- land *your* native place.'

His prejudice against Scotland appeared remarkably strong at

---

[1] [*Croker*[1] gives the date of the lady's letter as 2 Oct. 1773.]

this time. When I talked of our advancement in literature, 'Sir, (said he,) you have learnt a little from us, and you think yourselves very great men. Hume would never have written History, had not Voltaire written it before him. He is an echo of Voltaire.' BOSWELL. 'But, Sir, we have Lord Kames.' JOHNSON. 'You *have* Lord Kames. Keep him; ha, ha, ha! We don't envy you him. Do you ever see Dr. Robertson?' BOSWELL. 'Yes, Sir.' JOHNSON. 'Does the dog talk of me?' BOSWELL. 'Indeed, Sir, he does, and loves you.' Thinking that I now had him in a corner, and being solicitous for the literary fame of my country, I pressed him for his opinion on the merit of Dr. Robertson's *History of Scotland*. But, to my surprize, he escaped.—'Sir, I love Robertson, and I won't talk of his book.'

It is but justice both to him and Dr. Robertson to add, that though he indulged himself in this sally of wit, he had too good taste not to be fully sensible of the merits of that admirable work.

An essay, written by Mr. Deane, a divine of the Church of England, maintaining the future life of brutes, by an explication of certain parts of the scriptures, was mentioned, and the doctrine insisted on by a gentleman[1] who seemed fond of curious speculation. Johnson, who did not like to hear of any thing concerning a future state which was not authorised by the regular canons of orthodoxy, discouraged this talk; and being offended at its continuation, he watched an opportunity to give the gentleman a blow of reprehension. So, when the poor speculatist, with a serious metaphysical pensive face, addressed him, 'But really, Sir, when we see a very sensible dog, we don't know what to think of him;' Johnson, rolling with joy at the thought which beamed in his eye, turned quickly round, and replied, 'True, Sir: and when we see a very foolish *fellow*, we don't know what to think of *him*.' He then rose up, strided to the fire, and stood for some time laughing and exulting.

I told him that I had several times, when in Italy, seen the experiment of placing a scorpion within a circle of burning coals; that it ran round and round in extreme pain; and finding no way to escape, retired to the centre, and like a true Stoick philosopher,

---

[1] [Boswell, *Boswell Papers*, vii. 176.]

darted its sting into its head, and thus at once freed itself from its woes. '*This must end 'em.*' I said, this was a curious fact, as it shewed deliberate suicide in a reptile. Johnson would not admit the fact. He said, Maupertuis[1] was of opinion that it does not kill itself, but dies of the heat; that it gets to the centre of the circle, as the coolest place; that its turning its tail in upon its head is merely a convulsion, and that it does not sting itself. He said he would be satisfied if the great anatomist Morgagni, after dissecting a scorpion on which the experiment had been tried, should certify that its sting had penetrated into its head.

He seemed pleased to talk of natural philosophy. 'That wood-cocks, (said he,) fly over to the northern countries is proved, because they have been observed at sea. Swallows certainly sleep all the winter. A number of them conglobulate together, by flying round and round, and then all in a heap throw themselves under water, and lye in the bed of a river.' He told us, one of his first essays was a Latin poem upon the glow-worm. I am sorry I did not ask where it was to be found.

Talking of the Russians and the Chinese, he advised me to read Bell's travels. I asked him whether I should read Du Halde's account of China. 'Why yes, (said he,) as one reads such a book; that is to say, consult it.'

He talked of the heinousness of the crime of adultery, by which the peace of families was destroyed. He said, 'Confusion of progeny constitutes the essence of the crime; and therefore a woman who breaks her marriage vows is much more criminal than a man who does it. A man, to be sure, is criminal in the

---

[1] I should think it impossible not to wonder at the variety of Johnson's reading, however desultory it may have been. Who could have imagined that the High Church of England-man would be so prompt in quoting *Maupertuis*, who, I am sorry to think, stands in the list of those unfortunate mistaken men, who call themselves *esprits forts*. I have, however, a high respect for that Philosopher whom the Great Frederick of Prussia loved and honoured, and addressed pathetically in one of his Poems,—

> '*Maupertuis, cher Maupertuis,*
> *Que notre vie est peu de chose!*'

There was in Maupertuis a vigour and yet a tenderness of sentiment, united with strong intellectual powers, and uncommon ardour of soul. Would he had been a Christian! I cannot help earnestly venturing to hope that he is one now.

sight of GOD: but he does not do his wife a very material injury, if he does not insult her; if, for instance, from mere wantonness of appetite, he steals privately to her chambermaid. Sir, a wife ought not greatly to resent this. I would not receive home a daughter who had run away from her husband on that account. A wife should study to reclaim her husband by more attention to please him. Sir, a man will not, once in a hundred instances, leave his wife and go to a harlot, if his wife has not been negligent of pleasing.'

Here he discovered that acute discrimination, that solid judgement, and that knowledge of human nature, for which he was upon all occasions remarkable. Taking care to keep in view the moral and religious duty, as understood in our nation, he shewed clearly from reason and good sense, the greater degree of culpability in the one sex deviating from it than the other; and, at the same time, inculcated a very useful lesson as to *the way to keep him.*

I asked him if it was not hard that one deviation from chastity should so absolutely ruin a young woman. JOHNSON. 'Why, no, Sir; it is the great principle which she is taught. When she has given up that principle, she has given up every notion of female honour and virtue, which are all included in chastity.'

A gentleman[1] talked to him of a lady whom he greatly admired and wished to marry, but was afraid of her superiority of talents. 'Sir, (said he,) you need not be afraid; marry her. Before a year goes about, you'll find that reason much weaker, and that wit not so bright.' Yet the gentleman may be justified in his apprehension by one of Dr. Johnson's admirable sentences in his life of Waller: 'He doubtless praised many whom he would have been afraid to marry; and, perhaps, married one whom he would have been ashamed to praise. Many qualities contribute to domestic happiness, upon which poetry has no colours to bestow; and many airs and sallies may delight imagination, which he who flatters them never can approve.'

He praised Signor Baretti. 'His account of Italy is a very entertaining book; and, Sir, I know no man who carried his head

[1] [Boswell and Isabelle de Zuylen (Zélide). *Boswell Papers*, vii. 179.]

higher in conversation than Baretti. There are strong powers in his mind. He has not, indeed, many hooks; but with what hooks he has, he grapples very forcibly.'

At this time I observed upon the dial-plate of his watch a short Greek inscription, taken from the New Testament, Νυξ γαρ ερχεται, being the first words of our SAVIOUR'S solemn admonition to the improvement of that time which is allowed us to prepare for eternity: 'the night cometh, when no man can work.' He sometime afterwards laid aside this dial-plate; and when I asked him the reason, he said, 'It might do very well upon a clock which a man keeps in his closet; but to have it upon his watch which he carries about with him, and which is often looked at by others, might be censured as ostentatious.' Mr. Steevens is now possessed of the dial-plate inscribed as above.

He remained at Oxford a considerable time; I was obliged to go to London, where I received his letter, which had been returned from Scotland.

'To JAMES BOSWELL, ESQ.

'MY DEAR BOSWELL,—I have omitted a long time to write to you, without knowing very well why. I could now tell why I should not write; for who would write to men who publish the letters of their friends, without their leave? Yet I write to you in spite of my caution, to tell you that I shall be glad to see you, and that I wish you would empty your head of Corsica, which I think has filled it rather too long. But, at all events, I shall be glad, very glad to see you. I am, Sir, yours affectionately,

'Oxford, March 23, 1768.'   'SAM. JOHNSON.'

I answered thus:—

'To MR. SAMUEL JOHNSON

'MY DEAR SIR,   'London, 26th April, 1768.

'I have received your last letter, which, though very short, and by no means complimentary, yet gave me real pleasure, because it contains these words, "I shall be glad, very glad to see you." Surely you have no reason to complain of my publishing a single paragraph of one of your letters; the temptation to it was so strong. An irrevocable grant of your friendship, and your dignifying my desire of visiting Corsica with the epithet of "a wise and noble curiosity," are to me more valuable than many of the grants of kings.

'But how can you bid me "empty my head of Corsica?" My noble-minded friend, do you not feel for an oppressed nation bravely struggling to be free? Consider fairly what is the case. The Corsicans never received any kindness from the Genoese. They never agreed to be subject to them. They owe them nothing; and when reduced to an abject state of slavery, by force, shall they not rise in the great cause of liberty, and break the galling yoke? And shall not every liberal soul be warm for them? Empty my head of Corsica! Empty it of honour, empty it of humanity, empty it of friendship, empty it of piety. No! while I live, Corsica and the cause of the brave islanders shall ever employ much of my attention, shall ever interest me in the sincerest manner. . . . I am, &c.   'JAMES BOSWELL.'

Upon his arrival in London in May, he surprized me one morning with a visit at my lodgings in Half-Moon-street, was quite satisfied with my explanation, and was in the kindest and most agreeable frame of mind. As he had objected to a part of one of his letters being published, I thought it right to take this opportunity of asking him explicitly whether it would be improper to publish his letters after his death. His answer was, 'Nay, Sir, when I am dead, you may do as you will.'

He talked in his usual style with a rough contempt of popular liberty. 'They make a rout about *universal* liberty, without considering that all that is to be valued, or indeed can be enjoyed by individuals, is *private* liberty. Political liberty is good only so far as it produces private liberty. Now, Sir, there is the liberty of the press, which you know is a constant topick. Suppose you and I and two hundred more were restrained from printing our thoughts: what then? What proportion would that restraint upon us bear to the private happiness of the nation?'

This mode of representing the inconveniences of restraint as light and insignificant, was a kind of sophistry in which he

delighted to indulge himself, in opposition to the extreme laxity
for which it has been fashionable for too many to argue, when it
is evident, upon reflection, that the very essence of government
is restraint; and certain it is, that as government produces
rational happiness, too much restraint is better than too little.
But when restraint is unnecessary, and so close as to gall those
who are subject to it, the people may and ought to remonstrate;
and, if relief is not granted, to resist. Of this manly and spirited
principle, no man was more convinced than Johnson himself.

About this time Dr. Kenrick attacked him, through my sides,
in a pamphlet, entitled *An Epistle to James Boswell, Esq., occasioned by his having transmitted the moral Writings of Dr. Samuel
Johnson to Pascal Paoli, General of the Corsicans.* I was at first
inclined to answer this pamphlet; but Johnson, who knew that
my doing so would only gratify Kenrick, by keeping alive what
would soon die away of itself, would not suffer me to take any
notice of it.

His sincere regard for Francis Barber, his faithful negro servant, made him so desirous of his further improvement, that he
now placed him at a school at Bishop Stortford, in Hertfordshire.
This humane attention does Johnson's heart much honour. Out
of many letters which Mr. Barber received from his master, he
has preserved three, which he kindly gave me, and which I shall
insert according to their dates.

'*To* Mr. Francis Barber

'Dear Francis,—I have been very much out of order. I am
glad to hear that you are well, and design to come soon to see
you. I would have you stay at Mrs. Clapp's for the present, till
I can determine what we shall do. Be a good boy.

'My compliments to Mrs. Clapp and to Mr. Fowler. I am,
your's affectionately,

'May 28, 1768.'　　　　　　　　　　'Sam. Johnson.'

Soon afterwards, he supped at the Crown and Anchor tavern,
in the Strand, with a company whom I collected to meet him.
They were Dr. Percy, now Bishop of Dromore, Dr. Douglas,

now Bishop of Salisbury, Mr. Langton, Dr. Robertson the Historian, Dr. Hugh Blair, and Mr. Thomas Davies, who wished
much to be introduced to these eminent Scotch *literati*; but on
the present occasion he had very little opportunity of hearing
them talk, for with an excess of prudence, for which Johnson
afterwards found fault with them, they hardly opened their lips,
and that only to say something which they were certain would
not expose them to the sword of Goliath; such was their anxiety
for their fame when in the presence of Johnson. He was this
evening in remarkable vigour of mind, and eager to exert himself in conversation, which he did with great readiness and
fluency; but I am sorry to find that I have preserved but a small
part of what passed.

He allowed high praise to Thomson as a poet; but when one
of the company said he was also a very good man, our moralist
contested this with great warmth, accusing him of gross sensuality and licentiousness of manners. I was very much afraid
that in writing Thomson's *Life*, Dr. Johnson would have treated
his private character with a stern severity, but I was agreeably
disappointed; and I may claim a little merit in it, from my having
been at pains to send him authentick accounts of the affectionate
and generous conduct of that poet to his sisters, one of whom,
the wife of Mr. Thomson, schoolmaster at Lanark, I knew, and
was presented by her with three of his letters, one of which
Dr. Johnson has inserted in his *Life*.

He was vehement against old Dr. Mounsey, of Chelsea College, as 'a fellow who swore and talked bawdy.' 'I have been
often in his company, (said Dr. Percy,) and never heard him
swear or talk bawdy.' Mr. Davies, who sat next to Dr. Percy,
having after this had some conversation aside with him, made
a discovery which, in his zeal to pay court to Dr. Johnson, he
eagerly proclaimed aloud from the foot of the table: 'O, Sir, I
have found out a very good reason why Dr. Percy never heard
Mounsey swear or talk bawdy; for he tells me, he never saw
him but at the Duke of Northumberland's table.' 'And so, Sir,
(said Johnson loudly, to Dr. Percy,) you would shield this man
from the charge of swearing and talking bawdy, because he did

not do so at the Duke of Northumberland's table. Sir, you might as well tell us that you had seen him hold up his hand at the Old Bailey, and he neither swore nor talked bawdy; or that you had seen him in the cart at Tyburn, and he neither swore nor talked bawdy. And is it thus, Sir, that you presume to controvert what I have related?' Dr. Johnson's animadversion was uttered in such a manner, that Dr. Percy seemed to be displeased, and soon afterwards left the company, of which Johnson did not at that time take any notice.

Swift having been mentioned, Johnson, as usual, treated him with little respect as an authour. Some of us endeavoured to support the Dean of St. Patrick's by various arguments. One in particular praised his *Conduct of the Allies*. JOHNSON. 'Sir, his *Conduct of the Allies* is a performance of very little ability.' 'Surely, Sir, (said Dr. Douglas,) you must allow it has strong facts.'[1] JOHNSON. 'Why yes, Sir; but what is that to the merit of the composition? In the Sessions-paper of the Old Bailey there are strong facts. Housebreaking is a strong fact; robbery is a strong fact; and murder is a *mighty* strong fact; but is great praise due to the historian of those strong facts? No, Sir. Swift has told what he had to tell distinctly enough, but that is all. He had to count ten, and he has counted it right.' Then recollecting that Mr. Davies, by acting as an *informer*, had been the occasion of his talking somewhat too harshly to his friend Dr. Percy, for which, probably, when the first ebullition was over, he felt some compunction, he took an opportunity to give him a hit; so added, with a preparatory laugh, 'Why, Sir, Tom Davies might have written *The Conduct of the Allies*.' Poor Tom being thus suddenly dragged into ludicrous notice in presence of the Scottish Doctors, to whom he was ambitious of appearing to advantage, was

---

[1] My respectable friend, upon reading this passage, observed, that he probably must have said not simply, 'strong facts,' but 'strong facts well arranged.' His lordship, however, knows too well the value of written documents to insist on setting his recollection against my notes taken at the time. He does not attempt to *traverse the record*. The fact, perhaps, may have been, either that the additional words escaped me in the noise of a numerous company, or that Dr. Johnson, from his impetuosity, and eagerness to seize an opportunity to make a lively retort, did not allow Dr. Douglas to finish his sentence.

grievously mortified. Nor did his punishment rest here; for upon subsequent occasions, whenever he, 'statesman all over,'[1] assumed a strutting importance, I used to hail him—'the Authour of *The Conduct of the Allies.*'

When I called upon Dr. Johnson next morning, I found him highly satisfied with his colloquial prowess the preceding evening. 'Well, (said he,) we had good talk.' BOSWELL. 'Yes, Sir; you tossed and gored several persons.'

The late Alexander, Earl of Eglintoune, who loved wit more than wine, and men of genius more than sycophants, had a great admiration of Johnson; but from the remarkable elegance of his own manners, was, perhaps, too delicately sensible of the roughness which sometimes appeared in Johnson's behaviour. One evening about this time, when his Lordship did me the honour to sup at my lodgings with Dr. Robertson and several other men of literary distinction, he regretted that Johnson had not been educated with more refinement, and lived more in polished society. 'No, no, my Lord, (said Signor Baretti,) do with him what you would, he would always have been a bear.' 'True, (answered the Earl, with a smile,) but he would have been a *dancing* bear.'

To obviate all the reflections which have gone round the world to Johnson's prejudice, by applying to him the epithet of a *bear*, let me impress upon my readers a just and happy saying of my friend Goldsmith, who knew him well: 'Johnson, to be sure, has a roughness in his manner; but no man alive has a more tender heart. *He has nothing of the bear but his skin.*'

1769: ÆTAT. 60.]—IN 1769, so far as I can discover, the publick was favoured with nothing of Johnson's composition, either for himself or any of his friends. His *Meditations* too strongly prove that he suffered much both in body and mind; yet was he perpetually striving against *evil*, and nobly endeavouring to advance his intellectual and devotional improvement. Every generous and grateful heart must feel for the distresses of so eminent a benefactor to mankind; and now that his unhappiness is certainly known, must respect that dignity of character which prevented him from complaining.

---

[1] See the hard drawing of him in Churchill's *Rosciad*.

His Majesty having the preceding year instituted the Royal Academy of Arts in London, Johnson had now the honour of being appointed Professor in Ancient Literature.[1] In the course of the year he wrote some letters to Mrs. Thrale, passed some part of the summer at Oxford and at Lichfield, and when at Oxford wrote the following letter:—

'*To* The Reverend Mr. Thomas Warton

'Dear Sir,—Many years ago, when I used to read in the library of your College, I promised to recompence the College for that permission, by adding to their books a Baskerville's *Virgil*. I have now sent it, and desire you to reposit it on the shelves in my name.[2]

'If you will be pleased to let me know when you have an hour of leisure, I will drink tea with you. I am engaged for the afternoon, to-morrow and on Friday: all my mornings are my own.[3] I am, &c.,

'May 31, 1769.'   'Sam. Johnson.'

I came to London in the autumn, and having informed him that I was going to be married in a few months, I wished to have as much of his conversation as I could before engaging in a state of life which would probably keep me more in Scotland, and

[1] In which place he has been succeeded by Bennet Langton, Esq. When that truly religious gentleman was elected to this honorary Professorship, at the same time that Edward Gibbon, Esq., noted for introducing a kind of sneering infidelity into his Historical Writings, was elected Professor in Ancient History, in the room of Dr. Goldsmith, I observed that it brought to my mind, 'Wicked Will Whiston and good Mr. Ditton.' I am now also of that admirable institution as Secretary for Foreign Correspondence, by the favour of the Academicians, and the approbation of the Sovereign.

[2] It has this inscription in a blank leaf:—'*Hunc librum D. D. Samuel Johnson, eo quod hic loci studiis interdum vacaret.*' ["The gift of Samuel Johnson, who was occasionally at leisure to study here."] Of this library, which is an old Gothick room, he was very fond. On my observing to him that some of the *modern* libraries of the University were more commodious and pleasant for study, as being more spacious and airy, he replied, 'Sir, if a man has a mind to *prance*, he must study at Christ-Church and All-Souls.'

[3] During this visit he seldom or never dined out. He appeared to be deeply engaged in some literary work. Miss Williams was now with him at Oxford.

prevent my seeing him so often as when I was a single man; but I found he was at Brighthelmstone with Mr. and Mrs. Thrale. I was very sorry that I had not his company with me at the Jubilee, in honour of Shakspeare, at Stratford-upon-Avon, the great poet's native town. Johnson's connection both with Shakspeare and Garrick founded a double claim to his presence; and it would have been highly gratifying to Mr. Garrick. Upon this occasion I particularly lamented that he had not that warmth of friendship for his brilliant pupil, which we may suppose would have had a benignant effect on both. When almost every man of eminence in the literary world was happy to partake in this festival of genius, the absence of Johnson could not but be wondered at and regretted. The only trace of him there, was in the whimsical advertisement of a haberdasher, who sold *Shakspearian ribbands* of various dyes; and, by way of illustrating their appropriation to the bard, introduced a line from the celebrated Prologue at the opening of Drury-lane theatre:

'Each change of *many-colour'd* life he drew.'

From Brighthelmstone Dr. Johnson wrote me the following letter, which they who may think that I ought to have suppressed, must have less ardent feelings than I have always avowed.[1]

---

[1] In the Preface to my *Account of Corsica*, published in 1768, I thus express myself:

'He who publishes a book affecting not to be an authour, and professing an indifference for literary fame, may possibly impose upon many people such an idea of his consequence as he wishes may be received. For my part, I should be proud to be known as an authour, and I have an ardent ambition for literary fame; for, of all possessions, I should imagine literary fame to be the most valuable. A man who has been able to furnish a book, which has been approved by the world, has established himself as a respectable character in distant society, without any danger of having that character lessened by the observation of his weaknesses. To preserve an uniform dignity among those who see us every day, is hardly possible; and to aim at it, must put us under the fetters of perpetual restraint. The authour of an approved book may allow his natural disposition an easy play, and yet indulge the pride of superior genius, when he considers that by those who know him only as an authour, he never ceases to be respected. Such an authour, when in his hours of gloom and discontent, may have the consolation to think, that his writings are, at that very time, giving pleasure to numbers; and such an authour may cherish the hope of being remembered after death, which has been a great object to the noblest minds in all ages.'

'*To* James Boswell, Esq.

'Dear Sir,—Why do you charge me with unkindness? I have omitted nothing that could do you good, or give you pleasure, unless it be that I have forborne to tell you my opinion of your *Account of Corsica.* I believe my opinion, if you think well of my judgement, might have given you pleasure; but when it is considered how much vanity is excited by praise, I am not sure that it would have done you good. Your History is like other histories, but your Journal is in a very high degree curious and delightful. There is between the History and the Journal that difference which there will always be found between notions borrowed from without, and notions generated within. Your History was copied from books; your Journal rose out of your own experience and observation. You express images which operated strongly upon yourself, and you have impressed them with great force upon your readers. I know not whether I could name any narrative by which curiosity is better excited, or better gratified.

'I am glad that you are going to be married; and as I wish you well in things of less importance, wish you well with proportionate ardour in this crisis of your life. What I can contribute to your happiness, I should be very unwilling to with-hold; for I have always loved and valued you, and shall love you and value you still more, as you become more regular and useful: effects which a happy marriage will hardly fail to produce.

'I did not find that I am likely to come back very soon from this place. I shall, perhaps, stay a fortnight longer; and a fortnight is a long time to a lover absent from his mistress. Would a fortnight ever have an end? I am, dear Sir, your most affectionate humble servant.

'Brighthelmstone, Sept. 9, 1769.'   'Sam. Johnson.'

After his return to town, we met frequently, and I continued the practice of making notes of his conversation, though not with so much assiduity as I wish I had done. At this time, indeed, I had a sufficient excuse for not being able to appropriate so much time to my Journal; for General Paoli, after Corsica had been overpowered by the monarchy of France, was now no longer at the head of his brave countrymen, but having with difficulty escaped from his native island, had sought an asylum in Great-Britain; and it was my duty, as well as my pleasure, to attend much upon him. Such particulars of Johnson's conversation at this period as I have committed to writing, I shall here introduce, without any strict attention to methodical arrangement. Sometimes short notes of different days shall be blended together, and sometimes a day may seem important enough to be separately distinguished.

He said, he would not have Sunday kept with rigid severity and gloom, but with a gravity and simplicity of behaviour.

I told him that David Hume had made a short collection of Scotticisms.[1] 'I wonder, (said Johnson,) that *he* should find them.'

He would not admit the importance of the question concerning the legality of general warrants. 'Such a power' (he observed,) 'must be vested in every government, to answer particular cases of necessity; and there can be no just complaint but when it is abused, for which those who administer government must be answerable. It is a matter of such indifference, a matter about which the people care so very little, that were a man to be sent over Britain to offer them an exemption from it at a halfpenny a piece, very few would purchase it.' This was a specimen of that laxity of talking, which I have heard him fairly acknowledge; for, surely, while the power of granting general warrants was supposed to be legal, and the apprehension of them hung over our heads, we did not possess that security of freedom, congenial to our happy constitution, and which, by the intrepid exertions of Mr. Wilkes, has been happily established.

He said, 'The duration of Parliament, whether for seven years or for the life of the King, appears to me so immaterial, that I would not give half a crown to turn the scale one way or the other. The *habeas corpus* is the single advantage which our government has over that of other countries.'

---

[1] The first edition of Hume's *History of England* was full of Scotticisms, many of which he corrected in subsequent editions. [M.]

On the 30th of September we dined together at the Mitre. I attempted to argue for the superior happiness of the savage life, upon the usual fanciful topicks. JOHNSON. 'Sir, there can be nothing more false. The savages have no bodily advantages beyond those of civilised men. They have not better health; and as to care or mental uneasiness, they are not above it, but below it, like bears. No, Sir; you are not to talk such paradox: let me have no more on't. It cannot entertain, far less can it instruct. Lord Monboddo, one of your Scotch Judges, talked a great deal of such nonsense. I suffered *him*; but I will not suffer *you.*'— BOSWELL. 'But, Sir, does not Rousseau talk such nonsense?' JOHNSON. 'True, Sir; but Rousseau *knows* he is talking nonsense, and laughs at the world for staring at him.' BOSWELL. 'How so, Sir?' JOHNSON. 'Why, Sir, a man who talks nonsense so well, must know that he is talking nonsense. But I am *afraid,* (chuckling and laughing,) Monboddo does *not* know that he is talking nonsense.'[1] BOSWELL. 'Is it wrong then, Sir, to affect singularity, in order to make people stare?' JOHNSON. 'Yes, if you do it by propagating errour: and, indeed, it is wrong in any way. There is in human nature a general inclination to make people stare; and every wise man has himself to cure of it, and does cure himself. If you wish to make people stare by doing better than others, why, make them stare till they stare their eyes out. But consider how easy it is to make people stare by being absurd. I may do it by going into a drawing-room without my shoes. You remember the gentleman in *The Spectator*, who had a commission of lunacy taken out against him for his extreme singularity, such as never wearing a wig, but a night-cap. Now, Sir, abstractedly, the night-cap was best; but, relatively, the advantage was overbalanced by his making the boys run after him.'

Talking of a London life, he said, 'The happiness of London is not to be conceived but by those who have been in it. I will

[1] His Lordship having frequently spoken in an abusive manner of Dr. Johnson, in my company, I on one occasion during the life-time of my illustrious friend could not refrain from retaliation, and repeated to him this saying. He has since published I don't know how many pages in one of his curious books, attempting, in much anger, but with pitiful effect, to persuade mankind that my illustrious friend was not the great and good man which they esteemed and ever will esteem him to be.

venture to say, there is more learning and science within the circumference of ten miles from where we now sit, than in all the rest of the kingdom.' BOSWELL. 'The only disadvantage is the great distance at which people live from one another.' JOHNSON. 'Yes, Sir; but that is occasioned by the largeness of it, which is the cause of all the other advantages.' BOSWELL. 'Sometimes I have been in the humour of wishing to retire to a desart.' JOHNSON. 'Sir, you have desart enough in Scotland.'

Although I had promised myself a great deal of instructive conversation with him on the conduct of the married state, of which I had then a near prospect, he did not say much upon that topick. Mr. Seward heard him once say, that 'a man has a very bad chance for happiness in that state, unless he marries a woman of very strong and fixed principles of religion.' He maintained to me, contrary to the common notion, that a woman would not be the worse wife for being learned; in which, from all that I have observed of *Artemisias*, I humbly differed from him. That a woman should be sensible and well informed, I allow to be a great advantage; and think that Sir Thomas Overbury,[1] in his rude versification, has very judiciously pointed out that degree of intelligence which is to be desired in a female companion:

> 'Give me, next *good*, an *understanding wife*,
>   By Nature *wise*, not *learned* by much art;
> Some *knowledge* on her side will all my life
>   More scope of conversation impart;
> Besides, her inborne virtue fortifie;
> They are most firmly good, who best know why.'

When I censured a gentleman[2] of my acquaintance for marrying a second time, as it shewed a disregard of his first wife, he said, 'Not at all, Sir. On the contrary, were he not to marry again, it might be concluded that his first wife had given him a disgust to marriage; but by taking a second wife he pays the highest compliment to the first, by shewing that she made him so happy as a married man, that he wishes to be so a second time.' So ingenious a turn did he give to this delicate question. And yet,

---

[1] *A Wife*, a poem, 1614.
[2] [Lord Auchinleck. *Boswell's Letters*, i. 177, ii. 307.]

on another occasion, he owned that he once had almost asked a promise of Mrs. Johnson that she would not marry again, but had checked himself. Indeed, I cannot help thinking, that in his case the request would have been unreasonable; for if Mrs. Johnson forgot, or thought it no injury to the memory of her first love,—the husband of her youth and the father of her children,— to make a second marriage, why should she be precluded from a third, should she be so inclined? In Johnson's persevering fond appropriation of his *Tetty*, even after her decease, he seems totally to have overlooked the prior claim of the honest Birmingham trader. I presume that her having been married before had, at times, given him some uneasiness; for I remember his observing upon the marriage of one of our common friends,[1] 'He has done a very foolish thing, Sir; he has married a widow, when he might have had a maid.'

We drank tea with Mrs. Williams. I had last year the pleasure of seeing Mrs. Thrale at Dr. Johnson's one morning, and had conversation enough with her to admire her talents, and to shew her that I was as Johnsonian as herself. Dr. Johnson had probably been kind enough to speak well of me, for this evening he delivered me a very polite card from Mr. Thrale and her, inviting me to Streatham.

On the 6th of October I complied with this obliging invitation, and found, at an elegant villa, six miles from town, every circumstance that can make society pleasing. Johnson, though quite at home, was yet looked up to with an awe, tempered by affection, and seemed to be equally the care of his host and hostess. I rejoiced at seeing him so happy.

He played off his wit against Scotland with a good humoured pleasantry, which gave me, though no bigot to national prejudices, an opportunity for a little contest with him. I having said that England was obliged to us for gardeners, almost all their good gardeners being Scotchmen. JOHNSON. 'Why, Sir, that is because gardening is much more necessary amongst you than with us, which makes so many of your people learn it. It is *all* gardening with you. Things which grow wild here, must be

[1] [Langton. *Powell.*]

cultivated with great care in Scotland. Pray now (throwing himself back in his chair, and laughing,) are you ever able to bring the *sloe* to perfection?'

I boasted that we had the honour of being the first to abolish the unhospitable, troublesome, and ungracious custom of giving vails to servants. JOHNSON. 'Sir, you abolished vails, because you were too poor to be able to give them.'

Mrs. Thrale disputed with him on the merit of Prior. He attacked him powerfully; said he wrote of love like a man who had never felt it: his love verses were college verses; and he repeated the song 'Alexis shunn'd his fellow swains,' &c., in so ludicrous a manner, as to make us all wonder how any one could have been pleased with such fantastical stuff. Mrs. Thrale stood to her gun with great courage, in defence of amorous ditties, which Johnson despised, till he at last silenced her by saying, 'My dear Lady, talk no more of this. Nonsense can be defended but by nonsense.'

Mrs. Thrale then praised Garrick's talent for light gay poetry; and, as a specimen, repeated his song in *Florizel and Perdita*, and dwelt with peculiar pleasure on this line:

'I'd smile with the simple, and feed with the poor.'

JOHNSON. 'Nay, my dear Lady, this will never do. Poor David! Smile with the simple! What folly is that! And who would feed with the poor that can help it? No, no; let me smile with the wise, and feed with the rich.' I repeated this sally to Garrick, and wondered to find his sensibility as a writer not a little irritated by it. To sooth him, I observed, that Johnson spared none of us; and I quoted the passage in Horace, in which he compares one who attacks his friends for the sake of a laugh, to a pushing ox, that is marked by a bunch of hay put upon his horns: *'fœnum habet in cornu.'*[1] 'Ay, (said Garrick vehemently,) he has a whole *mow* of it.'

Talking of history, Johnson said, 'We may know historical facts to be true, as we may know facts in common life to be true. Motives are generally unknown. We cannot trust to the characters

---

[1] ['he carries hay on his horns.' Horace, *Satires*, i. iv. 34.]

we find in history, unless when they are drawn by those who knew the persons; as those, for instance, by Sallust and by Lord Clarendon.'

He would not allow much merit to Whitefield's oratory. 'His popularity, Sir, (said he,) is chiefly owing to the peculiarity of his manner. He would be followed by crowds were he to wear a night-cap in the pulpit, or were he to preach from a tree.'

I know not from what spirit of contradiction he burst out into a violent declamation against the Corsicans, of whose heroism I talked in high terms. 'Sir, (said he,) what is all this rout about the Corsicans? They have been at war with the Genoese for upwards of twenty years, and have never yet taken their fortified towns. They might have battered down their walls, and reduced them to powder in twenty years. They might have pulled the walls in pieces, and cracked the stones with their teeth in twenty years.' It was in vain to argue with him upon the want of artillery: he was not to be resisted for the moment.

On the evening of October 10, I presented Dr. Johnson to General Paoli. I had greatly wished that two men, for whom I had the highest esteem, should meet. They met with a manly ease, mutually conscious of their own abilities, and of the abilities of each other. The General spoke Italian, and Dr. Johnson English, and understood one another very well, with a little aid of interpretation from me, in which I compared myself to an isthmus which joins two great continents. Upon Johnson's approach, the General said, 'From what I have read of your works, Sir, and from what Mr. Boswell has told me of you, I have long held you in great veneration.' The General talked of languages being formed on the particular notions and manners of a people, without knowing which, we cannot know the language. We may know the direct signification of single words; but by these no beauty of expression, no sally of genius, no wit is conveyed to the mind. All this must be by allusion to other ideas. 'Sir, (said Johnson,) you talk of language, as if you had never done any thing else but study it, instead of governing a nation.' The General said, '*Questo e un troppo gran complimento;*' this is too great a compliment. Johnson answered, 'I should have thought

so, Sir, if I had not heard you talk.' The General asked him,
what he thought of the spirit of infidelity which was so prevalent.
JOHNSON. 'Sir, this gloom of infidelity, I hope, is only a transient cloud passing through the hemisphere, which will soon be
dissipated, and the sun break forth with his usual spendour.' 'You
think then, (said the General,) that they will change their principles like their clothes.' JOHNSON. 'Why, Sir, if they bestow
no more thought on principles than on dress, it must be so.' The
General said, that 'a great part of the fashionable infidelity was
owing to a desire of shewing courage. Men who have no opportunities of shewing it as to things in this life, take death and
futurity as objects on which to display it.' JOHNSON. 'That is
mighty foolish affectation. Fear is one of the passions of human
nature, of which it is impossible to divest it. You remember that
the Emperour Charles V, when he read upon the tomb-stone of
a Spanish nobleman. "Here lies one who never knew fear,"
wittily said, "Then he never snuffed a candle with his fingers." '

He talked a few words of French to the General; but finding
he did not do it with facility, he asked for pen, ink, and paper,
and wrote the following note:—

'*J'ai lu dans la geographie de Lucas de Linda un Paternoster
écrit dans une langue tout à-fait differente de l'Italienne, et de toutes
autres lesquelles se derivent du Latin. L'auteur l'appelle* linguam
Corsicæ rusticam; *elle a peut-etre passé, peu à peu; mais elle a cer-
tainement prevalue autrefois dans les montagnes et dans la campagne.
Le même auteur dit la même chose en parlant de Sardaigne; qu'il y
a deux langues dans l'Isle, une des villes, l'autre de la campagne.*'

The General immediately informed him that the *lingua rustica*
was only in Sardinia.

Dr. Johnson went home with me, and drank tea till late in the
night. He said, 'General Paoli had the loftiest port of any man
he had ever seen.' He denied that military men were always the
best bred men. 'Perfect good breeding,' he observed, 'consists
in having no particular mark of any profession, but a general
elegance of manners; whereas, in a military man, you can commonly distinguish the *brand* of a soldier, *l'homme d'épée.*'

Dr. Johnson shunned to-night any discussion of the perplexed question of fate and free will, which I attempted to agitate. 'Sir, (said he,) we *know* our will is free, and *there's* an end on't.'

He honoured me with his company at dinner on the 16th of October, at my lodgings in Old Bond-street, with Sir Joshua Reynolds, Mr. Garrick, Dr. Goldsmith, Mr. Murphy, Mr. Bickerstaff, and Mr. Thomas Davies. Garrick played round him with a fond vivacity, taking hold of the breasts of his coat, and, looking up in his face with a lively archness, complimented him on the good health which he seemed then to enjoy; while the sage, shaking his head, beheld him with a gentle complacency. One of the company[1] not being come at the appointed hour, I proposed, as usual upon such occasions, to order dinner to be served; adding, 'Ought six people to be kept waiting for one?' 'Why, yes, (answered Johnson, with a delicate humanity,) if the one will suffer more by your sitting down, than the six will do by waiting.' Goldsmith, to divert the tedious minutes, strutted about, bragging of his dress, and I believe was seriously vain of it, for his mind was wonderfully prone to such impressions. 'Come, come, (said Garrick,) talk no more of that. You are, perhaps, the worst—eh, eh!'—Goldsmith was eagerly attempting to interrupt him, when Garrick went on, laughing ironically, 'Nay, you will always *look* like a gentleman; but I am talking of being well or ill *drest*.' 'Well, let me tell you, (said Goldsmith,) when my tailor brought home my bloom-coloured coat, he said, "Sir, I have a favour to beg of you. When any body asks you who made your clothes, be pleased to mention John Filby, at the Harrow, in Water-lane."' JOHNSON. 'Why, Sir, that was because he knew the strange colour would attract crowds to gaze at it, and thus they might hear of him, and see how well he could make a coat even of so absurd a colour.'

After dinner our conversation first turned upon Pope. Johnson said, his characters of men were admirably drawn, those of women not so well. He repeated to us, in his forcible melodious manner, the concluding lines of the *Dunciad*. While he was talking loudly in praise of those lines, one of the company[2] ventured

---

[1] [Possibly Reynolds. *Powell.*]
[2] [Boswell. *Isham Coll.*, No. 20.]

to say, 'Too fine for such a poem:—a poem on what?' JOHN-
SON, (with a disdainful look,) 'Why, on *dunces*. It was worth
while being a dunce then. Ah, Sir, hadst *thou* lived in those days!
It is not worth while being a dunce now, when there are no wits.'
Bickerstaff observed, as a peculiar circumstance, that Pope's
fame was higher when he was alive than it was then. Johnson
said, his Pastorals were poor things, though the versification
was fine. He told us, with high satisfaction, the anecdote of
Pope's inquiring who was the authour of his *London*, and saying,
he will be soon *déterré*. He observed, that in Dryden's poetry
there were passages drawn from a profundity which Pope could
never reach. He repeated some fine lines on love, by the former,
(which I have now forgotten,) and gave great applause to the
character of Zimri. Goldsmith said, that Pope's character of
Addison shewed a deep knowledge of the human heart. Johnson
said, that the description of the temple, in the *Mourning Bride*,
was the finest poetical passage he had ever read; he recollected
none in Shakspeare equal to it. 'But, (said Garrick, all alarmed
for the 'god of his idolatry,') we know not the extent and variety
of his powers. We are to suppose there are such passages in his
works. Shakspeare must not suffer from the badness of our
memories.' Johnson, diverted by this enthusiastick jealousy, went
on with greater ardour: 'No, Sir; Congreve has *nature*;' (smiling
on the tragick eagerness of Garrick;) but composing himself, he
added, 'Sir, this is not comparing Congreve on the whole, with
Shakspeare on the whole; but only maintaining that Congreve
has one finer passage than any that can be found in Shakspeare.
Sir, a man may have no more than ten guineas in the world, but
he may have those ten guineas in one piece; and so may have a
finer piece than a man who has ten thousand pounds: but then he
has only one ten-guinea piece. What I mean is, that you can
shew me no passage where there is simply a description of
material objects, without any intermixture of moral notions,
which produces such an effect.' Mr. Murphy mentioned Shakspeare's description of the night before the battle of Agincourt;
but it was observed, it had *men* in it. Mr. Davies suggested the
speech of Juliet, in which she figures herself awaking in the tomb

of her ancestors. Some one mentioned the description of Dover Cliff. JOHNSON. 'No, Sir; it should be all precipice,—all vacuum. The crows impede your fall. The diminished appearance of the boats, and other circumstances, are all very good description; but do not impress the mind at once with the horrible idea of immense height. The impression is divided; you pass on by computation, from one stage of the tremendous space to another. Had the girl in *The Mourning Bride* said, she could not cast her shoe to the top of one of the pillars in the temple, it would not have aided the idea, but weakened it.'

Talking of a Barrister who had a bad utterance, some one,[1] (to rouse Johnson,) wickedly said, that he was unfortunate in not having been taught oratory by Sheridan. JOHNSON. 'Nay, Sir, if he had been taught by Sheridan, he would have cleared the room.' GARRICK. 'Sheridan has too much vanity to be a good man.' We shall now see Johnson's mode of *defending* a man; taking him into his own hands, and discriminating. JOHNSON. 'No, Sir. There is, to be sure, in Sheridan, something to reprehend, and every thing to laugh at; but, Sir, he is not a bad man. No, Sir; were mankind to be divided into good and bad, he would stand considerably within the ranks of good. And, Sir, it must be allowed that Sheridan excels in plain declamation, though he can exhibit no character.'

I should, perhaps, have suppressed this disquisition concerning a person of whose merit and worth I think with respect, had he not attacked Johnson so outrageously in his *Life of Swift*, and, at the same time, treated us, his admirers, as a set of pigmies. He who has provoked the lash of wit, cannot complain that he smarts from it.

Mrs. Montagu, a lady distinguished for having written an Essay on Shakspeare, being mentioned; REYNOLDS. 'I think that essay does her honour.' JOHNSON. 'Yes, Sir; it does *her* honour, but it would do nobody else honour. I have, indeed, not read it all. But when I take up the end of a web, and find it packthread, I do not expect, by looking further, to find embroidery. Sir, I will venture to say, there is not one sentence of true criti-

---

[1] [Probably Boswell. *Powell.*]

cism in her book.' GARRICK. 'But, Sir, surely it shews how much
Voltaire has mistaken Shakspeare, which nobody else has done.'
JOHNSON. 'Sir, nobody else has thought it worth while. And
what merit is there in that? You may as well praise a schoolmaster for whipping a boy who has construed ill. No, Sir, there
is no real criticism in it: none shewing the beauty of thought, as
formed on the workings of the human heart.'

The admirers of this Essay[1] may be offended at the slighting
manner in which Johnson spoke of it; but let it be remembered,
that he gave his honest opinion unbiassed by any prejudice, or
any proud jealousy of a woman intruding herself into the chair
of criticism; for Sir Joshua Reynolds has told me, that when the
Essay first came out, and it was not known who had written it,
Johnson wondered how Sir Joshua could like it. At this time Sir
Joshua himself had received no information concerning the
authour, except being assured by one of our most eminent
literati,[2] that it was clear its authour did not know the Greek
tragedies in the original. One day at Sir Joshua's table, when it
was related that Mrs. Montagu, in an excess of compliment to
the authour[3] of a modern tragedy, had exclaimed, 'I tremble for
Shakspeare;' Johnson said, 'When Shakspeare has got —— for
his rival, and Mrs. Montagu for his defender, he is in a poor
state indeed.'

Johnson proceeded: 'The Scotchman[4] has taken the right
method in his *Elements of Criticism*. I do not mean that he has
taught us any thing; but he has told us old things in a new way.'
MURPHY. 'He seems to have read a great deal of French criticism, and wants to make it his own; as if he had been for years

---

[1] Of whom I acknowledge myself to be one, considering it as a piece of
the secondary or comparative species of criticism; and not of that profound
species which alone Dr. Johnson would allow to be 'real criticism.' It is,
besides, clearly and elegantly expressed, and has done effectually what it
professed to do, namely, vindicated Shakspeare from the misrepresentations
of Voltaire; and considering how many young people were misled by his
witty, though false observations, Mrs. Montagu's Essay was of service to
Shakspeare with a certain class of readers, and is, therefore, entitled to
praise. Johnson, I am assured, allowed the merit which I have stated, saying,
(with reference to Voltaire,) 'it is conclusive *ad hominem* ['to the man'].'

[2] [Perhaps Malone. *Powell.*]

[3] [Jephson. *Mrs. Thrale and Steevens.*]   [4] [Lord Kames.]

anatomising the heart of man, and peeping into every cranny of it.' GOLDSMITH. 'It is easier to write that book, than to read it.' JOHNSON. 'We have an example of true criticism in Burke's *Essay on the Sublime and Beautiful*; and, if I recollect, there is also Du Bos; and Bouhours, who shews all beauty to depend on truth. There is no great merit in telling how many plays have ghosts in them, and how this Ghost is better than that. You must shew how terrour is impressed on the human heart. In the description of night in *Macbeth*, the beetle and the bat detract from the general idea of darkness,—inspissated gloom.'

Politicks being mentioned, he said, 'This petitioning is a new mode of distressing government, and a mighty easy one. I will undertake to get petitions either against quarter-guineas or half-guineas, with the help of a little hot wine. There must be no yielding to encourage this. The object is not important enough. We are not to blow up half a dozen palaces, because one cottage is burning.'

The conversation then took another turn. JOHNSON. 'It is amazing what ignorance of certain points one sometimes finds in men of eminence. A wit[1] about town, who wrote Latin bawdy verses, asked me, how it happened that England and Scotland, which were once two kingdoms, were now one:—and Sir Fletcher Norton did not seem to know that there were such publications as the Reviews.'

'The ballad of Hardyknute has no great merit, if it be really ancient. People talk of nature. But mere obvious nature may be exhibited with very little power of mind.'

On Thursday, October 19, I passed the evening with him at his house. He advised me to complete a Dictionary of words peculiar to Scotland, of which I shewed him a specimen. 'Sir, (said he,) Ray has made a collection of north-country words. By collecting those of your country, you will do a useful thing towards the history of the language. He bade me also go on with collections which I was making upon the antiquities of Scotland. 'Make a large book; a folio.' BOSWELL. 'But of what use will it be, Sir?' JOHNSON. 'Never mind the use; do it.'

---

[1] [Perhaps the Rev. B. Loveling. *Powell.*]

I complained that he had not mentioned Garrick in his Preface to Shakspeare; and asked him if he did not admire him. JOHN-SON. 'Yes, as "a poor player, who frets and struts his hour upon the stage;"—as a shadow.' BOSWELL. 'But has he not brought Shakspeare into notice?' JOHNSON. 'Sir, to allow that, would be to lampoon the age. Many of Shakspeare's plays are the worse for being acted: *Macbeth*, for instance.' BOSWELL. 'What, Sir, is nothing gained by decoration and action? Indeed, I do wish that you had mentioned Garrick.' JOHNSON. 'My dear Sir, had I mentioned him, I must have mentioned many more: Mrs. Pritchard, Mrs. Cibber,—nay, and Mr. Cibber too; he too altered Shakspeare.' BOSWELL. 'You have read his apology, Sir?' JOHNSON. 'Yes, it is very entertaining. But as for Cibber himself, taking from his conversation all that he ought not to have said, he was a poor creature. I remember when he brought me one of his Odes to have my opinion of it; I could not bear such nonsense, and would not let him read it to the end; so little respect had I for *that great man*! (laughing.) Yet I remember Richardson wondering that I could treat him with familiarity.'

I mentioned to him that I had seen the execution of several convicts at Tyburn, two days before, and that none of them seemed to be under any concern. JOHNSON. 'Most of them, Sir, have never thought at all.' BOSWELL. 'But is not the fear of death natural to man?' JOHNSON. 'So much so, Sir, that the whole of life is but keeping away the thoughts of it.' He then, in a low and earnest tone, talked of his meditating upon the aweful hour of his own dissolution, and in what manner he should conduct himself upon that occasion: 'I know not (said he,) whether I should wish to have a friend by me, or have it all between GOD and myself.'

Talking of our feeling for the distresses of others;—JOHN-SON. 'Why, Sir, there is much noise made about it, but it is greatly exaggerated. No, Sir, we have a certain degree of feeling to prompt us to do good: more than that, Providence does not intend. It would be misery to no purpose.' BOSWELL. 'But suppose now, Sir, that one of your intimate friends were appre-hended for an offence for which he might be hanged.' JOHN-

SON. 'I should do what I could to bail him, and give him any other assistance; but if he were once fairly hanged, I should not suffer.' BOSWELL. 'Would you eat your dinner that day, Sir?' JOHNSON. 'Yes, Sir; and eat it as if he were eating it with me. Why, there's Baretti, who is to be tried for his life to-morrow, friends have risen up for him on every side; yet if he should be hanged, none of them will eat a slice of plumb-pudding the less. Sir, that sympathetic feeling goes a very little way in depressing the mind.'

I told him that I had dined lately at Foote's, who shewed me a letter which he had received from Tom Davies, telling him that he had not been able to sleep from the concern which he felt on account of '*This sad affair of Baretti*,' begging of him to try if he could suggest any thing that might be of service; and, at the same time, recommending to him an industrious young man who kept a pickle-shop. JOHNSON. 'Ay, Sir, here you have a specimen of human sympathy; a friend hanged, and a cucumber pickled. We know not whether Baretti or the pickle-man has kept Davies from sleep; nor does he know himself. And as to his not sleeping, Sir: Tom Davies is a very great man; Tom has been upon the stage, and knows how to do those things. I have not been upon the stage, and cannot do those things.' BOSWELL. 'I have often blamed myself, Sir, for not feeling for others as sensibly as many say they do.' JOHNSON. 'Sir, don't be duped by them any more. You will find these very feeling people are not very ready to do you good. They *pay* you by *feeling*.'

BOSWELL. 'Foote has a great deal of humour?' JOHNSON. 'Yes, Sir.' BOSWELL. 'He has a singular talent of exhibiting character.' JOHNSON. 'Sir, it is not a talent; it is a vice; it is what others abstain from. It is not comedy, which exhibits the character of a species, as that of a miser gathered from many misers: it is farce, which exhibits individuals.' BOSWELL. 'Did not he think of exhibiting you, Sir?' JOHNSON. 'Sir, fear restrained him; he knew I would have broken his bones. I would have saved him the trouble of cutting off a leg; I would not have left him a leg to cut off.' BOSWELL. 'Pray, Sir, is not Foote an infidel?' JOHNSON. 'I do not know, Sir, that the fellow is an infidel; but if he be an infidel, he is an infidel as a dog is an infidel; that is to say, he has never thought upon the subject.'[1] BOSWELL. 'I suppose, Sir, he has thought superficially, and seized the first notions which occurred to his mind.' JOHNSON. 'Why then, Sir, still he is like a dog, that snatches the piece next him. Did you never observe that dogs have not the power of comparing? A dog will take a small bit of meat as readily as a large, when both are before him.'

'Buchanan (he observed,) has fewer *centos* than any modern Latin poet. He not only had great knowledge of the Latin language, but was a great poetical genius. Both the Scaligers praise him.'

He again talked of the passage in Congreve with high commendation, and said, 'Shakspeare never has six lines together without a fault. Perhaps you may find seven, but this does not refute my general assertion. If I come to an orchard, and say there's no fruit here, and then comes a poring man, who finds two apples and three pears, and tells me, "Sir, you are mistaken, I have found both apples and pears," I should laugh at him: what would that be to the purpose?'

BOSWELL. 'What do you think of Dr. Young's *Night Thoughts*, Sir?' JOHNSON. 'Why, Sir, there are very fine things in them.' BOSWELL. 'Is there not less religion in the nation now, Sir, than there was formerly?' JOHNSON. 'I don't know, Sir, that there is.' BOSWELL. 'For instance, there used to be a chaplain in every great family, which we do not find now.' JOHNSON. 'Neither do you find many of the state servants which great

[1] When Mr. Foote was at Edinburgh, he thought fit to entertain a numerous Scotch company, with a great deal of coarse jocularity, at the expense of Dr. Johnson, imagining it would be acceptable. I felt this as not civil to me; but sat very patiently till he had exhausted his merriment on that subject; and then observed, that surely Johnson must be allowed to have some sterling wit, and that I had heard him say a very good thing of Mr. Foote himself. 'Ah, my old friend Sam (cried Foote,) no man says better things; do let us have it.' Upon which I told the above story, which produced a very loud laugh from the company. But I never saw Foote so disconcerted. He looked grave and angry, and entered into a serious refutation of the justice of the remark. 'What, Sir, (said he,) talk thus of a man of liberal education;—a man who for years was at the University of Oxford;—a man who has added sixteen new characters to the English drama of his country!'

families used formerly to have. There is a change of modes in the whole department of life.'

Next day, October 20, he appeared, for the only time I suppose in his life, as a witness in a Court of Justice, being called to give evidence to the character of Mr. Baretti, who having stabbed a man in the street, was arraigned at the Old Bailey for murder. Never did such a constellation of genius enlighten the aweful Sessions-House, emphatically called JUSTICE HALL; Mr. Burke, Mr. Garrick, Mr. Beauclerk, and Dr. Johnson: and undoubtedly their favourable testimony had due weight with the Court and Jury. Johnson gave his evidence in a slow, deliberate, and distinct manner, which was uncommonly impressive. It is well known that Mr. Baretti was acquitted.

On the 26th of October, we dined together at the Mitre tavern. I found fault with Foote for indulging his talent of ridicule at the expence of his visitors, which I colloquially termed making fools of his company. JOHNSON. 'Why, Sir, when you go to see Foote, you do not go to see a saint: you go to see a man who will be entertained at your house, and then bring you on a publick stage; who will entertain you at his house, for the very purpose of bringing you on a publick stage. Sir, he does not make fools of his company; they whom he exposes are fools already: he only brings them into action.'

Talking of trade, he observed, 'It is a mistaken notion that a vast deal of money is brought into a nation by trade. It is not so. Commodities come from commodities: but trade produces no capital accession of wealth. However, though there should be little profit in money, there is a considerable profit in pleasure, as it gives to one nation the productions of another; as we have wines and fruits, and many other foreign articles, brought to us.' BOSWELL. 'Yes, Sir, and there is a profit in pleasure, by its furnishing occupation to such numbers of mankind.' JOHNSON. 'Why, Sir, you cannot call that pleasure to which all are averse, and which none begin but with the hope of leaving off; a thing which men dislike before they have tried it, and when they have tried it.' BOSWELL. 'But, Sir, the mind must be employed, and we grow weary when idle.' JOHNSON. 'That is, Sir, because, others being busy, we want company; but if we were all idle, there would be no growing weary; we should all entertain one another. There is, indeed, this in trade:—it gives men an opportunity of improving their situation. If there were no trade, many who are poor would always remain poor. But no man loves labour for itself.' BOSWELL. 'Yes, Sir, I know a person who does. He is a very laborious Judge,[1] and he loves the labour.' JOHNSON. 'Sir, that is because he loves respect and distinction. Could he have them without labour, he would like it less.' BOSWELL. 'He tells me he likes it for itself.'—'Why, Sir, he fancies so, because he is not accustomed to abstract.'

We went home to his house to tea. Mrs. Williams made it with sufficient dexterity, notwithstanding her blindness, though her manner of satisfying herself that the cups were full enough appeared to me a little aukward; for I fancied she put her finger down a certain way, till she felt the tea touch it.[2] In my first elation at being allowed the privilege of attending Dr. Johnson at his late visits to this lady, which was like being *è secretioribus consiliis*[3], I willingly drank cup after cup, as if it had been the Heliconian spring. But as the charm of novelty went off, I grew more fastidious; and besides, I discovered that she was of a peevish temper.

There was a pretty large circle this evening. Dr. Johnson was in very good humour, lively, and ready to talk upon all subjects. Mr. Fergusson, the self-taught philosopher, told him of a new-invented machine which went without horses: a man who sat in it turned a handle, which worked a spring that drove it forward. 'Then, Sir, (said Johnson,) what is gained is, the man has his choice whether he will move himself alone, or himself and the machine too.' Dominicetti being mentioned, he would not allow him any merit. 'There is nothing in all this boasted system. No, Sir; medicated baths can be no better than warm water: their

---

[1] [Lord Auchinleck. *Croker*[3].]

[2] I have since had reason to think that I was mistaken; for I have been informed by a lady, who was long intimate with her, and likely to be a more accurate observer of such matters, that she had acquired such a niceness of touch, as to know, by the feeling on the outside of the cup, how near it was to being full.   [3] ['one of his inner cabinet.']

only effect can be that of tepid moisture.' One of the company[1] took the other side, maintaining that medicines of various sorts, and some too of most powerful effect, are introduced into the human frame by the medium of the pores; and, therefore, when warm water is impregnated with salutiferous substances, it may produce great effects as a bath. This appeared to me very satisfactory. Johnson did not answer it; but talking for victory, and determined to be master of the field, he had recourse to the device which Goldsmith imputed to him in the witty words of one of Cibber's comedies: 'There is no arguing with Johnson; for when his pistol misses fire, he knocks you down with the butt end of it.' He turned to the gentleman, 'Well, Sir, go to Dominicetti, and get thyself fumigated; but be sure that the steam be directed to thy *head*, for *that* is the *peccant part.*' This produced a triumphant roar of laughter from the motley assembly of philosophers, printers, and dependents, male and female.

I know not how so whimsical a thought came into my mind, but I asked, 'If, Sir, you were shut up in a castle, and a newborn child with you, what would you do?' JOHNSON. 'Why, Sir, I should not much like my company.' BOSWELL. 'But would you take the trouble of rearing it?' He seemed, as may well be supposed, unwilling to pursue the subject: but upon my persevering in my question, replied, 'Why yes, Sir, I would; but I must have all conveniences. If I had no garden, I would make a shed on the roof, and take it there for fresh air. I should feed it, and wash it much, and with warm water to please it, not with cold water to give it pain.' BOSWELL. 'But, Sir, does not heat relax?' JOHNSON. 'Sir, you are not to imagine the water is to be very hot. I would not *coddle* the child. No, Sir, the hardy method of treating children does no good. I'll take you five children from London, who shall cuff five Highland children. Sir, a man bred in London will carry a burthen, or run, or wrestle, as well as a man brought up in the hardiest manner in the country.' BOSWELL. 'Good living, I suppose, makes the Londoners strong.' JOHNSON. 'Why, Sir, I don't know that it does. Our chairmen from Ireland, who are as strong men as any, have been brought up

---

[1] [Boswell. *Mrs. Piozzi*; *Croker*[1].]

upon potatoes. Quantity makes up for quality.' BOSWELL.
'Would you teach this child that I have furnished you with, any
thing?' JOHNSON. 'No, I should not be apt to teach it.' Bos-
WELL. 'Would not you have a pleasure in teaching it?' JOHNSON.
'No, Sir, I should *not* have a pleasure in teaching it.' BOSWELL.
'Have you not a pleasure in teaching men?—*There* I have you.
You have the same pleasure in teaching men, that I should have
in teaching children.' JOHNSON. 'Why, something about that.'

BOSWELL. 'Do you think, Sir, that what is called natural
affection is born with us? It seems to me to be the effect of habit,
or of gratitude for kindness. No child has it for a parent whom
it has not seen.' JOHNSON. 'Why, Sir, I think there is an instinctive natural affection in parents towards their children.'

Russia being mentioned as likely to become a great empire,
by the rapid increase of population:—JOHNSON. 'Why, Sir, I see
no prospect of their propagating more. They can have no more
children than they can get. I know of no way to make them breed
more than they do. It is not from reason and prudence that people
marry, but from inclination. A man is poor; he thinks, "I cannot
be worse, and so I'll e'en take Peggy." ' BOSWELL. 'But have
not nations been more populous at one period than another?'
JOHNSON. 'Yes, Sir; but that has been owing to the people
being less thinned at one period than another, whether by
emigrations, war, or pestilence, not by their being more or less
prolifick. Births at all times bear the same proportion to the
same number of people.' BOSWELL. 'But, to consider the state
of our own country;—does not throwing a number of farms into
one hand hurt population?' JOHNSON. 'Why no, Sir; the same
quantity of food being produced, will be consumed by the same
number of mouths, though the people may be disposed of in
different ways. We see, if corn be dear, and butchers' meat cheap,
the farmers all apply themselves to the raising of corn, till it
becomes plentiful and cheap, and then butchers' meat becomes
dear; so that an equality is always preserved. No, Sir, let fanciful
men do as they will, depend upon it, it is difficult to disturb the
system of life.' BOSWELL. 'But, Sir, is it not a very bad thing
for landlords to oppress their tenants, by raising their rents?'

JOHNSON. 'Very bad. But, Sir, it never can have any general influence; it may distress some individuals. For, consider this: landlords cannot do without tenants. Now tenants will not give more for land, than land is worth. If they can make more of their money by keeping a shop, or any other way, they'll do it, and so oblige landlords to let land come back to a reasonable rent, in order that they may get tenants. Land, in England, is an article of commerce. A tenant who pays his landlord his rent, thinks himself no more obliged to him than you think yourself obliged to a man in whose shop you buy a piece of goods. He knows the landlord does not let him have his land for less than he can get from others, in the same manner as the shopkeeper sells his goods. No shopkeeper sells a yard of ribband for sixpence when seven-pence is the current price.' BOSWELL. 'But, Sir, is it not better that tenants should be dependant on landlords?' JOHNSON. 'Why, Sir, as there are many more tenants than landlords, perhaps, strictly speaking, we should wish not. But if you please you may let your lands cheap, and so get the value, part in money and part in homage. I should agree with you in that.' BOSWELL. 'So, Sir, you laugh at schemes of political improvement.' JOHNSON. 'Why, Sir, most schemes of political improvement are very laughable things.'

He observed, 'Providence has wisely ordered that the more numerous men are, the more difficult it is for them to agree in any thing, and so they are governed. There is no doubt, that if the poor should reason, "We'll be the poor no longer, we'll make the rich take their turn," they could easily do it, were it not that they can't agree. So the common soldiers, though so much more numerous than their officers, are governed by them for the same reason.'

He said, 'Mankind have a strong attachment to the habitations to which they have been accustomed. You see the inhabitants of Norway do not with one consent quit it, and go to some part of America, where there is a mild climate, and where they may have the same produce from land, with the tenth part of the labour. No, Sir; their affection for their old dwellings, and the terrour of a general change, keep them at home. Thus, we see many of the finest spots in the world thinly inhabited, and many rugged spots well inhabited.'

The London Chronicle, which was the only news-paper he constantly took in, being brought, the office of reading it aloud was assigned to me. I was diverted by his impatience. He made me pass over so many parts of it, that my task was very easy. He would not suffer one of the petitions to the King about the Middlesex election to be read.

I had hired a Bohemian as my servant while I remained in London, and being much pleased with him, I asked Dr. Johnson whether his being a Roman Catholick should prevent my taking him with me to Scotland. JOHNSON. 'Why no, Sir, if *he* has no objection, you can have none.' BOSWELL. 'So, Sir, you are no great enemy to the Roman Catholick religion.' JOHNSON. 'No more, Sir, than to the Presbyterian religion.' BOSWELL. 'You are joking.' JOHNSON. 'No, Sir, I really think so. Nay, Sir, of the two, I prefer the Popish.' BOSWELL. 'How so, Sir?' JOHNSON. 'Why, Sir, the Presbyterians have no church, no apostolical ordination.' BOSWELL. 'And do you think that absolutely essential, Sir?' JOHNSON. 'Why, Sir, as it was an apostolical institution, I think it is dangerous to be without it. And, Sir, the Presbyterians have no public worship: they have no form of prayer in which they know they are to join. They go to hear a man pray, and are to judge whether they will join with him.' BOSWELL. 'But, Sir, their doctrine is the same with that of the Church of England. Their confession of faith, and the thirty-nine articles, contain the same points, even the doctrine of predestination.' JOHNSON. 'Why yes, Sir, predestination was a part of the clamour of the times, so it is mentioned in our articles, but with as little positiveness as could be.' BOSWELL. 'Is it necessary, Sir, to believe all the thirty-nine articles?' JOHNSON. 'Why, Sir, that is a question which has been much agitated. Some have thought it necessary that they should all be believed; others have considered them to be only articles of peace, that is to say, you are not to preach against them.' BOSWELL. 'It appears to me, Sir, that predestination, or what is equivalent to it, cannot be avoided, if we hold an universal prescience in the Deity.' JOHNSON.

'Why, Sir, does not GOD every day see things going on without preventing them?' BOSWELL. 'True, Sir; but if a thing be *certainly* foreseen, it must be fixed, and cannot happen otherwise; and if we apply this consideration to the human mind, there is no free will, nor do I see how prayer can be of any avail.' He mentioned Dr. Clarke, and Bishop Bramhall on *Liberty and Necessity,* and bid me read South's *Sermons on Prayer*; but avoided the question which has excruciated philosophers and divines, beyond any other. I did not press it further, when I perceived that he was displeased, and shrunk from any abridgement of an attribute usually ascribed to the Divinity, however irreconcileable in its full extent with the grand system of moral government. His supposed orthodoxy here cramped the vigorous powers of his understanding. He was confined by a chain which early imagination and long habit made him think massy and strong, but which, had he ventured to try, he could at once have snapt asunder.

I proceeded: 'What do you think, Sir, of Purgatory, as believed by the Roman Catholicks?' JOHNSON. 'Why, Sir, it is a very harmless doctrine. They are of opinion that the generality of mankind are neither so obstinately wicked as to deserve everlasting punishment, nor so good as to merit being admitted into the society of blessed spirits; and therefore that God is graciously pleased to allow of a middle state, where they may be purified by certain degrees of suffering. You see, Sir, there is nothing unreasonable in this.' BOSWELL. 'But then, Sir, their masses for the dead?' JOHNSON. 'Why, Sir, if it be once established that there are souls in purgatory, it is as proper to pray for *them,* as for our brethren of mankind who are yet in this life.' BOSWELL. 'The idolatry of the Mass?' JOHNSON. 'Sir, there is no idolatry in the Mass. They believe GOD to be there, and they adore him.' BOSWELL. 'The worship of Saints?' JOHNSON. 'Sir, they do not worship saints; they invoke them; they only ask their prayers. I am talking all this time of the *doctrines* of the Church of Rome. I grant you that in *practice,* Purgatory is made a lucrative imposition, and that the people do become idolatrous as they recommend themselves to the tutelary protection of particular saints.

I think their giving the sacrament only in one kind is criminal, because it is contrary to the express institution of CHRIST, and I wonder how the Council of Trent admitted it.' BOSWELL. 'Confession?' JOHNSON. 'Why, I don't know but that is a good thing. The scripture says, "Confess your faults one to another," and the priests confess as well as the laity. Then it must be considered that their absolution is only upon repentance, and often upon penance also. You think your sins may be forgiven without penance, upon repentance alone.'

I thus ventured to mention all the common objections against the Roman Catholick Church, that I might hear so great a man upon them. What he said is here accurately recorded. But it is not improbable that if one had taken the other side he might have reasoned differently.

I must however mention, that he had a respect for '*the old religion,*' as the mild Melancthon called that of the Roman Catholick Church, even while he was exerting himself for its reformation in some particulars. Sir William Scott informs me, that he heard Johnson say, 'A man who is converted from Protestantism to Popery may be sincere: he parts with nothing: he is only superadding to what he already had. But a convert from Popery to Protestantism gives up so much of what he has held as sacred as any thing that he retains; there is so much *laceration of mind* in such a conversion, that it can hardly be sincere and lasting.' The truth of this reflection may be confirmed by many and eminent instances, some of which will occur to most of my readers.

When we were alone, I introduced the subject of death, and endeavoured to maintain that the fear of it might be got over. I told him that David Hume said to me, he was no more uneasy to think he should *not be* after this life, than that he *had not been* before he began to exist. JOHNSON. 'Sir, if he really thinks so, his perceptions are disturbed; he is mad: if he does not think so, he lies. He may tell you, he holds his finger in the flame of a candle, without feeling pain; would you believe him? When he dies, he at least gives up all he has.' BOSWELL. 'Foote, Sir, told me, that when he was very ill he was not afraid to die.' JOHN-

SON. 'It is not true, Sir. Hold a pistol to Foote's breast, or to Hume's breast, and threaten to kill them, and you'll see how they behave.' BOSWELL. 'But may we not fortify our minds for the approach of death?' Here I am sensible I was in the wrong, to bring before his view what he ever looked upon with horrour; for although when in a celestial frame, in his 'Vanity of human Wishes', he has supposed death to be 'kind Nature's signal for retreat,' from this state of being to 'a happier seat,' his thoughts upon this aweful change were in general full of dismal apprehensions. His mind resembled the vast amphitheatre, the Colisæum at Rome. In the centre stood his judgement, which, like a mighty gladiator, combated those apprehensions that, like the wild beasts of the *Arena*, were all around in cells, ready to be let out upon him. After a conflict, he drove them back into their dens; but not killing them, they were still assailing him. To my question, whether we might not fortify our minds for the approach of death, he answered, in a passion, 'No, Sir, let it alone. It matters not how a man dies, but how he lives. The act of dying is not of importance, it lasts so short a time.' He added, (with an earnest look,) 'A man knows it must be so, and submits. It will do him no good to whine.'

I attempted to continue the conversation. He was so provoked, that he said, 'Give us no more of this;' and was thrown into such a state of agitation, that he expressed himself in a way that alarmed and distressed me; shewed an impatience that I should leave him, and when I was going away, called to me sternly, 'Don't let us meet to-morrow.'

I went home exceedingly uneasy. All the harsh observations which I had ever heard made upon his character, crowded into my mind; and I seemed to myself like the man who had put his head into the lion's mouth a great many times with perfect safety, but at last had it bit off.

Next morning I sent him a note, stating, that I might have been in the wrong, but it was not intentionally; he was therefore, I could not help thinking, too severe upon me. That notwithstanding our agreement not to meet that day, I would call on him in my way to the city, and stay five minutes by my watch.

'You are, (said I,) in my mind, since last night, surrounded with cloud and storm. Let me have a glimpse of sunshine, and go about my affairs in serenity and chearfulness.'

Upon entering his study, I was glad that he was not alone, which would have made our meeting more awkward. There were with him, Mr. Steevens and Mr. Tyers, both of whom I now saw for the first time. My note had, on his own reflection, softened him, for he received me very complacently; so that I unexpectedly found myself at ease, and joined in the conversation.

He said, the criticks had done too much honour to Sir Richard Blackmore, by writing so much against him. That in his 'Creation' he had been helped by various wits, a line by Phillips and a line by Tickell; so that by their aid, and that of others, the poem had been made out.

I defended Blackmore's supposed lines, which have been ridiculed as absolute nonsense:—

> 'A painted vest Prince Voltiger had on,
> Which from a naked Pict his grandsire won.'[1]

I maintained it to be a poetical conceit. A Pict being painted, if he is slain in battle, and a vest is made of his skin, it is a painted vest won from him, though he was naked.

---

[1] An acute correspondent of the *European Magazine*, April, 1792, has completely exposed a mistake which has been unaccountably frequent in ascribing these lines to Blackmore, notwithstanding that Sir Richard Steele, in that very popular work, *The Spectator*, mentions them as written by the Authour of *The British Princes*, the Honourable Edward Howard. The correspondent above mentioned, shews this mistake to be so inveterate, that not only *I* defended the lines as Blackmore's, in the presence of Dr. Johnson, without any contradiction or doubt of their authenticity, but that the Reverend Mr. Whitaker has asserted in print, that he understands they were *suppressed* in the late edition or editions of Blackmore. 'After all (says this intelligent writer) it is not unworthy of particular observation, that these lines so often quoted do not exist either in Blackmore or Howard.' In *The British Princes*, 8vo. 1669, now before me, p. 96, they stand thus:—

> 'A vest as admir'd Voltiger had on,
> Which, from this Island's foes, his grandsire won,
> Whose artful colour pass'd the Tyrian dye,
> Oblig'd to triumph in this legacy.'

It is probable, I think, that some wag, in order to make Howard still more ridiculous than he really was, has formed the couplet as it now circulates.

Johnson spoke unfavourably of a certain pretty voluminous authour, saying, 'He used to write anonymous books, and then other books commending those books, in which there was something of rascality.'

I whispered him, 'Well, Sir, you are now in good humour.' JOHNSON. 'Yes, Sir.' I was going to leave him, and had got as far as the staircase. He stopped me, and smiling, said, 'Get you gone *in*;' a curious mode of inviting me to stay, which I accordingly did for some time longer.

This little incidental quarrel and reconciliation, which, perhaps, I may be thought to have detailed too minutely, must be esteemed as one of many proofs which his friends had, that though he might be charged with *bad humour* at times, he was always a *good-natured* man; and I have heard Sir Joshua Reynolds, a nice and delicate observer of manners, particularly remark, that when upon any occasion Johnson had been rough to any person in company, he took the first opportunity of reconciliation, by drinking to him, or addressing his discourse to him; but if he found his dignified indirect overtures sullenly neglected, he was quite indifferent, and considered himself as having done all that he ought to do, and the other as now in the wrong.

Being to set out for Scotland on the 10th of November, I wrote to him at Streatham, begging that he would meet me in town on the 9th; but if this should be very inconvenient to him, I would go thither. His answer was as follows:—

'*To* JAMES BOSWELL, ESQ.

'DEAR SIR,—Upon balancing the inconveniences of both parties, I find it will less incommode you to spend your night here, than me to come to town. I wish to see you, and am ordered by the lady of this house to invite you hither. Whether you can come or not, I shall not have any occasion of writing to you again before your marriage, and therefore tell you now, that with great sincerity I wish you happiness. I am, dear Sir, your most affectionate humble servant,

'Nov. 9, 1769.'   'SAM. JOHNSON.'

I was detained in town till it was too late on the ninth, so went to him early on the morning of the tenth of November. 'Now (said he,) that you are going to marry, do not expect more from life, than life will afford. You may often find yourself out of humour, and you may often think your wife not studious enough to please you; and yet you may have reason to consider yourself as upon the whole very happily married.'

Talking of marriage in general, he observed, 'Our marriage service is too refined. It is calculated only for the best kind of marriages; whereas, we should have a form for matches of convenience, of which there are many.' He agreed with me that there was no absolute necessity for having the marriage ceremony performed by a regular clergyman, for this was not commanded in scripture.

I was volatile enough to repeat to him a little epigrammatick song of mine, on matrimony, which Mr. Garrick had a few days before procured to be set to musick by the very ingenious Mr. Dibden.

'A MATRIMONIAL THOUGHT.

'IN the blithe days of honey-moon,
    With Kate's allurements smitten,
I lov'd her late, I lov'd her soon,
    And call'd her dearest kitten.

'But now my kitten's grown a cat,
    And cross like other wives,
O! by my soul, my honest Mat,
    I fear she has nine lives.'

My illustrious friend said, 'It is very well, Sir; but you should not swear.' Upon which I altered 'O! by my soul,' to 'Alas, alas!'

He was so good as to accompany me to London, and see me into the post-chaise which was to carry me on my road to Scotland. And sure I am, that, however inconsiderable many of the particulars recorded at this time may appear to some, they will be esteemed by the best part of my readers as genuine traits of his character, contributing together to give a full, fair, and distinct view of it.

1770: ÆTAT. 61.]—IN 1770 he published a political pamphlet, entitled *The False Alarm*, intended to justify the conduct of ministry and their majority in the House of Commons, for having virtually assumed it as an axiom, that the expulsion of a Member of Parliament was equivalent to exclusion, and thus having declared Colonel Lutterel to be duly elected for the county of Middlesex, notwithstanding Mr. Wilkes had a great majority of votes. This being justly considered as a gross violation of the right of election, an alarm for the constitution extended itself all over the kingdom. To prove this alarm to be false, was the purpose of Johnson's pamphlet; but even his vast powers were inadequate to cope with constitutional truth and reason, and his argument failed of effect; and the House of Commons have since expunged the offensive resolution from their Journals. That the House of Commons might have expelled Mr. Wilkes repeatedly, and as often as he should be re-chosen, was not denied; but incapacitation cannot be but by an act of the whole legislature. It was wonderful to see how a prejudice in favour of government in general, and an aversion to popular clamour, could blind and contract such an understanding as Johnson's, in this particular case; yet the wit, the sarcasm, the eloquent vivacity which this pamphlet displayed, made it be read with great avidity at the time, and it will ever be read with pleasure, for the sake of its composition. That it endeavoured to infuse a narcotick indifference, as to publick concerns, into the minds of the people, and that it broke out sometimes into an extreme coarseness of contemptuous abuse, is but too evident.

It must not, however, be omitted, that when the storm of his violence subsides, he takes a fair opportunity to pay a grateful compliment to the King, who had rewarded his merit: 'These low-born rulers have endeavoured, surely without effect, to alienate the affections of the people from the only King who for almost a century has much appeared to desire, or much endeavoured to deserve them.' And, 'Every honest man must lament, that the faction has been regarded with frigid neutrality by the Tories, who being long accustomed to signalise their principles by opposition to the Court, do not yet consider, that

they have at last a King who knows not the name of party, and
who wishes to be the common father of all his people.'

To this pamphlet, which was at once discovered to be Johnson's, several answers came out, in which, care was taken to
remind the publick of his former attacks upon government, and
of his now being a pensioner, without allowing for the honourable terms upon which Johnson's pension was granted and
accepted, or the change of system which the British court had
undergone upon the accession of his present Majesty. He was,
however, soothed in the highest strain of panegyrick, in a poem
called 'The Remonstrance', by the Rev. Mr. Stockdale, to whom
he was, upon many occasions, a kind protector.

The following admirable minute made by him describes so
well his own state, and that of numbers to whom self-examination is habitual, that I cannot omit it:—

'June 1, 1770. Every man naturally persuades himself that he
can keep his resolutions, nor is he convinced of his imbecility
but by length of time and frequency of experiment. This opinion
of our own constancy is so prevalent, that we always despise him
who suffers his general and settled purpose to be overpowered
by an occasional desire. They, therefore, whom frequent failures
have made desperate, cease to form resolutions; and they who
are become cunning, do not tell them. Those who do not make
them are very few, but of their effect little is perceived; for
scarcely any man persists in a course of life planned by choice,
but as he is restrained from deviation by some external power.
He who may live as he will, seldom lives long in the observation of his own rules.'[1]

Of this year I have obtained the following letters:—

'*To* THE REVEREND DR. FARMER, *Cambridge*

'SIR,—As no man ought to keep wholly to himself any possession that may be useful to the publick, I hope you will not
think me unreasonably intrusive, if I have recourse to you for
such information as you are more able to give me than any other
man.

[1] *Pr. and Med.* p. 95. [p. 101].

432

'In support of an opinion which you have already placed above the need of any more support, Mr. Steevens, a very ingenious gentleman, lately of King's College, has collected an account of all the translations which Shakspeare might have seen and used. He wishes his catalogue to be perfect, and therefore intreats that you will favour him by the insertion of such additions as the accuracy of your inquiries has enabled you to make. To this request, I take the liberty of adding my own solicitation.

'We have no immediate use for this catalogue, and therefore do not desire that it should interrupt or hinder your more important employments. But it will be kind to let us know that you receive it. I am, Sir, &c.

'Johnson's-court, Fleet-street,   'SAM. JOHNSON.'
    March 21, 1770.'

'*To* THE REVEREND MR. THOMAS WARTON

'DEAR SIR,—The readiness with which you were pleased to promise me some notes on Shakspeare, was a new instance of your friendship. I shall not hurry you; but am desired by Mr. Steevens, who helps me in this edition, to let you know, that we shall print the tragedies first, and shall therefore want first the notes which belong to them. We think not to incommode the readers with a supplement; and therefore, what we cannot put into its proper place, will do us no good. We shall not begin to print before the end of six weeks, perhaps not so soon. I am, &c.

'London, June 23, 1770.'   'SAM. JOHNSON.'

'*To* THE REV. DR. JOSEPH WARTON

'DEAR SIR,—I am revising my edition of Shakspeare, and remember that I formerly misrepresented your opinion of Lear. Be pleased to write the paragraph as you would have it, and send it. If you have any remarks of your own upon that or any other play, I shall gladly receive them.

'Make my compliments to Mrs. Warton. I sometimes think of wandering for a few days to Winchester, but am apt to delay. I am, Sir, your most humble servant,

'Sept. 27, 1770.'   'SAM. JOHNSON.'

Tuesday, 25 *September*, *Friday*, 7 *December* 1770

'*To* MR. FRANCIS BARBER, *at Mrs. Clapp's, Bishop-Stortford Hertfordshire*

'DEAR FRANCIS,—I am at last sat down to write to you, and should very much blame myself for having neglected you so long, if I did not impute that and many other failings to want of health. I hope not to be so long silent again. I am very well satisfied with your progress, if you can really perform the exercises which you are set; and I hope Mr. Ellis does not suffer you to impose on him, or on yourself.

'Make my compliments to Mr. Ellis, and to Mrs. Clapp, and Mr. Smith.

'Let me know what English books you read for your entertainment. You can never be wise unless you love reading.

'Do not imagine that I shall forget or forsake you; for if, when I examine you, I find that you have not lost your time, you shall want no encouragement from yours affectionately,

'London, Sept. 25, 1770.'   'SAM. JOHNSON.'

To THE SAME

'DEAR FRANCIS,—I hope you mind your business. I design you shall stay with Mrs. Clapp these holidays. If you are invited out you may go, if Mr. Ellis gives leave. I have ordered you some clothes, which you will receive, I believe, next week. My compliments to Mrs. Clapp and to Mr. Ellis, and Mr. Smith, &c. I am your affectionate,

'December 7, 1770.'   'SAM. JOHNSON.'

During this year there was a total cessation of all correspondence between Dr. Johnson and me, without any coldness on either side, but merely from procrastination, continued from day to day; and as I was not in London, I had no opportunity of enjoying his company and recording his conversation. To supply this blank, I shall present my readers with some *Collectanea*, obligingly furnished to me by the Rev. Dr. Maxwell, of Falkland, in Ireland, some time assistant preacher at the Temple, and for many years the social friend of Johnson, who spoke of him with a very kind regard.

'My acquaintance with that great and venerable character commenced in the year 1754. I was introduced to him by Mr. Grierson,[1] his Majesty's printer at Dublin, a gentleman of uncommon learning, and great wit and vivacity. Mr. Grierson died in Germany, at the age of twenty-seven. Dr. Johnson highly respected his abilities, and often observed, that he possessed more extensive knowledge than any man of his years he had ever known. His industry was equal to his talents; and he particularly excelled in every species of philological learning, and was, perhaps, the best critick of the age he lived in.

'I must always remember with gratitude my obligation to Mr. Grierson, for the honour and happiness of Dr. Johnson's acquaintance and friendship, which continued uninterrupted and undiminished to his death: a connection, that was at once the pride and happiness of my life.

'What pity it is, that so much wit and good sense as he continually exhibited in conversation, should perish unrecorded! Few persons quitted his company without perceiving themselves wiser and better than they were before. On serious subjects he flashed the most interesting conviction upon his auditors; and upon lighter topicks, you might have supposed—*Albano musas de monte locutas.*[2]

'Though I can hope to add but little to the celebrity of so exalted a character, by any communications I can furnish, yet out of pure respect to his memory, I will venture to transmit to you some anecdotes concerning him, which fell under my own observation. The very *minutiæ* of such a character must be interesting, and may be compared to the filings of diamonds.

'In politicks he was deemed a Tory, but certainly was not so in the obnoxious or party sense of the term; for while he asserted the legal and salutary prerogatives of the crown, he no less respected the constitutional liberties of the people. Whiggism, at the time of the Revolution, he said, was accompanied with

---

[1] Son of the learned Mrs. Grierson, who was patronised by the late Lord Granville, and was the editor of several of the Classicks.

[2] [*Dictitet Albano* . . . 'They had come from the lips of the Muses on the Alban hill.' Horace, *Epistles,* ii. i. 26. (Wickham.)]

certain principles; but latterly, as a mere party distinction under Walpole and the Pelhams, was no better than the politicks of stock-jobbers, and the religion of infidels.

'He detested the idea of governing by parliamentary corruption, and asserted most strenuously, that a prince steadily and conspicuously pursuing the interests of his people, could not fail of parliamentary concurrence. A prince of ability, he contended, might and should be the directing soul and spirit of his own administration; in short, his own minister, and not the mere head of a party: and then, and not till then, would the royal dignity be sincerely respected.

'Johnson seemed to think, that a certain degree of crown influence over the Houses of Parliament, (not meaning a corrupt and shameful dependence,) was very salutary, nay, even necessary, in our mixed government. "For, (said he,) if the members were under no crown influence, and disqualified from receiving any gratification from Court, and resembled, as they possibly might, Pym and Haslerig, and other stubborn and sturdy members of the long Parliament, the wheels of government would be totally obstructed. Such men would oppose, merely to shew their power, from envy, jealousy, and perversity of disposition; and not gaining themselves, would hate and oppose all who did: not loving the person of the prince, and conceiving they owed him little gratitude, from the mere spirit of insolence and contradiction, they would oppose and thwart him upon all occasions."

'The inseparable imperfection annexed to all human governments consisted, he said, in not being able to create a sufficient fund of virtue and principle to carry the laws into due and effectual execution. Wisdom might plan, but virtue alone could execute. And where could sufficient virtue be found? A variety of delegated, and often discretionary, powers must be entrusted somewhere; which, if not governed by integrity and conscience, would necessarily be abused, till at last the constable would sell his for a shilling.

'This excellent person was sometimes charged with abetting slavish and arbitrary principles of government. Nothing in my opinion could be a grosser calumny and misrepresentation; for how can it be rationally supposed, that he should adopt such pernicious and absurd opinions, who supported his philosophical character with so much dignity, was extremely jealous of his personal liberty and independence, and could not brook the smallest appearance of neglect or insult, even from the highest personages?

'But let us view him in some instances of more familiar life.

'His general mode of life, during my acquaintance, seemed to be pretty uniform. About twelve o'clock I commonly visited him, and frequently found him in bed, or declaiming over his tea, which he drank very plentifully. He generally had a levee of morning visitors, chiefly men of letters; Hawkesworth, Goldsmith, Murphy, Langton, Steevens, Beauclerk, &c. &c., and sometimes learned ladies, particularly I remember a French lady[1] of wit and fashion doing him the honour of a visit. He seemed to me to be considered as a kind of publick oracle, whom every body thought they had a right to visit and consult; and doubtless they were well rewarded. I never could discover how he found time for his compositions. He declaimed all the morning, then went to dinner at a tavern, where he commonly staid late, and then drank his tea at some friend's house, over which he loitered a great while, but seldom took supper. I fancy he must have read and wrote chiefly in the night, for I can scarcely recollect that he ever refused going with me to a tavern, and he often went to Ranelagh, which he deemed a place of innocent recreation.

'He frequently gave all the silver in his pocket to the poor, who watched him, between his house and the tavern where he dined. He walked the streets at all hours, and said he was never robbed, for the rogues knew he had little money, nor had the appearance of having much.

'Though the most accessible and communicative man alive, yet when he suspected he was invited to be exhibited, he constantly spurned the invitation.

'Two young women from Staffordshire visited him when I was present, to consult him on the subject of Methodism, to which they were inclined. "Come, (said he,) you pretty fools, dine with Maxwell and me at the Mitre, and we will talk over

[1] [Mme de Boufflers. *Mrs. Piozzi*; *Croker*[1].]

that subject;' which they did, and after dinner he took one of
them upon his knee, and fondled her for half an hour together.

'Upon a visit to me at a country lodging near Twickenham,
he asked what sort of society I had there. I told him, but indifferent; as they chiefly consisted of opulent traders, retired from
business. He said, he never much liked that class of people; "For,
Sir, (said he,) they have lost the civility of tradesmen, without
acquiring the manners of gentlemen."

'Johnson was much attached to London: he observed, that a
man stored his mind better there, than any where else; and that
in remote situations a man's body might be feasted, but his mind
was starved, and his faculties apt to degenerate, from want of
exercise and competition. No place, (he said,) cured a man's
vanity or arrogance so well as London; for as no man was either
great or good *per se*, but as compared with others not so good or
great, he was sure to find in the metropolis many his equals, and
some his superiours. He observed, that a man in London was in
less danger of falling in love indiscreetly, than any where else;
for there the difficulty of deciding between the conflicting pretensions of a vast variety of objects, kept him safe. He told me,
that he had frequently been offered country preferment, if he
would consent to take orders; but he could not leave the improved society of the capital, or consent to exchange the ex-
hilarating joys and splendid decorations of publick life, for the
obscurity, insipidity, and uniformity of remote situations.

'Speaking of Mr. Harte, Canon of Windsor, and writer of *The
History of Gustavus Adolphus*, he much commended him as a
scholar, and a man of the most companionable talents he had
ever known. He said, the defects in his history proceeded not
from imbecility, but from foppery.

'He loved, he said, the old black letter books; they were rich
in matter, though their style was inelegant; wonderfully so, considering how conversant the writers were with the best models of
antiquity.

'Burton's *Anatomy of Melancholy*, he said, was the only book
that ever took him out of bed two hours sooner than he wished
to rise.

'He frequently exhorted me to set about writing a History of Ireland, and archly remarked, there had been some good Irish writers, and that one Irishman might at least aspire to be equal to another. He had great compassion for the miseries and distresses of the Irish nation, particularly the Papists; and severely reprobated the barbarous debilitating policy of the British government, which, he said, was the most detestable mode of persecution. To a gentleman, who hinted such policy might be necessary to support the authority of the English government, he replied by saying, "Let the authority of the English government perish, rather than be maintained by iniquity. Better would it be to restrain the turbulence of the natives by the authority of the sword, and to make them amenable to law and justice by an effectual and vigorous police, than to grind them to powder by all manner of disabilities and incapacities. Better (said he,) to hang or drown people at once, than by an unrelenting persecution to beggar and starve them." The moderation and humanity of the present times have, in some measure, justified the wisdom of his observations.

'Dr. Johnson was often accused of prejudices, nay, antipathy, with regard to the natives of Scotland. Surely, so illiberal a prejudice never entered his mind: and it is well known, many natives of that respectable country possessed a large share in his esteem; nor were any of them ever excluded from his good offices, as far as opportunity permitted. True it is, he considered the Scotch, nationally, as a crafty, designing people, eagerly attentive to their own interest, and too apt to overlook the claims and pretentions of other people. "While they confine their benevolence, in a manner, exclusively to those of their own country, they expect to share in the good offices of other people. Now (said Johnson,) this principle is either right or wrong; if right, we should do well to imitate such conduct; if wrong, we cannot too much detest it."

'Being solicited to compose a funeral sermon for the daughter of a tradesman, he naturally enquired into the character of the deceased; and being told she was remarkable for her humility and condescension to inferiours, he observed, that those were very laudable qualities, but it might not be so easy to discover who the lady's inferiours were.

'Of a certain player[1] he remarked, that his conversation usually threatened and announced more than it performed; that he fed you with a continual renovation of hope, to end in a constant succession of disappointment.

'When exasperated by contradiction, he was apt to treat his opponents with too much acrimony: as, "Sir, you don't see your way through that question:"—"Sir, you talk the language of ignorance." On my observing to him that a certain gentleman had remained silent the whole evening, in the midst of a very brilliant and learned society, "Sir, (said he,) the conversation overflowed, and drowned him."

'His philosophy, though austere and solemn, was by no means morose and cynical, and never blunted the laudable sensibilities of his character, or exempted him from the influence of the tender passions. Want of tenderness, he always alledged, was want of parts, and was no less a proof of stupidity than depravity.

'Speaking of Mr. Hanway, who published *An Eight Days' Journey from London to Portsmouth*, "Jonas, (said he,) acquired some reputation by travelling abroad, but lost it all by travelling at home."

'Of the passion of love he remarked, that its violence and ill effects were much exaggerated; for who knows any real sufferings on that head, more than from the exorbitancy of any other passion?

'He much commended Law's *Serious Call*, which he said was the finest piece of hortatory theology in any language. "Law, (said he,) fell latterly into the reveries of Jacob Behmen, whom Law alledged to have been somewhat in the same state with St. Paul, and to have seen *unutterable things*. Were it even so, (said Johnson,) Jacob would have resembled St. Paul still more, by not attempting to utter them."

'He observed, that the established clergy in general did not preach plain enough; and that polished periods and glittering sentences flew over the heads of the common people, without any

---

[1] [Thomas Sheridan. *Works* (1787); *Croker*[1].]

impression upon their hearts. Something might be necessary, he observed, to excite the affections of the common people, who were sunk in languor and lethargy, and therefore he supposed that the new concomitants of methodism might probably produce so desirable an effect. The mind, like the body, he observed, delighted in change and novelty, and even in religion itself, courted new appearances and modifications. Whatever might be thought of some methodist teachers, he said, he could scarcely doubt the sincerity of that man, who travelled nine hundred miles in a month, and preached twelve times a week; for no adequate reward, merely temporal, could be given for such indefatigable labour.

'Of Dr. Priestley's theological works, he remarked, that they tended to unsettle every thing, and yet settled nothing.

'He was much affected by the death of his mother, and wrote to me to come and assist him to compose his mind, which indeed I found extremely agitated. He lamented that all serious and religious conversation was banished from the society of men, and yet great advantages might be derived from it. All acknowledged, he said, what hardly any body practised, the obligation we were under of making the concerns of eternity the governing principles of our lives. Every man, he observed, at last wishes for retreat: he sees his expectations frustrated in the world, and begins to wean himself from it, and to prepare for everlasting separation.

'He observed, that the influence of London now extended every where, and that from all manner of communication being opened, there shortly would be no remains of the ancient simplicity, or places of cheap retreat to be found.

'He was no admirer of blank-verse, and said it always failed, unless sustained by the dignity of the subject. In blank-verse, he said, the language suffered more distortion, to keep it out of prose, than any inconvenience or limitation to be apprehended from the shackles and circumscription of rhyme.

'He reproved me once for saying grace without mention of the name of our LORD JESUS CHRIST, and hoped in future I would be more mindful of the apostolical injunction.

'He refused to go out of a room before me at Mr. Langton's house, saying, he hoped he knew his rank better than to presume to take place of a Doctor in Divinity. I mention such little anecdotes, merely to shew the peculiar turn and habit of his mind.

'He used frequently to observe, that there was more to be endured than enjoyed, in the general condition of human life; and frequently quoted those lines of Dryden:

"Strange cozenage! none would live past years again,
    Yet all hope pleasure from what still remain."

For his part, he said, he never passed that week in his life which he would wish to repeat, were an angel to make the proposal to him.

'He was of opinion, that the English nation cultivated both their soil and their reason better than any other people: but admitted that the French, though not the highest, perhaps, in any department of literature, yet in every department were very high. Intellectual pre-eminence, he observed, was the highest superiority; and that every nation derived their highest reputation from the splendour and dignity of their writers. Voltaire, he said, was a good narrator, and that his principal merit consisted in a happy selection and arrangement of circumstances.

'Speaking of the French novels, compared with Richardson's, he said, they might be pretty baubles, but a wren was not an eagle.

'In a Latin conversation with the Père Boscovitch, at the house of Mrs. Cholmondeley, I heard him maintain the superiority of Sir Isaac Newton over all foreign philosophers,[1] with a dignity and eloquence that surprized that learned foreigner. It being observed to him, that a rage for every thing English prevailed much in France after Lord Chatham's glorious war, he said, he did not wonder at it, for that we had drubbed those fellows into a proper reverence for us, and that their national petulance required periodical chastisement.

[1] In a Discourse by Sir William Jones, addressed to the Asiatick Society [in Calcutta], Feb. 24, 1785, is the following passage:—'One of the most sagacious men in this age who continues, I hope, to improve and adorn it, Samuel Johnson [he had been dead ten weeks], remarked in my hearing, that if Newton had flourished in ancient Greece, he would have been worshipped as a Divinity.' [M.]

'Lord Lyttelton's Dialogues he deemed a nugatory performance. "That man, (said he,) sat down to write a book, to tell
the world what the world had all his life been telling him."

'Somebody observing that the Scotch Highlanders, in the year
1745, had made surprising efforts, considering their numerous
wants and disadvantages: "Yes, Sir, (said he,) their wants were
numerous; but you have not mentioned the greatest of them all,
—the want of law."

'Speaking of the *inward light*, to which some methodists pretended, he said, it was a principle utterly incompatible with social
or civil security. "If a man (said he,) pretends to a principle of
action of which I can know nothing, nay, not so much as that he
has it, but only that he pretends to it; how can I tell what that
person may be prompted to do? When a person professes to be
governed by a written ascertained law, I can then know where
to find him."

'The poem of *Fingal*, he said, was a mere unconnected rhapsody, a tiresome repetition of the same images. "In vain shall
we look for the *lucidus ordo*,[1] where there is neither end or object,
design or moral, *nec certa recurrit imago*."[2]

'Being asked by a young nobleman, what was become of the
gallantry and military spirit of the old English nobility, he
replied, "Why, my Lord, I'll tell you what is become of it; it is
gone into the city to look for a fortune."

'Speaking of a dull tiresome fellow, whom he chanced to meet,
he said, "That fellow seems to me to possess but one idea, and
that is a wrong one."

'Much enquiry having been made concerning a gentleman,
who had quitted a company where Johnson was, and no information being obtained; at last Johnson observed, that "he did not
care to speak ill of any man behind his back, but he believed the
gentleman was an *attorney*."

'He spoke with much contempt of the notice taken of Woodhouse, the poetical shoemaker. He said, it was all vanity and
childishness: and that such objects were, to those who patronised

[1] ['clearness of order'. Horace, *Ars Poetica*, l. 41.]
[2] ['no definite image recurs'.]

them, mere mirrours of their own superiority. "They had better (said he,) furnish the man with good implements for his trade, than raise subscriptions for his poems. He may make an excellent shoemaker, but can never make a good poet. A school-boy's exercise may be a pretty thing for a school-boy; but is no treat for a man."

'Speaking of Boetius, who was the favourite writer of the middle ages, he said it was very surprizing, that upon such a subject, and in such a situation, he should be *magis philosophus quam Christianus.*[1]

'Speaking of Arthur Murphy, whom he very much loved, "I don't know (said he,) that Arthur can be classed with the very first dramatick writers; yet at present I doubt much whether we have any thing superiour to Arthur."

'Speaking of the national debt, he said, it was an idle dream to suppose that the country could sink under it. Let the public creditors be ever so clamorous, the interest of millions must ever prevail over that of thousands.

'Of Dr. Kennicott's Collations, he observed, that though the text should not be much mended thereby, yet it was no small advantage to know, that we had as good a text as the most consummate industry and diligence could procure.

'Johnson observed, that so many objections might be made to every thing, that nothing could overcome them but the necessity of doing something. No man would be of any profession, as simply opposed to not being of it: but every one must do something.

'He remarked, that a London parish was a very comfortless thing; for the clergyman seldom knew the face of one out of ten of his parishioners.

'Of the late Mr. Mallet he spoke with no great respect: said, he was ready for any dirty job: that he had written against Byng at the instigation of the ministry, and was equally ready to write for him, provided he found his account in it.

'A gentleman who had been very unhappy in marriage, married immediately after his wife died: Johnson said, it was the triumph of hope over experience.

[1] ['more of a philosopher than of a Christian.']

'He observed, that a man of sense and education should meet a suitable companion in a wife. It was a miserable thing when the conversation could only be such as, whether the mutton should be boiled or roasted, and probably a dispute about that.

'He did not approve of late marriages, observing, that more was lost in point of time, than compensated for by any possible advantages. Even ill assorted marriages were preferable to cheerless celibacy.

'Of old Sheridan he remarked, that he neither wanted parts nor literature; but that his vanity and Quixotism obscured his merits.

'He said, foppery was never cured; it was the bad stamina of the mind, which, like those of the body, were never rectified: once a coxcomb, and always a coxcomb.

'Being told that Gilbert Cowper called him the Caliban of literature; "Well, (said he,) I must dub him the Punchinello."

'Speaking of the old Earl of Corke and Orrery, he said, "that man spent his life in catching at an object, [literary eminence,] which he had not power to grasp."

'To find a substitution for violated morality, he said, was the leading feature in all perversions of religion.'

'He often used to quote, with great pathos, those fine lines of Virgil:

> *"Optima quæque dies miseris mortalibus ævi*
> *Prima fugit; subeunt morbi, tristisque senectus,*
> *Et labor, et duræ rapit inclementia mortis."*[1]

'Speaking of Homer, whom he venerated as the prince of poets, Johnson remarked that the advice given to Diomed by his father, when he sent him to the Trojan war, was the noblest exhortation that could be instanced in any heathen writer, and comprised in a single line:

> Αἰὲν ἀριστεύειν, καὶ ὑπείροχον ἔμμεναι ἄλλων·[2]

---

[1] ['It is ever the brightest day of life that is first to bid adieu to our hapless mortality: disease and gloomy eld steal upon us, and anon suffering, and the ruthless tyranny of death, sweep us away.' *Georgics*, iii. 66. (Jackson.)]

[2] ['Be ever best and o'ertop other men.' *Iliad*, vi. 208. (Marris.)]

which, if I recollect well, is translated by Dr. Clarke thus: *semper appetere præstantissima, et omnibus aliis antecellere.*

'He observed, "it was a most mortifying reflexion for any man to consider, *what he had done*, compared with what *he might have done*."

'He said few people had intellectual resources sufficient to forego the pleasures of wine. They could not otherwise contrive how to fill the interval between dinner and supper.

'He went with me, one Sunday, to hear my old Master, Gregory Sharpe, preach at the Temple. In the prefatory prayer, Sharpe ranted about *Liberty*, as a blessing most fervently to be implored, and its continuance prayed for. Johnson observed, that our *liberty* was in no sort of danger:—he would have done much better, to pray against our *licentiousness.*

'One evening at Mrs. Montagu's, where a splendid company was assembled, consisting of the most eminent literary characters, I thought he seemed highly pleased with the respect and attention that were shewn him, and asked him on our return home if he was not highly *gratified* by his visit: "No, Sir, (said he,) not highly *gratified*; yet I do not recollect to have passed many evenings *with fewer objections.*"

'Though of no high extraction himself, he had much respect for birth and family, especially among ladies. He said, "adventitious accomplishments may be possessed by all ranks; but one may easily distinguish the *born gentlewoman.*"

'He said, "the poor in England were better provided for, than in any other country of the same extent: he did not mean little Cantons, or petty Republicks. Where a great proportion of the people (said he,) are suffered to languish in helpless misery, that country must be ill policed, and wretchedly governed: a decent provision for the poor is the true test of civilization.— Gentlemen of education, he observed, were pretty much the same in all countries; the condition of the lower orders, the poor especially, was the true mark of national discrimination."

'When the corn laws were in agitation in Ireland, by which that country has been enabled not only to feed itself, but to export corn to a large amount; Sir Thomas Robinson observed, that those laws might be prejudicial to the corn-trade of England. "Sir Thomas, (said he,) you talk the language of a savage: what, Sir? would you prevent any people from feeding themselves, if by any honest means they can do it?"

'It being mentioned, that Garrick assisted Dr. Brown, the authour of the *Estimate*, in some dramatick composition, "No, Sir, (said Johnson,) he would no more suffer Garrick to write a line in his play, than he would suffer him to mount his pulpit."

'Speaking of Burke, he said, "It was commonly observed, he spoke too often in parliament; but nobody could say he did not speak well, though too frequently and too familiarly."

'Speaking of economy, he remarked, it was hardly worth while to save anxiously twenty pounds a year. If a man could save to that degree, so as to enable him to assume a different rank in society, then indeed, it might answer some purpose.

'He observed, a principal source of erroneous judgement was, viewing things partially and only on *one side*: as for instance, *fortune-hunters*, when they contemplated the fortunes *singly* and *separately*, it was a dazzling and tempting object; but when they came to possess the wives and their fortunes *together*, they began to suspect that they had not made quite so good a bargain.

'Speaking of the late Duke of Northumberland living very magnificently when Lord Lieutenant of Ireland, somebody remarked it would be difficult to find a suitable successor to him: then exclaimed Johnson, *he is only fit to succeed himself*.

'He advised me, if possible, to have a good orchard. He knew, he said, a clergyman of small income, who brought up a family very reputably which he chiefly fed with apple dumplins.

'He said, he had known several good scholars among the Irish gentlemen; but scarcely any of them correct in *quantity*. He extended the same observation to Scotland.

'Speaking of a certain Prelate,[1] who exerted himself very laudably in building churches and parsonage-houses; "however, said he, I do not find that he is esteemed a man of much professional learning, or a liberal patron of it;—yet, it is well, where a man possesses any strong positive excellence.—Few have all

---

[1] [Perhaps Dr. R. Robinson, Abp. of Armagh. *Croker*[1].]

kinds of merit belonging to their character. We must not examine matters too deeply—No, Sir, a *fallible being will fail some-where.*"

'Talking of the Irish clergy, he said, Swift was a man of great parts, and the instrument of much good to his country.—Berkeley was a profound scholar, as well as a man of fine imagination; but Usher, he said, was the great luminary of the Irish church; and a greater, he added, no church could boast of; at least in modern times.

'We dined *tête à tête* at the Mitre, as I was preparing to return to Ireland, after an absence of many years. I regretted much leaving London, where I had formed many agreeable connexions: "Sir, (said he,) I don't wonder at it; no man, fond of letters, leaves London without regret. But remember, Sir, you have seen and enjoyed a great deal;—you have seen life in its highest decorations, and the world has nothing new to exhibit. No man is so well qualifyed to leave publick life as he who has long tried it and known it well. We are always hankering after untried situations, and imagining greater felicity from them than they can afford. No, Sir, knowledge and virtue may be acquired in all countries, and your local consequence will make you some amends for the intellectual gratifications you relinquish." Then he quoted the following lines with great pathos:—

> "He who has early known the pomps of state,
> (For things unknown, 'tis ignorance to condemn;)
> And after having viewed the gaudy bait,
> Can boldly say, the trifle I contemn;
> With such a one contented could I live,
> Contented could I die;"—[1]

[1] These lines have been discovered by the author's second son in the *London Magazine* for July, 1732, where they form part of a poem on *Retirement*, copied, with some slight variations, from one of Walsh's smaller poems, entitled *The Retirement.* They exhibit another proof that Johnson retained in his memory fragments of neglected poetry. In quoting verses of that description, he appears by a slight variation to have sometimes given them a moral turn, and to have dexterously adapted them to his own senti-ments, where the original had a very different tendency. In 1782, when he was at Brighthelmstone, he repeated to Mr. Metcalfe, some verses, as very characteristick of a celebrated historian [Gibbon. *Mrs. Piozzi*; *Croker*[2]]. They are found among some anonymous poems appended to the second volume

'He then took a m⁰ st affecting leave of me; said, he knew, it was a point of *duty* that called me away. "We shall all be sorry to lose you," said he: *"laudo tamen."* '[1]

1771: ÆTAT. 6 .]—IN 1771 he published another political pamphlet, entitled *Thoughts on the late Transactions respecting Falkland's Islands*, in which, upon materials furnished to him by ministry, and upon general topicks expanded in his richest style, he successfully endeavoured to persuade the nation that it was wise and laudable to suffer the question of right to remain undecided, rather than involve our country in another war. It has been suggested by some, with what truth I shall not take upon me to decide, that he rated the consequence of those islands to Great-Britain too low. But however this may be, every humane mind must surely applaud the earnestness with which he averted the calamity of war; a calamity so dreadful, that it is astonishing how civilised, nay, Christian nations, can deliberately continue to renew it. His description of its miseries in this pamphlet, is one of the finest pieces of eloquence in the English language. Upon this occasion, too, we find Johnson lashing the party in opposition with unbounded severity, and making the fullest use of what he ever reckoned a most effectual argumentative instrument,—contempt. His character of their very able mysterious champion, JUNIUS, is executed with all the force of his genius, and finished with the highest care. He seems to have exulted in

of a collection frequently printed by Lintot, under the title of *Pope's Miscellanies*:—

'See how the wand'ring Danube flows,
    Realms and religions parting;
A friend to all true christian foes,
    To Peter, Jack, and Martin.
Now Protestant, and Papist now,
    Not constant long to either,
At length an infidel does grow,
    And ends his journey neither.
Thus many a youth I've known set out,
    Half Protestant, half Papist,
And rambling long the world about,
    Turn infidel or atheist.'   [M.]

[1] [See p. 231, note 1.]

sallying forth to single combat against the boasted and formidable hero, who bade defiance to 'principalities and powers, and
the rulers of this world.'

This pamphlet, it is observable, was softened in one particular,
after the first edition; for the conclusion of Mr. George Gren-
ville's character stood thus: 'Let him not, however, be depreciated in his grave. He had powers not universally possessed:
could he have enforced payment of the Manilla ransom, *he could
have counted it.*' Which, instead of retaining its sly sharp point,
was reduced to a mere flat unmeaning expression, or, if I may
use the word,—*truism*: 'He had powers not universally possessed: and if he sometimes erred, he was likewise sometimes
right.'

'*To* BENNET LANGTON, ESQ.

'DEAR SIR,—After much lingering of my own, and much of
the ministry, I have at length got out my paper.[1] But delay is
not yet at an end: Not many had been dispersed, before Lord
North ordered the sale to stop. His reasons I do not distinctly
know. You may try to find them in the perusal.[2] Before his order,
a sufficient number were dispersed to do all the mischief, though,
perhaps, not to make all the sport that might be expected from it.

'Soon after your departure, I had the pleasure of finding all
the danger past with which your navigation was threatened. I
hope nothing happens at home to abate your satisfaction; but
that Lady Rothes, and Mrs. Langton, and the young ladies, are
all well.

'I was last night at THE CLUB. Dr. Percy has written a long
ballad in many *fits*; it is pretty enough. He has printed, and will
soon publish it. Goldsmith is at Bath, with Lord Clare. At Mr.
Thrale's, where I am now writing, all are well. I am, dear Sir,
your most humble servant,

'March 20, 1771.'   'SAM. JOHNSON.'

---

[1] *Thoughts on the late Transactions respecting Falkland's Islands.*
[2] By comparing the first with the subsequent editions, this curious circumstance of ministerial authorship may be discovered.

Mr. Strahan, the printer, who had been long in intimacy with Johnson, in the course of his literary labours, who was at once his friendly agent in receiving his pension for him, and his banker in supplying him with money when he wanted it; who was himself now a Member of Parliament, and who loved much to be employed in political negociation; thought he should do eminent service both to government and Johnson, if he could be the means of his getting a seat in the House of Commons. With this view, he wrote a letter to one of the Secretaries of the Treasury,[1] of which he gave me a copy in his own hand-writing, which is as follows:—

'SIR,—You will easily recollect, when I had the honour of waiting upon you some time ago, I took the liberty to observe to you, that Dr. Johnson would make an excellent figure in the House of Commons, and heartily wished he had a seat there. My reasons are briefly these:

'I know his perfect good affection to his Majesty, and his government, which I am certain he wishes to support by every means in his power.

'He possesses a great share of manly, nervous, and ready eloquence; is quick in discerning the strength and weakness of an argument; can express himself with clearness and precision, and fears the face of no man alive.

'His known character, as a man of extraordinary sense and unimpeached virtue, would secure him the attention of the House, and could not fail to give him a proper weight there.

'He is capable of the greatest application, and can undergo any degree of labour, where he sees it necessary, and where his heart and affections are strongly engaged. His Majesty's ministers might therefore securely depend on his doing, upon every proper occasion, the utmost that could be expected from him. They would find him ready to vindicate such measures as tended to promote the stability of government, and resolute and steady in carrying them into execution. Nor is any thing to be apprehended from the supposed impetuosity of his temper. To the friends of the King you will find him a lamb, to his enemies a lion.

[1] [Either Sir Grey Cooper or John Robinson. *Powell.*]

'For these reasons, I humbly apprehend that he would be a very able and useful member. And I will venture to say, the employment would not be disagreeable to him; and knowing, as I do, his strong affection to the King, his ability to serve him in that capacity, and the extreme ardour with which I am convinced he would engage in that service, I must repeat, that I wish most heartily to see him in the House.

'If you think this worthy of attention, you will be pleased to take a convenient opportunity of mentioning it to Lord North. If his Lordship should happily approve of it, I shall have the satisfaction of having been, in some degree, the humble instrument of doing my country, in my opinion, a very essential service. I know your good-nature, and your zeal for the publick welfare, will plead my excuse for giving you this trouble. I am, with the greatest respect, Sir, your most obedient and humble servant,

'New-street, March 30, 1771.'   'WILLIAM STRAHAN.'

This recommendation, we know, was not effectual; but how, or for what reason, can only be conjectured. It is not to be believed that Mr. Strahan would have applied, unless Johnson had approved of it. I never heard him mention the subject; but at a later period of his life, when Sir Joshua Reynolds told him that Mr. Edmund Burke had said, that if he had come early into parliament, he certainly would have been the greatest speaker that ever was there, Johnson exclaimed, 'I should like to try my hand now.'

It has been much agitated among his friends and others, whether he would have been a powerful speaker in Parliament, had he been brought in when advanced in life. I am inclined to think that his extensive knowledge, his quickness and force of mind, his vivacity and richness of expression, his wit and humour, and above all his poignancy of sarcasm, would have had great effect in a popular assembly; and that the magnitude of his figure, and striking peculiarity of his manner, would have aided the effect. But I remember it was observed by Mr. Flood, that Johnson, having been long used to sententious brevity and the short flights of conversation, might have failed in that continued and expanded kind of argument, which is requisite in stating complicated matters in publick speaking; and as a proof of this he mentioned the supposed speeches in Parliament written by him for the magazine, none of which, in his opinion, were at all like real debates. The opinion of one who was himself so eminent an orator, must be allowed to have great weight. It was confirmed by Sir William Scott, who mentioned that Johnson had told him that he had several times tried to speak in the Society of Arts and Sciences, but 'had found he could not get on.' From Mr. William Gerrard Hamilton I have heard that Johnson, when observing to him that it was prudent for a man who had not been accustomed to speak in publick, to begin his speech in as simple a manner as possible, acknowledged that he rose in that society to deliver a speech which he had prepared; 'but (said he,) all my flowers of oratory forsook me.' I however cannot help wishing, that he *had* 'tried his hand' in Parliament; and I wonder that ministry did not make the experiment.

I at length renewed a correspondence which had been too long discontinued:—

'*To* DR. JOHNSON

 'My DEAR SIR,   'Edinburgh, April 18, 1771.

 'I can now fully understand those intervals of silence in your correspondence with me, which have often given me anxiety and uneasiness; for although I am conscious that my veneration and love for Mr. Johnson have never in the least abated, yet I have deferred for almost a year and a half to write to him.' . . .

In the subsequent part of this letter, I gave him an account of my comfortable life as a married man, and a lawyer in practice at the Scotch bar; invited him to Scotland, and promised to attend him to the Highlands, and Hebrides.

'*To* JAMES BOSWELL, ESQ.

 'DEAR SIR,—If you are now able to comprehend that I might

neglect to write without diminution of affection, you have taught
me, likewise, how that neglect may be uneasily felt without
resentment. I wished for your letter a long time, and when it
came, it amply recompensed the delay. I never was so much
pleased as now with your account of yourself; and sincerely hope,
that between publick business, improving studies, and domestick
pleasures, neither melancholy nor caprice will find any place for
entrance. Whatever philosophy may determine of material
nature, it is certainly true of intellectual nature, that it *abhors a
vacuum*: our minds cannot be empty; and evil will break in upon
them, if they are not pre-occupied by good. My dear Sir, mind
your studies, mind your business, make your lady happy, and be
a good Christian. After this,

> "——————— *tristitiam et metus*
> *Trades protervis in mare Creticum*
> *Portare ventis.*"[1]

'If we perform our duty, we shall be safe and steady, *"Sive
per,"* &c.,[2] whether we climb the Highlands, or are tost among
the Hebrides; and I hope the time will come when we may try
our powers both with cliffs and water. I see but little of Lord
Elibank, I know not why; perhaps by my own fault. I am this
day going into Staffordshire and Derbyshire for six weeks. I am,
dear Sir, your most affectionate, and most humble servant,

'London, June 20, 1771.'   'SAM. JOHNSON.'

'*To* SIR JOSHUA REYNOLDS, *in Leicester-fields*

'DEAR SIR,—When I came to Lichfield, I found that my portrait had been much visited, and much admired. Every man has
a lurking wish to appear considerable in his native place; and I
was pleased with the dignity conferred by such a testimony of
your regard.

---

[1] ['Sadness and fears I will commit to the wild winds to take with them
to the Cretan sea.' Horace, *Odes*, I. xxvi. 1. (Wickham.)]
[2] [*Sive per Syrtis iter aestuosas . . . facturus &c.,* 'whether he be going to
make his way through the surf of the Syrtes, or . .' Horace, *Odes* I. xxii. 5.
(Wickham.)]

'Be pleased, therefore, to accept the thanks of, Sir, your most obliged and most humble servant,

'Ashbourn in Derbyshire,   'SAM. JOHNSON.'
    July 17, 1771.'
'Compliments to Miss Reynolds.'

'*To* DR. JOHNSON

'MY DEAR SIR,   'Edinburgh, July 27, 1771.

'The bearer of this, Mr. Beattie, Professor of Moral Philosophy at Aberdeen, is desirous of being introduced to your acquaintance. His genius and learning, and labours in the service of virtue and religion, render him very worthy of it; and as he has a high esteem of your character, I hope you will give him a favourable reception. I ever am, &c.

'JAMES BOSWELL.'

'*To* BENNET LANGTON, ESQ., *at Langton, near Spilsby, Lincolnshire*

'DEAR SIR,—I am lately returned from Staffordshire and Derbyshire. The last letter mentions two others which you have written to me since you received my pamphlet. Of these two I never had but one, in which you mentioned a design of visiting Scotland, and, by consequence, put my journey to Langton out of my thoughts. My summer wanderings are now over, and I am engaging in a very great work, the revision of my *Dictionary*; from which I know not, at present, how to get loose.

'If you have observed, or been told, any errours or omissions, you will do me a great favour by letting me know them.

'Lady Rothes, I find, has disappointed you and herself. Ladies will have these tricks. The Queen and Mrs. Thrale, both ladies of experience, yet both missed their reckoning this summer. I hope, a few months will recompence your uneasiness.

'Please to tell Lady Rothes how highly I value the honour of her invitation, which it is my purpose to obey as soon as I have disengaged myself. In the mean time I shall hope to hear often of her Ladyship, and every day better news and better, till I hear

that you have both the happiness, which to both is very sincerely
wished, by, Sir, your most affectionate, and most humble servant,
'August 29, 1771.'   'SAM. JOHNSON.'

In October I again wrote to him, thanking him for his last
letter, and his obliging reception of Mr. Beattie; informing him
that I had been at Alnwick lately, and had good accounts of him
from Dr. Percy.

In his religious record of this year, we observe that he was
better than usual, both in body and mind, and better satisfied
with the regularity of his conduct. But he is still 'trying his ways'
too rigorously. He charges himself with not rising early enough;
yet he mentions what was surely a sufficient excuse for this, supposing it to be a duty seriously required, as he all his life appears
to have thought it. 'One great hindrance is want of rest; my
nocturnal complaints grow less troublesome towards morning;
and I am tempted to repair the deficiencies of the night.'[1] Alas!
how hard would it be if this indulgence were to be imputed to a
sick man as a crime. In his retrospect on the following Easter-
Eve, he says, 'When I review the last year, I am able to recollect
so little done, that shame and sorrow, though perhaps too
weakly, come upon me.' Had he been judging of any one else in
the same circumstances, how clear would he have been on the
favourable side. How very difficult, and in my opinion almost
constitutionally impossible it was for him to be raised early, even
by the strongest resolutions, appears from a note in one of his
little paper-books, (containing words arranged for his *Dictionary*,) written, I suppose, about 1753: 'I do not remember
that since I left Oxford I ever rose early by mere choice, but
once or twice at Edial, and two or three times for the *Rambler*.'
I think he had fair ground enough to have quieted his mind on
this subject, by concluding that he was physically incapable of
what is at best but a commodious regulation.

In 1772 he was altogether quiescent as an authour; but it will
be found from the various evidences which I shall bring together
that his mind was acute, lively, and vigorous.

[1] *Pr. and Med.* p. 101 [105].

'*To* Sir Joshua Reynolds

'Dear Sir,—Be pleased to send to Mr. Banks, whose place of residence I do not know, this note, which I have sent open, that, if you please, you may read it.

'When you send[1] it, do not use your own seal. I am, Sir, your most humble servant,

'Feb. 27, 1772.'   'Sam. Johnson'

'*To* Joseph Banks, Esq.

"*Perpetua*[2] *ambitâ bis terrâ præmia lactis*
Hæc habet altrici Capra secunda Jovis."[3]

'Sir,—I return thanks to you and to Dr. Solander for the pleasure which I received in yesterday's conversation. I could not recollect a motto for your Goat, but have given her one. You, Sir, may perhaps have an epick poem from some happier pen than, Sir, your most humble servant,

'Johnson's-court, Fleet-street,   'Sam. Johnson.'
    February 27, 1772.'

'*To* Dr. Johnson

'My Dear Sir,   'Edinburgh, March 3, 1772.

'It is hard that I cannot prevail on you to write to me oftener. But I am convinced that it is in vain to expect from you a private correspondence with any regularity. I must, therefore, look upon you as a fountain of wisdom, from whence few rills are communicated to a distance, and which must be approached at its source, to partake fully of its virtues. . . .

'I am coming to London soon, and am to appear in an appeal from the Court of Session in the House of Lords. A schoolmaster in Scotland was, by a court of inferiour jurisdiction, deprived of

---

[1] [Johnson wrote *seal*.]
[2] [Johnson wrote *Perpetui*.]
[3] Thus translated by a friend:—

'In fame scarce second to the nurse of Jove,
This Goat, who twice the world had traversed round,
Deserving both her master's care and love,
Ease and perpetual pasture now has found.'

457

his office, for being somewhat severe in the chastisement of his scholars. The Court of Session, considering it to be dangerous to the interest of learning and education, to lessen the dignity of teachers, and make them afraid of too indulgent parents, instigated by the complaints of their children, restored him. His enemies have appealed to the House of Lords, though the salary is only twenty pounds a year. I was Counsel for him here. I hope there will be little fear of a reversal; but I must beg to have your aid in my plan of supporting the decree. It is a general question, and not a point of particular law. . . . I am, &c.,

'JAMES BOSWELL.'

'*To* JAMES BOSWELL, ESQ.

'DEAR SIR,—That you are coming so soon to town I am very glad; and still more glad that you are coming as an advocate. I think nothing more likely to make your life pass happily away, than that consciousness of your own value, which eminence in your profession will certainly confer. If I can give you any collateral help, I hope you do not suspect that it will be wanting. My kindness for you has neither the merit of singular virtue, nor the reproach of singular prejudice. Whether to love you be right or wrong, I have many on my side: Mrs. Thrale loves you, and Mrs. Williams loves you, and what would have inclined me to love you, if I had been neutral before, you are a great favourite of Dr. Beattie.

'Of Dr. Beattie I should have thought much, but that his lady puts him out of my head; she is a very lovely woman.

'The ejection which you come hither to oppose, appears very cruel, unreasonable, and oppressive. I should think there could not be much doubt of your success.

'My health grows better, yet I am not fully recovered. I believe it is held, that men do not recover very fast after three-score. I hope yet to see Beattie's College: and have not given up the western voyage. But however all this may be or not, let us try to make each other happy when we meet, and not refer our pleasure to distant times or distant places.

'How comes it that you tell me nothing of your lady? I hope to see her some time, and till then shall be glad to hear of her. I am, dear Sir, &c.

'March 15, 1772.'   'SAM. JOHNSON.'

'*To* BENNET LANGTON, ESQ., *near Spilsby, Lincolnshire*

'DEAR SIR,—I congratulate you and Lady Rothes[1] on your little man, and hope you will all be many years happy together.

'Poor Miss Langton can have little part in the joy of her family. She this day called her aunt Langton to receive the sacrament with her; and made me talk yesterday on such subjects as suit her condition. It will probably be her *viaticum*. I surely need not mention again that she wishes to see her mother. I am, Sir, your most humble servant,

'March 14, 1772.'   'SAM. JOHNSON.'

On the 21st of March, I was happy to find myself again in my friend's study, and was glad to see my old acquaintance, Mr. Francis Barber, who was now returned home. Dr. Johnson received me with a hearty welcome; saying, 'I am glad you are come, and glad you are come upon such an errand:' (alluding to the cause of the schoolmaster.) BOSWELL. 'I hope, Sir, he will be in no danger. It is a very delicate matter to interfere between a master and his scholars: nor do I see how you can fix the degree of severity that a master may use.' JOHNSON. 'Why, Sir, till you can fix the degree of obstinacy and negligence of the scholars, you cannot fix the degree of severity of the master. Severity must be continued until obstinacy be subdued, and negligence be cured.' He mentioned the severity of Hunter, his own Master. 'Sir, (said I,) Hunter is a Scotch name: so it should seem this schoolmaster who beat you so severely was a Scotchman. I can now account for your prejudice against the Scotch.' JOHNSON. 'Sir, he was not Scotch; and abating his brutality, he was a very good master.'

We talked of his two political pamphlets, *The False Alarm*, and *Thoughts concerning Falkland's Islands*. JOHNSON. 'Well, Sir, which of them did you think the best?' BOSWELL. 'I liked

[1] Mr. Langton married the Countess Dowager of Rothes.

the second best.' JOHNSON. 'Why, Sir, I liked the first best; and
Beattie liked the first best. Sir, there is a subtlety of disquisition
in the first, that is worth all the fire of the second.' BOSWELL.
Pray, Sir, is it true that Lord North paid you a visit, and that
you got two hundred a year in addition to your pension?' JOHN-
SON. 'No, Sir. Except what I had from the bookseller, I did not
get a farthing by them. And, between you and me, I believe Lord
North is no friend to me.' BOSWELL. 'How so, Sir?' JOHNSON.
'Why, Sir, you cannot account for the fancies of men. Well, how
does Lord Elibank? and how does Lord Monboddo?' BOSWELL.
'Very well, Sir. Lord Monboddo still maintains the superiority
of the savage life.' JOHNSON. 'What strange narrowness of
mind now is that, to think the things we have not known, are
better than the things which we have known.' BOSWELL. 'Why,
Sir, that is a common prejudice.' JOHNSON. 'Yes, Sir; but a
common prejudice should not be found in one whose trade it is
to rectify errour.'

A gentleman having come in who was to go as a mate in the
ship along with Mr. Banks and Dr. Solander, Dr. Johnson asked
what were the names of the ships destined for the expedition.
The gentleman answered, they were once to be called the Drake
and the Ralegh, but now they were to be called the Resolution
and the Adventure. JOHNSON. 'Much better; for had the Ralegh
returned without going round the world, it would have been
ridiculous. To give them the names of the Drake and the Ralegh
was laying a trap for satire.' BOSWELL. 'Had not you some
desire to go upon this expedition, Sir?' JOHNSON. 'Why yes,
but I soon laid it aside. Sir, there is very little of intellectual, in
the course. Besides, I see but at a small distance. So it was not
worth my while to go to see birds fly, which I should not have
seen fly; and fishes swim, which I should not have seen swim.'

The gentleman being gone, and Dr. Johnson having left the
room for some time, a debate arose between the Reverend Mr.
Stockdale and Mrs. Desmoulins, whether Mr. Banks and Dr.
Solander were entitled to any share of glory from their expedition. When Dr. Johnson returned to us, I told him the subject
of their dispute. JOHNSON. 'Why, Sir, it was properly for botany

that they went out: I believe they thought only of culling of simples.'

I thanked him for showing civilities to Beattie. 'Sir, (said he,) I should thank *you.* We all love Beattie. Mrs. Thrale says, if ever she has another husband, she'll have Beattie. He sunk upon us[1] that he was married; else we should have shewn his lady more civilities. She is a very fine woman. But how can you shew civilities to a nonentity? I did not think he had been married. Nay, I did not think about it one way or other; but he did not tell us of his lady till late.'

He then spoke of St. Kilda, the most remote of the Hebrides. I told him, I thought of buying it. JOHNSON. 'Pray do, Sir. We will go and pass a winter amid the blasts there. We shall have fine fish, and we will take some dried tongues with us, and some books. We will have a strong built vessel, and some Orkney men to navigate her. We must build a tolerable house:

[1] 'TO JAMES BOSWELL, ESQ.

'MY DEAR SIR,—   '*Edinburgh, May* 3, 1792.

'As I suppose your great work will soon be reprinted, I beg leave to trouble you with a remark on a passage of it, in which I am a little misrepresented. Be not alarmed; the misrepresentation is not imputable to you. Not having the book at hand, I cannot specify the page, but I suppose you will easily find it. Dr. Johnson says, speaking of Mrs. Thrale's family, "Dr. Beattie *sunk upon us* that he was married," or words to that purpose. I am not sure that I understand *sunk upon us,* which is a very uncommon phrase, but it seems to me to imply, (and others, I find, have understood it in the same sense,) *studiously concealed from us his being married.* Now, Sir, this was by no means the case. I could have no motive to conceal a circumstance, of which I never was nor can be ashamed; and of which Dr. Johnson seemed to think, when he afterwards became acquainted with Mrs. Beattie, that I had, as was true, reason to be proud. So far was I from concealing her, that my wife had at that time almost as numerous an acquaintance in London as I had myself; and was, not very long after, kindly invited and elegantly entertained at Streatham by Mr. and Mrs. Thrale.

'My request, therefore, is, that you would rectify this matter in your new edition. You are at liberty to make what use you please of this letter.

'My best wishes ever attend you and your family. Believe me to be, with the utmost regard and esteem, dear Sir,

'Your obliged and affectionate humble servant,   'J. BEATTIE.'

I have, from my respect for my friend Dr. Beattie, and regard to his extreme sensibility, inserted the foregoing letter, though I cannot but wonder at his considering as any imputation a phrase commonly used among the best friends.

461

but we may carry with us a wooden house ready made, and requiring nothing but to be put up. Consider, Sir, by buying St. Kilda, you may keep the people from falling into worse hands. We must give them a clergyman, and he shall be one of Beattie's choosing. He shall be educated at Marischal College. I'll be your Lord Chancellor, or what you please.' BOSWELL. 'Are you serious, Sir, in advising me to buy St. Kilda? for if you should advise me to go to Japan, I believe I should do it.' JOHNSON. 'Why yes, Sir, I am serious.' BOSWELL. 'Why then, I'll see what can be done.'

I gave him an account of the two parties in the Church of Scotland, those for supporting the rights of patrons, independent of the people, and those against it. JOHNSON. 'It should be settled one way or other. I cannot wish well to a popular election of the clergy, when I consider that it occasions such animosities, such unworthy courting of the people, such slanders between the contending parties, and other disadvantages. It is enough to allow the people to remonstrate against the nomination of a minister for solid reasons.' (I suppose he meant heresy or immorality.)

He was engaged to dine abroad, and asked me to return to him in the evening, at nine, which I accordingly did.

We drank tea with Mrs. Williams, who told us a story of second sight, which happened in Wales where she was born. He listened to it very attentively, and said he should be glad to have some instances of that faculty well authenticated. His elevated wish for more and more evidence for spirit, in opposition to the groveling belief of materialism, led him to a love of such mysterious disquisitions. He again justly observed, that we could have no certainty of the truth of supernatural appearances, unless something was told us which we could not know by ordinary means, or something done which could not be done but by supernatural power; that Pharaoh in reason and justice required such evidence from Moses; nay, that our Saviour said, 'If I had not done among them the works which none other man did, they had not had sin.' He had said in the morning, that Macaulay's *History of St. Kilda* was very well written, except some foppery about liberty and slavery. I mentioned to him that

Macaulay told me, he was advised to leave out of his book the wonderful story that upon the approach of a stranger all the inhabitants catch cold;[1] but that it had been so well authenticated, he determined to retain it. JOHNSON. 'Sir, to leave things out of a book, merely because people tell you they will not be believed, is meanness. Macaulay acted with more magnanimity.'

We talked of the Roman Catholick religion, and how little difference there was in essential matters between ours and it. JOHNSON. 'True, Sir; all denominations of Christians have really little difference in point of doctrine, though they may differ widely in external forms. There is a prodigious difference between the external form of one of your Presbyterian churches in Scotland, and a church in Italy; yet the doctrine taught is essentially the same.'

I mentioned the petition to Parliament for removing the subscription to the Thirty-nine Articles. JOHNSON. 'It was soon thrown out. Sir, they talk of not making boys at the University subscribe to what they do not understand; but they ought to consider, that our Universities were founded to bring up members for the Church of England, and we must not supply our enemies with arms from our arsenal. No, Sir, the meaning of subscribing is, not that they fully understand all the articles, but that they will adhere to the Church of England. Now take it in this way, and suppose that they should only subscribe their adherence to the Church of England, there would be still the same difficulty; for still the young men would be subscribing to what they do not understand. For if you should ask them, what do you mean by the Church of England? Do you know in what it differs from the Presbyterian Church? from the Romish Church? from the Greek Church? from the Coptic Church? they could not tell you. So, Sir, it comes to the same thing.' BOSWELL. 'But, Sir, would it not be sufficient to subscribe the Bible?' JOHNSON. 'Why no, Sir; for all sects will subscribe the Bible; nay, the Mahometans will subscribe the Bible; for the Mahometans acknowledge JESUS CHRIST, as well as Moses, but maintain that GOD sent Mahomet as a still greater prophet than either.'

[1] See p. 390.

I mentioned the motion which had been made in the House of Commons, to abolish the fast of the 30th of January. JOHNSON. 'Why, Sir, I could have wished that it had been a temporary act, perhaps, to have expired with the century. I am against abolishing it; because that would be declaring it was wrong to establish it; but I should have no objection to make an act, continuing it for another century, and then letting it expire.'

He disapproved of the Royal Marriage Bill; 'Because (said he) I would not have the people think that the validity of marriage depends on the will of man, or that the right of a King depends on the will of man. I should not have been against making the marriage of any of the royal family, without the approbation of King and Parliament, highly criminal.'

In the morning we had talked of old families, and the respect due to them. JOHNSON. 'Sir, you have a right to that kind of respect, and are arguing for yourself. I am for supporting the principle, and am disinterested in doing it, as I have no such right.' BOSWELL. 'Why, Sir, it is one more incitement to a man to do well.' JOHNSON. 'Yes, Sir, and it is a matter of opinion, very necessary to keep society together. What is it but opinion, by which we have a respect for authority, that prevents us, who are the rabble, from rising up and pulling down you who are gentlemen from your places, and saying, "We will be gentlemen in our turn?" Now, Sir, that respect for authority is much more easily granted to a man whose father has had it, than to an upstart, and so Society is more easily supported.' BOSWELL. 'Perhaps, Sir, it might be done by the respect belonging to office, as among the Romans, where the dress, the *toga*, inspired reverence.' JOHNSON. 'Why, Sir, we know very little about the Romans. But, surely, it is much easier to respect a man who has always had respect, than to respect a man who we know was last year no better than ourselves, and will be no better next year. In republicks there is not a respect for authority, but a fear of power.' BOSWELL. 'At present, Sir, I think riches seem to gain most respect.' JOHNSON. 'No, Sir, riches do not gain hearty respect; they only procure external attention. A very rich man, from low beginnings, may buy his election in a borough; but, *cæteris paribus*, a man of family will be preferred. People will prefer a man for whose father their fathers have voted, though they should get no more money, or even less. That shows that the respect for family is not merely fanciful, but has an actual operation. If gentlemen of family would allow the rich upstarts to spend their money profusely, which they are ready enough to do, and not vie with them in expence, the upstarts would soon be at an end, and the gentlemen would remain: but if the gentlemen will vie in expence with the upstarts, which is very foolish, they must be ruined.'

I gave him an account of the excellent mimickry of a friend[1] of mine in Scotland; observing, at the same time, that some people thought it a very mean thing. JOHNSON. 'Why, Sir, it is making a very mean use of a man's powers. But to be a good mimick, requires great powers, great acuteness of observation, great retention of what is observed, and great pliancy of organs, to represent what is observed. I remember a lady of quality in this town, Lady —— ——,[2] who was a wonderful mimick, and used to make me laugh immoderately. I have heard she is now gone mad.' BOSWELL. 'It is amazing how a mimick can not only give you the gestures and voice of a person whom he represents; but even what a person would say on any particular subject.' JOHNSON. 'Why, Sir, you are to consider that the manner and some particular phrases of a person do much to impress you with an idea of him, and you are not sure that he would say what the mimick says in his character.' BOSWELL. 'I don't think Foote a good mimick, Sir.' JOHNSON. 'No, Sir; his imitations are not like. He gives you something different from himself, but not the character which he means to assume. He goes out of himself, without going into other people. He cannot take off any person unless he is strongly marked, such as George Faulkner. He is like a painter, who can draw the portrait of a man who has a wen upon his face, and who, therefore, is easily known. If a man hops upon one leg, Foote can hop upon one leg. But he has not that nice discrimination which your friend seems to possess. Foote is,

---

[1] [Lord Cullen. *Croker*[2]. Cf. *Boswell Papers*, ix. 253.]

[2] [Lady Emily Hervey. *Mrs. Piozzi*.]

however, very entertaining, with a kind of conversation between wit and buffoonery.'

On Monday, March 23, I found him busy, preparing a fourth edition of his folio Dictionary. Mr. Peyton, one of his original amanuenses, was writing for him. I put him in mind of a meaning of the word *side*, which he had omitted, viz. relationship; as father's side, mother's side. He inserted it. I asked him if *humiliating* was a good word. He said, he had seen it frequently used, but he did not know it to be legitimate English. He would not admit *civilization*, but only *civility*. With great deference to him, I thought *civilization*, from *to civilize* better in the sense opposed to *barbarity*, than *civility*; as it is better to have a distinct word for each sense, than one word with two senses, which *civility* is, in his way of using it.

He seemed also to be intent on some sort of chymical operation. I was entertained by observing how he contrived to send Mr. Peyton on an errand, without seeming to degrade him. 'Mr. Peyton,—Mr. Peyton, will you be so good as to take a walk to Temple-Bar? You will there see a chymist's shop; at which you will be pleased to buy for me an ounce of oil of vitriol; not spirit of vitriol, but oil of vitriol. It will cost three half-pence.' Peyton immediately went, and returned with it, and told him it cost but a penny.

I then reminded him of the schoolmaster's cause, and proposed to read to him the printed papers concerning it. 'No, Sir, (said he,) I can read quicker than I can hear.' So he read them to himself.

After he had read for some time, we were interrupted by the entrance of Mr. Kristrom, a Swede, who was tutor to some young gentlemen in the city. He told me, that there was a very good History of Sweden, by Daline. Having at that time an intention of writing the history of that country, I asked Dr. Johnson whether one might write a history of Sweden, without going thither. 'Yes, Sir, (said he,) one for common use.'

We talked of languages. Johnson observed, that Leibnitz had made some progress in a work, tracing all languages up to the Hebrew. 'Why, Sir, (said he,) you would not imagine that the

French *jour*, day, is derived from the Latin *dies*, and yet nothing is more certain; and the intermediate steps are very clear. From *dies*, comes *diurnus*. *Diu* is, by inaccurate ears, or inaccurate pronunciation, easily confounded with *giu*; then the Italians form a substantive of the ablative of an adjective, and thence *giurno*, or, as they make it, *giorno*; which is readily contracted into *giour*, or *jour*.' He observed, that the Bohemian language was true Sclavonick. The Swede said, it had some similarity with the German. JOHNSON. 'Why, Sir, to be sure, such parts of Sclavonia as confine with Germany, will borrow German words; and such parts as confine with Tartary will borrow Tartar words.'

He said, he never had it properly ascertained that the Scotch Highlanders and the Irish understood each other. I told him that my cousin Colonel Graham, of the Royal Highlanders, whom I met at Drogheda, told me they did. JOHNSON. 'Sir, if the Highlanders understood Irish, why translate the New Testament into Erse, as was done lately at Edinburgh, when there is an Irish translation?' BOSWELL. 'Although the Erse and Irish are both dialects of the same language, there may be a good deal of diversity between them, as between the different dialects in Italy.'—The Swede went away, and Mr. Johnson continued his reading of the papers. I said, 'I am afraid, Sir, it is troublesome to you.' 'Why, Sir, (said he,) I do not take much delight in it; but I'll go through it.'

We went to the Mitre, and dined in the room where he and I first supped together. He gave me great hopes of my cause. 'Sir, (said he,) the government of a schoolmaster is somewhat of the nature of military government; that is to say, it must be arbitrary, it must be exercised by the will of one man, according to particular circumstances. You must shew some learning upon this occasion. You must shew, that a schoolmaster has a prescriptive right to beat; and that an action of assault and battery cannot be admitted against him, unless there is some great excess, some barbarity. This man has maimed none of his boys. They are all left with the full exercise of their corporeal faculties. In our schools in England, many boys have been maimed; yet I never heard of an action against a schoolmaster on that account.

Puffendorf, I think, maintains the right of a schoolmaster to beat his scholars.'

On Saturday, March 27 [*sic.*], I introduced to him Sir Alexander Macdonald, with whom he had expressed a wish to be acquainted. He received him very courteously.

Sir Alexander observed, that the Chancellors in England are chosen from views much inferiour to the office, being chosen from temporary political views. JOHNSON. 'Why, Sir, in such a government as ours, no man is appointed to an office because he is the fittest for it, nor hardly in any other government; because there are so many connections and dependencies to be studied. A despotick prince may choose a man to an office, merely because he is the fittest for it. The King of Prussia may do it.' SIR A. 'I think, Sir, almost all great lawyers, such at least as have written upon law, have known only law, and nothing else.' JOHNSON. 'Why no, Sir; Judge Hále was a great lawyer, and wrote upon law; and yet he knew a great many other things, and has written upon other things. Selden too.' SIR A. 'Very true, Sir; and Lord Bacon. But was not Lord Coke a mere lawyer?' JOHNSON. 'Why, I am afraid he was; but he would have taken it very ill if you had told him so. He would have prosecuted you for scandal.' BOSWELL. 'Lord Mansfield is not a mere lawyer.' JOHNSON. 'No, Sir. I never was in Lord Mansfield's company; but, Lord Mansfield was distinguished at the University. Lord Mansfield, when he first came to town, "drank champagne with the wits," as Prior says. He was the friend of Pope.' SIR A. 'Barristers, I believe, are not so abusive now as they were formerly. I fancy they had less law long ago, and so were obliged to take to abuse, to fill up the time. Now they have such a number of precedents, they have no occasion for abuse.' JOHNSON. 'Nay, Sir, they had more law long ago than they have now. As to precedents, to be sure they will increase in course of time; but the more precedents there are, the less occasion is there for law; that is to say, the less occasion is there for investigating principles.' SIR A. 'I have been correcting several Scotch accents in my friend Boswell. I doubt, Sir, if any Scotchman ever attains to a perfect English pronunciation.' JOHNSON. 'Why, Sir, few of them do, because they do not persevere after acquiring a certain degree of it. But, Sir, there can be no doubt that they may attain to a perfect English pronunciation, if they will. We find how near they come to it; and certainly, a man who conquers nineteen parts of the Scottish accent, may conquer the twentieth. But, Sir, when a man has got the better of nine tenths, he grows weary, he relaxes his diligence, he finds he has corrected his accent so far as not to be disagreeable, and he no longer desires his friends to tell him when he is wrong; nor does he choose to be told. Sir, when people watch me narrowly, and I do not watch myself, they will find me out to be of a particular county. In the same manner, Dunning may be found out to be a Devonshire man. So most Scotchmen may be found out. But, Sir, little aberrations are of no disadvantage. I never catched Mallet in a Scotch accent; and yet Mallet, I suppose, was past five-and-twenty before he came to London.'

Upon another occasion I talked to him on this subject, having myself taken some pains to improve my pronunciation, by the aid of the late Mr. Love, of Drury-lane theatre, when he was a player at Edinburgh, and also of old Mr. Sheridan. Johnson said to me, 'Sir, your pronunciation is not offensive.' With this concession I was pretty well satisfied; and let me give my countrymen of North-Britain an advice not to aim at absolute perfection in this respect; not to speak *High English*, as we are apt to call what is far removed from the *Scotch*, but which is by no means *good English*, and makes, 'the fools who use it,' truly ridiculous. Good English is plain, easy, and smooth in the mouth of an unaffected English Gentleman. A studied and factitious pronunciation, which requires perpetual attention and imposes perpetual constraint, is exceedingly disgusting. A small intermixture of provincial peculiarities may, perhaps, have an agreeable effect, as the notes of different birds concur in the harmony of the grove, and please more than if they were all exactly alike. I could name some gentlemen of Ireland, to whom a slight proportion of the accent and recitative of that country is an advantage. The same observation will apply to the gentlemen of Scotland. I do not mean that we should speak as broad as a certain prosperous

member of Parliament[1] from that country; though it has been
well observed, that 'it has been of no small use to him; as it
rouses the attention of the House by its uncommonness; and is
equal to tropes and figures in a good English speaker.' I would
give as an instance of what I mean to recommend to my countrymen, the pronunciation of the late Sir Gilbert Elliot; and may I
presume to add that of the present Earl of Marchmont, who told
me, with great good humour, that the master of a shop in London, where he was not known, said to him, 'I suppose, Sir, you
are an American.' 'Why so, Sir?' (said his Lordship.) 'Because,
Sir, (replied the shopkeeper,) you speak neither English nor
Scotch, but something different from both, which I conclude is
the language of America.'

  BOSWELL. 'It may be of use, Sir, to have a Dictionary to
ascertain the pronunciation.' JOHNSON. 'Why, Sir, my Dictionary shows you the accents of words, if you can but remember
them.' BOSWELL. 'But, Sir, we want marks to ascertain the
pronunciation of the vowels. Sheridan, I believe, has finished
such a work.' JOHNSON. 'Why, Sir, consider how much easier
it is to learn a language by the ear, than by any marks. Sheridan's
Dictionary may do very well; but you cannot always carry it
about with you: and, when you want the word, you have not the
Dictionary. It is like a man who has a sword that will not draw.
It is an admirable sword, to be sure: but while your enemy is
cutting your throat, you are unable to use it. Besides, Sir, what
entitles Sheridan to fix the pronunciation of English? He has, in
the first place, the disadvantage of being an Irishman: and if he
says he will fix it after the example of the best company, why
they differ among themselves. I remember an instance: when I
published the Plan for my Dictionary, Lord Chesterfield told me
that the word *great* should be pronounced so as to rhyme to
state; and Sir William Yonge sent me word that it should be
pronounced so as to rhyme to *seat*, and that none but an Irishman
would pronounce it *grait*. Now here were two men of the highest
rank, the one, the best speaker in the House of Lords, the other,
the best speaker in the House of Commons, differing entirely.'

  [1] [Henry Dundas. *Croker*[1].]

I again visited him at night. Finding him in a very good humour, I ventured to lead him to the subject of our situation in a future state, having much curiosity to know his notions on that point. JOHNSON. 'Why, Sir, the happiness of an unembodied spirit will consist in a consciousness of the favour of GOD, in the contemplation of truth, and in the possession of felicitating ideas.' BOSWELL. 'But, Sir, is there any harm in our forming to ourselves conjectures as to the particulars of our happiness, though the scripture has said but very little on the subject? "We know not what we shall be." ' JOHNSON. 'Sir, there is no harm. What philosophy suggests to us on this topick is probable: what scripture tells us is certain. Dr. Henry More has carried it as far as philosophy can. You may buy both his theological and philosophical works in two volumes folio, for about eight shillings.' BOSWELL. 'One of the most pleasing thoughts is, that we shall see our friends again.' JOHNSON. 'Yes, Sir; but you must consider, that when we are become purely rational, many of our friendships will be cut off. Many friendships are formed by a community of sensual pleasures: all these will be cut off. We form many friendships with bad men, because they have agreeable qualities, and they can be useful to us; but, after death, they can no longer be of use to us. We form many friendships by mistake, imagining people to be different from what they really are. After death, we shall see every one in a true light. Then, Sir, they talk of our meeting our relations: but then all relationship is dissolved; and we shall have no regard for one person more than another, but for their real value. However, we shall either have the satisfaction of meeting our friends, or be satisfied without meeting them.' BOSWELL. 'Yet, Sir, we see in scripture, that Dives still retained an anxious concern about his brethren.' JOHNSON. 'Why, Sir, we must either suppose that passage to be metaphorical, or hold with many divines, and all the Purgatorians, that departed souls do not all at once arrive at the utmost perfection of which they are capable.' BOSWELL. 'I think, Sir, that is a very rational supposition.' JOHNSON. 'Why, yes, Sir; but we do not know it is a true one. There is no harm in believing it: but you must not compel others to make it an article of faith;

for it is not revealed,' BOSWELL. 'Do you think, Sir, it is wrong
in a man who holds the doctrine of purgatory, to pray for the
souls of his deceased friends?' JOHNSON. 'Why, no, Sir.' BOS-
WELL. 'I have been told, that in the Liturgy of the Episcopal
Church of Scotland, there was a form of prayer for the dead.'
JOHNSON. 'Sir, it is not in the liturgy which Laud framed for the
Episcopal Church of Scotland: if there is a liturgy older than that,
I should be glad to see it.' BOSWELL. 'As to our employment
in a future state, the sacred writings say little. The Revelation,
however, of St. John gives us many ideas, and particularly mentions musick.' JOHNSON. 'Why, Sir, ideas must be given you
by means of something which you know: and as to musick, there
are some philosophers and divines who have maintained that we
shall not be spiritualized to such a degree, but that something of
matter, very much refined, will remain. In that case, musick may
make a part of our future felicity.'

BOSWELL. 'I do not know whether there are any well-attested
stories of the appearance of ghosts. You know there is a famous
story of the appearance of Mrs. Veal, prefixed to *Drelincourt on
Death.*' JOHNSON. 'I believe, Sir, that is given up. I believe
the woman declared upon her death-bed that it was a lie.'[1]
BOSWELL. 'This objection is made against the truth of ghosts
appearing: that if they are in a state of happiness, it would be a
punishment to them to return to this world; and if they are in
a state of misery, it would be giving them a respite.' JOHNSON.
'Why, Sir, as the happiness or misery of unembodied spirits does
not depend upon place, but is intellectual, we cannot say that
they are less happy or less miserable by appearing upon earth.'

We went down between twelve and one to Mrs. Williams's
room, and drank tea. I mentioned that we were to have the
remains of Mr. Gray, in prose and verse, published by Mr.
Mason. JOHNSON. 'I think we have had enough of Gray. I see
they have published a splendid edition of Akenside's works. One
bad ode may be suffered; but a number of them together makes

---

[1] This fiction is known to have been invented by Daniel Defoe, and was
added to Drelincourt's book, to make it sell. The first edition had it not.
[M.]

one sick.' BOSWELL. 'Akenside's distinguished poem is his
Pleasures of Imagination: but, for my part, I never could admire
it so much as most people do.' JOHNSON. 'Sir, I could not read
it through.' BOSWELL. 'I have read it through; but I did not
find any great power in it.'

I mentioned Elwal, the heretick, whose trial Sir John Pringle
had given me to read. JOHNSON. 'Sir, Mr. Elwal was, I think,
an ironmonger at Wolverhampton; and he had a mind to make
himself famous, by being the founder of a new sect, which he
wished much should be called *Elwallians*. He held, that every
thing in the Old Testament that was not typical, was to be of
perpetual observance; and so he wore a ribband in the plaits of
his coat, and he also wore a beard. I remember I had the honour
of dining in company with Mr. Elwal. There was one Barter, a
miller, who wrote against him; and so you had the controversy
between Mr. ELWAL and Mr. BARTER. To try to make himself
distinguished, he wrote a letter to King George the Second,
challenging him to dispute with him, in which he said, "George,
if you be afraid to come by yourself, to dispute with a poor old
man, you may bring a thousand of your *black*-guards with you;
and if you should still be afraid, you may bring a thousand of
your *red*-guards." The letter had something of the impudence
of Junius to our present King. But the men of Wolverhampton
were not so inflammable as the Common-Council of London; so
Mr. Elwal failed in his scheme of making himself a man of great
consequence.'

On Tuesday, March 31, he and I dined at General Paoli's.
A question was started, whether the state of marriage was
natural to man. JOHNSON. 'Sir, it is so far from being natural
for a man and woman to live in a state of marriage, that we find
all the motives which they have for remaining in that connection,
and the restraints which civilized society imposes to prevent
separation, are hardly sufficient to keep them together.' The
General said, that in a state of nature a man and woman uniting
together would form a strong and constant affection, by the
mutual pleasure each would receive; and that the same causes
of dissention would not arise between them, as occur between

husband and wife in a civilized state. JOHNSON. 'Sir, they would have dissentions enough, though of another kind. One would choose to go a hunting in this wood, the other in that; one would choose to go a fishing in this lake, the other in that; or, perhaps, one would choose to go a hunting, when the other would choose to go a fishing; and so they would part. Besides, Sir, a savage man and a savage woman meet by chance; and when the man sees another woman that pleases him better, he will leave the first.'

We then fell into a disquisition whether there is any beauty independent of utility. The General maintained there was not. Dr. Johnson maintained that there was; and he instanced a coffee-cup which he held in his hand, the painting of which was of no real use, as the cup would hold the coffee equally well if plain; yet the painting was beautiful.

We talked of the strange custom of swearing in conversation. The General said, that all barbarous nations swore from a certain violence of temper, that could not be confined to earth, but was always reaching at the powers above. He said, too, that there was greater variety of swearing, in proportion as there was a greater variety of religious ceremonies.

Dr. Johnson went home with me to my lodgings in Conduit-street and drank tea, previous to our going to the Pantheon, which neither of us had seen before.

He said, 'Goldsmith's *Life of Parnell* is poor; not that it is poorly written, but that he had poor materials; for nobody can write the life of a man, but those who have eat and drunk and lived in social intercourse with him.'

I said, that if it was not troublesome and presuming too much, I would request him to tell me all the little circumstances of his life; what schools he attended, when he came to Oxford, when he came to London, &c. &c. He did not disapprove of my curiosity as to these particulars; but said, 'They'll come out by degrees as we talk together.'

He censured Ruffhead's *Life of Pope*; and said, 'he knew nothing of Pope, and nothing of poetry.' He praised Dr. Joseph Warton's *Essay on Pope*; but said, he supposed we should have no more of it, as the authour had not been able to persuade the world to think of Pope as he did. BOSWELL. 'Why, Sir, should that prevent him from continuing his work? He is an ingenious Counsel, who has made the most of his cause: he is not obliged to gain it.' JOHNSON. 'But, Sir, there is a difference when the cause is of a man's own making.'

We talked of the proper use of riches. JOHNSON. 'If I were a man of a great estate, I would drive all the rascals whom I did not like out of the county at an election.'

I asked him how far he thought wealth should be employed in hospitality. JOHNSON. 'You are to consider that ancient hospitality, of which we hear so much, was in an uncommercial country, when men being idle, were glad to be entertained at rich men's tables. But in a commercial country, a busy country, time becomes precious, and therefore hospitality is not so much valued. No doubt there is still room for a certain degree of it; and a man has a satisfaction in seeing his friends eating and drinking around him. But promiscuous hospitality is not the way to gain real influence. You must help some people at table before others; you must ask some people how they like their wine oftener than others. You therefore offend more people than you please. You are like the French statesman, who said, when he granted a favour, *"J'ai fait dix mécontents et un ingrat."* Besides, Sir, being entertained ever so well at a man's table, impresses no lasting regard or esteem. No, Sir, the way to make sure of power and influence is, by lending money confidentially to your neighbours at a small interest, or, perhaps, at no interest at all, and having their bonds in your possession.' BOSWELL. 'May not a man, Sir, employ his riches to advantage in educating young men of merit?' JOHNSON. 'Yes, Sir, if they fall in your way; but if it is understood that you patronize young men of merit, you will be harassed with solicitations. You will have numbers forced upon you who have no merit; some will force them upon you from mistaken partiality; and some from downright interested motives, without scruple; and you will be disgraced.'

'Were I a rich man, I would propagate all kinds of trees that will grow in the open air. A greenhouse is childish. I would introduce foreign animals into the country; for instance the reindeer.'[1]

The conversation now turned on critical subjects. JOHNSON. 'Bayes, in *The Rehearsal*, is a mighty silly character. If it was intended to be like a particular man, it could only be diverting while that man was remembered. But I question whether it was meant for Dryden, as has been reported; for we know some of the passages said to be ridiculed, were written since *The Rehearsal*; at least a passage mentioned in the Preface[2] is of a later date.' I maintained that it had merit as a general satire on the self-importance of dramatick authours. But even in this light he held it very cheap.

We then walked to the Pantheon. The first view of it did not strike us so much as Ranelagh, of which he said, the *'coup d'œil* was the finest thing he had ever seen.' The truth is, Ranelagh is of a more beautiful form; more of it, or rather indeed the whole *rotunda*, appears at once, and it is better lighted. However, as Johnson observed, we saw the Pantheon in time of mourning, when there was a dull uniformity; whereas we had seen Ranelagh when the view was enlivened with a gay profusion of colours. Mrs. Bosville, of Gunthwait, in Yorkshire, joined us, and entered into conversation with us. Johnson said to me afterwards, 'Sir, this is a mighty intelligent lady.'

I said there was not half a guinea's worth of pleasure in seeing this place. JOHNSON. 'But, Sir, there is half a guinea's worth of inferiority to other people in not having seen it.' BOSWELL. 'I doubt, Sir, whether there are many happy people here.' JOHNSON. 'Yes, Sir, there are many happy people here. There are many people here who are watching hundreds, and who think hundreds are watching them.'

[1] This project has since been realized. Sir Henry Liddel, who made a spirited tour into Lapland, brought two reindeer to his estate in Northumberland, where they bred; but the race has unfortunately perished.

[2] Dr. Johnson seems to have meant the Address to the Reader with a KEY subjoined to it; which have been prefixed to the modern editions of that play. He did not know, it appears, that several additions were made to *The Rehearsal* after the first edition. [M.]

Happening to meet Sir Adam Fergusson, I presented him to
Dr. Johnson. Sir Adam expressed some apprehension that the
Pantheon would encourage luxury. 'Sir, (said Johnson,) I am
a great friend to publick amusements; for they keep people from
vice. You now (addressing himself to me,) would have been
with a wench, had you not been here.—O! I forgot you were
married.'

Sir Adam suggested, that luxury corrupts a people, and
destroys the spirit of liberty. JOHNSON. 'Sir, that is all visionary.
I would not give half a guinea to live under one form of government rather than another. It is of no moment to the happiness of
an individual. Sir, the danger of the abuse of power is nothing
to a private man. What Frenchman is prevented from passing
his life as he pleases?' SIR ADAM. 'But, Sir, in the British constitution it is surely of importance to keep up a spirit in the
people, so as to preserve a balance against the crown.' JOHN-
SON. 'Sir, I perceive you are a vile Whig. Why all this childish
jealousy of the power of the crown? The crown has not power
enough. When I say that all governments are alike, I consider
that in no government power can be abused long. Mankind will
not bear it. If a sovereign oppresses his people to a great degree,
they will rise and cut off his head. There is a remedy in human
nature against tyranny, that will keep us safe under every form
of government. Had not the people of France thought themselves honoured as sharing in the brilliant actions of Lewis XIV,
they would not have endured him; and we may say the same of
the King of Prussia's people.' Sir Adam introduced the ancient
Greeks and Romans. JOHNSON. 'Sir, the mass of both of them
were barbarians. The mass of every people must be barbarous
where there is no printing, and consequently knowledge is not
generally diffused. Knowledge is diffused among our people by
the news-papers.' Sir Adam mentioned the orators, poets, and
artists of Greece. JOHNSON. 'Sir, I am talking of the mass of
the people. We see even what the boasted Athenians were. The
little effect which Demosthenes's orations had upon them, shews
that they were barbarians.'

Sir Adam was unlucky in his topicks; for he suggested a doubt of the propriety of Bishops having seats in the House of Lords. JOHNSON. 'How so, Sir? Who is more proper for having the dignity of a peer, than a Bishop, provided a Bishop be what he ought to be; and if improper Bishops be made, that is not the fault of the Bishops, but of those who make them.'

On Sunday, April 5, after attending divine service at St. Paul's church, I found him alone. Of a schoolmaster[1] of his acquaintance, a native of Scotland, he said, 'He has a great deal of good about him; but he is also very defective in some respects. His inner part is good, but his outer part is mighty aukward. You in Scotland do not attain that nice critical skill in languages, which we get in our schools in England. I would not put a boy to him, whom I intended for a man of learning. But for the sons of citizens, who are to learn a little, get good morals, and then go to trade, he may do very well.'

I mentioned a cause in which I had appeared as counsel at the bar of the General Assembly of the Church of Scotland, where a *Probationer*,[2] (as one licensed to preach, but not yet ordained, is called,) was opposed in his application to be inducted, because it was alledged that he had been guilty of fornication five years before. JOHNSON. 'Why, Sir, if he has repented, it is not a sufficient objection. A man who is good enough to go to heaven, is good enough to be a clergyman.' This was a humane and liberal sentiment. But the character of a clergyman is more sacred than that of an ordinary Christian. As he is to instruct with authority, he should be regarded with reverence, as one upon whom divine truth has had the effect to set him above such transgressions, as men less exalted by spiritual habits, and yet upon the whole not to be excluded from heaven, have been betrayed into by the predominance of passion. That clergymen may be considered as sinners in general, as all men are, cannot be denied; but this reflection will not counteract their good precepts so much, as the absolute knowledge of their having been guilty of certain specifick immoral acts. I told him, that by the rules of the Church of Scotland, in their *Book of Discipline*, if

[1] [James Elphinston. *Croker*[1].]
[2] [William MacMaster. *Boswell's Fee Book*, 23 and 28 May 1771.]

a *scandal,* as it is called, is not prosecuted for five years, it cannot afterwards be proceeded upon, 'unless it be *of a heinous nature,* or again become flagrant;' and that hence a question arose, whether fornication was a sin of a heinous nature; and that I had maintained, that it did not deserve that epithet, in as much as it was not one of those sins which argue very great depravity of heart: in short, was not, in the general acceptation of mankind, a heinous sin. JOHNSON. 'No, Sir, it is not a heinous sin. A heinous sin is that for which a man is punished with death or banishment.' BOSWELL. 'But, Sir, after I had argued that it was not a heinous sin, an old clergyman rose up, and repeating the text of scripture denouncing judgement against whoremongers, asked, whether, considering this, there could be any doubt of fornication being a heinous sin.' JOHNSON. 'Why, Sir, observe the word *whoremonger.* Every sin, if persisted in, will become heinous. Whoremonger is a dealer in whores, as ironmonger is a dealer in iron. But as you don't call a man an ironmonger for buying and selling a penknife; so you don't call a man a whoremonger for getting one wench with child.'[1]

I spoke of the inequality of the livings of the clergy in England, and the scanty provisions of some of the Curates. JOHNSON. 'Why yes, Sir; but it cannot be helped. You must consider, that the revenues of the clergy are not at the disposal of the state, like the pay of the army. Different men have founded different churches; and some are better endowed, some worse. The State cannot interfere and make an equal division of what has been particularly appropriated. Now when a clergyman has but a small living, or even two small livings, he can afford very little to a curate.'

He said, he went more frequently to church when there were prayers only, than when there was also a sermon, as the people required more an example for the one than the other; it being much easier for them to hear a sermon, than to fix their minds on prayer.

---

[1] It must not be presumed that Dr. Johnson meant to give any countenance to licentiousness, though in the character of an Advocate he made a just and subtle distinction between occasional and habitual transgression.

On Monday, April 6, I dined with him at Sır Alexander Macdonald's, where was a young officer in the regimentals of the Scots Royal, who talked with a vivacity, fluency, and precision so uncommon, that he attracted particular attention. He proved to be the Honourable Thomas Erskine, youngest brother to the Earl of Buchan, who has since risen into such brilliant reputation at the bar in Westminster-hall.

Fielding being mentioned, Johnson exclaimed, 'he was a blockhead;' and upon my expressing my astonishment at so strange an assertion, he said, 'What I mean by his being a blockhead is that he was a barren rascal.' BOSWELL. 'Will you not allow, Sir, that he draws very natural pictures of human life?' JOHNSON. 'Why, Sir, it is of very low life. Richardson used to say, that had he not known who Fielding was, he should have believed he was an ostler. Sir, there is more knowledge of the heart in one letter of Richardson's, than in all *Tom Jones*. I, indeed, never read *Joseph Andrews*.' ERSKINE. 'Surely, Sir, Richardson is very tedious.' JOHNSON. 'Why, Sir, if you were to read Richardson for the story, your impatience would be so much fretted that you would hang yourself. But you must read him for the sentiment, and consider the story as only giving occasion to the sentiment.'—I have already given my opinion of Fielding; but I cannot refrain from repeating here my wonder at Johnson's excessive and unaccountable depreciation of one of the best writers that England has produced. *Tom Jones* has stood the test of publick opinion with such success, as to have established its great merit, both for the story, the sentiments, and the manners, and also the varieties of diction, so as to leave no doubt of its having an animated truth of execution throughout.

A book of travels, lately published under the title of *Coriat Junior*, and written by Mr. Paterson,[1] was mentioned. Johnson said, this book was an imitation of Sterne,[2] and not of Coriat, whose name Paterson had chosen as a whimsical one. 'Tom Coriat, (said he,) was a humorist about the court of James

---

[1] Mr. Samuel Paterson, eminent for his knowledge of books.

[2] Mr. Paterson, in a pamphlet, produced some evidence to show that his work was written before Sterne's *Sentimental Journey* appeared.

the First. He had a mixture of learning, of wit, and of buffoonery. He first travelled through Europe, and published his travels. He afterwards travelled on foot through Asia, and had made many remarks; but he died at Mandoa, and his remarks were lost.'

We talked of gaming, and animadverted on it with severity. JOHNSON. 'Nay, gentlemen, let us not aggravate the matter. It is not roguery to play with a man who is ignorant of the game, while you are master of it, and so win his money; for he thinks he can play better than you, as you think you can play better than he; and the superiour skill carries it.' ERSKINE. 'He is a fool, but you are not a rogue.' JOHNSON. 'That's much about the truth, Sir. It must be considered, that a man who only does what every one of the society to which he belongs would do, is not a dishonest man. In the republick of Sparta, it was agreed, that stealing was not dishonourable, if not discovered. I do not commend a society where there is an agreement that what would not otherwise be fair, shall be fair; but I maintain, that an individual of any society, who practises what is allowed, is not a dishonest man.' BOSWELL. 'So then, Sir, you do not think ill of a man who wins perhaps forty thousand pounds in a winter?' JOHNSON. 'Sir, I do not call a gamester a dishonest man; but I call him an unsocial man, an unprofitable man. Gaming is a mode of transferring property without producing any intermediate good. Trade gives employment to numbers, and so produces intermediate good.'

Mr. Erskine told us, that when he was in the island of Minorca, he not only read prayers, but preached two sermons to the regiment. He seemed to object to the passage in scripture where we are told that the angel of the Lord smote in one night forty thousand Assyrians. 'Sir, (said Johnson,) you should recollect that there was a supernatural interposition; they were destroyed by pestilence. You are not to suppose that the angel of the LORD went about and stabbed each of them with a dagger, or knocked them on the head, man by man.'

After Mr. Erskine was gone, a discussion took place, whether the present Earl of Buchan, when Lord Cardross, did right to refuse to go Secretary of the Embassy to Spain, when Sir James

Gray, a man of inferiour rank, went Ambassadour. Dr. Johnson said, that perhaps in point of interest he did wrong; but in point of dignity he did well. Sir Alexander insisted that he was wrong; and said that Mr. Pitt intended it as an advantageous thing for him. 'Why, Sir, (said Johnson,) Mr. Pitt might think it an advantageous thing for him to make him a vintner, and get him all the Portugal trade; but he would have demeaned himself strangely had he accepted of such a situation. Sir, had he gone Secretary while his inferiour was Ambassadour, he would have been a traitor to his rank and family.'

I talked of the little attachment which subsisted between near relations in London. 'Sir, (said Johnson,) in a country so commercial as ours, where every man can do for himself, there is not so much occasion for that attachment. No man is thought the worse of here, whose brother was hanged. In uncommercial countries, many of the branches of a family must depend on the stock; so, in order to make the head of the family take care of them, they are represented as connected with his reputation, that, self-love being interested, he may exert himself to promote their interest. You have first large circles, or clans; as commerce increases, the connection is confined to families. By degrees, that too goes off, as having become unnecessary, and there being few opportunities of intercourse. One brother is a merchant in the city, and another is an officer in the guards. How little intercourse can these two have!'

I argued warmly for the old feudal system. Sir Alexander opposed it, and talked of the pleasure of seeing all men free and independent. JOHNSON. 'I agree with Mr. Boswell that there must be a high satisfaction in being a feudal Lord; but we are to consider, that we ought not to wish to have a number of men unhappy for the satisfaction of one.'—I maintained that numbers, namely, the vassals or followers, were not unhappy; for that there was a reciprocal satisfaction between the Lord and them: he being kind in his authority over them; they being respectful and faithful to him.

On Thursday, April 9, I called on him to beg he would go and dine with me at the Mitre tavern. He had resolved not to dine at all this day, I know not for what reason; and I was so unwilling to be deprived of his company, that I was content to submit to suffer a want, which was at first somewhat painful, but he soon made me forget it; and a man is always pleased with himself when he finds his intellectual inclinations predominate.

He observed, that to reason too philosophically on the nature of prayer, was very unprofitable.

Talking of ghosts, he said, he knew one friend, who was an honest man and a sensible man, who told him he had seen a ghost, old Mr. Edward Cave, the printer at St. John's Gate. He said, Mr. Cave did not like to talk of it, and seemed to be in great horrour whenever it was mentioned. BOSWELL. 'Pray, Sir, what did he say was the appearance?' JOHNSON. 'Why, Sir, something of a shadowy being.'

I mentioned witches, and asked him what they properly meant. JOHNSON. 'Why, Sir, they properly mean those who make use of the aid of evil spirits.' BOSWELL. 'There is no doubt, Sir, a general report and belief of their having existed.' JOHNSON. 'Sir, you have not only the general report and belief, but you have many voluntary solemn confessions.' He did not affirm anything positively upon a subject which it is the fashion of the times to laugh at as a matter of absurd credulity. He only seemed willing, as a candid enquirer after truth, however strange and inexplicable, to shew that he understood what might be urged for it.[1]

On Friday, April 10, I dined with him at General Oglethorpe's, where we found Dr. Goldsmith.

Armorial bearings having been mentioned, Johnson said, they were as ancient as the siege of Thebes, which he proved by a passage in one of the tragedies of Euripides.

I started the question whether duelling was consistent with moral duty. The brave old General fired at this, and said, with a lofty air, 'Undoubtedly a man has a right to defend his honour.' GOLDSMITH. (turning to me,) 'I ask you first, Sir, what would you do if you were affronted?' I answered I should think it

---

[1] See this curious question treated by him with most acute ability, *Journal of a Tour to the Hebrides,* 3rd edit. p. 33. [Aug. 16.]

necessary to fight. 'Why then, (replied Goldsmith,) that solves the question.' JOHNSON. 'No, Sir, it does not solve the question. It does not follow that what a man would do is therefore right.' I said, I wished to have it settled, whether duelling was contrary to the laws of Christianity. Johnson immediately entered on the subject, and treated it in a masterly manner; and so far as I have been able to recollect, his thoughts were these: 'Sir, as men become in a high degree refined, various causes of offence arise; which are considered to be of such importance, that life must be staked to atone for them, though in reality they are not so. A body that has received a very fine polish may be easily hurt. Before men arrive at this artificial refinement, if one tells his neighbour he lies, his neighbour tells him he lies; if one gives his neighbour a blow, his neighbour gives him a blow: but in a state of highly polished society, an affront is held to be a serious injury. It must, therefore, be resented, or rather a duel must be fought upon it; as men have agreed to banish from their society one who puts up with an affront without fighting a duel. Now, Sir, it is never unlawful to fight in self-defence. He, then, who fights a duel, does not fight from passion against his antagonist, but out of self-defence; to avert the stigma of the world, and to prevent himself from being driven out of society. I could wish there was not that superfluity of refinement; but while such notions prevail, no doubt a man may lawfully fight a duel.'

Let it be remembered, that this justification is applicable only to the person who *receives* an affront. All mankind must condemn the aggressor.

The General told us, that when he was a very young man, I think only fifteen, serving under Prince Eugene of Savoy, he was sitting in a company at table with a Prince of Wirtemberg. The Prince took up a glass of wine, and, by a fillip, made some of it fly in Oglethorpe's face. Here was a nice dilemma. To have challenged him instantly, might have fixed a quarrelsome character upon the young soldier: to have taken no notice of it might have been considered as cowardice. Oglethorpe, therefore, keeping his eye upon the Prince, and smiling all the time, as if he took what his Highness had done in jest, said '*Mon Prince,*—'

(I forget the French words he used, the purport however was,) 'That's a good joke; but we do it much better in England;' and threw a whole glass of wine in the Prince's face. An old General who sat by, said, '*Il a bien fait, mon Prince, vous l'avez commencé:*' and thus all ended in good humour.

Dr. Johnson said, 'Pray, General, give us an account of the siege of Belgrade.' Upon which the General, pouring a little wine upon the table, described every thing with a wet finger: 'Here we were, here werc the Turks,' &c. &c. Johnson listened with the closest attention.

A question was started, how far people who disagree in any capital point can live in friendship together. Johnson said they might. Goldsmith said they could not, as they had not the *idem velle atque idem nolle*—the same likings and the same aversions. JOHNSON. 'Why, Sir, you must shun the subject as to which you disagree. For instance, I can live very well with Burke: I love his knowledge, his genius, his diffusion, and affluence of conversation; but I would not talk to him of the Rockingham party.' GOLDSMITH. 'But, Sir, when people live together who have something as to which they disagree, and which they want to shun, they will be in the situation mentioned in the story of Bluebeard: "You may look into all the chambers but one." But we should have the greatest inclination to look into that chamber, to talk of that subject.' JOHNSON. (with a loud voice,) 'Sir, I am not saying that *you* could live in friendship with a man from whom you differ as to some point: I am only saying that *I* could do it. You put me in mind of Sappho in Ovid.'

Goldsmith told us, that he was now busy in writing a natural history, and, that he might have full leisure for it, he had taken lodgings, at a farmer's house, near to the six mile-stone, on the Edgeware road, and had carried down his books in two returned post-chaises. He said, he believed the farmer's family thought him an odd character, similar to that in which the *Spectator* appeared to his landlady and her children: he was *The Gentleman*. Mr. Mickle, the translator of *The Lusiad*, and I went to visit him at this place a few days afterwards. He was not at home; but having a curiosity to see his apartment, we went in and found curious scraps of descriptions of animals, scrawled upon the walls with a black lead pencil.

The subject of ghosts being introduced, Johnson repeated what he had told me of a friend of his, an honest man and a man of sense, having asserted to him, that he had seen an apparition. Goldsmith told us, he was assured by his brother, the Reverend Mr. Goldsmith, that he also had seen one. General Oglethorpe told us, that Prendergast, an officer in the Duke of Marlborough's army, had mentioned to many of his friends, that he should die on a particular day. That upon that day a battle took place with the French; that after it was over, and Prendergast was still alive, his brother officers, while they were yet in the field, jestingly asked him, where was his prophecy now. Prendergast gravely answered, 'I shall die, notwithstanding what you see.' Soon afterwards, there came a shot from a French battery, to which the orders for a cessation of arms had not yet reached, and he was killed upon the spot. Colonel Cecil, who took possession of his effects, found in his pocket-book the following solemn entry:

[Here the date.] 'Dreamt—or————[1] Sir John Friend meets me:' (here the very day on which he was killed, was mentioned.) Prendergast had been connected with Sir John Friend, who was executed for high treason. General Oglethorpe said, he was in company with Colonel Cecil when Pope came and enquired into the truth of this story, which made a great noise at the time, and was then confirmed by the Colonel.

On Saturday, April 11, he appointed me to come to him in the evening, when he should be at leisure to give me some assistance for the defence of Hastie, the schoolmaster of Campbelltown, for whom I was to appear in the House of Lords. When I came, I found him unwilling to exert himself. I pressed him to write down his thoughts upon the subject. He said, 'There's no occasion for my writing. I'll talk to you.' He was, however, at last prevailed on to dictate to me, while I wrote as follows:—

[1] Here was a blank, which may be filled up thus:—'*was told by an apparition*;'—the writer being probably uncertain whether he was asleep or awake, when his mind was impressed with the solemn presentiment with which the fact afterwards happened so wonderfully to correspond.

'The charge is, that he has used immoderate and cruel correction. Correction, in itself, is not cruel; children, being not reasonable, can be governed only by fear. To impress this fear, is therefore one of the first duties of those who have the care of children. It is the duty of a parent; and has never been thought inconsistent with parental tenderness. It is the duty of a master, who is in his highest exaltation when he is *loco parentis*.[1] Yet, as good things become evil by excess, correction, by being immoderate, may become cruel. But when is correction immoderate? When it is more frequent or more severe than is required *ad monendum et docendum*, for reformation and instruction. No severity is cruel which obstinacy makes necessary; for the greatest cruelty would be to desist, and leave the scholar too careless for instruction, and too much hardened for reproof. Locke, in his treatise of Education, mentions a mother, with applause, who whipped an infant eight times before she had subdued it; for had she stopped at the seventh act of correction, her daughter, says he, would have been ruined. The degrees of obstinacy in young minds are very different; as different must be the degrees of persevering severity. A stubborn scholar must be corrected till he is subdued. The discipline of a school is military. There must be either unbounded licence or absolute authority. The master, who punishes, not only consults the future happiness of him who is the immediate subject of correction; but he propagates obedience through the whole school; and establishes regularity by exemplary justice. The victorious obstinacy of a single boy would make his future endeavours of reformation or instruction totally ineffectual. Obstinacy, therefore, must never be victorious. Yet, it is well known, that there sometimes occurs a sullen and hardy resolution, that laughs at all common punishment, and bids defiance to all common degrees of pain. Correction must be proportioned to occasions. The flexible will be reformed by gentle discipline, and the refractory must be subdued by harsher methods. The degrees of scholastick as of military punishment, no stated rules can ascertain. It must be enforced till it overpowers

---

[1] ['in the place of a parent'.]

temptation; till stubbornness becomes flexible, and perverseness regular. Custom and reason have, indeed, set some bounds to scholastick penalties. The schoolmaster inflicts no capital punishments; nor enforces his edicts by either death or mutilation. The civil law has wisely determined, that a master who strikes at a scholar's eye shall be considered as criminal. But punishments, however severe, that produce no lasting evil, may be just and reasonable, because they may be necessary. Such have been the punishments used by the respondent. No scholar has gone from him either blind or lame, or with any of his limbs or powers injured or impaired. They were irregular, and he punished them: they were obstinate, and he enforced his punishment. But, however provoked, he never exceeded the limits of moderation, for he inflicted nothing beyond present pain; and how much of that was required, no man is so little able to determine as those who have determined against him;—the parents of the offenders. It has been said, that he used unprecedented and improper instruments of correction. Of this accusation the meaning is not very easy to be found. No instrument of correction is more proper than another, but as it is better adapted to produce present pain without lasting mischief. Whatever were his instruments, no lasting mischief has ensued; and therefore, however unusual, in hands so cautious they were proper. It has been objected, that the respondent admits the charge of cruelty, by producing no evidence to confute it. Let it be considered, that his scholars are either dispersed at large in the world, or continue to inhabit the place in which they were bred. Those who are dispersed cannot be found; those who remain are the sons of his persecutors, and are not likely to support a man to whom their fathers are enemies. If it be supposed that the enmity of their fathers proves the justice of the charge, it must be considered how often experience shews us, that men who are angry on one ground will accuse on another; with how little kindness, in a town of low trade, a man who lives by learning is regarded; and how implicitly, where the inhabitants are not very rich, a rich man is hearkened to and followed. In a place like Campbelltown, it is easy for one of the principal inhabitants to make a party. It is easy for that party to heat themselves with imaginary grievances. It is easy for them to oppress a man poorer than themselves; and natural to assert the dignity of riches, by persisting in oppression. The argument which attempts to prove the impropriety of restoring him to his school, by alledging that he has lost the confidence of the people, is not the subject of juridical consideration; for he is to suffer, if he must suffer, not for their judgement, but for his own actions. It may be convenient for them to have another master; but it is a convenience of their own making. It would be likewise convenient for him to find another school; but this convenience he cannot obtain. The question is not what is now convenient, but what is generally right. If the people of Campbelltown be distressed by the restoration of the respondent, they are distressed only by their own fault; by turbulent passions and unreasonable desires; by tyranny, which law has defeated, and by malice, which virtue has surmounted.'

'This, Sir, (said he,) you are to turn in your mind, and make the best use of it you can in your speech.'

Of our friend, Goldsmith, he said, 'Sir, he is so much afraid of being unnoticed, that he often talks merely lest you should forget that he is in the company.' BOSWELL. 'Yes, he stands forward.' JOHNSON. 'True, Sir; but if a man is to stand forward, he should wish to do it not in an aukward posture, not in rags, not so as that he shall only be exposed to ridicule.' BOSWELL. 'For my part, I like very well to hear honest Goldsmith talk away carelessly.' JOHNSON. 'Why yes, Sir; but he should not like to hear himself.'

On Tuesday, April 14, the decree of the Court of Session in the schoolmaster's cause was reversed in the House of Lords, after a very eloquent speech by Lord Mansfield, who shewed himself an adept in school discipline, but I thought was too rigorous towards my client. On the evening of the next day I supped with Dr. Johnson, at the Crown and Anchor tavern, in the Strand, in company with Mr. Langton and his brother-in-law, Lord Binning. I repeated a sentence of Lord Mansfield's speech, of which, by the aid of Mr. Longlands, the solicitor on the other side, who obligingly allowed me to compare his note with my own, I have a full copy: 'My Lords, severity is not the way to govern either boys or men.' 'Nay, (said Johnson,) it is the way to *govern* them. I know not whether it be the way to *mend* them.'

I talked of the recent expulsion of six students from the University of Oxford, who were methodists, and would not desist from publickly praying and exhorting. JOHNSON. 'Sir, that expulsion was extremely just and proper. What have they to do at an University who are not willing to be taught, but will presume to teach? Where is religion to be learnt but at an University? Sir, they were examined, and found to be mighty ignorant fellows.' BOSWELL. 'But, was it not hard, Sir, to expel them, for I am told they were good beings?' JOHNSON. 'Sir, I believe they might be good beings; but they were not fit to be in the University of Oxford. A cow is a very good animal in the field; but we turn her out of a garden.' Lord Elibank used to repeat this as an illustration uncommonly happy.

Desirous of calling Johnson forth to talk, and exercise his wit, though I should myself be the object of it, I resolutely ventured to undertake the defence of convivial indulgence in wine, though he was not to-night in the most genial humour. After urging the common plausible topicks, I at last had recourse to the maxim, *in vino veritas*; a man who is well warmed with wine will speak truth. JOHNSON. 'Why, Sir, that may be an argument for drinking, if you suppose men in general to be liars. But, Sir, I would not keep company with a fellow, who lyes as long as he is sober, and whom you must make drunk before you can get a word of truth out of him.'

Mr. Langton told us he was about to establish a school upon his estate, but it had been suggested to him, that it might have a tendency to make the people less industrious. JOHNSON. 'No, Sir. While learning to read and write is a distinction, the few who have that distinction may be the less inclined to work; but when every body learns to read and write, it is no longer a distinction. A man who has a laced waistcoat is too fine a man to work; but if every body had laced waistcoats, we should have people working in laced waistcoats. There are no people what-

ever more industrious, none who work more, than our manu-
facturers; yet they have all learnt to read and write. Sir, you
must not neglect doing a thing immediately good, from fear of
remote evil;—from fear of its being abused. A man who has
candles may sit up too late, which he would not do if he had not
candles; but nobody will deny that the art of making candles, by
which light is continued to us beyond the time that the sun gives
us light, is a valuable art, and ought to be preserved.' BOSWELL.
'But, Sir, would it not be better to follow Nature; and go to bed
and rise just as nature gives us light or with-holds it?' JOHN-
SON. 'No, Sir; for then we should have no kind of equality in the
partition of our time between sleeping and waking. It would be
very different in different seasons and in different places. In some
of the northern parts of Scotland how little light is there in the
depth of winter!'

We talked of Tacitus, and I hazarded an opinion, that with
all his merit for penetration, shrewdness of judgement, and
terseness of expression, he was too compact, too much broken
into hints, as it were, and therefore too difficult to be understood.
To my great satisfaction, Dr. Johnson sanctioned this opinion.
'Tacitus, Sir, seems to me rather to have made notes for an historical work, than to have written a history.'[1]

At this time it appears from his *Prayers and Meditations*, that
he had been more than commonly diligent in religious duties,
particularly in reading the Holy Scriptures. It was Passion Week,
that solemn season which the Christian world has appropriated
to the commemoration of the mysteries of our redemption, and
during which, whatever embers of religion are in our breasts,
will be kindled into pious warmth.

I paid him short visits both on Friday and Saturday, and seeing
his large folio Greek Testament before him, beheld him with a
reverential awe, and would not intrude upon his time. While he
was thus employed to such good purpose, and while his friends

---

[1] It is remarkable, that Lord Monboddo, whom, on account of his
resembling Dr. Johnson in some particulars, Foote called an Elzevir edition
of him, has, by coincidence, made the very same remark. *Origin and Progress
of Language*, vol. iii. 2nd edit. p. 219.

in their intercourse with him constantly found a vigorous intellect and a lively imagination, it is melancholy to read in his private register, 'My mind is unsettled and my memory confused. I have of late turned my thoughts with a very useless earnestness upon past incidents. I have yet got no command over my thoughts; an unpleasing incident is almost certain to hinder my rest.'[1] What philosophick heroism was it in him to appear with such manly fortitude to the world, while he was inwardly so distressed! We may surely believe that the mysterious principle of being 'made perfect through suffering' was to be strongly exemplified in him.

On Sunday, April 19, being Easter-day, General Paoli and I paid him a visit before dinner. We talked of the notion that blind persons can distinguish colours by the touch. Johnson said, that Professor Sanderson mentions his having attempted to do it, but that he found he was aiming at an impossibility; that to be sure a difference in the surface makes the difference of colours; but that difference is so fine, that it is not sensible to the touch. The General mentioned jugglers and fraudulent gamesters, who could know cards by the touch. Dr. Johnson said, 'the cards used by such persons must be less polished than ours commonly are.'

We talked of sounds. The General said, there was no beauty in a simple sound, but only in an harmonious composition of sounds. I presumed to differ from this opinion, and mentioned the soft and sweet sound of a fine woman's voice. JOHNSON. 'No, Sir, if a serpent or a toad uttered it, you would think it ugly.' BOSWELL. 'So you would think, Sir, were a beautiful tune to be uttered by one of those animals.' JOHNSON. 'No, Sir, it would be admired. We have seen fine fiddlers whom we liked as little as toads,' (laughing).

Talking on the subject of taste in the arts, he said, that difference of taste was, in truth, difference of skill. BOSWELL. 'But, Sir, is there not a quality called taste, which consists merely in perception or in liking? For instance, we find people differ much as to what is the best style of English composition. Some think Swift's the best; others prefer a fuller and grander way of writ-

[1] *Pr. and Med.* p. 111.

ing.' JOHNSON. 'Sir, you must first define what you mean by style, before you can judge who has a good taste in style, and who has a bad. The two classes of persons whom you have mentioned don't differ as to good and bad. They both agree that Swift has a good neat style; but one loves a neat style, another loves a style of more splendour. In like manner, one loves a plain coat, another loves a laced coat; but neither will deny that each is good in its kind.'

While I remained in London this spring, I was with him at several other times, both by himself and in company. I dined with him one day at the Crown and Anchor tavern, in the Strand, with Lord Elibank, Mr. Langton, and Dr. Vansittart of Oxford. Without specifying each particular day, I have preserved the following memorable things.

I regretted the reflection in his Preface to Shakspeare against Garrick, to whom we cannot but apply the following passage: 'I collated such copies as I could procure, and wished for more, but have not found the collectors of these rarities very communicative.' I told him, that Garrick had complained to me of it, and had vindicated himself by assuring me, that Johnson was made welcome to the full use of his collection, and that he left the key of it with a servant, with orders to have a fire and every convenience for him. I found Johnson's notion was, that Garrick wanted to be courted for them, and that, on the contrary, Garrick should have courted him, and sent him the plays of his own accord. But, indeed, considering the slovenly and careless manner in which books were treated by Johnson, it could not be expected that scarce and valuable editions should have been lent to him.

A gentleman[1] having to some of the usual arguments for drinking added this: 'You know, Sir, drinking drives away care, and makes us forget whatever is disagreeable. Would not you allow a man to drink for that reason?' JOHNSON. 'Yes, Sir, if he sat next *you*.'

I expressed a liking for Mr. Francis Osborne's works, and asked him what he thought of that writer. He answered, 'A conceited fellow. Were a man to write so now, the boys would

[1] [Boswell. *Boswell Papers,* ix. 88.]

throw stones at him.' He, however, did not alter my opinion of a favourite authour, to whom I was first directed by his being quoted in *The Spectator*, and in whom I have found much shrewd and lively sense, expressed indeed in a style somewhat quaint, which, however, I do not dislike. His book has an air of origin-ality. We figure to ourselves an ancient gentleman talking to us.

When one of his friends[1] endeavoured to maintain that a country gentleman might contrive to pass his life very agreeably, 'Sir, (said he,) you cannot give me an instance of any man who is permitted to lay out his own time, contriving not to have tedious hours.' This observation, however, is equally applicable to gentlemen who live in cities, and are of no profession.

He said, 'there is no permanent national character; it varies according to circumstances. Alexander the Great swept India: now the Turks sweep Greece.'

A learned gentleman[2] who in the course of conversation wished to inform us of this simple fact, that the Counsel upon the circuit at Shrewsbury were much bitten by fleas, took, I suppose, seven or eight minutes in relating it circumstantially. He in a plenitude of phrase told us, that large bales of woollen cloth were lodged in the town-hall;—that by reason of this, fleas nestled there in prodigious numbers; that the lodgings of the counsel were near to the town-hall;—and that those little animals moved from place to place with wonderful agility. Johnson sat in great im-patience till the gentleman had finished his tedious narrative, and then burst out (playfully however,) 'It is a pity, Sir, that you have not seen a lion; for a flea has taken you such a time, that a lion must have served you a twelve-month.'[3]

He would not allow Scotland to derive any credit from Lord Mansfield; for he was educated in England. 'Much (said he,) may be made of a Scotchman, if he be *caught* young.'

Talking of a modern historian and a modern moralist,[4] he said, 'There is more thought in the moralist than in the his-

---

[1] [Perhaps Boswell. *Boswell Papers*, ix. 95.]
[2] [Dr. Robert Vansittart. *Croker*[1]. See *Boswell Papers*, ix. 256.]
[3] Mrs. Piozzi, to whom I told this anecdote, has related it, as if the gentleman had given 'the *natural history* of the *mouse*.' *Anec.* p. 191.
[4] [Robertson and Beattie. *Boswell Papers*, ix. 257.]

torian. There is but a shallow stream of thought in history.'
BOSWELL. 'But surely, Sir, an historian has reflection.' JOHN-
SON. 'Why yes, Sir; and so has a cat when she catches a mouse
for her kitten. But she cannot write like *******; neither can
*********.'

He said, 'I am very unwilling to read the manuscripts of
authours, and give them my opinion. If the authours who apply
to me have money, I bid them boldly print without a name; if
they have written in order to get money, I tell them to go to the
booksellers, and make the best bargain they can.' BOSWELL.
'But, Sir, if a bookseller should bring you a manuscript to look
at?' JOHNSON. 'Why, Sir, I would desire the bookseller to take
it away.'

I mentioned a friend of mine[1] who had resided long in Spain,
and was unwilling to return to Britain. JOHNSON. 'Sir, he is
attached to some woman.' BOSWELL. 'I rather believe, Sir, it is
the fine climate which keeps him there.' JOHNSON. 'Nay, Sir,
how can you talk so? What is *climate* to happiness? Place me in
the heart of Asia, should I not be exiled? What proportion does
climate bear to the complex system of human life? You may
advise me to go to live at Bologna to eat sausages. The sausages
there are the best in the world; they lose much by being carried.'

On Saturday, May 9, Mr. Dempster and I had agreed to dine
by ourselves at the British Coffee-house. Johnson, on whom I
happened to call in the morning, said he would join us, which he
did, and we spent a very agreeable day, though I recollect but
little of what passed.

He said, 'Walpole was a minister given by the King to the
people: Pitt was a minister given by the people to the King,—
as an adjunct.'

'The misfortune of Goldsmith in conversation is this: he goes
on without knowing how he is to get off. His genius is great,
but his knowledge is small. As they say of a generous man, it is
a pity he is not rich, we may say of Goldsmith, it is a pity he is
not knowing. He would not keep his knowledge to himself.'

Before leaving London this year, I consulted him upon a

[1] [Boswell's brother David. *Ib.* 258.]

question purely of Scotch law. It was held of old, and continued
for a long period, to be an established principle in that law, that
whoever intermeddled with the effects of a person deceased,
without the interposition of legal authority to guard against
embezzlement, should be subjected to pay all the debts of the
deceased, as having been guilty of what was technically called
vicious intromission. The Court of Session had gradually relaxed
the strictness of this principle, where the interference proved
had been inconsiderable. In a case[1] which came before that Court
the preceding winter, I had laboured to persuade the Judges to
return to the ancient law. It was my own sincere opinion, that
they ought to adhere to it; but I had exhausted all my powers
of reasoning in vain. Johnson thought as I did; and in order to
assist me in my application to the Court for a revision and alteration of the judgement, he dictated to me the following argument:—

'This, we are told, is a law which has its force only from
the long practice of the Court: and may, therefore, be suspended
or modified as the Court shall think proper.

'Concerning the power of the Court to make or to suspend a
law, we have no intention to inquire. It is sufficient for our purpose that every just law is dictated by reason; and that the practice of every legal Court is regulated by equity. It is the quality
of reason to be invariable and constant; and of equity, to give to
one man what, in the same case, is given to another. The advantage which humanity derives from law is this: that the law gives
every man a rule of action, and prescribes a mode of conduct
which shall entitle him to the support and protection of society.
That the law may be a rule of action, it is necessary that it be
known; it is necessary that it be permanent and stable. The law
is the measure of civil right; but if the measure be changeable,
the extent of the thing measured never can be settled.

'To permit a law to be modified at discretion, is to leave the
community without law. It is to withdraw the direction of that
publick wisdom, by which the deficiencies of private understanding are to be supplied. It is to suffer the rash and ignorant to act

[1] Wilson against Smith and Armour.

at discretion, and then to depend for the legality of that action on the sentence of the Judge. He that is thus governed, lives not by law, but by opinion: not by a certain rule to which he can apply his intention before he acts, but by an uncertain and variable opinion, which he can never know but after he has committed the act on which that opinion shall be passed. He lives by a law, (if a law it be,) which he can never know before he has offended it. To this case may be justly applied that important principle, *misera est servitus ubi jus est aut incognitum aut vagum.*[1] If Intromission be not criminal till it exceeds a certain point, and that point be unsettled, and consequently different in different minds, the right of Intromission, and the right of the Creditor arising from it, are all *jura vaga*, and, by consequence, are *jura incognita*; and the result can be no other than a *misera servitus*, an uncertainty concerning the event of action, a servile dependence on private opinion.

'It may be urged, and with great plausibility, that there may be Intromission without fraud; which, however true, will by no means justify an occasional and arbitrary relaxation of the law. The end of law is protection as well as vengeance. Indeed, vengeance is never used but to strengthen protection. That society only is well governed, where life is freed from danger and from suspicion; where possession is so sheltered by salutary prohibitions, that violation is prevented more frequently than punished. Such a prohibition was this, while it operated with its original force. The creditor of the deceased was not only without loss, but without fear. He was not to seek a remedy for an injury suffered; for injury was warded off.

'As the law has been sometimes administered, it lays us open to wounds, because it is imagined to have the power of healing. To punish fraud when it is detected, is the proper act of vindictive justice; but to prevent frauds, and make punishment unnecessary, is the great employment of legislative wisdom. To permit Intromission, and to punish fraud, is to make law no better than a pitfall. To tread upon the brink is safe; but to come a step further

[1] ['A society in which rights are unknown or doubtful is no better than slavery.']

is destruction. But, surely, it is better to enclose the gulf, and hinder all access, than by encouraging us to advance a little, to entice us afterwards a little further, and let us perceive our folly only by our destruction.

'As law supplies the weak with adventitious strength, it likewise enlightens the ignorant with extrinsick understanding. Law teaches us to know when we commit injury, and when we suffer it. It fixes certain marks upon actions, by which we are admonished to do or to forbear them. *Qui sibi bene temperat in licitis*, says one of the fathers, *nunquam cadet in illicita*.[1] He who never intromits at all, will never intromit with fraudulent intentions.

'The relaxation of the law against vicious intromission has been very favourably represented by a great master of jurisprudence,[2] whose words have been exhibited with unnecessary pomp, and seem to be considered as irresistibly decisive. The great moment of his authority makes it necessary to examine his position. "Some ages ago, (says he,) before the ferocity of the inhabitants of this part of the island was subdued, the utmost severity of the civil law was necessary, to restrain individuals from plundering each other. Thus, the man who intermeddled irregularly with the moveables of a person deceased, was subjected to all the debts of the deceased without limitation. This makes a branch of the law of Scotland, known by the name of *vicious intromission*; and so rigidly was this regulation applied in our Courts of Law, that the most trifling moveable abstracted *malâ fide*, subjected the intermeddler to the foregoing consequences, which proved in many instances a most rigorous punishment. But this severity was necessary, in order to subdue the undisciplined nature of our people. It is extremely remarkable, that in proportion to our improvement in manners, this regulation has been gradually softened, and applied by our sovereign Court with a sparing hand."

'I find myself under a necessity of observing, that this learned and judicious writer has not accurately distinguished the de-

---

[1] ['Whoso is temperate in lawful pleasures will never fall into those that are unlawful.']

[2] Lord Kames, in his *Historical Law Tracts*.

ficiencies and demands of the different conditions of human life, which, from a degree of savageness and independence, in which all laws are vain, passes or may pass, by innumerable gradations, to a state of reciprocal benignity, in which laws shall be no longer necessary. Men are first wild and unsocial, living each man to himself, taking from the weak, and losing to the strong. In their first coalitions of society, much of this original savageness is retained. Of general happiness, the product of general confidence, there is yet no thought. Men continue to prosecute their own advantages by the nearest way; and the utmost severity of the civil law is necessary to restrain individuals from plundering each other. The restraints then necessary, are restraints from plunder, from acts of publick violence, and undisguised oppressions. The ferocity of our ancestors, as of all other nations, produced not fraud, but rapine. They had not yet learned to cheat, and attempted only to rob. As manners grow more polished, with the knowledge of good, men attain likewise dexterity in evil. Open rapine becomes less frequent, and violence gives way to cunning. Those who before invaded pastures and stormed houses, now begin to enrich themselves by unequal contracts and fraudulent intromissions. It is not against the violence of ferocity, but the circumventions of deceit, that this law was framed; and I am afraid the increase of commerce, and the incessant struggle for riches which commerce excites, give us no prospect of an end speedily to be expected of artifice and fraud. It therefore seems to be no very conclusive reasoning, which connects those two propositions;—"the nation is become less ferocious, and therefore the laws against fraud and *covin* shall be relaxed."

'Whatever reason may have influenced the Judges to a relaxation of the law, it was not that the nation was grown less fierce; and, I am afraid, it cannot be affirmed, that it is grown less fraudulent.

'Since this law has been represented as rigorously and unreasonably penal, it seems not improper to consider what are the conditions and qualities that make the justice or propriety of a penal law.

'To make a penal law reasonable and just, two conditions are necessary, and two proper. It is necessary that the law should be adequate to its end; that, if it be observed, it shall prevent the evil against which it is directed. It is, secondly, necessary that the end of the law be of such importance, as to deserve the security of a penal sanction. The other conditions of a penal law, which though not absolutely necessary, are to a very high degree fit, are, that to the moral violation of the law there are many temptations, and that of the physical observance there is great facility.

'All these conditions apparently concur to justify the law which we are now considering. Its end is the security of property; and property very often of great value. The method by which it effects the security is efficacious, because it admits, in its original rigour, no gradations of injury; but keeps guilt and innocence apart, by a distinct and definite limitation. He that intromits, is criminal; he that intromits not, is innocent. Of the two secondary considerations it cannot be denied that both are in our favour. The temptation to intromit is frequent and strong; so strong and so frequent, as to require the utmost activity of justice, and vigilance of caution, to withstand its prevalence; and the method by which a man may entitle himself to legal intromission, is so open and so facile, that to neglect it is a proof of fraudulent intention: for why should a man omit to do (but for reasons which he will not confess,) that which he can do so easily, and that which he knows to be required by the law? If temptation were rare, a penal law might be deemed unnecessary. If the duty enjoined by the law were of difficult performance, omission, though it could not be justified, might be pitied. But in the present case, neither equity nor compassion operate against it. A useful, a necessary law is broken, not only without a reasonable motive, but with all the inducements to obedience that can be derived from safety and facility.

'I therefore return to my original position, that a law, to have its effect, must be permanent and stable. It may be said, in the language of the schools, *Lex non recipit majus et minus*,[1]—we may have a law, or we may have no law, but we cannot have half a law. We must either have a rule of action, or be permitted

[1] ['Law does not admit degrees.']

500

to act by discretion and by chance. Deviations from the law must be uniformly punished, or no man can be certain when he shall be safe.

'That from the rigour of the original institution this Court has sometimes departed, cannot be denied. But, as it is evident that such deviations, as they make law uncertain, make life unsafe, I hope, that of departing from it there will now be an end; that the wisdom of our ancestors will be treated with due reverence; and that consistent and steady decisions will furnish the people with a rule of action, and leave fraud and fraudulent intromission no future hope of impunity or escape.'

With such comprehension of mind, and such clearness of penetration, did he thus treat a subject altogether new to him, without any other preparation than my having stated to him the arguments which had been used on each side of the question. His intellectual powers appeared with peculiar lustre, when tried against those of a writer of so much fame as Lord Kames, and that too in his Lordship's own department.

This masterly argument, after being prefaced and concluded with some sentences of my own, and garnished with the usual formularies, was actually printed and laid before the Lords of Session, but without success. My respected friend Lord Hailes, however, one of that honourable body, had critical sagacity enough to discover a more than ordinary hand in the *Petition*. I told him Dr. Johnson had favoured me with his pen. His Lordship, with wonderful *acumen*, pointed out exactly where his composition began, and where it ended. But that I may do impartial justice, and conform to the great rule of Courts, *Suum cuique tribuito*,[1] I must add, that their Lordships in general, though they were pleased to call this 'a well-drawn paper,' preferred the former very inferiour petition which I had written; thus confirming the truth of an observation made to me by one of their number, in a merry mood: 'My dear Sir, give yourself no trouble in the composition of the papers you present to us; for, indeed, it is casting pearls before swine.'

I renewed my solicitations that Dr. Johnson would this year accomplish his long-intended visit to Scotland.

[1] ['To render to every one his due.' Justinian, *Institutes*, I. i. 1.]

'*To* James Boswell, Esq.

'Dear Sir,—The regret has not been little with which I have missed a journey so pregnant with pleasing expectations, as that in which I could promise myself not only the gratification of curiosity, both rational and fanciful, but the delight of seeing those whom I love and esteem. * * * * * * *. But such has been the course of things, that I could not come; and such has been, I am afraid, the state of my body, that it would not well have seconded my inclination. My body, I think, grows better, and I refer my hopes to another year; for I am very sincere in my design to pay the visit, and take the ramble. In the mean time, do not omit any opportunity of keeping up a favourable opinion of me in the minds of any of my friends. Beattie's book is, I believe, every day more liked; at least, I like it more, as I look more upon it.

'I am glad if you got credit by your cause, and am yet of opinion, that our cause was good, and that the determination ought to have been in your favour. Poor Hastie, I think, had but his deserts.

'You promised to get me a little *Pindar*, you may add to it a little *Anacreon*.

'The leisure which I cannot enjoy, it will be a pleasure to hear that you employ upon the antiquities of the feudal establishment. The whole system of ancient tenures is gradually passing away; and I wish to have the knowledge of it preserved adequate and complete. For such an institution makes a very important part of the history of mankind. Do not forget a design so worthy of a scholar who studies the laws of his country, and of a gentleman who may naturally be curious to know the condition of his own ancestors. I am, dear Sir, your's with great affection,

'August 31, 1772.'   'Sam. Johnson.'

'*To* Dr. Johnson

'My Dear Sir,   'Edinburgh, Dec. 25, 1772.

'. . . I was much disappointed that you did not come to Scotland last autumn. However, I must own that your letter prevents me from complaining; not only because I am sensible that the state of your health was but too good an excuse, but because you write in a strain which shews that you have agreeable views of the scheme which we have so long proposed. . . .

'I communicated to Beattie what you said of his book in your last letter to me. He writes to me thus:—"You judge very rightly in supposing that Dr. Johnson's favourable opinion of my book must give me great delight. Indeed it is impossible for me to say how much I am gratified by it; for there is not a man upon earth whose good opinion I would be more ambitious to cultivate. His talents and his virtues I reverence more than any words can express. The extraordinary civilities (the paternal attentions I should rather say,) and the many instructions I have had the honour to receive from him, will to me be a perpetual source of pleasure in the recollection,

> *Dum memor ipse mei, dum spiritus hos reget artus.*[1]

"I had still some thoughts, while the summer lasted, of being obliged to go to London on some little business; otherwise I should certainly have troubled him with a letter several months ago, and given some vent to my gratitude and admiration. This I intend to do, as soon as I am left a little at leisure. Mean time, if you have occasion to write to him, I beg you will offer him my most respectful compliments, and assure him of the sincerity of my attachment and the warmth of my gratitude." . . . I am, &c.

'JAMES BOSWELL.'

1773: ÆTAT. 64.]—IN 1773 his only publication was an edition of his folio *Dictionary*, with additions and corrections; nor did he, so far as is known, furnish any productions of his fertile pen to any of his numerous friends or dependants, except the Preface[2] to his old amanuensis Macbean's *Dictionary of Ancient Geography*.

---

[1] ['While yet I have remembrance of myself and the breath governs these limbs.' *Aeneid*, iv. 336. (Jackson.)]

[2] He, however, wrote, or partly wrote, an Epitaph on Mrs. Bell, wife of his friend John Bell, Esq., brother of the Reverend Dr. Bell, Prebendary of Westminster, which is printed in his *Works* [i. 151]. It is in English prose, and has so little of his manner, that I did not believe he had any hand in it, till I was satisfied of the fact by the authority of Mr. Bell.

His *Shakspeare*, indeed, which had been received with high approbation by the publick, and gone through several editions, was
this year re-published by George Steevens, Esq., a gentleman
not only deeply skilled in ancient learning, and of very extensive
reading in English literature, especially the early writers, but
at the same time of acute discernment and elegant taste. It is
almost unnecessary to say, that by his great and valuable additions to Dr. Johnson's work, he justly obtained considerable
reputation:

'*Divisum imperium cum Jove Cæsar habet.*'[1]

'*To* JAMES BOSWELL, ESQ.

'DEAR SIR,—I have read your kind letter much more than the
elegant *Pindar* which it accompanied. I am always glad to find
myself not forgotten; and to be forgotten by you would give me
great uneasiness. My northern friends have never been unkind
to me: I have from you, dear Sir, testimonies of affection, which
I have not often been able to excite; and Dr. Beattie rates the
testimony which I was desirous of paying to his merit, much
higher than I should have thought it reasonable to expect.

'I have heard of your masquerade.[2] What says your synod to
such innovations? I am not studiously scrupulous, nor do I think
a masquerade either evil in itself, or very likely to be the occasion of evil; yet as the world thinks it a very licentious relaxation
of manners, I would not have been one of the *first* masquers in
a country where no masquerade had ever been before.[3]

A new edition of my great *Dictionary* is printed, from a copy
which I was persuaded to revise; but having made no preparation, I was able to do very little. Some superfluities I have expunged, and some faults I have corrected, and here and there
have scattered a remark; but the main fabrick of the work
remains as it was. I had looked very little into it since I wrote it,
and, I think, I found it full as often better, as worse, than I
expected.

[1] ['Caesar has divided the empire with Jove.' From an epigram in the
Life of Virgil ascribed to Donatus.]
[2] Given by a lady at Edinburgh.
[3] There had been masquerades in Scotland; but not for a very long time.

'Baretti and Davies have had a furious quarrel; a quarrel, I think, irreconcileable. Dr. Goldsmith has a new comedy, which is expected in the spring. No name is yet given it. The chief diversion arises from a stratagem by which a lover is made to mistake his future father-in-law's house for an inn. This, you see, borders upon farce. The dialogue is quick and gay, and the incidents are so prepared as not to seem improbable.

'I am sorry that you lost your cause of Intromission, because I yet think the arguments on your side unanswerable. But you seem, I think, to say that you gained reputation even by your defeat; and reputation you will daily gain, if you keep Lord Auchinleck's precept in your mind, and endeavour to consolidate in your mind a firm and regular system of law, instead of picking up occasional fragments.

'My health seems in general to improve; but I have been troubled for many weeks with a vexatious catarrh, which is sometimes sufficiently distressful. I have not found any great effects from bleeding and physick; and am afraid, that I must expect help from brighter days and softer air.

'Write to me now and then; and whenever any good befalls you, make haste to let me know it, for no one will rejoice at it more than, dear Sir, your most humble servant,

'London, Feb. 24, 1773.'   'SAM. JOHNSON.'

'You continue to stand very high in the favour of Mrs. Thrale.'

While a former edition of my work was passing through the press, I was unexpectedly favoured with a packet from Philadelphia, from Mr. James Abercrombie, a gentleman of that country, who is pleased to honour me with very high praise of my *Life of Dr. Johnson.* To have the fame of my illustrious friend, and his faithful biographer, echoed from the New World is extremely flattering; and my grateful acknowledgements shall be wafted across the Atlantick. Mr. Abercrombie has politely conferred on me a considerable additional obligation, by transmitting to me copies of two letters from Dr. Johnson to American gentlemen. 'Gladly, Sir, (says he,) would I have sent you the originals; but being the only relicks of the kind in America, they are considered by the possessors of such inestimable value, that no possible consideration would induce them to part with them. In some future publication of yours relative to that great and good man, they may perhaps be thought worthy of insertion.'

'*To* Mr. B——d[1]

'Sir,—That in the hurry of a sudden departure you should yet find leisure to consult my convenience, is a degree of kindness, and an instance of regard, not only beyond my claims, but above my expectation. You are not mistaken in supposing that I set a high value on my American friends, and that you should confer a very valuable favour upon me by giving me an opportunity of keeping myself in their memory.

'I have taken the liberty of troubling you with a packet, to which I wish a safe and speedy conveyance, because I wish a safe and speedy voyage to him that conveys it. I am, Sir, your most humble servant,

'London, Johnson's-court,   'Sam. Johnson.'
Fleet-street, March 4, 1773.'

'*To* The Reverend Mr. White[2]

'Dear Sir,—Your kindness for your friends accompanies you across the Atlantick. It was long since observed by Horace, that no ship could leave care behind; you have been attended in your voyage by other[3] powers,—by benevolence and constancy; and I hope care did not often shew her face in their company.

'I received the copy of *Rasselas*.[4] The impression is not magnificent, but it flatters an authour, because the printer seems to have expected that it would be scattered among the people. The

[1] This gentleman [Bond*], who now resides in America in a publick character of considerable dignity [consul], desired that his name might not be transcribed at full length.

[2] Now Doctor White, and Bishop of the Episcopal Church in Pennsylvania. During his first visit to England in 1771, as a candidate for holy orders, he was several times in company with Dr. Johnson, who expressed a wish to see the edition of his *Rasselas*, which Dr. White told him had been printed in America. Dr. White, on his return immediately sent him a copy.

[3] [Johnson wrote *better*.]

[4] [This Philadelphia edition (1768) is described in the imprint as 'Printed for every purchaser'.]

* [*Letters of Johnson*, 1822.]

little book has been well received, and is translated into Italian, French, German, and Dutch. It has now one honour more by an American edition.

'I know not that much has happened since your departure that can engage your curiosity. Of all publick transactions the whole world is now informed by the news-papers. Opposition seems to despond; and the dissenters, though they have taken advantage of unsettled times, and a government much enfeebled, seem not likely to gain any immunities.

'Dr. Goldsmith has a new comedy[1] in rehearsal at Covent-Garden, to which the manager predicts ill success. I hope he will be mistaken. I think it deserves a very kind reception.

'I shall soon publish a new edition of my large *Dictionary*: I have been persuaded to revise it, and have mended some faults, but added little to its usefulness.

'No book has been published since your departure, of which much notice is taken. Faction only fills the town with pamphlets, and greater subjects are forgotten in the noise of discord.

'Thus have I written, only to tell you how little I have to tell. Of myself I can only add, that having been afflicted many weeks with a very troublesome cough, I am now recovered.

'I take the liberty which you give me of troubling you with a letter, of which you will please to fill up the direction. I am, Sir, your most humble servant,

'Johnson's-court, Fleet-street,   'SAM. JOHNSON.'
    London, March 4, 1773.'

On Saturday, April 3, the day after my arrival in London this year, I went to his house late in the evening, and sat with Mrs. Williams till he came home. I found in the *London Chronicle*, Dr. Goldsmith's apology to the publick for beating Evans, a bookseller, on account of a paragraph in a news-paper published by him, which Goldsmith thought impertinent to him and to a lady of his acquaintance. The apology was written so much in Dr. Johnson's manner, that both Mrs. Williams and I supposed it to be his; but when he came home, he soon undeceived us.

---

[1] [*She Stoops to Conquer.*]

When he said to Mrs. Williams, 'Well, Dr. Goldsmith's *manifesto* has got into your paper;' I asked him if Dr. Goldsmith had written it, with an air that made him see I suspected it was his, though subscribed by Goldsmith. JOHNSON. 'Sir, Dr. Goldsmith would no more have asked me to write such a thing as that for him, than he would have asked me to feed him with a spoon, or to do anything else that denoted his imbecility. I as much believe that he wrote it, as if I had seen him do it. Sir, had he shewn it to any one friend, he would not have been allowed to publish it. He has, indeed, done it very well; but it is a foolish thing well done. I suppose he has been so much elated with the success of his new comedy, that he has thought every thing that concerned him must be of importance to the publick.' BOSWELL. 'I fancy, Sir, this is the first time that he has been engaged in such an adventure.' JOHNSON. 'Why, Sir, I believe it is the first time he has *beat*; he may have *been beaten* before. This, Sir, is a new plume to him.'

I mentioned Sir John Dalrymple's *Memoirs of Great-Britain and Ireland*, and his discoveries to the prejudice of Lord Russel and Algernon Sydney. JOHNSON. 'Why, Sir, every body who had just notions of government thought them rascals before. It is well that all mankind now see them to be rascals.' BOSWELL. 'But, Sir, may not those discoveries be true without their being rascals?' JOHNSON. 'Consider, Sir; would any of them have been willing to have had it known that they intrigued with France? Depend upon it, Sir, he who does what he is afraid should be known, has something rotten about him. This Dalrymple seems to be an honest fellow; for he tells equally what makes against both sides. But nothing can be poorer than his mode of writing: it is the mere bouncing of a school-boy. Great He! but greater She! and such stuff.'

I could not agree with him in this criticism; for though Sir John Dalrymple's style is not regularly formed in any respect, and one cannot help smiling sometimes at his affected *grandiloquence*, there is in his writing a pointed vivacity, and much of a gentlemanly spirit.

At Mr. Thrale's, in the evening, he repeated his usual paradoxical declamation against action in publick speaking. 'Action can have no effect upon reasonable minds. It may augment noise, but it never can enforce argument. If you speak to a dog, you use action; you hold up your hand thus, because he is a brute; and in proportion as men are removed from brutes, action will have the less influence upon them.' MRS. THRALE. 'What then, Sir, becomes of Demosthenes's saying? "Action, action, action!" ' JOHNSON. 'Demosthenes, Madam, spoke to an assembly of brutes; to a barbarous people.'

I thought it extraordinary, that he should deny the power of rhetorical action upon human nature, when it is proved by innumerable facts in all stages of society. Reasonable beings are not solely reasonable. They have fancies which may be pleased, passions which may be roused.

Lord Chesterfield being mentioned, Johnson remarked, that almost all of that celebrated nobleman's witty sayings were puns. He, however, allowed the merit of good wit to his Lordship's saying of Lord Tyrawley and himself, when both very old and infirm: 'Tyrawley and I have been dead these two years; but we don't choose to have it known.'

He talked with approbation of an intended edition of *The Spectator*, with notes; two volumes of which had been prepared by a gentleman eminent in the literary world,[1] and the materials which he had collected for the remainder had been transferred to another hand.[2] He observed, that all works which describe manners, require notes in sixty or seventy years, or less; and told us, he had communicated all he knew that could throw light upon *The Spectator*. He said, 'Addison had made his Sir Andrew Freeport a true Whig, arguing against giving charity to beggars, and throwing out other such ungracious sentiments; but that he had thought better, and made amends by making him found an hospital for decayed farmers.' He called for the volume of *The Spectator*, in which that account is contained, and read it aloud to us. He read so well, that every thing acquired additional weight and grace from his utterance.

[1] [Percy. *Boswell Papers*, vi. 96.]
[2] [Dr. John Calder. *Ib.*]

The conversation having turned on modern imitations of ancient ballads, and some one having praised their simplicity, he treated them with that ridicule which he always displayed when this subject was mentioned.

He disapproved of introducing scripture phrases into secular discourse. This seemed to me a question of some difficulty. A scripture expression may be used, like a highly classical phrase, to produce an instantaneous strong impression; and it may be done without being at all improper. Yet I own there is danger, that applying the language of our sacred book to ordinary subjects may tend to lessen our reverence for it. If therefore it be introduced at all, it should be with very great caution.

On Thursday, April 8, I sat a good part of the evening with him, but he was very silent. He said, 'Burnet's *History of his own times* is very entertaining. The style, indeed, is mere chit-chat. I do not believe that Burnet intentionally lyed; but he was so much prejudiced, that he took no pains to find out the truth. He was like a man who resolves to regulate his time by a certain watch; but will not inquire whether the watch is right or not.'

Though he was not disposed to talk, he was unwilling that I should leave him; and when I looked at my watch, and told him it was twelve o'clock, he cried, 'What's that to you and me?' and ordered Frank to tell Mrs. Williams that we were coming to drink tea with her, which we did. It was settled that we should go to church together next day.

On the 9th of April, being Good Friday, I breakfasted with him on tea and cross-buns; *Doctor* Levet, as Frank called him, making the tea. He carried me with him to the church of St. Clement Danes, where he had his seat; and his behaviour was, as I had imaged to myself, solemnly devout. I never shall forget the tremulous earnestness with which he pronounced the awful petition in the Litany: 'In the hour of death, and at the day of judgement, good LORD deliver us.'

We went to church both in the morning and evening. In the interval between the two services we did not dine; but he read in the Greek New Testament, and I turned over several of his books.

In Archbishop Laud's Diary, I found the following passage, which I read to Dr. Johnson:—

'1623. February 1, Sunday. I stood by the most illustrious Prince Charles,[1] at dinner. He was then very merry, and talked occasionally of many things with his attendants. Among other things, he said, that if he were necessitated to take any particular profession of life, he could not be a lawyer, adding his reasons: "I cannot (saith he,) defend a bad, nor yield in a good cause." '

JOHNSON. 'Sir, this is false reasoning; because every cause has a bad side: and a lawyer is not overcome, though the cause which he has endeavoured to support be determined against him.'

I told him that Goldsmith had said to me a few days before, 'As I take my shoes from the shoemaker, and my coat from the taylor, so I take my religion from the priest.' I regretted this loose way of talking. JOHNSON. 'Sir, he knows nothing; he has made up his mind about nothing.'

To my great surprize he asked me to dine with him on Easter-day. I never supposed that he had a dinner at his house; for I had not then heard of any one of his friends having been entertained at his table. He told me, 'I generally have a meat pye on Sunday: it is baked at a publick oven, which is very properly allowed, because one man can attend it; and thus the advantage is obtained of not keeping servants from church to dress dinners.'

April 11, being Easter-Sunday, after having attended Divine Service at St. Paul's, I repaired to Dr. Johnson's. I had gratified my curiosity much in dining with JEAN JACQUES ROUSSEAU, while he lived in the wilds of Neufchatel: I had as great a curiosity to dine with DR. SAMUEL JOHNSON, in the dusky recess of a court in Fleet-street. I supposed we should scarcely have knives and forks, and only some strange, uncouth, ill-drest dish: but I found every thing in very good order. We had no other company but Mrs. Williams and a young woman[2] whom I did not know. As a dinner here was considered as a singular phænomenon, and as I was frequently interrogated on the subject, my readers may perhaps be desirous to know our bill of fare. Foote, I remember,

---

[1] Afterwards Charles I.
[2] [Perhaps Miss Carmichael. *Mrs. Piozzi* (1816).]

in allusion to Francis, the *negro*, was willing to suppose that our repast was *black broth*. But the fact was, that we had a very good soup, a boiled leg of lamb and spinach, a veal pye, and a rice pudding.

Of Dr. John Campbell, the authour, he said, 'He is a very inquisitive and a very able man, and a man of good religious principles, though I am afraid he has been deficient in practice. Campbell is radically right; and we may hope, that in time there will be good practice.'

He owned that he thought Hawkesworth was one of his imitators, but he did not think Goldsmith was. Goldsmith, he said, had great merit. Boswell. 'But, Sir, he is much indebted to you for his getting so high in the publick estimation.' Johnson. 'Why, Sir, he has perhaps got *sooner* to it by his intimacy with me.'

Goldsmith, though his vanity often excited him to occasional competition, had a very high regard for Johnson, which he at this time expressed in the strongest manner in the Dedication of his comedy, entitled, *She Stoops to Conquer*.[1]

Johnson observed, that there were very few books printed in Scotland before the Union. He had seen a complete collection of them in the possession of the Hon. Archibald Campbell, a nonjuring Bishop.[2] I wish this collection had been kept entire. Many of them are in the library of the Faculty of Advocates at Edinburgh. I told Dr. Johnson that I had some intention to write the life of the learned and worthy Thomas Ruddiman. He said, 'I should take pleasure in helping you to do honour to him. But his farewell letter to the Faculty of Advocates, when he resigned the office of their Librarian, should have been in Latin.'

I put a question to him upon a fact in common life, which he could not answer, nor have I found any one else who could.

[1] 'By inscribing this slight performance to you, I do not mean so much to compliment you as myself. It may do me some honour to inform the publick, that I have lived many years in intimacy with you. It may serve the interests of mankind also to inform them, that the greatest wit may be found in a character, without impairing the most unaffected piety.'

[2] See an account of this learned and respectable gentleman, and of his curious work on the *Middle State*, *Journal of a Tour to the Hebrides*, 3rd edit. p. 371. [Oct. 25.]

What is the reason that women servants, though obliged to be at the expense of purchasing their own clothes, have much lower wages than men servants, to whom a great proportion of that article is furnished, and when in fact our female house servants work much harder than the male?

He told me, that he had twelve or fourteen times attempted to keep a journal of his life, but never could persevere. He advised me to do it. 'The great thing to be recorded, (said he,) is the state of your own mind; and you should write down every thing that you remember, for you cannot judge at first what is good or bad; and write immediately while the impression is fresh, for it will not be the same a week afterwards.'

I again solicited him to communicate to me the particulars of his early life. He said, 'You shall have them all for twopence. I hope you shall know a great deal more of me before you write my Life.' He mentioned to me this day many circumstances, which I wrote down when I went home, and have interwoven in the former part of this narrative.

On Tuesday, April 13, he and Dr. Goldsmith and I dined at General Oglethorpe's. Goldsmith expatiated on the common topick, that the race of our people was degenerated, and that this was owing to luxury. JOHNSON. 'Sir, in the first place, I doubt the fact. I believe there are as many tall men in England now, as ever there were. But, secondly, supposing the stature of our people to be diminished, that is not owing to luxury; for, Sir, consider to how very small a proportion of our people luxury can reach. Our soldiery, surely, are not luxurious, who live on six-pence a day; and the same remark will apply to almost all the other classes. Luxury, so far as it reaches the poor, will do good to the race of people; it will strengthen and multiply them. Sir, no nation was ever hurt by luxury; for, as I said before, it can reach but to a very few. I admit that the great increase of com-merce and manufactures hurts the military spirit of a people; because it produces a competition for something else than martial honours,—a competition for riches. It also hurts the bodies of the people; for you will observe, there is no man who works at any particular trade, but you may know him from his appearance

to do so. One part or other of his body being more used than the
rest, he is in some degree deformed: but, Sir, that is not luxury.
A tailor sits cross-legged; but that is not luxury. GOLDSMITH.
'Come, you're just going to the same place by another road.'
JOHNSON. 'Nay, Sir, I say that is not *luxury*. Let us take a walk
from Charing-cross to Whitechapel, through, I suppose, the
greatest series of shops in the world; what is there in any of
these shops (if you except gin-shops,) that can do any human
being any harm?' GOLDSMITH. 'Well, Sir, I'll accept your challenge. The very next shop to Northumberland-house is a pickle-
shop.' JOHNSON. 'Well, Sir: do we not know that a maid can in
one afternoon make pickles sufficient to serve a whole family for
a year? nay, that five pickle-shops can serve all the kingdom?
Besides, Sir, there is no harm done to any body by the making
of pickles, or the eating of pickles.'

We drank tea with the ladies; and Goldsmith sung Tony
Lumpkin's song in his comedy, *She Stoops to Conquer*, and a very
pretty one, to an Irish tune,[1] which he had designed for Miss
Hardcastle; but as Mrs. Bulkeley, who played the part, could not
sing, it was left out. He afterwards wrote it down for me, by which
means it was preserved, and now appears amongst his poems.
Dr Johnson, in his way home, stopped at my lodgings in Picca-
dilly, and sat with me, drinking tea a second time, till a late hour.

I told him that Mrs. Macaulay said, she wondered how he
could reconcile his political principles with his moral; his notions
of inequality and subordination with wishing well to the happiness of all mankind, who might live so agreeably, had they all
their portions of land, and none to domineer over another.
JOHNSON. 'Why, Sir, I reconcile my principles very well, because mankind are happier in a state of inequality and subordination. Were they to be in this pretty state of equality, they would
soon degenerate into brutes;—they would become Monboddo's
nation;—their tails would grow. Sir, all would be losers were
all to work for all:—they would have no intellectual improvement. All intellectual improvement arises from leisure; all leisure
arises from one working for another.'

[1] The humours of Ballamagairy.

Talking of the family of Stuart, he said, 'It should seem that
the family at present on the throne has now established as good
a right as the former family, by the long consent of the people;
and that to disturb this right might be considered as culpable.
At the same time I own, that it is a very difficult question, when
considered with respect to the house of Stuart. To oblige people
to take oaths as to the disputed right, is wrong. I know not
whether I could take them: but I do not blame those who do.'
So conscientious and so delicate was he upon this subject, which
has occasioned so much clamour against him.

Talking of law cases, he said, 'The English reports, in general,
are very poor: only the half of what has been said is taken down;
and of that half, much is mistaken. Whereas, in Scotland, the
arguments on each side are deliberately put in writing, to be
considered by the Court. I think a collection of your cases upon
subjects of importance, with the opinions of the Judges upon
them, would be valuable.'

On Thursday, April 15, I dined with him and Dr. Goldsmith
at General Paoli's. We found here Signor Martinelli, of Florence,
authour of a *History of England*, in Italian, printed at London.

I spoke of Allan Ramsay's *Gentle Shepherd*, in the Scottish
dialect, as the best pastoral that had ever been written; not only
abounding with beautiful rural imagery, and just and pleasing
sentiments, but being a real picture of manners; and I offered to
teach Dr. Johnson to understand it. 'No, Sir, (said he,) I won't
learn it. You shall retain your superiority by my not knowing it.'

This brought on a question whether one man is lessened by
another's acquiring an equal degree of knowledge with him.
Johnson asserted the affirmative. I maintained that the position
might be true in those kinds of knowledge which produce wisdom,
power, and force, so as to enable one man to have the government of others; but that a man is not in any degree lessened by
others knowing as well as he what ends in mere pleasure:—
eating fine fruits, drinking delicious wines, reading exquisite
poetry.

The General observed, that Martinelli was a Whig. JOHN-
SON. 'I am sorry for it. It shows the spirit of the times: he is

obliged to temporise.' BOSWELL. 'I rather think, Sir, that Tory-ism prevails in this reign.' JOHNSON. 'I know not why you should think so, Sir. You see your friend Lord Lyttelton, a nobleman, is obliged in his *History* to write the most vulgar Whiggism.'

An animated debate took place whether Martinelli should continue his *History of England* to the present day. GOLD-SMITH. 'To be sure he should.' JOHNSON. 'No, Sir; he would give great offence. He would have to tell of almost all the living great what they do not wish told.' GOLDSMITH. 'It may, per-haps, be necessary for a native to be more cautious; but a foreigner who comes among us without prejudice, may be con-sidered as holding the place of a Judge, and may speak his mind freely.' JOHNSON. 'Sir, a foreigner, when he sends a work from the press, ought to be on his guard against catching the errour and mistaken enthusiasm of the people among whom he happens to be.' GOLDSMITH. 'Sir, he wants only to sell his history, and to tell truth; one an honest, the other a laudable motive.' JOHN-SON. 'Sir, they are both laudable motives. It is laudable in a man to wish to live by his labours; but he should write so as he may *live* by them, not so as he may be knocked on the head. I would advise him to be at Calais before he publishes his history of the present age. A foreigner who attaches himself to a political party in this country, is in the worst state that can be imagined: he is looked upon as a mere intermeddler. A native may do it from interest.' BOSWELL. 'Or principle.' GOLDSMITH. 'There are people who tell a hundred political lies every day, and are not hurt by it. Surely, then, one may tell truth with safety.' JOHN-SON. 'Why, Sir, in the first place, he who tells a hundred lies has disarmed the force of his lies. But besides; a man had rather have a hundred lies told of him, than one truth which he does not wish should be told.' GOLDSMITH. 'For my part, I'd tell truth, and shame the devil.' JOHNSON. 'Yes, Sir; but the devil will be angry. I wish to shame the devil as much as you do, but I should choose to be out of the reach of his claws.' GOLDSMITH. 'His claws can do you no harm, when you have the shield of truth.'

It having been observed that there was little hospitality in

London;—JOHNSON. 'Nay, Sir, any man who has a name, or who has the power of pleasing, will be very generally invited in London. The man, Sterne, I have been told, has had engagements for three months.' GOLDSMITH. 'And a very dull fellow.' JOHNSON. 'Why no, Sir.'

Martinelli told us, that for several years he lived much with Charles Townshend, and that he ventured to tell him he was a bad joker. JOHNSON. 'Why, Sir, thus much I can say upon the subject. One day he and a few more agreed to go and dine in the country, and each of them was to bring a friend in his carriage with him. Charles Townshend asked Fitzherbert to go with him, but told him, "You must find somebody to bring you back: I can only carry you there." Fitzherbert did not much like this arrangement. He however consented, observing sarcastically, "It will do very well; for then the same jokes will serve you in returning as in going."'

An eminent publick character[1] being mentioned;—JOHNSON. 'I remember being present when he shewed himself to be so corrupted, or at least something so different from what I think right, as to maintain, that a member of parliament should go along with his party right or wrong. Now, Sir, this is so remote from native virtue, from scholastick virtue, that a good man must have undergone a great change before he can reconcile himself to such a doctrine. It is maintaining that you may lie to the publick; for you lie when you call that right which you think wrong, or the reverse. A friend of ours,[2] who is too much an echo of that gentleman, observed, that a man who does not stick uniformly to a party, is only waiting to be bought. Why then, said I, he is only waiting to be what that gentleman is already.'

We talked of the King's coming to see Goldsmith's new play. —'I wish he would,' said Goldsmith; adding, however, with an affected indifference, 'Not that it would do me the least good.' JOHNSON. 'Well then, Sir, let us say it would do *him* good, (laughing.) No, Sir, this affectation will not pass;—it is mighty idle. In such a state as ours, who would not wish to please the

---

[1] [Burke. *Boswell Papers,* vi. 145.]
[2] [Reynolds. *Ib.*]

Chief Magistrate?' GOLDSMITH. 'I *do* wish to please him. I remember a line in Dryden,—

> "And every poet is the monarch's friend."

It ought to be reversed.' JOHNSON. 'Nay, there are finer lines in Dryden on this subject:—

> "For colleges on bounteous Kings depend,
> And never rebel was to arts a friend." '

General Paoli observed, that 'successful rebels might.' MARTINELLI. 'Happy rebellions.' GOLDSMITH. 'We have no such phrase.' GENERAL PAOLI. 'But have you not the *thing?*' GOLDSMITH. 'Yes; all our *happy* revolutions. They have hurt our constitution, and will hurt it, till we mend it by another HAPPY REVOLUTION.' I never before discovered that my friend Goldsmith had so much of the old prejudice in him.

General Paoli, talking of Goldsmith's new play, said, '*Il a fait un compliment très gracieux à une certaine grande dame*;[1] meaning a Duchess of the first rank.

I expressed a doubt whether Goldsmith intended it, in order that I might hear the truth from himself. It, perhaps, was not quite fair to endeavour to bring him to a confession, as he might not wish to avow positively his taking part against the Court. He smiled and hesitated. The General at once relieved him, by this beautiful image: '*Monsieur Goldsmith est comme la mer, qui jette des perles et beaucoup d'autres belles choses, sans s'en appercevoir.*' GOLDSMITH. '*Très bien dit, et très élégamment.*'

A person[2] was mentioned, who it was said could take down in short hand the speeches in parliament with perfect exactness. JOHNSON. 'Sir, it is impossible. I remember one, Angel, who came to me to write for him a Preface or Dedication to a book upon short hand, and he professed to write as fast as a man could speak. In order to try him, I took down a book, and read while he wrote; and I favoured him, for I read more deliberately than usual. I had proceeded but a very little way, when he begged I would desist, for he could not follow me.' Hearing now for the

---

[1] [The Duchess of Cumberland, *Boswell Papers*, vi. between pp. 144–5.]
[2] [Cavendish, *Boswell Papers*, vi. 145.]

first time of this Preface or Dedication, I said, 'What an expense, Sir, do you put us to in buying books, to which you have written Prefaces or Dedications.' JOHNSON. 'Why, I have dedicated to the Royal family all round; that is to say, to the last generation of the Royal family.' GOLDSMITH. 'And perhaps, Sir, not one sentence of wit in a whole Dedication.' JOHNSON. 'Perhaps not, Sir.' BOSWELL. 'What then is the reason for applying to a particular person to do that which any one may do as well?' JOHNSON. 'Why, Sir, one man has greater readiness at doing it than another.'

I spoke of Mr. Harris, of Salisbury, as being a very learned man, and in particular an eminent Grecian. JOHNSON. 'I am not sure of that. His friends give him out as such, but I know not who of his friends are able to judge of it.' GOLDSMITH. 'He is what is much better: he is a worthy humane man.' JOHNSON. 'Nay, Sir, that is not to the purpose of our argument: that will as much prove that he can play upon the fiddle as well as Giardini, as that he is an eminent Grecian.' GOLDSMITH. 'The greatest muscial performers have but small emoluments. Giardini, I am told, does not get above seven hundred a year.' JOHNSON. 'That is, indeed, but little for a man to get, who does best that which so many endeavour to do. There is nothing, I think, in which the power of art is shown so much as in playing on the fiddle. In all other things we can do something at first. Any man will forge a bar of iron, if you give him a hammer; not so well as a smith, but tolerably. A man will saw a piece of wood, and make a box, though a clumsy one; but give him a fiddle and a fiddle-stick, and he can do nothing.'

On Monday, April 19, he called on me with Mrs. Williams, in Mr. Strahan's coach, and carried me out to dine with Mr. Elphinston, at his academy at Kensington. A printer having acquired a fortune sufficient to keep his coach, was a good topick for the credit of literature. Mrs. Williams said, that another printer, Mr. Hamilton, had not waited so long as Mr. Strahan, but had kept his coach several years sooner. JOHNSON. 'He was in the right. Life is short. The sooner that a man begins to enjoy his wealth the better.'

Mr. Elphinston talked of a new book that was much admired, and asked Dr. Johnson if he had read it. JOHNSON. 'I have looked into it.' 'What, (said Elphinston,) have you not read it through?' Johnson, offended at being thus pressed, and so obliged to own his cursory mode of reading, answered tartly, 'No, Sir, do *you* read books *through?*'

He this day again defended duelling, and put his argument upon what I have ever thought the most solid basis; that if publick war be allowed to be consistent with morality, private war must be equally so. Indeed we may observe what strained arguments are used, to reconcile war with the Christian religion. But, in my opinion, it is exceedingly clear that duelling, having better reasons for its barbarous violence, is more justifiable than war, in which thousands go forth without any cause of personal quarrel, and massacre each other.

On Wednesday, April 21, I dined with him at Mr. Thrale's. A gentleman[1] attacked Garrick for being vain. JOHNSON. 'No wonder, Sir, that he is vain; a man who is perpetually flattered in every mode that can be conceived. So many bellows have blown the fire, that one wonders he is not by this time become a cinder.' BOSWELL. 'And such bellows too. Lord Mansfield with his cheeks like to burst: Lord Chatham like an Æolus. I have read such notes from them to him, as were enough to turn his head.' JOHNSON. 'True. When he whom every body else flatters, flatters me, I then am truly happy.' MRS. THRALE. 'The sentiment is in Congreve, I think.' JOHNSON. 'Yes, Madam, in *The Way of the World*:

> "If there's delight in love, 'tis when I see
> That heart which others bleed for, bleed for me."

No, Sir, I should not be surprised though Garrick chained the ocean, and lashed the winds.' BOSWELL. 'Should it not be, Sir, lashed the ocean and chained the winds?' JOHNSON. 'No, Sir, recollect the original:

> "*In Corum atque Eurum solitus sævire flagellis*

---

[1] [Murphy. *Boswell Papers*, vi. 120.]

Barbarus, Æolio nunquam hoc in carcere passos,
Ipsum compedibus qui vinxerat Ennosigæum.'' [1]

This does very well, when both the winds and the sea are per-
sonified, and mentioned by their mythological names, as in
Juvenal; but when they are mentioned in plain language, the
application of the epithets suggested by me, is the most obvious;
and accordingly my friend himself, in his imitation of the passage
which describes Xerxes, has

'The waves he lashes, and enchains the wind.'

The modes of living in different countries, and the various
views with which men travel in quest of new scenes, having been
talked of, a learned gentleman[2] who holds a considerable office
in the law, expatiated on the happiness of a savage life; and mentioned an instance of an officer who had actually lived for some
time in the wilds of America, of whom, when in that state, he
quoted this reflection with an air of admiration, as if it had been
deeply philosophical: 'Here am I, free and unrestrained, amidst
the rude magnificence of Nature, with this Indian woman by my
side, and this gun with which I can procure food when I want it:
what more can be desired for human happiness?' It did not require
much sagacity to foresee that such a sentiment would not be
permitted to pass without due animadversion. JOHNSON. 'Do not
allow yourself, Sir, to be imposed upon by such gross absurdity.
It is sad stuff; it is brutish. If a bull could speak, he might as well
exclaim,—Here am I with this cow and this grass; what being
can enjoy greater felicity?'

We talked of the melancholy end of a gentleman[3] who had
destroyed himself. JOHNSON. 'It was owing to imaginary difficulties in his affairs, which, had he talked with any friend, would
soon have vanished.' BOSWELL. 'Do you think, Sir, that all who
commit suicide are mad?' JOHNSON. 'Sir, they are often not
universally disordered in their intellects, but one passion presses

---

[1] ['But how did he return, this haughty brave, Who whipt the winds,
and made the sea his slave? (Tho' Neptune took unkindly to be bound; And
Eurus never such hard usage found In his Æolian Prisons under ground).'
Juvenal, x. 180. (Dryden.)]

[2] [Probably W. W. Pepys. *Boswell Papers*, ix. 260.]

[3] [William Fitzherbert. *Ib.* vi, between pp. 146–7; xiii. 19.]

so upon them, that they yield to it, and commit suicide, as a
passionate man will stab another.' He added, 'I have often
thought, that after a man has taken the resolution to kill himself,
it is not courage in him to do any thing, however desperate,
because he has nothing to fear.' GOLDSMITH. 'I don't see that.'
JOHNSON. 'Nay but, my dear Sir, why should not you see what
every one else sees?' GOLDSMITH. 'It is for fear of something
that he has resolved to kill himself; and will not that timid disposition restrain him?' JOHNSON. 'It does not signify that the
fear of something made him resolve; it is upon the state of his
mind, after the resolution is taken, that I argue. Suppose a man,
either from fear, or pride, or conscience, or whatever motive,
has resolved to kill himself; when once the resolution is taken,
he has nothing to fear. He may then go and take the King of
Prussia by the nose, at the head of his army. He cannot fear the
rack, who is resolved to kill himself. When Eustace Budgel was
walking down to the Thames, determined to drown himself, he
might, if he pleased, without any apprehension of danger, have
turned aside, and first set fire to St. James's palace.'

On Tuesday, April 27, Mr. Beauclerk and I called on him in
the morning. As we walked up Johnson's-court, I said, 'I have
a veneration for this court;' and was glad to find that Beauclerk
had the same reverential enthusiasm. We found him alone. We
talked of Mr. Andrew Stuart's elegant and plausible Letters to
Lord Mansfield: a copy of which had been sent by the authour
to Dr. Johnson. JOHNSON. 'They have not answered the end.
They have not been talked of; I have never heard of them. This
is owing to their not being sold. People seldom read a book which
is given to them; and few are given. The way to spread a work
is to sell it at a low price. No man will send to buy a thing that
costs even sixpence, without an intention to read it.' BOSWELL.
'May it not be doubted, Sir, whether it be proper to publish
letters, arraigning the ultimate decision of an important cause
by the supreme judicature of the nation?' JOHNSON. 'No, Sir,
I do not think it was wrong to publish these letters. If they are
thought to do harm, why not answer them? But they will do no
harm. If Mr. Douglas be indeed the son of Lady Jane, he cannot

be hurt: if he be not her son, and yet has the great estate of the family of Douglas, he may well submit to have a pamphlet against him by Andrew Stuart. Sir, I think such a publication does good, as it does good to show us the possibilities of human life. And Sir, you will not say that the Douglas cause was a cause of easy decision, when it divided your Court as much as it could do, to be determined at all. When your Judges were seven and seven, the casting vote of the President must be given on one side or other: no matter, for my argument, on which; one or the other *must* be taken: as when I am to move, there is no matter which leg I move first. And then, Sir, it was otherwise determined here. No, Sir, a more dubious determination of any question cannot be imagined.'[1]

He said, 'Goldsmith should not be for ever attempting to shine in conversation: he has not temper for it, he is so much mortified when he fails. Sir, a game of jokes is composed partly of skill, partly of chance. A man may be beat at times by one who has not the tenth part of his wit. Now Goldsmith's putting himself against another, is like a man laying a hundred to one who cannot spare the hundred. It is not worth a man's while. A man should not lay a hundred to one, unless he can easily spare it, though he has a hundred chances for him: he can get but a guinea, and he may lose a hundred. Goldsmith is in this state. When he contends, if he gets the better, it is a very little addition to a man of his literary reputation: if he does not get the better, he is miserably vexed.'

Johnson's own superlative power of wit set him above any risk of such uneasiness. Garrick had remarked to me of him, a few days before, 'Rabelais and all other wits are nothing compared with him. You may be diverted by them; but Johnson

[1] I regretted that Dr. Johnson never took the trouble to study a question which interested nations. He would not even read a pamphlet which I wrote upon it, entitled *The Essence of the Douglas Cause*; which, I have reason to flatter myself, had considerable effect in favour of Mr. Douglas; of whose legitimate filiation I was then, and am still, firmly convinced. Let me add, that no fact can be more respectably ascertained, than by the judgement of the most august tribunal in the world; a judgement, in which Lord Mansfield and Lord Camden united in 1769, and from which only five of a numerous body entered a protest.

gives you a forcible hug, and shakes laughter out of you, whether you will or no.'

Goldsmith, however, was often very fortunate in his witty contests, even when he entered the lists with Johnson himself. Sir Joshua Reynolds was in company with them one day, when Goldsmith said, that he thought he could write a good fable, mentioned the simplicity which that kind of composition requires, and observed, that in most fables the animals introduced seldom talk in character. 'For instance, (said he,) the fable of the little fishes, who saw birds fly over their heads, and envying them, petitioned Jupiter to be changed into birds. The skill (continued he,) consists in making them talk like little fishes.' While he indulged himself in this fanciful reverie, he observed Johnson shaking his sides, and laughing. Upon which he smartly proceeded, 'Why, Dr. Johnson, this is not so easy as you seem to think; for if you were to make little fishes talk, they would talk like WHALES.'

Johnson, though remarkable for his great variety of composition, never exercised his talents in fable, except we allow his beautiful tale published in Mrs. Williams's *Miscellanies* to be of that species. I have, however, found among his manuscript collections the following sketch of one:—

'Glow-worm[1] lying in the garden saw a candle in a neighbouring palace,—and complained of the littleness of his own light;— another observed—wait a little;—soon dark;—have outlasted πολλ [*many*] of these glaring lights which are only brighter as they haste to nothing.'

On Thursday, April 29, I dined with him at General Oglethorpe's, where were Sir Joshua Reynolds, Mr. Langton, Dr. Goldsmith, and Mr. Thrale. I was very desirous to get Dr. Johnson absolutely fixed in his resolution to go with me to the Hebrides this year; and I told him that I had received a letter from Dr. Robertson the historian, upon the subject, with which he was much pleased; and now talked in such a manner of his

---

[1] It has already been observed (*ante,* 393), that one of his first Essays was a Latin Poem on a glow-worm; but whether it be any where extant, has not been ascertained. [M.]

long-intended tour, that I was satisfied he meant to fulfil his engagement.

The custom of eating dogs at Otaheite being mentioned, Goldsmith observed, that this was also a custom in China; that a dog-butcher is as common there as any other butcher; and that when he walks abroad all the dogs fall on him. JOHNSON. 'That is not owing to his killing dogs, Sir. I remember a butcher at Lichfield, whom a dog that was in the house where I lived, always attacked. It is the smell of carnage which provokes this, let the animals he has killed be what they may.' GOLDSMITH. 'Yes, there is a general abhorrence in animals at the signs of massacre. If you put a tub full of blood into a stable, the horses are like to go mad.' JOHNSON. 'I doubt that.' GOLDSMITH. 'Nay, Sir, it is a fact well authenticated.' THRALE. 'You had better prove it before you put it into your book on natural history. You may do it in my stable if you will.' JOHNSON. 'Nay, Sir, I would not have him prove it. If he is content to take his information from others, he may get through his book with little trouble, and without much endangering his reputation. But if he makes experiments for so comprehensive a book as his, there would be no end to them; his erroneous assertions would then fall upon himself, and he might be blamed for not having made experiments as to every particular.'

The character of Mallet having been introduced, and spoken of slightingly by Goldsmith; JOHNSON. 'Why, Sir, Mallet had talents enough to keep his literary reputation alive as long as he himself lived; and that, let me tell you, is a good deal.' GOLD-SMITH. 'But I cannot agree that it was so. His literary reputation was dead long before his natural death. I consider an authour's literary reputation to be alive only while his name will ensure a good price for his copy from the booksellers. I will get you (to Johnson,) a hundred guineas for any thing whatever that you shall write, if you put your name to it.'

Dr. Goldsmith's new play, *She Stoops to Conquer,* being mentioned; JOHNSON. 'I know of no comedy for many years that has so much exhilarated an audience, that has answered so much the great end of comedy—making an audience merry.'

Goldsmith having said, that Garrick's compliment to the Queen, which he introduced into the play of *The Chances*, which he had altered and revised this year, was mean and gross flattery; JOHNSON. 'Why, Sir, I would not *write*, I would not give solemnly under my hand, a character beyond what I thought really true; but a speech on the stage, let it flatter ever so extravagantly, is formular. It has always been formular to flatter Kings and Queens; so much so, that even in our church-service we have "our most religious King," used indiscriminately, whoever is King. Nay, they even flatter themselves;—"we have been graciously pleased to grant." No modern flattery, however, is so gross as that of the Augustan age, where the Emperour was deified. "*Præsens Divus habebitur Augustus.*"[1] And as to meanness, (rising into warmth,) how is it mean in a player,—a showman, —a fellow who exhibits himself for a shilling, to flatter his Queen? The attempt, indeed, was dangerous; for if it had missed, what became of Garrick, and what became of the Queen? As Sir William Temple says of a great General, it is necessary not only that his designs should be formed in a masterly manner, but that they should be attended with success. Sir, it is right, at a time when the Royal Family is not generally liked, to let it be seen that the people like at least one of them.' SIR JOSHUA REYNOLDS. 'I do not perceive why the profession of a player should be despised; for the great and ultimate end of all the employments of mankind is to produce amusement. Garrick produces more amusement than any body.' BOSWELL. 'You say, Dr. Johnson, that Garrick exhibits himself for a shilling. In this respect he is only on a footing with a lawyer who exhibits himself for his fee, and even will maintain any nonsense or absurdity, if the case requires it. Garrick refuses a play or a part which he does not like; a lawyer never refuses.' JOHNSON. 'Why, Sir, what does this prove? only that a lawyer is worse. Boswell is now like Jack in *The Tale of a Tub*, who, when he is puzzled by an argument, hangs himself. He thinks I shall cut him down, but I'll let him hang,' (laughing vociferously.) SIR JOSHUA REYNOLDS. 'Mr.

[1] ['Augustus shall prove himself a God on earth.' Horace, *Odes*, III. v. 2. (Wickham.)]

Boswell thinks that the profession of a lawyer being unquestionably honourable, if he can show the profession of a player to be more honourable, he proves his argument.'

On Friday, April 30, I dined with him at Mr. Beauclerk's, where were Lord Charlemont, Sir Joshua Reynolds, and some more members of the LITERARY CLUB, whom he had obligingly invited to meet me, as I was this evening to be balloted for as candidate for admission into that distinguished society. Johnson had done me the honour to propose me, and Beauclerk was very zealous for me.

Goldsmith being mentioned; JOHNSON. 'It is amazing how little Goldsmith knows. He seldom comes where he is not more ignorant than any one else.' SIR JOSHUA REYNOLDS. 'Yet there is no man whose company is more liked.' JOHNSON. 'To be sure, Sir. When people find a man of the most distinguished abilities as a writer, their inferiour while he is with them, it must be highly gratifying to them. What Goldsmith comically says of himself is very true,—he always gets the better when he argues alone; meaning, that he is master of a subject in his study, and can write well upon it; but when he comes into company, grows confused, and unable to talk. Take him as a poet, his *Traveller* is a very fine performance; ay, and so is his *Deserted Village*, were it not sometimes too much the echo of his *Traveller*. Whether, indeed, we take him as a poet,—as a comick writer,—or as an historian, he stands in the first class.' BOSWELL. 'An historian! My dear Sir, you surely will not rank his compilation of the Roman History with the works of other historians of this age?' JOHNSON. 'Why, who are before him?' BOSWELL. 'Hume,— Robertson,—Lord Lyttelton.' JOHNSON (his antipathy to the Scotch beginning to rise). 'I have not read Hume; but, doubtless, Goldsmith's *History* is better than the *verbiage* of Robertson, or the foppery of Dalrymple.' BOSWELL. 'Will you not admit the superiority of Robertson, in whose *History* we find such penetration—such painting?' JOHNSON. 'Sir, you must consider how that penetration and that painting are employed. It is not history, it is imagination. He who describes what he never saw, draws from fancy. Robertson paints minds as Sir Joshua paints faces in a history-piece: he imagines an heroic countenance. You must look upon Robertson's work as romance, and try it by that standard. History it is not. Besides, Sir, it is the great excellence of a writer to put into his book as much as his book will hold. Goldsmith has done this in his *History*. Now Robertson might have put twice as much into his book. Robertson is like a man who has packed gold in wool: the wool takes up more room than the gold. No, Sir; I always thought Robertson would be crushed by his own weight,— would be buried under his own ornaments. Goldsmith tells you shortly all you want to know: Robertson detains you a great deal too long. No man will read Robertson's cumbrous detail a second time; but Goldsmith's plain narrative will please again and again. I would say to Robertson what an old tutor of a college said to one of his pupils: "Read over your compositions, and where ever you meet with a passage which you think is particularly fine, strike it out." Goldsmith's abridgement is better than that of Lucius Florus or Eutropius; and I will venture to say, that if you compare him with Vertot, in the same places of the Roman History, you will find that he excels Vertot. Sir, he has the art of compiling, and of saying every thing he has to say in a pleasing manner. He is now writing a Natural History and will make it as entertaining as a Persian Tale.'

I cannot dismiss the present topick without observing, that it is probable that Dr. Johnson, who owned that he often 'talked for victory,' rather urged plausible objections to Dr. Robertson's excellent historical works, in the ardour of contest, than expressed his real and decided opinion; for it is not easy to suppose, that he should so widely differ from the rest of the literary world.

JOHNSON. 'I remember once being with Goldsmith in Westminster-abbey. While we surveyed the Poets' Corner, I said to him,

> "*Forsitan et nostrum nomen miscebitur istis.*"[1]

When we got to Temple-bar he stopped me, pointed to the heads upon it, and slily whispered me,

[1] Ovid. de Art. Amand. i. iii. v. 13 [339]. ['It may be that our names too will mingle with these.']

"Forsitan et nostrum nomen miscebitur ISTIS." [1]

Johnson praised John Bunyan highly. 'His *Pilgrim's Progress* has great merit, both for invention, imagination, and the conduct of the story; and it has had the best evidence of its merit, the general and continued approbation of mankind. Few books, I believe, have had a more extensive sale. It is remarkable, that it begins very much like the poem of Dante; yet there was no translation of Dante when Bunyan wrote. There is reason to think that he had read Spenser.'

A proposition which had been agitated, that monuments to eminent persons should, for the time to come, be erected in St. Paul's church as well as in Westminster-abbey, was mentioned; and it was asked, who should be honoured by having his monument first erected there. Somebody suggested Pope. JOHNSON. 'Why, Sir, as Pope was a Roman Catholick, I would not have his to be first. I think Milton's rather should have the precedence.[2] I think more highly of him now than I did at twenty. There is more thinking in him and in Butler, than in any of our poets.'

Some of the company expressed a wonder why the authour of so excellent a book as *The Whole Duty of Man* should conceal himself. JOHNSON. 'There may be different reasons assigned for this, any one of which would be very sufficient. He may have been a clergyman, and may have thought that his religious counsels would have less weight when known to come from a man whose profession was Theology. He may have been a man whose practice was not suitable to his principles, so that his character might injure the effect of his book, which he had written in a season of penitence. Or he may have been a man of rigid self-denial, so that he would have no reward for his pious labours while in this world, but refer it all to a future state.'

The gentlemen went away to their club, and I was left at

---

[1] In allusion to Dr. Johnson's supposed political principles, and perhaps his own.

[2] Here is another instance of his high admiration of Milton as a Poet, notwithstanding his just abhorrence of that sour Republican's political principles. His candour and discrimination are equally conspicuous. Let us hear no more of his 'injustice to Milton'.

Beauclerk's till the fate of my election should be announced to me. I sat in a state of anxiety which even the charming conversation of Lady Di Beauclerk could not entirely dissipate. In a short time I received the agreeable intelligence that I was chosen. I hastened to the place of meeting, and was introduced to such a society as can seldom be found. Mr. Edmund Burke, whom I then saw for the first time, and whose splendid talents had long made me ardently wish for his acquaintance; Dr. Nugent, Mr. Garrick, Dr. Goldsmith, Mr. (afterwards Sir William) Jones, and the company with whom I had dined. Upon my entrance, Johnson placed himself behind a chair, on which he leaned as on a desk or pulpit, and with humorous formality gave me a *Charge*, pointing out the conduct expected from me as a good member of this club.

Goldsmith produced some very absurd verses which had been publickly recited to an audience for money. JOHNSON. 'I can match this nonsense. There was a poem called *Eugenio*, which came out some years ago, and concludes thus:

> "And now, ye trifling, self-assuming elves,
>   Brimful of pride, of nothing, of yourselves,
>   Survey Eugenio, view him o'er and o'er,
>   Then sink into yourselves, and be no more."[1]

Nay, Dryden in his poem on the Royal Society, has these lines:

> "Then we upon our globe's last verge shall go,
>   And see the ocean leaning on the sky;

[1] Dr. Johnson's memory here was not perfectly accurate: *Eugenio* does not conclude thus. There are eight more lines after the last of those quoted by him; and the passage which he meant to recite is as follows:—
> 'Say now ye fluttering, poor assuming elves,
>   Stark full of pride, of folly, of—yourselves;
>   Say where's the wretch of all your impious crew
>   Who dares confront his character to view?
>   Behold Eugenio, view him o'er and o'er,
>   Then sink into yourselves, and be no more.'

Mr. Reed informs me that the Authour of *Eugenio*, a Wine Merchant at Wrexham in Denbighshire, soon after its publication, viz. 17th May, 1737, cut his own throat; and that it appears by Swift's *Works* that the poem had been shewn to him, and received some of his corrections. Johnson had read *Eugenio* on his first coming to town, for we see it mentioned in one of his letters to Mr. Cave, which has been inserted in this work [*ante*, p. 89].

> From thence our rolling neighbours we shall know,
>   And on the lunar world securely pry." '

Talking of puns, Johnson, who had a great contempt for that species of wit, deigned to allow that there was one good pun in *Menagiana*, I think on the word *corps*.[1]

Much pleasant conversation passed, which Johnson relished with great good humour. But his conversation alone, or what led to it, or was interwoven with it, is the business of this work.

On Saturday, May 1, we dined by ourselves at our old rendez-vous, the Mitre tavern. He was placid, but not much disposed to talk. He observed that 'The Irish mix better with the English than the Scotch do; their language is nearer to English; as a proof of which, they succeed very well as players, which Scotchmen do not. Then, Sir, they have not that extreme nationality which we find in the Scotch. I will do you, Boswell, the justice to say, that you are the most *unscottified* of your countrymen. You are almost the only instance of a Scotchman that I have known, who did not at every other sentence bring in some other Scotchman.'

We drank tea with Mrs. Williams. I introduced a question which has been much agitated in the Church of Scotland, whether the claim of lay-patrons to present ministers to parishes be well founded; and supposing it to be well founded, whether it ought to be exercised without the concurrence of the people? That Church is composed of a series of judicatures: a Presbytery, a

[1] I formerly thought that I had perhaps mistaken the word, and imagined it to be *Corps*, from its similarity of sound to the real one. For an accurate and shrewd unknown gentleman, to whom I am indebted for some remarks on my work, observes on this passage—'Q. if not on the word *Fort*? A vociferous French preacher said of Bourdaloue, "Il prêche *fort bien*, et moi *bien fort*."—Menagiana. See also Anecdotes Littéraires, Article Bourdaloue.' But my ingenious and obliging correspondent, Mr. Abercrombie of Philadelphia, has pointed out to me the following passage in *Menagiana*; which renders the preceding conjecture unnecessary, and confirms my original statement:

'Madme de Bourdonne, Chanoinesse de Remiremont, venoit d'entendre un discours plein de feu et d'esprit, mais fort peu solide, et très-irrégulier. Une de ses amies, qui y prenoit intérêt pour l'orateur, lui dit en sortant, "Eh bien, Madme, que vous semble-t-il de ce que vous venez d'entendre?— Qu'il y a d'esprit?"—"Il y a tant, répondit Madme de Bourdonne, que je n'y ai pas vu de *corps*." '—Menagiana, tome ii. p. 64. Amsterd. 1713.

Synod, and, finally, a General Assembly; before all of which, this matter may be contended: and in some cases the Presbytery having refused to induct or *settle*, as they call it, the person presented by the patron, it has been found necessary to appeal to the General Assembly. He said, I might see the subject well treated in the *Defence of Pluralities*; and although he thought that a patron should exercise his right with tenderness to the inclinations of the people of a parish, he was very clear as to his right. Then supposing the question to be pleaded before the General Assembly, he dictated to me what follows:

'Against the right of patrons is commonly opposed, by the inferiour judicatures, the plea of conscience. Their conscience tells them, that the people ought to choose their pastor; their conscience tells them that they ought not to impose upon a congregation a minister ungrateful and unacceptable to his auditors. Conscience is nothing more than a conviction felt by ourselves of something to be done, or something to be avoided; and in questions of simple unperplexed morality, conscience is very often a guide that may be trusted. But before conscience can determine, the state of the question is supposed to be completely known. In questions of law, or of fact, conscience is very often confounded with opinion. No man's conscience can tell him the rights of another man; they must be known by rational investigation or historical enquiry. Opinion, which he that holds it may call his conscience, may teach some men that religion would be promoted, and quiet preserved, by granting to the people universally the choice of their ministers. But it is a conscience very ill informed that violates the rights of one man, for the convenience of another. Religion cannot be promoted by injustice: and it was never yet found that a popular election was very quietly transacted.

'That justice would be violated by transferring to the people the right of patronage, is apparent to all who know whence that right had its original. The right of patronage was not at first a privilege torn by power from unresisting poverty. It is not an authority at first usurped in times of ignorance, and established only by succession and by precedents. It is not a grant capriciously made from a higher tyrant to a lower. It is a right dearly purchased by the first possessors, and justly inherited by those that succeeded them. When Christianity was established in this island, a regular mode of publick worship was prescribed. Publick worship requires a publick place; and the proprietors of lands, as they were converted, built churches for their families and their vassals. For the maintenance of ministers, they settled a certain portion of their lands; and a district, through which each minister was required to extend his care, was, by that circumscription, constituted a parish. This is a position so generally received in England, that the extent of a manor and of a parish are regularly received for each other. The churches which the proprietors of lands had thus built and thus endowed, they justly thought themselves entitled to provide with ministers; and where the episcopal government prevails, the Bishop has no power to reject a man nominated by the patron, but for some crime that might exclude him from the priesthood. For the endowment of the church being the gift of the landlord, he was consequently at liberty to give it according to his choice, to any man capable of performing the holy offices. The people did not choose him, because the people did not pay him.

'We hear it sometimes urged, that this original right is passed out of memory, and is obliterated and obscured by many translations of property and changes of government; that scarce any church is now in the hands of the heirs of the builders; and that the present persons have entered subsequently upon the pretended rights by a thousand accidental and unknown causes. Much of this, perhaps, is true. But how is the right of patronage extinguished? If the right followed the lands, it is possessed by the same equity by which the lands are possessed. It is, in effect, part of the manor, and protected by the same laws with every other privilege. Let us suppose an estate forfeited by treason, and granted by the Crown to a new family. With the lands were forfeited all the rights appendant to those lands; by the same power that grants the lands, the rights also are granted. The right lost to the patron falls not to the people, but is either retained by the Crown, or what to the people is the same thing, is by the Crown given away. Let it change hands ever so often, it is possessed by him that receives it with the same right as it was conveyed. It may, indeed, like all our possessions, be forcibly seized or fraudulently obtained. But no injury is still done to the people; for what they never had, they have never lost. Caius may usurp the right of Titius; but neither Caius nor Titius injure the people; and no man's conscience, however tender or however active, can prompt him to restore what may be proved to have been never taken away. Supposing, what I think cannot be proved, that a popular election of ministers were to be desired, our desires are not the measure of equity. It were to be desired that power should be only in the hands of the merciful, and riches in the possession of the generous; but the law must leave both riches and power where it finds them: and must often leave riches with the covetous, and power with the cruel. Convenience may be a rule in little things, where no other rule has been established. But as the great end of government is to give every man his own, no inconvenience is greater than that of making right uncertain. Nor is any man more an enemy to publick peace, than he who fills weak heads with imaginary claims, and breaks the series of civil subordination, by inciting the lower classes of mankind to encroach upon the higher.

'Having thus shown that the right of patronage, being originally purchased, may be legally transferred, and that it is now in the hands of lawful possessors, at least as certainly as any other right;—we have left to the advocates of the people no other plea than that of convenience. Let us, therefore, now consider what the people would really gain by a general abolition of the right of patronage. What is most to be desired by such a change is, that the country should be supplied with better ministers. But why should we suppose that the parish will make a wiser choice than the patron? If we suppose mankind actuated by interest, the patron is more likely to choose with caution, because he will suffer more by choosing wrong. By the deficiencies of his minister, or by his vices, he is equally offended with the rest of the congregation; but he will have this reason more to lament them, that they will be imputed to his absurdity or corruption. The qualifications of a minister are well known to be learning and piety. Of his learning the patron is probably the only judge in the parish; and of his piety not less a judge than others; and is more likely to enquire minutely and diligently before he gives a presentation, than one of the parochial rabble, who can give nothing but a vote. It may be urged, that though the parish might not choose better ministers, they would at least choose ministers whom they like better, and who would therefore officiate with greater efficacy. That ignorance and perverseness should always obtain what they like, was never considered as the end of government; of which it is the great and standing benefit, that the wise see for the simple, and the regular act for the capricious. But that this argument supposes the people capable of judging, and resolute to act according to their best judgements, though this be sufficiently absurd, it is not all its absurdity. It supposes not only wisdom, but unanimity in those, who upon no other occasions are unanimous or wise. If by some strange concurrence all the voices of a parish should unite in the choice of any single man, though I could not charge the patron with injustice for presenting a minister, I should censure him as unkind and injudicious. But, it is evident, that as in all other popular elections there will be contrariety of judgement and acrimony of passion, a parish upon every vacancy would break into factions, and the contest for the choice of a minister would set neighbours at variance, and bring discord into families. The minister would be taught all the arts of a candidate, would flatter some, and bribe others; and the electors, as in all other cases, would call for holidays and ale, and break the heads of each other during the jollity of the canvas. The time must, however, come at last, when one of the factions must prevail, and one of the ministers get possession of the church. On what terms does he enter upon his ministry but those of enmity with half his parish? By what prudence or what diligence can he hope to conciliate the affections of that party by whose defeat he has obtained his living? Every man who voted against him will enter the church with hanging head and downcast eyes, afraid to encounter that neighbour by whose vote and influence he has been overpowered.

He will hate his neighbour for opposing him, and his minister for having prospered by the opposition; and as he will never see him but with pain, he will never see him but with hatred. Of a minister presented by the patron, the parish has seldom any thing worse to say than that they do not know him. Of a minister chosen by a popular contest, all those who do not favour him, have nursed up in their bosoms principles of hatred and reasons of rejection. Anger is excited principally by pride. The pride of a common man is very little exasperated by the supposed usurpation of an acknowledged superiour. He bears only his little share of a general evil, and suffers in common with the whole parish; but when the contest is between equals, the defeat has many aggravations; and he that is defeated by his next neighbour, is seldom satisfied without some revenge; and it is hard to say what bitterness of malignity would prevail in a parish where these elections should happen to be frequent, and the enmity of opposition should be re-kindled before it had cooled.'

Though I present to my readers Dr. Johnson's masterly thoughts on this subject, I think it proper to declare, that notwithstanding I am myself a lay patron, I do not entirely subscribe to his opinion.

On Friday, May 7, I breakfasted with him at Mr. Thrale's in the Borough. While we were alone, I endeavoured as well as I could to apologise for a lady[1] who had been divorced from her husband by act of Parliament. I said, that he had used her very ill, had behaved brutally to her, and that she could not continue to live with him without having her delicacy contaminated; that all affection for him was thus destroyed; that the essence of conjugal union being gone, there remained only a cold form, a mere civil obligation; that she was in the prime of life, with qualities to produce happiness; that these ought not to be lost; and, that the gentleman[2] on whose account she was divorced had gained her heart while thus unhappily situated. Seduced, perhaps, by the charms of the lady in question, I thus attempted to palliate what I was sensible could not be justified; for, when I had

---

[1] [Lady Diana Beauclerk. *Boswell Papers,* vi. 132.]
[2] [Topham Beauclerk. *Ib.*]

finished my harangue, my venerable friend gave me a proper check: 'My dear Sir, never accustom your mind to mingle virtue and vice. The woman's a whore, and there's an end on't.'

He described the father[1] of one of his friends thus: 'Sir, he was so exuberant a talker at publick meetings, that the gentlemen of his county were afraid of him. No business could be done for his declamation.'

He did not give me full credit when I mentioned that I had carried on a short conversation by signs with some Esquimaux who were then in London, particularly with one of them who was a priest. He thought I could not make them understand me. No man was more incredulous as to particular facts, which were at all extraordinary; and therefore no man was more scrupulously inquisitive, in order to discover the truth.

I dined with him this day at the house of my friends, Messieurs Edward and Charles Dilly, booksellers in the Poultry: there were present, their elder brother Mr. Dilly of Bedfordshire, Dr. Goldsmith, Mr. Langton, Mr. Claxton, Reverend Dr. Mayo a dissenting minister, the Reverend Mr. Toplady, and my friend the Reverend Mr. Temple.

Hawkesworth's compilation of the voyages to the South Sea being mentioned; JOHNSON. 'Sir, if you talk of it as a subject of commerce, it will be gainful; if as a book that is to increase human knowledge, I believe there will not be much of that. Hawkesworth can tell only what the voyagers have told him; and they have found very little, only one new animal, I think.' BOSWELL. 'But many insects, Sir.' JOHNSON. 'Why, Sir, as to insects, Ray reckons of British insects twenty thousand species. They might have staid at home and discovered enough in that way.'

Talking of birds, I mentioned Mr. Daines Barrington's ingenious Essay against the received notion of their migration. JOHNSON. 'I think we have as good evidence for the migration of woodcocks as can be desired. We find they disappear at a certain time of the year, and appear again at a certain time of the year; and some of them, when weary in their flight, have been

[1] [Old Mr. Langton. *Ib.* pp. 132–3.]

known to alight on the rigging of ships far out at sea.' One of
the company observed, that there had been instances of some of
them found in summer in Essex. JOHNSON. 'Sir, that strengthens
our argument. *Exceptio probat regulam.*[1] Some being found shews,
that, if all remained, many would be found. A few sick or lame
ones may be found.' GOLDSMITH. 'There is a partial migration
of the swallows; the stronger ones migrate, the others do not.'

BOSWELL. 'I am well assured that the people of Otaheite who
have the bread tree, the fruit of which serves them for bread,
laughed heartily when they were informed of the tedious process
necessary with us to have bread;—plowing, sowing, harrowing,
reaping, threshing, grinding, baking.' JOHNSON. 'Why, Sir,
all ignorant savages will laugh when they are told of the advantages of civilized life. Were you to tell men who live without
houses, how we pile brick upon brick, and rafter upon rafter, and
that after a house is raised to a certain height, a man tumbles off
a scaffold, and breaks his neck, they would laugh heartily at our
folly in building; but it does not follow that men are better without houses. No, Sir, (holding up a slice of a good loaf,) this is
better than the bread tree.'

He repeated an argument, which is to be found in his *Rambler*,
against the notion that the brute creation is endowed with the
faculty of reason: 'birds build by instinct; they never improve;
they build their first nest as well as any one that they ever build.'
GOLDSMITH. 'Yet we see if you take away a bird's nest with
the eggs in it, she will make a slighter nest and lay again.'
JOHNSON. 'Sir, that is because at first she has full time and makes
her nest deliberately. In the case you mention she is pressed to
lay, and must therefore make her nest quickly, and consequently
it will be slight.' GOLDSMITH. 'The nidification of birds is what
is least known in natural history, though one of the most curious
things in it.'

I introduced the subject of toleration. JOHNSON. 'Every
society has a right to preserve publick peace and order, and
therefore has a good right to prohibit the propagation of opinions
which have a dangerous tendency. To say the *magistrate* has this

[1] ['The exception proves the rule.']

right, is using an inadequate word: it is the *society* for which the magistrate is agent. He may be morally or theologically wrong in restraining the propagation of opinions which he thinks dangerous, but he is politically right.' M A Y O. 'I am of opinion, Sir, that every man is entitled to liberty of conscience in religion; and that the magistrate cannot restrain that right.' J O H N S O N. 'Sir, I agree with you. Every man has a right to liberty of conscience, and with that the magistrate cannot interfere. People confound liberty of thinking with liberty of talking; nay, with liberty of preaching. Every man has a physical right to think as he pleases; for it cannot be discovered how he thinks. He has not a moral right; for he ought to inform himself, and think justly. But, Sir, no member of a society has a right to *teach* any doctrine contrary to what that society holds to be true. The magistrate, I say, may be wrong in what he thinks: but, while he thinks himself right, he may and ought to enforce what he thinks.' M A Y O. 'Then, Sir, we are to remain always in errour, and truth never can prevail; and the magistrate was right in persecuting the first Christians.' J O H N S O N. 'Sir, the only method by which religious truth can be established is by martyrdom. The magistrate has a right to enforce what he thinks; and he who is conscious of the truth has a right to suffer. I am afraid there is no other way of ascertaining the truth, but by persecution on the one hand and enduring it on the other.' G O L D S M I T H. 'But how is a man to act, Sir? Though firmly convinced of the truth of his doctrine, may he not think it wrong to expose himself to persecution? Has he a right to do so? Is it not, as it were, committing voluntary suicide?' J O H N S O N. 'Sir, as to voluntary suicide, as you call it, there are twenty thousand men in an army who will go without scruple to be shot at, and mount a breach for five-pence a day.' G O L D S M I T H. 'But have they a moral right to do this?' J O H N S O N. 'Nay, Sir, if you will not take the universal opinion of mankind, I have nothing to say. If mankind cannot defend their own way of thinking, I cannot defend it. Sir, if a man is in doubt whether it would be better for him to expose himself to martyrdom or not, he should not do it. He must be convinced that he has a delegation from heaven.' G O L D S M I T H. 'I would consider whether there is the greater chance of good or evil upon the whole. If I see a man who had fallen into a well, I would wish to help him out; but if there is a greater probability that he shall pull me in, than that I shall pull him out, I would not attempt it. So were I to go to Turkey, I might wish to convert the Grand Signor to the Christian faith; but when I considered that I should probably be put to death without effectuating my purpose in any degree, I should keep myself quiet.' JOHNSON. 'Sir, you must consider that we have perfect and imperfect obligations. Perfect obligations, which are generally not to do something, are clear and positive; as, "thou shalt not kill". But charity, for instance, is not definable by limits. It is a duty to give to the poor; but no man can say how much another should give to the poor, or when a man has given too little to save his soul. In the same manner, it is a duty to instruct the ignorant, and of consequence to convert infidels to Christianity; but no man in the common course of things is obliged to carry this to such a degree as to incur the danger of martyrdom, as no man is obliged to strip himself to the shirt in order to give charity. I have said, that a man must be persuaded that he has a particular delegation from heaven.' GOLDSMITH. 'How is this to be known? Our first reformers, who were burnt for not believing bread and wine to be CHRIST'—JOHNSON. (interrupting him,) 'Sir, they were not burnt for not believing bread and wine to be CHRIST, but for insulting those who did believe it. And, Sir, when the first reformers began, they did not intend to be martyred: as many of them ran away as could.' BOSWELL. 'But, Sir, there was your countryman, Elwal, who you told me challenged King George with his black-guards, and his red-guards.' JOHNSON. 'My countryman, Elwal, Sir, should have been put in the stocks; a proper pulpit for him; and he'd have had a numerous audience. A man who preaches in the stocks will always have hearers enough.' BOSWELL. 'But Elwal thought himself in the right.' JOHNSON. 'We are not providing for mad people; there are places for them in the neighbourhood,' (meaning Moorfields.) MAYO. 'But, Sir, is it not very hard that I should not be allowed to teach my children what I really believe to be the truth?'

JOHNSON. 'Why, Sir, you might contrive to teach your children *extrà scandalum*;[1] but, Sir, the magistrate, if he knows it, has a right to restrain you. Suppose you teach your children to be thieves?' MAYO. 'This is making a joke of the subject.' JOHNSON. 'Nay, Sir, take it thus:—that you teach them the community of goods; for which there are as many plausible arguments as for most erroneous doctrines. You teach them that all things at first were in common, and that no man had a right to any thing but as he laid his hands upon it; and that this still is, or ought to be, the rule amongst mankind. Here, Sir, you sap a great principle in society,—property. And don't you think the magistrate would have a right to prevent you? Or, suppose you should teach your children the notions of the Adamites, and they should run naked into the streets, would not the magistrate have a right to flog 'em into their doublets?' MAYO. 'I think the magistrate has no right to interfere till there is some overt act.' BOSWELL. 'So, Sir, though he sees an enemy to the state charging a blunderbuss, he is not to interefere till it is fired off?' MAYO. 'He must be sure of its direction against the state.' JOHNSON. 'The magistrate is to judge of that.—He has no right to restrain your thinking, because the evil centers in yourself. If a man were sitting at this table, and chopping off his fingers, the magistrate, as guardian of the community, has no authority to restrain him, however he might do it from kindness as a parent.—Though, indeed, upon more consideration, I think he may; as it is probable, that he who is chopping off his own fingers, may soon proceed to chop off those of other people. If I think it right to steal Mr. Dilly's plate, I am a bad man; but he can say nothing to me. If I make an open declaration that I think so, he will keep me out of his house. If I put forth my hand, I shall be sent to Newgate. This is the gradation of thinking, preaching, and acting: if a man thinks erroneously, he may keep his thoughts to himself, and nobody will trouble him; if he preaches erroneous doctrine, society may expel him; if he acts in consequence of it, the law takes place, and he is hanged.' MAYO. 'But, Sir, ought not Christians to have liberty of conscience?' JOHNSON. 'I have already

[1] ['without offence.']

541

told you so, Sir. You are coming back to where you were.'
BOSWELL. 'Dr. Mayo is always taking a return post-chaise, and
going the stage over again. He has it at half price.' JOHNSON.
'Dr. Mayo, like other champions for unlimited toleration, has
got a set of words.[1] Sir, it is no matter, politically, whether the
magistrate be right or wrong. Suppose a club were to be formed,
to drink confusion to King George the Third, and a happy
restoration to Charles the Third, this would be very bad with
respect to the State; but every member of that club must either
conform to its rules, or be turned out of it. Old Baxter, I remember, maintains, that the magistrate should "tolerate all things
that are tolerable." This is no good definition of toleration upon
any principle; but it shews that he thought some things were not
tolerable.' TOPLADY. 'Sir, you have untwisted this difficult subject with great dexterity.'

During this argument, Goldsmith sat in restless agitation,
from a wish to get in and *shine*. Finding himself excluded, he had
taken his hat to go away, but remained for some time with it in
his hand, like a gamester, who at the close of a long night, lingers
for a little while, to see if he can have a favourable opening to
finish with success. Once when he was beginning to speak, he
found himself overpowered by the loud voice of Johnson, who
was at the opposite end of the table, and did not perceive Goldsmith's attempt. Thus disappointed of his wish to obtain the
attention of the company, Goldsmith in a passion threw down his
hat, looking angrily at Johnson, and exclaiming in a bitter tone,
'*Take it*.' When Toplady was going to speak, Johnson uttered
some sound, which led Goldsmith to think that he was beginning
again, and taking the words from Toplady. Upon which, he
seized this oportunity of venting his own envy and spleen, under
the pretext of supporting another person: 'Sir, (said he to Johnson,) the gentleman has heard you patiently for an hour; pray

[1] Dr. Mayo's calm temper and steady perseverance rendered him an
admirable subject for the exercise of Dr. Johnson's powerful abilities. He
never flinched; but, after reiterated blows, remained seemingly unmoved
as at the first. The scintillations of Johnson's genius flashed every time he
was struck, without his receiving any injury. Hence he obtained the epithet
of THE LITERARY ANVIL.

allow us now to hear him.' JOHNSON. (sternly,) 'Sir, I was not interrupting the gentleman. I was only giving him a signal of my attention. Sir, you are impertinent.' Goldsmith made no reply, but continued in the company for some time.

A gentleman present[1] ventured to ask Dr. Johnson if there was not a material difference as to toleration of opinions which lead to action, and opinions merely speculative; for instance, would it be wrong in the magistrate to tolerate those who preach against the doctrine of the TRINITY? Johnson was highly offended, and said, 'I wonder, Sir, how a gentleman of your piety can introduce this subject in a mixed company.' He told me afterwards, that the impropriety was, that perhaps some of the company might have talked on the subject in such terms as would have shocked him; or he might have been forced to appear in their eyes a narrow-minded man. The gentleman, with submissive deference, said, he had only hinted at the question from a desire to hear Dr. Johnson's opinion upon it. JOHNSON. 'Why then, Sir, I think that permitting men to preach any opinion contrary to the doctrine of the established church tends, in a certain degree, to lessen the authority of the church, and, consequently, to lessen the influence of religion.' 'It may be considered, (said the gentleman,) whether it would not be politick to tolerate in such a case.' JOHNSON. 'Sir, we have been talking of *right*: this is another question. *I* think it is *not* politick to tolerate in such a case.'

Though he did not think it fit that so aweful a subject should be introduced in a mixed company, and therefore at this time waved the theological question; yet his own orthodox belief in the sacred mystery of the TRINITY is evinced beyond doubt, by the following passage in his private devotions:—

'O LORD, hear my prayers, for JESUS CHRIST's sake; to whom with thee and the HOLY GHOST, *three persons and one* GOD, be all honour and glory, world without end. Amen.'[2]

BOSWELL. 'Pray, Mr. Dilly, how does Dr. Leland's *History of Ireland* sell?' JOHNSON. (bursting forth with a generous

---

[1] [Langton. *Boswell Papers*, vi. 138.]
[2] *Pr. and Med.* p. 40.

indignation,) 'The Irish are in a most unnatural state; for we see there the minority prevailing over the majority. There is no instance, even in the ten persecutions, of such severity as that which the Protestants of Ireland have exercised against the Catholicks. Did we tell them we have conquered them, it would be above board: to punish them by confiscation and other penalties, as rebels, was monstrous injustice. King William was not their lawful sovereign: he had not been acknowledged by the Parliament of Ireland, when they appeared in arms against him.'

I here suggested something favourable of the Roman Catholicks. TOPLADY. 'Does not their invocation of saints suppose omnipresence in the saints?' JOHNSON. 'No, Sir, it supposes only pluri-presence; and when spirits are divested of matter, it seems probable that they should see with more extent than when in an embodied state. There is, therefore, no approach to an invasion of any of the divine attributes, in the invocation of saints. But I think it is will-worship, and presumption. I see no command for it, and therefore think it is safer not to practise it.'

He and Mr. Langton and I went together to THE CLUB, where we found Mr. Burke, Mr. Garrick, and some other members, and amongst them our friend Goldsmith, who sat silently brooding over Johnson's reprimand to him after dinner. Johnson perceived this, and said aside to some of us, 'I'll make Goldsmith forgive me;' and then called to him in a loud voice, 'Dr. Goldsmith,—something passed to-day where you and I dined; I ask your pardon.' Goldsmith answered placidly, 'It must be much from you, Sir, that I take ill.' And so at once the difference was over, and they were on as easy terms as ever, and Goldsmith rattled away as usual.

In our way to the club to-night, when I regretted that Goldsmith would, upon every occasion, endeavour to shine, by which he often exposed himself, Mr. Langton observed, that he was not like Addison, who was content with the fame of his writings, and did not aim also at excellency in conversation, for which he found himself unfit; and that he said to a lady, who complained of his having talked little in company, 'Madam, I have but nine-

pence in ready money, but I can draw for a thousand pounds.'
I observed, that Goldsmith had a great deal of gold in his cabinet,
but, not content with that, was always taking out his purse.
JOHNSON. 'Yes, Sir, and that so often an empty purse!'

Goldsmith's incessant desire of being conspicuous in company,
was the occasion of his sometimes appearing to such disadvantage
as one should hardly have supposed possible in a man of his
genius. When his literary reputation had risen deservedly high,
and his society was much courted, he became very jealous of the
extraordinary attention which was every where paid to Johnson.
One evening, in a circle of wits, he found fault with me for talking
of Johnson as entitled to the honour of unquestionable superiority.
'Sir, (said he,) you are for making a monarchy of what should
be a republick.'

He was still more mortified, when talking in a company with
fluent vivacity, and, as he flattered himself, to the admiration of
all who were present; a German[1] who sat next him, and perceived Johnson rolling himself, as if about to speak, suddenly
stopped him, saying, 'Stay, stay,—Toctor Shonson is going to
say something.' This was, no doubt, very provoking, especially
to one so irritable as Goldsmith, who frequently mentioned it
with strong expressions of indignation.

It may also be observed, that Goldsmith was sometimes content to be treated with an easy familiarity, but, upon occasions,
would be consequential and important. An instance of this occurred in a small particular. Johnson had a way of contracting
the names of his friends; as Beauclerk, Beau; Boswell, Bozzy;
Langton, Lanky; Murphy, Mur; Sheridan, Sherry. I remember
one day, when Tom Davies was telling that Dr. Johnson said,
'We are all in labour for a name to *Goldy's* play,' Goldsmith
seemed displeased that such a liberty should be taken with his
name, and said, 'I have often desired him not to call me *Goldy*.'
Tom was remarkably attentive to the most minute circumstance
about Johnson. I recollect his telling me once, on my arrival in
London, 'Sir, our great friend has made an improvement on his
appellation of old Mr. Sheridan. He calls him now *Sherry derry*.'

[1] [G. R. Moser, a Swiss. *Mrs. Piozzi.*]

'*To* The Reverend Mr. Bagshaw, *at Bromley*[1]

'Sir,—I return you my sincere thanks for your additions to my *Dictionary*; but the new edition has been published some time, and therefore I cannot now make use of them. Whether I shall ever revise it more, I know not. If many readers had been as judicious, as diligent, and as communicative as yourself, my work had been better. The world must at present take it as it is. I am, Sir, your most obliged and most humble servant,

    'May 8, 1773.'   'Sam. Johnson.'

On Sunday, May 8,[2] I dined with Johnson at Mr. Langton's with Dr. Beattie and some other company. He descanted on the subject of Literary Property. 'There seems (said he,) to be in authours a stronger right of property than that by occupancy; a metaphysical right, a right, as it were, of creation, which should from its nature be perpetual; but the consent of nations is against it, and indeed reason and the interests of learning are against it; for were it to be perpetual, no book, however useful, could be universally diffused amongst mankind, should the proprietor take it into his head to restrain its circulation. No book could have the advantage of being edited with notes, however necessary to its elucidation, should the proprietor perversely oppose it. For the general good of the world, therefore, whatever valuable work has once been created by an authour, and issued out by him, should be understood as no longer in his power, but as belonging to the publick; at the same time the authour is entitled to an

---

[1] The Reverend Thomas Bagshaw, M.A., who died on November 20, 1787, in the seventy-seventh year of his age, Chaplain of Bromley College, in Kent, and Rector of Southfleet. He had resigned the cure of Bromley Parish some time before his death. For this, and another letter from Dr. Johnson in 1784, to the same truely respectable man, I am indebted to Dr. John Loveday, of the Commons, a son of the late learned and pious John Loveday, Esq., of Caversham in Berkshire, who obligingly transcribed them for me from the originals in his possession. This worthy gentleman, having retired from business, now lives in Warwickshire. The world has been lately obliged to him as the Editor of the late Rev. Dr. Townson's excellent work, modestly entitled, *A Discourse on the Evangelical History, from the Interment to the Ascension of our Lord and Saviour Jesus Christ*; to which is prefixed, a truly interesting and pleasing account of the authour, by the Reverend Mr Ralph Churton.   [2] [Sunday was May 9.]

adequate reward. This he should have by an exclusive right to his work for a considerable number of years.'

He attacked Lord Monboddo's strange speculation on the primitive state of human nature; observing, 'Sir, it is all conjecture about a thing useless, even were it known to be true. Knowledge of all kinds is good. Conjecture, as to things useful, is good; but conjecture as to what it would be useless to know, such as whether men went upon all four, is very idle.'

On Monday, May 9 [10], as I was to set out on my return to Scotland next morning, I was desirous to see as much of Dr. Johnson as I could. But I first called on Goldsmith to take leave of him. The jealousy and envy which, though possessed of many most amiable qualities, he frankly avowed, broke out violently at this interview. Upon another occasion, when Goldsmith confessed himself to be of an envious disposition, I contended with Johnson that we ought not to be angry with him, he was so candid in owning it. 'Nay, Sir, (said Johnson,) we must be angry that a man has such a superabundance of an odious quality, that he cannot keep it within his own breast, but it boils over.' In my opinion, however, Goldsmith had not more of it than other people have, but only talked of it freely.

He now seemed very angry that Johnson was going to be a traveller; said, 'he would be a dead weight for me to carry, and that I should never be able to lug him along through the Highlands and Hebrides.' Nor would he patiently allow me to enlarge upon Johnson's wonderful abilities; but exclaimed, 'Is he like Burke, who winds into a subject like a serpent?' 'But, (said I,) Johnson is the Hercules who strangled serpents in his cradle.'

I dined with Dr. Johnson at General Paoli's. He was obliged, by indisposition, to leave the company early; he appointed me, however, to meet him in the evening at Mr. (now Sir Robert) Chambers's in the Temple, where he accordingly came, though he continued to be very ill. Chambers, as is common on such occasions, prescribed various remedies to him. JOHNSON. (fretted by pain,) 'Pr'ythee don't tease me. Stay till I am well, and then you shall tell me how to cure myself.' He grew better, and talked with a noble enthusiasm of keeping up the representation of respectable families. His zeal on this subject was a circumstance in his character exceedingly remarkable, when it is considered that he himself had no pretensions to blood. I heard him once say, 'I have great merit in being zealous for subordination and the honours of birth; for I can hardly tell who was my grand-father.' He maintained the dignity and propriety of male succession, in opposition to the opinion of one of our friends,[1] who had that day employed Mr. Chambers to draw his will, devising his estate to his three sisters, in preference to a remote heir male. Johnson called them 'three *dowdies*,' and said, with as high a spirit as the boldest Baron in the most perfect days of the feudal system, 'An ancient estate should always go to males. It is mighty foolish to let a stranger have it because he marries your daughter, and takes your name. As for an estate newly acquired by trade, you may give it, if you will, to the dog *Towser*, and let him keep his *own* name.'

I have known him at times exceedingly diverted at what seemed to others a very small sport. He now laughed immoder-ately, without any reason that we could perceive, at our friend's making his will; called him the *testator*, and added, 'I dare say, he thinks he has done a mighty thing. He won't stay till he gets home to his seat in the country, to produce this wonderful deed: he'll call up the landlord of the first inn on the road; and, after a suitable preface upon mortality and the uncertainty of life, will tell him that he should not delay making his will; and here, Sir, will he say, is my will, which I have just made, with the assist-ance of one of the ablest lawyers in the kingdom; and he will read it to him (laughing all the time). He believes he has made this will; but he did not make it: you, Chambers, made it for him. I trust you have had more conscience than to make him say, "being of sound understanding;" ha, ha, ha! I hope he has left me a legacy. I'd have his will turned into verse, like a ballad.'

In this playful manner did he run on, exulting in his own pleasantry, which certainly was not such as might be expected from the authour of *The Rambler*, but which is here preserved,

[1] [Langton. *Boswell Papers*, vi. 141.]

that my readers may be acquainted even with the slightest occasional characteristicks of so eminent a man.

Mr. Chambers did not by any means relish this jocularity upon a matter of which *pars magna fuit*,[1] and seemed impatient till he got rid of us. Johnson could not stop his merriment, but continued it all the way till we got without the Temple-gate. He then burst into such a fit of laughter, that he appeared to be almost in a convulsion; and, in order to support himself, laid hold of one of the posts at the side of the foot pavement, and sent forth peals so loud, that in the silence of the night his voice seemed to resound from Temple-bar to Fleet-ditch.

This most ludicrous exhibition of the aweful, melancholy, and venerable Johnson, happened well to counteract the feelings of sadness which I used to experience when parting with him for a considerable time. I accompanied him to his door, where he gave me his blessing.

He records of himself this year, 'Between Easter and Whitsuntide, having always considered that time as propitious to study, I attempted to learn the Low Dutch language.'[2] It is to be observed, that he here admits an opinion of the human mind being influenced by seasons, which he ridicules in his writings. His progress, he says, was interrupted by a fever, 'which, by the imprudent use of a small print, left an inflammation in his useful eye.' We cannot but admire his spirit when we know, that amidst a complication of bodily and mental distress, he was still animated with the desire of intellectual improvement. Various notes of his studies appear on different days, in his manuscript diary of this year, such as,

'*Inchoavi lectionem Pentateuchi—Finivi lectionem Conf. Fab. Burdonum.—Legi primum actum Troadum.—Legi Dissertationem Clerici postremam de Pent.—2 of Clark's Sermons.—L. Appolonii pugnam Betriciam.—L. centum versus Homeri.*'[3]

Let this serve as a specimen of what accessions of literature

[1] ['he was no small part.' Cf. *Aeneid* ii. 6.]
[2] *Pr. and Med*. p. 129.
[3] ['Began reading the Pentateuch. Finished the *Confutatio Fabulae Burdonum*. Read the first Act of *Troades*. Read Clarke's last Dissertation on the Pentateuch. Two of Clark's Sermons. Read the Bebrycian (*sic*; Betriciam is a misreading) in Apollonius. Read a hundred lines of Homer.']

he was perpetually infusing into his mind, while he charged himself with idleness.

This year died Mrs. Salusbury, (mother of Mrs. Thrale,) a lady whom he appears to have esteemed much, and whose memory he honoured with an Epitaph.[1]

In a letter from Edinburgh, dated the 29th of May, I pressed him to persevere in his resolution to make this year the projected visit to the Hebrides, of which he and I had talked for many years, and which I was confident would afford us much entertainment.

'To James Boswell, Esq.

'Dear Sir,—When your letter came to me, I was so darkened by an inflammation in my eye, that I could not for some time read it. I can now write without trouble, and can read large prints. My eye is gradually growing stronger; and I hope will be able to take some delight in the survey of a Caledonian loch.

'Chambers is going a Judge, with six thousand a year, to Bengal. He and I shall come down together as far as Newcastle, and thence I shall easily get to Edinburgh. Let me know the exact time when your Courts intermit. I must conform a little to Chambers's occasions, and he must conform a little to mine. The time which you shall fix, must be the common point to which we will come as near as we can. Except this eye, I am very well.

'Beattie is so caressed, and invited, and treated, and liked, and flattered, by the great, that I can see nothing of him. I am in great hope that he will be well provided for, and then we will live upon him at the Marischal College, without pity or modesty.

'——[2] left the town without taking leave of me, and is gone in deep dudgeon to ——.[3] Is not this very childish? Where is now my legacy?

'I hope your dear lady and her dear baby are both well. I shall see them too when I come; and I have that opinion of your choice,

---

[1] Mrs. Piozzi's *Anecdotes of Johnson*, p. 131.
[2] [Langton. *Croker*[1].]   [3] [Langton, in Lincolnshire.]

as to suspect that when I have seen Mrs. Boswell, I shall be less willing to go away. I am, dear Sir, your affectionate humble servant,

    'Johnson's-court, Fleet-street,   'SAM. JOHNSON.'
       July 5, 1773.'

    'Write to me as soon as you can. Chambers is now at Oxford.'

I again wrote to him, informing him that the Court of Session rose on the twelfth of August, hoping to see him before that time, and expressing perhaps in too extravagant terms, my admiration of him, and my expectation of pleasure from our intended tour.

'*To* JAMES BOSWELL, ESQ.

    'DEAR SIR,—I shall set out from London on Friday the sixth of this month, and purpose not to loiter much by the way. Which day I shall be at Edinburgh, I cannot exactly tell. I suppose I must drive to an inn, and send a porter to find you.

    'I am afraid Beattie will not be at his College soon enough for us, and I shall be sorry to miss him; but there is no staying for the concurrence of all conveniences. We will do as well as we can. I am, Sir, your most humble servant,

    'August 3, 1773.'   'SAM. JOHNSON.'

To THE SAME

    'DEAR SIR,—Not being at Mr. Thrale's when your letter came, I had written the enclosed paper and sealed it; bringing it hither for a frank, I found yours. If any thing could repress my ardour, it would be such a letter as yours. To disappoint a friend is unpleasing; and he that forms expectations like yours, must be disappointed. Think only when you see me, that you see a man who loves you, and is proud and glad that you love him. I am, Sir, your most affectionate,

    'August 3, 1773.'   'SAM. JOHNSON.'

To THE SAME

'DEAR SIR,   'Newcastle, Aug. 11, 1773.
'I came hither last night, and hope, but do not absolutely promise, to be in Edinburgh on Saturday. Beattie will not come so soon. I am, Sir, your most humble servant,
'My compliments to your lady.'   'SAM. JOHNSON.'

To THE SAME

'Mr. Johnson sends his compliments to Mr. Boswell, being just arrived at Boyd's.—Saturday night.'

His stay in Scotland was from the 18th of August, on which day he arrived, till the 22nd of November, when he set out on his return to London; and I believe ninety-four days were never passed by any man in a more vigorous exertion.

He came by the way of Berwick upon Tweed to Edinburgh, where he remained a few days, and then went by St. Andrew's, Aberdeen, Inverness, and Fort Augustus, to the Hebrides, to visit which was the principal object he had in view. He visited the isles of Sky, Rasay, Col, Mull, Inchkenneth, and Icolmkill. He travelled through Argyleshire by Inverary, and from thence by Lochlomond and Dunbarton to Glasgow, then by Loudon to Auchinleck in Ayrshire, the seat of my family, and then by Hamilton, back to Edinburgh, where he again spent some time. He thus saw the four Universities of Scotland, its three principal cities, and as much of the Highland and insular life as was sufficient for his philosophical contemplation. I had the pleasure of accompanying him during the whole of this journey. He was respectfully entertained by the great, the learned, and the elegant, wherever he went; nor was he less delighted with the hospitality which he experienced in humbler life.

His various adventures, and the force and vivacity of his mind, as exercised during this peregrination, upon innumerable topicks, have been faithfully, and to the best of my abilities, displayed in my *Journal of a Tour to the Hebrides*, to which, as the publick has been pleased to honour it by a very extensive circulation, I beg leave to refer, as to a separate and remarkable portion of his life,[1] which may be there seen in detail, and which exhibits as striking a view of his powers in conversation, as his works do of his excellence in writing. Nor can I deny to myself the very flattering gratification of inserting here the character which my friend Mr. Courtenay has been pleased to give of that work:

> 'With Reynolds' pencil, vivid, bold, and true,
> So fervent Boswell gives him to our view:
> In every trait we see his mind expand;
> The master rises by the pupil's hand;
> We love the writer, praise his happy vein,
> Grac'd with the naiveté of the sage Montaigne.
> Hence not alone are brighter parts display'd,
> But e'en the specks of character pourtray'd:
> We *see* the Rambler with fastidious smile
> Mark the lone tree, and note the heath-clad isle;
> But when th' heroick tale of Flora charms,
> Deck'd in a kilt, he wields a chieftain's arms:
> The tuneful piper sounds a martial strain,
> And Samuel sings, "The King shall have his *ain*." '

During his stay at Edinburgh, after his return from the Hebrides, he was at great pains to obtain information concerning Scotland; and it will appear from his subsequent letters, that he was not less solicitous for intelligence on this subject after his return to London.

'*To* JAMES BOSWELL, ESQ.

'DEAR SIR,—I came home last night, without any incommodity, danger, or weariness, and am ready to begin a new journey. I shall go to Oxford on Monday. I know Mrs. Boswell

---

[1] The authour was not a small gainer by this extraordinary Journey; for Dr. Johnson thus writes to Mrs. Thrale, Nov. 3, 1773:—'Boswell will praise my resolution and perseverance, and I shall in return celebrate his good humour and perpetual cheerfulness. He has better faculties than I had imagined; more justness of discernment, and more fecundity of images. It is very convenient to travel with him; for there is no house where he is not received with kindness and respect.' Let. 90, to Mrs. Thrale. [M.]

wished me well to go;[1] her wishes have not been disappointed. Mrs. Williams has received Sir A's[2] letter.

'Make my compliments to all those to whom my compliments may be welcome.

'Let the box[3] be sent as soon as it can, and let me know when to expect it.

'Enquire, if you can, the order of the Clans: Macdonald is first, Maclean second; further I cannot go. Quicken Dr. Webster.[4] I am, Sir, yours affectionately,

'Nov. 27, 1773.'   'SAM. JOHNSON.'

'MR. BOSWELL *to* DR. JOHNSON

'Edinburgh, Dec. 2, 1773.

'. . . You shall have what information I can procure as to the order of the Clans. A gentleman of the name of Grant tells me, that there is no settled order among them; and he says, that the Macdonalds were not placed upon the right of the army at Culloden; the Stuarts were. I shall, however, examine witnesses of every name that I can find here. Dr. Webster shall be quickened too. I like your little memorandums; they are symptoms of your being in earnest with your book of northern travels.

'Your box shall be sent next week by sea. You will find in it some pieces of the broom bush, which you saw growing on the old castle of Auchinleck. The wood has a curious appearance

---

[1] In this he shewed a very acute penetration. My wife paid him the most assiduous and respectful attention, while he was our guest; so that I wonder how he discovered her wishing for his departure. The truth is, that his irregular hours and uncouth habits, such as turning the candles with their heads downwards, when they did not burn bright enough, and letting the wax drop upon the carpet, could not but be disagreeable to a lady. Besides, she had not that high admiration of him which was felt by most of those who knew him; and what was very natural to a female mind, she thought he had too much influence over her husband. She once in a little warmth, made, with more point than justice, this remark upon that subject: 'I have seen many a bear led by a man: but I never before saw a man led by a bear.'

[2] Sir Alexander Gordon, one of the Professors at Aberdeen.

[3] This was a box containing a number of curious things which he had picked up in Scotland, particularly some horn spoons.

[4] The Rev. Dr. Alexander Webster, one of the ministers of Edinburgh, a man of distinguished abilities, who had promised him information concerning the Highlands and Islands of Scotland.

when sawn across. You may either have a little writing-standish
made of it, or get it formed into boards for a treatise on witch-
craft, by way of a suitable binding.' . . .

'MR. BOSWELL *to* DR. JOHNSON
                                              'Edinburgh, Dec. 18, 1773.
'. . . You promised me an inscription for a print to be taken
from an historical picture of Mary Queen of Scots being forced
to resign her crown, which Mr. Hamilton at Rome has painted
for me. The two following have been sent to me:

   "*Maria Scotorum Regina meliori seculo digna, jus regium civibus
seditiosis invita resignat.*"

   "*Cives seditiosi Mariam Scotorum Reginam sese muneri abdicare
invitam cogunt.*"[1]

'Be so good as to read the passage in Robertson, and see if
you cannot give me a better inscription. I must have it both in
Latin and English; so if you should not give me another Latin
one, you will at least choose the best of these two, and send a
translation of it.' . . .

His humane forgiving disposition was put to a pretty strong
test on his return to London, by a liberty which Mr. Thomas
Davies had taken with him in his absence, which was, to publish
two volumes, entitled, *Miscellaneous and fugitive Pieces*, which he
advertised in the news-papers, 'By the Authour of the Rambler.'
In this collection, several of Dr. Johnson's acknowledged writings, several of his anonymous performances, and some which
he had written for others, were inserted; but there were also
some in which he had no concern whatever. He was at first very
angry, as he had good reason to be. But, upon consideration of
his poor friend's narrow circumstances, and that he had only a
little profit in view, and meant no harm, he soon relented, and
continued his kindness to him as formerly.

In the course of his self-examination with retrospect to this

---

[1] ['Mary Queen of Scots, worthy of a better age, reluctantly surrenders
her rights to her rebellious people.
   'Rebellious subjects force Mary Queen of Scots against her will to abdicate
her office.']

year, he seems to have been much dejected; for he says, January 1, 1774, 'This year has passed with so little improvement, that I doubt whether I have not rather impaired than increased my learning';[1] and yet we have seen how he *read*, and we know how he *talked* during that period.

He was now seriously engaged in writing an account of our travels in the Hebrides, in consequence of which I had the pleasure of a more frequent correspondence with him.

'To JAMES BOSWELL, ESQ.

'DEAR SIR,—My operations have been hindered by a cough; at least I flatter myself, that if my cough had not come, I should have been further advanced. But I have had no intelligence from Dr. W——, [Webster,] nor from the Excise-office, nor from you. No account of the little borough.[2] Nothing of the Erse language. I have yet heard nothing of my box.

'You must make haste and gather me all you can, and do it quickly, or I will and shall do without it.

'Make my compliments to Mrs. Boswell, and tell her that I do not love her the less for wishing me away. I gave her trouble enough, and shall be glad, in recompense, to give her any pleasure.

'I would send some porter into the Hebrides, if I knew which way it could be got to my kind friends there. Enquire, and let me know.

'Make my compliments to all the Doctors of Edinburgh, and to all my friends, from one end of Scotland to the other.

'Write to me, and send me what intelligence you can: and if any thing is too bulky for the post, let me have it by the carrier. I do not like trusting winds and waves. I am, dear Sir, your most, &c.

'Jan. 29, 1774.'   'SAM. JOHNSON.'

To THE SAME

'DEAR SIR,—In a day or two after I had written the last discontented letter, I received my box, which was very welcome.

---

[1] *Pr. and Med.* p. 129.   [2] The ancient Burgh of Prestwick, in Ayrshire.

But still I must entreat you to hasten Dr. Webster, and continue to pick up what you can that may be useful.

'Mr. Oglethorpe was with me this morning. You know his errand. He was not unwelcome.

'Tell Mrs. Boswell that my good intentions towards her still continue. I should be glad to do any thing that would either benefit or please her.

'Chambers is not yet gone, but so hurried, or so negligent, or so proud, that I rarely see him. I have, indeed, for some weeks past, been very ill of a cold and cough, and have been at Mrs. Thrale's, that I might be taken care of. I am much better: *novæ redeunt in prælia vires*;[1] but I am yet tender, and easily disordered. How happy it was that neither of us were ill in the Hebrides.

'The question of Literary Property is this day before the Lords. Murphy drew up the Appellants' case, that is, the plea against the perpetual right. I have not seen it, nor heard the decision. I would not have the right perpetual.

'I will write to you as any thing occurs, and do you send me something about my Scottish friends. I have very great kindness for them. Let me know likewise how fees come in, and when we are to see you. I am, Sir, yours affectionately,

'London, Feb. 7, 1774.'   'SAM. JOHNSON.'

He at this time wrote the following letters to Mr. Steevens, his able associate in editing Shakspeare:—

'*To* GEORGE STEEVENS, ESQ., *in Hampstead*

'SIR,—If I am asked when I have seen Mr. Steevens, you know what answer I must give; if I am asked when I shall see him, I wish you would tell me what to say.

'If you have Lesley's *History of Scotland*, or any other book about Scotland, except Boetius and Buchanan, it will be a kindness if you send them to, Sir, your humble servant,

'Feb. 7, 1774.'   'SAM. JOHNSON.'

---

[1] [Perhaps Johnson imperfectly remembered '*novae rediere in pristina vires*, new-born strength returned to its whilom vigour.' *Aeneid*, xii. 424. (Jackson.)]

To THE SAME

'SIR,—We are thinking to augment our club and I am desirous of nominating you, if you care to stand the ballot, and can attend on Friday nights at least twice in five weeks: less than that is too little, and rather more will be expected. Be pleased to let me know before Friday. I am, Sir, your most, &c.,

'Feb. 21, 1774.'   'SAM. JOHNSON.'

To THE SAME

'SIR,—Last night you became a member of the club; if you call on me on Friday, I will introduce you. A gentleman,[1] proposed after you, was rejected.

'I thank you for *Neander*, but wish he were not so fine. I will take care of him. I am, Sir, your humble servant,

'March 5, 1774.'   'SAM. JOHNSON.'

'*To* JAMES BOSWELL, ESQ.

'DEAR SIR,—Dr. Webster's informations were much less exact and much less determinate than I expected: they are, indeed, much less positive than, if he can trust his own book[2] which he laid before me, he is able to give. But I believe it will always be found, that he who calls much for information will advance his work but slowly.

'I am, however, obliged to you, dear Sir, for your endeavours to help me, and hope, that between us something will some time be done, if not on this, on some occasion.

'Chambers is either married, or almost married, to Miss Wilton, a girl of sixteen, exquisitely beautiful, whom he has, with his lawyer's tongue, persuaded to take her chance with him in the East.

'We have added to the club, Charles Fox, Sir Charles Bunbury, Dr. Fordyce, and Mr. Steevens.

[1] [Gibbon. *Garrick.*]
[2] A manuscript account drawn up by Dr. Webster of all the parishes in Scotland, ascertaining their length, breadth, number of inhabitants, and distinguishing Protestants and Roman Catholicks. This book had been transmitted to government, and Dr. Johnson saw a copy of it in Dr. Webster's possession.

'Return my thanks to Dr. Webster. Tell Dr. Robertson I have not much to reply to his censure of my negligence; and tell Dr. Blair, that since he has written hither what I said to him, we must now consider ourselves as even, forgive one another, and begin again. I care not how soon, for he is a very pleasing man. Pay my compliments to all my friends, and remind Lord Elibank of his promise to give me all his works.

'I hope Mrs. Boswell and little Miss are well.—When shall I see them again? She is a sweet lady, only she was so glad to see me go, that I have almost a mind to come again, that she may again have the same pleasure.

'Enquire if it be practicable to send a small present of a cask of porter to Dunvegan, Rasay, and Col. I would not wish to be thought forgetful of civilities. I am, Sir, your humble servant,

'March 5, 1774.'   'SAM. JOHNSON.'

On the 5th of March I wrote to him, requesting his counsel whether I should this spring come to London. I stated to him on the one hand some pecuniary embarrassments, which, together with my wife's situation at that time, made me hesitate; and, on the other, the pleasure and improvement which my annual visit to the metropolis always afforded me; and particularly mentioned a peculiar satisfaction which I experienced in celebrating the festival of Easter in St. Paul's cathedral; that to my fancy it appeared like going up to Jerusalem at the feast of the Passover; and that the strong devotion which I felt on that occasion diffused its influence on my mind through the rest of the year.

'To JAMES BOSWELL, ESQ.

                              [*Not dated, but written about
                              the* 15*th of March.*]
'DEAR SIR,

'I am ashamed to think that since I received your letter I have passed so many days without answering it.

'I think there is no great difficulty in resolving your doubts. The reasons for which you are inclined to visit London, are, I think, not of sufficient strength to answer the objections. That you should delight to come once a year to the fountain of intelligence and pleasure, is very natural; but both information and pleasure must be regulated by propriety. Pleasure, which cannot be obtained but by unseasonable or unsuitable expence, must always end in pain; and pleasure, which must be enjoyed at the expence of another's pain, can never be such as a worthy mind can fully delight in.

'What improvement you might gain by coming to London, you may easily supply, or easily compensate, by enjoining yourself some particular study at home, or opening some new avenue to information. Edinburgh is not yet exhausted; and I am sure you will find no pleasure here which can deserve either that you should anticipate any part of your future fortune, or that you should condemn yourself and your lady to penurious frugality for the rest of the year.

'I need not tell you what regard you owe to Mrs. Boswell's entreaties; or how much you ought to study the happiness of her who studies yours with so much diligence, and of whose kindness you enjoy such good effects. Life cannot subsist in society but by reciprocal concessions. She permitted you to ramble last year, you must permit her now to keep you at home.

'Your last reason is so serious, that I am unwilling to oppose it. Yet you must remember, that your image of worshipping once a year in a certain place, in imitation of the Jews, is but a comparison; and *simile non est idem*; if the annual resort to Jerusalem was a duty to the Jews, it was a duty because it was commanded; and you have no such command, therefore no such duty. It may be dangerous to receive too readily, and indulge too fondly, opinions, from which, perhaps, no pious mind is wholly disengaged, of local sanctity and local devotion. You know what strange effects they have produced over a great part of the Christian world. I am now writing, and you, when you read this, are reading under the Eye of Omnipresence.

'To what degree fancy is to be admitted into religious offices, it would require much deliberation to determine. I am far from intending totally to exclude it. Fancy is a faculty bestowed by our Creator, and it is reasonable that all His gifts should be used to His glory, that all our faculties should co-operate in His worship; but they are to co-operate according to the will of Him that gave them, according to the order which His wisdom has established. As ceremonies prudential or convenient are less obligatory than positive ordinances, as bodily worship is only the token to others or ourselves of mental adoration, so Fancy is always to act in subordination to Reason. We may take Fancy for a companion, but must follow Reason as our guide. We may allow Fancy to suggest certain ideas in certain places; but Reason must always be heard, when she tells us, that those ideas and those places have no natural or necessary relation. When we enter a church we habitually recall to mind the duty of adoration, but we must not omit adoration for want of a temple; because we know, and ought to remember, that the Universal Lord is every where present; and that, therefore, to come to Jona,[1] or to Jerusalem, though it may be useful, cannot be necessary.

'Thus I have answered your letter, and have not answered it negligently. I love you too well to be careless when you are serious.

'I think I shall be very diligent next week about our travels, which I have too long neglected. I am, dear Sir, your most, &c.,

'Compliments to Madam and Miss.'   'SAM. JOHNSON.'

To THE SAME

'DEAR SIR,—The lady who delivers this has a lawsuit, in which she desires to make use of your skill and eloquence, and she seems to think that she shall have something more of both for a recommendation from me; which, though I know how little you want any external incitement to your duty, I could not refuse her, because I know that at least it will not hurt her, to tell you that I wish her well. I am, Sir, your most humble servant,

'May 10, 1774.'   'SAM. JOHNSON.'

'MR. BOSWELL *to* DR. JOHNSON

                           'Edinburgh, May 12, 1774.

'Lord Hailes has begged of me to offer you his best respects,

                 [1] Iona.

and to transmit to you specimens of *Annals of Scotland, from the Accession of Malcolm Kenmore to the Death of James V,* in drawing up which, his Lordship has been engaged for some time. His Lordship writes to me thus: "If I could procure Dr. Johnson's criticisms, they would be of great use to me in the prosecution of my work, as they would be judicious and true. I have no right to ask that favour of him. If you could, it would highly oblige me."

'Dr. Blair requests you may be assured that he did not write to London what you said to him, and that neither by word nor letter has he made the least complaint of you; but, on the contrary, has a high respect for you, and loves you much more since he saw you in Scotland. It would both divert and please you to see his eagerness about this matter.'

'*To* JAMES BOSWELL, ESQ.

'DEAR SIR,   'Streatham, June 21, 1774.

'Yesterday I put the first sheets of the *Journey to the Hebrides* to the press. I have endeavoured to do you some justice in the first paragraph. It will be one volume in octavo, not thick.

'It will be proper to make some presents in Scotland. You shall tell me to whom I shall give; and I have stipulated twenty-five for you to give in your own name. Some will take the present better from me, others better from you. In this, you who are to live in the place ought to direct. Consider it. Whatever you can get for my purpose send me; and make my compliments to your lady and both the young ones. I am, Sir, your, &c.,

                                        'SAM. JOHNSON.'

'MR. BOSWELL *to* DR. JOHNSON

                                        'Edinburgh, June 24, 1774.

'You do not acknowledge the receipt of the various packets which I have sent to you. Neither can I prevail with you to *answer* my letters, though you honour me with *returns.* You have said nothing to me about poor Goldsmith,[1] nothing about Langton.

'I have received for you, from the Society for propagating Christian Knowledge in Scotland, the following Erse books:—

[1] Dr. Goldsmith died April 4, this year.

The New Testament; Baxter's Call; The Confession of Faith of the Assembly of Divines at Westminster; The Mother's Catechism; A Gaelick and English Vocabulary.[1]

'*To* JAMES BOSWELL, ESQ.

'DEAR SIR,—I wish you could have looked over my book before the printer, but it could not easily be. I suspect some mistakes; but as I deal, perhaps, more in notions than in facts, the matter is not great, and the second edition will be mended, if any such there be. The press will go on slowly for a time, because I am going into Wales to-morrow.

'I should be very sorry if I appeared to treat such a character as that of Lord Hailes otherwise than with high respect. I return the sheets,[2] to which I have done what mischief I could; and finding it so little, thought not much of sending them. The narrative is clear, lively, and short.

'I have done worse to Lord Hailes than by neglecting his sheets: I have run him in debt. Dr. Horne, the President of Magdalen College in Oxford, wrote to me about three months ago, that he purposed to reprint *Walton's Lives,* and desired me to contribute to the work: my answer was, that Lord Hailes intended the same publication; and Dr. Horne has resigned it to him. His Lordship must now think seriously about it.

'Of poor dear Dr. Goldsmith there is little to be told, more than the papers have made publick. He died of a fever, made, I am afraid, more violent by uneasiness of mind. His debts began to be heavy, and all his resources were exhausted. Sir Joshua is of opinion that he owed not less than two thousand pounds. Was ever poet so trusted before?

'You may, if you please, put the inscription thus:—

'"*Maria Scotorum Regina nata* 15—, *a suis in exilium acta* 15—, *ab hospitâ neci data* 15—."[3] You must find the years.

---

[1] These books Dr. Johnson presented to the Bodleian Library.

[2] On the cover enclosing them, Dr. Johnson wrote, 'If my delay has given any reason for supposing that I have not a very deep sense of the honour done me by asking my judgement, I am very sorry.'

[3] ['Mary Queen of Scots, born 15—, driven into exile by her countrymen 15—, executed by her hostess 15—.']

'Of your second daughter you certainly gave the account yourself, though you have forgotten it. While Mrs. Boswell is well, never doubt of a boy. Mrs. Thrale brought, I think, five girls running, but while I was with you she had a boy.

'I am obliged to you for all your pamphlets, and of the last I hope to make some use. I made some of the former. I am, dear Sir, your most affectionate servant,

'July 4, 1774.'   'SAM. JOHNSON.'

'My compliments to all the three ladies.'

'*To* BENNET LANGTON, ESQ., *at Langton, near Spilsby, Lincolnshire*

'DEAR SIR,—You have reason to reproach me that I have left your last letter so long unanswered, but I had nothing particular to say. Chambers, you find, is gone far, and poor Goldsmith is gone much further. He died of a fever, exasperated, as I believe, by the fear of distress. He had raised money and squandered it, by every artifice of acquisition, and folly of expence. But let not his frailties be remembered; he was a very great man.

'I have just begun to print my *Journey to the Hebrides*, and am leaving the press to take another journey into Wales, whither Mr. Thrale is going, to take possession of, at least, five hundred a year, fallen to his lady. All at Streatham, that are alive, are well.

'I have never recovered from the last dreadful illness, but flatter myself that I grow gradually better; much, however, yet remains to mend. Κύριε ἐλέησον.[1]

'If you have the Latin version of *Busy, curious, thirsty fly*, be so kind as to transcribe and send it; but you need not be in haste, for I shall be I know not where, for at least five weeks. I wrote the following tetastrick on poor Goldsmith:—

> Τὸν τάφον εἰσοράας τὸν Ὀλιβάροιο.[2] κονίην
> Ἄφροσι μὴ σεμνήν, Ξεῖνε, πόδεσσι πάτει·
> Οἶσι μέμηλε φύσις, μέτρων χάρις, ἔργα παλαιῶν,
> Κλαίετε ποιητήν, ἱστορικόν, φυσικόν.[3]

[1] ['Lord, have mercy upon us.']   [2] [Johnson wrote Ὀλιβαρίοιο.]
[3] ['You behold, Stranger, the tomb of Oliver Goldsmith; tread not on his hallowed ashes with careless feet; if you have any care for nature, for the beauty of verse, for antiquity, weep for a poet, an historian, a naturalist.']

'Please to make my most respectful compliments to all the ladies, and remember me to young George and his sisters. I reckon George begins to shew a pair of heels.

'Do not be sullen now, but let me find a letter when I come back. I am, dear Sir, your affectionate, humble servant,

'July 5, 1774.'   'SAM. JOHNSON.'

'*To* MR. ROBERT LEVET

'Llewenny, in Denbighshire, Aug. 16, 1774.

'DEAR SIR,—Mr. Thrale's affairs have kept him here a great while, nor do I know exactly when we shall come hence. I have sent you a bill upon Mr. Strahan.

'I have made nothing of the Ipecacuanha, but have taken abundance of pills, and hope that they have done me good.

'Wales, so far as I have yet seen of it, is a very beautiful and rich country, all enclosed, and planted. Denbigh is not a mean town. Make my compliments to all my friends, and tell Frank I hope he remembers my advice. When his money is out, let him have more. I am, Sir, your humble servant,

'SAM. JOHNSON.'

'MR. BOSWELL *to* DR. JOHNSON

'Edinburgh, Aug. 30, 1774.

'You have given me an inscription for a portrait of Mary Queen of Scots, in which you, in a short and striking manner, point out her hard fate. But you will be pleased to keep in mind, that my picture is a representation of a particular scene in her history; her being forced to resign her crown, while she was imprisoned in the castle of Lochlevin. I must, therefore, beg that you will be kind enough to give me an inscription suited to that particular scene; or determine which of the two formerly transmitted to you is the best; and, at any rate, favour me with an English translation. It will be doubly kind if you comply with my request speedily.

'Your critical notes on the specimen of Lord Hailes's *Annals of Scotland* are excellent. I agreed with you in every one of them. He himself objected only to the alteration of *free* to *brave*, in the

565

passage where he says that Edward "departed with the glory due to the conquerour of a free people." He says, "to call the Scots brave would only add to the glory of their conquerour." You will make allowance for the national zeal of our annalist. I now send a few more leaves of the *Annals*, which I hope you will peruse, and return with observations, as you did upon the former occasion. Lord Hailes writes to me thus:—"Mr. Boswell will be pleased to express the grateful sense which Sir David Dalrymple has of Dr. Johnson's attention to his little specimen. The further specimen will show, that

> "Even in an *Edward* he can see desert."

'It gives me much pleasure to hear that a republication of *Isaac Walton's Lives* is intended. You have been in a mistake in thinking that Lord Hailes had it in view. I remember one morning, while he sat with you in my house, he said, that there should be a new edition of *Walton's Lives*; and you said, that "they should be benoted a little." This was all that passed on that subject. You must, therefore, inform Dr. Horne, that he may resume his plan. I enclose a note concerning it; and if Dr. Horne will write to me, all the attention that I can give shall be cheerfully bestowed, upon what I think a pious work, the preservation and elucidation of Walton, by whose writings I have been most pleasingly edified.' . . .

'MR. BOSWELL *to* DR. JOHNSON

'Edinburgh, Sept. 16, 1774.

'Wales has probably detained you longer than I supposed. You will have become quite a mountaineer, by visiting Scotland one year and Wales another. You must next go to Switzerland. Cambria will complain, if you do not honour her also with some remarks. And I find *concessere columnæ*,[1] the booksellers expect another book. I am impatient to see your *Tour to Scotland and the Hebrides*. Might you not send me a copy by the post as soon as it is printed off?' . . .

[1] [Horace, *Ars Poetica*, l. 373. See p. 618 for Horace's context.]

'*To* JAMES BOSWELL, ESQ.

'DEAR SIR,—Yesterday I returned from my Welch journey. I was sorry to leave my book suspended so long; but having an opportunity of seeing, with so much convenience, a new part of the island, I could not reject it. I have been in five of the six counties of North Wales; and have seen St. Asaph and Bangor, the two seats of their Bishops; have been upon Penmanmaur and Snowden, and passed over into Anglesea. But Wales is so little different from England, that it offers nothing to the speculation of the traveller.

'When I came home, I found several of your papers, with some pages of Lord Hailes's *Annals*, which I will consider. I am in haste to give you some account of myself, lest you should suspect me of negligence in the pressing business which I find recommended to my care, and which I knew nothing of till now, when all care is vain.[1]

'In the distribution of my books I purpose to follow your advice, adding such as shall occur to me. I am not pleased with your notes of remembrance added to your names, for I hope I shall not easily forget them.

'I have received four Erse books, without any direction, and suspect that they are intended for the Oxford library. If that is the intention, I think it will be proper to add the metrical psalms, and whatever else is printed in *Erse*, that the present may be complete. The donor's name should be told.

'I wish you could have read the book before it was printed, but our distance does not easily permit it.

'I am sorry Lord Hailes does not intend to publish *Walton*; I am afraid it will not be done so well, if it be done at all.

'I purpose now to drive the book forward. Make my compliments to Mrs. Boswell, and let me hear often from you. I am, dear Sir, your affectionate humble servant,

'London, Octob. 1, 1774.'   'SAM. JOHNSON.'

This tour to Wales, which was made in company with Mr.

---

[1] I had written to him, to request his interposition in behalf of a convict [John Reid. *Boswell Papers*, ix. 167 ff.], who I thought was very unjustly condemned.

and Mrs. Thrale, though it no doubt contributed to his health
and amusement, did not give occasion to such a discursive exercise of his mind as our tour to the Hebrides. I do not find that he
kept any journal or notes of what he saw there. All that I heard
him say of it was, that 'instead of bleak and barren mountains,
there were green and fertile ones; and that one of the castles in
Wales would contain all the castles that he had seen in Scotland.'

Parliament having been dissolved, and his friend Mr. Thrale,
who was a steady supporter of government, having again to
encounter the storm of a contested election, he wrote a short
political pamphlet, entitled *The Patriot*,* addressed to the electors of Great-Britain; a title which, to factious men, who consider
a patriot only as an opposer of the measures of government, will
appear strangely misapplied. It was, however, written with
energetick vivacity; and, except those passages in which it endeavours to vindicate the glaring outrage of the House of
Commons in the case of the Middlesex election, and to justify
the attempt to reduce our fellow-subjects in America to unconditional submission, it contained an admirable display of the properties of a real patriot, in the original and genuine sense;—a
sincere, steady, rational, and unbiassed friend to the interests
and prosperity of his King and country. It must be acknowledged, however, that both in this and his two former pamphlets,
there was, amidst many powerful arguments, not only a considerable portion of sophistry, but a contemptuous ridicule of his
opponents, which was very provoking.

'*To* Mr. Perkins[1]

'Sir,—You may do me a very great favour. Mrs. Williams,
a gentlewoman whom you may have seen at Mr. Thrale's, is a

---

[1] Mr. Perkins was for a number of years the worthy superintendant of
Mr. Thrale's great brewery, and after his death became one of the proprietors of it; and now resides in Mr. Thrale's house in Southwark, which
was the scene of so many literary meetings, and in which he continues the
liberal hospitality for which it was eminent. Dr. Johnson esteemed him
much. He hung up in the counting-house a fine proof of the admirable
mezzotinto of Dr. Johnson, by Doughty; and when Mrs. Thrale asked him
somewhat flippantly, 'Why do you put him up in the counting-house?' he

petitioner for Mr. Hetherington's charity: petitions are this day issued at Christ's Hospital.

'I am a bad manager of business in a crowd; and if I should send a mean man, he may be put[1] away without his errand. I must therefore intreat that you will go, and ask for a petition for Anna Williams, whose paper of enquiries was delivered with answers at the counting-house of the hospital on Thursday the 20th. My servant will attend you thither, and bring the petition home[2] when you have it.

'The petition, which they are to give us, is a form which they deliver to every petitioner, and which the petitioner is afterwards to fill up, and return to them again. This we must have, or we cannot proceed according to their directions. You need, I believe, only ask for a petition; if they enquire for whom you ask, you can tell them.

'I beg pardon for giving you this trouble; but it is a matter of great importance. I am, Sir, your most humble servant,

'October 25, 1774.'   'SAM. JOHNSON.'

'*To* JAMES BOSWELL, ESQ.

'DEAR SIR,—There has appeared lately in the papers an account of a boat overset between Mull and Ulva, in which many passengers were lost, and among them Maclean of Col. We, you know, were once drowned;[3] I hope, therefore, that the story is either wantonly or erroneously told. Pray satisfy me by the next post.

'I have printed two hundred and forty pages. I am able to do nothing much worth doing to dear Lord Hailes's book. I will, however, send back the sheets; and hope, by degrees, to answer all your reasonable expectations.

'Mr. Thrale has happily surmounted a very violent and acrimonious opposition; but all joys have their abatements: Mrs.

answered, 'Because, Madam, I wish to have one wise man there.' 'Sir,' (said Johnson,) 'I thank you. It is a very handsome compliment, and I believe you speak sincerely.'

[1] [Johnson wrote *sent.*]   [2] [Johnson wrote *to me.*]
[3] In the news-papers.

Thrale has fallen from her horse, and hurt herself very much.
The rest of our friends, I believe, are well. My compliments to
Mrs. Boswell. I am, Sir, your most affectionate servant,
    'London, Octob. 27, 1774.'   'SAM. JOHNSON.'

This letter, which shews his tender concern for an amiable
young gentleman to whom we had been very much obliged in
the Hebrides, I have inserted according to its date, though before
receiving it I had informed him of the melancholy event that the
young Laird of Col was unfortunately drowned.

'*To* JAMES BOSWELL, ESQ.

'DEAR SIR,—Last night I corrected the last page of our *Journey
to the Hebrides*. The printer has detained it all this time, for I had,
before I went into Wales, written all except two sheets. *The
Patriot* was called for by my political friends on Friday, was
written on Saturday, and I have heard little of it. So vague are
conjectures at a distance.[1] As soon as I can, I will take care that
copies be sent to you, for I would wish that they might be given
before they are bought; but I am afraid that Mr. Strahan will
send to you and to the booksellers at the same time. Trade is as
diligent as courtesy. I have mentioned all that you recommended.
Pray make my compliments to Mrs. Boswell and the younglings.
The club has, I think, not yet met.

'Tell me, and tell me honestly, what you think and what
others say of our travels. Shall we touch the continent?[2] I am,
dear Sir, your most humble servant,
    'No. 26, 1774.'   'SAM. JOHNSON.'

In his manuscript diary of this year, there is the following
entry:—
    'Nov. 27. Advent Sunday. I considered that this day, being
the beginning of the ecclesiastical year, was a proper time for a

---

[1] Alluding to a passage in a letter of mine, where speaking of his *Journey
to the Hebrides*, I say, 'But has not *The Patriot* been an interruption, by the
time taken to write it, and the time luxuriously spent in listening to its
applauses?'
[2] We had projected a voyage together up the Baltick, and talked of visiting some of the more northern regions.

new course of life. I began to read the Greek Testament regularly at 160 verses every Sunday. This day I began the Acts.

'In this week I read Virgil's *Pastorals*. I learned to repeat the *Pollio* and *Gallus*. I read carelessly the first *Georgick*.'

Such evidences of his unceasing ardour, both for 'divine and human lore,' when advanced into his sixty-fifth year, and notwithstanding his many disturbances from disease, must make us at once honour his spirit, and lament that it should be so grievously clogged by its material tegument. It is remarkable, that he was very fond of the precision which calculation produces. Thus we find in one of his manuscript diaries, '12 pages in 4to. Gr. Test. and 30 pages in Beza's folio, comprize the whole in 40 days.'

'Dr JOHNSON *to* JOHN HOOLE, Esq.

'DEAR SIR,—I have returned your play,[1] which you will find underscored with red, where there was a word which I did not like. The red will be washed off with a little water.

'The plot is so well framed, the intricacy so artful, and the disentanglement so easy, the suspense so affecting, and the passionate parts so properly interposed, that I have no doubt of its success. I am, Sir, your most humble servant,

'December 19, 1774.'   'SAM. JOHNSON.'

1775: ÆTAT. 66.]—THE first effort of his pen in 1775 was, 'Proposals for publishing the Works of Mrs. Charlotte Lennox,'† in three volumes quarto. In his diary, January 2, I find this entry: 'Wrote Charlotte's Proposals.' But, indeed, the internal evidence would have been quite sufficient. Her claim to the favour of the publick was thus enforced:—

'Most of the pieces, as they appeared singly, have been read with approbation, perhaps above their merit, but of no great advantage to the writer. She hopes, therefore, that she shall not be considered as too indulgent to vanity, or too studious of interest, if, from that labour which has hitherto been chiefly gainful to others, she endeavours to obtain at last some profit

---

[1] *Cleonice.*

for herself and her children. She cannot decently enforce her claim by the praise of her own performances; nor can she suppose, that, by the most artful and laboured address, any additional notice could be procured to a publication, of which Her MAJESTY has condescended to be the PATRONESS.'

He this year also wrote the Preface to Baretti's *Easy Lessons in Italian and English.*†

'*To* JAMES BOSWELL, ESQ.

DEAR SIR,—You never did ask for a book by the post till now, and I did not think on it. You see now it is done. I sent one to the King, and I hear he likes it.

'I shall send a parcel into Scotland for presents, and intend to give to many of my friends. In your catalogue you left out Lord Auchinleck.

'Let me know, as fast as you read it, how you like it; and let me know if any mistake is committed, or any thing important left out. I wish you could have seen the sheets. My compliments to Mrs. Boswell, and to Veronica, and to all my friends. I am, Sir, your most humble servant,

'January 14, 1775.'   'SAM. JOHNSON.'

'MR. BOSWELL *to* DR. JOHNSON

                                                    'Edinburgh, Jan. 19, 1775.

'Be pleased to accept of my best thanks for your *Journey to the Hebrides*, which came to me by last night's post. I did really ask the favour twice; but you have been even with me by granting it so speedily. Bis *dat qui cito dat.*[1] Though ill of a bad cold, you kept me up the greatest part of the last night; for I did not stop till I had read every word of your book. I looked back to our first talking of a visit to the Hebrides, which was many years ago, when sitting by ourselves in the Mitre tavern, in London, I think about *witching time o' night*; and then exulted in contemplating our scheme fulfilled, and a *monumentum perenne*[2] of it erected by your superiour abilities. I shall only say, that your

---

[1] ['He gives twice who gives quickly.']
[2] ['an enduring monument.' Horace, *Odes* III. xxx. 1.]

book has afforded me a high gratification. I shall afterwards give you my thoughts on particular passages. In the mean time, I hasten to tell you of your having mistaken two names, which you will correct in London, as I shall do here, that the gentlemen who deserve the valuable compliments which you have paid them, may enjoy their honours. In page 106, for *Gordon* read *Murchison*; and in page 357, for *Maclean* read *Macleod*. . . .

'But I am now to apply to you for immediate aid in my profession, which you have never refused to grant when I requested it. I enclose you a petition for Dr. Memis, a physician at Aberdeen, in which Sir John Dalrymple has exerted his talents, and which I am to answer as Counsel for the managers of the Royal Infirmary in that city. Mr. Jopp, the Provost, who delivered to you your freedom, is one of my clients, and, *as a citizen of Aberdeen*, you will support him.

'The fact is shortly this. In a translation of the charter of the Infirmary from Latin into English, made under the authority of the managers, the same phrase in the original is in one place rendered *Physician*, but when applied to Dr. Memis is rendered *Doctor of Medicine*. Dr. Memis complained of this before the translation was printed, but was not indulged with having it altered; and he has brought an action for damages, on account of a supposed injury, as if the designation given to him were an inferiour one, tending to make it be supposed he is *not a Physician*, and, consequently, to hurt his practice. My father has dismissed the action as groundless, and now he has appealed to the whole Court.'[1]

'*To* JAMES BOSWELL, ESQ.

'DEAR SIR,—I long to hear how you like the book; it is, I think, much liked here. But Macpherson is very furious; can you

---

[1] In the Court of Session of Scotland an action is first tried by one of the Judges, who is called the Lord Ordinary; and if either party is dissatisfied, he may appeal to the whole Court, consisting of fifteen, the Lord President and fourteen other Judges, who have both in and out of Court the title of Lords, from the name of their estates; as, Lord Auchinleck, Lord Monboddo, &c.

give me any more intelligence about him, or his Fingal? Do what you can, and do it quickly. Is Lord Hailes on our side?

'Pray let me know what I owed you when I left you, that I may send it to you.

'I am going to write about the Americans. If you have picked up any hints among your lawyers, who are great masters of the law of nations, or if your own mind suggests any thing, let me know. But mum, it is a secret.

'I will send your parcel of books as soon as I can; but I cannot do as I wish. However, you find every thing mentioned in the book which you recommended.

'Langton is here; we are all that ever we were. He is a worthy fellow, without malice, though not without resentment.

'Poor Beauclerk is so ill, that his life is thought to be in danger. Lady Di nurses him with very great assiduity.

'Reynolds has taken too much to strong liquor,[1] and seems to delight in his new character.

'This is all the news that I have; but as you love verses, I will send you a few which I made upon Inchkenneth;[2] but remember the condition, that you shall not show them, except to Lord Hailes, whom I love better than any man whom I know so little. If he asks you to transcribe them for him, you may do it, but I think he must promise not to let them be copied again, nor to show them as mine.

'I have at last sent back Lord Hailes's sheets. I never think about returning them, because I alter nothing. You will see that I might as well have kept them. However, I am ashamed of my delay; and if I have the honour of receiving any more, promise punctually to return them by the next post. Make my compliments to dear Mrs. Boswell, and to Miss Veronica. I am, dear Sir, yours most faithfully,

'Jan. 21, 1775.'

'SAM. JOHNSON.'[3]

---

[1] It should be recollected, that this fanciful description of his friend was given by Johnson after he himself had become a water-drinker.

[2] See them in *Journal of a Tour to the Hebrides*, 3rd edit. p. 337 [Oct. 17].

[3] He now sent me a Latin inscription for my historical picture of Mary

'Mr. Boswell *to* Dr. Johnson

'Edinburgh, Jan. 27, 1775.

'. . . You rate our lawyers here too high, when you call them great masters of the law of nations. . . .

'As for myself, I am ashamed to say that I have read little and thought little on the subject of America. I will be much obliged to you, if you will direct me where I shall find the best information of what is to be said on both sides. It is a subject vast in its present extent and future consequences. The imperfect hints which now float in my mind, tend rather to the formation of an opinion that our government has been precipitant and severe in the resolutions taken against the Bostonians. Well do you know that I have no kindness for that race. But nations, or bodies of men, should, as well as individuals, have a fair trial, and not be condemned on character alone. Have we not express contracts with our colonies, which afford a more certain foundation of judgement, than general political speculations on the mutual rights of States and their provinces or colonies? Pray let me know immediately what to read, and I shall diligently endeavour to gather for you any thing that I can find. Is Burke's speech on American taxation published by himself? Is it authentick? I remember to have heard you say, that you had never considered East-Indian affairs; though, surely,

Queen of Scots, and afterwards favoured me with an English translation. Mr. Alderman Boydell, that eminent Patron of the Arts, has subjoined them to the engraving from my picture.

> '*Maria Scotorum Regina*
> *Hominum seditiosorum*
> *Contumeliis lassata,*
> *Minis territa, clamoribus victa,*
> *Libello, per quem*
> *Regno cedit,*
> *Lacrimans trepidansque*
> *Nomen apponit.*'

> 'Mary Queen of Scots,
> Harassed, terrified, and overpowered
> By the insults, menaces,
> And clamours
> Of her rebellious subjects,
> Sets her hand,
> With tears and confusion,
> To a resignation of the kingdom.'

they are of much importance to Great-Britain. Under the recollection of this, I shelter myself from the reproach of ignorance about
the Americans. If you write upon the subject I shall certainly
understand it. But, since you seem to expect that I should know
something of it, without your instruction, and that my own mind
should suggest something, I trust you will put me in the way. . . .

'What does Becket mean by the *Originals* of Fingal and other
poems of Ossian, which he advertises to have lain in his shop?'. . .

'*To* JAMES BOSWELL, ESQ.

'DEAR SIR,—You sent me a case to consider, in which I have
no facts but which are against us, nor any principles on which to
reason. It is vain to try to write thus without materials. The fact
seems to be against you; at least I cannot know nor say any
thing to the contrary. I am glad that you like the book so well.
I hear no more of Macpherson. I shall long to know what Lord
Hailes says of it. Lend it him privately. I shall send the parcel as
soon as I can. Make my compliments to Mrs. Boswell. I am,
Sir, &c.,

'Jan. 28, 1775.'   'SAM. JOHNSON.'

'MR. BOSWELL *to* DR. JOHNSON

'Edinburgh, Feb. 2, 1775.

'. . . As to Macpherson, I am anxious to have from yourself a
full and pointed account of what has passed between you and
him. It is confidently told here, that before your book came out
he sent to you, to let you know that he understood you meant to
deny the authenticity of Ossian's poems; that the originals were
in his possession; that you might have inspection of them, and
might take the evidence of people skilled in the Erse language;
and that he hoped, after this fair offer, you would not be so
uncandid as to assert that he had refused reasonable proof. That
you paid no regard to his message, but published your strong
attack upon him; that then he wrote a letter to you, in such terms
as he thought suited to one who had not acted as a man of
veracity. You may believe it gives me pain to hear your conduct
represented as unfavourable, while I can only deny what is said,

on the ground that your character refutes it, without having any
information to oppose. Let me, I beg it of you, be furnished with
a sufficient answer to any calumny upon this occasion.

'Lord Hailes writes to me, (for we correspond more than we
talk together,) "As to Fingal, I see a controversy arising, and
purpose to keep out of its way. There is no doubt that I might
mention some circumstances; but I do not choose to commit
them to paper." What his opinion is, I do not know. He says,
"I am singularly obliged to Dr. Johnson for his accurate and
useful criticisms. Had he given some strictures on the general
plan of the work, it would have added much to his favours." He
is charmed with your verses on Inchkenneth, says they are very
elegant, but bids me tell you he doubts whether

"Legitimas faciunt pectora pura preces"[1]

be according to the rubrick: but that is your concern; for, you
know, he is a Presbyterian.' . . .

'*To* Dr. LAWRENCE.[2]

'SIR,   'Feb. 7, 1775.

'One of the Scotch physicians is now prosecuting a corporation that in some publick instrument have stiled him *Doctor of
Medicine* instead of *Physician*. Boswell desires, being advocate
for the corporation, to know whether *Doctor of Medicine* is[3] not
a legitimate title, and whether it may[4] be considered as a disadvantageous distinction. I am to write to-night; be pleased to
tell me. I am, Sir, your most, &c.,

'SAM. JOHNSON.'

'*To* JAMES BOSWELL, ESQ.

'MY DEAR BOSWELL,—I am surprized that, knowing as you
do the disposition of your countrymen to tell lies in favour of
each other,[5] you can be at all affected by any reports that circulate among them. Macpherson never in his life offered me the

---

[1] ["Pure hearts make lawful prayers.']
[2] The learned and worthy Dr. Lawrence, whom Dr. Johnson respected
and loved as his physician and friend.
[3] [Johnson wrote *be*.]   [4] [Johnson wrote *can*.]
[5] My friend has, in this letter, relied upon my testimony, with a confidence, of which the ground has escaped my recollection.

sight of any original or of any evidence of any kind; but thought
only of intimidating me by noise and threats, till my last answer,
—that I would not be deterred from detecting what I thought a
cheat, by the menaces of a ruffian—put an end to our correspondence.

'The state of the question is this. He, and Dr. Blair, whom I
consider as deceived, say, that he copied the poem from old
manuscripts. His copies, if he had them, and I believe him to
have none, are nothing. Where are the manuscripts? They can
be shewn if they exist, but they were never shewn. *De non
existentibus et non apparentibus*, says our law, *eadem est ratio*.[1] No
man has a claim to credit upon his own word, when better
evidence, if he had it, may be easily produced. But, so far as we
can find, the Erse language was never written till very lately for
the purposes of religion. A nation that cannot write, or a language
that was never written, has no manuscripts.

'But whatever he has, he never offered to show. If old manuscripts should now be mentioned, I should, unless there were
more evidence than can be easily had, suppose them another
proof of Scotch conspiracy in national falsehood.

'Do not censure the expression; you know it to be true.

'Dr. Memis's question is so narrow as to allow no speculation; and I have no facts before me but those which his advocate
has produced against you.

'I consulted this morning the President of the London College
of Physicians, who says, that with us, *Doctor of Physick* (we do
not say *Doctor of Medicine*) is the highest title that a practicer
of physick can have; that *Doctor* implies not only *Physician*, but
teacher of physick; that every *Doctor* is legally a *Physician*; but
no man, not a *Doctor*, can *practice physick* but by *licence* particularly
granted. The Doctorate is a licence of itself. It seems to us a very
slender cause of prosecution. . . .

'I am now engaged, but in a little time I hope to do all you
would have. My compliments to Madam and Veronica. I am, Sir,
your most humble servant,

'February 7, 1775.'   'SAM. JOHNSON.'

[1] 'It is presumed that what does not appear does not exist.'

What words were used by Mr. Macpherson in his letter to the venerable Sage, I have never heard; but they are generally said to have been of a nature very different from the language of literary contest. Dr. Johnson's answer appeared in the newspapers of the day, and has since been frequently re-published; but not with perfect accuracy. I give it as dictated to me by himself, written down in his presence, and authenticated by a note in his own hand-writing, '*This, I think, is a true copy.*'[1]

'Mr. James Macpherson,—I received your foolish and impudent letter. Any violence offered me I shall do my best to repel; and what I cannot do for myself, the law shall do for me. I hope I shall never be deterred from detecting what I think a cheat, by the menaces of a ruffian.

'What would you have me retract? I thought your book an imposture; I think it an imposture still. For this opinion I have given my reasons to the publick, which I here dare you to refute. Your rage I defy. Your abilities, since your Homer, are not so formidable; and what I hear of your morals, inclines me to pay regard not to what you shall say, but to what you shall prove. You may print this if you will.

'Sam. Johnson.'

Mr. Macpherson little knew the character of Dr. Johnson, if he supposed that he could be easily intimidated; for no man was ever more remarkable for personal courage. He had, indeed, an aweful dread of death, or rather, 'of something after death;' and what rational man, who seriously thinks of quitting all that he has ever known, and going into a new and unknown state of being, can be without that dread? But his fear was from reflection; his courage natural. His fear, in that one instance, was the result of philosophical and religious consideration. He feared death, but he feared nothing else, not even what might occasion death. Many instances of his resolution may be mentioned. One day, at Mr. Beauclerk's house in the country, when two large dogs were fighting, he went up to them, and beat them till they separated;

---

[1] I have deposited it in the British Museum. [Not found there.]

and at another time, when told of the danger there was that a
gun might burst if charged with many balls, he put in six or
seven, and fired it off against a wall. Mr. Langton told me, that
when they were swimming together near Oxford, he cautioned
Dr. Johnson against a pool, which was reckoned particularly
dangerous; upon which Johnson directly swam into it. He told
me himself that one night he was attacked in the street by four
men, to whom he would not yield, but kept them all at bay, till
the watch came up, and carried both him and them to the round-
house. In the playhouse at Lichfield, as Mr. Garrick informed
me, Johnson having for a moment quitted a chair which was
placed for him between the side-scenes, a gentleman took possession of it, and when Johnson on his return civilly demanded
his seat, rudely refused to give it up; upon which Johnson laid
hold of it, and tossed him and the chair into the pit. Foote, who
so successfully revived the old comedy, by exhibiting living
characters, had resolved to imitate Johnson on the stage, expecting great profits from his ridicule of so celebrated a man. Johnson being informed of his intention, and being at dinner at Mr.
Thomas Davies's the bookseller, from whom I had the story, he
asked Mr. Davies 'what was the common price of an oak stick;'
and being answered six-pence, 'Why then, Sir, (said he,) give
me leave to send your servant to purchase me a shilling one.
I'll have a double quantity; for I am told Foote means to *take me
off*, as he calls it, and I am determined the fellow shall not do it
with impunity.' Davies took care to acquaint Foote of this,
which effectually checked the wantonness of the mimick. Mr.
Macpherson's menaces made Johnson provide himself with the
same implement of defence; and had he been attacked, I have no
doubt that, old as he was, he would have made his corporal
prowess be felt as much as his intellectual.

His *Journey to the Western Islands of Scotland** is a most
valuable performance. It abounds in extensive philosophical
views of society, and in ingenious sentiments and lively description. A considerable part of it, indeed, consists of speculations,
which many years before he saw the wild regions which we
visited together, probably had employed his attention, though

the actual sight of those scenes undoubtedly quickened and augmented them. Mr. Orme, the very able historian, agreed with
me in this opinion, which he thus strongly expressed:—'There
are in that book thoughts, which, by long revolution in the great
mind of Johnson, have been formed and polished like pebbles
rolled in the ocean!'

That he was to some degree of excess a *true-born Englishman*,
so as to have ever entertained an undue prejudice against both
the country and the people of Scotland, must be allowed. But it
was a prejudice of the head, and not of the heart. He had no ill-
will to the Scotch; for, if he had been conscious of that, he would
never have thrown himself into the bosom of their country, and
trusted to the protection of its remote inhabitants with a fearless
confidence. His remark upon the nakedness of the country, from
its being denuded of trees, was made after having travelled two
hundred miles along the eastern coast, where certainly trees are
not to be found near the road; and he said it was 'a map of the
road' which he gave. His disbelief of the authenticity of the
poems ascribed to Ossian, a Highland bard, was confirmed in
the course of his journey, by a very strict examination of the
evidence offered for it; and although their authenticity was made
too much a national point by the Scotch, there were many
respectable persons in that country, who did not concur in this;
so that his judgement upon the question ought not to be decried,
even by those who differ from him. As to myself, I can only say,
upon a subject now become very uninteresting, that when the
fragments of Highland poetry first came out, I was much pleased
with their wild peculiarity, and was one of those who subscribed
to enable their editor, Mr. Macpherson, then a young man, to
make a search in the Highlands and Hebrides for a long poem in
the Erse language, which was reported to be preserved somewhere in those regions. But when there came forth an Epick
Poem in six books, with all the common circumstances of former
compositions of that nature; and when, upon an attentive examination of it, there was found a perpetual recurrence of the same
images which appear in the fragments; and when no ancient
manuscript, to authenticate the work, was deposited in any

publick library, though that was insisted on as a reasonable proof, *who* could forbear to doubt?

Johnson's grateful acknowledgements of kindnesses received in the course of this tour, completely refute the brutal reflections which have been thrown out against him, as if he had made an ungrateful return; and his delicacy in sparing in his book those who we find from his letters to Mrs. Thrale were just objects of censure, is much to be admired. His candour and amiable disposition is conspicuous from his conduct, when informed by Mr. Macleod, of Rasay, that he had committed a mistake, which gave that gentleman some uneasiness. He wrote him a courteous and kind letter, and inserted in the news-papers an advertisement, correcting the mistake.[1]

The observations of my friend Mr. Dempster in a letter written to me, soon after he had read Dr. Johnson's book, are so just and liberal, that they cannot be too often repeated:—

'. . . There is nothing in the book, from beginning to end, that a Scotchman need to take amiss. What he says of the country is true; and his observations on the people are what must naturally occur to a sensible, observing, and reflecting inhabitant of a convenient metropolis, where a man on thirty pounds a year may be better accommodated with all the little wants of life, than Col or Sir Allan.

'I am charmed with his researches concerning the Erse language, and the antiquity of their manuscripts. I am quite convinced; and I shall rank Ossian and his Fingals and Oscars amongst the nursery tales, not the true history of our country, in all time to come.

'Upon the whole, the book cannot displease, for it has no pretensions. The authour neither says he is a geographer, nor an antiquarian, nor very learned in the history of Scotland, nor a naturalist, nor a fossilist. The manners of the people, and the face of the country, are all he attempts to describe, or seems to have thought of. Much were it to be wished, that they who have travelled into more remote, and of course more curious regions, had all possessed his good sense. Of the state of learning, his

[1] See *Journal of a Tour to the Hebrides*, 3rd edit. p. 520 [p. 431].

observations on Glasgow University show he has formed a very
sound judgement. He understands our climate too; and he has
accurately observed the changes, however slow and imperceptible
to us, which Scotland has undergone, in consequence of the
blessings of liberty and internal peace.' . . .

Mr. Knox, another native of Scotland, who has since made the
same tour, and published an account of it, is equally liberal.

'I have read (says he,) his book again and again, travelled
with him from Berwick to Glenelg, through countries with
which I am well acquainted; sailed with him from Glenelg to
Rasay, Sky, Rum, Col, Mull, and Icolmkill, but have not been
able to correct him in any matter of consequence. I have often
admired the accuracy, the precision, and the justness of what he
advances, respecting both the country and the people.

'The Doctor has every where delivered his sentiments with
freedom, and in many instances with a seeming regard for the
benefit of the inhabitants and the ornament of the country. His
remarks on the want of trees and hedges for shade, as well as for
shelter to the cattle, are well founded, and merit the thanks, not the
illiberal censure of the natives. He also felt for the distresses of the
Highlanders, and explodes, with great propriety, the bad management of the grounds, and the neglect of timber in the Hebrides.'

Having quoted Johnson's just compliments on the Rasay
family, he says: 'On the other hand, I found this family equally
lavish in their encomiums upon the Doctor's conversation, and
his subsequent civilities to a young gentleman of that country,
who, upon waiting upon him at London, was well received, and
experienced all the attention and regard that a warm friend
could bestow. Mr. Macleod having also been in London, waited
upon the Doctor, who provided a magnificent and expensive
entertainment in honour of his old Hebridean acquaintance.'
And talking of the military road by Fort Augustus, he says: 'By
this road, though one of the most rugged in Great Britain, the
celebrated Dr. Johnson passed from Inverness to the Hebride
Isles. His observations on the country and people are extremely
correct, judicious, and instructive.'[1]

[1] Page 103.

Mr. Tytler, the acute and able vindicator of Mary Queen of Scots, in one of his letters to Mr. James Elphinstone, published in that gentleman's *Forty Years' Correspondence*, says:

'I read Dr. Johnson's Tour with very great pleasure. Some few errours he has fallen into, but of no great importance, and those are lost in the numberless beauties of his work.

'If I had leisure, I could perhaps point out the most exceptionable places; but at present I am in the country, and have not his book at hand. It is plain he meant to speak well of Scotland; and he has in my apprehension done us great honour in the most capital article, the character of the inhabitants.'

His private letters to Mrs. Thrale, written during the course of his journey, which therefore may be supposed to convey his genuine feelings at the time, abound in such benignant sentiments towards the people who showed him civilities, that no man whose temper is not very harsh and sour, can retain a doubt of the goodness of his heart.

It is painful to recollect with what rancour he was assailed by numbers of shallow irritable North Britons, on account of his supposed injurious treatment of their country and countrymen, in his *Journey*. Had there been any just ground for such a charge, would the virtuous and candid Dempster have given his opinion of the book, in the terms which I have quoted? Would the patriotick Knox[1] have spoken of it as he has done? Would Mr. Tytler, surely

'—— a *Scot*, if ever *Scot* there were,'

have expressed himself thus? And let me add, that, citizen of the world as I hold myself to be, I have that degree of predilection for my *natale solum*,[2] nay, I have that just sense of the merit of an ancient nation, which has been ever renowned for its valour, which in former times maintained its independence against a powerful neighbour, and in modern times has been equally distinguished for its ingenuity and industry in civilized life, that I

---

[1] I observed with much regret, while the first edition of this work was passing through the press (Aug. 1790), that this ingenious gentleman was dead.

[2] ['native soil'.]

should have felt a generous indignation at any injustice done to it. Johnson treated Scotland no worse than he did even his best friends, whose characters he used to give as they appeared to him, both in light and shade. Some people, who had not exercised their minds sufficiently, condemned him for censuring his friends. But Sir Joshua Reynolds, whose philosophical penetration and justness of thinking were not less known to those who lived with him, than his genius in his art is admired by the world, explained his conduct thus: 'He was fond of discrimination, which he could not shew without pointing out the bad as well as the good in every character; and as his friends were those whose characters he knew best, they afforded him the best opportunity for showing the acuteness of his judgement.'

He expressed to his friend Mr. Windham of Norfolk, his wonder at the extreme jealousy of the Scotch, and their resentment at having their country described by him as it really was; when, to say that it was a country as good as England, would have been a gross falsehood. 'None of us, (said he,) would be offended if a foreigner who has travelled here should say, that vines and olives don't grow in England.' And as to his prejudice against the Scotch, which I always ascribed to that nationality which he observed in *them*, he said to the same gentleman, 'When I find a Scotchman, to whom an Englishman is as a Scotchman, that Scotchman shall be as an Englishman to me.' His intimacy with many gentlemen of Scotland, and his employing so many natives of that country as his amanuenses, prove that his prejudice was not virulent; and I have deposited in the British Museum,[1] amongst other pieces of his writing, the following note in answer to one from me, asking if he would meet me at dinner at the Mitre, though a friend of mine, a Scotchman, was to be there:—

'Mr. Johnson does not see why Mr. Boswell should suppose a Scotchman less acceptable than any other man. He will be at the Mitre.'

My much-valued friend Dr. Barnard, now Bishop of Killaloe, having once expressed to him an apprehension, that if he should

---

[1] [Not found there.]

visit Ireland he might treat the people of that country more unfavourably than he had done the Scotch, he answered, with strong
pointed double-edged wit, 'Sir, you have no reason to be afraid
of me. The Irish are not in a conspiracy to cheat the world by
false representations of the merits of their countrymen. No, Sir;
the Irish are a FAIR PEOPLE;—they never speak well of one
another.'

Johnson told me of an instance of Scottish nationality, which
made a very unfavourable impression upon his mind. A Scotchman, of some consideration in London, solicited him to recommend, by the weight of his learned authority, to be master of an
English school, a person of whom he who recommended him
confessed he knew no more but that he was his countryman.
Johnson was shocked at this unconscientious conduct.

All the miserable cavillings against his *Journey*, in news-
papers, magazines, and other fugitive publications, I can speak
from certain knowledge, only furnished him with sport. At last
there came out a scurrilous volume, larger than Johnson's own,
filled with malignant abuse, under a name, real or fictitious, of
some low man[1] in an obscure corner of Scotland, though supposed to be the work of another Scotchman,[2] who has found
means to make himself well known both in Scotland and England. The effect which it had upon Johnson was, to produce this
pleasant observation to Mr. Seward, to whom he lent the book:
'This fellow must be a blockhead. They don't know how to go
about their abuse. Who will read a five shilling book against
me? No, Sir, if they had wit, they should have kept pelting me
with pamphlets.'

'MR. BOSWELL *to* DR. JOHNSON

'Edinburgh, Feb. 18, 1775.
'You would have been very well pleased if you had dined with
me to-day. I had for my guests, Macquharrie, young Maclean
of Col, the successor of our friend, a very amiable man, though
not marked with such active qualities as his brother; Mr. Maclean of Torloisk in Mull, a gentleman of Sir Allan's family; and

---

[1] [Rev. Donald McNicol. *Powell*.]   [2] [James Macpherson. *Croker*[1].]

586

two of the clan Grant; so that the Highland and Hebridean genius reigned. We had a great deal of conversation about you, and drank your health in a bumper. The toast was not proposed by me, which is a circumstance to be remarked, for I am now so connected with you, that any thing that I can say or do to your honour has not the value of an additional compliment. It is only giving you a guinea out of that treasure of admiration which already belongs to you, and which is no hidden treasure; for I suppose my admiration of you is co-existent with the knowledge of my character.

'I find that the Highlanders and Hebrideans in general are much fonder of your *Journey* than the low-country or *hither* Scots. One of the Grants said to-day, that he was sure you were a man of a good heart, and a candid man, and seemed to hope he should be able to convince you of the antiquity of a good proportion of the poems of Ossian. After all that has passed, I think the matter is capable of being proved to a certain degree. I am told that Macpherson got one old Erse MS. from Clanranald, for the restitution of which he executed a formal obligation; and it is affirmed, that the Gaelick (call it Erse or call it Irish,) has been written in the Highlands and Hebrides for many centuries. It is reasonable to suppose, that such of the inhabitants as acquired any learning, possessed the art of writing as well as their Irish neighbours, and Celtick cousins; and the question is, can sufficient evidence be shewn of this?

'Those who are skilled in ancient writings can determine the age of MSS. or at least can ascertain the century in which they were written; and if men of veracity, who are so skilled, shall tell us that MSS. in the possession of families in the Highlands and isles are the works of a remote age, I think we should be convinced by their testimony.

'There is now come to this city, Ranald Macdonald from the Isle of Egg, who has several MSS. of Erse poetry, which he wishes to publish by subscription. I have engaged to take three copies of the book, the price of which is to be six shillings, as I would subscribe for all the Erse that can be printed, be it old or new, that the language may be preserved. This man says, that some of his manuscripts are ancient; and, to be sure, one of them which was shewn to me does appear to have the duskyness of antiquity. . . .

'The enquiry is not yet quite hopeless, and I should think that the exact truth may be discovered, if proper means be used. I am, &c.

'JAMES BOSWELL.'

'*To* JAMES BOSWELL, ESQ.

'DEAR SIR,—I am sorry that I could get no books for my friends in Scotland. Mr. Strahan has at last promised to send two dozen to you. If they come, put the names of my friends into them; you may cut them out,[1] and paste them with a little starch in the book.

'You then are going wild about Ossian. Why do you think any part can be proved? The dusky manuscript of Egg is probably not fifty years old; if it be an hundred, it proves nothing. The tale of Clanranald has no proof. Has Clanranald told it? Can he prove it? There are, I believe, no Erse manuscripts. None of the old families had a single letter in Erse that we heard of. You say it is likely that they could write. The learned, if any learned there were, could; but knowing by that learning, some written language, in that language they wrote, as letters had never been applied to their own. If there are manuscripts, let them be shewn, with some proof that they are not forged for the occasion. You say many can remember parts of Ossian. I believe all those parts are versions of the English; at least there is no proof of their antiquity.

'Macpherson is said to have made some translations himself; and having taught a boy to write it, ordered him to say that he had learnt it of his grandmother. The boy, when he grew up, told the story. This Mrs. Williams heard at Mr. Strahan's table. Do not be credulous; you know how little a Highlander can be trusted. Macpherson is, so far as I know, very quiet. Is not that proof enough? Every thing is against him. No visible manuscript; no inscription in the language: no correspondence among friends:

[1] From a list in his hand-writing.

no transaction of business, of which a single scrap remains in the ancient families. Macpherson's pretence is, that the character was Saxon. If he had not talked unskilfully of *manuscripts*, he might have fought with oral tradition much longer. As to Mr. Grant's information, I suppose he knows much less of the matter than ourselves.

'In the mean time, the bookseller says that the sale[1] is sufficiently quick. They printed four thousand. Correct your copy wherever it is wrong, and bring it up. Your friends will all be glad to see you. I think of going myself into the country about May.

'I am sorry that I have not managed to send the books sooner. I have left four for you, and do not restrict you absolutely to follow my directions in the distribution. You must use your own discretion.

'Make my compliments to Mrs. Boswell: I suppose she is now just beginning to forgive me. I am, dear Sir, your humble servant, 'Feb. 25, 1775.'   'SAM. JOHNSON.'

On Tuesday, March 21, I arrived in London; and on repairing to Dr. Johnson's before dinner, found him in his study, sitting with Mr. Peter Garrick, the elder brother of David, strongly resembling him in countenance and voice, but of more sedate and placid manners. Johnson informed me, that 'though Mr. Beauclerk was in great pain, it was hoped he was not in danger, and that he now wished to consult Dr. Heberden to try the effect of a *new understanding*.' Both at this interview, and in the evening at Mr. Thrale's, where he and Mr. Peter Garrick and I met again, he was vehement on the subject of the Ossian controversy; observing, 'We do not know that there are any ancient Erse manuscripts; and we have no other reason to disbelieve that there are men with three heads, but that we do not know that there are any such men.' He also was outrageous, upon his supposition that my countrymen 'loved Scotland better than truth,' saying, 'All of them,—nay not all,—but *droves* of them, would come up, and attest any thing for the honour of Scotland.' He

[1] Of his *Journey to the Western Islands of Scotland.*

also persevered in his wild allegation, that he questioned if there was a tree between Edinburgh and the English border older than himself. I assured him he was mistaken, and suggested that the proper punishment would be that he should receive a stripe at every tree above a hundred years old, that was found within that space. He laughed, and said, 'I believe I might submit to it for a *baubee*!'

The doubts which, in my correspondence with him, I had ventured to state as to the justice and wisdom of the conduct of Great-Britain towards the American colonies, while I at the same time requested that he would enable me to inform myself upon that momentous subject, he had altogether disregarded; and had recently published a pamphlet, entitled, *Taxation no Tyranny; an answer to the Resolutions and Address of the American Congress.* *

He had long before indulged most unfavourable sentiments of our fellow-subjects in America. For, as early as 1769, I was told by Dr. John Campbell, that he had said of them, 'Sir, they are a race of convicts, and ought to be thankful for any thing we allow them short of hanging.'

Of this performance I avoided to talk with him; for I had now formed a clear and settled opinion, that the people of America were well warranted to resist a claim that their fellow-subjects in the mother-country should have the entire command of their fortunes, by taxing them without their own consent; and the extreme violence which it breathed, appeared to me so unsuitable to the mildness of a Christian philosopher, and so directly opposite to the principles of peace which he had so beautifully recommended in his pamphlet respecting Falkland's Islands, that I was sorry to see him appear in so unfavourable a light. Besides, I could not perceive in it that ability of argument, or that felicity of expression, for which he was, upon other occasions, so eminent. Positive assertion, sarcastical severity, and extravagant ridicule, which he himself reprobated as a test of truth, were united in this rhapsody.

That this pamphlet was written at the desire of those who were then in power, I have no doubt; and, indeed, he owned to me, that it had been revised and curtailed by some of them. He told me, that they had struck out one passage, which was to this effect:—'That the Colonists could with no solidity argue from their not having been taxed while in their infancy, that they should not now be taxed. We do not put a calf into the plow; we wait till he is an ox.' He said, 'They struck it out either critically as too ludicrous, or politically as too exasperating. I care not which. It was their business. If an architect says, I will build five stories, and the man who employs him says, I will have only three, the employer is to decide.' 'Yes, Sir, (said I,) in ordinary cases. But should it be so when the architect gives his skill and labour *gratis?*'

Unfavourable as I am constrained to say my opinion of this pamphlet was, yet, since it was congenial with the sentiments of numbers at that time, and as everything relating to the writings of Dr. Johnson is of importance in literary history, I shall therefore insert some passages which were struck out, it does not appear why, either by himself or those who revised it. They appear printed in a few proof leaves of it in my possession, marked with corrections in his own handwriting. I shall distinguish them by *Italicks*.

In the paragraph where he says the Americans were incited to resistance by European intelligence from 'Men whom they thought their friends, but who were friends only to themselves,' there followed,—'*and made by their selfishness, the enemies of their country.*'

And the next paragraph ran thus:—'On the original contrivers of mischief, *rather than on those whom they have deluded*, let an insulted nation pour out its vengeance.'

The paragraph which came next was in these words:—'*Unhappy is that country in which men can hope for advancement by favouring its enemies. The tranquillity of stable government is not always easily preserved against the machinations of single innovators; but what can be the hope of quiet, when factions hostile to the legislature can be openly formed and openly avowed?*'

After the paragraph which now concludes the pamphlet, there followed this, in which he certainly means the great Earl of Chatham, and glances at a certain popular Lord Chancellor.[1]

---

[1] [Lord Camden. *Croker*[1].]

'*If, by the fortune of war, they drive us utterly away, what they will do next can only be conjectured. If a new monarchy is erected, they will want a* King. *He who first takes into his hand the sceptre of America, should have a name of good omen.* William *has been known both as conqueror and deliverer; and perhaps England, however contemned, might yet supply them with* another William. *Whigs, indeed, are not willing to be governed; and it is possible that* King William *may be strongly inclined to guide their measures: but Whigs have been cheated like other mortals, and suffered their leader to become their tyrant, under the name of their* Protector. *What more they will receive from England, no man can tell. In their rudiments of empire they may want a* Chancellor.'

Then came this paragraph:—

'*Their numbers are, at present, not quite sufficient for the greatness which, in some form of government or other, is to rival the ancient monarchies; but by Dr. Franklin's rule of progression, they will, in a century and a quarter, be more than equal to the inhabitants of Europe. When the Whigs of America are thus multiplied, let the Princes of the earth tremble in their palaces. If they should continue to double and to double, their own hemisphere would not contain them. But let not our boldest oppugners of authority look forward with delight to this futurity of Whiggism.*'

How it ended I know not, as it is cut off abruptly at the foot of the last of these proof pages.

His pamphlets in support of the measures of administration were published on his own account, and he afterwards collected them into a volume, with the title of *Political Tracts, by the Authour of the Rambler*, with this motto:—

> '*Fallitur egregio quisquis sub Principe credit*
> *Servitium; nunquam libertas gratior extat*
> *Quam sub Rege pio.*'   Claudianus.[1]

These pamphlets drew upon him numerous attacks. Against the common weapons of literary warfare he was hardened; but

---

[1] [He errs who deems obedience to a prince
Slav'ry—a happier freedom never reigns
Than with a pious monarch.
            Consulatus Stilichonis, 3, 133. (Croker.)]

there were two instances of animadversion which I communicated to him, and from what I could judge, both from his silence and his looks, appeared to me to impress him much.

One was, *A Letter to Dr. Samuel Johnson, occasioned by his late political Publications.* It appeared previous to his *Taxation no Tyranny,* and was written by Dr. Joseph Towers. In that performance, Dr. Johnson was treated with the respect due to so eminent a man, while his conduct as a political writer was boldly and pointedly arraigned, as inconsistent with the character of one, who, if he did employ his pen upon politics, 'It might reasonably be expected should distinguish himself, not by party violence and rancour, but by moderation and by wisdom.'

It concluded thus:—'I would, however, wish you to remember, should you again address the publick under the character of a political writer, that luxuriance of imagination or energy of language will ill compensate for the want of candour, of justice, and of truth. And I shall only add, that should I hereafter be disposed to read, as I heretofore have done, the most excellent of all your performances, *The Rambler,* the pleasure which I have been accustomed to find in it will be much diminished by the reflection that the writer of so moral, so elegant, and so valuable a work, was capable of prostituting his talents in such productions as *The False Alarm,* the *Thoughts on the Transactions respecting Falkland's Islands,* and *The Patriot.*'

I am willing to do justice to the merit of Dr. Towers, of whom I will say, that although I abhor his Whiggish democratical notions and propensities, (for I will not call them principles,) I esteem him as an ingenious, knowing, and very convivial man.

The other instance was a paragraph of a letter to me, from my old and most intimate friend, the Reverend Mr. Temple, who wrote the character of Gray, which has had the honour to be adopted both by Mr. Mason and Dr. Johnson in their accounts of that poet. The words were,—'How can your great, I will not say your *pious,* but your *moral* friend, support the barbarous measures of administration, which they have not the face to ask even their infidel pensioner Hume to defend.'

However confident of the rectitude of his own mind, Johnson

may have felt sincere uneasiness that his conduct should be erroneously imputed to unworthy motives, by good men; and that the influence of his valuable writings should on that account be in any degree obstructed or lessened.

He complained to a Right Honourable friend[1] of distinguished talents and very elegant manners, with whom he maintained a long intimacy, and whose generosity towards him will afterwards appear, that his pension having been given to him as a literary character, he had been applied to by administration to write political pamphlets; and he was even so much irritated, that he declared his resolution to resign his pension. His friend shewed him the impropriety of such a measure, and he afterwards expressed his gratitude, and said he had received good advice. To that friend he once signified a wish to have his pension secured to him for his life; but he neither asked nor received from government any reward whatsoever for his political labours.

On Friday, March 24, I met him at the LITERARY CLUB, where were Mr. Beauclerk, Mr. Langton, Mr. Colman, Dr. Percy, Mr. Vesey, Sir Charles Bunbury, Dr. George Fordyce, Mr. Steevens, and Mr. Charles Fox. Before he came in, we talked of his *Journey to the Western Islands*, and of his coming away 'willing to believe the second sight,'[2] which seemed to excite some ridicule. I was then so impressed with the truth of many of the stories of it which I had been told, that I avowed my conviction, saying, 'He is only *willing* to believe: I *do* believe. The evidence is enough for me, though not for his great mind. What will not fill a quart bottle will fill a pint bottle. I am filled with belief.' 'Are you? (said Colman,) then cork it up.'

I found his *Journey* the common topick of conversation in London at this time, wherever I happened to be. At one of Lord Mansfield's formal Sunday evening conversations, strangely called *Levées*, his Lordship addressed me, 'We have all been reading your travels, Mr. Boswell.' I answered, 'I was but the humble attendant of Dr. Johnson.' The Chief Justice replied,

---

[1] [William Gerard Hamilton. *Croker*[1].]
[2] Johnson's *Journey to the Western Islands of Scotland*, ed. 1775, p. 256.

with that air and manner which none, who ever saw and heard him, can forget, 'He speaks ill of nobody but Ossian.'

Johnson was in high spirits this evening at the club, and talked with great animation and success. He attacked Swift, as he used to do upon all occasions. The *Tale of a Tub* is so much superiour to his other writings, that one can hardly believe he was the authour of it.[1] 'There is in it such a vigour of mind, such a swarm of thoughts, so much of nature, and art, and life.' I wondered to hear him say of *Gulliver's Travels*, 'When once you have thought of big men and little men, it is very easy to do all the rest.' I endeavoured to make a stand for Swift, and tried to rouse those who were much more able to defend him; but in vain. Johnson at last, of his own accord, allowed very great merit to the inventory of articles found in the pockets of *the Man Mountain*, particularly the description of his watch, which it was conjectured was his GOD, as he consulted it upon all occasions. He observed, that 'Swift put his name to but two things, (after he had a name to put,) *The Plan for the Improvement of the English Language*, and the last *Drapier's Letter*.'

From Swift, there was an easy transition to Mr. Thomas Sheridan.—JOHNSON. 'Sheridan is a wonderful admirer of the tragedy of *Douglas*, and presented its authour with a gold medal. Some years ago, at a coffee-house in Oxford, I called to him, "Mr. Sheridan, Mr. Sheridan, how came you to give a gold medal to Home, for writing that foolish play?" This, you see,

---

[1] This doubt has been much agitated on both sides, I think without good reason. See Addison's *Freeholder*, May 4, 1714;—*An Apology for the Tale of a Tub*;—Dr. Hawkesworth's Preface to Swift's *Works*, and Swift's Letter to Tooke the Printer, and Tooke's Answer, in that collection;—Sheridan's *Life of Swift*;—Mr. Courtenay's note on p. 3 of his *Poetical Review of the Literary and Moral Character of Dr. Johnson*; and Mr. Cooksey's *Essay on the Life and Character of John Lord Somers, Baron of Evesham*.

Dr. Johnson here speaks only to the *internal evidence*. I take leave to differ from him, having a very high estimation of the powers of Dr. Swift. His *Sentiments of a Church-of-England-man*, his *Sermon on the Trinity*, and other serious pieces, prove his learning as well as his acuteness in logick and metaphysicks; and his various compositions of a different cast exhibit not only wit, humour, and ridicule; but a knowledge 'of nature, and art, and life:' a combination therefore of those powers, when (as the *Apology* says,) 'the authour was young, his invention at the heighth, and his reading fresh in his head,' might surely produce *The Tale of a Tub*.

was wanton and insolent; but I *meant* to be wanton and insolent. A medal has no value but as a stamp of merit. And was Sheridan to assume to himself the right of giving that stamp? If Sheridan was magnificent enough to bestow a gold medal as an honorary reward of dramatick excellence, he should have requested one of the Universities to choose the person on whom it should be conferred. Sheridan had no right to give a stamp of merit: it was counterfeiting Apollo's coin.'

On Monday, March 27, I breakfasted with him at Mr. Strahan's. He told us, that he was engaged to go that evening to Mrs. Abington's benefit. 'She was visiting some ladies whom I was visiting, and begged that I would come to her benefit. I told her I could not hear: but she insisted so much on my coming, that it would have been brutal to have refused her.' This was a speech quite characteristical. He loved to bring forward his having been in the gay circles of life; and he was, perhaps, a little vain of the solicitations of this elegant and fashionable actress. He told us, the play was to be *The Hypocrite*, altered from Cibber's *Nonjuror*, so as to satirize the Methodists. 'I do not think (said he,) the character of *The Hypocrite* justly applicable to the Methodists, but it was very applicable to the Nonjurors. I once said to Dr. Madan, a clergyman of Ireland, who was a great Whig, that perhaps a Nonjuror would have been less criminal in taking the oaths imposed by the ruling power, than refusing them; because refusing them, necessarily laid him under almost an irresistible temptation to be more criminal; for, a man *must* live, and if he precludes himself from the support furnished by the establishment, will probably be reduced to very wicked shifts to maintain himself.'[1] BOSWELL. 'I should think, Sir, that a man who took the oaths contrary to his principles, was a deter-

---

[1] This was not merely a cursory remark; for in his *Life of Fenton* he observes, 'With many other wise and virtuous men, who at that time of discord and debate (about the beginning of this century) consulted conscience [whether] well or ill informed, more than interest, he doubted the legality of the government; and refusing to qualify himself for publick employment, by taking the oaths required, left the University without a degree.' This conduct Johnson calls 'perverseness of integrity.'

The question concerning the morality of taking oaths, of whatever kind, imposed by the prevailing power at the time, rather than to be excluded

mined wicked man, because he was sure he was committing perjury; whereas a Nonjuror might be insensibly led to do what was
wrong, without being so directly conscious of it.' JOHNSON,
'Why, Sir, a man who goes to bed to his patron's wife is pretty
sure that he is committing wickedness.' BOSWELL. 'Did the
nonjuring clergymen do so, Sir?' JOHNSON. 'I am afraid many
of them did.'

I was startled at his argument, and could by no means think it
convincing. Had not his own father complied with the requisition
of government, (as to which he once observed to me, when I
pressed him upon it, '*That*, Sir, he was to settle with himself,')
he would probably have thought more unfavourably of a Jacobite
who took the oaths:

> '———— had he not resembled
> My father as he *swore*————.'

Mr. Strahan talked of launching into the great ocean of London, in order to have a chance for rising into eminence; and,
observing that many men were kept back from trying their fortunes there, because they were born to a competency, said, 'Small
certainties are the bane of men of talents;' which Johnson confirmed. Mr. Strahan put Johnson in mind of a remark which he
had made to him; 'There are few ways in which a man can be
more innocently employed than in getting money.' 'The more
one thinks of this, (said Strahan,) the juster it will appear.'

Mr. Strahan had taken a poor boy[1] from the country as an

from all consequence, or even any considerable usefulness in society, has
been agitated with all the acuteness of casuistry. It is related, that he who
devised the oath of abjuration, profligately boasted that he had framed a
test which should 'damn one half of the nation, and starve the other.' Upon
minds not exalted to inflexible rectitude, or minds in which zeal for a party
is predominant to excess, taking that oath against conviction may have been
palliated under the plea of necessity, or ventured upon in heat, as upon the
whole producing more good than evil.

At a county election in Scotland, many years ago, when there was a warm
contest between the friends of the Hanoverian succession, and those against
it, the oath of abjuration having been demanded, the freeholders upon one
side rose to go away. Upon which a very sanguine gentleman, one of their
number, ran to the door to stop them, calling out with much earnestness,
'Stay, stay, my friends, and let us swear the rogues out of it!'

[1] [William Davenport. *Johnson's Letters*, No. 387.]

apprentice, upon Johnson's recommendation. Johnson having enquired after him, said, 'Mr. Strahan, let me have five guineas on
account, and I'll give this boy one. Nay, if a man recommends
a boy, and does nothing for him, it is sad work. Call him
down.'

I followed him into the court-yard, behind Mr. Strahan's
house; and there I had a proof of what I had heard him profess,
that he talked alike to all. 'Some people (said he), tell you that
they let themselves down to the capacity of their hearers. I never
do that. I speak uniformly, in as intelligible a manner as I can.'

'Well, my boy, how do you go on?'—'Pretty well, Sir; but
they are afraid I an't strong enough for some parts of the business.' JOHNSON. 'Why, I shall be sorry for it; for when you
consider with how little mental power and corporeal labour a
printer can get a guinea a week, it is a very desirable occupation
for you. Do you hear,—take all the pains you can; and if this
does not do, we must think of some other way of life for you.
There's a guinea.'

Here was one of the many, many instances of his active benevolence. At the same time, the slow and sonorous solemnity with
which, while he bent himself down, he addressed a little thick
short-legged boy, contrasted with the boy's aukwardness and
awe, could not but excite some ludicrous emotions.

I met him at Drury-lane play-house in the evening. Sir Joshua
Reynolds, at Mrs. Abington's request, had promised to bring a
body of wits to her benefit; and having secured forty places in
the front boxes, had done me the honour to put me in the group.
Johnson sat on the seat directly behind me; and as he could
neither see nor hear at such a distance from the stage, he was
wrapped up in grave abstraction, and seemed quite a cloud,
amidst all the sunshine of glitter and gaiety. I wondered at his
patience in sitting out a play of five acts, and a farce of two. He
said very little; but after the prologue to *Bon Ton* had been
spoken, which he could hear pretty well from the more slow and
distinct utterance, he talked of prologue-writing, and observed,
'Dryden has written prologues superiour to any that David
Garrick has written; but David Garrick has written more good

prologues than Dryden has done. It is wonderful that he has been able to write such a variety of them.'

At Mr. Beauclerk's, where I supped, was Mr. Garrick, whom I made happy with Johnson's praise of his prologues; and I suppose, in gratitude to him, he took up one of his favourite topicks, the nationality of the Scotch, which he maintained in his pleasant manner, with the aid of a little poetical fiction. 'Come, come, don't deny it: they are really national. Why, now, the Adams are as liberal-minded men as any in the world: but, I don't know how it is, all their workmen are Scotch. You are, to be sure, wonderfully free from that nationality: but so it happens, that you employ the only Scotch shoe-black in London.' He imitated the manner of his old master with ludicrous exaggeration; repeating, with pauses and half-whistlings interjected,

> '*Os homini sublime dedit,—cælumque tueri*
> *Jussit,—et erectos ad sidera—tollere vultus*;'[1]

looking downwards all the time, and, while pronouncing the four last words, absolutely touching the ground with a kind of contorted gesticulation.

Garrick, however, when he pleased, could imitate Johnson very exactly; for that great actor, with his distinguished powers of expression which were so universally admired, possessed also an admirable talent of mimickry. He was always jealous that Johnson spoke lightly of him. I recollect his exhibiting him to me one day, as if saying, 'Davy has some convivial pleasantry about him, but 'tis a futile fellow;' which he uttered perfectly with the tone and air of Johnson.

I cannot too frequently request of my readers, while they peruse my account of Johnson's conversation, to endeavour to keep in mind his deliberate and strong utterance. His mode of speaking was indeed very impressive;[2] and I wish it could be

---

[1]   ['Man looks aloft, and with uplifted eyes
             Beholds his own hereditary skies.'
                        Ovid, *Meta.* i. 85. (Dryden.)]
[2] My noble friend Lord Pembroke said once to me at Wilton, with a happy pleasantry and some truth, that 'Dr. Johnson's sayings would not appear so extraordinary, were it not for his *bow-wow way*.' The sayings themselves are generally of sterling merit; but, doubtless, his *manner* was an addition to

preserved as musick is written, according to the very ingenious
method of Mr. Steele,[1] who has shewn how the recitation of Mr.
Garrick, and other eminent speakers, might be transmitted to
posterity *in score*.[2]

Next day I dined with Johnson at Mr. Thrale's. He attacked
Gray, calling him a 'dull fellow.' BOSWELL. 'I understand he
was reserved, and might appear dull in company; but surely he
was not dull in poetry.' JOHNSON. 'Sir, he was dull in company,
dull in his closet, dull every where. He was dull in a new way,
and that made many people think him GREAT. He was a mechanical poet.' He then repeated some ludicrous lines, which have
escaped my memory, and said, 'Is not that GREAT, like his Odes?'
Mrs. Thrale maintained that his Odes were melodious; upon
which he exclaimed,

> 'Weave the warp, and weave the woof;'—

I added, in a solemn tone,

> 'The winding-sheet of Edward's race.'

'*There* is a good line.' 'Ay, (said he,) and the next line is a good
one,' (pronouncing it contemptuously;)

> 'Give ample verge and room enough.'—

'No, Sir, there are but two good stanzas in Gray's poetry, which
are in his *Elegy in a Country Church-yard*.' He then repeated the
stanza,

> 'For who to dumb forgetfulness a prey,' &c.

their effect; and therefore should be attended to as much as may be. It is
necessary, however, to guard those who were not acquainted with him,
against overcharged imitations or caricatures of his manner, which are
frequently attempted, and many of which are second-hand copies from the
late Mr. Henderson the actor, who, though a good mimick of some persons,
did not represent Johnson correctly.

[1] See '*Prosodia Rationalis*; or, an Essay towards establishing the Melody
and Measure of Speech, to be expressed and perpetuated by peculiar
Symbols.' London, 1779.

[2] I use the phrase *in score*, as Dr. Johnson has explained it in his Dictionary:—'*A song in* SCORE, the words with the musical notes of a song
annexed.' But I understand that in scientifick propriety it means all the
parts of a musical composition noted down in the characters by which it is
exhibited to the eye of the skilful.

mistaking one word; for instead of *precincts* he said *confines*. He added, 'The other stanza I forget.'

A young lady who had married a man[1] much her inferiour in rank being mentioned, a question arose how a woman's relations should behave to her in such a situation; and, while I recapitulate the debate, and recollect what has since happened, I cannot but be struck in a manner that delicacy forbids me to express. While I contended that she ought to be treated with an inflexible steadiness of displeasure, Mrs. Thrale was all for mildness and forgiveness, and, according to the vulgar phrase, 'making the best of a bad bargain.' Johnson. 'Madam, we must distinguish. Were I a man of rank, I would not let a daughter starve who had made a mean marriage; but having voluntarily degraded herself from the station which she was originally entitled to hold, I would support her only in that which she herself had chosen; and would not put her on a level with my other daughters. You are to consider, Madam, that it is our duty to maintain the subordination of civilized society; and when there is a gross and shameful deviation from rank, it should be punished so as to deter others from the same perversion.'

After frequently considering this subject, I am more and more confirmed in what I then meant to express, and which was sanctioned by the authority, and illustrated by the wisdom, of Johnson; and I think it of the utmost consequence to the happiness of Society, to which subordination is absolutely necessary. It is weak, and contemptible, and unworthy, in a parent to relax in such a case. It is sacrificing general advantage to private feelings. And let it be considered, that the claim of a daughter who has acted thus, to be restored to her former situation, is either fantastical or unjust. If there be no value in the distinction of rank, what does she suffer by being kept in the situation to which she has descended? If there be a value in that distinction, it ought to be steadily maintained. If indulgence be shewn to such conduct, and the offenders know that in a longer or shorter time they shall be received as well as if they had not contaminated their blood by a base alliance, the great check upon that inordinate

[1] [Lady Susan Fox and William O'Brien. *Boswell Papers,* x. 160.]

caprice which generally occasions low marriages will be removed, and the fair and comfortable order of improved life will be miserably disturbed.

Lord Chesterfield's Letters being mentioned, Johnson said, 'It was not to be wondered at that they had so great a sale, considering that they were the letters of a statesman, a wit, one who had been so much in the mouths of mankind, one long accustomed *virûm volitare per ora*.'[1]

On Friday, March 31, I supped with him and some friends at a tavern. One of the company[2] attempted, with too much forwardness, to rally him on his late appearance at the theatre; but had reason to repent of his temerity. 'Why, Sir, did you go to Mrs. Abington's benefit? Did you see?' J O H N S O N. 'No, Sir.' 'Did you hear?' J O H N S O N. 'No, Sir.' 'Why then, Sir, did you go?' J O H N - S O N. 'Because, Sir, she is a favourite of the publick; and when the publick cares the thousandth part for you that it does for her, I will go to your benefit too.'

Next morning I won a small bet from Lady Diana Beauclerk, by asking him as to one of his particularities, which her Ladyship laid I durst not do. It seems he had been frequently observed at the Club to put into his pocket the Seville oranges, after he had squeezed the juice of them into the drink which he made for himself. Beauclerk and Garrick talked of it to me, and seemed to think that he had a strange unwillingness to be discovered. We could not divine what he did with them; and this was the bold question to be put. I saw on his table the spoils of the preceding night, some fresh peels nicely scraped and cut into pieces. 'O, Sir, (said I,) I now partly see what you do with the squeezed oranges which you put into your pocket at the Club.' J O H N S O N. 'I have a great love for them.' B O S W E L L. 'And pray, Sir, what do you do with them? You scrape them, it seems, very neatly, and what next?' J O H N S O N. 'I let them dry, Sir.' B O S - W E L L. 'And what next?' J O H N S O N. 'Nay, Sir, you shall know their fate no further.' B O S W E L L. 'Then the world must be left

---

[1] ['to flit conqueror through the mouths of men.' Virgil, *Georgics*, iii. 9. (Jackson.)]

[2] [Boswell. *Boswell Papers*, x. 168.]

in the dark. It must be said (assuming a mock solemnity,) he scraped them, and let them dry, but what he did with them next, he never could be prevailed upon to tell.' JOHNSON. 'Nay, Sir, you should say it more emphatically:—he could not be prevailed upon, even by his dearest friends, to tell.'

He had this morning received his Diploma as Doctor of Laws from the University of Oxford. He did not vaunt of his new dignity, but I understood he was highly pleased with it. I shall here insert the progress and completion of that high academical honour, in the same manner as I have traced his obtaining that of Master of Arts.

To the Reverend Dr. FOTHERGILL, *Vice-Chancellor of the University of* Oxford, *to be communicated to the Heads of Houses, and proposed in Convocation.*

'MR. VICE-CHANCELLOR AND GENTLEMEN,

'THE honour of the degree of M.A. by diploma, formerly conferred upon MR. SAMUEL JOHNSON, in consequence of his having eminently distinguished himself by the publication of a series of Essays, excellently calculated to form the manners of the people, and in which the cause of religion and morality has been maintained and recommended by the strongest powers of argument and elegance of language, reflected an equal degree of lustre upon the University itself.

'The many learned labours which have since that time employed the attention and displayed the abilities of that great man, so much to the advancement of literature and the benefit of the community, render him worthy of more distinguished honours in the Republick of letters: and I persuade myself, that I shall act agreeably to the sentiments of the whole University, in desiring that it may be proposed in Convocation to confer on him the degree of Doctor in Civil Law by diploma, to which I readily give my consent; and am, Mr. Vice-Chancellor and Gentlemen, your affectionate friend and servant,

    'Downing-street, March 23, 1775.'   'NORTH.'[1]

---

[1] Extracted from the Convocation Register, Oxford.

DIPLOMA.

'*CANCELLARIUS, Magistri, et Scholares Universitatis Oxonien-*
sis omnibus ad quos præsentes Literæ pervenerint, Salutem in
Domino Sempiternam.

'SCIATIS, *virum illustrem,* SAMUELEM JOHNSON, *in omni*
humaniorum literarum genere eruditum, omniumque scientiarum
comprehensione felicissimum, scriptis suis, ad popularium mores for-
mandos summâ verborum elegantiâ ac sententiarum gravitate com-
positis, ita olim inclaruisse, ut dignus videretur cui ab Academiâ
suâ eximia quædam laudis præmia deferentur [*deferrentur*] *quique*
[*in*] *venerabilem Magistrorum Ordinem summâ cum dignitate co-*
optaretur:

Cùm verò eundem clarissimum virum tot posteà tantique labores,
in patriâ præsertim linguâ ornandâ et stabiliendâ feliciter impensi,
ita insigniverint, ut in Literarum Republicâ PRINCEPS *jam et*
PRIMARIUS *jure habeatur; Nos* CANCELLARIUS, *Magistri, et Scholares*
Universitatis Oxoniensis, quò talis viri merita pari honoris remunera-
tione exæquentur, et perpetuum suæ simul laudis, nostræque ergà
literas propensissimæ voluntatis extet monumentum, in solenni Con-
vocatione Doctorum et Magistrorum Regentium, et non Regentium,
prædictum SAMUELEM JOHNSON *Doctorem in Jure Civili renuncia-*
vimus et constituimus, eumque virtute præsentis Diplomatis singulis
juribus, privilegiis et honoribus, ad istum gradum quàquà pertinenti-
bus, frui et gaudere jussimus. In cujus rei testimonium commune
Universitatis Oxoniensis sigillum præsentibus apponi fecimus.

'*Datum in Domo nostræ Convocationis die tricesimo Mensis*
Martii, Anno Domini Millesimo septingentesimo, septuagesimo
quinto.'[1]

[1] ['You must know that the illustrious Samuel Johnson, a man learned in
all humane letters and happy in his grasp of the sciences, long since became
so famous for his writings, eminently calculated in form and matter to
improve the manners of his countrymen, that the University thought him
worthy of signal honour and so enrolled him among its honoured Masters.
'Now whereas this distinguished man has won such repute by his subsequent labours, notably in refining and fixing our language, that he is
justly reckoned a chief and leader in the republic of letters, therefore we the
Chancellor, Master, and Scholars of the University of Oxford, wishing at
once to honour him as he deserves, and to record our own devotion to
letters, have in our solemn Convocation of Doctors and Masters made the

'*Viro Reverendo* THOMÆ FOTHERGILL, *S.T.P. Universitatis Oxoniensis Vice-Cancellario.*

'*S. P. D.*

'SAM. JOHNSON.

'*MULTIS non est opus, ut testimonium quo, te præside, Oxonienses nomen meum posteris commendârunt, quali animo acceperim compertum faciam. Nemo sibi placens non lætatur; nemo sibi non placet, qui vobis, literarum arbitris, placere potuit. Hoc tamen habet incommodi tantum beneficium, quod mihi nunquam posthâc sine vestræ famæ detrimento vel labi liceat vel cessare; semperque sit timendum, ne quod mihi tam eximiæ laudi est, vobis aliquando fiat opprobrio. Vale.*'[1]

'7 *Id. Apr.*, 1775.'

said Samuel Johnson a Doctor of Civil Law, and have by the present diploma made him free of all the rights and privileges that belong to that degree.']

The original is in my possession. He shewed me the Diploma, and allowed me to read it, but would not consent to my taking a copy of it, fearing perhaps that I should blaze it abroad in his life-time. His objection to this appears from his 99th letter to Mrs. Thrale, whom in that letter he thus scolds for the grossness of her flattery of him:—'The other Oxford news is, that they have sent me a degree of Doctor of Laws, with such praises in the Diploma as perhaps ought to make me ashamed: they are very like your praises. I wonder whether I shall ever shew it to you.'

It is remarkable that he never, so far as I know, assumed his title of *Doctor,* but called himself *Mr.* Johnson, as appears from many of his cards or notes to myself; and I have seen many from him to other persons, in which he uniformly takes that designation. I once observed on his table a letter directed to him with the addition of *Esquire,* and objected to it as being a designation inferiour to that of Doctor; but he checked me, and seemed pleased with it, because, as I conjectured, he liked to be sometimes taken out of the class of literary men, and to be merely *genteel,—un gentilhomme comme un autre.*

[1] ['I need not use many words to tell you how I receive the commendation with which the University over which you preside has transmitted my name to posterity. Every man is glad to think well of himself; and that man must think well of himself, of whom you, the arbiters of letters, can think well. But the good you have done me has one drawback: henceforth any fault of mine, of commission or omission, will hurt your reputation; I must always fear that what is a signal honour to me may one day bring discredit upon you.']

'The original is in the hands of Dr. Fothergill, then Vice-Chancellor, who made this transcript.' T. WARTON.

He revised some sheets of Lord Hailes's *Annals of Scotland*, and wrote a few notes on the margin with red ink, which he bade me tell his Lordship did not sink into the paper, and might be wiped off with a wet sponge, so that he did not spoil his manuscript. I observed to him that there were very few of his friends so accurate as that I could venture to put down in writing what they told me as his sayings. JOHNSON. 'Why should you write down *my* sayings?' BOSWELL. 'I write them when they are good.' JOHNSON. 'Nay, you may as well write down the sayings of any one else that are good.' But *where*, I might with great propriety have added, can I find such?

I visited him by appointment in the evening, and we drank tea with Mrs. Williams. He told me that he had been in the company of a gentleman[1] whose extraordinary travels had been much the subject of conversation. But I found that he had not listened to him with that full confidence, without which there is little satisfaction in the society of travellers. I was curious to hear what opinion so able a judge as Johnson had formed of his abilities, and I asked if he was not a man of sense. JOHNSON. 'Why, Sir, he is not a distinct relater; and I should say, he is neither abounding nor deficient in sense. I did not perceive any superiority of understanding.' BOSWELL. 'But will you not allow him a nobleness of resolution, in penetrating into distant regions?' JOHNSON. 'That, Sir, is not to the present purpose. We are talking of his sense. A fighting cock has a nobleness of resolution.'

Next day, Sunday, April 2, I dined with him at Mr. Hoole's. We talked of Pope. JOHNSON. 'He wrote his *Dunciad* for fame. That was his primary motive. Had it not been for that, the dunces might have railed against him till they were weary, without his troubling himself about them. He delighted to vex them, no doubt; but he had more delight in seeing how well he could vex them.'

The *Odes to Obscurity and Oblivion*, in ridicule of 'cool Mason and warm Gray,' being mentioned, Johnson said, 'They are Colman's best things.' Upon its being observed that it was believed these Odes were made by Colman and Lloyd jointly;—

[1] [James Bruce. *Boswell Papers*, x. 170, 174.]

JOHNSON. 'Nay, Sir, how can two people make an Ode? Perhaps one made one of them, and one the other.' I observed that two people had made a play, and quoted the anecdote of Beaumont and Fletcher, who were brought under suspicion of treason, because while concerting the plan of a tragedy when sitting together at a tavern, one of them was overheard saying to the other, 'I'll kill the King.' JOHNSON. 'The first of these Odes is the best: but they are both good. They exposed a very bad kind of writing.' BOSWELL. 'Surely, Sir, Mr. Mason's *Elfrida* is a fine Poem: at least you will allow there are some good passages in it.' JOHNSON. 'There are now and then some good imitations of Milton's bad manner.'

I often wondered at his low estimation of the writings of Gray and Mason. Of Gray's poetry I have in a former part of this work expressed my high opinion; and for that of Mr. Mason I have ever entertained a warm admiration. His *Elfrida* is exquisite, both in poetical description and moral sentiment; and his *Caractacus* is a noble drama. Nor can I omit paying my tribute of praise to some of his smaller poems, which I have read with pleasure, and which no criticism shall persuade me not to like. If I wondered at Johnson's not tasting the works of Mason and Gray, still more have I wondered at their not tasting his works; that they should be insensible to his energy of diction, to his splendour of images, and comprehension of thought. Tastes may differ as to the violin, the flute, the hautboy, in short all the lesser instruments: but who can be insensible to the powerful impressions of the majestick organ?

His *Taxation no Tyranny* being mentioned, he said, 'I think I have not been attacked enough for it. Attack is the re-action; I never think I have hit hard, unless it rebounds.' BOSWELL. 'I don't know, Sir, what you would be at. Five or six shots of small arms in every newspaper, and repeated cannonading in pamphlets, might, I think, satisfy you. But, Sir, you'll never make out this match, of which we have talked, with a certain political lady,[1] since you are so severe against her principles.' JOHNSON. 'Nay, Sir, I have the better chance for that. She is like the Amazons of

[1] [Mrs. Macaulay. *Ib.* 178.]

old; she must be courted by the sword. But I have not been severe upon her.' BOSWELL. 'Yes, Sir, you have made her ridiculous.' JOHNSON. 'That was already done, Sir. To endeavour to make *her* ridiculous, is like blacking the chimney.'

I put him in mind that the landlord at Ellon in Scotland said, that he heard he was the greatest man in England,—next to Lord Mansfield. 'Ay, Sir, (said he,) the exception defined the idea. A Scotchman could go no farther:

"The force of Nature could no farther go."

Lady Miller's collection of verses by fashionable people, which were put into her Vase at Batheaston villa, near Bath, in competition for honorary prizes, being mentioned, he held them very cheap: '*Bouts rimés* (said he,) is a mere conceit, and an *old* conceit *now*; I wonder how people were persuaded to write in that manner for this lady.' I named a gentleman[1] of his acquaintance who wrote for the Vase. JOHNSON. 'He was a blockhead for his pains.' BOSWELL. 'The Duchess of Northumberland wrote.' JOHNSON. 'Sir, the Duchess of Northumberland may do what she pleases: nobody will say anything to a lady of her high rank. But I should be apt to throw ******'s verses in his face.'

I talked of the cheerfulness of Fleet-street, owing to the constant quick succession of people which we perceive passing through it. JOHNSON. 'Why, Sir, Fleet-street has a very animated appearance; but I think the full tide of human existence is at Charing-cross.'

He made the common remark on the unhappiness which men who have led a busy life experience, when they retire in expectation of enjoying themselves at ease, and that they generally languish for want of their habitual occupation, and wish to return to it. He mentioned as strong an instance of this as can well be imagined. 'An eminent tallow-chandler in London, who had acquired a considerable fortune, gave up the trade in favour of his foreman, and went to live at a country-house near town. He soon grew weary, and paid frequent visits to his old shop, where he

---

[1] [Captain Constantine Phipps, later Baron Mulgrave. *Boswell Papers*, x. 179.]

desired they might let him know their *melting-days*, and he would come and assist them; which he accordingly did. Here, Sir, was a man, to whom the most disgusting circumstance in the business to which he had been used was a relief from idleness.'

On Wednesday, April 5, I dined with him at Messieurs Dilly's, with Mr. John Scott of Amwell, the Quaker, Mr. Langton, Mr. Miller, (now Sir John,) and Dr. Thomas Campbell, an Irish clergyman, whom I took the liberty of inviting to Mr. Dilly's table, having seen him at Mr. Thrale's, and been told that he had come to England chiefly with a view to see Dr. Johnson, for whom he entertained the highest veneration. He has since published *A Philosophical Survey of the South of Ireland*, a very entertaining book, which has, however, one fault;—that it assumes the fictitious character of an Englishman.

We talked of publick speaking.—JOHNSON. 'We must not estimate a man's powers by his being able or not able to deliver his sentiments in publick. Isaac Hawkins Browne, one of the first wits of this country, got into Parliament, and never opened his mouth. For my own part, I think it is more disgraceful never to try to speak, than to try it and fail; as it is more disgraceful not to fight, than to fight and be beaten.' This argument appeared to me fallacious; for if a man has not spoken, it may be said that he would have done very well if he had tried; whereas, if he has tried and failed, there is nothing to be said for him. 'Why then, (I asked,) is it thought disgraceful for a man not to fight, and not disgraceful not to speak in publick?' JOHNSON. 'Because there may be other reasons for a man's not speaking in publick than want of resolution: he may have nothing to say, (laughing.) Whereas, Sir, you know courage is reckoned the greatest of all virtues; because, unless a man has that virtue, he has no security for preserving any other.'

He observed, that 'the statutes against bribery were intended to prevent upstarts with money from getting into Parliament;' adding, that 'if he were a gentleman of landed property, he would turn out all his tenants who did not vote for the candidate whom he supported.' LANGTON. 'Would not that, Sir, be checking the freedom of election?' JOHNSON. 'Sir, the law does not mean that the privilege of voting should be independent of old family interest; of the permanent property of the country.'

On Thursday, April 6, I dined with him at Mr. Thomas Davies's, with Mr. Hicky, the painter, and my old acquaintance Mr. Moody, the player.

Dr. Johnson, as usual, spoke contemptuously of Colley Cibber. 'It is wonderful that a man, who for forty years had lived with the great and the witty, should have acquired so ill the talents of conversation: and he had but half to furnish; for one half of what he said was oaths.' He, however, allowed considerable merit to some of his comedies, and said there was no reason to believe that the *Careless Husband* was not written by himself. Davies said, he was the first dramatick writer who introduced genteel ladies upon the stage. Johnson refuted this observation by instancing several such characters in comedies before his time. DAVIES. (trying to defend himself from a charge of ignorance,) 'I mean genteel moral characters.' 'I think (said Hicky,) gentility and morality are inseparable.' BOSWELL. 'By no means, Sir. The genteelest characters are often the most immoral. Does not Lord Chesterfield give precepts for uniting wickedness and the graces? A man, indeed, is not genteel when he gets drunk; but most vices may be committed very genteelly: a man may debauch his friend's wife genteelly: he may cheat at cards genteelly.' HICKY. 'I do not think *that* is genteel.' BOSWELL. 'Sir, it may not be like a gentleman, but it may be genteel.' JOHNSON. 'You are meaning two different things. One means exteriour grace; the other honour. It is certain that a man may be very immoral with exteriour grace. Lovelace, in *Clarissa*, is a very genteel and a very wicked character. Tom Hervey, who died t'other day, though a vicious man, was one of the genteelest men that ever lived.' Tom Davies instanced Charles the Second. JOHNSON. (taking fire at any attack upon that Prince, for whom he had an extraordinary partiality,) 'Charles the Second was licentious in his practice; but he always had a reverence for what was good. Charles the Second knew his people, and rewarded merit. The Church was at no time better filled than in his reign. He was the best King we have had from his time till the reign of his present

Majesty, except James the Second, who was a very good King, but unhappily believed that it was necessary for the salvation of his subjects that they should be Roman Catholicks. *He* had the merit of endeavouring to do what he thought was for the salvation of the souls of his subjects, till he lost a great Empire. *We*, who thought that we should *not* be saved if we were Roman Catholicks, had the merit of maintaining our religion, at the expence of submitting ourselves to the government of King William, (for it could not be done otherwise,)—to the government of one of the most worthless scoundrels that ever existed. No; Charles the Second was not such a man as ——, (naming another King[1]). He did not destroy his father's will. He took money, indeed, from France: but he did not betray those over whom he ruled: he did not let the French fleet pass ours. George the First knew nothing, and desired to know nothing; did nothing, and desired to do nothing: and the only good thing that is told of him is, that he wished to restore the crown to its hereditary successor.' He roared with prodigious violence against George the Second. When he ceased, Moody interjected, in an Irish tone, and with a comick look, 'Ah! poor George the Second.'

I mentioned that Dr. Thomas Campbell had come from Ireland to London, principally to see Dr. Johnson. He seemed angry at this observation. DAVIES. 'Why, you know, Sir, there came a man from Spain to see Livy;[2] and Corelli came to England to see Purcell, and when he heard he was dead, went directly back again to Italy.' JOHNSON. 'I should not have wished to be dead to disappoint Campbell, had he been so foolish as you represent him; but I should have wished to have been a hundred miles off.' This was apparently perverse; and I do believe it was not his real way of thinking: he could not but like a man who came so far to see him. He laughed with some complacency, when I told him Campbell's odd expression to me concerning him: 'That having seen such a man, was a thing to talk of a century hence,'—as if he could live so long.

We got into an argument whether the Judges who went to

---

[1] [George II. *Croker*[1].]   [2] Plin. *Epist.* lib. ii. ep. 3.

India might with propriety engage in trade. Johnson warmly
maintained that they might. 'For why (he urged,) should not
Judges get riches, as well as those who deserve them less?' I
said, they should have sufficient salaries, and have nothing to
take off their attention from the affairs of the publick. JOHNSON.
'No Judge, Sir, can give his whole attention to his office; and it
is very proper that he should employ what time he has to himself, for his own advantage, in the most profitable manner.'
'Then, Sir, (said Davies, who enlivened the dispute by making
it somewhat dramatick,) he may become an insurer; and when
he is going to the bench, he may be stopped,—"Your Lordship
cannot go yet: here is a bunch of invoices: several ships are about
to sail." ' JOHNSON. 'Sir, you may as well say a Judge should
not have a house; for they may come and tell him, "Your Lordship's house is on fire;" and so, instead of minding the business
of his Court, he is to be occupied in getting the engine with the
greatest speed. There is no end of this. Every Judge who has
land, trades to a certain extent in corn or in cattle; and in the
land itself, undoubtedly. His steward acts for him, and so do
clerks for a great merchant. A Judge may be a farmer; but he is
not to geld his own pigs. A Judge may play a little at cards for
his amusement; but he is not to play at marbles, or at chuck-
farthing in the Piazza. No, Sir; there is no profession to which a
man gives a very great proportion of this time. It is wonderful,
when a calculation is made, how little the mind is actually employed in the discharge of any profession. No man would be a
Judge, upon the condition of being obliged to be totally a Judge.
The best employed lawyer has his mind at work but for a small
proportion of his time: a great deal of his occupation is merely
mechanical. I once wrote for a magazine: I made a calculation,
that if I should write but a page a day, at the same rate, I should,
in ten years, write nine volumes in folio, of an ordinary size and
print.' BOSWELL. 'Such as Carte's*History*?' JOHNSON. 'Yes, Sir.
When a man writes from his own mind, he writes very rapidly.[1]

[1] Johnson certainly did, who had a mind stored with knowledge, and
teeming with imagery: but the observation is not applicable to writers in
general.

The greatest part of a writer's time is spent in reading, in order to write: a man will turn over half a library to make one book.'

I argued warmly against the Judges trading, and mentioned Hale as an instance of a perfect Judge, who devoted himself entirely to his office. JOHNSON. 'Hale, Sir, attended to other things besides law: he left a great estate.' BOSWELL. 'That was, because what he got, accumulated without any exertion and anxiety on his part.'

While the dispute went on, Moody once tried to say something upon our side. Tom Davies clapped him on the back, to encourage him. Beauclerk, to whom I mentioned this circumstance, said, 'that he could not conceive a more humiliating situation than to be clapped on the back by Tom Davies.'

We spoke of Rolt, to whose *Dictionary of Commerce* Dr. Johnson wrote the Preface. JOHNSON. 'Old Gardner the bookseller employed Rolt and Smart to write a monthly miscellany, called *The Universal Visitor*. There was a formal written contract, which Allen the printer saw. Gardner thought as you do of the Judge. They were bound to write nothing else; they were to have, I think, a third of the profits of this sixpenny pamphlet; and the contract was for ninety-nine years. I wish I had thought of giving this to Thurlow, in the cause about Literary Property. What an excellent instance would it have been of the oppression of booksellers towards poor authours!'[1] (smiling.) Davies, zealous for the honour of *the Trade*, said, Gardner was not properly a bookseller. JOHNSON. 'Nay, Sir; he certainly was a bookseller. He had served his time regularly, was a member of the Stationers' company, kept a shop in the face of mankind, purchased copyright, and was a *bibliopole*, Sir, in every sense. I wrote for some months in *The Universal Visitor*, for poor Smart, while he was mad, not then knowing the terms on which he was engaged to write, and thinking I was doing him good. I hoped his wits

---

[1] There has probably been some mistake as to the terms of this supposed extraordinary contract, the recital of which from hearsay afforded Johnson so much play for his sportive acuteness. Or if it was worded as he supposed, it is so strange that I should conclude it was a joke. Mr. Gardner, I am assured, was a worthy and a liberal man.

would soon return to him. Mine returned to me, and I wrote in
The Universal Visitor no longer.'

Friday, April 7, I dined with him at a Tavern, with a numerous
company. JOHNSON. 'I have been reading Twiss's *Travels in
Spain*, which are just come out. They are as good as the first
book of travels that you will take up. They are as good as those
of Keysler or Blainville; nay, as Addison's, if you except the
learning. They are not so good as Brydone's, but they are better
than Pococke's. I have not, indeed, cut the leaves yet; but I have
read in them where the pages are open, and I do not suppose that
what is in the pages which are closed is worse than what is in the
open pages. It would seem (he added,) that Addison had not
acquired much Italian learning, for we do not find it introduced
into his writings. The only instance that I recollect, is his quoting "*Stavo bene; per star meglio, sto qui.*" '[1]

I mentioned Addison's having borrowed many of his classical
remarks from Leandro Alberti. Mr. Beauclerk said, 'It was
alledged that he had borrowed also from another Italian authour.'[2]
JOHNSON. 'Why, Sir, all who go to look for what the Classicks
have said of Italy, must find the same passages; and I should
think it would be one of the first things the Italians would do on
the revival of learning, to collect all that the Roman authours
have said of their country.'

Ossian being mentioned;—JOHNSON. 'Supposing the Irish
and Erse languages to be the same, which I do not believe, yet
as there is no reason to suppose that the inhabitants of the Highlands and Hebrides ever wrote their native language, it is not
to be credited that a long poem was preserved among them. If
we had no evidence of the art of writing being practised in one of
the counties of England, we should not believe that a long poem
was preserved *there*, though in the neighbouring counties, where
the same language was spoken, the inhabitants could write.
BEAUCLERK. 'The ballad of *Lilliburlero* was once in the mouths

---

[1] 'I was well; I would be better; and here I am.'
Addison does not mention where this epitaph, which has eluded a very
diligent inquiry, is found. [M.]
[2] [Capaccio or Cappaccio, G. C. *Boswell Papers*, x. 194.]

of all the people of this country, and is said to have had a great effect in bringing about the Revolution. Yet I question whether any body can repeat it now; which shews how improbable it is that much poetry should be preserved by tradition.'

One of the company[1] suggested an internal objection to the antiquity of the poetry said to be Ossian's, that we do not find the wolf in it, which must have been the case had it been of that age.

The mention of the wolf had led Johnson to think of other wild beasts; and while Sir Joshua Reynolds and Mr. Langton were carrrying on a dialogue about something which engaged them earnestly, he, in the midst of it, broke out, 'Pennant tells of Bears—' [what he added, I have forgotten.] They went on, which he being dull of hearing, did not perceive, or, if he did, was not willing to break off his talk; so he continued to vociferate his remarks, and *Bear* ('like a word in a catch' as Beauclerk said,) was repeatedly heard at intervals, which coming from him who, by those who did not know him, had been so often assimilated to that ferocious animal, while we who were sitting around could hardly stifle laughter, produced a very ludicrous effect. Silence having ensued, he proceeded: 'We are told, that the black bear is innocent; but I should not like to trust myself with him.' Mr. Gibbon muttered, in a low tone of voice, 'I should not like to trust myself with *you*.' This piece of sarcastick pleasantry was a prudent resolution, if applied to a competition of abilities.

Patriotism having become one of our topicks, Johnson suddenly uttered, in a strong determined tone, an apophthegm, at which many will start: 'Patriotism is the last refuge of a scoundrel.' But let it be considered, that he did not mean a real and generous love of our country, but that pretended patriotism which so many, in all ages and countries, have made a cloak for self-interest. I maintained, that certainly all patriots were not scoundrels. Being urged, (not by Johnson,) to name one exception, I mentioned an eminent person,[2] whom we all greatly admired. JOHNSON. 'Sir, I do not say that he is *not* honest; but

[1] [Percy. *Ib.* 46.]
[2] [Burke. *Ib.* 197.]

we have no reason to conclude from his political conduct that he *is* honest. Were he to accept of a place from this ministry, he would lose that character of firmness which he has, and might be turned out of his place in a year. This ministry is neither stable, not grateful to their friends, as Sir Robert Walpole was, so that he may think it more for his interest to take his chance of his party coming in.'

Mrs. Pritchard being mentioned, he said, 'Her playing was quite mechanical. It is wonderful how little mind she had. Sir, she had never read the tragedy of *Macbeth* all through. She no more thought of the play out of which her part was taken, than a shoemaker thinks of the skin, out of which the piece of leather, of which he is making a pair of shoes, is cut.'

On Saturday, May 8,[1] I dined with him at Mr. Thrale's, where we met the Irish Dr. Campbell. Johnson had supped the night before at Mrs. Abington's, with some fashionable people whom he named; and he seemed much pleased with having made one in so elegant a circle. Nor did he omit to pique his *mistress* a little with jealousy of her housewifery; for he said, (with a smile,) 'Mrs. Abington's jelly, my dear lady, was better than yours.'

Mrs. Thrale, who frequently practised a coarse mode of flattery, by repeating his *bon-mots* in his hearing, told us that he had said, a certain celebrated actor[2] was just fit to stand at the door of an auction-room with a long pole, and cry 'Pray gentlemen, walk in;' and that a certain authour,[3] upon hearing this, had said, that another still more celebrated actor[4] was fit for nothing better than that, and would pick your pocket after you came out. Johnson. 'Nay, my dear lady, there is no wit in what our friend added; there is only abuse. You may as well say of any man that he will pick a pocket. Besides, the man who is stationed at the door does not pick people's pockets; that is done within, by the auctioneer.'

Mrs. Thrale told us, that Tom Davies repeated, in a very bald manner, the story of Dr. Johnson's first repartee to me, which

---

[1] [This should be April 8.]
[2] [Barry. *Boswell Papers*, x. 199.]
[3] [Murphy. *Ib.*]   [4] [Garrick. *Ib.*]

I have related exactly.[1] He made me say, 'I *was born* in Scotland,' instead of 'I *come from* Scotland;' so that Johnson saying, 'That, Sir, is what a great many of your countrymen cannot help,' had no point, or even meaning: and that upon this being mentioned to Mr. Fitzherbert, he observed, 'It is not every man that can *carry* a *bon mot*.'

On Monday, April 10, I dined with him at General Oglethorpe's, with Mr. Langton and the Irish Dr. Campbell, whom the General had obligingly given me leave to bring with me. This learned gentleman was thus gratified with a very high intellectual feast, by not only being in company with Dr. Johnson, but with General Oglethorpe, who had been so long a celebrated name both at home and abroad.[2]

I must, again and again, intreat of my readers not to suppose that my imperfect record of conversation contains the whole of what was said by Johnson, or other eminent persons who lived with him. What I have preserved, however, has the value of the most perfect authenticity.

He this day enlarged upon Pope's melancholy remark,

'Man never *is*, but always *to be* blest.'

He asserted that *the present* was never a happy state to any human being; but that, as every part of life, of which we are conscious, was at some point of time a period yet to come, in

---

[1] See *ante*, p. 277.

[2] Let me here be allowed to pay my tribute of most sincere gratitude to the memory of that excellent person, my intimacy with whom was the more valuable to me, because my first acquaintance with him was unexpected and unsolicited. Soon after the publication of my *Account of Corsica*, he did me the honour to call on me, and, approaching me with a frank courteous air, said, 'My name, Sir, is Oglethorpe, and I wish to be acquainted with you.' I was not a little flattered to be thus addressed by an eminent man, of whom I had read in Pope, from my early years,

'Or, driven by strong benevolence of soul,
    Will fly, like Oglethorpe, from pole to pole.'

I was fortunate enough to be found worthy of his good opinion, insomuch, that I not only was invited to make one in the many respectable companies whom he entertained at his table, but had a cover at his hospitable board every day when I happened to be disengaged; and in his society I never failed to enjoy learned and animated conversation, seasoned with genuine sentiments of virtue and religion.

which felicity was expected, there was some happiness produced by hope. Being pressed upon this subject, and asked if he really was of opinion, that though, in general, happiness was very rare in human life, a man was not sometimes happy in the moment that was present, he answered, 'Never, but when he is drunk.'

He urged General Oglethorpe to give the world his Life. He said, 'I know no man whose Life would be more interesting. If I were furnished with materials, I should be very glad to write it.'[1]

Mr. Scott of Amwell's *Elegies* were lying in the room. Dr. Johnson observed, 'They are very well; but such as twenty people might write.' Upon this I took occasion to controvert Horace's maxim,

> '——— *mediocribus esse poetis*
> *Non Di, non homines, non concessére columnæ.*'[2]

For here, (I observed,) was a very middle-rate poet, who pleased many readers, and therefore poetry of a middle sort was entitled to some esteem; nor could I see why poetry should not, like every thing else, have different gradations of excellence, and consequently of value. Johnson repeated the common remark, that, 'as there is no necessity for our having poetry at all, it being merely a luxury, an instrument of pleasure, it can have no value, unless when exquisite in its kind.' I declared myself not satisfied. 'Why then, Sir, (said he,) Horace and you must settle it.' He was not much in the humour of talking.

No more of his conversation for some days appears in my journal, except that when a gentleman[3] told him he had bought a suit of laces for his lady, he said, 'Well, Sir, you have done a good thing and a wise thing.' 'I have done a good thing, (said

---

[1] The General seemed unwilling to enter upon it at this time; but upon a subsequent occasion he communicated to me a number of particulars, which I have committed to writing; but I was not sufficiently diligent in obtaining more from him, not apprehending that his friends were so soon to lose him; for, notwithstanding his great age, he was very healthy and vigorous, and was at last carried off by a violent fever, which is often fatal at any period of life.

[2] ['To poets to be second-rate is a privilege which neither men nor gods nor bookstalls ever allowed.' Horace *Ars Poetica*, l. 372. (Wickham.)]

[3] [Boswell. *Boswell Papers*, x. 208–9.]

the gentleman,) but I do not know that I have done a wise thing.'
JOHNSON. 'Yes, Sir; no money is better spent than what is laid
out for domestick satisfaction. A man is pleased that his wife is
drest as well as other people; and a wife is pleased that she
is drest.'

On Friday, April 14, being Good-Friday, I repaired to him in
the morning, according to my usual custom on that day, and
breakfasted with him. I observed that he fasted so very strictly,
that he did not even taste bread, and took no milk with his tea;
I suppose because it is a kind of animal food.

He entered upon the state of the nation, and thus discoursed:
'Sir, the great misfortune now is, that government has too little
power. All that it has to bestow, must of necessity be given to
support itself; so that it cannot reward merit. No man, for
instance, can now be made a Bishop for his learning and piety;[1]
his only chance for promotion is his being connected with somebody who has parliamentary interest. Our several ministries in
this reign have outbid each other in concessions to the people.
Lord Bute, though a very honourable man,—a man who meant
well,—a man who had his blood full of prerogative,—was a theoretical statesman,—a book-minister,—and thought this country
could be governed by the influence of the Crown alone. Then,
Sir, he gave up a great deal. He advised the King to agree that
the Judges should hold their places for life, instead of losing them
at the accession of a new King. Lord Bute, I suppose, thought to
make the King popular by this concession; but the people never
minded it; and it was a most impolitick measure. There is no
reason why a Judge should hold his office for life, more than any
other person in publick trust. A Judge may be partial otherwise
than to the Crown: we have seen Judges partial to the populace.
A Judge may become corrupt, and yet there may not be legal
evidence against him. A Judge may become froward from age.
A Judge may grow unfit for his office in many ways. It was
desirable that there should be a possibility of being delivered
from him by a new King. That is now gone by an act of Parliament *ex gratia* of the Crown. Lord Bute advised the King to give

[1] From this too just observation there are some eminent exceptions.

up a very large sum of money,[1] for which nobody thanked him. It was of consequence to the King, but nothing to the publick, among whom it was divided. When I say Lord Bute advised, I mean, that such acts were done when he was minister, and we are to suppose that he advised them.—Lord Bute shewed an undue partiality to Scotchmen. He turned out Dr. Nichols, a very eminent man, from being physician to the King, to make room for one of his countrymen, a man very low in his profession.[2] He had ************[3] and ****[4] to go on errands for him. He had occasion for people to go on errands for him; but he should not have had Scotchmen; and, certainly, he should not have suffered them to have access to him before the first people in England.'

I told him, that the admission of one of them before the first people in England, which had given the greatest offence, was no more than what happens at every minister's levee, where those who attend are admitted in the order that they have come, which is better than admitting them according to their rank; for if that were to be the rule, a man who has waited all the morning might have the mortification to see a peer, newly come, go in before him, and keep him waiting still. JOHNSON. 'True, Sir; but **** should not have come to the levee, to be in the way of people of consequence. He saw Lord Bute at all times; and could have said what he had to say at any time, as well as at the levee. There is now no Prime Minister: there is only an agent for government in the House of Commons. We are governed by the Cabinet:

[1] The money arising from the property of the prizes taken before the declaration of war, which were given to his Majesty by the peace of Paris, and amounted to upwards of £700,000, and from the lands in the ceded islands, which were estimated at £200,000 more. Surely there was a noble munificence in this gift from a Monarch to his people. And let it be remembered, that during the Earl of Bute's administration, the King was graciously pleased to give up the hereditary revenues of the Crown, and to accept, instead of them, of the limited sum of £800,000 a year; upon which Blackstone observes, that 'The hereditary revenues, being put under the same management as the other branches of the publick patrimony, will produce more, and be better collected than heretofore; and the publick is a gainer of upwards of £100,000 *per annum* by this disinterested bounty of his Majesty.' Book I. Chap. viii. p. 330.

[2] [Dr. W. Duncan. *Boswell Papers*, x. 212.]
[3] [Wedderburn(e). *Ib.*]   [4] [Home (the author of *Douglas*). *Ib.*]

but there is no one head there, as in Sir Robert Walpole's time.'
Boswell. 'What then, Sir, is the use of Parliament?' Johnson. 'Why, Sir, Parliament is a larger council to the King; and
the advantage of such a council is, having a great number of men
of property concerned in the legislature, who, for their own
interest, will not consent to bad laws. And you must have observed, Sir, that administration is feeble and timid, and cannot
act with that authority and resolution which is necessary. Were
I in power, I would turn out every man who dared to oppose me.
Government has the distribution of offices, that it may be enabled
to maintain its authority.'

'Lord Bute (he added,) took down too fast, without building
up something new.' Boswell. 'Because, Sir, he found a rotten
building. The political coach was drawn by a set of bad horses:
it was necessary to change them.' Johnson. 'But he should have
changed them one by one.'

I told him that I had been informed by Mr. Orme, that many
parts of the East-Indies were better mapped than the Highlands
of Scotland. Johnson. 'That a country may be mapped, it must
be travelled over.' 'Nay, (said I, meaning to laugh with him at
one of his prejudices,) can't you say, it is not *worth* mapping?'

As we walked to St. Clement's church, and saw several shops
open upon this most solemn fast-day of the Christian world, I
remarked, that one disadvantage arising from the immensity of
London, was, that nobody was heeded by his neighbour; there
was no fear of censure for not observing Good-Friday, as it
ought to be kept, and as it is kept in country-towns. He said, it
was, upon the whole, very well observed even in London. He,
however, owned, that London was too large; but added, 'It is
nonsense to say the head is too big for the body. It would be as
much too big, though the body were ever so large; that is to say,
though the country were ever so extensive. It has no similarity
to a head connected with a body.'

Dr. Wetherell, Master of University College, Oxford, accompanied us home from church; and after he was gone, there came
two other gentlemen,[1] one of whom uttered the commonplace

[1] [Edward Dilly and Sir John Miller. *Boswell Papers*, x. 214.]

complaints, that by the increase of taxes, labour would be dear, other nations would undersell us, and our commerce would be ruined. JOHNSON. (smiling,) 'Never fear, Sir. Our commerce is in a very good state; and suppose we had no commerce at all, we could live very well on the produce of our own country.' I cannot omit to mention, that I never knew any man who was less disposed to be querulous than Johnson. Whether the subject was his own situation, or the state of the publick, or the state of human nature in general, though he saw the evils, his mind was turned to resolution, and never to whining or complaint.

We went again to St. Clement's in the afternoon. He had found fault with the preacher in the morning[1] for not choosing a text adapted to the day. The preacher in the afternoon[2] had chosen one extremely proper: 'It is finished.'

After the evening service, he said, 'Come, you shall go home with me, and sit just an hour.' But he was better than his word; for after we had drunk tea with Mrs. Williams, he asked me to go up to his study with him, where we sat a long while together in a serene undisturbed frame of mind, sometimes in silence, and sometimes conversing, as we felt ourselves inclined, or more properly speaking, as *he* was inclined; for during all the course of my long intimacy with him, my respectful attention never abated, and my wish to hear him was such, that I constantly watched every dawning of communication from that great and illuminated mind.

He observed, 'All knowledge is of itself of some value. There is nothing so minute or inconsiderable, that I would not rather know it than not. In the same manner, all power, of whatever sort, is of itself desirable. A man would not submit to learn to hem a ruffle, of his wife, or his wife's maid; but if a mere wish could attain it, he would rather wish to be able to hem a ruffle.'

He again advised me to keep a journal fully and minutely, but not to mention such trifles as, that meat was too much or too little done, or that the weather was fair or rainy. He had, till very near his death, a contempt for the notion that the weather affects the human frame.

---

[1] [The Rector [John Burrows]. *Boswell Papers*, x. 213–14.]
[2] [The Curate [S. Popham]. *Ib.*]

I told him that our friend Goldsmith had said to me, that he had come too late into the world, for that Pope and other poets had taken up the places in the Temple of Fame; so that, as but a few at any period can possess poetical reputation, a man of genius can now hardly acquire it. JOHNSON. 'That is one of the most sensible things I have ever heard of Goldsmith. It is difficult to get literary fame, and it is every day growing more difficult. Ah, Sir, that should make a man think of securing happiness in another world, which all who try sincerely for it may attain. In comparison of that, how little are all other things! The belief of immortality is impressed upon all men, and all men act under an impression of it, however they may talk, and though, perhaps, they may be scarcely sensible of it.' I said, it appeared to me that some people had not the least notion of immortality; and I mentioned a distinguished gentleman of our acquaintance.[1] JOHNSON. 'Sir, if it were not for the notion of immortality, he would cut a throat to fill his pockets.' When I quoted this to Beauclerk, who knew much more of the gentleman than we did, he said, in his acid manner, 'He would cut a throat to fill his pockets, if it were not for fear of being hanged.'

Dr. Johnson proceeded: 'Sir, there is a great cry about infidelity; but there are, in reality, very few infidels. I have heard a person, originally a Quaker, but now, I am afraid, a Deist,[2] say, that he did not believe there were, in all England, above two hundred infidels.'

He was pleased to say, 'If you come to settle here, we will have one day in the week on which we will meet by ourselves. That is the happiest conversation where there is no competition, no vanity, but a calm quiet interchange of sentiments.' In his private register this evening is thus marked, 'Boswell sat with me till night; we had some serious talk.'[3] It also appears from the same record, that after I left him he was occupied in religious duties, in 'giving Francis, his servant, some directions for preparation to communicate; in reviewing his life, and resolving on better conduct.' The humility and piety which he discovers on

---

[1] [Fox. *Boswell Papers*, x. 216.]
[2] [Dr. Brocklesby. *Ib.*]   [3] *Pr. and Med.* p. 138.

such occasions, is truely edifying. No saint, however, in the course of his religious warfare, was more sensible of the unhappy failure of pious resolves, than Johnson. He said one day, talking to an acquaintance[1] on this subject, 'Sir, Hell is paved with good intentions.'[2]

On Sunday, April 16, being Easter Day, after having attended the solemn service at St. Paul's, I dined with Dr. Johnson and Mrs. Williams. I maintained that Horace was wrong in placing happiness in *Nil admirari*,[3] for that I thought admiration one of the most agreeable of all our feelings; and I regretted that I had lost much of my disposition to admire, which people generally do as they advance in life. JOHNSON. 'Sir, as a man advances in life, he gets what is better than admiration—judgement, to estimate things at their true value.' I still insisted that admiration was more pleasing than judgement, as love is more pleasing than friendship. The feeling of friendship is like that of being comfortably filled with roast beef; love, like being enlivened with champagne. JOHNSON. 'No, Sir; admiration and love are like being intoxicated with champagne; judgement and friendship like being enlivened. Waller has hit upon the same thought with you:[4] but I don't believe you have borrowed from Waller. I wish you would enable yourself to borrow more.'

He then took occasion to enlarge on the advantages of reading, and combated the idle superficial notion, that knowledge enough may be acquired in conversation. 'The foundation (said he,) must be laid by reading. General principles must be had from books, which, however, must be brought to the test of real life. In conversation you never get a system. What is said upon a

[1] [Probably Boswell. *Powell.*]
[2] This is a proverbial sentence. 'Hell,' says Herbert, 'is full of good meanings and wishings.' *Jacula Prudentum*, p. 11, edit. 1651. [M.]
[3] ['Nought to admire.' Horace *Epistles* I. vi. 1.]
[4]
     'Amoret's as sweet and good,
     As the most delicious food;
     Which but tasted does impart
     Life and gladness to the heart.
     Sacharissa's beauty's wine,
     Which to madness does incline;
     Such a liquor as no brain
     That is mortal can sustain.'

subject is to be gathered from a hundred people. The parts of a truth, which a man gets thus, are at such a distance from each other that he never attains to a full view.'

'*To* BENNET LANGTON, ESQ.

'DEAR SIR,—I have enquired more minutely about the medicine for the rheumatism, which I am sorry to hear that you still want. The receipt is this:

'Take equal quantities of flour of sulphur, and *flour* of mustardseed, make them an electuary with honey or treacle; and take a bolus as big as a nutmeg several times a day, as you can bear it: drinking after it a quarter of a pint of the infusion of the root of Lovage.

'Lovage, in Ray's *Nomenclature*, is Levisticum: perhaps the Botanists may know the Latin name.

'Of this medicine I pretend not to judge. There is all the appearance of its efficacy, which a single instance can afford: the patient was very old, the pain very violent, and the relief, I think, speedy and lasting.

'My opinion of alterative medicine is not high, but *quid tentasse nocebit?*[1] if it does harm, or does no good, it may be omitted; but that it may do good, you have, I hope, reason to think is desired by, Sir, your most affectionate, humble servant,

'April 17, 1775.'   'SAM. JOHNSON.'

On Tuesday, April 18, he and I were engaged to go with Sir Joshua Reynolds to dine with Mr. Cambridge, at his beautiful villa on the banks of the Thames, near Twickenham. Dr. Johnson's tardiness was such, that Sir Joshua, who had an appointment at Richmond, early in the day, was obliged to go by himself on horseback, leaving his coach to Johnson and me. Johnson was in such good spirits, that every thing seemed to please him as we drove along.

Our conversation turned on a variety of subjects. He thought portrait-painting an improper employment for a woman. 'Publick practice of any art, (he observed,) and staring in men's faces, is very indelicate in a female.' I happened to start a ques-

[1] ['It can do no harm to try.']

tion of propriety, whether, when a man knows that some of his intimate friends are invited to the house of another friend, with whom they are all equally intimate, he may join them without an invitation. JOHNSON. 'No, Sir; he is not to go when he is not invited. They may be invited on purpose to abuse him' (smiling).

As a curious instance how little a man knows, or wishes to know, his own character in the world, or, rather, as a convincing proof that Johnson's roughness was only external, and did not proceed from his heart, I insert the following dialogue. JOHNSON. 'It is wonderful, Sir, how rare a quality good humour is in life. We meet with very few good humoured men.' I mentioned four of our friends,[1] none of whom he would allow to be good humoured. One was *acid*, another was *muddy*, and to the others he had objections which have escaped me. Then, shaking his head and stretching himself at his ease in the coach, and smiling with much complacency, he turned to me and said, 'I look upon *myself* as a good humoured fellow.' The epithet *fellow*, applied to the great Lexicographer, the stately Moralist, the masterly Critick, as if he had been *Sam* Johnson, a mere pleasant companion, was highly diverting; and this light notion of himself struck me with wonder. I answered, also smiling, 'No, no, Sir; that will *not* do. You are good natured, but not good humoured: you are irascible. You have not patience with folly and absurdity. I believe you would pardon them, if there were time to deprecate your vengeance; but punishment follows so quick after sentence, that they cannot escape.'

I had brought with me a great bundle of Scotch magazines and news-papers, in which his *Journey to the Western Islands* was attacked in every mode; and I read a great part of them to him, knowing they would afford him entertainment. I wish the writers of them had been present: they would have been sufficiently vexed. One ludicrous imitation of his style, by Mr. Maclaurin, now one of the Scotch Judges, with the title of Lord Dreghorn, was distinguished by him from the rude mass. 'This (said he,) is the best. But I could caricature my own style much better

---

[1] [Reynolds, Burke, Beauclerk (acid), Langton (muddy). *Boswell Papers*, vi. 41, 46.]

myself.' He defended his remark upon the general insufficiency of education in Scotland; and confirmed to me the authenticity of his witty saying on the learning of the Scotch;—'Their learning is like bread in a besieged town: every man gets a little, but no man gets a full meal.' 'There is (said he,) in Scotland, a diffusion of learning, a certain portion of it widely and thinly spread. A merchant there has as much learning as one of their clergy.'

He talked of Isaac Walton's *Lives*, which was one of his most favourite books. Dr. Donne's *Life*, he said, was the most perfect of them. He observed, that 'it was wonderful that Walton, who was in a very low situation in life, should have been familiarly received by so many great men, and that at a time when the ranks of society were kept more separate than they are now.' He supposed that Walton had then given up his business as a linendraper and sempster, and was only an authour; and added, 'that he was a great panegyrist.' BOSWELL. 'No quality will get a man more friends than a disposition to admire the qualities of others. I do not mean flattery, but a sincere admiration.' JOHNSON. 'Nay, Sir, flattery pleases very generally. In the first place, the flatterer may think what he says to be true: but, in the second place, whether he thinks so or not, he certainly thinks those whom he flatters of consequence enough to be flattered.'

No sooner had we made our bow to Mr. Cambridge, in his library, than Johnson ran eagerly to one side of the room, intent on poring over the backs of the books. Sir Joshua observed, (aside,) 'He runs to the books, as I do to the pictures: but I have the advantage. I can see much more of the pictures than he can of the books.' Mr. Cambridge, upon this, politely said, 'Dr. Johnson, I am going, with your pardon, to accuse myself, for I have the same custom which I perceive you have. But it seems odd that one should have such a desire to look at the backs of books.' Johnson, ever ready for contest, instantly started from his reverie, wheeled about, and answered, 'Sir, the reason is very plain. Knowledge is of two kinds. We know a subject ourselves, or we know where we can find information upon it. When we enquire into any subject, the first thing we have to do is to know what books have treated of it. This leads us to look at catalogues,

and at the backs of books in libraries.' Sir Joshua observed to me
the extraordinary promptitude with which Johnson flew upon an
argument. 'Yes, (said I,) he has no formal preparation, no
flourishing with his sword; he is through your body in an
instant.'

Johnson was here solaced with an elegant entertainment, a
very accomplished family, and much good company; among
whom was Mr. Harris of Salisbury, who paid him many compliments on his *Journey to the Western Islands.*

The common remark as to the utility of reading history being
made;—JOHNSON. 'We must consider how very little history
there is; I mean real authentick history. That certain Kings
reigned, and certain battles were fought, we can depend upon as
true; but all the colouring, all the philosophy, of history is conjecture.' BOSWELL. 'Then, Sir, you would reduce all history to
no better than an almanack, a mere chronological series of remarkable events.' Mr. Gibbon, who must at that time have been
employed upon his *History,* of which he published the first
volume in the following year, was present; but did not step forth
in defence of that species of writing. He probably did not like to
trust himself with JOHNSON![1]

Johnson observed, that the force of our early habits was so
great, that though reason approved, nay, though our senses
relished a different course, almost every man returned to them.
I do not believe there is any observation upon human nature
better founded than this; and, in many cases, it is a very painful
truth; for where early habits have been mean and wretched, the
joy and elevation resulting from better modes of life must be
damped by the gloomy consciousness of being under an almost
inevitable doom to sink back into a situation which we recollect
with disgust. It surely may be prevented, by constant attention
and unremitting exertion to establish contrary habits of superiour
efficacy.

The Beggar's Opera, and the common question, whether it was
pernicious in its effects, having been introduced;—JOHNSON.
'As to this matter, which has been very much contested, I myself

[1] See *ante,* p. 615.

am of opinion, that more influence has been ascribed to *The Beggar's Opera*, than it in reality ever had; for I do not believe that any man was ever made a rogue by being present at its representation. At the same time I do not deny that it may have some influence, by making the character of a rogue familiar, and in some degree pleasing.'[1] Then collecting himself as it were, to give a heavy stroke: 'There is in it such a *labefactation* of all principles, as may be injurious to morality.'

While he pronounced this response, we sat in a comical sort of restraint, smothering a laugh, which we were afraid might burst out. In his *Life of Gay*, he has been still more decisive as to the inefficiency of *The Beggar's Opera* in corrupting society. But I have ever thought somewhat differently; for, indeed, not only are the gaiety and heroism of a highwayman very captivating to a youthful imagination, but the arguments for adventurous depredation are so plausible, the allusions so lively, and the contrasts with the ordinary and more painful modes of acquiring property are so artfully displayed, that it requires a cool and strong judgement to resist so imposing an aggregate: yet, I own, I should be very sorry to have *The Beggar's Opera* suppressed; for there is in it so much of real London life, so much brilliant wit, and such a variety of airs, which, from early association of ideas, engage, soothe, and enliven the mind, that no performance which the theatre exhibits, delights me more.

The late *'worthy'* Duke of Queensberry, as Thomson, in his *Seasons*, justly characterises him, told me, that when Gay first shewed him *The Beggar's Opera*, his Grace's observation was, 'This is a very odd thing, Gay; I am satisfied that it is either a

---

[1] A very eminent physician [perhaps Sir John Pringle. *Powell*], whose discernment is as acute and penetrating in judging of the human character as it is in his own profession, remarked once at a club where I was, that a lively young man, fond of pleasure, and without money, would hardly resist a solicitation from his mistress to go upon the highway, immediately after being present at the representation of *The Beggar's Opera*. I have been told of an ingenious observation by Mr. Gibbon, that '*The Beggar's Opera* may, perhaps, have sometimes increased the number of highwaymen; but that it has had a beneficial effect in refining that class of men, making them less ferocious, more polite, in short, more like gentlemen.' Upon this Mr. Courtenay said, that 'Gay was the Orpheus of highwaymen.'

very good thing, or a very bad thing.' It proved the former,
beyond the warmest expectations of the authour or his friends.
Mr. Cambridge, however, shewed us to-day, that there was good
reason enough to doubt concerning its success. He was told by
Quin, that during the first night of its appearance it was long in
a very dubious state; that there was a disposition to damn it,
and that it was saved by the song,

'Oh ponder well! be not severe!'

the audience being much affected by the innocent looks of Polly,
when she came to those two lines, which exhibit at once a painful
and ridiculous image,

'For on the rope that hangs my Dear,
Depends poor Polly's life.'

Quin himself had so bad an opinion of it, that he refused the part
of Captain Macheath, and gave it to Walker, who acquired great
celebrity by his grave yet animated performance of it.

We talked of a young gentleman's marriage with an eminent
singer,[1] and his determination that she should no longer sing in
publick, though his father was very earnest she should, because
her talents would be liberally rewarded, so as to make her a good
fortune. It was questioned whether the young gentleman, who
had not a shilling in the world, but was blest with very uncommon
talents, was not foolishly delicate, or foolishly proud, and his
father truely rational without being mean. Johnson, with all the
high spirit of a Roman senator, exclaimed, 'He resolved wisely
and nobly to be sure. He is a brave man. Would not a gentleman
be disgraced by having his wife singing publickly for hire? No,
Sir, there can be no doubt here. I know not if I should not *prepare*
myself for a publick singer, as readily as let my wife be one.'

Johnson arraigned the modern politicks of this country, as
entirely devoid of all principle of whatever kind. 'Politicks (said
he,) are now nothing more than means of rising in the world.
With this sole view do men engage in politicks, and their whole
conduct proceeds upon it. How different in that respect is the
state of the nation now from what it was in the time of Charles

---

[1] [R. B. Sheridan and Elizabeth Linley. *Boswell Papers*, vi. 45.]

the First, during the Usurpation, and after the Restoration, in the time of Charles the Second. *Hudibras* affords a strong proof how much hold political principles had then upon the minds of men. There is in *Hudibras* a great deal of bullion which will always last. But to be sure the brightest strokes of his wit owed their force to the impression of the characters, which was upon men's minds at the time; to their knowing them, at table and in the street; in short, being familiar with them; and above all, to his satire being directed against those whom a little while before they had hated and feared. The nation in general has ever been loyal, has been at all times attached to the monarch, though a few daring rebels have been wonderfully powerful for a time. The murder of Charles the First was undoubtedly not committed with the approbation or consent of the people. Had that been the case, Parliament would not have ventured to consign the regicides to their deserved punishment. And we know what exuberance of joy there was when Charles the Second was restored. If Charles the Second had bent all his mind to it, had made it his sole object, he might have been as absolute as Louis the Fourteenth.' A gentleman[1] observed he would have done no harm if he had. JOHNSON. 'Why, Sir, absolute princes seldom do any harm. But they who are governed by them are governed by chance. There is no security for good government.' CAMBRIDGE. 'There have been many sad victims to absolute power.' JOHNSON. 'So, Sir, have there been to popular factions.' BOSWELL. 'The question is, which is worst, one wild beast or many?'

Johnson praised *The Spectator*, particularly the character of Sir Roger de Coverley. He said, 'Sir Roger did not die a violent death, as has been generally fancied. He was not killed; he died only because others were to die, and because his death afforded an opportunity to Addison for some very fine writing. We have the example of Cervantes making Don Quixote die.—I never could see why Sir Roger is represented as a little cracked. It appears to me that the story of the widow was intended to have something superinduced upon it: but the superstructure did not come.'

---

[1] [Boswell. *Boswell Papers*, vi. 45.]

Somebody[1] found fault with writing verses in a dead language, maintaining that they were merely arrangements of so many words, and laughed at the Universities of Oxford and Cambridge, for sending forth collections of them not only in Greek and Latin, but even in Syriac, Arabick, and other more unknown tongues. JOHNSON. 'I would have as many of these as possible; I would have verses in every language that there are the means of acquiring. Nobody imagines that an University is to have at once two hundred poets; but it should be able to show two hundred scholars. Pieresc's death was lamented, I think, in forty languages. And I would have at every coronation, and every death of a King, every *Gaudium*, and every *Luctus*, University verses, in as many languages as can be acquired. I would have the world to be thus told, "Here is a school where every thing may be learnt."'

Having set out next day on a visit to the Earl of Pembroke, at Wilton, and to my friend, Mr. Temple,[2] at Mamhead, in Devonshire, and not having returned to town till the second of May, I did not see Dr. Johnson for a considerable time, and during the remaining part of my stay in London, kept very imperfect notes of his conversation, which had I according to my usual custom written out at large soon after the time, much might have been preserved, which is now irretrievably lost. I can now only record some particular scenes, and a few fragments of his *memorabilia*. But to make some amends for my relaxation of diligence in one respect, I have to present my readers with arguments upon two law cases, with which he favoured me.

On Saturday, the sixth of May, we dined by ourselves at the Mitre, and he dictated to me what follows, to obviate the complaint already mentioned,[3] which had been made in the form of an action in the Court of Session, by Dr. Memis, of Aberdeen, that in the same translation of a charter in which *physicians* were mentioned, he was called *Doctor of Medicine*.

'There are but two reasons for which a physician can decline the title of *Doctor of Medicine*, because he supposes himself dis-

---

[1] [Reynolds. *Boswell Papers*, vi. 46.]
[2] See *ante*, p. 593.   [3] See *ante*, p. 573.

632

graced by the doctorship, or supposes the doctorship disgraced by himself. To be disgraced by a title which he shares in common with every illustrious name of his profession, with Boerhaave, with Arbuthnot, and with Cullen, can surely diminish no man's reputation. It is, I suppose, to the doctorate, from which he shrinks, that he owes his right of practising physick. A Doctor of Medicine is a physician under the protection of the laws, and by the stamp of authority. The physician, who is not a Doctor, usurps a profession, and is authorised only by himself to decide upon health and sickness, and life and death. That this gentleman is a Doctor, his diploma makes evident; a diploma not obtruded upon him, but obtained by solicitation, and for which fees were paid. With what countenance any man can refuse the title which he has either begged or bought, is not easily discovered.

'All verbal injury must comprise in it either some false position, or some unnecessary declaration of defamatory truth. That in calling him Doctor, a false appellation was given him, he himself will not pretend, who at the same time that he complains of the title, would be offended if we supposed him to be not a Doctor. If the title of Doctor be a defamatory truth, it is time to dissolve our colleges; for why should the publick give salaries to men whose approbation is reproach? It may likewise deserve the notice of the publick to consider what help can be given to the professors of physick, who all share with this unhappy gentleman the ignominious appellation, and of whom the very boys in the street are not afraid to say, *There goes the Doctor*.

'What is implied by the term Doctor is well known. It distinguishes him to whom it is granted, as a man who has attained such knowledge of his profession as qualifies him to instruct others. A Doctor of Laws is a man who can form lawyers by his precepts. A Doctor of Medicine is a man who can teach the art of curing diseases. There is an old axiom which no man has yet thought fit to deny, *Nil dat quod non habet*.[1] Upon this principle to be Doctor implies skill, for *nemo docet quod non didicit*.[2] In

---

[1] ['No one can give what he lacks.']
[2] ['No one can teach what he has not learned.']

England, whoever practises physick, not being a Doctor, must practise by a licence: but the doctorate conveys a licence in itself.

'By what accident it happened that he and the other physicians were mentioned in different terms, where the terms themselves were equivalent, or where in effect that which was applied to him was the more honourable, perhaps they who wrote the paper cannot now remember. Had they expected a lawsuit to have been the consequence of such petty variation, I hope they would have avoided it.[1] But, probably, as they meant no ill, they suspected no danger, and, therefore, consulted only what appeared to them propriety or convenience.'

A few days afterwards I consulted him upon a cause, *Paterson and others* against *Alexander and others*, which had been decided by a casting vote in the Court of Session, determining that the Corporation of Stirling was corrupt, and setting aside the election of some of their officers, because it was proved that three of the leading men who influenced the majority had entered into an unjustifiable compact, of which, however, the majority were ignorant. He dictated to me, after a little consideration, the following sentences upon the subject:—

'There is a difference between majority and superiority; majority is applied to number, and superiority to power; and power, like many other things, is to be estimated *non numero sed pondere*.[2] Now though the greater *number* is not corrupt, the greater *weight* is corrupt, so that corruption predominates in the borough, taken *collectively*, though, perhaps, taken *numerically*, the greater part may be uncorrupt. That borough, which is so constituted as to act corruptly, is in the eye of reason corrupt, whether it be by the uncontrolable power of a few, or by an accidental pravity of the multitude. The objection, in which is urged the injustice of making the innocent suffer with the guilty, is an objection not only against society, but against the possibility of society. All societies, great and small, subsist upon this

---

[1] In justice to Dr. Memis, though I was against him as an Advocate, I must mention, that he objected to the variation very earnestly, before the translation was printed off.

[2] ['Not by number but by weight.']

condition; that as the individuals derive advantages from union, they may likewise suffer inconveniences; that as those who do nothing, and sometimes those who do ill, will have the honours and emoluments of general virtue and general prosperity, so those likewise who do nothing, or perhaps do well, must be involved in the consequences of predominant corruption.'

This in my opinion was a very nice case; but the decision was affirmed in the House of Lords.

On Monday, May 8, we went together and visited the mansions of Bedlam. I had been informed that he had once been there before with Mr. Wedderburne, (now Lord Loughborough,) Mr. Murphy, and Mr. Foote; and I had heard Foote give a very entertaining account of Johnson's happening to have his attention arrested by a man who was very furious, and who, while beating his straw, supposed it to be William Duke of Cumberland, whom he was punishing for his cruelties in Scotland, in 1746.[1] There was nothing peculiarly remarkable this day; but the general contemplation of insanity was very affecting. I accompanied him home, and dined and drank tea with him.

Talking of an acquaintance of ours,[2] distinguished for knowing an uncommon variety of miscellaneous articles both in antiquities and polite literature, he observed, 'You know, Sir, he runs about with little weight upon his mind.' And talking of another very ingenious gentleman,[3] who from the warmth of his temper was at variance with many of his acquaintance, and wished to avoid them, he said, 'Sir, he leads the life of an outlaw.'

On Friday, May 12, as he had been so good as to assign me a room in his house, where I might sleep occasionally, when I happened to sit with him to a late hour, I took possession of it this night, found every thing in excellent order, and was attended by honest Francis with a most civil assiduity. I asked

[1] My very honourable friend General Sir George Howard, who served in the Duke of Cumberland's army, has assured me that the cruelties were not imputable to his Royal Highness.
[2] [*Croker*[1] *suggests* Percy. Possibly Dr. Michael Lort or Lait.]
[3] [Steevens. *Croker*[1].]

Johnson whether I might go to a consultation with another
lawyer upon Sunday, as that appeared to me to be doing work
as much in my way, as if an artisan should work on the day
appropriated for religious rest. JOHNSON. 'Why, Sir, when you
are of consequence enough to oppose the practice of consulting
upon Sunday, you should do it: but you may go now. It is not
criminal, though it is not what one should do, who is anxious for
the preservation and increase of piety, to which a peculiar observance of Sunday is a great help. The distinction is clear
between what is of moral and what is of ritual obligation.'

On Saturday, May 13, I breakfasted with him by invitation,
accompanied by Mr. Andrew Crosbie, a Scotch Advocate, whom
he had seen at Edinburgh, and the Hon. Colonel (now General)
Edward Stopford, brother to Lord Courtown, who was desirous
of being introduced to him. His tea and rolls and butter, and
whole breakfast apparatus were all in such decorum, and his
behaviour was so courteous, that Colonel Stopford was quite
surprized, and wondered at his having heard so much said of
Johnson's slovenliness and roughness. I have preserved nothing
of what passed, except that Crosbie pleased him much by talking
learnedly of alchymy, as to which Johnson was not a positive
unbeliever, but rather delighted in considering what progress
had actually been made in the transmutation of metals, what near
approaches there had been to the making of gold; and told us
that it was affirmed, that a person in the Russian dominions had
discovered the secret, but died without revealing it, as imagining
it would be prejudicial to society. He added, that it was not
impossible but it might in time be generally known.

It being asked whether it was reasonable for a man to be angry
at another whom a woman had preferred to him;—JOHNSON. 'I
do not see, Sir, that it is reasonable for a man to be angry at
another, whom a woman has preferred to him: but angry he is,
no doubt; and he is loath to be angry at himself.'

Before setting out for Scotland on the 23rd, I was frequently
in his company at different places, but during this period have
recorded only two remarks: one concerning Garrick: 'He has
not Latin enough. He finds out the Latin by the meaning, rather

than the meaning by the Latin.' And another concerning writers of travels, who, he observed, 'were more defective than any other writers.'

I passed many hours with him on the 17th, of which I find all my memorial is, 'much laughing.' It should seem he had that day been in a humour for jocularity and merriment, and upon such occasions I never knew a man laugh more heartily. We may suppose, that the high relish of a state so different from his habitual gloom, produced more than ordinary exertions of that distinguishing faculty of man, which has puzzled philosophers so much to explain. Johnson's laugh was as remarkable as any circumstance in his manner. It was a kind of good humoured growl. Tom Davies described it drolly enough: 'He laughs like a rhinoceros.'

'*To* BENNET LANGTON, ESQ.

'DEAR SIR,—I have an old amanuensis[1] in great distress. I have given what I think I can give, and begged till I cannot tell where to beg again. I put into his hands this morning four guineas. If you could collect three guineas more, it would clear him from his present difficulty. I am, Sir, your most humble servant,

'May 21, 1775.'　　　　　　　　　　　　'SAM. JOHNSON.'

'*To* JAMES BOSWELL, ESQ.

'DEAR SIR,—I make no doubt but you are now safely lodged in your own habitation, and have told all your adventures to Mrs. Boswell and Miss Veronica. Pray teach Veronica to love me. Bid her not mind mamma.

'Mrs. Thrale has taken cold, and been very much disordered, but I hope is grown well. Mr. Langton went yesterday to Lincolnshire, and has invited Nicolaida[2] to follow him. Beauclerk talks of going to Bath. I am to set out on Monday; so there is nothing but dispersion.

'I have returned Lord Hailes's entertaining sheets, but must

---

[1] [Probably Peyton. *Powell.*]　　　　　　　　　　[2] A learned Greek.

stay till I come back for more, because it will be inconvenient to send them after me in my vagrant state.

'I promised Mrs. Macaulay[1] that I would try to serve her son at Oxford. I have not forgotten it, nor am unwilling to perform it. If they desire to give him an English education, it should be considered whether they cannot send him for a year or two to an English school. If he comes immediately from Scotland, he can make no figure in our Universities. The schools in the north, I believe, are cheap; and, when I was a young man, were eminently good.

'There are two little books published by the Foulis, Telemachus and Collins's *Poems*, each a shilling: I would be glad to have them.

'Make my compliments to Mrs. Boswell, though she does not love me. You see what perverse things ladies are, and how little fit to be trusted with feudal estates. When she mends and loves me, there may be more hope of her daughters.

'I will not send compliments to my friends by name, because I would be loath to leave any out in the enumeration. Tell them, as you see them, how well I speak of Scotch politeness, and Scotch hospitality, and Scotch beauty, and of every thing Scotch, but Scotch oat-cakes, and Scotch prejudices.

'Let me know the answer of Rasay, and the decision relating to Sir Allan.[2] I am, my dearest Sir, with great affection, your most obliged, and most humble servant,

'May 27, 1775.'   'SAM. JOHNSON.'

After my return to Scotland, I wrote three letters to him, from which I extract the following passages:—

'I have seen Lord Hailes since I came down. He thinks it wonderful that you are pleased to take so much pains in revising his *Annals*. I told him that you said you were well rewarded by the entertainment which you had in reading them.'

---

[1] Wife of the Rev. Mr. Kenneth Macaulay, authour of *The History of St. Kilda*.
[2] A law-suit carried on by Sir Allan Maclean, Chief of his Clan, to recover certain parts of his family estates from the Duke of Argyle.

'There has been a numerous flight of Hebrideans in Edinburgh this summer, whom I have been happy to entertain at my house. Mr. Donald Macqueen[1] and Lord Monboddo supped with me one evening. They joined in controverting your proposition, that the Gaelick of the Highlands and Isles of Scotland was not written till of late.'

'My mind has been somewhat dark this summer. I have need of your warming and vivifying rays; and I hope I shall have them frequently. I am going to pass some time with my father at Auchinleck.'

'*To* James Boswell, Esq.

'Dear Sir,—I am now returned from the annual ramble into the middle counties. Having seen nothing I had not seen before, I have nothing to relate. Time has left that part of the island few antiquities; and commerce has left the people no singularities. I was glad to go abroad, and, perhaps, glad to come home; which is, in other words, I was, I am afraid, weary of being at home, and weary of being abroad. Is not this the state of life? But, if we confess this weariness, let us not lament it, for all the wise and all the good say, that we may cure it.

'For the black fumes which rise in your mind, I can prescribe nothing but that you disperse them by honest business or innocent pleasure, and by reading, sometimes easy and sometimes serious. Change of place is useful; and I hope that your residence at Auchinleck will have many good effects. . . .

'That I should have given pain to Rasay, I am sincerely sorry; and am therefore very much pleased that he is no longer uneasy. He still thinks that I have represented him as personally giving up the Chieftainship. I meant only that it was no longer contested between the two houses, and supposed it settled, perhaps, by the cession of some remote generation, in the house of Dunvegan. I am sorry the advertisement was not continued for three or four times in the paper.

---

[1] A very learned minister in the Isle of Sky, whom both Dr. Johnson and I have mentioned with regard.

'That Lord Monboddo and Mr. Macqueen should controvert a position contrary to the imaginary interest of literary or national prejudice, might be easily imagined; but of a standing fact there ought to be no controversy: If there are men with tails, catch an *homo caudatus*;[1] if there was writing of old in the Highlands or Hebrides, in the Erse language, produce the manuscripts. Where men write, they will write to one another, and some of their letters, in families studious of their ancestry, will be kept. In Wales there are many manuscripts.

'I have now three parcels of Lord Hailes's history, which I purpose to return all the next week: that his respect for my little observations should keep his work in suspense, makes one of the evils of my journey. It is in our language, I think, a new mode of history, which tells all that is wanted, and, I suppose, all that is known, without laboured splendour of language, or affected subtilty of conjecture. The exactness of his dates raises my wonder. He seems to have the closeness of Henault without his constraint.

'Mrs. Thrale was so entertained with your *Journal*,[2] that she almost read herself blind. She has a great regard for you.

'Of Mrs. Boswell, though she knows in her heart that she does not love me, I am always glad to hear any good, and hope that she and the little dear ladies will have neither sickness nor any other affliction. But she knows that she does not care what becomes of me, and for that she may be sure that I think her very much to blame.

'Never, my dear Sir, do you take it into your head to think that I do not love you; you may settle yourself in full confidence both of my love and my esteem; I love you as a kind man, I value you as a worthy man, and hope in time to reverence you as a man of exemplary piety. I hold you, as Hamlet has it, 'in my heart of hearts,' and therefore, it is little to say, that I am, Sir, your affectionate humble servant,

'London, Aug. 27, 1775.'   'SAM. JOHNSON.'

---

[1] ['A man with a tail.']
[2] My *Journal of a Tour to the Hebrides,* which that lady read in the original manuscript.

To THE SAME

'SIR,—If in these papers[1] there is little alteration attempted, do not suppose me negligent. I have read them perhaps more closely than the rest; but I find nothing worthy of an objection.

'Write to me soon, and write often, and tell me all your honest heart. I am, Sir, yours affectionately,

'Aug. 30, 1775.'   'SAM. JOHNSON.'

To THE SAME

'MY DEAR SIR,—I now write to you, lest in some of your freaks and humours you should fancy yourself neglected. Such fancies I must entreat you never to admit, at least never to indulge: for my regard for you is so radicated and fixed, that it is become part of my mind, and cannot be effaced but by some cause uncommonly violent; therefore, whether I write or not, set your thoughts at rest. I now write to tell you that I shall not very soon write again, for I am to set out to-morrow on another journey. . . .

'Your friends are all well at Streatham, and in Leicester-fields.[2] Make my compliments to Mrs. Boswell, if she is in good humour with me. I am, Sir, &c.

'September 14, 1775.'   'SAM. JOHNSON.'

What he mentions in such light terms as, 'I am to set out to-morrow on another journey,' I soon afterwards discovered was no less than a tour to France with Mr. and Mrs. Thrale. This was the only time in his life that he went upon the Continent.

'*To* MR. ROBERT LEVET

'DEAR SIR,   'Sept. 18, 1775. Calais.

'We are here in France, after a very pleasing passage of no more than six hours. I know not when I shall write again, and therefore I write now, though you cannot suppose that I have much to say. You have seen France yourself. From this place we are going to Rouen, and from Rouen to Paris, where Mr. Thrale

---

[1] Another parcel of Lord Hailes's *Annals of Scotland.*
[2] Where Sir Joshua Reynolds lived.

designs to stay about five or six weeks. We have a regular recommendation to the English resident, so we shall not be taken for vagabonds. We think to go one way and return another, and see as much as we can. I will try to speak a little French; I tried hitherto but little, but I spoke sometimes. If I heard better, I suppose I should learn faster. I am, Sir, your humble servant,

'SAM. JOHNSON.'

To THE SAME

'DEAR SIR,   'Paris, Oct. 22, 1775.

'We are still here, commonly very busy in looking about us. We have been to-day at Versailles. You have seen it, and I shall not describe it. We came yesterday from Fontainbleau, where the Court is now. We went to see the King and Queen at dinner, and the Queen was so impressed by Miss,[1] that she sent one of the Gentlemen to enquire who she was. I find all true that you have ever told me of Paris. Mr. Thrale is very liberal, and keeps us two coaches, and a very fine table; but I think our cookery very bad. Mrs. Thrale got into a convent of English nuns, and I talked with her through the grate, and I am very kindly used by the English Benedictine friars. But upon the whole I cannot make much acquaintance here; and though the churches, palaces, and some private houses are very magnificent, there is no very great pleasure after having seen many, in seeing more; at least the pleasure, whatever it be, must some time have an end, and we are beginning to think when we shall come home. Mr. Thrale calculates that, as we left Streatham on the fifteenth of September, we shall see it again about the fifteenth of November.

'I think I had not been on this side of the sea five days before I found a sensible improvement in my health. I ran a race in the rain this day, and beat Baretti. Baretti is a fine fellow, and speaks French, I think, quite as well as English.

'Make my compliments to Mrs. Williams; and give my love to Francis; and tell my friends that I am not lost. I am, dear Sir, your affectionate humble, &c.   'SAM. JOHNSON.'

[1] Miss Thrale.

'*To* Dr. Samuel Johnson

  'My Dear Sir,   'Edinburgh, Oct. 24, 1775.

  'If I had not been informed that you were at Paris, you should have had a letter from me by the earliest opportunity, announcing the birth of my son, on the 9th instant; I have named him Alexander, after my father. I now write, as I suppose your fellow traveller, Mr. Thrale, will return to London this week, to attend his duty in Parliament, and that you will not stay behind him.

  'I send another parcel of Lord Hailes's *Annals.* I have undertaken to solicit you for a favour to him, which he thus requests in a letter to me: "I intend soon to give you *The Life of Robert Bruce*, which you will be pleased to transmit to Dr. Johnson. I wish that you could assist me in a fancy which I have taken, of getting Dr. Johnson to draw a character of Robert Bruce, from the account that I give of that prince. If he finds materials for it in my work, it will be a proof that I have been fortunate in selecting the most striking incidents."

  'I suppose by *The Life of Robert Bruce*, his Lordship means that part of his *Annals* which relates the history of that prince, and not a separate work.

  'Shall we have *A Journey to Paris* from you in the winter? You will, I hope, at any rate be kind enough to give me some account of your French travels very soon, for I am very impatient. What a different scene have you viewed this autumn, from that which you viewed in autumn 1773! I ever am, my dear Sir, your much obliged and affectionate humble servant,

                               'James Boswell.'

'*To* James Boswell, Esq.

  'Dear Sir,—I am glad that the young Laird is born, and an end, as I hope, put to the only difference that you can ever have with Mrs. Boswell.[1] I know that she does not love me; but I intend to persist in wishing her well till I get the better of her.

  'Paris is, indeed, a place very different from the Hebrides, but

  [1] This alludes to my old feudal principle of preferring male to female succession.

it is to a hasty traveller not so fertile of novelty, nor affords so many opportunities of remark. I cannot pretend to tell the publick any thing of a place better known to many of my readers than to myself. We can talk of it when we meet.

'I shall go next week to Streatham, from whence I purpose to send a parcel of the *History* every post. Concerning the character of Bruce, I can only say, that I do not see any great reason for writing it; but I shall not easily deny what Lord Hailes and you concur in desiring.

'I have been remarkably healthy all the journey, and hope you and your family have known only that trouble and danger which has so happily terminated. Among all the congratulations that you may receive, I hope you believe none more warm or sincere, than those of, dear Sir, your most affectionate,

'November 16, 1775.'   'SAM. JOHNSON.'

'To MRS. LUCY PORTER, *in Lichfield*[1]

'DEAR MADAM,—This week I came home from Paris. I have brought you a little box, which I thought pretty; but I know not whether it is properly a snuff-box, or a box for some other use. I will send it, when I can find an opportunity. I have been through the whole journey remarkably well. My fellow-travellers were the same whom you saw at Lichfield, only we took Baretti with us. Paris is not so fine a place as you would expect. The palaces and churches, however, are very splendid and magnificent; and what would please you, there are many very fine pictures; but I do not think their way of life commodious or pleasant.

'Let me know how your health has been all this while. I hope the fine summer has given you strength sufficient to encounter the winter.

'Make my compliments to all my friends; and, if your fingers will let you, write to me, or let your maid write, if it be troublesome to you. I am, dear Madam, your most affectionate humble servant,

'November 16, 1775.'   'SAM. JOHNSON.'

[1] There can be no doubt that many years previous to 1775 he corresponded with this lady, who was his step-daughter, but none of his earlier letters to her have been preserved. [Many have been published since.]

To The Same

'Dear Madam,—Some weeks ago I wrote to you, to tell you that I was just come home from a ramble, and hope that I should have heard from you. I am afraid winter has laid hold on your fingers, and hinders you from writing. However, let somebody write, if you cannot, and tell me how you do, and a little of what has happened at Lichfield among our friends. I hope you are all well.

'When I was in France, I thought myself growing young, but am afraid that cold weather will take part of my new vigour from me. Let us, however, take care of ourselves, and lose no part of our health by negligence.

'I never knew whether you received the *Commentary on the New Testament* and the *Travels*, and the glasses.

'Do, my dear love, write to me; and do not let us forget each other. This is the season of good wishes, and I wish you all good. I have not lately seen Mr. Porter,[1] nor heard of him. Is he with you?

'Be pleased to make my compliments to Mrs. Adey, and Mrs. Cobb, and all my friends; and when I can do any good, let me know. I am, dear Madam, yours most affectionately,

'December, 1775.'   'Sam. Johnson.'

It is to be regretted that he did not write an account of his travels in France; for as he is reported to have once said, that 'he could write the Life of a Broomstick,' so, notwithstanding so many former travellers have exhausted almost every subject for remark in that great kingdom, his very accurate observation, and peculiar vigour of thought and illustration, would have produced a valuable work. During his visit to it, which lasted but about two months, he wrote notes or minutes of what he saw. He promised to show me them, but I neglected to put him in mind of it; and the greatest part of them has been lost, or perhaps, destroyed in a precipitate burning of his papers a few days before his death, which must ever be lamented. One small paperbook, however, entitled 'France II,' has been preserved, and is

[1] Son of Mrs. Johnson, by her first husband.

in my possession. It is a diurnal register of his life and observations, from the 10th of October to the 4th of November, inclusive, being twenty-six days, and shews an extraordinary attention to various minute particulars. Being the only memorial of this tour that remains, my readers, I am confident, will peruse it with pleasure, though his notes are very short, and evidently written only to assist his own recollection.

'Oct. 10. Tuesday. We saw the *Ecole Militaire*, in which one hundred and fifty young boys are educated for the army. They have arms of different sizes, according to the age;—flints of wood. The building is very large, but nothing fine, except the council-room. The French have large squares in the windows;—they make good iron palisades. Their meals are gross.

'We visited the Observatory, a large building of a great height. The upper stones of the parapet very large, but not cramped with iron. The flat on the top is very extensive; but on the insulated part there is no parapet. Though it was broad enough, I did not care to go upon it. Maps were printing in one of the rooms.

'We walked to a small convent of the Fathers of the Oratory. In the reading-desk of the refectory lay the lives of the Saints.

'Oct. 11. Wednesday. We went to see *Hôtel de Chatlois*,[1] a house not very large, but very elegant. One of the rooms was gilt to a degree that I never saw before. The upper part for servants and their masters was pretty.

'Thence we went to Mr. Monville's, a house divided into small apartments, furnished with effeminate and minute elegance. —Porphyry.

'Thence we went to St. Roque's church, which is very large; —the lower part of the pillars incrusted with marble.—Three chapels behind the high altar;—the last a mass of low arches.— Altars, I believe, all round.

'We passed through *Place de Vendôme*, a fine square, about as big as Hanover-square.—Inhabited by the high families.— Lewis XIV. on horse-back in the middle.

---

[1] [Chatelet *MS.*, *recte.*]

'Monville is the son of a farmer-general. In the house of Chatlois[1] is a room furnished with japan, fitted up in Europe.

'We dined with Boccage,[2] the Marquis Blanchetti, and his lady.—The sweetmeats taken by the Marchioness Blanchetti, after observing that they were dear.—Mr. Le Roy, Count Manucci, the Abbé, the Prior, and Father Wilson, who staid with me, till I took him home in the coach.

'Bathiani is gone.

'The French have no laws for the maintenance of their poor.— Monk not necessarily a priest.—Benedictines rise at four; are at church an hour and half; at church again half an hour before, half an hour after, dinner; and again from half an hour after seven to eight. They may sleep eight hours.—Bodily labour wanted in monasteries.

'The poor taken to hospitals, and miserably kept.—Monks in the convent fifteen:—accounted poor.

'Oct. 12. Thursday. We went to the Gobelins.—Tapestry makes a good picture;—imitates flesh exactly.—One piece with a gold ground;—the birds not exactly coloured.—Thence we went to the King's cabinet;—very neat, not, perhaps, perfect. —Gold ore.—Candles of the candle-tree.—Seeds.—Woods. Thence to Gagnier's[3] house, where I saw rooms nine, furnished with a profusion of wealth and elegance which I never had seen before.—Vases.—Pictures.—The Dragon china.—The lustre said to be of crystal, and to have cost 3,500l.—The whole furniture said to have cost 125,000l.—Damask hangings covered with pictures.—Porphyry.—This house struck me.—Then we waited on the ladies to Monville's.—Captain Irwin with us.[4]— Spain. County towns all beggars.—At Dijon he could not find the way to Orleans.—Cross roads of France very bad.—Five soldiers.—Woman.—Soldiers escaped.——The Colonel would not lose five men for the death of one woman.—The magistrate cannot seize a soldier but by the Colonel's permission.—Good inn at Nismes.—Moors of Barbary fond of Englishmen.—

---

[1] [Chatelet *MS.*, *recte.*]   [2] [Bocage *MS.*]   [3] [Gagni's *MS.*]
[4] The rest of this paragraph appears to be a minute of what was told by Captain Irwin.

Gibraltar eminently healthy;—It has beef from Barbary;—
There is a large garden.—Soldiers sometimes fall from the rock.

'Oct. 13. Friday. I staid at home all day, only went to find the
Prior, who was not at home.—I read something in Canus.[1]—
Nec admiror, nec multum laudo.[2]

'Oct. 14. Saturday. We went to the house of Mr. Argenson,
which was almost wainscotted with looking-glasses, and covered
with gold.—The ladies' closet wainscotted with large squares of
glass over painted paper. They always place mirrours to reflect
their rooms.

'Then we went to Julien's, the Treasurer of the Clergy:—
30,000l. a year.—The house has no very large room, but is set
with mirrours, and covered with gold.—Books of wood here,
and in another library.

'At D*********'s[3] I looked into the books in the lady's
closet, and, in contempt, shewed them to Mr. T.—*Prince Titi;
Bibl. des Fées*, and other books.—She was offended, and shut up,
as we heard afterwards, her apartment.

'Then we went to Julien Le Roy, the King's watchmaker, a
man of character in his business, who shewed a small clock made
to find the longitude.—A decent man.

'Afterwards we saw the *Palais Marchand*, and the Courts of
Justice, civil and criminal.—Queries[4] on the *Sellette*.—This building has the old Gothick passages, and a great appearance of
antiquity.—Three hundred prisoners sometimes in the gaol.

'Much disturbed; hope no ill will be.[5]

'In the afternoon I visited Mr. Freron the journalist. He spoke
Latin very scantily, but seemed to understand me.—His house
not splendid, but of commodious size.—His family, wife, son,
and daughter, not elevated but decent.—I was pleased with my
reception.—He is to translate my book, which I am to send him
with notes.

[1] Melchior Canus, a celebrated Spanish Dominican, who died at Toledo
in 1560. He wrote a treatise *De Locis Theologicis*, in twelve books.
[2] ['I do not admire it, nor much commend it.']
[3] [D'Argenson's ⟨*MS.*⟩]   [4] [Queeney *MS.*]
[5] This passage, which some may think superstitious, reminds me of
Archbishop Laud's Diary.

'Oct. 15. Sunday. At Choisi, a royal palace on the banks of the Seine, about 7 m. from Paris.—The terrace noble along the river.—The rooms numerous and grand, but not discriminated from other palaces.—The chapel beautiful, but small.—China globes.—Inlaid table.—Labyrinth.—Sinking table.—Toilet tables.

'Oct. 16. Monday. The Palais Royal very grand, large, and lofty.—A very great collection of pictures.—Three of Raphael.—Two Holy Family.—One small piece of M. Angelo.—One room of Rubens—I thought the pictures of Raphael fine.

'The Thuilleries.[1]—Statues.—Venus.—Æn. and Anchises in his arms.—Nilus.—Many more. The walks not open to mean persons.—Chairs at night hired for two sous apiece.—Pont tournant.

'Austin Nuns.—Grate.—Mrs. Fermor, Abbess.—She knew Pope, and thought him disagreeable.—Mrs. —— has many books;—has seen life.—Their frontlet disagreeable.—Their hood.—Their life easy.—Rise about five; hour and half in chapel.—Dine at ten.—Another hour and half at chapel; half an hour about three, and half an hour more at seven:—four hours in chapel.—A large garden.—Thirteen pensioners.—Teacher complained.

'At the Boulevards[2] saw nothing, yet was glad to be there.—Rope-dancing and farce.—Egg dance.

'N. [Note.] Near Paris, whether on week-days or Sundays, the roads empty.

'Oct. 17. Tuesday. At the Palais Marchand I bought

A snuff-box	24 L.
——————	6
Table book	15
Scissars 3 p [pair]	18
	———
	63—2 12 6

'We heard the lawyers plead.—N. As many killed at Paris as there are days in the year. *Chambre de question.*—Tournelle at the Palais Marchand.—An old venerable building.

[1] [Tuilleries *MS.*]   [2] [Boulevard *MS.*]

'The Palais Bourbon, belonging to the Prince of Condé. Only one small wing shown;—lofty;—splendid;—gold and glass.— The battles of the great Condé are painted in one of the rooms. The present Prince a grandsire at thirty-nine.

'The sight of palaces, and other great buildings, leaves no very distinct images, unless to those who talk of them and impress them. As I entered, my wife was in my mind:[1] she would have been pleased. Having now nobody to please, I am little pleased.

'N. In France there is no middle rank.

'So many shops open, that Sunday is little distinguished at Paris.—The palaces of Louvre and Thuilleries[2] granted out in lodgings.

'In the *Palais de Bourbon*, gilt globes of metal at the fire-place.

'The French beds commended.—Much of the marble, only paste.

'The Colosseum a mere wooden building, at least much of it.

'Oct. 18. Wednesday. We went to Fontainebleau, which we found a large mean town, crouded with people.—The forest thick with woods, very extensive.—Manucci secured us lodging.—The appearance of the country pleasant.—No hills, few streams, only one hedge.—I remember no chapels nor crosses on the road.—Pavement still, and rows of trees.

'N. Nobody but mean people walk in Paris.

'Oct. 19. Thursday. At Court, we saw the apartments;—the King's bed-chamber and council-chamber extremely splendid— Persons of all ranks in the external[3] rooms through which the family passes:—servants and masters.—Brunet with us the second time.

'The introductor came to us;—civil to me.—Presenting.—I had scruples.—Not necessary.—We went and saw the King and Queen at dinner.—We saw the other ladies at dinner—Madame Elizabeth, with the Princess of Guimené.—At night we went to

---

[1] His tender affection for his departed wife, of which there are many evidences in his *Prayers and Meditations*, appears very feelingly in this passage.

[2] [Tuilleries *MS.*]   [3] [outward *MS.*]

a comedy. I neither saw nor heard.—Drunken women.—Mrs. Th. preferred one to the other.

'Oct. 20. Friday. We saw the Queen mount in the forest.—Brown habit; rode aside: one lady rode aside.—The Queen's horse light grey; martingale.—She galloped.—We then went to the apartments, and admired them.—Then wandered through the palace.—In the passages, stalls and shops.—Painting in Fresco by a great master, worn out.—We saw the King's horses and dogs.—The dogs almost all English.—Degenerate.

'The horses not much commended.—The stables cool; the kennel filthy.

'At night the ladies went to the opera. I refused, but should have been welcome.

'The King fed himself with his left hand as we.

'Saturday, 21. In the night I got ground.—We came home to Paris.—I think we did not see the chapel.—Tree broken by the wind.—The French chairs made all of boards painted.

'N. Soldiers at the court of justice.—Soldiers not amenable to the magistrates.—Dijon woman.[1]

'Faggots in[2] the palace.—Every thing slovenly, except in chief rooms.—Trees in the roads, some tall, none old, many very young and small.

'Women's saddles seem ill made.—Queen's bridle woven with silver.—Tags to strike the horse.

'Sunday, Oct. 22. To Versailles, a mean town. Carriages of business passing.—Mean shops against the wall.—Our way lay through Sêve,[3] where the China manufacture.—Wooden bridge at Sêve, in the way to Versailles.—The palace of great extent. —The front long; I saw it not perfectly.—The Menagerie. Cygnets dark; their black feet; on the ground; tame.—Halcyons, or gulls.—Stag and hind, young.—Aviary, very large; the net, wire.—Black stag of China, small.—Rhinoceros, the horn broken and pared away, which, I suppose, will grow; the basis, I think, four inches 'cross; the skin folds like loose cloth doubled over his body, and cross his hips; a vast animal, though young; as big, perhaps, as four oxen.—The young elephant, with his tusks

[1] See p. 647.   [2] [Fagot *MS.*]   [3] [Sevre *MS.*]

just appearing.—The brown bear put out his paws;—all very tame.—The lion.—The tigers I did not well view.—The camel, or dromedary with two bunches called the Huguin,[1] taller than any horse.—Two camels with one bunch.—Among the birds was a pelican, who being let out, went to a fountain, and swam about to catch fish. His feet well webbed: he dipped his head, and turned his long bill sidewise. He caught two or three fish, but did not eat them.

'Trianon is a kind of retreat appendant to Versailles. It has an open portico; the pavement, and, I think, the pillars, of marble. —There are many rooms, which I do not distinctly remember— A table of porphyry, about five feet long, and between two and three broad, given to Lewis XIV. by the Venetian State.—In the council-room almost all that was not door or window, was, I think, looking-glass.—Little Trianon is a small palace like a gentleman's house.—The upper floor paved with brick.—Little Vienne.—The court is ill paved.—The rooms at the top are small, fit to sooth the imagination with privacy. In the front of Versailles are small basons of water on the terrace, and other basons, I think, below them. There are little courts.—The great gallery is wainscotted with mirrors, not very large, but joined by frames. I suppose the large plates were not yet made.—The play-house was very large.—The chapel I do not remember if we saw.—We saw one chapel, but I am not certain whether there or at Trianon.—The foreign office paved with bricks.— The dinner half a Louis[2] each, and, I think, a Louis[2] over.— Money given at Menagerie, three livres; at palace,[3] six livres.

'Oct. 23. Monday. Last night I wrote to Levet.——We went to see the looking-glasses wrought. They come from Normandy in cast plates, perhaps the third of an inch thick. At Paris they are ground upon a marble table, by rubbing one plate on another with grit between them. The various sands, of which there are said to be five, I could not learn. The handle, by which the upper glass is moved, has the form of a wheel, which may be moved in

---

[1] This epithet should be applied to this animal, with one bunch. [Lewis *MS.*]   [3] [elsewhere *MS.*]

all directions. The plates are sent up with their surfaces ground, but not polished, and so continue till they are bespoken, lest time should spoil the surface, as we were told. Those that are to be polished, are laid on a table, covered with several thick cloths, hard strained, that the resistance may be equal; they are then rubbed with a hand rubber, held down hard by a contrivance which I did not well understand. The powder which is used last seemed to me to be iron dissolved in aqua fortis: they called it, as Baretti said, *marc*[1] *de l'eau forte,* which he thought was dregs. They mentioned vitriol and saltpetre. The cannon ball swam in the quicksilver. To silver them, a leaf of beaten tin is laid, and rubbed with quicksilver, to which it unites. Then more quicksilver is poured upon it, which, by its mutual [attraction] rises very high. Then a paper is laid at the nearest end of the plate, over which the glass is slided till it lies upon the plate, having driven much of the quicksilver before it. It is then, I think, pressed upon cloths, and then set sloping to drop the superfluous mercury; the slope is daily heightened towards a perpendicular.

'In the way I saw the Grêve, the Mayor's house, and the Bastile.

'We then went to Sans-terre, a brewer. He brews with about as much malt as Mr. Thrale, and sells his beer at the same price, though he pays no duty for malt, and little more than half as much for beer. Beer is sold retail at 6p. a bottle. He brews 4,000 barrels a year. There are seventeen brewers in Paris, of whom none is supposed to brew more than he:—reckoning them at 3,000 each, they make 51,000 a year.—They make their malt, for malting is here no trade.

'The moat of the Bastile is dry.

'Oct. 24. Tuesday. We visited the King's library—I saw the *Speculum humanæ Salvationis,* rudely printed, with ink, sometimes pale, sometimes black; part supposed to be with wooden types, and part with pages cut on boards.—The Bible, supposed to be older than that of Mentz, in 62 [1462]: it has no date; it is supposed to have been printed with wooden types.—I am in doubt;

[1] [Mar *MS.* (a phonetic spelling).]

the print is large and fair, in two folios.—Another book was shewn me, supposed to have been printed with wooden types;—I think, *Durandi Sanctuarium* in 58 [1458]. This is inferred from the difference of form sometimes seen in the same letter, which might be struck with different puncheons.—The regular similitude of most letters proves better that they are metal.—I saw nothing but the *Speculum* which I had not seen, I think, before.

'Thence to the Sorbonne.—The library very large, not in lattices like the King's. *Marbone*[1] and *Durandi*,[2] q. collection 14 vol.[3] *Scriptores de rebus Gallicis*, many folios.—*Histoire Généalogique of France*, 9 vol.—*Gallia Christiana*, the first edition, 4to.[4] the last, f. 12 vol.[3]—The Prior and Librarian dined [with us]:—I waited on them home.—Their garden pretty, with covered walks, but small; yet may hold many students.—The Doctors of the Sorbonne are all equal:—choose those who succeed to vacancies.—Profit little.

'Oct. 25. Wednesday. I went with the Prior to St. Cloud, to see Dr. Hooke.—We walked round the palace, and had some talk.—I dined with our whole company at the Monastery.—In the library, *Beroald*,—*Cymon*,—*Titus*, from Boccace.—*Oratio Proverbialis* to the Virgin, from Petrarch; Falkland to Sandys; Dryden's Preface to the third vol. of Miscellanies.[5]

'Oct. 26. Thursday. We saw the china at Sêve,[6] cut, glazed, painted. Bellevue, a pleasing house, not great: fine prospect.—Meudon, an old palace.—Alexander, in Porphyry: hollow between eyes and nose, thin cheeks.—Plato and Aristotle—Noble terrace overlooks the town.—St. Cloud.—Gallery not very high, nor grand, but pleasing.—In the rooms, Michael Angelo, drawn by himself, Sir Thomas More, Des Cartes, Bochart, Naudæus, Mazarine.—Gilded wainscot, so common that it is not minded. —Gough and Keene.—Hooke came to us at the inn.—A message from Drumgold.

'Oct. 27. Friday. I staid at home.—Gough and Keene, and

---

[1] [Martene *MS.*]   [2] [Durand's *MS.*]
[3] [fol. *MS.*]   [4] [4 *MS.*]
[5] He means, I suppose, that he read these different pieces while he remained in the library.
[6] [Sevre *MS.*]

Mrs. S———'s[1] friend dined with us.—This day we began to have a fire.—The weather is grown very cold, and I fear, has a bad effect upon my breath, which has grown much more free and easy in this country.

'Sat., Oct. 28. I visited the Grand Chartreux[2] built by St. Louis.[3]—It is built for forty, but contains only twenty-four, and will not maintain more. The friar that spoke to us had a pretty apartment.—Mr. Baretti says four rooms; I remember but three.—His books seemed to be French.—His garden was neat; he gave me grapes.—We saw the Place de Victoire, with the statues of the King, and the captive nations.

'We saw the palace and gardens of Luxembourg, but the gallery was shut.—We climbed to the top stairs.—I dined with Colbrooke, who had much company:—Foote, Sir George Rodney, Motteux, Udson, Taaf.—Called on the Prior, and found him in bed.

'Hotel—a guinea a day.—Coach, three guineas a week.—Valet de place, three l. a day.—*Avantcoureur*, a guinea a week.—Ordinary dinner, six l. a head.—Our ordinary seems to be about five guineas a day.—Our extraordinary expences, as diversions, gratuities, clothes, I cannot reckon.—Our travelling is ten guineas a day.

'White stockings,[4] 18 l.—Wig.—Hat.

'Sunday, Oct. 29. We saw the boarding-school.—The *Enfans trouvés.*—A room with about eighty-six children in cradles, as sweet as a parlour.—They lose a third; take in to perhaps more than seven [years old]; put them to trades; pin to them the papers sent with them.—Want nurses.—Saw their chapel.

'Went to St. Eustatia; saw an innumerable company of girls catechised, in many bodies, perhaps 100 to a catechist.—Boys taught at one time, girls at another.—The sermon; the preacher wears a cap, which he takes off at the name:—his action uniform, not very violent.

---

[1] [Mrs. Strickland and Capt. Killpatrick. *Croker*[1] and Tyson and Guppy, *French Journals*, p. 183.]
[2] [Chartreuse *MS.*]   [3] [St. Lewis *MS.*]
[4] [stockens *MS.*]

'Oct. 30. Monday. We saw the library of St. Germain.—A very
noble collection.—*Codex Divinorum Officiorum*, 1459:—a letter,
square like that of the *Offices,* perhaps the same.—The *Codex,* by
Fust and Gernsheym[a].—*Meursius,* 12 v. fol.—*Amadis,* in French,
3 v. fol.—CATHOLICON *sine colophone,* but of 1460.—Two other
editions,[1] one by . . . . *Augustin. de Civitate Dei,* without name,
date, or place, but of Fust's square letter as it seems.

'I dined with Col. Drumgold;—had a pleasing afternoon.

'Some of the books of St. Germain's stand in presses from the
wall, like those at Oxford.

'Oct. 31. Tuesday. I lived at the Benedictines; meagre day;
soup meagre, herrings, eels, both with sauce; fryed fish; lentils,
tasteless in themselves. In[2] the library; where I found *Maffeus's
de Historiâ Indicâ: Promontorium flectere, to double the Cape.* I
parted very tenderly from the Prior and Friar Wilkes.

'*Maitre es Arts,* 2 y.—*Bacc. Theol.* 3 y.—*Licentiate,* 2 y.—
Doctor Th. 2 y. in all 9 years.—For the Doctorate three disputa-
tions, *Major, Minor, Sorbonica.*—Several colleges suppressed,
and transferred to that which was the Jesuits' College.

'Nov. 1. Wednesday. We left Paris.—St. Denis, a large town;
the church not very large, but the middle isle is very lofty and
aweful.—On the left are chapels built beyond the line of the wall,
which destroy the symmetry of the sides. The organ is higher
above the pavement than any[3] I have ever seen.—The gates are
of brass.—On the middle gate[4] is the history of our Lord.—The
painted windows are historical, and said to be eminently beautiful.—We were at another church belonging to a convent, of
which the portal is a dome; we could not enter further, and it
was almost dark.

'Nov. 2. Thursday. We came this day to Chantilly, a seat
belonging to the Prince of Condé.—This place is eminently

[a] [Gernshein *MS.*]

[1] I have looked in vain into De Bure, Meerman, Mattaire, and other
typographical books, for the two editions of the *Catholicon,* which Dr. Johnson mentions here, with *names* which I cannot make out. I read 'one by
Latinius [Lathomi], one by *Boedinus* [Badius].' I have deposited the
original MS. in the British Museum, where the curious may see it. My
grateful acknowledgements are due to Mr. Planta for the trouble he was
pleased to take in aiding my researches.

[2] [To *MS.*]   [3] [any *not in MS.*]   [4] [gates *MS.*]

beautified by all varieties of waters[1] starting up in fountains, falling in cascades, running in streams, and spread in lakes.— The water seems to be too near the house.—All this water is brought from a source or river[2] three leagues off, by an artificial canal, which for one league is carried under ground.—The house is magnificent.—The cabinet seems well stocked: what I remember was, the jaws of a hippopotamus, and a young hippopotamus preserved, which, however, is so small, that I doubt its reality. —It seems too hairy for an abortion, and too small for a mature birth.—Nothing was in spirits;[3] all was dry.—The dog; the deer; the ant-bear with long snout.—The toucan, long broad beak.—The stables were of very great length.—The kennel had no scents.—There was a mockery of a village.—The Menagerie had few animals.[4]—Two faussans,[5] or Brasilian weasels, spotted, very wild.—There is a forest, and, I think, a park.—I walked till I was very weary, and next morning felt my feet battered, and[6] with pains in the toes.

'Nov. 3. Friday. We came to Compiegne, a very large town, with a royal palace built round a pentagonal court.—The court is raised upon vaults, and has, I suppose, an entry on one side by a gentle rise.—Talk of painting.—The church is not very large, but very elegant and splendid.—I had at first great difficulty to walk, but motion grew continually easier.—At night we came to Noyon, an episcopal city.—The cathedral is very beautiful, the pillars alternately Gothick and Corinthian.—We entered a very noble parochial church.—Noyon is walled, and is said to be three miles round.

---

[1] [water *MS.*]   [2] [a river *MS.*]   [3] [spirit *MS.*]

[4] The writing is so bad here, that the names of several of the animals could not be decyphered without much more acquaintance with natural history than I possess.—Dr. Blagden, with his usual politeness, most obligingly examined the MS. To that gentleman, and to Dr. Gray, of the British Museum, who also very readily assisted me, I beg leave to express my best thanks.

[5] It is thus written by Johnson, from the French pronunciation of *fossane*. It should be observed, that the person who shewed this Menagerie was mistaken in supposing the *fossane* and the Brasilian weasel to be the same, the *fossane* being a different animal, and a native of Madagascar. I find them, however, upon one plate in Pennant's *Synopsis of Quadrupeds.*

[6] [and sore *MS.*]

'Nov. 4. Saturday. We rose very early, and came through St. Quintin to Cambray, not long after three.—We went to an English nunnery, to give a letter to Father Welch, the confessor, who came to visit us in the evening.

'Nov. 5. Sunday. We saw the cathedral.—It is very beautiful, with chapels on each side.—The choir splendid.— The balustrade in one part brass.—The Neff very high and grand.—The altar silver as far as it is seen.—The vestments very splendid.——At the Benedictines church——'

Here his Journal[1] ends abruptly. Whether he wrote any more after this time, I know not; but probably not much, as he arrived in England about the 12th of November. These short notes of his tour, though they may seem minute taken singly, make together a considerable mass of information, and exhibit such an ardour of enquiry and acuteness of examination, as, I believe, are found in but few travellers, especially at an advanced age. They completely refute the idle notion which has been propagated, *that he could not see*; and, if he had taken the trouble to revise and digest them, he undoubtedly could have expanded them into a very entertaining narrative.

When I met him in London the following year, the account which he gave me of his French tour, was, 'Sir, I have seen all the visibilities of Paris, and around it; but to have formed an acquaintance with the people there, would have required more time than I could stay. I was just beginning to creep into acquaintance by means of Colonel Drumgold, a very high man, Sir, head of *L'Ecole Militaire*, a most complete character, for he had first been a professor of rhetorick, and then became a soldier. And, Sir, I was very kindly treated by the English Benedictines, and have a cell appropriated to me in their convent.'

He observed, 'The great in France live very magnificently, but the rest very miserably. There is no happy middle state as in England. The shops of Paris are mean; the meat in the markets

---

[1] My worthy and ingenious friend, Mr. Andrew Lumisden, by his accurate acquaintance with France, enabled me to make out many proper names, which Dr. Johnson had written indistinctly, and sometimes spelt erroneously.

is such as would be sent to a gaol in England: and Mr. Thrale
justly observed, that the cookery of the French was forced upon
them by necessity; for they could not eat their meat, unless they
added some taste to it. The French are an indelicate people;
they will spit upon any place. At Madame ————'s,[1] a literary
lady of rank, the footman took the sugar in his fingers, and threw
it into my coffee. I was going to put it aside; but hearing it was
made on purpose for me, I e'en tasted Tom's fingers. The same
lady would needs make tea *à l'Angloise*. The spout of the tea-pot
did not pour freely; she bad the footman blow into it. France is
worse than Scotland in every thing but climate. Nature has done
more for the French; but they have done less for themselves than
the Scotch have done.'

It happened that Foote was at Paris at the same time with
Dr. Johnson, and his description of my friend while there, was
abundantly ludicrous. He told me, that the French were quite
astonished at his figure and manner, and at his dress, which he
obstinately continued exactly as in London;—his brown clothes,
black stockings, and plain shirt. He mentioned, that an Irish
gentleman[2] said to Johnson, 'Sir, you have not seen the best
French players.' JOHNSON. 'Players, Sir! I look on them as no
better than creatures set upon tables and joint-stools to make
faces and produce laughter, like dancing dogs.'—'But, Sir, you
will allow that some players are better than others?' JOHNSON.
'Yes, Sir, as some dogs dance better than others.'

While Johnson was in France, he was generally very resolute
in speaking Latin. It was a maxim with him that a man should
not let himself down, by speaking a language which he speaks
imperfectly. Indeed, we must have often observed how inferiour,
how much like a child a man appears, who speaks a broken
tongue. When Sir Joshua Reynolds, at one of the dinners of the
Royal Academy, presented him to a Frenchman[3] of great distinction, he would not deign to speak French, but talked Latin,
though his Excellency did not understand it, owing, perhaps, to

---

[1] ⌈Madame du Boccage. *Mrs. Piozzi. Croker*[1].⌉
[2] ⌈Perhaps Capt. Killpatrick. *Powell.*⌉
[3] ⌈Probably the French Ambassador. *Powell.*⌉

Johnson's English pronunciation: yet upon another occasion he
was observed to speak French to a Frenchman of high rank, who
spoke English; and being asked the reason, with some expression of surprise,—he answered, 'because I think my French is as
good as his English.' Though Johnson understood French perfectly, he could not speak it readily, as I have observed at his
first interview with General Paoli, in 1769; yet he wrote it, I
imagine, pretty well, as appears from some of his letters in Mrs.
Piozzi's collection, of which I shall transcribe one:—

> *A Madame La Comtesse de* ———.

'July 16, 1775.[1]

'Oui, *Madame, le moment est arrivé, et il faut que je parte. Mais
pourquoi faut-il partir? Est-ce que je m'ennuye? Je m'ennuyerai
ailleurs. Est-ce que je cherche ou quelque plaisir, ou quelque soulage-
ment? Je ne cherche rien, je n'espere rien. Aller voir ce que jai vû,
etre un peu rejoué, un peu degouté, me resouvenir que la vie se passe
en vain, me plaindre de moi, m'endurcir aux dehors; voici le tout de
ce qu'on compte pour les delices de l'année. Que Dieu vous donne,
Madame, tous les agrémens de la vie, avec un esprit qui peut en
jouir sans s'y livrer trop.'*

Here let me not forget a curious anecdote, as related to me by
Mr. Beauclerk, which I shall endeavour to exhibit as well as I
can in that gentleman's lively manner; and in justice to him it is
proper to add, that Dr. Johnson told me I might rely both on the
correctness of his memory, and the fidelity of his narrative.
'When Madame de Boufflers was first in England, (said Beauclerk,) she was desirous to see Johnson. I accordingly went with
her to his chambers in the Temple, where she was entertained
with his conversation for some time. When our visit was over,
she and I left him, and were got into Inner Temple-lane, when
all at once I heard a noise like thunder. This was occasioned by
Johnson, who it seems, upon a little recollection, had taken it
into his head that he ought to have done the honours of his

---

[1] [Madame de Boufflers. *Mrs. Piozzi.* The original is dated May 16,
1776.]

literary residence to a foreign lady of quality, and eager to show himself a man of gallantry, was hurrying down the stair-case in violent agitation. He overtook us before we reached the Temple-gate, and brushing in between me and Madame de Boufflers, seized her hand, and conducted her to her coach. His dress was a rusty brown morning suit, a pair of old shoes by way of slippers, a little shrivelled wig sticking on the top of his head, and the sleeves of his shirt and the knees of his breeches hanging loose. A considerable crowd of people gathered round, and were not a little struck by this singular appearance.'

He spoke Latin with wonderful fluency and elegance. When Pere Boscovich was in England, Johnson dined in company with him at Sir Joshua Reynolds's, and at Dr. Douglas's, now Bishop of Salisbury. Upon both occasions that celebrated foreigner expressed his astonishment at Johnson's Latin conversation. When at Paris, Johnson thus characterised Voltaire to Freron the Journalist: *'Vir est acerrimi ingenii et paucarum literarum.'*[1]

'To Dr. Samuel Johnson

'My Dear Sir,   'Edinburgh, Dec. 5, 1775.

'Mr. Alexander Maclean, the present young Laird of Col, being to set out to-morrow for London, I give him this letter to introduce him to your acquaintance. The kindness which you and I experienced from his brother, whose unfortunate death we sincerely lament, will make us always desirous to shew attention to any branch of the family. Indeed, you have so much of the true Highland cordiality, that I am sure you would have thought me to blame if I had neglected to recommend to you this Hebridean prince, in whose island we were hospitably entertained. I ever am with respectful attachment, my dear Sir, your most obliged and most humble servant,

'James Boswell.'

Mr. Maclean returned with the most agreeable accounts of the polite attention with which he was received by Dr. Johnson. In the course of this year Dr. Burney informs me, that 'he very

[1] ['A man of very acute intellect and little literature.']

frequently met Dr. Johnson at Mr. Thrale's, at Streatham, where they had many long conversations, often sitting up as long as the fire and candles lasted, and much longer than the patience of the servants subsisted.'

A few of Johnson's sayings, which that gentleman recollects, shall here be inserted.

'I never take a nap after dinner but when I have had a bad night, and then the nap takes me.'

'The writer of an epitaph should not be considered as saying nothing but what is strictly true. Allowance must be made for some degree of exaggerated praise. In lapidary inscriptions a man is not upon oath.'

'There is now less flogging in our great schools than formerly, but then less is learned there; so that what the boys get at one end, they lose at the other.'

'More is learned in publick than in private schools, from emulation; there is the collision of mind with mind, or the radiation of many minds pointing to one centre. Though few boys make their own exercises, yet if a good exercise is given up, out of a great number of boys, it is made by somebody.'

'I hate by-roads in education. Education is as well known, and has long been as well known, as ever it can be. Endeavouring to make children prematurely wise is useless labour. Suppose they have more knowledge at five or six years old than other children, what use can be made of it? It will be lost before it is wanted, and the waste of so much time and labour of the teacher can never be repaid. Too much is expected from precocity, and too little performed. Miss ——[1] was an instance of early cultivation, but in what did it terminate? In marrying a little Presbyterian parson,[2] who keeps an infant boarding-school, so that all her employment now is,

"To suckle fools, and chronicle small-beer."

She tells the children, "This is a cat, and that is a dog, with four legs and a tail; see there! you are much better than a cat or a dog, for you can speak." If I had bestowed such an education on

[1] [Miss Aikin. *Croker*[1].]   [2] [Rev. R. Barbauld. *Ib.*]

a daughter, and had discovered that she thought of marrying such a fellow, I would have sent her to the *Congress.*'

'After having talked slightingly of musick, he was observed to listen very attentively while Miss Thrale played on the harpsichord, and with eagerness he called to her, "Why don't you dash away like Burney?" Dr. Burney upon this said to him, "I believe, Sir, we shall make a musician of you at last." Johnson with candid complacency replied, "Sir, I shall be glad to have a new sense given to me."'

'He had come down one morning to the breakfast-room, and been a considerable time by himself before any body appeared. When, on a subsequent day, he was twitted by Mrs. Thrale for being very late, which he generally was, he defended himself by alluding to the extraordinary morning, when he had been too early, "Madam, I do not like to come down to *vacuity.*"'

'Dr. Burney having remarked that Mr. Garrick was beginning to look old, he said, "Why, Sir, you are not to wonder at that; no man's face has had more wear and tear."'

Not having heard from him for a longer time than I supposed he would be silent, I wrote to him December 18, not in good spirits:—

'Sometimes I have been afraid that the cold which has gone over Europe this year like a sort of pestilence has seized you severely: sometimes my imagination, which is upon occasions prolifick of evil, hath figured that you may have somehow taken offence at some part of my conduct.'

'To JAMES BOSWELL, ESQ.

'DEAR SIR,—Never dream of any offence. How should you offend me? I consider your friendship as a possession, which I intend to hold till you take it from me, and to lament if ever by my fault I should lose it. However, when such suspicions find their way into your mind, always give them vent; I shall make haste to disperse them; but hinder their first ingress if you can. Consider such thoughts as morbid.

'Such illness as may excuse my omission to Lord Hailes, I cannot honestly plead. I have been hindered, I know not how,

by a succession of petty obstructions. I hope to mend immediately, and to send next post to his Lordship. Mr. Thrale would
have written to you if I had omitted; he sends his compliments
and wishes to see you.

'You and your lady will now have no more wrangling about
feudal inheritance. How does the young Laird of Auchinleck?
I suppose Miss Veronica is grown a reader and discourser.

'I have just now got a cough, but it has never yet hindered me
from sleeping: I have had quieter nights than are common
with me.

'I cannot but rejoice that Joseph[1] has had the wit to find the
way back. He is a fine fellow, and one of the best travellers in
the world.

'Young Col brought me your letter. He is a very pleasing
youth. I took him two days ago to the Mitre, and we dined
together. I was as civil as I had the means of being.

'I have had a letter from Rasay, acknowledging, with great
appearance of satisfaction, the insertion in the Edinburgh paper.
I am very glad that it was done.

'My compliments to Mrs. Boswell, who does not love me;
and of all the rest, I need only send them to those that do: and
I am afraid it will give you very little trouble to distribute them.
I am, my dear, dear Sir, your affectionate humble servant,

'December 23, 1775.'   'SAM. JOHNSON.'

1776: ÆTAT. 67.]—IN 1776, Johnson wrote, so far as I can
discover, nothing for the publick: but that his mind was still
ardent, and fraught with generous wishes to attain to still higher
degrees of literary excellence, is proved by his private notes of
this year, which I shall insert in their proper place.

'To JAMES BOSWELL, ESQ.

'DEAR SIR,—I have at last sent you all Lord Hailes's papers.
While I was in France, I looked very often into Henault; but

---

[1] Joseph Ritter, a Bohemian, who was in my service many years, and
attended Dr. Johnson and me in our Tour to the Hebrides. After having
left me for some time, he had now returned to me.

Lord Hailes, in my opinion, leaves him far and far behind. Why I did not dispatch so short a perusal sooner, when I look back, I am utterly unable to discover: but human moments are stolen away by a thousand petty impediments which leave no trace behind them. I have been afflicted, through the whole Christmas, with the general disorder, of which the worst effect was a cough, which is now much mitigated, though the country, on which I look from a window at Streatham, is now covered with a deep snow. Mrs. Williams is very ill: every body else is as usual.

'Among the papers, I found a letter to you, which I think you had not opened; and a paper for *The Chronicle*, which I suppose it not necessary now to insert. I return them both.

'I have, within these few days, had the honour of receiving Lord Hailes's first volume, for which I return my most respectful thanks.

'I wish you, my dearest friend, and your haughty lady, (for I know she does not love me,) and the young ladies, and the young Laird, all happiness. Teach the young gentleman, in spite of his mamma, to think and speak well of, Sir, your affectionate humble servant,

'Jan. 10, 1776.'   'Sam. Johnson.'

At this time was in agitation a matter of great consequence to me and my family, which I should not obtrude upon the world, were it not that the part which Dr. Johnson's friendship for me made him take in it, was the occasion of an exertion of his abilities, which it would be injustice to conceal. That what he wrote upon the subject may be understood, it is necessary to give a state of the question, which I shall do as briefly as I can.

In the year 1504, the barony or manour of Auchinleck, (pronounced *Affléck*,) in Ayrshire, which belonged to a family of the same name with the lands, having fallen to the Crown by forfeiture, James the Fourth, King of Scotland, granted it to Thomas Boswell, a branch of an ancient family in the county of Fife, stiling him in the charter, *dilecto familiari nostro*;[1] and assigning,

---

[1] ['Our beloved kinsman.']

as the cause of the grant, *pro bono et fideli servitio nobis præstito*.[1] Thomas Boswell was slain in battle, fighting along with his Sovereign, at the fatal field of Floddon, in 1513.

From this very honourable founder of our family, the estate was transmitted, in a direct series of heirs male, to David Boswell, my father's great grand uncle, who had no sons, but four daughters, who were all respectably married, the eldest to Lord Cathcart.

David Boswell, being resolute in the military feudal principle of continuing the male succession, passed by his daughters, and settled the estate on his nephew by his next brother, who approved of the deed, and renounced any pretensions which he might possibly have, in preference to his son. But the estate having been burthened with large portions to the daughters, and other debts, it was necessary for the nephew to sell a considerable part of it, and what remained was still much encumbered.

The frugality of the nephew preserved, and, in some degree, relieved the estate. His son, my grandfather, an eminent lawyer, not only re-purchased a great part of what had been sold, but acquired other lands; and my father, who was one of the Judges of Scotland, and had added considerably to the estate, now signified his inclination to take the privilege allowed by our law,[2] to secure it to his family in perpetuity by an entail, which, on account of marriage articles, could not be done without my consent.

In the plan of entailing the estate, I heartily concurred with him, though I was the first to be restrained by it; but we unhappily differed as to the series of heirs which should be established, or in the language of our law, called to the succession. My father had declared a predilection for heirs general, that is, males and females indiscriminately. He was willing, however, that all males descending from his grandfather should be preferred to females; but would not extend that privilege to males deriving their descent from a higher source. I, on the other hand,

---

[1] ['For good and faithful service rendered us.']
[2] Acts of Parliament of Scotland, 1685, cap. 22.

had a zealous partiality for heirs male, however remote, which I maintained by arguments which appeared to me to have considerable weight.[1] And in the particular case of our family, I apprehended that we were under an implied obligation, in honour and good faith, to transmit the estate by the same tenure which we held it, which was as heirs male, excluding nearer females. I therefore, as I thought conscientiously, objected to my father's scheme.

My opposition was very displeasing to my father, who was entitled to great respect and deference; and I had reason to apprehend disagreeable consequences from my non-compliance with his wishes. After much perplexity and uneasiness, I wrote to Dr. Johnson, stating the case, with all its difficulties, at full length, and earnestly requesting that he would consider it at leisure, and favour me with his friendly opinion and advice.

[1] As first, the opinion of some distinguished naturalists, that our species is transmitted through males only, the female being all along no more than a *nidus*, or nurse, as Mother Earth is to plants of every sort; which notion seems to be confirmed by that text of scripture, 'He was yet *in the loins of his* FATHER when Melchisedeck met him' (Heb. vii. 10); and consequently, that a man's grandson by a daughter, instead of being his *surest* descendant as is vulgarly said, has in reality no connection whatever with his blood.—And secondly, independent of this theory, (which, if true, should completely exclude heirs general,) that if the preference of a male to a female, without regard to primogeniture, (as a son, though much younger, nay, even a grandson by a son, to a daughter,) be once admitted, as it universally is, it must be equally reasonable and proper in the most remote degree of descent from an original proprietor of an estate, as in the nearest; because,—however distant from the representative at the time,—that remote heir male, upon the failure of those nearer to the *original proprietor* than he is, becomes in fact the nearest male to *him*, and is, therefore, preferable as *his* representative, to a female descendant.—A little extension of mind will enable us easily to perceive that a son's son, in continuation to whatever length of time, is preferable to a son's daughter, in the succession to an ancient inheritance; in which regard should be had to the representation of the original proprietor, and not to that of one of his descendants.

I am aware of Blackstone's admirable demonstration of the reasonableness of the legal succession, upon the principle of there being the greatest probability that the nearest heir of the person who last dies proprietor of an estate, is of the blood of the first purchaser. But supposing a pedigree to be carefully authenticated through all its branches, instead of mere *probability* there will be a *certainty* that *the nearest heir male, at whatever period*, has the same right of blood with the first heir male, namely, *the original purchaser's eldest son*.

'*To* JAMES BOSWELL, ESQ.

'DEAR SIR,—I was much impressed by your letter, and, if I can form upon your case any resolution satisfactory to myself, will very gladly impart it: but whether I am quite equal to it, I do not know. It is a case compounded of law and justice, and requires a mind versed in juridical disquisitions. Could you not tell your whole mind to Lord Hailes? He is, you know, both a Christian and a Lawyer. I suppose he is above partiality, and above loquacity: and, I believe, he will not think the time lost in which he may quiet a disturbed, or settle a wavering mind. Write to me, as any thing occurs to you; and if I find myself stopped by want of facts necessary to be known, I will make inquiries of you as my doubts arise.

' If your former resolutions should be found only fanciful, you decide rightly in judging that your father's fancies may claim the preference; but whether they are fanciful or rational, is the question. I really think Lord Hailes could help us.

'Make my compliments to dear Mrs. Boswell; and tell her, that I hope to be wanting in nothing that I can contribute to bring you all out of your troubles. I am, dear Sir, most affectionately, your humble servant,

'London, Jan. 15, 1776.'   'SAM. JOHNSON.'

To THE SAME

'DEAR SIR,—I am going to write upon a question which requires more knowledge of local law, and more acquaintance with the general rules of inheritance, than I can claim; but I write, because you request it.

'Land is, like any other possession, by natural right wholly in the power of its present owner; and may be sold, given, or bequeathed, absolutely or conditionally, as judgement shall direct, or passion incite.

'But natural right would avail little without the protection of law; and the primary notion of law is restraint in the exercise of natural right. A man is therefore, in society, not fully master of what he calls his own, but he still retains all the power which law does not take from him.

'In the exercise of the right which law either leaves or gives, regard is to be paid to moral obligations.

'Of the estate which we are now considering, your father still retains such possession, with such power over it, that he can sell it, and do with the money what he will, without any legal impediment. But when he extends his power beyond his own life, by settling the order of succession, the law makes your consent necessary.

'Let us suppose that he sells the land to risk the money in some specious adventure, and in that adventure loses the whole; his posterity would be disappointed; but they could not think themselves injured or robbed. If he spent it upon vice or pleasure, his successors could only call him vicious and voluptuous; they could not say that he was injurious or unjust.

'He that may do more, may do less. He that, by selling or squandering, may disinherit a whole family, may certainly disinherit part, by a partial settlement.

'Laws are formed by the manners and exigencies of particular times, and it is but accidental that they last longer than their causes: the limitation of feudal succession to the male arose from the obligation of the tenant to attend his chief in war.

'As times and opinions are always changing, I know not whether it be not usurpation to prescribe rules to posterity, by presuming to judge of what we cannot know: and I know not whether I fully approve either your design or your father's, to limit that succession which descended to you unlimited. If we are to leave *sartum tectum*[1] to posterity, what we have without any merit of our own received from our ancestors, should not choice and free-will be kept unviolated? Is land to be treated with more reverence than liberty?—If this consideration should restrain your father from disinheriting some of the males, does it leave you the power of disinheriting all the females?

'Can the possessor of a feudal estate make any will? Can he appoint, out of the inheritance, any portions to his daughters? There seems to be a very shadowy difference between the power of leaving land, and of leaving money to be raised from land;

[1] [The technical term in Roman law for a building in good repair.]

669

between leaving an estate to females, and leaving the male heir, in effect, only their steward.

'Suppose at one time a law that allowed only males to inherit, and during the continuance of this law many estates to have descended, passing by the females, to remoter heirs. Suppose afterwards the law repealed in correspondence with a change of manners, and women made capable of inheritance; would not then the tenure of estates be changed? Could the women have no benefit from a law made in their favour? Must they be passed by upon moral principles for ever, because they were once excluded by a legal prohibition? Or may that which passed only to males by one law, pass likewise to females by another?

'You mention your resolution to maintain the right of your brothers:[1] I do not see how any of their rights are invaded.

'As your whole difficulty arises from the act of your ancestor, who diverted the succession from the females, you enquire, very properly, what were his motives, and what was his intention; for you certainly are not bound by his act more than he intended to bind you, nor hold your land on harder or stricter terms than those on which it was granted.

'Intentions must be gathered from acts. When he left the estate to his nephew, by excluding his daughters, was it, or was it not, in his power to have perpetuated the succession to the males? If he could have done it, he seems to have shewn, by omitting it, that he did not desire it to be done; and, upon your own principles, you will not easily prove your right to destroy that capacity of succession which your ancestors have left.

'If your ancestor had not the power of making a perpetual settlement; and if, therefore, we cannot judge distinctly of his intentions, yet his act can only be considered as an example; it makes not an obligation. And, as you observe, he set no example of rigorous adherence to the line of succession. He that overlooked a brother, would not wonder that little regard is shewn to remote relations.

'As the rules of succession are, in a great part, purely legal, no man can be supposed to bequeath any thing, but upon legal

[1] Which term I applied to all the heirs male.

terms; he can grant no power which the law denies; and if he makes no special and definite limitation, he confers all the powers which the law allows.

'Your ancestor, for some reason, disinherited his daughters; but it no more follows that he intended his act as a rule for posterity, than the disinheriting of his brother.

'If, therefore, you ask by what right your father admits daughters to inheritance, ask yourself, first, by what right you require them to be excluded?

'It appears, upon reflection, that your father excludes nobody; he only admits nearer females to inherit before males more remote; and the exclusion is purely consequential.

'These, dear Sir, are my thoughts, immethodical and deliberative; but, perhaps, you may find in them some glimmering of evidence.

'I cannot, however, but again recommend to you a conference with Lord Hailes, whom you know to be both a Lawyer and a Christian.

'Make my compliments to Mrs. Boswell, though she does not love me. I am, Sir, your affectionate servant,

'Feb. 3, 1773.'[1]   'SAM. JOHNSON.'

I had followed his recommendation and consulted Lord Hailes, who upon this subject had a firm opinion contrary to mine. His Lordship obligingly took the trouble to write me a letter, in which he discussed with legal and historical learning, the points in which I saw much difficulty, maintaining that 'the succession of heirs general was the succession, by the law of Scotland, from the throne to the cottage, as far as we can learn it by record;' observing that the estate of our family had not been limited to heirs male; and that though an heir male had in one instance been chosen in preference to nearer females, that had been an arbitrary act, which had seemed to be best in the embarrassed state of affairs at that time; and the fact was, that upon a fair computation of the value of land and money at the time, applied to the estate and the burthens upon it, there was nothing given to the heir male but the skeleton of an estate. 'The plea of con-

---

[1] [In error for 1776.]

science (said his Lordship,) which you put, is a most respectable one, especially when *conscience* and *self* are on different sides. But I think that conscience is not well informed, and that *self* and *she* ought on this occasion to be of a side.'

This letter, which had considerable influence upon my mind, I sent to Dr. Johnson, begging to hear from him again, upon this interesting question.

'To JAMES BOSWELL, ESQ.

'DEAR SIR,—Having not any acquaintance with the laws or customs of Scotland, I endeavoured to consider your question upon general principles, and found nothing of much validity that I could oppose to this position: "He who inherits a fief unlimited by his ancestors inherits the power of limiting it according to his own judgement or opinion." If this be true, you may join with your father.

'Further consideration produced another conclusion: "He who receives a fief unlimited by his ancestors, gives his heirs some reason to complain, if he does not transmit it unlimited to posterity. For why should he make the state of others worse than his own, without reason?" If this be true, though neither you nor your father are about to do what is quite right, but as your father violates (I think) the legal succession least, he seems to be nearer the right than yourself.

'It cannot but occur that "Women have natural and equitable claims as well as men, and these claims are not to be capriciously or lightly superseded or infringed." When fiefs implied military service, it is easily discerned why females could not inherit them; but that reason is now at an end. As manners make laws, manners likewise repeal them.

'These are the general conclusions which I have attained. None of them are very favourable to your scheme of entail, nor perhaps to any scheme. My observation, that only he who acquires an estate may bequeath it capriciously,[1] if it contains any conviction, includes this position likewise, that only he who acquires an estate may entail it capriciously. But I think it may be safely

[1] I had reminded him of his observation mentioned, *ante*, p. 548.

presumed, that "he who inherits an estate, inherits all the power legally concomitant;" and that "He who gives or leaves unlimited an estate legally limitable, must be presumed to give that power of limitation which he omitted to take away, and to commit future contingencies to future prudence." In these two positions I believe Lord Hailes will advise you to rest; every other notion of possession seems to me full of difficulties and embarrassed with scruples.

'If these axioms be allowed, you have arrived now at full liberty without the help of particular circumstances, which, however, have in your case great weight. You very rightly observe, that he who passing by his brother gave the inheritance to his nephew, could limit no more than he gave; and by Lord Hailes's estimate of fourteen years' purchase, what he gave was no more than you may easily entail according to your own opinion, if that opinion should finally prevail.

'Lord Hailes's suspicion that entails are encroachments on the dominion of Providence, may be extended to all hereditary privileges and all permanent institutions; I do not see why it may not be extended to any provision but for the present hour, since all care about futurity proceeds upon a supposition, that we know at least in some degree what will be future. Of the future we certainly know nothing; but we may form conjectures from the past; and the power of forming conjectures, includes, in my opinion, the duty of acting in conformity to that probability which we discover. Providence gives the power, of which reason teaches the use. I am, dear Sir, your most faithful servant,

'Feb. 9, 1776.'   'SAM. JOHNSON.'

'I hope I shall get some ground now with Mrs. Boswell; make my compliments to her, and to the little people.

'Don't burn papers; they may be safe enough in your own box,—you will wish to see them hereafter.'

To THE SAME

'DEAR SIR,—To the letters which I have written about your great question I have nothing to add. If your conscience is satisfied, you have now only your prudence to consult. I long for a letter, that I may know how this troublesome and vexatious question is at last decided.[1] I hope that it will at last end well. Lord Hailes's letter was very friendly, and very seasonable, but I think his aversion from entails has something in it like superstition. Providence is not counteracted by any means which Providence puts into our power. The continuance and propagation of families makes a great part of the Jewish law, and is by no means prohibited in the Christian institution, though the necessity of it continues no longer. Hereditary tenures are established in all civilized countries, and are accompanied in most with hereditary authority. Sir William Temple considers our constitution as defective, that there is not an unalienable estate in land connected with a peerage; and Lord Bacon mentions as a proof that the Turks are Barbarians, their want of *Stirpes*,[2] as he calls them, or hereditary rank. Do not let your mind, when it is freed from the supposed necessity of a rigorous entail, be entangled with contrary objections, and think all entails unlawful, till you have cogent arguments, which I believe you will never find. I am afraid of scruples.

'I have now sent all Lord Hailes's papers; part I found hidden in a drawer in which I had laid them for security, and had forgotten them. Part of these are written twice: I have returned both the copies. Part I had read before.

'Be so kind as to return Lord Hailes my most respectful thanks for his first volume; his accuracy strikes me with wonder; his narrative is far superiour to that of Henault, as I have formerly mentioned.

'I am afraid that the trouble, which my irregularity and delay

[1] The entail framed by my father with various judicious clauses, was executed by him and me, settling the estate upon the heirs male of his grandfather, which I found had been already done by my grandfather, imperfectly, but so as to be defeated only by selling the lands. I was freed by Dr. Johnson from scruples of conscientious obligation, and could, therefore, gratify my father. But my opinion and partiality for male succession, in its full extent, remained unshaken. Yet let me not be thought harsh or unkind to daughters: for my notion is, that they should be treated with great affection and tenderness, and always participate of the prosperity of the family.

[2] [family, good birth.]

has cost him, is greater, far greater, than any good that I can do him will ever recompense; but if I have any more copy, I will try to do better.

'Pray let me know if Mrs. Boswell is friends with me, and pay my respects to Veronica, and Euphemia, and Alexander. I am, Sir, your most humble servant,

'February 15, 1776.'   'SAM. JOHNSON.'

'MR. BOSWELL *to* DR. JOHNSON
                                        'Edinburgh, Feb. 20, 1776.

'. . . You have illuminated my mind and relieved me from imaginary shackles of conscientious obligation. Were it necessary, I could immediately join in an entail upon the series of heirs approved by my father; but it is better not to act too suddenly.'

'DR. JOHNSON *to* MR. BOSWELL

'DEAR SIR,—I am glad that what I could think or say has at all contributed to quiet your thoughts. Your resolution not to act, till your opinion is confirmed by more deliberation, is very just. If you have been scrupulous, do not now be rash. I hope that as you think more, and take opportunities of talking with men intelligent in questions of property, you will be able to free yourself from every difficulty.

'When I wrote last, I sent, I think, ten packets. Did you receive them all?

'You must tell Mrs. Boswell that I suspected her to have written without your knowledge,[1] and therefore did not return any answer, lest a clandestine correspondence should have been perniciously discovered. I will write to her soon. . . . I am, dear Sir, most affectionately yours,

'Feb. 24, 1776.'   'SAM. JOHNSON.'

Having communicated to Lord Hailes what Dr. Johnson wrote concerning the question which perplexed me so much, his Lordship wrote to me: 'Your scruples have produced more fruit than

---

[1] A letter to him on the interesting subject of the family settlement, which I had read.

I ever expected from them; an excellent dissertation on general principles of morals and law.'

I wrote to Dr. Johnson on the 20th[1] of February, complaining of melancholy, and expressing a strong desire to be with him; informing him that the ten packets came all safe; that Lord Hailes was much obliged to him, and said he had almost wholly removed his scruples against entails.

'*To* JAMES BOSWELL, ESQ.

'DEAR SIR,—I have not had your letter half an hour; as you lay so much weight upon my notions, I should think it not just to delay my answer.

'I am very sorry that your melancholy should return, and should be sorry likewise if it could have no relief but from company. My counsel you may have when you are pleased to require it; but of my company you cannot in the next month have much, for Mr. Thrale will take me to Italy, he says, on the first of April.

'Let me warn you very earnestly against scruples. I am glad that you are reconciled to your settlement, and think it a great honour to have shaken Lord Hailes's opinion of entails. Do not, however, hope wholly to reason away your troubles; do not feed them with attention, and they will die imperceptibly away. Fix your thoughts upon your business, fill your intervals with company, and sunshine will again break in upon your mind. If you will come to me, you must come very quickly; and even then I know not but we may scour the country together, for I have a mind to see Oxford and Lichfield, before I set out on this long journey. To this I can only add, that I am, dear Sir, your most affectionate humble servant,

'March 5, 1776.'   'SAM. JOHNSON.'

To THE SAME

'DEAR SIR,—Very early in April we leave England, and in the beginning of the next week I shall leave London for a short time; of this I think it necessary to inform you, that you may not

[1] [A misprint for 29th, as Boswell's journal shows.]

be disappointed in any of your enterprises. I had not fully resolved to go into the country before this day.

'Please to make my compliments to Lord Hailes; and mention very particularly to Mrs. Boswell my hope that she is reconciled to, Sir, your faithful servant,

'March 12, 1776.'   'SAM. JOHNSON.'

Above thirty years ago, the heirs of Lord Chancellor Clarendon presented the University of Oxford with the continuation of his *History*, and such other of his Lordship's manuscripts as had not been published, on condition that the profits arising from their publication should be applied to the establishment of a *Manège* in the University. The gift was accepted in full convocation. A person[1] being now recommended to Dr. Johnson, as fit to superintend this proposed riding-school, he exerted himself with that zeal for which he was remarkable upon every similar occasion. But, on enquiry into the matter, he found that the scheme was not likely to be soon carried into execution; the profits arising from the Clarendon press being, from some mismanagement, very scanty. This having been explained to him by a respectable dignitary of the church,[2] who had good means of knowing it, he wrote a letter upon the subject, which at once exhibits his extraordinary precision and acuteness, and his warm attachment to his ALMA MATER.

'*To* THE REVEREND DR. WETHERELL, *Master of University College, Oxford*

'DEAR SIR,—Few things are more unpleasant than the transaction of business with men who are above knowing or caring what they have to do; such as the trustees for Lord Cornbury's institution will, perhaps, appear, when you have read Dr. *******'s[3] letter.

'The last part of the Doctor's letter is of great importance.

---

[1] [Mr. Carter. *Johnson's Letters*, Nos. 379, 383, 384.1, 386.]
[2] [Dr. John Douglas. *Powell*.]
[3] [Boswell's copy at Yale has the name, Douglas.]

The complaint[1] which he makes I have heard long ago, and did not know but it was redressed. It is unhappy that a practice so erroneous has not yet been altered; for altered it must be, or our press will be useless, with all its privileges. The booksellers, who, like all other men, have strong prejudices in their own favour, are enough inclined to think the practice of printing and selling books by any but themselves, an encroachment on the rights of their fraternity; and have need of stronger inducements to circulate academical publications than those of one another; for, of that mutual co-operation by which the general trade is carried on, the University can bear no part. Of those whom he neither loves nor fears, and from whom he expects no reciprocation of good offices, why should any man promote the interest but for profit? I suppose, with all our scholastick ignorance of mankind, we are still too knowing to expect that the booksellers will erect themselves into patrons, and buy and sell under the influence of a disinterested zeal for the promotion of learning.

'To the booksellers, if we look for either honour or profit from our press, not only their common profit, but something more must be allowed; and if books, printed at Oxford, are expected to be rated at a high price, that price must be levied on the publick, and paid by the ultimate purchaser, not by the intermediate agents. What price shall be set upon the book, is, to the booksellers, wholly indifferent, provided that they gain a proportionate profit by negociating the sale.

'Why books printed at Oxford should be particularly dear, I am, however, unable to find. We pay no rent; we inherit many of our instruments and materials; lodging and victuals are cheaper than at London; and, therefore, workmanship ought, at least, not to be dearer. Our expences are naturally less than those of booksellers; and, in most cases, communities are content with less profit than individuals.

'It is, perhaps, not considered through how many hands a book often passes, before it comes into those of the reader; or

---

[1] I suppose the complaint was, that the trustees of the Oxford Press did not allow the London booksellers a sufficient profit upon vending their publications.

what part of the profit each hand must retain, as a motive for transmitting it to the next.

'We will call our primary agent in London, Mr. Cadell, who receives our books from us, gives them room in his warehouse, and issues them on demand; by him they are sold to Mr. Dilly a wholesale bookseller, who sends them into the country; and the last seller is the country bookseller. Here are three profits to be paid between the printer and the reader, or in the style of commerce, between the manufacturer and the consumer; and if any of these profits is too penuriously distributed, the process of commerce is interrupted.[1]

'We are now come to the practical question, what is to be done? You will tell me, with reason, that I have said nothing, till I declare how much, according to my opinion, of the ultimate price ought to be distributed through the whole succession of sale.

'The deduction, I am afraid, will appear very great: but let it be considered before it is refused. We must allow, for profit, between thirty and thirty-five *per cent.*, between six and seven shillings in the pound; that is, for every book which costs the last buyer twenty shillings, we must charge Mr. Cadell with something less than fourteen. We must set the copies at fourteen shillings each, and superadd what is called the quarterly-book, or for every hundred books so charged we must deliver an hundred and four.

'The profits will then stand thus:—

'Mr. Cadell, who runs no hazard, and gives no credit, will be paid for warehouse room and attendance by a shilling profit on each book, and his chance of the quarterly-book.

'Mr. Dilly, who buys the book for fifteen shillings, and who will expect the quarterly-book if he takes five and twenty, will send it to his country customer at sixteen and six, by which, at the hazard of loss, and the certainty of long credit, he gains the regular profit of ten *per cent.* which is expected in the wholesale trade.

'The country bookseller, buying at sixteen and sixpence, and commonly trusting a considerable time, gains but three and six-

[1] [Boswell's copy at Yale has *intercepted.*]

679

pence, and if he trusts a year, not much more than two and six-
pence; otherwise than as he may, perhaps, take as long credit as
he gives.

'With less profit than this, and more you see he cannot have,
the country bookseller cannot live; for his receipts are small, and
his debts sometimes bad.

'Thus, dear Sir, I have been incited by Dr. *******'s letter
to give you a detail of the circulation of books, which, perhaps,
every man has not had opportunity of knowing; and which those
who know it, do not, perhaps, always distinctly consider.
I am, &c.

'March 12, 1776.'   'SAM. JOHNSON.'[1]

Having arrived in London late on Friday, the 15th of March,
I hastened next morning to wait on Dr. Johnson, at his house;
but found he was removed from Johnson's-court, No. 7, to Bolt-
court, No. 8, still keeping to his favourite Fleet-street. My
reflection at the time upon this change as marked in my Journal,
is as follows: 'I felt a foolish regret that he had left a court which
bore his name;[2] but it was not foolish to be affected with some
tenderness of regard for a place in which I had seen him a great
deal, from whence I had often issued a better and a happier man
than when I went in, and which had often appeared to my
imagination while I trod its pavement, in the solemn darkness of
the night, to be sacred to wisdom and piety.' Being informed
that he was at Mr. Thrale's, in the Borough, I hastened thither,
and found Mrs. Thrale and him at breakfast. I was kindly welcomed. In a moment he was in a full glow of conversation, and
I felt myself elevated as if brought into another state of being.
Mrs. Thrale and I looked to each other while he talked, and our
looks expressed our congenial admiration and affection for him.
I shall ever recollect this scene with great pleasure. I exclaimed

---

[1] I am happy in giving this full and clear statement to the publick, to
vindicate, by the authority of the greatest authour of his age, that respectable body of men, the Booksellers of London, from vulgar reflections, as if
their profits were exorbitant, when, in truth, Dr. Johnson has here allowed
them more than they usually demand.

[2] He said, when in Scotland, that he was *Johnson of that Ilk*.

to her, 'I am now, intellectually, *Hermippus redivivus*,[1] I am quite restored by him, by transfusion of *mind*.'[2] 'There are many (she replied) who admire and respect Mr. Johnson; but you and I *love* him.'

He seemed very happy in the near prospect of going to Italy with Mr. and Mrs. Thrale. 'But, (said he,) before leaving England I am to take a jaunt to Oxford, Birmingham, my native city Lichfield, and my old friend, Dr. Taylor's, at Ashbourn, in Derbyshire. I shall go in a few days, and you, Boswell, shall go with me.' I was ready to accompany him; being willing even to leave London to have the pleasure of his conversation.

I mentioned with much regret the extravagance of the representative[3] of a great family in Scotland, by which there was danger of its being ruined; and as Johnson respected it for its antiquity, he joined with me in thinking it would be happy if this person should die. Mrs. Thrale seemed shocked at this, as feudal barbarity; and said, 'I do not understand this preference of the estate to its owner; of the land to the man who walks upon that land.' JOHNSON. 'Nay, Madam, it is not a preference of the land to its owner, it is the preference of a family to an individual. Here is an establishment in a country, which is of importance for ages, not only to the chief but to his people; an establishment which extends upwards and downwards; that this should be destroyed by one idle fellow is a sad thing.'

He said, 'Entails are good, because it is good to preserve in a country, serieses of men, to whom the people are accustomed to look up as to their leaders. But I am for leaving a quantity of land in commerce, to excite industry, and keep money in the country; for if no land were to be bought in a country, there would be no encouragement to acquire wealth, because a family could not be founded there; or if it were acquired, it must be carried away to another country where land may be bought. And although the land in every country will remain the same, and be as fertile where there is no money, as where there is, yet all that portion of the happiness of civil life, which is produced by money

---

[1] ['restored']   [2] See *ante*, p. 295.
[3] [Norman Macleod, 20th Chief of Macleod. *Boswell Papers*, xi. 135.]

circulating in a country, would be lost.' BOSWELL. 'Then, Sir, would it be for the advantage of a country that all its lands were sold at once?' JOHNSON. 'So far, Sir, as money produces good, it would be an advantage; for, then that country would have as much money circulating in it as it is worth. But to be sure this would be counterbalanced by disadvantages attending a total change of proprietors.'

I expressed my opinion that the power of entailing should be limited thus: 'That there should be one third, or perhaps one half of the land of a country kept free for commerce; that the proportion allowed to be entailed, should be parcelled out so that no family could entail above a certain quantity. Let a family according to the abilities of its representatives, be richer or poorer in different generations, or always rich if its representatives be always wise: but let its absolute permanency be moderate. In this way we should be certain of there being always a number of established roots; and as in the course of nature, there is in every age an extinction of some families, there would be continual openings for men ambitious of perpetuity, to plant a stock in the entail ground.'[1] JOHNSON. 'Why, Sir, mankind will be better able to regulate the system of entails, when the evil of too much land being locked up by them is felt, than we can do at present when it is not felt.'

I mentioned Dr. Adam Smith's book on *The Wealth of Nations*, which was just published, and that Sir John Pringle had observed to me, that Dr. Smith, who had never been in trade, could not be expected to write well on that subject any more than a lawyer upon physick. JOHNSON. 'He is mistaken, Sir: a man who has never been engaged in trade himself may undoubtedly write well upon trade, and there is nothing which requires more to

---

[1] The privilege of perpetuating in a family an estate and arms *indefeasibly* from generation to generation, is enjoyed by none of his Majesty's subjects except in Scotland, where the legal fiction of *fine* and *recovery* is unknown. It is a privilege so proud, that I should think it would be proper to have the exercise of it dependent on the royal prerogative. It seems absurd to permit the power of perpetuating their representation, to men, who having had no eminent merit, have truly no name. The King, as the impartial father of his people, would never refuse to grant the privilege to those who deserved it.

be illustrated by philosophy than trade does. As to mere wealth, that is to say, money, it is clear that one nation or one individual cannot increase its store but by making another poorer: but trade procures what is more valuable, the reciprocation of the peculiar advantages of different countries. A merchant seldom thinks but of his own particular trade. To write a good book upon it, a man must have extensive views. It is not necessary to have practised, to write well upon a subject.' I mentioned law as a subject on which no man could write well without practice. JOHNSON. 'Why, Sir, in England, where so much money is to be got by the practice of the law, most of our writers upon it have been in practice; though Blackstone had not been much in practice when he published his *Commentaries*. But upon the Continent, the great writers on law have not all been in practice: Grotius, indeed, was; but Puffendorf was not, Burlamaqui was not.'

When we had talked of the great consequence which a man acquired by being employed in his profession, I suggested a doubt of the justice of the general opinion, that it is improper in a lawyer to solicit employment; for why, I urged, should it not be equally allowable to solicit that as the means of consequence, as it is to solicit votes to be elected a member of Parliament? Mr. Strahan had told me that a countryman of his and mine,[1] who had risen to eminence in the law, had, when first making his way, solicited him to get him employed in city causes. JOHNSON. 'Sir, it is wrong to stir up law-suits; but when once it is certain that a law-suit is to go on, there is nothing wrong in a lawyer's endeavouring that he shall have the benefit, rather than another.' BOSWELL. 'You would not solicit employment, Sir, if you were a lawyer.' JOHNSON. 'No, Sir, but not because I should think it wrong, but because I should disdain it.' This was a good distinction, which will be felt by men of just pride. He proceeded: 'However, I would not have a lawyer to be wanting to himself in using fair means. I would have him to inject a little hint now and then, to prevent his being overlooked.'

[1] [Wedderburn. *Croker.*[1]]

Lord Mountstuart's bill for a Scotch Militia, in supporting which his Lordship had made an able speech in the House of Commons, was now a pretty general topick of conversation. JOHNSON. 'As Scotland contributes so little land-tax towards the general support of the nation, it ought not to have a militia paid out of the general fund, unless it should be thought for the general interest, that Scotland should be protected from an invasion, which no man can think will happen; for what enemy would invade Scotland, where there is nothing to be got? No, Sir; now that the Scotch have not the pay of English soldiers spent among them, as so many troops are sent abroad, they are trying to get money another way, by having a militia paid. If they are afraid, and seriously desire to have an armed force to defend them, they should pay for it. Your scheme is to retain a part of your little land-tax, by making us pay and clothe your militia.' BOSWELL. 'You should not talk of *we* and *you*, Sir: there is now an *Union*.' JOHNSON. 'There must be a distinction of interest, while the proportions of land-tax are so unequal. If Yorkshire should say, "Instead of paying our land-tax, we will keep a greater number of militia," it would be unreasonable.' In this argument my friend was certainly in the wrong. The land-tax is as unequally proportioned between different parts of England, as between England and Scotland; nay, it is considerably unequal in Scotland itself. But the land-tax is but a small part of the numerous branches of publick revenue, all of which Scotland pays precisely as England does. A French invasion made in Scotland would soon penetrate into England.

He thus discoursed upon supposed obligations in settling estates:—'Where a man gets the unlimited property of an estate, there is no obligation upon him in *justice* to leave it to one person rather than to another. There is a motive of preference from *kindness*, and this kindness is generally entertained for the nearest relation. If I *owe* a particular man a sum of money, I am obliged to let that man have the next money I get, and cannot in justice let another have it: but if I owe money to no man, I may dispose of what I get as I please. There is not a *debitum justitiæ*[1] to a

[1] ['a debt in law.']

man's next heir; there is only a *debitum caritatis*.[1] It is plain, then, that I have morally a choice, according to my liking. If I have a brother in want, he has a claim from affection to my assistance; but if I have also a brother in want, whom I like better, he has a preferable claim. The right of an heir at law is only this, that he is to have the succession to an estate, in case no other person is appointed to it by the owner. His right is merely preferable to that of the King.'

We got into a boat to cross over to Black-friars; and as we moved along the Thames, I talked to him of a little volume, which, altogether unknown to him, was advertised to be published in a few days, under the title of *Johnsoniana, or Bon-Mots of Dr. Johnson.* JOHNSON. 'Sir, it is a mighty impudent thing.' BOSWELL. 'Pray, Sir, could you have no redress if you were to prosecute a publisher for bringing out, under your name, what you never said, and ascribing to you dull stupid nonsense, or making you swear profanely, as many ignorant relaters of your *bon-mots* do?' JOHNSON. 'No, Sir; there will always be some truth mixed with the falsehood, and how can it be ascertained how much is true and how much is false? Besides, Sir, what damages would a jury give me for having been represented as swearing?' BOSWELL. 'I think, Sir, you should at least disavow such a publication, because the world and posterity might with much plausible foundation say, "Here is a volume which was publickly advertised and came out in Dr. Johnson's own time, and, by his silence, was admitted by him to be genuine."' JOHNSON. 'I shall give myself no trouble about the matter.'

He was, perhaps, above suffering from such spurious publications; but I could not help thinking, that many men would be much injured in their reputation, by having absurd and vicious sayings imputed to them; and that redress ought in such cases to be given.

He said, 'The value of every story depends on its being true. A story is a picture either of an individual or of human nature in general: if it be false, it is a picture of nothing. For instance: suppose a man should tell that Johnson, before setting out for

[1] ['a debt of kindness.']

Italy, as he had to cross the Alps, sat down to make himself wings. This many people would believe; but it would be a picture of nothing. *******[1] (naming a worthy friend of ours,) used to think a story, a story, till I shewed him that truth was essential to it.' I observed, that Foote entertained us with stories which were not true; but that, indeed, it was properly not as narratives that Foote's stories pleased us, but as collections of ludicrous images. JOHNSON. 'Foote is quite impartial, for he tells lies of every body.'

The importance of strict and scrupulous veracity cannot be too often inculcated. Johnson was known to be so rigidly attentive to it, that even in his common conversation the slightest circumstance was mentioned with exact precision. The knowledge of his having such a principle and habit made his friends have a perfect reliance on the truth of every thing that he told, however it might have been doubted if told by many others. As an instance of this, I may mention an odd incident which he related as having happened to him one night in Fleet-street. 'A gentlewoman (said he) begged I would give her my arm to assist her in crossing the street, which I accordingly did; upon which she offered me a shilling, supposing me to be the watchman. I perceived that she was somewhat in liquor.' This, if told by most people, would have been thought an invention; when told by Johnson, it was believed by his friends as much as if they had seen what passed.

We landed at the Temple-stairs, where we parted.

I found him in the evening in Mrs. Williams's room. We talked of religious orders. He said, 'It is as unreasonable for a man to go into a Carthusian convent for fear of being immoral, as for a man to cut off his hands for fear he should steal. There is, indeed, great resolution in the immediate act of dismembering himself; but when that is once done, he has no longer any merit: for though it is out of his power to steal, yet he may all his life be a thief in his heart. So when a man has once become a Carthusian, he is obliged to continue so, whether he chooses it or not. Their silence, too, is absurd. We read in the Gospel of the

---

[1] [Langton. *Boswell Papers*, xi. 141.]

apostles being sent to preach, but not to hold their tongues. All severity that does not tend to increase good, or prevent evil, is idle. I said to the Lady Abbess[1] of a convent, "Madam, you are here, not for the love of virtue, but the fear of vice." She said, "She should remember this as long as she lived." ' I thought it hard to give her this view of her situation, when she could not help it; and, indeed, I wondered at the whole of what he now said; because, both in his *Rambler* and *Idler*, he treats religious austerities with much solemnity of respect.

Finding him still persevering in his abstinence from wine, I ventured to speak to him of it.—JOHNSON. 'Sir, I have no objection to a man's drinking wine, if he can do it in moderation. I found myself apt to go to excess in it, and therefore, after having been for some time without it, on account of illness, I thought it better not to return to it. Every man is to judge for himself, according to the effects which he experiences. One of the fathers tells us, he found fasting made him so peevish that he did not practise it.'

Though he often enlarged upon the evil of intoxication, he was by no means harsh and unforgiving to those who indulged in occasional excess in wine. One of his friends,[2] I well remember, came to sup at a tavern with him and some other gentlemen, and too plainly discovered that he had drunk too much at dinner. When one who loved mischief,[3] thinking to produce a severe censure, asked Johnson, a few days afterwards, 'Well, Sir, what did your friend say to you, as an apology for being in such a situation?' Johnson answered, 'Sir, he said all that a man *should* say: he said he was sorry for it.'

I heard him once give a very judicious practical advice upon this subject: 'A man, who has been drinking wine at all freely, should never go into a new company. With those who have partaken of wine with him, he may be pretty well in unison; but he will probably be offensive, or appear ridiculous, to other people.'

He allowed very great influence to education. 'I do not deny,

---

[1] [Mrs. Fermor. *Powell.*]
[2] [Boswell. *Boswell Papers,* x. 168, 170.]
[3] [Colman. *Ib.* 170, *n.* 2.]

Sir, but there is some original difference in minds; but it is nothing in comparison of what is formed by education. We may instance the science of *numbers*, which all minds are equally capable of attaining; yet we find a prodigious difference in the powers of different men, in that respect, after they are grown up, because their minds have been more or less exercised in it: and I think the same cause will explain the difference of excellence in other things, gradations admitting always some difference in the first principles.'

This is a difficult subject; but it is best to hope that diligence may do a great deal. We are *sure* of what it can do, in increasing our mechanical force and dexterity.

I again visited him on Monday. He took occasion to enlarge, as he often did, upon the wretchedness of a sea-life. 'A ship is worse than a gaol. There is, in a gaol, better air, better company, better conveniency of every kind; and a ship has the additional disadvantage of being in danger. When men come to like a sea-life, they are not fit to live on land.'—'Then (said I) it would be cruel in a father to breed his son to the sea.' JOHNSON. 'It would be cruel in a father who thinks as I do. Men go to sea, before they know the unhappiness of that way of life; and when they have come to know it, they cannot escape from it, because it is then too late to choose another profession; as indeed is generally the case with men, when they have once engaged in any particular way of life.'

On Tuesday, March 19, which was fixed for our proposed jaunt, we met in the morning at the Somerset coffee-house in the Strand, where we were taken up by the Oxford coach. He was accompanied by Mr. Gwyn, the architect; and a gentleman of Merton College,[1] whom we did not know, had the fourth seat. We soon got into conversation; for it was very remarkable of Johnson, that the presence of a stranger was no restraint upon his talk. I observed that Garrick, who was about to quit the stage, would soon have an easier life. JOHNSON. 'I doubt that, Sir.' BOSWELL. 'Why, Sir, he will be Atlas with the burthen off his back.' JOHNSON. 'But I know not, Sir, if he will be so

---

[1] ['A young gentleman of Gloucestershire.' *Boswell Papers*, xi. 165.]

steady without his load. However, he should never play any
more, but be entirely the gentleman, and not partly the player:
he should no longer subject himself to be hissed by a mob, or to
be insolently treated by performers, whom he used to rule with
a high hand, and who would gladly retaliate.' BOSWELL. 'I
think he should play once a year for the benefit of decayed actors,
as it has been said he means to do.' JOHNSON. 'Alas, Sir! he
will soon be a decayed actor himself.'

Johnson expressed his disapprobation of ornamental architecture, such as magnificent columns supporting a portico, or expensive pilasters supporting merely their own capitals, 'because it
consumes labour disproportionate to its utility.' For the same
reason he satyrised statuary. 'Painting (said he) consumes
labour not disproportionate to its effect; but a fellow will hack
half a year at a block of marble to make something in stone that
hardly resembles a man. The value of statuary is owing to its
difficulty. You would not value the finest head cut upon a carrot.'
Here he seemed to me to be strangely deficient in taste; for
surely statuary is a noble art of imitation, and preserves a
wonderful expression of the varieties of the human frame; and
although it must be allowed that the circumstances of difficulty
enhance the value of a marble head, we should consider, that if
it requires a long time in the performance, it has a proportionate
value in durability.

Gwyn was a fine lively rattling fellow. Dr. Johnson kept him
in subjection, but with a kindly authority. The spirit of the artist,
however, rose against what he thought a Gothick attack, and he
made a brisk defence. 'What, Sir, will you allow no value to
beauty in architecture or in statuary? Why should we allow it
then in writing? Why do you take the trouble to give us so many
fine allusions, and bright images, and elegant phrases? You
might convey all your instruction without these ornaments.'
Johnson smiled with complacency; but said, 'Why, Sir, all these
ornaments are useful, because they obtain an easier reception
for truth; but a building is not at all more convenient for being
decorated with superfluous carved work.'

Gwyn at last was lucky enough to make one reply to Dr.

Johnson, which he allowed to be excellent. Johnson censured him for taking down a church which might have stood many years, and building a new one at a different place, for no other reason but that there might be a direct road to a new bridge; and his expression was, 'You are taking a church out of the way, that the people may go in a straight line to the bridge.'—'No, Sir, (said Gwyn,) I am putting the church *in* the way, that the people may not *go out of the way.*' Johnson. (with a hearty loud laugh of approbation,) 'Speak no more. Rest your colloquial fame upon this.'

Upon our arrival at Oxford, Dr. Johnson and I went directly to University College, but were disappointed on finding that one of the fellows, his friend Mr. Scott, who accompanied him from Newcastle to Edinburgh, was gone to the country. We put up at the Angel inn, and passed the evening by ourselves in easy and familiar conversation. Talking of constitutional melancholy, he observed, 'A man so afflicted, Sir, must divert distressing thoughts, and not combat with them.' Boswell. 'May not he think them down, Sir?' Johnson. 'No, Sir. To attempt to *think them down* is madness. He should have a lamp constantly burning in his bed-chamber during the night, and if wakefully disturbed, take a book, and read, and compose himself to rest. To have the management of the mind is a great art, and it may be attained in a considerable degree by experience and habitual exercise.' Boswell. 'Should not he provide amusements for himself? Would it not, for instance, be right for him to take a course of chymistry?' Johnson. 'Let him take a course of chymistry, or a course of rope-dancing, or a course of any thing to which he is inclined at the time. Let him contrive to have as many retreats for his mind as he can, as many things to which it can fly from itself. Burton's *Anatomy of Melancholy* is a valuable work. It is, perhaps, overloaded with quotation. But there is great spirit and great power in what Burton says, when he writes from his own mind.'

Next morning we visited Dr. Wetherell, Master of University College, with whom Dr. Johnson conferred on the most advantageous mode of disposing of the books printed at the

Clarendon press, on which subject his letter has been inserted in a former page. I often had occasion to remark, Johnson loved business, loved to have his wisdom actually operate on real life. Dr. Wetherell and I talked of him without reserve in his own presence. WETHERELL. 'I would have given him a hundred guineas if he would have written a preface to his *Political Tracts*, by way of a Discourse on the British Constitution.' BOSWELL. 'Dr. Johnson, though in his writings, and upon all occasions a great friend to the constitution both in church and state, has never written expressly in support of either. There is really a claim upon him for both. I am sure he could give a volume of no great bulk upon each, which would comprise all the substance, and with his spirit would effectually maintain them. He should erect a fort on the confines of each.' I could perceive that he was displeased with this dialogue. He burst out, 'Why should *I* be always writing?' I hoped he was conscious that the debt was just, and meant to discharge it, though he disliked being dunned.

We then went to Pembroke College, and waited on his old friend Dr. Adams, the master of it, whom I found to be a most polite, pleasing, communicative man. Before his advancement to the headship of his college, I had intended to go and visit him at Shrewsbury, where he was rector of St. Chad's, in order to get from him what particulars he could recollect of Johnson's academical life. He now obligingly gave me part of that authentick information, which, with what I afterwards owed to his kindness, will be found incorporated in its proper place in this work.

Dr. Adams had distinguished himself by an able answer to David Hume's *Essay on Miracles*. He told me he had once dined in company with Hume in London; that Hume shook hands with him, and said, 'You have treated me much better than I deserve;' and that they exchanged visits. I took the liberty to object to treating an infidel writer with smooth civility. Where there is a controversy concerning a passage in a classick authour, or concerning a question in antiquities, or any other subject in which human happiness is not deeply interested, a man may treat his antagonist with politeness and even respect. But where the controversy is concerning the truth of religion, it is of such vast importance to him who maintains it, to obtain the victory, that the person of an opponent ought not to be spared. If a man firmly believes that religion is an invaluable treasure, he will consider a writer who endeavours to deprive mankind of it as a *robber*; he will look upon him as *odious*, though the infidel might think himself in the right. A robber who reasons as the gang do in the *Beggar's Opera*, who call themselves *practical* philosophers, and may have as much sincerity as pernicious *speculative* philosophers, is not the less an object of just indignation. An abandoned profligate may think that it is not wrong to debauch my wife, but shall I, therefore, not detest him? And if I catch him in making an attempt, shall I treat him with politeness? No, I will kick him down stairs, or run him through the body; that is, if I really love my wife, or have a true rational notion of honour. An Infidel then shall not be treated handsomely by a Christian, merely because he endeavours to rob with ingenuity. I do declare, however, that I am exceedingly unwilling to be provoked to anger, and could I be persuaded that truth would not suffer from a cool moderation in its defenders, I should wish to preserve good humour, at least, in every controversy; nor, indeed, do I see why a man should lose his temper while he does all he can to refute an opponent. I think ridicule may be fairly used against an infidel; for instance, if he be an ugly fellow,[1] and yet absurdly vain of his person, we may contrast his appearance with Cicero's beautiful image of Virtue, could she be seen. Johnson coincided with me and said, 'When a man voluntarily engages in an important controversy, he is to do all he can to lessen his antagonist, because authority from personal respect has much weight with most people, and often more than reasoning. If my antagonist writes bad language, though that may not be essential to the question, I will attack him for his bad language.' ADAMS. 'You would not jostle a chimney-sweeper.' JOHNSON. 'Yes, Sir, if it were necessary to jostle him *down*.'

Dr. Adams told us, that in some of the Colleges at Oxford, the fellows had excluded the students from social intercourse with them in the common room. JOHNSON. 'They are in the right,

[1] [Probably Gibbon. *Powell*.]

Sir, for there can be no real conversation, no fair exertion of mind amongst them, if the young men are by; for a man who has a character does not choose to stake it in their presence.' BOSWELL. 'But, Sir, may there not be very good conversation without a contest for superiority?' JOHNSON. 'No animated conversation, Sir, for it cannot be but one or other will come off superiour. I do not mean that the victor must have the better of the argument, for he may take the weak side; but his superiority of parts and knowledge will necessarily appear: and he to whom he thus shews himself superiour is lessened in the eyes of the young men. You know it was said, *"Mallem cum Scaligero errare quam cum Clavio rectè sapere."*[1] In the same manner take Bentley's and Jason de Nores' Comments upon Horace, you will admire Bentley more when wrong, than Jason when right.'

We walked with Dr. Adams into the master's garden, and into the common room. JOHNSON. (after a reverie of meditation,) 'Ay! Here I used to play at draughts with Phil. Jones and Fludyer. Jones loved beer, and did not get very forward in the church. Fludyer turned out a scoundrel, a Whig, and said he was ashamed of having been bred at Oxford. He had a living at Putney, and got under the eye of some retainers to the court at that time, and so became a violent Whig: but he had been a scoundrel all along, to be sure.' BOSWELL. 'Was he a scoundrel, Sir, in any other way than that of being a political scoundrel? Did he cheat at draughts?' JOHNSON. 'Sir, we never played for *money*.'

He then carried me to visit Dr. Bentham, Canon of Christ-Church, and Divinity Professor, with whose learned and lively conversation we were much pleased. He gave us an invitation to dinner, which Dr. Johnson told me was a high honour. 'Sir, it is a great thing to dine with the Canons of Christ-Church.' We could not accept his invitation, as we were engaged to dine at University College. We had an excellent dinner there, with the Master and Fellows, it being St. Cuthbert's day, which is kept by them as a festival, as he was a saint of Durham, with which this college is much connected.

We drank tea with Dr. Horne, late President of Magdalen

---

[1] ['Better to err with Scaliger than to be right with Clavio.']

College, and Bishop of Norwich, of whose abilities, in different respects, the publick has had eminent proofs, and the esteem annexed to whose character was increased by knowing him personally. He had talked of publishing an edition of Walton's *Lives*, but had laid aside that design, upon Dr. Johnson's telling him, from mistake, that Lord Hailes intended to do it. I had wished to negociate between Lord Hailes and him, that one or other should perform so good a work. J o h n s o n. 'In order to do it well, it will be necessary to collect all the editions of Walton's *Lives*. By way of adapting the book to the taste of the present age, they have, in a later edition, left out a vision which he relates Dr. Donne had, but it should be restored; and there should be a critical catalogue given of the works of the different persons whose lives were written by Walton, and therefore their works must be carefully read by the editor.'

We then went to Trinity College, where he introduced me to Mr. Thomas Warton, with whom we passed a part of the evening. We talked of biography.—J o h n s o n. 'It is rarely well executed. They only who live with a man can write his life with any genuine exactness and discrimination; and few people who have lived with a man know what to remark about him. The chaplain of a late Bishop,[1] whom I was to assist in writing some memoirs of his Lordship, could tell me scarcely any thing.'[2]

I said, Mr. Robert Dodsley's life should be written, as he had been so much connected with the wits of his time, and by his literary merit had raised himself from the station of a footman. Mr. Warton said, he had published a little volume under the title of *The Muse in Livery*. J o h n s o n. 'I doubt whether Dodsley's brother would thank a man who should write his life: yet Dodsley himself was not unwilling that his original low

[1] [Rev. John Darby and Bp. Zachary Pearce. *Boswell Papers*, xi. 174.]
[2] It has been mentioned to me by an accurate English friend,* that Dr. Johnson could never have used the phrase *almost nothing*, as not being English; and therefore I have put another in its place. At the same time, I am not quite convinced it is not good English. For the best writers use the phrase '*Little or nothing*;' i.e. almost so little as to be nothing.

* [The phrase was objected to as a Scotticism by 'G' in the *Monthly Review*, 1792, viii. 79.]

condition should be recollected. When Lord Lyttelton's *Dialogues of the Dead* came out, one of which is between Apicius, an ancient epicure, and Dartineuf, a modern epicure, Dodsley said to me, "I knew Dartineuf well, for I was once his footman." '

Biography led us to speak of Dr. John Campbell, who had written a considerable part of the *Biographia Britannica.* Johnson, though he valued him highly, was of opinion that there was not so much in his great work, *A Political Survey of Great Britain,* as the world had been taught to expect;[1] and had said to me, that he believed Campbell's disappointment, on account of the bad success of that work, had killed him. He this evening observed of it, 'That work was his death.' Mr. Warton, not adverting to his meaning, answered, 'I believe so; from the great attention he bestowed on it.' JOHNSON. 'Nay, Sir, he died of *want* of attention, if he died at all by that book.'

We talked of a work much in vogue at that time, written in a very mellifluous style, but which, under pretext of another subject, contained much artful infidelity. I said it was not fair to attack us thus unexpectedly; he should have warned us of our danger, before we entered his garden of flowery eloquence, by advertising, 'Spring-guns and men-traps set here.' The authour[2] had been an Oxonian, and was remembered there for having 'turned Papist'. I observed, that as he had changed several times —from the Church of England to the Church of Rome,—from the Church of Rome to infidelity,—I did not despair yet of seeing him a methodist preacher. JOHNSON. (laughing,) 'It is said, that his range has been more extensive, and that he has once been Mahometan. However, now that he has published his infidelity, he will probably persist in it.' BOSWELL. 'I am not quite sure of that, Sir.'

I mentioned Sir Richard Steele having published his *Christian Hero,* with the avowed purpose of obliging himself to lead a religious life; yet, that his conduct was by no means strictly suitable. JOHNSON. 'Steele, I believe, practised the lighter vices.'

---

[1] Yet surely it is a very useful work, and of wonderful research and labour for one man to have executed.

[2] [Gibbon. *Boswell Papers*, xi. 175, 177.]

Mr. Warton, being engaged, could not sup with us at our inn; we had therefore another evening by ourselves. I asked Johnson, whether a man's[1] being forward in making himself known to eminent people, and seeing as much of life, and getting as much information as he could in every way, was not yet lessening himself by his forwardness. JOHNSON. 'No, Sir; a man always makes himself greater as he increases his knowledge.'

I censured some ludicrous fantastick dialogues between two coach-horses, and other such stuff, which Baretti had lately published. He joined with me, and said, 'Nothing odd will do long. *Tristram Shandy* did not last.' I expressed a desire to be acquainted with a lady who had been much talked of,[2] and universally celebrated for extraordinary address and insinuation. JOHNSON. 'Never believe extraordinary characters which you hear of people. Depend upon it, Sir, they are exaggerated. You do not see one man shoot a great deal higher than another.' I mentioned Mr. Burke. JOHNSON. 'Yes; Burke *is* an extraordinary man. His stream of mind is perpetual.' It is very pleasing to me to record, that Johnson's high estimation of the talents of this gentleman was uniform from their early acquaintance. Sir Joshua Reynolds informs me, that when Mr. Burke was first elected a member of Parliament, and Sir John Hawkins expressed a wonder at his attaining a seat, Johnson said, 'Now we who know Burke, know, that he will be one of the first men in this country.' And once, when Johnson was ill, and unable to exert himself as much as usual without fatigue, Mr. Burke having been mentioned, he said, 'That fellow calls forth all my powers. Were I to see Burke now, it would kill me.' So much was he accustomed to consider conversation as a contest, and such was his notion of Burke as an opponent.

Next morning, Thursday, March 21, we set out in a post-chaise to pursue our ramble. It was a delightful day, and we drove through Blenheim park. When I looked at the magnificent bridge built by John Duke of Marlborough, over a small rivulet, and recollected the Epigram made upon it—

[1] [Boswell. *Boswell Papers*, xi. 176.]
[2] [Mrs. Caroline Rudd. *Ib.* 202.]

> 'The lofty arch his high ambition shows,
> The stream, an emblem of his bounty flows:'

and saw that now, by the genius of Brown, a magnificent body of water was collected, I said, 'They have *drowned* the Epigram.' I observed to him, while in the midst of the noble scene around us, 'You and I, Sir, have, I think, seen together the extremes of what can be seen in Britain:—the wild rough island of Mull, and Blenheim Park.'

We dined at an excellent inn at Chapel-house, where he expatiated on the felicity of England in its taverns and inns, and triumphed over the French for not having, in any perfection, the tavern life. 'There is no private house, (said he,) in which people can enjoy themselves so well, as at a capital tavern. Let there be ever so great plenty of good things, ever so much grandeur, ever so much elegance, ever so much desire that every body should be easy; in the nature of things it cannot be: there must always be some degree of care and anxiety. The master of the house is anxious to entertain his guests; the guests are anxious to be agreeable to him: and no man, but a very impudent dog indeed, can as freely command what is in another man's house, as if it were his own. Whereas, at a tavern, there is a general freedom from anxiety. You are sure you are welcome: and the more noise you make, the more trouble you give, the more good things you call for, the welcomer you are. No servants will attend you with the alacrity which waiters do, who are incited by the prospect of an immediate reward in proportion as they please. No, Sir; there is nothing which has yet been contrived by man, by which so much happiness is produced as by a good tavern or inn.'[1] He then repeated, with great emotion, Shenstone's lines:—

> 'Whoe'er has travell'd life's dull round,
> Where'er his stages may have been,

[1] Sir John Hawkins has preserved very few *Memorabilia* of Johnson. There is, however, to be found, in his bulky tome [p. 87], a very excellent one upon this subject:—'In contradiction to those, who, having a wife and children, prefer domestick enjoyments to those which a tavern affords, I have heard him assert, *that a tavern chair was the throne of human felicity.*— "As soon," said he, "as I enter the door of a tavern, I experience an oblivion

> May sigh to think he still has found
> The warmest welcome at an inn.'[1]

My illustrious friend, I thought, did not sufficiently admire Shenstone. That ingenious and elegant gentleman's opinion of Johnson appears in one of his letters to Mr. Graves, dated Feb. 9, 1760. 'I have lately been reading one or two volumes of *The Rambler*; who, excepting against some few hardnesses[2] in his manner, and the want of more examples to enliven, is one of the most nervous, most perspicuous, most concise, [and] most harmonious prose writers I know. A learned diction improves by time.'

In the afternoon, as we were driven rapidly along in the post-chaise, he said to me 'Life has not many things better than this.'

We stopped at Stratford-upon-Avon, and drank tea and coffee; and it pleased me to be with him upon the classick ground of Shakspeare's native place.

He spoke slightingly of Dyer's *Fleece.*—'The subject, Sir, cannot be made poetical. How can a man write poetically of serges and druggets? Yet you will hear many people talk to you gravely of that *excellent* poem, *The Fleece.*' Having talked of Grainger's *Sugar-Cane*, I mentioned to him Mr. Langton's having told me, that this poem, when read in manuscript at Sir Joshua Reynolds's, had made all the assembled wits burst into a laugh, when, after much blank-verse pomp, the poet began a new paragraph thus:—

> 'Now, Muse, let's sing of *rats.*'

of care, and a freedom from solicitude: when I am seated, I find the master courteous, and the servants obsequious to my call; anxious to know and ready to supply my wants: wine there exhilarates my spirits, and prompts me to free conversation and an interchange of discourse with those whom I most love: I dogmatise and am contradicted, and in this conflict of opinions and sentiments I find delight." '

[1] We happened to lie this night at the inn at Henley, where Shenstone wrote these lines. I give them as they are found in the corrected edition of his Works, published after his death. In Dodsley's collection the stanza ran thus:—

> 'Whoe'er has travell'd life's dull round,
> Whate'er his *various tour has* been,
> May sigh to think *how oft* he found
> *His* warmest welcome at an Inn.'

[2] 'He too often makes use of the *abstract* for the *concrete.*' SHENSTONE.

And what increased the ridicule was, that one of the company, who slily overlooked the reader, perceived that the word had been originally *mice*, and had been altered to *rats*, as more dignified.[1]

This passage does not appear in the printed work. Dr. Grainger, or some of his friends, it should seem, having become sensible that introducing even *Rats* in a grave poem, might be liable to banter. He, however, could not bring himself to relinquish the idea; for they are thus, in a still more ludicrous manner, periphrastically exhibited in his poem as it now stands:

> 'Nor with less waste the whisker'd vermin race
> A countless clan despoil the lowland cane.'

Johnson said, that Dr. Grainger was an agreeable man; a man who would do any good that was in his power. His translation of *Tibullus*, he thought, was very well done; but *The Sugar-Cane*, a poem, did not please him;[2] for, he exclaimed, 'What could he make of a sugar-cane? One might as well write the "Parsley-bed, a Poem;" or "The Cabbage-garden, a Poem." ' BOSWELL. 'You must then *pickle* your cabbage with the *sal atticum*.'[3] JOHNSON.

---

[1] Such is this little laughable incident, which has been often related. Dr. Percy, the Bishop of Dromore, who was an intimate friend of Dr. Grainger, and has a particular regard for his memory, has communicated to me the following explanation:—

'The passage in question was originally not liable to such a perversion; for the authour having occasion in that part of his work to mention the havock made by rats and mice, had introduced the subject in a kind of mock heroick, and a parody of Homer's battle of the frogs and mice, invoking the Muse of the old Grecian bard in an elegant and well-turned manner. In that state I had seen it; but afterwards, unknown to me and other friends, he had been persuaded, contrary to his own better judgement, to alter it, so as to produce the unlucky effect above-mentioned.'

The above was written by the Bishop when he had not the Poem itself to recur to; and though the account given was true of it at one period, yet as Dr. Grainger afterwards altered the passage in question, the remarks in the text do not now apply to the printed poem.

The Bishop gives this character of Dr. Grainger:—'He was not only a man of genius and learning, but had many excellent virtues; being one of the most generous, friendly, and benevolent men I ever knew.'

[2] Dr. Johnson said to me, 'Percy, Sir, was angry with me for laughing at *The Sugar-Cane*: for he had a mind to make a great thing of Grainger's rats.'

[3] [Attic salt.]

'You know there is already *The Hop-Garden*, a Poem: and, I think, one could say a great deal about cabbage. The poem might begin with the advantages of civilized society over a rude state, exemplified by the Scotch, who had no cabbages till Oliver Cromwell's soldiers introduced them, and one might thus shew how arts are propagated by conquest, as they were by the Roman arms.' He seemed to be much diverted with the fertility of his own fancy.

I told him, that I heard Dr. Percy was writing the history of the wolf in Great-Britain. JOHNSON. 'The wolf, Sir! why the wolf? Why does he not write of the bear, which we had formerly? Nay, it is said we had the beaver. Or why does he not write of the grey rat, the Hanover rat, as it is called, because it is said to have come into this country about the time that the family of Hanover came? I should like to see *The History of the Grey Rat, by Thomas Percy, D.D., Chaplain in Ordinary to His Majesty*,' (laughing immoderately). BOSWELL. 'I am afraid a court chaplain could not decently write of the grey rat.' JOHNSON. 'Sir, he need not give it the name of the Hanover rat.' Thus could he indulge a luxuriant sportive imagination, when talking of a friend whom he loved and esteemed.

He mentioned to me the singular history of an ingenious acquaintance.[1] 'He had practised physick in various situations with no great emolument. A West-India gentleman,[1] whom he delighted by his conversation, gave him a bond for a handsome annuity during his life, on the condition of his accompanying him to the West-Indies, and living with him there for two years. He accordingly embarked with the gentleman; but upon the voyage fell in love with a young woman[1] who happened to be one of the passengers, and married the wench. From the imprudence of his disposition he quarrelled with the gentleman, and declared he would have no connection with him. So he forfeited the annuity. He settled as a physician in one of the Leeward Islands. A man was sent out to him merely to compound his medicines. This fellow set up as a rival to him in his practice of physick, and got so much the better of him in the opinion of the people of the

[1] [James Grainger, Mr. Bourryau, and Miss Burt. *Boswell Papers*, xi. 180.]

island that he carried away all the business, upon which he returned to England, and soon after died.'

On Friday, March 22, having set out early from Henley, where we had lain the preceding night, we arrived at Birmingham about nine o'clock, and, after breakfast, went to call on his old school-fellow Mr. Hector.[1] A very stupid maid, who opened the door, told us, that 'her master was gone out; he was gone to the country; she could not tell when he would return.' In short, she gave us a miserable reception; and Johnson observed, 'She would have behaved no better to people who wanted him in the way of his profession.' He said to her, 'My name is Johnson; tell him I called. Will you remember the name?' She answered with rustick simplicity, in the Warwickshire pronunciation, 'I don't understand you, Sir.'—'Blockhead, (said he,) I'll write.' I never heard the word *blockhead* applied to a woman before, though I do not see why it should not, when there is evident occasion for it.[2] He, however, made another attempt to make her understand him, and roared loud in her ear, '*Johnson*,' and then she catched the sound.

We next called on Mr. Lloyd, one of the people called Quakers. He too was not at home; but Mrs. Lloyd was, and received us courteously, and asked us to dinner. Johnson said to me, 'After the uncertainty of all human things at Hector's, this invitation came very well.' We walked about the town, and he was pleased to see it increasing.

[1] Mr. Hector's house was in the Square—now known as the Old Square. It afterwards formed part of the Stork Hotel, but it was pulled down when Corporation Street was made. A marble tablet had been placed on the house at the suggestion of the late Mr. George Dawson, marking the spot where 'Edmund Hector was the host, Samuel Johnson the guest.' This tablet, together with the wainscoting, the door, and the mantelpiece of one of the rooms, was set up in Aston Hall, at the Johnson Centenary, in a room that is to be known as Dr. Johnson's Room.

[2] My worthy friend Mr. Langton, to whom I am under innumerable obligations in the course of my Johnsonian History, has furnished me with a droll illustration of this question. An honest carpenter, after giving some anecdote in his presence of the ill-treatment which he had received from a clergyman's wife, who was a noted termagant, and whom he accused of unjust dealing in some transaction with him, added, 'I took care to let her know what I thought of her.' And being asked, 'What did you say?' answered, 'I told her she was a *scoundrel*.'

I talked of legitimation by subsequent marriage, which obtained in the Roman law, and still obtains in the law of Scotland. JOHNSON. 'I think it a bad thing; because the chastity of women being of the utmost importance, as all property depends upon it, they who forfeit it should not have any possibility of being restored to good character; nor should the children, by an illicit connection, attain the full rights of lawful children, by the posteriour consent of the offending parties.' His opinion upon this subject deserves consideration. Upon his principle there may, at times, be a hardship, and seemingly a strange one, upon individuals; but the general good of society is better secured. And, after all, it is unreasonable in an individual to repine that he has not the advantage of a state which is made different from his own, by the social institution under which he is born. A woman does not complain that her brother, who is younger than her, gets their common father's estate. Why then should a natural son complain that a younger brother, by the same parents lawfully begotten, gets it? The operation of law is similar in both cases. Besides, an illegitimate son, who has a younger legitimate brother by the same father and mother, has no stronger claim to the father's estate, than if that legitimate brother had only the same father, from whom alone the estate descends.

Mr. Lloyd joined us in the street; and in a little while we met *Friend Hector*, as Mr. Lloyd called him. It gave me pleasure to observe the joy which Johnson and he expressed on seeing each other again. Mr. Lloyd and I left them together, while he obligingly shewed me some of the manufactures of this very curious assemblage of artificers. We all met at dinner at Mr. Lloyd's, where we were entertained with great hospitality. Mr. and Mrs. Lloyd had been married the same year with their Majesties, and, like them, had been blessed with a numerous family of fine children, their numbers being exactly the same. Johnson said, 'Marriage is the best state for man in general; and every man is a worse man, in proportion as he is unfit for the married state.'

I have always loved the simplicity of manners, and the spiritual-mindedness of the Quakers; and talking with Mr. Lloyd, I observed, that the essential part of religion was piety, a devout intercourse with the Divinity; and that many a man was a Quaker without knowing it.

As Dr. Johnson had said to me in the morning, while we walked together, that he liked individuals among the Quakers, but not the sect; when we were at Mr. Lloyd's, I kept clear of introducing any question concerning the peculiarities of their faith. But I having asked to look at Baskerville's edition of *Barclay's Apology*, Johnson laid hold of it; and the chapter on baptism happening to open, Johnson remarked, 'He says there is neither precept nor practice for baptism, in the scriptures; that is false.' Here he was the aggressor, by no means in a gentle manner; and the good Quakers had the advantage of him; for he had read negligently, and had not observed that Barclay speaks of *infant* baptism; which they calmly made him perceive. Mr. Lloyd, however, was in as great a mistake; for when insisting that the rite of baptism by water was to cease, when the *spiritual* administration of CHRIST began, he maintained, that John the Baptist said, '*My baptism* shall decrease, but *his* shall increase.' Whereas the words are, '*He* must increase, but *I* must decrease.'[1]

One of them having objected to the 'observance of days, and months, and years,' Johnson answered, 'The Church does not superstitiously observe days, merely as days, but as memorials of important facts. Christmas might be kept as well upon one day of the year as another; but there should be a stated day for commemorating the birth of our Saviour, because there is danger that what may be done on any day, will be neglected.'

He said to me at another time, 'Sir, the holidays observed by our church are of great use in religion.' There can be no doubt of this, in a limited sense, I mean if the number of such consecrated portions of time be not too extensive. The excellent Mr. Nelson's *Festivals and Fasts*, which has, I understand, the greatest sale of any book ever printed in England, except the Bible, is a most valuable help to devotion; and in addition to it I would recommend two sermons on the same subject, by Mr. Pott, Archdeacon of St. Alban's, equally distinguished for piety and elegance. I am sorry to have it to say, that Scotland is the

---

[1] *John* iii. 30.

only Christian country, Catholick or Protestant, where the great events of our religion are not solemnly commemorated by its ecclesiastical establishment, on days set apart for the purpose.

Mr. Hector was so good as to accompany me to see the great works of Mr. Bolton, at a place which he has called Soho, about two miles from Birmingham, which the very ingenious proprietor shewed me himself to the best advantage. I wish that Johnson had been with us: for it was a scene which I should have been glad to contemplate by his light. The vastness and the contrivance of some of the machinery would have 'matched his mighty mind'. I shall never forget Mr. Bolton's expression to me: 'I sell here, Sir, what all the world desires to have—POWER.' He had about seven hundred people at work. I contemplated him as an *iron chieftain*, and he seemed to be a father to his tribe. One of them came to him, complaining grievously of his landlord for having distrained his goods. 'Your landlord is in the right, Smith, (said Bolton). But I'll tell you what: find you a friend who will lay down one half of your rent, and I'll lay down the other half; and you shall have your goods again.'

From Mr. Hector I now learnt many particulars of Dr. Johnson's early life, which, with others that he gave me at different times since, have contributed to the formation of this work.

Dr. Johnson said to me in the morning, 'You will see, Sir, at Mr. Hector's, his sister, Mrs. Careless, a clergyman's widow. She was the first woman with whom I was in love. It dropt out of my head imperceptibly; but she and I shall always have a kindness for each other.' He laughed at the notion that a man never can be really in love but once, and considered it as a mere romantick fancy.

On our return from Mr. Bolton's, Mr. Hector took me to his house, where we found Johnson sitting placidly at tea, with his *first love*; who, though now advanced in years, was a genteel woman, very agreeable, and well-bred.

Johnson lamented to Mr. Hector the state of one of their school-fellows, Mr. Charles Congreve, a clergyman, which he thus described: 'He obtained, I believe, considerable preferment in Ireland, but now lives in London, quite as a valetudinarian, afraid to go into any house but his own. He takes a short airing in his post-chaise every day. He has an elderly woman, whom he calls cousin, who lives with him, and jogs his elbow when his glass has stood too long empty, and encourages him in drinking, in which he is very willing to be encouraged; not that he gets drunk, for he is a very pious man, but he is always muddy. He confesses to one bottle of port every day, and he probably drinks more. He is quite unsocial; his conversation is monosyllabical: and when, at my last visit, I asked him what a clock it was? that signal of my departure had so pleasing an effect on him, that he sprung up to look at his watch, like a greyhound bounding at a hare.' When Johnson took leave of Mr. Hector, he said, 'Don't grow like Congreve; nor let me grow like him, when you are near me.'

When he again talked of Mrs. Careless to-night, he seemed to have had his affection revived; for he said, 'If I had married her, it might have been as happy for me.' Boswell. 'Pray, Sir, do you not suppose that there are fifty women in the world, with any one of whom a man may be as happy, as with any one woman in particular?' Johnson. 'Ay, Sir, fifty thousand.' Boswell. 'Then, Sir, you are not of opinion with some who imagine that certain men and certain women are made for each other; and that they cannot be happy if they miss their counterparts?' Johnson. 'To be sure not, Sir. I believe marriages would in general be as happy, and often more so, if they were all made by the Lord Chancellor, upon a due consideration of characters and circumstances, without the parties having any choice in the matter.'

I wished to have staid at Birmingham to-night, to have talked more with Mr. Hector; but my friend was impatient to reach his native city; so we drove on that stage in the dark, and were long pensive and silent. When we came within the focus of the Lichfield lamps, 'Now (said he,) we are getting out of a state of death.' We put up at the Three Crowns, not one of the great inns, but a good old fashioned one, which was kept by Mr. Wilkins, and was the very next house to that in which Johnson was born and brought up, and which was still his own property.[1]

[1] I went through the house where my illustrious friend was born, with

We had a comfortable supper, and got into high spirits. I felt all my Toryism glow in this old capital of Staffordshire. I could have offered incense *genio loci*;[1] and I indulged in libations of that ale, which Boniface, in *The Beaux Stratagem,* recommends with such an eloquent jollity.

Next morning he introduced me to Mrs. Lucy Porter, his step-daughter. She was now an old maid, with much simplicity of manner. She had never been in London. Her brother, a Captain in the navy, had left her a fortune of ten thousand pounds; about a third of which she had laid out in building a stately house, and making a handsome garden, in an elevated situation in Lichfield. Johnson, when here by himself, used to live at her house. She reverenced him, and he had a parental tenderness for her.

We then visited Mr. Peter Garrick, who had that morning received a letter from his brother David, announcing our coming to Lichfield. He was engaged to dinner, but asked us to tea, and to sleep at his house. Johnson, however, would not quit his old acquaintance Wilkins, of the Three Crowns. The family likeness of the Garricks was very striking; and Johnson thought that David's vivacity was not so peculiar to himself as was supposed. 'Sir, (said he,) I don't know but if Peter had cultivated all the arts of gaiety as much as David has done, he might have been as brisk and lively. Depend upon it, Sir, vivacity is much an art, and depends greatly on habit.' I believe there is a good deal of truth in this, notwithstanding a ludicrous story told me by a lady abroad,[2] of a heavy German baron, who had lived much with the young English at Geneva, and was ambitious to be as lively as they; with which view, he, with assiduous exertion, was jumping over the tables and chairs in his lodgings; and when the people of the house ran in and asked, with surprize, what was the matter, he answered, '*Sh' apprens t'etre fif.*'

We dined at our inn, and had with us a Mr. Jackson, one of

a reverence with which it doubtless will long be visited. An engraved view of it, with the adjacent buildings, is in *The Gent. Mag.* for Feb. 1785.

[1] [To the presiding spirit of the place.']

[2] [Isabelle de Zuylen (Zélide). *Boswelliana,* p. 220.]

Johnson's schoolfellows, whom he treated with much kindness, though he seemed to be a low man, dull and untaught. He had a coarse grey coat, black waistcoat, greasy leather breeches, and a yellow uncurled wig; and his countenance had the ruddiness which betokens one who is in no haste to 'leave his can.' He drank only ale. He had tried to be a cutler at Birmingham, but had not succeeded; and now he lived poorly at home, and had some scheme of dressing leather in a better manner than common; to his indistinct account of which, Dr. Johnson listened with patient attention, that he might assist him with his advice. Here was an instance of genuine humanity and real kindness in this great man, who has been most unjustly represented as altogether harsh and destitute of tenderness. A thousand such instances might have been recorded in the course of his long life; though, that his temper was warm and hasty, and his manner often rough, cannot be denied.

I saw here, for the first time, *oat ale*; and oat cakes not hard as in Scotland, but soft like a Yorkshire cake, were served at breakfast. It was pleasant to me to find, that *Oats*, the *food of horses*, were so much used as the *food of the people* in Dr. Johnson's own town. He expatiated in praise of Lichfield and its inhabitants, who, he said, were 'the most sober, decent people in England, the genteelest in proportion to their wealth, and spoke the purest English.' I doubted as to the last article of this eulogy: for they had several provincial sounds; as, *there*, pronounced like *fear*, instead of like *fair*; *once* pronounced *woonse*, instead of *wunse*, or *wonse*. Johnson himself never got entirely free of those provincial accents. Garrick sometimes used to take him off, squeezing a lemon into a punch-bowl, with uncouth gesticulations, looking round the company, and calling out, 'Who's for *poonsh*?'

Very little business appeared to be going forward in Lichfield. I found however two strange manufactures for so inland a place, sail-cloth and streamers for ships; and I observed them making some saddle-cloths, and dressing sheepskins: but upon the whole, the busy hand of industry seemed to be quite slackened. 'Surely, Sir, (said I,) you are an idle set of people.' 'Sir, (said

Johnson,) we are a city of philosophers: we work with our heads, and make the boobies of Birmingham work for us with their hands.'

There was at this time a company of players performing at Lichfield. The manager, Mr. Stanton, sent his compliments, and begged leave to wait on Dr. Johnson. Johnson received him very courteously, and he drank a glass of wine with us. He was a plain decent well-behaved man, and expressed his gratitude to Dr. Johnson for having once got him permission from Dr. Taylor at Ashbourne to play there upon moderate terms. Garrick's name was soon introduced. J O H N S O N. 'Garrick's conversation is gay and grotesque. It is a dish of all sorts, but all good things. There is no solid meat in it: there is a want of sentiment in it. Not but that he has sentiment sometimes, and sentiment, too, very powerful and very pleasing: but it has not its full proportion in his conversation.'

When we were by ourselves he told me, 'Forty years ago, Sir, I was in love with an actress here, Mrs. Emmet, who acted Flora, in *Hob in the Well*.' What merit this lady had as an actress, or what was her figure, or her manner, I have not been informed: but, if we may believe Mr. Garrick, his old master's taste in theatrical merit was by no means refined; he was not an *elegans formarum spectator*.[1] Garrick used to tell, that Johnson said of an actor, who played Sir Harry Wildair at Lichfield, 'There is a courtly vivacity about the fellow;' when in fact, according to Garrick's account, 'he was the most vulgar ruffian that ever went upon *boards*.'

We had promised Mr. Stanton to be at his theatre on Monday. Dr. Johnson jocularly proposed me to write a Prologue for the occasion: 'A Prologue, by James Boswell, Esq. from the Hebrides.' I was really inclined to take the hint. Methought, 'Prologue, spoken before Dr. Samuel Johnson, at Lichfield, 1776;' would have sounded as well as, 'Prologue, spoken before the Duke of York, at Oxford,' in Charles the Second's time. Much might have been said of what Lichfield had done for

---

[1] ['A nice observer of the female form.' Terence, *Eunuchus*, iii. 5. (*Croker*.)]

Shakspeare, by producing Johnson and Garrick. But I found he was averse to it.

We went and viewed the museum of Mr. Richard Green, apothecary here, who told me he was proud of being a relation of Dr. Johnson's. It was, truely, a wonderful collection, both of antiquities and natural curiosities, and ingenious works of art. He had all the articles accurately arranged, with their names upon labels, printed at his own little press; and on the staircase leading to it was a board, with the names of contributors marked in gold letters. A printed catalogue of the collection was to be had at a bookseller's. Johnson expressed his admiration of the activity and diligence and good fortune of Mr. Green, in getting together, in his situation, so great a variety of things; and Mr. Green told me that Johnson once said to him, 'Sir, I should as soon have thought of building a man of war, as of collecting such a museum.' Mr. Green's obliging alacrity in shewing it was very pleasing. His engraved portrait, with which he has favoured me, has a motto truely characteristical of his disposition, '*Nemo sibi vivat.*'[1]

A physician[2] being mentioned who had lost his practice, because his whimsically changing his religion had made people distrustful of him, I maintained that this was unreasonable, as religion is unconnected with medical skill. JOHNSON. 'Sir, it is not unreasonable; for when people see a man absurd in what they understand, they may conclude the same of him in what they do not understand. If a physician were to take to eating of horse-flesh, nobody would employ him; though one may eat horse-flesh, and be a very skilful physician. If a man were educated in an absurd religion, his continuing to profess it would not hurt him, though his changing to it would.'

We drank tea and coffee at Mr. Peter Garrick's, where was Mrs. Aston, one of the maiden sisters of Mrs. Walmsley, wife of Johnson's first friend, and sister also of the lady of whom Johnson used to speak with the warmest admiration, by the name of Molly Aston, who was afterwards married to Captain Brodie of the navy.

---

[1] ['Let no man live for himself.']
[2] [Dr. John Boswell. J. B.'s uncle. *Boswell Papers*, xi. 192.]

On Sunday, March 24, we breakfasted with Mrs. Cobb, a widow lady, who lived in an agreeable sequestered place close by the town, called the Friary, it having been formerly a religious house. She and her niece, Miss Adey, were great admirers of Dr. Johnson; and he behaved to them with a kindness and easy pleasantry, such as we see between old and intimate acquaintance. He accompanied Mrs. Cobb to St. Mary's church, and I went to the cathedral, where I was very much delighted with the musick, finding it to be peculiarly solemn and accordant with the words of the service.

We dined at Mr. Peter Garrick's, who was in a very lively humour, and verified Johnson's saying, that if he had cultivated gaiety as much as his brother David, he might have equally excelled in it. He was to-day quite a London narrator, telling us a variety of anecdotes with that earnestness and attempt at mimicry which we usually find in the wits of the metropolis. Dr. Johnson went with me to the cathedral in the afternoon. It was grand and pleasing to contemplate this illustrious writer, now full of fame, worshipping in the 'solemn temple' of his native city.

I returned to tea and coffee at Mr. Peter Garrick's, and then found Dr. Johnson at the Reverend Mr. Seward's, Canon Residentiary, who inhabited the Bishop's palace, in which Mr. Walmsley lived, and which had been the scene of many happy hours in Johnson's early life. Mr. Seward had, with ecclesiastical hospitality and politeness, asked me in the morning, merely as a stranger, to dine with him; and in the afternoon, when I was introduced to him, he asked Dr. Johnson and me to spend the evening and sup with him. He was a genteel well-bred dignified clergyman, had travelled with Lord Charles Fitzroy, uncle of the present Duke of Grafton, who died when abroad, and he had lived much in the great world. He was an ingenious and literary man, had published an edition of Beaumont and Fletcher, and written verses in Dodsley's collection. His lady was the daughter of Mr. Hunter, Johnson's first schoolmaster. And now, for the first time, I had the pleasure of seeing his celebrated daughter, Miss Anna Seward, to whom I have since been indebted for many civilities, as well as some obliging communications concerning Johnson.

Mr. Seward mentioned to us the observations which he had made upon the strata of earth in volcanos, from which it appeared, that they were so very different in depth at different periods, that no calculation whatever could be made as to the time required for their formation. This fully refuted an anti-mosaical remark introduced into Captain Brydone's entertaining tour, I hope heedlessly, from a kind of vanity which is too common in those who have not sufficiently studied the most important of all subjects. Dr. Johnson, indeed, had said before, independent of this observation, 'Shall all the accumulated evidence of the history of the world;—shall the authority of what is unquestionably the most ancient writing, be overturned by an uncertain remark such as this?'

On Monday, March 25, we breakfasted at Mrs. Lucy Porter's. Johnson had sent an express to Dr. Taylor's, acquainting him of our being at Lichfield, and Taylor had returned an answer that his postchaise should come for us this day. While we sat at breakfast, Dr. Johnson received a letter by the post, which seemed to agitate him very much. When he had read it, he exclaimed, 'One of the most dreadful things that has happened in my time.' The phrase *my time*, like the word *age*, is usually understood to refer to an event of a publick or general nature. I imagined something like an assassination of the King—like a gunpowder plot carried into execution—or like another fire of London. When asked, 'What is it, Sir?' he answered, 'Mr. Thrale has lost his only son!' This was, no doubt, a very great affliction to Mr. and Mrs. Thrale, which their friends would consider accordingly; but from the manner in which the intelligence of it was communicated by Johnson, it appeared for the moment to be comparatively small. I, however, soon felt a sincere concern, and was curious to observe, how Dr. Johnson would be affected. He said, 'This is a total extinction to their family, as much as if they were sold into captivity.' Upon my mentioning that Mr. Thrale had daughters, who might inherit his wealth;— 'Daughters, (said Johnson, warmly,) he'll no more value his daughters than—' I was going to speak.—'Sir, (said he,) don't you know how you yourself think? Sir, he wishes to propagate his name.' In short, I saw male succession strong in his mind, even where there was no name, no family of any long standing. I said, it was lucky he was not present when this misfortune happened. JOHNSON. 'It is lucky for *me*. People in distress never think that you feel enough.' BOSWELL. 'And Sir, they will have the hope of seeing you, which will be a relief in the mean time; and when you get to them, the pain will be so far abated, that they will be capable of being consoled by you, which, in the first violence of it, I believe, would not be the case.' JOHNSON. 'No, Sir; violent pain of mind, like violent pain of body, *must* be severely felt.' BOSWELL. 'I own, Sir, I have not so much feeling for the distress of others, as some people have, or pretend to have: but I know this, that I would do all in my power to relieve them.' JOHNSON. 'Sir, it is affectation to pretend to feel the distress of others, as much as they do themselves. It is equally so, as if one should pretend to feel as much pain while a friend's leg is cutting off, as he does. No, Sir; you have expressed the rational and just nature of sympathy. I would have gone to the extremity of the earth to have preserved this boy.'

He was soon quite calm. The letter was from Mr. Thrale's clerk, and concluded, 'I need not say how much they wish to see you in London.' He said, 'We shall hasten back from Taylor's.'

Mrs. Lucy Porter and some other ladies of the place talked a great deal of him when he was out of the room, not only with veneration but affection. It pleased me to find that he was so much *beloved* in his native city.

Mrs. Aston, whom I had seen the preceding night, and her sister, Mrs. Gastrel, a widow lady, had each a house and garden, and pleasure-ground, prettily situated upon Stowhill, a gentle eminence adjoining to Lichfield. Johnson walked away to dinner there, leaving me by myself without any apology; I wondered at this want of that facility of manners, from which a man has no difficulty in carrying a friend to a house where he is intimate; I felt it very unpleasant to be thus left in solitude in a country town, where I was an entire stranger, and began to think myself unkindly deserted: but I was soon relieved, and convinced that my friend, instead of being deficient in delicacy, had conducted the matter with perfect propriety, for I received the following note in his handwriting: 'Mrs. Gastrel, at the lower house on Stowhill, desires Mr. Boswell's company to dinner at two.' I accepted of the invitation, and had here another proof how amiable his character was in the opinion of those who knew him best. I was not informed, till afterwards, that Mrs. Gastrel's husband was the clergyman who, while he lived at Stratford upon Avon, where he was proprietor of Shakspeare's garden, with Gothick barbarity cut down his mulberry-tree,[1] and, as Dr. Johnson told me, did it to vex his neighbours. His lady, I have reason to believe, on the same authority, participated in the guilt of what the enthusiasts for our immortal bard deem almost a species of sacrilege.

After dinner Dr. Johnson wrote a letter to Mrs. Thrale on the death of her son. I said it would be very distressing to Thrale, but she would soon forget it, as she had so many things to think of. JOHNSON. 'No, Sir, Thrale will forget it first. *She* has many things that she *may* think of. *He* has many things that he *must* think of.' This was a very just remark upon the different effect of those light pursuits which occupy a vacant and easy mind, and those serious engagements which arrest attention, and keep us from brooding over grief.

He observed of Lord Bute, 'It was said of Augustus, that it would have been better for Rome that he had never been born, or had never died. So it would have been better for this nation if Lord Bute had never been minister, or had never resigned.'

In the evening we went to the Town-hall, which was converted into a temporary theatre, and saw *Theodosius*, with *The Stratford Jubilee*. I was happy to see Dr. Johnson sitting in a conspicuous part of the pit, and receiving affectionate homage from all his acquaintance. We were quite gay and merry. I afterwards mentioned to him that I condemned myself for being so, when poor

[1] See an accurate and animated statement of Mr. Gastrel's barbarity, by Mr. Malone, in a note on *Some account of the Life of William Shakspeare*, prefixed to his admirable edition of that poet's works, vol. i. p. 118.

Mr. and Mrs. Thrale were in such distress. JOHNSON. 'You are wrong, Sir; twenty years hence Mr. and Mrs. Thrale will not suffer much pain from the death of their son. Now, Sir, you are to consider, that distance of place, as well as distance of time, operates upon the human feelings. I would not have you be gay in the presence of the distressed, because it would shock them; but you may be gay at a distance. Pain for the loss of a friend, or of a relation whom we love, is occasioned by the want which we feel. In time the vacuity is filled with something else; or, sometimes the vacuity closes up of itself.'

Mr. Seward and Mr. Pearson, another clergyman here, supt with us at our inn, and after they left us, we sat up late as we used to do in London.

Here I shall record some fragments of my friend's conversation during this jaunt.

'Marriage, Sir, is much more necessary to a man than to a woman; for he is much less able to supply himself with domestick comforts. You will recollect my saying to some ladies the other day, that I had often wondered why young women should marry, as they have so much more freedom, and so much more attention paid to them while unmarried, than when married. I indeed did not mention the *strong* reason for their marrying—the *mechanical* reason.' BOSWELL. 'Why, that *is* a strong one. But does not imagination make it seem much more important than it is in reality? Is it not, to a certain degree, a delusion in us as well as in women?' JOHNSON. 'Why yes, Sir; but it is a delusion that is always beginning again.' BOSWELL. 'I don't know but there is upon the whole more misery than happiness produced by that passion.' JOHNSON. 'I don't think so, Sir.'

'Never speak of a man in his own presence. It is always indelicate, and may be offensive.'

'Questioning is not the mode of conversation among gentlemen. It is assuming a superiority, and it is particularly wrong to question a man concerning himself. There may be parts of his former life which he may not wish to be made known to other persons, or even brought to his own recollection.'

'A man should be careful never to tell tales of himself to his own disadvantage. People may be amused and laugh at the time, but they will be remembered, and brought out against him upon some subsequent occasion.'

'Much may be done if a man puts his whole mind to a particular object. By doing so, Norton[1] has made himself the great lawyer that he is allowed to be.'

I mentioned an acquaintance of mine,[2] a sectary, who was a very religious man, who not only attended regularly on publick worship with those of his communion, but made a particular study of the Scriptures, and even wrote a commentary on some parts of them, yet was known to be very licentious in indulging himself with women; maintaining that men are to be saved by faith alone, and that the Christian religion had not prescribed any fixed rule for the intercourse between the sexes. JOHNSON. 'Sir, there is no trusting to that crazy piety.'

I observed that it was strange how well Scotchmen were known to one another in their own country, though born in very distant counties; for we do not find that the gentlemen of neighbouring counties in England are mutually known to each other. Johnson, with his usual acuteness, at once saw and explained the reason of this; 'Why, Sir, you have Edinburgh, where the gentlemen from all your counties meet, and which is not so large but that they are all known. There is no such common place of collection in England, except London, where from its great size and diffusion, many of those who reside in contiguous counties of England, may long remain unknown to each other.'

On Tuesday, March 26, there came for us an equipage properly suited to a wealthy well-beneficed clergyman;—Dr. Taylor's large roomy post-chaise, drawn by four stout plump horses, and driven by two steady jolly postillions, which conveyed us to Ashbourne; where I found my friend's schoolfellow living upon an establishment perfectly corresponding with his substantial creditable equipage: his house, garden, pleasure-grounds, table, in short every thing good, and no scantiness appearing. Every

---

[1] Sir Fletcher Norton, afterwards Speaker of the House of Commons, and in 1782 created Baron Grantley. [M.]

[2] [Dr. John Boswell. *Boswell Papers*, xi. 193.]

man should form such a plan of living as he can execute completely. Let him not draw an outline wider than he can fill up.
I have seen many skeletons of shew and magnificence which
excite at once ridicule and pity. Dr. Taylor had a good estate of
his own, and good preferment in the church, being a prebendary
of Westminster, and rector of Bosworth. He was a diligent justice of the peace, and presided over the town of Ashbourne, to
the inhabitants of which I was told he was very liberal; and as a
proof of this it was mentioned to me, he had the preceding winter
distributed two hundred pounds among such of them as stood
in need of his assistance. He had consequently a considerable
political interest in the county of Derby, which he employed to
support the Devonshire family; for though the schoolfellow and
friend of Johnson, he was a Whig. I could not perceive in his
character much congeniality of any sort with that of Johnson,
who, however, said to me, 'Sir, he has a very strong understanding.' His size, and figure, and countenance, and manner, were
that of a hearty English 'Squire, with the parson superinduced:
and I took particular notice of his upper servant, Mr. Peters, a
decent grave man, in purple clothes, and a large white wig, like
the butler or *major domo* of a Bishop.

Dr. Johnson and Dr. Taylor met with great cordiality; and
Johnson soon gave him the same sad account of their school-
fellow, Congreve, that he had given to Mr. Hector; adding a
remark of such moment to the rational conduct of a man in the
decline of life, that it deserves to be imprinted upon every mind:
'There is nothing against which an old man should be so much
upon his guard as putting himself to nurse.' Innumerable have
been the melancholy instances of men once distinguished for
firmness, resolution, and spirit, who in their latter days have
been governed like children, by interested female artifice.

Dr. Taylor commended a physician[1] who was known to him
and Dr. Johnson, and said, 'I fight many battles for him, as many
people in the country dislike him.' JOHNSON. 'But you should
consider, Sir, that by every one of your victories he is a loser;
for, every man of whom you get the better, will be very angry,

[1] [Dr. Butter, *Boswell Papers*, xi. 204.]

and will resolve not to employ him; whereas if people get the better of you in argument about him, they'll think, "We'll send for Dr. ****** nevertheless."' This was an observation deep and sure in human nature.

Next day we talked of a book in which an eminent judge[1] was arraigned before the bar of the publick, as having pronounced an unjust decision in a great cause. Dr. Johnson maintained that this publication would not give any uneasiness to the judge. 'For (said he,) either he acted honestly, or he meant to do injustice. If he acted honestly, his own consciousness will protect him; if he meant to do injustice, he will be glad to see the man who attacks him, so much vexed.'

Next day, as Dr. Johnson had acquainted Dr. Taylor of the reason for his returning speedily to London, it was resolved that we should set out after dinner. A few of Dr. Taylor's neighbours were his guests that day.

Dr. Johnson talked with approbation of one who had attained to the state of the philosophical wise man, that is, to have no want of any thing. 'Then, Sir, (said I,) the savage is a wise man.' 'Sir, (said he,) I do not mean simply being without,—but not having a want.' I maintained, against this proposition, that it was better to have fine clothes, for instance, than not to feel the want of them. JOHNSON. 'No, Sir; fine clothes are good only as they supply the want of other means of procuring respect. Was Charles the Twelfth, think you, less respected for his coarse blue coat and black stock? And you find the King of Prussia dresses plain, because the dignity of his character is sufficient.' I here brought myself into a scrape, for I heedlessly said, 'Would not *you*, Sir, be the better for velvet and embroidery?' JOHNSON. 'Sir, you put an end to all argument when you introduce your opponent himself. Have you no better manners? There is *your want*.' I apologised by saying, I had mentioned him as an instance of one who wanted as little as any man in the world, and yet, perhaps, might receive some additional lustre from dress.

Having left Ashbourne in the evening, we stopped to change horses at Derby, and availed ourselves of a moment to enjoy the

---

[1] [Lord Mansfield, *Boswell Papers*, xi. 213.]

conversation of my countryman, Dr. Butter, then physician there. He was in great indignation because Lord Mountstuart's bill for a Scotch militia had been lost. Dr. Johnson was as violent against it. 'I am glad, (said he,) that Parliament has had the spirit to throw it out. You wanted to take advantage of the timidity of our scoundrels;' (meaning, I suppose, the ministry). It may be observed, that he used the epithet scoundrel very commonly, not quite in the sense in which it is generally understood, but as a strong term of disapprobation; as when he abruptly answered Mrs. Thrale, who had asked him how he did, 'Ready to become a scoundrel, Madam; with a little more spoiling you will, I think, make me a complete rascal:'[1] he meant, easy to become a capricious and self-indulgent valetudinarian; a character for which I have heard him express great disgust.

Johnson had with him upon this jaunt, *Il Palmerino d'Inghilterra*, a romance praised by Cervantes; but did not like it much. He said, he read it for the language, by way of preparation for his Italian expedition.—We lay this night at Loughborough.

On Thursday, March 28, we pursued our journey. I mentioned that old Mr. Sheridan complained of the ingratitude of Mr. Wedderburne and General Fraser, who had been much obliged to him when they were young Scotchmen entering upon life in England. JOHNSON. 'Why, Sir, a man is very apt to complain of the ingratitude of those who have risen far above him. A man when he gets into a higher sphere, into other habits of life, cannot keep up all his former connections. Then, Sir, those who knew him formerly upon a level with themselves, may think that they ought still to be treated as on a level, which cannot be; and an acquaintance in a former situation may bring out things which it would be very disagreeable to have mentioned before higher company, though, perhaps, every body knows of them.' He placed this subject in a new light to me, and shewed that a man who has risen in the world, must not be condemned too harshly for being distant to former acquaintance, even though he may have been much obliged to them. It is, no doubt, to be wished that a proper degree of attention should be shewn by

[1] *Anecdotes of Johnson*, p. 176.

great men to their early friends. But if either from obtuse insensibility to difference of situation, or presumptuous forwardness, which will not submit even to an exteriour observance of it, the dignity of high place cannot be preserved, when they are admitted into the company of those raised above the state in which they once were, encroachment must be repelled, and the kinder feelings sacrificed. To one of the very fortunate persons whom I have mentioned, namely, Mr. Wedderburne, now Lord Loughborough, I must do the justice to relate, that I have been assured by another early acquaintance of his, old Mr. Macklin, who assisted him in improving his pronunciation, that he had found him very grateful. Macklin, I suppose, had not pressed upon his elevation with so much eagerness as the gentleman who complained of him. Dr. Johnson's remark as to the jealousy entertained of our friends who rise far above us, is certainly very just. By this was withered the early friendship between Charles Townshend and Akenside; and many similar instances might be adduced.

He said, 'It is commonly a weak man who marries for love.' We then talked of marrying women of fortune; and I mentioned a common remark, that a man may be, upon the whole, richer by marrying a woman with a very small portion, because a woman of fortune will be proportionally expensive; whereas a woman who brings none will be very moderate in expenses. JOHNSON. 'Depend upon it, Sir, this is not true. A woman of fortune being used to the handling of money, spends it judiciously; but a woman who gets the command of money for the first time upon her marriage, has such a gust in spending it, that she throws it away with great profusion.'

He praised the ladies of the present age, insisting that they were more faithful to their husbands, and more virtuous in every respect, than in former times, because their understandings were better cultivated. It was an undoubted proof of his good sense and good disposition, that he was never querulous, never prone to inveigh against the present times, as is so common when superficial minds are on the fret. On the contrary, he was willing to speak favourably of his own age; and, indeed, maintained its

superiority in every respect, except in its reverence for government; the relaxation of which he imputed, as its grand cause, to
the shock which our monarchy received at the Revolution, though
necessary; and secondly, to the timid concessions made to faction
by successive administrations in the reign of his present Majesty.
I am happy to think, that he lived to see the Crown at last recover
its just influence.

At Leicester we read in the newspaper that Dr. James was
dead. I thought that the death of an old school-fellow, and one
with whom he had lived a good deal in London, would have
affected my fellow-traveller much: but he only said, 'Ah! poor
Jamy.' Afterwards, however, when we were in the chaise, he
said, with more tenderness, 'Since I set out on this jaunt, I have
lost an old friend and a young one;—Dr. James, and poor Harry,'
(meaning Mr. Thrale's son.)

Having lain at St. Alban's on Thursday, March 28, we breakfasted the next morning at Barnet. I expressed to him a weakness
of mind which I could not help; an uneasy apprehension that my
wife and children, who were at a great distance from me, might,
perhaps, be ill. 'Sir, (said he,) consider how foolish you would
think it in *them* to be apprehensive that *you* are ill.' This sudden
turn relieved me for the moment; but I afterwards perceived it
to be an ingenious fallacy. I might, to be sure, be satisfied that
they had no reason to be apprehensive about me, because I *knew*
that I myself was well: but we might have a mutual anxiety,
without the charge of folly; because each was, in some degree,
uncertain as to the condition of the other.

I enjoyed the luxury of our approach to London, that metropolis which we both loved so much, for the high and varied
intellectual pleasure which it furnishes. I experienced immediate
happiness while whirled along with such a companion, and said
to him, 'Sir, you observed one day at General Oglethorpe's, that
a man is never happy for the present, but when he is drunk. Will
you not add,—or when driving rapidly in a post-chaise?' JOHN-
SON. 'No, Sir, you are driving rapidly *from* something, or *to*
something.'

Talking of melancholy, he said, 'Some men, and very thinking

720

men too, have not those vexing thoughts.[1] Sir Joshua Reynolds
is the same all the year round. Beauclerk, except when ill and in
pain, is the same. But I believe most men have them in the degree
in which they are capable of having them. If I were in the country,
and were distressed by that malady, I would force myself to take a
book; and every time I did it I should find it the easier. Melancholy, indeed, should be diverted by every means but drinking.'

We stopped at Messieurs Dillys, booksellers in the Poultry;
from whence he hurried away, in a hackney coach, to Mr.
Thrale's, in the Borough. I called at his house in the evening,
having promised to acquaint Mrs. Williams of his safe return;
when, to my surprize, I found him sitting with her at tea, and,
as I thought, not in a very good humour: for, it seems, when he
had got to Mr. Thrale's, he found the coach was at the door
waiting to carry Mrs. and Miss Thrale, and Signor Baretti, their
Italian master, to Bath. This was not shewing the attention
which might have been expected to the 'Guide, Philosopher, and
Friend,' the *Imlac* who had hastened from the country to console
a distressed mother, who he understood was very anxious for his
return. They had, I found, without ceremony, proceeded on their
intended journey. I was glad to understand from him that it was
still resolved that his tour to Italy with Mr. and Mrs. Thrale
should take place, of which he had entertained some doubt, on
account of the loss which they had suffered; and his doubts afterwards proved to be well-founded. He observed, indeed very
justly, that 'their loss was an additional reason for their going

[1] The phrase 'vexing thoughts,' is, I think, very expressive. It has been
familiar to me from my childhood; for it is to be found in the *Psalms in
Metre*, used in the churches (I believe I should say *kirks*) of Scotland, *Psal.*
xliii. v. 5;

> 'Why art thou then cast down, my soul?
> What should discourage thee?
> And why with *vexing thoughts* art thou
> Disquieted in me?'

Some allowance must no doubt be made for early prepossession. But at a
maturer period of life, after looking at various metrical versions of the
Psalms, I am well satisfied that the version used in Scotland is, upon the
whole, the best; and that it is vain to think of having a better. It has in
general a simplicity and *unction* of sacred Poesy; and in many parts its
transfusion is admirable.

abroad; and if it had not been fixed that he should have been one of the party, he would force them out; but he would not advise them unless his advice was asked, lest they might suspect that he recommended what he wished on his own account.' I was not pleased that his intimacy with Mr. Thrale's family, though it no doubt contributed much to his comfort and enjoyment, was not without some degree of restraint. Not, as has been grossly suggested, that it was required of him as a task to talk for the entertainment of them and their company; but that he was not quite at his ease; which, however, might partly be owing to his own honest pride—that dignity of mind which is always jealous of appearing too compliant.

On Sunday, March 31, I called on him, and shewed him as a curiosity which I had discovered, his *Translation of Lobo's Account of Abyssinia,* which Sir John Pringle had lent me, it being then little known as one of his works. He said, 'Take no notice of it,' or 'don't talk of it.' He seemed to think it beneath him, though done at six-and-twenty. I said to him, 'Your style, Sir, is much improved since you translated this.' He answered with a sort of triumphant smile, 'Sir, I hope it is.'

On Wednesday, April 3, in the morning I found him very busy putting his books in order, and as they were generally very old ones, clouds of dust were flying around him. He had on a pair of large gloves, such as hedgers use. His present appearance put me in mind of my uncle, Dr. Boswell's description of him, 'A robust genius, born to grapple with whole libraries.'

I gave him an account of a conversation which had passed between me and Captain Cook, the day before, at dinner at Sir John Pringle's; and he was much pleased with the conscientious accuracy of that celebrated circumnavigator, who set me right as to many of the exaggerated accounts given by Dr. Hawkesworth of his Voyages. I told him that while I was with the Captain, I catched the enthusiasm of curiosity and adventure, and felt a strong inclination to go with him on his next voyage. JOHNSON. 'Why, Sir, a man *does* feel so, till he considers how very little he can learn from such voyages.' BOSWELL. 'But one is carried away with the general grand and indistinct notion of

A Voyage round the World.' Johnson. 'Yes, Sir, but a man is to guard himself against taking a thing in general.' I said I was certain that a great part of what we are told by the travellers to the South Sea must be conjecture, because they had not enough of the language of those countries to understand so much as they have related. Objects falling under the observation of the senses might be clearly known; but every thing intellectual, every thing abstract—politicks, morals, and religion, must be darkly guessed. Dr. Johnson was of the same opinion. He upon another occasion, when a friend[1] mentioned to him several extraordinary facts, as communicated to him by the circumnavigators, slily observed, 'Sir, I never before knew how much I was respected by these gentlemen; they told *me* none of these things.'

He had been in company with Omai, a native of one of the South Sea Islands, after he had been some time in this country. He was struck with the elegance of his behaviour, and accounted for it thus: 'Sir, he had passed his time, while in England, only in the best company; so that all that he had acquired of our manners was genteel. As a proof of this, Sir, Lord Mulgrave and he dined one day at Streatham; they sat with their backs to the light fronting me, so that I could not see distinctly; and there was so little of the savage in Omai, that I was afraid to speak to either, lest I should mistake one for the other.'

We agreed to dine to-day at the Mitre-tavern, after the rising of the House of Lords, where a branch of the litigation concerning the Douglas Estate, in which I was one of the counsel, was to come on. I brought with me Mr. Murray, Solicitor-General of Scotland, now one of the Judges of the Court of Session, with the title of Lord Henderland. I mentioned Mr. Solicitor's relation, Lord Charles Hay, with whom I knew Dr. Johnson had been acquainted. Johnson. 'I wrote something for Lord Charles; and I thought he had nothing to fear from a court-martial. I suffered a great loss when he died; he was a mighty pleasing man in conversation, and a reading man. The character of a soldier is high. They who stand forth the foremost in danger, for the community, have the respect of mankind. An officer is

---

[1] [James Hutton, the Moravian, *Boswell's Note, teste H. W. Liebert.*]

much more respected than any other man who has as little money. In a commercial country, money will always purchase respect. But you find, an officer, who has, properly speaking, no money, is every where well received and treated with attention. The character of a soldier always stands him in stead.' BOSWELL. 'Yet, Sir, I think that common soldiers are worse thought of than other men in the same rank of life; such as labourers.' JOHNSON. 'Why, Sir, a common soldier is usually a very gross man, and any quality which procures respect may be overwhelmed by grossness. A man of learning may be so vicious or so ridiculous that you cannot respect him. A common soldier too, generally eats more than he can pay for. But when a common soldier is civil in his quarters, his red coat procures him a degree of respect.' The peculiar respect paid to the military character in France was mentioned. BOSWELL. 'I should think that where military men are so numerous, they would be less valued as not being rare.' JOHNSON. 'Nay, Sir, wherever a particular character or profession is high in the estimation of a people, those who are of it will be valued above other men. We value an Englishman highly in this country, and yet Englishmen are not rare in it.'

Mr. Murray praised the ancient philosophers for the candour and good humour with which those of different sects disputed with each other. JOHNSON. 'Sir, they disputed with good humour, because they were not in earnest as to religion. Had the ancients been serious in their belief, we should not have had their Gods exhibited in the manner we find them represented in the Poets. The people would not have suffered it. They disputed with good humour upon their fanciful theories, because they were not interested in the truth of them: when a man has nothing to lose, he may be in good humour with his opponent. Accordingly you see in Lucian, the Epicurean, who argues only negatively, keeps his temper; the Stoick, who has something positive to preserve, grows angry. Being angry with one who controverts an opinion which you value, is a necessary consequence of the uneasiness which you feel. Every man who attacks my belief, diminishes in some degree my confidence in it, and therefore makes me uneasy; and I am angry with him who makes me uneasy. Those only who believed in revelation have been angry at having their faith called in question; because they only had something upon which they could rest as matter of fact.' MURRAY. 'It seems to me that we are not angry at a man for controverting an opinion which we believe and value; we rather pity him.' JOHNSON. 'Why, Sir; to be sure when you wish a man to have that belief which you think is of infinite advantage, you wish well to him; but your primary consideration is your own quiet. If a madman were to come into this room with a stick in his hand, no doubt we should pity the state of his mind; but our primary consideration would be to take care of ourselves. We should knock him down first, and pity him afterwards. No, Sir; every man will dispute with great good humour upon a subject in which he is not interested. I will dispute very calmly upon the probability of another man's son being hanged; but if a man zealously enforces the probability that my own son will be hanged, I shall certainly not be in a very good humour with him.' I added this illustration, 'If a man endeavours to convince me that my wife, whom I love very much, and in whom I place great confidence, is a disagreeable woman, and is even unfaithful to me, I shall be very angry, for he is putting me in fear of being unhappy.' MURRAY. 'But, Sir, truth will always bear an examination.' JOHNSON. 'Yes, Sir, but it is painful to be forced to defend it. Consider, Sir, how should you like, though conscious of your innocence, to be tried before a jury for a capital crime, once a week.'

We talked of education at great schools; the advantages and disadvantages of which Johnson displayed in a luminous manner; but his arguments preponderated so much in favour of the benefit which a boy of good parts might receive at one of them, that I have reason to believe Mr. Murray was very much influenced by what he had heard to-day, in his determination to send his own son to Westminster school.—I have acted in the same manner with regard to my own two sons; having placed the eldest at Eton, and the second at Westminster. I cannot say which is best. But in justice to both those noble seminaries, I with high satisfaction declare, that my boys have derived from them a great deal of good, and no evil: and I trust they will, like Horace, be grateful to their father for giving them so valuable an education.

I introduced the topick, which is often ignorantly urged, that the Universities of England are too rich;[1] so that learning does not flourish in them as it would do, if those who teach had smaller salaries, and depended on their assiduity for a great part of their income. JOHNSON. 'Sir, the very reverse of this is the truth; the English Universities are not rich enough. Our fellowships are only sufficient to support a man during his studies to fit him for the world, and accordingly in general they are held no longer than till an opportunity offers of getting away. Now and then, perhaps, there is a fellow who grows old in his college; but this is against his will, unless he be a man very indolent indeed. A hundred a year is reckoned a good fellowship, and that is no more than is necessary to keep a man decently as a scholar. We do not allow our fellows to marry, because we consider academical institutions as preparatory to a settlement in the world. It is only by being employed as a tutor, that a fellow can obtain any thing more than a livelihood. To be sure a man, who has enough without teaching, will probably not teach; for we would all be idle if we could. In the same manner, a man who is to get nothing by teaching, will not exert himself. Gresham College was intended as a place of instruction for London; able professors were to read lectures gratis, they contrived to have no scholars; whereas, if they had been allowed to receive but sixpence a lecture from each scholar, they would have been emulous to have had many scholars. Every body will agree that it should be the interest of those who teach to have scholars; and this is the case in our Universities. That they are too rich is certainly not true; for they have nothing good enough to keep a man of eminent learning with them for his life. In the foreign Universities a professorship is a high thing. It is as much almost as a man can make by his learning; and therefore we find the most learned men abroad

[1] Dr. Adam Smith, who was for some time a Professor in the University of Glasgow, has uttered, in his *Wealth of Nations*, some reflections upon this subject which are certainly not well founded, and seem to be invidious.

are in the Universities. It is not so with us. Our Universities are impoverished of learning, by the penury of their provisions. I wish there were many places of a thousand a-year at Oxford, to keep first-rate men of learning from quitting the University.' Undoubtedly if this were the case, Literature would have a still greater dignity and splendour at Oxford, and there would be grander living sources of instruction.

I mentioned Mr. Maclaurin's uneasiness on account of a degree of ridicule carelessly thrown on his deceased father, in Goldsmith's *History of Animated Nature*, in which that celebrated mathematician is represented as being subject to fits of yawning so violent as to render him incapable of proceeding in his lecture; a story altogether unfounded, but for the publication of which the law would give no reparation.[1] This led us to agitate the question, whether legal redress could be obtained, even when a man's deceased relation was calumniated in a publication. Mr. Murray maintained there should be reparation, unless the authour could justify himself by proving the fact. JOHNSON. 'Sir, it is of so much more consequence that truth should be told, than that individuals should not be made uneasy, that it is much better that the law does not restrain writing freely concerning the characters of the dead. Damages will be given to a man who is calumniated in his life-time, because he may be hurt in his worldly interest, or at least hurt in his mind: but the law does not regard that uneasiness which a man feels on having his ancestor calumniated. That is too nice. Let him deny what is said, and let the matter have a fair chance by discussion. But, if a man could say nothing against a character but what he can prove, history could not be written; for a great deal is known of men of which proof cannot be brought. A minister may be notoriously known to take bribes, and yet you may not be able to prove it.' Mr. Murray suggested, that the authour should be obliged to shew some sort of evidence, though he would not

[1] Dr. Goldsmith was dead before Mr. Maclaurin discovered the ludicrous errour. But Mr. Nourse, the bookseller, who was the proprietor of the work, upon being applied to by Sir John Pringle, agreed very handsomely to have the leaf on which it was contained cancelled, and re-printed without it, at his own expence.

require a strict legal proof: but Johnson firmly and resolutely opposed any restraint whatever, as adverse to a free investigation of the characters of mankind.[1]

1 What Dr. Johnson has here said, is undoubtedly good sense; yet I am afraid that law, though defined by *Lord Coke* 'the perfection of reason,' is not altogether *with him*; for it is held in the books, that an attack on the reputation even of a dead man, may be punished as a libel, because tending to a breach of the peace. There is, however, I believe, no modern decided case to that effect. In the King's Bench, Trinity Term, 1790, the question occurred on occasion of an indictment, *The King* v. *Topham,* who, as a *proprietor* of a news-paper entitled *The World,* was found guilty of a libel against Earl Cowper, deceased, because certain injurious charges against his Lordship were published in that paper. An arrest of Judgement having been moved for, the case was afterwards solemnly argued. My friend Mr. Const, whom I delight in having an opportunity to praise, not only for his abilities but his manners; a gentleman whose ancient German blood has been mellowed in England, and who may be truely said to unite the *Baron* and the *Barrister,* was one of the Counsel for Mr. Topham. He displayed much learning and ingenuity upon the general question; which, however, was not decided, as the Court granted an arrest chiefly on the informality of the indictment. No man has a higher reverence for the law of England than I have; but, with all deference I cannot help thinking, that prosecution by indictment, if a defendant is never to be allowed to justify, must often be very oppressive, unless Juries, whom I am more and more confirmed in holding to be judges of law as well as of fact, resolutely interpose. Of late an act of Parliament has passed declaratory of their full right to one as well as the other, in matter of libel; and the bill having been brought in by a popular gentleman, * many of his party have in most extravagant terms declaimed on the wonderful acquisition to the liberty of the press. For my own part I ever was clearly of opinion that this right was inherent in the very constitution of a Jury, and indeed in sense and reason inseparable from their important function. To establish it, therefore, by Statute, is, I think, narrowing its foundation, which is the broad and deep basis of Common Law. Would it not rather weaken the right of primogeniture, or any other old and universally-acknowledged right, should the legislature pass an act in favour of it? In my *Letter to the People of Scotland, against diminishing the number of the Lords of Session,* published in 1785, there is the following passage, which, as a concise, and I hope a fair and rational state of the matter, I presume to quote: 'The Juries of England are Judges of *law* as well as of *fact,* in *many civil,* and in *all criminal* trials. That my principles of *resistance* may not be misapprehended any more than my principles of *submission,* I protest that I should be the last man in the world to encourage Juries to contradict rashly, wantonly, or perversely, the opinion of the Judges. On the contrary, I would have them listen respectfully to the advice they receive from the Bench, by which they may be often well directed in forming *their own opinion*; which, "and not another's," is the opinion they are to return *upon their oaths.* But where, after due attention to

* [Fox. *Powell.*]

On Thursday, April 4, having called on Dr. Johnson, I said, it was a pity that truth was not so firm as to bid defiance to all attacks, so that it might be shot at as much as people chose to attempt, and yet remain unhurt. JOHNSON. 'Then, Sir, it would not be shot at. Nobody attempts to dispute that two and two make four: but with contests concerning moral truth, human passions are generally mixed, and therefore it must ever be liable to assault and misrepresentation.'

On Friday, April 5, being Good Friday, after having attended the morning service at St. Clement's Church, I walked home with Johnson. We talked of the Roman Catholick religion. JOHNSON. 'In the barbarous ages, Sir, priests and people were equally deceived; but afterwards there were gross corruptions introduced by the clergy, such as indulgencies to priests to have concubines, and the worship of images, not, indeed, inculcated, but knowingly permitted.' He strongly censured the licensed stews at Rome. BOSWELL. 'So then, Sir, you would allow of no irregular intercourse whatever between the sexes?' JOHNSON. 'To be sure I would not, Sir. I would punish it much more than is done, and so restrain it. In all countries there has been fornication, as in all countries there has been theft; but there may be more or less of the one, as well as of the other, in proportion to the force of law. All men will naturally commit fornication, as all men will naturally steal. And, Sir, it is very absurd to argue, as has been often done, that prostitutes are necessary to prevent the violent effects of appetite from violating the decent order of life; nay, should be permitted, in order to preserve the chastity of our wives and daughters. Depend upon it, Sir, severe laws, steadily enforced, would be sufficient against those evils, and would promote marriage.'

I stated to him this case:—'Suppose a man has a daughter, who he knows has been seduced, but her misfortune is concealed from the world: should he keep her in his house? Would he not, by doing so, be accessary to imposition? And, perhaps, a worthy,

all that the Judge has said, they are decidedly of a different opinion from him, they have not only a *power* and a *right*, but they are *bound in conscience* to bring in a verdict accordingly.'

unsuspecting man might come and marry this woman, unless the
father inform him of the truth.' JOHNSON. 'Sir, he is accessary
to no imposition. His daughter is in his house; and if a man
courts her, he takes his chance. If a friend, or, indeed, if any man
asks his opinion whether he should marry her, he ought to advise
him against it, without telling why, because his real opinion is
then required. Or, if he has other daughters who know of her
frailty, he ought not to keep her in his house. You are to consider the state of life is this; we are to judge of one another's
characters as well as we can; and a man is not bound, in honesty
or honour, to tell us the faults of his daughter or of himself. A
man who has debauched his friend's daughter is not obliged to
say to every body—"Take care of me; don't let me into your
houses without suspicion. I once debauched a friend's daughter:
I may debauch yours."'

Mr. Thrale called upon him, and appeared to bear the loss of
his son with a manly composure. There was no affectation about
him; and he talked, as usual, upon indifferent subjects. He seemed
to me to hesitate as to the intended Italian tour, on which, I
flattered myself, he and Mrs. Thrale and Dr. Johnson were soon
to set out; and, therefore, I pressed it as much as I could.
I mentioned, that Mr. Beauclerk had said, that Baretti, whom
they were to carry with them, would keep them so long in the
little towns of his own district, that they would not have time
to see Rome. I mentioned this, to put them on their guard.
JOHNSON. 'Sir, we do not thank Mr. Beauclerk for supposing
that we are to be directed by Baretti. No, Sir; Mr. Thrale is to
go, by my advice, to Mr. Jackson,[1] (the all-knowing) and get
from him a plan for seeing the most that can be seen in the time
that we have to travel. We must, to be sure, see Rome, Naples,
Florence, and Venice, and as much more as we can.' (Speaking
with a tone of animation.)

When I expressed an earnest wish for his remarks on Italy,
he said, 'I do not see that I could make a book upon Italy; yet

---

[1] A gentleman, who from his extraordinary stores of knowledge, has
been stiled *omniscient*. Johnson, I think very properly, altered it to all-
knowing, as it is a *verbum solenne*, appropriated to the Supreme Being.

I should be glad to get two hundred pounds, or five hundred pounds, by such a work.' This shewed both that a journal of his Tour upon the Continent was not wholly out of his contemplation, and that he uniformly adhered to that strange opinion, which his indolent disposition made him utter: 'No man but a blockhead ever wrote, except for money.' Numerous instances to refute this will occur to all who are versed in the history of literature.

He gave us one of the many sketches of character which were treasured in his mind, and which he was wont to produce quite unexpectedly in a very entertaining manner. 'I lately, (said he,) received a letter from the East Indies, from a gentleman[1] whom I formerly knew very well; he had returned from that country with a handsome fortune, as it was reckoned, before means were found to acquire those immense sums which have been brought from thence of late; he was a scholar, and an agreeable man, and lived very prettily in London, till his wife died. After her death, he took to dissipation and gaming, and lost all he had. One evening he lost a thousand pounds to a gentleman whose name I am sorry I have forgotten. Next morning he sent the gentleman five hundred pounds, with an apology that it was all he had in the world. The gentleman sent the money back to him, declaring he would not accept of it; and adding, that if Mr. ———— had occasion for five hundred pounds more, he would lend it to him. He resolved to go out again to the East Indies, and make his fortune anew. He got a considerable appointment, and I had some intention of accompanying him. Had I thought then as I do now, I should have gone: but, at that time, I had objections to quitting England.'

It was a very remarkable circumstance about Johnson, whom shallow observers have supposed to have been ignorant of the world, that very few men had seen greater variety of characters; and none could observe them better, as was evident from the strong, yet nice portraits which he often drew. I have frequently thought that if he had made out what the French call *une catalogue raisonnée* of all the people who had passed under his

[1] [Joseph Fowke. *Boswell Papers*, xi. 227.]

observation, it would have afforded a very rich fund of instruction and entertainment. The suddenness with which his accounts of some of them started out in conversation, was not less pleasing than surprising. I remember he once observed to me, 'It is wonderful, Sir, what is to be found in London. The most literary conversation that I ever enjoyed, was at the table of Jack Ellis, a money-scrivener behind the Royal Exchange, with whom I at one period used to dine generally once a week.'[1]

Volumes would be required to contain a list of his numerous and various acquaintance, none of whom he ever forgot; and could describe and discriminate them all with precision and vivacity. He associated with persons the most widely different in manners, abilities, rank, and accomplishments. He was at once the companion of the brilliant Colonel Forrester of the Guards, who wrote *The Polite Philosopher*, and of the aukward and uncouth Robert Levet; of Lord Thurlow, and Mr. Sastres, the Italian master; and has dined one day with the beautiful, gay, and fascinating Lady Craven,[2] and the next with good Mrs. Gardiner, the tallow-chandler, on Snow-hill.

On my expressing my wonder at his discovering so much of the knowledge peculiar to different professions, he told me, 'I

[1] This Mr. Ellis was, I believe, the last of that profession called *Scriveners*, which is one of the London companies, but of which the business is no longer carried on separately, but is transacted by attornies and others. He was a man of literature and talents. He was the authour of a Hudi-brastick version of Maphæus's *Canto*, in addition to the *Æneid*; of some poems in Dodsley's *Collections*; and various other small pieces; but being a very modest man, never put his name to anything. He shewed me a transla-tion which he had made of Ovid's *Epistles*, very prettily done. There is a good engraved portrait of him by Pether, from a picture by Fry, which hangs in the hall of the Scriveners' company. I visited him October 4, 1790, in his ninety-third year, and found his judgement distinct and clear, and his memory, though faded so as to fail him occasionally, yet, as he assured me, and I indeed perceived, able to serve him very well, after a little recollection. It was agreeable to observe, that he was free from the discontent and fret-fulness which too often molest old age. He in the summer of that year walked to Rotherhithe, where he dined, and walked home in the evening. He died on the 31st of December, 1791.

[2] Lord Macartney, who with his other distinguished qualities, is re-markable also for an elegant pleasantry, told me, that he met Johnson at Lady Craven's, and that he seemed jealous of any interference: 'So, (said his Lordship, smiling,) *I kept back*.'

learnt what I know of law, chiefly from Mr. Ballow,[1] a very able man. I learnt some, too, from Chambers; but was not so teachable then. One is not willing to be taught by a young man.' When I expressed a wish to know more about Mr. Ballow, Johnson said, 'Sir, I have seen him but once these twenty years. The tide of life has driven us different ways.' I was sorry at the time to hear this; but whoever quits the creeks of private connections, and fairly gets into the great ocean of London, will, by imperceptible degrees, unavoidably experience such cessations of acquaintance.

'My knowledge of physick, (he added,) I learnt from Dr. James, whom I helped in writing the proposals for his *Dictionary* and also a little in the *Dictionary* itself.[2] I also learnt some from Dr. Lawrence, but was then grown more stubborn.'

A curious incident happened to-day, while Mr. Thrale and I sat with him. Francis announced that a large packet was brought to him from the post-office, said to have come from Lisbon, and it was charged *seven pounds ten shillings*. He would not receive it, supposing it to be some trick, nor did he even look at it. But upon enquiry afterwards he found that it was a real packet for him, from that very friend in the East Indies of whom he had been speaking; and the ship which carried it having come to Portugal, this packet, with others, had been put into the post-office at Lisbon.

I mentioned a new gaming-club, of which Mr. Beauclerk had given me an account, where the members played to a desperate extent. JOHNSON. 'Depend upon it, Sir, this is mere talk. *Who* is ruined by gaming? You will not find six instances in an age. There is a strange rout made about deep play: whereas you have many more people ruined by adventurous trade, and yet we do not hear such an outcry against it.' THRALE. 'There may be few people absolutely ruined by deep play; but very many are much hurt in their circumstances by it.' JOHNSON. 'Yes, Sir, and so are very many by other kinds of expence.' I had heard him talk

---

[1] There is an account of him in Sir John Hawkins's *Life of Johnson*.

[2] I have in vain endeavoured to find out what parts Johnson wrote for Dr. James. Perhaps medical men may.

once before in the same manner; and at Oxford he said, 'he wished he had learnt to play at cards.' The truth, however, is, that he loved to display his ingenuity in argument; and therefore would sometimes in conversation maintain opinions which he was sensible were wrong, but in supporting which, his reasoning and wit would be most conspicuous. He would begin thus: 'Why, Sir, as to the good or evil of card-playing—' 'Now, (said Garrick,) he is thinking which side he shall take.' He appeared to have a pleasure in contradiction, especially when any opinion whatever was delivered with an air of confidence; so that there was hardly any topick, if not one of the great truths of Religion and Morality, that he might not have been incited to argue, either for or against it. Lord Elibank[1] had the highest admiration of his powers. He once observed to me, 'Whatever opinion Johnson maintains, I will not say that he convinces me; but he never fails to shew me, that he has good reasons for it.' I have heard Johnson pay his Lordship this high compliment: 'I never was in Lord Elibank's company without learning something.'

We sat together till it was too late for the afternoon service. Thrale said he had come with intention to go to church with us. We went at seven to evening prayers at St. Clement's church, after having drank coffee; an indulgence, which I understood Johnson yielded to on this occasion, in compliment to Thrale.

On Sunday, April 7, Easter-day, after having been at St. Paul's cathedral, I came to Dr. Johnson, according to my usual custom. It seemed to me, that there was always something peculiarly mild and placid in his manner upon this holy festival, the commemoration of the most joyful event in the history of our world, the resurrection of our LORD and SAVIOUR, who, having triumphed over death and the grave, proclaimed immortality to mankind.

I repeated to him an argument of a lady[2] of my acquaintance, who maintained, that her husband's having been guilty of numberless infidelities, released her from conjugal obligations, because they were reciprocal. JOHNSON. 'This is miserable stuff, Sir.

---

[1] Patrick, Lord Elibank, who died in 1778.
[2] *[Prof. Pottle and Dr. Bennett suggest* Jane, Countess of Eglinton. See *Boswell Papers,* xi. 277.*]*

To the contract of marriage, besides the man and wife, there is a third party—Society; and, if it be considered as a vow—GOD: and, therefore, it cannot be dissolved by their consent alone. Laws are not made for particular cases, but for men in general. A woman may be unhappy with her husband; but she cannot be freed from him without the approbation of the civil and ecclesiastical power. A man may be unhappy, because he is not so rich as another; but he is not to seize upon another's property with his own hand.' BOSWELL. 'But, Sir, this lady does not want that the contract should be dissolved; she only argues that she may indulge herself in gallantries with equal freedom as her husband does, provided she takes care not to introduce a spurious issue into his family. You know, Sir, what Macrobius has told us of Julia.'[1] JOHNSON. 'This lady of yours, Sir, I think, is very fit for a brothel.'

Mr. Macbean, authour of the *Dictionary of ancient Geography*, came in. He mentioned that he had been forty years absent from Scotland. 'Ah, Boswell! (said Johnson, smiling,) what would you give to be forty years from Scotland?' I said, 'I should not like to be so long absent from the seat of my ancestors.' This gentleman, Mrs. Williams, and Mr. Levett, dined with us.

Dr. Johnson made a remark, which both Mr. Macbean and I thought new. It was this: that 'the law against usury is for the protection of creditors as well as of debtors; for if there were no such check, people would be apt, from the temptation of great interest, to lend to desperate persons, by whom they would lose their money. Accordingly there are instances of ladies being ruined, by having injudiciously sunk their fortunes for high annuities, which, after a few years, ceased to be paid, in consequence of the ruined circumstances of the borrower.'

Mrs. Williams was very peevish; and I wondered at Johnson's patience with her now, as I had often done on similar occasions. The truth is, that his humane consideration of the forlorn and indigent state in which this lady was left by her father, induced him to treat her with the utmost tenderness, and even to be

---

[1] '*Nunquam enim nisi navi plenâ tollo vectorem.*' ['I never take on a passenger but when the ship is full.'] Lib. ii. c. vi.

desirous of procuring her amusement, so as sometimes to incommode many of his friends, by carrying her with him to their houses, where, from her manner of eating, in consequence of her blindness, she could not but offend the delicacy of persons of nice sensations.

After coffee, we went to afternoon service in St. Clement's church. Observing some beggars in the street as we walked along, I said to him I supposed there was no civilised country in the world, where the misery of want in the lowest classes of the people was prevented. JOHNSON. 'I believe, Sir, there is not; but it is better that some should be unhappy, than that none should be happy, which would be the case in a general state of equality.'

When the service was ended, I went home with him, and we sat quietly by ourselves. He recommended Dr. Cheyne's books. I said, I thought Cheyne had been reckoned whimsical. 'So he was, (said he,) in some things; but there is no end of objections. There are few books to which some objection or other may not be made.' He added, 'I would not have you read anything else of Cheyne, but his book on Health, and his *English Malady*.'

Upon the question whether a man[1] who had been guilty of vicious actions would do well to force himself into solitude and sadness; JOHNSON. 'No, Sir, unless it prevent him from being vicious again. With some people, gloomy penitence is only madness turned upside down. A man may be gloomy, till, in order to be relieved from gloom, he has recourse again to criminal indulgencies.'

On Wednesday, April 10, I dined with him at Mr. Thrale's, where were Mr. Murphy and some other company. Before dinner, Dr. Johnson and I passed some time by ourselves. I was sorry to find it was now resolved that the proposed journey to Italy should not take place this year. He said, 'I am disappointed, to be sure; but it is not a great disappointment.' I wondered to see him bear, with a philosophical calmness, what would have made most people peevish and fretful. I perceived, however, that he had so warmly cherished the hope of enjoying classical scenes,

[1] [Boswell. *Powell.*]

that he could not easily part with the scheme; for he said, 'I shall probably contrive to get to Italy some other way. But I won't mention it to Mr. and Mrs. Thrale, as it might vex them.' I suggested, that going to Italy might have done Mr. and Mrs. Thrale good. JOHNSON. 'I rather believe not, Sir. While grief is fresh, every attempt to divert only irritates. You must wait till grief be *digested*, and then amusement will dissipate the remains of it.'

At dinner, Mr. Murphy entertained us with the history of Mr. Joseph Simpson, a schoolfellow of Dr. Johnson's, a barrister at law, of good parts, but who fell into a dissipated course of life, incompatible with that success in his profession which he once had, and would otherwise have deservedly maintained; yet he still preserved a dignity in his deportment. He wrote a tragedy on the story of Leonidas, entitled *The Patriot.* He read it to a company of lawyers, who found so many faults, that he wrote it over again: so then there were two tragedies on the same subject and with the same title. Dr. Johnson told us, that one of them was still in his possession. This very piece was, after his death, published by some person who had been about him, and, for the sake of a little hasty profit, was fallaciously advertised, so as to make it be believed to have been written by Johnson himself.

I said, I disliked the custom which some people had of bringing their children into company, because it in a manner forced us to pay foolish compliments to please their parents. JOHNSON. 'You are right, Sir. We may be excused for not caring much about other people's children, for there are many who care very little about their own children. It may be observed, that men, who from being engaged in business, or from their course of life in whatever way, seldom see their children, do not care much about them. I myself should not have had much fondness for a child of my own.' MRS. THRALE. 'Nay, Sir, how can you talk so?' JOHNSON. 'At least, I never wished to have a child.'

Mr. Murphy mentioned Dr. Johnson's having a design to publish an edition of Cowley. Johnson said, he did not know but he should; and he expressed his disapprobation of Dr. Hurd, for having published a mutilated edition under the title of *Select*

Works of Abraham Cowley. Mr. Murphy thought it a bad precedent; observing that any authour might be used in the same
manner; and that it was pleasing to see the variety of an authour's
compositions, at different periods.

We talked of Flatman's Poems; and Mrs. Thrale observed,
that Pope had partly borrowed from him *The dying Christian to
his Soul*. Johnson repeated Rochester's verses upon Flatman,
which I think by much too severe:

> 'Nor that slow drudge in swift Pindarick strains,
> Flatman, who Cowley imitates with pains,
> And rides a jaded Muse, whipt with lose reins.'

I like to recollect all the passages that I heard Johnson repeat:
it stamps a value on them.

He told us, that the book entitled *The Lives of the Poets*, by
Mr. Cibber, was entirely compiled by Mr. Shiels, a Scotchman,
one of his amanuenses. 'The bookseller (said he,) gave Theo-
philus Cibber, who was then in prison, ten guineas, to allow
Mr. Cibber to be put upon the title-page, as the authour; by this,
a double imposition was intended: in the first place, that it was
the work of a Cibber at all; and, in the second place, that it was
the work of old Cibber.'[1]

[1] In the *Monthly Review* for May, 1792, there is such a correction of the
above passage, as I should think myself very culpable not to subjoin. 'This
account is very inaccurate. The following statement of facts we know to be
true, in every material circumstance:—Shiels was the principal collector and
digester of the materials for the work: but as he was very raw in authourship, an indifferent writer in prose, and his language full of Scotticisms,
Cibber, who was a clever, lively fellow, and then soliciting employment
among the booksellers, was engaged to correct the style and diction of the
whole work, then intended to make only four volumes, with power to alter,
expunge, or add, as he liked. He was also to supply *notes*, occasionally,
especially concerning those dramatick poets with whom he had been chiefly
conversant. He also engaged to write several of the Lives; which, (as we
are told,) he, accordingly, performed. He was farther useful in striking out
the Jacobitical and Tory sentiments, which Shiels had industriously interspersed wherever he could bring them in:—and, as the success of the work
appeared, after all, very doubtful, he was content with twenty-one pounds
for his labour beside a few sets of the books, to disperse among his friends.—
Shiels had nearly seventy pounds, beside the advantage of many of the best
Lives in the work being communicated by friends to the undertaking; and for
which Mr. Shiels had the same consideration as for the rest, being paid by
the sheet, for the whole. He was, however, so angry with his Whiggish

Mr. Murphy said, that *The Memoirs of Gray's Life* set him much higher in his estimation than his poems did; for you there saw a man constantly at work in literature. Johnson acquiesced in this; but depreciated the book, I thought, very unreasonably. For he said, 'I forced myself to read it, only because it was a

supervisor, (Theo., like his father, being a violent stickler for the political principles which prevailed in the Reign of George the Second,) for so unmercifully mutilating his copy, and scouting his politicks, that he wrote Cibber a challenge: but was prevented from sending it, by the publisher, who fairly laughed him out of his fury. The proprietors, too, were discontented, in the end, on account of Mr. Cibber's unexpected industry; for his corrections and alterations in the proof-sheets were so numerous and considerable, that the printer made for them a grievous addition to his bill; and, in fine, all parties were dissatisfied. On the whole, the work was productive of no profit to the undertakers, who had agreed, in case of success, to make Cibber a present of some addition to the twenty guineas which he had received, and for which his receipt is now in the booksellers' hands. We are farther assured, that he actually obtained an additional sum; when he, soon after, (in the year 1758,) unfortunately embarked for Dublin, on an engagement for one of the theatres there: but the ship was cast away, and every person on board perished. There were about sixty passengers, among whom was the Earl of Drogheda, with many other persons of consequence and property.

'As to the alledged design of making the compilement pass for the work of old Mr. Cibber, the charges seem to have been founded on a somewhat uncharitable construction. We are assured that the thought was not harboured by some of the proprietors, who are still living; and we hope that it did not occur to the first designer of the work, who was also the printer of it, and who bore a respectable character.

'We have been induced to enter thus circumstantially into the foregoing detail of facts relating to *The Lives of the Poets*, compiled by Messrs. Cibber and Shiels, from a sincere regard to that sacred principle of Truth, to which Dr. Johnson so rigidly adhered, according to the best of his knowledge; and which we believed, *no consideration* would have prevailed on him to violate. In regard to the matter, which we now dismiss, he had, no doubt, been misled by partial and wrong information: Shiels was the Doctor's amanuensis; he had quarrelled with Cibber; it is natural to suppose that he told his story in his own way; and it is certain that *he* was not "a very sturdy moralist".' This explanation appears to me very satisfactory. It is, however, to be observed, that the story told by Johnson does not rest solely upon my record of his conversation; for he himself has published it in his *Life of Hammond,* where he says, 'the manuscript of Shiels is now in my possession.' Very probably he had trusted to Shiels's word, and never looked at it so as to compare it with *The Lives of the Poets,* as published under Mr. Cibber's name. What became of that manuscript I know not. I should have liked much to examine it. I suppose it was thrown into the fire in that impetuous combustion of papers, which Johnson I think rashly executed, when *moribundus.*

common topick of conversation. I found it mighty dull; and, as to the style, it is fit for the second table.' Why he thought so I was at a loss to conceive. He now gave it as his opinion, that 'Akenside was a superiour poet both to Gray and Mason.'

Talking of the Reviews, Johnson said, 'I think them very impartial: I do not know an instance of partiality.' He mentioned what had passed upon the subject of the *Monthly* and *Critical Reviews*, in the conversation with which his Majesty had honoured him. He expatiated a little more on them this evening. 'The Monthly Reviewers (said he,) are not Deists; but they are Christians with as little christianity as may be; and are for pulling down all establishments. The Critical Reviewers are for supporting the constitution, both in church and state. The Critical Reviewers, I believe, often review without reading the books through; but lay hold of a topick, and write chiefly from their own minds. The Monthly Reviewers are duller men, and are glad to read the books through.'

He talked of Lord Lyttelton's extreme anxiety as an authour; observing, that 'he was thirty years in preparing his *History*, and that he employed a man to point it for him; as if (laughing) another man could point his sense better than himself.' Mr. Murphy said, he understood, his history was kept back several years for fear of Smollet. JOHNSON. 'This seems strange to Murphy and me, who never felt that anxiety, but sent what we wrote to the press, and let it take its chance.' MRS. THRALE. 'The time has been, Sir, when you felt it.' JOHNSON. 'Why really, Madam, I do not recollect a time when that was the case.'

Talking of *The Spectator*, he said, 'It is wonderful that there is such a proportion of bad papers, in the half of the work which was not written by Addison; for there was all the world to write that half, yet not a half of that half is good. One of the finest pieces in the English language is the paper on Novelty, yet we do not hear it talked of. It was written by Grove, a dissenting *teacher*.' He would not, I perceived, call him a *clergyman*, though he was candid enough to allow very great merit to his composition. Mr. Murphy said, he remembered when there were several people alive in London, who enjoyed a considerable reputation

merely from having written a paper in *The Spectator*. He mentioned particularly Mr. Ince, who used to frequent Tom's coffee-
house. 'But (said Johnson,) you must consider how highly Steele
speaks of Mr. Ince.' He would not allow that the paper on carrying a boy to travel, signed *Philip Homebred*, which was reported
to be written by the Lord Chancellor Hardwicke, had merit. He
said, 'it was quite vulgar, and had nothing luminous.'

Johnson mentioned Dr. Barry's[1] System of Physick. 'He was
a man (said he,) who had acquired a high reputation in Dublin,
came over to England, and brought his reputation with him, but
had not great success. His notion was, that pulsation occasions
death by attrition; and that, therefore, the way to preserve life
is to retard pulsation. But we know that pulsation is strongest
in infants, and that we increase in growth while it operates in its
regular course; so it cannot be the cause of destruction.' Soon
after this, he said something very flattering to Mrs. Thrale,
which I do not recollect; but it concluded with wishing her
long life. 'Sir, (said I,) if Dr. Barry's system be true, you have
now shortened Mrs. Thrale's life, perhaps, some minutes, by
accelerating her pulsation.'

On Thursday, April 11, I dined with him at General Paoli's,
in whose house I now resided, and where I had ever afterwards
the honour of being entertained with the kindest attention as his
constant guest, while I was in London, till I had a house of my
own there. I mentioned my having that morning introduced to
Mr. Garrick, Count Neni, a Flemish Nobleman of great rank and
fortune, to whom Garrick talked of Abel Drugger as *a small part*;
and related, with pleasant vanity, that a Frenchman who had
seen him in one of his low characters, exclaimed, *'Comment! je ne
le crois pas. Ce n'est pas Monsieur Garrick, ce Grand Homme!'*
Garrick added, with an appearance of grave recollection, 'If I
were to begin life again, I think I should not play those low
characters.' Upon which I observed, 'Sir, you would be in the
wrong; for your great excellence is your variety of playing, your
representing so well, characters so very different.' JOHNSON.
'Garrick, Sir, was not in earnest in what he said; for, to be sure,

[1] Sir Edward Barry, Baronet.

his peculiar excellence is his variety: and, perhaps, there is not any one character which has not been as well acted by somebody else, as he could do it.' BOSWELL. 'Why then, Sir, did he talk so?' JOHNSON. 'Why, Sir, to make you answer as you did.' BOSWELL. 'I don't know, Sir; he seemed to dip deep into his mind for the reflection.' JOHNSON. 'He had not far to dip, Sir: he said the same thing, probably, twenty times before.'

Of a nobleman[1] raised at a very early period to high office, he said, 'His parts, Sir, are pretty well for a Lord; but would not be distinguished in a man who had nothing else but his parts.'

A journey to Italy was still in his thoughts. He said, 'A man who has not been in Italy, is always conscious of an inferiority, from his not having seen what it is expected a man should see. The grand object of travelling is to see the shores of the Mediterranean. On those shores were the four great Empires of the world; the Assyrian, the Persian, the Grecian, and the Roman.— All our religion, almost all our law, almost all our arts, almost all that sets us above savages, has come to us from the shores of the Mediterranean.' The General observed, that 'THE MEDITERRANEAN would be a noble subject for a poem.'

We talked of translation. I said, I could not define it, nor could I think of a similitude to illustrate it; but that it appeared to me the translation of poetry could be only imitation. JOHNSON. 'You may translate books of science exactly. You may also translate history, in so far as it is not embellished with oratory, which is poetical. Poetry, indeed, cannot be translated; and, therefore, it is the poets that preserve languages; for we would not be at the trouble to learn a language, if we could have all that is written in it just as well in a translation. But as the beauties of poetry cannot be preserved in any language except that in which it was originally written, we learn the language.'

A gentleman[2] maintained that the art of printing had hurt real learning, by disseminating idle writings.—JOHNSON. 'Sir, if it had not been for the art of printing, we should now have **no learning** at all; for books would have perished faster than

---

[1] [Lord Shelburne, *Boswell Papers*, xi. 242.]
[2] [Paoli, *Ib.* 243.]

they could have been transcribed.' This observation seems not just, considering for how many ages books were preserved by writing alone.

The same gentleman maintained, that a general diffusion of knowledge among a people was a disadvantage; for it made the vulgar rise above their humble sphere. JOHNSON. 'Sir, while knowledge is a distinction, those who are possessed of it will naturally rise above those who are not. Merely to read and write was a distinction at first; but we see when reading and writing have become general, the common people keep their stations. And so, were higher attainments to become general the effect would be the same.'

'Goldsmith (he said,) referred every thing to vanity; his virtues, and his vices too, were from that motive. He was not a social man. He never exchanged mind with you.'

We spent the evening at Mr. Hoole's. Mr. Mickle, the excellent translator of *The Lusiad*, was there. I have preserved little of the conversation of this evening. Dr. Johnson said, 'Thomson had a true poetical genius, the power of viewing every thing in a poetical light. His fault is such a cloud of words sometimes, that the sense can hardly peep through. Shiels, who compiled *Cibber's Lives of the Poets*,[1] was one day sitting with me. I took down Thomson, and read aloud a large portion of him, and then asked, —Is not this fine? Shiels having expressed the highest admiration. Well, Sir, (said I,) I have omitted every other line.'

I related a dispute between Goldsmith and Mr. Robert Dodsley, one day when they and I were dining at Tom Davies's, in 1762. Goldsmith asserted, that there was no poetry produced in this age. Dodsley appealed to his own *Collection*, and maintained, that though you could not find a palace like Dryden's *Ode on St. Cecilia's Day*, you had villages composed of very pretty houses; and he mentioned particularly *The Spleen*. JOHNSON. 'I think Dodsley gave up the question. He and Goldsmith said the same thing; only he said it in a softer manner than Goldsmith did; for he acknowledged that there was no poetry, nothing that towered above the common mark. You may find wit and

[1] See *ante*, note, p. 738.

humour in verse, and yet no poetry. *Hudibras* has a profusion of
these; yet it is not to be reckoned a poem. *The Spleen*, in Dodsley's *Collection*, on which you say he chiefly rested, is not poetry.'
BOSWELL. 'Does not Gray's poetry, Sir, tower above the common mark?' JOHNSON. 'Yes, Sir; but we must attend to the
difference between what men in general cannot do if they would,
and what every man may do if he would. Sixteen-string Jack[1]
towered above the common mark.' BOSWELL. 'Then, Sir, what
is poetry?' JOHNSON. 'Why, Sir, it is much easier to say what
it is not. We all *know* what light is; but it is not easy to *tell*
what it is.'

On Friday, April 12, I dined with him at our friend Tom
Davies's, where we met Mr. Cradock, of Leicestershire, authour
of *Zobeide*, a tragedy; a very pleasing gentleman, to whom my
friend Dr. Farmer's very excellent *Essay on the Learning of
Shakspeare* is addressed; and Dr. Harwood, who has written and
published various works; particularly a fantastical translation of
the New Testament, in modern phrase, and with a Socinian
twist.

I introduced Aristotle's doctrine in his *Art of Poetry*, of 'the
κάθαρσις τῶν παθημάτων, the purging of the passions,' as the purpose of tragedy.[2] 'But how are the passions to be purged by
terrour and pity?' (said I, with an assumed air of ignorance, to
incite him to talk, for which it was often necessary to employ
some address). JOHNSON. 'Why, Sir, you are to consider what
is the meaning of purging in the original sense. It is to expel
impurities from the human body. The mind is subject to the
same imperfection. The passions are the great movers of human
actions; but they are mixed with such impurities, that it is necessary they should be purged or refined by means of terrour and
pity. For instance, ambition is a noble passion; but by seeing
upon the stage, that a man who is so excessively ambitious as to

[1] A noted highwayman, who after having been several times tried and
acquitted, was at last hanged. He was remarkable for foppery in his dress,
and particularly for wearing a bunch of sixteen strings at the knees of his
breeches.
[2] See an ingenious Essay on this subject by the late Dr. Moor, Greek
Professor at Glasgow.

raise himself by injustice, is punished, we are terrified at the fatal consequences of such a passion. In the same manner a certain degree of resentment is necessary; but if we see that a man carries it too far, we pity the object of it, and are taught to moderate that passion.' My record upon this occasion does great injustice to Johnson's expression, which was so forcible and brilliant, that Mr. Cradock whispered me, 'O that his words were written in a book!'

I observed the great defect of the tragedy of *Othello* was, that it had not a moral; for that no man could resist the circumstances of suspicion which were artfully suggested to Othello's mind. JOHNSON. 'In the first place, Sir, we learn from *Othello* this very useful moral, not to make an unequal match; in the second place, we learn not to yield too readily to suspicion. The handkerchief is merely a trick, though a very pretty trick; but there are no other circumstances of reasonable suspicion, except what is related by Iago of Cassio's warm expressions concerning Desdemona in his sleep; and that depended entirely upon the assertion of one man. No, Sir, I think *Othello* has more moral than almost any play.'

Talking of a penurious gentleman[1] of our acquaintance, Johnson said, 'Sir, he is narrow, not so much from avarice, as from impotence to spend his money. He cannot find in his heart to pour out a bottle of wine; but he would not much care if it should sour.'

He said, he wished to see John Dennis's *Critical Works* collected. Davies said they would not sell. Dr. Johnson seemed to think otherwise.

Davies said of a well-known dramatick authour,[2] that 'he lived upon *potted stories*, and that he made his way as Hannibal did, by vinegar; having begun by attacking people; particularly the players.'

He reminded Dr. Johnson of Mr. Murphy's having paid him the highest compliment that ever was paid to a layman, by asking his pardon for repeating some oaths in the course of telling a story.

[1] [Sir Alexander MacDonald. *Powell.*]   [2] [Murphy, *Croker*[2].]

Johnson and I supt this evening at the Crown and Anchor tavern, in company with Sir Joshua Reynolds, Mr. Langton, Mr. Nairne, now one of the Scotch Judges, with the title of Lord Dunsinan, and my very worthy friend, Sir William Forbes, of Pitsligo.

We discussed the question whether drinking improved conversation and benevolence. Sir Joshua maintained it did. JOHNSON. 'No, Sir: before dinner men meet with great inequality of understanding; and those who are conscious of their inferiority, have the modesty not to talk. When they have drunk wine, every man feels himself happy, and loses that modesty, and grows impudent and vociferous: but he is not improved; he is only not sensible of his defects.' Sir Joshua said the Doctor was talking of the effects of excess in wine; but that a moderate glass enlivened the mind, by giving a proper circulation to the blood. 'I am (said he,) in very good spirits when I get up in the morning. By dinnertime I am exhausted; wine puts me in the same state as when I got up; and I am sure that moderate drinking makes people talk better.' JOHNSON. 'No, Sir; wine gives not light, gay, ideal hilarity; but tumultuous, noisy, clamorous merriment. I have heard none of those drunken,—nay, drunken is a coarse word,—none of those *vinous* flights.' SIR JOSHUA. 'Because you have sat by, quite sober, and felt an envy of the happiness of those who were drinking.' JOHNSON. 'Perhaps, contempt.—And, Sir, it is not necessary to be drunk one's self, to relish the wit of drunkenness. Do we not judge of the drunken wit of the dialogue between Iago and Cassio, the most excellent in its kind, when we are quite sober? Wit is wit, by whatever means it is produced; and, if good, will appear so at all times. I admit that the spirits are raised by drinking, as by the common participation of any pleasure: cock-fighting, or bear-baiting, will raise the spirits of a company, as drinking does, though surely they will not improve conversation. I also admit, that there are some sluggish men who are improved by drinking; as there are fruits which are not good till they are rotten. There are such men, but they are medlars. I indeed allow that there have been a very few men of talents who were improved by drinking; but

I maintain that I am right as to the effects of drinking in general: and let it be considered, that there is no position, however false in its universality, which is not true of some particular man.' Sir William Forbes said, 'Might not a man warmed with wine be like a bottle of beer, which is made brisker by being set before the fire?'—'Nay, (said Johnson, laughing,) I cannot answer that: that is too much for me.'

I observed, that wine did some people harm, by inflaming, confusing, and irritating their minds; but that the experience of mankind had declared in favour of moderate drinking. JOHNSON. 'Sir, I do not say it is wrong to produce self-complacency by drinking; I only deny that it improves the mind. When I drank wine, I scorned to drink it when in company. I have drunk many a bottle by myself; in the first place, because I had need of it to raise my spirits; in the second place, because I would have nobody to witness its effects upon me.'

He told us, 'almost all his *Ramblers* were written just as they were wanted for the press; that he sent a certain portion of the copy of an essay, and wrote the remainder, while the former part of it was printing. When it was wanted, and he had fairly sat down to it, he was sure it would be done.'

He said, that for general improvement, a man should read whatever his immediate inclination prompts him to; though, to be sure, if a man has a science to learn, he must regularly and resolutely advance. He added, 'what we read with inclination makes a much stronger impression. If we read without inclination, half the mind is employed in fixing the attention; so there is but one half to be employed on what we read.' He told us, he read Fielding's *Amelia* through without stopping.[1] He said, 'if a man begins to read in the middle of a book, and feels an inclination to go on, let him not quit it, to go to the beginning. He may, perhaps, not feel again the inclination.'

Sir Joshua mentioned Mr. Cumberland's *Odes*, which were just published. JOHNSON. 'Why, Sir, they would have been

---

[1] We have here an involuntary testimony to the excellence of this admirable writer, to whom we have seen that Dr. Johnson *directly* allowed so little merit.

thought as good as Odes commonly are, if Cumberland had not put his name to them; but a name immediately draws censure, unless it be a name that bears down everything before it. Nay, Cumberland has made his *Odes* subsidiary to the fame of another man.[1] They might have run well enough by themselves; but he has not only loaded them with a name, but has made them carry double.'

We talked of the Reviews, and Dr. Johnson spoke of them as he did at Thrale's.[2] Sir Joshua said, what I have often thought, that he wondered to find so much good writing employed in them, when the authours were to remain unknown, and so could not have the motive of fame. JOHNSON. 'Nay, Sir, those who write in them, write well, in order to be paid well.'

Soon after this day, he went to Bath with Mr. and Mrs. Thrale. I had never seen that beautiful city, and wished to take the opportunity of visiting it, while Johnson was there. Having written to him, I received the following answer.

'*To* JAMES BOSWELL, ESQ.

'DEAR SIR,—Why do you talk of neglect? When did I neglect you? If you will come to Bath, we shall all be glad to see you. Come, therefore, as soon as you can.

'But I have a little business for you at London. Bid Francis look in the paper-drawer of the chest of drawers in my bed-chamber, for two cases; one for the Attorney-General, and one for the Solicitor-General. They lie, I think, at the top of my papers; otherwise they are somewhere else, and will give me more trouble.

'Please to write to me immediately, if they can be found. Make my compliments to all our friends round the world, and to Mrs. Williams at home. I am, Sir, your, &c.

'SAM. JOHNSON.'

'Search for the papers as soon as you can, that, if it is necessary, I may write to you again before you come down.'

---

[1] Mr. Romney, the painter, who has now deservedly established a high reputation.

[2] See *ante*, p. 740.

On the 26th of April, I went to Bath; and on my arrival at the Pelican inn, found lying for me an obliging invitation from Mr. and Mrs. Thrale, by whom I was agreeably entertained almost constantly during my stay. They were gone to the rooms; but there was a kind note from Dr. Johnson, that he should sit at home all the evening. I went to him directly, and before Mr. and Mrs. Thrale returned, we had by ourselves some hours of tea-drinking and talk.

I shall group together such of his sayings as I preserved during the few days that I was at Bath.

Of a person[1] who differed from him in politicks, he said, 'In private life he is a very honest gentleman; but I will not allow him to be so in publick life. People *may* be honest, though they are doing wrong: that is between their Maker and them. But *we*, who are suffering by their pernicious conduct, are to destroy them. We are sure that ——— acts from interest. We know what his genuine principles were. They who allow their passions to confound the distinctions between right and wrong, are criminal. They may be convinced; but they have not come honestly by their conviction.'

It having been mentioned, I know not with what truth, that, a certain female political writer,[2] whose doctrines he disliked, had of late become very fond of dress, sat hours together at her toilet, and even put on rouge:—JOHNSON. 'She is better employed at her toilet, than using her pen. It is better she should be reddening her own cheeks, than blackening other people's characters.'

He told us that 'Addison wrote Budgell's papers in the *Spectator*, at least mended them so much, that he made them almost his own; and that Draper, Tonson's partner, assured Mrs. Johnson, that the much admired Epilogue to *The Distressed Mother*, which came out in Budgell's name, was in reality written by Addison.'

'The mode of government by one may be ill adapted to a small society, but is best for a great nation. The characteristic of our

[1] [Burke, *Croker*[1].]
[2] [Mrs. Catherine Macaulay, *Mrs. Piozzi: Croker*[2].]

own government at present is imbecility. The magistrate dare not call the guards for fear of being hanged. The guards will not come, for fear of being given up to the blind rage of popular juries.'

Of the father[1] of one of our friends, he observed, 'He never clarified his notions, by filtrating them through other minds. He had a canal upon his estate, where at one place the bank was too low.—I dug the canal deeper, said he.'

He told me that 'so long ago as 1748 he had read "*The Grave*, a Poem,"[2] but did not like it much.' I differed from him, for though it is not equal throughout, and is seldom elegantly correct, it abounds in solemn thought, and poetical imagery beyond the common reach. The world has differed from him; for the poem has passed through many editions, and is still much read by people of a serious cast of mind.

A literary lady of large fortune[3] was mentioned, as one who did good to many, but by no means 'by stealth,' and instead of 'blushing to find it fame,' acted evidently from vanity. JOHNSON. 'I have seen no beings who do as much good from benevolence, as she does, from whatever motive. If there are such under the earth, or in the clouds, I wish they would come up, or come down. What Soame Jenyns says upon this subject is not to be minded; he is a wit. No, Sir; to act from pure benevolence is not possible for finite beings. Human benevolence is mingled with vanity, interest, or some other motive.'

He would not allow me to praise a lady[4] then at Bath; observing, 'She does not gain upon me, Sir; I think her empty-headed.' He was, indeed, a stern critick upon characters and

---

[1] [Old Mr. Langton, *Boswell Papers*, xi. 265.]
[2] I am sorry that there are no memoirs of the Reverend Robert Blair, the authour of this poem. He was the representative of the ancient family of Blair, of Blair, in Ayrshire, but the estate had descended to a female, and afterwards passed to the son of her husband by another marriage. He was minister of the parish of Athelstanford, where Mr. John Home was his successor; so that it may truely be called classick ground. His son, who is of the same name, and a man eminent for talents and learning, is now, with universal approbation, Solicitor-General of Scotland.
[3] [Mrs. Montagu, *Boswell Papers*, xi. 265.]
[4] [Miss Peggy Owen, *Ib.*]

manners. Even Mrs. Thrale did not escape his friendly animadversion at times. When he and I were one day endeavouring
to ascertain, article by article, how one of our friends[1] could
possibly spend as much money in his family as he told us he did,
she interrupted us by a lively extravagant sally, on the expence
of clothing his children, describing it in a very ludicrous and
fanciful manner. Johnson looked a little angry, and said, 'Nay,
Madam, when you are declaiming, declaim; and when you are
calculating, calculate.' At another time, when she said, perhaps
affectedly, 'I don't like to fly.' JOHNSON. 'With *your* wings,
Madam, you *must* fly: but have a care, there are *clippers* abroad.'
How very well was this said, and how fully has experience proved
the truth of it! But have they not *clipped* rather *rudely*, and gone
a great deal *closer* than was necessary?

A gentleman[2] expressed a wish to go and live three years at
Otaheité, or New-Zealand, in order to obtain a full acquaintance
with people, so totally different from all that we have ever known,
and be satisfied what pure nature can do for man. JOHNSON.
'What could you learn, Sir? What can savages tell, but what
they themselves have seen? Of the past, or the invisible, they can
tell nothing. The inhabitants of Otaheité and New-Zealand are
not in a state of pure nature; for it is plain they broke off from
some other people. Had they grown out of the ground, you might
have judged of a state of pure nature. Fanciful people may talk
of a mythology being amongst them; but it must be invention.
They have once had religion, which has been gradually debased.
And what account of their religion can you suppose to be learnt
from savages? Only consider, Sir, our own state: our religion is
in a book; we have an order of men whose duty it is to teach it;
we have one day in the week set apart for it, and this is in general
pretty well observed: yet ask the first ten gross men you meet,
and hear what they can tell of their religion.'

On Monday, April 29, he and I made an excursion to Bristol,
where I was entertained with seeing him enquire upon the spot,
into the authenticity of 'Rowley's Poetry,' as I had seen him
enquire upon the spot into the authenticity of 'Ossian's Poetry.'

[1] [Langton. *Ib.*]   [2] [Boswell, *Ib.* 267.]

George Catcot, the pewterer, who was as zealous for Rowley, as Dr. Hugh Blair was for Ossian, (I trust my Reverend friend will excuse the comparison,) attended us at our inn, and with a triumphant air of lively simplicity called out, 'I'll make Dr. Johnson a convert.' Dr. Johnson, at his desire, read aloud some of Chatterton's fabricated verses, while Catcot stood at the back of his chair, moving himself like a pendulum, and beating time with his feet, and now and then looking into Dr. Johnson's face, wondering that he was not yet convinced. We called on Mr. Barret, the surgeon, and saw some of the *originals* as they were called, which were executed very artificially; but from a careful inspection of them, and a consideration of the circumstances with which they were attended, we were quite satisfied of the imposture, which, indeed, has been clearly demonstrated from internal evidence, by several able criticks.[1]

Honest Catcot seemed to pay no attention whatever to any objections, but insisted, as an end of all controversy, that we should go with him to the tower of the church of St. Mary, Redcliff, and *view with our own eyes* the ancient chest in which the manuscripts were found. To this, Dr. Johnson good-naturedly agreed; and though troubled with a shortness of breathing, laboured up a long flight of steps, till we came to the place where the wonderous chest stood. '*There,* (said Catcot, with a bouncing confident credulity,) *there* is the very chest itself.' After this *ocular demonstration,* there was no more to be said. He brought to my recollection a Scotch Highlander, a man of learning too, and who had seen the world, attesting, and at the same time giving his reasons for the authenticity of Fingal:—'I have heard all that poem when I was young.'—'Have you, Sir? Pray what have you heard?'—'I have heard Ossian, Oscar, and *every one of them.*'

Johnson said of Chatterton, 'This is the most extraordinary young man that has encountered my knowledge. It is wonderful how the whelp has written such things.'

We were by no means pleased with our inn at Bristol. 'Let us see now, (said I,) how we should describe it.' Johnson was

---

[1] Mr. Tyrwhitt, Mr. Warton, Mr. Malone.

ready with his raillery. 'Describe it, Sir?—Why, it was so bad that Boswell wished to be in Scotland!'

After Dr. Johnson's return to London, I was several times with him at his house, where I occasionally slept, in the room that had been assigned to me. I dined with him at Dr. Taylor's, at General Oglethorpe's, and at General Paoli's. To avoid a tedious minuteness, I shall group together what I have preserved of his conversation during this period also, without specifying each scene where it passed, except one, which will be found so remarkable as certainly to deserve a very particular relation. Where the place or the persons do not contribute to the zest of the conversation, it is unnecessary to encumber my page with mentioning them. To know of what vintage our wine is, enables us to judge of its value, and to drink it with more relish: but to have the produce of each vine of one vineyard, in the same year, kept separate, would serve no purpose. To know that our wine, (to use an advertising phrase,) is 'of the stock of an Ambassadour lately deceased,' heightens its flavour: but it signifies nothing to know the bin where each bottle was once deposited.

'Garrick (he observed,) does not play the part of Archer in *The Beaux Stratagem* well. The gentleman should break out through the footman, which is not the case as he does it.'

'Where there is no education, as in savage countries, men will have the upper hand of women. Bodily strength, no doubt, contributes to this; but it would be so, exclusive of that; for it is mind that always governs. When it comes to dry understanding, man has the better.'

'The little volumes entitled *Respublicæ*, which are very well done, were a bookseller's work.'

'There is much talk of the misery which we cause to the brute creation; but they are recompensed by existence. If they were not useful to man, and therefore protected by him, they would not be nearly so numerous.' This argument is to be found in the able and benignant Hutchinson's[1] *Moral Philosophy*. But the question is, whether the animals who endure such sufferings of various kinds, for the service and entertainment of man, would

[1] [Francis Hutcheson.]

accept of existence upon the terms on which they have it. Madame Sévigné, who, though she had many enjoyments, felt with delicate sensibility the prevalence of misery, complains of the task of existence having been imposed upon her without her consent.

'That man is never happy for the present is so true, that all his relief from unhappiness is only forgetting himself for a little while. Life is a progress from want to want, not from enjoyment to enjoyment.'

'Though many men are nominally entrusted with the administration of hospitals and other publick institutions, almost all the good is done by one man, by whom the rest are driven on; owing to confidence in him, and indolence in them.'

'Lord Chesterfield's *Letters to his Son*, I think, might be made a very pretty book. Take out the immorality, and it should be put into the hands of every young gentleman. An elegant manner and easiness of behaviour are acquired gradually and imperceptibly. No man can say "I'll be genteel." There are ten genteel women for one genteel man, because they are more restrained. A man without some degree of restraint is insufferable; but we are all less restrained than women. Were a woman sitting in company to put out her legs before her as most men do, we should be tempted to kick them in.'

No man was a more attentive and nice observer of behaviour in those in whose company he happened to be, than Johnson; or, however strange it may seem to many, had a higher estimation of its refinements. Lord Eliot informs me, that one day when Johnson and he were at dinner at a gentleman's house in London, upon Lord Chesterfield's Letters being mentioned, Johnson surprized the company by this sentence: 'Every man of any education would rather be called a rascal, than accused of deficiency in *the graces*.' Mr. Gibbon, who was present, turned to a lady[1] who knew Johnson well, and lived much with him, and in his quaint manner, tapping his box, addressed her thus: 'Don't you think, Madam, (looking towards Johnson,) that among *all* your acquaintance, you could find *one* exception?' The lady smiled, and seemed to acquiesce.

[1] [Perhaps Mrs. Thrale. *Powell.*]

'I read (said he,) Sharpe's letters on Italy over again, when I was at Bath. There is a great deal of matter in them.'

'Mrs. Williams was angry that Thrale's family did not send regularly to her every time they heard from me while I was in the Hebrides. Little people are apt to be jealous: but they should not be jealous; for they ought to consider, that superiour attention will necessarily be paid to superiour fortune or rank. Two persons may have equal merit, and on that account may have an equal claim to attention; but one of them may have also fortune and rank, and so may have a double claim.'

Talking of his notes on Shakspeare, he said, 'I despise those who do not see that I am right in the passage where *as* is repeated, and "asses of great charge" introduced. That on "To be, or not to be," is disputable.'[1]

A gentleman,[2] whom I found sitting with him one morning, said, that in his opinion the character of an infidel was more detestable than that of a man notoriously guilty of an atrocious crime. I differed from him, because we are surer of the odiousness of the one, than of the errour of the other. JOHNSON. 'Sir, I agree with him; for the infidel would be guilty of any crime if he were inclined to it.'

'Many things which are false are transmitted from book to book, and gain credit in the world. One of these is the cry against the evil of luxury. Now the truth is, that luxury produces much good. Take the luxury of building in London. Does it not produce real advantage in the conveniency and elegance of accommodation, and this all from the exertion of industry? People will tell you, with a melancholy face, how many builders are in gaol. It is plain they are in gaol, not for building; for rents are not fallen.—A man gives half a guinea for a dish of green peas. How much gardening does this occasion? how many labourers must the competition to have such things early in the market, keep in

---

[1] It may be observed, that Mr. Malone, in his very valuable edition of Shakspeare, has fully vindicated Dr. Johnson from the idle censures which the first of these notes has given rise to. The interpretation of the other passage, which Dr. Johnson allows to be *disputable*, he has clearly shown to be erroneous.

[2] [George Steevens. *Boswell Papers*, vi. 51; xi, 275.]

employment? You will hear it said, very gravely, "Why was not the half-guinea, thus spent in luxury, given to the poor? To how many might it have afforded a good meal?" Alas! has it not gone to the *industrious* poor, whom it is better to support than the *idle* poor? You are much surer that you are doing good when you *pay* money to those who work, as the recompence of their labour, than when you *give* money merely in charity. Suppose the ancient luxury of a dish of peacock's brains were to be revived, how many carcases would be left to the poor at a cheap rate? And as to the rout that is made about people who are ruined by extravagance, it is no matter to the nation that some individuals suffer. When so much general productive exertion is the consequence of luxury, the nation does not care though there are debtors in gaol; nay, they would not care though their creditors were there too.'

The uncommon vivacity of General Oglethorpe's mind, and variety of knowledge, having sometimes made his conversation seem too desultory, Johnson observed, 'Oglethorpe, Sir, never *completes* what he has to say.'

He on the same account made a similar remark on Patrick Lord Elibank: 'Sir, there is nothing *conclusive* in his talk.'

When I complained of having dined at a splendid table[1] without hearing one sentence of conversation worthy of being remembered, he said, 'Sir, there seldom is any such conversation.' BOSWELL. 'Why then meet at table?' JOHNSON. 'Why, to eat and drink together, and to promote kindness; and, Sir, this is better done when there is no solid conversation; for when there is, people differ in opinion, and get into bad humour, or some of the company who are not capable of such conversation, are left out, and feel themselves uneasy. It was for this reason, Sir Robert Walpole said, he always talked bawdy at his table, because in that all could join.'

Being irritated by hearing a gentleman[2] ask Mr. Levett a variety of questions concerning him, when he was sitting by, he broke out, 'Sir, you have but two topicks, yourself and me. I am sick of both.' 'A man, (said he,) should not talk of himself,

---

[1] [The Earl of Pembroke's at Wilton. *Boswell Papers*, xi. 288.]
[2] [Boswell. *Ib.* 280.]

nor much of any particular person. He should take care not to be made a proverb; and, therefore, should avoid having any one topick of which people can say, "We shall hear him upon it." There was a Dr. Oldfield, who was always talking of the Duke of Marlborough. He came into a coffee-house one day, and told that his Grace had spoken in the House of Lords for half an hour. "Did he indeed speak for half an hour?" (said Belchier, the surgeon,)—"Yes."—"And what did he say of Dr. Oldfield?"—"Nothing."—"Why then, Sir, he was very ungrateful; for Dr. Oldfield could not have spoken for a quarter of an hour, without saying something of him." '

'Every man is to take existence on the terms on which it is given to him. To some men it is given on condition of not taking liberties, which other men may take without much harm. One man may drink wine, and be nothing the worse for it; on another, wine may have effects so inflammatory as to injure him both in body and mind, and perhaps, make him commit something for which he may deserve to be hanged.'

'Lord Hailes's *Annals of Scotland* have not that painted form which is the taste of this age; but it is a book which will always sell, it has such a stability of dates, such a certainty of facts, and such a punctuality of citation. I never before read Scotch history with certainty.'

I asked him whether he would advise me to read the Bible with a commentary, and what commentaries he would recommend. JOHNSON. 'To be sure, Sir, I would have you read the Bible with a commentary; and I would recommend Lowth and Patrick on the Old Testament, and Hammond on the New.'

During my stay in London this spring, I solicited his attention to another law case, in which I was engaged. In the course of a contested election for the Borough of Dumfermline, which I attended as one of my friend Colonel (afterwards Sir Archibald) Campbell's counsel; one of his political agents,[1] who was charged with having been unfaithful to his employer, and having deserted to the opposite party for a pecuniary reward—attacked very rudely in a news-paper the Reverend Mr. James Thomson, one

[1] [Robert Scotland. *Ib.* x. 91–93.]

of the ministers of that place, on account of a supposed allusion
to him in one of his sermons. Upon this the minister, on a subsequent Sunday, arraigned him by name from the pulpit with
some severity; and the agent, after the sermon was over, rose
up and asked the minister aloud, 'What bribe he had received
for telling so many lies from the chair of verity.' I was present
at this very extraordinary scene. The person arraigned, and his
father and brother, who had also had a share both of the reproof
from the pulpit, and in the retaliation, brought an action against
Mr. Thomson, in the Court of Session, for defamation and
damages, and I was one of the counsel for the reverend defendant.
The *Liberty of the Pulpit* was our great ground of defence; but
we argued also on the provocation of the previous attack, and on
the instant retaliation. The Court of Session, however, the
fifteen Judges, who are at the same time the Jury, decided against
the minister, contrary to my humble opinion; and several of
them expressed themselves with indignation against him. He
was an aged gentleman, formerly a military chaplain, and a man
of high spirit and honour. Johnson was satisfied that the judgement was wrong, and dictated to me the following argument in
confutation of it:—

'Of the censure pronounced from the pulpit, our determination must be formed, as in other cases, by a consideration of the
action itself, and the particular circumstances with which it is
invested.

'The right of censure and rebuke seems necessarily appendant
to the pastoral office. He, to whom the care of a congregation is
entrusted, is considered as the shepherd of a flock, as the teacher
of a school, as the father of a family. As a shepherd tending not
his own sheep but those of his master, he is answerable for those
that stray, and that lose themselves by straying. But no man can
be answerable for losses which he has not power to prevent, or
for vagrancy which he has not authority to restrain.

'As a teacher giving instruction for wages, and liable to reproach, if those whom he undertakes to inform make no proficiency, he must have the power of enforcing attendance, of
awakening negligence, and repressing contradiction.

'As a father, he possesses the paternal authority of admonition, rebuke, and punishment. He cannot, without reducing his office to an empty name, be hindered from the exercise of any practice necessary to stimulate the idle, to reform the vicious, to check the petulant, and correct the stubborn.

'If we enquire into the practice of the primitive Church, we shall, I believe, find the ministers of the word exercising the whole authority of this complicated character. We shall find them not only encouraging the good by exhortation, but terrifying the wicked by reproof and denunciation. In the earliest ages of the Church, while religion was yet pure from secular advantages, the punishment of sinners was publick censure, and open penance; penalties inflicted merely by ecclesiastical authority, at a time while the Church had yet no help from the civil power; while the hand of the magistrate lifted only the rod of persecution; and when governours were ready to afford a refuge to all those who fled from clerical authority.

'That the Church, therefore, had once a power of publick censure is evident, because that power was frequently exercised. That it borrowed not its power from the civil authority, is likewise certain, because civil authority was at that time its enemy.

'The hour came at length, when after three hundred years of struggle and distress, Truth took possession of imperial power, and the civil laws lent their aid to the ecclesiastical constitutions. The magistrate from that time co-operated with the priest, and clerical sentences were made efficacious by secular force. But the State, when it came to the assistance of the Church, had no intention to diminish its authority. Those rebukes and those censures which were lawful before, were lawful still. But they had hitherto operated only upon voluntary submission. The refractory and contemptuous were at first in no danger of temporal severities, except what they might suffer from the reproaches of conscience, or the detestation of their fellow Christians. When religion obtained the support of law, if admonitions and censures had no effect, they were seconded by the magistrates with coercion and punishment.

'It therefore appears from ecclesiastical history, that the right of inflicting shame by publick censure, has been always considered as inherent in the Church; and that this right was not conferred by the civil power; for it was exercised when the civil power operated against it. By the civil power it was never taken away; for the Christian magistrate interposed his office, not to rescue sinners from censure, but to supply more powerful means of reformation; to add pain where shame was insufficient; and when men were proclaimed unworthy of the society of the faithful, to restrain them by imprisonment, from spreading abroad the contagion of wickedness.

'It is not improbable that from this acknowledged power of publick censure, grew in time the practice of auricular confession. Those who dreaded the blast of publick reprehension, were willing to submit themselves to the priest, by a private accusation of themselves; and to obtain a reconciliation with the Church by a kind of clandestine absolution and invisible penance; conditions with which the priest would in times of ignorance and corruption easily comply, as they increased his influence, by adding the knowledge of secret sins to that of notorious offences, and enlarged his authority, by making him the sole arbiter of the terms of reconcilement.

'From this bondage the Reformation set us free. The minister has no longer power to press into the retirements of conscience, to torture us by interrogatories, or put himself in possession of our secrets and our lives. But though we have thus controlled his usurpations, his just and original power remains unimpaired. He may still see, though he may not pry: he may yet hear, though he may not question. And that knowledge which his eyes and ears force upon him it is still his duty to use, for the benefit of his flock. A father who lives near a wicked neighbour, may forbid a son to frequent his company. A minister who has in his congregation a man of open and scandalous wickedness, may warn his parishioners to shun his conversation. To warn them is not only lawful, but not to warn them would be criminal. He may warn them one by one in friendly converse, or by a parochial visitation. But if he may warn each man singly, what shall forbid him to warn them altogether? Of that which is to be made known to all, how is there any difference whether it be communicated to each singly, or to all together? What is known to all, must necessarily be publick. Whether it shall be public at once, or publick by degrees, is the only question. And of a sudden and solemn publication the impression is deeper, and the warning more effectual.

'It may easily be urged, if a minister be thus left at liberty to delate sinners from the pulpit, and to publish at will the crimes of a parishioner, he may often blast the innocent, and distress the timorous. He may be suspicious, and condemn without evidence; he may be rash, and judge without examination; he may be severe, and treat slight offences with too much harshness; he may be malignant and partial, and gratify his private interest or resentment under the shelter of his pastoral character.

'Of all this there is possibility, and of all this there is danger. But if possibility of evil be to exclude good, no good ever can be done. If nothing is to be attempted in which there is danger, we must all sink into hopeless inactivity. The evils that may be feared from this practice arise not from any defect in the institution, but from the infirmities of human nature. Power, in whatever hands it is placed, will be sometimes improperly exerted; yet courts of law must judge, though they will sometimes judge amiss. A father must instruct his children, though he himself may often want instruction. A minister must censure sinners, though his censure may be sometimes erroneous by want of judgement, and sometimes unjust by want of honesty.

'If we examine the circumstances of the present case, we shall find the sentence neither erroneous nor unjust; we shall find no breach of private confidence, no intrusion into secret transactions. The fact was notorious and indubitable; so easy to be proved, that no proof was desired. The act was base and treacherous, the perpetration insolent and open, and the example naturally mischievous. The minister however, being retired and recluse, had not yet heard what was publickly known throughout the parish; and on occasion of a publick election, warned his people, according to his duty, against the crimes which publick elections frequently produce. His warning was felt by one of his parishioners, as pointed particularly at himself. But instead of producing, as might be wished, private compunction and immediate reformation, it kindled only rage and resentment. He charged his minister, in a publick paper, with scandal, defamation, and falsehood. The minister, thus reproached, had his own character to vindicate, upon which his pastoral authority must necessarily depend. To be charged with a defamatory lie is an injury which no man patiently endures in common life. To be charged with polluting the pastoral office with scandal and falsehood, was a violation of character still more atrocious, as it affected not only his personal but his clerical veracity. His indignation naturally rose in proportion to his honesty, and with all the fortitude of injured honesty, he dared this calumniator in the church, and at once exonerated himself from censure, and rescued his flock from deception and from danger. The man whom he accuses pretends not to be innocent; or at least only pretends; for he declines a trial. The crime of which he is accused has frequent opportunities and strong temptations. It has already spread far, with much depravation of private morals, and much injury to publick happiness. To warn the people, therefore, against it was not wanton and officious, but necessary and pastoral.

'What then is the fault with which this worthy minister is charged? He has usurped no dominion over conscience. He has exerted no authority in support of doubtful and controverted opinions. He has not dragged into light a bashful and corrigible sinner. His censure was directed against a breach of morality, against an act which no man justifies. The man who appropriated this censure to himself, is evidently and notoriously guilty. His consciousness of his own wickedness incited him to attack his faithful reprover with open insolence and printed accusations. Such an attack made defence necessary; and we hope it will be at last decided that the means of defence were just and lawful.'

When I read this to Mr. Burke, he was highly pleased, and exclaimed, 'Well; he does his work in a workman-like manner.'[1]

---

[1] As a proof of Dr. Johnson's extraordinary powers of composition, it appears from the original manuscript of this excellent dissertation, of which he dictated the first eight paragraphs on the 10th of May, and the remainder

Mr. Thomson wished to bring the cause by appeal before the House of Lords, but was dissuaded by the advice of the noble person who lately presided so ably in that Most Honourable House, and who was then Attorney-General. As my readers will no doubt be glad also to read the opinion of this eminent man upon the same subject, I shall here insert it.

CASE.

'There is herewith laid before you,

'1. Petition for the Reverend Mr. James Thomson, minister of Dumfermline.

'2. Answers thereto.

'3. Copy of the judgement of the Court of Session upon both.

'4. Notes of the opinions of the Judges, being the reasons upon which their decree is grounded.

'These papers you will please to peruse, and give your opinion,

'Whether there is a probability of the above decree of the Court of Session's being reversed, if Mr. Thomson should appeal from the same?'

'I don't think the appeal adviseable: not only because the value of the judgement is in no degree adequate to the expence; but because there are many chances, that upon the general complexion of the case, the impression will be taken to the disadvantage of the appellant.

'It is impossible to approve the style of that sermon. But the *complaint* was not less ungracious from that man, who had behaved so ill by his original libel, and, at the time, when he received the reproach he complains of. In the last article, all the plaintiffs are equally concerned. It struck me also with some wonder, that the Judges should think so much fervour apposite to the occasion of reproving the defendant for a little excess.

'Upon the matter, however, I agree with them in condemning the behaviour of the minister; and in thinking it a subject fit for

on the 13th, that there are in the whole only seven corrections, or rather variations, and those not considerable. Such were at once the vigorous and accurate emanations of his mind.

ecclesiastical censure; and even for an action, if any individual could qualify[1] a wrong, and a damage arising from it. But this I doubt. The circumstance of publishing the reproach in a pulpit, though extremely indecent, and culpable in another view, does not constitute a different sort of wrong, or any other rule of law, than would have obtained, if the same words had been pronounced elsewhere. I don't know, whether there be any difference in the law of Scotland, in the definition of slander, before the Commissaries, or the Court of Session. The common law of England does not give way to actions for every reproachful word. An action cannot be brought for general damages, upon any words which import less than an offence cognisable by law; consequently no action could have been brought here for the words in question. Both laws admit the truth to be a justification in actions *for words*; and the law of England does the same in actions for libels. The judgement, therefore, seems to me to have been wrong, in that the Court repelled that defence.

'E. Thurlow.'

I am now to record a very curious incident in Dr. Johnson's Life, which fell under my own observation; of which *pars magna fui*,[2] and which I am persuaded will, with the liberal-minded, be much to his credit.

My desire of being acquainted with celebrated men of every description, had made me, much about the same time, obtain an introduction to Dr. Samuel Johnson and to John Wilkes, Esq. Two men more different could perhaps not be selected out of all mankind. They had even attacked one another with some asperity in their writings; yet I lived in habits of friendship with both. I could fully relish the excellence of each; for I have ever delighted in that intellectual chymistry, which can separate good qualities from evil in the same person.

Sir John Pringle, 'mine own friend and my Father's friend,'

[1] It is curious to observe that Lord Thurlow has here, perhaps in compliment to North Britain, made use of a term of the Scotch Law, which to an English reader may require explanation. To *qualify* a wrong, is to point out and establish it.

[2] ['I was no small part.' *Aeneid* ii. 5.]

between whom and Dr. Johnson I in vain wished to establish an acquaintance, as I respected and lived in intimacy with both of them, observed to me once, very ingeniously, 'It is not in friendship as in mathematicks, where two things, each equal to a third, are equal between themselves. You agree with Johnson as a middle quality, and you agree with me as a middle quality; but Johnson and I should not agree.' Sir John was not sufficiently flexible; so I desisted; knowing, indeed, that the repulsion was equally strong on the part of Johnson; who, I know not from what cause, unless his being a Scotchman, had formed a very erroneous opinion of Sir John. But I conceived an irresistible wish, if possible, to bring Dr. Johnson and Mr. Wilkes together. How to manage it, was a nice and difficult matter.

My worthy booksellers and friends, Messieurs Dilly in the Poultry, at whose hospitable and well-covered table I have seen a greater number of literary men, than at any other, except that of Sir Joshua Reynolds, had invited me to meet Mr. Wilkes and some more gentlemen on Wednesday, May 15. 'Pray (said I,) let us have Dr. Johnson.'—'What, with Mr. Wilkes? not for the world, (said Mr. Edward Dilly:) Dr. Johnson would never forgive me.'—'Come, (said I,) if you'll let me negociate for you, I will be answerable that all shall go well.' DILLY. 'Nay, if you will take it upon you, I am sure I shall be very happy to see them both here.'

Notwithstanding the high veneration which I entertained for Dr. Johnson, I was sensible that he was sometimes a little actuated by the spirit of contradiction, and by means of that I hoped I should gain my point. I was persuaded that if I had come upon him with a direct proposal, 'Sir, will you dine in company with Jack Wilkes?' he would have flown into a passion, and would probably have answered, 'Dine with Jack Wilkes, Sir! I'd as soon dine with Jack Ketch.'[1] I therefore, while we were sitting quietly by ourselves at his house in an evening, took occasion to open my plan thus:—'Mr. Dilly, Sir, sends his respectful compliments to you, and would be happy if you would do him the honour to

---

[1] This has been circulated as if actually said by Johnson; when the truth is, it was only *supposed* by me.

dine with him on Wednesday next along with me, as I must soon
go to Scotland.' JOHNSON. 'Sir, I am obliged to Mr. Dilly. I
will wait upon him—' BOSWELL. 'Provided, Sir, I suppose, that
the company which he is to have, is agreeable to you.' JOHNSON.
'What do you mean, Sir? What do you take me for? Do you think
I am so ignorant of the world, as to imagine that I am to prescribe to a gentleman what company he is to have at his table?'
BOSWELL. 'I beg your pardon, Sir, for wishing to prevent you
from meeting people whom you might not like. Perhaps he may
have some of what he calls his patriotick friends with him.'
JOHNSON. 'Well, Sir, and what then? What care *I* for his
patriotick friends? Poh!' BOSWELL. 'I should not be surprized
to find Jack Wilkes there.' JOHNSON. 'And if Jack Wilkes
should be there, what is that to *me*, Sir? My dear friend, let us
have no more of this. I am sorry to be angry with you; but really
it is treating me strangely to talk to me as if I could not meet
any company whatever, occasionally.' BOSWELL. 'Pray forgive
me, Sir: I meant well. But you shall meet whoever comes, for
me.' Thus I secured him, and told Dilly that he would find him
very well pleased to be one of his guests on the day appointed.

Upon the much-expected Wednesday, I called on him about
half an hour before dinner, as I often did when we were to dine
out together, to see that he was ready in time, and to accompany
him. I found him buffeting his books, as upon a former occasion,[1]
covered with dust, and making no preparation for going abroad.
'How is this, Sir? (said I.) Don't you recollect that you are to
dine at Mr. Dilly's?' JOHNSON. 'Sir, I did not think of going to
Dilly's: it went out of my head. I have ordered dinner at home
with Mrs. Williams.' BOSWELL. 'But, my dear Sir, you know
you were engaged to Mr. Dilly, and I told him so. He will expect
you, and will be much disappointed if you don't come.' JOHN-
SON. 'You must talk to Mrs. Williams about this.'

Here was a sad dilemma. I feared that what I was so confident
I had secured would yet be frustrated. He had accustomed himself to shew Mrs. Williams such a degree of humane attention,
as frequently imposed some restraint upon him; and I knew that

[1] See p. 722.

766

if she should be obstinate, he would not stir. I hastened down stairs to the blind lady's room, and told her I was in great uneasiness, for Dr. Johnson had engaged to me to dine this day at Mr. Dilly's, but that he had told me he had forgotten his engagement, and had ordered dinner at home. 'Yes, Sir, (said she, pretty peevishly,) Dr. Johnson is to dine at home.'— 'Madam, (said I,) his respect for you is such, that I know he will not leave you unless you absolutely desire it. But as you have so much of his company, I hope you will be good enough to forego it for a day; as Mr. Dilly is a very worthy man, has frequently had agreeable parties at his house for Dr. Johnson, and will be vexed if the Doctor neglects him to-day. And then, Madam, be pleased to consider my situation; I carried the message, and I assured Mr. Dilly that Dr. Johnson was to come, and no doubt he has made a dinner, and invited a company, and boasted of the honour he expected to have. I shall be quite disgraced if the Doctor is not there.' She gradually softened to my solicitations, which were certainly as earnest as most entreaties to ladies upon any occasion, and was graciously pleased to empower me to tell Dr. Johnson, 'That all things considered, she thought he should certainly go.' I flew back to him, still in dust, and careless of what should be the event, 'indifferent in his choice to go or stay;' but as soon as I had announced to him Mrs. Williams's consent, he roared, 'Frank, a clean shirt,' and was very soon drest. When I had him fairly seated in a hackney-coach with me, I exulted as much as a fortune-hunter who has got an heiress into a post-chaise with him to set out for Gretna-Green.

When we entered Mr. Dilly's drawing room, he found himself in the midst of a company he did not know. I kept myself snug and silent, watching how he would conduct himself. I observed him whispering to Mr. Dilly, 'Who is that gentleman, Sir?'—'Mr. Arthur Lee.'—JOHNSON. 'Too, too, too,' (under his breath,) which was one of his habitual mutterings. Mr. Arthur Lee could not but be very obnoxious to Johnson, for he was not only a *patriot* but an *American*. He was afterwards minister from the United States at the court of Madrid. 'And who is the gentleman in lace?'—'Mr. Wilkes, Sir.' This information confounded him still more; he had some difficulty to restrain himself, and taking up a book, sat down upon a window-seat and read, or at least kept his eye upon it intently for some time, till he composed himself. His feelings, I dare say, were aukward enough. But he no doubt recollected his having rated me for supposing that he could be at all disconcerted by any company, and he, therefore, resolutely set himself to behave quite as an easy man of the world, who could adapt himself at once to the disposition and manners of those whom he might chance to meet.

The cheering sound of 'Dinner is upon the table,' dissolved his reverie, and we *all* sat down without any symptom of ill humour. There were present, besides Mr. Wilkes, and Mr. Arthur Lee, who was an old companion of mine when he studied physick at Edinburgh, Mr. (now Sir John) Miller, Dr. Lettsom, and Mr. Slater the druggist. Mr. Wilkes placed himself next to Dr. Johnson, and behaved to him with so much attention and politeness, that he gained upon him insensibly. No man eat more heartily than Johnson, or loved better what was nice and delicate. Mr. Wilkes was very assiduous in helping him to some fine veal. 'Pray give me leave, Sir:—It is better here—A little of the brown—Some fat, Sir—A little of the stuffing—Some gravy—Let me have the pleasure of giving you some butter— Allow me to recommend a squeeze of this orange;—or the lemon, perhaps, may have more zest.'—'Sir, Sir, I am obliged to you, Sir,' cried Johnson, bowing, and turning his head to him with a look for some time of 'surly virtue,'[1] but, in a short while, of complacency.

Foote being mentioned, Johnson said, 'He is not a good mimick.' One of the company[2] added, 'A merry Andrew, a buffoon.' JOHNSON. 'But he has wit too, and is not deficient in ideas, or in fertility and variety of imagery, and not empty of reading; he has knowledge enough to fill up his part. One species of wit he has in an eminent degree, that of escape. You drive him into a corner with both hands; but he's gone, Sir, when you think you have got him—like an animal that jumps

[1] Johnson's *London, a poem*, v. 145.
[2] [Edward Dilly, *Boswell Papers*, xi. 284.]

over your head. Then he has a great range for his wit; he never lets truth stand between him and a jest, and he is sometimes mighty coarse. Garrick is under many restraints from which Foote is free.' WILKES. 'Garrick's wit is more like Lord Chesterfield's.' JOHNSON. 'The first time I was in company with Foote was at Fitzherbert's. Having no good opinion of the fellow, I was resolved not to be pleased; and it is very difficult to please a man against his will. I went on eating my dinner pretty sullenly, affecting not to mind him. But the dog was so very comical, that I was obliged to lay down my knife and fork, throw myself back upon my chair, and fairly laugh it out. No, Sir, he was irresistible.[1] He upon one occasion experienced, in an extraordinary degree, the efficacy of his powers of entertaining. Amongst the many and various modes which he tried of getting money, he became a partner with a small-beer brewer, and he was to have a share of the profits for procuring customers amongst his numerous acquaintance. Fitzherbert was one who took his small-beer; but it was so bad that the servants resolved not to drink it. They were at some loss how to notify their resolution, being afraid of offending their master, who they knew liked Foote much as a companion. At last they fixed upon a little black boy, who was rather a favourite, to be their deputy, and deliver their remonstrance; and having invested him with the whole authority of the kitchen, he was to inform Mr. Fitzherbert, in all their names, upon a certain day, that they would drink Foote's small-beer no longer. On that day Foote happened to dine at Fitzherbert's, and this boy served at table; he was so delighted with Foote's stories, and merriment, and grimace, that when he went down stairs, he told them, "This is the finest man I have ever seen. I will not deliver your message. I will drink his small-beer." '

Somebody observed that Garrick could not have done this. WILKES. 'Garrick would have made the small-beer still smaller. He is now leaving the stage; but he will play *Scrub* all his life.' I knew that Johnson would let nobody attack Garrick but him-

---

[1] Foote told me that Johnson said of him, 'For loud obstreperous broad-faced mirth, I know not his equal.'

self, as Garrick once said to me, and I had heard him praise his liberality; so to bring out his commendation of his celebrated pupil, I said, loudly, 'I have heard Garrick is liberal.' JOHNSON. 'Yes, Sir, I know that Garrick has given away more money than any man in England that I am acquainted with, and that not from ostentatious views. Garrick was very poor when he began life; so when he came to have money, he probably was very unskilful in giving away, and saved when he should not. But Garrick began to be liberal as soon as he could; and I am of opinion, the reputation of avarice which he has had, has been very lucky for him, and prevented his having many enemies. You despise a man for avarice, but do not hate him. Garrick might have been much better attacked for living with more splendour than is suitable to a player: if they had had the wit to have assaulted him in that quarter, they might have galled him more. But they have kept clamouring about his avarice, which has rescued him from much obloquy and envy.'

Talking of the great difficulty of obtaining authentick information for biography, Johnson told us, 'When I was a young fellow I wanted to write the *Life of Dryden*, and in order to get materials, I applied to the only two persons then alive who had seen him; these were old Swinney, and old Cibber. Swinney's information was no more than this, "That at Will's coffee-house Dryden had a particular chair for himself, which was set by the fire in winter, and was then called his winter-chair; and that it was carried out for him to the balcony in summer, and was then called his summer-chair." Cibber could tell no more but "That he remembered him a decent old man, arbiter of critical disputes at Will's." You are to consider that Cibber was then at a great distance from Dryden, had perhaps one leg only in the room, and durst not draw in the other.' BOSWELL. 'Yet Cibber was a man of observation?' JOHNSON. 'I think not.' BOSWELL. 'You will allow his *Apology* to be well done.' JOHNSON. 'Very well done, to be sure, Sir. That book is a striking proof of the justice of Pope's remark:

> "Each might his several province well command,
>   Would all but stoop to what they understand." '

Boswell. 'And his plays are good.' Johnson. 'Yes; but that was his trade; *l'esprit du corps*: he had been all his life among players and play-writers. I wondered that he had so little to say in conversation, for he had kept the best company, and learnt all that can be got by the ear. He abused Pindar to me, and then shewed me an Ode of his own, with an absurd couplet, making a linnet soar on an eagle's wing.[1] I told him that when the ancients made a simile, they always made it like something real.'

Mr. Wilkes remarked, that 'among all the bold flights of Shakspeare's imagination, the boldest was making Birnamwood march to Dunsinane; creating a wood where there never was a shrub; a wood in Scotland! ha! ha! ha!' And he also observed, that 'the clannish slavery of the Highlands of Scotland was the single exception to Milton's remark of "The Mountain Nymph, sweet Liberty," being worshipped in all hilly countries.'— 'When I was at Inverary (said he,) on a visit to my old friend, Archibald, Duke of Argyle, his dependents congratulated me on being such a favourite of his Grace. I said, "It is then, gentlemen, truely lucky for me; for if I had displeased the Duke, and he had wished it, there is not a Campbell among you but would have been ready to bring John Wilkes's head to him in a charger. It would have been only

       "Off with his head! So much for Aylesbury."

I was then member for Aylesbury.'

Dr. Johnson and Mr. Wilkes talked of the contested passage in Horace's *Art of Poetry*, '*Difficile est propriè communia dicere.*'[2] Mr. Wilkes according to my note, gave the interpretation thus; 'It is difficult to speak with propriety of common things; as, if a poet had to speak of Queen Caroline drinking tea, he must endeavour to avoid the vulgarity of cups and saucers.' But upon reading my note, he tells me that he meant to say, that 'the word *communia*, being a Roman law term, signifies here things *communis juris*, that is to say, what have never yet been treated by any body; and this appears clearly from what followed,

[1] See *ante*, p. 285.

[2] [Line 128. For translation see note 2, p. 772.]

> "———*Tuque*
> *Rectiùs Iliacum carmen deducis in actus,*
> *Quàm si proferres ignota indictaque primus.*"[1]

You will easier make a tragedy out of the *Iliad* than on any
subject not handled before.'[2] JOHNSON. 'He means that it is

[1] [Lines 128 to 130. For translation see note 2.]

[2] My very pleasant friend himself, as well as others *who remember old
stories,* will no doubt be surprized, when I observe that *John Wilkes* here
shews himself to be of the WARBURTONIAN SCHOOL. It is nevertheless true,
as appears from Dr. Hurd the Bishop of Worcester's very elegant commentary and notes on the '*Epistola ad Pisones.*'

It is necessary to a fair consideration of the question, that the whole
passage in which the words occur should be kept in view:

> '*Si quid inexpertum scenæ committis, et audes*
> *Personam formare novam, servetur ad imum*
> *Qualis ab incepto processerit, et sibi constet.*
> *Difficile est propriè communia dicere: tuque*
> *Rectiùs Iliacum carmen deducis in actus,*
> *Quàm si proferres ignota indictaque primus.*
> *Publica materies privati juris erit, si*
> *Non circa vilem patulumque moraberis orbem,*
> *Nec verbum verbo curabis reddere fidus*
> *Interpres; nec desilies imitator in artum*
> *Unde pedem proferre pudor vetet aut operis lex.*'.

['If you trust a new venture on the stage, and have the boldness to frame
a fresh character, see that it is kept to the end such as it starts at the beginning and is self-consistent.

'It is a hard task to treat what is common in a way of your own; and you
are doing more rightly in breaking the tale of Troy into acts than in giving
the world a new story of your own telling. You may acquire private rights
in common ground, provided you will neither linger in the one hackneyed
and easy round; nor trouble to render word for word with the faithfulness
of a translator; nor by your mode of imitating take the "leap into the pit"
out of which very shame, if not the law of your work, will forbid you to stir
hand or foot to escape.' Lines 125 to 135 (Wickham).]

The 'Commentary' thus illustrates it: 'But the formation of quite *new
characters* is a work of great difficulty and hazard. For here there is no
generally received and fixed *archetype* to work after, but every one *judges* of
common right, according to the extent and comprehension of his own idea;
therefore he advises to labour and refit *old characters and subjects,* particularly
those made known and authorised by the practice of Homer and the Epick
writers.'

The 'Note' is,

'*Difficile* EST PROPRIÈ COMMUNIA DICERE.' Lambin's Comment is '*Communia hoc loco appellat Horatius argumenta fabularum à nullo adhuc tractata:
et ita, quæ cuivis exposita sunt et in medio quodammodo posita, quasi vacua et à
nemine occupata.*' And that this is the true meaning of *communia* is evidently

difficult to appropriate to particular persons qualities which are common to all mankind, as Homer has done.'

fixed by the words *ignota indictaque*, which are explanatory of it; so that the sense given it in the commentary is unquestionably the right one. Yet, notwithstanding the clearness of the case, a late critick has this strange passage: '*Difficile quidem esse propriè communia dicere, hoc est, materiam vulgarem, notam et è medio petitam, ita immutare atque exornare, ut nova et scriptori propria videatur, ultro concedimus; et maximi procul dubio ponderis ista est observatio. Sed omnibus utrinque collatis, et tum difficilis, tum venusti, tam judicii quam ingenii ratione habitâ, major videtur esse gloria fabulam formare penitùs novam, quàm veterem, utcunque mutatam, de novo exhibere.*' (Poet. Præl. v. ii. p. 164.) Where, having first put a wrong construction on the word *communia*, he employs it to introduce an impertinent criticism. For where does the poet prefer the glory of refitting *old* subjects to that of inventing new ones? The contrary is implied in what he urges about the superiour difficulty of the latter, from which he dissuades his countrymen, only in respect of their abilities and inexperience in these matters; and in order to cultivate in them, which is the main view of the Epistle, a spirit of correctness, by sending them to the old subjects, treated by the Greek writers.'

For my own part (with all deference for Dr. Hurd, who thinks the *case clear,*) I consider the passage, '*Difficile est propriè communia dicere,*' to be a *crux* for the criticks on Horace.

The explication which My Lord of Worcester treats with so much contempt, is nevertheless countenanced by authority which I find quoted by the learned Baxter in his edition of Horace: '*Difficile est propriè communia dicere, h. e. res vulgares disertis verbis enarrare, vel humile thema cum dignitate tractare. Difficile est communes res propriis explicare verbis.* Vet. Schol.' I was much disappointed to find that the great critick, Dr. Bentley, has no note upon this very difficult passage, as from his vigorous and illuminated mind I should have expected to receive more satisfaction than I have yet had.

Sanadon thus treats of it: '*Propriè communia dicere; c'est à dire, qu'il n'est pas aisé de former à ces personnages d'imagination, des caractères particuliers et cependant vraisemblables. Comme l'on a été le maitre de les former tels qu'on a voulu, les fautes que l'on fait en cela sont moins pardonnables. C'est pourquoi Horace conseille de prendre toujours des sujets connus tels que sont par exemple ceux que l'on peut tirer des poèmes d'Homere.*'

And *Dacier* observes upon it, '*Apres avoir marqué les deux qualités qu'il faut donner aux personnages qu'on invente, il conseille aux Poëtes tragiques, de n'user pas trop facilement de cette liberté quils ont d'en inventer, car il est trés difficile de reussir dans ces nouveaux caractéres. Il est mal aisé, dit Horace, de traiter proprement, c'est à dire* convenablement, *des* sujets communs; *c'est à dire, des sujets inventés, et qui n'ont aucun fondement ni dans l'Histoire ni dans la Fable; et il les appelle* communs, *parce qu'ils sont en disposition à tout le monde, et que tout le monde a le droit de les inventer, et qu'ils sont, comme on dit, au premier occupant.*' See his observations at large on this expression and the following.

After all, I cannot help entertaining some doubt whether the words, *Difficile est propriè communia dicere,* may not have been thrown in by Horace to form a *separate* article in a 'choice of difficulties' which a poet has to encounter, who chooses a new subject; in which case it must be uncertain which

WILKES. 'We have no City-Poet now: that is an office which has gone into disuse. The last was Elkanah Settle. There is something in *names* which one cannot help feeling. Now *Elkanah Settle* sounds so *queer*, who can expect much from that name? We should have no hesitation to give it for John Dryden, in preference to Elkanah Settle, from the names only, without knowing their different merits.' JOHNSON. 'I suppose, Sir, Settle did as well for Aldermen in his time, as John Home could do now. Where did Beckford and Trecothick learn English?'

Mr. Arthur Lee mentioned some Scotch who had taken possession of a barren part of America, and wondered why they should choose it. JOHNSON. 'Why, Sir, all barrenness is comparative. The *Scotch* would not know it to be barren.' BOSWELL. 'Come, come, he is flattering the English. You have now been in Scotland, Sir, and say if you did not see meat and drink enough there.' JOHNSON. 'Why yes, Sir; meat and drink enough to give the inhabitants sufficient strength to run away from home.' All these quick and lively sallies were said sportively, quite in jest, and with a smile, which showed that he meant only wit. Upon this topick he and Mr. Wilkes could perfectly assimilate; here was a bond of union between them, and I was conscious that as both of them had visited Caledonia, both were fully satisfied of the strange narrow ignorance of those who imagine that it is a land of famine. But they amused themselves with persevering in the old jokes. When I claimed a superiority for Scotland over England in one respect, that no man can be arrested there for a debt merely because another swears it against him; but there must first be the judgement of a court of

of the various explanations is the true one, and every reader has a right to decide as it may strike his own fancy. And even should the words be understood as they generally are, to be connected both with what goes before and what comes after, the exact sense cannot be absolutely ascertained; for instance, whether *proprie* is meant to signify *in an appropriated manner*, as Dr. Johnson here understands it, or, as it is often used by Cicero, *with propriety*, or *elegantly*. In short, it is a rare instance of a defect in perspicuity in an admirable writer, who with almost every species of excellence, is peculiarly remarkable for that quality. The length of this note perhaps requires an apology. Many of my readers, I doubt not, will admit that a critical discussion of a passage in a favourite classick is very engaging. [Boswell's French in this note is left as he printed it.]

law ascertaining its justice; and that a seizure of the person, before judgement is obtained, can take place only, if his creditor should swear that he is about to fly from the country, or, as it is technically expressed, is *in meditatione fugæ*:[1] WILKES. 'That, I should think, may be safely sworn of all the Scotch nation.' JOHNSON. (to Mr. Wilkes,) 'You must know, Sir, I lately took my friend Boswell and shewed him genuine civilised life in an English provincial town. I turned him loose at Lichfield, my native city, that he might see for once real civility: for you know he lives among savages in Scotland, and among rakes in London.' WILKES. 'Except when he is with grave, sober, decent people like you and me.' JOHNSON. (smiling,) 'And we ashamed of him.'

They were quite frank and easy. Johnson told the story of his asking Mrs. Macaulay to allow her footman to sit down with them, to prove the ridiculousness of the argument for the equality of mankind; and he said to me afterwards, with a nod of satisfaction, 'You saw Mr. Wilkes acquiesced.' Wilkes talked with all imaginable freedom of the ludicrous title given to the Attorney-General, *Diabolus Regis*;[2] adding, 'I have reason to know something about that officer; for I was prosecuted for a libel.' Johnson, who many people would have supposed must have been furiously angry at hearing this talked of so lightly, said not a word. He was now, *indeed*, 'a good-humoured fellow.'

After dinner we had an accession of Mrs. Knowles, the Quaker lady, well known for her various talents, and of Mr. Alderman Lee. Amidst some patriotick groans, somebody (I think the Alderman) said, 'Poor old England is lost.' JOHNSON. 'Sir, it is not so much to be lamented that Old England is lost, as that the Scotch have found it.'[3] WILKES. 'Had Lord Bute governed Scotland only, I should not have taken the trouble to write his eulogy, and dedicate *Mortimer* to him.'

Mr. Wilkes held a candle to shew a fine print of a beautiful

---

[1] ['meditating flight.']
[2] ['The King's Devil.']
[3] It would not become me to expatiate on this strong and pointed remark, in which a very great deal of meaning is condensed.

female figure which hung in the room, and pointed out the elegant contour of the bosom with the finger of an arch connoisseur. He afterwards, in a conversation with me, waggishly insisted, that all the time Johnson shewed visible signs of a fervent admiration of the corresponding charms of the fair Quaker.

This record, though by no means so perfect as I could wish, will serve to give a notion of a very curious interview, which was not only pleasing at the time, but had the agreeable and benignant effect of reconciling any animosity, and sweetening any acidity, which in the various bustle of political contest, had been produced in the minds of two men, who though widely different, had so many things in common—classical learning, modern literature, wit, and humour, and ready repartee—that it would have been much to be regretted if they had been for ever at a distance from each other.

Mr. Burke gave me much credit for this successful *negociation*; and pleasantly said, that 'there was nothing to equal it in the whole history of the *Corps Diplomatique.*'

I attended Dr. Johnson home, and had the satisfaction to hear him tell Mrs. Williams how much he had been pleased with Mr. Wilkes's company, and what an agreeable day he had passed.

I talked a good deal to him of the celebrated Margaret Caroline Rudd, whom I had visited, induced by the fame of her talents, address, and irresistible power of fascination. To a lady who disapproved of my visiting her, he said on a former occasion, 'Nay, Madam, Boswell is in the right; I should have visited her myself, were it not that they have now a trick of putting every thing into the news-papers.' This evening he exclaimed, 'I envy him his acquaintance with Mrs. Rudd.'

I mentioned a scheme which I had of making a tour to the Isle of Man, and giving a full account of it; and that Mr. Burke had playfully suggested as a motto,

'The proper study of mankind is MAN.'

JOHNSON. 'Sir, you will get more by the book than the jaunt

will cost you; so you will have your diversion for nothing, and add to your reputation.'

On the evening of the next day I took leave of him, being to set out for Scotland. I thanked him with great warmth for all his kindness. 'Sir, (said he,) you are very welcome. Nobody repays it with more.'

How very false is the notion which has gone round the world of the rough, and passionate, and harsh manners of this great and good man. That he had occasional sallies of heat of temper, and that he was sometimes, perhaps, too 'easily provoked' by absurdity and folly, and sometimes too desirous of triumph in colloquial contest, must be allowed. The quickness both of his perception and sensibility disposed him to sudden explosions of satire; to which his extraordinary readiness of wit was a strong and almost irresistible incitement. To adopt one of the finest images in Mr. Home's *Douglas*,

> 'On each glance of thought
> Decision followed, as the thunderbolt
> Pursues the flash!'

I admit that the beadle within him was often so eager to apply the lash, that the Judge had not time to consider the case with sufficient deliberation.

That he was occasionally remarkable for violence of temper may be granted: but let us ascertain the degree, and not let it be supposed that he was in a perpetual rage, and never without a club in his hand, to knock down every one who approached him. On the contrary, the truth is, that by much the greatest part of his time he was civil, obliging, nay, polite in the true sense of the word; so much so, that many gentlemen, who were long acquainted with him, never received, or even heard a strong expression from him.

The following letters concerning an Epitaph which he wrote for the monument of Dr. Goldsmith, in Westminster-Abbey, afford at once a proof of his unaffected modesty, his carelessness as to his own writings, and of the great respect which he enter-tained for the taste and judgement of the excellent and eminent person to whom they are addressed:

'*To* Sir Joshua Reynolds

'Dear Sir,—I have been kept away from you, I know not well how, and of these vexatious hindrances I know not when there will be an end. I therefore send you the poor dear Doctor's epitaph. Read it first yourself; and if you then think it right, shew it to the Club. I am, you know, willing to be corrected. If you think any thing much amiss, keep it to yourself, till we come together. I have sent two copies, but prefer the card. The dates must be settled by Dr. Percy. I am, Sir, your most humble servant,

'May 16, 1776.'   'Sam. Johnson.'

To The Same

'Sir,—Miss Reynolds has a mind to send the Epitaph to Dr. Beattie; I am very willing, but having no copy, cannot immediately recollect it. She tells me you have lost it. Try to recollect and put down as much as you retain; you perhaps may have kept what I have dropped. The lines for which I am at a loss are something of *rerum civilium sivè naturalium*.[1] It was a sorry trick to lose it; help me if you can. I am, Sir, your most humble servant,

'June 22, 1776.'   'Sam. Johnson.'

'The gout grows better but slowly.'

It was, I think, after I had left London this year, that this Epitaph gave occasion to a *Remonstrance* to the Monarch of Literature, for an account of which I am indebted to Sir William Forbes, of Pitsligo.

That my readers may have the subject more fully and clearly before them, I shall first insert the Epitaph.

Olivarii Goldsmith,

Poetæ, Physici, Historici,
Qui nullum ferè scribendi genus
Non tetigit,
Nullum quod tetigit non ornavit:

[1] These words must have been in the other copy. They are not in that which was preferred.

Sive risus essent movendi,
Sive lacrymæ,
Affectuum potens at lenis dominator:
Ingenio sublimis, vividus, versatilis,
Oratione grandis, nitidus, venustus:
Hoc monumento memoriam coluit
Sodalium amor,
Amicorum fides,
Lectorum veneratio.
Natus in Hiberniâ Forniæ Longfordiensis,
In loco cui nomen Pallas,
Nov. XXIX. MDCCXXXI;
Eblanæ literis institutus;
Obiit Londini,
April IV, MDCCLXXIV.'[1]

Sir William Forbes writes to me thus:—

'I enclose the *Round Robin.* This *jeu d'esprit* took its rise one day at dinner at our friend Sir Joshua Reynolds's. All the company present, except myself, were friends and acquaintance of Dr. Goldsmith. The Epitaph, written for him by Dr. Johnson, became the subject of conversation, and various emendations were suggested, which it was agreed should be submitted to the Doctor's consideration. But the question was, who should have the courage to propose them to him? At last it was hinted, that there could be no way so good as that of a *Round Robin,* as the sailors call it, which they make use of when they enter into a conspiracy, so as not to let it be known who puts his name first or last to the paper. This proposition was instantly assented to; and Dr. Barnard, Dean of Derry, now Bishop of Killaloe, drew up an address to Dr. Johnson on the occasion, replete with wit and humour, but which it was feared the Doctor might think

---

[1] ['Oliver Goldsmith, Poet, Naturalist, Historian; who touched almost every kind of writing, and touched none that he did not adorn. A powerful but kindly master of the emotions, whether he would move to tears or to laughter. Of genius lofty, lively, versatile; in style great, graceful, and charming.This monument to his memory has been raised by the love of his companions, the fidelity of his friends, the veneration of his readers.

'He was born at Palla in County Longford, 29 Nov. 1731, educated at Dublin, and died in London, 4 April 1774.']

treated the subject with too much levity. Mr. Burke then proposed the address as it stands in the paper in writing, to which
I had the honour to officiate as clerk.

'Sir Joshua agreed to carry it to Dr. Johnson, who received it
with much good humour,[1] and desired Sir Joshua to tell the
gentlemen, that he would alter the Epitaph in any manner they
pleased, as to the sense of it; but *he would never consent to disgrace
the walls of Westminster Abbey with an English inscription.*

'I consider this *Round Robin* as a species of literary curiosity
worth preserving, as it marks, in a certain degree, Dr. Johnson's
character.'

My readers are presented with a faithful transcript of a paper,
which I doubt not of their being desirous to see.[2]

Sir William Forbes's observation is very just. The anecdote

---

[1] He however, upon seeing Dr. Warton's name to the suggestion, that
the Epitaph should be in English, observed to Sir Joshua, 'I wonder that Joe
Warton, a scholar by profession, should be such a fool.' He said too, 'I
should have thought Mund Burke would have had more sense.' Mr. Langton,
who was one of the company at Sir Joshua's, like a sturdy scholar, resolutely
refused to sign the *Round Robin*. The Epitaph is engraved upon Dr. Goldsmith's monument without any alteration. At another time, when somebody
[possibly Reynolds. *Powell.*] endeavoured to argue in favour of its being in
English, Johnson said, 'The language of the country of which a learned man
was a native, is not the language fit for his epitaph, which should be in
ancient and permanent language. Consider, Sir; how you should feel, were
you to find at Rotterdam an epitaph upon Erasmus *in Dutch*!' For my own
part I think it would be best to have Epitaphs written both in a learned
language, and in the language of the country; so that they might have the
advantage of being more universally understood, and at the same time be
secured of classical stability. I cannot, however, but be of opinion, that it is
not sufficiently discriminative. Applying to Goldsmith equally the epithets of
'*Poetæ, Historici, Physici*,' is surely not right; for as to his claim to the last
of those epithets, I have heard Johnson himself say, 'Goldsmith, Sir, will
give us a very fine book upon the subject; but if he can distinguish a cow
from a horse, that, I believe, may be the extent of his knowledge of natural
history.' His book is indeed an excellent performance, though in some
instances he appears to have trusted too much to Buffon, who, with all his
theoretical ingenuity and extraordinary eloquence, I suspect had little actual
information in the science on which he wrote so admirably. For instance, he
tells us that the *cow* sheds her horns every two years; a most palpable
errour, which Goldsmith has faithfully transferred into his book. It is
wonderful that Buffon, who lived so much in the country, at his noble seat,
should have fallen into such a blunder. I suppose he has confounded the *cow*
with the *deer*.   [2] A reproduction of the document is here omitted.

now related proves, in the strongest manner, the reverence and awe with which Johnson was regarded, by some of the most eminent men of his time, in various departments, and even by such of them as lived most with him; while it also confirms what I have again and again inculcated, that he was by no means of that ferocious and irascible character which has been ignorantly imagined.

This hasty composition is also to be remarked as one of a thousand instances which evince the extraordinary promptitude of Mr. Burke; who while he is equal to the greatest things, can adorn the least; can, with equal facility, embrace the vast and complicated speculations of politicks, or the ingenious topicks of literary investigation.[1]

'DR. JOHNSON *to* MRS. BOSWELL

'MADAM,—You must not think me uncivil in omitting to answer the letter with which you favoured me some time ago. I imagined it to have been written without Mr. Boswell's knowledge, and therefore supposed the answer to require, what I could not find, a private conveyance.

'The difference with Lord Auchinleck is now over; and since young Alexander has appeared, I hope no more difficulties will arise among you; for I sincerely wish you all happy. Do not teach the young ones to dislike me, as you dislike me yourself; but let me at least have Veronica's kindness, because she is my acquaintance.

'You will now have Mr. Boswell home; it is well that you have him; he has led a wild life. I have taken him to Lichfield, and he has followed Mr. Thrale to Bath. Pray take care of him, and tame him. The only thing in which I have the honour to agree with you is, in loving him; and while we are so much of a mind in a matter of so much importance, our other quarrels will, I hope, produce no great bitterness. I am, Madam, your most humble servant,

'May 16, 1776.'   'SAM. JOHNSON.'

[1] Beside this Latin Epitaph, Johnson honoured the memory of his friend Goldsmith with a short one in Greek. See *ante*, July 5, 1774.

'Mr. Boswell *to* Dr. Johnson
'Edinburgh, June 25, 1776.

'You have formerly complained that my letters were too long. There is no danger of that complaint being made at present; for I find it difficult for me to write to you at all. [Here an account of having been afflicted with a return of melancholy or bad spirits.]

'The boxes of books[1] which you sent to me are arrived; but I have not yet examined the contents. . . .

'I send you Mr. Maclaurin's paper for the negro, who claims his freedom in the Court of Session.'

'Dr. Johnson *to* Mr. Boswell

'Dear Sir,—These black fits, of which you complain, perhaps hurt your memory as well as your imagination. When did I complain that your letters were too long?[2] Your last letter, after a very long delay, brought very bad news. [Here a series of reflections upon melancholy, and—what I could not help thinking strangely unreasonable in him who had suffered so much from it himself,—a good deal of severity and reproof, as if it were owing to my own fault, or that I was, perhaps, affecting it from a desire of distinction.]

'Read Cheyne's *English Malady*; but do not let him teach you a foolish notion that melancholy is a proof of acuteness. . . .

'To hear that you have not opened your boxes of books is very offensive. The examination and arrangement of so many volumes might have afforded you an amusement very seasonable at present, and useful for the whole of life. I am, I confess, very angry that you manage yourself so ill. . . .

'I do not now say any more, than that I am, with great kindness, and sincerity, dear Sir, your humble servant,

'July 2, 1776.'   'Sam. Johnson.'

[1] Upon a settlement of our account of expences on a Tour to the Hebrides, there was a balance due to me, which Dr. Johnson chose to discharge by sending books.
[2] Baretti told me that Johnson complained of my writing very long letters to him when I was upon the continent; which was most certainly true; but it seems my friend did not remember it.

'It was last year determined by Lord Mansfield, in the Court of King's Bench, that a negro cannot be taken out of the kingdom without his own consent.'

'DR. JOHNSON *to* MR. BOSWELL

'DEAR SIR,—I make haste to write again, lest my last letter should give you too much pain. If you are really oppressed with overpowering and involuntary melancholy, you are to be pitied rather than reproached. . . .

'Now, my dear Bozzy, let us have done with quarrels and with censure. Let me know whether I have not sent you a pretty library. There are, perhaps, many books among them which you never need read through; but there are none which it is not proper for you to know, and sometimes to consult. Of these books, of which the use is only occasional, it is often sufficient to know the contents, that, when any question arises, you may know where to look for information.

'Since I wrote, I have looked over Mr. Maclaurin's plea, and think it excellent. How is the suit carried on? If by subscription, I commission you to contribute, in my name, what is proper. Let nothing be wanting in such a case. Dr. Drummond,[1] I see, is superseded. His father would have grieved; but he lived to obtain the pleasure of his son's election, and died before that pleasure was abated.

'Langton's lady has brought him a girl, and both are well; I dined with him the other day. . . .

'It vexes me to tell you, that on the evening of the 29th of May I was seized by the gout, and am not quite well. The pain has not been violent, but the weakness and tenderness were very troublesome, and what is said to be very uncommon, it has not alleviated my other disorders. Make use of youth and health

---

[1] The son of Johnson's old friend, Mr. William Drummond. (See pp. 376–9.) He was a young man of such distinguished merit, that he was nominated to one of the medical professorships in the College of Edinburgh without solicitation while he was at Naples. Having other views, he did not accept of the honour, and soon afterwards died.

while you have them; make my compliments to Mrs. Boswell.
I am, my dear Sir, your most affectionate
   'July 6, 1776.'   'SAM. JOHNSON.'

'MR. BOSWELL *to* DR. JOHNSON

   'MY DEAR SIR,   'Edinburgh, July 18, 1776.
   'Your letter of the second of this month was rather a harsh
medicine; but I was delighted with that spontaneous tenderness,
which, a few days afterwards, sent forth such balsam as your
next brought me. I found myself for some time so ill that all I
could do was to preserve a decent appearance, while all within
was weakness and distress. Like a reduced garrison that has some
spirit left, I hung out flags, and planted all the force I could
muster, upon the walls. I am now much better, and I sincerely
thank you for your kind attention and friendly counsel. . . .
   'Count Manucci[1] came here last week from travelling in Ireland. I have shewn him what civilities I could on his own
account, on your's, and on that of Mr. and Mrs. Thrale. He has
had a fall from his horse, and been much hurt. I regret this
unlucky accident, for he seems to be a very amiable man.'

   As the evidence of what I have mentioned at the beginning
of this year, I select from his private register the following
passage:

   'July 25, 1776. O GOD, who hast ordained that whatever is to
be desired should be sought by labour, and who, by thy blessing,
bringest honest labour to good effect, look with mercy upon my
studies and endeavours. Grant me, O LORD, to design only what
is lawful and right; and afford me calmness of mind, and steadiness of purpose, that I may so do thy will in this short life, as
to obtain happiness in the world to come, for the sake of JESUS
CHRIST our Lord. Amen.'

   It appears from a note subjoined, that this was composed when

---

[1] A Florentine nobleman, mentioned by Johnson in his *Notes of his Tour
in France*. I had the pleasure of becoming acquainted with him in London,
in the spring of this year.

he 'purposed to apply vigorously to study, particularly of the Greek and Italian tongues.'

Such a purpose, so expressed, at the age of sixty-seven, is admirable and encouraging; and it must impress all the thinking part of my readers with a consolatory confidence in habitual devotion, when they see a man of such enlarged intellectual powers as Johnson, thus in the genuine earnestness of secrecy, imploring the aid of that Supreme Being, 'from whom cometh down every good and every perfect gift.'

'*To* SIR JOSHUA REYNOLDS

'SIR,—A young man, whose name is Paterson, offers himself this evening to the Academy. He is the son of a man for whom I have long had a kindness, and who is now abroad in distress. I shall be glad that you will be pleased to shew him any little countenance, or pay him any small distinction. How much it is in your power to favour or to forward a young man I do not know; nor do I know how much this candidate deserves favour by his personal merit, or what hopes his proficiency may now give of future eminence. I recommend him as the son of my friend. Your character and station enable you to give a young man great encouragement by very easy means. You have heard of a man who asked no other favour of Sir Robert Walpole, than that he would bow to him at his levee. I am, Sir, your most humble servant,

'Aug. 3, 1776.'   'SAM. JOHNSON.'

'MR. BOSWELL *to* DR. JOHNSON

'Edinburgh, August 30, 1776.

[After giving him an account of my having examined the chests of books which he had sent to me, and which contained what may be truely called a numerous and miscellaneous *Stall Library*, thrown together at random:—]

'Lord Hailes was against the decree in the case of my client, the minister; not that he justified the minister, but because the parishioner both provoked and retorted. I sent his Lordship your able argument upon the case for his perusal. His observation upon it in a letter to me was, "Dr. Johnson's *Suasorium*[1] is pleasantly[2] and artfully composed. I suspect, however, that he has not convinced himself; for, I believe that he is better read in ecclesiastical history, than to imagine that a Bishop or a Presbyter has a right to begin censure or discipline *è cathedrá*. . . ."[3]

'For the honour of Count Manucci, as well as to observe that exactness of truth which you have taught me, I must correct what I said in a former letter. He did not fall from his horse, which might have been an imputation on his skill as an officer of cavalry; his horse fell with him.

'I have, since I saw you, read every word of Granger's *Biographical History*. It has entertained me exceedingly, and I do not think him the *Whig* that you supposed. Horace Walpole's being his patron is, indeed, no good sign of his political principles. But he denied to Lord Mountstuart that he was a Whig, and said he had been accused by both parties of partiality. It seems he was like Pope,

> "While Tories call me Whig, and Whigs a Tory."

I wish you would look more into his book; and as Lord Mountstuart wishes much to find a proper person to continue the work upon Granger's plan, and has desired I would mention it to you; if such a man occurs, please to let me know. His Lordship will give him generous encouragement.'

'*To* MR. ROBERT LEVETT

'DEAR SIR,—Having spent about six weeks at this place, we have at length resolved upon returning. I expect to see you all in Fleet-street on the 30th of this month.

'I did not go into the sea till last Friday, but think to go most

---

[1] ['pleading'.]

[2] Why his Lordship uses the epithet *pleasantly*, when speaking of a grave piece of reasoning, I cannot conceive. But different men have different notions of pleasantry. I happened to sit by a gentleman one evening at the Opera-house in London, who, at the moment when *Medea* appeared to be in great agony at the thought of killing her children, turned to me with a smile, and said, '*funny* enough.'

[3] Dr. Johnson afterwards told me, that he was of opinion that a clergyman had this right.

of this week, though I know not that it does me any good. My nights are very restless and tiresome, but I am otherwise well.

'I have written word of my coming to Mrs. Williams. Remember me kindly to Francis and Betsy. I am, Sir, your humble servant,

    'Brighthelmstone, Oct. 21, 1776.'   'SAM. JOHNSON.'[1]

I again wrote to Dr. Johnson on the 21st of October, informing him, that my father had, in the most liberal manner, paid a large debt for me, and that I had now the happiness of being upon very good terms with him; to which he returned the following answer.

'*To* JAMES BOSWELL, ESQ.

'DEAR SIR,—I had great pleasure in hearing that you are at last on good terms with your father. Cultivate his kindness by all honest and manly means. Life is but short; no time can be afforded but for the indulgence of real sorrow, or contests upon questions seriously momentous. Let us not throw away any of our days upon useless resentment, or contend who shall hold out longest in stubborn malignity. It is best not to be angry; and best, in the next place, to be quickly reconciled. May you and your father pass the remainder of your time in reciprocal benevolence! . . .

'Do you ever hear from Mr. Langton? I visit him sometimes, but he does not talk. I do not like his scheme of life; but, as I am not permitted to understand it, I cannot set any thing right that is wrong. His children are sweet babies.

'I hope my irreconcileable enemy, Mrs. Boswell, is well. Desire her not to transmit her malevolence to the young people. Let me have Alexander, and Veronica, and Euphemia, for my friends.

'Mrs. Williams, whom you may reckon as one of your well-wishers, is in a feeble and languishing state, with little hope of growing better. She went for some part of the autumn into the

[1] For this and Dr. Johnson's other letters to Mr. Levett, I am indebted to my old acquaintance Mr. Nathaniel Thomas, whose worth and ingenuity have been long known to a respectable, though not a wide circle; and whose collection of medals would do credit to persons of greater opulence.

country, but is little benefited; and Dr. Lawrence confesses that his art is at an end. Death is, however, at a distance; and what more than that can we say of ourselves? I am sorry for her pain, and more sorry for her decay. Mr. Levett is sound, wind and limb.

'I was some weeks this autumn at Brighthelmstone. The place was very dull, and I was not well; the expedition to the Hebrides was the most pleasant journey that I ever made. Such an effort annually would give the world a little diversification.

'Every year, however, we cannot wander, and must therefore endeavour to spend our time at home as well as we can. I believe it is best to throw life into a method, that every hour may bring its employment, and every employment have its hour. Xenophon observes, in his *Treatise of Oeconomy*, that if every thing be kept in a certain place, when any thing is worn out or consumed, the vacuity which it leaves will shew what is wanting; so if every part of time has its duty, the hour will call into remembrance its proper engagement.

'I have not practised all this prudence myself, but I have suffered much for want of it; and I would have you, by timely recollection and steady resolution, escape from those evils which have lain heavy upon me. I am, my dearest Boswell, your most humble servant,

'Bolt-court, Nov. 16, 1776.'   'SAM. JOHNSON.'

On the 16th of November I informed him that Mr. Strahan had sent me *twelve* copies of the *Journey to the Western Islands*, handsomely bound, instead of the *twenty* copies which were stipulated; but which, I supposed, were to be only in sheets; requested to know how they should be distributed: and mentioned that I had another son born to me, who was named David, and was a sickly infant.

'To JAMES BOSWELL, ESQ.

'DEAR SIR,—I have been for some time ill of a cold, which, perhaps, I made an excuse to myself for not writing, when in reality I knew not what to say.

'The books you must at last distribute as you think best, in my name, or your own, as you are inclined, or as you judge most proper. Every body cannot be obliged; but I wish that nobody may be offended. Do the best you can.

'I congratulate you on the increase of your family, and hope that little David is by this time well, and his mamma perfectly recovered. I am much pleased to hear of the re-establishment of kindness between you and your father. Cultivate his paternal tenderness as much as you can. To live at variance at all is un-comfortable. Besides that, in the whole dispute you have the wrong side; at least you gave the first provocations, and some of them very offensive. Let it now be all over. As you have no reason to think that your new mother has shewn you any foul play, treat her with respect, and with some degree of confidence; this will secure your father. When once a discordant family has felt the pleasure of peace, they will not willingly lose it. If Mrs. Boswell would but be friends with me, we might now shut the temple of Janus.

'What came of Dr. Memis's cause? Is the question about the negro determined? Has Sir Allan any reasonable hopes? What is become of poor Macquarry? Let me know the event of all these litigations. I wish particularly well to the negro and Sir Allan.

'Mrs. Williams has been much out of order; and though she is something better, is likely, in her physician's opinion, to endure her malady for life, though she may, perhaps, die of some other. Mrs. Thrale is big, and fancies that she carries a boy; if it were very reasonable to wish much about it, I should wish her not to be disappointed. The desire of male heirs is not appendant only to feudal tenures. A son is almost necessary to the continuance of Thrale's fortune; for what can misses do with a brewhouse? Lands are fitter for daughters than trades.

'Baretti went away from Thrale's in some whimsical fit of disgust, or ill-nature, without taking any leave. It is well if he finds in any other place as good an habitation, and as many conveniencies. He has got five-and-twenty guineas by trans-lating Sir Joshua's *Discourses* into Italian, and Mr. Thrale gave him an hundred in the spring; so that he is yet in no difficulties.

'Colman has bought Foote's patent, and is to allow Foote for life sixteen hundred pounds a year, as Reynolds told me, and to allow him to play so often on such terms that he may gain four hundred pounds more. What Colman can get by this bargain, but trouble and hazard, I do not see. I am, dear Sir, your humble servant,

'Dec. 21, 1776.'   'SAM. JOHNSON.'

The Reverend Dr. Hugh Blair, who had long been admired as a preacher at Edinburgh, thought now of diffusing his excellent sermons more extensively, and encreasing his reputation, by publishing a collection of them. He transmitted the manuscript to Mr. Strahan, the printer, who after keeping it for some time, wrote a letter to him, discouraging the publication. Such at first was the unpropitious state of one of the most successful theological books that has ever appeared. Mr. Strahan, however, had sent one of the sermons to Dr. Johnson for his opinion; and after his unfavourable letter to Dr. Blair had been sent off, he received from Johnson on Christmas-eve, a note in which was the following paragraph: 'I have read over Dr. Blair's first sermon with more than approbation; to say it is good, is to say too little.'

I believe Mr. Strahan had very soon after this time a conversation with Dr. Johnson concerning them; and then he very candidly wrote again to Dr. Blair, enclosing Johnson's note, and agreeing to purchase the volume, for which he and Mr. Cadell gave one hundred pounds. The sale was so rapid and extensive, and the approbation of the publick so high, that to their honour be it recorded, the proprietors made Dr. Blair a present first of one sum, and afterwards of another, of fifty pounds, thus voluntarily doubling the stipulated price; and when he prepared another volume, they gave him at once three hundred pounds, being in all five hundred pounds, by an agreement to which I am a subscribing witness; and now for a third octavo volume he has received no less than six hundred pounds.

1777: ÆTAT. 68.]—IN 1777, it appears from his *Prayers and*

Meditations, that Johnson suffered much from a state of mind 'unsettled and perplexed,' and from that constitutional gloom, which, together with his extreme humility and anxiety with regard to his religious state, made him contemplate himself through too dark and unfavourable a medium. It may be said of him, that he 'saw GOD in clouds.' Certain we may be of his injustice to himself in the following lamentable paragraph, which it is painful to think came from the contrite heart of this great man, to whose labours the world is so much indebted: 'When I survey my past life, I discover nothing but a barren waste of time, with some disorders of body, and disturbances of the mind, very near to madness, which I hope He that made me will suffer to extenuate many faults, and excuse many deficiencies.'[1] But we find his devotions in this year eminently fervent; and we are comforted by observing intervals of quiet, composure, and gladness.

On Easter-day we find the following emphatick prayer:

'Almighty and most merciful Father, who seest all our miseries, and knowest all our necessities, look down upon me, and pity me. Defend me from the violent incursion [incursions] of evil thoughts, and enable me to form and keep such resolutions as may conduce to the discharge of the duties which thy providence shall appoint me; and so help me, by thy Holy Spirit, that my heart may surely there be fixed, where true joys are to be found, and that I may serve thee with pure affection and a cheerful mind. Have mercy upon me, O GOD, have mercy upon me; years and infirmities oppress me, terrour and anxiety beset me. Have mercy upon me, my Creator and my Judge. [In all dangers protect me.] In all perplexities relieve and free me; and so help me by thy Holy Spirit, that I may now so commemorate the death of thy Son our Saviour JESUS CHRIST, as that when this short and painful life shall have an end, I may, for his sake, be received to everlasting happiness. Amen.'[2]

While he was at church, the agreeable impressions upon his mind are thus commemorated:

[1] *Pr. and Med.* p. 155.   [2] *Ib.* p. 158.

'I was for some time distressed, but at last obtained, I hope from the GOD of Peace, more quiet than I have enjoyed for a long time. I had made no resolution, but as my heart grew lighter, my hopes revived, and my courage increased; and I wrote with my pencil in my Common Prayer Book,

> "*Vita ordinanda.*
> *Biblia legenda.*
> *Theologiæ opera danda.*
> *Serviendum et lætandum.*" '[1]

Mr. Steevens, whose generosity is well known, joined Dr. Johnson in kind assistance to a female relation of Dr. Goldsmith, and desired that on her return to Ireland she would procure authentick particulars of the life of her celebrated relation. Concerning her there is the following letter:—

'*To* GEORGE STEEVENS, ESQ.

'DEAR SIR,—You will be glad to hear that from Mrs. Goldsmith, whom we lamented as drowned, I have received a letter full of gratitude to us all, with promise to make the enquiries which we recommended to her.

'I would have had the honour of conveying this intelligence to Miss Caulfield, but that her letter is not at hand, and I know not the direction. You will tell the good news. I am, Sir, your most, &c.

'February 25, 1777.'   'SAM. JOHNSON.'

'MR. BOSWELL *to* DR. JOHNSON

'MY DEAR SIR,   'Edinburgh, Feb. 14, 1777.

'My state of epistolary accounts with you at present is extraordinary. The balance, as to number, is on your side. I am indebted to you for two letters; one dated the 16th of November, upon which very day I wrote to you, so that our letters were exactly exchanged, and one dated the 21st of December last.

'My heart was warmed with gratitude by the truely kind contents of both of them; and it is amazing and vexing that I have

[1] ['Resolved: to order my life; to read the Bible; to study theology; to serve God with gladness'.]

allowed so much time to elapse without writing to you. But
delay is inherent in me, by nature or by bad habit. I waited till
I should have an opportunity of paying you my compliments on a
new year. I have procrastinated till the year is no longer new. . . .

'Dr. Memis's cause was determined against him, with £40
costs. The Lord President, and two other of the Judges, dissented
from the majority, upon this ground;—that although there may
have been no intention to injure him by calling him *Doctor of
Medicine,* instead of *Physician,* yet, as he remonstrated against
the designation before the charter was printed off, and represented that it was disagreeable, and even hurtful to him, it was
ill-natured to refuse to alter it, and let him have the designation
to which he was certainly entitled. My own opinion is, that our
court has judged wrong. The defendants were *in malâ fide,* to
persist in naming him in a way that he disliked. You remember
poor Goldsmith, when he grew important, and wished to appear
Doctor Major, could not bear your calling him *Goldy.* Would it
not have been wrong to have named him so in your *Preface to
Shakspeare,* or in any serious permanent writing of any sort?
The difficulty is, whether an action should be allowed on such
petty wrongs. *De minimis non curat lex.*[1]

'The Negro cause is not yet decided. A memorial is preparing
on the side of slavery. I shall send you a copy as soon as it is
printed. Maclaurin is made happy by your approbation of his
memorial for the black.

'Macquarry was here in the winter, and we passed an evening
together. The sale of his estate cannot be prevented.

'Sir Allan Maclean's suit against the Duke of Argyle, for
recovering the ancient inheritance of his family, is now fairly
before all our judges. I spoke for him yesterday, and Maclaurin
to-day; Crosbie spoke to-day against him. Three more counsel
are to be heard, and next week the cause will be determined.
I send you the *Informations,* or *Cases,* on each side, which I hope
you will read. You said to me when we were under Sir Allan's
hospitable roof, "I will help him with my pen." You said it
with a generous glow; and though his Grace of Argyle did

[1] ['The law does not concern itself about trifles.']

afterwards mount you upon an excellent horse, upon which "you looked like a Bishop," you must not swerve from your purpose at Inchkenneth. I wish you may understand the points at issue, amidst our Scotch law principles and phrases.

[Here followed a full state of the case, in which I endeavoured to make it as clear as I could to an Englishman, who had no knowledge of the formularies and technical language of the law of Scotland.]

'I shall inform you how the cause is decided here. But as it may be brought under the review of our Judges, and is certainly to be carried by appeal to the House of Lords, the assistance of such a mind as yours will be of consequence. Your paper on *Vicious Intromission* is a noble proof of what you can do even in Scotch law. . . .

'I have not yet distributed all your books. Lord Hailes and Lord Monboddo have each received one, and return you thanks. Monboddo dined with me lately, and having drank tea, we were a good while by ourselves, and as I knew that he had read the *Journey* superficially, as he did not talk of it as I wished, I brought it to him, and read aloud several passages; and then he talked so, that I told him he was to have a copy *from the authour*. He begged *that* might be marked on it. . . . I ever am, my dear Sir, your most faithful, and affectionate humble servant,

'JAMES BOSWELL'

'SIR ALEXANDER DICK *to* DR. SAMUEL JOHNSON
    'SIR,   'Prestonfield, Feb. 17, 1777.
    'I had yesterday the honour of receiving your book of your *Journey to the Western Islands of Scotland*, which you was so good as to send me, by the hands of our mutual friend, Mr. Boswell, of Auchinleck; for which I return you my most hearty thanks; and after carefully reading it over again, shall deposit in my little collection of choice books, next our worthy friend's *Journey to Corsica*. As there are many things to admire in both performances, I have often wished that no Travels or Journeys should be published but those undertaken by persons of integrity and capacity to judge well, and describe faithfully, and in good

language, the situation, condition, and manners of the countries past through. Indeed our country of Scotland, in spite of the union of the crowns, is still in most places so devoid of clothing, or cover from hedges and plantations, that it was well you gave your readers a sound *Monitoire* with respect to that circumstance. The truths you have told, and the purity of the language in which they are expressed, as your *Journey* is universally read, may, and already appear to have a very good effect. For a man of my acquaintance, who has the largest nursery for trees and hedges in this country, tells me, that of late the demand upon him for these articles is doubled, and sometimes tripled. I have, therefore, listed Dr. Samuel Johnson in some of my memorandums of the principal planters and favourers of the enclosures, under a name which I took the liberty to invent from the Greek, *Papadendrion.*[1] Lord Auchinleck and some few more are of the list. I am told that one gentleman in the shire of Aberdeen, *viz.* Sir Archibald Grant, has planted above fifty millions of trees on a piece of very wild ground at Monimusk: I must enquire if he has fenced them well, before he enters my list; for, that is the soul of enclosing. I began myself to plant a little, our ground being too valuable for much, and that is now fifty years ago; and the trees, now in my seventy-fourth year, I look up to with reverence, and shew them to my eldest son, now in his fifteenth year, and they are full the height of my country-house here, where I had the pleasure of receiving you, and hope again to have that satisfaction with our mutual friend, Mr. Boswell. I shall always continue, with the truest esteem, dear Doctor, your much obliged, and obedient humble servant,

'ALEXANDER DICK.'[2]

'*To* JAMES BOSWELL, ESQ.

'DEAR SIR,—It is so long since I heard any thing from you,[3] that I am not easy about it; write something to me next post.

---

[1] ['Father of plantations.']
[2] For a character of this very amiable man, see *Journal of a Tour to the Hebrides,* 3rd edit. p. 36. [Aug. 17].
[3] By the then course of the post, my long letter of the 14th had not yet reached him.

When you sent your last letter, every thing seemed to be mending; I hope nothing has lately grown worse. I suppose young
Alexander continues to thrive, and Veronica is now very pretty
company. I do not suppose the lady is yet reconciled to me, yet
let her know that I love her very well, and value her very much.

'Dr. Blair is printing some sermons. If they are all like the
first, which I have read, they are *sermones aurei, ac auro magis
aurei.*[1] It is excellently written both as to doctrine and language.
Mr. Watson's book[2] seems to be much esteemed. . . .

'Poor Beauclerk still continues very ill. Langton lives on as
he is used to do. His children are very pretty, and, I think, his
lady loses her Scotch. Paoli I never see.

'I have been so distressed by difficulty of breathing, that I lost,
as was computed, six-and-thirty ounces of blood in a few days.
I am better, but not well.

'I wish you would be vigilant and get me Graham's *Telemachus* that was printed at Glasgow, a very little book; and
Johnstoni Poemata, another little book, printed at Middleburgh.

'Mrs. Williams sends her compliments, and promises that
when you come hither, she will accommodate you as well as
ever she can in the old room. She wishes to know whether you
sent her book to Sir Alexander Gordon.

'My dear Boswell, do not neglect to write to me; for your
kindness is one of the pleasures of my life, which I should be
sorry to lose. I am, Sir, your humble servant,

'February 18, 1777.'   'SAM JOHNSON.'

'*To* DR. SAMUEL JOHNSON

'DEAR SIR,   'Edinburgh, Feb. 24, 1777.
'Your letter dated the 18th instant, I had the pleasure to
receive last post. Although my late long neglect, or rather delay,
was truely culpable, I am tempted not to regret it, since it has
produced me so valuable a proof of your regard. I did, indeed,
during that inexcusable silence, sometimes divert the reproaches
of my own mind, by fancying that I should hear again from you,

---

[1] ["Golden sermons; nay, more golden than gold.']
[2] *History of Philip the Second.*

inquiring with some anxiety about me, because, for aught you knew, I might have been ill.

'You are pleased to shew me, that my kindness is of some consequence to you. My heart is elated at the thought. Be assured, my dear Sir, that my affection and reverence for you are exalted and steady. I do not believe that a more perfect attachment ever existed in the history of mankind. And it is a noble attachment; for the attractions are Genius, Learning, and Piety.

'Your difficulty of breathing alarms me, and brings into my imagination an event, which although in the natural course of things, I must expect at some period, I cannot view with composure. . . .

'My wife is much honoured by what you say of her. She begs you may accept of her best compliments. She is to send you some marmalade of oranges of her own making. . . . I ever am, my dear Sir, your most obliged and faithful humble servant,

'JAMES BOSWELL.'

'*To* JAMES BOSWELL, ESQ.

'DEAR SIR,—I have been much pleased with your late letter, and am glad that my old enemy, Mrs. Boswell, begins to feel some remorse. As to Miss Veronica's Scotch, I think it cannot be helped. An English maid you might easily have; but she would still imitate the greater number, as they would be likewise those whom she must most respect. Her dialect will not be gross. Her Mamma has not much Scotch, and you have yourself very little. I hope she knows my name, and does not call me *Johnston*.[1]

'The immediate cause of my writing is this:—One Shaw, who seems a modest and a decent man, has written an *Erse Grammar*, which a very learned Highlander, Macbean, has, at my request, examined and approved.

'The book is very little, but Mr. Shaw has been persuaded by his friends to set it at half a guinea, though I had advised only a crown, and thought myself liberal. You, whom the authour

---

[1] John*son* is the most common English formation of the Sirname from *John*; John*ston* the Scotch. My illustrious friend observed that many North Britons pronounced his name in their own way.

considers as a great encourager of ingenious men, will receive
a parcel of his proposals and receipts. I have undertaken to give
you notice of them, and to solicit your countenance. You must
ask no poor man, because the price is really too high. Yet such
a work deserves patronage.

'It is proposed to augment our club from twenty to thirty, of
which I am glad; for as we have several in it whom I do not
much like to consort with,[1] I am for reducing it to a mere
miscellaneous collection of conspicuous men, without any determinate character. . . . I am, dear Sir, most affectionately your's,
    'March 11, 1777.'   'SAM. JOHNSON.'

'My respects to Madam, to Veronica, to Alexander, to Euphemia, to David.'

'MR. BOSWELL *to* DR. JOHNSON

                                        'Edinburgh, April 4, 1777.
[After informing him of the death of my little son David, and
that I could not come to London this spring:—]
'I think it hard that I should be a whole year without seeing
you. May I presume to petition for a meeting with you in the
autumn? You have, I believe, seen all the cathedrals in England,
except that of Carlisle. If you are to be with Dr. Taylor, at
Ashbourne, it would not be a great journey to come thither. We
may pass a few most agreeable days there by ourselves, and I
will accompany you a good part of the way to the southward
again. Pray think of this.

'You forget that Mr. Shaw's *Erse Grammar* was put into
your hands by myself last year. Lord Eglintoune put it into
mine. I am glad that Mr. Macbean approves of it. I have
received Mr. Shaw's Proposals for its publication, which I can
perceive are written *by the hand of a* MASTER. . . .

'Pray get for me all the editions of *Walton's Lives*: I have a
notion that the republication of them with Notes will fall upon
me, between Dr. Horne and Lord Hailes.'

---

[1] On account of their differing from him as to religion and politicks.

Mr. Shaw's Proposals † for *An Analysis of the Scotch Celtick Language*, were thus illuminated by the pen of Johnson:

'Though the Erse dialect of the Celtick language has, from the earliest times, been spoken in Britain, and still subsists in the northern parts and adjacent islands, yet, by the negligence of a people rather warlike than lettered, it has hitherto been left to the caprice and judgement of every speaker, and has floated in the living voice, without the steadiness of analogy, or direction of rules. An Erse Grammar is an addition to the stores of literature; and its authour hopes for the indulgence always shewn to those that attempt to do what was never done before. If his work shall be found defective, it is at least all his own: he is not like other grammarians, a compiler or transcriber; what he delivers, he has learned by attentive observation among his countrymen, who perhaps will be themselves surprized to see that speech reduced to principles, which they have used only by imitation.

'The use of this book will, however, not be confined to the mountains and islands; it will afford a pleasing and important subject of speculation, to those whose studies lead them to trace the affinity of languages, and the migrations of the ancient races of mankind.'

'*To* Dr. Samuel Johnson

'My Dear Sir,   'Glasgow, April 24, 1777.

'Our worthy friend Thrale's death having appeared in the news-papers, and been afterwards contradicted, I have been placed in a state of very uneasy uncertainty, from which I hoped to be relieved by you: but my hopes have as yet been vain. How could you omit to write to me on such an occasion? I shall wait with anxiety.

'I am going to Auchinleck to stay a fortnight with my father. It is better not to be there very long at one time. But frequent renewals of attention are agreeable to him.

'Pray tell me about this edition of "*The English Poets*, with a Preface, biographical and critical, to each Authour, by Samuel Johnson, LL.D." which I see advertised. I am delighted with

the prospect of it. Indeed I am happy to feel that I am capable of
being so much delighted with literature. But is not the charm
of this publication chiefly owing to the *magnum nomen*[1] in the
front of it?

'What do you say of Lord Chesterfield's *Memoirs and last
Letters*?

'My wife has made marmalade of oranges for you. I left her
and my daughters and Alexander all well yesterday. I have
taught Veronica to speak of you thus;—Dr. John*son*, not John*-
ston*. I remain, my dear Sir, your most affectionate, and obliged
humble servant,　　　　　　　　　　　　　'JAMES BOSWELL.'

'*To* JAMES BOSWELL, ESQ.

'DEAR SIR,—The story of Mr. Thrale's death, as he had
neither been sick nor in any other danger, made so little impression upon me, that I never thought about obviating its effects on
any body else. It is supposed to have been produced by the
English custom of making April fools, that is, of sending one
another on some foolish errand on the first of April.

'Tell Mrs. Boswell that I shall taste her marmalade cautiously
at first. *Timeo Danaos et dona ferentes.*[2] Beware, says the Italian
proverb, of a reconciled enemy. But when I find it does me no
harm, I shall then receive it and be thankful for it, as a pledge of
firm, and, I hope, of unalterable kindness. She is, after all, a
dear, dear lady.

'Please to return Dr. Blair thanks for his sermons. The
Scotch write English wonderfully well. . . .

'Your frequent visits to Auchinleck, and your short stay there,
are very laudable and very judicious. Your present concord with
your father gives me great pleasure; it was all that you seemed
to want.

'My health is very bad, and my nights are very unquiet.
What can I do to mend them? I have for this summer nothing
better in prospect than a journey into Staffordshire and Derbyshire, perhaps with Oxford and Birmingham in my way.

[1] ['great name.']
[2] ['I fear the Danaans, though their hands proffer gifts.' *Aeneid*, II, i. 49.
(Jackson.).]

'Make my compliments to Miss Veronica; I must leave it to *her* philosophy to comfort you for the loss of little David. You must remember, that to keep three out of four is more than your share. Mrs. Thrale has but four out of eleven.

'I am engaged to write little Lives, and little Prefaces, to a little edition of *The English Poets*. I think I have persuaded the booksellers to insert something of Thomson; and if you could give me some information about him, for the life which we have is very scanty, I should be glad. I am, dear Sir, your most affectionate humble servant,

'May 3, 1777.'   'SAM. JOHNSON.'

To those who delight in tracing the progress of works of literature, it will be an entertainment to compare the limited design with the ample execution of that admirable performance, *The Lives of the English Poets*, which is the richest, most beautiful, and indeed most perfect production of Johnson's pen. His notion of it at this time appears in the preceding letter. He has a memorandum in this year, '29 May, Easter Eve, I treated with booksellers on a bargain, but the time was not long[1].' The bargain was concerning that undertaking; but his tender conscience seems alarmed lest it should have intruded too much on his devout preparation for the solemnity of the ensuing day. But, indeed, very little time was necessary for Johnson's concluding a treaty with the booksellers; as he had, I believe, less attention to profit from his labours than any man to whom literature has been a profession. I shall here insert from a letter to me from my late worthy friend Mr. Edward Dilly, though of a later date, an account of this plan so happily conceived; since it was the occasion of procuring for us an elegant collection of the best biography and criticism of which our language can boast.

'To JAMES BOSWELL, ESQ.

'DEAR SIR,   'Southill, Sept. 26, 1777.

'You will find by this letter, that I am still in the same calm

[1] *Pr. and Med.* p. 155.

retreat, from the noise and bustle of London, as when I wrote to you last. I am happy to find you had such an agreeable meeting with your old friend Dr. Johnson; I have no doubt your stock is much increased by the interview; few men, nay I may say, scarcely any man, has got that fund of knowledge and entertainment as Dr. Johnson in conversation. When he opens freely, every one is attentive to what he says, and cannot fail of improvement as well as pleasure.

'The edition of *The Poets*, now printing, will do honour to the English press; and a concise account of the life of each authour, by Dr. Johnson, will be a very valuable addition, and stamp the reputation of this edition superiour to any thing that is gone before. The first cause that gave rise to this undertaking, I believe, was owing to the little trifling edition of *The Poets*, printing by the Martins, at Edinburgh, and to be sold by Bell, in London. Upon examining the volumes which were printed, the type was found so extremely small, that many persons could not read them; not only this inconvenience attended it, but the inaccuracy of the press was very conspicuous. These reasons, as well as the idea of an invasion of what we call our Literary Property, induced the London Booksellers to print an elegant and accurate edition of all the English Poets of reputation, from Chaucer to the present time.

'Accordingly a select number of the most respectable booksellers met on the occasion; and, on consulting together, agreed, that all the proprietors of copy-right in the various Poets should be summoned together; and when their opinions were given, to proceed immediately on the business. Accordingly a meeting was held, consisting of about forty of the most respectable booksellers of London, when it was agreed that an elegant and uniform edition of *The English Poets* should be immediately printed, with a concise account of the life of each authour, by Dr. Samuel Johnson; and that three persons should be deputed to wait upon Dr. Johnson, to solicit him to undertake the Lives, *viz.*, T. Davies, Strahan, and Cadell. The Doctor very politely undertook it, and seemed exceedingly pleased with the proposal. As to the terms, it was left entirely to the Doctor to name his own:

he mentioned two hundred guineas:[1] it was immediately agreed to; and a farther compliment, I believe, will be made him. A committee was likewise appointed to engage the best engravers, *viz.*, Bartolozzi, Sherwin, Hall, etc. Likewise another committee for giving directions about the paper, printing, etc., so that the whole will be conducted with spirit, and in the best manner, with respect to authourship, editorship, engravings, etc., etc. My brother will give you a list of the Poets we mean to give, many of which are within the time of the Act of Queen Anne, which Martin and Bell cannot give, as they have no property in them; the proprietors are almost all the booksellers in London, of consequence. I am, dear Sir, ever your's,

'EDWARD DILLY.'

I shall afterwards have occasion to consider the extensive and varied range which Johnson took, when he was once led upon ground which he trod with a peculiar delight, having long been intimately acquainted with all the circumstances of it that could interest and please.

'DR. JOHNSON *to* CHARLES O'CONNOR, ESQ.[2]

'SIR,—Having had the pleasure of conversing with Dr. Campbell about your character and your literary undertaking, I am resolved to gratify myself by renewing a correspondence which

---

[1] Johnson's moderation in demanding so small a sum is extraordinary. Had he asked one thousand, or even fifteen hundred guineas, the booksellers, who knew the value of his name, would doubtless have readily given it. They have probably got five thousand guineas by this work in the course of twenty-five years. [M].

[2] Mr. Joseph Cooper Walker, of the Treasury, Dublin, who obligingly communicated to me this and a former letter from Dr. Johnson to the same gentleman (for which see p. 227), writes to me as follows:—'Perhaps it would gratify you to have some account of Mr. O'Connor. He is an amiable, learned, venerable old gentleman, of an independent fortune, who lives at Belanagar, in the county of Roscommon; he is an admired writer, and Member of the Irish Academy.—The above Letter is alluded to in the Preface to the 2nd edit. of his *Dissert.* p. 3.'—Mr. O'Connor afterwards died at the age of eighty-two. See a well-drawn character of him in the *Gent. Mag.* for August 1791.

began and ended a great while ago, and ended, I am afraid, by my fault; a fault which, if you have not forgotten it, you must now forgive.

'If I have ever disappointed you, give me leave to tell you, that you have likewise disappointed me. I expected great discoveries in Irish antiquity, and large publications in the Irish language; but the world still remains as it was, doubtful and ignorant. What the Irish language is in itself, and to what languages it has affinity, are very interesting questions, which every man wishes to see resolved that has any philological or historical curiosity. Dr. Leland begins his history too late: the ages which deserve an exact enquiry are those times (for such there were) when Ireland was the school of the west, the quiet habitation of sanctity and literature. If you could give a history, though imperfect, of the Irish nation, from its conversion to Christianity to the invasion from England, you would amplify knowledge with new views and new objects. Set about it therefore, if you can: do what you can easily do without anxious exactness. Lay the foundation, and leave the superstructure to posterity. I am, Sir, your most humble servant,

'May 19, 1777.'   'SAM. JOHNSON.'

Early in this year came out, in two volumes quarto, the post-humous works of the learned Dr. Zachary Pearce, Bishop of Rochester; being *A Commentary, with Notes, on the four Evangelists and the Acts of the Apostles*, with other theological pieces. Johnson had now an opportunity of making a grateful return to that excellent prelate, who, we have seen, was the only person who gave him any assistance in the compilation of his *Dictionary*. The Bishop had left some account of his life and character, written by himself. To this Johnson made some valuable additions,† and also furnished to the editor, the Reverend Mr. Derby, a Dedication,† which I shall here insert, both because it will appear at this time with peculiar propriety; and because it will tend to propagate and increase that 'fervour of *Loyalty*,' which in me, who boast of the name of TORY, is not only a principle, but a passion.

'To The King

'Sir,—I presume to lay before your Majesty the last labours of a learned Bishop, who died in the toils and duties of his calling. He is now beyond the reach of all earthly honours and rewards; and only the hope of inciting others to imitate him, makes it now fit to be remembered, that he enjoyed in his life the favour of your Majesty.

'The tumultuary life of Princes seldom permits them to survey the wide extent of national interest, without losing sight of private merit; to exhibit qualities which may be imitated by the highest and the humblest of mankind; and to be at once amiable and great.

'Such characters, if now and then they appear in history, are contemplated with admiration. May it be the ambition of all your subjects to make haste with their tribute of reverence: and as posterity may learn from your Majesty how Kings should live, may they learn, likewise, from your people, how they should be honoured. I am, may it please your Majesty, with the most profound respect, your Majesty's most dutiful and devoted

'Subject and Servant.'

In the summer he wrote a Prologue* which was spoken before *A Word to the Wise*, a comedy by Mr. Hugh Kelly, which had been brought upon the stage in 1770; but he being a writer for ministry, in one of the news-papers, it fell a sacrifice to popular fury, and in the playhouse phrase, was *damned*. By the generosity of Mr. Harris, the proprietor of Covent Garden theatre, it was now exhibited for one night, for the benefit of the authour's widow and children. To conciliate the favour of the audience was the intention of Johnson's Prologue, which, as it is not long, I shall here insert, as a proof that his poetical talents were in no degree impaired.

> 'This night presents a play, which publick rage,
> Or right or wrong, once hooted from the stage:
> From zeal or malice, now no more we dread,
> For English vengeance *wars not with the dead*.
> A generous foe regards with pitying eye
> The man whom Fate has laid where all must lie.

To wit, reviving from its author's dust,
Be kind, ye judges, or at least be just:
Let no renewed hostilities invade
Th' oblivious grave's inviolable shade.
Let one great payment every claim appease,
And him who cannot hurt, allow to please;
To please by scenes, unconscious of offence,
By harmless merriment, or useful sense.
Where aught of bright or fair the piece displays,
Approve it only;—'tis too late to praise.
If want of skill or want of care appear,
Forbear to hiss;—the poet cannot hear.
By all, like him, must praise and blame be found,
At last, a fleeting gleam, or empty sound;
Yet then shall calm reflection bless the night,
When liberal pity dignified delight;
When pleasure fir'd her touch at virtue's flame,
And mirth was bounty with an humbler name.'

A circumstance which could not fail to be very pleasing to
Johnson occurred this year. The Tragedy of *Sir Thomas Overbury*, written by his early companion in London, Richard Savage,
was brought out with alterations at Drury-lane theatre.[1] The
Prologue to it was written by Mr. Richard Brinsley Sheridan;
in which, after describing very pathetically the wretchedness of

'Ill-fated Savage, at whose birth was giv'n
No parent but the Muse, no friend but Heav'n:'

he introduced an elegant compliment to Johnson on his *Dictionary*, that wonderful performance which cannot be too often or
too highly praised; of which Mr. Harris, in his *Philological
Inquiries*,[2] justly and liberally observes:'Such is its merit, that our
language does not possess a more copious, learned, and valuable
work.' The concluding lines of this Prologue were these:—

'So pleads the tale[3] that gives to future times
The son's misfortunes and the parent's crimes;

[1] It was not at Drury-lane, but at Covent Garden theatre, that it was
acted. [M.]
[2] Part First, Chap. 4.   [3] *Life of Richard Savage*, by Dr. Johnson.

There shall his fame (if own'd to-night) survive,
Fix'd by THE HAND THAT BIDS OUR LANGUAGE LIVE.'

Mr. Sheridan here at once did honour to his taste and to his
liberality of sentiment, by shewing that he was not prejudiced
from the unlucky difference which had taken place between his
worthy father and Dr. Johnson. I have already mentioned, that
Johnson was very desirous of reconciliation with old Mr. Sheridan. It will, therefore, not seem at all surprizing that he was
zealous in acknowledging the brilliant merit of his son. While
it had as yet been displayed only in the drama, Johnson proposed
him as a member of THE LITERARY CLUB, observing, that 'He
who has written the two best comedies of his age, is surely a
considerable man.' And he had, accordingly, the honour to be
elected; for an honour it undoubtedly must be allowed to be,
when it is considered of whom that society consists, and that a
single black ball excludes a candidate.

'MR. BOSWELL *to* DR. JOHNSON

'MY DEAR SIR,   'July 9, 1777.[1]
'For the health of my wife and children I have taken the
little country-house at which you visited my uncle, Dr. Boswell,
who, having lost his wife, is gone to live with his son. We took
possession of our villa about a week ago; we have a garden of
three quarters of an acre, well stocked with fruit-trees and
flowers, and gooseberries and currants, and peas and beans, and
cabbages, &c. &c., and my children are quite happy. I now write
to you in a little study, from the window of which I see around
me a verdant grove, and beyond it the lofty mountain called
Arthur's Seat.

'Your last letter, in which you desire me to send you some
additional information concerning Thomson, reached me very
fortunately just as I was going to Lanark, to put my wife's two
nephews, the young Campbells, to school there, under the care
of Mr. Thomson, the master of it, whose wife is sister to the
authour of *The Seasons*. She is an old woman; but her memory is
very good; and she will with pleasure give me for you every

[1] [Actually *June* 9.]

807

particular that you wish to know, and she can tell. Pray then take
the trouble to send me such questions as may lead to biographical materials. You say that the *Life* which we have of Thomson
is scanty. Since I received your letter I have read his *Life*, published under the name of Cibber, but as you told me, really
written by a Mr. Shiels;[1] that written by Dr. Murdoch; one
prefixed to an edition of the *Seasons*, published at Edinburgh,
which is compounded of both, with the addition of an anecdote
of Quin's relieving Thomson from prison; the abridgement of
Murdoch's account of him, in the *Biographia Britannica*, and
another abridgement of it in the *Biographical Dictionary*, enriched with Dr. Joseph Warton's critical panegyrick on the
Seasons in his *Essay on the Genius and Writings of Pope*: from all
these it appears to me that we have a pretty full account of this
poet. However, you will, I doubt not, shew me many blanks,
and I shall do what can be done to have them filled up. As Thomson never returned to Scotland, (which *you* will think very wise,)
his sister can speak from her own knowledge only as to the early
part of his life. She has some letters from him, which may
probably give light as to his more advanced progress, if she will
let us see them, which I suppose she will. I believe George Lewis
Scott[2] and Dr. Armstrong are now his only surviving companions, while he lived in and about London; and they, I dare
say, can tell more of him than is yet known. My own notion is,
that Thomson was a much coarser man than his friends are
willing to acknowledge. His *Seasons* are indeed full of elegant
and pious sentiments: but a rank soil, nay a dunghill, will produce beautiful flowers.

'Your edition of *The English Poets*[3] will be very valuable, on
account of the *Prefaces* and *Lives*. But I have seen a specimen of
an edition of *The Poets* at the Apollo press, at Edinburgh, which,
for excellence in printing and engraving, highly deserves a
liberal encouragement.

[1] See *ante*, p. 738.
[2] Formerly Sub-preceptor to his present Majesty, and afterwards a
Commissioner of Excise. [M.]
[3] Dr. Johnson was not the *editor* of this Collection of *The English Poets*;
he merely furnished the biographical prefaces. [M.]

'Most sincerely do I regret the bad health and bad rest with which you have been afflicted; and I hope you are better. I cannot believe that the Prologue which you generously gave to Mr. Kelly's widow and children the other day, is the effusion of one in sickness and in disquietude: but external circumstances are never sure indications of the state of man. I send you a letter which I wrote to you two years ago at Wilton; and did not send at the time, for fear of being reproved as indulging too much tenderness; and one written to you at the tomb of Melancthon, which I kept back, lest I should appear at once too superstitious and too enthusiastick. I now imagine that perhaps they may please you.

'You do not take the least notice of my proposal for our meeting at Carlisle.[1] Though I have meritoriously refrained from visiting London this year, I ask you if it would not be wrong that I should be two years without having the benefit of your conversation, when, if you come down as far as Derbyshire, we may meet at the expence of a few days' journeying, and not many pounds. I wish you to see Carlisle, which made me mention that place. But if you have not a desire to complete your tour of the English cathedrals, I will take a larger share of the road between this place and Ashbourne. So tell me *where* you will fix for our passing a few days by ourselves. Now don't cry "foolish fellow," or "idle dog." Chain your humour, and let your kindness play.

'You will rejoice to hear that Miss Macleod, of Rasay, is married to Colonel Mure Campbell, an excellent man, with a pretty good estate of his own, and the prospect of having the

[1] Dr. Johnson had himself talked of our seeing Carlisle together. *High* was a favourite word of his to denote a person of rank. He said to me, 'Sir, I believe we may meet at the house of a Roman Catholick lady in Cumberland; a high lady, Sir.' I afterwards discovered that he meant Mrs. Strickland, sister of Charles Townley, Esq., whose very noble collection of statues and pictures is not more to be admired, than his extraordinary and polite readiness in shewing it, which I and several of my friends have agreeably experienced. They who are possessed of valuable stores of gratification to persons of taste, should exercise their benevolence in imparting the pleasure. Grateful acknowledgments are due to Welbore Ellis Agar, Esq., for the liberal access which he is pleased to allow to his exquisite collection of pictures.

Earl of Loudoun's fortune and honours. Is not this a noble lot for our fair Hebridean? How happy am I that she is to be in Ayrshire. We shall have the Laird of Rasay, and old Malcolm, and I know not how many gallant Macleods, and bagpipes, &c. &c. at Auchinleck. Perhaps you may meet them all there.

'Without doubt you have read what is called *The Life* of David Hume, written by himself, with the letter from Dr. Adam Smith subjoined to it. Is not this an age of daring effrontery? My friend Mr. Anderson, Professor of Natural Philosophy at Glasgow, at whose house you and I supped, and to whose care Mr. Windham, of Norfolk, was entrusted at that University, paid me a visit lately; and after we had talked with indignation and contempt of the poisonous productions with which this age is infested, he said there was now an excellent opportunity for Dr. Johnson to step forth. I agreed with him that you might knock Hume's and Smith's heads together, and make vain and ostentatious infidelity exceedingly ridiculous. Would it not be worth your while to crush such noxious weeds in the moral garden?

'You have said nothing to me of Dr. Dodd. I know not how you think on that subject; though the news-papers give us a saying of your's in favour of mercy to him. But I own I am very desirous that the royal prerogative of remission of punishment should be employed to exhibit an illustrious instance of the regard which GOD's VICEGERENT will ever shew to piety and virtue. If for ten righteous men the ALMIGHTY would have spared Sodom, shall not a thousand acts of goodness done by Dr. Dodd counterbalance one crime? Such an instance would do more to encourage goodness, than his execution would do to deter from vice. I am not afraid of any bad consequence to society; for who will persevere for a long course of years in a distinguished discharge of religious duties, with a view to commit a forgery with impunity?

'Pray make my best compliments acceptable to Mr. and Mrs. Thrale, by assuring them of my hearty joy that the *Master*, as you call him, is alive. I hope I shall often taste his Champagne —*soberly*.

'I have not heard from Langton for a long time. I suppose he is as usual,

>"Studious the busy moments to deceive."

'. . . I remain, my dear Sir, your most affectionate, and faithful humble servant,   'JAMES BOSWELL.'

On the 23rd of June, I again wrote to Dr. Johnson, enclosing a ship-master's receipt for a jar of orange-marmalade, and a large packet of Lord Hailes's *Annals of Scotland*.

'*To* JAMES BOSWELL, ESQ.

'DEAR SIR,—I have just received your packet from Mr. Thrale's, but have not day-light enough to look much into it. I am glad that I have credit enough with Lord Hailes to be trusted with more copy. I hope to take more care of it than of the last. I return Mrs. Boswell my affectionate thanks for her present, which I value as a token of reconciliation.

'Poor Dodd was put to death yesterday, in opposition to the recommendation of the jury—the petition of the city of London —and a subsequent petition signed by three-and-twenty thousand hands. Surely the voice of the publick, when it calls so loudly, and calls only for mercy, ought to be heard.

'The saying that was given me in the papers I never spoke; but I wrote many of his petitions, and some of his letters. He applied to me very often. He was, I am afraid, long flattered with hopes of life; but I had no part in the dreadful delusion; for, as soon as the King had signed his sentence, I obtained from Mr. Chamier an account of the disposition of the court towards him, with a declaration that there *was no hope even of a respite*. This letter immediately was laid before Dodd; but he believed those whom he wished to be right, as it is thought, till within three days of his end. He died with pious composure and resolution. I have just seen the Ordinary that attended him. His address to his fellow-convicts offended the Methodists; but he had a Moravian[1] with him much of his time. His moral character is

---

[1] [The Rev. Benjamin Latrobe. *Review of English Studies*, 1948, xxiv. 145.]

very bad: I hope all is not true that is charged upon him. Of his behaviour in prison an account will be published.

'I give you joy of your country-house, and your pretty garden; and hope some time to see you in your felicity. I was much pleased with your two letters that had been kept so long in store;[1] and rejoice at Miss Rasay's advancement, and wish Sir Allan success.

[1] Since they have been so much honoured by Dr. Johnson I shall here insert them:—

'*To* MR. SAMUEL JOHNSON.

'MY EVER DEAR AND MUCH-RESPECTED SIR,—You know my solemn enthusiasm of mind. You love me for it, and I respect myself for it, because in so far I resemble Mr. Johnson. You will be agreeably surprized when you learn the reason of my writing this letter. I am at Wittemberg in Saxony. I am in the old church where the Reformation was first preached, and where some of the reformers lie interred. I cannot resist the serious pleasure of writing to Mr. Johnson from the Tomb of Melancthon. My paper rests upon the gravestone of that great and good man, who was undoubtedly the worthiest of all the reformers. He wished to reform abuses which had been introduced into the Church; but had no private resentment to gratify. So mild was he, that when his aged mother consulted him with anxiety on the perplexing disputes of the times, he advised her "to keep to the old religion." At this tomb, then, my ever dear and respected friend! I vow to thee an eternal attachment. It shall be my study to do what I can to render your life happy; and, if you die before me, I shall endeavour to do honour to your memory; and, elevated by the remembrance of you, persist in noble piety. May GOD, the Father of all beings, ever bless you! and may you continue to love, your most affectionate friend, and devoted servant,

'Sunday, Sept. 30, 1764.'   JAMES BOSWELL.'

'*To* DR. SAMUEL JOHNSON.

'MY DEAR SIR,   'Wilton-house, April 22, 1775.

'Every scene of my life confirms the truth of what you have told me, "there is no certain happiness in this state of being."—I am here, amidst all that you know is at Lord Pembroke's; and yet I am weary and gloomy. I am just setting out for the house of an old friend in Devonshire, and shall not get back to London for a week yet. You said to me last Good-Friday, with a cordiality that warmed my heart, that if I came to settle in London, we should have a day fixed every week, to meet by ourselves and talk freely. To be thought worthy of such a privilege cannot but exalt me. During my present absence from you, while, notwithstanding the gaiety which you allow me to possess, I am darkened by temporary clouds, I beg to have a few lines from you; a few lines merely of kindness, as a *viaticum* till I see you again. In your *Vanity of Human Wishes*, and in Parnell's *Contentment*, I find the only sure means of enjoying happiness; or, at least, the hopes of happiness. I ever am, with reverence and affection, most faithfully yours,

'JAMES BOSWELL.'

'I hope to meet you somewhere towards the north, but am loath to come quite to Carlisle. Can we not meet at Manchester? But we will settle it in some other letters.

'Mr. Seward,[1] a great favourite at Streatham, has been, I think, enkindled by our travels with a curiosity to see the Highlands. I have given him letters to you and Beattie. He desires that a lodging may be taken for him at Edinburgh, against his arrival. He is just setting out.

'Langton has been exercising the militia. Mrs. Williams is, I fear, declining. Dr. Lawrence says he can do no more. She is gone to summer in the country, with as many conveniences about her as she can expect; but I have no great hope. We must all die: may we all be prepared!

'I suppose Miss Boswell reads her book, and young Alexander takes to his learning. Let me hear about them; for every thing that belongs to you, belongs in a more remote degree, and not, I hope, very remote, to, dear Sir, yours affectionately,

'June 28, 1777.'   'SAM. JOHNSON.'

To THE SAME

'DEAR SIR,—This gentleman is a great favourite at Streatham, and therefore you will easily believe that he has very valuable qualities. Our narrative has kindled him with a desire of visiting the Highlands, after having already seen a great part of Europe. You must receive him as a friend, and when you have directed him to the curiosities of Edinburgh, give him instructions and recommendations for the rest of his journey. I am, dear Sir, your most humble servant,

'June 24, 1777.'   'SAM. JOHNSON.'

Johnson's benevolence to the unfortunate was, I am confident, as steady and active as that of any of those who have been most eminently distinguished for that virtue. Innumerable proofs of it I have no doubt will be for ever concealed from mortal eyes.

---

[1] William Seward, Esq., F.R.S., editor of *Anecdotes of some distinguished persons*, etc., in four volumes, 8vo., well known to a numerous and valuable acquaintance for his literature, love of the fine arts, and social virtues. I am indebted to him for several communications concerning Johnson.

We may, however, form some judgement of it, from the many
and very various instances which have been discovered. One,
which happened in the course of this summer, is remarkable
from the name and connection of the person who was the object
of it. The circumstance to which I allude is ascertained by two
letters, one to Mr. Langton, and another to the Reverend
Dr. Vyse, rector of Lambeth, son of the respectable clergyman
at Lichfield, who was contemporary with Johnson, and in whose
father's family Johnson had the happiness of being kindly
received in his early years.

'Dr. Johnson *to* Bennet Langton, Esq.

'Dear Sir,—I have lately been much disordered by a difficulty
of breathing, but am now better. I hope your house is well.

'You know we have been talking lately of St. Cross, at
Winchester; I have an old acquaintance whose distress makes
him very desirous of an hospital, and I am afraid I have not
strength enough to get him into the Chartreux. He is a painter,
who never rose higher than to get his immediate living, and
from that, at eighty-three, he is disabled by a slight stroke of
the palsy, such as does not make him at all helpless on common
occasions, though his hand is not steady enough for his art.

'My request is, that you will try to obtain a promise of the
next vacancy, from the Bishop of Chester. It is not a great thing
to ask, and I hope we shall obtain it. Dr. Warton has promised
to favour him with his notice, and I hope he may end his days in
peace. I am, Sir, your most humble servant,

'June 29, 1777.'   'Sam. Johnson.'

'*To* The Reverend Dr. Vyse, *at Lambeth*

'Sir,—I doubt not but you will readily forgive me for taking
the liberty of requesting your assistance in recommending an old
friend to his Grace the Archbishop, as Governour of the Charter-
house.

'His name is De Groot; he was born at Gloucester; I have
known him many years. He has all the common claims to
charity, being old, poor, and infirm, in a great degree. He has

likewise another claim, to which no scholar can refuse attention; he is by several descents the nephew of Hugo Grotius; of him, from whom perhaps every man of learning has learnt something. Let it not be said that in any lettered country a nephew of Grotius asked a charity and was refused. I am, reverend Sir, your most humble servant,

'July 19, 1777.'   'SAM. JOHNSON.'

'REVEREND DR. VYSE *to* MR. BOSWELL
    'SIR,   'Lambeth, June 9, 1787.
    'I have searched in vain for the letter which I spoke of, and which I wished, at your desire, to communicate to you. It was from Dr. Johnson, to return me thanks for my application to Archbishop Cornwallis in favour of poor De Groot. He rejoices at the success it met with, and is lavish in the praise he bestows upon his favourite, Hugo Grotius. I am really sorry that I cannot find this letter, as it is worthy of the writer. That which I send you enclosed[1] is at your service. It is very short, and will not perhaps be thought of any consequence, unless you should judge proper to consider it as a proof of the very humane part which Dr. Johnson took in behalf of a distressed and deserving person. I am, Sir, your most obedient humble servant,
                                              'W. VYSE.'

'DR. JOHNSON *to* MR. EDWARD DILLY[2]
    'SIR,—To the collection of *English Poets*, I have recommended the volume of Dr. Watts to be added; his name has long been held by me in veneration, and I would not willingly be reduced to tell of him only that he was born and died. Yet of his life I know very little, and therefore must pass him in a manner very unworthy of his character, unless some of his friends will favour me with the necessary information; many of them must be known to you; and by your influence, perhaps I may obtain some instruction. My plan does not exact much; but I wish to

---

    [1] The preceding letter.
    [2] [Really to William Sharp.]

distinguish Watts, a man who never wrote but for a good purpose. Be pleased to do for me what you can. I am, Sir, your
humble servant,   'SAM. JOHNSON.'

'Bolt-Court, Fleet-street, July 7, 1777.'

'*To* DR. SAMUEL JOHNSON

'MY DEAR SIR,   'Edinburgh, July 15, 1777.
'The fate of poor Dr. Dodd made a dismal impression upon
my mind. . . .

'I had sagacity enough to divine that you wrote his speech to
the Recorder, before sentence was pronounced. I am glad you
have written so much for him; and I hope to be favoured with an
exact list of the several pieces when we meet.

'I received Mr. Seward as the friend of Mr. and Mrs. Thrale,
and as a gentleman recommended by Dr. Johnson to my attention. I have introduced him to Lord Kames, Lord Monboddo,
and Mr. Nairne. He is gone to the Highlands with Dr. Gregory;
when he returns I shall do more for him.

'Sir Allan Maclean has carried that branch of his cause, of
which we had good hopes: the President and one other Judge
only were against him. I wish the House of Lords may do as
well as the Court of Session has done. But Sir Allan has not the
lands of *Brolos* quite cleared by this judgement, till a long
account is made up of debts and interests on the one side, and
rents on the other. I am, however, not much afraid of the
balance.

'Macquarry's estates, Staffa and all, were sold yesterday,
and bought by a Campbell. I fear he will have little or nothing
left out of the purchase money.

'I send you the case against the negro, by Mr. Cullen, son to
Dr. Cullen, in opposition to Maclaurin's for liberty, of which
you have approved. Pray read this, and tell me what you think
as a *Politician*, as well as a *Poet*, upon the subject.

'Be so kind as to let me know how your time is to be distributed next autumn. I will meet you at Manchester, or where
you please; but I wish you would complete your tour of the

cathedrals, and come to Carlisle, and I will accompany you a part of the way homewards. I am ever, most faithfully yours,

'JAMES BOSWELL.'

'*To* JAMES BOSWELL, ESQ.

'DEAR SIR,—Your notion of the necessity of an yearly interview is very pleasing to both my vanity and tenderness. I shall, perhaps, come to Carlisle another year; but my money has not held out so well as it used to do. I shall go to Ashbourne, and I purpose to make Dr. Taylor invite you. If you live awhile with me at his house, we shall have much time to ourselves, and our stay will be no expence to us or him. I shall leave London the 28th; and after some stay at Oxford and Lichfield, shall probably come to Ashbourne about the end of your Session, but of all this you shall have notice. Be satisfied we will meet somewhere.

'What passed between me and poor Dr. Dodd you shall know more fully when we meet.

'Of lawsuits there is no end; poor Sir Allan must have another trial, for which, however, his antagonist cannot be much blamed, having two Judges on his side. I am more afraid of the debts than of the House of Lords. It is scarcely to be imagined to what debts will swell, that are daily increasing by small additions, and how carelessly in a state of desperation debts are contracted. Poor Macquarry was far from thinking that when he sold his islands he should receive nothing. For what were they sold? And what was their yearly value? The admission of money into the Highlands will soon put an end to the feudal modes of life, by making those men landlords who were not chiefs. I do not know that the people will suffer by the change; but there was in the patriarchal authority something venerable and pleasing. Every eye must look with pain on a *Campbell* turning the *Macquarries* at will out of their *sedes avitæ*,[1] their hereditary island.

'Sir Alexander Dick is the only Scotsman liberal enough not to be angry that I could not find trees, where trees were not. I was much delighted by his kind letter.

'I remember Rasay with too much pleasure not to partake of

[1] ['ancestral seat'.]

817

the happiness of any part of that amiable family. Our ramble in the islands hangs upon my imagination, I can hardly help imagining that we shall go again. Pennant seems to have seen a great deal which we did not see: when we travel again let us look better about us.

'You have done right in taking your uncle's house. Some change in the form of life, gives from time to time a new epocha of existence. In a new place there is something new to be done, and a different system of thoughts rises in the mind. I wish I could gather currants in your garden. Now fit up a little study, and have your books ready at hand; do not spare a little money, to make your habitation pleasing to yourself.

'I have dined lately with poor dear ———.[1] I do not think he goes on well. His table is rather coarse, and he has his children too much about him.[2] But he is a very good man.

'Mrs. Williams is in the country to try if she can improve her health; she is very ill. Matters have come so about that she is in the country with very good accommodation; but, age and sickness, and pride, have made her so peevish that I was forced to bribe the maid to stay with her, by a secret stipulation of half a crown a week over her wages.

'Our CLUB ended its session about six weeks ago. We now only meet to dine once a fortnight. Mr. Dunning, the great lawyer, is one of our members. The Thrales are well.

'I long to know how the Negro's cause will be decided. What is the opinion of Lord Auchinleck, or Lord Hailes, or Lord Monboddo? I am, dear Sir, your most affectionate, &c.

'July 22, 1777.'   'SAM. JOHNSON.'

'DR. JOHNSON *to* MRS. BOSWELL

'MADAM,—Though I am well enough pleased with the taste

---

[1] [Langton. *Mrs. Piozzi*; *Croker*[1].]

[2] This very just remark I hope will be constantly held in remembrance by parents, who are in general too apt to indulge their own fond feelings for their children at the expence of their friends. The common custom of introducing them after dinner is highly injudicious. It is agreeable enough that they should appear at any other time; but they should not be suffered to poison the moments of festivity by attracting the attention of the company, and in a manner compelling them from politeness to say what they do not think.

of sweetmeats, very little of the pleasure which I received at the arrival of your jar of marmalade arose from eating it. I received it as a token of friendship, as a proof of reconciliation, things much sweeter than sweetmeats, and upon this consideration I return you, dear Madam, my sincerest thanks. By having your kindness I think I have a double security for the continuance of Mr. Boswell's, which it is not to be expected that any man can long keep, when the influence of a lady so highly and so justly valued operates against him. Mr. Boswell will tell you that I was always faithful to your interest, and always endeavoured to exalt you in his estimation. You must now do the same for me. We must all help one another, and you must now consider me, as, dear Madam, your most obliged, and most humble servant,

'July 22, 1777.'   'SAM. JOHNSON.'

'MR. BOSWELL *to* DR. JOHNSON

'MY DEAR SIR,   'Edinburgh, July 28, 1777.
'This is the day on which you were to leave London, and I have been amusing myself in the intervals of my law-drudgery, with figuring you in the Oxford post-coach. I doubt, however, if you have had so merry a journey as you and I had in that vehicle last year, when you made so much sport with Gwyn, the architect. Incidents upon a journey are recollected with peculiar pleasure; they are preserved in brisk spirits, and come up again in our minds, tinctured with that gaiety, or at least that animation with which we first perceived them.' . . .

[I added, that something had occurred, which I was afraid might prevent me from meeting him; and that my wife had been affected with complaints which threatened a consumption, but was now better.]

'*To* JAMES BOSWELL, ESQ.

'DEAR SIR,—Do not disturb yourself about our interviews; I hope we shall have many; nor think it any thing hard or unusual, that your design of meeting me is interrupted. We have both endured greater evils, and have greater evils to expect.

'Mrs. Boswell's illness makes a more serious distress. Does the blood rise from her lungs or from her stomach? From little vessels broken in the stomach there is no danger. Blood from the lungs is, I believe, always frothy, as mixed with wind. Your physicians know very well what is to be done. The loss of such a lady would, indeed, be very afflictive, and I hope she is in no danger. Take care to keep her mind as easy as is possible.

'I have left Langton in London. He has been down with the militia, and is again quiet at home, talking to his little people, as, I suppose, you do sometimes. Make my compliments to Miss Veronica. The rest are too young for ceremony.

'I cannot but hope that you have taken your country-house at a very seasonable time, and that it may conduce to restore, or establish Mrs. Boswell's health, as well as provide room and exercise for the young ones. That you and your lady may both be happy, and long enjoy your happiness, is the sincere and earnest wish of, dear Sir, your most, &c.

'Oxford, Aug. 4, 1777.'   'SAM. JOHNSON.'

'MR. BOSWELL *to* DR. JOHNSON

[Informing him that my wife had continued to grow better, so that my alarming apprehensions were relieved: and that I hoped to disengage myself from the other embarrassment which had occurred, and therefore requesting to know particularly when he intended to be at Ashbourne.]

'*To* JAMES BOSWELL, ESQ.

'DEAR SIR,—I am this day come to Ashbourne, and have only to tell you, that Dr. Taylor says you shall be welcome to him, and you know how welcome you will be to me. Make haste to let me know when you may be expected.

'Make my compliments to Mrs. Boswell, and tell her, I hope we shall be at variance no more. I am, dear Sir, your most humble servant,

'August 30, 1777.'   'SAM. JOHNSON.'

'*To* JAMES BOSWELL, ESQ.

'DEAR SIR,—On Saturday I wrote a very short letter, immediately upon my arrival hither, to shew you that I am not less desirous of the interview than yourself. Life admits not of delays; when pleasure can be had, it is fit to catch it. Every hour takes away part of the things that please us, and perhaps part of our disposition to be pleased. When I came to Lichfield, I found my old friend Harry Jackson dead. It was a loss, and a loss not to be repaired, as he was one of the companions of my childhood. I hope we may long continue to gain friends, but the friends which merit or usefulness can procure us, are not able to supply the place of old acquaintance, with whom the days of youth may be retraced, and those images revived which gave the earliest delight. If you and I live to be much older, we shall take great delight in talking over the Hebridean Journey.

'In the mean time it may not be amiss to contrive some other little adventure, but what it can be I know not; leave it, as Sidney says,

"To virtue, fortune, wine, and woman's breast;"[1]

for I believe Mrs. Boswell must have some part in the consultation.

[1] By an odd mistake, in the first three editions we find a reading in this line to which Dr. Johnson would by no means have subscribed, *wine* having been substituted for *time*. That error probably was a mistake in the transcript of Johnson's original letter. The other deviation in the beginning of the line (*virtue* instead of *nature*) must be attributed to his memory having deceived him. The verse quoted is the concluding line of a sonnet of Sidney's:—

> 'Who doth desire that chast his wife should bee,
>   First be he true, for truth doth truth deserve,
> Then be he such, as she his worth may see,
>   And, alwaies one, credit with her preserve:
> Not toying kynd nor causelessly unkynd,
>   Nor stirring thoughts, nor yet denying right,
> Nor spying faults, nor in plaine errors blind,
>   Never hard hand, nor ever rayns (reins) too light;
> As far from want, as far from vaine expence,
>   Th' one doth enforce, the t'other doth entice:
> Allow good companie, but drive from thence
>   All filthie mouths that glorie in their vice:
> This done, thou hast no more but leave the rest
>   To *nature*, fortune, *time*, and woman's breast.'

[M.]

'One thing you will like. The Doctor, so far as I can judge, is likely to leave us enough to ourselves. He was out to-day before I came down, and, I fancy, will stay out till dinner. I have brought the papers about poor Dodd, to show you, but you will soon have dispatched them.

'Before I came away I sent poor Mrs. Williams into the country, very ill of a pituitous defluxion, which wastes her gradually away, and which her physician declares himself unable to stop. I supplied her as far as could be desired, with all conveniences to make her excursion and abode pleasant and useful. But I am afraid she can only linger a short time in a morbid state of weakness and pain.

'The Thrales, little and great, are all well, and purpose to go to Brighthelmstone at Michaelmas. They will invite me to go with them, and perhaps I may go, but I hardly think I shall like to stay the whole time; but of futurity we know but little.

'Mrs. Porter is well; but Mrs. Aston, one of the ladies at Stowhill, has been struck with a palsy, from which she is not likely ever to recover. How soon may such a stroke fall upon us!

'Write to me, and let us know when we may expect you. I am, dear Sir, your most humble servant,

'Ashbourne, Sept. 1, 1777.'   'SAM. JOHNSON.'

'MR. BOSWELL *to* DR. JOHNSON

'Edinburgh, Sept. 9, 1777.

[After informing him that I was to set out next day, in order to meet him at Ashbourne:—]

'I have a present for you from Lord Hailes; the fifth book of *Lactantius*, which he has published with Latin notes. He is also to give you a few anecdotes for your *Life of Thomson*, who I find was private tutor to the present Earl of Hadington, Lord Hailes's cousin, a circumstance not mentioned by Dr. Murdoch. I have keen expectations of delight from your edition of *The English Poets*.

'I am sorry for poor Mrs. Williams's situation. You will,

however, have the comfort of reflecting on your kindness to her. Mr. Jackson's death, and Mrs. Aston's palsy, are gloomy circumstances. Yet surely we should be habituated to the uncertainty of life and health. When my mind is unclouded by melancholy, I consider the temporary distresses of this state of being, as "light afflictions," by stretching my mental view into that glorious after-existence, when they will appear to be as nothing. But present pleasures and present pains must be felt. I lately read *Rasselas* over again with great satisfaction.

'Since you are desirous to hear about Macquarry's sale I shall inform you particularly. The gentleman who purchased Ulva is Mr. Campbell, of Auchnaba: our friend Macquarry was proprietor of two-thirds of it, of which the rent was £156 5s. 1½d. This parcel was set up at £4,069 5s. 1d., but it sold for no less than £5,540. The other third of Ulva, with the island of Staffa, belonged to Macquarry of Ormaig. Its rent, including that of Staffa, £83 12s. 2½d.—set up at £2,178 16s. 4d.—sold for no less than £3,540. The Laird of Col wished to purchase Ulva, but he thought the price too high. There may, indeed, be great improvements made there, both in fishing and agriculture; but the interest of the purchase-money exceeds the rent so very much, that I doubt if the bargain will be profitable. There is an island called Little Colonsay, of £10 yearly rent, which I am informed has belonged to the Macquarrys of Ulva for many ages, but which was lately claimed by the Presbyterian Synod of Argyll, in consequence of a grant made to them by Queen Anne. It is believed that their claim will be dismissed, and that Little Colonsay will also be sold for the advantage of Macquarry's creditors. What think you of purchasing this island, and endowing a school or college there, the master to be a clergyman of the Church of England? How venerable would such an institution make the name of DR. SAMUEL JOHNSON in the Hebrides! I have, like yourself, a wonderful pleasure in recollecting our travels in those islands. The pleasure is, I think, greater than it reasonably should be, considering that we had not much either of beauty or elegance to charm our imaginations, or of rude novelty to astonish. Let us, by all means, have another expedition. I shrink a little from our scheme of going up the Baltick.[1] I am sorry you have already been in Wales; for I wish to see it. Shall we go to Ireland, of which I have seen but little? We shall try to strike out a plan when we are at Ashbourne. I am ever, your most faithful humble servant,

'JAMES BOSWELL.'

'*To* JAMES BOSWELL, ESQ.

'DEAR SIR,—I write to be left at Carlisle, as you direct me; but you cannot have it. Your letter, dated Sept. 6, was not at this place till this day, Thursday, Sept. 11; and I hope you will be here before this is at Carlisle.[2] However, what you have not going, you may have returning; and as I believe I shall not love you less after our interview, it will then be as true as it is now, that I set a very high value upon your friendship, and count your kindness as one of the chief felicities of my life. Do not fancy that an intermission of writing is a decay of kindness. No man is always in a disposition to write; nor has any man at all times something to say.

[1] It appears that Johnson, now in his sixty-eighth year, was seriously inclined to realise the project of our going up the Baltick, which I had started when we were in the Isle of Sky; for he thus writes to Mrs. Thrale; *Letters*, vol. i. p. 366:—

'Ashbourne, Sept. 13, 1777.
'Boswell, I believe, is coming. He talks of being here to day. I shall be glad to see him. But he shrinks from the Baltick expedition, which I think is the best scheme in our power. What we shall substitute I know not. He wants to see Wales; but, except the woods of *Bachycraigh*, what is there in Wales, that can fill the hunger of ignorance, or quench the thirst of curiosity? We may, perhaps, form some scheme or other; but, in the phrase of *Hockley in the Hole*, it is a pity he has not a *better bottom*.'

Such an ardour of mind, and vigour of enterprise, is admirable at any age: but more particularly so at the advanced period at which Johnson was then arrived. I am sorry now that I did not insist on our executing that scheme. Besides the other objects of curiosity and observation, to have seen my illustrious friend received, as he probably would have been, by a Prince so eminently distinguished for his variety of talents and acquisitions as the late King of Sweden; and by the Empress of Russia, whose extraordinary abilities, information, and magnanimity, astonish the world, would have afforded a noble subject for contemplation and record. This reflection may possibly be thought too visionary by the more sedate and cold-blooded part of my readers; yet I own, I frequently indulge it with an earnest, unavailing regret.

[2] It so happened. The letter was forwarded to my house at Edinburgh.

'That distrust which intrudes so often on your mind is a mode of melancholy, which, if it be the business of a wise man to be happy, it is foolish to indulge; and if it be a duty to preserve our faculties entire for their proper use, it is criminal. Suspicion is very often an useless pain. From that, and all other pains, I wish you free and safe; for I am, dear Sir, most affectionately yours,

'Ashbourne, Sept. 11, 1777.'   'SAM. JOHNSON.'

On Sunday evening, September 14, I arrived at Ashbourne, and drove directly up to Dr. Taylor's door. Dr. Johnson and he appeared before I had got out of the post-chaise, and welcomed me cordially.

I told them that I had travelled all the preceding night, and gone to bed at Leek, in Staffordshire; and that when I rose to go to church in the afternoon, I was informed there had been an earthquake, of which, it seems, the shock had been felt, in some degree, at Ashbourne. JOHNSON. 'Sir, it will be much exaggerated in popular talk: for, in the first place, the common people do not accurately adapt their thoughts to the objects; nor, secondly, do they accurately adapt their words to their thoughts: they do not mean to lie; but, taking no pains to be exact, they give you very false accounts. A great part of their language is proverbial. If anything rocks at all, they say *it rocks like a cradle*; and in this way they go on.'

The subject of grief for the loss of relations and friends being introduced, I observed that it was strange to consider how soon it in general wears away. Dr. Taylor mentioned a gentleman[1] of the neighbourhood as the only instance he had ever known of a person who had endeavoured to *retain* grief. He told Dr. Taylor, that after his Lady's death, which affected him deeply, he *resolved* that the grief, which he cherished with a kind of sacred fondness, should be lasting; but that he found he could not keep it long. JOHNSON. 'All grief for what cannot in the course of nature be helped, soon wears away; in some sooner, indeed, in some later; but it never continues very long, unless where there

---

[1] [Littleton Poyntz Meynell. *Boswell Papers*, xiii. 16.]

is madness, such as will make a man have pride so fixed in his mind, as to imagine himself a King; or any other passion in an unreasonable way: for all unnecessary grief is unwise, and therefore will not be long retained by a sound mind. If, indeed, the cause of our grief is occasioned by our own misconduct, if grief is mingled with remorse of conscience, it should be lasting.' Boswell. 'But, Sir, we do not approve of a man who very soon forgets the loss of a wife or a friend.' Johnson. 'Sir, we disapprove of him, not because he soon forgets his grief, for the sooner it is forgotten the better, but because we suppose, that if he forgets his wife or his friend soon, he has not had much affection for them.'

I was somewhat disappointed in finding that the edition of *The English Poets*, for which he was to write Prefaces and Lives, was not an undertaking directed by him: but that he was to furnish a Preface and Life to any poet the booksellers pleased. I asked him if he would do this to any dunce's works, if they should ask him. Johnson. 'Yes, Sir, and *say* he was a dunce.' My friend seemed now not much to relish talking of this edition.

On Monday, September 15, Dr. Johnson observed, that every body commended such parts of his *Journey to the Western Islands*, as were in their own way. 'For instance, (said he,) Mr. Jackson (the all-knowing) told me there was more good sense upon trade in it, than he should hear in the House of Commons in a year, except from Burke. Jones commended the part which treats of language; Burke that which describes the inhabitants of mountainous countries.'

After breakfast, Johnson carried me to see the garden belonging to the school of Ashbourne, which is very prettily formed upon a bank, rising gradually behind the house. The Reverend Mr. Langley, the head-master, accompanied us.

While we sat basking in the sun upon a seat here, I introduced a common subject of complaint, the very small salaries which many curates have, and I maintained, 'that no man should be invested with the character of a clergyman, unless he has a security for such an income as will enable him to appear respectable; that, therefore, a clergyman should not be allowed to have a curate, unless he gives him a hundred pounds a year; if he cannot do that, let him perform the duty himself.' JOHNSON. 'To be sure, Sir, it is wrong that any clergyman should be without a reasonable income; but as the church revenues were sadly diminished at the Reformation, the clergy who have livings cannot afford, in many instances, to give good salaries to curates, without leaving themselves too little; and, if no curate were to be permitted unless he had a hundred pounds a year, their number would be very small, which would be a disadvantage, as then there would not be such choice in the nursery for the church, curates being candidates for the higher ecclesiastical offices, according to their merit and good behaviour.' He explained the system of the English Hierarchy exceedingly well. 'It is not thought fit (said he,) to trust a man with the care of a parish till he has given proof as a curate that he shall deserve such a trust.' This is an excellent *theory*; and if the *practice* were according to it, the Church of England would be admirable indeed. However, as I have heard Dr. Johnson observe as to the Universities, bad practice does not infer that the *constitution* is bad.

We had with us at dinner several of Dr. Taylor's neighbours, good civil gentlemen, who seemed to understand Dr. Johnson very well, and not to consider him in the light that a certain person[1] did, who being struck, or rather stunned by his voice and manner, when he was afterwards asked what he thought of him, answered, 'He's a tremendous companion.'

Johnson told me, that 'Taylor was a very sensible acute man, and had a strong mind; that he had great activity in some respects, and yet such a sort of indolence, that if you should put a pebble upon his chimney-piece, you would find it there, in the same state, a year afterwards.'

And here is the proper place to give an account of Johnson's humane and zealous interference in behalf of the Reverend Dr. William Dodd, formerly Prebendary of Brecon, and chaplain in ordinary to his Majesty; celebrated as a very popular preacher, an encourager of charitable institutions, and authour of a variety of works, chiefly theological. Having unhappily contracted

[1] [George Garrick. *Mrs. Piozzi*; *Murphy*; *Croker*[1].]

expensive habits of living, partly occasioned by licentiousness of manners, he in an evil hour, when pressed by want of money, and dreading an exposure of his circumstances, forged a bond of which he attempted to avail himself to support his credit, flattering himself with hopes that he might be able to repay its amount without being detected. The person, whose name he thus rashly and criminally presumed to falsify, was the Earl of Chesterfield, to whom he had been tutor, and who, he perhaps, in the warmth of his feelings, flattered himself would have generously paid the money in case of an alarm being taken, rather than suffer him to fall a victim to the dreadful consequences of violating the law against forgery, the most dangerous crime in a commercial country; but the unfortunate divine had the mortification to find that he was mistaken. His noble pupil appeared against him, and he was capitally convicted.

Johnson told me that Dr. Dodd was very little acquainted with him, having been but once in his company, many years previous to this period (which was precisely the state of my own acquaintance with Dodd); but in his distress he bethought himself of Johnson's persuasive power of writing, if haply it might avail to obtain for him the Royal Mercy. He did not apply to him directly, but, extraordinary as it may seem, through the late Countess of Harrington, who wrote a letter to Johnson, asking him to employ his pen in favour of Dodd. Mr. Allen, the printer, who was Johnson's landlord and next neighbour in Bolt-court, and for whom he had much kindness, was one of Dodd's friends, of whom, to the credit of humanity be it recorded, that he had many who did not desert him, even after his infringement of the law had reduced him to the state of a man under sentence of death. Mr. Allen told me that he carried Lady Harrington's letter to Johnson, that Johnson read it walking up and down his chamber, and seemed much agitated, after which he said, 'I will do what I can;'—and certainly he did make extraordinary exertions.

He this evening, as he had obligingly promised in one of his letters, put into my hands the whole series of his writings upon this melancholy occasion, and I shall present my readers with the abstract which I made from the collection; in doing which I studied to avoid copying what had appeared in print, and now make part of the edition of *Johnson's Works*, published by the Booksellers of London, but taking care to mark Johnson's variations in some of the pieces there exhibited.

Dr. Johnson wrote in the first place, Dr. Dodd's *Speech to the Recorder of London*, at the Old-Bailey, when sentence of death was about to be pronounced upon him.

He wrote also *The Convict's Address to his unhappy Brethren*, a sermon delivered by Dr. Dodd, in the chapel of Newgate. According to Johnson's manuscript it began thus after the text, *What shall I do to be saved?*—

'These were the words with which the keeper, to whose custody Paul and Silas were committed by their prosecutors, addressed his prisoners, when he saw them freed from their bonds by the perceptible agency of divine favour, and was, therefore, irresistibly convinced that they were not offenders against the laws, but martyrs to the truth.'

Dr. Johnson was so good as to mark for me with his own hand, on a copy of this sermon which is now in my possession, such passages as were added by Dr. Dodd. They are not many: whoever will take the trouble to look at the printed copy, and attend to what I mention, will be satisfied of this.

There is a short introduction by Dr. Dodd, and he also inserted this sentence, 'You see with what confusion and dishonour I now stand before you;—no more in the pulpit of instruction, but on this humble seat with yourselves.' The *notes* are entirely Dodd's own, and Johnson's writing ends at the words, 'the thief whom he pardoned on the cross.' What follows was supplied by Dr. Dodd himself.

The other pieces written by Johnson in the above-mentioned collection, are two letters, one to the Lord Chancellor Bathurst, (not Lord North, as is erroneously supposed,) and one to Lord Mansfield;—A Petition from Dr. Dodd to the King;—A Petition from Mrs. Dodd to the Queen;—Observations of some length inserted in the newspapers, on occasion of Earl Percy's having presented to his Majesty a petition for mercy to Dodd, signed by twenty thousand people, but all in vain. He told me that he had also written a petition from the city of London; 'but (said he, with a significant smile) they *mended* it.'[1]

The last of these articles which Johnson wrote is *Dr. Dodd's last solemn Declaration*, which he left with the sheriff at the place of execution. Here also my friend marked the variations on a copy of that piece now in my possession. Dodd inserted, 'I never knew or attended to the calls of frugality, or the needful minuteness of painful œconomy;' and in the next sentence he introduced the words which I distinguish by *Italicks*; 'My life for some *few unhappy* years past has been *dreadfully erroneous.*' Johnson's expression was *hypocritical*; but his remark on the margin is 'With this he said he could not charge himself.'

Having thus authentically settled what part of the *Occasional Papers*, concerning Dr. Dodd's miserable situation, came from the pen of Johnson, I shall proceed to present my readers with my record of the unpublished writings relating to that extraordinary and interesting matter.

I found a letter to Dr. Johnson from Dr. Dodd, May 23, 1777, in which *The Convict's Address* seems clearly to be meant:—

[1] Having unexpectedly, by the favour of Mr. Stone, of London Field, Hackney, seen the original in Johnson's hand-writing, of 'The Petition of the City of London to his Majesty, in favour of Dr. Dodd,' I now present it to my readers, with such passages as were omitted inclosed in crotchets, and the additions or variations marked in Italicks.

'That William Dodd, Doctor of Laws, now lying under sentence of death *in your Majesty's gaol of Newgate*, for the crime of forgery, has for a great part of his life set a useful and laudable example of diligence in his calling, [and as we have reason to believe, has exercised his ministry with great fidelity and efficacy,] *which, in many instances, has produced the most happy effect.*

'That he has been the first institutor, [or] *and* a very earnest and active promoter of several modes of useful charity, and [that] therefore [he] may be considered as having been on many occasions a benefactor to the publick.

'[That when they consider his past life, they are willing to suppose his late crime to have been not the consequence of habitual depravity, but the suggestion of some sudden and violent temptation.]

'[That] *Your Petitioners* therefore considering his case as in some of its circumstances unprecedented and peculiar, *and encouraged by your Majesty's known clemency*, [they] most humbly recommend the said William Dodd to [his] *your* Majesty's most gracious consideration, in hopes that he will be found not altogether [unfit] *unworthy* to stand an example of Royal Mercy.'

'I am so penetrated, my ever dear Sir, with a sense of your extreme benevolence towards me, that I cannot find words equal to the sentiments of my heart. . . .

'You are too conversant in the world to need the slightest hint from me, of what infinite utility the Speech[1] on the aweful day has been to me. I experience, every hour, some good effect from it. I am sure that effects still more salutary and important must follow from *your kind and intended favour*. I will labour,— God being my helper,—to do justice to it from the pulpit. I am sure, had I your sentiments constantly to deliver from thence, in all their mighty force and power, not a soul could be left unconvinced and unpersuaded.' . . .

He added:—'May God Almighty bless and reward, with his choicest comforts, your philanthropick actions, and enable me at all times to express what I feel of the high and uncommon obligations which I owe to the *first man* in our times.'

On Sunday, June 22, he writes, begging Dr. Johnson's assistance in framing a supplicatory letter to his Majesty:—

'If his Majesty could be moved of his royal clemency to spare me and my family the horrours and ignominy of a *publick death*, which the *publick* itself is solicitous to wave, and to grant me in some silent distant corner of the globe, to pass the remainder of my days in penitence and prayer, I would bless his clemency and be humbled.'

This letter was brought to Dr. Johnson when in church. He stooped down and read it, and wrote, when he went home, the following letter for Dr. Dodd to the King:—

'Sir,—May it not offend your Majesty, that the most miserable of men applies himself to your clemency, as his last hope and his last refuge; that your mercy is most earnestly and humbly implored by a clergyman, whom your Laws and Judges have condemned to the horrour and ignominy of a publick execution.

'I confess the crime, and own the enormity of its consequences, and the danger of its example. Nor have I the confidence to petition for impunity; but humbly hope, that publick security

---

[1] His Speech at the Old Bailey, when found guilty.

may be established, without the spectacle of a clergyman dragged through the streets, to a death of infamy, amidst the derision of the profligate and profane; and that justice may be satisfied with irrevocable exile, perpetual disgrace, and hopeless penury.

'My life, Sir, has not been useless to mankind. I have benefited many. But my offences against GOD are numberless, and I have had little time for repentance. Preserve me, Sir, by your prerogative of mercy, from the necessity of appearing unprepared at that tribunal, before which Kings and Subjects must stand at last together. Permit me to hide my guilt in some obscure corner of a foreign country, where, if I can ever attain confidence to hope that my prayers will be heard, they shall be poured with all the fervour of gratitude for the life and happiness of your Majesty. I am, Sir, your Majesty's, &c.'

Subjoined to it was written as follows:—

'*To* DR. DODD

'SIR,—I most[1] seriously enjoin you not to let it be at all known that I have written this letter, and to return the copy to Mr. Allen in a cover to me. I hope I need not tell you, that I wish it success.—But do not indulge hope.—Tell nobody.'

It happened luckily that Mr. Allen was pitched on to assist in this melancholy office, for he was a great friend of Mr. Akerman, the keeper of Newgate. Dr. Johnson never went to see Dr. Dodd. He said to me, 'it would have done *him* more harm, than good to Dodd, who once expressed a desire to see him, but not earnestly.'

Dr. Johnson, on the 20th June, wrote the following letter:—

'*To* THE RIGHT HONOURABLE CHARLES JENKINSON

'SIR,—Since the conviction and condemnation of Dr. Dodd, I have had, by the intervention of a friend, some intercourse with him, and I am sure I shall lose nothing in your opinion by tenderness and commiseration. Whatever be the crime, it is not easy to have any knowledge of the delinquent, without a wish that his life may be spared; at least when no life has been taken away by him. I will, therefore, take the liberty of suggesting

[1] [Johnson probably wrote *must*.]

some reasons for which I wish this unhappy being to escape the utmost rigour of his sentence.

'He is, so far as I can recollect, the first clergyman of our church who has suffered publick execution for immorality; and I know not whether it would not be more for the interest of religion to bury such an offender in the obscurity of perpetual exile, than to expose him in a cart, and on the gallows, to all who for any reason are enemies to the clergy.

'The supreme power has, in all ages, paid some attention to the voice of the people; and that voice does not least deserve to be heard, when it calls out for mercy. There is now a very general desire that Dodd's life should be spared. More is not wished; and, perhaps, this is not too much to be granted.

'If you, Sir, have any opportunity of enforcing these reasons, you may, perhaps, think them worthy of consideration: but whatever you determine, I most respectfully intreat that you will be pleased to pardon for this intrusion, Sir, your most obedient and most humble servant,

'SAM. JOHNSON.'

It has been confidently circulated, with invidious remarks, that to this letter no attention whatever was paid by Mr. Jenkinson (afterwards Earl of Liverpool), and that he did not even deign to shew the common civility of owning the receipt of it. I could not but wonder at such conduct in the noble Lord, whose own character and just elevation in life, I thought, must have impressed him with all due regard for great abilities and attainments. As the story had been much talked of, and apparently from good authority, I could not but have animadverted upon it in this work, had it been as was alledged; but from my earnest love of truth, and having found reason to think that there might be a mistake, I presumed to write to his Lordship, requesting an explanation; and it is with the sincerest pleasure that I am enabled to assure the world, that there is no foundation for it, the fact being, that owing to some neglect, or accident, Johnson's letter never came to Lord Hawkesbury's hands. I should have thought it strange indeed, if that noble Lord had undervalued my illustrious friend; but instead of this being the case, his Lordship, in the very polite answer with which he was pleased immediately to honour me, thus expresses himself:—'I have always respected the memory of Dr. Johnson, and admire his writings; and I frequently read many parts of them with pleasure and great improvement.'

All applications for the Royal Mercy having failed, Dr. Dodd prepared himself for death; and, with a warmth of gratitude, wrote to Dr. Johnson as follows:—

'June 25, *Midnight*.

'Accept, thou *great* and *good* heart, my earnest and fervent thanks and prayers for all thy benevolent and kind efforts in my behalf.—Oh! Dr. Johnson! as I sought your knowledge at an early hour in life, would to heaven I had cultivated the love and acquaintance of so excellent a man!—I pray GOD most sincerely to bless you with the highest transports—the infelt satisfaction of *humane* and benevolent exertions!—And admitted, as I trust I shall be, to the realms of bliss before you, I shall hail *your* arrival there with transport, and rejoice to acknowledge that you was my Comforter, my Advocate, and my *Friend*! GOD *be ever* with *you*!'

Dr. Johnson lastly wrote to Dr. Dodd this solemn and soothing letter:—

'*To* THE REVEREND DR. DODD

'DEAR SIR,—That which is appointed to all men is now coming upon you. Outward circumstances, the eyes and the thoughts of men, are below the notice of an immortal being about to stand the trial for eternity, before the Supreme Judge of heaven and earth. Be comforted: your crime, morally or religiously considered, has no very deep dye of turpitude. It corrupted no man's principles; it attacked no man's life. It involved only a temporary and reparable injury. Of this, and of all other sins, you are earnestly to repent; and may GOD, who knoweth our frailty, and desireth not our death, accept your repentance, for the sake of his Son JESUS CHRIST our Lord.

'In requital of those well-intended offices which you are pleased so emphatically to acknowledge, let me beg that you make in your devotions one petition for my eternal welfare. I am, dear Sir, your affectionate servant,

'June 26, 1777.'   'SAM. JOHNSON.'

Under the copy of this letter I found written, in Johnson's own hand, 'Next day, June 27, he was executed.'

To conclude this interesting episode with an useful application, let us now attend to the reflections of Johnson at the end of the *Occasional Papers*, concerning the unfortunate Dr. Dodd:—

'Such were the last thoughts of a man whom we have seen exulting in popularity, and sunk in shame. For his reputation, which no man can give to himself, those who conferred it are to answer. Of his publick ministry the means of judging were sufficiently attainable. He must be allowed to preach well, whose sermons strike his audience with forcible conviction. Of his life, those who thought it consistent with his doctrine, did not originally form false notions. He was at first what he endeavoured to make others; but the world broke down his resolution, and he in time ceased to exemplify his own instructions.

'Let those who are tempted to his faults, tremble at his punishment; and those whom he impressed from the pulpit with religious sentiments, endeavour to confirm them, by considering the regret and self-abhorrence with which he reviewed in prison his deviations from rectitude.'

Johnson gave us this evening, in his happy discriminative manner, a portrait of the late Mr. Fitzherbert, of Derbyshire. 'There was (said he,) no sparkle, no brilliancy in Fitzherbert; but I never knew a man who was so generally acceptable. He made every body quite easy, overpowered nobody by the superiority of his talents, made no man think worse of himself by being his rival, seemed always to listen, did not oblige you to hear much from him, and did not oppose what you said. Every body liked him; but he had no friend, as I understand the word, nobody with whom he exchanged intimate thoughts. People were willing to think well of every thing about him.

A gentleman was making an affected rant, as many people do, of great feelings about "his dear son," who was at school near London; how anxious he was lest he might be ill, and what he would give to see him. "Can't you (said Fitzherbert), take a post-chaise and go to him." This, to be sure, *finished* the affected man, but there was not much in it.[1] However, this was circulated as wit for a whole winter, and I believe part of a summer too; a proof that he was no very witty man. He was an instance of the truth of the observation, that a man will please more upon the whole by negative qualities than by positive; by never offending, than by giving a great deal of delight. In the first place, men hate more steadily than they love; and if I have said something to hurt a man once, I shall not get the better of this by saying many things to please him.'

Tuesday, September 16, Dr. Johnson having mentioned to me the extraordinary size and price of some cattle reared by Dr. Taylor, I rode out with our host, surveyed his farm, and was shown one cow which he had sold for a hundred and twenty guineas, and another for which he had been offered a hundred and thirty. Taylor thus described to me his old schoolfellow and friend, Johnson: 'He is a man of a very clear head, great power of words, and a very gay imagination; but there is no disputing with him. He will not hear you, and having a louder voice than you, must roar you down.'

In the afternoon I tried to get Dr. Johnson to like the Poems of Mr. Hamilton of Bangour, which I had brought with me: I had been much pleased with them at a very early age; the impression still remained on my mind; it was confirmed by the opinion of my friend the Honourable Andrew Erskine, himself

[1] Dr. Gisborne, Physician to his Majesty's Household, has obligingly communicated to me a fuller account of this story than had reached Dr. Johnson. The affected Gentleman was the late John Gilbert Cooper, Esq., author of a *Life of Socrates*, and of some poems in Dodsley's *Collection*. Mr. Fitzherbert found him one morning, apparently, in such violent agitation, on account of the indisposition of his son, as to seem beyond the power of comfort. At length, however, he exclaimed, 'I'll write an Elegy.' Mr. Fitzherbert being satisfied, by this, of the sincerity of his emotions, slyly said, 'Had not you better take a post-chaise and go and see him?' It was the shrewdness of the insinuation which made the story be circulated.

both a good poet and a good critick, who thought Hamilton as true a poet as ever wrote, and that his not having fame was unaccountable. Johnson, upon repeated occasions, while I was at Ashbourne, talked slightingly of Hamilton. He said there was no power of thinking in his verses, nothing that strikes one, nothing better than what you generally find in magazines; and that the highest praise they deserved was, that they were very well for a gentleman to hand about among his friends. He said the imitation of *Ne sit ancillæ tibi amor, &c.*[1] was too solemn; he read part of it at the beginning. He read the beautiful pathetick song, *Ah the poor shepherd's mournful fate,* and did not seem to give attention to what I had been used to think tender elegant strains, but laughed at the rhyme, in Scotch pronunciation, *wishes* and *blushes*, reading *wushes*—and there he stopped. He owned that the epitaph on Lord Newhall was pretty well done. He read the *Inscription in a Summer-house*, and a little of the imitations of Horace's *Epistles*; but said, he found nothing to make him desire to read on. When I urged that there were some good poetical passages in the book. 'Where (said he,) will you find so large a collection without some?' I thought the description of Winter might obtain his approbation:

> 'See Winter, from the frozen north
> Drives his iron chariot forth!
> His grisly hand in icy chains
> Fair Tweeda's silver flood constrains,' &c.

He asked why an *'iron* chariot'? and said 'icy chains' was an old image. I was struck with the uncertainty of taste, and somewhat sorry that a poet whom I had long read with fondness, was not approved by Dr. Johnson. I comforted myself with thinking that the beauties were too delicate for his robust perceptions. Garrick maintained that he had not a taste for the finest productions of genius: but I was sensible, that when he took the trouble to analyse critically, he generally convinced us that he was right.

    In the evening, the Reverend Mr. Seward, of Lichfield, who was passing through Ashbourne in his way home, drank tea with

---

[1] ['Your love for a handmaid need cost you no blushes.' Horace, *Odes* II. iv. 1. (Wickham.)]

us. Johnson described him thus:—'Sir, his ambition is to be a fine talker; so he goes to Buxton, and such places, where he may find companies to listen to him. And, Sir, he is a valetudinarian, one of those who are always mending themselves. I do not know a more disagreeable character than a valetudinarian, who thinks he may do any thing that is for his ease, and indulges himself in the grossest freedoms: Sir, he brings himself to the state of a hog in a stye.'

Dr. Taylor's nose happening to bleed, he said, it was because he had omitted to have himself blooded four days after a quarter of a year's interval. Dr. Johnson, who was a great dabbler in physick, disapproved much of periodical bleeding. 'For (said he,) you accustom yourself to an evacuation which Nature cannot perform of herself, and therefore she cannot help you, should you, from forgetfulness or any other cause, omit it; so you may be suddenly suffocated. You may accustom yourself to other periodical evacuations, because should you omit them, Nature can supply the omission; but Nature cannot open a vein to blood you.'—'I do not like to take an emetick, (said Taylor,) for fear of breaking some small vessels.'—'Poh! (said Johnson,) if you have so many things that will break, you had better break your neck at once, and there's an end on't. You will break no small vessels:' (blowing with high derision.)

I mentioned to Dr. Johnson, that David Hume's persisting in his infidelity, when he was dying, shocked me much. JOHNSON. 'Why should it shock you, Sir? Hume owned he had never read the New Testament with attention. Here then was a man, who had been at no pains to inquire into the truth of religion, and had continually turned his mind the other way. It was not to be expected that the prospect of death would alter his way of thinking, unless GOD should send an angel to set him right.' I said, I had reason to believe that the thought of annihilation gave Hume no pain. JOHNSON. 'It was not so, Sir. He had a vanity in being thought easy. It is more probable that he should assume an appearance of ease, than that so very improbable a thing should be, as a man not afraid of going (as, in spite of his delusive theory, he cannot be sure but he may go,) into an unknown state, and not being uneasy at leaving all he knew. And you are to consider, that upon his own principle of annihilation he had no motive to speak the truth.' The horrour of death which I had always observed in Dr. Johnson, appeared strong to-night. I ventured to tell him, that I had been, for moments in my life, not afraid of death; therefore I could suppose another man in that state of mind for a considerable space of time. He said, 'he never had a moment in which death was not terrible to him.' He added, that it had been observed, that scarce any man dies in publick, but with apparent resolution; from that desire of praise which never quits us. I said, Dr. Dodd seemed to be willing to die, and full of hopes of happiness. 'Sir, (said he,) Dr. Dodd would have given both his hands and both his legs to have lived. The better a man is, the more afraid he is of death, having a clearer view of infinite purity.' He owned, that our being in an unhappy uncertainty as to our salvation, was mysterious; and said, 'Ah! we must wait till we are in another state of being, to have many things explained to us.' Even the powerful mind of Johnson seemed foiled by futurity. But I thought, that the gloom of uncertainty in solemn religious speculation, being mingled with hope, was yet more consolatory than the emptiness of infidelity. A man can live in thick air, but perishes in an exhausted receiver.

Dr. Johnson was much pleased with a remark which I told him was made to me by General Paoli:—'That it is impossible not to be afraid of death; and that those who at the time of dying are not afraid, are not thinking of death, but of applause, or something else, which keeps death out of their sight: so that all men are equally afraid of death when they see it; only some have a power of turning their sight away from it better than others.'

On Wednesday, September 17, Dr. Butter, physician at Derby, drank tea with us; and it was settled that Dr. Johnson and I should go on Friday and dine with him. Johnson said, 'I'm glad of this.' He seemed weary of the uniformity of life at Dr. Taylor's.

Talking of biography, I said, in writing a life, a man's

peculiarities should be mentioned, because they mark his character. JOHNSON. 'Sir, there is no doubt as to peculiarities: the question is, whether a man's vices should be mentioned; for instance, whether it should be mentioned that Addison and Parnell drank too freely: for people will probably more easily indulge in drinking from knowing this; so that more ill may be done by the example than good by telling the whole truth.' Here was an instance of his varying from himself in talk; for when Lord Hailes and he sat one morning calmly conversing in my house at Edinburgh, I well remember that Dr. Johnson maintained, that 'If a man is to write *A Panegyrick*, he may keep vices out of sight; but if he professes to write *A Life*, he must represent it really as it was:' and when I objected to the danger of telling that Parnell drank to excess, he said, that 'it would produce an instructive caution to avoid drinking, when it was seen, that even the learning and genius of Parnell could be debased by it.' And in the Hebrides he maintained, as appears from my *Journal*,[1] that a man's intimate friend should mention his faults, if he writes his life.

He had this evening, partly, I suppose, from the spirit of contradiction to his Whig friend, a violent argument with Dr. Taylor, as to the inclinations of the people of England at this time towards the Royal Family of Stuart. He grew so outrageous as to say, 'that, if England were fairly polled, the present King would be sent away to-night, and his adherents hanged to-morrow.' Taylor, who was as violent a Whig as Johnson was a Tory, was roused by this to a pitch of bellowing. He denied, loudly, what Johnson said; and maintained, that there was an abhorrence against the Stuart family, though he admitted that the people were not much attached to the present King.[2] JOHNSON. 'Sir, the state of the country is this: the people knowing it to be agreed on all hands that this King has not the hereditary

---

[1] *Journal of a Tour to the Hebrides.* 3rd edit. p. 240 [Sept. 22].

[2] Dr. Taylor was very ready to make this admission, because the party with which he was connected was not in power. There was then some truth in it, owing to the pertinacity of factious clamour. Had he lived till now, it would have been impossible for him to deny that his Majesty possesses the warmest affection of his people.

right to the crown, and there being no hope that he who has it can be restored, have grown cold and indifferent upon the subject of loyalty, and have no warm attachment to any King. They would not, therefore, risk any thing to restore the exiled family. They would not give twenty shillings a piece to bring it about. But, if a mere vote could do it, there would be twenty to one; at least, there would be a very great majority of voices for it. For, Sir, you are to consider, that all those who think a King has a right to his crown, as a man has to his estate, which is the just opinion, would be for restoring the King who certainly has the hereditary right, could he be trusted with it; in which there would be no danger now, when laws and every thing else are so much advanced: and every King will govern by the laws. And you must also consider, Sir, that there is nothing on the other side to oppose to this; for it is not alledged by any one that the present family has any inherent right: so that the Whigs could not have a contest between two rights.'

Dr. Taylor admitted, that if the question as to hereditary right were to be tried by a poll of the people of England, to be sure the abstract doctrine would be given in favour of the family of Stuart; but he said, the conduct of that family, which occasioned their expulsion, was so fresh in the minds of the people, that they would not vote for a restoration. Dr. Johnson, I think, was contented with the admission as to the hereditary right, leaving the original point in dispute, *viz.* what the people upon the whole would do, taking in right and affection; for he said, people were afraid of a change, even though they think it right. Dr. Taylor said something of the slight foundation of the hereditary right of the house of Stuart. 'Sir, (said Johnson,) the house of Stuart succeeded to the full right of both the houses of York and Lancaster, whose common source had the undisputed right. A right to a throne is like a right to any thing else. Possession is sufficient, where no better right can be shown. This was the case with the Royal Family of England, as it is now with the King of France: for as to the first beginning of the right, we are in the dark.'

Thursday, September 18. Last night Dr. Johnson had proposed

that the crystal lustre, or chandelier, in Dr. Taylor's large
room, should be lighted up some time or other. Taylor said, it
should be lighted up next night. 'That will do very well, (said
I,) for it is Dr. Johnson's birth-day.' When we were in the Isle
of Sky, Johnson had desired me not to mention his birth-day.
He did not seem pleased at this time that I mentioned it, and
said (somewhat sternly,) 'he would *not* have the lustre lighted
the next day.'

Some ladies, who had been present yesterday when I mentioned his birth-day, came to dinner to-day, and plagued him
unintentionally, by wishing him joy. I know not why he disliked
having his birth-day mentioned, unless it were that it reminded
him of his approaching nearer to death, of which he, had a
constant dread.

I mentioned to him a friend of mine[1] who was formerly gloomy
from low spirits, and much distressed by the fear of death, but
was now uniformly placid, and contemplated his dissolution
without any perturbation. 'Sir, (said Johnson,) this is only a
disordered imagination taking a different turn.'

We talked of a collection being made of all the English Poets
who had published a volume of poems. Johnson told me 'that a
Mr. Coxeter, whom he knew, had gone the greatest length
towards this; having collected, I think, about five hundred
volumes of poets whose works were little known; but that upon
his death Tom Osborne bought them, and they were dispersed,
which he thought a pity, as it was curious to see any series
complete; and in every volume of poems something good may
be found.'

He observed, that a gentleman of eminence in literature[2] had
got into a bad style of poetry of late. 'He puts (said he,) a very
common thing in a strange dress till he does not know it himself,
and thinks other people do not know it.' BOSWELL. 'That is
owing to his being so much versant in old English poetry.'
JOHNSON. 'What is that to the purpose, Sir? If I say a man is
drunk, and you tell me it is owing to his taking much drink, the

[1] [George Dempster. *Boswell Papers*, xiii. 29.]
[2] [Tom Warton. *Ib.* 30.]

matter is not mended. No, Sir, ———— has taken to an odd mode.
For example, he'd write thus:

> "Hermit hoar, in solemn cell,
> Wearing out life's evening gray."

Gray evening is common enough; but *evening gray* he'd think
fine.—Stay;—we'll make out the stanza:

> "Hermit hoar, in solemn cell,
> Wearing out life's evening gray;
> Smite thy bosom, sage, and tell,
> What is bliss? and which the way?" '

BOSWELL. 'But why smite his bosom, Sir?' JOHNSON. 'Why, to
shew he was in earnest,' (smiling.)—He at an after period
added the following stanza:

> 'Thus I spoke; and speaking sigh'd;
> —Scarce repress'd the starting tear;—
> When the smiling sage reply'd—
> —Come, my lad, and drink some beer.'[1]

I cannot help thinking the first stanza very good solemn poetry,
as also the three first lines of the second. Its last line is an
excellent burlesque surprise on gloomy sentimental enquirers.
And, perhaps, the advice is as good as can be given to a low-
spirited dissatisfied being:—'Don't trouble your head with
sickly thinking: take a cup, and be merry.'

    Friday, September 19, after breakfast Dr. Johnson and I set

---

[1] As some of my readers may be gratified by reading the progress of this
little composition, I shall insert it from my notes. 'When Dr. Johnson and I
were sitting *tête-à-tête* at the Mitre tavern, May 9, 1778, he said "*Where* is
bliss," would be better. He then added a ludicrous stanza, but would not
repeat it, lest I should take it down. It was somewhat as follows; the last
line I am sure I remember:

> "While I thus   cried,
>   seer,
> The hoary   reply'd,
>   Come, my lad, and drink some beer."

In spring, 1779, when in better humour, he made the second stanza, as in
the text. There was only one variation afterwards made on my suggestion,
which was changing *hoary* in the third line to *smiling*, both to avoid a sameness with the epithet in the first line, and to describe the hermit in his
pleasantry. He was then very well pleased that I should preserve it.'

out in Dr. Taylor's chaise to go to Derby. The day was fine, and
we resolved to go by Keddlestone, the seat of Lord Scarsdale,
that I might see his Lordship's fine house. I was struck with the
magnificence of the building; and the extensive park, with the
finest verdure, covered with deer, and cattle, and sheep, delighted
me. The number of old oaks, of an immense size, filled me with
a sort of respectful admiration: for one of them sixty pounds was
offered. The excellent smooth gravel roads; the large piece of
water formed by his Lordship from some small brooks, with a
handsome barge upon it; the venerable Gothick church, now the
family chapel, just by the house; in short, the grand group of
objects agitated and distended my mind in a most agreeable
manner. 'One should think (said I,) that the proprietor of all
this *must* be happy.'—'Nay, Sir, (said Johnson,) all this excludes
but one evil—poverty.'[1]

Our names were sent up, and a well-drest elderly housekeeper, a most distinct articulator, shewed us the house; which
I need not describe, as there is an account of it published in
Adam's Works in Architecture. Dr. Johnson thought better of it
to-day than when he saw it before; for he had lately attacked it
violently, saying, 'It would do excellently for a town-hall. The
large room with the pillars (said he,) would do for the Judges
to sit in at the assizes; the circular room for a jury-chamber; and
the rooms above for prisoners.' Still he thought the large room
ill lighted, and of no use but for dancing in; and the bed-chambers
but indifferent rooms; and that the immense sum which it cost
was injudiciously laid out. Dr. Taylor had put him in mind of
his *appearing* pleased with the house. 'But (said he,) that was
when Lord Scarsdale was present. Politeness obliges us to
appear pleased with a man's works when he is present. No man

[1] When I mentioned Dr. Johnson's remark to a lady of admirable good
sense and quickness of understanding, she observed, 'It is true, all this
excludes only one evil; but how much good does it let in?'———To this
observation much praise has been justly given. Let me then now do myself
the honour to mention that the lady who made it was the late Margaret
Montgomerie, my very valuable wife, and the very affectionate mother of
my children, who, if they inherit her good qualities, will have no reason to
complain of their lot. *Dos magna parentum virtus.* ['Their ample dowry is
their parents' worth.' Horace, *Odes* iii, xxiv. 21. (Wickham.).]

will be so ill bred as to question you. You may therefore pay compliments without saying what is not true. I should say to Lord Scarsdale of his large room, "My Lord, this is the most *costly* room that I ever saw;" which is true.'

Dr. Manningham, physician in London, who was visiting at Lord Scarsdale's, accompanied us through many of the rooms, and soon afterwards my Lord himself, to whom Dr. Johnson was known, appeared, and did the honours of the house. We talked of Mr. Langton. Johnson, with a warm vehemence of affectionate regard, exclaimed, 'The earth does not bear a worthier man than Bennet Langton.' We saw a good many fine pictures, which I think are described in one of *Young's Tours*. There is a printed catalogue of them which the housekeeper put into my hand; I should like to view them at leisure. I was much struck with Daniel interpreting Nebuchadnezzar's dream by Rembrandt. We were shown a pretty large library. In his Lordship's dressing-room lay Johnson's small *Dictionary*: he shewed it to me, with some eagerness, saying, 'Look'ye! *Quæ terra nostri non plena laboris.*'[1] He observed, also, Goldsmith's *Animated Nature*; and said, 'Here's our friend! The poor Doctor would have been happy to hear of this.'

In our way, Johnson strongly expressed his love of driving fast in a post-chaise. 'If (said he,) I had no duties, and no reference to futurity, I would spend my life in driving briskly in a post-chaise with a pretty woman; but she should be one who could understand me, and would add something to the conversation.' I observed, that we were this day to stop just where the Highland army did in 1745. JOHNSON. 'It was a noble attempt.' BOSWELL. 'I wish we could have an authentick history of it.' JOHNSON. 'If you were not an idle dog you might write it, by collecting from every body what they can tell, and putting down your authorities.' BOSWELL. 'But I could not have the advantage of it in my life-time.' JOHNSON. 'You might have the satisfaction of its fame, by printing it in Holland; and as to profit, consider how long it was before writing came to be considered in a

---

[1] [*Quae regio in terris* . . . 'Is there any land of all the lands, that is not yet rife with our tale of sorrow?' *Aeneid* i. 460. (Jackson.)]

pecuniary view. Baretti says, he is the first man that ever received copy-money in Italy.' I said that I would endeavour to do what Dr. Johnson suggested; and I thought that I might write so as to venture to publish my *History of the Civil War in Great-Britain in 1745 and 1746*, without being obliged to go to a foreign press.[1]

When we arrived at Derby, Dr. Butter accompanied us to see the manufactory of china there. I admired the ingenuity and delicate art with which a man fashioned clay into a cup, a saucer, or a tea-pot, while a boy turned round a wheel to give the mass rotundity. I thought this as excellent in its species of power, as making good verses in *its* species. Yet I had no respect for this potter. Neither, indeed, has a man of any extent of thinking for a mere verse-maker, in whose numbers, however perfect, there is no poetry, no mind. The china was beautiful, but Dr. Johnson justly observed it was too dear; for that he could have vessels of silver, of the same size, as cheap as what were here made of porcelain.

I felt a pleasure in walking about Derby such as I always have in walking about any town to which I am not accustomed. There is an immediate sensation of novelty; and one speculates on the way in which life is passed in it, which, although there is a sameness every where upon the whole, is yet minutely diversified. The minute diversities in every thing are wonderful. Talking of shaving the other night at Dr. Taylor's, Dr. Johnson said, 'Sir, of a thousand shavers, two do not shave so much alike as not to be distinguished.' I thought this not possible, till he specified so many of the varieties in shaving;—holding the razor more or less perpendicular;—drawing long or short strokes;—beginning at the upper part of the face, or the under;—at the right side or the left side. Indeed, when one considers what variety of sounds can be uttered by the windpipe, in the compass of a very small aperture, we may be convinced how many degrees of difference there may be in the application of a razor.

---

[1] I am now happy to understand, that Mr. John Home, who was himself gallantly in the field for the reigning family, in that interesting warfare, but is generous enough to do justice to the other side, is preparing an account of it for the press.

We dined with Dr. Butter, whose lady is daughter of my cousin, Sir John Douglas, whose grandson is now presumptive heir of the noble family of Queensberry. Johnson and he had a good deal of medical conversation. Johnson said, he had somewhere or other given an account of Dr. Nichols's discourse *De Animâ Medicâ*. He told us 'that whatever a man's distemper was, Dr. Nichols would not attend him as a physician, if his mind was not at ease; for he believed that no medicines would have any influence. He once attended a man in trade, upon whom he found none of the medicines he prescribed had any effect: he asked the man's wife privately whether his affairs were not in a bad way? She said no. He continued his attendance some time, still without success. At length the man's wife told him, she had discovered that her husband's affairs *were* in a bad way. When Goldsmith was dying, Dr. Turton said to him, "Your pulse is in greater disorder than it should be, from the degree of fever which you have: is your mind at ease?" Goldsmith answered it was not.'

After dinner, Mrs. Butter went with me to see the silk-mill which Mr. John Lombe had[1] had a patent for, having brought away the contrivance from Italy. I am not very conversant with mechanicks; but the simplicity of this machine, and its multiplied operations, struck me with an agreeable surprize. I had learnt from Dr. Johnson, during this interview, not to think with a dejected indifference of the works of art, and the pleasures of life, because life is uncertain and short; but to consider such indifference as a failure of reason, a morbidness of mind; for happiness should be cultivated as much as we can, and the objects which are instrumental to it should be steadily considered as of importance, with a reference not only to ourselves, but to multitudes in successive ages. Though it is proper to value small parts, as

'Sands make the mountain, moments make the year;'[2]

yet we must contemplate, collectively, to have a just estimation

[1] See Hutton's *History of Derby*, a book which is deservedly esteemed for its information, accuracy, and good narrative. Indeed the age in which we live is eminently distinguished by topographical excellence.

[2] Young. ['Love of Fame', Satire vi. 194: 'Small sands the mountain, moments, &c.']

of objects. One moment's being uneasy or not, seems of no consequence; yet this may be thought of the next, and the next, and so on, till there is a large portion of misery. In the same way one must think of happiness, of learning, of friendship. We cannot tell the precise moment when friendship is formed. As in filling a vessel drop by drop, there is at last a drop which makes it run over; so in a series of kindnesses there is at last one which makes the heart run over. We must not divide objects of our attention into minute parts, and think separately of each part. It is by contemplating a large mass of human existence, that a man, while he sets a just value on his own life, does not think of his death as annihilating all that is great and pleasing in the world, as if actually *contained in his mind*, according to Berkeley's reverie. If his imagination be not sickly and feeble, it 'wings its distant way' far beyond himself, and views the world in unceasing activity of every sort. It must be acknowledged, however, that Pope's plaintive reflection, that all things would be as gay as ever, on the day of his death, is natural and common. We are apt to transfer to all around us our own gloom, without considering that at any given point of time there is, perhaps, as much youth and gaiety in the world as at another. Before I came into this life, in which I have had so many pleasant scenes, have not thousands and ten thousands of deaths and funerals happened, and have not families been in grief for their nearest relations? But have those dismal circumstances at all affected *me*? Why then should the gloomy scenes which I experience, or which I know, affect others? Let us guard against imagining that there is an end of felicity upon earth, when we ourselves grow old, or are unhappy.

Dr. Johnson told us at tea, that when some of Dr. Dodd's pious friends were trying to console him by saying that he was going to leave 'a wretched world,' he had honesty enough not to join in the cant:—'No, no, (said he,) it has been a very agreeable world to me.' Johnson added, 'I respect Dodd for thus speaking the truth; for, to be sure, he had for several years enjoyed a life of great voluptuousness.'

He told us, that Dodd's city friends stood by him so, that a thousand pounds were ready to be given to the gaoler, if he would let him escape. He added, that he knew a friend of Dodd's, who walked about Newgate for some time on the evening before the day of his execution, with five hundred pounds in his pocket, ready to be paid to any of the turnkeys who could get him out: but it was too late; for he was watched with much circumspection. He said, Dodd's friends had an image of him made of wax, which was to have been left in his place; and he believed it was carried into the prison.

Johnson disapproved of Dr. Dodd's leaving the world persuaded that *The Convict's Address to his unhappy Brethren* was of his own writing. 'But, Sir, (said I,) you contributed to the deception; for when Mr. Seward expressed a doubt to you that it was not Dodd's own, because it had a great deal more force of mind in it than any thing known to be his, you answered,— "Why should you think so? Depend upon it, Sir, when a man knows he is to be hanged in a fortnight, it concentrates his mind wonderfully." ' JOHNSON. 'Sir, as Dodd got it from me to pass as his own, while that could do him any good, there was an *implied promise* that I should not own it. To own it, therefore, would have been telling a lie, with the addition of breach of promise, which was worse than simply telling a lie to make it be believed it was Dodd's. Besides, Sir, I did not *directly* tell a lie: I left the matter uncertain. Perhaps I thought that Seward would not believe it the less to be mine for what I said; but I would not put it in his power to say I had owned it.'

He praised Blair's sermons: 'Yet,' said he, (willing to let us see he was aware that fashionable fame, however deserved, is not always the most lasting,) 'perhaps, they may not be reprinted after seven years; at least not after Blair's death.'

He said, 'Goldsmith was a plant that flowered late. There appeared nothing remarkable about him when he was young; though when he had got high in fame, one of his friends[1] began to recollect something of his being distinguished at College. Goldsmith in the same manner recollected more of that friend's early years, as he grew a greater man.'

[1] [Burke. *Boswell Papers*, xiii. 38.]

I mentioned that Lord Monboddo told me, he awaked every morning at four, and then for his health got up and walked in his room naked, with the window open, which he called taking *an air bath*; after which he went to bed again, and slept two hours more. Johnson, who was always ready to beat down any thing that seemed to be exhibited with disproportionate importance, thus observed: 'I suppose, Sir, there is no more in it than this, he awakes at four, and cannot sleep till he chills himself, and makes the warmth of the bed a grateful sensation.'

I talked of the difficulty of rising in the morning. Dr. Johnson told me, 'that the learned Mrs. Carter, at that period when she was eager in study, did not awake as early as she wished, and she therefore had a contrivance, that, at a certain hour, her chamber-light should burn a string to which a heavy weight was suspended, which then fell with a strong sudden noise: this roused her from sleep, and then she had no difficulty in getting up.' But I said *that* was my difficulty; and wished there could be some medicine invented which would make one rise without pain, which I never did, unless after lying in bed a very long time. Perhaps there may be something in the stores of Nature which could do this. I have thought of a pulley to raise me gradually; but that would give me pain, as it would counteract my internal inclination. I would have something that can dissipate the *vis inertiæ*[1] and give elasticity to the muscles. As I imagine that the human body may be put, by the operation of other substances, into any state in which it has ever been; and as I have experienced a state in which rising from bed was not disagreeable, but easy, nay, sometimes agreeable; I suppose that this state may be produced, if we knew by what. We can heat the body, we can cool it; we can give it tension or relaxation; and surely it is possible to bring it into a state in which rising from bed will not be a pain.

Johnson observed, that 'a man should take a sufficient quantity of sleep, which Dr. Mead says is between seven and nine hours.' I told him, that Dr. Cullen said to me, that a man should not take more sleep than he can take at once. JOHNSON. 'This rule,

[1] ["The power of inertness."]

Sir, cannot hold in all cases; for many people have their sleep broken by sickness; and surely, Cullen would not have a man to get up, after having slept but an hour. Such a regimen would soon end in a *long sleep*.'[1] Dr. Taylor remarked, I think very justly, that 'a man who does not feel an inclination to sleep at the ordinary time, instead of being stronger than other people, must not be well; for a man in health has all the natural inclinations to eat, drink, and sleep, in a strong degree.'

Johnson advised me to-night not to *refine* in the education of my children. 'Life (said he,) will not bear refinement: you must do as other people do.'

As we drove back to Ashbourne, Dr. Johnson recommended to me, as he had often done, to drink water only: 'For (said he,) you are then sure not to get drunk; whereas if you drink wine you are never sure.' I said, drinking wine was a pleasure which I was unwilling to give up. 'Why, Sir, (said he,) there is no doubt that not to drink wine is a great deduction from life; but it may be necessary.' He however owned, that in his opinion a free use of wine did not shorten life; and said, he would not give less for the life of a certain Scotch Lord (whom he named)[2] celebrated for hard drinking, than for that of a sober man. 'But stay, (said he, with his usual intelligence, and accuracy of enquiry,) does it take much wine to make him drunk?' I answered, 'a great deal either of wine or strong punch.'—'Then (said he,) that is the worse.' I presume to illustrate my friend's observation thus: 'A fortress which soon surrenders has its

---

[1] This regimen was, however, practised by Bishop Ken, of whom Hawkins (*not Sir John*) in his life of that venerable Prelate, p. 4, tells us; 'And that neither his study might be the aggressor on his hours of instruction, or what he judged his duty prevent his improvements; or both, his closet addresses to his GOD; he strictly accustomed himself to but one sleep, which often obliged him to rise at one or two of the clock in the morning, and sometimes sooner; and grew so habitual, that it continued with him almost till his last illness. And so lively and chearful was his temper, that he would be very facetious and entertaining to his friends in the evening, even when it was perceived that with difficulty he kept his eyes open; and then seemed to go to rest with no other purpose than the refreshing and enabling him with more vigour and chearfulness to sing his morning hymn, as he then used to do to his lute before he put on his cloaths.'

[2] [Archibald, 11th Earl of Eglinton. *Boswell Papers*, xiii. 37.]

walls less shattered than when a long and obstinate resistance
is made.'

I ventured to mention a person[1] who was as violent a Scotsman as he was an Englishman; and literally had the same contempt for an Englishman compared with a Scotsman, that he
had for a Scotsman compared with an Englishman; and that he
would say of Dr. Johnson, 'Damned rascal! to talk as he does of
the Scotch.' This seemed, for a moment, 'to give him pause.'
It, perhaps, presented his extreme prejudice against the Scotch
in a point of view somewhat new to him, by the effect of *contrast*.

By the time when we returned to Ashbourne, Dr. Taylor was
gone to bed. Johnson and I sat up a long time by ourselves.

He was much diverted with an article which I shewed him in
the *Critical Review* of this year, giving an account of a curious
publication, entitled, *A Spiritual Diary and Soliloquies*, by John
Rutty, M.D. Dr. Rutty was one of the people called Quakers,
a physician of some eminence in Dublin, and authour of several
works. This Diary, which was kept from 1753 to 1775, the year
in which he died, and was now published in two volumes octavo,
exhibited, in the simplicity of his heart, a minute and honest
register of the state of his mind; which, though frequently
laughable enough, was not more so than the history of many
men would be, if recorded with equal fairness.

The following specimens were extracted by the Reviewers:—
'Tenth month, 1753.

23. Indulgence in bed an hour too long.

Twelfth month, 17. An hypochondriack obnubilation from
wind and indigestion.

Ninth month, 28. An over-dose of whisky.

29. A dull, cross, cholerick [sickish] day.

First month, 1757—22. A little swinish at dinner and repast.

31. Dogged on provocation.

Second month, 5. Very dogged or snappish.

14. Snappish on fasting.

26. Cursed snappishness to those under me, on a bodily
indisposition.

[1] [Archibald, 11th Earl of Eglinton. *Boswell Papers*, xiii. 37.]

Third month, 11. On a provocation, exercised a dumb resentment for two days, instead of scolding.

22. Scolded too vehemently.

23. Dogged again.

Fourth month, 29. Mechanically and sinfully dogged.'

Johnson laughed heartily at this good Quietist's self-condemning minutes; particularly at his mentioning, with such a serious regret, occasional instances of '*swinishness* in eating, and *doggedness of temper.*' He thought the observations of the Critical Reviewers upon the importance of a man to himself so ingenious and so well expressed, that I shall here introduce them.

After observing, that 'There are few writers who have gained any reputation by recording their own actions,' they say:—

'We may reduce the egotists to four classes. In the *first* we have Julius Cæsar: he relates his own transactions; but he relates them with peculiar grace and dignity, and his narrative is supported by the greatness of his character and atchievements. In the *second* class we have Marcus Antoninus: this writer has given us a series of reflections on his own life; but his sentiments are so noble, his morality so sublime, that his meditations are universally admired. In the *third* class we have some others of tolerable credit, who have given importance to their own private history by an intermixture of literary anecdotes, and the occurrences of their own times: the celebrated *Huetius* has published an entertaining volume upon this place "*De rebus ad eum pertinentibus.*"[1] In the *fourth* class we have the journalists, temporal and spiritual: Elias Ashmole, William Lilly, George Whitefield, John Wesley, and a thousand other old women and fanatick writers of memoirs and meditations.'

I mentioned to him that Dr. Hugh Blair, in his lectures on Rhetorick and Belles Lettres, which I heard him deliver at Edinburgh, had animadverted on the Johnsonian style as too pompous; and attempted to imitate it, by giving a sentence of Addison in *The Spectator*, No. 411, in the manner of Johnson. When treating of the utility of the pleasures of imagination in

---

[1] ['On matters that concerned him.']

preserving us from vice, it is observed of those 'who know not how to be idle and innocent,' that 'their very first step out of business is into vice or folly;' which Dr. Blair supposed would have been expressed in *The Rambler* thus: 'Their very first step out of the regions of business is into the perturbation of vice, or the vacuity of folly.'[1] JOHNSON. 'Sir, these are not the words I should have used. No, Sir; the imitators of my style have not hit it. Miss Aikin has done it the best; for she has imitated the sentiment as well as the diction.'

I intend, before this work is concluded, to exhibit specimens of imitation of my friend's style in various modes; some caricaturing or mimicking it, and some formed upon it, whether intentionally or with a degree of similarity to it, of which, perhaps, the writers were not conscious.[2]

In Baretti's Review, which he published in Italy, under the title of *Frusta Letteraria*, it is observed, that Dr. Robertson the historian had formed his style upon that of *Il celebre Samuele Johnson*. My friend himself was of that opinion; for he once said to me, in a pleasant humour, 'Sir, if Robertson's style be faulty, he owes it to me; that is, having too many words, and those too big ones.'

I read to him a letter which Lord Monboddo had written to me, containing some critical remarks upon the style of his *Journey to the Western Islands of Scotland*. His Lordship praised the very fine passage upon landing at Icolmkill;[3] but his own

---

[1] When Dr. Blair published his *Lectures*, he was invidiously attacked for having omitted his censure on Johnson's style, and, on the contrary, praising it highly. But before that time Johnson's *Lives of the Poets* had appeared, in which his style was considerably easier than when he wrote *The Rambler*. It would, therefore, have been uncandid in Blair, even supposing his criticism to have been just, to have preserved it.

[2] See p. 1370.

[3] 'We were now treading that illustrious island, which was once the luminary of the Caledonian regions, whence savage clans and roving barbarians derived the benefits of knowledge, and the blessings of religion. To abstract the mind from all local emotion would be impossible if it were endeavoured, and would be foolish if it were possible. Whatever withdraws us from the power of our senses, whatever makes the past, the distant, or the future, predominate over the present, advances us in the dignity of thinking beings. Far from me, and from my friends, be such frigid philosophy, as may conduct us, indifferent and unmoved, over any ground which has been dignified by wisdom, bravery, or virtue. The man is little to be envied,

style being exceedingly dry and hard, he disapproved of the richness of Johnson's language, and of his frequent use of metaphorical expressions. J O H N S O N. 'Why, Sir, this criticism would be just, if in my style, superfluous words, or words too big for the thoughts, could be pointed out; but this I do not believe can be done. For instance; in the passage which Lord Monboddo admires, 'We were now treading that illustrious region,' the word *illustrious*, contributes nothing to the mere narration; for the fact might be told without it: but it is not, therefore, superfluous; for it wakes the mind to peculiar attention, where something of more than usual importance is to be presented. "Illustrious!" for what? and then the sentence proceeds to expand the circumstances connected with Iona. And, Sir, as to metaphorical expression, that is a great excellence in style, when it is used with propriety, for it gives you two ideas for one;—conveys the meaning more luminously, and generally with a perception of delight.'

He told me, that he had been asked to undertake the new edition of the *Biographia Britannica*, but had declined it; which he afterwards said to me he regretted. In this regret many will join, because it would have procured us more of Johnson's most delightful species of writing; and although my friend Dr. Kippis has hitherto discharged the task judiciously, distinctly, and with more impartiality than might have been expected from a Separatist, it were to have been wished that the superintendence of this literary Temple of Fame had been assigned to 'a friend to the constitution in Church and State.' We should not then have had it too much crowded with obscure dissenting teachers, doubtless men of merit and worth, but not quite to be numbered amongst 'the most eminent persons who have flourished in Great-Britain and Ireland.'[1]

whose patriotism would not gain force upon the plain of Marathon, or whose piety would not grow warmer among the ruins of Iona.'

Had our Tour produced nothing else but this sublime passage, the world must have acknowledged that it was not made in vain. Sir Joseph Banks, the present respectable President of the Royal Society, told me, he was so much struck on reading it, that he clasped his hands together, and remained for some time in an attitude of silent admiration.

[1] In this censure which has been carelessly uttered, I carelessly joined.

On Saturday, September 20, after breakfast, when Taylor was
gone out to his farm, Dr. Johnson and I had a serious conversation by ourselves on melancholy and madness; which he was,
I always thought, erroneously inclined to confound together.
Melancholy, like 'great wit,' may be 'near allied to madness;'
but there is, in my opinion, a distinct separation between them.
When he talked of madness, he was to be understood as speaking
of those who were in any great degree disturbed, or as it is
commonly expressed, 'troubled in mind.' Some of the ancient
philosophers held, that all deviations from right reason were
madness; and whoever wishes to see the opinions both of
ancients and moderns upon this subject, collected and illustrated
with a variety of curious facts, may read Dr. Arnold's very
entertaining work.[1]

But in justice to Dr. Kippis, who with that manly candid good temper which
marks his character, set me right, I now with pleasure retract it; and I
desire it may be particularly observed, as pointed out by him to me, that
'The new lives of dissenting Divines, in the first four volumes of the second
edition of the *Biographia Britannica* are those of John Abernethy, Thomas
Amory, George Benson, Hugh Broughton, the learned Puritan, Simon
Browne, Joseph Boyse of Dublin, Thomas Cartwright the learned Puritan,
and Samuel Chandler. The only doubt I have ever heard suggested is,
whether there should have been an article of Dr. Amory. But I was con-
vinced, and am still convinced, that he was entitled to one, from the reality
of his learning, and the excellent and candid nature of his practical writings.
'The new lives of clergymen of the Church of England, in the same four
volumes, are as follows: John Balguy, Edward Bentham, George Berkley
Bishop of Cloyne, William Berriman, Thomas Birch, William Borlase,
Thomas Bott, James Bradley, Thomas Broughton, John Brown, John
Burton, Joseph Butler Bishop of Durham, Thomas Carte, Edmund Castell,
Edmund Chishull, Charles Churchill, William Clarke, Robert Clayton
Bishop of Clogher, John Conybeare Bishop of Bristol, George Costard, and
Samuel Croxhall.—"I am not conscious (says Dr. Kippis,) of any partiality
in conducting the work. I would not willingly insert a Dissenting Minister
that does not justly deserve to be noticed, or omit an established Clergyman
that does. At the same time, I shall not be deterred from introducing Dissenters into the *Biographia*, when I am satisfied that they are entitled to that
distinction, from their writings, learning, and merit." '
Let me add that the expression 'A friend to the constitution in Church and
State,' was not meant by me, as any reflection upon this reverend gentleman,
as if he were an enemy to the political constitution of his country, as established at the revolution, but, from my steady and avowed predilection for a
Tory, was quoted from Johnson's *Dictionary*, where that distinction is so
defined.

[1] *Observations on Insanity*, by Thomas Arnold, M.D., London, 1782.

Johnson said, 'A madman loves to be with people whom he fears; not as a dog fears the lash; but of whom he stands in awe.' I was struck with the justice of this observation. To be with those of whom a person, whose mind is wavering and dejected, stands in awe, represses and composes an uneasy tumult of spirits, and consoles him with the contemplation of something steady, and at least comparatively great.

He added, 'Madmen are all sensual in the lower stages of the distemper. They are eager for gratifications to sooth their minds, and divert their attention from the misery which they suffer: but when they grow very ill, pleasure is too weak for them, and they seek for pain.[1] Employment, Sir, and hardships, prevent melancholy. I suppose in all our army in America there was not one man who went mad.'

We entered seriously upon a question of much importance to me, which Johnson was pleased to consider with friendly attention. I had long complained to him that I felt myself discontented in Scotland, as too narrow a sphere, and that I wished to make my chief residence in London, the great scene of ambition, instruction, and amusement: a scene, which was to me, comparatively speaking, a heaven upon earth. JOHNSON. 'Why, Sir, I never knew any one who had such a *gust* for London as you have: and I cannot blame you for your wish to live there: yet, Sir, were I in your father's place, I should not consent to your settling there; for I have the old feudal notions, and I should be afraid that Auchinleck would be deserted, as you would soon find it more desirable to have a country-seat in a better climate.

---

[1] We read in the Gospels, that those unfortunate persons who were possessed with evil spirits (which, after all, I think is the most probable cause of madness, as was first suggested to me by my respectable friend Sir John Pringle), had recourse to pain, tearing themselves, and jumping sometimes into the fire, sometimes into the water. Mr. Seward has furnished me with a remarkable anecdote in confirmation of Dr. Johnson's observation. A tradesman, who had acquired a large fortune in London, retired from business, and went to live at Worcester. His mind, being without its usual occupation, and having nothing else to supply its place, preyed upon itself, so that existence was a torment to him. At last he was seized with the stone; and a friend who found him in one of its severest fits, having expressed his concern, 'No, no, Sir, (said he,) don't pity me: what I now feel is ease compared with that torture of mind from which it relieves me.'

I own, however, that to consider it as a *duty* to reside on a family estate is a prejudice; for we must consider, that working-people get employment equally, and the produce of land is sold equally, whether a great family resides at home or not; and if the rents of an estate be carried to London, they return again in the circulation of commerce; nay, Sir, we must perhaps allow, that carrying the rents to a distance is a good, because it contributes to that circulation. We must, however, allow, that a well-regulated great family may improve a neighbourhood in civility and elegance, and give an example of good order, virtue, and piety; and so its residence at home may be of much advantage. But if a great family be disorderly and vicious, its residence at home is very pernicious to a neighbourhood. There is not now the same inducement to live in the country as formerly; the pleasures of social life are much better enjoyed in town; and there is no longer in the country that power and influence in proprietors of land which they had in old times, and which made the country so agreeable to them. The Laird of Auchinleck now is not near so great a man as the Laird of Auchinleck was a hundred years ago.'

I told him, that one of my ancestors never went from home without being attended by thirty men on horseback. Johnson's shrewdness and spirit of enquiry were exerted upon every occasion. 'Pray (said he,) how did your ancestor support his thirty men and thirty horses, when he went at a distance from home, in an age when there was hardly any money in circulation?' I suggested the same difficulty to a friend, who mentioned Douglas's going to the Holy Land with a numerous train of followers. Douglas could, no doubt, maintain followers enough while living upon his own lands, the produce of which supplied them with food; but he could not carry that food to the Holy Land; and as there was no commerce by which he could be supplied with money, how could he maintain them in foreign countries?

I suggested a doubt, that if I were to reside in London, the exquisite zest with which I relished it in occasional visits might go off, and I might grow tired of it. JOHNSON. 'Why, Sir, you find no man, at all intellectual, who is willing to leave London. No, Sir, when a man is tired of London, he is tired of life; for there is in London all that life can afford.'

To obviate his apprehension, that by settling in London I might desert the seat of my ancestors, I assured him, that I had old feudal principles to a degree of enthusiasm; and that I felt all the *dulcedo* of the *natale solum.*[1] I reminded him, that the Laird of Auchinleck had an elegant house, in front of which he could ride ten miles forward upon his own territories, upon which he had upwards of six hundred people attached to him; that the family seat was rich in natural romantick beauties of rock, wood, and water; and that in my 'morn of life,' I had appropriated the finest descriptions in the ancient Classicks to certain scenes there, which were thus associated in my mind. That when all this was considered, I should certainly pass a part of the year at home, and enjoy it the more from variety, and from bringing with me a share of the intellectual stores of the metropolis. He listened to all this, and kindly 'hoped it might be as I now supposed.'

He said, 'A country gentleman should bring his lady to visit London as soon as he can, that they may have agreeable topicks for conversation when they are by themselves.'

As I meditated trying my fortune in Westminster Hall, our conversation turned upon the profession of the law in England. JOHNSON. 'You must not indulge too sanguine hopes, should you be called to our bar. I was told, by a very sensible lawyer, that there are a great many chances against any man's success in the profession of the law; the candidates are so numerous, and those who get large practice so few. He said, it was by no means true that a man of good parts and application is sure of having business, though he, indeed, allowed that if such a man could but appear in a few causes, his merit would be known, and he would get forward; but that the great risk was, that a man might pass half a life-time in the Courts, and never have an opportunity of shewing his abilities.'[2]

[1] ['sweetness of the native soil.' Ovid, *Ep. ex Ponto* I. iii. 35.]
[2] Now, at the distance of fifteen years since this conversation passed, the

We talked of employment being absolutely necessary to preserve the mind from wearying and growing fretful, especially
in those who have a tendency to melancholy; and I mentioned
to him a saying which somebody[1] had related of an American
savage, who, when an European was expatiating on all the
advantages of money, put this question: 'Will it purchase
occupation?' JOHNSON. 'Depend upon it, Sir, this saying is too
refined for a savage. And, Sir, money *will* purchase occupation;
it will purchase all the conveniences of life; it will purchase
variety of company; it will purchase all sorts of entertainment.'

I talked to him of Forster's *Voyage to the South Seas,* which
pleased me; but I found he did not like it. 'Sir, (said he,) there
is a great affectation of fine writing in it.' BOSWELL. 'But he
carries you along with him.' JOHNSON. 'No, Sir; he does not
carry *me* along with him: he leaves me behind him: or rather,
indeed, he sets me before him; for he makes me turn over many
leaves at a time.'

On Sunday, September 21, we went to the church of Ashbourne, which is one of the largest and most luminous that I
have seen in any town of the same size. I felt great satisfaction
in considering that I was supported in my fondness for solemn
publick worship by the general concurrence and munificence of
mankind.

Johnson and Taylor were so different from each other, that
I wondered at their preserving such an intimacy. Their having
been at school and college together, might, in some degree,
account for this; but Sir Joshua Reynolds has furnished me with
a stronger reason; for Johnson mentioned to him, that he had
been told by Taylor he was to be his heir. I shall not take upon
me to animadvert upon this; but certain it is, that Johnson paid
great attention to Taylor. He now, however, said to me, 'Sir,
observation which I have had an opportunity of making in Westminster
Hall has convinced me, that, however true the opinion of Dr. Johnson's legal
friend may have been some time ago, the same certainty of success cannot
now be promised to the same display of merit. The reasons, however, of the
rapid rise of some, and the disappointment of others equally respectable, are
such as it might seem invidious to mention, and would require a longer
detail than would be proper for this work.

[1] [J. B. forgot his name. *Boswell Papers,* xiii. 45.]

I love him; but I do not love him more; my regard for him does not increase. As it is said in the Apocrypha, "his talk is of bullocks:"[1] I do not suppose he is very fond of my company. His habits are by no means sufficiently clerical: this he knows that I see; and no man likes to live under the eye of perpetual disapprobation.'

I have no doubt that a good many sermons were composed for Taylor by Johnson. At this time I found, upon his table, a part of one which he had newly begun to write: and *Concio pro Tayloro*[2] appears in one of his diaries. When to these circumstances we add the internal evidence from the power of thinking and style, in the collection which the Reverend Mr. Hayes has published, with the *significant* title of 'Sermons *left for publication* by the Reverend John Taylor, LL.D.,' our conviction will be complete.

I, however, would not have it thought, that Dr. Taylor, though he could not write like Johnson, (as, indeed, who could?) did not sometimes compose sermons as good as those which we generally have from very respectable divines. He shewed me one with notes on the margin in Johnson's hand-writing; and I was present when he read another to Johnson, that he might have his opinion of it, and Johnson said it was 'very well.' These, we may be sure, were not Johnson's; for he was above little arts, or tricks of deception.

Johnson was by no means of opinion, that every man of a learned profession should consider it as incumbent upon him, or as necessary to his credit, to appear as an authour. When in the ardour of ambition for literary fame, I regretted to him one day that an eminent Judge[3] had nothing of it, and therefore would leave no perpetual monument of himself to posterity. 'Alas, Sir, (said Johnson,) what a mass of confusion should we have, if every Bishop, and every Judge, every Lawyer, Physician, and Divine, were to write books.'

---

[1] *Ecclesiasticus*, ch. xxxviii. verse 25. The whole chapter may be read as an admirable illustration of the superiority of cultivated minds over the gross and illiterate.

[2] ['A Sermon for Taylor'.]

[3] [Probably Lord Auchinleck. *Powell.*]

I mentioned to Johnson a respectable person[1] of a very strong mind, who had little of that tenderness which is common to human nature; as an instance of which, when I suggested to him that he should invite his son,[2] who had been settled ten years in foreign parts, to come home and pay him a visit, his answer was, 'No, no, let him mind his business.' J O H N S O N. 'I do not agree with him, Sir, in this. Getting money is not all a man's business: to cultivate kindness is a valuable part of the business of life.'

In the evening, Johnson, being in very good spirits, entertained us with several characteristical portraits. I regret that any of them escaped my retention and diligence. I found, from experience, that to collect my friend's conversation so as to exhibit it with any degree of its original flavour, it was necessary to write it down without delay. To record his sayings, after some distance of time, was like preserving or pickling long-kept and faded fruits, or other vegetables, which, when in that state, have little or nothing of their taste when fresh.

I shall present my readers with a series of what I gathered this evening from the Johnsonian garden.

'My friend, the late Earl of Corke, had a great desire to maintain the literary character of his family: he was a genteel man, but did not keep up the dignity of his rank. He was so generally civil, that nobody thanked him for it.'

'Did we not hear so much said of Jack Wilkes, we should think more highly of his conversation. Jack has great variety of talk, Jack is a scholar, and Jack has the manners of a gentleman. But after hearing his name sounded from pole to pole, as the phœnix of convivial felicity, we are disappointed in his company. He has always been *at me*: but I would do Jack a kindness, rather than not. The contest is now over.'

'Garrick's gaiety of conversation has delicacy and elegance: Foote makes you laugh more; but Foote has the air of a buffoon paid for entertaining the company. He indeed, well deserves his hire.'

'Colley Cibber once consulted me as to one of his birth-day

[1] [Lord Auchinleck. *Boswell Papers*, xiii. 48.]   [2] [David Boswell, *Ib.*]

Odes, a long time before it was wanted. I objected very freely to several passages. Cibber lost patience, and would not read his Ode to an end. When we had done with criticism, we walked over to Richardson's, the authour of *Clarissa*, and I wondered to find Richardson displeased that I "did not treat Cibber with more *respect*." Now, Sir, to talk of *respect* for a *player*!' (smiling disdainfully.) BOSWELL. 'There, Sir, you are always heretical: you never will allow merit to a player.' JOHNSON. 'Merit, Sir! what merit? Do you respect a rope-dancer, or a ballad-singer?' BOSWELL. 'No, Sir: but we respect a great player, as a man who can conceive lofty sentiments, and can express them gracefully.' JOHNSON. 'What, Sir, a fellow who claps a hump on his back, and a lump on his leg, and cries *"I am Richard the Third"*? Nay, Sir, a ballad-singer is a higher man, for he does two things; he repeats and he sings: there is both recitation and musick in his performance: the player only recites.' BOSWELL. 'My dear Sir! you may turn anything into ridicule. I allow, that a player of farce is not entitled to respect; he does a little thing: but he who can represent exalted characters, and touch the noblest passions, has very respectable powers; and mankind have agreed in admiring great talents for the stage. We must consider, too, that a great player does what very few are capable to do: his art is a very rare faculty. *Who* can repeat Hamlet's soliloquy, "To be, or not to be," as Garrick does it?' JOHNSON. 'Any body may. Jemmy,[1] there (there a boy about eight years old, who was in the room,) will do it as well in a week.' BOSWELL. 'No, no, Sir: and as a proof of the merit of great acting, and of the value which mankind set upon it, Garrick has got a hundred thousand pounds.' JOHNSON. 'Is getting a hundred thousand pounds a proof of excellence? That has been done by a scoundrel commissary.'[2]

This was most fallacious reasoning. I was *sure*, for once, that I had the best side of the argument. I boldly maintained the just distinction between a tragedian and a mere theatrical droll; between those who rouse our terrour and pity, and those who

---

[1] [James Fieldhouse. *Boswell Papers*, xiii. 51.]
[2] [Robert Paris Taylor. *Ib.*]

only make us laugh. 'If (said I,) Betterton and Foote were to walk into this room, you would respect Betterton much more than Foote.' J O H N S O N. 'If Betterton were to walk into this room with Foote, Foote would soon drive him out of it. Foote, Sir, *quatenùs* Foote, has powers superiour to them all.'

On Monday, September 22, when at breakfast, I unguardedly said to Dr. Johnson, 'I wish I saw you and Mrs. Macaulay together.' He grew very angry; and, after a pause, while a cloud gathered on his brow, he burst out, 'No, Sir; you would not see us quarrel, to make you sport. Don't you know that it is very uncivil to *pit* two people against one another?' Then, checking himself, and wishing to be more gentle, he added, 'I do not say you should be hanged or drowned for this; but it *is* very uncivil.' Dr. Taylor thought him in the wrong, and spoke to him privately of it; but I afterwards acknowledged to Johnson that I was to blame, for I candidly owned, that I meant to express a desire to see a contest between Mrs. Macaulay and him; but then I knew how the contest would end; so that I was to see him triumph. J O H N S O N. 'Sir, you cannot be sure how a contest will end; and no man has a right to engage two people in a dispute by which their passions may be inflamed, and they may part with bitter resentment against each other. I would sooner keep company with a man from whom I must guard my pockets, than with a man who contrives to bring me into a dispute with somebody that he may hear it. This is the great fault of ———, (naming one of our friends,)[1] endeavouring to introduce a subject upon which he knows two people in the company differ.' B O S W E L L. 'But he told me, Sir, he does it for instruction.' J O H N S O N. 'Whatever the motive be, Sir, the man who does so, does very wrong. He has no more right to instruct himself at such a risk, than he has to make two people fight a duel, that he may learn how to defend himself.'

He found great fault with a gentleman[1] of our acquaintance for keeping a bad table. 'Sir, (said he,) when a man is invited to dinner, he is disappointed if he does not get something good. I advised Mrs. Thrale, who has no card-parties at her house, to

[1] [Langton. *Boswell Papers*, xiii. 52, 53.]

give sweet-meats, and such good things, in an evening, as are not commonly given, and she would find company enough come to her; for every body loves to have things which please the palate put in their way, without trouble or preparation.' Such was his attention to the *minutiæ* of life and manners.

He thus characterised the Duke of Devonshire, grandfather of the present representative of that very respectable family: 'He was not a man of superiour abilities, but he was a man strictly faithful to his word. If, for instance, he had promised you an acorn, and none had grown that year in his woods, he would not have contented himself with that excuse; he would have sent to Denmark for it. So unconditional was he in keeping his word; so high as to the point of honour.' This was a liberal testimony from the Tory Johnson to the virtue of a great Whig nobleman.

Mr. Burke's *Letter to the Sheriffs of Bristol, on the affairs of America,* being mentioned, Johnson censured the composition much, and he ridiculed the definition of a free government, *viz.* 'For any practical purpose, it is what the people think so.'[1]— 'I will let the King of France govern me on those conditions, (said he,) for it is to be governed just as I please.' And when Dr. Taylor talked of a girl being sent to a parish workhouse, and asked how much she could be obliged to work, 'Why, (said Johnson,) as much as is reasonable: and what is that? as much as *she thinks* reasonable.'

Dr. Johnson obligingly proposed to carry me to see Islam, a romantick scene, now belonging to a family of the name of Port, but formerly the seat of the Congreves. I suppose it is well described in some of the Tours. Johnson described it distinctly and vividly, at which I could not but express to him my wonder; because, though my eyes, as he observed, were better than his, I could not by any means equal him in representing visible objects. I said, the difference between us in this respect was as that between a man who has a bad instrument, but plays well on it, and a man who has a good instrument, on which he can play very imperfectly.

[1] 2nd edit. p. 53.

I recollect a very fine amphitheatre, surrounded with hills covered with woods, and walks neatly formed along the side of a rocky steep, on the quarter next the house, with recesses under projections of rock, overshadowed with trees; in one of which recesses, we were told, Congreve wrote his *Old Bachelor*. We viewed a remarkable natural curiosity at Islam; two rivers bursting near each other from the rock, not from immediate springs, but after having run for many miles under ground. Plott, in his *History of Staffordshire*,[1] gives an account of this curiosity; but Johnson would not believe it, though we had the attestation of the gardener, who said, he had put in corks, where the river *Manyfold* sinks into the ground, and had catched them in a net, placed before one of the openings where the water bursts out. Indeed, such subterraneous courses of water are found in various parts of our globe.[2]

Talking of Dr. Johnson's unwillingness to believe extraordinary things, I ventured to say, 'Sir, you come near Hume's argument against miracles, "That it is more probable witnesses should lie, or be mistaken, than that they should happen."' JOHNSON. 'Why, Sir, Hume, taking the proposition simply, is right. But the Christian revelation is not proved by the miracles alone, but as connected with prophecies, and with the doctrines in confirmation of which the miracles were wrought.'

He repeated his observation, that the differences among Christians are really of no consequence. 'For instance (said he,) if a Protestant objects to a Papist, "You worship images;" the Papist can answer, "I do not insist on *your* doing it; you may be a very good Papist without it: I do it only as a help to my devotion."' I said, the great article of Christianity is the revelation of immortality. Johnson admitted it was.

In the evening, a gentleman-farmer,[3] who was on a visit at Dr. Taylor's, attempted to dispute with Johnson in favour of Mungo Campbell, who shot Alexander, Earl of Eglintoune,

---

[1] Page 89.

[2] See Plott's *History of Staffordshire*, p. 88, and the authorities referred to by him.

[3] [Walter John Fieldhouse. *Boswell Papers*, vi. 211, xiii. 55.]

upon his having fallen, when retreating from his Lordship, who he believed was about to seize his gun, as he had threatened to do. He said, he should have done just as Campbell did. JOHNSON. 'Whoever would do as Campbell did, deserves to be hanged; not that I could, as a juryman, have found him legally guilty of murder; but I am glad they found means to convict him.' The gentleman-farmer said, 'A poor man has as much honour as a rich man; and Campbell had *that* to defend.' Johnson exclaimed, 'A poor man has no honour.' The English yeoman, not dismayed, proceeded: 'Lord Eglintoune was a damned fool to run on upon Campbell, after being warned that Campbell would shoot him if he did.' Johnson, who could not bear any thing like swearing, angrily replied, 'He was *not* a *damned* fool: he only thought too well of Campbell. He did not believe Campbell would be such a *damned* scoundrel, as to do so *damned* a thing.' His emphasis on *damned*, accompanied with frowning looks, reproved his opponent's want of decorum in *his* presence.

Talking of the danger of being mortified by rejection, when making approaches to the acquaintance of the great, I observed: 'I am, however, generally for trying, "Nothing venture, nothing have." ' JOHNSON. 'Very true, Sir; but I have always been more afraid of failing, than hopeful of success.' And, indeed, though he had all just respect for rank, no man ever less courted the favour of the great.

During this interview at Ashbourne, Johnson seemed to be more uniformly social, cheerful, and alert, than I had almost ever seen him. He was prompt on great occasions and on small. Taylor, who praised every thing of his own to excess; in short, 'whose geese were all swans,' as the proverb says, expatiated on the excellence of his bull-dog, which, he told us, was 'perfectly well shaped.' Johnson, after examining the animal attentively, thus repressed the vain-glory of our host:—'No, Sir, he is *not* well shaped; for there is not the quick transition from the thickness of the fore-part, to the *tenuity*—the thin part—behind, which a bull-dog ought to have.' This *tenuity* was the only *hard word* that I heard him use during this interview, and it will be observed, he instantly put another expression in its place. Taylor said, a small bull-dog was as good as a large one. JOHNSON. 'No, Sir; for, in proportion to his size, he has strength: and your argument would prove, that a good bull-dog may be as small as a mouse.' It was amazing how he entered with perspicuity and keenness upon every thing that occurred in conversation. Most men, whom I know, would no more think of discussing a question about a bull-dog, than of attacking a bull.

I cannot allow any fragment whatever that floats in my memory concerning the great subject of this work to be lost. Though a small particular may appear trifling to some, it will be relished by others; while every little spark adds something to the general blaze: and to please the true, candid, warm admirers of Johnson, and in any degree increase the splendour of his reputation, I bid defiance to the shafts of ridicule, or even of malignity. Showers of them have been discharged at my *Journal of a Tour to the Hebrides*; yet it still sails unhurt along the stream of time, and, as an attendant upon Johnson,

'Pursues the triumph, and partakes the gale.'

One morning after breakfast, when the sun shone bright, we walked out together, and 'pored' for some time with placid indolence upon an artificial water-fall, which Dr. Taylor had made by building a strong dyke of stone across the river behind his garden. It was now somewhat obstructed by branches of trees and other rubbish, which had come down the river, and settled close to it. Johnson, partly from a desire to see it play more freely, and partly from that inclination to activity which will animate, at times, the most inert and sluggish mortal, took a long pole which was lying on the bank, and pushed down several parcels of this wreck with painful assiduity, while I stood quietly by, wondering to behold the sage thus curiously employed, and smiling with an humorous satisfaction each time when he carried his point. He worked till he was quite out of breath; and having found a large dead cat so heavy that he could not move it after several efforts, 'Come,' said he, (throwing down the pole,) '*you* shall take it now;' which I accordingly did, and being a fresh man, soon made the cat tumble over the cascade. This may be laughed at as too trifling to record; but it is a small characteristick trait in the Flemish picture which I give of my friend, and in which, therefore I mark the most minute particulars. And let it be remembered, that *Æsop at play* is one of the instructive apologues of antiquity.

I mentioned an old gentleman[1] of our acquaintance whose memory was beginning to fail. JOHNSON. 'There must be a diseased mind, where there is a failure of memory at seventy. A man's head, Sir, must be morbid, if he fails so soon.' My friend, being now himself sixty-eight, might think thus: but I imagine, that *threescore and ten*, the Psalmist's period of sound human life, in later ages may have a failure, though there be no disease in the constitution.

Talking of Rochester's Poems, he said, he had given them to Mr. Steevens to castrate for the edition of the poets, to which he was to write Prefaces. Dr. Taylor (the only time I ever heard him say any thing witty)[2] observed, that 'if Rochester had been castrated himself, his exceptionable poems would not have been written.' I asked if Burnet had not given a good Life of Rochester. JOHNSON. 'We have a good *Death*: there is not much *Life*.' I asked whether Prior's Poems were to be printed entire: Johnson said they were. I mentioned Lord Hailes's censure of Prior, in his Preface to a collection of *Sacred Poems*, by various hands, published by him at Edinburgh a great many years ago, where he mentions, 'those impure tales which will be the eternal opprobrium of their ingenious authour.' JOHNSON. 'Sir, Lord Hailes has forgot. There is nothing in Prior that will excite to lewdness. If Lord Hailes thinks there is, he must be more combustible than other people.' I instanced the tale of *Paulo Purganti and his Wife*. JOHNSON. 'Sir, there is nothing there, but that his wife wanted to be kissed when poor Paulo was out of pocket. No, Sir, Prior is a lady's book. No lady is ashamed to have it standing in her library.'

The hypochondriack disorder being mentioned, Dr. Johnson

---

[1] [Lord Auchinleck. *Boswell Papers*, vi. 191, xiii. 56.]

[2] I am told that Horace, Earl of Orford, has a collection of *Bon-Mots* by persons who never said but one.

did not think it so common as I supposed. 'Dr. Taylor (said he,) is the same one day as another. Burke and Reynolds are the same. Beauclerk, except when in pain, is the same. I am not so myself; but this I do not mention commonly.'

I complained of a wretched changefulness, so that I could not preserve, for any long continuance, the same views of any thing. It was most comfortable to me to experience, in Dr. Johnson's company, a relief from this uneasiness. His steady vigorous mind held firm before me those objects which my own feeble and tremulous imagination frequently presented, in such a wavering state, that my reason could not judge well of them.

Dr. Johnson advised me to-day, to have as many books about me as I could; that I might read upon any subject upon which I had a desire for instruction at the time. 'What you read *then* (said he,) you will remember; but if you have not a book immediately ready, and the subject moulds in your mind, it is a chance if you again have a desire to study it.' He added, 'If a man never has an eager desire for instruction, he should prescribe a task for himself. But it is better when a man reads from immediate inclination.'

He repeated a good many lines of Horace's *Odes*, while we were in the chaise. I remember particularly the Ode *Eheu fugaces*.[1]

He said, the dispute as to the comparative excellence of Homer or Virgil[2] was inaccurate. 'We must consider (said he,) whether Homer was not the greatest poet, though Virgil may have produced the finest poem. Virgil was indebted to Homer for the whole invention of the structure of an epick poem, and for many of his beauties.'

He told me that Bacon was a favourite authour with him; but he had never read his works till he was compiling the *English*

---

[1] [*Eheu fugaces . . . Labuntur anni*. 'Ah me, the fleeting years are slipping by.' Horace, *Odes* ii. xiv. (Wickham.)]

[2] I am informed by Mr. Langton, that a great many years ago he was present when this question was agitated between Dr. Johnson and Mr. Burke; and, to use Johnson's phrase, they 'talked their best;' Johnson for Homer, Burke for Virgil. It may well be supposed to have been one of the ablest and most brilliant contests that ever was exhibited. How much must we regret that it has not been preserved.

Dictionary, in which, he said, I might see Bacon very often quoted. Mr. Seward recollects his having mentioned, that a Dictionary of the English Language might be compiled from Bacon's writings alone, and that he had once an intention of giving an edition of Bacon, at least of his English works, and writing the Life of that great man. Had he executed this intention, there can be no doubt that he would have done it in a most masterly manner. Mallet's *Life of Bacon* has no inconsiderable merit as an acute and elegant dissertation relative to its subject; but Mallet's mind was not comprehensive enough to embrace the vast extent of Lord Verulam's genius and research. Dr. Warburton therefore observed, with witty justness, 'that Mallet, in his *Life of Bacon*, had forgotten that he was a philosopher; and if he should write the Life of the Duke of Marlborough, which he had undertaken to do, he would probably forget that he was a general.'

Wishing to be satisfied what degree of truth there was in a story which a friend[1] of Johnson's and mine had told me to his disadvantage, I mentioned it to him in direct terms; and it was to this effect: that a gentleman[2] who had lived in great intimacy with him, shewn him much kindness, and even relieved him from a spunging-house, having afterwards fallen into bad circumstances, was one day, when Johnson was at dinner with him, seized for debt, and carried to prison; that Johnson sat still undisturbed, and went on eating and drinking; upon which the gentleman's sister, who was present, could not suppress her indignation: 'What, Sir, (said she,) are you so unfeeling, as not even to offer to go to my brother in his distress; you who have been so much obliged to him?' And that Johnson answered, 'Madam, I owe him no obligation; what he did for me he would have done for a dog.'

Johnson assured me, that the story was absolutely false: but like a man conscious of being in the right, and desirous of completely vindicating himself from such a charge, he did not arrogantly rest on a mere denial, and on his general character, but

[1] [Beauclerk, *Boswell's Note Book*, p. 16.]
[2] [The Hon. Henry Hervey. *Ib.* pp. 16, 17.]

proceeded thus:—'Sir, I was very intimate with that gentleman, and was once relieved by him from an arrest; but I never was present when he was arrested, never knew that he was arrested, and I believe he never was in difficulties after the time when he relieved me. I loved him much; yet, in talking of his general character, I may have said, though I do not remember that I ever did say so, that as his generosity proceeded from no principle, but was a part of his profusion, he would do for a dog what he would do for a friend: but I never applied this remark to any particular instance, and certainly not to his kindness to me. If a profuse man, who does not value his money, and gives a large sum to a whore, gives half as much, or an equally large sum to relieve a friend, it cannot be esteemed as virtue. This was all that I could say of that gentleman; and, if said at all, it must have been said after his death. Sir, I would have gone to the world's end to relieve him. The remark about the dog, if made by me, was such a sally as might escape one when painting a man highly.'

On Tuesday, September 23, Johnson was remarkably cordial to me. It being necessary for me to return to Scotland soon, I had fixed on the next day for my setting out, and I felt a tender concern at the thought of parting with him. He had, at this time, frankly communicated to me many particulars, which are inserted in this work in their proper places; and once, when I happened to mention that the expence of my jaunt would come to much more than I had computed, he said, 'Why, Sir, if the expence were to be an inconvenience, you would have reason to regret it: but, if you have had the money to spend, I know not that you could have purchased as much pleasure with it in any other way.'

During this interview at Ashbourne, Johnson and I frequently talked with wonderful pleasure of mere trifles which had occurred in our tour to the Hebrides; for it had left a most agreeable and lasting impression upon his mind.

He found fault with me for using the phrase to *make* money. 'Don't you see (said he,) the impropriety of it? To *make* money is to *coin* it: you should say *get* money.' The phrase, however, is,

I think, pretty current. But Johnson was at all times jealous of infractions upon the genuine English language, and prompt to repress colloquial barbarisms; such as, *pledging myself*, for *undertaking*; *line*, for *department* or *branch*, as, the *civil line*, the *banking line*. He was particularly indignant against the almost universal use of the word *idea* in the sense of *notion* or *opinion*, when it is clear that *idea* can only signify something of which an image can be formed in the mind. We may have an *idea* or *image* of a mountain, a tree, a building; but we cannot surely have an *idea* or *image* of an *argument* or *proposition*. Yet we hear the sages of the law 'delivering their *ideas* upon the question under consideration;' and the first speakers in parliament 'entirely coinciding in the *idea* which has been ably stated by an honourable member;'—or 'reprobating an *idea* unconstitutional, and fraught with the most dangerous consequences to a great and free country.' Johnson called this 'modern cant.'

I perceived that he pronounced the word *heard*, as if spelt with a double *e*, *heerd*, instead of sounding it *herd*, as is most usually done. He said, his reason was, that if it were pronounced *herd*, there would be a single exception from the English pronunciation of the syllable *ear*, and he thought it better not to have that exception.

He praised Grainger's *Ode on Solitude*, in Dodsley's *Collection*, and repeated, with great energy, the exordium:—

> 'O Solitude, romantick maid,
> Whether by nodding towers you tread;
> Or haunt the desart's trackless gloom,
> Or hover o'er the yawning tomb;
> Or climb the Andes' clifted side,
> Or by the Nile's coy source abide;
> Or, starting from your half-year's sleep,
> From Hecla view the thawing deep;
> Or, at the purple dawn of day,
> Tadnor's marble wastes survey';

observing, 'This, Sir, is very noble.'

In the evening our gentleman-farmer, and two others, entertained themselves and the company with a great number of tunes on the fiddle. Johnson desired to have 'Let ambition fire thy mind,' played over again, and appeared to give a patient attention to it; though he owned to me that he was very insensible to the power of musick. I told him, that it affected me to such a degree, as often to agitate my nerves painfully, producing in my mind alternate sensations of pathetick dejection, so that I was ready to shed tears; and of daring resolution, so that I was inclined to rush into the thickest part of the battle. 'Sir, (said he,) I should never hear it, if it made me such a fool.'

Much of the effect of musick, I am satisfied, is owing to the association of ideas. That air, which instantly and irresistibly excites in the Swiss, when in a foreign land, the *maladie du pais*, has, I am told, no intrinsick power of sound. And I know from my own experience, that Scotch reels, though brisk, make me melancholy, because I used to hear them in my early years, at a time when Mr. Pitt called for soldiers 'from the mountains of the north,' and numbers of brave Highlanders were going abroad, never to return. Whereas the airs in *The Beggar's Opera*, many of which are very soft, never fail to render me gay, because they are associated with the warm sensations and high spirits of London. This evening, while some of the tunes of ordinary composition were played with no great skill, my frame was agitated, and I was conscious of a generous attachment to Johnson, as my preceptor and friend, mixed with an affectionate regret that he was an old man, whom I should probably lose in a short time. I thought I could defend him at the point of my sword. My reverence and affection for him were in full glow. I said to him, 'My dear Sir, we must meet every year, if you don't quarrel with me.' JOHNSON. 'Nay, Sir, you are more likely to quarrel with me, than I with you. My regard for you is greater almost than I have words to express; but I do not choose to be always repeating it; write it down in the first leaf of your pocket-book, and never doubt of it again.'

I talked to him of misery being 'the doom of man' in this life, as displayed in his *Vanity of Human Wishes*. Yet I observed that things were done upon the supposition of happiness; grand houses were built, fine gardens were made, splendid places of publick amusement were contrived, and crowded with company. JOHNSON. 'Alas, Sir, these are all only struggles for happiness. When I first entered Ranelagh, it gave an expansion and gay sensation to my mind, such as I never experienced any where else. But, as Xerxes wept when he viewed his immense army, and considered that not one of that great multitude would be alive a hundred years afterwards, so it went to my heart to consider that there was not one in all that brilliant circle, that was not afraid to go home and think; but that the thoughts of each individual there, would be distressing when alone.' This reflection was experimentally just. The feeling of languor,[1] which succeeds the animation of gaiety, is itself a very severe pain; and when the mind is then vacant, a thousand disappointments and vexations rush in and excruciate. Will not many even of my fairest readers allow this to be true?

I suggested, that being in love, and flattered with hopes of success; or having some favourite scheme in view for the next day, might prevent that wretchedness of which we had been talking. JOHNSON. 'Why, Sir, it may sometimes be so as you suppose; but my conclusion is in general but too true.'

While Johnson and I stood in calm conference by ourselves in Dr. Taylor's garden, at a pretty late hour in a serene autumn night, looking up to the heavens, I directed the discourse to the subject of a future state. My friend was in a placid and most benignant frame. 'Sir, (said he,) I do not imagine that all things will be made clear to us immediately after death, but that the ways of Providence will be explained to us very gradually.' I ventured to ask him whether, although the words of some texts of Scripture seemed strong in support of the dreadful doctrine of an eternity of punishment, we might not hope that the denunciation was figurative, and would not literally be executed.

---

[1] Pope mentions,
    'Stretch'd on the rack of a too easy chair.' [*Dunciad* iv. 342.]
But I recollect a couplet quite apposite to my subject in *Virtue, an Ethick Epistle*, a beautiful and instructive poem, by an anonymous writer, in 1758; who, treating of pleasure in excess, says:—
      'Till languor, suffering on the rack of bliss,
      Confess that man was never made for this.'

J O H N S O N . 'Sir, you are to consider the intention of punishment in a future state. We have no reason to be sure that we shall then be no longer liable to offend against GOD. We do not know that even the angels are quite in a state of security; nay we know that some of them have fallen. It may, therefore, perhaps be necessary, in order to preserve both men and angels in a state of rectitude, that they should have continually before them the punishment of those who have deviated from it; but we may hope that by some other means a fall from rectitude may be prevented. Some of the texts of Scripture upon this subject are, as you observe, indeed strong; but they may admit of a mitigated interpretation.' He talked to me upon this awful and delicate question in a gentle tone, and as if afraid to be decisive.

After supper I accompanied him to his apartment, and at my request he dictated to me an argument in favour of the negro who was then claiming his liberty, in an action in the Court of Session in Scotland. He had always been very zealous against slavery in every form, in which I, with all deference, thought that he discovered 'a zeal without knowledge.' Upon one occasion, when in company with some very grave men at Oxford, his toast was, 'Here's to the next insurrection of the negroes in the West Indies.' His violent prejudice against our West Indian and American settlers appeared whenever there was an opportunity. Towards the conclusion of his *Taxation no Tyranny,* he says, 'how is it that we hear the loudest *yelps* for liberty among the drivers of negroes?' and in his conversation with Mr. Wilkes, he asked, 'Where did Beckford and Trecothick learn English?'[1] That Trecothick could both speak and write good English is well known. I myself was favoured with his correspondence concerning the brave Corsicans. And that Beckford could speak it with a spirit of honest resolution even to his Majesty, as his 'faithful Lord-Mayor of London,' is commemorated by the noble monument erected to him in Guildhall.

The argument dictated by Dr. Johnson was as follows:—

'It must be agreed that in most ages many countries have had part of their inhabitants in a state of slavery; yet it may be

[1] See *ante,* p. 774.

doubted whether slavery can ever be supposed the natural condition of man. It is impossible not to conceive that men in their original state were equal; and very difficult to imagine how one would be subjected to another but by violent compulsion. An individual may, indeed, forfeit his liberty by a crime; but he cannot by that crime forfeit the liberty of his children. What is true of a criminal seems true likewise of a captive. A man may accept life from a conquering enemy on condition of perpetual servitude; but it is very doubtful whether he can entail that servitude on his descendants; for no man can stipulate without commission for another. The condition which he himself accepts, his son or grandson perhaps would have rejected. If we should admit, what perhaps may with more reason be denied, that there are certain relations between man and man which may make slavery necessary and just, yet it can never be proved that he who is now suing for his freedom ever stood in any of those relations. He is certainly subject by no law, but that of violence, to his present master; who pretends no claim to his obedience, but that he bought him from a merchant of slaves, whose right to sell him never was examined. It is said that, according to the constitutions of Jamaica, he was legally enslaved; these constitutions are merely positive; and apparently injurious to the rights of mankind, because whoever is exposed to sale is condemned to slavery without appeal; by whatever fraud or violence he might have been originally brought into the merchant's power. In our own time Princes have been sold, by wretches to whose care they were entrusted, that they might have an European education; but when once they were brought to a market in the plantations, little would avail either their dignity or their wrongs. The laws of Jamaica afford a Negro no redress. His colour is considered as a sufficient testimony against him. It is to be lamented that moral right should ever give way to political convenience. But if temptations of interest are sometimes too strong for human virtue, let us at least retain a virtue where there is no temptation to quit it. In the present case there is apparent right on one side, and no convenience on the other. Inhabitants of this island can neither gain riches nor power by taking away the liberty of any part of the human species. The sum of the argument is this:—No man is by nature the property of another: The defendant is, therefore, by nature free: The rights of nature must be some way forfeited before they can be justly taken away: That the defendant has by any act forfeited the rights of nature we require to be proved; and if no proof of such forfeiture can be given, we doubt not but the justice of the court will declare him free.'

I record Dr. Johnson's argument fairly upon this particular case; where, perhaps, he was in the right. But I beg leave to enter my most solemn protest against his general doctrine with respect to the *Slave Trade*. For I will resolutely say—that his unfavourable notion of it was owing to prejudice, and imperfect or false information. The wild and dangerous attempt which has for some time been persisted in to obtain an act of our Legislature, to abolish so very important and necessary a branch of commercial interest, must have been crushed at once, had not the insignificance of the zealots who vainly took the lead in it, made the vast body of Planters, Merchants, and others, whose immense properties are involved in that trade, reasonably enough suppose that there could be no danger. The encouragement which the attempt has received excites my wonder and indignation: and though some men of superiour abilities have supported it; whether from a love of temporary popularity, when prosperous; or a love of general mischief, when desperate, my opinion is unshaken. To abolish a *status*, which in all ages GOD has sanctioned, and man has continued, would not only be *robbery* to an innumerable class of our fellow-subjects; but it would be extreme cruelty to the African Savages, a portion of whom it saves from massacre, or intolerable bondage in their own country, and introduces into a much happier state of life; especially now when their passage to the West-Indies and their treatment there is humanely regulated. To abolish that trade would be to

'—— shut the gates of mercy on mankind.'[1]

Whatever may have passed elsewhere concerning it, The HOUSE OF LORDS is wise and independent:

[1] Gray's *Elegy*, 68.

'*Intaminatis fulget honoribus;*
Nec sumit aut ponit secures
Arbitrio popularis auræ.[1]

I have read, conversed, and thought much upon the subject, and would recommend to all who are capable of conviction, an excellent Tract by my learned and ingenious friend John Ranby, Esq. entitled *Doubts on the Abolition of the Slave Trade.* To Mr. Ranby's *Doubts* I will apply Lord Chancellor Hardwicke's expression in praise of a Scotch Law Book, called *Dirleton's Doubts*; 'HIS *Doubts*, (said his Lordship,) are better than most people's *Certainties.*'

When I said now to Johnson, that I was afraid I kept him too late up. 'No, Sir, (said he,) I don't care though I sit all night with you.' This was an animated speech from a man in his sixty-ninth year.

Had I been as attentive not to displease him as I ought to have been, I know not but this vigil might have been fulfilled; but I unluckily entered upon the controversy concerning the right of Great-Britain to tax America, and attempted to argue in favour of our fellow-subjects on the other side of the Atlantick. I insisted that America might be very well governed, and made to yield sufficient revenue by the means of *influence*, as exemplified in Ireland, while the people might be pleased with the imagination of their participating of the British constitution, by having a body of representatives, without whose consent money could not be exacted from them. Johnson could not bear my thus opposing his avowed opinion, which he had exerted himself with an extreme degree of heat to enforce; and the violent agitation into which he was thrown, while answering, or rather reprimanding me, alarmed me so, that I heartily repented of my having unthinkingly introduced the subject. I myself, however, grew warm, and the change was great, from the calm state of philosophical discussion in which we had a little before been pleasingly employed.

---

[1] ['Virtue, which cannot know the disgrace of rejection, shines bright with honours that have no stain on them, nor takes nor resigns the rods at the shifting breath of the people's pleasure.' Horace, *Odes* III. ii. (Wickham.)]

I talked of the corruption of the British Parliament, in which I alledged that any question, however unreasonable or unjust, might be carried by a venal majority; and I spoke with high admiration of the Roman Senate, as if composed of men sincerely desirous to resolve what they should think best for their country. My friend would allow no such character to the Roman Senate; and he maintained that the British Parliament was not corrupt, and that there was no occasion to corrupt its members; asserting, that there was hardly ever any question of great importance before Parliament, any question in which a man might not very well vote either upon one side or the other. He said there had been none in his time except that respecting America.

We were fatigued by the contest, which was produced by my want of caution; and he was not then in the humour to slide into easy and cheerful talk. It therefore so happened, that we were after an hour or two very willing to separate and go to bed.

On Wednesday, September 24, I went into Dr. Johnson's room before he got up, and finding that the storm of the preceding night was quite laid, I sat down upon his bed-side, and he talked with as much readiness and good-humour as ever. He recommended to me to plant a considerable part of a large moorish farm which I had purchased, and he made several calculations of the expence and profit: for he delighted in exercising his mind on the science of numbers. He pressed upon me the importance of planting at the first in a very sufficient manner, quoting the saying '*In bello non licet bis errare:*'[1] and adding, 'this is equally true in planting.'

I spoke with gratitude of Dr. Taylor's hospitality; and, as evidence that it was not on account of his good table alone that Johnson visited him often, I mentioned a little anecdote which had escaped my friend's recollection, and at hearing which repeated, he smiled. One evening, when I was sitting with him, Frank delivered this message: 'Sir, Dr. Taylor sends his compliments to you, and begs you will dine with him to-morrow. He has got a hare.'—'My compliments (said Johnson,) and I'll dine with him—hare or rabbit.'

---

[1] ['In war it is not permitted to make a mistake twice.']

After breakfast I departed, and pursued my journey north-wards. I took my post-chaise from the Green Man, a very good inn at Ashbourne, the mistress of which, a mighty civil gentle-woman, courtseying very low, presented me with an engraving of the sign of her house; to which she had subjoined, in her own hand-writing, an address in such singular simplicity of style, that I have preserved it pasted upon one of the boards of my original Journal at this time, and shall here insert it for the amusement of my readers:—

'*M. KILLINGLEY's duty waits upon* Mr. Boswell, *is exceed-ingly obliged to him for this favour; whenever he comes this way, hopes for a continuance of the same. Would* Mr. Boswell *name the house to his extensive acquaintance, it would be a singular favour confer'd on one who has it not in her power to make any other return but her most grateful thanks, and sincerest prayers for his happiness in time, and in a blessed eternity.—Tuesday morn.*'

From this meeting at Ashbourne I derived a considerable accession to my Johnsonian store. I communicated my original Journal to Sir William Forbes, in whom I have always placed deserved confidence; and what he wrote to me concerning it is so much to my credit as the biographer of Johnson, that my readers will, I hope, grant me their indulgence for here inserting it: 'It is not once or twice going over it (says Sir William,) that will satisfy me; for I find in it a high degree of instruction as well as entertainment; and I derive more benefit from Dr. John-son's admirable discussions than I should be able to draw from his personal conversation; for, I suppose there is not a man in the world to whom he discloses his sentiments so freely as to yourself.'

I cannot omit a curious circumstance which occurred at Edensor-inn, close by Chatsworth, to survey the magnificence of which I had gone a considerable way out of my road to Scotland. The inn was then kept by a very jolly landlord, whose name, I think, was Malton. He happened to mention that 'the celebrated Dr. Johnson had been in his house.' I inquired *who* this Dr. Johnson was, that I might hear mine host's notion of him. 'Sir, (said he,) Johnson, the great writer; *Oddity*, as they call him. He's the greatest writer in England; he writes for the ministry; he has a correspondence abroad, and lets them know what's going on.'

My friend, who had a thorough dependance upon the authenticity of my relation without any *embellishment*, as *falsehood* or *fiction* is too gently called, laughed a good deal at this representation of himself.

'MR. BOSWELL *to* DR. JOHNSON

'MY DEAR SIR,   'Edinburgh, Sept. 29, 1777.
    'By the first post I inform you of my safe arrival at my own house, and that I had the comfort of finding my wife and children all in good health.

'When I look back upon our late interview, it appears to me to have answered expectation better than almost any scheme of happiness that I ever put in execution. My Journal is stored with wisdom and wit; and my memory is filled with the recollection of lively and affectionate feelings, which now, I think, yield me more satisfaction than at the time when they were first excited. I have experienced this upon other occasions. I shall be obliged to you if you will explain it to me; for it seems wonderful that pleasure should be more vivid at a distance than when near. I wish you may find yourself in the humour to do me this favour; but I flatter myself with no strong hope of it; for I have observed, that unless upon very serious occasions, your letters to me are not *answers* to those which I write.'

[I then expressed much uneasiness that I had mentioned to him the name of the gentleman[1] who had told me the story so much to his disadvantage, the truth of which he had completely refuted; for that my having done so might be interpreted as a breach of confidence, and offend one whose society I valued:—therefore earnestly requesting that no notice might be taken of it to any body, till I should be in London, and have an opportunity to talk it over with the gentleman.]

                    [1] Topham Beauclerk, see *ante*, p. 871.

'*To* JAMES BOSWELL, ESQ.

'DEAR SIR,—You will wonder, or you have wondered, why no letter has come from me. What you wrote at your return, had in it such a strain of cowardly caution as gave me no pleasure. I could not well do what you wished; I had no need to vex you with a refusal. I have seen Mr. ———, and as to him have set all right, without any inconvenience, so far as I know, to you. Mrs. Thrale had forgot the story. You may now be at ease.

'And at ease I certainly wish you, for the kindness that you shewed in coming so long a journey to see me. It was pity to keep you so long in pain, but, upon reviewing the matter, I do not see what I could have done better than as I did.

'I hope you found at your return my dear enemy and all her little people quite well, and had no reason to repent of your journey. I think on it with great gratitude.

'I was not well when you left me at the Doctor's, and I grew worse; yet I staid on, and at Lichfield was very ill. Travelling, however, did not make me worse; and when I came to London, I complied with a summons to go to Brighthelmston, where I saw Beauclerk, and staid three days.

'Our CLUB has recommenced last Friday, but I was not there. Langton has another wench.[1] Mrs. Thrale is in hopes of a young brewer. They got by their trade last year a very large sum, and their expenses are proportionate.

'Mrs. Williams's health is very bad. And I have had for some time a very difficult and laborious respiration; but I am better by purges, abstinence, and other methods. I am yet, however, much behind-hand in my health and rest.

'Dr. Blair's Sermons are now universally commended; but let him think that I had the honour of first finding and first praising his excellencies. I did not stay to add my voice to that of the publick.

'My dear friend, let me thank you once more for your visit; you did me great honour, and I hope met with nothing that displeased you. I staid long at Ashbourne, not much pleased, yet aukward at departing. I then went to Lichfield, where I

[1] A daughter born to him.

883

found my friend at Stow-hill[1] very dangerously diseased. Such is life. Let us try to pass it well, whatever it be, for there is surely something beyond it.

'Well, now I hope all is well, write as soon as you can to, dear Sir, your affectionate servant,

'London, Nov. 25, 1777.'   'SAM. JOHNSON.'

'*To* DR. SAMUEL JOHNSON

'MY DEAR SIR,   'Edinburgh, Nov. 29, 1777.

'This day's post has at length relieved me from much uneasiness, by bringing me a letter from you. I was, indeed, doubly uneasy;—on my own account and yours. I was very anxious to be secured against any bad consequences from my imprudence in mentioning the gentleman's name who had told me a story to your disadvantage; and as I could hardly suppose it possible, that you would delay so long to make me easy, unless you were ill, I was not a little apprehensive about you. You must not be offended when I venture to tell you that you appear to me to have been too rigid upon this occasion. "The *cowardly caution which gave you no pleasure*," was suggested to me by a friend[2] here, to whom I mentioned the strange story and the detection of its falsity, as an instance how one may be deceived by what is apparently very good authority. But, as I am still persuaded, that as I might have obtained the truth, without mentioning the gentleman's name, it was wrong in me to do it, I cannot see that you are just in blaming my caution. But if you were ever so just in your disapprobation, might you not have dealt more tenderly with me?

'I went to Auchinleck about the middle of October, and passed some time with my father very comfortably. . . .

'I am engaged in a criminal prosecution against a country schoolmaster, for indecent behaviour to his female scholars. There is no statute against such abominable conduct; but it is punishable at common law. I shall be obliged to you for your

---

[1] Mrs. Aston.
[2] [*Prof. Pottle suggests* John Johnston of Grange. See *Boswell Papers*, xiii. 67.]

assistance in this extraordinary trial. I ever am, my dear Sir, your faithful humble servant,

'JAMES BOSWELL.'

About this time I wrote to Johnson, giving him an account of the decision of the *Negro cause*, by the court of Session, which by those who hold even the mildest and best regulated slavery in abomination, (of which number I do not hesitate to declare that I am one,) should be remembered with high respect, and to the credit of Scotland; for it went upon a much broader ground than the case of *Somerset*, which was decided in England;[1] being truly the general question, whether a perpetual obligation of service to one master in any mode should be sanctified by the law of a free country. A negro, then called *Joseph Knight*, a native of Africa, who having been brought to Jamaica in the usual course of the slave trade, and purchased by a Scotch gentleman in that island, had attended his master to Scotland, where it was officiously suggested to him that he would be found entitled to his liberty without any limitation. He accordingly brought his action, in the course of which the advocates on both sides did themselves great honour. Mr. Maclaurin has had the praise of Johnson, for his argument[2] in favour of the negro, and Mr. Macconochie distinguished himself on the same side, by his ingenuity and extraordinary research. Mr. Cullen, on the part of the master, discovered good information and sound reasoning; in which he was well supported by Mr. James Fergusson, remarkable for a manly understanding, and a knowledge both of books and of the world. But I cannot too highly praise the speech which Mr. Henry Dundas generously contributed to the cause

---

[1] See *State Trials*, vol. xi. p. 339, and Mr. Hargrave's argument.
[2] The motto to it was happily chosen:—
        '*Quamvis ille niger, quamvis tu candidus esses.*'
['Though he was swart and thou art fair.' Virgil, *Eclogues* ii. 16. (Jackson.)] I cannot avoid mentioning a circumstance no less strange than true, that a brother Advocate [Alexander Wight, *according to Scott, but the identification is very doubtful*] in considerable practice, but of whom it certainly cannot be said, *Ingenuas didicit fideliter artes*, ['A careful study of the liberal arts.' Ovid, *Epistles* ii. ix. 47.] asked Mr. Maclaurin, with a face of flippant assurance, 'Are these words your own?'

of the sooty stranger. Mr. Dundas's Scottish accent, which has
been so often in vain obtruded as an objection to his powerful
abilities in parliament, was no disadvantage to him in his own
country. And I do declare, that upon this memorable question he
impressed me, and I believe all his audience, with such feelings
as were produced by some of the most eminent orations of antiquity. This testimony I liberally give to the excellence of an old
friend, with whom it has been my lot to differ very widely upon
many political topicks; yet I persuade myself without malice. A
great majority of the Lords of Session decided for the negro.
But four of their number, the Lord President, Lord Elliock,
Lord Monboddo, and Lord Covington, resolutely maintained
the lawfulness of a *status*, which has been acknowledged in all
ages and countries, and that when freedom flourished, as in old
Greece and Rome.

'*To* JAMES BOSWELL, ESQ.

'DEAR SIR,—This is the time of the year in which all express
their good wishes to their friends, and I send mine to you and
your family. May your lives be long, happy, and good. I have
been much out of order, but, I hope, do not grow worse.

'The crime of the schoolmaster whom you are engaged to
prosecute is very great, and may be suspected to be too common.
In our law it would be a breach of the peace, and a misdemea-
nour: that is, a kind of indefinite crime, not capital, but punishable at the discretion of the Court. You cannot want matter: all
that needs to be said will easily occur.

'Mr. Shaw, the authour of the *Gaelick Grammar*, desires me
to make a request for him to Lord Eglintoune, that he may be
appointed Chaplain to one of the new-raised regiments.

'All our friends are as they were; little has happened to them
of either good or bad. Mrs. Thrale ran a great black hair-
dressing pin into her eye; but by great evacuation she kept it
from inflaming, and it is almost well. Miss Reynolds has been
out of order, but is better. Mrs. Williams is in a very poor state
of health.

'If I should write on, I should, perhaps, write only complaints, and therefore I will content myself with telling you, that I love to think on you, and to hear from you; and that I am, dear Sir, yours faithfully,

'December 27, 1777.'   'SAM. JOHNSON.'

'*To* DR. SAMUEL JOHNSON

'DEAR SIR,   'Edinburgh, Jan. 8, 1778.

'Your congratulations upon a new year are mixed with complaint: mine must be so too. My wife has for some time been very ill, having been confined to the house these three months by a severe cold, attended with alarming symptoms.

[Here I gave a particular account of the distress which the person, upon every account most dear to me, suffered; and of the dismal state of apprehension in which I now was: adding that I never stood more in need of his consoling philosophy.]

'Did you ever look at a book written by Wilson, a Scotsman,[1] under the Latin name of *Volusenus*, according to the custom of literary men at a certain period. It is entitled *De Animi Tranquillitate*.[2] I earnestly desire tranquillity. *Bona res quies*:[3] but I fear I shall never attain it: for, when unoccupied, I grow gloomy, and occupation agitates me to feverishness. . . . I am, dear Sir, your most affectionate humble servant, 'JAMES BOSWELL.'

'*To* JAMES BOSWELL, ESQ.

'DEAR SIR,—To a letter so interesting as your last, it is proper to return some answer, however little I may be disposed to write.

'Your alarm at your lady's illness was reasonable, and not disproportionate to the appearance of the disorder. I hope your physical friend's[4] conjecture is now verified, and all fear of a consumption at an end: a little care and exercise will then restore her. London is a good air for ladies; and if you bring

[1] [Scotsman 1; Scotchman 2, 3.]
[2] ['Concerning peace of mind.']
[3] ['Peace of mind is good.']
[4] [Probably Dr. Alexander Wood. *R. W. Chapman*.]

her hither, I will do for her what she did for me—I will retire
from my apartments, for her accommodation. Behave kindly to
her, and keep her cheerful.

'You always seem to call for tenderness. Know then, that in
the first month of the present year I very highly esteem and
very cordially love you. I hope to tell you this at the beginning
of every year as long as we live; and why should we trouble
ourselves to tell or hear it oftener?

'Tell Veronica, Euphemia, and Alexander, that I wish them,
as well as their parents, many happy years.

'You have ended the negro's cause much to my mind. Lord
Auchinleck and dear Lord Hailes were on the side of liberty.
Lord Hailes's name reproaches me; but if he saw my languid
neglect of my own affairs, he would rather pity than resent my
neglect of his. I hope to mend, *ut et mihi vivam et amicis*.[1] I am,
dear Sir, your's affectionately,

'January 24, 1778.'   'SAM. JOHNSON.'

'My service to my fellow-traveller, Joseph.'

Johnson maintained a long and intimate friendship with Mr.
Welch, who succeeded the celebrated Henry Fielding as one of
his Majesty's Justices of the Peace for Westminster; kept a
regular office for the police of that great district; and discharged
his important trust, for many years, faithfully and ably. Johnson,
who had an eager and unceasing curiosity to know human life
in all its variety, told me, that he attended Mr. Welch in his
office for a whole winter, to hear the examinations of the cul-
prits; but that he found an almost uniform tenor of misfortune,
wretchedness and profligacy. Mr. Welch's health being impaired,
he was advised to try the effect of a warm climate; and Johnson,
by his interest with Mr. Chamier, procured him leave of absence
to go to Italy, and a promise that the pension or salary of two
hundred pounds a year, which Government allowed him, should
not be discontinued. Mr. Welch accordingly went abroad,
accompanied by his daughter Anne, a young lady of uncommon
talents and literature.

[1] ["That I may live for my own good and my friends'."]

'*To* Saunders Welch, Esq., *at the English Coffee-House, Rome*

'Dear Sir,—To have suffered one of my best and dearest friends to pass almost two years in foreign countries without a letter, has a very shameful appearance of inattention. But the truth is, that there was no particular time in which I had any thing particular to say; and general expressions of good will, I hope, our long friendship is grown too solid to want.

'Of publick affairs you have information from the newspapers wherever you go, for the English keep no secret; and of other things, Mrs. Nollekens informs you. My intelligence could therefore be of no use; and Miss Nancy's letters made it unnecessary to write to you for information: I was likewise for some time out of humour, to find that motion, and nearer approaches to the sun, did not restore your health so fast as I expected. Of your health, the accounts have lately been more pleasing; and I have the gratification of imaging to myself a length of years which I hope you have gained, and of which the enjoyment will be improved by a vast accession of images and observations which your journeys and various residence have enabled you to make and accumulate. You have travelled with this felicity, almost peculiar to yourself, that your companion is not to part from you at your journey's end; but you are to live on together, to help each other's recollection, and to supply each other's omissions. The world has few greater pleasures than that which two friends enjoy, in tracing back, at some distant time, those transactions and events through which they have passed together. One of the old man's miseries is, that he cannot easily find a companion able to partake with him of the past. You and your fellow-traveller have this comfort in store, that your conversation will be not easily exhausted; one will always be glad to say what the other will always be willing to hear.

'That you may enjoy this pleasure long, your health must have your constant attention. I suppose you purpose to return this year. There is no need of haste: do not come hither before the height of summer, that you may fall gradually into the inconveniences of your native clime. July seems to be the proper month. August and September will prepare you for the winter. After having travelled so far to find health, you must take care not to lose it at home; and I hope a little care will effectually preserve it.

'Miss Nancy has doubtless kept a constant and copious journal. She must not expect to be welcome when she returns, without a great mass of information. Let her review her journal often, and set down what she finds herself to have omitted, that she may trust to memory as little as possible, for memory is soon confused by a quick succession of things; and she will grow every day less confident of the truth of her own narratives, unless she can recur to some written memorials. If she has satisfied herself with hints, instead of full representations, let her supply the deficiencies now while her memory is yet fresh, and while her father's memory may help her. If she observes this direction, she will not have travelled in vain; for she will bring home a book with which she may entertain herself to the end of life. If it were not now too late, I would advise her to note the impression which the first sight of any thing new and wonderful made upon her mind. Let her now set her thoughts down as she can recollect them; for faint as they may already be, they will grow every day fainter.

'Perhaps I do not flatter myself unreasonably when I imagine that you may wish to know something of me. I can gratify your benevolence with no account of health. The hand of time, or of disease, is very heavy upon me. I pass restless and uneasy nights, harassed with convulsions of my breast, and flatulencies at my stomach; and restless nights make heavy days. But nothing will be mended by complaints, and therefore I will make an end. When we meet, we will try to forget our cares and our maladies, and contribute, as we can, to the chearfulness of each other. If I had gone with you, I believe I should have been better; but I do not know that it was in my power. I am, dear Sir, your most humble servant,

'Feb. 3, 1778.'   'SAM. JOHNSON.'

This letter, while it gives admirable advice how to travel to the best advantage, and will therefore be of very general use, is another eminent proof of Johnson's warm and affectionate heart.[1]

'*To* DR. SAMUEL JOHNSON

'MY DEAR SIR,   'Edinburgh, Feb. 26, 1778.

'Why I have delayed, for near a month, to thank you for your last affectionate letter, I cannot say; for my mind has been in better health these three weeks than for some years past. I believe I have evaded till I could send you a copy of Lord Hailes's opinion on the negro's cause, which he wishes you to read, and correct any errours that there may be in the language; for, says he, "we live in a critical, though not a learned age; and I seek to screen myself under the shield of Ajax." I communicated to him your apology for keeping the sheets of his *Annals* so long. He says, "I am sorry to see that Dr. Johnson is in a state of languor. Why should a sober Christian, neither an enthusiast nor a fanatick, be very merry or very sad?" I envy his Lordship's comfortable constitution: but well do I know that languor and dejection will afflict the best, however excellent their principles. I am in possession of Lord Hailes's opinion in his own hand-writing, and have had it for some time. My excuse then for procrastination must be, that I wanted to have it copied; and I have now put that off so long, that it will be better to bring it with me than send it, as I shall probably get you to look at it sooner, when I solicit you in person.

'My wife, who is, I thank GOD, a good deal better, is much obliged to you for your very polite and courteous offer of your apartment: but, if she goes to London, it will be best for her to have lodgings in the more airy vicinity of Hyde-Park. I, however, doubt much if I shall be able to prevail with her to accompany me to the metropolis; for she is so different from you and me, that she dislikes travelling; and she is so anxious about her

[1] The friendship between Mr. Welch and him was unbroken. Mr. Welch died not many months before him, and bequeathed him five guineas for a ring, which Johnson received with tenderness, as a kind memorial. His regard was constant for his friend Mr. Welch's daughters; of whom, Jane is married to Mr. Nollekens the statuary, whose merit is too well known to require any praise from me.

children, that she thinks she should be unhappy if at a distance
from them. She therefore wishes rather to go to some country
place in Scotland, where she can have them with her.

'I purpose being in London about the 20th of next month, as
I think it creditable to appear in the House of Lords as one of
Douglas's Counsel, in the great and last competition between
Duke Hamilton and him. . . .

'I am sorry poor Mrs. Williams is so ill: though her temper
is unpleasant, she has always been polite and obliging to me.
I wish many happy years to good Mr. Levett, who I suppose
holds his usual place at your breakfast table.[1] I ever am, my dear
Sir, your affectionate humble servant,

'JAMES BOSWELL.'

To THE SAME

'MY DEAR SIR,   'Edinburgh, Feb. 28, 1778.
'You are at present busy amongst the English poets, preparing, for the publick instruction and entertainment, Prefaces,
biographical and critical. It will not, therefore, be out of season
to appeal to you for the decision of a controversy which has
arisen between a lady and me concerning a passage in Parnell.
That poet tells us, that his Hermit quitted his cell

"——— to know the world by sight,
To find if *books* or *swains* report it right;
(For yet by *swains alone* the world he knew,
Whose feet came wand'ring o'er the nightly dew.")

I maintain, that there is an inconsistency here; for as the Hermit's notions of the world were formed from the reports both of
books and *swains*, he could not justly be said to know by *swains
alone*. Be pleased to judge between us, and let us have your
reasons.[2]

---

[1] Dr. Percy, the Bishop of Dromore, humorously observed, that Levett
used to breakfast on the crust of a roll, which Johnson, after tearing out the
crumb for himself, threw to his humble friend. BOSWELL. [Perhaps the word
threw is here too strong. Dr. Johnson never treated Levett with contempt.
—M.]
[2] See this subject discussed in a subsequent page, under May 3, 1779 [p.
1024].

'What do you say to *Taxation no Tyranny*, now, after Lord North's declaration, or confession, or whatever else his conciliatory speech should be called? I never differed from you in politicks but upon two points,—the Middlesex Election, and the Taxation of the Americans by the British *Houses of Representatives*. There is a *charm* in the word *Parliament*, so I avoid it. As I am a steady and a warm Tory, I regret that the King does not see it to be better for him to receive constitutional supplies from his American subjects by the voice of their own assemblies, where his Royal Person is represented, than through the medium of his British subjects. I am persuaded that the power of the Crown, which I wish to increase, would be greater when in contact with all its dominions, than if "the rays of regal bounty"[1] were to "shine" upon America through that dense and troubled body, a modern British Parliament. But, enough of this subject; for your angry voice at Ashbourne upon it, still sounds aweful "in my mind's *ears*." I ever am, my dear Sir, your most affectionate humble servant,

'JAMES BOSWELL.'

To THE SAME

'MY DEAR SIR,   'Edinburgh, March 12, 1778.

'The alarm of your late illness distressed me but a few hours; for on the evening of the day that it reached me, I found it contradicted in *The London Chronicle*, which I could depend upon as authentick concerning you, Mr. Strahan being the printer of it. I did not see the paper in which "the approaching extinction of a bright luminary" was announced. Sir William Forbes told me of it; and he says, he saw me so uneasy, that he did not give me the report in such strong terms as he had read it. He afterwards sent me a letter from Mr. Langton to him, which relieved me much. I am, however, not quite easy, as I have not heard from you; and now I shall not have that comfort before I see you, for I set out for London to-morrow before the

---

[1] Alluding to a line in his *Vanity of Human Wishes*, describing Cardinal Wolsey in his state of elevation:—
'Through him the rays of regal bounty shine.'

post comes in. I hope to be with you on Wednesday morning; and I ever am, with the highest veneration, my dear Sir, your much obliged, faithful, and affectionate, humble servant.

'JAMES BOSWELL.'

On Wednesday, March 18, I arrived in London, and was informed by good Mr. Francis that his master was better, and was gone to Mr. Thrale's at Streatham, to which place I wrote to him, begging to know when he would be in town. He was not expected for some time; but next day having called on Dr. Taylor, in Dean's-yard, Westminster, I found him there, and was told he had come to town for a few hours. He met me with his usual kindness, but instantly returned to the writing of something on which he was employed when I came in, and on which he seemed much intent. Finding him thus engaged, I made my visit very short, and had no more of his conversation, except his expressing a serious regret that a friend of ours[1] was living at too much expence, considering how poor an appearance he made: 'If (said he,) a man has splendour from his expence, if he spends his money in pride or in pleasure, he has value: but if he lets others spend it for him, which is most commonly the case, he has no advantage from it.'

On Friday, March 20, I found him at his own house, sitting with Mrs. Williams, and was informed that the room formerly allotted to me was now appropriated to a charitable purpose; Mrs. Desmoulins,[2] and I think her daughter, and a Miss Carmichael, being all lodged in it. Such was his humanity, and such his generosity, that Mrs. Desmoulins herself told me, he allowed her half-a-guinea a week. Let it be remembered, that this was above a twelfth part of his pension.

His liberality, indeed, was at all periods of his life very remarkable. Mr. Howard, of Lichfield, at whose father's house Johnson had in his early years been kindly received, told me, that when he was a boy at the Charter-House, his father wrote

[1] [Langton. *Boswell Papers*, xiii. 109.]
[2] Daughter of Dr. Swinfen, Johnson's godfather, and widow of Mr. Desmoulins, a writing-master.

to him to go and pay a visit to Mr. Samuel Johnson, which he accordingly did, and found him in an upper room, of poor appearance. Johnson received him with much courteousness, and talked a great deal to him, as to a school-boy, of the course of his education, and other particulars. When he afterwards came to know and understand the high character of this great man, he recollected his condescension with wonder. He added, that when he was going away, Mr. Johnson presented him with half-a-guinea; and this, said Mr. Howard, was at a time when he probably had not another.

We retired from Mrs. Williams to another room. Tom Davies soon after joined us. He had now unfortunately failed in his circumstances, and was much indebted to Dr. Johnson's kindness for obtaining for him many alleviations of his distress. After he went away, Johnson blamed his folly in quitting the stage, by which he and his wife got five hundred pounds a year. I said, I believed it was owing to Churchill's attack upon him,

'He mouths a sentence, as curs mouth a bone.'

JOHNSON. 'I believe so too, Sir. But what a man is he, who is to be driven from the stage by a line? Another line would have driven him from his shop.'

I told him, that I was engaged as Counsel at the bar of the House of Commons to oppose a road-bill in the county of Stirling, and asked him what mode he would advise me to follow in addressing such an audience. JOHNSON. 'Why, Sir, you must provide yourself with a good deal of extraneous matter, which you are to produce occasionally, so as to fill up the time; for you must consider, that they do not listen much. If you begin with the strength of your cause, it may be lost before they begin to listen. When you catch a moment of attention, press the merits of the question upon them.' He said, as to one point of the merits, that he thought 'it would be a wrong thing to deprive the small landholders of the privilege of assessing themselves for making and repairing the high roads; *it was destroying a certain portion of liberty, without a good reason, which was always a bad thing.*' When I mentioned this observation next day to Mr. Wilkes, he pleasantly said, 'What! does *he* talk of liberty?

Liberty is as ridiculous in *his* mouth as *Religion* in *mine*.' Mr. Wilkes's advice, as to the best mode of speaking at the bar of the House of Commons, was not more respectful towards the senate, than that of Dr. Johnson. 'Be as impudent as you can, as merry as you can, and say whatever comes uppermost. Jack Lee is the best heard there of any Counsel; and he is the most impudent dog, and always abusing us.'

In my interview with Dr. Johnson this evening, I was quite easy, quite as his companion; upon which I find in my Journal the following reflection: 'So ready is my mind to suggest matter for dissatisfaction, that I felt a sort of regret that I was so easy. I missed that aweful reverence with which I used to contemplate Mr. Samuel Johnson, in the complex magnitude of his literary, moral, and religious character. I have a wonderful superstitious love of *mystery*; when, perhaps, the truth is, that it is owing to the cloudy darkness of my own mind. I should be glad that I am more advanced in my progress of being, so that I can view Dr. Johnson with a steadier and clearer eye. My dissatisfaction to-night was foolish. Would it not be foolish to regret that we shall have less mystery in a future state? That we "now see in a glass darkly," but shall "then see face to face"? ' This reflection, which I thus freely communicate, will be valued by the thinking part of my readers, who may have themselves experienced a similar state of mind.

He returned next day to Streatham, to Mr. Thrale's; where, as Mr. Strahan once complained to me, 'he was in a great measure absorbed from the society of his old friends.' I was kept in London by business, and wrote to him on the 27th, that a separation from him for a week, when we were so near, was equal to a separation for a year, when we were at four hundred miles distance. I went to Streatham on Monday, March 30. Before he appeared, Mrs. Thrale made a very characteristical remark:—'I do not know for certain what will please Dr. Johnson: but I know for certain that it will displease him to praise any thing, even what he likes, extravagantly.'

At dinner he laughed at querulous declamations against the age, on account of luxury,—increase of London,—scarcity of provisions,—and other such topicks. 'Houses (said he,) will be built till rents fall: and corn is more plentiful now than ever it was.'

I had before dinner repeated a ridiculous story told me by an old man who had been a passenger with me in the stage-coach to-day. Mrs. Thrale, having taken occasion to allude to it in talking to me, called it 'The story told you by the old *woman*.'— 'Now, Madam, (said I,) give me leave to catch you in the fact; it was not an old *woman*, but an old *man*, whom I mentioned as having told me this.' I presumed to take an opportunity, in presence of Johnson, of shewing this lively lady how ready she was, unintentionally, to deviate from exact authenticity of narration.

Thomas à Kempis (he observed,) must be a good book, as the world has opened its arms to receive it. It is said to have been printed, in one language or other, as many times as there have been months since it first came out.[1] I always was struck with this sentence in it: 'Be not angry that you cannot make others as you wish them to be, since you cannot make yourself as you wish to be.'

He said, 'I was angry with Hurd about Cowley, for having published a selection of his works: but, upon better consideration, I think there is no impropriety in a man's publishing as much as he chooses of any authour, if he does not put the rest out of the way. A man, for instance, may print the *Odes* of Horace alone.' He seemed to be in a more indulgent humour, than when this subject was discussed between him and Mr. Murphy.[2]

When we were at tea and coffee, there came in Lord Trimlestown, in whose family was an ancient Irish peerage, but it suffered by taking the generous side in the troubles of the last century.[3] He was a man of pleasing conversation, and was accompanied by a young gentleman, his son.

[1] The first edition was in 1492. Between that period and 1792, according to this account, there were 3600 editions. But this is very improbable. [M.]
[2] See *ante*, p. 737.
[3] Since this was written the attainder has been reversed; and Nicholas Barnewall is now a peer of Ireland with this title. The person mentioned in

I mentioned that I had in my possession the Life of Sir Robert Sibbald, the celebrated Scottish antiquary, and founder of the Royal College of Physicians at Edinburgh, in the original manuscript in his own handwriting; and that it was I believed the most natural and candid account of himself that ever was given by any man. As an instance, he tells that the Duke of Perth, then Chancellor of Scotland, pressed him very much to come over to the Roman Catholic faith: that he resisted all his Grace's arguments for a considerable time, till one day he felt himself, as it were, instantaneously convinced, and with tears in his eyes ran into the Duke's arms, and embraced the ancient religion; that he continued very steady in it for some time, and accompanied his Grace to London one winter, and lived in his household; that there he found the rigid fasting prescribed by the church very severe upon him; that this disposed him to reconsider the controversy, and having then seen that he was in the wrong, he returned to Protestantism. I talked of some time or other publishing this curious life. MRS. THRALE. 'I think you had as well let alone that publication. To discover such weakness, exposes a man when he is gone.' JOHNSON. 'Nay, it is an honest picture of human nature. How often are the primary motives of our greatest actions as small as Sibbald's, for his re-conversion.' MRS. THRALE. 'But may they not as well be forgotten?' JOHN-SON. 'No, Madam, a man loves to review his own mind. That is the use of a diary, or journal.' LORD TRIMLESTOWN. 'True, Sir. As the ladies love to see themselves in a glass; so a man likes to see himself in his journal.' BOSWELL. 'A very pretty allusion.' JOHNSON. 'Yes, indeed.' BOSWELL. 'And as a lady adjusts her dress before a mirror, a man adjusts his character by looking at his journal.' I next year found the very same thought in Atterbury's *Funeral Sermon on Lady Cutts*; where, having mentioned her *Diary*, he says, 'In this glass she every day dressed her mind.' This is a proof of coincidence, and not of plagiarism; for I had never read that sermon before.

Next morning, while we were at breakfast, Johnson gave a

the text had studied physick, and prescribed *gratis* to the poor. Hence arose the subsequent conversation. [M.]

very earnest recommendation of what he himself practised with the utmost conscientiousness: I mean a strict attention to truth, even in the most minute particulars. 'Accustom your children (said he,) constantly to this; if a thing happened at one window, and they, when relating it, say that it happened at another, do not let it pass, but instantly check them; you do not know where deviation from truth will end.' BOSWELL. 'It may come to the door: and when once an account is at all varied in one circumstance, it may by degrees be varied so as to be totally different from what really happened.' Our lively hostess, whose fancy was impatient of the rein, fidgeted at this, and ventured to say, 'Nay, this is too much. If Mr. Johnson should forbid me to drink tea, I would comply, as I should feel the restraint only twice a day; but little variations in narrative must happen a thousand times a day, if one is not perpetually watching.' JOHNSON. 'Well, Madam, and you *ought* to be perpetually watching. It is more from carelessness about truth than from intentional lying, that there is so much falsehood in the world.'

In his review of Dr. Warton's *Essay on the Writings and Genius of Pope*, Johnson has given the following salutary caution upon this subject:—

'Nothing but experience could evince the frequency of false information, or enable any man to conceive that so many groundless reports should be propagated, as every man of eminence may hear of himself. Some men relate what they think, as what they know; some men of confused memories and habitual inaccuracy, ascribe to one man what belongs to another; and some talk on, without thought or care. A few men are sufficient to broach falsehoods, which are afterwards innocently diffused by successive relaters.'[1]

Had he lived to read what Sir John Hawkins and Mrs. Piozzi have related concerning himself, how much would he have found his observation illustrated. He was indeed so much impressed with the prevalence of falsehood, voluntary or unintentional, that I never knew any person who upon hearing an extraordinary circumstance told, discovered more of the *incredulus odi*. He

[1] *Literary Magazine*, 1756, p. 37.

would say, with a significant look and decisive tone, 'It is not so. Do not tell this again.'[1] He inculcated upon all his friends the importance of perpetual vigilance against the slightest degrees of falsehood; the effect of which, as Sir Joshua Reynolds observed to me, has been, that all who were of his *school* are distinguished for a love of truth and accuracy, which they would not have possessed in the same degree, if they had not been acquainted with Johnson.

Talking of ghosts, he said, 'It is wonderful that five thousand years have now elapsed since the creation of the world, and still it is undecided whether or not there has ever been an instance of the spirit of any person appearing after death. All argument is against it; but all belief is for it.'

He said, 'John Wesley's conversation is good, but he is never at leisure. He is always obliged to go at a certain hour. This is very disagreeable to a man who loves to fold his legs and have out his talk, as I do.'

On Friday, April 3, I dined with him in London, in a company where were present several eminent men, whom I shall not name, but distinguish their parts in the conversation by different letters.[2]

F. 'I have been looking at this famous antique marble dog of Mr. Jennings, valued at a thousand guineas, said to be Alcibiades's dog.' JOHNSON. 'His tail then must be docked. That was the mark of Alcibiades's dog.' E. 'A thousand guineas! The representation of no animal whatever is worth so much. At this rate a dead dog would indeed be better than a living lion.' JOHNSON. 'Sir, it is not the worth of the thing, but of the skill

---

[1] The following plausible but overprudent counsel on this subject is given by an Italian writer [Dante], quoted by '*Rhedi de generatione insectarum,*' with the epithet of '*divini poetæ*:'

> '*Sempre a quel ver ch'ha faccia di menzogna*
> *De' l'uom chiuder le labbra fin ch'el pote,*
> *Però che senza colpa fa vergogna.*'

Dante, *Inf.* xi. 124

['Always to that truth which has the appearance of a lie a man should close his lips as much as he can, lest, without sin, be he put to shame.']

[2] [C = Chemist (Fordyce), E = Edmund (Burke), F = Fitzpatrick (Lord Upper Ossory), I or J = Infidel (Gibbon), P = Painter (Reynolds), R = R. B. Sheridan. J. B.'s *Memorandum.* The occasion was a meeting of the Literary Club.]

in forming it which is so highly estimated. Every thing that enlarges the sphere of human powers, that shows man he can do what he thought he could not do, is valuable. The first man who balanced a straw upon his nose; Johnson, who rode upon three horses at a time; in short, all such men deserved the applause of mankind, not on account of the use of what they did, but of the dexterity which they exhibited.' Boswell. 'Yet a misapplication of time and assiduity is not to be encouraged. Addison, in one of his *Spectators*, commends the judgement of a King, who, as a suitable reward to a man that by long perseverance had attained to the art of throwing a barley-corn through the eye of a needle, gave him a bushel of barley.' Johnson. 'He must have been a King of Scotland, where barley is scarce.' F. 'One of the most remarkable antique figures of an animal is the boar at Florence.' Johnson. 'The first boar that is well made in marble should be preserved as a wonder. When men arrive at a facility of making boars well, then the workmanship is not of such value, but they should however be preserved as examples, and as a greater security for the restoration of the art, should it be lost.'

E. 'We hear prodigious complaints at present of emigration. I am convinced that emigration makes a country more populous.' J. 'That sounds very much like a paradox.' E. 'Exportation of men, like exportation of all other commodities, makes more be produced.' Johnson. 'But there would be more people were there not emigration, provided there were food for more.' E. 'No; leave a few breeders, and you'll have more people than if there were no emigration.' Johnson. 'Nay, Sir, it is plain there will be more people, if there are more breeders. Thirty cows in good pasture will produce more calves than ten cows, provided they have good bulls.' E. 'There are bulls enough in Ireland.' Johnson. (smiling,) 'So, Sir, I should think from your argument.' Boswell. 'You said, exportation of men, like exportation of other commodities, makes more be produced. But a bounty is given to encourage the exportation of corn, and no bounty is given for the exportation of men; though, indeed, those who go, gain by it.' R. 'But the bounty on the exportation

of corn is paid at home.' E. 'That's the same thing.' JOHNSON.
'No, Sir.' R. 'A man who stays at home, gains nothing by his
neighbours emigrating.' BOSWELL. 'I can understand that
emigration may be the cause that more people may be produced
in a country; but the country will not therefore be the more
populous; for the people issue from it. It can only be said that
there is a flow of people. It is an encouragement to have children,
to know that they can get a living by emigration.' R. 'Yes, if
there were an emigration of children under six years of age. But
they don't emigrate till they could earn their livelihood in some
way at home.' C. 'It is remarkable that the most unhealthy
countries, where there are the most destructive diseases, such
as Egypt and Bengal, are the most populous.' JOHNSON.
'Countries which are the most populous have the most destructive diseases. *That* is the true state of the proposition.' C. 'Holland is very unhealthy, yet it is exceedingly populous.' JOHN-
SON. 'I know not that Holland is unhealthy. But its populousness
is owing to an influx of people from all other countries. Disease
cannot be the cause of populousness, for it not only carries off a
great proportion of the people, but those who are left are
weakened and unfit for the purposes of increase.'

R. 'Mr. E., I don't mean to flatter, but when posterity reads
one of your speeches in Parliament, it will be difficult to believe
that you took so much pains, knowing with certainty that it
could produce no effect, that not one vote would be gained by
it.' E. 'Waiving your compliment to me, I shall say in general,
that it is very well worth while for a man to take pains to speak
well in Parliament. A man, who has vanity, speaks to display
his talents; and if a man speaks well, he gradually establishes a
certain reputation and consequence in the general opinion, which
sooner or later will have its political reward. Besides, though
not one vote is gained, a good speech has its effect. Though an
act which has been ably opposed passes into a law, yet in its
progress it is modelled, it is softened in such a manner, that we
see plainly the Minister has been told, that the Members attached
to him are so sensible of its injustice or absurdity from what they
have heard, that it must be altered.' JOHNSON. 'And, Sir, there

is a gratification of pride. Though we cannot out-vote them we will out-argue them. They shall not do wrong without its being shown both to themselves and to the world.' E. 'The House of Commons is a mixed body. (I except the Minority, which I hold to be pure, [smiling,] but I take the whole House.) It is a mass by no means pure; but neither is it wholly corrupt, though there is a large proportion of corruption in it. There are many members who generally go with the Minister, who will not go all lengths. There are many honest well-meaning country gentle-men who are in parliament only to keep up the consequence of their families. Upon most of these a good speech will have influence.' JOHNSON. 'We are all more or less governed by interest. But interest will not make us do every thing. In a case which admits of doubt, we try to think on the side which is for our interest, and generally bring ourselves to act accordingly. But the subject must admit of diversity of colouring; it must receive a colour on that side. In the House of Commons there are members enough who will not vote what is grossly unjust or absurd. No, Sir, there must always be right enough, or appearance of right, to keep wrong in countenance.' BOSWELL. 'There is surely always a majority in parliament who have places, or who want to have them, and who therefore will be generally ready to support government without requiring any pretext.' E. 'True, Sir; that majority will always follow

"Quo clamor vocat et turba faventium." '[1]

BOSWELL. 'Well now, let us take the common phrase, Place-hunters. I thought they had hunted without regard to any thing, just as their huntsmen, the Minister, leads, looking only to the prey.'[2] J. 'But taking your metaphor, you know that in hunting there are few so desperately keen as to follow without reserve.

---

[1] ['Whither the shouting calls us and the applauding populace'. Horace, *Odes* III. xxiv. 46. (Wickham.)]
[2] Lord Bolingbroke, who, however detestable as a metaphysician, must be allowed to have had admirable talents as a political writer, thus describes the House of Commons, in his 'Letter to Sir William Wyndham:'—'You know the nature of that assembly; they grow, like hounds, fond of the man who shews them game, and by whose halloo they are used to be encouraged.'

Some do not choose to leap ditches and hedges and risk their necks, or gallop over steeps, or even to dirty themselves in bogs and mire.' BOSWELL. 'I am glad there are some good, quiet, moderate political hunters.' E. 'I believe, in any body of men in England, I should have been in the Minority; I have always been in the Minority.' P. 'The House of Commons resembles a private company. How seldom is any man convinced by another's argument; passion and pride rise against it.' R. 'What would be the consequence, if a Minister, sure of a majority in the House of Commons, should resolve that there should be no speaking at all upon his side.' E. 'He must soon go out. That has been tried; but it was found it would not do.'

E. 'The Irish language is not primitive; it is Teutonick, a mixture of the northern tongues: it has much English in it.' JOHNSON. 'It may have been radically Teutonick; but English and High Dutch have no similarity to the eye, though radically the same. Once, when looking into Low Dutch, I found, in a whole page, only one word similar to English; *stroem*, like *stream*, and it signified *tide*.' E. 'I remember having seen a Dutch Sonnet, in which I found this word, *roesnopies*. Nobody would at first think that this could be English; but, when we enquire, we find *roes*, rose, and *nopie*, knob; so we have *rosebuds*.'

JOHNSON. 'I have been reading Thicknesse's travels, which I think are entertaining.' BOSWELL. 'What, Sir, a good book?' JOHNSON. 'Yes, Sir, to read once; I do not say you are to make a study of it, and digest it; and I believe it to be a true book in his intention. All travellers generally mean to tell truth; though Thicknesse observes, upon Smollet's account of his alarming a whole town in France by firing a blunderbuss, and frightening a French nobleman till he made him tie on his portmanteau, that he would be loth to say Smollet had told two lies in one page; but he had found the only town in France where these things could have happened. Travellers must often be mistaken. In every thing, except where mensuration can be applied, they may honestly differ. There has been, of late, a strange turn in travellers to be displeased.'

E. 'From the experience which I have had,—and I have had a

great deal,—I have learnt to think *better* of mankind.' JOHNSON. 'From my experience I have found them worse in commercial dealings, more disposed to cheat, than I had any notion of; but more disposed to do one another good than I had conceived.' J. 'Less just and more beneficent.' JOHNSON. 'And really it is wonderful, considering how much attention is necessary for men to take care of themselves, and ward off immediate evils which press upon them, it is wonderful how much they do for others. As it is said of the greatest liar, that he tells more truth than falsehood; so it may be said of the worst man, that he does more good than evil.' BOSWELL. 'Perhaps from experience men may be found *happier* than we suppose.' JOHNSON. 'No, Sir; the more we enquire, we shall find men the less happy.' P. 'As to thinking better or worse of mankind from experience, some cunning people will not be satisfied unless they have put men to the test, as they think. There is a very good story told of Sir Godfrey Kneller, in his character of a Justice of the peace. A gentleman brought his servant before him, upon an accusation of having stolen some money from him; but it having come out that he had laid it purposely in the servant's way, in order to try his honesty, Sir Godfrey sent the master to prison.'[1] JOHNSON. 'To resist temptation once, is not a sufficient proof of honesty. If a servant, indeed, were to resist the continued temptation of silver lying in a window, as some people let it lye, when he is sure his master does not know how much there is of it, he would give a strong proof of honesty. But this is a proof to which you have no right to put a man. You know, humanly speaking, there is a certain degree of temptation which will overcome any virtue. Now, in so far as you approach temptation to a man, you do him an injury; and, if he is overcome, you share his guilt.' P. 'And, when once overcome, it is easier for him to be got the better of again.' BOSWELL. 'Yes, you are his seducer; you have

---

[1] Pope thus introduces this story:
> 'Faith in such case if you should prosecute,
> I think Sir Godfrey should decide the suit,
> Who sent the thief who [that] stole the cash away,
> And punish'd him that put it in his way.'
>   *Imitations of Horace,* book II. epist, ii.

debauched him. I have known a man[1] resolve to put friendship to the test, by asking a friend to lend him money merely with that view, when he did not want it.' JOHNSON. 'That is very wrong, Sir. Your friend may be a narrow man, and yet have many good qualities: narrowness may be his only fault. Now you are trying his general character as a friend, by one particular singly, in which he happens to be defective, when, in truth, his character is composed of many particulars.'

E. 'I understand the hogshead of claret, which this society was favoured with by our friend the Dean, is nearly out; I think he should be written to, to send another of the same kind. Let the request be made with a happy ambiguity of expression, so that we may have the chance of his sending *it* also as a present.' JOHNSON. 'I am willing to offer my services as secretary on this occasion.' P. 'As many as are for Dr. Johnson being secretary hold up your hands.—Carried unanimously.' BOSWELL. 'He will be our Dictator.' JOHNSON. 'No, the company is to dictate to me. I am only to write for wine; and I am quite disinterested, as I drink none; I shall not be suspected of having forged the application. I am no more than humble *scribe*.' E. 'Then you shall *pre*scribe.' BOSWELL. 'Very well. The first play of words to-day.' J. 'No, no; the *bulls* in Ireland.' JOHNSON. 'Were I your Dictator you should have no wine. It would be my business *cavere ne quid detrimenti Respublica caperet*,[2] and wine is dangerous. Rome was ruined by luxury,' (smiling.) E. 'If you allow no wine as Dictator, you shall not have me for your master of horse.'

On Saturday, April 4, I drank tea with Johnson at Dr. Taylor's, where he had dined. He entertained us with an account of a tragedy written by a Dr. Kennedy, (not the Lisbon physician.) 'The catastrophe of it (said he,) was, that a King, who was jealous of his Queen with his prime-minister, castrated himself.[3]

---

[1] [Boswell. *Powell.*]

[2] ['To take care that the State suffer no harm.']

[3] The reverse of the story of *Combabus*, on which Mr. David Hume told Lord Macartney, that a friend of his had written a tragedy. It is, however, possible that I may have been inaccurate in my perception of what Dr. Johnson related, and that he may have been talking of the same ludicrous

This tragedy was actually shewn about in manuscript to several people, and, amongst others, to Mr. Fitzherbert, who repeated to me two lines of the Prologue:

> "Our hero's fate we have but gently touch'd;
> The fair might blame us, if it were less couch'd."

It is hardly to be believed what absurd and indecent images men will introduce into their writings, without being sensible of the absurdity and indecency. I remember Lord Orrery told me, that there was a pamphlet written against Sir Robert Walpole, the whole of which was an allegory on the PHALLICK OBSCENITY. The Duchess of Buckingham asked Lord Orrery *who* this person was? He answered, he did not know. She said, she would send to Mr. Pulteney, who, she supposed, could inform her. So then, to prevent her from making herself ridiculous, Lord Orrery sent her Grace a note, in which he gave her to understand what was meant.'

He was very silent this evening; and read in a variety of books: suddenly throwing down one, and taking up another.

He talked of going to Streatham that night. TAYLOR. 'You'll be robbed if you do: or you must shoot a highwayman. Now I would rather be robbed than do that; I would not shoot a highwayman.' JOHNSON. 'But I would rather shoot him in the instant when he is attempting to rob me, than afterwards swear against him at the Old-Bailey, to take away his life, after he has robbed me. I am surer I am right in the one case than in the other. I may be mistaken as to the man, when I swear: I cannot be mistaken, if I shoot him in the act. Besides, we feel less reluctance to take away a man's life, when we are heated by the injury, than to do it at a distance of time by an oath, after we have cooled.' BOSWELL. 'So, Sir, you would rather act from the motive of private passion, than that of publick advantage.' JOHNSON. 'Nay, Sir, when I shoot the highwayman I act from both.' BOSWELL. 'Very well, very well.—There is no catching him.' JOHNSON. 'At the

tragical subject that Mr. Hume had mentioned. [The story of Combabus, which was originally told by Lucian, may be found in Bayle's *Dictionary*. —M.]

same time one does not know what to say. For perhaps one may, a year after, hang himself from uneasiness for having shot a man.[1] Few minds are fit to be trusted with so great a thing.' BOSWELL. 'Then, Sir, you would not shoot him?' JOHNSON. 'But I might be vexed afterwards for that too.'

Thrale's carriage not having come for him, as he expected, I accompanied him some part of the way home to his own house. I told him, that I had talked of him to Mr. Dunning a few days before, and had said, that in his company we did not so much interchange conversation, as listen to him; and that Dunning observed, upon this, 'One is always willing to listen to Dr. Johnson:' to which I answered, 'That is a great deal from you, Sir.'—'Yes, Sir, (said Johnson,) a great deal indeed. Here is a man willing to listen, to whom the world is listening all the rest of the year.' BOSWELL. 'I think, Sir, it is right to tell one man of such a handsome thing, which has been said of him by another. It tends to increase benevolence.' JOHNSON. 'Undoubtedly it is right, Sir.'

On Tuesday, April 7, I breakfasted with him at his house. He said, 'nobody was content.' I mentioned to him a respectable person[2] in Scotland whom he knew; and I asserted, that I really believed he was always content. JOHNSON. 'No, Sir, he is not content with the present; he has always some new scheme, some new plantation, something which is future. You know he was not content as a widower; for he married again.' BOSWELL. 'But he is not restless.' JOHNSON. 'Sir, he is only locally at rest. A chymist is locally at rest; but his mind is hard at work. This gentleman has done with external exertions. It is too late for

[1] The late Duke of Montrose was generally said to have been uneasy on that account; but I can contradict the report from his Grace's own authority. As he used to admit me to very easy conversation with him, I took the liberty to introduce the subject. His Grace told me, that when riding one night near London, he was attacked by two highwaymen on horseback, and that he instantly shot one of them, upon which the other galloped off; that his servant, who was very well mounted, proposed to pursue him and take him, but that his Grace said, 'No, we have had blood enough: I hope the man may live to repent.' His Grace, upon my presuming to put the question, assured me, that his mind was not at all clouded by what he had thus done in self-defence.

[2] [Lord Auchinleck. *Boswell's 1778 Journal.*]

him to engage in distant projects.' BOSWELL. 'He seems to amuse himself quite well; to have his attention fixed, and his tranquillity preserved by very small matters. I have tried this; but it would not do with me.' JOHNSON. (laughing,) 'No, Sir; it must be born with a man to be contented to take up with little things. Women have a great advantage that they may take up with little things, without disgracing themselves: a man cannot, except with fiddling. Had I learnt to fiddle, I should have done nothing else.' BOSWELL. 'Pray, Sir, did you ever play on any musical instrument?' JOHNSON. 'No, Sir. I once bought me a flagelet; but I never made out a tune.' BOSWELL. 'A flagelet, Sir!—so small an instrument?[1] I should have liked to hear you play on the violoncello. *That* should have been *your* instrument.' JOHNSON. 'Sir, I might as well have played on the violoncello as another; but I should have done nothing else. No, Sir; a man would never undertake great things, could he be amused with small. I once tried knotting. Dempster's sister undertook to teach me; but I could not learn it.' BOSWELL. 'So, Sir; it will be related in pompous narrative, "Once for his amusement he tried knotting; nor did this Hercules disdain the distaff." ' JOHNSON. 'Knitting of stockings is a good amusement. As a freeman of Aberdeen I should be a knitter of stockings.' He asked me to go down with him and dine at Mr. Thrale's at Streatham, to which I agreed. I had lent him *An Account of Scotland, in 1702*, written by a man of various enquiry,[2] an English chaplain to a regiment stationed there. JOHNSON. 'It is sad stuff, Sir, miserably written, as books in general then were. There is now an elegance of style universally diffused. No man now writes so ill as Martin's *Account of the Hebrides* is written. A man could not write so ill, if he should try. Set a merchant's clerk now to write, and he'll do better.'

He talked to me with serious concern of a certain female

---

[1] When I told this to Miss Seward, she smiled, and repeated, with admirable readiness, from *Acis and Galatea*,
> 'Bring me a hundred reeds of ample growth,
> To make a pipe for my CAPACIOUS MOUTH.'

[2] [The Rev. Thomas Morer. The second edition, 1715, gives the author's name.]

friend's[1] 'laxity of narration, and inattention to truth.'—'I am as much vexed (said he,) at the ease with which she hears it mentioned to her, as at the thing itself. I told her, "Madam, you are contented to hear every day said to you, what the highest of mankind have died for, rather than bear."—You know, Sir, the highest of mankind have died rather than bear to be told they had uttered a falsehood. Do talk to her of it: I am weary.'

BOSWELL. 'Was not Dr. John Campbell a very inaccurate man in his narrative, Sir? He once told me, that he drank thirteen bottles of port at a sitting.'[2] JOHNSON. 'Why, Sir, I do not know that Campbell ever lied with pen and ink; but you could not entirely depend on any thing he told you in conversation, if there was fact mixed with it. However, I loved Campbell: he was a solid orthodox man: he had a reverence for religion. Though defective in practice, he was religious in principle; and he did nothing grossly wrong that I have heard.'

I told him, that I had been present the day before, when Mrs. Montagu, the literary lady, sat to Miss Reynolds for her picture; and that she said, 'she had bound up Mr. Gibbon's *History* without the last two offensive chapters; for that she thought the book so far good, as it gave, in an elegant manner, the substance of the bad writers *medii ævi*,[3] which the late Lord Lyttelton advised her to read.' JOHNSON. 'Sir, she has not read them: she shews none of this impetuosity to me: she does not know Greek, and, I fancy, knows little Latin. She is willing you should think

---

[1] [Mrs. Thrale, *Boswell's 1788 Journal.*]

[2] Lord Macartney observes upon this passage, 'I have heard him tell many things, which, though embellished by their mode of narrative, had their foundation in truth; but I never remember any thing approaching to this. If he had written it, I should have supposed some wag had put the figure of one before the three.'—I am, however, absolutely certain that Dr. Campbell told me it, and I gave particular attention to it, being myself a lover of wine, and therefore curious to hear whatever is remarkable concerning drinking. There can be no doubt that some men can drink, without suffering any injury, such a quantity as to others appears incredible. It is but fair to add, that Dr. Campbell told me, he took a very long time to this great potation; and I have heard Dr. Johnson say, 'Sir, if a man drinks very slowly, and lets one glass evaporate before he takes another, I know not how long he may drink.' Dr. Campbell mentioned a Colonel of Militia who sat with him all the time, and drank equally.

[3] ['of the middle ages'.]

910

she knows them; but she does not say she does.' BOSWELL. 'Mr. Harris, who was present, agreed with her.' JOHNSON. 'Harris was laughing at her, Sir. Harris is a sound sullen scholar; he does not like interlopers. Harris, however, is a prig, and a bad prig.[1] I looked into his book, and thought he did not understand his own system.' BOSWELL. 'He says plain things in a formal and abstract way, to be sure: but his method is good: for to have clear notions upon any subject, we must have recourse to analytick arrangement.' JOHNSON. 'Sir, it is what every body does, whether they will or no. But sometimes things may be made darker by definition. I see a *cow*, I define her, *Animal quadrupes ruminans cornutum.*[2] But a goat ruminates, and a cow may have no horns. *Cow* is plainer.' BOSWELL. 'I think Dr. Franklin's definition of *Man* a good one—"A tool-making animal."' JOHNSON. 'But many a man never made a tool; and suppose a man without arms, he could not make a tool.'

Talking of drinking wine, he said, 'I did not leave off wine because I could not bear it; I have drunk three bottles of port without being the worse for it. University College has witnessed this.' BOSWELL. 'Why then, Sir, did you leave it off?' JOHNSON. 'Why, Sir, because it is so much better for a man to be sure that he is never to be intoxicated, never to lose the power over himself. I shall not begin to drink wine again, till I grow old, and want it.' BOSWELL. 'I think, Sir, you once said to me, that not to drink wine was a great deduction from life.' JOHNSON. 'It is a diminution of pleasure, to be sure; but I do not say a diminution of happiness. There is more happiness in being rational.' BOSWELL. 'But if we could have pleasure always, should not we be happy? The greatest part of men would compound for pleasure.' JOHNSON. 'Supposing we could have

---

[1] What my friend meant by these words concerning the amiable philosopher of Salisbury, I am at a loss to understand. A friend suggests, that Johnson thought his *manner* as a writer affected, while at the same time the *matter* did not compensate for that fault. In short, that he meant to make a remark quite different from that which a *celebrated gentleman** made on a very eminent physician†: 'He is a coxcomb, but a *satisfactory coxcomb.*'

     * [W. G. Hamilton. *Boswell Papers*, xvii. 76.]
     † [Dr. Richard Warren. *Ib.*]
[2] ['A quadruped which chews the cud and has horns.']

pleasure always, an intellectual man would not compound for it. The greatest part of men would compound, because the greatest part of men are gross.' BOSWELL. 'I allow there may be greater pleasure than from wine. I have had more pleasure from your conversation, I have indeed; I assure you I have.' JOHNSON. 'When we talk of pleasure, we mean sensual pleasure. When a man says, he had pleasure with a woman, he does not mean conversation, but something of a very different nature. Philosophers tell you, that pleasure is *contrary* to happiness. Gross men prefer animal pleasure. So there are men who have preferred living among savages. Now what a wretch must he be, who is content with such conversation as can be had among savages! You may remember an officer at Fort Augustus, who had served in America, told us of a woman whom they were obliged to *bind*, in order to get her back from savage life.' BOSWELL. 'She must have been an animal, a beast.' JOHNSON. 'Sir, she was a speaking cat.'

I mentioned to him that I had become very weary in a company where I heard not a single intellectual sentence, except that 'a man who had been settled ten years in Minorca was become a much inferiour man to what he was in London, because a man's mind grows narrow in a narrow place.' JOHNSON. 'A man's mind grows narrow in a narrow place, whose mind is enlarged only because he has lived in a large place: but what is got by books and thinking is preserved in a narrow place as well as in a large place. A man cannot know modes of life as well in Minorca as in London; but he may study mathematicks as well in Minorca.' BOSWELL. 'I don't know, Sir: if you had remained ten years in the Isle of Col, you would not have been the man that you now are.' JOHNSON. 'Yes, Sir, if I had been there from fifteen to twenty-five; but not if from twenty-five to thirty-five.' BOSWELL. 'I own, Sir, the spirits which I have in London make me do every thing with more readiness and vigour. I can talk twice as much in London as any where else.'

Of Goldsmith he said, 'He was not an agreeable companion, for he talked always for fame. A man who does so never can be pleasing. The man who talks to unburthen his mind is the man to delight you. An eminent friend of ours[1] is not so agreeable as the variety of his knowledge would otherwise make him, because he talks partly from ostentation.'

Soon after our arrival at Thrale's, I heard one of the maids calling eagerly on another, to go to Dr. Johnson. I wondered what this could mean. I afterwards learnt, that it was to give her a Bible, which he had brought from London as a present to her.

He was for a considerable time occupied in reading *Mémoires de Fontenelle*, leaning and swinging upon the low gate into the court, without his hat.

I looked into Lord Kames's *Sketches of the History of Man*; and mentioned to Dr. Johnson his censure of Charles the Fifth, for celebrating his funeral obsequies in his life-time, which, I told him, I had been used to think a solemn and affecting act. Johnson. 'Why, Sir, a man may dispose his mind to think so of that act of Charles; but it is so liable to ridicule, that if one man out of ten thousand laughs at it, he'll make the other nine thousand nine hundred and ninety-nine laugh too.' I could not agree with him in this.

Sir John Pringle had expressed a wish that I would ask Dr. Johnson's opinion what were the best English sermons for style. I took an opportunity to-day of mentioning several to him.— '*Atterbury?*' Johnson. 'Yes, Sir, one of the best.' Boswell. '*Tillotson?*' Johnson. 'Why, not now. I should not advise a preacher at this day to imitate Tillotson's style: though I don't know; I should be cautious of objecting to what has been applauded by so many suffrages.—*South* is one of the best, if you except his peculiarities, and his violence, and sometimes coarseness of language.—*Seed* has a very fine style; but he is not very theological.—*Jortin's* sermons are very elegant.— *Sherlock's* style too is very elegant, though he has not made it his principal study.—And you may add *Smallridge*. All the latter preachers have a good style. Indeed, nobody now talks much of style: every body composes pretty well. There are no such unharmonious periods as there were a hundred years ago. I should recommend Dr. *Clarke's* sermons, were he orthodox.

[1] [Burke. *Mrs. Piozzi, Boswell's 1778 Journal.*]

However, it is very well known *where* he was not orthodox, which was upon the doctrine of the Trinity, as to which he is a condemned heretick; so one is aware of it.' BOSWELL. 'I like Ogden's *Sermons on Prayer* very much, both for neatness of style and subtilty of reasoning.' JOHNSON. 'I should like to read all that Ogden has written.' BOSWELL. 'What I wish to know is, what sermons afford the best specimen of English pulpit eloquence.' JOHNSON. 'We have no sermons addressed to the passions that are good for any thing; if you mean that kind of eloquence.' A CLERGYMAN:[1] (whose name I do not recollect.) 'Were not Dodd's sermons addressed to the passions?' JOHNSON. 'They were nothing, Sir, be they addressed to what they may.'

At dinner, Mrs. Thrale expressed a wish to go and see Scotland. JOHNSON. 'Seeing Scotland, Madam, is only seeing a worse England. It is seeing the flower gradually fade away to the naked stalk. Seeing the Hebrides, indeed, is seeing quite a different scene.'

Our poor friend, Mr. Thomas Davies, was soon to have a benefit at Drury-lane theatre, as some relief to his unfortunate circumstances. We were all warmly interested for his success, and had contributed to it. However, we thought there was no harm in having our joke, when he could not be hurt by it. I proposed that he should be brought on to speak a Prologue upon the occasion; and I began to mutter fragments of what it might be: as, that when now grown *old*, he was obliged to cry, 'Poor Tom's *a-cold*;'—that he owned he had been driven from the stage by a Churchill, but that this was no disgrace, for a Churchill had beat the French;—that he had been satyrised as 'mouthing a sentence as curs mouth a bone,' but he was now glad of a bone to pick.—'Nay, (said Johnson,) I would have him to say,

"Mad Tom is come to see the world again."'

He and I returned to town in the evening. Upon the road, I endeavoured to maintain, in argument, that a landed gentleman

[1] [Mr. Embry, *Mrs. Piozzi.*]

is not under any obligation to reside upon his estate; and that by living in London he does no injury to his country. J O H N S O N. 'Why, Sir, he does no injury to his country in general, because the money which he draws from it gets back again in circulation; but to his particular district, his particular parish, he does an injury. All that he has to give away is not given to those who have the first claim to it. And though I have said that the money circulates back, it is a long time before that happens. Then, Sir, a man of family and estate ought to consider himself as having the charge of a district, over which he is to diffuse civility and happiness.'

Next day I found him at home in the morning. He praised Delany's *Observations on Swift*; said that his book and Lord Orrery's might both be true, though one viewed Swift more, and the other less favourably; and that, between both, we might have a complete notion of Swift.

Talking of a man's resolving to deny himself the use of wine, from moral and religious considerations, he said, 'He must not doubt about it. When one doubts as to pleasure, we know what will be the conclusion. I now no more think of drinking wine, than a horse does. The wine upon the table is no more for me, than for the dog that is under the table.'

On Thursday, April 9, I dined with him at Sir Joshua Reynolds's, with the Bishop of St. Asaph, (Dr. Shipley,) Mr. Allan Ramsay, Mr. Gibbon, Mr. Cambridge, and Mr. Langton. Mr. Ramsay had lately returned from Italy, and entertained us with his observations upon Horace's villa, which he had examined with great care. I relished this much, as it brought fresh into my mind what I had viewed with great pleasure thirteen years before. The Bishop, Dr. Johnson, and Mr. Cambridge, joined with Mr. Ramsay, in recollecting the various lines in Horace relating to the subject.

Horace's journey to Brundusium being mentioned, Johnson observed, that the brook which he describes is to be seen now, exactly as at that time, and that he had often wondered how it happened, that small brooks, such as this, kept the same situation for ages, notwithstanding earthquakes, by which even mountains have been changed, and agriculture, which produces such a variation upon the surface of the earth. CAMBRIDGE. 'A Spanish writer[1] has this thought in a poetical conceit. After observing that most of the solid structures of Rome are totally perished, while the Tiber remains the same, he adds,

> "*Lo que èra Firme huió solamente,*
> *Lo Fugitivo permanece y dura.*" '[2]

JOHNSON. 'Sir, that is taken from *Janus Vitalis*:

> "——————————— *immota labescunt;*
> *Et quæ perpetuò sunt agitata manent.*" '[3]

The Bishop said, it appeared from Horace's writings that he was a cheerful contented man. JOHNSON. 'We have no reason to believe that, my Lord. Are we to think Pope was happy, because he says so in his writings? We see in his writings what he wished the state of his mind to appear. Dr. Young, who pined for preferment, talks with contempt of it in his writings, and affects to despise every thing that he did not despise.' BISHOP OF ST. ASAPH. 'He was like other chaplains, looking for vacancies: but that is not peculiar to the clergy. I remember when I was with the army, after the battle of Lafeldt, the officers seriously grumbled that no general was killed.' CAMBRIDGE. 'We may believe Horace more when he says,

> "*Romæ Tibur amem, ventosus Tibure Romam;*"[4]

than when he boasts of his consistency:

> "*Me constare mihi scis, et decedere tristem,*
> *Quandocunque trahunt invisa negotia Romam.*" '[5]

---

[1] [Quevedo y Villegas.]

[2] ['Only that which was static disappeared; what is fugitive remains and endures.']

[3] [*labescunt* should be *labascunt.* 'The motionless disappears; what is in constant motion abides.']

[4] ['At Rome I love Tibur, fickle as the wind, at Tibur Rome. *Epistles* I. viii. 12. (Wickham.)]

[5] ['You know that I am consistent, and that it is with a heavy heart that I go away whenever the business which I hate draws me to Rome.' *Ib.* xiv. 16.]

BOSWELL. 'How hard is it that man can never be at rest.'
RAMSAY. 'It is not in his nature to be at rest. When he is at
rest, he is in the worst state that he can be in; for he has nothing
to agitate him. He is then like the man in the Irish song,

> "There liv'd a young man in Ballinacrazy.
> Who wanted a wife for to make him un*ai*sy." '

Goldsmith being mentioned, Johnson observed, that it was
long before his merit came to be acknowledged. That he once
complained to him, in ludicrous terms of distress, 'Whenever I
write any thing, the publick *make a point* to know nothing about
it:' but that his *Traveller* brought him into high reputation.
LANGTON. 'There is not one bad line in that poem; not one of
Dryden's careless verses.' SIR JOSHUA. 'I was glad to hear
Charles Fox say, it was one of the finest poems in the English
language.' LANGTON. 'Why was you glad? You surely had no
doubt of this before.' JOHNSON. 'No; the merit of *The Traveller*
is so well established, that Mr. Fox's praise cannot augment it,
nor censure diminish it.' SIR JOSHUA. 'But his friends may suspect they had too great a partiality for him.' JOHNSON. 'Nay,
Sir, the partiality of his friends was all against him. It was with
difficulty we could give him a hearing. Goldsmith had no settled
notions upon any subject; so he talked always at random. It
seemed to be his intention to blurt out whatever was in his mind,
and see what would become of it. He was angry too, when
catched in an absurdity; but it did not prevent him from falling
into another the next minute. I remember Chamier, after talking
with him for some time, said, "Well, I do believe he wrote this
poem himself: and, let me tell you, that is believing a great
deal." Chamier once asked him, what he meant by *slow*, the last
word in the first line of *The Traveller*,

> "Remote, unfriended, melancholy, slow."

Did he mean tardiness of locomotion? Goldsmith, who would
say something without consideration, answered, "Yes." I was
sitting by, and said, "No, Sir; you do not mean tardiness of
locomotion; you mean, that sluggishness of mind which comes
upon a man in solitude." Chamier believed then that I had

written the line as much as if he had seen me write it. Goldsmith, however, was a man, who, whatever he wrote, did it better than any other man could do. He deserved a place in Westminster-Abbey, and every year he lived, would have deserved it better. He had, indeed, been at no pains to fill his mind with knowledge. He transplanted it from one place to another; and it did not settle in his mind; so he could not tell what was in his own books.'

We talked of living in the country. JOHNSON. 'No wise man will go to live in the country, unless he has something to do which can be better done in the country. For instance: if he is to shut himself up for a year to study a science, it is better to look out to the fields, than to an opposite wall. Then, if a man walks out in the country, there is nobody to keep him from walking in again: but if a man walks out in London, he is not sure when he shall walk in again. A great city is, to be sure, the school for studying life; and "The proper study of mankind is man," as Pope observes.' BOSWELL. 'I fancy London is the best place in the world for society; though I have heard that the very first society of Paris is still beyond any thing that we have here.' JOHNSON. 'Sir, I question if in Paris such a company as is sitting round this table could be got together in less than half a year. They talk in France of the felicity of men and women living together: the truth is, that there the men are not higher than the women, they know no more than the women do, and they are not held down in their conversation by the presence of women.' RAMSAY. 'Literature is upon the growth, it is in its spring in France. Here it is rather *passée*.' JOHNSON. 'Literature was in France long before we had it. Paris was the second city for the revival of letters: Italy had it first, to be sure. What have we done for literature, equal to what was done by the Stephani and others in France? Our literature came to us through France. Caxton printed only two books, Chaucer and Gower, that were not translations from the French; and Chaucer, we know, took much from the Italians. No, Sir, if literature be in its spring in France, it is a second spring; it is after a winter. We are now before the French in literature; but we had it long after them. In England, any man who wears a sword and a powdered wig is ashamed to be illiterate. I believe it is not so in France. Yet there is, probably, a great deal of learning in France, because they have such a number of religious establishments; so many men who have nothing else to do but to study. I do not know this; but I take it upon the common principles of chance. Where there are many shooters, some will hit.'

We talked of old age. Johnson (now in his seventieth year,) said, 'It is a man's own fault, it is from want of use, if his mind grows torpid in old age.' The Bishop asked, if an old man does not lose faster than he gets. JOHNSON. 'I think not, my Lord, if he exerts himself.' One of the company[1] rashly observed, that he thought it was happy for an old man that insensibility comes upon him. JOHNSON. (with a noble elevation and disdain,) 'No Sir, I should never be happy by being less rational.' BISHOP OF ST. ASAPH. 'Your wish then, Sir, is γηράσκειν διδασκόμενος.'[2] JOHNSON. 'Yes, my Lord.'

His Lordship mentioned a charitable establishment in Wales, where people were maintained, and supplied with every thing, upon the condition of their contributing the weekly produce of their labour; and he said, they grew quite torpid for want of property. JOHNSON. 'They have no object for hope. Their condition cannot be better. It is rowing without a port.'

One of the company[3] asked him the meaning of the expression in Juvenal, *unius lacertæ.* JOHNSON. 'I think it clear enough; as much ground as one may have a chance to find a lizard upon.'

Commentators have differed as to the exact meaning of the expression by which the Poet intended to enforce the sentiment contained in the passage where these words occur. It is enough that they mean to denote even a very small possession, provided it be a man's own:

> '*Est aliquid quocunque loco quocunque recessu,*
> *Unius sese dominum fecisse lacertæ.*'[4]

[1] [R. O. Cambridge. *Boswell's 1778 Journal.*]
[2] [γηράσκω δ᾽ αἰεὶ πολλὰ διδασκόμενος 'I grow in learning as I grow in years.' Solon *ap.* Plutarch, *Solon,* ch. 31.]
[3] [R. O. Cambridge. *Boswell's 1778 Journal.*]
[4] ['Tis somewhat to be lord of some small ground In which a lizard may at least turn round.' Juvenal iii. 230. (Dryden.)]

This season there was a whimsical fashion in the newspapers of applying Shakspeare's words to describe living persons well known in the world; which was done under the title of *Modern Characters from Shakspeare*; many of which were admirably adapted. The fancy took so much, that they were afterwards collected into a pamphlet. Somebody[1] said to Johnson, across the table, that he had not been in those characters. 'Yes (said he,) I have. I should have been sorry to be left out.' He then repeated what had been applied to him,

'I must borrow GARAGANTUA's mouth.'[2]

Miss Reynolds not perceiving at once the meaning of this, he was obliged to explain it to her, which had something of an aukward and ludicrous effect. 'Why, Madam, it has a reference to me, as using big words, which require the mouth of a giant to pronounce them. Garagantua is the name of a giant in Rabelais.' BOSWELL. 'But, Sir, there is another amongst them for you:

"He would not flatter Neptune for his trident,
Or Jove for his power to thunder." '

JOHNSON. 'There is nothing marked in that. No, Sir, Garagantua is the best.' Notwithstanding this ease and good humour, when I, a little while afterwards, repeated his sarcasm on Kenrick,[3] which was received with applause, he asked, '*Who* said that?' and on my suddenly answering, *Garagantua*, he looked serious, which was a sufficient indication that he did not wish it to be kept up.

When we went to the drawing-room there was a rich assemblage. Besides the company who had been at dinner, there were Mr. Garrick, Mr. Harris of Salisbury, Dr. Percy, Dr. Burney, Honourable Mrs. Cholmondeley, Miss Hannah More, &c. &c.

After wandering about in a kind of pleasing distraction for some time, I got into a corner, with Johnson, Garrick, and Harris. GARRICK. (to Harris,) 'Pray, Sir, have you read Potter's *Æschylus*?' HARRIS. 'Yes; and think it pretty.' GARRICK. (to Johnson,) 'And what think you, Sir, of it?' JOHNSON.

---

[1] [Not yet identified.]   [2] [*As You Like It*, III. ii.]   [3] See p. 351.

'I thought what I read of it *verbiage*: but upon Mr. Harris's recommendation, I will read a play. (To Mr. Harris,) Don't prescribe two.' Mr. Harris suggested one, I do not remember which. JOHNSON. 'We must try its effect as an English poem; that is the way to judge of the merit of a translation. Translations are, in general, for people who cannot read the original.' I mentioned the vulgar saying, that Pope's *Homer* was not a good representation of the original. JOHNSON. 'Sir, it is the greatest work of the kind that has ever been produced.' BOSWELL. 'The truth is, it is impossible perfectly to translate poetry. In a different language it may be the same tune, but it has not the same tone. Homer plays it on a bassoon; Pope on a flagelet.' HARRIS. 'I think Heroick poetry is best in blank verse; yet it appears that rhyme is essential to English poetry, from our deficiency in metrical quantities. In my opinion, the chief excellence of our language is numerous prose.' JOHNSON. 'Sir William Temple was the first writer who gave cadence to English prose. Before his time they were careless of arrangement, and did not mind whether a sentence ended with an important word or an insignificant word, or with what part of speech it was concluded.' Mr. Langton, who now had joined us, commended Clarendon. JOHNSON. 'He is objected to for his parentheses, his involved clauses, and his want of harmony. But he is supported by his matter. It is, indeed, owing to a plethory of matter that his style is so faulty. Every *substance*, (smiling to Mr. Harris,) has so many *accidents.*—To be distinct, we must talk *analytically*. If we analyse language, we must speak of it grammatically; if we analyse argument, we must speak of it logically.' GARRICK. 'Of all the translations that ever were attempted, I think Elphinston's *Martial* the most extraordinary. He consulted me upon it, who am a little of an epigrammatist myself, you know. I told him freely, "You don't seem to have that turn." I asked him if he was serious; and finding he was, I advised him against publishing. Why, his translation is more difficult to understand than the original. I thought him a man of some talents; but he seems crazy in this.' JOHNSON. 'Sir, you have done what I had not courage to do. But he did not ask my

advice, and I did not force it upon him, to make him angry with
me.' GARRICK. 'But as a friend, Sir—.' JOHNSON. 'Why, such
a friend as I am with him—no.' GARRICK. 'But if you see a
friend going to tumble over a precipice?' JOHNSON. 'That is an
extravagant case, Sir. You are sure a friend will thank you for
hindering him from tumbling over a precipice; but, in the other
case, I should hurt his vanity, and do him no good. He would
not take my advice. His brother-in-law, Strahan, sent him a
subscription of fifty pounds, and said he would send him fifty
more, if he would not publish.' GARRICK. 'What! eh! is Strahan
a good judge of an Epigram? Is not he rather an *obtuse* man, eh?'
JOHNSON. 'Why, Sir, he may not be a judge of an Epigram: but
you see he is a judge of what is *not* an Epigram.' BOSWELL. 'It
is easy for you, Mr. Garrick, to talk to an authour as you talked
to Elphinston; you, who have been so long the manager of a
theatre, rejecting the plays of poor authours. You are an old
Judge, who have often pronounced sentence of death. You are a
practiced surgeon, who have often amputated limbs; and though
this may have been for the good of your patients, they cannot
like you. Those who have undergone a dreadful operation are
not very fond of seeing the operator again.' GARRICK. 'Yes, I
know enough of that. There was a reverend gentleman, (Mr.
Hawkins,) who wrote a tragedy, the SIEGE of something,[1] which
I refused.' HARRIS. 'So, the siege was raised.' JOHNSON. 'Ay,
he came to me and complained; and told me, that Garrick said
his play was wrong in the *concoction*. Now, what is the concoction of a play?' (Here Garrick started, and twisted himself,
and seemed sorely vexed; for Johnson told me, he believed the
story was true.) GARRICK. 'I—I—I— said *first* concoction.'
JOHNSON. (smiling,) 'Well, he left out *first*. And Rich, he said,
refused him *in false English*: he could shew it under his hand.'
GARRICK. 'He wrote to me in violent wrath, for having refused
his play: "Sir, this is growing a very serious and terrible affair.
I am resolved to publish my play. I will appeal to the world;

[1] It was called *The Siege of Aleppo*. Mr. Hawkins, the authour of it, was
formerly Professor of Poetry at Oxford. It is printed in his *Miscellanies*, 3
vols. octavo.

and how will your judgement appear?" I answered, "Sir, notwithstanding all the seriousness, and all the terrours, I have no objection to your publishing your play; and as you live at a great distance, (Devonshire, I believe,) if you will send it to me, I will convey it to the press." I never heard more of it, ha! ha! ha!'

On Friday, April 10, I found Johnson at home in the morning. We resumed the conversation of yesterday. He put me in mind of some of it which had escaped my memory, and enabled me to record it more perfectly than I otherwise could have done. He was much pleased with my paying so great attention to his recommendation in 1763, the period when our acquaintance began, that I should keep a journal; and I could perceive he was secretly pleased to find so much of the fruit of his mind preserved; and as he had been used to imagine and say that he always laboured when he said a good thing—it delighted him, on a review, to find that his conversation teemed with point and imagery.

I said to him, 'You were yesterday, Sir, in remarkably good humour: but there was nothing to offend you, nothing to produce irritation or violence. There was no bold offender. There was not one capital conviction. It was a maiden assize. You had on your white gloves.'

He found fault with our friend Langton for having been too silent. 'Sir, (said I,) you will recollect, that he very properly took up Sir Joshua for being glad that Charles Fox had praised Goldsmith's *Traveller*, and you joined him.' JOHNSON. 'Yes, Sir, I knocked Fox on the head, without ceremony. Reynolds is too much under Fox and Burke at present. He is under the *Fox star* and the *Irish constellation*. He is always under some planet.' BOSWELL. 'There is no Fox star.' JOHNSON. 'But there is a dog star.' BOSWELL. 'They say, indeed, a fox and a dog are the same animal.'

I reminded him of a gentleman,[1] who, Mrs. Cholmondeley said, was first talkative from affectation, and then silent from the same cause; that he first thought, 'I shall be celebrated as the liveliest man in every company;' and then, all at once, 'O!

[1] [Langton. *Boswell's 1778 Journal.*]

it is much more respectable to be grave and look wise.' 'He has
reversed the Pythagorean discipline, by being first talkative,
and then silent. He reverses the course of Nature too: he was
first the gay butterfly, and then the creeping worm.' Johnson
laughed loud and long at this expansion and illustration of what
he himself had told me.

We dined together with Mr. Scott (now Sir William Scott,
his Majesty's Advocate General,) at his chambers in the Temple,
nobody else there. The company being small, Johnson was not
in such spirits as he had been the preceding day, and for a considerable time little was said. At last he burst forth, 'Subordination is sadly broken down in this age. No man, now, has the
same authority which his father had,—except a gaoler. No
master has it over his servants: it is diminished in our colleges;
nay, in our grammar-schools.' BOSWELL. 'What is the cause of
this, Sir?' JOHNSON. 'Why, the coming in of the Scotch,' (laughing sarcastically.) BOSWELL. 'That is to say, things have been
turned topsy turvey.—But your serious cause.' JOHNSON. 'Why,
Sir, there are many causes, the chief of which is, I think, the
great increase of money. No man now depends upon the Lord
of a Manour, when he can send to another country, and fetch
provisions. The shoe-black at the entry of my court does not
depend on me. I can deprive him but of a penny a day, which he
hopes somebody else will bring him; and that penny I must
carry to another shoe-black, so the trade suffers nothing. I have
explained, in my *Journey to the Hebrides*, how gold and silver
destroy feudal subordination. But, besides, there is a general
relaxation of reverence. No son now depends upon his father as
in former times. Paternity used to be considered as of itself a
great thing, which had a right to many claims. That is, in
general, reduced to very small bounds. My hope is, that as
anarchy produces tyranny, this extreme relaxation will produce
freni strictio.'[1]

Talking of fame, for which there is so great a desire, I observed how little there is of it in reality, compared with the
other objects of human attention. 'Let every man recollect, and

[1] ['a tight rein'.]

he will be sensible how small a part of his time is employed in talking or thinking of Shakspeare, Voltaire, or any of the most celebrated men that have ever lived, or are now supposed to occupy the attention and admiration of the world. Let this be extracted and compressed; into what a narrow space will it go!' I then slily introduced Mr. Garrick's fame, and his assuming the airs of a great man. JOHNSON. 'Sir, it is wonderful how *little* Garrick assumes. No, Sir, Garrick *fortunam reverenter habet.*[1] Consider, Sir: celebrated men, such as you have mentioned, have had their applause at a distance; but Garrick had it dashed in his face, sounded in his ears, and went home every night with the plaudits of a thousand in his *cranium*. Then, Sir, Garrick did not *find*, but *made* his way to the tables, the levees, and almost the bed-chambers of the great. Then, Sir, Garrick had under him a numerous body of people; who, from fear of his power, and hopes of his favour, and admiration of his talents, were constantly submissive to him. And here is a man who has advanced the dignity of his profession. Garrick has made a player a higher character.' SCOTT. 'And he is a very sprightly writer too.' JOHNSON. 'Yes, Sir; and all this supported by great wealth of his own acquisition. If all this had happened to me, I should have had a couple of fellows with long poles walking before me, to knock down every body that stood in the way. Consider, if all this had happened to Cibber or Quin, they'd have jumped over the moon.—Yet Garrick speaks to *us*.' (smiling.) BOSWELL. 'And Garrick is a very good man, a charitable man.' JOHNSON. 'Sir, a liberal man. He has given away more money than any man in England. There may be a little vanity mixed; but he has shewn, that money is not his first object.' BOSWELL. 'Yet Foote used to say of him, that he walked out with an intention to do a generous action; but, turning the corner of a street, he met with the ghost of a half-penny, which frightened him.' JOHNSON. 'Why, Sir, that is very true, too; for I never knew a man of whom it could be said with less certainty to-day, what he will do to-morrow, than Garrick; it depends so much on his

[1] ['treats his good fortune with deference'. AUSONIUS, *Epigrammata* ii. [viii.] 7.]

humour at the time.' SCOTT. 'I am glad to hear of his liberality. He has been represented as very saving.' JOHNSON. 'With his domestick saving we have nothing to do. I remember drinking tea with him long ago, when Peg Woffington made it, and he grumbled at her for making it too strong.[1] He had then begun to feel money in his purse, and did not know when he should have enough of it.'

On the subject of wealth, the proper use of it, and the effects of that art which is called œconomy, he observed, 'It is wonderful to think how men of very large estates not only spend their yearly income, but are often actually in want of money. It is clear, they have not value for what they spend. Lord Shelburne told me, that a man of high rank, who looks into his own affairs, may have all that he ought to have, all that can be of any use, or appear with any advantage, for five thousand pounds a year. Therefore, a great proportion must go in waste; and, indeed, this is the case with most people, whatever their fortune is.' BOSWELL. 'I have no doubt, Sir, of this. But how is it? What is waste?' JOHNSON. 'Why, Sir, breaking bottles, and a thousand other things. Waste cannot be accurately told, though we are sensible how destructive it is. Œconomy on the one hand, by which a certain income is made to maintain a man genteely, and waste on the other, by which, on the same income, another man lives shabbily, cannot be defined. It is a very nice thing: as one man wears his coat out much sooner than another, we cannot tell how.'

We talked of war. JOHNSON. 'Every man thinks meanly of himself for not having been a soldier, or not having been at sea.' BOSWELL. 'Lord Mansfield does not.' JOHNSON. 'Sir, if Lord Mansfield were in a company of General Officers and Admirals who have been in service, he would shrink; he'd wish to creep under the table.' BOSWELL. 'No; he'd think he could *try* them all.' JOHNSON. 'Yes, if he could catch them: but they'd try him much sooner. No, Sir; were Socrates and Charles the

---

[1] When Johnson told this little anecdote to Sir Joshua Reynolds, he mentioned a circumstance which he omitted to-day:—'Why, (said Garrick,) it is as red as blood.'

Twelfth of Sweden both present in any company, and Socrates to say, "Follow me, and hear a lecture on philosophy;" and Charles, laying his hand on his sword, to say, "Follow me, and dethrone the Czar;" a man would be ashamed to follow Socrates. Sir, the impression is universal; yet it is strange. As to the sailor, when you look down from the quarter deck to the space below, you see the utmost extremity of human misery; such crouding, such filth, such stench!' BOSWELL. 'Yet sailors are happy.' JOHNSON. 'They are happy as brutes are happy, with a piece of fresh meat,—with the grossest sensuality. But, Sir, the profession of soldiers and sailors has the dignity of danger. Mankind reverence those who have got over fear, which is so general a weakness.' SCOTT. 'But is not courage mechanical, and to be acquired?' JOHNSON. 'Why yes, Sir, in a collective sense. Soldiers consider themselves only as parts of a great machine.' SCOTT. 'We find people fond of being sailors.' JOHNSON. 'I cannot account for that, any more than I can account for other strange perversions of imagination.'

His abhorrence of the profession of a sailor was uniformly violent; but in conversation he always exalted the profession of a soldier. And yet I have, in my large and various collection of his writings, a letter[1] to an eminent friend, in which he expresses himself thus: 'My god-son called on me lately. He is weary, and rationally weary, of a military life. If you can place him in some other state, I think you may increase his happiness, and secure his virtue. A soldier's time is passed in distress and danger, or in idleness and corruption.' Such was his cool reflection in his study; but whenever he was warmed and animated by the presence of company, he, like other philosophers, whose minds are impregnated with poetical fancy, caught the common enthusiasm for splendid renown.

He talked of Mr. Charles Fox, of whose abilities he thought highly, but observed, that he did not talk much at our CLUB. I have heard Mr. Gibbon remark, 'that Mr. Fox could not be

[1] [The letter from which Boswell printed extracts, here and at p. 1249 was found at Fettercairn. We now know that the 'eminent friend' was John Mudge, and that Johnson's godson was his son William—who stuck it out to become a major-general.—*R.W.C.*]

afraid of Dr. Johnson; yet he certainly was very shy of saying any thing in Dr. Johnson's presence.' Mr. Scott now quoted what was said of Alcibiades by a Greek poet, to which Johnson assented.

He told us, that he had given Mrs. Montagu a catalogue of all Daniel Defoe's works of imagination; most, if not all of which, as well as of his other works, he now enumerated, allowing a considerable share of merit to a man, who, bred a tradesman, had written so variously and so well. Indeed, his *Robinson Crusoe* is enough of itself to establish his reputation.

He expressed great indignation at the imposture of the Cock-lane Ghost, and related, with much satisfaction, how he had assisted in detecting the cheat, and had published an account of it in the news-papers. Upon this subject I incautiously offended him, by pressing him with too many questions, and he shewed his displeasure. I apologised, saying that 'I asked questions in order to be instructed and entertained; I repaired eagerly to the fountain; but that the moment he gave me a hint, the moment he put a lock upon the well, I desisted.'—'But, Sir, (said he,) that is forcing one to do a disagreeable thing:' and he continued to rate me. 'Nay, Sir, (said I,) when you have put a lock upon the well, so that I can no longer drink, do not make the fountain of your wit play upon me and wet me.'

He sometimes could not bear being teazed with questions. I was once present when a gentleman[1] asked so many as, 'What did you do, Sir?' 'What did you say, Sir?' that he at last grew enraged, and said, 'I will not be put to the *question*. Don't you consider, Sir, that these are not the manners of a gentleman? I will not be baited with *what*, and *why*; what is this? what is that? why is a cow's tail long? why is a fox's tail bushy?' The gentle-man, who was a good deal out of countenance, said, 'Why, Sir, you are so good, that I venture to trouble you.' JOHNSON. 'Sir, my being so *good* is no reason why you should be so *ill*.'

Talking of the Justitia hulk at Woolwich, in which criminals were punished, by being confined to labour, he said, 'I do not see that they are punished by this: they must have worked equally had they never been guilty of stealing. They now only

[1] [Boswell. *Boswell's 1778 Journal.*]

work; so, after all, they have gained; what they stole is clear gain to them; the confinement is nothing. Every man who works is confined: the smith to his shop, the tailor to his garret.' Bos-well. 'And Lord Mansfield to his Court.' Johnson. 'Yes, Sir, you know the notion of confinement may be extended, as in the song, "Every island is a prison." There is, in Dodsley's *Collection*, a copy of verses to the authour of that song.'

Smith's[1] Latin verses on Pococke,[2] the great traveller, were mentioned. He repeated some of them, and said they were Smith's best verses.

He talked with an uncommon animation of travelling into distant countries; that the mind was enlarged by it, and that an acquisition of dignity of character was derived from it. He expressed a particular enthusiasm with respect to visiting the wall of China. I catched it for the moment, and said I really believed I should go and see the wall of China had I not children, of whom it was my duty to take care. 'Sir, (said he,) by doing so, you would do what would be of importance in raising your children to eminence. There would be a lustre reflected upon them from your spirit and curiosity. They would be at all times regarded as the children of a man who had gone to view the wall of China. I am serious, Sir.'

When we had left Mr. Scott's, he said, 'Will you go home with me?' 'Sir, (said I,) it is late; but I'll go with you for three minutes.' Johnson. 'Or *four*.' We went to Mrs. Williams's room, where we found Mr. Allen the printer, who was the land-lord of his house in Bolt-court, a worthy obliging man, and his very old acquaintance; and what was exceedingly amusing, though he was of a very diminutive size, he used, even in John-son's presence, to imitate the stately periods and slow and solemn utterance of the great man.—I this evening boasted, that although I did not write what is called stenography, or short-hand, in appropriated characters devised for the purpose, I had a method of my own of writing half words, and leaving out some altogether, so as yet to keep the substance and language of any discourse which I had heard so much in view, that I could

---

[1] [Edmund Smith (1672–1710).]

[2] It was Pococke the Orientalist, on whom Smith wrote.

give it very completely soon after I had taken it down. He defied me, as he had once defied an actual short-hand writer, and he made the experiment by reading slowly and distinctly a part of Robertson's *History of America*, while I endeavoured to write it in my way of taking notes. It was found that I had it very imperfectly; the conclusion from which was, that its excellence was principally owing to a studied arrangement of words, which could not be varied or abridged without an essential injury.

On Sunday, April 12, I found him at home before dinner; Dr. Dodd's poem entitled *Thoughts in Prison* was lying upon his table. This appearing to me an extraordinary effort by a man who was in Newgate for a capital crime, I was desirous to hear Johnson's opinion of it: to my surprize, he told me he had not read a line of it. I took up the book and read a passage to him. JOHNSON. 'Pretty well, if you are previously disposed to like them.' I read another passage, with which he was better pleased. He then took the book into his own hands, and having looked at the prayer at the end of it, he said, 'What *evidence* is there that this was composed the night before he suffered? *I* do not believe it.' He then read aloud where he prays for the King, &c. and observed, 'Sir, do you think that a man the night before he is to be hanged cares for the succession of a royal family?— Though, he *may* have composed this prayer, then. A man who has been canting all his life, may cant to the last.—And yet a man who has been refused a pardon after so much petitioning, would hardly be praying thus fervently for the King.'

He and I, and Mrs. Williams, went to dine with the Reverend Dr. Percy. Talking of Goldsmith, Johnson said, he was very envious. I defended him, by observing that he owned it frankly upon all occasions. JOHNSON. 'Sir, you are enforcing the charge. He had so much envy, that he could not conceal it. He was so full of it that he overflowed. He talked of it to be sure often enough. Now, Sir, what a man avows, he is not ashamed to think; though many a man thinks, what he is ashamed to avow. We are all envious naturally; but by checking envy, we get the better of it. So we are all thieves naturally; a child always tries to get at what it wants, the nearest way; by good instruction and

good habits this is cured, till a man has not even an inclination
to seize what is another's; has no struggle with himself about it.'

And here I shall record a scene of too much heat between
Dr. Johnson and Dr. Percy, which I should have suppressed
were it not that it gave occasion to display the truely tender
and benevolent heart of Johnson, who, as soon as he found a
friend was at all hurt by any thing which he had 'said in his
wrath,' was not only prompt and desirous to be reconciled, but
exerted himself to make ample reparation.

Books of Travels having been mentioned, Johnson praised
Pennant very highly, as he did at Dunvegan, in the Isle of Sky.[1]
Dr. Percy, knowing himself to be the heir male of the ancient
Percies,[2] and having the warmest and most dutiful attachment
to the noble House of Northumberland, could not sit quietly
and hear a man praised, who had spoken disrespectfully of
Alnwick-Castle and the Duke's pleasure grounds, especially as
he thought meanly of his travels. He therefore opposed Johnson
eagerly. JOHNSON. 'Pennant in what he has said of Alnwick,
has done what he intended; he has made you very angry.'
PERCY. 'He has said the garden is *trim,* which is representing
it like a citizen's parterre, when the truth is, there is a very large
extent of fine turf and gravel walks.' JOHNSON. 'According to
your own account, Sir, Pennant is right. It *is* trim. Here is grass
cut close, and gravel rolled smooth. Is not that trim? The extent

---

[1] *Journal of a Tour to the Hebrides,* 3rd edit., p. 221 [Sept. 17].

[2] See this accurately stated, and the descent of his family from the Earls
of Northumberland clearly deduced in the Reverend Dr. Nash's excellent
History of Worcestershire, vol. ii. p. 318. The Doctor has subjoined a note,
in which he says, 'The Editor hath seen and carefully examined the proofs
of all the particulars above-mentioned, now in the possession of the Reverend
Thomas Percy.' The same proofs I have also myself carefully examined, and
have seen some additional proofs which have occurred since the Doctor's
book was published; and both as a Lawyer accustomed to the consideration
of evidence, and as a Genealogist versed in the study of pedigrees, I am
fully satisfied. I cannot help observing, as a circumstance of no small
moment, that in tracing the Bishop of Dromore's genealogy, essential aid
was given by the late Elizabeth Duchess of Northumberland, Heiress of that
illustrious House; a lady not only of high dignity of spirit, such as became
her noble blood, but of excellent understanding and lively talents. With a
fair pride I can boast of the honour of her Grace's correspondence, specimens
of which adorn my archives. [Percy's claim was groundless.]

is nothing against that; a mile may be as trim as a square yard. Your extent puts me in mind of the citizen's enlarged dinner, two pieces of roast-beef, and two puddings. There is no variety, no mind exerted in laying out the ground, no trees.' PERCY. 'He pretends to give the natural history of Northumberland, and yet takes no notice of the immense number of trees planted there of late.' JOHNSON. 'That, Sir, has nothing to do with the *natural* history; that is *civil* history. A man who gives the natural history of the oak, is not to tell how many oaks have been planted in this place or that. A man who gives the natural history of the cow, is not to tell how many cows are milked at Islington. The animal is the same, whether milked in the Park or at Islington.' PERCY. 'Pennant does not describe well; a carrier who goes along the side of Loch-lomond would describe it better.' JOHNSON. 'I think he describes very well.' PERCY. 'I travelled after him.' JOHNSON. 'And *I* travelled after him.' PERCY. 'But, my good friend, you are short-sighted, and do not see so well as I do.' I wondered at Dr. Percy's venturing thus. Dr. Johnson said nothing at the time; but inflammable particles were collecting for a cloud to burst. In a little while Dr. Percy said something more in disparagement of Pennant. JOHNSON. (pointedly,) 'This is the resentment of a narrow mind, because he did not find every thing in Northumberland.' PERCY. (feeling the stroke,) 'Sir, you may be as rude as you please.' JOHNSON. 'Hold, Sir! Don't talk of rudeness; remember, Sir, you told me (puffing hard with passion struggling for a vent,) I was short-sighted. We have done with civility. We are to be as rude as we please.' PERCY. 'Upon my honour, Sir, I did not mean to be uncivil.' JOHNSON. 'I cannot say so, Sir; for I *did* mean to be uncivil, thinking *you* had been uncivil.' Dr. Percy rose, ran up to him, and taking him by the hand, assured him affectionately that his meaning had been misunderstood; upon which a reconciliation instantly took place. JOHNSON. 'My dear Sir, I am willing you shall *hang* Pennant.' PERCY. (resuming the former subject,) 'Pennant complains that the helmet is not hung out to invite to the hall of hospitality. Now I never heard that it was a custom to hang out a *helmet*.' JOHNSON. 'Hang him up, hang him up.'

BOSWELL. (humouring the joke,) 'Hang out his skull instead of a helmet, and you may drink ale out of it in your hall of Odin, as he is your enemy; that will be truly ancient. *There* will be *Northern Antiquities*.'[1] JOHNSON. 'He's a *Whig*, Sir; a *sad dog*. (smiling at his own violent expressions, merely for *political* difference of opinion.) But he's the best traveller I ever read; he observes more things than any one else does.'

I could not help thinking that this was too high praise of a writer who had traversed a wide extent of country in such haste, that he could put together only curt frittered fragments of his own, and afterwards procured supplemental intelligence from parochial ministers, and others not the best qualified or most impartial narrators, whose ungenerous prejudice against the house of Stuart glares in misrepresentation; a writer, who at best treats merely of superficial objects, and shews no philosophical investigation of character and manners, such as Johnson has exhibited in his masterly *Journey*, over part of the same ground; and who it should seem from a desire of ingratiating himself with the Scotch, has flattered the people of North-Britain so inordinately and with so little discrimination, that the judicious and candid amongst them must be disgusted, while they value more the plain, just, yet kindly report of Johnson.

Having impartially censured Mr. Pennant, as a Traveller in Scotland, let me allow him, from authorities much better than mine, his deserved praise as an able Zoologist; and let me also from my own understanding and feelings, acknowledge the merit of his *London*, which, though said to be not quite accurate in some particulars, is one of the most pleasing topographical performances that ever appeared in any language. Mr. Pennant, like his countrymen in general, has the true spirit of a *Gentleman*. As a proof of it, I shall quote from his *London* the passage, in which he speaks of my illustrious friend. 'I must by no means omit *Bolt-court*, the long residence of Doctor SAMUEL JOHNSON, a man of the strongest natural abilities, great learning, a most retentive memory, of the deepest and most unaffected piety and morality, mingled with those numerous weaknesses and prejudices which

---

[1] The title of a book translated by Dr. Percy [1770].

his friends have kindly taken care to draw from their dread abode.[1] I brought on myself his transient anger, by observing that in his tour in *Scotland*, he once had "long and woeful experience of oats being the food of men in *Scotland* as they were of horses in *England*." It was a national reflection unworthy of him, and I shot my bolt. In return he gave me a tender hug. *Con amore* he also said of me "*The dog is a Whig;*" I admired the virtues of Lord *Russell*, and pitied his fall. I should have been a Whig at the Revolution. There have been periods since, in which I should have been, what I now am, a moderate Tory, a supporter, as far as my little influence extends, of a well-poised balance between the crown and people: but should the scale preponderate against the *Salus populi*, that moment may it be said "*The* dog's a *Whig!*" '

We had a calm after the storm, staid the evening and supped, and were pleasant and gay. But Dr. Percy told me he was very uneasy at what had passed; for there was a gentleman[2] there who was acquainted with the Northumberland family, to whom he hoped to have appeared more respectable, by shewing how intimate he was with Dr. Johnson, and who might now, on the contrary, go away with an opinion to his disadvantage. He begged I would mention this to Dr. Johnson, which I afterwards did. His observation upon it was, 'This comes of *stratagem*; had he told me that he wished to appear to advantage before that gentleman, he should have been at the top of the house, all the time.' He spoke of Dr. Percy in the handsomest terms. 'Then, Sir, (said I,) may I be allowed to suggest a mode by which you may effectually counteract any unfavourable report of what passed. I will write a letter to you upon the subject of the unlucky contest of that day, and you will be kind enough to put in writing as an answer to that letter, what you have now said, and as Lord Percy is to dine with us at General Paoli's soon, I will take an opportunity to read the correspondence in his Lord-

[1] This is the common cant against faithful Biography. Does the worthy gentleman mean that I, who was taught discrimination of character by Johnson, should have omitted his frailties, and, in short, have *bedawbed* him as the worthy gentleman has bedawbed Scotland?

[2] [Perhaps Norton Nicholls. *See* p. 965 *infra.*]

ship's presence.' This friendly scheme was accordingly carried into execution without Dr. Percy's knowledge. Johnson's letter placed Dr. Percy's unquestionable merit in the fairest point of view; and I contrived that Lord Percy should hear the correspondence, by introducing it at General Paoli's, as an instance of Dr. Johnson's kind disposition towards one in whom his Lordship was interested. Thus every unfavourable impression was obviated that could possibly have been made on those by whom he wished most to be regarded. I breakfasted the day after with him, and informed him of my scheme, and its happy completion, for which he thanked me in the warmest terms, and was highly delighted with Dr. Johnson's letter in his praise, of which I gave him a copy. He said, 'I would rather have this than degrees from all the Universities in Europe. It will be for me, and my children and grand-children.' Dr. Johnson having afterwards asked me if I had given him a copy of it, and being told I had, was offended, and insisted that I should get it back, which I did. As, however, he did not desire me to destroy either the original or the copy, or forbid me to let it be seen, I think myself at liberty to apply to it his general declaration to me concerning his other letters, 'That he did not choose they should be published in his lifetime; but had no objection to their appearing after his death.' I shall therefore insert this kindly correspondence, having faithfully narrated the circumstances accompanying it.

'*To* DR. SAMUEL JOHNSON

'MY DEAR SIR,—I beg leave to address you in behalf of our friend Dr. Percy, who was much hurt by what you said to him that day we dined at his house;[1] when, in the course of the dispute as to Pennant's merit as a traveller, you told Percy that "he had the resentment of a narrow mind against Pennant, because he did not find every thing in Northumberland." Percy is sensible that you did not mean to injure him; but he is vexed to think that your behaviour to him upon that occasion may be interpreted as a proof that he is despised by you, which I know is not

[1] Sunday, April 12, 1778.

the case. I have told him, that the charge of being narrow-minded was only as to the particular point in question; and that he had the merit of being a martyr to his noble family.

'Earl Percy is to dine with General Paoli next Friday; and I should be sincerely glad to have it in my power to satisfy his Lordship how well you think of Dr. Percy, who, I find, apprehends that your good opinion of him may be of very essential consequence; and who assures me, that he has the highest respect and the warmest affection for you.

'I have only to add, that my suggesting this occasion for the exercise of your candour and generosity, is altogether unknown to Dr. Percy, and proceeds from my good-will towards him, and my persuasion that you will be happy to do him an essential kindness. I am, more and more, my dear Sir, your most faithful and affectionate humble servant,

                                         'JAMES BOSWELL.'

'To JAMES BOSWELL, ESQ.

'Sir,—The debate between Dr. Percy and me is one of those foolish controversies, which begin upon a question of which neither party cares how it is decided, and which is, nevertheless, continued to acrimony, by the vanity with which every man resists confutation. Dr. Percy's warmth proceeded from a cause which, perhaps, does him more honour than he could have derived from juster criticism. His abhorrence of Pennant proceeded from his opinion that Pennant had wantonly and indecently censured his patron. His anger made him resolve, that, for having been once wrong, he never should be right. Pennant has much in his notions that I do not like; but still I think him a very intelligent traveller. If Percy is really offended, I am sorry; for he is a man whom I never knew to offend any one. He is a man very willing to learn, and very able to teach; a man, out of whose company I never go without having learned something. It is sure that he vexes me sometimes, but I am afraid it is by making me feel my own ignorance. So much extension of mind, and so much minute accuracy of enquiry, if you survey your whole circle of acquaintance, you will find so scarce, if you find it at all, that you will value Percy by comparison. Lord Hailes is somewhat like him: but Lord Hailes does not, perhaps, go beyond him in research; and I do not know that he equals him in elegance. Percy's attention to poetry has given grace and splendour to his studies of antiquity. A mere antiquarian is a rugged being.

'Upon the whole, you see that what I might say in sport or petulance to him, is very consistent with full conviction of his merit. I am, dear Sir, your most, &c.,

    'April 23, 1778.'   'SAM. JOHNSON.'

'*To* THE REVEREND DR. PERCY, *Northumberland-House.*

'DEAR SIR,—I wrote to Dr. Johnson on the subject of the *Pennantian* controversy; and have received from him an answer which will delight you. I read it yesterday to Dr. Robertson, at the Exhibition; and at dinner to Lord Percy, General Oglethorpe, &c. who dined with us at General Paoli's; who was also a witness to the high *testimony* to your honour.

'General Paoli desires the favour of your company next Tuesday to dinner, to meet Dr. Johnson. If I can, I will call on you to-day. I am, with sincere regard, your most obedient humble servant,

    'South Audley-street, April 25.'   'JAMES BOSWELL.'[1]

On Monday, April 13, I dined with Johnson at Mr. Langton's, where were Dr. Porteus, then Bishop of Chester, now of London, and Dr. Stinton. He was at first in a very silent mood. Before dinner he said nothing but 'Pretty baby,' to one of the children. Langton said very well to me afterwards, that he could repeat Johnson's conversation before dinner, as Johnson had said that he could repeat a complete chapter of *The Natural History of*

---

[1] Though the Bishop of Dromore kindly answered the letters which I wrote to him, relative to Dr. Johnson's early history; yet, in justice to him, I think it proper to add, that the account of the foregoing conversation and the subsequent transaction, as well as some other conversations in which he is mentioned, has been given to the publick without previous communication with his Lordship.

Iceland, from the Danish of *Horrebow*, the whole of which was exactly thus:—

> 'CHAP. LXXII. *Concerning snakes.*
> 'There are no snakes to be met with throughout the whole island.'

At dinner we talked of another mode in the newspapers of giving modern characters in sentences from the classicks, and of the passage

> *'Parcus deorum cultor, et infrequens,*
> *Insanientis dum sapientiæ*
> *Consultus erro, nunc retrorsùm*
> *Vela dare, atque iterare cursus*
>   *Cogor relictos:'*[1]

being well applied to Soame Jenyns; who, after having wandered in the wilds of infidelity, had returned to the Christian faith. Mr. Langton asked Johnson as to the propriety of *sapientiæ consultus.* JOHNSON. 'Though *consultus* was primarily an adjective, like *amicus* it came to be used as a substantive. So we have *Juris consultus*, a consult in law.'

We talked of the styles of different painters, and how certainly a connoisseur could distinguish them; I asked, if there was as clear a difference of styles in language as in painting, or even as in hand-writing, so that the composition of every individual may be distinguished? JOHNSON. 'Yes. Those who have a style of eminent excellence, such as Dryden and Milton, can always be distinguished.' I had no doubt of this, but what I wanted to know was, whether there was really a peculiar style to every man whatever, as there is certainly a peculiar hand-writing, a peculiar countenance, not widely different in many, yet always enough to be distinctive:—

> '———— ————*facies non omnibus una,*
>   *Nec diversa tamen.'*[2]

The Bishop thought not; and said, he supposed that many pieces

---

[1] ['A grudging and infrequent worshipper of the gods, whilst I strayed, the professor of a wisdom that is folly, I have been forced now to turn my sails backward and steer again in the course which I had abandoned.'
                 Horace, *Odes* I. xxxiv. 1. (Wickham.)]

[2] ['features not the same in all, nor yet the difference great'.
                 Ovid, *Metamorphoses* ii. 13.]

in Dodsley's collection of poems, though all very pretty, had nothing appropriated in their style, and in that particular could not be at all distinguished. JOHNSON. 'Why, Sir, I think every man whatever has a peculiar style, which may be discovered by nice examination and comparison with others: but a man must write a great deal to make his style obviously discernible. As logicians say, this appropriation of style is infinite *in potestate*, limited *in actu.*'[1]

Mr. Topham Beauclerk came in the evening, and he and Dr. Johnson and I staid to supper. It was mentioned that Dr. Dodd had once wished to be a member of THE LITERARY CLUB. JOHNSON. 'I should be sorry if any of our Club were hanged. I will not say but some of them deserve it.'[2] Beauclerk (supposing this to be aimed at persons for whom he had at that time a wonderful fancy, which, however, did not last long,) was irritated, and eagerly said, 'You, Sir, have a friend, (naming him)[3] who deserves to be hanged; for he speaks behind their backs against those with whom he lives on the best terms, and attacks them in the news-papers. *He* certainly ought to be *kicked.*' JOHNSON. 'Sir, we all do this in some degree, *"Veniam petimus damusque vicissim."*[4] To be sure it may be done so much, that a man may deserve to be kicked.' BEAUCLERK. 'He is very malignant.' JOHNSON. 'No, Sir; he is not malignant. He is mischievous, if you will. He would do no man an essential injury; he may, indeed, love to make sport of people by vexing their vanity. I, however, once knew an old gentleman[5] who was absolutely malignant. He really wished evil to others, and rejoiced at it.' BOSWELL. 'The gentleman, Mr. Beauclerk, against whom you are so violent, is, I know, a man of good principles.' BEAUCLERK. 'Then he does not wear them out in practice.'

Dr. Johnson, who, as I have observed before, delighted in

---

[1] ['potentially . . . actually'.]
[2] See note, *ante*, p. 798.
[3] [George Steevens. *Boswell Papers*, xiv. 178.]
[4] ['This liberty we claim for ourselves and [*petimusque*] give again to others.' Horace, *Ars Poetica* 11. (Wickham.)]
[5] [Littleton Poyntz Meynell. *Boswell's* 1778 *Journal.*]

discrimination of character, and having a masterly knowledge of human nature, was willing to take men as they are, imperfect and with a mixture of good and bad qualities, I suppose thought he had said enough in defence of his friend, of whose merits, notwithstanding his exceptional points, he had a just value; and added no more on the subject.

On Tuesday, April 14, I dined with him at General Oglethorpe's, with General Paoli and Mr. Langton. General Oglethorpe declaimed against luxury. JOHNSON. 'Depend upon it, Sir, every state of society is as luxurious as it can be. Men always take the best they can get.' OGLETHORPE. 'But the best depends much upon ourselves; and if we can be as well satisfied with plain things, we are in the wrong to accustom our palates to what is high-seasoned and expensive. What says Addison in his *Cato*, speaking of the Numidian?

> "Coarse are his meals, the fortune of the chace,
> Amid the running stream he slakes his thirst,
> Toils all the day, and at the approach of night,
> On the first friendly bank he throws him down,
> Or rests his head upon a rock till morn;
> And if the following day he chance to find
> A new repast, or an untasted spring,
> Blesses his stars, and thinks it luxury."

Let us have *that* kind of luxury, Sir, if you will.' JOHNSON. 'But hold, Sir; to be merely satisfied is not enough. It is in refinement and elegance that the civilized man differs from the savage. A great part of our industry, and all our ingenuity is exercised in procuring pleasure; and, Sir, a hungry man has not the same pleasure in eating a plain dinner, that a hungry man has in eating a luxurious dinner. You see I put the case fairly. A hungry man may have as much, nay, more pleasure in eating a plain dinner, than a man grown fastidious has in eating a luxurious dinner. But I suppose the man who decides between the two dinners, to be equally a hungry man.'

Talking of different governments,—JOHNSON. 'The more contracted that power is, the more easily it is destroyed. A country governed by a despot is an inverted cone. Government there cannot be so firm, as when it rests upon a broad basis gradually contracted, as the government of Great Britain, which is founded on the parliament, then is in the privy council, then in the King.' Boswell. 'Power, when contracted into the person of a despot, may be easily destroyed, as the prince may be cut off. So Caligula wished that the people of Rome had but one neck, that he might cut them off at a blow.' Oglethorpe. 'It was of the Senate he wished that. The Senate by its usurpation controuled both the Emperour and the people. And don't you think that we see too much of that in our own Parliament?'

Dr. Johnson endeavoured to trace the etymology of Maccaronick verses, which he thought were of Italian invention from Maccaroni; but on being informed that this would infer that they were the most common and easy verses, maccaroni being the most ordinary and simple food, he was at a loss; for he said, 'He rather should have supposed it to import in its primitive signification, a composition of several things; for Maccaronick verses are verses made out of a mixture of different languages, that is, of one language with the termination of another.' I suppose we scarcely know of a language in any country where there is any learning, in which that motley ludicrous species of composition may not be found. It is particularly droll in Low Dutch. The *Polemomiddinia* of Drummond of Hawthornden, in which there is a jumble of many languages moulded, as if it were all in Latin, is well known. Mr. Langton made us laugh heartily at one in the Grecian mould, by Joshua Barnes, in which are to be found such comical *Anglo-Ellenisms* as Κλυββοισιν εβανχθεν: they were banged with clubs.

On Wednesday, April 15, I dined with Dr. Johnson at Mr. Dilly's, and was in high spirits, for I had been a good part of the morning with Mr. Orme, the able and eloquent historian of Hindostan, who expressed a great admiration of Johnson. 'I do not care (said he,) on what subject Johnson talks; but I love better to hear him talk than any body. He either gives you new thoughts, or a new colouring. It is a shame to the nation that he has not been more liberally rewarded. Had I been George the Third, and thought as he did about America, I would have given Johnson three hundred a year for his *Taxation no Tyranny* alone.' I repeated this, and Johnson was much pleased with such praise from such a man as Orme.

At Mr. Dilly's to-day were Mrs. Knowles, the ingenious Quaker lady,[1] Miss Seward, the poetess of Lichfield, the Reverend Dr. Mayo, and the Rev. Mr. Beresford, Tutor to the Duke of Bedford. Before dinner Dr. Johnson seized upon Mr. Charles Sheridan's *Account of the late Revolution in Sweden*, and seemed to read it ravenously, as if he devoured it, which was to all appearance his method of studying. 'He knows how to read better than any one (said Mrs. Knowles;) he gets at the substance of a book directly; he tears out the heart of it.' He kept it wrapt up in the table-cloth in his lap during the time of dinner, from an avidity to have one entertainment in readiness when he should have finished another; resembling (if I may use so coarse a simile) a dog who holds a bone in his paws in reserve, while he eats something else which has been thrown to him.

The subject of cookery having been very naturally introduced at a table where Johnson, who boasted of the niceness of his palate, owned that 'he always found a good dinner,' he said, 'I could write a better book of cookery than has ever yet been written; it should be a book upon philosophical principles. Pharmacy is now made much more simple. Cookery may be made so too. A prescription which is now compounded of five ingredients, had formerly fifty in it. So in cookery, if the nature of the ingredients be well known, much fewer will do. Then as you cannot make bad meat good, I would tell what is the best butcher's meat, the best beef, the best pieces; how to choose young fowls; the proper season of different vegetables; and then how to roast and boil, and compound.' DILLY. 'Mrs. Glasse's *Cookery*, which is the best, was written by Dr. Hill. Half the *trade*[2] know this.' JOHNSON. 'Well, Sir. This shews how much

---

[1] Dr. Johnson, describing her needle-work in one of his letters to Mrs. Thrale, i, p. 326, uses the learned word *sutile*; which Mrs. Thrale has mistaken, and made the phrase injurious by writing '*futile* pictures.' [See *post*, p. 952.]

[2] As Physicians are called *the Faculty*, and Counsellors at Law *the Profession*; the Booksellers of London are denominated *the Trade*. Johnson disapproved of these denominations.

better the subject of cookery may be treated by a philosopher.
I doubt if the book be written by Dr. Hill; for, in Mrs. Glasse's
Cookery, which I have looked into, salt-petre and sal-prunella are
spoken of as different substances, whereas sal-prunella is only
salt-petre burnt on charcoal; and Hill could not be ignorant of
this. However, as the greatest part of such a book is made by
transcription, this mistake may have been carelessly adopted.
But you shall see what a Book of Cookery I shall make! I shall
agree with Mr. Dilly for the copy-right.' Miss Seward. 'That
would be Hercules with the distaff indeed.' Johnson. 'No,
Madam. Women can spin very well; but they cannot make a
good book of Cookery.'

Johnson. 'O! Mr. Dilly—you must know that an English
Benedictine Monk[1] at Paris has translated *The Duke of Berwick's
Memoirs*, from the original French, and has sent them to me to
sell. I offered them to Strahan, who sent them back with this
answer:—"That the first book he had published was the *Duke
of Berwick's Life*, by which he had lost: and he hated the name."
—Now I honestly tell you, that Strahan has refused them; but
I also honestly tell you, that he did it upon no principle, for he
never looked into them.' Dilly. 'Are they well translated, Sir?'
Johnson. 'Why, Sir, very well—in a style very current and
very clear. I have written to the Benedictine to give me an
answer upon two points—What evidence is there that the
letters are authentick? (for if they are not authentick they are
nothing;)— And how long will it be before the original French
is published? For if the French edition is not to appear for a considerable time, the translation will be almost as valuable as an
original book. They will make two volumes in octavo; and I
have undertaken to correct every sheet as it comes from the
press.' Mr. Dilly desired to see them, and said he would send
for them. He asked Dr. Johnson if he would write a Preface to
them. Johnson. 'No, Sir. The Benedictines were very kind to
me, and I'll do what I undertook to do; but I will not mingle my
name with them. I am to gain nothing by them. I'll turn them
loose upon the world, and let them take their chance.' Dr.

[1] [Abbé Hooke. *Croker*[1].]

MAYO. 'Pray, Sir, are Ganganelli's letters authentick?' JOHN-
SON. 'No, Sir. Voltaire put the same question to the editor of
them, that I did to Macpherson—Where are the originals?'

Mrs. Knowles affected to complain that men had much more
liberty allowed them than women. JOHNSON. 'Why, Madam,
women have all the liberty they should wish to have. We have
all the labour and the danger, and the women all the advantage.
We go to sea, we build houses, we do everything, in short, to
pay our court to the women.' MRS. KNOWLES. 'The Doctor
reasons very wittily, but not convincingly. Now, take the
instance of building; the mason's wife, if she is ever seen in
liquor, is ruined; the mason may get himself drunk as often as
he pleases, with little loss of character; nay, may let his wife
and children starve.' JOHNSON. 'Madam, you must consider, if
the mason does get himself drunk, and let his wife and children
starve, the parish will oblige him to find security for their
maintenance. We have different modes of restraining evil.
Stocks for the men, a ducking-stool for women, and a pound for
beasts. If we require more perfection from women than from
ourselves, it is doing them honour. And women have not the
same temptations that we have: they may always live in virtuous
company; men must mix in the world indiscriminately. If a
woman has no inclination to do what is wrong being secured
from it is no restraint to her. I am at liberty to walk into the
Thames; but if I were to try it, my friends would restrain me
in Bedlam, and I should be obliged to them.' MRS. KNOWLES.
'Still, Doctor, I cannot help thinking it a hardship that more
indulgence is allowed to men than to women. It gives a superiority
to men, to which I do not see how they are entitled.' JOHNSON.
'It is plain, Madam, one or other must have the superiority. As
Shakspeare says, "If two men ride on a horse, one must ride
behind."' DILLY. 'I suppose, Sir, Mrs. Knowles would have
them to ride in panniers, one on each side.' JOHNSON. 'Then,
Sir, the horse would throw them both.' MRS. KNOWLES. 'Well,
I hope that in another world the sexes will be equal.' BOSWELL.
'That is being too ambitious, Madam. *We* might as well desire
to be equal with the angels. We shall all, I hope, be happy in a

future state, but we must not expect to be all happy in the same degree. It is enough if we be happy according to our several capacities. A worthy carman will get to heaven as well as Sir Isaac Newton. Yet, though equally good, they will not have the same degrees of happiness.' JOHNSON. 'Probably not.'

Upon this subject I had once before sounded him, by mentioning the late Reverend Mr. Brown, of Utrecht's, image; that a great and small glass, though equally full, did not hold an equal quantity; which he threw out to refute David Hume's saying, that a little miss, going to dance at a ball, in a fine new dress, was as happy as a great oratour, after having made an eloquent and applauded speech. After some thought, Johnson said, 'I come over to the parson.' As an instance of coincidence of thinking, Mr. Dilly told me, that Dr. King, a late dissenting minister in London, said to him, upon the happiness in a future state of good men of different capacities, 'A pail does not hold so much as a tub; but, if it be equally full, it has no reason to complain. Every Saint in heaven will have as much happiness as he can hold.' Mr. Dilly thought this a clear, though a familiar illustration of the phrase, 'One star differeth from another in brightness.'

Dr. Mayo having asked Johnson's opinion of Soame Jenyns's *View of the Internal Evidence of the Christian Religion;*—JOHNSON. 'I think it a pretty book; not very theological indeed; and there seems to be an affectation of ease and carelessness, as if it were not suitable to his character to be very serious about the matter.' BOSWELL. 'He may have intended this to introduce his book the better among genteel people, who might be unwilling to read too grave a treatise. There is a general levity in the age. We have physicians now with bag-wigs; may we not have airy divines, at least somewhat less solemn in their appearance than they used to be?' JOHNSON. 'Jenyns might mean as you say.' BOSWELL. '*You* should like his book, Mrs. Knowles, as it maintains, as you *friends* do, that courage is not a Christian virtue.' MRS. KNOWLES. 'Yes, indeed, I like him there; but I cannot agree with him, that friendship is not a Christian virtue.' JOHNSON. 'Why, Madam, strictly speaking, he is right.

All friendship is preferring the interest of a friend, to the neglect, or, perhaps, against the interest of others; so that an old
Greek said, "He that has *friends* has *no friend.*" Now Christianity recommends universal benevolence, to consider all men as
our brethren, which is contrary to the virtue of friendship, as
described by the ancient philosophers. Surely, Madam, your sect
must approve of this; for, you call all men *friends.*' M RS.
KNOWLES. 'We are commanded to do good to all men, "but
especially to them who are of the household of Faith." ' JOHN-
SON. 'Well, Madam. The household of Faith is wide enough.'
MRS. KNOWLES. 'But, Doctor, our Saviour had twelve Apostles,
yet there was *one* whom he *loved.* John was called "the disciple
whom JESUS loved." ' JOHNSON. (with eyes sparkling benignantly,) 'Very well, indeed, Madam. You have said very well.'
BOSWELL. 'A fine application. Pray, Sir, had you ever thought
of it?' JOHNSON. 'I had not, Sir.'

From this pleasing subject, he, I know not how or why, made
a sudden transition to one upon which he was a violent aggressor; for he said, 'I am willing to love all mankind, *except an
American:*' and his inflammable corruption bursting into horrid
fire, he 'breathed out threatenings and slaughter;' calling them,
'Rascals—Robbers—Pirates;' and exclaiming, he'd 'burn and
destroy them.' Miss Seward, looking to him with mild but
steady astonishment, said, 'Sir, this is an instance that we are
always most violent against those whom we have injured.'—He
was irritated still more by this delicate and keen reproach; and
roared out another tremendous volley, which one might fancy
could be heard across the Atlantick. During this tempest I sat
in great uneasiness, lamenting his heat of temper; till, by
degrees, I diverted his attention to other topicks.

DR. MAYO. (to Dr. Johnson,) 'Pray, Sir, have you read
Edwards, of New England, on *Grace?*' JOHNSON. 'No, Sir.'
BOSWELL. 'It puzzled me so much as to the freedom of the
human will, by stating, with wonderful acute ingenuity, our
being actuated by a series of motives which we cannot resist,
that the only relief I had was to forget it.' MAYO. 'But he
makes the proper distinction between moral and physical neces-

sity.' BOSWELL. 'Alas, Sir, they come both to the same thing. You may be bound as hard by chains when covered by leather, as when the iron appears. The argument for the moral necessity of human actions is always, I observe, fortified by supposing universal prescience to be one of the attributes of the Deity.' JOHNSON. 'You are surer that you are free, than you are of prescience; you are surer that you can lift up your finger or not as you please, than you are of any conclusion from a deduction of reasoning. But let us consider a little the objection from prescience. It is certain I am either to go home to-night or not; that does not prevent my freedom.' BOSWELL. 'That it is certain you are *either* to go home or not, does not prevent your freedom; because the liberty of choice between the two is compatible with that certainty. But if *one* of these events be certain *now*, you have no *future* power of volition. If it be certain you are to go home to-night, you *must* go home.' JOHNSON. 'If I am well acquainted with a man, I can judge with great probability how he will act in any case, without his being restrained by my judging. GOD may have this probability increased to certainty.' BOSWELL. 'When it is increased to *certainty*, freedom ceases, because that cannot be certainly foreknown, which is not certain at the time; but if it be certain at the time, it is a contradiction in terms to maintain that there can be afterwards any *contingency* dependent upon the exercise of will or any thing else.' JOHNSON. 'All theory is against the freedom of the will; all experience for it.'— I did not push the subject any farther. I was glad to find him so mild in discussing a question of the most abstract nature, involved with theological tenets, which he generally would not suffer to be in any degree opposed.[1]

He as usual defended luxury; 'You cannot spend money in luxury without doing good to the poor. Nay, you do more good to them by spending it in luxury, than by giving it: for by spending it in luxury, you make them exert industry, whereas

---

[1] If any of my readers are disturbed by this thorny question, I beg leave to recommend to them Letter 69 of Montesquieu's *Lettres Persanes*; and the late Mr. John Palmer of Islington's Answer to Dr. Priestley's mechanical arguments for what he absurdly calls 'Philosophical Necessity.'

by giving it, you keep them idle. I own, indeed, there may be more virtue in giving it immediately in charity, than in spending it in luxury; though there may be a pride in that too.' Miss Seward asked, if this was not Mandeville's doctrine of 'private vices publick benefits.' JOHNSON. 'The fallacy of that book is, that Mandeville defines neither vices nor benefits. He reckons among vices everything that gives pleasure. He takes the narrowest system of morality, monastick morality, which holds pleasure itself to be a vice, such as eating salt with our fish, because it makes it taste better; and he reckons wealth as a publick benefit, which is by no means always true. Pleasure of itself is not a vice. Having a garden, which we all know to be perfectly innocent, is a great pleasure. At the same time, in this state of being there are many pleasures vices, which however are so immediately agreeable that we can hardly abstain from them. The happiness of Heaven will be, that pleasure and virtue will be perfectly consistent. Mandeville puts the case of a man who gets drunk in an ale-house; and says it is a publick benefit, because so much money is got by it to the publick. But it must be considered, that all the good gained by this, through the gradation of alehouse-keeper, brewer, maltster, and farmer, is overbalanced by the evil caused to the man and his family by his getting drunk. This is the way to try what is vicious, by ascertaining whether more evil than good is produced by it upon the whole, which is the case in all vice. It may happen that good is produced by vice; but not as vice; for instance, a robber may take money from its owner, and give it to one who will make a better use of it. Here is good produced; but not by the robbery as robbery, but as translation of property. I read Mandeville forty, or, I believe, fifty years ago. He did not puzzle me; he opened my views into real life very much. No, it is clear that the happiness of society depends on virtue. In Sparta, theft was allowed by general consent: theft, therefore, was *there* not a crime, but then there was no security; and what a life must they have had, when there was no security. Without truth there must be a dissolution of society. As it is, there is so little truth, that we are almost afraid to trust our ears; but how should we be,

if falsehood were multiplied ten times? Society is held together
by communication and information; and I remember this remark
of Sir Thomas Brown's, "Do the devils lie? No; for then Hell
could not subsist." '[1]

Talking of Miss ————,[2] a literary lady, he said, 'I was
obliged to speak to Miss Reynolds, to let her know that I
desired she would not flatter me so much.' Somebody now
observed, 'She flatters Garrick.' JOHNSON. 'She is in the right
to flatter Garrick. She is in the right for two reasons; first,
because she has the world with her, who have been praising
Garrick these thirty years; and secondly, because she is rewarded
for it by Garrick. Why should she flatter *me*? I can do nothing
for her. Let her carry her praise to a better market. (Then
turning to Mrs. Knowles.) You, Madam, have been flattering
me all the evening; I wish you would give Boswell a little now.
If you knew his merit as well as I do, you would say a great
deal; he is the best travelling companion in the world.'

Somebody mentioned the Reverend Mr. Mason's prosecution
of Mr. Murray, the bookseller, for having inserted in a collection
of *Gray's Poems*, only fifty lines, of which Mr. Mason had still
the exclusive property, under the statute of Queen Anne; and
that Mr. Mason had persevered, notwithstanding his being
requested to name his own terms of compensation.[3] Johnson
signified his displeasure at Mr. Mason's conduct very strongly;
but added, by way of shewing that he was not surprized at it,
'Mason's a Whig.' MRS. KNOWLES. (not hearing distinctly)
'What! a Prig, Sir?' JOHNSON. 'Worse, Madam; a Whig! But
he is both.'

I expressed a horrour at the thought of death. MRS.
KNOWLES. 'Nay, thou should'st not have a horrour for what is
the gate of life.' JOHNSON. (standing upon the hearth rolling
about, with a serious, solemn, and somewhat gloomy air,) 'No
rational man can die without uneasy apprehension.' MRS.
KNOWLES. 'The Scriptures tell us, "The righteous shall have

[1] [*Pseud. Epidem.* (1646), I. xi. 16, and *Adventurer*, 50.]
[2] [Hannah More. *Mrs. Piozzi*; Croker[1]; *Boswell's 1778 Journal*.]
[3] [See *A Letter to W Mason, A.M. from J. Murray, Bookseller in London*;
2nd edit. p 29.]

hope in his death."' JOHNSON. 'Yes, Madam; that is, he shall not have despair. But, consider, his hope of salvation must be founded on the terms on which it is promised that the mediation of our SAVIOUR shall be applied to us,—namely, obedience; and where obedience has failed, then, as suppletory to it, repentance. But what man can say that his obedience has been such, as he would approve of in another, or even in himself upon close examination, or that his repentance has not been such as to require being repented of? No man can be sure that his obedience and repentance will obtain salvation.' MRS. KNOWLES. 'But divine intimation of acceptance may be made to the soul.' JOHNSON. 'Madam, it may; but I should not think the better of a man who should tell me on his death-bed he was sure of salvation. A man cannot be sure himself that he has divine intimation of acceptance; much less can he make others sure that he has it.' BOSWELL. 'Then, Sir, we must be contented to acknowledge that death is a terrible thing.' JOHNSON. 'Yes, Sir. I have made no approaches to a state which can look on it as not terrible.' MRS. KNOWLES. (seeming to enjoy a pleasing serenity in the persuasion of benignant divine light,) 'Does not St. Paul say, "I have fought the good fight of faith, I have finished my course; henceforth is laid up for me a crown of life?"' JOHNSON. 'Yes, Madam; but here was a man inspired, a man who had been converted by supernatural interposition.' BOSWELL. 'In prospect death is dreadful; but in fact we find that people die easy.' JOHNSON. 'Why, Sir, most people have not *thought* much of the matter, so cannot *say* much, and it is supposed they die easy. Few believe it certain they are then to die; and those who do, set themselves to behave with resolution, as a man does who is going to be hanged. He is not the less unwilling to be hanged.' MISS SEWARD. 'There is one mode of the fear of death, which is certainly absurd; and that is the dread of annihilation, which is only a pleasing sleep without a dream.' JOHNSON. 'It is neither pleasing, nor sleep; it is nothing. Now mere existence is so much better than nothing, that one would rather exist even in pain, than not exist.' BOSWELL. 'If annihilation be nothing, then existing in pain is not a comparative state, but is a positive evil, which I cannot think we should choose. I must be allowed to differ here; and it would lessen the hope of a future state founded on the argument, that the Supreme Being, who is good as he is great, will hereafter compensate for our present sufferings in this life. For if existence, such as we have it here, be comparatively a good, we have no reason to complain, though no more of it should be given to us. But if our only state of existence were in this world, then we might with some reason complain that we are so dissatisfied with our enjoyments compared with our desires.' JOHNSON. 'The lady confounds annihilation, which is nothing, with the apprehension of it, which is dreadful. It is in the apprehension of it that the horrour of annihilation consists.'

Of John Wesley, he said, 'He can talk well on any subject.' BOSWELL. 'Pray, Sir, what has he made of his story of a ghost?' JOHNSON. 'Why, Sir, he believes it; but not on sufficient authority. He did not take time enough to examine the girl. It was at Newcastle, where the ghost was said to have appeared to a young woman several times, mentioning something about the right to an old house, advising application to be made to an attorney, which was done; and, at the same time, saying the attorney would do nothing, which proved to be the fact. "This (says John,) is a proof that a ghost knows our thoughts." Now (laughing,) it is not necessary to know our thoughts, to tell that an attorney will sometimes do nothing. Charles Wesley, who is a more stationary man, does not believe the story. I am sorry that John did not take more pains to inquire into the evidence for it.' MISS SEWARD. (with an incredulous smile,) 'What, Sir! about a ghost?' JOHNSON. (with solemn vehemence,) 'Yes, Madam: this is a question which, after five thousand years, is yet undecided; a question, whether in theology or philosophy, one of the most important that can come before the human understanding.'

Mrs. Knowles mentioned, as a proselyte to Quakerism, Miss ————,[1] a young lady well known to Dr. Johnson, for whom he had shewn much affection; while she ever had, and still

[1] [Jane Harry, the natural daughter of Thomas Hibbert. *Croker*[1].]

retained, a great respect for him. Mrs. Knowles at the same time took an opportunity of letting him know 'that the amiable young creature was sorry at finding that he was offended at her leaving the Church of England and embracing a simpler faith;' and, in the gentlest and most persuasive manner, solicited his kind indulgence for what was sincerely a matter of conscience. JOHNSON, (frowning very angrily,) 'Madam, she is an odious wench. She could not have any proper conviction that it was her duty to change her religion, which is the most important of all subjects, and should be studied with all care, and with all the helps we can get. She knew no more of the Church which she left, and that which she embraced, than she did of the difference between the Copernican and Ptolemaick systems.' MRS. KNOWLES. 'She had the New Testament before her.' JOHNSON. 'Madam, she could not understand the New Testament, the most difficult book in the world, for which the study of a life is required.' MRS. KNOWLES. 'It is clear as to essentials.' JOHNSON. 'But not as to controversial points. The heathens were easily converted, because they had nothing to give up; but we ought not, without very strong conviction indeed, to desert the religion in which we have been educated. That is the religion given you, the religion in which it may be said Providence has placed you. If you live conscientiously in that religion, you may be safe. But errour is dangerous indeed, if you err when you choose a religion for yourself.' MRS. KNOWLES. 'Must we then go by implicit faith?' JOHNSON. 'Why, Madam, the greatest part of our knowledge is implicit faith; and as to religion, have we heard all that a disciple of Confucius, all that a Mahometan, can say for himself?' He then rose again into passion, and attacked the young proselyte in the severest terms of reproach, so that both the ladies seemed to be much shocked.[1]

[1] Mrs. Knowles, not satisfied with the fame of her needlework, the '*sutile pictures*' mentioned by Johnson, in which she has indeed displayed much dexterity, nay, with the fame of reasoning better than women generally do, as I have fairly shewn her to have done, communicated to me a Dialogue of considerable length, which after many years had elapsed, she wrote down as having passed between Dr. Johnson and herself at this interview. As I had not the least recollection of it, and did not find the smallest trace of it in my

We remained together till it was pretty late. Notwithstanding occasional explosions of violence, we were all delighted upon the whole with Johnson. I compared him at this time to a warm West-Indian climate, where you have a bright sun, quick vegetation, luxuriant foliage, luscious fruits; but where the same heat sometimes produces thunder, lightning, earthquakes, in a terrible degree.

April 17, being Good Friday, I waited on Johnson, as usual. I observed at breakfast that although it was a part of his abstemious discipline on this most solemn fast, to take no milk in his tea, yet when Mrs. Desmoulins inadvertently poured it in, he did not reject it. I talked of the strange indecision of mind, and imbecility in the common occurrences of life, which we may observe in some people. JOHNSON. 'Why, Sir, I am in the habit of getting others to do things for me.' BOSWELL. 'What, Sir! have you that weakness?' JOHNSON. 'Yes, Sir. But I always think afterwards I should have done better for myself.'

I told him that at a gentleman's[1] house where there was thought to be such extravagance or bad management, that he was living much beyond his income, his lady had objected to the cutting of a pickled mango, and that I had taken an opportunity to ask the price of it, and found it was only two shillings; so here was a very poor saving. JOHNSON. 'Sir, that is the blundering œconomy of a narrow understanding. It is stopping one hole in a sieve.'

I expressed some inclination to publish an account of my *Travels* upon the continent of Europe, for which I had a variety of materials collected. JOHNSON. 'I do not say, Sir, you may not publish your travels; but I give you my opinion, that you would lessen yourself by it. What can you tell of countries so well

Record taken at the time, I could not in consistency with my firm regard to authenticity, insert it in my work. It has, however, been published in *The Gent. Mag.* for June 1791. It chiefly relates to the principles of the sect called *Quakers*; and no doubt the Lady appears to have greatly the advantage of Dr. Johnson in argument as well as expression. From what I have now stated, and from the internal evidence of the paper itself, any one who may have the curiosity to peruse it, will judge whether it was wrong in me to reject it, however willing to gratify Mrs. Knowles.

[1] [Langton. *Mrs Piozzi*; *Croker*[1].]

known as those upon the continent of Europe, which you have visited?' Boswell. 'But I can give an entertaining narrative, with many incidents, anecdotes, *jeux d'esprit*, and remarks, so as to make very pleasant reading.' Johnson. 'Why, Sir, most modern travellers in Europe who have published their travels, have been laughed at: I would not have you added to the number.[1] The world is now not contented to be merely entertained by a traveller's narrative; they want to learn something. Now some of my friends asked me, why I did not give some account of my travels in France. The reason is plain; intelligent readers had seen more of France than I had. *You* might have liked my travels in France, and The Club might have liked them; but, upon the whole, there would have been more ridicule than good produced by them.' Boswell. 'I cannot agree with you, Sir. People would like to read what you say of any thing. Suppose a face has been painted by fifty painters before; still we love to see it done by Sir Joshua.' Johnson. 'True, Sir, but Sir Joshua cannot paint a face when he has not time to look on it.' Boswell. 'Sir, a sketch of any sort by him is valuable. And, Sir, to talk to you in your own style (raising my voice, and shaking my head,) you *should* have given us your travels in France. I am *sure* I am right, and *there's an end on't*.'

I said to him that it was certainly true, as my friend Dempster had observed in his letter to me upon the subject, that a great part of what was in his *Journey to the Western Islands of Scotland* had been in his mind before he left London. Johnson. 'Why yes, Sir, the topicks were; and books of travels will be good in proportion to what a man has previously in his mind; his knowing what to observe; his power of contrasting one mode of life with another. As the Spanish proverb says, "He, who would bring home the wealth of the Indies, must carry the wealth of the Indies with him." So it is in travelling; a man must carry knowledge with him, if he would bring home knowledge.' Boswell. 'The proverb, I suppose, Sir, means, he must carry a large stock with him to trade with.' Johnson. 'Yes, Sir.'

---

[1] I believe, however, I shall follow my own opinion; for the world has shewn a very flattering partiality to my writings, on many occasions.

It was a delightful day: as we walked to St. Clement's church, I again remarked that Fleet-street was the most cheerful scene in the world. 'Fleet-street (said I,) is in my mind more delightful than Tempé.' JOHNSON. 'Ay, Sir; but let it be compared with Mull.'

There was a very numerous congregation to-day at St. Clement's church, which Dr. Johnson said he observed with pleasure.

And now I am to give a pretty full account of one of the most curious incidents in Johnson's life, of which he himself has made the following minute on this day: 'In my return from church, I was accosted by Edwards, an old fellow-collegian, who had not seen me since 1729. He knew me, and asked if I remembered one Edwards; I did not at first recollect the name, but gradually as we walked along, recovered it, and told him a conversation that had passed at an ale-house between us. My purpose is to continue our acquaintance[1].'

It was in Butcher-row that this meeting happened. Mr. Edwards, who was a decent-looking elderly man in grey clothes, and a wig of many curls, accosted Johnson with familiar confidence, knowing who he was, while Johnson returned his salutation with a courteous formality, as to a stranger. But as soon as Edwards had brought to his recollection their having been at Pembroke-College together nine-and-forty years ago, he seemed much pleased, asked where he lived, and said he should be glad to see him in Bolt-court. EDWARDS. 'Ah, Sir! we are old men now.' JOHNSON. (who never liked to think of being old,) 'Don't let us discourage one another.' EDWARDS. 'Why, Doctor, you look stout and hearty, I am happy to see you so; for the news papers told us you were very ill.' JOHNSON. 'Ay, Sir, they are always telling lies of *us old fellows.*'

Wishing to be present at more of so singular a conversation as that between two fellow-collegians, who had lived forty years in London without ever having chanced to meet, I whispered to Mr. Edwards that Dr. Johnson was going home, and that he had better accompany him now. So Edwards walked along with

[1] *Pr. and Med.* p. 164.

us, I eagerly assisting to keep up the conversation. Mr. Edwards informed Dr. Johnson that he had practised long as a solicitor in Chancery, but that he now lived in the country upon a little farm, about sixty acres, just by Stevenage in Hertfordshire, and that he came to London (to Barnard's Inn, No. 6), generally twice a week. Johnson appearing to be in a reverie, Mr. Edwards addressed himself to me, and expatiated on the pleasure of living in the country. BOSWELL. 'I have no notion of this, Sir. What you have to entertain you, is, I think, exhausted in half an hour.' EDWARDS. 'What? don't you love to have hope realized? I see my grass, and my corn, and my trees growing. Now, for instance, I am curious to see if this frost has not nipped my fruit-trees.' JOHNSON. (who we did not imagine was attending,) 'You find, Sir, you have fears as well as hopes.'—So well did he see the whole, when another saw but the half of a subject.

When we got to Dr. Johnson's house, and were seated in his library, the dialogue went on admirably. EDWARDS. 'Sir, I remember you would not let us say *prodigious* at College. For even then, Sir, (turning to me,) he was delicate in language, and we all feared him.'[1] JOHNSON. (to Edwards,) 'From your having practised the law long, Sir, I presume you must be rich.' EDWARDS. 'No, Sir; I got a good deal of money; but I had a number of poor relations to whom I gave a great part of it.' JOHNSON. 'Sir, you have been rich in the most valuable sense of the word.' EDWARDS. 'But I shall not die rich.' JOHNSON. 'Nay, sure, Sir, it is better to *live* rich than to *die* rich.' EDWARDS. 'I wish I had continued at College.' JOHNSON. 'Why do you wish that, Sir?' EDWARDS. 'Because I think I should have had a much easier life than mine has been. I should have been a parson, and had a good living, like Bloxam and several others, and lived comfortably.' JOHNSON. 'Sir, the life of a parson, of a conscientious clergyman, is not easy. I have always considered a clergyman as the father of a larger family than he is able to maintain. I would rather have Chancery suits upon my hands

---

[1] Johnson said to me afterwards, 'Sir, they respected me for my literature; and yet it was not great but by comparison. Sir, it is amazing how little literature there is in the world.'

than the cure of souls. No, Sir, I do not envy a clergyman's life as an easy life, nor do I envy the clergyman who makes it an easy life.' Here taking himself up all of a sudden, he exclaimed, 'O! Mr. Edwards! I'll convince you that I recollect you. Do you remember our drinking together at an alehouse near Pembroke gate? At that time, you told me of the Eton boy, who, when verses on our SAVIOUR's turning water into wine were prescribed as an exercise, brought up a single line, which was highly admired,—

> *"Vidit et erubuit lympha pudica* DEUM,"[1]

and I told you of another fine line in Camden's *Rèmains*, an eulogy upon one of our Kings, who was succeeded by his son, a prince of equal merit:—

> *"Mira cano, Sol occubuit, nox nulla secuta est."* [2]

EDWARDS. 'You are a philosopher, Dr. Johnson. I have tried too in my time to be a philosopher; but, I don't know how, cheerfulness was always breaking in.'—Mr. Burke, Sir Joshua Reynolds, Mr. Courtenay, Mr. Malone, and, indeed, all the eminent men to whom I have mentioned this, have thought it an exquisite trait of character. The truth is, that philosophy, like religion, is too generally supposed to be hard and severe, at least so grave as to exclude all gaiety.

EDWARDS. 'I have been twice married, Doctor. You, I suppose, have never known what it was to have a wife.' JOHNSON. 'Sir, I have known what it was to have a wife, and (in a solemn, tender, faultering tone) I have known what it was to *lose a wife*. —It had almost broke my heart.'

---

[1] ['The modest nymph saw her God and blushed.'] This line has frequently been attributed to Dryden, when a King's Scholar at Westminster. But neither Eton nor Westminster have in truth any claim to it, the line being borrowed, with a slight change, from an Epigram by Crashaw:—

> 'JOANN. 2,
> 'Aquæ in vinum versæ.
> 'Unde rubor vestris et non sua purpura lymphis?
> Quæ rosa mirantes tam nova mutat aquas?
> Numen, convivæ, præsens agnoscite numen,
> Nympha pudica DEUM vidit, et erubuit.'   [M.]

[2] ['I sing a marvel: the sun set, but no night followed.' (Perhaps by Giraldus Cambrensis.)]

EDWARDS. 'How do you live, Sir? For my part, I must have my regular meals, and a glass of good wine. I find I require it.' JOHNSON. 'I now drink no wine, Sir. Early in life I drank wine: for many years I drank none. I then for some years drank a great deal.' EDWARDS. 'Some hogsheads, I warrant you.' JOHNSON. 'I then had a severe illness, and left it off, and I have never begun it again. I never felt any difference upon myself from eating one thing rather than another, nor from one kind of weather rather than another. There are people, I believe, who feel a difference; but I am not one of them. And as to regular meals, I have fasted from the Sunday's dinner to the Tuesday's dinner, without any inconvenience. I believe it is best to eat just as one is hungry: but a man who is in business, or a man who has a family, must have stated meals. I am a straggler. I may leave this town and go to Grand Cairo, without being missed here or observed there.' EDWARDS. 'Don't you eat supper, Sir?' JOHNSON. 'No, Sir.' EDWARDS. 'For my part, now, I consider supper as a turnpike through which one must pass, in order to get to bed.'[1]

JOHNSON. 'You are a lawyer, Mr. Edwards. Lawyers know life practically. A bookish man should always have them to converse with. They have what he wants.' EDWARDS. 'I am grown old: I am sixty-five.' JOHNSON. 'I shall be sixty-eight next birth-day. Come, Sir, drink water, and put in for a hundred.'

Mr. Edwards mentioned a gentleman[2] who had left his whole fortune to Pembroke College. JOHNSON. 'Whether to leave one's whole fortune to a College be right, must depend upon circumstances. I would leave the interest of the fortune I bequeathed to a College to my relations or my friends, for their lives. It is the same thing to a College, which is a permanent society, whether it gets the money now or twenty years hence; and I would wish to make my relations or friends feel the benefit of it.'

This interview confirmed my opinion of Johnson's most humane and benevolent heart. His cordial and placid behaviour

---

[1] I am not absolutely sure but this was my own suggestion, though it is truly in the character of Edwards.

[2] [The Rev. James Phipps. Macleane's *Pembroke College*.]

to an old fellow-collegian, a man so different from himself; and
his telling him that he would go down to his farm and visit him,
showed a kindliness of disposition very rare at an advanced age.
He observed, 'how wonderful it was that they had both been in
London forty years, without having ever once met, and both
walkers in the street too!' Mr. Edwards, when going away,
again recurred to his consciousness of senility, and looking full
in Johnson's face, said to him, 'You'll find in Dr. Young,

> "O my coevals! remnants of yourselves!" '[1]

Johnson did not relish this at all; but shook his head with
impatience. Edwards walked off, seemingly highly pleased with
the honour of having been thus noticed by Dr. Johnson. When
he was gone, I said to Johnson, I thought him but a weak man.
JOHNSON. 'Why, yes, Sir. Here is a man who has passed
through life without experience: yet I would rather have him
with me than a more sensible man who will not talk readily.
This man is always willing to say what he has to say.' Yet Dr.
Johnson had himself by no means that willingness which he
praised so much, and I think so justly; for who has not felt the
painful effect of the dreary void, when there is a total silence in
a company, for any length of time; or, which is as bad, or perhaps worse, when the conversation is with difficulty kept up by
a perpetual effort?

Johnson once observed to me, 'Tom Tyers described me the
best: "Sir, (said he,) you are like a ghost: you never speak till
you are spoken to." '

The gentleman whom he thus familiarly mentioned was
Mr. Thomas Tyers, son of Mr. Jonathan Tyers, the founder
of that excellent place of publick amusement, Vauxhall Gardens,
which must ever be an estate to its proprietor, as it is peculiarly
adapted to the taste of the English nation; there being a mixture
of curious show,—gay exhibition, musick, vocal and instrumental, not too refined for the general ear;—for all which only a
shilling is paid;[2] and, though last, not least, good eating and

---

[1] [*Night Thoughts*: Night, iv. 109.]
[2] In summer 1792, additional and more expensive decorations having
been introduced, the price of admission was raised to two shillings. I cannot

drinking for those who choose to purchase that regale. Mr.
Thomas Tyers was bred to the law; but having a handsome
fortune, vivacity of temper, and eccentricity of mind, he could
not confine himself to the regularity of practice. He therefore
ran about the world with a pleasant carelessness, amusing everybody by his desultory conversation. He abounded in anecdote,
but was not sufficiently attentive to accuracy. I therefore cannot
venture to avail myself much of a biographical sketch of Johnson
which he published, being one among the various persons ambitious of appending their names to that of my illustrious friend.
That sketch is, however, an entertaining little collection of fragments. Those which he published of Pope and Addison are of
higher merit; but his fame must chiefly rest upon his *Political
Conferences,* in which he introduces several eminent persons
delivering their sentiments in the way of dialogue, and discovers
a considerable share of learning, various knowledge, and discernment of character. This much may I be allowed to say of a man
who was exceedingly obliging to me, and who lived with Dr.
Johnson in as easy a manner as almost any of his very numerous
acquaintance.

Mr. Edwards had said to me aside, that Dr. Johnson should
have been of a profession. I repeated the remark to Johnson that
I might have his own thoughts on the subject. JOHNSON. 'Sir,
it *would* have been better that I had been of a profession. I ought
to have been a lawyer.' BOSWELL. 'I do not think, Sir, it would
have been better, for we should not have had the *English Dictionary.*' JOHNSON. 'But you would have had *Reports.*' BOSWELL.
'Ay; but there would not have been another, who could have
written the *Dictionary.* There have been many very good Judges.
Suppose you had been Lord Chancellor; you would have
delivered opinions with more extent of mind, and in a more
ornamented manner, than perhaps any Chancellor ever did, or
ever will do. But, I believe, causes have been as judiciously

approve of this. The company may be more select; but a number of the
honest commonalty are, I fear, excluded from sharing in elegant and innocent entertainment. An attempt to abolish the one-shilling gallery at the
playhouse has been very properly counteracted.

decided as you could have done.' JOHNSON. 'Yes, Sir. Property has been as well settled.'

Johnson, however, had a noble ambition floating in his mind, and had, undoubtedly, often speculated on the possibility of his supereminent powers being rewarded in this great and liberal country by the highest honours of the state. Sir William Scott informs me, that upon the death of the late Lord Lichfield, who was Chancellor of the University of Oxford, he said to Johnson, 'What a pity it is, Sir, that you did not follow the profession of the law. You might have been Lord Chancellor of Great Britain, and attained to the dignity of the peerage; and now that the title of Lichfield, your native city, is extinct, you might have had it.' Johnson, upon this, seemed much agitated; and, in an angry tone, exclaimed, 'Why will you vex me by suggesting this, when it is too late?'

But he did not repine at the prosperity of others. The late Dr. Thomas Leland told Mr. Courtenay, that when Mr. Edmund Burke shewed Johnson his fine house and lands near Beaconsfield, Johnson coolly said, *'Non equidem invideo; miror magis.'*[1]

---

[1] ['I grudge thee not—rather I marvel.'—Virgil, *Eclogues* i. 11. (Wickham.)] I am not entirely without suspicion that Johnson may have felt a little momentary envy; for no man loved the good things of this life better than he did; and he could not but be conscious that he deserved a much larger share of them, than he ever had. I attempted in a newspaper to comment on the above passage, in the manner of Warburton, who must be allowed to have shewn uncommon ingenuity, in giving to any authour's text whatever meaning he chose it should carry. As this imitation may amuse my readers, I shall here introduce it:—

'No saying of Dr. Johnson's has been more misunderstood than his applying to Mr. Burke when he first saw him at his fine place at Beaconsfield, *Non equidem invideo; miror magis.* These two celebrated men had been friends for many years before Mr. Burke entered on his parliamentary career. They were both writers, both members of THE LITERARY CLUB; when, therefore, Dr. Johnson saw Mr. Burke in a situation so much more splendid than that to which he himself had attained, he did not mean to express that he thought it a disproportionate prosperity; but while he, as a philosopher, asserted an exemption from envy, *non equidem invideo*, he went on in the words of the poet *miror magis*; thereby signifying, either that he was occupied in admiring what he was glad to see; or, perhaps, that considering the general lot of men of superiour abilities, he wondered that Fortune, who is represented as blind, should, in this instance, have been so just.'

Yet no man had a higher notion of the dignity of literature than Johnson, or was more determined in maintaining the respect which he justly considered as due to it. Of this, besides the general tenor of his conduct in society, some characteristical instances may be mentioned.

He told Sir Joshua Reynolds, that once when he dined in a numerous company of booksellers, where the room being small, the head of the table, at which he sat, was almost close to the fire, he persevered in suffering a great deal of inconvenience from the heat, rather than quit his place, and let one of them sit above him.

Goldsmith, in his diverting simplicity, complained one day, in a mixed company, of Lord Camden. 'I met him (said he,) at Lord Clare's house in the country, and he took no more notice of me than if I had been an ordinary man.' The company having laughed heartily, Johnson stood forth in defence of his friend. 'Nay, Gentlemen, (said he,) Dr. Goldsmith is in the right. A nobleman ought to have made up to such a man as Goldsmith; and I think it is much against Lord Camden that he neglected him.'

Nor could he patiently endure to hear that such respect as he thought due only to higher intellectual qualities, should be bestowed on men of slighter, though perhaps more amusing talents. I told him, that one morning, when I went to breakfast with Garrick, who was very vain of his intimacy with Lord Camden, he accosted me thus:—'Pray now, did you—did you meet a little lawyer turning the corner, eh?'—'No, Sir, (said I.) Pray what do you mean by the question?'—'Why, (replied Garrick, with an affected indifference, yet as if standing on tip-toe,) Lord Camden has this moment left me. We have had a long walk together.' JOHNSON. 'Well, Sir, Garrick talked very properly. Lord Camden *was* a *little lawyer* to be associating so familiarly with a player.'

Sir Joshua Reynolds observed, with great truth, that Johnson considered Garrick to be as it were his *property*. He would allow no man either to blame or to praise Garrick in his presence, without contradicting him.

Having fallen into a very serious frame of mind, in which
mutual expressions of kindness passed between us, such as
would be thought too vain in me to repeat, I talked with regret
of the sad inevitable certainty that one of us must survive the
other. JOHNSON. 'Yes, Sir, that is an affecting consideration. I
remember Swift, in one of his letters to Pope, says, "I intend to
come over, that we may meet once more; and when we must
part, it is what happens to all human beings." ' BOSWELL. 'The
hope that we shall see our departed friends again must support
the mind.' JOHNSON. 'Why yes, Sir.' BOSWELL. 'There is a
strange unwillingness to part with life, independent of serious
fears as to futurity. A reverend friend[1] of ours (naming him)
tells me, that he feels an uneasiness at the thoughts of leaving
his house, his study, his books.' JOHNSON. 'This is foolish in
*****. A man need not be uneasy on these grounds; for, as he
will retain his consciousness, he may say with the philosopher,
Omnia mea mecum porto.'[2] BOSWELL. 'True, Sir: we may carry
our books in our heads; but still there is something painful in
the thought of leaving for ever what has given us pleasure. I
remember, many years ago, when my imagination was warm,
and I happened to be in a melancholy mood, it distressed me to
think of going into a state of being in which Shakspeare's poetry
did not exist. A lady whom I then much admired, a very amiable
woman, humoured my fancy, and relieved me by saying, "The
first thing you will meet in the other world, will be an elegant
copy of Shakspeare's works presented to you." ' Dr. Johnson
smiled benignantly at this, and did not appear to disapprove of
the notion.

We went to St. Clement's church again in the afternoon, and
then returned and drank tea and coffee in Mrs. Williams's room;
Mrs. Desmoulins doing the honours of the tea-table. I observed
that he would not even look at a proof-sheet of his *Life of Waller*
on Good-Friday.

Mr. Allen, the printer, brought a book on agriculture, which
was printed, and was soon to be published. It was a very strange

---

[1] [Dr. Blair. *Boswell's 1787 Journal.*]
[2] ['All that is mine I carry with me.' Cicero *Paradoxa* i.]

performance, the authour[1] having mixed in it his own thoughts upon various topicks, along with his remarks on ploughing, sowing, and other farming operations. He seemed to be an absurd profane fellow, and had introduced in his book many sneers at religion, with equal ignorance and conceit. Dr. Johnson permitted me to read some passages aloud. One was, that he resolved to work on Sunday, and did work, but he owned he felt *some* weak compunction; and he had this very curious reflection:—'I was born in the wilds of Christianity, and the briars and thorns still hang about me.' Dr. Johnson could not help laughing at this ridiculous image, yet was very angry at the fellow's impiety. 'However, (said he,) the Reviewers will make him hang himself.' He, however, observed, 'that formerly there might have been a dispensation obtained for working on Sunday in the time of harvest.' Indeed in ritual observances, were all the ministers of religion what they should be, and what many of them are, such a power might be wisely and safely lodged with the Church.

On Saturday, April 14,[2] I drank tea with him. He praised the late Mr. Duncombe,[3] of Canterbury, as a pleasing man. 'He used to come to me: I did not seek much after *him*. Indeed I never sought much after any body.' BOSWELL. 'Lord Orrery, I suppose.' JOHNSON. 'No, Sir; I never went to him but when he sent for me.' BOSWELL. 'Richardson?' JOHNSON. 'Yes, Sir. But I sought after George Psalmanazar the most. I used to go and sit with him at an alehouse in the city.'

I am happy to mention another instance which I discovered of his *seeking after* a man of merit. Soon after the Honourable Daines Barrington had published his excellent *Observations on the Statutes*, Johnson waited on that worthy and learned gentleman; and, having told him his name, courteously said, 'I have read your book, Sir, with great pleasure, and wish to be better

---

[1] [William Marshall, *Minutes of Agriculture. Croker*[1], confirmed by J.B.'s Journal which reads *Minutes of Ag*.]

[2] [actually, April 18.]

[3] William Duncombe, Esq. He married the sister of John Hughes the poet; was the authour of two tragedies and other ingenious productions; and died 26th Feb. 1769, aged 79. [M.]

known to you.' Thus began an acquaintance, which was continued with mutual regard as long as Johnson lived.

Talking of a recent seditious delinquent,[1] he said, 'They should set him in the pillory, that he may be punished in a way that would disgrace him.' I observed, that the pillory does not always disgrace. And I mentioned an instance of a gentleman[2] who I thought was not dishonoured by it. JOHNSON. 'Ay, but he was, Sir. He could not mouth and strut as he used to do, after having been there. People are not very willing to ask a man to their tables who has stood in the pillory.'

The Gentleman who had dined with us at Dr. Percy's[3] came in. Johnson attacked the Americans with intemperate vehemence of abuse. I said something in their favour; and added, that I was always sorry when he talked on that subject. This, it seems, exasperated him; though he said nothing at the time. The cloud was charged with sulphureous vapour, which was afterwards to burst in thunder.—We talked of a gentleman[4] who was running out his fortune in London; and I said, 'We must get him out of it. All his friends must quarrel with him, and that will soon drive him away.' JOHNSON. 'Nay, Sir; we'll send *you* to him. If your company does not drive a man out of his house, nothing will.' This was a horrible shock, for which there was no visible cause. I afterwards asked him why he had said so harsh a thing. JOHNSON. 'Because, Sir, you made me angry about the Americans.' BOSWELL. 'But why did you not take your revenge directly?' JOHNSON. (smiling,) 'Because, Sir, I had nothing ready. A man cannot strike till he has his weapons.' This was a candid and pleasant confession.

He shewed me to-night his drawing-room, very genteelly fitted up; and said, 'Mrs. Thrale sneered when I talked of my having asked you and your lady to live at my house. I was obliged to tell her, that you would be in as respectable a situation in my house as in hers. Sir, the insolence of wealth will creep out.' BOSWELL. 'She has a little both of the insolence of wealth,

---

[1] [Horne Tooke. *Boswell's 1778 Journal.*]
[2] [John Shebbeare. *Ib.*]　　　　　[3] [The Rev. Norton Nicholls. *Ib.*]
[4] [Langton. *Mrs. Piozzi*; *Croker*[1].]

and the conceit of parts.' JOHNSON. 'The insolence of wealth is a wretched thing; but the conceit of parts has some foundation. To be sure it should not be. But who is without it?' BOSWELL. 'Yourself, Sir.' JOHNSON. 'Why, I play no tricks: I lay no traps.' BOSWELL. 'No, Sir. You are six feet high, and you only do not stoop.'

We talked of the numbers of people that sometimes have composed the household of great families. I mentioned that there were a hundred in the family of the present Earl of Eglintoune's father. Dr. Johnson seeming to doubt it, I began to enumerate. 'Let us see: my Lord and my Lady two.' JOHNSON. 'Nay, Sir, if you are to count by twos, you may be long enough.' BOSWELL. 'Well, but now I add two sons and seven daughters, and a servant for each, that will make twenty; so we have the fifth part already.' JOHNSON. 'Very true. You get at twenty pretty readily; but you will not so easily get further on. We grow to five feet pretty readily; but it is not so easy to grow to seven.'

On Sunday, April 19, being Easter-day, after the solemnities of the festival in St. Paul's Church, I visited him, but could not stay to dinner. I expressed a wish to have the arguments for Christianity always in readiness, that my religious faith might be as firm and clear as any proposition whatever, so that I need not be under the least uneasiness, when it should be attacked. JOHNSON. 'Sir, you cannot answer all objections. You have demonstration for a First Cause: you see he must be good as well as powerful, because there is nothing to make him otherwise, and goodness of itself is preferable. Yet you have against this, what is very certain, the unhappiness of human life. This, however, gives us reason to hope for a future state of compensation, that there may be a perfect system. But of that we were not sure, till we had a positive revelation.' I told him, that his *Rasselas* had often made me unhappy; for it represented the misery of human life so well, and so convincingly to a thinking mind, that if at any time the impression wore off, and I felt myself easy, I began to suspect some delusion.

On Monday, April 20, I found him at home in the morning.

We talked of a gentleman[1] who we apprehended was gradually involving his circumstances by bad management. JOHNSON. 'Wasting a fortune is evaporation by a thousand imperceptible means. If it were a stream, they'd stop it. You must speak to him. It is really miserable. Were he a gamester, it could be said he had hopes of winning. Were he a bankrupt in trade, he might have grown rich; but he has neither spirit to spend nor resolution to spare. He does not spend fast enough to have pleasure from it. He has the crime of prodigality, and the wretchedness of parsimony. If a man is killed in a duel, he is killed as many a one has been killed; but it is a sad thing for a man to lie down and die; to bleed to death, because he has not fortitude enough to sear the wound, or even to stitch it up.' I cannot but pause a moment to admire the fecundity of fancy, and choice of language, which in this instance, and, indeed, on almost all occasions, he displayed. It was well observed by Dr. Percy, now Bishop of Dromore, 'The conversation of Johnson is strong and clear, and may be compared to an antique statue, where every vein and muscle is distinct and bold. Ordinary conversation resembles an inferiour cast.'

On Saturday, April 25, I dined with him at Sir Joshua Reynolds's, with the learned Dr. Musgrave, Counsellor Leland of Ireland, son to the historian, Mrs. Cholmondeley, and some more ladies. *The Project,* a new poem,[2] was read to the company by Dr. Musgrave. JOHNSON. 'Sir, it has no power. Were it not for the well-known names with which it is filled, it would be nothing: the names carry the poet, not the poet the names.' MUSGRAVE. 'A temporary poem always entertains us.' JOHNSON. 'So does an account of the criminals hanged yesterday entertain us.'

He proceeded:—'Demosthenes Taylor, as he was called, (that is, the Editor of Demosthenes) was the most silent man, the merest statue of a man that I have ever seen. I once dined in company with him, and all he said during the whole time was no more than *Richard.* How a man should say only Richard, it is not easy to imagine. But it was thus: Dr. Douglas was talking

[1] [Langton. *Boswell's* 1778 *Journal.*]   [2] By Richard Tickell.

of Dr. Zachary Grey, and ascribing to him something that was written by Dr. Richard Grey. So, to correct him, Taylor said, (imitating his affected sententious emphasis and nod,) *"Rich-ard."* '

Mrs. Cholmondeley, in a high flow of spirits, exhibited some lively sallies of hyperbolical compliment to Johnson, with whom she had been long acquainted, and was very easy. He was quick in catching the *manner* of the moment, and answered her some-what in the style of the hero of a romance, 'Madam, you crown me with unfading laurels.'

I happened, I know not how, to say that a pamphlet meant a prose piece. JOHNSON. 'No, Sir. A few sheets of poetry unbound are a pamphlet,[1] as much as a few sheets of prose.' MUSGRAVE. 'A pamphlet may be understood to mean a poetical piece in Westminster-Hall, that is, in formal language; but in common language it is understood to mean prose.' JOHNSON. (and here was one of the many instances of his knowing clearly and telling exactly how a thing is,) 'A pamphlet is understood in common language to mean prose, only from this, that there is so much more prose written than poetry; as when we say a *book*, prose is understood for the same reason, though a book may as well be in poetry as in prose. We understand what is most general, and we name what is less frequent.'

We talked of a lady's[2] verses on Ireland. MISS REYNOLDS. 'Have you seen them, Sir?' JOHNSON. 'No, Madam. I have seen a translation from Horace, by one of her daughters. She shewed it me.' MISS REYNOLDS. 'And how was it, Sir?' JOHNSON. 'Why, very well for a young Miss's verses;—that is to say, compared with excellence, nothing; but, very well, for the per-son who wrote them. I am vexed at being shewn verses in that manner.' MISS REYNOLDS. 'But if they should be good, why not give them hearty praise?' JOHNSON. 'Why, Madam, because

---

[1] Dr. Johnson is supported by the usage of preceding writers. So in *Musarum Deliciæ,* 8vo. 1656 (the writer is speaking of Suckling's play entitled *Aglaura,* printed in folio):—

'This great voluminous *pamphlet* may be said
To be like one that hath more hair than head.'   [M.]

[2] [Lady Lucan and her daughter. *Boswell's 1778 Journal.*]

I have not then got the better of my bad humour from having been shewn them. You must consider, Madam; beforehand they may be bad, as well as good. Nobody has a right to put another under such a difficulty, that he must either hurt the person by telling the truth, or hurt himself by telling what is not true.' BOSWELL. 'A man often shews his writings to people of eminence, to obtain from them, either from their good-nature, or from their not being able to tell the truth firmly, a commendation, of which he may afterwards avail himself.' JOHNSON. 'Very true, Sir. Therefore a man, who is asked by an authour, what he thinks of his work, is put to the torture, and is not obliged to speak the truth; so that what he says is not considered as his opinion; yet he has said it, and cannot retract it; and this authour, when mankind are hunting him with a cannister at his tail, can say, "I would not have published, had not Johnson, or Reynolds, or Musgrave, or some other good judge commended the work." Yet I consider it as a very difficult question in conscience, whether one should advise a man not to publish a work, if profit be his object; for the man may say, "Had it not been for you, I should have had the money." Now you cannot be sure; for you have only your own opinion, and the publick may think very differently.' SIR JOSHUA REYNOLDS. 'You must upon such an occasion have two judgements; one as to the real value of the work, the other as to what may please the general taste at the time.' JOHNSON. 'But you can be *sure* of neither; and therefore I should scruple much to give a suppressive vote. Both Goldsmith's comedies were once refused; his first by Garrick, his second by Colman, who was prevailed on at last by much solicitation, nay, a kind of force, to bring it on. His *Vicar of Wakefield* I myself did not think would have had much success. It was written and sold to a bookseller before his *Traveller*; but published after; so little expectation had the bookseller from it. Had it been sold after *The Traveller*, he might have had twice as much money for it, though sixty guineas was no mean price. The bookseller had the advantage of Goldsmith's reputation from *The Traveller* in the sale, though Goldsmith had it not in selling the copy.' SIR JOSHUA REYNOLDS. '*The Beggar's Opera*

affords a proof how strangely people will differ in opinion about
a literary performance. Burke thinks it has no merit.' JOHNSON.
'It was refused by one of the houses; but I should have thought
it would succeed, not from any great excellence in the writing,
but from the novelty, and the general spirit and gaiety of the
piece, which keeps the audience always attentive, and dismisses
them in good humour.'

We went to the drawing-room, where was a considerable
increase of company. Several of us got round Dr. Johnson, and
complained that he would not give us an exact catalogue of his
works, that there might be a complete edition. He smiled, and
evaded our entreaties. That he intended to do it, I have no doubt,
because I have heard him say so; and I have in my possession an
imperfect list, fairly written out, which he entitles *Historia
Studiorum*. I once got from one of his friends[1] a list, which there
was pretty good reason to suppose was accurate, for it was
written down in his presence by this friend, who enumerated
each article aloud, and had some of them mentioned to him by
Mr. Levett, in concert with whom it was made out; and
Johnson, who heard all this, did not contradict it. But when I
shewed a copy of this list to him, and mentioned the evidence for
its exactness, he laughed, and said, 'I was willing to let them go
on as they pleased, and never interfered.' Upon which I read it
to him, article by article, and got him positively to own or
refuse; and then, having obtained certainty so far, I got some
other articles confirmed by him directly; and afterwards, from
time to time, made additions under his sanction.

His friend Edward Cave having been mentioned, he told us,
'Cave used to sell ten thousand of *The Gentleman's Magazine*;
yet such was then his minute attention and anxiety that the sale
should not suffer the smallest decrease, that he would name a
particular person who he heard had talked of leaving off the
Magazine, and would say, "Let us have something good next
month." '

It was observed, that avarice was inherent in some dispositions. JOHNSON. 'No man was born a miser, because no man

[1] [Percy. *Boswell's Letters*, ii. 281.]

was born to possession. Every man is born *cupidus*—desirous of getting; but not *avarus*—desirous of keeping.' BOSWELL. 'I have heard old Mr. Sheridan maintain, with much ingenuity, that a complete miser is a happy man; a miser who gives himself wholly to the one passion of saving.' JOHNSON. 'That is flying in the face of all the world, who have called an avaricious man a *miser*, because he is miserable. No, Sir; a man who both spends and saves money is the happiest man, because he has both enjoyments.'

The conversation having turned on *Bon-Mots,* he quoted, from one of the *Ana,* an exquisite instance of flattery in a maid of honour in France, who being asked by the Queen what o'clock it was, answered, 'What your Majesty pleases.' He admitted that Mr. Burke's classical pun upon Mr. Wilkes's being carried on the shoulders[1] of the mob,—

> '———————— *Numerisque fertur*
>   *Lege solutus,*'[2]

was admirable; and though he was strangely unwilling to allow to that extraordinary man the talent of wit,[3] he also laughed with approbation at another of his playful conceits; which was, that 'Horace has in one line given a description of a good desirable manour:—

> "*Est modus in rebus, sunt certi denique fines;*"[4]

that is to say, a *modus* as to the tithes and certain *fines.*'

He observed, 'A man cannot with propriety speak of himself, except he relates simple facts; as, "I was at Richmond:" or what

---

[1] ['on the shoulders': *humeris*].

[2] ['As he pours along in lawless rhythms.' Horace (of Pindar), *Odes* IV. ii. 11. (Wickham.)]

[3] See this question fully investigated in the Notes upon my *Journal of a Tour to the Hebrides,* 3rd edit. p. 21, *et seq.* [Aug. 15]. And ere, as a lawyer mindful of the maxim *Suum cuique tribuito,* I cannot forbear to mention, that the additional Note beginning with 'I find since the former edition,' is not mine, but was obligingly furnished by Mr. Malone, who was so kind as to superintend the press while I was in Scotland, and the first part of the second edition was printing. He would not allow me to ascribe it to its proper authour; but, as it is exquisitely acute and elegant, I take this opportunity, without his knowledge, to do him justice.

[4] ['There is measure in everything, there are fixed limits.' Horace, *Satires* I, i. 106. (Wickham.)]

depends on mensuration; as, "I am six feet high." He is sure
he has been at Richmond; he is sure he is six feet high: but he
cannot be sure he is wise, or that he has any other excellence.
Then, all censure of a man's self is oblique praise. It is in order
to shew how much he can spare. It has all the invidiousness of
self-praise, and all the reproach of falsehood.' BOSWELL. 'Sometimes it may proceed from a man's strong consciousness of his
faults being observed. He knows that others would throw him
down, and therefore he had better lye down softly of his own
accord.'

On Tuesday, April 28, he was engaged to dine at General
Paoli's, where, as I have already observed, I was still entertained
in elegant hospitality, and with all the ease and comfort of a
home. I called on him, and accompanied him in a hackney-coach.
We stopped first at the bottom of Hedge-lane, into which he
went to leave a letter, 'with good news for a poor man[1] in distress', as he told me. I did not question him particularly as to
this. He himself often resembled Lady Bolingbroke's lively
description of Pope; that 'he was *un politique aux choux et aux
raves.*' He would say, 'I dine to-day in Grosvenor-square;' this
might be with a Duke: or, perhaps, 'I dine to-day at the other
end of the town:' or, 'A gentleman of great eminence called on
me yesterday.' He loved thus to keep things floating in conjecture: *Omne ignotum pro magnifico est.*[2] I believe I ventured to
dissipate the cloud, to unveil the mystery, more freely and frequently than any of his friends. We stopped again at Wirgman's,
the well-known *toy-shop*, in St. James's-street, at the corner of
St. James's-place, to which he had been directed, but not clearly,
for he searched about some time, and could not find it at first;
and said, 'To direct one only to a corner shop is *toying* with one.'
I suppose he meant this as a play upon the word *toy*: it was the
first time that I knew him stoop to such sport. After he had been
some time in the shop, he sent for me to come out of the coach,
and help him to choose a pair of silver buckles, as those he had

[1] ⌈Mauritius Lowe. *Croker*[3].⌉
[2] 'The unknown always passes for something peculiarly grand.' Tacitus,
Agricola, ch. xxx.

were too small. Probably this alteration in dress had been suggested by Mrs. Thrale, by associating with whom, his external appearance was much improved. He got better cloaths; and the dark colour, from which he never deviated, was enlivened by metal buttons. His wigs, too, were much better; and during their travels in France, he was furnished with a Paris-made wig, of handsome construction. This choosing of silver buckles was a negociation: 'Sir, (said he,) I will not have the ridiculous large ones now in fashion; and I will give no more than a guinea for a pair.' Such were the *principles* of the business; and, after some examination, he was fitted. As we drove along, I found him in a talking humour, of which I availed myself. BOSWELL. 'I was this morning in Ridley's shop, Sir; and was told, that the collection called *Johnsoniana* has sold very much.' JOHNSON. 'Yet the *Journey to the Hebrides* has not had a great sale.'[1] BOSWELL. 'That is strange.' JOHNSON. 'Yes, Sir; for in that book I have told the world a great deal that they did not know before.'

BOSWELL. 'I drank chocolate, Sir, this morning with Mr. Eld; and, to my no small surprize, found him to be a *Staffordshire Whig*, a being which I did not believe had existed.' JOHNSON. 'Sir, there are rascals in all countries.' BOSWELL. 'Eld said, a Tory was a creature generated between a non-juring parson and one's grandmother.' JOHNSON. 'And I have always said, the first Whig was the Devil.' BOSWELL. 'He certainly was, Sir. The Devil was impatient of subordination; he was the first who resisted power:—

"Better to reign in Hell, than serve in Heaven." '[2]

At General Paoli's were Sir Joshua Reynolds, Mr. Langton, Marchese Gherardi of Lombardy, and Mr. John Spottiswoode the younger, of Spottiswoode,[3] the solicitor. At this time fears

[1] Here he either was mistaken, or had a different notion of an extensive sale from what is generally entertained: for the fact is, that four thousand copies of that excellent work were sold very quickly. A new edition has been printed since his death, besides that in the collection of his works.

[2] [*Paradise Lost*, i. 263.]

[3] In the phraseology of Scotland, I should have said, 'Mr. John Spottiswoode the younger, *of that ilk*.' Johnson knew that sense of the word very well, and has thus explained it in his *Dictionary*, *voce* ILK:—'It also signifies " the same;" as, *Mackintosh of that ilk*, denotes a gentleman whose surname and the title of his estate are the same.'

of an invasion were circulated; to obviate which, Mr. Spottis-woode observed, that Mr. Fraser the engineer, who had lately come from Dunkirk, said, that the French had the same fears of us. JOHNSON. 'It is thus that mutual cowardice keeps us in peace. Were one half of mankind brave, and one half cowards, the brave would be always beating the cowards. Were all brave, they would lead a very uneasy life; all would be continually fighting: but being all cowards, we go on very well.'

We talked of drinking wine. JOHNSON. 'I require wine, only when I am alone. I have then often wished for it, and often taken it.' SPOTTISWOODE. 'What, by way of a companion, Sir?' JOHNSON. 'To get rid of myself, to send myself away. Wine gives great pleasure; and every pleasure is of itself a good. It is a good, unless counterbalanced by evil. A man may have a strong reason not to drink wine; and that may be greater than the pleasure. Wine makes a man better pleased with himself. I do not say that it makes him more pleasing to others. Sometimes it does. But the danger is, that while a man grows better pleased with himself, he may be growing less pleasing to others.[1] Wine gives a man nothing. It neither gives him knowledge nor wit; it only animates a man, and enables him to bring out what a dread of the company has repressed. It only puts in motion what has been locked up in frost. But this may be good, or it may be bad.' SPOTTISWOODE. 'So, Sir, wine is a key which opens a box; but this box may be either full or empty.' JOHNSON. 'Nay, Sir, conversation is the key: wine is a pick-lock, which forces open the box and injures it. A man should cultivate his mind so as to have that confidence and readiness without wine, which wine gives.' BOSWELL. 'The great difficulty of resisting wine is from benevolence. For instance, a good worthy man asks you to taste his wine, which he has had twenty years in his cellar.' JOHNSON. 'Sir, all this notion about benevolence arises from a

---

[1] It is observed in Waller's *Life*, in the *Biographia Britannica*, that he drank only water; and that while he sat in a company who were drinking wine, 'he had the dexterity to accommodate his discourse to the pitch of theirs as it *sunk*.' If excess in drinking be meant, the remark is acutely just. But surely, a moderate use of wine gives a gaiety of spirits which water-drinkers know not.

man's imagining himself to be of more importance to others, than he really is. They don't care a farthing whether he drinks wine or not.' SIR JOSHUA REYNOLDS. 'Yes, they do for the time.' JOHNSON. 'For the time!—If they care this minute, they forget it the next. And as for the good worthy man; how do you know he is good and worthy? No good and worthy man will insist upon another man's drinking wine. As to the wine twenty years in the cellar,—of ten men, three say this, merely because they must say something;—three are telling a lie, when they say they have had the wine twenty years;—three would rather save the wine;—one, perhaps, cares. I allow it is something to please one's company: and people are always pleased with those who partake pleasure with them. But after a man has brought himself to relinquish the great personal pleasure which arises from drinking wine, any other consideration is a trifle. To please others by drinking wine, is something, only if there be nothing against it. I should, however, be sorry to offend worthy men:—

> "Curst be the verse, how well so e'er it flow,
> That tends to make one worthy man my foe." '[1]

BOSWELL. 'Curst be the *spring*, the *water*.' JOHNSON. 'But let us consider what a sad thing it would be, if we were obliged to drink or do any thing else that may happen to be agreeable to the company where we are.' LANGTON. 'By the same rule you must join with a gang of cut-purses.' JOHNSON. 'Yes, Sir: but yet we must do justice to wine; we must allow it the power it possesses. To make a man pleased with himself, let me tell you, is doing a very great thing;

> "*Si patriæ volumus, si* Nobis *vivere cari.*" '[2]

I was at this time myself a water-drinker, upon trial, by Johnson's recommendation. JOHNSON. 'Boswell is a bolder combatant than Sir Joshua: he argues for wine without the help of wine; but Sir Joshua with it.' SIR JOSHUA REYNOLDS. 'But to please one's company is a strong motive.' JOHNSON. (who, from

---

[1] [Pope, *Epistle to Arbuthnot*, 283.]
[2] ['If we could make our life of value to our country *and to ourselves*.' Horace, *Epistles* i. 3. 29. (Wickham.)]

drinking only water, supposed every body who drank wine to
be elevated,) 'I won't argue any more with you, Sir. You are
too far gone.' SIR JOSHUA. 'I should have thought so indeed,
Sir, had I made such a speech as you have now done.' JOHNSON.
(drawing himself in, and, I really thought blushing,) 'Nay, don't
be angry. I did not mean to offend you.' SIR JOSHUA. 'At first
the taste of wine was disagreeable to me; but I brought myself
to drink it, that I might be like other people. The pleasure of
drinking wine is so connected with pleasing your company, that
altogether there is something of social goodness in it.' JOHNSON.
'Sir, this is only saying the same thing over again.' SIR JOSHUA.
'No, this is new.' JOHNSON. 'You put it in new words, but it is
an old thought. This is one of the disadvantages of wine. It
makes a man mistake words for thoughts.' BOSWELL. 'I think
it is a new thought; at least, it is in a new *attitude*.' JOHNSON.
'Nay, Sir, it is only in a new coat; or an old coat with a new
facing. (Then laughing heartily,) It is the old dog in a new
doublet.—An extraordinary instance however may occur where
a man's patron will do nothing for him, unless he will drink:
there may be a good reason for drinking.'

I mentioned a nobleman,[1] who I believed was really uneasy
if his company would not drink hard. JOHNSON. 'That is from
having had people about him whom he has been accustomed to
command.' BOSWELL. 'Supposing I should be *tête-a-tête* with
him at table.' JOHNSON. 'Sir, there is no more reason for your
drinking with *him*, than his being sober with *you*.' BOSWELL.
'Why, that is true; for it would do him less hurt to be sober,
than it would do me to get drunk.' JOHNSON. 'Yes, Sir; and
from what I have heard of him, one would not wish to sacrifice
himself to such a man. If he must always have somebody to
drink with him, he should buy a slave, and then he would be
sure to have it. They who submit to drink as another pleases,
make themselves his slaves.' BOSWELL. 'But, Sir, you will
surely make allowance for the duty of hospitality. A gentleman
who loves drinking, comes to visit me.' JOHNSON. 'Sir, a man

[1] [Archibald, 11th Earl of Eglinton. *Boswell's 1778 Journal*. Cf. *Boswell*
Papers, xii. 301; xiii. 184; xiv. 27; xv. 229.]

knows whom he visits; he comes to the table of a sober man.' BOSWELL. 'But, Sir, you and I should not have been so well received in the Highlands and Hebrides, if I had not drunk with our worthy friends. Had I drunk water only as you did, they would not have been so cordial.' JOHNSON. 'Sir William Temple mentions that in his travels through the Netherlands he had two or three gentlemen with him; and when a bumper was necessary, he put it on *them*. Were I to travel again through the islands, I would have Sir Joshua with me to take the bumpers.' BOSWELL. 'But, Sir, let me put a case. Suppose Sir Joshua should take a jaunt into Scotland; he does me the honour to pay me a visit at my house in the country; I am overjoyed at seeing him; we are quite by ourselves, shall I unsociably and churlishly let him sit drinking by himself? No, no, my dear Sir Joshua, you shall not be treated so, I *will* take a bottle with you.'

The celebrated Mrs. Rudd being mentioned. JOHNSON. 'Fifteen years ago I should have gone to see her.' SPOTTISWOODE. 'Because she was fifteen years younger?' JOHNSON. 'No, Sir; but now they have a trick of putting every thing into the newspapers.'

He begged of General Paoli to repeat one of the introductory stanzas of the first book of Tasso's *Jerusalem*, which he did, and then Johnson found fault with the simile of sweetening the edges of a cup for a child, being transferred from Lucretius into an epick poem. The General said he did not imagine Homer's poetry was so ancient as is supposed, because he ascribes to a Greek colony circumstances of refinement not found in Greece itself at a later period, when Thucydides wrote. JOHNSON. 'I recollect but one passage quoted by Thucydides from Homer, which is not to be found in our copies of Homer's works; I am for the antiquity of Homer, and think that a Grecian colony, by being nearer Persia, might be more refined than the mother country.'

On Wednesday, April 29, I dined with him at Mr. Allan Ramsay's, where were Lord Binning, Dr. Robertson the historian, Sir Joshua Reynolds, and the Honourable Mrs. Boscawen, widow of the Admiral, and mother of the present Viscount

Falmouth; of whom, if it be not presumptuous in me to praise
her, I would say, that her manners are the most agreeable, and
her conversation the best, of any lady with whom I ever had
the happiness to be acquainted. Before Johnson came we talked
a good deal of him; Ramsay said he had always found him a very
polite man, and that he treated him with great respect, which he
did very sincerely. I said I worshipped him. ROBERTSON.
'But some of you spoil him; you should not worship him; you
should worship no man.' BOSWELL. 'I cannot help worshipping
him, he is so much superiour to other men.' ROBERTSON. 'In
criticism, and in wit in conversation, he is no doubt very excellent; but in other respects he is not above other men; he will
believe any thing, and will strenuously defend the most minute
circumstance connected with the Church of England.' BOSWELL.
'Believe me, Doctor, you are much mistaken as to this; for when
you talk with him calmly in private, he is very liberal in his way
of thinking.' ROBERTSON. 'He and I have been always very
gracious; the first time I met him was one evening at Strahan's,
when he had just had an unlucky altercation with Adam Smith,
to whom he had been so rough, that Strahan, after Smith was
gone, had remonstrated with him, and told him that I was
coming soon, and that he was uneasy to think that he might
behave in the same manner to me. "No, no, Sir, (said Johnson,)
I warrant you Robertson and I shall do very well." Accordingly
he was gentle and good-humoured, and courteous with me the
whole evening; and he has been so upon every occasion that we
have met since. I have often said (laughing,) that I have been
in a great measure indebted to Smith for my good reception.'
BOSWELL. 'His power of reasoning is very strong, and he has a
peculiar art of drawing characters, which is as rare as good portrait painting.' SIR JOSHUA REYNOLDS. 'He is undoubtedly
admirable in this; but, in order to mark the characters which
he draws, he overcharges them, and gives people more than they
really have, whether of good or bad.'

No sooner did he, of whom we had been thus talking so easily,
arrive, than we were all as quiet as a school upon the entrance
of the head-master; and were very soon set down to a table

covered with such variety of good things, as contributed not a little to dispose him to be pleased.

RAMSAY. 'I am old enough to have been a contemporary of Pope. His poetry was highly admired in his life-time, more a great deal than after his death.' JOHNSON. 'Sir, it has not been less admired since his death; no authours ever had so much fame in their own life-time as Pope and Voltaire; and Pope's poetry has been as much admired since his death as during his life; it has only not been as much talked of, but that is owing to its being now more distant, and people having other writings to talk of. Virgil is less talked of than Pope, and Homer is less talked of than Virgil; but they are not less admired. We must read what the world reads at the moment. It has been maintained that this superfœtation, this teeming of the press in modern times, is prejudicial to good literature, because it obliges us to read so much of what is of inferiour value, in order to be in the fashion; so that better works are neglected for want of time, because a man will have more gratification of his vanity in conversation, from having read modern books, than from having read the best works of antiquity. But it must be considered, that we have now more knowledge generally diffused; all our ladies read now, which is a great extension. Modern writers are the moons of literature; they shine with reflected light, with light borrowed from the ancients. Greece appears to me to be the fountain of knowledge; Rome of elegance.' RAMSAY. 'I suppose Homer's *Iliad* to be a collection of pieces which had been written before his time. I should like to see a translation of it in poetical prose like the book of Ruth or Job.' ROBERTSON. 'Would you, Dr. Johnson, who are master of the English language, but try your hand upon a part of it.' JOHNSON. 'Sir, you could not read it without the pleasure of verse.'[1]

We talked of antiquarian researches. JOHNSON. 'All that is really *known* of the ancient state of Britain is contained in a few

[1] This experiment which Madame Dacier made in vain, has since been tried in our own language, by the editor of *Ossian*, and we must either think very meanly of his abilities, or allow that Dr. Johnson was in the right. And Mr. Cowper, a man of real genius, has miserably failed in his blank verse translation.

pages. We *can* know no more than what the old writers have told us; yet what large books have we upon it, the whole of which, excepting such parts as are taken from those old writers, is all a dream, such as Whitaker's *Manchester*. I have heard Henry's *History of Britain* well spoken of: I am told it is carried on in separate divisions, as the civil, the military, the religious history: I wish much to have one branch well done, and that is the history of manners, of common life.' ROBERTSON. 'Henry should have applied his attention to that alone, which is enough for any man; and he might have found a great deal scattered in various books, had he read solely with that view. Henry erred in not selling his first volume at a moderate price to the booksellers, that they might have pushed him on till he had got reputation. I sold my *History of Scotland* at a moderate price, as a work by which the booksellers might either gain or not; and Cadell has told me that Millar and he have got six thousand pounds by it. I afterwards received a much higher price for my writings. An authour should sell his first work for what the booksellers will give, till it shall appear whether he is an authour of merit, or, which is the same thing as to purchase-money, an authour who pleases the publick.'

Dr. Robertson expatiated on the character of a certain nobleman;[1] that he was one of the strongest-minded men that ever lived; that he would sit in company quite sluggish, while there was nothing to call forth his intellectual vigour; but the moment that any important subject was started, for instance, how this country is to be defended against a French invasion, he would rouse himself, and shew his extraordinary talents with the most powerful ability and animation. JOHNSON. 'Yet this man cut his own throat. The true strong and sound mind is the mind that can embrace equally great things and small. Now I am told the King of Prussia will say to a servant, "Bring me a bottle of such a wine, which came in such a year; it lies in such a corner of the cellars." I would have a man great in great things, and elegant in little things.' He said to me afterwards, when we were by ourselves, 'Robertson was in a mighty romantick humour, he

[1] [Lord Clive. *Croker*[1]. *Boswell's 1778 Journal*.]

talked of one whom he did not know; but I *downed* him with the King of Prussia.' 'Yes, Sir, (said I,) you threw a *bottle* at his head.'

An ingenious gentleman[1] was mentioned, concerning whom both Robertson and Ramsay agreed that he had a constant firmness of mind; for after a laborious day, and amidst a multiplicity of cares and anxieties, he would sit down with his sisters and be quite cheerful and good-humoured. Such a disposition, it was observed, was a happy gift of nature. Johnson. 'I do not think so; a man has from nature a certain portion of mind; the use he makes of it depends upon his own free will. That a man has always the same firmness of mind I do not say; because every man feels his mind less firm at one time than at another; but I think a man's being in a good or bad humour depends upon his will.' I, however, could not help thinking that a man's humour is often uncontroulable by his will.

Johnson harangued against drinking wine. 'A man (said he,) may choose whether he will have abstemiousness and knowledge, or claret and ignorance.' Dr. Robertson, (who is very companionable,) was beginning to dissent as to the proscription of claret. Johnson. (with a placid smile,) 'Nay, Sir, you shall not differ with me; as I have said that the man is most perfect who takes in the most things, I am for knowledge and claret.' Robertson. (holding a glass of generous claret in his hand,) 'Sir, I can only drink your health.' Johnson. 'Sir, I should be sorry if *you* should be ever in such a state as to be able to do nothing more.' Robertson. 'Dr. Johnson, allow me to say, that in one respect I have the advantage of you; when you were in Scotland you would not come to hear any of our preachers, whereas, when I am here, I attend your publick worship without scruple, and indeed, with great satisfaction.' Johnson. 'Why, Sir, that is not so extraordinary: the King of Siam sent ambassadors to Louis the Fourteenth; but Louis the Fourteenth sent none to the King of Siam.'[2]

---

[1] [Robert Adam. *Boswell's 1778 Journal* which reads 'Robert Adams'.]
[2] Mrs. Piozzi confidently mentions this as having passed in Scotland. *Anecdotes*, p. 62.

Here my friend for once discovered a want of knowledge or forgetfulness; for Louis the Fourteenth did send an embassy to the King of Siam, and the Abbé Choisi, who was employed in it, published an account of it in two volumes.

Next day, Thursday, April 30, I found him at home by himself. JOHNSON. 'Well, Sir, Ramsay gave us a splendid dinner. I love Ramsay. You will not find a man in whose conversation there is more instruction, more information, and more elegance, than in Ramsay's.' BOSWELL. 'What I admire in Ramsay, is his continuing to be so young.' JOHNSON. 'Why, yes, Sir, it is to be admired. I value myself upon this, that there is nothing of the old man in my conversation. I am now sixty-eight, and I have no more of it than at twenty-eight.' BOSWELL. 'But, Sir, would not you wish to know old age? He who is never an old man, does not know the whole of human life; for old age is one of the divisions of it.' JOHNSON. 'Nay, Sir, what talk is this?' BOSWELL. 'I mean, Sir, the Sphinx's description of it;—morning, noon, and night. I would know night, as well as morning and noon.' JOHNSON. 'What, Sir, would you know what it is to feel the evils of old age? Would you have the gout? Would you have decrepitude?'—Seeing him heated, I would not argue any farther; but I was confident that I was in the right. I would, in due time, be a Nestor, an elder of the people; and there *should* be some difference between the conversation of twenty-eight and sixty-eight. A grave picture should not be gay. There is a serene, solemn, placid old age. JOHNSON. 'Mrs. Thrale's mother said of me what flattered me much. A clergyman was complaining of want of society in the country where he lived; and said, "They talk of *runts*;" (that is, young cows). "Sir, (said Mrs. Salusbury,) Mr. Johnson would learn to talk of runts:" meaning that I was a man who would make the most of my situation, whatever it was.' He added, 'I think myself a very polite man.'

On Saturday, May 2, I dined with him at Sir Joshua Reynolds's, where there was a very large company, and a great deal of conversation; but owing to some circumstance which I cannot now recollect, I have no record of any part of it, except that

there were several people there by no means of the Johnsonian
school; so that less attention was paid to him than usual, which
put him out of humour; and upon some imaginary offence from
me, he attacked me with such rudeness, that I was vexed and
angry, because it gave those persons an opportunity of enlarging
upon his supposed ferocity, and ill treatment of his best friends.
I was so much hurt, and had my pride so much roused, that I
kept away from him for a week; and, perhaps, might have kept
away much longer, nay, gone to Scotland without seeing him
again, had not we fortunately met and been reconciled. To such
unhappy chances are human friendships liable.

On Friday, May 8, I dined with him at Mr. Langton's. I was
reserved and silent, which I suppose he perceived, and might
recollect the cause. After dinner when Mr. Langton was called
out of the room, and we were by ourselves, he drew his chair
near to mine, and said, in a tone of conciliating courtesy, 'Well,
how have you done?' BOSWELL. 'Sir, you have made me very
uneasy by your behaviour to me when we were last at Sir
Joshua Reynolds's. You know, my dear Sir, no man has a
greater respect and affection for you, or would sooner go to the
end of the world to serve you. Now to treat me so—.' He
insisted that I had interrupted him, which I assured him was
not the case; and proceeded—'But why treat me so before
people who neither love you nor me?' JOHNSON. 'Well, I am
sorry for it. I'll make it up to you twenty different ways, as you
please.' BOSWELL. 'I said to-day to Sir Joshua, when he observed
that you *tossed* me sometimes—I don't care how often, or how
high he tosses me, when only friends are present, for then I fall
upon soft ground: but I do not like falling on stones, which is the
case when enemies are present.—I think this a pretty good image,
Sir.' JOHNSON. 'Sir, it is one of the happiest I have ever heard.'

The truth is, there was no venom in the wounds which he
inflicted at any time, unless they were irritated by some malignant infusion by other hands. We were instantly as cordial again
as ever, and joined in hearty laugh at some ludicrous but innocent peculiarities of one of our friends.[1] BOSWELL. 'Do you

[1] [Perhaps Langton. *Powell.*]

think, Sir, it is always culpable to laugh at a man to his face?'
JOHNSON. 'Why, Sir, that depends upon the man and the thing.
If it is a slight man, and a slight thing, you may; for you take
nothing valuable from him.'

He said, 'I read yesterday Dr. Blair's sermon on Devotion,
from the text *"Cornelius, a devout man."*[1] His doctrine is the best
limited, the best expressed: there is the most warmth without
fanaticism, the most rational transport. There is one part of it
which I disapprove, and I'd have him correct it; which is, that
"he who does not feel joy in religion is far from the kingdom of
heaven!" There are many good men whose fear of GOD predominates over their love. It may discourage. It was rashly said.
A noble sermon it is indeed. I wish Blair would come over to the
Church of England.'

When Mr. Langton returned to us, the 'flow of talk' went on.
An eminent authour[2] being mentioned;—JOHNSON. 'He is not
a pleasant man. His conversation is neither instructive nor brilliant. He does not talk as if impelled by any fulness of knowledge
or vivacity of imagination. His conversation is like that of any
other sensible man. He talks with no wish either to inform or to
hear, but only because he thinks it does not become ————
———— to sit in a company and say nothing.'

Mr. Langton having repeated the anecdote of Addison having
distinguished between his powers in conversation and in writing,
by saying 'I have only nine-pence in my pocket; but I can draw
for a thousand pounds;'—JOHNSON. 'He had not that retort
ready, Sir; he had prepared it before-hand.' LANGTON. (turning
to me,) 'A fine surmise. Set a thief to catch a thief.'

Johnson called the East-Indians barbarians. BOSWELL. 'You
will except the Chinese, Sir?' JOHNSON. 'No, Sir.' BOSWELL.
'Have they not arts?' JOHNSON. 'They have pottery.' BOSWELL.
'What do you say to the written characters of their language?'
JOHNSON. 'Sir, they have not an alphabet. They have not been
able to form what all other nations have formed.' BOSWELL.
'There is more learning in their language than in any other,
from the immense number of their characters.' JOHNSON. 'It is

[1] [*Acts* x. 1.]   [2] [*Croker*[1] *suggests* Robertson, *Hill* Blair.]

only more difficult from its rudeness; as there is more labour in hewing down a tree with a stone than with an axe.'

He said, 'I have been reading Lord Kames's *Sketches of the History of Man*. In treating of severity of punishment, he mentions that of Madame Lapouchin, in Russia, but he does not give it fairly; for I have looked at *Chappe D'Auteroche*, from whom he has taken it. He stops where it is said that the spectators thought her innocent, and leaves out what follows; that she nevertheless was guilty. Now this is being as culpable as one can conceive, to misrepresent fact in a book, and for what motive? It is like one of those lies which people tell, one cannot see why. The woman's life was spared; and no punishment was too great for the favourite of an Empress who had conspired to dethrone her mistress.' BOSWELL. 'He was only giving a picture of the lady in her sufferings.' JOHNSON. 'Nay, don't endeavour to palliate this. Guilt is a principal feature in the picture. Kames is puzzled with a question that puzzled me when I was a very young man. Why is it that the interest of money is lower, when money is plentiful; for five pounds has the same proportion of value to a hundred pounds when money is plentiful, as when it is scarce? A lady explained it to me. "It is (said she,) because when money is plentiful there are so many more who have money to lend, that they bid down one another. Many have then a hundred pounds; and one says,—Take mine rather than another's, and you shall have it at four *per cent*." ' BOSWELL. 'Does Lord Kames decide the question?' JOHNSON. 'I think he leaves it as he found it.' BOSWELL. 'This must have been an extraordinary lady who instructed you, Sir. May I ask who she was?' JOHNSON. 'Molly Aston,[1] Sir, the sister of those ladies with whom

---

[1] Johnson had an extraordinary admiration of this lady, notwithstanding she was a violent Whig. In answer to her high-flown speeches for *Liberty*, he addressed to her the following Epigram, of which I presume to offer a translation:—

> '*Liber ut esse velim suasisti pulchra Maria,*
> *Ut maneam liber pulchra Maria vale.*'
> Adieu, Maria! since you'd have me free;
> For, who beholds thy charms a slave must be.

A correspondent of *The Gentleman's Magazine*, who subscribes himself SCIOLUS, to whom I am indebted for several excellent remarks, observes, you dined at Lichfield. I shall be at home to-morrow.' BOSWELL. 'Then let us dine by ourselves at the Mitre, to keep up the old custom, "the custom of the manor," the custom of the mitre.' JOHNSON. 'Sir, so it shall be.'

On Saturday, May 9, we fulfilled our purpose of dining by ourselves at the Mitre, according to old custom. There was, on these occasions, a little circumstance of kind attention to Mrs. Williams, which must not be omitted. Before coming out, and leaving her to dine alone, he gave her her choice of a chicken, a sweetbread, or any other little nice thing, which was carefully sent to her from the tavern, ready-drest.

Our conversation to-day, I know not how, turned, (I think for the only time at any length, during our long acquaintance,) upon the sensual intercourse between the sexes, the delight of which he ascribed chiefly to imagination. 'Were it not for imagination, Sir, (said he,) a man would be as happy in the arms of a chambermaid as of a Duchess. But such is the adventitious charm of fancy, that we find men who have violated the best principles of society, and ruined their fame and their fortune, that they might possess a woman of rank.' It would not be proper to record the particulars of such a conversation in moments of unreserved frankness, when nobody was present on whom it could have any hurtful effect. That subject, when philosophically treated, may surely employ the mind in as curious discussion, and as innocently, as anatomy; provided that those who do treat it keep clear of inflammatory incentives.

'From grave to gay, from lively to severe,'—we were soon engaged in very different speculation; humbly and reverently considering and wondering at the universal mystery of all

'The turn of Dr. Johnson's lines to Miss Aston, whose Whig principles he had been combating, appears to me to be taken from an ingenious epigram in the *Menagiana* on a young lady who appeared at a masquerade, *habillée en Jésuite*, during the fierce contentions of the followers of Molinos [Luis Molina] and Jansenius concerning free-will:—

> "On s'étonne ici que Caliste
> Ait pris l'habit de Moliniste.
> Puisque cette jeune beauté
> Ote à chacun sa liberté,
> N'est-ce pas une Janséniste?" '

things, as our imperfect faculties can now judge of them. 'There are (said he,) innumerable questions to which the inquisitive mind can in this state receive no answer: Why do you and I exist? Why was this world created? Since it was to be created, why was it not created sooner?'

On Sunday, May 10, I supped with him at Mr. Hoole's, with Sir Joshua Reynolds. I have neglected the memorial of this evening, so as to remember no more of it than two particulars; one, that he strenuously opposed an argument by Sir Joshua, that virtue was preferable to vice, considering this life only; and that a man would be virtuous were it only to preserve his character: and that he expressed much wonder at the curious formation of the bat, a mouse with wings; saying, that 'it was almost as strange a thing in physiology, as if the fabulous dragon could be seen.'

On Tuesday, May 12, I waited on the Earl of Marchmont, to know if his Lordship would favour Dr. Johnson with information concerning Pope, whose *Life* he was about to write. Johnson had not flattered himself with the hopes of receiving any civility from this nobleman; for he said to me, when I mentioned Lord Marchmont as one who could tell him a great deal about Pope,— 'Sir, he will tell *me* nothing.' I had the honour of being known to his Lordship, and applied to him of myself, without being commissioned by Johnson. His Lordship behaved in the most polite and obliging manner, promised to tell all he recollected about Pope, and was so very courteous as to say, 'Tell Dr. Johnson I have a great respect for him, and am ready to shew it in any way I can. I am to be in the city to-morrow, and will call at his house as I return.' His Lordship however asked, 'Will he write the Lives of the Poets impartially? He was the first that brought Whig and Tory into a Dictionary. And what do you think of his definition of Excise? Do you know the history of his aversion to the word *transpire*?' Then taking down the folio *Dictionary*, he shewed it with this censure on its secondary sense: ' "To escape from secrecy to notice; a sense lately innovated from France, without necessity." The truth was Lord Bolingbroke, who left the Jacobites, first used it; therefore, it was to

be condemned. He should have shewn what word would do for
it, if it was unnecessary.' I afterwards put the question to
Johnson: 'Why, Sir, (said he,) *get abroad*.' BOSWELL. 'That,
Sir, is using two words.' JOHNSON. 'Sir, there is no end of this.
You may as well insist to have a word for old age.' BOSWELL.
'Well, Sir, *Senectus*.' JOHNSON. 'Nay, Sir, to insist always that
there should be one word to express a thing in English, because
there is one in another language, is to change the language.'

I availed myself of this opportunity to hear from his Lordship
many particulars both of Pope and Lord Bolingbroke, which I
have in writing.

I proposed to Lord Marchmont that he should revise Johnson's
Life of Pope: 'So (said his Lordship,) you would put me in a
dangerous situation. You know he knocked down Osborne the
bookseller.'

Elated with the success of my spontaneous exertion to procure
material and respectable aid to Johnson for his very favourite
work, *The Lives of the Poets*, I hastened down to Mr. Thrale's
at Streatham, where he now was, that I might insure his being
at home next day; and after dinner, when I thought he would
receive the good news in the best humour, I announced it
eagerly: 'I have been at work for you to-day, Sir. I have been
with Lord Marchmont. He bade me tell you he has a great
respect for you, and will call on you to-morrow at one o'clock,
and communicate all he knows about Pope.'—Here I paused, in
full expectation that he would be pleased with this intelligence,
would praise my active merit, and would be alert to embrace
such an offer from a nobleman. But whether I had shewn an
over-exultation, which provoked his spleen; or whether he was
seized with a suspicion that I had obtruded him on Lord Marchmont, and had humbled him too much; or whether there was
any thing more than an unlucky fit of ill-humour, I know not;
but, to my surprize, the result was,—JOHNSON. 'I shall not be
in town to-morrow. I don't care to know about Pope.' MRS.
THRALE. (surprized as I was, and a little angry) 'I suppose,
Sir, Mr. Boswell thought, that as you are to write Pope's *Life*,
you would wish to know about him.' JOHNSON. 'Wish! why yes.

If it rained knowledge I'd hold out my hand; but I would not give myself the trouble to go in quest of it.' There was no arguing with him at the moment. Some time afterwards he said, 'Lord Marchmont will call on me, and then I shall call on Lord Marchmont.' Mr. Thrale was uneasy at his unaccountable caprice; and told me, that if I did not take care to bring about a meeting between Lord Marchmont and him, it would never take place, which would be a great pity. I sent a card to his Lordship, to be left at Johnson's house, acquainting him, that Dr. Johnson could not be in town next day, but would do himself the honour of waiting on him at another time. I give this account fairly, as a specimen of that unhappy temper with which this great and good man had occasionally to struggle, from something morbid in his constitution. Let the most censorious of my readers suppose himself to have a violent fit of the tooth-ach, or to have received a severe stroke on the shin-bone, and when in such a state to be asked a question; and if he has any candour, he will not be surprized at the answers which Johnson sometimes gave in moments of irritation, which, let me assure them, is exquisitely painful. But it must not be erroneously supposed that he was, in the smallest degree, careless concerning any work which he undertook, or that he was generally thus peevish. It will be seen, that in the following year he had a very agreeable interview with Lord Marchmont, at his Lordship's house; and this very afternoon he soon forgot any fretfulness, and fell into conversation as usual.

I mentioned a reflection having been thrown out against four Peers for having presumed to rise in opposition to the opinion of the twelve Judges, in a cause in the House of Lords, as if that were indecent. JOHNSON. 'Sir, there is no ground for censure. The Peers are Judges themselves; and supposing them really to be of a different opinion, they might from duty be in opposition to the Judges, who were there only to be consulted.'

In this observation I fully concurred with him; for, unquestionably, all the Peers are vested with the highest judicial powers; and, when they are confident that they understand a cause, are not obliged, nay ought not to acquiesce in the opinion of the ordinary Law Judges, or even in that of those who from their studies and experience are called the Law Lords. I consider the Peers in general as I do a Jury, who ought to listen with respectful attention to the sages of the law; but, if after hearing them, they have a firm opinion of their own, are bound, as honest men, to decide accordingly. Nor is it so difficult for them to understand even law questions, as is generally thought; provided they will bestow sufficient attention upon them. This observation was made by my honoured relation the late Lord Cathcart, who had spent his life in camps and courts; yet assured me, that he could form a clear opinion upon most of the causes that came before the House of Lords, 'as they were so well enucleated in the Cases.'

Mrs. Thrale told us, that a curious clergyman[1] of our acquaintance had discovered a licentious stanza, which Pope had originally in his *Universal Prayer*, before the stanza,

> 'What conscience dictates to be done,
>   Or warns us not to do,' &c.

It was this:—

> 'Can sins of moment claim the rod
>   Of everlasting fires?
> And that offend great Nature's GOD,
>   Which Nature's self inspires?'

and that Dr. Johnson observed, 'it had been borrowed from *Guarini*.' There are, indeed, in *Pastor Fido*, many such flimsy superficial reasonings, as that in the last two lines of this stanza.

BOSWELL. 'In that stanza of Pope's, *"rod of fires"* is certainly a bad metaphor.' MRS. THRALE. 'And "sins of *moment*" is a faulty expression; for its true import is *momentous*, which cannot be intended.' JOHNSON. 'It must have been written "of *moments.*" Of *moment*, is *momentous*; of *moments*, *momentary*. I warrant you, however, Pope wrote this stanza, and some friend struck it out. Boileau wrote some such thing, and Arnaud struck it out, saying, *"Vous gagnerez deux ou trois impies, et perdrez je ne scais combien des honnettes gens."* These fellows want to say

[1] [Dr. Michael Lort. *Boswell's 1778 Journal.*]

a daring thing, and don't know how to go about it. Mere poets know no more of fundamental principles than—.' Here he was interrupted somehow. Mrs. Thrale mentioned Dryden. JOHNSON. 'He puzzled himself about predestination.—How foolish was it in Pope to give all his friendship to Lords, who thought they honoured him by being with him; and to choose such Lords as Burlington, and Cobham, and Bolingbroke! Bathurst was negative, a pleasing man; and I have heard no ill of Marchmont; and then always saying, "I do not value you for being a Lord;" which was a sure proof that he did. I never say, I do not value Boswell more for being born to an estate, because I do not care.' BOSWELL. 'Nor for being a Scotchman?' JOHNSON. 'Nay, Sir, I do value you more for being a Scotchman. You are a Scotchman without the faults of a Scotchman. You would not have been so valuable as you are, had you not been a Scotchman.'

Talking of divorces, I asked if Othello's doctrine was not plausible?

> 'He that is robb'd, not wanting what is stolen,
> Let him not know't, and he's not robb'd at all.'[1]

Dr. Johnson and Mrs. Thrale joined against this. JOHNSON. 'Ask any man if he'd wish not to know of such an injury.' BOSWELL. 'Would you tell your friend to make him unhappy?' JOHNSON. 'Perhaps, Sir, I should not; but that would be from prudence on my own account. A man would tell his father.' BOSWELL. 'Yes; because he would not have spurious children to get any share of the family inheritance.' MRS. THRALE. 'Or he would tell his brother.' BOSWELL. 'Certainly his *elder* brother.' JOHNSON. 'You would tell your friend of a woman's infamy, to prevent his marrying a whore: there is the same reason to tell him of his wife's infidelity, when he is married, to prevent the consequences of imposition. It is a breach of confidence not to tell a friend.' BOSWELL. 'Would you tell Mr. ————?' (naming a gentleman[2] who assuredly was not in the least danger of such a miserable disgrace, though married to a fine woman.) JOHNSON. 'No, Sir; because it would do no good:

---

[1] [*Othello*, III. iii. 343–4.]   [2] [Langton. *Boswell's 1778 Journal.*]

he is so sluggish, he'd never go to parliament and get through a divorce.'

He said of one of our friends,[1] 'He is ruining himself without pleasure. A man who loses at play, or who runs out his fortune at court, makes his estate less, in hopes of making it bigger: (I am sure of this word, which was often used by him:) but it is a sad thing to pass through the quagmire of parsimony, to the gulph of ruin. To pass over the flowery path of extravagance is very well.'

Amongst the numerous prints pasted on the walls of the dining-room at Streatham, was Hogarth's 'Modern Midnight Conversation.' I asked him what he knew of Parson Ford, who makes a conspicuous figure in the riotous group. JOHNSON. 'Sir, he was my acquaintance and relation, my mother's nephew. He had purchased a living in the country, but not simoniacally. I never saw him but in the country. I have been told he was a man of great parts; very profligate, but I never heard he was impious.' BOSWELL. 'Was there not a story of his ghost having appeared?' JOHNSON. 'Sir, it was believed. A waiter at the Hummums, in which house Ford died, had been absent for some time, and returned, not knowing that Ford was dead. Going down to the cellar, according to the story, he met him; going down again he met him a second time. When he came up, he asked some of the people of the house what Ford could be doing there. They told him Ford was dead. The waiter took a fever, in which he lay for some time. When he recovered, he said he had a message to deliver to some women from Ford; but he was not to tell what, or to whom. He walked out; he was followed; but somewhere about St. Paul's they lost him. He came back, and said he had delivered the message, and the women exclaimed, "Then we are all undone!" Dr. Pellet, who was not a credulous man, inquired into the truth of this story, and he said, the evidence was irresistible. My wife went to the Hummums; (it is a place where people get themselves cupped.) I believe she went with intention to hear about this story of Ford. At first they were unwilling to tell her; but, after they had talked to her, she

[1] [Mr. Langton. See *ante*, p. 967.]

came away satisfied that it was true. To be sure the man had a fever; and this vision may have been the beginning of it. But if the message to the women, and their behaviour upon it, were true as related, there was something supernatural. That rests upon his word; and there it remains.'

After Mrs. Thrale was gone to bed, Johnson and I sat up late. We resumed Sir Joshua Reynolds's argument on the preceding Sunday, that a man would be virtuous though he had no other motive than to preserve his character. JOHNSON. 'Sir, it is not true: for as to this world vice does not hurt a man's character.' BOSWELL. 'Yes, Sir, debauching a friend's wife will.' JOHNSON. 'No, Sir. Who thinks the worse of ————[1] for it?' BOSWELL. 'Lord ————[2] was not his friend.' JOHNSON. 'That is only a circumstance, Sir; a slight distinction. He could not get into the house but by Lord ————. A man is chosen Knight of the shire, not the less for having debauched ladies.' BOSWELL. 'What, Sir, if he debauched the ladies of gentlemen in the county, will not there be a general resentment against him?' JOHNSON. 'No, Sir. He will lose those particular gentlemen; but the rest will not trouble their heads about it.' (warmly.) BOSWELL. 'Well, Sir, I cannot think so.' JOHNSON. 'Nay, Sir, there is no talking with a man who will dispute what every body knows, (angrily.) Don't you know this?' BOSWELL. 'No, Sir; and I wish to think better of your country than you represent it. I knew in Scotland a gentleman obliged to leave it for debauching a lady; and in one of our counties an Earl's brother[3] lost his election, because he had debauched the lady of another Earl in that county, and destroyed the peace of a noble family.'

Still he would not yield. He proceeded: 'Will you not allow, Sir, that vice does not hurt a man's character so as to obstruct his prosperity in life, when you know that ———— ————[4] was loaded with wealth and honours; a man who had acquired his fortune by such crimes, that his consciousness of them impelled him to cut his own throat.' BOSWELL. 'You will

---

[1] [Beauclerk. *Boswell's 1778 Journal.*]
[2] [Frederick St. John, 2nd Viscount Bolingbroke, *Ib.*]
[3] ['A brother of Lord Rothes.' *Ib.*]
[4] [Lord Clive. *Mrs. Piozzi.*]

recollect, Sir, that Dr. Robertson said, he cut his throat because
he was weary of still life; little things not being sufficient to
move his great mind.' JOHNSON. (very angry,) 'Nay, Sir, what
stuff is this! You had no more this opinion after Robertson said
it, than before. I know nothing more offensive than repeating
what one knows to be foolish things, by way of continuing a
dispute, to see what a man will answer,—to make him your
butt!' (angrier still.) BOSWELL. 'My dear Sir, I had no such
intention as you seem to suspect; I had not indeed. Might not
this nobleman have felt every thing "weary, stale, flat, and
unprofitable," as Hamlet says?' JOHNSON. 'Nay, if you are to
bring in gabble, I'll talk no more. I will not, upon my honour.'—
My readers will decide upon this dispute.

Next morning I stated to Mrs. Thrale at breakfast, before he
came down, the dispute of last night as to the influence of
character upon success in life. She said he was certainly wrong;
and told me, that a Baronet[1] lost an election in Wales, because
he had debauched the sister of a gentleman in the county, whom
he made one of his daughters invite as her companion at his
seat in the country, when his lady and his other children were in
London. But she would not encounter Johnson upon the subject.

I staid all this day with him at Streatham. He talked a great
deal, in very good humour.

Looking at Messrs. Dilly's splendid edition of Lord Chesterfield's miscellaneous works, he laughed, and said, 'Here now are
two speeches ascribed to him, both of which were written by me:
and the best of it is, they have found out that one is like Demosthenes, and the other like Cicero.'

He censured Lord Kames's *Sketches of the History of Man*, for
misrepresenting Clarendon's account of the appearance of Sir
George Villiers's ghost, as if Clarendon were weakly credulous;
when the truth is, that Clarendon only says, that the story was
upon a better foundation of credit, than usually such discourses
are founded upon; nay, speaks thus of the person who was
reported to have seen the vision, 'the poor man, *if he had been
at all waking*;' which Lord Kames has omitted. He added, 'in

[1] [Sir Nicholas Bayley. *Boswell's 1778 Journal.*]

this book it is maintained that virtue is natural to man, and that if we would but consult our own hearts we should be virtuous. Now after consulting our own hearts all we can, and with all the helps we have, we find how few of us are virtuous. This is saying a thing which all mankind know not to be true.' Boswell. 'Is not modesty natural?' Johnson. 'I cannot say, Sir, as we find no people quite in a state of nature; but I think the more they are taught, the more modest they are. The French are a gross, ill-bred, untaught people; a lady there will spit on the floor and rub it with her foot. What I gained by being in France was, learning to be better satisfied with my own country. Time may be employed to more advantage from nineteen to twenty-four almost in any way than in travelling; when you set travelling against mere negation, against doing nothing, it is better to be sure; but how much more would a young man improve were he to study during those years. Indeed, if a young man is wild, and must run after women and bad company, it is better this should be done abroad, as, on his return, he can break off such connections, and begin at home a new man, with a character to form, and acquaintances to make. How little does travelling supply to the conversation of any man who has travelled? how little to Beauclerk?' Boswell. 'What say you to Lord ————?'[1] Johnson. 'I never but once heard him talk of what he had seen, and that was of a large serpent in one of the Pyramids of Egypt.' Boswell. 'Well, I happened to hear him tell the same thing, which made me mention him.'

I talked of a country life. Johnson. 'Were I to live in the country, I would not devote myself to the acquisition of popularity; I would live in a much better way, much more happily; I would have my time at my own command.' Boswell. 'But, Sir, is it not a sad thing to be at a distance from all our literary friends?' Johnson. 'Sir, you will by and by have enough of this conversation, which now delights you so much.'

As he was a zealous friend of subordination, he was at all times watchful to repress the vulgar cant against the manners of the great; 'High people, Sir, (said he,) are the best; take a hundred

[1] [Lord Charlemont. *Croker*[1]. *Boswell's 1778 Journal.*]

ladies of quality, you'll find them better wives, better mothers, more willing to sacrifice their own pleasure to their children than a hundred other women. Tradeswomen (I mean the wives of tradesmen) in the city, who are worth from ten to fifteen thousand pounds, are the worst creatures upon the earth, grossly ignorant, and thinking viciousness fashionable. Farmers, I think, are often worthless fellows. Few lords will cheat; and, if they do, they'll be ashamed of it: farmers cheat and are not ashamed of it: they have all the sensual vices too of the nobility, with cheating into the bargain. There is as much fornication and adultery among farmers as amongst noblemen.' BOSWELL. 'The notion of the world, Sir, however is, that the morals of women of quality are worse than those in lower stations.' JOHNSON. 'Yes, Sir, the licentiousness of one woman of quality makes more noise than that of a number of women in lower stations; then, Sir, you are to consider the malignity of women in the city against women of quality, which will make them believe any thing of them, such as that they call their coachmen to bed. No, Sir, so far as I have observed, the higher in rank, the richer ladies are, they are the better instructed and the more virtuous.'

This year the Reverend Mr. Horne published his *Letter to Mr. Dunning on the English Particle*; Johnson read it, and though not treated in it with sufficient respect, he had candour enough to say to Mr. Seward, 'Were I to make a new edition of my *Dictionary*, I would adopt several[1] of Mr. Horne's etymologies; I hope they did not put the dog in the pillory for his libel; he has too much literature for that.'

On Saturday, May 16, I dined with him at Mr. Beauclerk's with Mr. Langton, Mr. Steevens, Dr. Higgins, and some others. I regret very feelingly every instance of my remissness in recording his *memorabilia*; I am afraid it is the condition of humanity (as Mr. Windham, of Norfolk, once observed to me, after having made an admirable speech in the House of Com-

---

[1] In Mr. Horne Tooke's enlargement of that *Letter*, which he has since published with the title of "Ἔπεα πτερόεντα ['winged words']; or, the *Diversions of Purley*; he mentions this compliment, as if Dr. Johnson instead of *several* of his etymologies had said *all*. His recollection having thus magnified it, shews how ambitious he was of the approbation of so great a man.

mons, which was highly applauded, but which he afterwards perceived might have been better:) 'that we are more uneasy from thinking of our wants, than happy in thinking of our acquisitions.' This is an unreasonable mode of disturbing our tranquillity, and should be corrected; let me then comfort myself with the large treasure of Johnson's conversation which I have preserved for my own enjoyment and that of the world, and let me exhibit what I have upon each occasion, whether more or less, whether a bulse, or only a few sparks of a diamond.

He said, 'Dr. Mead lived more in the broad sunshine of life than almost any man.'

The disaster of General Burgoyne's army was then the common topic of conversation. It was asked why piling their arms was insisted upon as a matter of such consequence, when it seemed to be a circumstance so inconsiderable in itself. JOHN-SON. 'Why, Sir, a French authour says, "*Il y a beaucoup de puérilités dans la guerre.*" All distinctions are trifles, because great things can seldom occur, and those distinctions are settled by custom. A savage would as willingly have his meat sent to him in the kitchen, as eat it at the table here; as men become civilized, various modes of denoting honourable preference are invented.'

He this day made the observations upon the similarity between *Rasselas* and *Candide*, which I have inserted in its proper place, when considering his admirable philosophical Romance. He said *Candide* he thought had more power in it than any thing that *Voltaire* had written.

He said, 'the lyrical part of Horace never can be perfectly translated; so much of the excellence is in the numbers and the expression. Francis has done it the best; I'll take his, five out of six, against them all.'

On Sunday, May 17, I presented to him Mr. Fullarton, of Fullarton, who has since distinguished himself so much in India, to whom he naturally talked of travels, as Mr. Brydone accompanied him in his tour to Sicily and Malta. He said, 'The information which we have from modern travellers is much more authentick than what we had from ancient travellers; ancient travellers guessed; modern travellers measure. The Swiss admit

that there is but one errour in Stanyan. If Brydone were more
attentive to his Bible, he would be a good traveller.'

He said, 'Lord Chatham was a Dictator; he possessed the
power of putting the State in motion; now there is no power, all
order is relaxed.' Boswell. 'Is there no hope of a change to the
better?' Johnson. 'Why, yes, Sir, when we are weary of this
relaxation. So the City of London will appoint its Mayors again
by seniority.' Boswell. 'But is not that taking a mere chance
for having a good or a bad Mayor?' Johnson. 'Yes, Sir; but
the evil of competition is greater than that of the worst Mayor
that can come; besides, there is no more reason to suppose that
the choice of a rabble will be right, than that chance will be
right.'

On Tuesday, May 19, I was to set out for Scotland in the
evening. He was engaged to dine with me at Mr. Dilly's, I
waited upon him to remind him of his appointment and attend
him thither; he gave me some salutary counsel, and recommended vigorous resolution against any deviation from moral
duty. Boswell. 'But you would not have me to bind myself by
a solemn obligation?' Johnson. (much agitated,) 'What! a
vow—O, no, Sir, a vow is a horrible thing, it is a snare for sin.
The man who cannot go to Heaven without a vow—may go—'
Here, standing erect, in the middle of his library, and rolling
grand, his pause was truly a curious compound of the solemn
and the ludicrous; he half-whistled in his usual way, when
pleasant, and he paused, as if checked by religious awe. Methought he would have added—to Hell—but was restrained. I
humoured the dilemma. 'What! Sir, (said I,) *In cælum jusseris
ibit?*[1] alluding to his imitation of it,—

'And bid him go to Hell, to Hell he goes.'

I had mentioned to him a slight fault in his noble *Imitation of
the Tenth Satire of Juvenal*, a too near recurrence of the verb
spread, in his description of the young Enthusiast at College:—

'Through all his veins the fever of renown,
   Spreads from the strong contagion of the gown;

[1] ['And bid him go to heaven, to heaven he will go.' Juvenal, *Satires* iii.
78. Johnson, *London*, 116.]

O'er Bodley's dome his future labours *spread*,
And Bacon's mansion trembles o'er his head.'

He had desired me to change *spreads* to *burns*, but for perfect
authenticity, I now had it done with his own hand.[1] I thought
this alteration not only cured the fault, but was more poetical,
as it might carry an allusion to the shirt by which Hercules was
inflamed.

We had a quiet comfortable meeting at Mr. Dilly's; nobody
there but ourselves. Mr. Dilly mentioned somebody having
wished that Milton's *Tractate on Education* should be printed
along with his Poems in the edition of *The English Poets* then
going on. JOHNSON. 'It would be breaking in upon the plan;
but would be of no great consequence. So far as it would be any
thing, it would be wrong. Education in England has been in
danger of being hurt by two of its greatest men, Milton and
Locke. Milton's plan is impracticable, and I suppose has never
been tried. Locke's, I fancy, has been tried often enough, but is
very imperfect; it gives too much to one side, and too little to
the other; it gives too little to literature.—I shall do what I
can for Dr. Watts; but my materials are very scanty. His poems
are by no means his best works; I cannot praise his poetry itself
highly; but I can praise its design.'

My illustrious friend and I parted with assurances of affectionate regard.

I wrote to him on the 25th of May, from Thorpe in Yorkshire,
one of the seats of Mr. Bosville, and gave him an account of my
having passed a day at Lincoln, unexpectedly, and therefore
without having any letters of introduction, but that I had been
honoured with civilities from the Reverend Mr. Simpson, an
acquaintance of his, and Captain Broadley, of the Lincolnshire
Militia; but more particularly from the Reverend Dr. Gordon,
the Chancellor, who first received me with great politeness as
a stranger, and when I informed him who I was, entertained me

---

[1] The slip of paper on which he made the correction is deposited by me
in the noble library to which it relates, and to which I have presented other
pieces of his hand-writing. ⟨The slip of paper was presented to the
Bodleian in 1947 by Lt.-Col. R. H. Isham.⟩

at his house with the most flattering attention; I also expressed
the pleasure with which I had found that our worthy friend
Langton was highly esteemed in his own county town.

'*To* DR. SAMUEL JOHNSON

'MY DEAR SIR,   'Edinburgh, June 18, 1778.
    '. . . Since my return to Scotland, I have been again at
Lanark, and have had more conversation with Thomson's sister.
It is strange that Murdoch, who was his intimate friend, should
have mistaken his mother's maiden name, which he says was
Hume, whereas Hume was the name of his grandmother by the
mother's side. His mother's name was Beatrix Trotter,[1] a
daughter of Mr. Trotter, of Fogo, a small proprietor of land.
Thomson had one brother, whom he had with him in England
as his amanuensis; but he was seized with a consumption, and
having returned to Scotland, to try what his native air would do
for him, died young. He had three sisters, one married to Mr.
Bell, minister of the parish of Strathaven; one to Mr. Craig,
father of the ingenious architect, who gave the plan of the New
Town of Edinburgh; and one to Mr. Thomson, master of the
grammar-school at Lanark. He was of a humane and benevolent
disposition; not only sent valuable presents to his sisters, but a
yearly allowance in money, and was always wishing to have it
in his power to do them more good. Lord Lyttelton's observation, that "he loathed much to write," was very true. His letters
to his sister, Mrs. Thomson, were not frequent, and in one of
them he says, "All my friends who know me, know how backward I am to write letters; and never impute the negligence of
my hand to the coldness of my heart." I send you a copy of the
last letter which she had from him; she never heard that he had
any intention of going into holy orders. From this late interview
with his sister, I think much more favourably of him, as I hope
you will. I am eager to see more of your Prefaces to the Poets;
I solace myself with the few proof-sheets which I have.

    [1] Dr. Johnson was by no means attentive to minute accuracy in his *Lives
of the Poets*; for notwithstanding my having detected this mistake, he has
continued it.

'I send another parcel of Lord Hailes's *Annals*, which you will please to return to me as soon as you conveniently can. He says, "he wishes you would cut a little deeper;" but he may be proud that there is so little occasion to use the critical knife. I ever am, my dear Sir, your faithful and affectionate, humble servant,

'JAMES BOSWELL.'

Mr. Langton has been pleased, at my request, to favour me with some particulars of Dr. Johnson's visit to Warley-camp, where this gentleman was at the time stationed as a Captain in the Lincolnshire militia. I shall give them in his own words in a letter to me.

'It was in the summer of the year 1778, that he complied with my invitation to come down to the Camp at Warley, and he staid with me about a week; the scene appeared, notwithstanding a great degree of ill health that he seemed to labour under, to interest and amuse him, as agreeing with the disposition that I believe you know he constantly manifested towards enquiring into subjects of the military kind. He sate, with a patient degree of attention, to observe the proceedings of a regimental court-martial, that happened to be called, in the time of his stay with us; and one night, as late as at eleven o'clock, he accompanied the Major of the regiment in going what are styled the *Rounds*, where he might observe the forms of visiting the guards, for the seeing that they and their sentries are ready in their duty on their several posts. He took occasion to converse at times on military topicks, one in particular, that I see the mention of, in your *Journal of a Tour to the Hebrides*, which lies open before me,[1] as to gun-powder; which he spoke of to the same effect, in part, that you relate.

'On one occasion, when the regiment were going through their exercise, he went quite close to the men at one of the extremities of it, and watched all their practices attentively; and, when he came away, his remark was, "The men indeed do load their muskets and fire with wonderful celerity." He was likewise particular in requiring to know what was the weight of the

[1] Third edition, p. 111 [Aug. 28].

musquet balls in use, and within what distance they might be expected to take effect when fired off.

'In walking among the tents, and observing the difference between those of the officers and private men, he said that the superiority of accommodation of the better conditions of life, to that of the inferiour ones, was never exhibited to him in so distinct a view. The civilities paid to him in the camp were, from the gentlemen of the Lincolnshire regiment, one of the officers of which accommodated him with a tent in which he slept; and from General Hall, who very courteously invited him to dine with him, where he appeared to be very well pleased with his entertainment, and the civilities he received on the part of the General;[1] the attention likewise, of the General's aide-de-camp, Captain Smith, seemed to be very welcome to him, as appeared by their engaging in a great deal of discourse together. The gentlemen of the East York regiment likewise on being informed of his coming, solicited his company at dinner, but by that time he had fixed his departure, so that he could not comply with the invitation.'

'*To* JAMES BOSWELL, ESQ.

'DEAR SIR,—I have received two letters from you, of which the second complains of the neglect shewn to the first. You must not tye your friends to such punctual correspondence. You have all possible assurances of my affection and esteem; and there ought to be no need of reiterated professions. When it may happen that I can give you either counsel or comfort, I hope it will never happen to me that I should neglect you; but you must not think me criminal or cold if I say nothing when I have nothing to say.

'You are now happy enough. Mrs. Boswell is recovered; and I congratulate you upon the probability of her long life. If general approbation will add anything to your enjoyment, I can tell you that I have heard you mentioned as *a man whom everybody likes*. I think life has little more to give.

[1] When I one day at Court expressed to General Hall my sense of the honour he had done my friend, he politely answered, 'Sir, I did *myself* honour.'

'————————[1] has gone to his regiment. He has laid down his coach, and talks of making more contractions of his expence: how he will succeed I know not. It is difficult to reform a household gradually; it may be better done by a system totally new. I am afraid he has always something to hide. When we pressed him to go to ————————,[2] he objected the necessity of attending his navigation; yet he could talk of going to Aberdeen, a place not much nearer his navigation. I believe he cannot bear the thought of living at ———————— in a state of diminution; and of appearing among the gentlemen of the neighbourhood *shorn of his beams*. This is natural, but it is cowardly. What I told him of the encreasing expence of a growing family seems to have struck him. He certainly had gone on with very confused views, and we have, I think, shown him that he is wrong; though, with the common deficience of advisers, we have not shown him how to do right.

'I wish you would a little correct or restrain your imagination, and imagine that happiness, such as life admits, may be had at other places as well as London. Without asserting[3] Stoicism, it may be said, that it is our business to exempt ourselves as much as we can from the power of external things. There is but one solid basis of happiness; and that is, the reasonable hope of a happy futurity. This may be had every where.

'I do not blame your preference of London to other places, for it is really to be preferred, if the choice is free; but few have the choice of their place, or their manner of life; and mere pleasure ought not to be the prime motive of action.

'Mrs. Thrale, poor thing, has a daughter. Mr. Thrale dislikes the times, like the rest of us. Mrs. Williams is sick; Mrs. Desmoulins is poor. I have miserable nights. Nobody is well but Mr. Levett. I am, dear Sir, your most, &c.

'London, July 3, 1778.'   'SAM. JOHNSON.'

In the course of this year there was a difference between him and his friend Mr. Strahan; the particulars of which it is unneces-

[1] [Langton. *Croker*[1]]
[2] [Probably Langton in Lincolnshire.]   [3] Perhaps *affecting*. [M.]

sary to relate. Their reconciliation was communicated to me in a letter from Mr. Strahan, in the following words:—

'The notes I shewed you that passed between him and me were dated in March last. The matter lay dormant till July 27, when he wrote to me as follows:

"*To* WILLIAM STRAHAN, ESQ.

"SIR,—It would be very foolish for us to continue strangers any longer. You can never by persistency make wrong right. If I resented too acrimoniously, I resented only to yourself. Nobody ever saw or heard what I wrote. You saw that my anger was over, for in a day or two I came to your house. I have given you longer time; and I hope you have made so good use of it, as to be no longer on evil terms with, Sir, your, &c.

"SAM. JOHNSON."

'On this I called upon him; and he has since dined with me.'

After this time, the same friendship as formerly continued between Dr. Johnson and Mr. Strahan. My friend mentioned to me a little circumstance of his attention, which, though we may smile at it, must be allowed to have its foundation in a nice and true knowledge of human life. 'When I write to Scotland, (said he,) I employ Strahan to frank my letters, that he may have the consequence of appearing a Parliament-man among his countrymen.'

'*To* CAPTAIN LANGTON,[1] *Warley-camp*

'DEAR SIR,—When I recollect how long ago I was received with so much kindness at Warley Common, I am ashamed that I have not made some enquiries after my friends.

'Pray how many sheep-stealers did you convict? and how did you punish them? When are you to be cantoned in better habitations? The air grows cold, and the ground damp. Longer stay in the camp cannot be without much danger to the health of the common men, if even the officers can escape.

[1] Dr. Johnson here addresses his worthy friend, Bennet Langton, Esq., by his title as Captain of the Lincolnshire militia, in which he has since been most deservedly raised to the rank of Major.

'You see that Dr. Percy is now Dean of Carlisle; about five hundred a year, with a power of presenting himself to some good living. He is provided for.

'The session of THE CLUB is to commence with that of the Parliament. Mr. Banks desires to be admitted; he will be a very honourable accession.

'Did the King please you? The Coxheath men, I think, have some reason to complain: Reynolds says your camp is better than theirs.

'I hope you find yourself able to encounter this weather. Take care of your own health; and, as you can, of your men. Be pleased to make my compliments to all the gentlemen whose notice I have had, and whose kindness I have experienced. I am, dear Sir, your most humble servant,

'October 31, 1778.'   'SAM. JOHNSON.'

I wrote to him on the 18th of August, the 18th of September, and the 6th of November; informing him of my having had another son born, whom I had called James; that I had passed some time at Auchinleck; that the Countess of Loudoun, now in her ninety-ninth year, was as fresh as when he saw her, and remembered him with respect; and that his mother by adoption, the Countess of Eglintoune, had said to me, 'Tell Mr. Johnson I love him exceedingly;' that I had again suffered much from bad spirits; and that as it was very long since I heard from him, I was not a little uneasy.

The continuance of his regard for his friend Dr. Burney, appears from the following letters:—

'*To* THE REVEREND DR. WHEELER, *Oxford*

'DEAR SIR,—Dr. Burney, who brings this paper, is engaged in a History of Musick; and having been told by Dr. Markham of some MSS. relating to his subject, which are in the library of your College, is desirous to examine them. He is my friend; and therefore I take the liberty of intreating your favour and assistance in his enquiry: and can assure you, with great confidence, that if you knew him he would not want any intervenient solicitation to obtain the kindness of one who loves learning and virtue as you love them.

'I have been flattering myself all the summer with the hope of paying my annual visit to my friends; but something has obstructed me: I still hope not to be long without seeing you. I should be glad of a little literary talk; and glad to shew you, by the frequency of my visits, how eagerly I love it, when you talk it. I am, dear Sir, your most humble servant,

'London, November 2, 1778.'   'SAM. JOHNSON.'

'*To* THE REVEREND DR. EDWARDS, *Oxford*

'SIR,—The bearer, DR. BURNEY, has had some account of a Welsh Manuscript in the Bodleian library, from which he hopes to gain some materials for his History of Musick; but, being ignorant of the language, is at a loss where to find assistance. I make no doubt but you, Sir, can help him through his difficulties, and therefore take the liberty of recommending him to your favour, as I am sure you will find him a man worthy of every civility that can be shewn, and every benefit that can be conferred.

'But we must not let Welsh drive us from Greek. What comes of Xenophon? If you do not like the trouble of publishing the book, do not let your commentaries be lost; contrive that they may be published somewhere. I am, Sir, your humble servant,

'London, November 2, 1778.'   'SAM. JOHNSON.'

These letters procured Dr. Burney great kindness and friendly offices from both of these gentlemen, not only on that occasion, but in future visits to the university. The same year Dr. Johnson not only wrote to Dr. Joseph Warton in favour of Dr. Burney's youngest son, who was to be placed in the college of Winchester, but accompanied him when he went thither.

We surely cannot but admire the benevolent exertions of this great and good man, especially when we consider how grievously he was afflicted with bad health, and how uncomfortable his home was made by the perpetual jarring of those whom he charitably accommodated under his roof. He has sometimes suffered me to talk jocularly of his group of females, and call them his *Seraglio*. He thus mentions them, together with honest Levett, in one of his letters to Mrs. Thrale:[1] 'Williams hates every body; Levett hates Desmoulins, and does not love Williams; Desmoulins hates them both; Poll[2] loves none of them.'

'*To* JAMES BOSWELL, ESQ.

'DEAR SIR,—It is indeed a long time since I wrote, and I think you have some reason to complain; however, you must not let small things disturb you, when you have such a fine addition to your happiness as a new boy, and I hope your lady's health restored by bringing him. It seems very probable that a little care will now restore her, if any remains of her complaints are left.

'You seem, if I understand your letter, to be gaining ground at Auchinleck, an incident that would give me great delight. . . .

'When any fit of anxiety, or gloominess, or perversion of mind, lays hold upon you, make it a rule not to publish it by complaints, but exert your whole care to hide it; by endeavouring to hide it, you will drive it away. Be always busy.

'THE CLUB is to meet with the Parliament; we talk of electing Banks, the traveller; he will be a reputable member.

'Langton has been encamped with his company of militia on Warley-common; I spent five days amongst them; he signalized himself as a diligent officer, and has very high respect in the regiment. He presided when I was there at a court-martial; he is now quartered in Hertfordshire; his lady and little ones are in Scotland. Paoli came to the camp and commended the soldiers.

'Of myself I have no great matter to say, my health is not restored, my nights are restless and tedious. The best night that I have had these twenty years was at Fort-Augustus. I hope soon to send you a few lives to read. I am, dear Sir, your most affectionate,

'November 21, 1778.'   'SAM. JOHNSON.'

About this time the Rev. Mr. John Hussey, who had been some time in trade, and was then a clergyman of the Church of

[1] Vol. ii, p. 38.   [2] Miss Carmichael.

England, being about to undertake a journey to Aleppo, and other parts of the East, which he accomplished, Dr. Johnson, (who had long been in habits of intimacy with him,) honoured him with the following letter:—

To MR. JOHN HUSSEY

'DEAR SIR,—I have sent you the *Grammar*, and have left you two books more, by which I hope to be remembered; write my name in them; we may perhaps see each other no more, you part with my good wishes, nor do I despair of seeing you return. Let no opportunities of vice corrupt you; let no bad example seduce you; let the blindness of Mahometans confirm you in Christianity. GOD bless you. I am, dear Sir, your affectionate humble servant,

'December 29, 1778.'   'SAM. JOHNSON.'

Johnson this year expressed great satisfaction at the publication of the first volume of *Discourses to the Royal Academy*, by Sir Joshua Reynolds, whom he always considered as one of his literary school. Much praise indeed is due to those excellent *Discourses*, which are so universally admired, and for which the authour received from the Empress of Russia a gold snuff-box, adorned with her profile in *bas relief*, set in diamonds; and containing what is infinitely more valuable, a slip of paper, on which are written with her Imperial Majesty's own hand, the following words: '*Pour le Chevalier Reynolds en témoignage du contentement que j'ai ressentie à la lecture de ses excellens discours sur la peinture.*'

In 1779, Johnson gave the world a luminous proof that the vigour of his mind in all its faculties, whether memory, judgement, or imagination, was not in the least abated; for this year came out the first four volumes of his *Prefaces, biographical and critical, to the most eminent of the English Poets*,* published by the booksellers of London. The remaining volumes came out in the year 1780 [1781]. The Poets were selected by the several booksellers who had the honorary copy right, which is still preserved among them by mutual compact, notwithstanding the decision of the House of Lords against the perpetuity of Literary Property. We have his own authority,[1] that by his recommendation the poems of Blackmore, Watts, Pomfret, and Yalden, were added to the collection. Of this work I shall speak more particularly hereafter.

On the 22nd of January, I wrote to him on several topicks, and mentioned that as he had been so good as to permit me to have the proof sheets of his *Lives of the Poets*, I had written to his servant, Francis, to take care of them for me.

'MR. BOSWELL *to* DR. JOHNSON

'MY DEAR SIR,   'Edinburgh, Feb. 2, 1779.

'Garrick's death is a striking event; not that we should be surprised with the death of any man, who has lived sixty-two years; but because there was a *vivacity* in our late celebrated friend, which drove away the thoughts of *death* from any association with *him*. I am sure you will be tenderly affected with his departure; and I would wish to hear from you upon the subject. I was obliged to him in my days of effervescence in London, when poor Derrick was my governour; and since that time I received many civilities from him. Do you remember how pleasing it was, when I received a letter from him at Inverary, upon our first return to civilized living after our Hebridean journey? I shall always remember him with affection as well as admiration.

'On Saturday last, being the 30th of January, I drank coffee and old port, and had solemn conversation with the Reverend Mr. Falconer, a nonjuring bishop, a very learned and worthy man. He gave two toasts, which you will believe I drank with cordiality, Dr. Samuel Johnson, and Flora Macdonald. I sat about four hours with him, and it was really as if I had been living in the last century. The Episcopal Church of Scotland, though faithful to the royal house of Stuart, has never accepted of any *congé d'élire*, since the Revolution; it is the only true Episcopal Church in Scotland, as it has its own succession of bishops. For as to the episcopal clergy who take the oaths to the present government, they indeed follow the rites of the Church

---

[1] *Life of Watts.*

of England, but, as Bishop Falconer observed, "they are not *Episcopals*; for they are under no bishop, as a bishop cannot have authority beyond his diocese." This venerable gentleman did me the honour to dine with me yesterday, and he laid his hands upon the heads of my little ones. We had a good deal of curious literary conversation, particularly about Mr. Thomas Ruddiman, with whom he lived in great friendship.

'Any fresh instance of the uncertainty of life makes one embrace more closely a valuable friend. My dear and much respected Sir, may GOD preserve you long in this world while I am in it. I am ever, your much obliged, and affectionate humble servant,   'JAMES BOSWELL.'

On the 23rd of February I wrote to him again, complaining of his silence, as I had heard he was ill, and had written to Mr. Thrale, for information concerning him; and I announced my intention of soon being again in London.

'*To* JAMES BOSWELL, ESQ.

'DEAR SIR,—Why should you take such delight to make a bustle, to write to Mr. Thrale that I am negligent, and to Francis to do what is so very unnecessary. Thrale, you may be sure, cared not about it; and I shall spare Francis the trouble, by ordering a set both of the *Lives* and *Poets* to dear Mrs. Boswell,[1] in acknowledgement of her marmalade. Persuade her to accept them, and accept them kindly. If I thought she would receive them scornfully, I would send them to Miss Boswell, who, I hope, has yet none of her mamma's ill-will to me.

'I would send sets of *Lives*, four volumes, to some other friends, to Lord Hailes first. His second volume lies by my bedside; a book surely of great labour, and to every just thinker of great delight. Write me word to whom I shall send besides; would it please Lord Auchinleck? Mrs. Thrale waits in the coach. I am, dear Sir, &c.,

'March 13, 1779.'   'SAM. JOHNSON.'

[1] He sent a set elegantly bound and gilt, which was received as a very handsome present.

This letter crossed me on the road to London, where I arrived on Monday, March 15, and next morning at a late hour, found Dr. Johnson sitting over his tea, attended by Mrs. Desmoulins, Mr. Levett, and a clergyman,[1] who had come to submit some poetical pieces to his revision. It is wonderful what a number and variety of writers, some of them even unknown to him, prevailed on his good-nature to look over their works, and suggest corrections and improvements. My arrival interrupted for a little while the important business of this true representative of Bayes; upon its being resumed, I found that the subject under immediate consideration was a translation, yet in manuscript, of the *Carmen Seculare* of Horace, which had this year been set to musick, and performed as a publick entertainment in London, for the joint benefit of Monsieur Philidor and Signor Baretti. When Johnson had done reading, the authour asked him bluntly, 'If upon the whole it was a good translation?' Johnson, whose regard for truth was uncommonly strict, seemed to be puzzled for a moment, what answer to make, as he certainly could not honestly commend the performance: with exquisite address he evaded the question thus, 'Sir, I do not say that it may not be made a very good translation.' Here nothing whatever in favour of the performance was affirmed, and yet the writer was not shocked. A printed *Ode to the Warlike Genius of Britain*, came next in review; the bard was a lank bony figure, with short black hair; he was writhing himself in agitation, while Johnson read, and shewing his teeth in a grin of earnestness, exclaimed in broken sentences, and in a keen sharp tone, 'Is that poetry, Sir?—Is it *Pindar*?' JOHNSON. 'Why, Sir, there is here a great deal of what is called poetry.' Then, turning to me, the poet cried, 'My muse has not been long upon the town, and (pointing to the *Ode*) it trembles under the hand of the great critick.' Johnson, in a tone of displeasure, asked him, 'Why do you praise Anson?' I did not trouble him by asking his reason for this question. He proceeded, 'Here is an errour, Sir; you have made Genius feminine.' 'Palpable, Sir; (cried the enthusiast,) I know it. But (in a lower tone,) it was to pay a compliment to

[1] [The Rev. William Tasker. *Boswell Papers*, xiii. 210.]

the Duchess of Devonshire, with which her Grace was pleased. She is walking across Coxheath, in the military uniform, and I suppose her to be the Genius of Britain.' JOHNSON. 'Sir, you are giving a reason for it; but that will not make it right. You may have a reason why two and two should make five; but they will still make but four.'

Although I was several times with him in the course of the following days, such it seems were my occupations, or such my negligence, that I have preserved no memorial of his conversation till Friday, March 26, when I visited him. He said he expected to be attacked on account of his *Lives of the Poets*. 'However (said he,) I would rather be attacked than unnoticed. For the worst thing you can do to an authour is to be silent as to his works. An assault upon a town is a bad thing; but starving it is still worse; an assault may be unsuccessful; you may have more men killed than you kill; but if you starve the town, you are sure of victory.'

Talking of a friend of ours[1] associating with persons of very discordant principles and characters; I said he was a very universal man, quite a man of the world. JOHNSON. 'Yes, Sir; but one may be so much a man of the world as to be nothing in the world. I remember a passage in Goldsmith's *Vicar of Wakefield*, which he was afterwards fool enough to expunge: "I do not love a man who is zealous for nothing." ' BOSWELL. 'That was a fine passage.' JOHNSON. 'Yes, Sir: there was another fine passage too, which he struck out: "When I was a young man, being anxious to distinguish myself, I was perpetually starting new propositions. But I soon gave this over; for, I found that generally what was new was false." ' I said I did not like to sit with people of whom I had not a good opinion. JOHNSON. 'But you must not indulge your delicacy too much; or you will be a *tête-à-tête* man all your life.'

During my stay in London this spring, I find I was unaccountably negligent in preserving Johnson's sayings, more so than at any time when I was happy enough to have an opportunity of hearing his wisdom and wit. There is no help for it now.

[1] [Perhaps Reynolds. *Croker*[1].]

I must content myself with presenting such scraps as I have. But I am nevertheless ashamed and vexed to think how much has been lost. It is not that there was a bad crop this year; but that I was not sufficiently careful in gathering it in. I, therefore, in some instances can only exhibit a few detached fragments.

Talking of the wonderful concealment of the authour of the celebrated letters signed *Junius*; he said, 'I should have believed Burke to be Junius, because I know no man but Burke who is capable of writing these letters; but Burke spontaneously denied it to me. The case would have been different had I asked him if he was the authour; a man so questioned, as to an anonymous publication, may think he has a right to deny it.'

He observed that his old friend, Mr. Sheridan, had been honoured with extraordinary attention in his own country, by having had an exception made in his favour in an Irish Act of Parliament concerning insolvent debtors. 'Thus to be singled out (said he,) by a legislature, as an object of publick consideration and kindness, is a proof of no common merit.'

At Streatham, on Monday, March 29, at breakfast he maintained that a father had no right to control the inclinations of his daughters in marriage.

On Wednesday, March 31, when I visited him, and confessed an excess of which I had very seldom been guilty; that I had spent a whole night in playing at cards, and that I could not look back on it with satisfaction; instead of a harsh animadversion, he mildly said, 'Alas, Sir, on how few things can we look back with satisfaction.'

On Thursday, April 1, he commended one of the Dukes of Devonshire for 'a dogged veracity.' He said too, 'London is nothing to some people; but to a man whose pleasure is intellectual, London is the place. And there is no place where œconomy can be so well practised as in London. More can be had here for the money, even by ladies, than any where else. You cannot play tricks with your fortune in a small place; you must make an uniform appearance. Here a lady may have well-furnished apartments, and elegant dress, without any meat in her kitchen.'

I was amused by considering with how much ease and coolness
he could write or talk to a friend, exhorting him not to suppose
that happiness was not to be found as well in other places as in
London; when he himself was at all times sensible of its being,
comparatively speaking, a heaven upon earth. The truth is, that
by those who from sagacity, attention, and experience, have
learnt the full advantage of London, its pre-eminence over every
other place, not only for variety of enjoyment, but for comfort,
will be felt with a philosophical exultation. The freedom from
remark and petty censure, with which life may be passed there,
is a circumstance which a man who knows the teazing restraint of
a narrow circle must relish highly. Mr. Burke, whose orderly
and amiable domestic habits might make the eye of observation
less irksome to him than to most men, said once very pleasantly,
in my hearing, 'Though I have the honour to represent Bristol,
I should not like to live there; I should be obliged to be so much
upon my good behaviour.' In London, a man may live in splendid
society at one time, and in frugal retirement at another, without
animadversion. There, and there alone, a man's own house is
truly his *castle*, in which he can be in perfect safety from intrusion
whenever he pleases. I never shall forget how well this was
expressed to me one day by Mr. Meynell: 'The chief advantage
of London (said he,) is, that a man is always *so near his burrow.'*

He said of one of his old acquaintances,[1] 'He is very fit for a
travelling governour. He knows French very well. He is a man of
good principles; and there would be no danger that a young gentleman should catch his manner; for it is so very bad, that it must
be avoided. In that respect he would be like the drunken Helot.'

A gentleman[2] has informed me, that Johnson said of the same
person, 'Sir, he has the most *inverted* understanding of any man
whom I have ever known.'

On Friday, April 2, being Good-Friday, I visited him in the
morning as usual; and finding that we insensibly fell into a train
of ridicule upon the foibles of one of our friends,[3] a very worthy

---

[1] [James Elphinston. *Boswell Papers*, xiii. 213–14.]
[2] [Probably William Strahan, Elphinston's brother-in-law. *Powell.*]
[3] [Langton. *Boswell Papers*, xiii. 214.]

man, I, by way of a check, quoted some good admonition from *The Government of the Tongue,* that very pious book. It happened also remarkably enough, that the subject of the sermon preached to us to-day by Dr. Burrows, the rector of St. Clement Danes, was the certainty that at the last day we must give an account of 'the deeds done in the body;' and, amongst various acts of culpability he mentioned evil-speaking. As we were moving slowly along in the crowd from church, Johnson jogged my elbow, and said, 'Did you attend to the sermon?' 'Yes, Sir, (said I,) it was very applicable to *us.*' He, however, stood upon the defensive. 'Why, Sir, the sense of ridicule is given us, and may be lawfully used. The authour of *The Government of the Tongue* would have us treat all men alike.'

In the interval between morning and evening service, he endeavoured to employ himself earnestly in devotional exercises; and, as he has mentioned in his *Prayers and Meditations,*[1] gave me *Les Pensées de Pascal,* that I might not interrupt him. I preserve the book with reverence. His presenting it to me is marked upon it with his own hand, and I have found in it a truly divine unction. We went to church again in the afternoon.

On Saturday, April 3, I visited him at night, and found him sitting in Mrs. Williams's room, with her, and one[2] who he afterwards told me was a natural son of the second Lord Southwell. The table had a singular appearance, being covered with a heterogeneous assemblage of oysters and porter for his company, and tea for himself. I mentioned my having heard an eminent physician,[3] who was himself a Christian, argue in favour of universal toleration, and maintain, that no man could be hurt by another man's differing from him in opinion. JOHNSON. 'Sir, you are to a certain degree hurt by knowing that even one man does not believe.'

On Easter-day, after solemn service at St. Paul's, I dined with him: Mr. Allen the printer was also his guest. He was uncommonly silent; and I have not written down any thing, except

---

[1] p. 173.
[2] [Mauritius Lowe. *Boswell Papers,* xiii. 215, xv. 181.]
[3] [Dr. Heberden. *Ib.* xiii. 215.]

a single curious fact, which, having the sanction of his inflexible veracity, may be received as a striking instance of human insensibility and inconsideration. As he was passing by a fishmonger who was skinning an eel alive, he heard him 'curse it, because it would not lye still.'

On Wednesday, April 7, I dined with him at Sir Joshua Reynolds's. I have not marked what company was there. Johnson harangued upon the qualities of different liquors; and spoke with great contempt of claret, as so weak, that 'a man would be drowned by it before it made him drunk.' He was persuaded to drink one glass of it, that he might judge, not from recollection, which might be dim, but from immediate sensation. He shook his head, and said, 'Poor stuff! No, Sir, claret is the liquor for boys; port, for men; but he who aspires to be a hero (smiling,) must drink brandy. In the first place, the flavour of brandy is most grateful to the palate; and then brandy will do soonest for a man what drinking *can* do for him. There are, indeed, few who are able to drink brandy. That is a power rather to be wished for than attained. And yet, (proceeded he,) as in all pleasure hope is a considerable part, I know not but fruition comes too quick by brandy. Florence wine I think the worst; it is wine only to the eye; it is wine neither while you are drinking it, nor after you have drunk it; it neither pleases the taste, nor exhilarates the spirits.' I reminded him how heartily he and I used to drink wine together, when we were first acquainted; and how I used to have a head-ache after sitting up with him. He did not like to have this recalled, or, perhaps, thinking that I boasted improperly, resolved to have a witty stroke at me: 'Nay, Sir, it was not the *wine* that made your head ache, but the *sense* that I put into it.' BOSWELL. 'What, Sir! will sense make the head ache?' JOHNSON. 'Yes, Sir, (with a smile,) when it is not used to it.'—No man who has a true relish of pleasantry could be offended at this; especially if Johnson in a long intimacy had given him repeated proofs of his regard and good estimation. I used to say, that as he had given me a thousand pounds in praise, he had a good right now and then to take a guinea from me.

On Thursday, April 8, I dined with him at Mr. Allan Ramsay's, with Lord Graham and some other company. We talked of Shakspeare's witches. JOHNSON. 'They are beings of his own creation; they are a compound of malignity and meanness, without any abilities; and are quite different from the Italian magician. King James says in his *Dæmonology*, 'Magicians command the devils: witches are their servants. The Italian magicians are elegant beings.' RAMSAY. 'Opera witches, not Drury-lane witches.' Johnson observed, that abilities might be employed in a narrow sphere, as in getting money, which he said he believed no man could do, without vigorous parts, though concentrated to a point. RAMSAY. 'Yes, like a strong horse in a mill; he pulls better.'

Lord Graham, while he praised the beauty of Lochlomond, on the banks of which is his family seat, complained of the climate, and said he could not bear it. JOHNSON. 'Nay, my Lord, don't talk so: you may bear it well enough. Your ancestors have borne it more years than I can tell.' This was a handsome compliment to the antiquity of the House of Montrose. His Lordship told me afterwards, that he had only affected to complain of the climate; lest, if he had spoken as favourably of his country as he really thought, Dr. Johnson might have attacked it. Johnson was very courteous to Lady Margaret Macdonald. 'Madam, (said he,) when I was in the Isle of Sky, I heard of the people running to take the stones off the road, lest Lady Margaret's horse should stumble.'

Lord Graham commended Dr. Drummond at Naples, as a man of extraordinary talents; and added, that he had a great love of liberty. JOHNSON. 'He is *young*, my Lord; (looking to his Lordship with an arch smile,) all *boys* love liberty, till experience convinces them they are not so fit to govern themselves as they imagined. We are all agreed as to our own liberty; we would have as much of it as we can get; but we are not agreed as to the liberty of others: for in proportion as we take, others must lose. I believe we hardly wish that the mob should have liberty to govern us. When that was the case some time ago, no man was at liberty not to have candles in his windows.' RAMSAY. 'The result is, that order is better than confusion.' JOHNSON. 'The result is, that order cannot be had but by subordination.'

On Friday, April 16, I had been present at the trial of the unfortunate Mr. Hackman, who, in a fit of frantick jealous love, had shot Miss Ray, the favourite of a nobleman.[1] Johnson, in whose company I dined to-day, with some other friends, was much interested by my account of what passed, and particularly with his prayer for the mercy of heaven. He said, in a solemn fervid tone, 'I hope he *shall* find mercy.'

This day a violent altercation arose between Johnson and Beauclerk, which having made much noise at the time, I think it proper, in order to prevent any future misrepresentation, to give a minute account of it.

In talking of Hackman, Johnson argued, as Judge Blackstone had done, that his being furnished with two pistols was a proof that he meant to shoot two persons. Mr. Beauclerk said, 'No; for that every wise man who intended to shoot himself, took two pistols, that he might be sure of doing it at once. Lord —————————'s[2] cook shot himself with one pistol, and lived ten days in great agony. Mr. —————,[3] who loved buttered muffins, but durst not eat them because they disagreed with his stomach, resolved to shoot himself; and then he eat three buttered muffins for breakfast, before shooting himself, knowing that he should not be troubled with indigestion: *he* had two charged pistols; one was found lying charged upon the table by him, after he had shot himself with the other.' 'Well, (said Johnson, with an air of triumph,) you see here one pistol was sufficient.' Beauclerk replied smartly, 'Because it happened to kill him.' And either then, or a very little afterwards, being piqued at Johnson's triumphant remark, added, 'This is what you don't know, and I do.' There was then a cessation of the dispute; and some minutes intervened, during which, dinner and the glass went on cheerfully; when Johnson suddenly and abruptly exclaimed, 'Mr.

---

[1] [John Montagu, 4th Earl of Sandwich. *Croker*[1].]
[2] [Lord Charles Spencer. *Johnson and Boswell Revised*, p. 49.]
[3] [Mr. Delmis. *Ib.* pp. 49–50.]

Beauclerk, how came you to talk so petulantly to me, as "This is what you don't know, but what I know"? One thing *I* know, which *you* don't seem to know, that you are very uncivil.' BEAUCLERK. 'Because *you* began by being uncivil, (which you always are.)' The words in parenthesis were, I believe, not heard by Dr. Johnson. Here again there was a cessation of arms. Johnson told me, that the reason why he waited at first some time without taking any notice of what Mr. Beauclerk said, was because he was thinking whether he should resent it. But when he considered that there were present a young Lord and an eminent traveller,[1] two men of the world with whom he had never dined before, he was apprehensive that they might think they had a right to take such liberties with him as Beauclerk did, and therefore resolved he would not let it pass; adding, that 'he would not appear a coward.' A little while after this, the conversation turned on the violence of Hackman's temper. Johnson then said, 'It was his business to *command* his temper, as my friend, Mr. Beauclerk, should have done some time ago.' BEAUCLERK. 'I should learn of *you*, Sir.' JOHNSON. 'Sir, you have given *me* opportunities enough of learning, when I have been in *your* company. No man loves to be treated with contempt.' BEAUCLERK. (with a polite inclination towards Johnson,) 'Sir, you have known me twenty years, and however I may have treated others, you may be sure I could never treat you with contempt.' JOHNSON. 'Sir, you have said more than was necessary.' Thus it ended; and Beauclerk's coach not having come for him till very late, Dr. Johnson and another gentleman[2] sat with him a long time after the rest of the company were gone; and he and I dined at Beauclerk's on the Saturday se'nnight following.

After this tempest had subsided, I recollect the following particulars of his conversation:—

'I am always for getting a boy forward in his learning; for that is a sure good. I would let him at first read *any* English book which happens to engage his attention; because you have

---

[1] [Viscount Althorp and Sir Joseph Banks. *Boswell Papers*, xiii. 227.]
[2] [Steevens. *Johnson and Boswell Revised*, p. 50.]

done a great deal when you have brought him to have entertainment from a book. He'll get better books afterwards.'

'Mallet, I believe, never wrote a single line of his projected
life of the Duke of Marlborough. He groped for materials;
and thought of it, till he had exhausted his mind. Thus it sometimes happens that men entangle themselves in their own
schemes.'

'To be contradicted, in order to force you to talk, is mighty
unpleasing. You *shine*, indeed; but it is by being *ground*.'

Of a gentleman who made some figure among the *Literati* of
his time, (Mr. Fitzherbert,) he said, 'What eminence he had
was by a felicity of manner; he had no more learning than what
he could not help.'

On Saturday, April 24, I dined with him at Mr. Beauclerk's,
with Sir Joshua Reynolds, Mr. Jones, (afterwards Sir William,)
Mr. Langton, Mr. Steevens, Mr. Paradise, and Dr. Higgins. I
mentioned that Mr. Wilkes had attacked Garrick to me, as a
man who had no friend. 'I believe he is right, Sir. Οἱ φίλοι, οὐ
φίλος—He had friends, but no friend.[1] Garrick was so diffused,
he had no man to whom he wished to unbosom himself. He found
people always ready to applaud him, and that always for the
same thing: so he saw life with great uniformity.' I took upon
me, for once, to fight with Goliath's weapons, and play the
sophist.—'Garrick did not need a friend, as he got from every
body all he wanted. What is a friend? One who supports you and
comforts you, while others do not. Friendship, you know, Sir,
is the cordial drop, "to make the nauseous draught of life go
down:" but if the draught be not nauseous, if it be all sweet,
there is no occasion for that drop.' JOHNSON. 'Many men would
not be content to live so. I hope I should not. They would wish
to have an intimate friend, with whom they might compare
minds, and cherish private virtues.' One of the company mentioned Lord Chesterfield, as a man who had no friend. JOHN-
SON. 'There were more materials to make friendship in Garrick,
had he not been so diffused.' BOSWELL. 'Garrick was pure gold,
but beat out to thin leaf. Lord Chesterfield was tinsel.' JOHNSON.

[1] See *ante*, pp. 148, 946.

'Garrick was a very good man, the cheerfullest man of his age; a decent liver in a profession which is supposed to give indulgence to licentiousness; and a man who gave away, freely, money acquired by himself. He began the world with a great hunger for money; the son of a half-pay officer, bred in a family, whose study was to make four-pence do as much as others made four-pence halfpenny do. But, when he had got money, he was very liberal.' I presumed to animadvert on his eulogy on Garrick, in his *Lives of the Poets.* 'You say, Sir, his death eclipsed the gaiety of nations.' JOHNSON. 'I could not have said more nor less. It is the truth; *eclipsed,* not *extinguished*; and his death *did* eclipse; it was like a storm.' BOSWELL. 'But why nations? Did his gaiety extend farther than his own nation?' JOHNSON. 'Why, Sir, some exaggeration must be allowed. Besides, nations may be said—if we allow the Scotch to be a nation, and to have gaiety,—which they have not. *You* are an exception, though. Come, gentlemen, let us candidly admit that there is one Scotchman who is cheerful.' BEAUCLERK. 'But he is a very unnatural Scotchman.' I, however, continued to think the compliment to Garrick hyperbolically untrue. His acting had ceased some time before his death; at any rate he had acted in Ireland but a short time, at an early period of his life, and never in Scotland. I objected also to what appears an anticlimax of praise, when contrasted with the preceding panegyrick,—'and diminished the public stock of harmless pleasure!'—'Is not *harmless pleasure* very tame?' JOHNSON. 'Nay, Sir, harmless pleasure is the highest praise. Pleasure is a word of dubious import; pleasure is in general dangerous, and pernicious to virtue; to be able therefore to furnish pleasure that is harmless, pleasure pure and unalloyed, is as great a power as man can possess.' This was, perhaps, as ingenious a defence as could be made; still, however, I was not satisfied.

A celebrated wit[1] being mentioned, he said, 'One may say of him as was said of a French wit,[2] *Il n'a de l'esprit que contre Dieu.* I have been several times in company with him, but never perceived any strong power of wit. He produces a general effect

[1] [Wilkes. *Boswell Papers*, xiii. 234.]   [2] [By Boileau.]

by various means; he has a cheerful countenance and a gay voice. Besides his trade is wit. It would be as wild in him to come into company without merriment, as for a highwayman to take the road without his pistols.'

Talking of the effects of drinking, he said, 'Drinking may be practised with great prudence; a man who exposes himself when he is intoxicated, has not the art of getting drunk; a sober man who happens occasionally to get drunk, readily enough goes into a new company, which a man who has been drinking should never do. Such a man will undertake any thing; he is without skill in inebriation. I used to slink home, when I had drunk too much. A man accustomed to self-examination will be conscious when he is drunk, though an habitual drunkard will not be conscious of it. I knew a physician[1] who for twenty years was not sober; yet in a pamphlet, which he wrote upon fevers, he appealed to Garrick and me for his vindication from a charge of drunkenness. A bookseller (naming him,)[2] who got a large fortune by trade, was so habitually and equably drunk, that his most intimate friends never perceived that he was more sober at one time than another.'

Talking of celebrated and successful irregular practisers in physick; he said, 'Taylor was the most ignorant man I ever knew; but sprightly. Ward the dullest. Taylor challenged me once to talk Latin with him; (laughing). I quoted some of Horace, which he took to be a part of my own speech. He said a few words well enough.' BEAUCLERK. 'I remember, Sir, you said that Taylor was an instance how far impudence could carry ignorance.' Mr. Beauclerk was very entertaining this day, and told us a number of short stories in a lively elegant manner, and with that air of *the world* which has I know not what impressive effect, as if there were something more than is expressed, or than perhaps we could perfectly understand. As Johnson and I accompanied Sir Joshua Reynolds in his coach, Johnson said, 'There is in Beauclerk a predominance over his company, that one does not like. But he is a man who has lived so much in the

---

[1] [Dr. Robert James. *Boswell Papers*, xiii. 235.]
[2] [Andrew Millar. *Ib.*]

world, that he has a short story on every occasion; he is always ready to talk, and is never exhausted.'

Johnson and I passed the evening at Miss Reynolds's, Sir Joshua's sister. I mentioned that an eminent friend of ours,[1] talking of the common remark, that affection descends, said, that 'this was wisely contrived for the preservation of mankind; for which it was not so necessary that there should be affection from children to parents, as from parents to children; nay, there would be no harm in that view though children should at a certain age eat their parents.' JOHNSON. 'But, Sir, if this were known generally to be the case, parents would not have affection for children.' BOSWELL. 'True, Sir; for it is in expectation of a return that parents are so attentive to their children; and I know a very pretty instance of a little girl[2] of whom her father was very fond, who once when he was in a melancholy fit, and had gone to bed, persuaded him to rise in good humour by saying, "My dear papa, please to get up, and let me help you on with your clothes, that I may learn to do it when you are an old man."'

Soon after this time a little incident occurred, which I will not suppress, because I am desirous that my work should be, as much as is consistent with the strictest truth, an antidote to the false and injurious notions of his character, which have been given by others, and therefore I infuse every drop of genuine sweetness into my biographical cup.

'*To* DR. JOHNSON

'MY DEAR SIR,—I am in great pain with an inflamed foot, and obliged to keep my bed, so am prevented from having the pleasure to dine at Mr. Ramsay's to-day, which is very hard; and my spirits are sadly sunk. Will you be so friendly as to come and sit an hour with me in the evening. I am ever your most faithful, and affectionate humble servant,

'South Audley-street,   'JAMES BOSWELL.'
    Monday, April 26.'

---

[1] [Burke. *Boswell Papers*, xiii. 236.]
[2] [J. B.'s daughter, Veronica. *Ib.* 192, 236.]

'*To* Mr. Boswell

'Mr. Johnson laments the absence of Mr. Boswell, and will come to him.—Harley-street.'

He came to me in the evening, and brought Sir Joshua Reynolds. I need scarcely say, that their conversation, while they sate by my bedside, was the most pleasing opiate to pain that could have been administered.

Johnson being now better disposed to obtain information concerning Pope than he was last year,[1] sent by me to my Lord Marchmont a present of those volumes of his *Lives of the Poets* which were at this time published, with a request to have permission to wait on him; and his Lordship, who had called on him twice, obligingly appointed Saturday, the first of May, for receiving us.

On that morning Johnson came to me from Streatham, and after drinking chocolate at General Paoli's, in South-Audley-street, we proceeded to Lord Marchmont's in Curzon-street. His Lordship met us at the door of his library, and with great politeness said to Johnson, 'I am not going to make an encomium upon *myself*, by telling you the high respect I have for *you*, Sir.' Johnson was exceedingly courteous; and the interview, which lasted about two hours, during which the Earl communicated his anecdotes of Pope, was as agreeable as I could have wished. When we came out, I said to Johnson, that considering his Lordship's civility, I should have been vexed if he had again failed to come. 'Sir, (said he,) I would rather have given twenty pounds than not have come.' I accompanied him to Streatham, where we dined, and returned to town in the evening.

On Monday, May 3, I dined with him at Mr. Dilly's; I pressed him this day for his opinion on the passage in Parnell, concerning which I had in vain questioned him in several letters, and at length obtained it in *due form of law*.

Case for Dr. Johnson's Opinion;
3rd of May, 1779.

'Parnell, in his *Hermit,* has the following passage:

---

[1] See *ante*, pp. 987–9.

'To clear this doubt, to know the world by sight,
To find if *books* and *swains* report it right:
(For yet by *swains alone* the world he knew,
Whose feet came wand'ring o'er the nightly dew.)'

Is there not a contradiction in its being *first* supposed that the *Hermit* knew *both* what books and swains reported of the world; yet *afterwards* said, that he knew it by swains *alone?*

'*I think it an inaccuracy.— He mentions two instructors in the first line, and says he had only one in the next.*'[1]

This evening I set out for Scotland.

'*To* Mrs. Lucy Porter, *in Lichfield*

'Dear Madam,—Mr. Green has informed me that you are much better; I hope I need not tell you that I am glad of it. I cannot boast of being much better; my old nocturnal complaint still pursues me, and my respiration is difficult, though much easier than when I left you the summer before last. Mr. and Mrs. Thrale are well; Miss has been a little indisposed; but she is got well again. They have since the loss of their boy had two daughters; but they seem likely to want a son.

'I hope you had some books which I sent you. I was sorry for poor Mrs. Adey's death, and am afraid you will be sometimes solitary; but endeavour, whether alone or in company, to keep

---

[1] 'I do not (says Mr. Malone,) see any difficulty in this passage, and wonder that Dr. Johnson should have acknowledged it to be *inaccurate.* The Hermit, it should be observed, had no actual experience of the world whatsoever: all his knowledge concerning it had been obtained in two ways; from *books*, and from the *relations* of those country swains, who had seen a little of it. The plain meaning, therefore, is, "To clear his doubts concerning Providence, and to obtain some knowledge of the world by actual experience; to see whether the accounts furnished by books, or by the oral communications of swains, were just representations of it; [I say, *swains*,] for his oral or *vivâ voce* information had been obtained from that part of mankind *alone*, &c." The word *alone* here does not relate to the whole of the preceding line, as has been supposed, but, by a common licence, to the words,—*of all mankind*, which are understood, and of which it is restrictive.'

Mr. Malone, it must be owned, has shewn much critical ingenuity in the explanation of this passage. His interpretation, however, seems to me much too recondite. The *meaning* of the passage may be certain enough; but surely the *expression* is confused, and one part of it contradictory to the other.

yourself cheerful. My friends likewise die very fast; but such is the state of man. I am, dear love, your most humble servant,

     'May 4, 1779.'   'SAM. JOHNSON.'

He had, before I left London, resumed the conversation concerning the appearance of a ghost at Newcastle upon Tyne, which Mr. John Wesley believed, but to which Johnson did not give credit. I was, however, desirous to examine the question closely, and at the same time wished to be made acquainted with Mr. John Wesley; for though I differed from him in some points, I admired his various talents, and loved his pious zeal. At my request, therefore, Dr. Johnson gave me a letter of introduction to him.

'*To* THE REVEREND MR. JOHN WESLEY

     'SIR,—Mr. Boswell, a gentleman who has been long known to me, is desirous of being known to you, and has asked this recommendation, which I give him with great willingness, because I think it very much to be wished that worthy and religious men should be acquainted with each other. I am, Sir, your most humble servant.

     'May 3, 1779.'   'SAM. JOHNSON.'

Mr. Wesley being in the course of his ministry at Edinburgh, I presented this letter to him, and was very politely received. I begged to have it returned to me, which was accordingly done. His state of the evidence as to the ghost did not satisfy me.

I did not write to Johnson, as usual, upon my return to my family, but tried how he would be affected by my silence. Mr. Dilly sent me a copy of a note which he received from him on the 13th of July, in these words:—

'*To* MR. DILLY

     'SIR,—Since Mr. Boswell's departure I have never heard from him; please to send word what you know of him, and whether you have sent my books to his lady. I am, &c.,

                                     'SAM. JOHNSON.'

My readers will not doubt that his solicitude about me was very flattering.

'*To* JAMES BOSWELL, ESQ.

'DEAR SIR,—What can possibly have happened, that keeps us two such strangers to each other? I expected to have heard from you when you came home; I expected afterwards. I went into the country and returned; and yet there is no letter from Mr. Boswell. No ill I hope has happened; and if ill should happen, why should it be concealed from him who loves you? Is it a fit of humour, that has disposed you to try who can hold out longest without writing? If it be, you have the victory. But I am afraid of something bad; set me free from my suspicions.

'My thoughts are at present employed in guessing the reason of your silence: you must not expect that I should tell you any thing, if I had any thing to tell. Write, pray write to me, and let me know what is, or what has been the cause of this long interruption. I am, dear Sir, your most affectionate humble servant,

'July 13, 1779.'   'SAM. JOHNSON.'

'*To* DR. SAMUEL JOHNSON

'MY DEAR SIR,   'Edinburgh, July 17, 1779.

'What may be justly denominated a supine indolence of mind has been my state of existence since I last returned to Scotland. In a livelier state I had often suffered severely from long intervals of silence on your part; and I had even been chid by you for expressing my uneasiness. I was willing to take advantage of my insensibility, and while I could bear the experiment, to try whether your affection for me would, after an unusual silence on my part, make you write first. This afternoon I have had very high satisfaction by receiving your kind letter of inquiry, for which I most gratefully thank you. I am doubtful if it was right to make the experiment; though I have gained by it. I was beginning to grow tender, and to upbraid myself, especially after having dreamt two nights ago that I was with you. I and my wife, and my four children, are all well. I would not delay one post to answer your letter; but as it is late, I have not time to do more. You shall soon hear from me, upon many and various particulars; and I shall never again put you to any test. I ever am, with veneration, my dear Sir, your much obliged, and faithful humble servant,

'JAMES BOSWELL.'

On the 22nd of July, I wrote to him again; and gave him an account of my last interview with my worthy friend, Mr. Edward Dilly, at his brother's house at Southill, in Bedfordshire, where he died soon after I parted from him, leaving me a very kind remembrance of his regard.

I informed him that Lord Hailes, who had promised to furnish him with some anecdotes for his *Lives of the Poets*, had sent me three instances of Prior's borrowing from *Gombauld*, in *Recueil des Poetes*, tome 3. Epigram *To John I owed great obligation*, p. 25. *To the Duke of Noailles*, p. 32. *Sauntering Jack and Idle Joan*, p. 25.

My letter was a pretty long one, and contained a variety of particulars; but he, it should seem, had not attended to it; for his next to me was as follows:—

'*To* JAMES BOSWELL, ESQ.

'MY DEAR SIR,—Are you playing the same trick again, and trying who can keep silence longest? Remember that all tricks are either knavish or childish; and that it is as foolish to make experiments upon the constancy of a friend, as upon the chastity of a wife.

'What can be the cause of this second fit of silence, I cannot conjecture; but after one trick, I will not be cheated by another, nor will harass my thoughts with conjectures about the motives of a man who, probably, acts only by caprice. I therefore suppose you are well, and that Mrs. Boswell is well too; and that the fine summer has restored Lord Auchinleck. I am much better than you left me; I think I am better than when I was in Scotland.

'I forgot whether I informed you that poor Thrale has been in great danger. Mrs. Thrale likewise has miscarried, and been

much indisposed. Every body else is well; Langton is in camp.
I intend to put Lord Hailes's description of Dryden[1] into another
edition, and as I know his accuracy, wish he would consider the
dates, which I could not always settle to my own mind.

'Mr. Thrale goes to Brighthelmston, about Michaelmas, to
be jolly and ride a hunting. I shall go to town, or perhaps to
Oxford. Exercise and gaiety, or rather carelessness, will, I hope,
dissipate all remains of his malady; and I likewise hope by the
change of place, to find some opportunities of growing yet better
myself. I am, dear Sir, your humble servant,

'Streatham, Sept. 9, 1779.'   'SAM. JOHNSON.'

My readers will not be displeased at being told every slight
circumstance of the manner in which Dr. Johnson contrived to
amuse his solitary hours. He sometimes employed himself in
chymistry, sometimes in watering and pruning a vine, and
sometimes in small experiments, at which those who may smile,
should recollect that there are moments which admit of being
soothed only by trifles.[2]

On the 20th of September I defended myself against his suspicion of me, which I did not deserve; and added, 'Pray let us write
frequently. A whim strikes me, that we should send off a sheet
once a week, like a stage-coach, whether it be full or not; nay,
though it should be empty. The very sight of your hand-writing

---

[1] Which I communicated to him from his Lordship, but it has not yet been
published. I have a copy of it. [The few notices concerning Dryden, which
Lord Hailes had collected, the authour afterwards gave to Mr. Malone.—
M.]

[2] In one of his manuscript Diaries, there is the following entry, which
marks his curious minute attention: 'July 26, 1768. I shaved my nail by
accident in whetting the knife, about an eighth of an inch from the bottom,
and about a fourth from the top. This I measure that I may know the growth
of nails; the whole is about five eighths of an inch.'

Another of the same kind appears, 'Aug. 7, 1779, *Partem brachii dextri
carpo proximam et cutem pectoris circa mamillam dextram rasi, ut notum fieret
quanto temporis pili renovarentur.*' ['I shaved my right arm next the wrist, and
the skin round the right nipple, to discover how soon the hair would grow
again.']

And, 'Aug. 15, 1773. I cut from the vine 41 leaves, which weighed five oz.
and a half, and eight scruples:—I lay them upon my book-case, to see what
weight they will lose by drying.'

would comfort me; and were a sheet to be thus sent regularly, we should much oftener convey something, were it only a few kind words.'

My friend Colonel James Stuart, second son of the Earl of Bute, who had distinguished himself as a good officer of the Bedfordshire militia, had taken a publick-spirited resolution to serve his country in its difficulties, by raising a regular regiment, and taking the command of it himself. This, in the heir of the immense property of Wortley, was highly honourable. Having been in Scotland recruiting, he obligingly asked me to accompany him to Leeds, then the head-quarters of his corps; from thence to London for a short time, and afterwards to other places to which the regiment might be ordered. Such an offer, at a time of the year when I had full leisure, was very pleasing; especially as I was to accompany a man of sterling good sense, information, discernment, and conviviality; and was to have a second crop, in one year, of London and Johnson. Of this I informed my illustrious friend, in characteristical warm terms, in a letter dated the 30th of September, from Leeds.

On Monday, October 4, I called at his house before he was up. He sent for me to his bedside, and expressed his satisfaction at this incidental meeting, with as much vivacity as if he had been in the gaiety of youth. He called briskly, 'Frank, go and get coffee, and let us breakfast *in splendour.*'

During this visit to London I had several interviews with him, which it is unnecessary to distinguish particularly. I consulted him as to the appointment of guardians to my children, in case of my death. 'Sir, (said he,) do not appoint a number of guardians. When there are many, they trust one to another, and the business is neglected. I would advise you to choose only one; let him be a man of respectable character, who, for his own credit, will do what is right; let him be a rich man, so that he may be under no temptation to take advantage; and let him be a man of business, who is used to conduct affairs with ability and expertness, to whom, therefore, the execution of the trust will not be burdensome.'

On Sunday, October 10, we dined together at Mr. Strahan's.

The conversation having turned on the prevailing practice of going to the East-Indies in quest of wealth;—JOHNSON. 'A man had better have ten thousand pounds at the end of ten years passed in England, than twenty thousand pounds at the end of ten years passed in India, because you must compute what you *give* for money; and a man who has lived ten years in India, has given up ten years of social comfort and all those advantages which arise from living in England. The ingenious Mr. Brown, distinguished by the name of *Capability Brown*, told me, that he was once at the seat of Lord Clive, who had returned from India with great wealth; and that he shewed him at the door of his bed-chamber a large chest, which he said he had once had full of gold; upon which Brown observed, "I am glad you can bear it so near your bed-chamber." '

We talked of the state of the poor in London.—JOHNSON. 'Saunders Welch, the Justice, who was once High-Constable of Holborn, and had the best opportunities of knowing the state of the poor, told me, that I under-rated the number, when I computed that twenty a week, that is, above a thousand a year, died of hunger; not absolutely of immediate hunger; but of the wasting and other diseases which are the consequences of hunger. This happens only in so large a place as London, where people are not known. What we are told about the great sums got by begging is not true: the trade is overstocked. And, you may depend upon it, there are many who cannot get work. A particular kind of manufacture fails: those who have been used to work at it, can, for some time, work at nothing else. You meet a man begging; you charge him with idleness: he says, "I am willing to labour. Will you give me work?"—"I cannot."—"Why, then you have no right to charge me with idleness." '

We left Mr. Strahan's at seven, as Johnson had said he intended to go to evening prayers. As we walked along, he complained of a little gout in his toe, and said, 'I shan't go to prayers to-night; I shall go to-morrow: Whenever I miss church on a Sunday, I resolve to go another day. But I do not always do it.' This was a fair exhibition of that vibration between pious resolutions and indolence, which many of us have too often experienced.

I went home with him, and we had a long quiet conversation.

I read him a letter from Dr. Hugh Blair concerning Pope, (in writing whose life he was now employed,) which I shall insert as a literary curiosity.[1]

'To JAMES BOSWELL, ESQ.

'DEAR SIR,—In the year 1763, being at London, I was carried by Dr. John Blair, Prebendary of Westminster, to dine at old Lord Bathurst's; where we found the late Mr. Mallet, Sir James Porter, who had been Ambassadour at Constantinople, the late Dr. Macaulay, and two or three more. The conversation turning on Mr. Pope, Lord Bathurst told us, that *The Essay on Man* was originally composed by Lord Bolingbroke in prose, and that Mr. Pope did no more than put it into verse: that he had read Lord Bolingbroke's manuscript in his own hand-writing; and remembered well, that he was at a loss whether most to admire the elegance of Lord Bolingbroke's prose, or the beauty of Mr. Pope's verse. When Lord Bathurst told this, Mr. Mallet bade me attend, and remember this remarkable piece of information; as, by the course of Nature, I might survive his Lordship, and be a witness of his having said so. The conversation was indeed too remarkable to be forgotten. A few days after, meeting with you, who were then also in London, you will remember that I mentioned to you what had passed on this subject, as I was much struck with this anecdote. But what ascertains my recollection

---

[1] The Rev. Dr. Law, Bishop of Carlisle, in the Preface to his valuable edition of Archbishop King's *Essay on the Origin of Evil*, mentions that the principles maintained in it had been adopted by Pope in his *Essay on Man*; and adds, 'The fact, notwithstanding such denial (Bishop Warburton's), might have been strictly verified by an unexceptionable testimony, viz. that of the late Lord Bathurst, who saw the very same system of the τὸ βέλτιον ['the better'] (taken from the Archbishop) in Lord Bolingbroke's own hand, lying before Mr. Pope, while he was composing his *Essay*.' This is respectable evidence; but that of Dr. Blair is more direct from the fountain-head, as well as more full. Let me add to it that of Dr. Joseph Warton; 'The late Lord Bathurst repeatedly assured me that he had read the whole scheme of *The Essay on Man*, in the hand-writing of Bolingbroke, and drawn up in a series of propositions, which Pope was to versify and illustrate.' *Essay on the Genius and Writings of Pope*, vol. ii. p. 62.

of it beyond doubt, is, that being accustomed to keep a journal of what passed when I was in London, which I wrote out every evening, I find the particulars of the above information, just as I have now given them, distinctly marked; and am thence enabled to fix this conversation to have passed on Friday, the 22nd of April, 1763.

'I remember also distinctly, (though I have not for this the authority of my journal,) that the conversation going on concerning Mr. Pope, I took notice of a report which had been sometimes propagated that he did not understand Greek. Lord Bathurst said to me, that he knew that to be false; for that part of the *Iliad* was translated by Mr. Pope in his house in the country; and that in the mornings when they assembled at breakfast, Mr. Pope used frequently to repeat, with great rapture, the Greek lines which he had been translating, and then to give them his version of them, and to compare them together.

'If these circumstances can be of any use to Dr. Johnson, you have my full liberty to give them to him. I beg you will, at the same time, present to him my most respectful compliments, with best wishes for his success and fame in all his literary undertakings. I am, with great respect, my dearest Sir, your most affectionate, and obliged humble servant,

'Broughton Park, Sept. 21, 1779.'   'HUGH BLAIR.'

JOHNSON. 'Depend upon it, Sir, this is too strongly stated. Pope may have had from Bolingbroke the philosophick *stamina* of his Essay; and admitting this to be true, Lord Bathurst did not intentionally falsify. But the thing is not true in the latitude that Blair seems to imagine; we are sure that the poetical imagery, which makes a great part of the poem, was Pope's own. It is amazing, Sir, what deviations there are from precise truth, in the account which is given of almost every thing. I told Mrs. Thrale, "You have so little anxiety about truth, that you never tax your memory with the exact thing." Now what is the use of the memory to truth, if one is careless of exactness? Lord Hailes's *Annals of Scotland* are very exact; but they contain mere dry particulars. They are to be considered as a Dictionary. You know such things are there; and may be looked at when you please. Robertson paints; but the misfortune is, you are sure he does not know the people whom he paints; so you cannot suppose a likeness. Characters should never be given by an historian, unless he knew the people whom he describes, or copies from those who knew them.'

BOSWELL. 'Why, Sir, do people play this trick which I observe now, when I look at your grate, putting the shovel against it to make the fire burn?' JOHNSON. 'They play the trick, but it does not make the fire burn. *There* is a better; (setting the poker perpendicularly up at right angles with the grate.) In days of superstition they thought, as it made a cross with the bars, it would drive away the witch.'

BOSWELL. 'By associating with you, Sir, I am always getting an accession of wisdom. But perhaps a man, after knowing his own character—the limited strength of his own mind, should not be desirous of having too much wisdom, considering, *quid valeant humeri*,[1] how little he can carry.' JOHNSON. 'Sir, be as wise as you can; let a man be *aliis lætus, sapiens sibi*:[2]

> "Though pleas'd to see the dolphins play,
> I mind my compass and my way."[3]

You may be wise in your study in the morning, and gay in company at a tavern in the evening. Every man is to take care of his own wisdom and his own virtue, without minding too much what others think.'

He said, 'Dodsley first mentioned to me the scheme of an English Dictionary; but I had long thought of it.' BOSWELL. 'You did not know what you were undertaking.' JOHNSON. 'Yes, Sir, I knew very well what I was undertaking,—and very well how to do it,—and have done it very well.' BOSWELL. 'An excellent climax! and it *has* availed you. In your Preface you say, "What would it avail me in this gloom of solitude?" You have been agreeably mistaken.'

---

[1] ["What your shoulders can bear.' Horace, *Ars Poetica* 1. 39.]
[2] ['happy with others, wise when alone']
[3] *The Spleen*, a Poem [by Matthew Green].

In his *Life of Milton* he observes, 'I cannot but remark a kind of respect, perhaps unconsciously, paid to this great man by his biographers: every house in which he resided is historically mentioned, as if it were an injury to neglect naming any place that he honoured by his presence.' I had, before I read this observation, been desirous of shewing that respect to Johnson, by various inquiries. Finding him this evening in a very good humour, I prevailed on him to give me an exact list of his places of residence, since he entered the metropolis as an authour, which I subjoin in a note.[1]

I mentioned to him a dispute between a friend of mine and his lady, concerning conjugal infidelity, which my friend had maintained was by no means so bad in the husband, as in the wife. JOHNSON. 'Your friend was in the right, Sir. Between a man and his Maker it is a different question: but between a man and his wife, a husband's infidelity is nothing. They are connected by children, by fortune, by serious considerations of community. Wise married women don't trouble themselves about infidelity in their husbands.' BOSWELL. 'To be sure there is a great difference between the offence of infidelity in a man and that of his wife.' JOHNSON. 'The difference is boundless. The man imposes no bastards upon his wife.'

Here it may be questioned whether Johnson was entirely in the right. I suppose it will not be controverted that the difference in the degree of criminality is very great, on account of consequences: but still it may be maintained, that, independent of moral obligation, infidelity is by no means a light offence in a husband; because it must hurt a delicate attachment, in which a mutual constancy is implied, with such refined sentiments as Massinger has exhibited in his play of *The Picture*.—Johnson probably at another time would have admitted this opinion. And let it be kept in remembrance, that he was very careful not to

---

[1] 1. Exeter-street, off Catherine-street, Strand. 2. Greenwich. 3. Woodstock-street, near Hanover-square. 4. Castle-street, Cavendish-square, No. 6. 5. Strand. 6. Boswell-court. 7. Strand, again. 8. Bow-street. 9. Holborn. 10. Fetter-lane. 11. Holborn, again. 12. Gough-square. 13. Staple Inn. 14. Gray's Inn. 15. Inner Temple-lane, No. 1. 16. Johnson's-court, No. 7. 17. Bolt-court, No. 8.

give any encouragement to irregular conduct. A gentleman,[1] not adverting to the distinction made by him upon this subject, supposed a case of singular perverseness in a wife, and heedlessly said, 'That then he thought a husband might do as he pleased with a safe conscience.' JOHNSON. 'Nay, Sir, this is wild indeed (smiling;) you must consider that fornication is a crime in a single man; and you cannot have more liberty by being married.'

He this evening expressed himself strongly against the Roman Catholicks; observing, 'In every thing in which they differ from us they are wrong.' He was even against the invocation of Saints; in short, he was in the humour of opposition.

Having regretted to him that I had learnt little Greek, as is too generally the case in Scotland; that I had for a long time hardly applied at all to the study of that noble language, and that I was desirous of being told by him what method to follow; he recommended to me as easy helps, Sylvanus's *First Book of the Iliad*; Dawson's *Lexicon to the Greek New Testament*; and *Hesiod*, with *Pasoris Lexicon* at the end of it.

On Tuesday, October 12, I dined with him at Mr. Ramsay's, with Lord Newhaven, and some other company, none of whom I recollect, but a beautiful Miss Graham,[2] a relation of his Lordship's, who asked Dr. Johnson to hob or nob with her. He was flattered by such pleasing attention, and politely told her, he never drank wine; but if she would drink a glass of water, he was much at her service. She accepted. 'Oho, Sir! (said Lord Newhaven) you are caught.' JOHNSON. 'Nay, I do not see *how* I am *caught*; but if I am caught, I don't want to get free again. If I am caught, I hope to be kept.' Then when the two glasses of water were brought, smiling placidly to the young lady, he said, 'Madam, let us *reciprocate*.'

Lord Newhaven and Johnson carried on an argument for some time, concerning the Middlesex election. Johnson said, 'Parliament may be considered as bound by law as a man is bound where there is nobody to tie the knot. As it is clear that the

---

[1] [Boswell. *Boswell's proofs.*]
[2] Now the Lady of Sir Henry Dashwood, Bart.

House of Commons may expel, and expel again and again, why not allow of the power to incapacitate for that parliament, rather than have a perpetual contest kept up between parliament and the people.' Lord Newhaven took the opposite side; but respectfully said, 'I speak with great deference to you, Dr. Johnson; I speak to be instructed.' This had its full effect on my friend. He bowed his head almost as low as the table, to a complimenting nobleman; and called out, 'My Lord, my Lord, I do not desire all this ceremony; let us tell our minds to one another quietly.' After the debate was over, he said, 'I have got lights on the subject to-day, which I had not before.' This was a great deal from him, especially as he had written a pamphlet[1] upon it.

He observed, 'The House of Commons was originally not a privilege of the people, but a check for the Crown on the House of Lords. I remember Henry the Eighth wanted them to do something; they hesitated in the morning, but did it in the afternoon. He told them, "It is well you did; or half your heads should have been upon Temple-bar." But the House of Commons is now no longer under the power of the crown, and therefore must be bribed.' He added, 'I have no delight in talking of publick affairs.'

Of his fellow-collegian, the celebrated Mr. George Whitefield, he said, 'Whitefield never drew as much attention as a mountebank does; he did not draw attention by doing better than others, but by doing what was strange. Were Astley to preach a sermon standing upon his head on a horse's back, he would collect a multitude to hear him; but no wise man would say he had made a better sermon for that. I never treated Whitefield's ministry with contempt; I believe he did good. He had devoted himself to the lower classes of mankind, and among them he was of use. But when familiarity and noise claim the praise due to knowledge, art, and elegance, we must beat down such pretensions.'

What I have preserved of his conversation during the remainder of my stay in London at this time, is only what follows: I told him that when I objected to keeping company with a

---

[1] *The False Alarm.*

notorious infidel,[1] a celebrated friend[2] of ours said to me, 'I do
not think that men who live laxly in the world, as you and I
do, can with propriety assume such an authority. Dr. Johnson
may, who is uniformly exemplary in his conduct. But it is not
very consistent to shun an infidel to-day, and get drunk to-
morrow.' JOHNSON. 'Nay, Sir, this is sad reasoning. Because a
man cannot be right in all things, is he to be right in nothing?
Because a man sometimes gets drunk, is he therefore to steal?
This doctrine would very soon bring a man to the gallows.'

After all, however, it is a difficult question how far sincere
Christians should associate with the avowed enemies of religion;
for in the first place, almost every man's mind may be more or
less 'corrupted by evil communications;'[3] secondly, the world may
very naturally suppose that they are not really in earnest in
religion, who can easily bear its opponents; and thirdly, if the
profane find themselves quite well received by the pious, one
of the checks upon an open declaration of their infidelity, and
one of the probable chances of obliging them seriously to reflect,
which their being shunned would do, is removed.

He, I know not why, shewed upon all occasions an aversion to
go to Ireland, where I proposed to him that we should make a
tour. JOHNSON. 'It is the last place where I should wish to
travel.' BOSWELL. 'Should you not like to see Dublin, Sir?'
JOHNSON. 'No, Sir; Dublin is only a worse capital.' BOSWELL.
'Is not the Giant's-Causeway worth seeing?' JOHNSON. 'Worth
seeing? yes; but not worth going to see.'

Yet he had a kindness for the Irish nation, and thus generously
expressed himself to a gentleman from that country, on the subject of an UNION which artful Politicians have often had in view—
'Do not make an union with us, Sir. We should unite with you,
only to rob you. We should have robbed the Scotch, if they had
had any thing of which we could have robbed them.'

Of an acquaintance of ours, whose manners and every thing
about him, though expensive, were coarse, he said, 'Sir, you see
in him vulgar prosperity.'

---

[1] [Probably Gibbon. *Powell*.]
[2] [Probably Beauclerk.]   [3] [I *Cor.* xv. 33.]

A foreign minister of no very high talents, who had been in his company for a considerable time quite overlooked, happened luckily to mention that he had read some of his *Rambler* in Italian, and admired it much. This pleased him greatly; he observed that the title had been translated, *Il Genio errante*, though I have been told it was rendered more ludicrously, *Il Vagabondo*; and finding that this minister gave such a proof of his taste, he was all attention to him, and on the first remark which he made, however simple, exclaimed, 'The Ambassadour says well —His Excellency observes—' And then he expanded and enriched the little that had been said, in so strong a manner, that it appeared something of consequence. This was exceedingly entertaining to the company who were present, and many a time afterwards it furnished a pleasant topick of merriment: '*The Ambassadour says well,*' became a laughable term of applause, when no mighty matter had been expressed.

I left London on Monday, October 18, and accompanied Colonel Stuart to Chester, where his regiment was to lye for some time.

'MR. BOSWELL *to* DR. JOHNSON

'MY DEAR SIR,   'Chester, October 22, 1779.

'It was not till one o'clock on Monday morning, that Colonel Stuart and I left London; for we chose to bid a cordial adieu to Lord Mountstuart, who was to set out on that day on his embassy to Turin. We drove on excellently, and reached Lichfield in good time enough that night. The Colonel had heard so preferable a character of the George, that he would not put up at the Three Crowns, so that I did not see our host Wilkins. We found at the George as good accommodation as we could wish to have, and I fully enjoyed the comfortable thought that *I was in Lichfield again.* Next morning it rained very hard; and as I had much to do in a little time, I ordered a post-chaise, and between eight and nine sallied forth to make a round of visits. I first went to Mr. Green, hoping to have had him to accompany me to all my other friends, but he was engaged to attend the

Bishop of Sodor and Man, who was then lying at Lichfield very
ill of the gout. Having taken a hasty glance at the additions to
Green's museum, from which it was not easy to break away, I
next went to the Friery, where I at first occasioned some tumult
in the ladies, who were not prepared to receive *company* so early:
but my *name*, which has by wonderful felicity come to be so
closely associated with yours, soon made all easy; and Mrs.
Cobb and Miss Adye re-assumed their seats at the breakfast-
table, which they had quitted with some precipitation. They
received me with the kindness of an old acquaintance; and after
we had joined in a cordial chorus to *your* praise, Mrs. Cobb gave
me the high satisfaction of hearing that you said, "Boswell is a
man who I believe never left a house without leaving a wish for
his return." And she afterwards added, that she bid you tell me,
that if ever I came to Lichfield, she hoped I would take a bed
at the Friery. From thence I drove to Peter Garrick's, where I
also found a very flattering welcome. He appeared to me to
enjoy his usual cheerfulness; and he very kindly asked me to
come when I could, and pass a week with him. From Mr.
Garrick's, I went to the Palace to wait on Mr. Seward. I was
first entertained by his lady and daughter, he himself being in
bed with a cold, according to his valetudinary custom. But he
desired to see me; and I found him drest in his black gown, with
a white flannel night-gown above it; so that he looked like a
Dominican friar. He was good-humoured and polite; and under
his roof too my reception was very pleasing. I then proceeded
to Stow-hill, and first paid my respects to Mrs. Gastrell, whose
conversation I was not willing to quit. But my sand-glass was
now beginning to run low, as I could not trespass too long on the
Colonel's kindness, who obligingly waited for me; so I hastened
to Mrs. Aston's, whom I found much better than I feared I
should; and there I met a brother-in-law of these ladies, who
talked much of you, and very well too, as it appeared to me. It
then only remained to visit Mrs. Lucy Porter, which I did, I
really believe, with sincere satisfaction on both sides. I am sure
I was glad to see her again; and, as I take her to be very honest,
I trust she was glad to see me again; for she expressed herself

so, that I could not doubt of her being in earnest. What a great key-stone of kindness, my dear Sir, were you that morning! for we were all held together by our common attachment to you. I cannot say that I ever passed two hours with more self-complacency than I did those two at Lichfield. Let me not entertain any suspicion that this is idle vanity. Will not you confirm me in my persuasion, that he who finds himself so regarded has just reason to be happy?

'We got to Chester about midnight on Tuesday; and here again I am in a state of much enjoyment. Colonel Stuart and his officers treat me with all the civility I could wish; and I play my part admirably. *Lætus aliis, sapiens sibi*, the classical sentence which you, I imagine, invented the other day,[1] is exemplified in my present existence. The Bishop, to whom I had the honour to be known several years ago, shews me much attention; and I am edified by his conversation. I must not omit to tell you, that his Lordship admires, very highly, your *Prefaces to the Poets*. I am daily obtaining an extension of agreeable acquaintance, so that I am kept in animated variety; and the study of the place itself, by the assistance of books, and of the Bishop, is sufficient occupation. Chester pleases my fancy more than any town I ever saw. But I will not enter upon it at all in this letter.

'How long I shall stay here, I cannot yet say. I told a very pleasing young lady,[2] niece to one of the Prebendaries,[3] at whose house I saw her, "I have come to Chester, Madam, I cannot tell how; and far less can I tell how I am to get away from it." Do not think me too juvenile. I beg it of you, my dear Sir, to favour me with a letter while I am here, and add to the happiness of a happy friend, who is ever, with affectionate veneration, most sincerely yours,

'JAMES BOSWELL.'

'If you do not write directly, so as to catch me here, I shall be disappointed. Two lines from you will keep my lamp burning bright.'

[1] [See p. 1034.]
[2] Miss Letitia Barnston.
[3] [The Rev. Roger Barnston. *Reade.*]

'*To* JAMES BOSWELL, ESQ.

'DEAR SIR,—Why should you importune me so earnestly to write? Of what importance can it be to hear of distant friends, to a man who finds himself welcome wherever he goes, and makes new friends faster than he can want them? If, to the delight of such universal kindness of reception, any thing can be added by knowing that you retain my good-will, you may indulge yourself in the full enjoyment of that small addition.

'I am glad that you made the round of Lichfield with so much success: the oftener you are seen, the more you will be liked. It was pleasing to me to read that Mrs. Aston was so well; and that Lucy Porter was so glad to see you.

'In the place where you now are, there is much to be observed; and you will easily procure yourself skilful directors. But what will you do to keep away the *black dog* that worries you at home? If you would, in compliance with your father's advice, enquire into the old tenures and old charters of Scotland, you would certainly open to yourself many striking scenes of the manners of the middle ages. The feudal system, in a country half-barbarous, is naturally productive of great anomalies in civil life. The knowledge of past times is naturally growing less in all cases not of publick record; and the past time of Scotland is so unlike the present, that it is already difficult for a Scotchman to image the œconomy of his grandfather. Do not be tardy nor negligent; but gather up eagerly what can yet be found.[1]

'We have, I think, once talked of another project, a *History of the late insurrection in Scotland*, with all its incidents. Many falsehoods are passing into uncontradicted history. Voltaire, who loved a striking story, has told what he could not find to be true.

'You may make collections for either of these projects, or for both, as opportunities occur, and digest your materials at leisure. The great direction which Burton has left to men dis-

[1] I have a valuable collection made by my Father, which, with some additions and illustrations of my own, I intend to publish. I have some hereditary claim to be an Antiquary; not only from my Father, but as being descended, by the mother's side, from the able and learned Sir John Skene, whose merit bids defiance to all the attempts which have been made to lessen his fame.

ordered like you, is this, *Be not solitary; be not idle*: which I
would thus modify;—If you are idle, be not solitary; if you are
solitary, be not idle.

'There is a letter for you, from your humble servant,

'London, October 27, 1779.' 'SAM. JOHNSON.'

'*To* DR. SAMUEL JOHNSON

'MY DEAR SIR, 'Carlisle, Nov. 7, 1779.

'That I should importune you to write to me at Chester,
is not wonderful, when you consider what an avidity I have for
delight; and that the *amor* of pleasure, like the *amor nummi*,[1]
increases in proportion with the quantity which we possess of it.
Your letter, so full of polite kindness and masterly counsel, came
like a large treasure upon me, while already glittering with
riches. I was quite enchanted at Chester, so that I could with
difficulty quit it. But the enchantment was the reverse of that
of Circé; for so far was there from being any thing sensual in
it, that I was *all mind*. I do not mean all reason only; for my
fancy was kept finely in play. And why not?—If you please I
will send you a copy, or an abridgement of my Chester journal,
which is truly a log-book of felicity.

'The Bishop treated me with a kindness which was very
flattering. I told him, that you regretted you had seen so little
of Chester. His Lordship bade me tell you, that he should be
glad to shew you more of it. I am proud to find the friendship
with which you honour me is known in so many places.

'I arrived here late last night. Our friend the Dean[2] has been
gone from hence some months; but I am told at my inn, that
he is very *populous* (popular). However, I found Mr. Law, the
Archdeacon, son to the Bishop, and with him I have breakfasted
and dined very agreeably. I got acquainted with him at the
assizes here, about a year and a half ago; he is a man of great
variety of knowledge, uncommon genius, and I believe, sincere
religion. I received the holy sacrament in the Cathedral in the
morning, this being the first Sunday in the month; and was at
prayers there in the evening. It is divinely cheering to me to

[1] ['love of money.' Juvenal, *Sat.* xiv. 139.] [2] Thomas Percy.

think that there is a Cathedral so near Auchinleck; and I now leave Old England in such a state of mind as I am thankful to GOD for granting me.

'The *black dog* that worries me at home I cannot but dread; yet as I have been for some time past in a military train, I trust I shall *repulse* him. To hear from you will animate me like the sound of a trumpet, I therefore hope, that soon after my return to the northern field, I shall receive a few lines from you.

'Colonel Stuart did me the honour to escort me in his carriage to shew me Liverpool, and from thence back again to Warrington, where we parted.[1] In justice to my valuable wife, I must inform you she wrote to me, that as I was so happy, she would not be so selfish as to wish me to return sooner than business absolutely required my presence. She made my clerk write to me a post or two after to the same purpose, by commission from her; and this day a kind letter from her met me at the Post-Office here, acquainting me that she and the little ones were well, and expressing all their wishes for my return home. I am, more and more, my dear Sir, your affectionate and obliged humble servant,   'JAMES BOSWELL.'

'*To* JAMES BOSWELL, ESQ.

'DEAR SIR,—Your last letter was not only kind but fond. But I wish you to get rid of all intellectual excesses, and neither to exalt your pleasures, nor aggravate your vexations, beyond their real and natural state. Why should you not be as happy at Edinburgh as at Chester? *In culpa est animus, qui se non effugit usquam.*[2] Please yourself with your wife and children, and studies, and practice.

'I have sent a petition[3] from Lucy Porter, with which I leave

---

[1] His regiment was afterwards ordered to Jamaica, where he accompanied it, and almost lost his life by the climate. This impartial order I should think a sufficient refutation of the idle rumour that 'there was still something behind the throne greater than the throne itself.'

[2] ['The true culprit is the mind, which can never run away from itself.' Horace, *Epistles* i. 14. 13. (Wickham.)]

[3] Requesting me to inquire concerning the family of a gentleman who was then paying his addresses to Miss Doxy. [James Susannah Patton.]

it to your discretion whether it is proper to comply. Return me her letter, which I have sent, that you may know the whole case, and not be seduced to any thing that you may afterwards repent. Miss Doxy perhaps you know to be Mr. Garrick's niece.

'If Dean Percy can be popular at Carlisle, he may be very happy. He has in his disposal two livings, each equal, or almost equal in value to the deanery; he may take one himself, and give the other to his son.

'How near is the Cathedral to Auchinleck, that you are so much delighted with it? It is, I suppose, at least an hundred and fifty miles off. However, if you are pleased, it is so far well.

'Let me know what reception you have from your father, and the state of his health. Please him as much as you can, and add no pain to his last years.

'Of our friends here I can recollect nothing to tell you. I have neither seen nor heard of Langton. Beauclerk is just returned from Brighthelmston, I am told, much better. Mr. Thrale and his family are still there; and his health is said to be visibly improved; he has not bathed, but hunted.

'At Bolt-court there is much malignity, but of late little open hostility.[1] I have had a cold, but it is gone.

'Make my compliments to Mrs. Boswell, &c. I am, Sir, your humble servant,'

'London, Nov. 13, 1779.'   'SAM. JOHNSON.'

On November 22, and December 21, I wrote to him from Edinburgh, giving a very favourable report of the family of Miss Doxy's lover;—that after a good deal of enquiry I had discovered the sister of Mr. Francis Stewart, one of his amanuenses when writing his *Dictionary*;—that I had, as desired by him, paid her a guinea for an old pocket-book of her brother's which he had retained; and that the good woman, who was in very moderate circumstances, but contented and placid, wondered at his scrupulous and liberal honesty, and received the guinea as if sent her by Providence.—That I had repeatedly begged of him to keep his promise to send me his letter to Lord Chesterfield, and that

[1] See *ante*, p. 1007.

this *memento*, like *Delenda est Carthago*,[1] must be in every letter that I should write to him, till I had obtained my object.

1780: ÆTAT. 71.]—IN 1780, the world was kept in impatience for the completion of his *Lives of the Poets*, upon which he was employed so far as his indolence allowed him to labour.

I wrote to him on January 1, and March 13, sending him my notes of Lord Marchmont's information concerning Pope;— complaining that I had not heard from him for almost four months, though he was two letters in my debt;—that I had suffered again from melancholy;—hoping that he had been in so much better company, (the Poets,) that he had not time to think of his distant friends; for if that were the case, I should have some recompence for my uneasiness;—that the state of my affairs did not admit of my coming to London this year; and begging he would return me Goldsmith's two poems, with his lines marked.

His friend Dr. Lawrence having now suffered the greatest affliction to which a man is liable, and which Johnson himself had felt in the most severe manner; Johnson wrote to him in an admirable strain of sympathy and pious consolation.

'To DR. LAWRENCE

'DEAR SIR,—At a time when all your friends ought to shew their kindness, and with a character which ought to make all that know you your friends, you may wonder that you have yet heard nothing from me.

'I have been hindered by a vexatious and incessant cough, for which within these ten days I have been bled[2] once, fasted four or five times, taken physick five times, and opiates, I think, six. This day it seems to remit.

'The loss, dear Sir, which you have lately suffered, I felt many years ago, and know therefore how much has been taken from you, and how little help can be had from consolation. He that outlives a wife whom he has long loved, sees himself disjoined from the only mind that has the same hopes, and fears, and

---

[1] ['Carthage must be destroyed.' Plutarch, *Life of Cato*.]
[2] [Johnson probably wrote *have bled*.]

interest; from the only companion with whom he has shared much good or evil; and with whom he could set his mind at liberty, to retrace the past or anticipate the future. The continuity of being is lacerated; the settled course of sentiment and action is stopped; and life stands suspended and motionless, till it is driven by external causes into a new channel. But the time of suspense is dreadful.

'Our first recourse in this distressed solitude, is, perhaps for want of habitual piety, to a gloomy acquiescence in necessity. Of two mortal beings, one must lose the other; but surely there is a higher and better comfort to be drawn from the consideration of that Providence which watches over all, and a belief that the living and the dead are equally in the hands of GOD, who will reunite those whom he has separated; or who sees that it is best not to reunite. I am, dear Sir, your most affectionate, and most humble servant,

    'January 20, 1780.'   'SAM. JOHNSON.'

'*To* JAMES BOSWELL, ESQ.

'DEAR SIR,—Well, I had resolved to send you the Chesterfield letter; but I will write once again without it. Never impose tasks upon mortals. To require two things is the way to have them both undone.

'For the difficulties which you mention in your affairs I am sorry; but difficulty is now very general: it is not therefore less grievous, for there is less hope of help. I pretend not to give you advice, not knowing the state of your affairs; and general counsels about prudence and frugality would do you little good. You are, however, in the right not to increase your own perplexity by a journey hither; and I hope that by staying at home you will please your father.

'Poor dear Beauclerk—*nec, ut soles, dabis joca.*[1] His wit and his folly, his acuteness and maliciousness, his merriment and reasoning, are now over. Such another will not often be found among mankind. He directed himself to be buried by the side

---

[1] ['Nor wilt thou play any longer as thou art wont'. Hadrian, 'Animula vagula, blandula' (Duff.)]

of his mother, an instance of tenderness which I hardly expected. He has left his children to the care of Lady Di, and if she dies, of Mr. Langton, and of Mr. Leicester his relation, and a man of good character. His library has been offered to sale to the Russian ambassador.[1]

'Dr. Percy, notwithstanding all the noise of the newspapers, has had no literary loss.[2] Clothes and moveables were burnt to the value of about one hundred pounds; but his papers, and I think his books, were all preserved.

'Poor Mr. Thrale has been in extreme danger from an apoplectical disorder, and recovered, beyond the expectation of his physicians; he is now at Bath, that his mind may be quiet, and Mrs. Thrale and Miss are with him.

'Having told you what has happened to your friends, let me say something to you of yourself. You are always complaining of melancholy, and I conclude from those complaints that you are fond of it. No man talks of that which he is desirous to conceal, and every man desires to conceal that of which he is ashamed. Do not pretend to deny it; *manifestum habemus furem*;[3] make it an invariable and obligatory law to yourself, never to mention your own mental diseases; if you are never to speak of them, you will think on them but little, and if you think little of them, they will molest you rarely. When you talk of them, it is plain that you want either praise or pity; for praise there is no room, and pity will do you no good; therefore, from this hour speak no more, think no more, about them.

'Your transaction with Mrs. Stewart gave me great satisfaction; I am much obliged to you for your attention. Do not lose sight of her; your countenance may be of great credit, and of consequence of great advantage to her. The memory of her brother is yet fresh in my mind; he was an ingenious and worthy man.

'Please to make my compliments to your lady, and to the

---

[1] Mr. Beauclerk's library was sold by publick auction in April and May 1781, for £5011. [M.]

[2] By a fire in Northumberland-house, where he had an apartment, in which I have passed many an agreeable hour.

[3] ['We have caught the thief in the act.']

young ladies. I should like to see them, pretty loves. I am, dear
Sir, yours affectionately,
'April 8, 1780.'   'SAM. JOHNSON.'

Mrs. Thrale being now at Bath with her husband, the correspondence between Johnson and her was carried on briskly. I
shall present my readers with one of her original letters to him
at this time, which will amuse them probably more than those
well-written but studied epistles which she has inserted in her
collection, because it exhibits the easy vivacity of their literary
intercourse. It is also of value as a key to Johnson's answer,
which she has printed by itself, and of which I shall subjoin
extracts.

'MRS. THRALE *to* DR. JOHNSON

'I had a very kind letter from you yesterday, dear Sir, with a
most circumstantial date. You took trouble with my circulating
letter, Mr. Evans writes me word, and I thank you sincerely for
so doing: one might do mischief else not being on the spot.

'Yesterday's evening was passed at Mrs. Montagu's: there
was Mr. Melmoth; I do not like him *though*, nor he me; it was
expected we should have pleased each other; he is, however,
just Tory enough to hate the Bishop of Peterborough[1] for
Whiggism, and Whig enough to abhor you for Toryism.

'Mrs. Montagu flattered him finely; so he had a good afternoon on't. This evening we spend at a concert. Poor Queeney's[2]
sore eyes have just released her; she had a long confinement,
and could neither read nor write, so my master[3] treated her very
good-naturedly with the visits of a young woman in this town,
a taylor's daughter,[4] who professes musick, and teaches so as
to give six lessons a day to ladies, at five and threepence a
lesson. Miss Burney says she is a great performer; and I respect

[1] Dr. John Hinchliffe.
[2] A kind of nick-name given to Mrs. Thrale's eldest daughter, whose
name being *Esther*, she might be assimilated to a *Queen*.
[3] Mr. Thrale.
[4] [Jenny Guest. *Mrs. Piozzi.*]

the wench for getting her living so prettily; she is very modest and pretty-mannered, and not seventeen years old.

'You live in a fine whirl indeed; if I did not write regularly you would half forget me, and that would be very wrong, for I *felt* my regard for you in my *face* last night, when the criticisms were going on.

'This morning it was all connoisseurship; we went to see some pictures painted by a gentleman-artist, Mr. Taylor, of this place; my master makes one, every where, and has got a good dawling[1] companion to ride with him now. . . .[2] He looks well enough, but I have no notion of health for a man whose mouth cannot be sewed up. Burney and I and Queeney teize him every meal he eats, and Mrs. Montagu is quite serious with him; but what *can* one do? He will eat, I think, and if he does eat I know he will not live; it makes me very unhappy, but I must bear it. Let me always have your friendship. I am, most sincerely, dear Sir, your faithful servant,

    'Bath, Friday, April 28.'   'H. L. T.'

'DR. JOHNSON *to* MRS. THRALE

'DEAREST MADAM,—Mr. Thrale never will live abstinently, till he can persuade himself to live by rule.[3] . . . Encourage, as you can, the musical girl.[4]

'Nothing is more common than mutual dislike, where mutual approbation is particularly expected. There is often on both sides a vigilance not over-benevolent; and as attention is strongly excited, so that nothing drops unheeded, any difference in taste or opinion, and some difference where there is no restraint will commonly appear, immediately generates dislike.

'Never let criticisms operate upon your face or your mind; it is very rarely that an authour is hurt by his criticks. The blaze of reputation cannot be blown out, but it often dies in the socket; a very few names may be considered as perpetual lamps that

---

[1] In Johnson's Dictionary is neither *dawling* nor *dawdling*. He uses *dawdle, post,* p. 1162.
[2] [The original has 'Captain Cotton who married Miss Aston'.]
[3] I have taken the liberty to leave out a few lines.
[4] [Jenny Guest, later well known as Mrs. Miles (note by Mrs. Piozzi).]

shine unconsumed. From the authour of *Fitzosborne's Letters* I
cannot think myself in much danger. I met him only once about
thirty years ago, and in some small dispute reduced him to
whistle; having not seen him since, that is the last impression.
Poor Moore, the fabulist, was one of the company.

'Mrs. Montagu's long stay, against her own inclination, is
very convenient. You would, by your own confession, want a
companion; and she is *par pluribus*;[1] conversing with her you
may *find variety in one*.'[2]

'London, May 1, 1780.'

On the 2nd of May I wrote to him, and requested that we
might have another meeting somewhere in the North of England, in the autumn of this year.

From Mr. Langton I received soon after this time a letter, of
which I extract a passage, relative both to Mr. Beauclerk and
Dr. Johnson.

'The melancholy information you have received concerning
Mr. Beauclerk's death is true. Had his talents been directed in
any sufficient degree as they ought, I have always been strongly
of opinion that they were calculated to make an illustrious figure;
and that opinion, as it had been in part formed upon Dr. Johnson's judgment, receives more and more confirmation by hearing
what, since his death, Dr. Johnson has said concerning them; a
few evenings ago, he was at Mr. Vesey's, where Lord Althorpe,
who was one of a numerous company there, addressed Dr.
Johnson on the subject of Mr. Beauclerk's death, saying, "Our
CLUB has had a great loss since we met last." He replied, "A
loss, that perhaps the whole nation could not repair!" The Doctor then went on to speak of his endowments, and particularly
extolled the wonderful ease with which he uttered what was
highly excellent. He said, that "no man ever was so free when
he was going to say a good thing, from a *look* that expressed
that it was coming; or, when he had said it, from a look that
expressed that it *had* come." At Mr. Thrale's, some days before,
when we were talking on the same subject, he said, referring to

[1] ['a host in herself.']   [2] *Spectator*, 470.

the same idea of his wonderful facility. "That Beauclerk's talents were those which he had felt himself more disposed to envy, than those of any whom he had known."

'On the evening I have spoken of above, at Mr. Vesey's, you would have been much gratified, as it exhibited an instance of the high importance in which Dr. Johnson's character is held, I think even beyond any I ever before was witness to. The company consisted chiefly of ladies, among whom were the Duchess Dowager of Portland, the Duchess of Beaufort, whom I suppose from her rank I must name before her mother Mrs. Boscawen, and her elder sister Mrs. Lewson, who was likewise there; Lady Lucan, Lady Clermont, and others of note both for their station and understandings. Among the gentlemen were Lord Althorpe, whom I have before named, Lord Macartney, Sir Joshua Reynolds, Lord Lucan, Mr. Wraxal, whose book you have probably seen, *The Tour to the Northern Parts of Europe*; a very agreeable ingenious man; Dr. Warren, Mr. Pepys, the Master in Chancery, whom I believe you know, and Dr. Barnard, the Provost of Eton. As soon as Dr. Johnson was come in and had taken a chair, the company began to collect round him, till they became not less than four, if not five, deep; those behind standing, and listening over the heads of those that were sitting near him. The conversation for some time was chiefly between Dr. Johnson and the Provost of Eton, while the others contributed occasionally their remarks. Without attempting to detail the particulars of the conversation, which perhaps if I did, I should spin my account out to a tedious length, I thought, my dear Sir, this general account of the respect with which our valued friend was attended to, might be acceptable.'

'*To* THE REVEREND DR. FARMER

'SIR,   'May 23, 1780.

'I know your disposition to second[1] any literary attempt, and therefore venture upon the liberty of entreating you to procure from College or University registers, all the dates, or other informations which they can supply, relating to Ambrose

---
[1] [*forward*, MS.]

Philips, Broome, and Gray, who were all of Cambridge, and of whose lives I am to give such accounts as I can gather. Be pleased to forgive this trouble from, Sir, your most humble servant,
'SAM. JOHNSON.'

While Johnson was thus engaged in preparing a delightful literary entertainment for the world, the tranquillity of the metropolis of Great-Britain was unexpectedly disturbed, by the most horrid series of outrage that ever disgraced a civilized country. A relaxation of some of the severe penal provisions against our fellow-subjects of the Catholick communion had been granted by the legislature, with an opposition so inconsiderable that the genuine mildness of Christianity, united with liberal policy, seemed to have become general in this island. But a dark and malignant spirit of persecution soon shewed itself, in an unworthy petition for the repeal of the wise and humane statute. That petition was brought forward by a mob, with the evident purpose of intimidation, and was justly rejected. But the attempt was accompanied and followed by such daring violence as is unexampled in history. Of this extraordinary tumult, Dr. Johnson has given the following concise, lively, and just account in his *Letters to Mrs. Thrale:*—[1]

'On Friday,[2] the good Protestants met in Saint George's-Fields, at the summons of Lord George Gordon, and marching to Westminster, insulted the Lords and Commons, who all bore it with great tameness. At night the outrages began by the demolition of the mass-house by Lincoln's-Inn.'

'An exact journal of a week's defiance of government I cannot give you. On Monday, Mr. Strahan, who had been insulted, spoke to Lord Mansfield, who had I think been insulted too, of the licentiousness of the populace; and his Lordship treated it as a very slight irregularity. On Tuesday night they pulled down Fielding's house, and burnt his goods in the street. They had gutted on Monday Sir George Savile's house, but the building

[1] Vol. ii, p. 148, *et seq.* I have selected passages from several letters, without mentioning dates.
[2] June 2.

was saved. On Tuesday evening, leaving Fielding's ruins, they went to Newgate to demand their companions who had been seized demolishing the chapel. The keeper could not release them but by the Mayor's permission, which he went to ask; at his return he found all the prisoners released, and Newgate in a blaze. They then went to Bloomsbury, and fastened upon Lord Mansfield's house, which they pulled down; and as for his goods, they totally burnt them. They have since gone to Caen-wood, but a guard was there before them. They plundered some Papists, I think, and burnt a mass-house in Moorfields the same night.'

'On Wednesday I walked with Dr. Scot to look at Newgate, and found it in ruins, with the fire yet glowing. As I went by, the Protestants were plundering the Sessions-house at the Old-Bailey. There were not, I believe, a hundred; but they did their work at leisure, in full security, without sentinels, without trepidation, as men lawfully employed, in full day. Such is the cowardice of a commercial place. On Wednesday they broke open the Fleet, and the King's-Bench, and the Marshalsea, and Wood-street Compter, and Clerkenwell Bridewell, and released all the prisoners.'

'At night they set fire to the Fleet, and to the King's-Bench, and I know not how many other places; and one might see the glare of conflagration fill the sky from many parts. The sight was dreadful. Some people were threatened: Mr. Strahan advised me to take care of myself. Such a time of terrour you have been happy in not seeing.'

'The King said in Council, "That the magistrates had not done their duty, but that he would do his own;" and a proclamation was published, directing us to keep our servants within doors, as the peace was now to be preserved by force. The soldiers were sent out to different parts, and the town is now [*June 9*] at quiet.'

'The soldiers are stationed so as to be every where within call: there is no longer any body of rioters, and the individuals are hunted to their holes, and led to prison; Lord George was last night sent to the Tower. Mr. John Wilkes was this day in my neighbourhood, to seize the publisher of a seditious paper.'

'Several chapels have been destroyed, and several inoffensive Papists have been plundered; but the high sport was to burn the gaols. This was a good rabble trick. The debtors and the criminals were all set at liberty; but of the criminals, as has always happened, many are already retaken; and two pirates have surrendered themselves, and it is expected that they will be pardoned.'

'Government now acts again with its proper force; and we are all under the protection of the King and the law. I thought that it would be agreeable to you and my master to have my testimony to the publick security; and that you would sleep more quietly when I told you that you are safe.'

'There has, indeed, been an universal panick, from which the King was the first that recovered. Without the concurrence of his ministers, or the assistance of the civil magistrate, he put the soldiers in motion, and saved the town from calamities, such as a rabble's government must naturally produce.'

'The publick has escaped a very heavy calamity. The rioters attempted the Bank on Wednesday night, but in no great number; and like other thieves, with no great resolution. Jack Wilkes headed the party that drove them away. It is agreed, that if they had seized the Bank on Tuesday, at the height of the panick, when no resistance had been prepared, they might have carried irrecoverably away whatever they had found. Jack, who was always zealous for order and decency, declares that if he be trusted with power, he will not leave a rioter alive. There is, however, now no longer any need of heroism or bloodshed; no blue ribband[1] is any longer worn.'

Such was the end of this miserable sedition, from which London was delivered by the magnanimity of the Sovereign himself. Whatever some may maintain, I am satisfied that there was no combination or plan, either domestick or foreign; but that the mischief spread by a gradual contagion of frenzy, augmented by the quantities of fermented liquors, of which the deluded populace possessed themselves in the course of their depredations.

[1] Lord George Gordon and his followers, during these outrages, wore blue ribbands in their hats. [M.]

I should think myself very much to blame, did I here neglect to do justice to my esteemed friend Mr. Akerman, the keeper of Newgate, who long discharged a very important trust with an uniform intrepid firmness, and at the same time a tenderness and a liberal charity, which entitle him to be recorded with distinguished honour.

Upon this occasion, from the timidity and negligence of magistracy on the one hand, and the almost incredible exertions of the mob on the other, the first prison of this great country was laid open, and the prisoners set free; but that Mr. Akerman, whose house was burnt, would have prevented all this, had proper aid been sent to him in due time, there can be no doubt.

Many years ago, a fire broke out in the brick part which was built as an addition to the old gaol of Newgate. The prisoners were in consternation and tumult, calling out, 'We shall be burnt—we shall be burnt! Down with the gate—down with the gate!' Mr. Akerman hastened to them, shewed himself at the gate, and having, after some confused vociferation of 'Hear him—hear him!' obtained a silent attention, he then calmly told them, that the gate must not go down; that they were under his care, and that they should not be permitted to escape: but that he could assure them, they need not be afraid of being burnt, for that the fire was not in the prison, properly so called, which was strongly built with stone; and that if they would engage to be quiet, he himself would come in to them, and conduct them to the further end of the building, and would not go out till they gave him leave. To this proposal they agreed; upon which Mr. Akerman, having first made them fall back from the gate, went in, and with a determined resolution, ordered the outer turnkey upon no account to open the gate, even though the prisoners (though he trusted they would not) should break their word, and by force bring himself to order it. 'Never mind me, (said he,) should that happen.' The prisoners peaceably followed him, while he conducted them through passages of which he had the keys, to the extremity of the gaol which was most distant from the fire. Having, by this very judicious conduct, fully satisfied them that there was no immediate risk, if any at all, he then addressed them thus: 'Gentlemen, you are now convinced that I told you true. I have no doubt that the engines will soon extinguish this fire; if they should not, a sufficient guard will come, and you shall all be taken out and lodged in the Compters. I assure you, upon my word and honour, that I have not a farthing insured. I have left my house, that I might take care of you. I will keep my promise, and stay with you, if you insist upon it; but if you will allow me to go out and look after my family and property, I shall be obliged to you.' Struck with his behaviour, they called out, 'Master Akerman, you have done bravely; it was very kind in you: by all means go and take care of your own concerns.' He did so accordingly, while they remained, and were all preserved.

Johnson has been heard to relate the substance of this story with high praise, in which he was joined by Mr. Burke. My illustrious friend, speaking of Mr. Akerman's kindness to his prisoners, pronounced this eulogy upon his character:—'He who has long had constantly in his view the worst of mankind, and is yet eminent for the humanity of his disposition, must have had it originally in a great degree, and continued to cultivate it very carefully.'

In the course of this month my brother David waited upon Dr. Johnson, with the following letter of introduction, which I had taken care should be lying ready on his arrival in London.

'*To* DR. SAMUEL JOHNSON

   'MY DEAR SIR,   'Edinburgh, April 29, 1780.

   'This will be delivered to you by my brother David, on his return from Spain. You will be glad to see the man who vowed to "stand by the old castle of Auchinleck, with heart, purse, and sword;" that romantick family solemnity devised by me, of which you and I talked with complacency upon the spot. I trust that twelve years of absence have not lessened his feudal attachment; and that you will find him worthy of being introduced to your acquaintance. I have the honour to be, with affectionate veneration, my dear Sir, your most faithful humble servant,

                                         'JAMES BOSWELL.'

Johnson received him very politely, and has thus mentioned him in a letter to Mrs. Thrale:[1] 'I have had with me a brother of Boswell's, a Spanish merchant,[2] whom the war has driven from his residence at Valencia; he is gone to see his friends, and will find Scotland but a sorry place after twelve years' residence in a happier climate. He is a very agreeable man, and speaks no Scotch.'

'*To* Dr. Beattie, *at Aberdeen*

'Sir,—More years than I have any delight to reckon, have past since you and I saw one another; of this, however, there is no reason for making any reprehensory complaint—*Sic fata ferunt*.[3] But methinks there might pass some small interchange of regard between us. If you say, that I ought to have written, I now write; and I write to tell you, that I have much kindness for you and Mrs. Beattie; and that I wish your health better, and your life long. Try change of air, and come a few degrees Southwards: a softer climate may do you both good; winter is coming on; and London will be warmer, and gayer, and busier, and more fertile of amusement than Aberdeen.

'My health is better; but that will be little in the balance, when I tell you that Mrs. Montagu has been very ill, and is I doubt now but weakly. Mr. Thrale has been very dangerously disordered; but is much better, and I hope will totally recover. He has withdrawn himself from business the whole summer. Sir Joshua and his sister are well; and Mr. Davies has had great success as an authour,[4] generated by the corruption of a bookseller. More news I have not to tell you, and therefore you must be contented with hearing, what I know not whether you much

---

[1] Vol. ii, p. 163. Mrs. Piozzi has omitted the name, she best knows why.
[2] Now settled in London.
[3] ['The fates wrought to this end.' Virgil, *Aeneid* ii. 34. (Jackson.)]
[4] Meaning his entertaining *Memoirs of David Garrick, Esq.*, of which Johnson (as Davies informed me) wrote the first sentence; thus giving, as it were, the key-note to the performance. It is, indeed, very characteristical of its authour, beginning with a maxim, and proceeding to illustrate.—'All excellence has a right to be recorded. I shall, therefore, think it superfluous to apologise for writing the life of a man, who by an uncommon assemblage of private virtues, adorned the highest eminence in a publick profession.'

wish to hear,[1] that I am, Sir, your most humble servant,

    'Bolt-court, Fleet-street,   'SAM. JOHNSON.'

      August 21, 1780.'

'*To* JAMES BOSWELL, ESQ.

'DEAR SIR,—I find you have taken one of your fits of taciturnity, and have resolved not to write till you are written to; it is but a peevish humour, but you shall have your way.

'I have sat at home in Bolt-court, all the summer, thinking to write the *Lives*, and a great part of the time only thinking. Several of them, however, are done, and I still think to do the rest.

'Mr. Thrale and his family have, since his illness, passed their time first at Bath, and then at Brighthelmston; but I have been at neither place. I would have gone to Lichfield, if I could have had time, and I might have had time, if I had been active; but I have missed much, and done little.

'In the late disturbances, Mr. Thrale's house and stock were in great danger; the mob was pacified at their first invasion, with about fifty pounds in drink and meat; and at their second, were driven away by the soldiers. Mr. Strahan got a garrison into his house, and maintained them a fortnight; he was so frighted that he removed part of his goods. Mrs. Williams took shelter in the country.

'I know not whether I shall get a ramble this autumn; it is now about the time when we were travelling. I have, however, better health than I had then, and hope you and I may yet shew ourselves on some part of Europe, Asia, or Africa.[2] In the mean time let us play no trick, but keep each other's kindness by all means in our power.

   [1] I wish he had omitted the suspicion expressed here, though I believe he meant nothing but jocularity; for though he and I differed sometimes in opinion, he well knew how much I loved and revered him. BEATTIE.

   [2] It will, no doubt, be remarked how he avoids the *rebellious* land of America. This puts me in mind of an anecdote, for which I am obliged to my worthy social friend, Governour Richard Penn: 'At one of Miss E. Hervey's assemblies, Dr. Johnson was following her up and down the room; upon which Lord Abingdon observed to her, "Your great friend is very fond of you; you can go no where without him."—"Ay, (said she,) he would follow me to any part of the world."—"Then (said the Earl,) ask him to go with you to *America*." '

'The bearer of this is Dr. Dunbar, of Aberdeen, who has written and published a very ingenious book,[1] and who I think has a kindness for me, and will, when he knows you, have a kindness for you.

'I suppose your little ladies are grown tall; and your son is become a learned young man. I love them all, and I love your naughty lady, whom I never shall persuade to love me. When the *Lives* are done, I shall send them to complete her collection, but must send them in paper, as for want of a pattern, I cannot bind them to fit the rest. I am, Sir, yours most affectionately,

    'London, Aug. 21, 1780.'   'Sam. Johnson.'

This year he wrote to a young clergyman[2] in the country, the following very excellent letter, which contains valuable advice to Divines in general:—

'Dear Sir,—Not many days ago Dr. Lawrence shewed me a letter, in which you make mention[3] of me: I hope, therefore, you will not be displeased that I endeavour to preserve your good-will by some observations which your letter suggested to me.

'You are afraid of falling into some improprieties in the daily service by reading to an audience that requires no exactness. Your fear, I hope, secures you from danger. They who contract absurd habits are such as have no fear. It is impossible to do the same thing very often, without some peculiarity of manner: but that manner may be good or bad, and a little care will at least preserve it from being bad: to make it good, there must, I think, be something of natural or casual felicity, which cannot be taught.

'Your present method of making your sermons seems very judicious. Few frequent preachers can be supposed to have sermons more their own than yours will be. Take care to register, somewhere or other, the authours from whom your several discourses are borrowed; and do not imagine that you shall always

---

[1] *Essays on the History of Mankind.*
[2] [The Rev. Charles Lawrence. *Johnson's Works*, 1789, xv. 496.]
[3] [Johnson wrote *kind mention*.]

remember, even what perhaps you now think it impossible to forget.

'My advice, however, is, that you attempt, from time to time, an original sermon; and in the labour of composition, do not burthen your mind with too much at once; do not exact from yourself at one effort of excogitation, propriety of thought and elegance of expression. Invent first, and then embellish. The production of something, where nothing was before, is an act of greater energy than the expansion or decoration of the thing produced. Set down diligently your thoughts as they rise, in the first words that occur; and, when you have matter, you will easily give it form: nor, perhaps, will this method be always necessary; for, by habit, your thoughts and diction will flow together.

'The composition of sermons is not very difficult: the divisions not only help the memory of the hearer, but direct the judgement of the writer; they supply sources of invention, and keep every part in its proper place.

'What I like least in your letter is your account of the manners of your parish; from which I gather, that it has been long neglected by the parson. The Dean of Carlisle,[1] who was then a little rector in Northamptonshire, told me, that it might be discerned whether or no there was a clergyman resident in a parish by the civil or savage manner of the people. Such a congregation as yours stands in much need of reformation; and I would not have you think it impossible to reform them. A very savage parish was civilised by a decayed gentlewoman, who came among them to teach a petty school. My learned friend Dr. Wheeler of Oxford, when he was a young man, had the care of a neighbouring parish for fifteen pounds a year, which he was never paid; but he counted it a convenience that it compelled him to make a sermon weekly. One woman he could not bring to the communion; and, when he reproved or exhorted her, she only answered, that she was no scholar. He was advised to set some good woman or man of the parish, a little wiser than herself, to talk to her in language level to her mind. Such honest,

[1] Dr. Percy, now Bishop of Dromore.

I may call them holy artifices, must be practised by every clergy-man; for all means must be tried by which souls may be saved. Talk to your people, however, as much as you can; and you will find, that the more frequently you converse with them upon religious subjects, the more willingly they will attend, and the more submissively they will learn. A clergyman's diligence always makes him venerable. I think I have now only to say, that in the momentous work you have undertaken, I pray GOD to bless you. I am, Sir, your most humble servant,

'Bolt-court, Aug. 30, 1780.'   'SAM. JOHNSON.'

My next letters to him were dated August 24, September 6, and October 1, and from them I extract the following passages:—

'My brother David and I find the long indulged fancy of our comfortable meeting again at Auchinleck, so well realised, that it in some degree confirms the pleasing hope of *O! preclarum diem!*[1] in a future state.'

'I beg that you may never again harbour a suspicion of my indulging a peevish humour, or playing tricks; you will recollect that when I confessed to you, that I had once been intentionally silent to try your regard, I gave you my word and honour that I would not do so again.'

'I rejoice to hear of your good state of health; I pray GOD to continue it long. I have often said, that I would willingly have ten years added to my life, to have ten taken from yours; I mean, that I would be ten years older, to have you ten years younger. But let me be thankful for the years during which I have enjoyed your friendship, and please myself with the hopes of enjoying it many years to come in this state of being, trusting always, that in another state, we shall meet never to be separated. Of this we can form no notion; but the thought, though indistinct, is delightful, when the mind is calm and clear.'

'The riots in London were certainly horrible; but you give me no account of your own situation, during the barbarous anarchy. A description of it by DR. JOHNSON would be a great painting;[2] you might write another *London, a Poem.*'

[1] ['Oh glorious day.' Cicero, *De Senectute* 84.]
[2] I had not then seen his letters to Mrs. Thrale.

'I am charmed with your condescending affectionate expression, "let us keep each other's kindness by all the means in our power;" my revered Friend! how elevating is it to my mind, that I am found worthy to be a companion to Dr. Samuel Johnson! All that you have said in grateful praise of Mr. Walmsley, I have long thought of you; but we are both Tories, which has a very general influence upon our sentiments. I hope that you will agree to meet me at York, about the end of this month; or if you will come to Carlisle, that would be better still, in case the Dean be there. Please to consider, that to keep each other's kindness, we should every year have that free and intimate communication of mind which can be had only when we are together. We should have both our solemn and our pleasant talk.'

'I write now for the third time, to tell you that my desire for our meeting this autumn, is much increased. I wrote to 'Squire Godfrey Bosville, my Yorkshire chief, that I should, perhaps, pay him a visit, as I was to hold a conference with Dr. Johnson at York. I give you my word and honour that I said not a word of his inviting you; but he wrote to me as follows:—

' "I need not tell you I shall be happy to see you here the latter end of this month, as you propose; and I shall likewise be in hopes that you will persuade Dr. Johnson to finish the conference here. It will add to the favour of your own company, if you prevail upon such an associate, to assist your observations. I have often been entertained with his writings, and I once belonged to a club of which he was a member, and I never spent an evening there, but I heard something from him well worth remembering."

'We have thus, my dear Sir, good comfortable quarters in the neighbourhood of York, where you may be assured we shall be heartily welcome. I pray you then resolve to set out; and let not the year 1780 be a blank in our social calendar, and in that record of wisdom and wit, which I keep with so much diligence, to your honour, and the instruction and delight of others.'

Mr. Thrale had now another contest for the representation in parliament of the borough of Southwark, and Johnson kindly

lent him his assistance, by writing advertisements and letters
for him. I shall insert one as a specimen:*

  '*To* THE WORTHY ELECTORS OF THE BOROUGH OF
                 SOUTHWARK

  'GENTLEMEN,—A new Parliament being now called, I again
solicit the honour of being elected for one of your representatives; and solicit it with the greater confidence, as I am not
conscious of having neglected my duty, or of having acted otherwise than as becomes the independent representative of independent constituents; superiour to fear, hope, and expectation, who
has no private purposes to promote, and whose prosperity is
involved in the prosperity of his country. As my recovery from
a very severe distemper is not yet perfect, I have declined to
attend the Hall, and hope an omission so necessary will not be
harshly censured.

  'I can only send my respectful wishes, that all your delibera-
tions may tend to the happiness of the kingdom, and the peace
of the borough. I am, Gentlemen, your most faithful and obedient servant,

  'Southwark, Sept. 5, 1780.'   'HENRY THRALE.'

  On his birth-day, Johnson has this note: 'I am now beginning
the seventy-second year of my life, with more strength of body,
and greater vigour of mind, than I think is common at that age.'
But still he complains of sleepless nights and idle days, and
forgetfulness, or neglect of resolutions. He thus pathetically
expresses himself,—'Surely I shall not spend my whole life with
my own total disapprobation.'[1]

  Mr. Macbean, whom I have mentioned more than once, as
one of Johnson's humble friends, a deserving but unfortunate
man, being now oppressed by age and poverty, Johnson solicited
the Lord Chancellor Thurlow, to have him admitted into the
Charter-house. I take the liberty to insert his Lordship's answer,
as I am eager to embrace every occasion of augmenting the
respectable notion which should ever be entertained of my illustrious friend:—

           [1] *Pr. and Med.* p. 185.

'*To* Dr. Samuel Johnson

'Sir,   'London, October 24, 1780.

'I have this moment received your letter, dated the 19th, and returned from Bath.

'In the beginning of the summer I placed one in the Chartreux, without the sanction of a recommendation so distinct and so authoritative as yours of Macbean; and I am afraid, that according to the establishment of the House, the opportunity of making the charity so good amends will not soon recur. But whenever a vacancy shall happen, if you'll favour me with notice of it, I will try to recommend him to the place, even though it should not be my turn to nominate. I am, Sir, with great regard, your most faithful and obedient servant,   'Thurlow.'

'*To* James Boswell, Esq.

'Dear Sir,—I am sorry to write you a letter that will not please you, and yet it is at last what I resolve to do. This year must pass without an interview; the summer has been foolishly lost, like many other of my summers and winters. I hardly saw a green field, but staid in town to work, without working much.

'Mr. Thrale's loss of health has lost him the election; he is now going to Brighthelmston, and expects me to go with him; and how long I shall stay, I cannot tell. I do not much like the place, but yet I shall go, and stay while my stay is desired. We must, therefore, content ourselves with knowing what we know as well as man can know the mind of man, that we love one another, and that we wish each other's happiness, and that the lapse of a year cannot lessen our mutual kindness.

'I was pleased to be told that I accused Mrs. Boswell unjustly, in supposing that she bears me ill-will. I love you so much, that I would be glad to love all that love you, and that you love; and I have love very ready for Mrs. Boswell, if she thinks it worthy of acceptance. I hope all the young ladies and gentlemen are well.

'I take a great liking to your brother. He tells me that his father received him kindly, but not fondly; however, you seem to have lived well enough at Auchinleck, while you staid. Make your father as happy as you can.

'You lately told me of your health: I can tell you in return, that my health has been for more than a year past, better than it has been for many years before. Perhaps it may please GOD to give us some time together before we are parted. I am, dear Sir, yours most affectionately,

'October 17, 1780.'   'SAM. JOHNSON.'

Being disappointed in my hopes of meeting Johnson this year, so that I could hear none of his admirable sayings, I shall compensate for this want by inserting a collection of them, for which I am indebted to my worthy friend Mr. Langton, whose kind communications have been separately interwoven in many parts of this work. Very few articles of this collection were committed to writing by himself, he not having that habit; which he regrets, and which those who know the numerous opportunities he had of gathering the rich fruits of *Johnsonian* wit and wisdom, must ever regret. I however found, in conversations with him, that a good store of *Johnsoniana* was treasured in his mind; and I compared it to Herculaneum, or some old Roman field, which, when dug, fully rewards the labour employed. The authenticity of every article is unquestionable. For the expression, I, who wrote them down in his presence, am partly answerable.

'Theocritus is not deserving of very high respect as a writer; as to the pastoral part, Virgil is very evidently superiour. He wrote when there had been a larger influx of knowledge into the world than when Theocritus lived. Theocritus does not abound in the description, though living in a beautiful country: the manners painted are coarse and gross. Virgil has much more description, more sentiment, more of Nature, and more of art. Some of the most excellent parts of Theocritus are, where Castor and Pollux, going with the other Argonauts, land on the Bebrycian coast, and there fall into a dispute with Amycus, the King of that country; which is as well conducted as Euripides could have done it; and the battle is well related. Afterwards they carry off a woman, whose two brothers come to recover her, and expostulate with Castor and Pollux on their injustice; but they pay no regard to the brothers, and a battle ensues, where Castor and his brother are triumphant. Theocritus seems not to have seen that the brothers have the advantage in their argument over his Argonaut heroes. *The Sicilian Gossips* is a piece of merit.'

'Callimachus is a writer of little excellence. The chief thing to be learned from him is his account of Rites and Mythology; which, though desirable to be known for the sake of understanding other parts of ancient authours, is the least pleasing or valuable part of their writings.'

'Mattaire's account of the Stephani is a heavy book. He seems to have been a puzzle-headed man, with a large share of scholarship, but with little geometry or logick in his head, without method, and possessed of little genius. He wrote Latin verses from time to time, and published a set in his old age, which he called '*Senilia;*' in which he shews so little learning or taste in writing, as to make *Carteret* a dactyl. In matters of genealogy it is necessary to give the bare names as they are; but in poetry, and in prose of any elegance in the writing, they require to have inflection given to them. His book of the Dialects is a sad heap of confusion; the only way to write on them is to tabulate them with Notes, added at the bottom of the page, and references.'

'It may be questioned, whether there is not some mistake as to the methods of employing the poor, seemingly on a supposition that there is a certain portion of work left undone for want of persons to do it; but if that is otherwise, and all the materials we have are actually worked up, or all the manufactures we can use or dispose of are already executed, then what is given to the poor, who are to be set at work, must be taken from some who now have it, as time must be taken for learning, according to Sir William Petty's observation; a certain part of those very materials that, as it is, are properly worked up, must be spoiled by the unskilfulness of novices. We may apply to well-meaning, but misjudging persons in particulars of this nature, what Giannone said to a monk, who wanted what he called to *convert* him: "*Tu sei santo, ma tu non sei filosofo.*"[1]—It is an unhappy

---

[1] ['You are a saint, but you are not a philosopher.']

circumstance that one might give away five hundred pounds in a year to those that importune in the streets, and not do any good.'

'There is nothing more likely to betray a man into absurdity than *condescension*; when he seems to suppose his understanding too powerful for his company.'

'Having asked Mr. Langton if his father and mother had sat for their pictures, which he thought it right for each generation of a family to do, and being told they had opposed it, he said, "Sir, among the anfractuosities of the human mind, I know not if it may not be one, that there is a superstitious reluctance to sit for a picture." '

'John Gilbert Cooper related, that soon after the publication of his *Dictionary*, Garrick being asked by Johnson what people said of it, told him, that among other animadversions, it was objected that he cited authorities which were beneath the dignity of such a work, and mentioned Richardson. "Nay, (said Johnson,) I have done worse than that: I have cited *thee*, David." '

'Talking of expence, he observed, with what munificence a great merchant will spend his money, both from his having it at command, and from his enlarged views by calculation of a good effect upon the whole. "Whereas (said he,) you will hardly ever find a country gentleman who is not a good deal disconcerted at an unexpected occasion for his being obliged to lay out ten pounds." '

'When in good humour he would talk of his own writings with a wonderful frankness and candour, and would even criticise them with the closest severity. One day, having read over one of his *Ramblers*, Mr. Langton asked him, how he liked that paper; he shook his head, and answered, "too wordy." At another time, when one was reading his tragedy of *Irene* to a company at a house in the country, he left the room; and somebody having asked him the reason of this, he replied, "Sir, I thought it had been better." '

'Talking of a point of delicate scrupulosity of moral conduct, he said to Mr. Langton, "Men of harder minds than ours will do many things from which you and I would shrink; yet, Sir, they will, perhaps, do more good in life than we. But let us try to help one another. If there be a wrong twist it may be set right. It is not probable that two people can be wrong the same way." '

'Of the Preface to Capel's *Shakspeare*, he said, "If the man would have come to me, I would have endeavoured to endow his purposes with words; for, as it is, he doth gabble monstrously."'[1]

'He related, that he had once in a dream a contest of wit with some other person, and that he was very much mortified by imagining that his opponent had the better of him. "Now, (said he,) one may mark here the effect of sleep in weakening the power of reflection; for had not my judgement failed me, I should have seen, that the wit of this supposed antagonist, by whose superiority I felt myself depressed, was as much furnished by me, as that which I thought I had been uttering in my own character." '

'One evening in company, an ingenious and learned gentleman read to him a letter of compliment which he had received from one of the Professors of a foreign University. Johnson, in an irritable fit, thinking there was too much ostentation, said, "I never receive any of these tributes of applause from abroad. One instance I recollect of a foreign publication, in which mention is made of *l'illustre Lockman*."'[2]

'Of Sir Joshua Reynolds, he said, "Sir, I know no man who has passed through life with more observation than Reynolds." '

'He repeated to Mr. Langton, with great energy, in the Greek, our SAVIOUR'S gracious expression concerning the forgiveness of Mary Magdalen, Ἡ πίστις σου σέσωκέ σε· πορεύου εἰς εἰρήνην. "Thy faith hath saved thee; go in peace."[3] He said, "the manner of this dismission is exceedingly affecting." '

'He thus defined the difference between physical and moral truth; "Physical truth, is, when you tell a thing as it actually is. Moral truth, is, when you tell a thing sincerely and precisely as it appears to you. I say such a one walked across the street; if he really did so, I told a physical truth. If I thought so, though I should have been mistaken, I told a moral truth." '

---

[1] [*Tempest*, I. ii.]

[2] Secretary to the British Herring Fishery, remarkable for an extraordinary number of occasional verses, not of eminent merit.

[3] *Luke* vii. 50.

'Huggins, the translator of Ariosto, and Mr. Thomas Warton, in the early part of his literary life, had a dispute concerning that poet, of whom Mr. Warton in his *Observations on Spencer's Fairy Queen*, gave some account, which Huggins attempted to answer with violence, and said, "I will *militate* no longer against his *nescience*." Huggins was master of the subject, but wanted expression. Mr. Warton's knowledge of it was then imperfect, but his manner lively and elegant. Johnson said, "It appears to me, that Huggins has ball without powder, and Warton powder without ball." '

'Talking of the Farce of *High Life below Stairs*,[1] he said, "Here is a Farce, which is really very diverting when you see it acted; and yet one may read it, and not know that one has been reading any thing at all." '

'He used at one time to go occasionally to the green room of Drury-lane Theatre, where he was much regarded by the players, and was very easy and facetious with them. He had a very high opinion of Mrs. Clive's comick powers, and conversed more with her than with any of them. He said, "Clive, Sir, is a good thing to sit by; she always understands what you say." And she said of him, "I love to sit by Dr. Johnson; he always entertains me." One night, when *The Recruiting Officer* was acted, he said to Mr. Holland, who had been expressing an apprehension that Dr. Johnson would disdain the works of Farquhar; "No, Sir, I think Farquhar a man whose writings have considerable merit." '

'His friend Garrick was so busy in conducting the drama, that they could not have so much intercourse as Mr. Garrick used to profess an anxious wish that there should be.[2] There might, indeed, be something in the contemptuous severity as to the merit of acting, which his old preceptor nourished in himself, that would mortify Garrick after the great applause which he received from the audience. For though Johnson said of him, "Sir, a man who has a nation to admire him every night, may well be expected to be somewhat elated;" yet he would treat theatrical matters with a ludicrous slight. He mentioned one

[1] [By Rev. James Townley.]
[2] In a letter written by Johnson to a friend in 1742–3, he says:—'I never see Garrick.' [M.]

evening, "I met David coming off the stage, drest in a woman's riding-hood, when he acted in *The Wonder*; I came full upon him, and I believe he was not pleased." '

'Once he asked Tom Davies, whom he saw drest in a fine suit of clothes, "And what art thou to-night?" Tom answered, "The Thane of Ross;" (which it will be recollected is a very inconsiderable character.) "O brave!" said Johnson.'

'Of Mr. Longley, at Rochester, a gentleman of very considerable learning, whom Dr. Johnson met there, he said, "My heart warms towards him. I was surprised to find in him such a nice acquaintance with the metre in the learned languages; though I was somewhat mortified that I had it not so much to myself, as I should have thought." '

'Talking of the minuteness with which people will record the sayings of eminent persons, a story was told, that when Pope was on a visit to Spence at Oxford, as they looked from the window they saw a Gentleman Commoner, who was just come in from riding, amusing himself with whipping at a post. Pope took occasion to say, "That young gentleman seems to have little to do." Mr. Beauclerk observed, "Then, to be sure, Spence turned round and wrote that down;" and went on to say to Dr. Johnson, "Pope, Sir, would have said the same of you, if he had seen you distilling." JOHNSON. "Sir, if Pope had told me of my distilling, I would have told him of his grotto." '

'He would allow no settled indulgence of idleness upon principle, and always repelled every attempt to urge excuses for it. A friend one day suggested, that it was not wholesome to study soon after dinner. JOHNSON. "Ah, Sir, don't give way to such a fancy. At one time of my life I had taken it into my head that it was not wholesome to study between breakfast and dinner." '

'Mr. Beauclerk one day repeated to Dr. Johnson Pope's lines,

"Let modest Foster, if he will, excel
Ten metropolitans in preaching well:"

Then asked the Doctor, "Why did Pope say this?" JOHNSON. "Sir, he hoped it would vex somebody." '

'Dr. Goldsmith, upon occasion of Mrs. Lennox's bringing out

a play, said to Dr. Johnson at THE CLUB, that a person[1] had advised
him to go and hiss it, because she had attacked Shakspeare in
her book called *Shakspeare Illustrated*. JOHNSON. "And did not
you tell him he was a rascal?" GOLDSMITH. "No, Sir, I did not.
Perhaps he might not mean what he said." JOHNSON. "Nay,
Sir, if he lied, it is a different thing." Colman slily said, (but it is
believed Dr. Johnson did not hear him,) "Then the proper
expression should have been,—Sir, if you don't lie, you're a
rascal." '

'His affection for Topham Beauclerk was so great, that when
Beauclerk was labouring under that severe illness which at last
occasioned his death, Johnson said, (with a voice faultering with
emotion,) "Sir, I would walk to the extent of the diameter of
the earth to save Beauclerk." '

'One night at THE CLUB he produced a translation of an Epitaph
which Lord Elibank had written in English, for his Lady, and
requested of Johnson to turn into Latin for him. Having read
Domina de North et Gray, he said to Dyer, "You see, Sir, what
barbarisms we are compelled to make use of, when modern
titles are to be specifically mentioned in Latin inscriptions."
When he had read it once aloud, and there had been a general
approbation expressed by the company, he addressed himself to
Mr. Dyer in particular, and said, "Sir, I beg to have your judgement, for I know your nicety." Dyer then very properly desired
to read it over again; which having done, he pointed out an
incongruity in one of the sentences. Johnson immediately
assented to the observation, and said, "Sir, this is owing to an
alteration of a part of the sentence, from the form in which I had
first written it; and I believe, Sir, you may have remarked, that
the making a partial change, without a due regard to the general
structure of the sentence, is a very frequent cause of errour in
composition." '

'Johnson was well acquainted with Mr. Dossie, authour of a
treatise on Agriculture; and said of him, "Sir, of the objects
which the Society of Arts have chiefly in view, the chymical
effects of bodies operating upon other bodies, he knows more

[1] [Richard Cumberland. *Mrs. Piozzi*; *Malone*.]

than almost any man." Johnson, in order to give Mr. Dossie his vote to be a member of this Society, paid up an arrear which had run on for two years. On this occasion he mentioned a circumstance as characteristick of the Scotch. "One of that nation, (said he,) who had been a candidate, against whom I had voted, came up to me with a civil salutation. Now, Sir, this is their way. An Englishman would have stomached it, and been sulky, and never have taken further notice of you; but a Scotchman, Sir, though you vote nineteen times against him, will accost you with equal complaisance after each time, and the twentieth time, Sir, he will get your vote." '

'Talking on the subject of toleration, one day when some friends were with him in his study, he made his usual remark, that the State has a right to regulate the religion of the people, who are the children of the State. A clergyman having readily acquiesced in this, Johnson, who loved discussion, observed, "But, Sir, you must go round to other States than your own. You do not know what a Bramin has to say for himself.[1] In short, Sir, I have got no further than this: Every man has a right to utter what he thinks truth, and every other man has a right to knock him down for it. Martyrdom is the test." '

'A man, he observed, should begin to write soon; for, if he waits till his judgement is matured, his inability, through want of practice to express his conceptions, will make the disproportion so great between what he sees, and what he can attain, that he will probably be discouraged from writing at all. As a proof of the justness of this remark, we may instance what is related of the great Lord Granville; that after he had written his letter, giving an account of the battle of Dettingen, he said, "Here is a letter, expressed in terms not good enough for a tallow-chandler to have used." '

'Talking of a Court-martial that was sitting upon a very momentous publick occasion, he expressed much doubt of an

---

[1] Here Lord Macartney remarks, 'A Bramin or any cast of the Hindoos will neither admit you to be of their religion, nor be converted to yours;—a thing which struck the Portuguese with the greatest astonishment, when they discovered the East Indies.'

enlightened decision; and said, that perhaps there was not a member of it, who in the whole course of his life, had ever spent an hour by himself in balancing probabilities.'

'Goldsmith one day brought to THE CLUB a printed Ode, which he, with others, had been hearing read by its authour[1] in a publick room at the rate of five shillings each for admission. One of the company[2] having read it aloud, Dr. Johnson said, "Bolder words and more timorous meaning, I think never were brought together." '

'Talking of Gray's *Odes*, he said, "They are forced plants raised in a hot-bed; and they are poor plants; they are but cucumbers after all." A gentleman present, who had been running down Ode-writing in general, as a bad species of poetry, unluckily said, "Had they been literally cucumbers, they had been better things than Odes."—"Yes, Sir, (said Johnson,) for a *hog*." '

'His distinction of the different degrees of attainment of learning was thus marked upon two occasions. Of Queen Elizabeth he said, "She had learning enough to have given dignity to a bishop;" and of Mr. Thomas Davies he said, "Sir, Davies has learning enough to give credit to a clergyman." '

'He used to quote, with great warmth, the saying of Aristotle recorded by Diogenes Laertius; that there was the same difference between one learned and unlearned, as between the living and the dead.'

'It is very remarkable, that he retained in his memory very slight and trivial, as well as important things. As an instance of this, it seems that an inferiour domestick of the Duke of Leeds had attempted to celebrate his Grace's marriage in such homely rhimes as he could make; and this curious composition having been sung to Dr. Johnson he got it by heart, and used to repeat it in a very pleasant manner. Two of the stanzas were these:—

"When the Duke of Leeds shall married be
To a fine young lady of high quality,

---

[1] [George Marriott. *Boswell Papers*, vi. 130.]
[2] [Burke. *Ib.*]

> How happy will that gentlewoman be
> In his Grace of Leeds's good company.
>
> She shall have all that's fine and fair,
> And the best of silk and sattin shall wear;
> And ride in a coach to take the air,
> And have a house in St. James's-square."[1]

To hear a man, of the weight and dignity of Johnson, repeating such humble attempts at poetry, had a very amusing effect. He, however, seriously observed of the last stanza repeated by him, that it nearly comprized all the advantages that wealth can give.'

'An eminent foreigner, when he was shewn the British Museum, was very troublesome with many absurd inquiries. "Now there, Sir, (said he,) is the difference between an Englishman and a Frenchman. A Frenchman must be always talking, whether he knows any thing of the matter or not; an Englishman is content to say nothing, when he has nothing to say." '

'His unjust contempt for foreigners was, indeed, extreme. One evening, at old Slaughter's coffee-house, when a number of them were talking loud about little matters, he said, "Does not this confirm old Meynell's observation—*For any thing I see, foreigners are fools.*" '

---

[1] The correspondent of *The Gentleman's Magazine* [1792, p. 214] who subscribes himself SCIOLUS furnishes the following supplement:—

'A lady of my acquaintance* remembers to have heard her uncle† sing those homely stanzas more than 45 years ago. He repeated the second thus;

> "She shall breed young lords and ladies fair,
> And ride abroad in a coach and three pair,
> And the best, &c.
> And have a house, &c."

And remembered a third which seems to have been the introductory one, and is believed to have been the only remaining one:—

> "When the Duke of Leeds shall have made his choice
> Of a charming young lady that's beautiful and wise,
> She'll be the happiest young gentlewoman under the skies,
> As long as the sun and moon shall rise,
> And how happy shall, &c." '

It is with pleasure I add that this stanza could never be more truly applied than at this present time.

* [Mrs. Thrale. *Mrs. Piozzi.*]   † [Sir Thomas Salusbury. *Ib.*]

'He said, that once, when he had a violent tooth-ach, a Frenchman accosted him thus:—"*Ah, Monsieur, vous etudiez trop.*" '

'Having spent an evening at Mr. Langton's with the Reverend Dr. Parr, he was much pleased with the conversation of that learned gentleman; and after he was gone, said to Mr. Langton, "Sir, I am obliged to you for having asked me this evening. Parr is a fair man. I do not know when I have had an occasion of such free controversy. It is remarkable how much of a man's life may pass without meeting with any instance of this kind of open discussion." '

'We may fairly institute a criticism between Shakspeare and Corneille, as they both had, though in a different degree, the lights of a latter age. It is not so just between the Greek dramatick writers and Shakspeare. It may be replied to what is said by one of the remarkers on Shakspeare, that though Darius's shade had *prescience*, it does not necessarily follow that he had all *past* particulars revealed to him.'

'Spanish plays, being wildly and improbably farcical, would please children here, as children are entertained with stories full of prodigies; their experience not being sufficient to cause them to be so readily startled at deviations from the natural course of life. The machinery of the Pagans is uninteresting to us: when a Goddess appears in Homer or Virgil, we grow weary; still more so in the Grecian tragedies, as in that kind of composition a nearer approach to Nature is intended. Yet there are good reasons for reading romances; as—the fertility of invention, the beauty of style and expression, the curiosity of seeing with what kind of performances the age and country in which they were written was delighted: for it is to be apprehended, that at the time when very wild improbable tales were well received, the people were in a barbarous state, and so on the footing of children, as has been explained.'

'It is evident enough that no one who writes now can use the Pagan deities and mythology; the only machinery, therefore, seems that of ministering spirits, the ghosts of the departed, witches, and fairies, though these latter, as the vulgar superstition concerning them (which, while in its force, infected at least the imagination of those that had more advantage in education, though their reason set them free from it,) is every day wearing out, seem likely to be of little further assistance in the machinery of poetry. As I recollect, Hammond introduces a hag or witch into one of his love elegies, where the effect is unmeaning and disgusting.'

'The man who uses his talent of ridicule in creating or grossly exaggerating the instances he gives, who imputes absurdities that did not happen, or when a man was a little ridiculous describes him as having been very much so, abuses his talents greatly. The great use of delineating absurdities is, that we may know how far human folly can go; the account, therefore, ought of absolute necessity to be faithful. A certain character (naming the person) as to the general cast of it, is well described by Garrick, but a great deal of the phraseology he uses in it, is quite his own, particularly in the proverbial comparisons, "obstinate as a pig," &c., but I don't know whether it might not be true of Lord ————,[1] that from a too great eagerness for praise and popularity, and a politeness carried to a ridiculous excess, he was likely, after asserting a thing in general, to give it up again in parts. For instance, if he had said Reynolds was the first of painters, he was capable enough of giving up, as objections might happen to be severally made, first his outline,—then the grace in form,—then the colouring,—and lastly, to have owned that he was such a mannerist, that the disposition of his pictures was all alike.'

'For hospitality, as formerly practised, there is no longer the same reason; heretofore the poorer people were more numerous, and from want of commerce, their means of getting a livelihood more difficult; therefore the supporting them was an act of great benevolence; now that the poor can find maintenance for themselves, and their labour is wanted, a general undiscerning hospitality tends to ill, by withdrawing them from their work to idleness and drunkenness. Then, formerly rents were received in kind, so that there was a great abundance of provisions in

[1] [John Boyle, 5th Earl of Cork and Orrery. *Mrs. Piozzi.*]

possession of the owners of the lands, which, since the plenty of money afforded by commerce, is no longer the case.'

'Hospitality to strangers and foreigners in our country is now almost at an end, since, from the increase of them that come to us, there have been a sufficient number of people that have found an interest in providing inns and proper accommodations, which is in general a more expedient method for the entertainment of travellers. Where the travellers and strangers are few, more of that hospitality subsists, as it has not been worth while to provide places of accommodation. In Ireland there is still hospitality to strangers, in some degree; in Hungary and Poland probably more.'

'Colman, in a note on his translation of *Terence*, talking of Shakspeare's learning, asks, "What says Farmer to this? What says Johnson?" Upon this he observed, "Sir, let Farmer answer for himself: *I* never engaged in this controversy. I always said, Shakspeare had Latin enough to grammaticise his English." '

'A clergyman,[1] whom he characterised as one who loved to say little oddities, was affecting one day, at a Bishop's table, a sort of slyness and freedom not in character, and repeated, as if part of *The Old Man's Wish*, a song by Dr. Walter Pope, a verse bordering on licentiousness. Johnson rebuked him in the finest manner, by first shewing him that he did not know the passage he was aiming at, and thus humbling him: "Sir, that is not the song: it is thus." And he gave it right. Then looking stedfastly on him, "Sir, there is a part of that song which I should wish to exemplify in my own life:—

"May I govern my passions with absolute sway!" '

'Being asked if Barnes knew a good deal of Greek, he answered, "I doubt, Sir, he was *unoculus inter cæcos*." '[2]

'He used frequently to observe, that men might be very eminent in a profession, without our perceiving any particular power of mind in them in conversation. "It seems strange (said he,) that a man should see so far to the right, who sees so short

---

[1] [Possibly Dr. Michael Lort. *Powell.*]
[2] ['the one-eyed man among the blind.']

a way to the left. Burke is the only man whose common conversation corresponds with the general fame which he has in the world. Take up whatever topick you please, he is ready to meet you." '

'A gentleman,[1] by no means deficient in literature, having discovered less acquaintance with one of the Classicks than Johnson expected, when the gentleman left the room, he observed, "You see, now, how little any body reads." Mr. Langton happening to mention his having read a good deal in Clenardus's *Greek Grammar*, "Why, Sir, (said he,) who is there in this town who knows any thing of Clenardus but you and I?" And upon Mr. Langton's mentioning that he had taken the pains to learn by heart the Epistle of St. Basil, which is given in that Grammar as a praxis, "Sir, (said he,) I never made such an effort to attain Greek." '

'Of Dodsley's *Publick Virtue, a Poem*, he said, "It was fine *blank* (meaning to express his usual contempt for blank verse); however, this miserable poem did not sell, and my poor friend Doddy said, Publick Virtue was not a subject to interest the age." '

'Mr. Langton, when a very young man, read Dodsley's *Cleone, a Tragedy*, to him, not aware of his extreme impatience to be read to. As it went on he turned his face to the back of his chair, and put himself into various attitudes, which marked his uneasiness. At the end of an act, however, he said, "Come let's have some more, let's go into the slaughter-house again, Lanky. But I am afraid there is more blood than brains." Yet he afterwards said, "When I heard you read it, I thought higher of its power of language: when I read it myself, I was more sensible of its pathetick effect;" and then he paid it a compliment which many will think very extravagant. "Sir, (said he,) if Otway had written this play, no other of his pieces would have been remembered." Dodsley himself, upon this being repeated to him, said, "It was too much:" it must be remembered, that Johnson always appeared not to be sufficiently sensible of the merit of Otway.'

[1] [*Professor Hilles suggests* Reynolds. *Lit. Career of Reynolds*, p. 106.]

'Snatches of reading (said he,) will not make a Bentley or a Clarke. They are, however, in a certain degree advantageous. I would put a child into a library (where no unfit books are) and let him read at his choice. A child should not be discouraged from reading any thing that he takes a liking to, from a notion that it is above his reach. If that be the case, the child will soon find it out and desist; if not, he of course gains the instruction; which is so much the more likely to come, from the inclination with which he takes up the study.'

'Though he used to censure carelessness with great vehemence, he owned, that he once, to avoid the trouble of locking up five guineas, hid them, he forgot where, so that he could not find them.'

'A gentleman who introduced his brother[1] to Dr. Johnson was earnest to recommend him to the Doctor's notice, which he did by saying, "When we have sat together some time, you'll find my brother grow very entertaining."—"Sir, (said Johnson,) I can wait." '

'When the rumour was strong that we should have a war, because the French would assist the Americans, he rebuked a friend with some asperity for supposing it, saying, "No, Sir, national faith is not yet sunk so low." '

'In the latter part of his life, in order to satisfy himself whether his mental faculties were impaired, he resolved that he would try to learn a new language, and fixed upon the Low Dutch, for that purpose, and this he continued till he had read about one half of 'Thomas à Kempis'; and finding that there appeared no abatement of his power of acquisition, he then desisted, as thinking the experiment had been duly tried. Mr. Burke justly observed, that this was not the most vigorous trial, Low Dutch being a language so near to our own; had it been one of the languages entirely different, he might have been very soon satisfied.'

'Mr. Langton and he having gone to see a Freemason's funeral procession, when they were at Rochester, and some solemn musick being played on French horns, he said, "This is the first time that I have ever been affected by musical sounds;"

[1] [Perhaps Boswell and his brother David. *Powell.*]

adding, "that the impression made upon him was of a melancholy kind." Mr. Langton saying, that this effect was a fine one,— JOHNSON. "Yes, if it softens the mind, so as to prepare it for the reception of salutary feelings, it may be good: but inasmuch as it is melancholy *per se*, it is bad." '

'Goldsmith had long a visionary project, that some time or other when his circumstances should be easier, he would go to Aleppo, in order to acquire a knowledge as far as might be, of any arts peculiar to the East, and introduce them into Britain. When this was talked of in Dr. Johnson's company, he said, "Of all men Goldsmith is the most unfit to go out upon such an inquiry; for he is utterly ignorant of such arts as we already possess, and consequently could not know what would be accessions to our present stock of mechanical knowledge. Sir, he would bring home a grinding-barrow, which you see in every street in London, and think that he had furnished a wonderful improvement." '

'Greek, Sir, (said he,) is like lace; every man gets as much of it as he can.'[1]

'When Lord Charles Hay, after his return from America, was preparing his defence to be offered to the Court-Martial which he had demanded, having heard Mr. Langton as high in expressions of admiration of Johnson, as he usually was, he requested that Dr. Johnson might be introduced to him; and Mr. Langton having mentioned it to Johnson, he very kindly and readily agreed; and being presented by Mr. Langton to his Lordship, while under arrest, he saw him several times; upon one of which occasions Lord Charles read to him what he had prepared, which Johnson signified his approbation of, saying, "It is a very good soldierly defence." Johnson said, that he had advised his Lordship, that as it was in vain to contend with those who were in possession of power, if they would offer him the rank of Lieutenant-General, and a government, it would be better judged to desist from urging his complaints. It is well known that his Lordship died before the sentence was made known.'

[1] It should be remembered, that this was said twenty-five or thirty years ago, when lace was very generally worn. [M. 1799.]

'Johnson one day gave high praise to Dr. Bentley's verses[1] in Dodsley's *Collection*, which he recited with his usual energy. Dr. Adam Smith, who was present, observed in his decisive professorial manner, "Very well—Very well." Johnson however added, "Yes, they *are* very well, Sir; but you may observe in what manner they are well. They are the forcible verses of a man of a strong mind, but not accustomed to write verse; for there is some uncouthness in the expression." [2]

[1] Dr. Johnson, in his *Life of Cowley*, says, that these are 'the only English verses which Bentley is known to have written.' I shall here insert them, and hope my readers will apply them.

'Who strives to mount Parnassus' hill,
    And thence poetick laurels bring,
Must first acquire due force and skill,
    Must fly with swan's or eagle's wing.

Who Nature's treasures would explore,
    Her mysteries and arcana know;
Must high as lofty Newton soar,
    Must stoop as delving Woodward low.

Who studies ancient laws and rites,
    Tongues, arts, and arms, and history;
Must drudge, like Selden, days and nights,
    And in the endless labour die.

Who travels in religious jars,
    (Truth mixt with errour, shades with rays;)
Like Whiston, wanting pyx or stars,
    In ocean wide or sinks or strays.

But grant our hero's hope, long toil
    And comprehensive genius crown,
All sciences, all arts his spoil,
    Yet what reward, or what renown?

Envy, innate in vulgar souls,
    Envy steps in and stops his rise,
Envy with poison'd tarnish fouls
    His lustre, and his worth decries.

He lives inglorious or in want,
    To college and old books confin'd;
Instead of learn'd he's call'd pedant,
    Dunces advanc'd, he's left behind:
Yet left content a genuine Stoick he,
Great without patron, rich without South Sea.

[2] The difference between Johnson and Smith is apparent even in this slight instance. Smith was a man of extraordinary application, and had his mind crowded with all manner of subjects; but the force, acuteness, and

'Drinking tea one day at Garrick's with Mr. Langton, he was questioned if he was not somewhat of a heretick as to Shakspeare; said Garrick, "I doubt he is a little of an infidel."— "Sir, (said Johnson,) I will stand by the lines I have written on Shakspeare in my Prologue at the opening of your Theatre." Mr. Langton suggested, that in the line

"And panting Time toil'd after him in vain,"

Johnson might have had in his eye the passage in *The Tempest*, where Prospero says of Miranda,

"———She will outstrip all praise,
And make it halt behind her."

Johnson said nothing. Garrick then ventured to observe, "I do not think that the happiest line in the praise of Shakspeare." Johnson exclaimed (smiling,) "Prosaical rogues! next time I write, I'll make both time and space pant." [1]

'It is well known that there was formerly a rude custom for those who were sailing upon the Thames, to accost each other

vivacity of Johnson were not to be found there. He had book-making so much in his thoughts, and was so chary of what might be turned to account in that way, that he once said to Sir Joshua Reynolds, that he made it a rule, when in company, never to talk of what he understood. Beauclerk had for a short time a pretty high opinion of Smith's conversation. Garrick, after listening to him for a while, as to one of whom his expectations had been raised, turned slyly to a friend,* and whispered him, 'What say you to this?—eh? *flabby*, I think.'

*[Perhaps Beauclerk. Cf. *Boswell Papers*, xi.. 148; xv. 12.]

[1] I am sorry to see in the *Transactions of the Royal Society of Edinburgh*, vol. ii, *An Essay on the Character of Hamlet*, written, I should suppose, by a very young man, though called 'Reverend';† who speaks with presumptuous petulance of the first literary character of his age. Amidst a cloudy confusion of words, (which hath of late too often passed in Scotland for *Metaphysicks*,) he thus ventures to criticise one of the noblest lines in our language:—'Dr. Johnson has remarked, that "time toil'd after him in vain." But I should apprehend, that this is *entirely to mistake the character*. Time toils after *every great man*, as well as after Shakspeare. The *workings* of an ordinary mind *keep pace*, indeed, with time; they move no faster; *they have their beginning, their middle, and their end*; but superiour natures can *reduce these into a point*. They do not, indeed, *suppress* them; but they *suspend*, or they *lock them up in the breast*.' The learned Society, under whose sanction such gabble is ushered into the world, would do well to offer a premium to any one who will discover its meaning.
†[The Rev. Thomas Robertson.]

as they passed, in the most abusive language they could invent, generally, however, with as much satirical humour as they were capable of producing. Addison gives a specimen of this ribaldry, in Number 383 of *The Spectator*, when Sir Roger de Coverly and he are going to Spring-garden. Johnson was once eminently successful in this species of contest; a fellow having attacked him with some coarse raillery, Johnson answered him thus, "Sir, your wife, *under pretence of keeping a bawdy-house*, is a receiver of stolen goods." One evening when he and Mr. Burke and Mr. Langton were in company together, and the admirable scolding of Timon of Athens was mentioned, this instance of Johnson's was quoted, and thought to have at least equal excellence.'

'As Johnson always allowed the extraordinary talents of Mr. Burke, so Mr. Burke was fully sensible of the wonderful powers of Johnson. Mr. Langton recollects having passed an evening with both of them, when Mr. Burke repeatedly entered upon topicks which it was evident he would have illustrated with extensive knowledge and richness of expression; but Johnson always seized upon the conversation, in which, however, he acquitted himself in a most masterly manner. As Mr. Burke and Mr. Langton were walking home, Mr. Burke observed that Johnson had been very great that night; Mr. Langton joined in this, but added, he could have wished to hear more from another person; (plainly intimating that he meant Mr. Burke.) "O, no (said Mr. Burke,) it is enough for me to have rung the bell to him." '

'Beauclerk having observed to him of one of their friends, that he was aukward at counting money, "Why, Sir, (said Johnson,) I am likewise aukward at counting money. But then, Sir, the reason is plain; I have had very little money to count." '

'He had an abhorrence of affectation. Talking of old Mr. Langton, of whom he said, "Sir, you will seldom see such a gentleman, such are his stores of literature, such his knowledge in divinity, and such his exemplary life;" he added, "and Sir, he has no grimace, no gesticulation, no bursts of admiration on trivial occasions; he never embraces you with an overacted cordiality." '

'Being in company with a gentleman who thought fit to maintain Dr. Berkeley's ingenious philosophy, that nothing exists but as perceived by some mind; when the gentleman was going away, Johnson said to him, "Pray, Sir, don't leave us; for we may perhaps forget to think of you, and then you will cease to exist." '

'Goldsmith, upon being visited by Johnson one day in the Temple, said to him with a little jealousy of the appearance of his accommodation, "I shall soon be in better chambers than these." Johnson at the same time checked him and paid him a handsome compliment, implying that a man of his talents should be above attention to such distinctions,—"Nay, Sir, never mind that. *Nil te quæsiveris extra.*" '[1]

'At the time when his pension was granted to him, he said, with a noble literary ambition, "Had this happened twenty years ago, I should have gone to Constantinople to learn Arabick, as Pococke did." '

'As an instance of the niceness of his taste, though he praised West's translation of Pindar, he pointed out the following passage as faulty, by expressing a circumstance so minute as to detract from the general dignity which should prevail:

"Down then from thy glittering *nail*,
'Take, O Muse, thy [the] Dorian lyre." '

'When Mr. Vesey was proposed as a member of the Literary Club, Mr. Burke began by saying that he was a man of gentle manners. "Sir, (said Johnson,) you need say no more. When you have said a man of gentle manners; you have said enough." '

'The late Mr. Fitzherbert told Mr. Langton that Johnson said to him, "Sir, a man has no more right to *say* an uncivil thing, than to *act* one; no more right to say a rude thing to another than to knock him down." '

'My dear friend Dr. Bathurst, (said he with a warmth of approbation,) declared he was glad that his father, who was a West-Indian planter, had left his affairs in total ruin, because

[1] [*Nec te* . . . 'Seek not thyself, without thyself to find.' Persius, *Satires* i. 7. (Dryden.)]

having no estate, he was not under the temptation of having slaves.'

'Richardson had little conversation, except about his own works, of which Sir Joshua Reynolds said he was always willing to talk, and glad to have them introduced. Johnson when he carried Mr. Langton to see him, professed that he could bring him out into conversation, and used this allusive expression, "Sir, I can make him *rear*." But he failed; for in that interview Richardson said little else than that there lay in the room a translation of his *Clarissa* into German.'[1]

'Once when somebody produced a newspaper in which there was a letter of stupid abuse of Sir Joshua Reynolds, of which Johnson himself came in for a share,—"Pray," said he, "let us have it read aloud from beginning to end;" which being done, he with a ludicrous earnestness, and not directing his look to any particular person, called out, "Are we alive after all this satire!"'

'He had a strong prejudice against the political character of Secker, one instance of which appeared at Oxford, where he expressed great dissatisfaction at his varying the old established toast, "Church and King." "The Archbishop of Canterbury," said he (with an affected smooth smiling grimace,) "drinks, 'Constitution in Church and State.'" Being asked what difference there was between the two toasts, he said, "Why, Sir, you may be sure he meant something." Yet when the life of that prelate, prefixed to his sermons by Dr. Porteus and Dr. Stinton

---

[1] A literary lady has favoured me with a characteristick anecdote of Richardson. One day at his country-house at Northend, where a large company was assembled at dinner, a gentleman who was just returned from Paris, willing to please Mr. Richardson, mentioned to him a very flattering circumstance,—that he had seen his *Clarissa* lying on the King's brother's table. Richardson observing that part of the company were engaged in talking to each other, affected then not to attend to it. But by and by, when there was a general silence, and he thought that the flattery might be fully heard, he addressed himself to the gentleman, 'I think, Sir, you were saying something about,—' pausing in a high flutter of expectation. The gentleman, provoked at his inordinate vanity, resolved not to indulge it, and with an exquisitely sly air of indifference answered, 'A mere trifle, Sir, not worth repeating.' The mortification of Richardson was visible, and he did not speak ten words more the whole day. Dr. Johnson was present, and appeared to enjoy it much.

his chaplains, first came out, he read it with the utmost avidity, and said, "It is a life well written, and that well deserves to be recorded." '

'Of a certain noble Lord,[1] he said, "Respect him, you could not; for he had no mind of his own. Love him you could not; for that which you could do with him, every one else could." '

'Of Dr. Goldsmith he said, "No man was more foolish when he had not a pen in his hand, or more wise when he had." '

'He told in his lively manner the following literary anecdote: "Green and Guthrie, an Irishman and a Scotchman, undertook a translation of Duhalde's *History of China*. Green said of Guthrie, that he knew no English, and Guthrie of Green, that he knew no French; and these two undertook to translate Duhalde's *History of China*. In this translation there was found "the twenty-sixth day of the new moon." Now as the whole age of the moon is but twenty-eight days, the moon instead of being new, was nearly as old as it could be. Their blunder arose from their mistaking the word *neuvième* ninth, for *nouvelle* or *neuve*, new." '

'Talking of Dr. Blagden's copiousness and precision of communication, Dr. Johnson said, "Blagden, Sir, is a delightful fellow." '

'On occasion of Dr. Johnson's publishing his pamphlet of *The False Alarm*, there came out a very angry answer[2] (by many supposed to be by Mr. Wilkes). Dr. Johnson determined on not answering it; but, in conversation with Mr. Langton, mentioned a particular or two, which if he *had* replied to it, he might perhaps have inserted. In the answerer's pamphlet, it had been said with solemnity, "Do you consider, Sir, that a House of Commons is to the people as a Creature is to its Creator?" To this question, said Dr. Johnson, I could have replied, that—in the first place— the idea of a CREATOR must be such as that He has a power to unmake or annihilate His creature.'

'Then it cannot be conceived that a creature can make laws for its CREATOR.'[3]

---

[1] [John Boyle, 5th Earl of Cork and Orrery, *Croker*[1].]
[2] *A Letter to Samuel Johnson LL.D.*, 1770 [by John Wilkes].
[3] His profound admiration of the GREAT FIRST CAUSE was such as to set him above that 'Philosophy and vain deceit' [*Colossians*, ii. 8] with which men of narrower conceptions have been infected. I have heard him strongly

'Depend upon it, said he, that if a man *talks* of his misfortunes, there is something in them that is not disagreeable to him; for where there is nothing but pure misery, there never is any recourse to the mention of it.'

'A man must be a poor beast that should *read* no more in quantity than he could *utter* aloud.'

'Imlac in *Rasselas*, I spelt with a *c* at the end, because it is less like English, which should always have the Saxon *k* added to the *c*.'[1]

'Many a man is mad in certain instances, and goes through life without having it perceived: for example, a madness has seized a person of supposing himself obliged literally to pray continually—had the madness turned the opposite way and the person thought it a crime ever to pray, it might not improbably have continued unobserved.'

'He apprehended that the delineation of *characters* in the end of the first Book of the *Retreat of the Ten Thousand*[2] was the first instance of the kind that was known.'

'Supposing (said he,) a wife to be of a studious or argumentative turn, it would be very troublesome: for instance,—if a woman should continually dwell upon the subject of the Arian heresy.'

'No man speaks concerning another, even suppose it be in his praise, if he thinks he does not hear him, exactly as he would, if he thought he was within hearing.'

' "The applause of a single human being is of great consequence:" This he said to me with great earnestness of manner, very near the time of his decease, on occasion of having desired me to read a letter addressed to him from some person in the North of England; which when I had done, and he asked me what the contents were, as I thought being particular upon it might fatigue him, it being of great length, I only told him in

maintain that 'what is right is not so from any natural fitness, but because God wills it to be right;' and it is certainly so, because He has predisposed the relations of things so as that which He wills must be right.

[1] I hope the authority of the great Master of our language will stop that curtailing innovation, by which we see *critic, public*, &c., frequently written instead of *critick, publick*, &c.   [2] [Xenophon's *Anabasis*.]

general that it was highly in his praise;—and then he expressed himself as above.'

'He mentioned with an air of satisfaction what Baretti had told him; that, meeting, in the course of his studying English, with an excellent paper in the *Spectator*, one of four that were written by the respectable Dissenting Minister, Mr. Grove of Taunton, and observing the genius and energy of mind that it exhibits, it greatly quickened his curiosity to visit our country; as he thought if such were the lighter periodical essays of our authours, their productions on more weighty occasions must be wonderful indeed!'

'He observed once, at Sir Joshua Reynolds's, that a beggar in the street will more readily ask alms from a *man*, though there should be no marks of wealth in his appearance, than from even a well-dressed *woman*;[1] which he accounted for from the greater degree of carefulness as to money that is to be found in women; saying farther upon it, that the opportunities in general that they possess of improving their condition are much fewer than men have; and adding, as he looked round the company, which consisted of men only,—there is not one of us who does not think he might be richer if he would use his endeavour.'

'He thus characterised an ingenious writer[2] of his acquaintance: "Sir, he is an enthusiast by rule." '

'"*He may hold up that* SHIELD *against all his enemies;*"—was an observation on Homer, in reference to his description of the shield of Achilles, made by Mrs. Fitzherbert, wife to his friend Mr. Fitzherbert of Derbyshire, and respected by Dr. Johnson as a very fine one. He had in general a very high opinion of that lady's understanding.'

'An observation of Bathurst's may be mentioned, which Johnson repeated, appearing to acknowledge it to be well founded, namely, it was somewhat remarkable how seldom, on occasion of coming into the company of any new person, one felt any wish or inclination to see him again.'

[1] Sterne is of a direct contrary opinion. See his *Sentimental Journey*, Article, 'The Mystery.'

[2] [*Hill suggests* Joseph Warton.]

This year the Reverend Dr. Franklin having published a translation of *Lucian*, inscribed to him the *Demonax* thus:—

'To Dr. Samuel Johnson, the Demonax of the present age, this piece is inscribed by a sincere admirer of his respectable talents,   'The Translator.'

Though upon a particular comparison of Demonax and Johnson, there does not seem to be a great deal of similarity between them, this Dedication is a just compliment from the general character given by Lucian of the ancient Sage, 'ἄριστον ὦν οἶδα ἐγὼ φιλοσόφων γενόμενον, the best philosopher whom I have ever seen or known.'

1781: Ætat. 72.]—In 1781 Johnson at last completed his *Lives of the Poets*, of which he gives this account: 'Some time in March I finished the *Lives of the Poets*, which I wrote in my usual way, dilatorily and hastily, unwilling to work, and working with vigour and haste.'[1] In a memorandum previous to this, he says of them: 'Written, I hope, in such a manner as may tend to the promotion of piety.'[2]

This is the work which of all Dr. Johnson's writings will perhaps be read most generally, and with most pleasure. Philology and biography were his favourite pursuits, and those who lived most in intimacy with him, heard him upon all occasions, when there was a proper opportunity, take delight in expatiating upon the various merits of the English Poets: upon the niceties of their characters, and the events of their progress through the world which they contributed to illuminate. His mind was so full of that kind of information, and it was so well arranged in his memory, that in performing what he had undertaken in this way, he had little more to do than to put his thoughts upon paper, exhibiting first each Poet's life, and then subjoining a critical examination of his genius and works. But when he began to write, the subject swelled in such a manner, that instead of prefaces to each poet, of no more than a few pages, as he had originally intended,[3] he produced an ample, rich, and most enter-

---

[1] *Pr. and Med.* p. 190.   [2] *Ib.* p. 174.
[3] His design is thus announced in his *Advertisement*: 'The Booksellers

taining view of them in every respect. In this he resembled
Quintilian, who tells us, that in the composition of his *Institutions of Oratory*, 'Latiùs se tamen aperiente materiâ, plus quàm
imponebatur oneris sponte suscepi.'[1] The booksellers, justly sensible of the great additional value of the copy-right, presented him
with another hundred pounds, over and above two hundred, for
which his agreement was to furnish such prefaces as he thought
fit.

This was, however, but a small recompence for such a collection of biography, and such principles and illustrations of criticism, as, if digested and arranged in one system, by some modern
Aristotle or Longinus, might form a code upon that subject,
such as no other nation can shew. As he was so good as to make
me a present of the greatest part of the original, and indeed only
manuscript of this admirable work, I have an opportunity of
observing with wonder the correctness with which he rapidly
struck off such glowing composition. He may be assimilated to
the Lady in Waller, who could impress with 'Love at first sight:'

> 'Some other nymphs with colours faint,
> And pencil slow may Cupid paint,
> And a weak heart in time destroy;
> She has a stamp, and prints the boy.'

That he, however, had a good deal of trouble, and some
anxiety in carrying on the work, we see from a series of letters
to Mr. Nichols the printer,[2] whose variety of literary inquiry

having determined to publish a body of English Poetry, I was persuaded to
promise them a Preface to the works of each authour; an undertaking, as
it was then presented to my mind, not very tedious or difficult.

'My purpose was only to have allotted to every poet an Advertisement,
like that [in original *those*] which we find in the French Miscellanies, containing a few dates, and a general character; but I have been led beyond my
intention, I hope by the honest desire of giving useful pleasure.'

[1] ['But as my matter grew under my hand, I voluntarily undertook a
bigger task than had been laid upon me.' Lib. i. Proem. 3.]

[2] Thus:—'In the *Life of Waller*, Mr. Nichols will find a reference to the
Parliamentary History from which a long quotation is to be inserted. If Mr.
Nichols cannot easily find the book, Mr. Johnson will send it from Streat-
ham.'

'Clarendon is here returned.'

'By some accident, I laid *your* note upon Duke up so safely, that I cannot

and obliging disposition, rendered him very useful to Johnson.
Mr. Steevens appears, from the papers in my possession, to have
supplied him with some anecdotes and quotations; and I observe
the fair hand of Mrs. Thrale as one of his copyists of select
passages. But he was principally indebted to my steady friend
Mr. Isaac Reed, of Staple-inn, whose extensive and accurate
knowledge of English literary history I do not express with
exaggeration, when I say it is wonderful; indeed his labours
have proved it to the world; and all who have the pleasure of his
acquaintance can bear testimony to the frankness of his communications in private society.

It is not my intention to dwell upon each of Johnson's *Lives
of the Poets*, or attempt an analysis of their merits, which, were
I able to do it, would take up too much room in this work; yet
I shall make a few observations upon some of them, and insert
a few various readings.

The Life of Cowley he himself considered as the best of the

find it. Your informations have been of great use to me. I must beg it again;
with another list of our authours, for I have laid that with the other. I have
sent Stepney's Epitaph. Let me have the revises as soon as can be. Dec. 1778.

'I have sent Philips, with his Epitaphs, to be inserted. The fragment of a
preface is hardly worth the impression, but that we may seem to do something. It may be added to the *Life of Philips*. The Latin page is to be added
to the *Life of Smith*. I shall be at home to revise the two sheets of Milton.
March 1, 1779.'

'Please to get me the last edition of Hughes's *Letters*; and try to get
Dennis upon *Blackmore*, and upon *Cato*, and any thing of the same writer
against Pope. Our materials are defective.'

'As Waller professed to have imitated Fairfax, do you think a few pages
of Fairfax would enrich our edition? Few readers have seen it, and it may
please them. But it is not necessary.'

' "An account of the Lives and works of some of the most eminent English
Poets. By," &c.—"The English Poets, biographically and critically considered, by SAM. JOHNSON."—Let Mr. Nichols take his choice, or make
another to his mind. May, 1781.'

'You somehow forgot the advertisement for the new edition. It was not
inclosed. Of Gay's *Letters* I see not that any use can be made, for they give
no information of any thing. That he was a member of the Philosophical
Society is something; but surely he could be but a corresponding member.
However, not having his life here, I know not how to put it in, and it is of
little importance.'

See several more in *The Gent. Mag.*, 1785. The Editor of that Miscellany,
in which Johnson wrote for several years, seems justly to think that every
fragment of so great a man is worthy of being preserved.

whole, on account of the dissertation which it contains on the *Metaphysical Poets*. Dryden, whose critical abilities were equal to his poetical, had mentioned them in his excellent Dedication of his Juvenal, but had barely mentioned them. Johnson has exhibited them at large, with such happy illustration from their writings, and in so luminous a manner, that indeed he may be allowed the full merit of novelty, and to have discovered to us, as it were, a new planet in the poetical hemisphere.

It is remarked by Johnson, in considering the works of a poet,[1] that 'amendments are seldom made without some token of a rent;' but I do not find that this is applicable to prose.[2] We shall see that though his amendments in this work are for the better, there is nothing of the *pannus assutus*;[3] the texture is uniform: and indeed, what had been there at first, is very seldom unfit to have remained.

Various Readings[4] *in the Life of* COWLEY.

'All [future votaries of] *that may hereafter pant for* solitude.

'To conceive and execute the [agitation or perception] *pains and the pleasures* of other minds.

'The wide effulgence of [the blazing] *a summer* noon.'

In the Life of WALLER, Johnson gives a distinct and animated narrative of publick affairs in that variegated period, with strong yet nice touches of character; and having a fair opportunity to display his political principles, does it with an unqualified manly confidence, and satisfies his readers how nobly he might have executed a *Tory History* of his country.

So easy is his style in these Lives, that I do not recollect more than three uncommon or learned words; one, when giving an account of the approach of Waller's mortal disease, he says, 'he

---

[1] *Life of Sheffield* [para. 25].

[2] See, however, p. 1072 of this volume, where the same remark is made and Johnson is there speaking of *prose*. [M.]

[3] [*Purpureus . . . unus et alter Assuitur pannus*, 'a purple patch or two is tacked on'. Horace, *Ars Poetica* l. 15 (Wickham).]

[4] The original reading is enclosed in crotchets, and the present one is printed in Italicks.

found his legs grow *tumid*;' by using the expression his legs *swelled*, he would have avoided this; and there would have been no impropriety in its being followed by the interesting question to his physician, 'What that *swelling* meant?' Another, when he mentions that Pope had *emitted* proposals; when *published* or *issued* would have been more readily understood; and a third, when he calls Orrery and Dr. Delany, writers both undoubtedly *veracious*; when *true, honest,* or *faithful,* might have been used. Yet, it must be owned, that none of these are *hard* or *too big* words; that custom would make them seem as easy as any others; and that a language is richer and capable of more beauty of expression, by having a greater variety of synonimes.

His dissertation upon the unfitness of poetry for the aweful subjects of our holy religion, though I do not entirely agree with him, has all the merit of originality, with uncommon force and reasoning.

Various Readings in the Life of WALLER.

'Consented to [the insertion of their names] *their own nomination*.

'[After] *paying* a fine of ten thousand pounds.

'Congratulating Charles the Second on his [coronation] *recovered right*.

'He that has flattery ready for all whom the vicissitudes of the world happen to exalt, must be [confessed to degrade his powers] *scorned as a prostituted mind*.

'The characters by which Waller intended to distinguish his writings are [elegance] *sprightliness* and dignity.

'Blossoms to be valued only as they [fetch] *foretell* fruits.

'Images such as the superficies of nature [easily] *readily* supplies.

'[His] *Some* applications [are sometimes] *may be thought* too remote and unconsequential.

'His images are [sometimes confused] *not always distinct*.'

Against his Life of MILTON, the hounds of Whiggism have opened in full cry. But of Milton's great excellence as a poet, where shall we find such a blazon as by the hand of Johnson? I shall select only the following passage concerning *Paradise Lost*:

'Fancy can hardly forbear to conjecture with what temper Milton surveyed the silent progress of his work, and marked his reputation stealing its way in a kind of subterraneous current, through fear and silence. I cannot but conceive him calm and confident, little disappointed, not at all dejected, relying on his own merit with steady consciousness, and waiting without impatience the vicissitudes of opinion, and the impartiality of a future generation.'

Indeed even Dr. Towers, who may be considered as one of the warmest zealots of *The Revolution Society* itself, allows, that 'Johnson has spoken in the highest terms of the abilities of that great poet, and has bestowed on his principal poetical compositions the most honourable encomiums.'[1]

That a man, who venerated the Church and Monarchy as Johnson did, should speak with a just abhorrence of Milton as a politician, or rather as a daring foe to good polity, was surely to be expected; and to those who censure him, I would recommend his commentary on Milton's celebrated complaint of his situation, when by the lenity of Charles the Second, 'a lenity of which (as Johnson well observes) the world has had perhaps no other example; he, who had written in justification of the murder of his Sovereign, was safe under an *Act of Oblivion*.'

[1] See *An Essay on the Life, Character, and Writings of Dr. Samuel Johnson*, London, 1787; which is very well written, making a proper allowance for the democratical bigotry of its authour; whom I cannot however but admire for his liberality in speaking thus of my illustrious friend:—

'He possessed extraordinary powers of understanding, which were much cultivated by study, and still more by meditation and reflection. His memory was remarkably retentive, his imagination uncommonly vigorous, and his judgement keen and penetrating. He had a strong sense of the importance of religion; his piety was sincere, and sometimes ardent; and his zeal for the interests of virtue was often manifested in his conversation and in his writings. The same energy which was displayed in his literary productions was exhibited also in his conversation, which was various, striking, and instructive; and perhaps no man ever equalled him for nervous and pointed repartees.'

'His *Dictionary*, his moral *Essays*, and his productions in polite literature, will convey useful instruction, and elegant entertainment, as long as the language in which they are written shall be understood.'

'No sooner is he safe than he finds himself in danger, *fallen on evil days and evil tongues, and with darkness and with danger compassed round.* This darkness, had his eyes been better employed, had undoubtedly deserved compassion; but to add the mention of danger was ungrateful and unjust. He was fallen, indeed, on *evil days*; the time was come in which regicides could no longer boast their wickedness. But of *evil tongues* for Milton to complain, required impudence at least equal to his other powers; Milton, whose warmest advocates must allow, that he never spared any asperity of reproach, or brutality of insolence.'

I have, indeed, often wondered how Milton, 'an acrimonious and surly Republican,'—a man 'who in his domestick relations was so severe and arbitrary,' and whose head was filled with the hardest and most dismal tenets of Calvinism, should have been such a poet; should not only have written with sublimity, but with beauty, and even gaiety; should have exquisitely painted the sweetest sensations of which our nature is capable; imaged the delicate raptures of connubial love; nay, seemed to be animated with all the spirit of revelry. It is a proof that in the human mind the departments of judgement and imagination, perception and temper, may sometimes be divided by strong partitions; and that the light and shade in the same character may be kept so distinct as never to be blended.[1]

In the *Life of Milton*, Johnson took occasion to maintain his own and the general opinion of the excellence of rhyme over blank verse, in English poetry; and quotes this apposite illustration of it by 'an ingenious critick,' that *it seems to be verse only to the eye.*[2] The gentleman whom he thus characterises, is (as he told Mr. Seward) Mr. Lock, of Norbury Park, in Surrey, whose knowledge and taste in the fine arts is universally celebrated; with whose elegance of manners the writer of the present

[1] Mr. Malone thinks it is rather a proof that he felt nothing of those cheerful sensations which he has described: that on these topicks it is the *poet*, and not the *man*, that writes.

[2] One of the most natural instances of the effect of blank verse occurred to the late Earl of Hopeton. His Lordship observed one of his shepherds poring in the fields upon Milton's *Paradise Lost*; and having asked him what book it was, the man answered, 'An't please your Lordship, this is a very odd sort of an authour: he would fain rhyme, but cannot get at it.

work has felt himself much impressed, and to whose virtues a common friend,[1] who has known him long, and is not much addicted to flattery, gives the highest testimony.

Various Readings in the Life of MILTON.

'I cannot find any meaning but this which [his most bigotted advocates] *even kindness and reverence* can give.

'[Perhaps no] *scarcely any* man ever wrote so much, and praised so few.

'A certain [rescue] *preservative* from oblivion.

'Let me not be censured for this digression, as [contracted] *pedantick* or paradoxical.

'Socrates rather was of opinion, that what we had to learn was how to [obtain and communicate happiness] *do good and avoid evil.*

'Its elegance [who can exhibit?] *is less attainable.*'

I could, with pleasure, expatiate upon the masterly execution of the Life of DRYDEN, which we have seen[2] was one of Johnson's literary projects at an early period, and which it is remarkable, that after desisting from it, from a supposed scantiness of materials, he should, at an advanced age, have exhibited so amply.

His defence of that great poet against the illiberal attacks upon him, as if his embracing the Roman Catholick communion had been a time-serving measure, is a piece of reasoning at once able and candid. Indeed, Dryden himself, in his *Hind and Panther*, hath given such a picture of his mind, that they who know the anxiety for repose as to the aweful subject of our state beyond the grave, though they may think his opinion ill-founded, must think charitably of his sentiment:—

> 'But, gracious GOD, how well dost thou provide
> For erring judgements an unerring guide!
> Thy throne is darkness in the abyss of light,
> A blaze of glory that forbids the sight.
> O! teach me to believe thee thus conceal'd,

[1] [Possibly Malone. *Powell.*]   [2] See p. 770.

> And search no farther than thyself reveal'd;
> But Her alone for my director take,
> Whom thou hast promis'd never to forsake.
> My thoughtless youth was wing'd with vain desires;
> My manhood, long misled by wand'ring fires,
> Follow'd false lights; and when their glimpse was gone,
> My pride struck out new sparkles of her own.
> Such was I, such by Nature still I am;
> Be thine the glory, and be mine the shame.
> Good life be now my task: my doubts are done;
> What more could shock my faith than Three in One?'

In drawing Dryden's character, Johnson has given, though I suppose unintentionally, some touches of his own. Thus:—'The power that predominated in his intellectual operations was rather strong reason than quick sensibility. Upon all occasions that were presented, he studied rather than felt; and produced sentiments not such as Nature enforces, but meditation supplies. With the simple and elemental passions as they spring separate in the mind, he seems not much acquainted. He is, therefore, with all his variety of excellence, not often pathetick; and had so little sensibility of the power of effusions purely natural, that he did not esteem them in others.' It may indeed be observed, that in all the numerous writings of Johnson, whether in prose or verse, and even in his Tragedy, of which the subject is the distress of an unfortunate Princess, there is not a single passage that ever drew a tear.

Various Readings in the Life of DRYDEN.

'The reason of this general perusal, Addison has attempted to [find in] *derive from* the delight which the mind feels in the investigation of secrets.

'His best actions are but [convenient] *inability of* wickedness.

'When once he had engaged himself in disputation, [matter] *thoughts* flowed in on either side.

'The abyss of an un-ideal [emptiness] *vacancy*.

'These, like [many other harlots,] *the harlots of other men*, had his love though not his approbation.

'He [sometimes displays] *descends to display* his knowledge with°pedantick ostentation.

'French words which [were then used in] *had then crept into* conversation.'

The Life of POPE was written by Johnson *con amore*, both from the early possession which that writer had taken of his mind, and from the pleasure which he must have felt, in for ever silencing all attempts to lessen his poetical fame by demonstrating his excellence, and pronouncing the following triumphant eulogium:—'After all this, it is surely superfluous to answer the question that has once been asked, Whether Pope was a poet? otherwise than by asking in return, If Pope be not a poet, where is poetry to be found? To circumscribe poetry by a definition, will only shew the narrowness of the definer; though a definition which shall exclude Pope will not easily be made. Let us look round upon the present time, and back upon the past; let us enquire to whom the voice of mankind has decreed the wreath of poetry; let their productions be examined, and their claims stated, and the pretensions of Pope will be no more disputed.'

I remember once to have heard Johnson say, 'Sir, a thousand years may elapse before there shall appear another man with a power of versification equal to that of Pope.' That power must undoubtedly be allowed its due share in enhancing the value of his captivating composition.

Johnson, who had done liberal justice to Warburton in his edition of *Shakspeare*, which was published during the life of that powerful writer, with still greater liberality took an opportunity, in the *Life of Pope*, of paying the tribute due to him when he was no longer in 'high place,' but numbered with the dead.[1]

---

[1] Of Johnson's conduct towards Warburton, a very honourable notice is taken by the editor* of *Tracts by Warburton and a Warburtonian, not admitted into the Collection of their respective Works*. After an able and 'fond, though not undistinguishing,' consideration of Warburton's character, he says, 'In two immortal works, Johnson has stood forth in the foremost rank of his admirers. By the testimony of such a man, impertinence must be

* [Dr. Parr. *Boswell's Letters*, ii. 357.]

It seems strange, that two such men as Johnson and Warburton, who lived in the same age and country, should not only not have been in any degree of intimacy, but been almost personally unacquainted. But such instances, though we must wonder at them, are not rare. If I am rightly informed, after a careful enquiry, they never met but once, which was at the house of Mrs. French, in London, well known for her elegant assemblies,

abashed, and malignity itself must be softened. Of literary merit, Johnson, as we all know, was a sagacious but a most severe judge. Such was his discernment, that he pierced into the most secret springs of human actions; and such was his integrity, that he always weighed the moral characters of his fellow-creatures in the "balance of the sanctuary." He was too courageous to propitiate a rival, and too proud to truckle to a superiour. Warburton he knew, as I know him, and as every man of sense and virtue would wish to be known,—I mean, both from his own writings, and from the writings of those who dissented from his principles, or who envied his reputation. But, as to favours, he had never received or asked any from the Bishop of Gloucester; and, if my memory fails me not, he had seen him only once, when they met almost without design, conversed without much effort, and parted without any lasting impressions of hatred or affection. Yet, with all the ardour of sympathetick genius, Johnson has done that spontaneously and ably, which, by some writers, had been before attempted injudiciously, and which, by others, from whom more successful attempts might have been expected, has not *hitherto* been done at all. He spoke well of Warburton, without insulting those whom Warburton despised. He suppressed not the imperfections of this extraordinary man, while he endeavoured to do justice to his numerous and transcendental excellencies. He defended him when living, amidst the clamours of his enemies; and praised him when dead, amidst the *silence of his friends.*'

Having availed myself of this editor's eulogy on my departed friend, for which I warmly thank him, let me not suffer the lustre of his reputation, honestly acquired by profound learning and vigorous eloquence, to be tarnished by a charge of illiberality. He has been accused of invidiously dragging again into light certain writings of a person respectable by his talents, his learning, his station and his age, which were published a great many years ago, and have since, it is said, been silently given up by their authour. But when it is considered that these writings were not *sins of youth*, but deliberate works of one well-advanced in life [Richard Hurd], overflowing at once with flattery to a great man of great interest in the Church, and with unjust and acrimonious abuse of two men of eminent merit; and that, though it would have been unreasonable to expect an humiliating recantation, no apology whatever has been made in the cool of the evening, for the oppressive fervour of the heat of the day; no slight relenting indication has appeared in any note, or any corner of later publications; is it not fair to understand him as superciliously persevering? When he allows the shafts to remain in the wounds, and will not stretch forth a lenient hand, is it wrong, is it not generous to become an indignant avenger?

and bringing eminent characters together. The interview proved to be mutually agreeable.

I am well informed, that Warburton said of Johnson, 'I admire him, but I cannot bear his style:' and that Johnson being told of this, said, 'That is exactly my case as to him.' The manner in which he expressed his admiration of the fertility of Warburton's genius and of the variety of his materials was, 'The table is always full, Sir. He brings things from the north, and the south, and from every quarter. In his *Divine Legation*, you are always entertained. He carries you round and round, without carrying you forward to the point; but then you have no wish to be carried forward.' He said to the Reverend Mr. Strahan, 'Warburton is perhaps the last man who has written with a mind full of reading and reflection.'

It is remarkable, that in the Life of Broome, Johnson takes notice of Dr. Warburton's using a mode of expression which he himself used, and that not seldom, to the great offence of those who did not know him. Having occasion to mention a note, stating the different parts which were executed by the associated translators of *The Odyssey*, he says, 'Dr. Warburton told me, in his warm language, that he thought the relation given in the note *a lie*.' The language is *warm* indeed; and, I must own, cannot be justified in consistency with a decent regard to the established forms of speech. Johnson had accustomed himself to use the word *lie*, to express a mistake or an errour in relation; in short, when the *thing was not so as told*, though the relator did not *mean* to deceive. When he thought there was intentional falsehood in the relator, his expression was, 'He *lies*, and he *knows* he *lies*.'

Speaking of Pope's not having been known to excel in conversation, Johnson observes, that 'traditional memory retains no sallies of raillery, or sentences of observation; nothing either pointed or solid, wise or merry; and that one apophthegm only is recorded.' In this respect, Pope differed widely from Johnson, whose conversation was, perhaps, more admirable than even his writings, however excellent. Mr. Wilkes has, however, favoured me with one repartee of Pope, of which Johnson was not informed. Johnson, after justly censuring him for having 'nursed in his mind a foolish dis-esteem of Kings,' tells us, 'yet a little regard shewn him by the Prince of Wales melted his obduracy; and he had not much to say when he was asked by his Royal Highness, *how he could love a Prince, while he disliked Kings?*' The answer which Pope made, was, 'The young lion is harmless, and even playful; but when his claws are full grown he becomes cruel, dreadful, and mischievous.'

But although we have no collection of Pope's sayings, it is not therefore to be concluded, that he was not agreeable in social intercourse; for Johnson has been heard to say, that 'the happiest conversation is that of which nothing is distinctly remembered but a general effect of pleasing impression.' The late Lord Somerville,[1] who saw much both of great and brilliant life, told me, that he had dined in company with Pope, and that after dinner the *little man*, as he called him, drank his bottle of Burgundy, and was exceedingly gay and entertaining.

I cannot with-hold from my great friend a censure of at least culpable inattention, to a nobleman, who, it has been shewn, behaved to him with uncommon politeness. He says, 'Except Lord Bathurst, none of Pope's noble friends were such as that a good man would wish to have his intimacy with them known to posterity.' This will not apply to Lord Mansfield, who was not ennobled in Pope's life-time; but Johnson should have recollected, that Lord Marchmont was one of those noble friends. He includes his Lordship along with Lord Bolingbroke, in a charge of neglect of the papers which Pope left by his will; when, in truth, as I myself pointed out to him, before he wrote that

[1] Let me here express my grateful remembrance of Lord Somerville's kindness to me, at a very early period. He was the first person of high rank that took particular notice of me in the way most flattering to a young man, fondly ambitious of being distinguished for his literary talents; and by the honour of his encouragement made me think well of myself, and aspire to deserve it better. He had a happy art of communicating his varied knowledge of the world, in short remarks and anecdotes, with a quiet pleasant gravity, that was exceedingly engaging. Never shall I forget the hours which I enjoyed with him at his apartments in the Royal Palace of Holy-Rood House, and at his seat near Edinburgh, which he himself had formed with an elegant taste.

poet's life, the papers were 'committed to *the sole care and judge-ment* of Lord Bolingbroke, unless he (Lord Bolingbroke) shall not survive me;' so that Lord Marchmont had no concern what-ever with them. After the first edition of the *Lives*, Mr. Malone, whose love of justice is equal to his accuracy, made, in my hear-ing, the same remark to Johnson; yet he omitted to correct the erroneous statement.[1] These particulars I mention, in the belief that there was only forgetfulness in my friend; but I owe this much to the Earl of Marchmont's reputation, who, were there no other memorials, will be immortalised by that line of Pope in the verses on his Grotto:

'And the bright flame was shot through Marchmont's soul.'

Various Readings in the Life of POPE.

'[Somewhat free] *sufficiently bold* in his criticisms.

'All the gay [niceties] *varieties* of diction.

'Strikes the imagination with far [more] *greater* force.

'It is [probably] *certainly* the noblest version of poetry which the world has ever seen.

'Every sheet enabled him to write the next with [less trouble] *more facility*.

'No man sympathizes with [vanity depressed] *the sorrows of vanity*.

'It had been [criminal] *less easily excused*.

'When he [threatened to lay down] *talked of laying down* his pen.

'Society [is so named emphatically in opposition to] *politically regulated, is a state contra-distinguished from* a state of nature.

'A fictitious life of an [absurd] *infatuated* scholar.

'A foolish [contempt, disregard,] *disesteem* of Kings.

'His hopes and fears, his joys and sorrows [were like those of other mortals] *acted strongly upon his mind*.

'Eager to pursue knowledge and attentive to [accumulate] *retain it*.

[1] This neglect did not arise from any ill-will towards Lord Marchmont, but from inattention; just as he neglected to correct his statement concerning the family of Thomson the poet, after it had been shewn to be erroneous (*ante*, p. 1000). [M.]

'A mind [excursive] *active*, ambitious, and adventurous.

'In its [noblest] *widest* researches still longing to go forward.

'He wrote in such a manner as might expose him to few [neglects] *hazards*.

'The [reasonableness] *justice* of my determination.

'A [favourite] *delicious* employment of the poets.

'More terrifick and more powerful [beings] *phantoms* perform on the stormy ocean.

'The inventor of [those] *this* petty [beings] *nation*.

'The [mind] *heart* naturally loves truth.'

In the Life of Addison we find an unpleasing account of his having lent Steele a hundred pounds, and 'reclaimed his loan by an execution.' In the new edition of the *Biographia Britannica*, the authenticity of this anecdote is denied. But Mr. Malone has obliged me with the following note concerning it:—

'Many persons having doubts concerning this fact, I applied to Dr. Johnson to learn on what authority he asserted it. He told me, he had it from Savage, who lived in intimacy with Steele, and who mentioned, that Steele told him the story with tears in his eyes.—Ben Victor, Dr. Johnson said, likewise informed him of this remarkable transaction, from the relation of Mr. Wilkes the comedian, who was also an intimate of Steele's.—Some, in defence of Addison, have said, that "the act was done with the good-natured view of rousing Steele, and correcting that profusion which always made him necessitous."—"If that were the case, (said Johnson,) and that he only wanted to alarm Steele, he would afterwards have *returned* the money to his friend, which it is not pretended he did."—"This too, (he added,) might be retorted by an advocate for Steele, who might alledge, that he did not repay the loan *intentionally*, merely to see whether Addison would be mean and ungenerous enough to make use of legal process to recover it. But of such speculations there is no end: we cannot dive into the hearts of men; but their actions are open to observation.'

'I then mentioned to him that some people thought that Mr. Addison's character was so pure, that the fact, *though true*, ought to have been suppressed. He saw no reason for this. "If nothing but the bright side of characters should be shewn, we should sit down in despondency, and think it utterly impossible to imitate them in *any thing*. The sacred writers, (he observed,) related the vicious as well as the virtuous actions of men; which had this moral effect, that it kept mankind from *despair*, into which otherwise they would naturally fall, were they not supported by the recollection that others had offended like themselves, and by penitence and amendment of life had been restored to the favour of Heaven."

'March 15, 1782.'   'E. M.'

The last paragraph of this note is of great importance; and I request that my readers may consider it with particular attention. It will be afterwards referred to in this work.

Various Readings in the Life of ADDISON.

'[But he was our first great example] *He was, however, one of our earliest examples* of correctness.

'And [overlook] *despise* their masters.

'His instructions were such as the [state] *character* of his [own time] *readers* made [necessary] *proper*.

'His purpose was to [diffuse] *infuse* literary curiosity by gentle and unsuspected conveyance [among] *into* the gay, the idle, and the wealthy.

'Framed rather for those that [wish] *are learning* to write.

'Domestick [manners] *scenes.*'

In his Life of PARNELL, I wonder that Johnson omitted to insert an Epitaph which he had long before composed for that amiable man, without ever writing it down, but which he was so good as, at my request, to dictate to me, by which means it has been preserved.

'*Hic requiescit* THOMAS PARNELL, *S. T. P.*

> *Qui sacerdos pariter et poeta,*
> *Utrasque partes ita implevit,*

> *Ut neque sacerdoti suavitas poetæ,*
> *Nec poetæ sacerdotis sanctitas, deesset.*'[1]

Various Readings in the Life of PARNELL.

'About three years [after] *afterwards.*

'[Did not much want] *was in no great need of* improvement.

'But his prosperity *did not last long* [was clouded by that which took away all his powers of enjoying either profit or pleasure, the death of his wife, whom he is said to have lamented with such sorrow, as hastened his end.][2] His end, whatever was the cause, was now approaching.

'In the Hermit, the [composition] *narrative*, as it is less airy, is less pleasing.'

In the Life of BLACKMORE, we find that writer's reputation generously cleared by Johnson from the cloud of prejudice which the malignity of contemporary wits had raised around it. In this spirited exertion of justice, he has been imitated by Sir Joshua Reynolds, in his praise of the architecture of Vanburgh.

We trace Johnson's own character in his observations on Blackmore's 'magnanimity as an authour.' 'The incessant attacks of his enemies, whether serious or merry, are never discovered to have disturbed his quiet, or to have lessened his confidence in himself.' Johnson, I recollect, once told me, laughing heartily, that he understood it had been said of him, 'He *appears* not to feel; but, when he is *alone*, depend upon it, he *suffers sadly.*' I am as certain as I can be of any man's real sentiments, that he *enjoyed* the perpetual shower of little hostile arrows, as evidence of his fame.

Various Readings in the Life of BLACKMORE.

'To [set] *engage* poetry [on the side] *in the cause* of virtue.

'He likewise [established] *enforced* the truth of Revelation.

---

[1] ['Here lies Thomas Parnell, D.D., who, at once priest and poet, so played both parts that the poet's sweetness was never false to the priest, nor the priest's piety false to the poet.']

[2] I should have thought that Johnson, who had felt the severe affliction from which Parnell never recovered, would have preserved this passage.

'[Kindness] *benevolence* was ashamed to favour.

'His practice, which was once [very extensive] *invidiously great.*

'There is scarcely any distemper of dreadful name [of] which he has not [shewn] *taught his reader* how [it is to be opposed] *to oppose.*

'Of this [contemptuous] *indecent* arrogance.

'[He wrote] *but produced* likewise a work of a different kind.

'At least [written] *compiled* with integrity.

'Faults which many tongues [were desirous] *would have made haste* to publish.

'But though he [had not] *could not boast of* much critical knowledge.

'He [used] *waited for* no felicities of fancy.

'Or had ever elevated his [mind] *views* to that ideal perfection which every [mind] *genius* born to excel is condemned always to pursue and never overtake.

'The [first great] *fundamental* principle of wisdom and of virtue.'

Various Readings in the Life of PHILIPS.

'His dreaded [rival] *antagonist* POPE.

'They [have not often much] *are not loaded with* thought.

'In his translations from Pindar, he [will not be denied to have reached] *found the art of reaching* all the obscurity of the Theban bard.'

Various Readings in the Life of CONGREVE.

'Congreve's conversation must surely have been *at least* equally pleasing with his writings.

'It apparently [requires] *pre-supposes* a familiar knowledge of many characters.

'Reciprocation of [similes] *conceits.*

'The dialogue is quick and [various] *sparkling.*

'Love for Love; a comedy [more drawn from life] *of nearer alliance to life.*

'The general character of his miscellanies is, that they shew little wit and [no] *little* virtue.

'[Perhaps] *certainly* he had not the fire requisite for the higher species of lyrick poetry.'

Various Readings in the Life of TICKELL.

'[Longed] *long wished* to peruse it.

'At the [accession] *arrival* of King George.

'Fiction [unnaturally] *unskilfully* compounded of Grecian deities and Gothick fairies.'

Various Readings in the Life of AKENSIDE.

'For [another] *a different* purpose.

'[A furious] *an unnecessary* and outrageous zeal.

'[Something which] *what* he called and thought liberty.

'A [favourer of innovation] *lover of contradiction.*

'Warburton's [censure] *objections.*

'His rage [for liberty] *of patriotism.*

'Mr. Dyson with [a zeal] *an ardour* of friendship.'

In the Life of LYTTELTON, Johnson seems to have been not favourably disposed towards that nobleman. Mrs. Thrale suggests that he was offended by *Molly Aston's*[1] preference of his Lordship to him.[2] I can by no means join in the censure bestowed

[1] [i.e. Hill Boothby. Boswell is in error; *Johns. Misc.* i. 257.]
[2] Let not my readers smile to think of Johnson's being a candidate for female favour; Mr. Peter Garrick assured me, that he was told by a lady, that in her opinion Johnson was 'a very *seducing man.*' Disadvantages of person and manner may be forgotten, where intellectual pleasure is communicated to a susceptible mind; and that Johnson was capable of feeling the most delicate and disinterested attachment, appears from the following letter, which is published by Mrs. Thrale [*Piozzi Letters*, ii. 391], with some others to the same person, of which the excellence is not so apparent:—

'*To* MISS BOOTHBY.

'DEAREST MADAM,   'January [1], 1755.
'Though I am afraid your illness leaves you little leisure for the reception of airy civilities, yet I cannot forbear to pay you my congratulations on the new year; and to declare my wishes that your years to come may be many and happy. In this wish, indeed, I include myself, who have none but you on whom my heart reposes; yet surely I wish your good, even though your situation were such as should permit you to communicate no gratifications to, dearest, dearest Madam, your, &c.

'SAM. JOHNSON.'

by Johnson on his Lordship, whom he calls 'poor Lyttelton,' for
returning thanks to the Critical Reviewers for having 'kindly
commended' his *Dialogues of the Dead*. Such 'acknowledgements
(says my friend,) never can be proper, since they must be paid
either for flattery or for justice.' In my opinion, the most upright
man, who has been tried on a false accusation, may, when he is
acquitted, make a bow to his jury. And when those who are so
much the arbiters of literary merit, as in a considerable degree
to influence the publick opinion, review an authour's work,
placido lumine,[1] when I am afraid mankind in general are better
pleased with severity, he may surely express a grateful sense of
their civility.

Various Readings in the Life of LYTTELTON.

'He solaced [himself] *his grief* by writing a long poem to her
memory.

'The production rather [of a mind that means well than thinks
vigorously] *as it seems of leisure than of study, rather effusions
than compositions*.

'His last literary [work] *production*.

'[Found the way] *undertook* to persuade.'

As the introduction to his critical examination of the genius
and writings of YOUNG, he did Mr. Herbert Croft, then a Barrister of Lincoln's-inn, now a clergyman, the honour to adopt a
Life of Young written by that gentleman, who was the friend of
Dr. Young's son, and wished to vindicate him from some very
erroneous remarks to his prejudice. Mr. Croft's performance
was subjected to the revision of Dr. Johnson, as appears from
the following note to Mr. John Nichols[2]:—

'This *Life of Dr. Young* was written by a friend of his son.
What is crossed with black is expunged[3] by the authour, what
is crossed with red is expunged[3] by me. If you find any thing
more that can be well omitted, I shall not be sorry to see it yet
shorter.'

---

[1] ['with kindly glance.' Horace, *Odes* iv. iii. 2.]
[2] *Gent. Mag.* vol. lv. p. 10.   [3] [Johnson wrote *erased* (bis).]

It has always appeared to me to have a considerable share of merit, and to display a pretty successful imitation of Johnson's style. When I mentioned this to a very eminent literary character,[1] he opposed me vehemently, exclaiming, 'No, no, it is *not* a good imitation of Johnson; it has all his pomp without his force; it has all the nodosities of the oak without its strength.' This was an image so happy, that one might have thought he would have been satisfied with it; but he was not. And setting his mind again to work, he added, with exquisite felicity, 'It has all the contortions of the Sybil, without the inspiration.'

Mr. Croft very properly guards us against supposing that Young was a gloomy man; and mentions, that 'his parish was indebted to the good-humour of the authour of the *Night Thoughts* for an Assembly and a Bowling-Green.' A letter from a noble foreigner is quoted, in which he is said to have been 'very pleasant in conversation.'

Mr. Langton, who frequently visited him, informs me, that there was an air of benevolence in his manner, but that he could obtain from him less information than he had hoped to receive from one who had lived so much in intercourse with the brightest men of what has been called the Augustan age of England; and that he shewed a degree of eager curiosity concerning the common occurrences that were then passing, which appeared somewhat remarkable in a man of such intellectual stores, of such an advanced age, and who had retired from life with declared disappointment in his expectations.

An instance at once of his pensive turn of mind, and his cheerfulness of temper, appeared in a little story which he himself told to Mr Langton, when they were walking in his garden: 'Here (said he,) I had put a handsome sun-dial, with this inscription, *Eheu fugaces!*[2] which (speaking with a smile) was sadly verified, for by the next morning my dial had been carried off.'[3]

---

[1] [Burke. *Boswell Papers*, xiv. 218.]
[2] [*Eheu fugaces . . . Labuntur anni*, 'Ah me . . . the fleeting years are slipping by.' Horace, *Odes* ii. xiv. 1. (Wickham.)]
[3] The late Mr. James Ralph told Lord Macartney, that he passed an evening with Dr. Young at Lord Melcombe's (then Mr. Dodington) at

It gives me much pleasure to observe, that however Johnson may have casually talked, yet when he sits, as 'an ardent judge zealous to his trust, giving sentence'[1] upon the excellent works of Young, he allows them the high praise to which they are justly entitled. 'The *Universal Passion* (says he,) is indeed a very great performance,—his distichs have the weight of solid sentiment, and his points the sharpness of resistless truth.'

But I was most anxious concerning Johnson's decision upon *Night Thoughts*, which I esteem as a mass of the grandest and richest poetry that human genius has ever produced; and was delighted to find this character of that work: 'In his *Night Thoughts*, he has exhibited a very wide display of original poetry, variegated with deep reflections and striking allusions; a wilderness of thought, in which the fertility of fancy scatters flowers of every hue and of every odour. This is one of the few poems in which blank verse could not be changed for rhime but with disadvantage.' And afterwards, 'Particular lines are not to be regarded; the power is in the whole; and in the whole there is a magnificence like that ascribed to Chinese plantation, the magnificence of vast extent and endless diversity.'

But there is in this Poem not only all that Johnson so well brings in view, but a power of the *Pathetick* beyond almost any example that I have seen. He who does not feel his nerves shaken, and his heart pierced by many passages in this extraordinary work, particularly by that most affecting one, which describes the gradual torment suffered by the contemplation of an object of affectionate attachment, visibly and certainly decaying into dissolution, must be of a hard and obstinate frame.

To all the other excellencies of *Night Thoughts* let me add the great and peculiar one, that they contain not only the noblest sentiments of virtue, and contemplations on immortality, but the *Christian Sacrifice*, the *Divine Propitiation*, with all its interesting circumstances, and consolations to 'a wounded spirit,' solemnly

Hammersmith. The Doctor happening to go out into the garden, Mr. Dodington observed to him, on his return, that it was a dreadful night, as in truth it was, there being a violent storm of rain and wind. 'No, Sir, (replied the Doctor,) it is a very fine night. The LORD is abroad.'

[1] [Pope, *Essays on Criticism*, 677.]

and poetically displayed in such imagery and language, as cannot fail to exalt, animate, and soothe the truly pious. No book whatever can be recommended to young persons, with better hopes of seasoning their minds with *vital religion*, than Young's *Night Thoughts*.

In the Life of Swift, it appears to me that Johnson had a certain degree of prejudice against that extraordinary man, of which I have elsewhere had occasion to speak. Mr. Thomas Sheridan imputed it to a supposed apprehension in Johnson, that Swift had not been sufficiently active in obtaining for him an Irish degree when it was solicited,[1] but of this there was not sufficient evidence; and let me not presume to charge Johnson with injustice, because he did not think so highly of the writings of this authour, as I have done from my youth upwards. Yet that he had an unfavourable bias is evident, were it only from that passage in which he speaks of Swift's practice of saving, as, 'first ridiculous and at last detestable;' and yet after some examination of circumstances, finds himself obliged to own, that 'it will perhaps appear that he only liked one mode of expence better than another, and saved merely that he might have something to give.'

One observation which Johnson makes in Swift's life should be often inculcated:—

'It may be justly supposed, that there was in his conversation what appears so frequently in his letters, an affectation of familiarity with the great, an ambition of momentary equality, sought and enjoyed by the neglect of those ceremonies which custom has established as the barriers between one order of society and another. This transgression of regularity was by himself and his admirers termed greatness of soul; but a great mind disdains to hold any thing by courtesy, and therefore never usurps what a lawful claimant may take away. He that encroaches on another's dignity puts himself in his power; he is either repelled with helpless indignity, or endured by clemency and condescension.'

[1] See p. 96.

Various Readings in the Life of Swift.

'Charity may be persuaded to think that it might be written by a man of *a* peculiar [opinions] *character*, without ill intention.

'He did not [disown] *deny* it.

'[To] *by* whose kindness it is not unlikely that he was [indebted for] *advanced to* his benefices.

'[With] *for* this purpose he had recourse to Mr. Harley.

'Sharpe, whom he [represents] *describes* as "the harmless tool of others' hate."

'Harley was slow because he was [irresolute] *doubtful*.

'When [readers were not many] *we were not yet a nation of readers*.

'[Every man who] *he that could say he* knew him.

'Every man of known influence has so many [more] petitions [than] *which* he [can] *cannot* grant, that he must necessarily offend more than he [can gratify] *gratifies*.

'Ecclesiastical [preferments] *benefices*.

'Swift [procured] *contrived* an interview.

'[As a writer] *In his works* he has given very different specimens.

'On all common occasions he habitually [assumes] *affects* a style of [superiority] *arrogance*.

'By the [omission] *neglect* of those ceremonies.

'That their merits filled the world [and] *or that* there was no [room for] *hope of* more.'

I have not confined myself to the order of the *Lives*, in making my few remarks. Indeed a different order is observed in the original publication, and in the collection of Johnson's *Works*. And should it be objected, that many of my various readings are inconsiderable, those who make the objection will be pleased to consider, that such small particulars are intended for those who are nicely critical in composition, to whom they will be an acceptable selection.

Spence's Anecdotes, which are frequently quoted and referred to in Johnson's *Lives of the Poets*, are in a manuscript collection, made by the Reverend Mr. Joseph Spence, containing a number of particulars concerning eminent men. To each anecdote is marked the name of the person on whose authority it is mentioned. This valuable collection is the property of the Duke of Newcastle, who upon the application of Sir Lucas Pepys, was pleased to permit it to be put into the hands of Dr. Johnson, who I am sorry to think made but an aukward return. 'Great assistance (says he,) has been given me by Mr. Spence's Collection, of which I consider the communication as a favour worthy of publick acknowledgement;' but he has not owned to whom he was obliged; so that the acknowledgement is unappropriated to his Grace.

While the world in general was filled with admiration of Johnson's *Lives of the Poets*, there were narrow circles in which prejudice and resentment were fostered, and from which attacks of different sorts issued against him.[1] By some violent Whigs he was arraigned of injustice to Milton; by some Cambridge men of depreciating Gray; and his expressing with a dignified freedom what he really thought of George, Lord Lyttelton, gave offence to some of the friends of that nobleman, and particularly produced a declaration of war against him from Mrs. Montagu, the ingenious Essayist on Shakspeare, between whom and his Lordship a commerce of reciprocal compliments had long been carried on. In this war the smaller powers in alliance with him were of course led to engage, at least on the defensive, and thus I for one was excluded from the enjoyment of 'A Feast of Reason,' such as Mr. Cumberland has described, with a keen, yet just and delicate pen, in his *Observer*. These minute inconveniencies gave not the least disturbance to Johnson. He nobly said, when I talked to him of the feeble, though shrill outcry which had been raised, 'Sir, I considered myself as entrusted with a certain portion of truth. I have given my opinion sincerely; let them shew where they think me wrong.'

[1] From this disreputable class, I except an ingenious though not satisfactory defence of HAMMOND, which I did not see till lately, by the favour of its authour, my amiable friend, the Reverend Mr. Bevill, who published it without his name. It is a juvenile performance, but elegantly written, with classical enthusiasm of sentiment, and yet with a becoming modesty, and great respect for Dr. Johnson.

While my friend is thus contemplated in the splendour derived from his last and perhaps most admirable work, I introduce him with peculiar propriety as the correspondent of WARREN HASTINGS, a man whose regard reflects dignity even upon JOHNSON; a man, the extent of whose abilities was equal to that of his power; and who, by those who are fortunate enough to know him in private life, is admired for his literature and taste, and beloved for the candour, moderation, and mildness of his character. Were I capable of paying a suitable tribute of admiration to him, I should certainly not withhold it at a moment[1] when it is not possible that I should be suspected of being an interested flatterer. But how weak would be my voice after that of the millions whom he governed. His condescending and obliging compliance with my solicitation, I with humble gratitude acknowledge; and while by publishing his letter to me, accompanying the valuable communication, I do eminent honour to my great friend, I shall entirely disregard any invidious suggestions, that as I in some degree participate in the honour, I have, at the same time, the gratification of my own vanity in view.

'*To* JAMES BOSWELL, ESQ.

'SIR,   'Park-lane, Dec. 2, 1790.

'I have been fortunately spared the troublesome suspense of a long search, to which, in performance of my promise, I had devoted this morning, by lighting upon the objects of it among the first papers that I laid my hands on: my veneration for your great and good friend, Dr. Johnson, and the pride, or I hope something of a better sentiment, which I indulged in possessing such memorials of his good will towards me, having induced me to bind them in a parcel containing other select papers, and labelled with the titles appertaining to them. They consist but of three letters, which I believe were all that I ever received from Dr. Johnson. Of these, one, which was written in quadruplicate, under the different dates of its respective dispatches, has already been made publick, but not from any communication of mine. This, however, I have joined to the rest; and have now

[1] January 1791.

the pleasure of sending them to you for the use to which you informed me it was your desire to destine them.

'My promise was pledged with the condition, that if the letters were found to contain any thing which should render them improper for the publick eye, you would dispense with the performance of it. You will have the goodness, I am sure, to pardon my recalling this stipulation to your recollection, as I should be loth to appear negligent of that obligation which is always implied in an epistolary confidence. In the reservation of that right I have read them over with the most scrupulous attention, but have not seen in them the slightest cause on that ground to withhold them from you. But, though not on that, yet on another ground I own I feel a little, yet but a little, reluctance to part with them: I mean on that of my own credit, which I fear will suffer by the information conveyed by them, that I was early in the possession of such valuable instructions for the beneficial employment of the influence of my late station, and (as it may seem,) have so little availed myself of them. Whether I could, if it were necessary, defend myself against such an imputation, it little concerns the world to know. I look only to the effect which these relicks may produce, considered as evidences of the virtues of their authour: and believing that they will be found to display an uncommon warmth of private friendship, and a mind ever attentive to the improvement and extension of useful knowledge, and solicitous for the interests of mankind, I can cheerfully submit to the little sacrifice of my own fame, to contribute to the illustration of so great and venerable a character. They cannot be better applied, for that end, than by being entrusted to your hands. Allow me, with this offering, to infer from it a proof of the very great esteem with which I have the honour to profess myself, Sir, your most obedient and most humble servant,

'WARREN HASTINGS.'

'*P.S.* At some future time, and when you have no further occasion for these papers, I shall be obliged to you if you would return them.'

The last of the three letters thus graciously put into my hands, and which has already appeared in publick, belongs to this year; but I shall previously insert the first two in the order of their dates. They altogether form a grand group in my biographical picture.

To THE HONOURABLE WARREN HASTINGS, ESQ.

'SIR,—Though I have had but little personal knowledge of you, I have had enough to make me wish for more; and though it be now a long time since I was honoured by your visit, I had too much pleasure from it to forget it. By those whom we delight to remember, we are unwilling to be forgotten; and therefore I cannot omit this opportunity of reviving myself in your memory by a letter which you will receive from the hands of my friend Mr. Chambers;[1] a man, whose purity of manners and vigour of mind are sufficient to make every thing welcome that he brings.

'That this is my only reason for writing, will be too apparent by the uselessness of my letter to any other purpose. I have no questions to ask; not that I want curiosity after either the ancient or present state of regions in which have been seen all the power and splendour of wide-extended empire; and which, as by some grant of natural superiority, supply the rest of the world with almost all that pride desires, and luxury enjoys. But my knowledge of them is too scanty to furnish me with proper topicks of enquiry; I can only wish for information; and hope, that a mind comprehensive like yours will find leisure, amidst the cares of your important station, to enquire into many subjects of which the European world either thinks not at all, or thinks with deficient intelligence and uncertain conjecture. I shall hope, that he who once intended to increase the learning of his country by the introduction of the Persian language, will examine nicely the traditions and histories of the East; that he will survey the wonders[2] of its ancient edifices, and trace the vestiges of its

---

[1] Afterwards Sir Robert Chambers, one of his Majesty's Judges in India.
[2] [Johnson wrote *remains.*]

ruined cities; and that, at his return, we shall know the arts and opinions of a race of men, from whom very little has been hitherto derived.

'You, Sir, have no need of being told by me, how much may be added by your attention and patronage to experimental knowledge and natural history. There are arts of manufacture practised in the countries in which you preside, which are yet very imperfectly known here, either to artificers or philosophers. Of the natural productions, animate and inanimate, we yet have so little intelligence, that our books are filled, I fear, with conjectures about things which an Indian peasant knows by his senses.

'Many of those things my first wish is to see; my second to know by such accounts as a man like you will be able to give.

'As I have not skill to ask proper questions, I have likewise no such access to great men as can enable me to send you any political information. Of the agitations of an unsettled government, and the struggles of a feeble ministry, care is doubtless taken to give you more exact accounts than I can obtain. If you are inclined to interest yourself much in publick transactions, it is no misfortune to you to be so distant from them.

'That literature is not totally forsaking us, and that your favourite language is not neglected, will appear from the book,[1] which I should have pleased myself more with sending, if I could have presented[2] it bound: but time was wanting. I beg, however, Sir, that you will accept it from a man very desirous of your regard; and that if you think me able to gratify you by any thing more important, you will employ me.

'I am now going to take leave, perhaps a very long leave, of my dear Mr. Chambers. That he is going to live where you govern, may justly alleviate the regret of parting; and the hope of seeing both him[3] and you again, which I am not willing to mingle with doubt, must at present comfort[4] as it can, Sir, your most humble servant,

'March 30, 1774.'   'SAM JOHNSON.'

---

[1] Jones's *Persian Grammar*.   [2] [Johnson wrote *procured*.]
[3] [Johnson wrote *them*.]   [4] [Johnson wrote *content*.]

To THE SAME

'SIR,—Being informed that by the departure of a ship, there is now an opportunity of writing to Bengal, I am unwilling to slip out of your memory by my own negligence, and therefore take the liberty of reminding you of my existence, by sending you a book which is not yet made publick.

'I have lately visited a region less remote, and less illustrious than India, which afforded some occasions for speculation; what has occurred to me, I have put into the volume,[1] of which I beg your acceptance.

'Men in your station seldom have presents totally disinterested; my book is received, let me now make my request.

'There is, Sir, somewhere within your government, a young adventurer, one Chauncey Lawrence, whose father is one of my oldest friends. Be pleased to shew the young man what countenance is fit, whether he wants to be restrained by your authority, or encouraged by your favour. His father is now President of the College of Physicians, a man venerable for his knowledge, and more venerable for his virtue.

'I wish you a prosperous government, a safe return, and a long enjoyment of plenty and tranquillity. I am, Sir, your most obedient and most humble servant,

'London, Dec. 20, 1774.'   'SAM. JOHNSON.'

To THE SAME

'SIR,   'Jan. 9[2], 1781.

'Amidst the importance and multiplicity of affairs in which your great office engages you, I take the liberty of recalling your attention for a moment to literature, and will not prolong the interruption by an apology, which your character makes needless.

'Mr. Hoole, a gentleman long known, and long esteemed in the India-House, after having translated Tasso, has undertaken Ariosto. How well he is qualified for his undertaking he has already shewn. He is desirous, Sir, of your favour in promoting

---

[1] *Journey to the Western Islands of Scotland.*
[2] [The holograph, in the British Museum, is dated Jan. 29.]

his proposals, and flatters me by supposing that my testimony may advance his interest.

'It is a new thing for a clerk of the India-House to translate poets;—it is new for a Governour of Bengal to patronize learning. That he may find his ingenuity rewarded, and that learning may flourish under your protection, is the wish of, Sir, your most humble servant,

'SAM. JOHNSON.'

I wrote to him in February, complaining of having been troubled by a recurrence of the perplexing question of Liberty and Necessity; and mentioning that I hoped soon to meet him again in London.

'To JAMES BOSWELL, ESQ.

'DEAR SIR,—I hoped you had got rid of all this hypocrisy of misery. What have you to do with Liberty and Necessity? Or what more than to hold your tongue about it? Do not doubt but I shall be most heartily glad to see you here again, for I love every part about you but your affectation of distress.

'I have at last finished my *Lives*, and have laid up for you a load of copy, all out of order, so that it will amuse you a long time to set it right. Come to me, my dear Bozzy, and let us be as happy as we can. We will go again to the Mitre, and talk old times over. I am, dear Sir, yours affectionately,

'March 14, 1781.'   'SAM. JOHNSON.'

On Monday, March 19, I arrived in London, and on Tuesday, the 20th, met him in Fleet-street, walking, or rather indeed moving along; for his peculiar march is thus described in a very just and picturesque manner, in a short Life[1] of him published very soon after his death:—'When he walked the streets, what

---

[1] Published by Kearsley, with this well-chosen motto:—

'From his cradle
He was a SCHOLAR, and a ripe and good one:
And to add greater honours to his age
Than man could give him, he died fearing Heaven.'

SHAKSPEARE.

with the constant roll of his head, and the concomitant motion of his body, he appeared to make his way by that motion, independent of his feet.' That he was often much stared at while he advanced in this manner, may easily be believed; but it was not safe to make sport of one so robust as he was. Mr. Langton saw him one day, in a fit of absence, by a sudden start, drive the load off a porter's back, and walk forward briskly, without being conscious of what he had done. The porter was very angry, but stood still, and eyed the huge figure with much earnestness, till he was satisfied that his wisest course was to be quiet, and take up his burthen again.

Our accidental meeting in the street after a long separation was a pleasing surprize to us both. He stepped aside with me into Falcon-court, and made kind inquiries about my family, and as we were in a hurry going different ways, I promised to call on him next day; he said he was engaged to go out in the morning. 'Early, Sir?' said I. JOHNSON. 'Why, Sir, a London morning does not go with the sun.'

I waited on him next evening, and he gave me a great portion of his original manuscript of his *Lives of the Poets*, which he had preserved for me.

I found on visiting his friend, Mr. Thrale, that he was now very ill, and had removed, I suppose by the solicitation of Mrs. Thrale, to a house in Grosvenor-square. I was sorry to see him sadly changed in his appearance.

He told me I might now have the pleasure to see Dr. Johnson drink wine again, for he had lately returned to it. When I mentioned this to Johnson, he said, 'I drink it now sometimes, but not socially.' The first evening that I was with him at Thrale's, I observed he poured a quantity of it into a large glass, and swallowed it greedily. Every thing about his character and manners was forcible and violent; there never was any moderation; many a day did he fast, many a year did he refrain from wine; but when he did eat, it was voraciously; when he did drink wine, it was copiously. He could practise abstinence, but not temperance.

Mrs. Thrale and I had a dispute, whether Shakspeare or

Milton had drawn the most admirable picture of a man.[1] I was for Shakspeare; Mrs. Thrale for Milton; and after a fair hearing, Johnson decided for my opinion.

I told him of one of Mr. Burke's playful sallies upon Dean Marlay: 'I don't like the Deanery of *Ferns*, it sounds so like a *barren* title.'—'Dr. *Heath* should have it;' said I. Johnson laughed, and condescending to trifle in the same mode of conceit, suggested Dr. *Moss*.

He said, 'Mrs. Montagu has dropt me. Now, Sir, there are people whom one should like very well to drop, but would not wish to be dropped by.' He certainly was vain of the society of ladies, and could make himself very agreeable to them, when he chose it; Sir Joshua Reynolds agreed with me that he could. Mr. Gibbon, with his usual sneer, controverted it, perhaps in resentment of Johnson's having talked with some disgust of his ugliness, which one would think a *philosopher* would not mind. Dean Marlay wittily observed, 'A lady may be vain when she can turn a wolf-dog into a lap-dog.'

The election for Ayrshire, my own county, was this spring tried upon a petition, before a Committee of the House of Commons. I was one of the Counsel for the sitting member, and took the liberty of previously stating different points to Johnson, who never failed to see them clearly, and to supply me with some good hints. He dictated to me the following note upon the registration of deeds:—

'All laws are made for the convenience of the community;

[1] Shakspeare makes Hamlet thus describe his father:—

> 'See what a grace was seated on this brow:
> Hyperion's curls, the front of Jove himself,
> An eye like Mars, to threaten and command;
> A station like the herald, Mercury,
> New-lighted on a heaven-kissing hill;
> A combination, and a form, indeed,
> Where every god did seem to set his seal,
> To give the world assurance of a man.' [III. iv.]

Milton thus pourtrays our first parent, Adam:—

> 'His fair large front and eye sublime declar'd
> Absolute rule; and hyacinthin locks
> Round from his parted forelock manly hung
> Clust'ring, but not beneath his shoulders broad.' [*Par. Lost*, iv. 300.]

what is legally done, should be legally recorded, that the state of things may be known, and that wherever evidence is requisite, evidence may be had. For this reason, the obligation to frame and establish a legal register is enforced by a legal penalty, which penalty is the want of that perfection and plenitude of right which a register would give. Thence it follows, that this is not an objection merely legal; for the reason on which the law stands being equitable, makes it an equitable objection.'

'This (said he,) you must enlarge on, when speaking to the Committee. You must not argue there as if you were arguing in the schools; close reasoning will not fix their attention; you must say the same thing over and over again, in different words. If you say it but once, they miss it in a moment of inattention. It is unjust, Sir, to censure lawyers for multiplying words when they argue; it is often *necessary* for them to multiply words.'

His notion of the duty of a member of Parliament, sitting upon an election-committee, was very high; and when he was told of a gentleman[1] upon one of those committees, who read the newspapers part of the time, and slept the rest, while the merits of a vote were examined by the counsel; and as an excuse, when challenged by the chairman for such behaviour, bluntly answered, 'I had made up my mind upon that case;'—Johnson, with an indignant contempt, said, 'If he was such a rogue as to make up his mind upon a case without hearing it, he should not have been such a fool as to tell it.' 'I think (said Mr. Dudley Long, now North,) the Doctor has pretty plainly made him out to be both rogue and fool.'

Johnson's profound reverence for the Hierarchy made him expect from bishops the highest degree of decorum; he was offended even at their going to taverns; 'A bishop[2] (said he,) has nothing to do at a tippling-house. It is not indeed immoral in him to go to a tavern; neither would it be immoral in him to whip a top in Grosvenor-square. But, if he did, I hope the boys would fall upon him and apply the whip to *him*. There are gradations in conduct; there is morality,—decency,—propriety. None of these should be violated by a bishop. A bishop should

---

[1] [William Strahan. *Boswell Papers*, xiv. 181.]
[2] [Bishop Shipley of St. Asaph is here glanced at.]

not go to a house where he may meet a young fellow leading out a wench.' BOSWELL. 'But, Sir, every tavern does not admit women.' JOHNSON. 'Depend upon it, Sir, any tavern will admit a well-drest man and a well-drest woman; they will not perhaps admit a woman whom they see every night walking by their door, in the street. But a well-drest man may lead in a well-drest woman to any tavern in London. Taverns sell meat and drink, and will sell them to any body who can eat and can drink. You may as well say that a mercer will not sell silks to a woman of the town.'

He also disapproved of bishops going to routs, at least of their staying at them longer than their presence commanded respect. He mentioned a particular bishop. 'Poh! (said Mrs. Thrale,) the Bishop of————[1] is never minded at a rout.' BOSWELL. 'When a bishop places himself in a situation where he has no distinct character, and is of no consequence, he degrades the dignity of his order.' JOHNSON. 'Mr. Boswell, Madam, has said it as correctly as could be.'

Nor was it only in the dignitaries of the Church that Johnson required a particular decorum and delicacy of behaviour; he justly considered that the clergy, as persons set apart for the sacred office of serving at the altar, and impressing the minds of men with the aweful concerns of a future state, should be somewhat more serious than the generality of mankind, and have a suitable composure of manners. A due sense of the dignity of their profession, independent of higher motives, will ever prevent them from losing their distinction in an indiscriminate sociality; and did such as affect this, know how much it lessens them in the eyes of those whom they think to please by it, they would feel themselves much mortified.

Johnson and his friend, Beauclerk, were once together in company with several clergymen, who thought that they should appear to advantage, by assuming the lax jollity of *men of the world*; which, as it may be observed in similar cases, they carried to noisy excess. Johnson, who they expected would be *entertained*, sat grave and silent for some time; at last, turning to Beauclerk,

---

[1] [Bp. Porteus of Chester. *Boswell Papers*, xiv. 175.]

he said, by no means in a whisper, 'This merriment of parsons is mighty offensive.'

Even the dress of a clergyman should be in character, and nothing can be more despicable than conceited attempts at avoiding the appearance of the clerical order; attempts, which are as ineffectual as they are pitiful. Dr. Porteus, now Bishop of London, in his excellent charge when presiding over the diocese of Chester, justly animadverts upon this subject; and observes of a reverend fop, that he 'can be but *half a beau.*'

Addison, in *The Spectator*,[1] has given us a fine portrait of a clergyman, who is supposed to be a member of his *Club*; and Johnson has exhibited a model, in the character of Mr. Mudge,[2] which has escaped the collectors of his works, but which he owned to me, and which indeed he shewed to Sir Joshua Reynolds at the time when it was written. It bears the genuine marks of Johnson's best manner, and is as follows:—

'The Reverend Mr. *Zacariah Mudge*, Prebendary of Exeter, and Vicar of St. Andrew's in Plymouth; a man equally eminent for his virtues and abilities, and at once beloved as a companion and reverenced as a pastor. He had that general curiosity to which no kind of knowledge is indifferent or superfluous; and that general benevolence by which no order of men is hated or despised.

'His principles both of thought and action were great and comprehensive. By a solicitous examination of objections, and judicious comparison of opposite arguments, he attained what enquiry never gives but to industry and perspicuity, a firm and unshaken settlement of conviction. But his firmness was without asperity; for, knowing with how much difficulty truth was sometimes found, he did not wonder that many missed it.

'The general course of his life was determined by his profession; he studied the sacred volumes in the original languages; with what diligence and success, his *Notes upon the Psalms* give sufficient evidence. He once endeavoured to add the knowledge of Arabick to that of Hebrew; but finding his thoughts too much diverted from other studies, after some time, desisted from his purpose.

[1] [No. 2.]   [2] See p. 267.

'His discharge of parochial duties was exemplary. How his *Sermons* were composed, may be learned from the excellent volume which he has given to the publick; but how they were delivered, can be known only to those that heard them; for as he appeared in the pulpit, words will not easily describe him. His delivery, though unconstrained was not negligent, and though forcible was not turbulent; disdaining anxious nicety of emphasis, and laboured artifice of action, it captivated the hearer by its natural dignity, it roused the sluggish, and fixed the volatile, and detained the mind upon the subject, without directing it to the speaker.

'The grandeur and solemnity of the preacher did not intrude upon his general behaviour; at the table of his friends he was a companion communicative and attentive, of unaffected manners, of manly cheerfulness, willing to please, and easy to be pleased. His acquaintance was universally solicited, and his presence obstructed no enjoyment which religion did not forbid. Though studious he was popular; though argumentative he was modest; though inflexible he was candid; and though metaphysical yet orthodox.'[1]

On Friday, March 30, I dined with him at Sir Joshua Reynolds's, with the Earl of Charlemont, Sir Annesley Stewart, Mr. Eliot of Port-Eliot, Mr. Burke, Dean Marlay, Mr. Langton; a most agreeable day, of which I regret that every circumstance is not preserved; but it is unreasonable to require such a multiplication of felicity.

Mr. Eliot, with whom Dr. Walter Harte had travelled, talked to us of his *History of Gustavus Adolphus*, which he said was a very good book in the German translation. J O H N S O N. 'Harte was excessively vain. He put copies of his book in manuscript into the hands of Lord Chesterfield and Lord Granville, that they might revise it. Now, how absurd was it to suppose that two such noblemen would revise so big a manuscript. Poor man! he left London the day of the publication of his book, that

---

[1] *London Chronicle*, May 2, 1769. This respectable man is there mentioned to have died on the 3rd of April, that year, at Cofflect [Coffleet], the seat of Thomas Veale, Esq. in his way to London.

he might be out of the way of the great praise he was to receive; and he was ashamed to return, when he found how ill his book had succeeded. It was unlucky in coming out on the same day with Robertson's *History of Scotland*. His husbandry, however, is good.' BOSWELL. 'So he was fitter for that than for heroick history: he did well when he turned his sword into a plough-share.'

Mr. Eliot mentioned a curious liquor peculiar to his country, which the Cornish fishermen drink. They call it *Mahogany*; and it is made of two parts gin, and one part treacle, well beaten together. I begged to have some of it made, which was done with proper skill by Mr. Eliot. I thought it very good liquor; and said it was a counterpart of what is called *Athol Porridge* in the Highlands of Scotland, which is a mixture of whisky and honey. Johnson said, 'that must be a better liquor than the Cornish, for both its component parts are better.' He also observed, '*Mahogany* must be a modern name; for it is not long since the wood called mahogany was known in this country.' I mentioned his scale of liquors;—claret for boys,—port for men,— brandy for heroes. 'Then (said Mr. Burke,) let me have claret: I love to be a boy; to have the careless gaiety of boyish days.' JOHNSON. 'I should drink claret too, if it would give me that; but it does not: it neither makes boys men, nor men boys. You'll be drowned by it, before it has any effect upon you.'

I ventured to mention a ludicrous paragraph in the news-papers, that Dr. Johnson was learning to dance of Vestris. Lord Charlemont, wishing to excite him to talk, proposed, in a whisper, that he should be asked, whether it was true. 'Shall I ask him?' said his Lordship. We were, by a great majority, clear for the experiment. Upon which his Lordship very gravely, and with a courteous air said, 'Pray, Sir, is it true that you are taking lessons of Vestris?' This was risking a good deal, and required the boldness of a General of Irish Volunteers to make the attempt. Johnson was at first startled, and in some heat answered, 'How can your Lordship ask so simple a question?' But immediately recovering himself, whether from unwillingness to be deceived, or to appear deceived, or whether from real good humour, he kept up the joke: 'Nay, but if any body were to answer the paragraph, and contradict it, I'd have a reply, and would say, that he who contradicted it was no friend either to Vestris or me. For why should not Dr. Johnson add to his other powers a little corporeal agility? Socrates learnt to dance at an advanced age, and Cato learnt Greek at an advanced age. Then it might proceed to say, that this Johnson, not content with dancing on the ground, might dance on the rope; and they might introduce the elephant dancing on the rope. A nobleman[1] wrote a play, called *Love in a hollow Tree*. He found out that it was a bad one, and therefore wished to buy up all the copies, and burn them. The Duchess of Marlborough had kept one; and when he was against her at an election, she had a new edition of it printed, and prefixed to it, as a frontispiece, an elephant dancing on a rope; to shew, that his Lordship's writing comedy was as aukward as an elephant dancing on a rope.'

On Sunday, April 1, I dined with him at Mr. Thrale's, with Sir Philip Jennings Clerk and Mr. Perkins,[2] who had the superintendence of Mr. Thrale's brewery, with a salary of five hundred pounds a year. Sir Philip had the appearance of a gentleman of ancient family, well advanced in life. He wore his own white hair in a bag of goodly size, a black velvet coat, with an embroidered waistcoat, and very rich laced ruffles; which Mrs. Thrale said were old fashioned, but which, for that reason, I thought the more respectable, more like a Tory; yet Sir Philip was then in Opposition in Parliament. 'Ah, Sir, (said Johnson,) ancient ruffles and modern principles do not agree.' Sir Philip defended the Opposition to the American war ably and with temper, and I joined him. He said, the majority of the nation was against the ministry. JOHNSON. '*I*, Sir, am against the ministry; but it is for having too little of that, of which Opposition thinks they have too much. Were I minister, if any man wagged his finger against me, he should be turned out; for that which it is in the power of Government to give at pleasure to one or to another, should be given to the supporters of Government. If you will not

---

[1] William, the first Viscount Grimston.
[2] See p. 568.

oppose at the expence of losing your place, your opposition will not be honest, you will feel no serious grievance; and the present opposition is only a contest to get what others have. Sir Robert Walpole acted as I would do. As to the American war, the *sense* of the nation is *with* the ministry. The majority of those who can *understand* is with it; the majority of those who can only *hear* is against it; and as those who can only hear are more numerous than those who can understand, and Opposition is always loudest, a majority of the rabble will be for Opposition.'

This boisterous vivacity entertained us; but the truth in my opinion was, that those who could understand the best were against the American war, as almost every man now is, when the question has been coolly considered.

Mrs. Thrale gave high praise to Mr. Dudley Long, (now North). JOHNSON. 'Nay, my dear lady, don't talk so. Mr. Long's character is very *short*. It is nothing. He fills a chair. He is a man of genteel appearance, and that is all.[1] I know nobody who blasts by praise as you do: for whenever there is exaggerated praise, every body is set against a character. They are provoked to attack it. Now there is Pepys;[2] you praised that man with such disproportion, that I was incited to lessen him, perhaps more than he deserves. His blood is upon your head. By the same principle, your malice defeats itself; for your censure is too violent. And yet, (looking to her with a leering smile,) she is the first woman in the world, could she but restrain that wicked tongue of hers;—she would be the only woman, could she but command that little whirligig.'

[1] Here Johnson condescended to play upon the words *Long* and *short*. But little did he know that, owing to Mr. Long's reserve in his presence, he was talking thus of a gentleman distinguished amongst his acquaintance for acuteness of wit; one to whom I think the French expression, '*Il pétille d'esprit*,' is particularly suited. He has gratified me by mentioning that he heard Dr. Johnson say, 'Sir, if I were to lose Boswell, it would be a limb amputated.'

[2] William Weller Pepys, Esq., one of the Masters in the High Court of Chancery, and well known in polite circles. My acquaintance with him is not sufficient to enable me to speak of him from my own judgement. But I know that both at Eton and Oxford he was the intimate friend of the late Sir James Macdonald, the *Marcellus* of Scotland, whose extraordinary talents, learning, and virtues, will ever be remembered with admiration and regret.

Upon the subject of exaggerated praise I took the liberty to say, that I thought there might be very high praise given to a known character which deserved it, and therefore it would not be exaggerated. Thus, one might say of Mr. Edmund Burke, He is a very wonderful man. JOHNSON. 'No, Sir, you would not be safe if another man had a mind perversely to contradict. He might answer, "Where is all the wonder? Burke is, to be sure, a man of uncommon abilities, with a great quantity of matter in his mind, and a great fluency of language in his mouth. But we are not to be stunned and astonished by him." So you see, Sir, even Burke would suffer, not from any fault of his own, but from your folly.'

Mrs. Thrale mentioned a gentleman[1] who had acquired a fortune of four thousand a year in trade, but was absolutely miserable, because he could not talk in company; so miserable, that he was impelled to lament his situation in the street to ******,[2] whom he hates, and who he knows despises him. 'I am a most unhappy man, (said he). I am invited to conversations. I go to conversations; but, alas! I have no conversation.' JOHNSON. 'Man commonly cannot be successful in different ways. This gentleman has spent, in getting four thousand pounds a year, the time in which he might have learnt to talk; and now he cannot talk.' Mr. Perkins made a shrewd and droll remark: 'If he had got his four thousand a year as a mountebank, he might have learnt to talk at the same time that he was getting his fortune.'

Some other gentlemen[3] came in. The conversation concerning the person whose character Dr. Johnson had treated so slightingly, as he did not know his merit, was resumed. Mrs. Thrale said, 'You think so of him, Sir, because he is quiet, and does not exert himself with force. You'll be saying the same thing of Mr. *****[4] there, who sits as quiet—.' This was not well-bred; and Johnson did not let it pass without correction. 'Nay, Madam, what right have you to talk thus? Both Mr. ***** and I have

---

[1] [Charles Selwyn. *Boswell Papers*, xiv. 186.]   [2] [William Seward. *Ib.*]
[3] [Seward, Sir John Lade, and Henry Smith. *Ib.* 187.]
[4] [Henry Smith. *Ib.*]

reason to take it ill. *You* may talk so of Mr. *****; but why do you make *me* do it? Have I said anything against Mr. *****? You have *set* him, that I might shoot him: but I have not shot him.'

One of the gentlemen[1] said, he had seen three folio volumes of Dr. Johnson's sayings collected by me. 'I must put you right, Sir, (said I,) for I am very exact in authenticity. You could not see folio volumes, for I have none: you might have seen some in quarto and octavo. This is inattention which one should guard against.' JOHNSON. 'Sir, it is a want of concern about veracity. He does not know that he saw *any* volumes. If he had seen them he could have remembered their size.'

Mr. Thrale appeared very lethargick to-day. I saw him again on Monday evening, at which time he was not thought to be in immediate danger; but early in the morning of Wednesday, the 4th, he expired. Johnson was in the house, and thus mentions the event: 'I felt almost the last flutter of his pulse, and looked for the last time upon the face that for fifteen years had never been turned upon me but with respect and benignity.'[2] Upon that day there was a *Call* of THE LITERARY CLUB; but Johnson apologised for his absence by the following note:—

'MR. JOHNSON knows that Sir Joshua Reynolds and the other gentlemen will excuse his incompliance with the Call, when they are told that Mr. Thrale died this morning.—Wednesday.'

Mr. Thrale's death was a very essential loss to Johnson, who, although he did not foresee all that afterwards happened, was sufficiently convinced that the comforts which Mr. Thrale's family afforded him, would now in a great measure cease. He, however, continued to shew a kind attention to his widow and children as long as it was acceptable; and he took upon him, with a very earnest concern, the office of one of his executors, the importance of which seemed greater than usual to him, from his circumstances having been always such, that he had scarcely any share in the real business of life. His friends of THE CLUB were in hopes that Mr. Thrale might have made a liberal

[1] [William Seward. *Ib.*]   [2] *Pr. and Med.* p. 191.

provision for him for his life, which, as Mr. Thrale left no son, and a very large fortune, it would have been highly to his honour to have done; and, considering Dr. Johnson's age, could not have been of long duration; but he bequeathed him only two hundred pounds, which was the legacy given to each of his executors. I could not but be somewhat diverted by hearing Johnson talk in a pompous manner of his new office, and particularly of the concerns of the brewery, which it was at last resolved should be sold. Lord Lucan tells a very good story, which, if not precisely exact, is certainly characteristical: that when the sale of Thrale's brewery was going forward, Johnson appeared bustling about, with an ink-horn and pen in his button-hole, like an excise-man; and on being asked what he really considered to be the value of the property which was to be disposed of, answered, 'We are not here to sell a parcel of boilers and vats, but the potentiality of growing rich, beyond the dreams of avarice.'

On Friday, April 6, he carried me to dine at a club, which, at his desire, had been lately formed at the Queen's Arms, in St. Paul's Church-yard. He told Mr. Hoole, that he wished to have a *City Club*, and asked him to collect one; but, said he, 'Don't let them be *patriots*.' The company to-day were very sensible, well-behaved men. I have preserved only two particulars of his conversation. He said he was glad Lord George Gordon had escaped, rather than that a precedent should be established for hanging a man for *constructive treason*; which, in consistency with his true, manly, constitutional Toryism, he considered would be a dangerous engine of arbitrary power. And upon its being mentioned that an opulent and very indolent Scotch nobleman, who totally resigned the management of his affairs to a man of knowledge and abilities, had claimed some merit by saying, 'The next best thing to managing a man's own affairs well is being sensible of incapacity, and not attempting it, but having full confidence in one who can do it.' JOHNSON. 'Nay, Sir, this is paltry. There is a middle course. Let a man give application; and depend upon it he will soon get above a despicable state of helplessness, and attain the power of acting for himself.'

On Saturday, April 7, I dined with him at Mr. Hoole's, with Governour Bouchier and Captain Orme, both of whom had been long in the East-Indies; and being men of good sense and observation, were very entertaining. Johnson defended the oriental regulation of different *casts* of men, which was objected to as totally destructive of the hopes of rising in society by personal merit. He shewed that there was a *principle* in it sufficiently plausible by analogy. 'We see (said he,) in metals that there are different species; and so likewise in animals, though one species may not differ very widely from another, as in the species of dogs,—the cur, the spaniel, the mastiff. The Bramins are the mastiffs of mankind.'

On Thursday, April 12, I dined with him at a Bishop's,[1] where were Sir Joshua Reynolds, Mr. Berrenger, and some more company. He had dined the day before at another Bishop's.[2] I have unfortunately recorded none of his conversation at the Bishop's where we dined together: but I have preserved his ingenious defence of his dining twice abroad in Passion-week; a laxity, in which I am convinced he would not have indulged himself at the time when he wrote his solemn paper in *The Rambler*, upon that aweful season. It appeared to me, that by being much more in company, and enjoying more luxurious living, he had contracted a keener relish of pleasure, and was consequently less rigorous in his religious rites. This he would not acknowledge; but he reasoned, with admirable sophistry, as follows: 'Why, Sir, a Bishop's calling company together in this week is, to use the vulgar phrase, not *the thing*. But you must consider laxity is a bad thing; but preciseness is also a bad thing; and your general character may be more hurt by preciseness than by dining with a Bishop in Passion-week. There might be a handle for reflection. It might be said, "He refused to dine with a Bishop in Passion-week, but was three Sundays absent from Church."' BOSWELL. 'Very true, Sir. But suppose a man to be uniformly of good conduct, would it not be better that he should refuse to dine with a Bishop in this week, and so not encourage

---

[1] [Porteus of Chester. *Boswell Papers*, xiv. 196.]
[2] [Shipley of St. Asaph. *Ib.*]

a bad practice by his example?' JOHNSON. 'Why, Sir, you are to consider whether you might not do more harm by lessening the influence of a Bishop's character by your disapprobation in refusing him, than by going to him.'

To MRS. LUCY PORTER, *in Lichfield*

'DEAR MADAM,—Life is full of troubles. I have just lost my dear friend Thrale. I hope he is happy; but I have had a great loss. I am otherwise pretty well. I require some care of myself, but that care is not ineffectual; and when I am out of order, I think it often my own fault.

'The spring is now making quick advances. As it is the season in which the whole world is enlivened and invigorated, I hope that both you and I shall partake of its benefits. My desire is to see Lichfield; but being left executor to my friend, I know not whether I can be spared; but I will try, for it is now long since we saw one another, and how little we can promise ourselves many more interviews, we are taught by hourly examples of mortality. Let us try to live so as that mortality may not be an evil. Write to me soon, my dearest; your letters will give me great pleasure.

'I am sorry that Mr. Porter has not had his box; but by sending it to Mr. Mathias, who very readily undertook its conveyance, I did the best I could, and perhaps before now he has it.

'Be so kind as to make my compliments to my friends; I have a great value for their kindness, and hope to enjoy it before summer is past. Do write to me. I am, dearest love, your most humble servant,

'London, April 12, 1781.'   'SAM. JOHNSON.'

On Friday, April 13, being Good-Friday, I went to St. Clement's church with him, as usual. There I saw again his old fellow-collegian, Edwards, to whom I said, 'I think, Sir, Dr. Johnson and you meet only at Church.'—'Sir, (said he,) it is the best place we can meet in, except Heaven, and I hope we shall meet there too.' Dr. Johnson told me, that there was very little communication between Edwards and him, after their unexpected renewal of acquaintance. 'But, (said he, smiling), he met me once, and said, "I am told you have written a very pretty book called *The Rambler*." I was unwilling that he should leave the world in total darkness, and sent him a set.'

Mr. Berenger[1] visited him to-day, and was very pleasing. We talked of an evening society for conversation at a house in town, of which we were all members, but of which Johnson said, 'It will never do, Sir. There is nothing served about there, neither tea, nor coffee, nor lemonade, nor any thing whatever; and depend upon it, Sir, a man does not love to go to a place from whence he comes out exactly as he went in.' I endeavoured, for argument's sake, to maintain that men of learning and talents might have very good intellectual society, without the aid of any little gratifications of the senses. Berenger joined with Johnson, and said, that without these any meeting would be dull and insipid. He would therefore have all the slight refreshments; nay, it would not be amiss to have some cold meat, and a bottle of wine upon a side-board. 'Sir, (said Johnson to me, with an air of triumph,) Mr. Berenger knows the world. Every body loves to have good things furnished to them without any trouble. I told Mrs. Thrale once, that as she did not choose to have card tables, she should have a profusion of the best sweet-meats, and she would be sure to have company enough come to her.' I agreed with my illustrious friend upon this subject; for it has pleased GOD to make man a composite animal, and where there is nothing to refresh the body, the mind will languish.

On Sunday, April 15, being Easter-day, after solemn worship in St. Paul's church, I found him alone; Dr. Scott, of the Commons, came in. He talked of its having been said, that Addison wrote some of his best papers in *The Spectator* when warm with wine. Dr. Johnson did not seem willing to admit this. Dr. Scott, as a confirmation of it, related, that Blackstone, a sober man, composed his *Commentaries* with a bottle of port before him;

[1] Richard Berenger, Esq., many years Gentleman of the Horse, and first equerry to his present Majesty. [M.] [See *ante*, p. 1133.]

and found his mind invigorated and supported in the fatigue of
his great work, by a temperate use of it.

I told him, that in a company where I had lately been, a
desire was expressed to know his authority for the shocking
story of Addison's sending an execution into Steele's house.[1]
'Sir, (said he,) it is generally known, it is known to all who are
acquainted with the literary history of that period. It is as well
known, as that he wrote *Cato*.' Mr. Thomas Sheridan once
defended Addison to me, by alledging that he did it in order to
cover Steele's goods from other creditors, who were going to
seize them.

We talked of the difference between the mode of education at
Oxford, and that in those Colleges where instruction is chiefly
conveyed by lectures. JOHNSON. Lectures were once useful;
but now, when all can read, and books are so numerous, lectures
are unnecessary. If your attention fails, and you miss a part of
a lecture, it is lost; you cannot go back as you do upon a book.'
Dr. Scott agreed with him. 'But yet (said I), Dr. Scott, you
yourself gave lectures at Oxford.' He smiled. 'You laughed
(then said I,) at those who came to you.'

Dr. Scott left us, and soon afterwards we went to dinner. Our
company consisted of Mrs. Williams, Mrs. Desmoulins, Mr.
Levett, Mr. Allen, the printer, and Mrs. Hall, sister of the
Reverend Mr. John Wesley, and resembling him, as I thought,
both in figure and manner. Johnson produced now, for the first
time, some handsome silver salvers, which he told me he had
bought fourteen years ago; so it was a great day. I was not a
little amused by observing Allen perpetually struggling to talk
in the manner of Johnson, like the little frog in the fable blowing
himself up to resemble the stately ox.

I mentioned a kind of religious Robinhood Society, which met
every Sunday evening, at Coachmakers'-hall, for free debate;
and that the subject for this night was, the text which relates,
with other miracles, which happened at our SAVIOUR's death,
'And the graves were opened, and many bodies of the saints
which slept arose, and came out of the graves after his resurrec-

[1] See this explained, *ante*, p. 1104.

tion, and went into the holy city, and appeared unto many.'
Mrs. Hall said it was a very curious subject, and she should like
to hear it discussed. JOHNSON. (somewhat warmly,) 'One
would not go to such a place to hear it,—one would not be seen
in such a place—to give countenance to such a meeting.' I,
however, resolved that I would go. 'But, Sir, (said she to
Johnson,) I should like to hear *you* discuss it.' He seemed reluc-
tant to engage in it. She talked of the resurrection of the human
race in general, and maintained that we shall be raised with the
same bodies. JOHNSON. 'Nay, Madam, we see that it is not to
be the same body; for the Scripture uses the illustration of grain
sown, and we know that the grain which grows is not the same
with what is sown. You cannot suppose that we shall rise with
a diseased body; it is enough if there be such a sameness as to
distinguish identity of person.' She seemed desirous of knowing
more, but he left the question in obscurity.

Of apparitions,[1] he observed, 'A total disbelief of them is
adverse to the opinion of the existence of the soul between death
and the last day; the question simply is, whether departed
spirits ever have the power of making themselves perceptible
to us; a man who thinks he has seen an apparition, can only be
convinced himself; his authority will not convince another, and
his conviction, if rational, must be founded on being told something which cannot be known but by supernatural means.'

He mentioned a thing as not unfrequent, of which I had never
heard before,—being *called*, that is, hearing one's name pronounced by the voice of a known person at a great distance, far
beyond the possibility of being reached by any sound uttered
by human organs. 'An acquaintance,[2] on whose veracity I can
depend, told me, that walking home one evening to Kilmarnock
he heard himself called from a wood, by the voice of a brother

---

[1] As this subject frequently recurs in these volumes, the reader may be
led erroneously to suppose that Dr. Johnson was so fond of such discussions,
as frequently to introduce them. But the truth is, that the authour himself
delighted in talking concerning ghosts, and what he has frequently denominated *the mysterious*; and therefore took every opportunity of *leading* Johnson
to converse on such subjects. [M.]

[2] [J. B.'s clerk, Brown. *Boswell Papers*, xiv. 200.]

who had gone to America; and the next packet brought accounts of that brother's death.' Macbean asserted that this inexplicable *calling* was a thing very well known. Dr. Johnson said, that one day at Oxford, as he was turning the key of his chamber, he heard his mother distinctly call *Sam*. She was then at Lichfield; but nothing ensued. This phænomenon is, I think, as wonderful as any other mysterious fact, which many people are very slow to believe, or rather, indeed, reject with an obstinate contempt.

Some time after this, upon his making a remark which escaped my attention, Mrs. Williams and Mrs. Hall were both together striving to answer him. He grew angry, and called out loudly, 'Nay, when you both speak at once, it is intolerable.' But checking himself, and softening, he said, 'This one may say, though you *are* ladies.' Then he brightened into gay humour, and addressed them in the words of one of the songs in *The Beggar's Opera*:—

'But two at a time there's no mortal can bear.'

'What, Sir, (said I,) are you going to turn Captain Macheath?' There was something as pleasantly ludicrous in this scene as can be imagined. The contrast between Macheath, Polly, and Lucy —and Dr. Samuel Johnson, blind, peevish Mrs. Williams, and lean, lank, preaching Mrs. Hall, was exquisite.

I stole away to Coachmakers'-hall, and heard the difficult text of which we had talked, discussed with great decency, and some intelligence, by several speakers. There was a difference of opinion as to the appearance of ghosts in modern times, though the arguments for it, supported by Mr. Addison's authority, preponderated. The immediate subject of debate was embarrassed by the *bodies* of the saints having been said to rise, and by the question what became of them afterwards; did they return again to their graves? or were they translated to heaven? Only one evangelist mentions the fact,[1] and the commentators whom I have looked at, do not make the passage clear. There is, however, no occasion for our understanding it farther, than to know that it was one of the extraordinary manifestations of

---

[1] *St. Matthew*, chap. xxvii. vv. 52, 53.

divine power, which accompanied the most important event that ever happened.

On Friday, April 20, I spent with him one of the happiest days that I remember to have enjoyed in the whole course of my life. Mrs. Garrick, whose grief for the loss of her husband was, I believe, as sincere as wounded affection and admiration could produce, had this day, for the first time since his death, a select party of his friends to dine with her. The company was Miss Hannah More, who lived with her, and whom she called her Chaplain; Mrs. Boscawen,[1] Mrs. Elizabeth Carter, Sir Joshua Reynolds, Dr. Burney, Dr. Johnson, and myself. We found ourselves very elegantly entertained at her house in the Adelphi, where I have passed many a pleasing hour with him 'who gladdened life.' She looked very well, talked of her husband with complacency, and while she cast her eyes on his portrait, which hung over the chimney-piece, said, that 'death was now the most agreeable object to her.' The very semblance of David Garrick was cheering. Mr. Beauclerk, with happy propriety, inscribed under that fine portrait of him, which by Lady Diana's kindness is now the property of my friend Mr. Langton, the following passage from his beloved Shakspeare:—

> 'A merrier man,
> Within the limit of becoming mirth,
> I never spent an hour's talk withal.
> His eye begets occasion for his wit;
> For every object that the one doth catch,
> The other turns to a mirth-moving jest;
> Which his fair tongue (Conceit's expositor)
> Delivers in such apt and gracious words,
> That aged ears play truant at his tales,
> And younger hearings are quite ravished:
> So sweet and voluble is his discourse.'

We were all in fine spirits; and I whispered to Mrs. Boscawen, 'I believe this is as much as can be made of life.' In addition to a splendid entertainment, we were regaled with Lichfield ale, which had a peculiar appropriated value. Sir

[1] See *ante,* p. 977.

Joshua, and Dr. Burney, and I, drank cordially of it to Dr. Johnson's health; and though he would not join us, he as cordially answered, 'Gentlemen, I wish you all as well as you do me.'

The general effect of this day dwells upon my mind in fond remembrance; but I do not find much conversation recorded. What I have preserved shall be faithfully given.

One of the company[1] mentioned Mr. Thomas Hollis, the strenuous Whig, who used to send over Europe presents of democratical books, with their boards stamped with daggers and caps of liberty. Mrs. Carter said, 'He was a bad man. He used to talk uncharitably.' JOHNSON. 'Poh! poh! Madam; who is the worse for being talked of uncharitably? Besides, he was a dull poor creature as ever lived: and I believe he would not have done harm to a man whom he knew to be of very opposite principles to his own. I remember once at the Society of Arts, when an advertisement was to be drawn up, he pointed me out as the man who could do it best. This, you will observe, was kindness to me. I however slipt away, and escaped it.'

Mrs. Carter having said of the same person, 'I doubt he was an Atheist.' JOHNSON. 'I don't know that. He might perhaps have become one, if he had had time to ripen, (smiling.) He might have *exuberated* into an Atheist.'

Sir Joshua Reynolds praised *Mudge's Sermons*.[2] JOHNSON. 'Mudge's Sermons are good, but not practical. He grasps more sense than he can hold; he takes more corn than he can make into meal; he opens a wide prospect, but it is so distant, it is indistinct. I love *Blair's Sermons*. Though the dog is a Scotchman, and a Presbyterian, and every thing he should not be, I was the first to praise them. Such was my candour,' (smiling.) MRS. BOSCAWEN. 'Such his great merit to get the better of all your prejudices.' JOHNSON. 'Why, Madam, let us compound the matter; let us ascribe it to my candour, and his merit.'

In the evening we had a large company in the drawing-room, several ladies, the Bishop of Killaloe, Dr. Percy, Mr. Chamber-

---

[1] [Probably Boswell. Cf. *Boswell Papers*, iv. 46.]
[2] See *ante*, p. 1126.

layne, of the Treasury, &c. &c. Somebody said the life of a mere literary man could not be very entertaining. JOHNSON. 'But it certainly may. This is a remark which has been made, and repeated, without justice; why should the life of a literary man be less entertaining than the life of any other man? Are there not as interesting varieties in such a life? As *a literary life* it may be very entertaining.' BOSWELL. 'But it must be better surely, when it is diversified with a little active variety—such as his having gone to Jamaica; or—his having gone to the Hebrides.' Johnson was not displeased at this.

Talking of a very respectable authour,[1] he told us a curious circumstance in his life, which was, that he had married a printer's devil. REYNOLDS. 'A printer's devil, Sir! Why, I thought a printer's devil was a creature with a black face and in rags.' JOHNSON. 'Yes, Sir. But I suppose, he had her face washed, and put clean clothes on her. (Then looking very serious, and very earnest.) And she did not disgrace him; the woman had a bottom of good sense.' The word *bottom* thus introduced, was so ludicrous when contrasted with his gravity, that most of us could not forbear tittering and laughing; though I recollect that the Bishop of Killaloe kept his countenance with perfect steadiness, while Miss Hannah More slyly hid her face behind a lady's back who sat on the same settee with her. His pride could not bear that any expression of his should excite ridicule, when he did not intend it; he therefore resolved to assume and exercise despotick power, glanced sternly around, and called out in a strong tone, 'Where's the merriment?' Then collecting himself, and looking aweful, to make us feel how he could impose restraint, and as it were searching his mind for a still more ludicrous word, he slowly pronounced, 'I say the *woman* was *fundamentally* sensible;' as if he had said, hear this now, and laugh if you dare. We all sat composed as at a funeral.

He and I walked away together; we stopped a little while by the rails of the Adelphi, looking on the Thames, and I said to him with some emotion that I was now thinking of two friends we had lost, who once lived in the buildings behind us, Beau-

[1] [Dr. John Campbell. *Boswell Papers*, xiv. 204.]

clerk and Garrick. 'Ay, Sir, (said he, tenderly,) and two such friends as cannot be supplied.'

For some time after this day I did not see him very often, and of the conversation which I did enjoy, I am sorry to find I have preserved but little. I was at this time engaged in a variety of other matters, which required exertion and assiduity, and necessarily occupied almost all my time.

One day having spoken very freely of those who were then in power, he said to me, 'Between ourselves, Sir, I do not like to give opposition the satisfaction of knowing how much I disapprove of the ministry.' And when I mentioned that Mr. Burke had boasted how quiet the nation was in George the Second's reign, when Whigs were in power, compared with the present reign, when Tories governed;—'Why, Sir, (said he,) you are to consider that Tories having more reverence for government, will not oppose with the same violence as Whigs, who being unrestrained by that principle, will oppose by any means.'

This month he lost not only Mr. Thrale, but another friend, Mr. William Strahan, Junior, printer, the eldest son of his old and constant friend, Printer to his Majesty.

'*To* Mrs. Strahan

'Dear Madam,—The grief which I feel for the loss of a very kind friend is sufficient to make me know how much you must suffer by the death of an amiable son; a man, of whom I think it may truly be said, that no one knew him who does not lament him. I look upon myself as having a friend, another friend, taken from me.

'Comfort, dear Madam, I would give you if I could, but I know how little the forms of consolation can avail. Let me, however, counsel you not to waste your health in unprofitable sorrow, but go to Bath, and endeavour to prolong your own life; but when we have all done all that we can, one friend must in time lose the other. I am, dear Madam, your most humble servant,

'April 23, 1781.'   'Sam. Johnson.'

On Tuesday, May 8, I had the pleasure of again dining with him and Mr. Wilkes, at Mr. Dilly's. No *negociation* was now required to bring them together; for Johnson was so well satisfied with the former interview, that he was very glad to meet Wilkes again, who was this day seated between Dr. Beattie and Dr. Johnson; (between *Truth* and *Reason*, as General Paoli said, when I told him of it.) WILKES. 'I have been thinking, Dr. Johnson, that there should be a bill brought into parliament that the controverted elections for Scotland should be tried in that country, at their own Abbey of Holy-Rood House, and not here; for the consequence of trying them here is, that we have an inundation of Scotchmen, who come up and never go back again. Now here is Boswell, who is come up upon the election for his own county, which will not last a fortnight.' JOHNSON. 'Nay, Sir, I see no reason why they should be tried at all; for, you know, one Scotchman is as good as another.' WILKES. 'Pray, Boswell, how much may be got in a year by an Advocate at the Scotch bar?' BOSWELL. 'I believe two thousand pounds.' WILKES. 'How can it be possible to spend that money in Scotland?' JOHNSON. 'Why, Sir, the money may be spent in England: but there is a harder question. If one man in Scotland gets possession of two thousand pounds, what remains for all the rest of the nation?' WILKES. 'You know, in the last war, the immense booty which Thurot carried off by the complete plunder of seven Scotch isles; he re-embarked with *three and six-pence.*' Here again Johnson and Wilkes joined in extravagant sportive raillery upon the supposed poverty of Scotland, which Dr. Beattie and I did not think it worth our while to dispute.

The subject of quotation being introduced, Mr. Wilkes censured it as pedantry. JOHNSON. 'No, Sir, it is a good thing; there is a community of mind in it. Classical quotation is the *parole* of literary men all over the world.' WILKES. 'Upon the continent they all quote the vulgate Bible. Shakspeare is chiefly quoted here; and we quote also Pope, Prior, Butler, Waller, and sometimes Cowley.'

We talked of Letter-writing. JOHNSON. 'It is now become so much the fashion to publish letters, that in order to avoid it, I put as little into mine as I can.' BOSWELL. 'Do what you will, Sir, you cannot avoid it. Should you even write as ill as you can, your letters would be published as curiosities:

> "Behold a miracle! instead of wit,
>   See two dull lines with Stanhope's pencil writ." '

He gave us an entertaining account of *Bet Flint*, a woman of the town, who, with some eccentrick talents and much effrontery, forced herself upon his acquaintance. 'Bet (said he,) wrote her own Life in verse,[1] which she brought to me, wishing that I would furnish her with a Preface to it. (Laughing.) I used to say of her that she was generally slut and drunkard; occasionally, whore and thief. She had, however, genteel lodgings, a spinnet on which she played, and a boy that walked before her chair. Poor Bet was taken up on a charge of stealing a counterpane, and tried at the Old Bailey. Chief Justice ————,[2] who loved a wench, summed up favourably, and she was acquitted. After which Bet said, with a gay and satisfied air, 'Now that the counterpane is *my own*, I shall make a petticoat of it.'

Talking of oratory, Mr. Wilkes described it as accompanied with all the charms of poetical expression. JOHNSON. 'No, Sir; oratory is the power of beating down your adversary's arguments, and putting better in their place.' WILKES. 'But this does not move the passions.' JOHNSON. 'He must be a weak man, who is to be so moved.' WILKES. (naming a celebrated orator,)[3] 'Amidst all the brilliancy of ————'s imagination, and the exuberance of his wit, there is a strange want of *taste*. It was observed of Apelles's Venus, that her flesh seemed as if she had been nourished by roses: his oratory would sometimes make one suspect that he eats potatoes and drinks whisky.'

---

[1] Johnson, whose memory was wonderfully retentive [see *ante*, p. 30], remembered the first four lines of this curious production, which have been communicated to me by a young lady* of his acquaintance:—

> 'When first I drew my vital breath,
>   A little minikin I came upon earth;
>   And then I came from a dark abode,
>   Into this gay and gaudy world.'

* [*Prof. Tinker suggests* Fanny Burney.]

[2] [Sir John Willes. *Croker*.[1]]

[3] [Burke. *Boswell Papers*, xi. 283, xiii. 232.]

Mr. Wilkes observed, how tenacious we are of forms in this country, and gave as an instance, the vote of the House of Commons for remitting money to pay the army in America *in Portugal pieces*, when, in reality, the remittance is made not in Portugal money, but in our own specie. JOHNSON. 'Is there not a law, Sir, against exporting the current coin of the realm?' WILKES. 'Yes, Sir: but might not the House of Commons, in case of real evident necessity, order our own current coin to be sent into our own colonies?' Here Johnson, with that quickness of recollection which distinguished him so eminently, gave the *Middlesex Patriot* an admirable retort upon his own ground. 'Sure, Sir, *you* don't think a *resolution of the House of Commons* equal to *the law of the land?*' WILKES. (at once perceiving the application,) 'GOD forbid, Sir.' To hear what had been treated with such violence in *The False Alarm*, now turned into pleasant repartee, was extremely agreeable. Johnson went on;—'Locke observes well, that a prohibition to export the current coin is impolitick; for when the balance of trade happens to be against a state, the current coin *must* be exported.'

Mr. Beauclerk's great library was this season sold in London by auction. Mr. Wilkes said, he wondered to find in it such a numerous collection of sermons; seeming to think it strange that a gentleman of Mr. Beauclerk's character in the gay world should have chosen to have many compositions of that kind. JOHNSON. 'Why, Sir, you are to consider, that sermons make a considerable branch of English literature; so that a library must be very imperfect if it has not a numerous collection of sermons:[1]

---

[1] Mr. Wilkes probably did not know that there is in an English sermon the most comprehensive and lively account of that entertaining faculty, for which he himself is so much admired. It is in Dr. Barrow's first volume, and fourteenth sermon, '*Against foolish Talking and Jesting.*' My old acquaintance, the late Corbyn Morris, in his ingenious *Essay on Wit, Humour, and Ridicule*, calls it 'a *profuse* description of Wit;' but I do not see how it could be curtailed, without leaving out some good circumstance of discrimination. As it is not generally known, and may perhaps dispose some to read sermons, from which they may receive real advantage, while looking only for entertainment, I shall here subjoin it:—

'But first (says the learned preacher) it may be demanded, what the thing we speak of is? Or what this facetiousness (or *wit* as he calls it before) doth import? To which questions I might reply, as Democritus did to him that and in all collections, Sir, the desire of augmenting it grows stronger in proportion to the advance in acquisition; as motion is accelerated by the continuance of the *impetus*. Besides, Sir, (looking at Mr. Wilkes with a placid but significant smile,) a man may collect sermons with intention of making himself better

asked the definition of a man, "'Tis that which we all see and know." Any one better apprehends what it is by acquaintance, than I can inform him by description. It is, indeed, a thing so versatile and multiform, appearing in so many shapes, so many postures, so many garbs, so variously apprehended by several eyes and judgements, that it seemeth no less hard to settle a clear and certain notion thereof, than to make a portrait of Proteus, or to define the figure of the fleeting air. Sometimes it lieth in pat allusion to a known story, or in seasonable application of a trivial saying, or in forging an apposite tale; sometimes it playeth in words and phrases, taking advantage from the ambiguity of their sense, or the affinity of their sound: sometimes it is wrapped in a dress of humourous expression: sometimes it lurketh under an odd similitude: sometimes it is lodged in a sly question, in a smart answer, in a quirkish reason, in a shrewd intimation, in cunningly diverting or cleverly retorting an objection: sometimes it is couched in a bold scheme of speech, in a tart irony, in a lusty hyperbole, in a startling metaphor, in a plausible reconciling of contradictions, or in acute nonsense: sometimes a scenical representation of persons or things, a counterfeit speech, a mimical look or gesture, passeth for it: sometimes an affected simplicity, sometimes a presumptuous bluntness giveth it being: sometimes it riseth only from a lucky hitting upon what is strange: sometimes from a crafty wresting obvious matter to the purpose. Often it consisteth in one knows not what, and springeth up one can hardly tell how. Its ways are unaccountable, and inexplicable; being answerable to the numberless rovings of fancy, and windings of language. It is, in short, a manner of speaking out of the simple and plain way, (such as reason teacheth and proveth things by,) which by a pretty surprizing uncouthness in conceit or expression, doth affect and amuse the fancy, stirring in it some wonder, and breeding some delight thereto. It raiseth admiration, as signifying a nimble sagacity of apprehension, a special felicity of invention, a vivacity of spirit, and reach of wit more than vulgar; it seeming to argue a rare quickness of parts, that one can fetch in remote conceits applicable; a notable skill, that he can dextrously accommodate them to the purpose before him; together with a lively briskness of humour, not apt to damp those sportful flashes of imagination. (Whence in Aristotle such persons are termed ἐπιδέξιοι, dextrous men, and εὔστροφοι, men of facile or versatile manners, who can easily turn themselves to all things, or turn all things to themselves.) It also procureth delight, by gratifying curiosity with its rareness, as semblance of difficulty: (as monsters, not for their beauty, but their rarity; as juggling tricks, not for their use, but their abstruseness, are beheld with pleasure:) by diverting the mind from its road of serious thoughts; by instilling gaiety and airiness of spirit; by provoking to such dispositions of spirit in way of emulation or complaisance; and by seasoning matters, otherwise distasteful or insipid, with an unusual and thence grateful tang.'

by them. I hope Mr. Beauclerk intended, that some time or other that should be the case with him.'

Mr. Wilkes said to me, loud enough for Dr. Johnson to hear, 'Dr. Johnson should make me a present of his *Lives of the Poets*, as I am a poor patriot, who cannot afford to buy them.' Johnson seemed to take no notice of this hint; but in a little while, he called to Mr. Dilly, 'Pray, Sir, be so good as to send a set of my *Lives* to Mr. Wilkes, with my compliments.' This was accordingly done; and Mr. Wilkes paid Dr. Johnson a visit, was courteously received, and sat with him a long time.

The company gradually dropped away. Mr. Dilly himself was called down stairs upon business; I left the room for some time; when I returned, I was struck with observing Dr. Samuel Johnson and John Wilkes, Esq., literally *tête-à-tête*; for they were reclined upon their chairs, with their heads leaning almost close to each other, and talking earnestly, in a kind of confidential whisper, of the personal quarrel between George the Second and the King of Prussia. Such a scene of perfectly easy sociality between two such opponents in the war of political controversy, as that which I now beheld, would have been an excellent subject for a picture. It presented to my mind the happy days which are foretold in Scripture, when the lion shall lie down with the kid.[1]

After this day there was another pretty long interval, during which Dr. Johnson and I did not meet. When I mentioned it to him with regret, he was pleased to say, 'Then, Sir, let us live double.'

About this time it was much the fashion for several ladies to have evening assemblies, where the fair sex might participate in conversation with literary and ingenious men, animated by a desire to please. These societies were denominated *Blue-stocking Clubs*, the origin of which title being little known, it may be worth while to relate it. One of the most eminent members of those societies, when they first commenced, was Mr. Stilling-

---

[1] When I mentioned this to the Bishop of Killaloe, 'With the *goat*,' said his Lordship. Such, however, is the engaging politeness and pleasantry of Mr. Wilkes, and such the social good humour of the Bishop, that when they dined together at Mr. Dilly's, where I also was, they were mutually agreeable.

fleet,[1] whose dress was remarkably grave, and in particular it was observed, that he wore blue stockings. Such was the excellence of his conversation, that his absence was felt as so great a loss, that it used to be said, 'We can do nothing without the *blue stockings*;' and thus by degrees the title was established. Miss Hannah More has admirably described a *Blue-stocking Club*, in her *Bas Bleu*, a poem in which many of the persons who were most conspicuous there are mentioned.

Johnson was prevailed with to come sometimes into these circles, and did not think himself too grave even for the lively Miss Monckton (now Countess of Corke), who used to have the finest *bit of blue* at the house of her mother, Lady Galway. Her vivacity enchanted the Sage, and they used to talk together with all imaginable ease. A singular instance happened one evening, when she insisted that some of Sterne's writings were very pathetick. Johnson bluntly denied it. 'I am sure (said she,) they have affected *me*.' 'Why, (said Johnson, smiling, and rolling himself about,) that is, because, dearest, you're a dunce.' When she some time afterwards mentioned this to him, he said with equal truth and politeness; 'Madam, if I had thought so, I certainly should not have said it.'

Another evening Johnson's kind indulgence towards me had a pretty difficult trial. I had dined at the Duke of Montrose's, with a very agreeable party, and his Grace, according to his usual custom, had circulated the bottle very freely. Lord Graham and I went together to Miss Monckton's, where I certainly was in extraordinary spirits, and above all fear or awe. In the midst of a great number of persons of the first rank, amongst whom I recollect with confusion, a noble lady of the most stately decorum, I placed myself next to Johnson, and thinking myself now fully his match, talked to him in a loud and boisterous manner, desirous to let the company know how I could contend with *Ajax*. I particularly remember pressing him upon the value of the pleasures of the imagination, and as an illustration of my argument, asking him, 'What, Sir, supposing I were to fancy

[1] Mr. Benjamin Stillingfleet, authour of tracts relating to natural history, &c.

that the ———— (naming the most charming Duchess[1] in his Majesty's dominions) were in love with me, should I not be very happy?' My friend with much address evaded my interrogatories, and kept me as quiet as possible; but it may easily be conceived how he must have felt.[2] However, when a few days afterwards I waited upon him and made an apology, he behaved with the most friendly gentleness.

While I remained in London this year, Johnson and I dined together at several places. I recollect a placid day at Dr. Butter's, who had now removed from Derby to Lower Grosvenor-street, London; but of his conversation on that and other occasions during this period, I neglected to keep any regular record, and shall therefore insert here some miscellaneous articles which I find in my Johnsonian notes.

His disorderly habits, when 'making provision for the day that was passing over him,' appear from the following anecdote, communicated to me by Mr. John Nichols:—'In the year 1763,

---

[1] [Georgina, Duchess of Devonshire. *Mrs. Piozzi.*]

[2] Next day I endeavoured to give what had happened the most ingenious turn I could, by the following verses:—

TO THE HONOURABLE MISS MONCKTON.

'Not that with th' excellent Montrose
    I had the happiness to dine;
Not that I late from table rose,
    From Graham's wit, from generous wine.
It was not these alone which led
    On sacred manners to encroach;
And made me feel what most I dread,
    JOHNSON's just frown, and self-reproach.
But when I enter'd, not abash'd,
    From your bright eyes were shot such rays,
At once intoxication flash'd,
    And all my frame was in a blaze.
But not a brilliant blaze I own,
    Of the dull smoke I'm yet asham'd;
I was a dreary ruin grown,
    And not enlighten'd though inflam'd.
Victim at once to wine and love,
    I hope, MÀRIA, you'll forgive;
While I invoke the powers above,
    That henceforth I may wiser live.'

The lady was generously forgiving, returned me an obliging answer, and I thus obtained an *Act of Oblivion*, and took care never to offend again.

a young bookseller, who was an apprentice to Mr. Whiston, waited on him with a subscription to his *Shakspeare*: and observing that the Doctor made no entry in any book of the subscriber's name, ventured diffidently to ask, whether he would please to have the gentleman's address, that it might be properly inserted in the printed list of subscribers. '*I shall print no list of subscribers*;' said Johnson, with great abruptness: but almost immediately recollecting himself, added, very complacently, 'Sir, I have two very cogent reasons for not printing any list of subscribers;—one, that I have lost all the names,—the other, that I have spent all the money.'

Johnson could not brook appearing to be worsted in argument, even when he had taken the wrong side, to shew the force and dexterity of his talents. When, therefore, he perceived that his opponent gained ground, he had recourse to some sudden mode of robust sophistry. Once when I was pressing upon him with visible advantage, he stopped me thus:—'My dear Boswell, let's have no more of this; you'll make nothing of it. I'd rather have you whistle a Scotch tune.'

Care, however, must be taken to distinguish between Johnson when he 'talked for victory,' and Johnson when he had no desire but to inform and illustrate. 'One of Johnson's principal talents (says an eminent friend of his)[1] was shewn in maintaining the wrong side of an argument, and in a splendid perversion of the truth. If you could contrive to have his fair opinion on a subject, and without any bias from personal prejudice, or from a wish to be victorious in argument, it was wisdom itself, not only convincing, but overpowering.'

He had, however, all his life habituated himself to consider conversation as a trial of intellectual vigour and skill; and to this, I think, we may venture to ascribe that unexampled richness and brilliancy which appeared in his own. As a proof at once of his eagerness for colloquial distinction, and his high notion of this eminent friend, he once addressed him thus:— '——, we now have been several hours together; and you have said but one thing for which I envied you.'

[1] [William Gerard Hamilton. *Boswell's Proofs* and *Letters*, ii. 424.]

He disliked much all speculative desponding considerations, which tended to discourage men from diligence and exertion. He was in this like Dr. Shaw, the great traveller, who, Mr. Daines Barrington told me, used to say, 'I hate a *cui bono*[1] man.' Upon being asked by a friend[2] what he should think of a man who was apt to say *non est tanti*;[3]—'That he's a stupid fellow, Sir; (answered Johnson): What would these *tanti* men be doing the while?' When I, in a low-spirited fit, was talking to him with indifference of the pursuits which generally engage us in a course of action, and inquiring a *reason* for taking so much trouble; 'Sir, (said he, in an animated tone) it is driving on the system of life.'

He told me, that he was glad that I had, by General Ogle-thorpe's means, become acquainted with Dr. Shebbeare. Indeed that gentleman, whatever objections were made to him, had knowledge and abilities much above the class of ordinary writers, and deserves to be remembered as a respectable name in litera-ture, were it only for his admirable *Letters on the English Nation*, under the name of 'Battista Angeloni, a Jesuit.'

Johnson and Shebbeare[4] were frequently named together, as having in former reigns had no predilection for the family of Hanover. The authour[5] of the celebrated *Heroick Epistle to Sir William Chambers*, introduces them in one line, in a list of those 'who tasted the sweets of his present Majesty's reign.' Such was Johnson's candid relish of the merit of that satire, that he allowed Dr. Goldsmith, as he told me, to read it to him from beginning to end, and did not refuse his praise to its execution.

Goldsmith could sometimes take adventurous liberties with him, and escape unpunished. Beauclerk told me that when Gold-smith talked of a project for having a third Theatre in London, solely for the exhibition of new plays, in order to deliver authours from the supposed tyranny of managers, Johnson treated it slightingly; upon which Goldsmith said, 'Ay, ay, this

---

[1] ['Who gains by it?']   [2] [*Hill suggests* Boswell.]
[3] ['It is not worth while.']
[4] I recollect a ludicrous paragraph in the newspapers, that the King had pensioned both a *He*-bear and a *She*-bear.   [5] [William Mason.]

may be nothing to you, who can now shelter yourself behind the corner of a pension;' and that Johnson bore this with good-humour.

Johnson praised the Earl of Carlisle's Poems, which his Lordship had published with his name, as not disdaining to be a candidate for literary fame. My friend was of opinion, that when a man of rank appeared in that character, he deserved to have his merit handsomely allowed.[1] In this I think he was more liberal than Mr. William Whitehead, in his *Elegy to Lord Villiers*, in which under the pretext of 'superiour toils, demanding all their care,' he discovers a jealousy of the great paying their court to the Muses:—

> '————————— to the chosen few
> Who dare excel, thy fost'ring aid afford,
> Their arts, their magick powers, with honours due
> Exalt;—but be thyself what they record.'

---

[1] Men of rank and fortune, however, should be pretty well assured of having a real claim to the approbation of the publick, as writers, before they venture to stand forth. Dryden, in his preface to *All for Love*, thus expresses himself:—

'Men of pleasant conversation (at least esteemed so) and endued with a trifling kind of fancy, perhaps helped out by [with] a smattering of Latin, are ambitious to distinguish themselves from the herd of gentlemen, by their poetry:

> "*Rarus enim fermè sensus communis in illa*
> *Fortuna.*"—[*Juvenal* viii. 73.*]

And is not this a wretched affectation, not to be contented with what fortune has done for them, and sit down quietly with their estates, but they must call their wits in question, and needlessly expose their nakedness to publick view? Not considering that they are not to expect the same approbation from sober men, which they have found from their flatterers after the third bottle: If a little glittering in discourse has passed them on us for witty men, where was the necessity of undeceiving the world? Would a man who has an ill title to an estate, but yet is in possession of it, would he bring it of his own accord to be tried at Westminster? We who write, if we want the talents [talent], yet have the excuse that we do it for a poor subs.stence; but what can be urged in their defence, who, not having the vocation of poverty to scribble, out of mere wantonness take pains to make themselves ridiculous? Horace was certainly in the right where he said, "That no man is satisfied with his own condition." A Poet is not pleased, because he is not rich; and the rich are discontented because the poets will not admit them of their number.'

* ['It is unusual to find men of humility among men of the highest fortune.']

Johnson had called twice on the Bishop of Killaloe before his Lordship set out for Ireland, having missed him the first time. He said, 'It would have hung heavy on my heart if I had not seen him. No man ever paid more attention to another than he has done to me;[1] and I have neglected him, not wilfully, but from being otherwise occupied. Always, Sir, set a high value on spontaneous kindness. He whose inclination prompts him to cultivate your friendship of his own accord, will love you more than one whom you have been at pains to attach to you.'

Johnson told me, that he was once much pleased to find that a carpenter, who lived near him, was very ready to shew him some things in his business which he wished to see: 'It was paying (said he,) respect to literature.'

I asked him if he was not dissatisfied with having so small a share of wealth, and none of those distinctions in the state which are the objects of ambition. He had only a pension of three hundred a year. Why was he not in such circumstances as to keep his coach? Why had he not some considerable office? JOHNSON. 'Sir, I have never complained of the world; nor do I think that I have reason to complain. It is rather to be wondered at that I have so much. My pension is more out of the usual course of things than any instance that I have known. Here, Sir, was a man avowedly no friend to Government at the time, who got a pension without asking for it. I never courted the great; they sent for me; but I think they now give me up. They are

---

[1] This gave me very great pleasure, for there had been once a pretty smart altercation between Dr. Barnard and him, upon a question, whether a man could improve himself after the age of forty-five; when Johnson in a hasty humour, expressed himself in a manner not quite civil. Dr. Barnard made it the subject of a copy of pleasant verses, in which he supposed himself to learn different perfections from different men. They concluded with delicate irony:—

> 'Johnson shall teach me how to place
> In fairest light each borrow'd grace;
>   From him I'll learn to write;
> Copy his clear familiar style,
> And by the roughness of his file
>   Grow, like *himself*, *polite*.'

I know not whether Johnson ever saw the poem, but I had occasion to find that as Dr. Barnard and he knew each other better, their mutual regard increased.

satisfied; they have seen enough of me.' Upon my observing that I could not believe this, for they must certainly be highly pleased by his conversation; conscious of his own superiority, he answered, 'No, Sir; great Lords and great Ladies don't love to have their mouths stopped.' This was very expressive of the effect which the force of his understanding and brilliancy of his fancy could not but produce; and, to be sure, they must have found themselves strangely diminished in his company. When I warmly declared how happy I was at all times to hear him;— 'Yes, Sir, (said he); but if you were Lord Chancellor, it would not be so: you would then consider your own dignity.'

There was much truth and knowledge of human nature in this remark. But certainly one should think, that in whatever elevated state of life a man who *knew* the value of the conversation of Johnson might be placed, though he might prudently avoid a situation in which he might appear lessened by comparison; yet he would frequently gratify himself in private with the participation of the rich intellectual entertainment which Johnson could furnish. Strange, however, it is, to consider how few of the great sought his society; so that if one were disposed to take occasion for satire on that account, very conspicuous objects present themselves. His noble friend, Lord Elibank, well observed, that if a great man procured an interview with Johnson, and did not wish to see him more, it shewed a mere idle curiosity, and a wretched want of relish for extraordinary powers of mind. Mrs. Thrale justly and wittily accounted for such conduct by saying, that Johnson's conversation was by much too strong for a person accustomed to obsequiousness and flattery; it was *mustard in a young child's mouth!*

One day, when I told him that I was a zealous Tory, but not enough 'according to knowledge,' and should be obliged to him for 'a reason,' he was so candid, and expressed himself so well, that I begged of him to repeat what he had said, and I wrote down as follows:—

Of Tory and Whig.

'A wise Tory and a wise Whig, I believe, will agree. Their principles are the same, though their modes of thinking are different. A high Tory makes government unintelligible: it is lost in the clouds. A violent Whig makes it impracticable: he is for allowing so much liberty to every man, that there is not power enough to govern any man. The prejudice of the Tory is for establishment; the prejudice of the Whig is for innovation. A Tory does not wish to give more real power to Government; but that Government should have more reverence. Then they differ as to the Church. The Tory is not for giving more legal power to the Clergy, but wishes they should have a considerable influence, founded on the opinion of mankind; the Whig is for limiting and watching them with a narrow jealousy.'

'*To* Mr. Perkins

'Sir,—However often I have seen you, I have hitherto forgotten the note, but I have now sent it: with my good wishes for the prosperity of you and your partner,[1] of whom, from our short conversation, I could not judge otherwise than favourably. I am, Sir, your most humble servant,

'June 2, 1781.'   'Sam. Johnson.'

On Saturday, June 2, I set out for Scotland, and had promised to pay a visit in my way, as I sometimes did, at Southill, in Bedfordshire, at the hospitable mansion of 'Squire Dilly, the elder brother of my worthy friends, the booksellers, in the Poultry. Dr. Johnson agreed to be of the party this year, with Mr. Charles Dilly and me, and to go and see Lord Bute's seat at Luton Hoe. He talked little to us in the carriage, being chiefly occupied in reading Dr. Watson's[2] second volume of *Chemical*

[1] Mr. Barclay, a descendant of Robert Barclay, of Ury, the celebrated apologist of the people called Quakers, and remarkable for maintaining the principles of his venerable progenitor, with as much of the elegance of modern manners, as is consistent with primitive simplicity.

[2] Now Bishop of Llandaff, one of the *poorest* Bishopricks in this kingdom. His Lordship has written with much zeal to show the propriety of *equalizing* the revenues of Bishops. He has informed us that he has burnt all his chemical papers. The friends of our excellent constitution, now assailed on every side by innovators and levellers, would have less regretted the suppression of some of his Lordship's other writings.

Essays, which he liked very well, and his own *Prince of Abyssinia,* on which he seemed to be intensely fixed; having told us, that he had not looked at it since it was first published. I happened to take it out of my pocket this day, and he seized upon it with avidity. He pointed out to me the following remarkable passage:—

'By what means (said the prince) are the Europeans thus powerful; or why, since they can so easily visit Asia and Africa for trade or conquest, cannot the Asiaticks and Africans invade their coasts, plant colonies in their ports, and give laws to their natural princes? The same wind that carries them back would bring us thither.' 'They are more powerful, Sir, than we, (answered Imlac,) because they are wiser. Knowledge will always predominate over ignorance, as man governs the other animals. But why their knowledge is more than ours, I know not what reason can be given, but the unsearchable will of the Supreme Being.'

He said, 'This, Sir, no man can explain otherwise.'

We stopped at Welwyn, where I wished much to see, in company with Dr. Johnson, the residence of the authour of *Night Thoughts,* which was then possessed by his son, Mr. Young. Here some address was requisite, for I was not acquainted with Mr. Young, and had I proposed to Dr. Johnson that we should send to him, he would have checked my wish, and perhaps been offended. I therefore concerted with Mr. Dilly, that I should steal away from Dr. Johnson and him, and try what reception I could procure from Mr. Young; if unfavourable, nothing was to be said; but if agreeable, I should return and notify it to them. I hastened to Mr. Young's, found he was at home, sent in word that a gentleman desired to wait upon him, and was shewn into a parlour, where he and a young lady, his daughter, were sitting. He appeared to be a plain, civil, country gentleman; and when I begged pardon for presuming to trouble him, but that I wished much to see his place, if he would give me leave; he behaved very courteously, and answered, 'By all means, Sir; we are just going to drink tea; will you sit down?' I thanked him, but said, that Dr. Johnson had come with me from London, and I must return to the inn and drink tea with him; that my name was Boswell, I had travelled with him in the Hebrides. 'Sir, (said he,) I should think it a great honour to see Dr. Johnson here. Will you allow me to send for him?' Availing myself of this opening, I said that 'I would go myself and bring him, when he had drunk tea; he knew nothing of my calling here.' Having been thus successful, I hastened back to the inn, and informed Dr. Johnson that 'Mr. Young, son of Dr. Young, the authour of *Night Thoughts*, whom I had just left, desired to have the honour of seeing him at the house where his father lived.' Dr. Johnson luckily made no inquiry how this invitation had arisen, but agreed to go, and when we entered Mr. Young's parlour, he addressed him with a very polite bow, 'Sir, I had a curiosity to come and see this place. I had the honour to know that great man, your father.' We went into the garden, where we found a gravel walk, on each side of which was a row of trees, planted by Dr. Young, which formed a handsome Gothick arch; Dr. Johnson called it a fine grove. I beheld it with reverence.

We sat some time in the summer-house, on the outside wall of which was inscribed, '*Ambulantis in horto audiebant vocem Dei*;'[1] and in reference to a brook by which it is situated, '*Vivendi rectè qui prorogat horam*, &c.'[2] I said to Mr. Young, that I had been told his father was cheerful. 'Sir, (said he,) he was too well-bred a man not to be cheerful in company; but he was gloomy when alone. He never was cheerful after my mother's death, and he had met with many disappointments.' Dr. Johnson observed to me afterwards, 'That this was no favourable account of Dr. Young; for it is not becoming in a man to have so little acquiescence in the ways of Providence, as to be gloomy because he has not obtained as much preferment as he expected; nor to continue gloomy for the loss of his wife. Grief has its time.' The last part of this censure was theoretically made. Practically, we know that grief for the loss of a wife may be continued very long,

[1] ['They heard the voice of the Lord God walking in the garden.' *Genesis* iii. 8.]

[2] ['He who keeps putting off the moment of reform is like the country-man waiting for the river to run by. But the river slides and rolls, and will slide and roll on to all time.' Horace, *Epistles* I. ii. 41. (Wickham.)]

in proportion as affection has been sincere. No man knew this better than Dr. Johnson.

We went into the church, and looked at the monument erected by Mr. Young to his father. Mr. Young mentioned an anecdote, that his father had received several thousand pounds of subscription-money for his *Universal Passion*, but had lost it in the South-Sea.[1] Dr. Johnson thought this must be a mistake; for he had never seen a subscription-book.

Upon the road we talked of the uncertainty of profit with which authours and booksellers engage in the publication of literary works. JOHNSON. 'My judgement I have found is no certain rule as to the sale of a book.' BOSWELL. 'Pray, Sir, have you been much plagued with authours sending you their works to revise?' JOHNSON. 'No, Sir; I have been thought a sour, surly fellow.' BOSWELL. 'Very lucky for you, Sir,—in that respect.' I must however observe, that notwithstanding what he now said, which he no doubt imagined at the time to be the fact, there was, perhaps, no man who more frequently yielded to the solicitations even of very obscure authours, to read their manuscripts, or more liberally assisted them with advice and correction.

He found himself very happy at 'Squire Dilly's, where there is always abundance of excellent fare, and hearty welcome.

On Sunday, June 3, we all went to Southill church, which is very near to Mr. Dilly's house. It being the first Sunday of the month, the holy sacrament was administered, and I staid to partake of it. When I came afterwards into Dr. Johnson's room, he said, 'You did right to stay and receive the communion; I had not thought of it.' This seemed to imply that he did not choose to approach the altar without a previous preparation, as to which good men entertain different opinions, some holding that it is irreverent to partake of that ordinance without considerable premeditation; others, that whoever is a sincere Christian, and in a proper frame of mind to discharge any other ritual duty of our religion, may, without scruple, discharge this most solemn

---

[1] This assertion is disproved by a comparison of dates. The first four satires of Young were published in 1725; the South Sea scheme (which appears to be meant,) was in 1720. [M.]

one. A middle notion I believe to be the just one, which is, that communicants need not think a long train of preparatory forms indispensably necessary; but neither should they rashly and lightly venture upon so aweful and mysterious an institution. Christians must judge each for himself, what degree of retirement and self-examination is necessary upon each occasion.

Being in a frame of mind which, I hope for the felicity of human nature, many experience,—in fine weather,—at the country house of a friend,—consoled and elevated by pious exercises,—I expressed myself with an unrestrained fervour to my 'Guide, Philosopher, and Friend;' 'My dear Sir, I would fain be a good man; and I am very good now. I fear GOD, and honour the King, I wish to do no ill, and to be benevolent to all mankind.' He looked at me with a benignant indulgence; but took occasion to give me wise and salutary caution. 'Do not, Sir, accustom yourself to trust to *impressions*. There is a middle state of mind between conviction and hypocrisy, of which many are conscious. By trusting to impressions, a man may gradually come to yield to them, and at length be subject to them, so as not to be a free agent, or what is the same thing in effect, to *suppose* that he is not a free agent. A man who is in that state, should not be suffered to live; if he declares he cannot help acting in a particular way, and is irresistibly impelled, there can be no confidence in him, no more than in a tyger. But, Sir, no man believes himself to be impelled irresistibly; we know that he who says he believes it, lies. Favourable impressions at particular moments, as to the state of our souls, may be deceitful and dangerous. In general no man can be sure of his acceptance with God; some, indeed, may have had it revealed to them. St. Paul, who wrought miracles, may have had a miracle wrought on himself, and may have obtained supernatural assurance of pardon, and mercy, and beatitude; yet St. Paul, though he expresses strong hope, also expresses fear, lest having preached to others, he himself should be a cast-away.'

The opinion of a learned Bishop[1] of our acquaintance, as to there being merit in religious faith, being mentioned;—JOHNSON.

[1] [Dr. Barnard, Bp of Killaloe. *Boswell Papers*, xiv. 245.]

'Why, yes, Sir, the most licentious man, were hell open
before him, would not take the most beautiful strumpet to his
arms. We must, as the Apostle says, live by faith, not by sight.'

I talked to him of original sin,[1] in consequence of the fall of
man, and of the atonement made by our SAVIOUR. After some
conversation, which he desired me to remember, he, at my
request, dictated to me as follows:—

'With respect to original sin, the inquiry is not necessary; for
whatever is the cause of human corruption, men are evidently
and confessedly so corrupt, that all the laws of heaven and earth
are insufficient to restrain them from crimes.

'Whatever difficulty there may be in the conception of vicarious punishments, it is an opinion which has had possession of
mankind in all ages. There is no nation that has not used the
practice of sacrifices. Whoever, therefore, denies the propriety
of vicarious punishments, holds an opinion which the sentiments
and practice of mankind have contradicted, from the beginning
of the world. The great sacrifice for the sins of mankind was
offered at the death of the MESSIAH, who is called in Scripture
"The Lamb of God, that taketh away the sins of the world." To
judge of the reasonableness of the scheme of redemption, it must
be considered as necessary to the government of the universe,
that GOD should make known his perpetual and irreconcileable
detestation of moral evil. He might indeed punish, and punish
only the offenders; but as the end of punishment is not revenge
of crimes, but propagation of virtue, it was more becoming the
Divine clemency to find another manner of proceeding, less
destructive to man, and at least equally powerful to promote
goodness. The end of punishment is to reclaim and warn. *That*

---

[1] Dr. Ogden, in his second sermon *On the Articles of the Christian Faith*,
with admirable acuteness thus addresses the opposers of that Doctrine,
which accounts for the confusion, sin and misery, which we find in this life:
'It would be severe in GOD, you think, to *degrade* us to such a sad state as
this, for the offence of our first parents: but you can allow him to *place* us
in it without any inducement. Are our calamities lessened for not being
ascribed to Adam? If your condition be unhappy, is it not still unhappy,
whatever was the occasion? with the aggravation of this reflection, that if
it was as good as it was at first designed, there seems to be somewhat the
less reason to look for its amendment.'

punishment will both reclaim and warn, which shews evidently such abhorrence of sin in GOD, as may deter us from it, or strike us with dread of vengeance when we have committed it. This is effected by vicarious punishment. Nothing could more testify the opposition between the nature of GOD and moral evil, or more amply display his justice, to men and angels, to all orders and successions of beings, than that it was necessary for the highest and purest nature, even for DIVINITY itself, to pacify the demands of vengeance, by a painful death; of which the natural effect will be, that when justice is appeased, there is a proper place for the exercise of mercy; and that such propitiation shall supply, in some degree, the imperfections of our obedience, and the inefficacy of our repentance: for, obedience and repentance, such as we can perform, are still necessary. Our SAVIOUR has told us, that he did not come to destroy the law, but to fulfill; to fulfill the typical law, by the performance of what those types had foreshewn; and the moral law, by precepts of greater purity and higher exaltation."

[Here he said, 'GOD bless you with it.' I acknowledged myself much obliged to him; but I begged that he would go on as to the propitiation being the chief object of our most holy faith. He then dictated this one other paragraph.]

'The peculiar doctrine of Christianity is, that of an universal sacrifice, and perpetual propitiation. Other prophets only proclaimed the will and the threatenings of GOD. CHRIST satisfied his justice.'

The Reverend Mr. Palmer,[1] Fellow of Queen's-College,

---

[1] This unfortunate person, whose full name was Thomas Fysche Palmer, afterwards went to Dundee, in Scotland, where he officiated as minister to a congregation of the sect who called themselves *Unitarians*, from a notion that they distinctively worship ONE GOD, because they *deny* the mysterious doctrine of the TRINITY. They do not advert that the great body of the Christian Church, in maintaining that mystery, maintain also the *Unity* of the GOD-HEAD; the 'TRINITY in UNITY!—three persons and ONE GOD.' The Church humbly adores the DIVINITY as exhibited in the holy Scriptures. The Unitarian sect vainly presumes to comprehend and define the ALMIGHTY. Mr. Palmer having heated his mind with political speculations, became so much dissatisfied with our excellent Constitution, as to compose, publish, and circulate writings, which were found to be so seditious and dangerous, that upon being found guilty by a Jury, the Court of Justiciary in Scotland

Cambridge, dined with us. He expressed a wish that a better
provision were made for parish-clerks. JOHNSON. 'Yes, Sir, a
parish-clerk should be a man who is able to make a will, or write
a letter for any body in the parish.'

I mentioned Lord Monboddo's notion[1] that the ancient Egyp-
tians, with all their learning, and all their arts, were not only
black, but woolly-haired. Mr. Palmer asked how did it appear
upon examining the mummies? Dr. Johnson approved of this
test.

Although upon most occasions I never heard a more strenuous
advocate for the advantages of wealth, than Dr. Johnson: he this
day, I know not from what caprice, took the other side. 'I have
not observed (said he,) that men of very large fortunes enjoy
any thing extraordinary that makes happiness. What has the
Duke of Bedford? What has the Duke of Devonshire? The only
great instance that I have ever known of the enjoyment of
wealth was, that of Jamaica Dawkins, who, going to visit
Palmyra, and hearing that the way was infested by robbers,
hired a troop of Turkish horse to guard him.'

Dr. Gibbons, the Dissenting minister, being mentioned, he
said, 'I took to Dr. Gibbons.' And addressing himself to Mr.
Charles Dilly, added, 'I shall be glad to see him. Tell him, if
he'll call on me, and dawdle over a dish of tea in an afternoon,
I shall take it kind.'

The Reverend Mr. Smith, Vicar of Southill, a very respectable
man, with a very agreeable family, sent an invitation to us to
drink tea. I remarked Dr. Johnson's very respectful politeness.
Though always fond of changing the scene, he said, 'We must
have Mr. Dilly's leave. We cannot go from your house, Sir,
without your permission.' We all went, and were well satisfied
with our visit. I however remember nothing particular, except a
nice distinction which Dr. Johnson made with respect to the
power of memory, maintaining that forgetfulness was a man's

sentenced him to transportation for fourteen [i.e. seven] years. A loud clamour
against this sentence was made by some Members of both Houses of Parliament; but both Houses approved of it by a great majority; and he was conveyed to the settlement for convicts in New South Wales.

own fault. 'To remember and to recollect (said he,) are different things. A man has not the power to recollect what is not in his mind; but when a thing is in his mind he may remember it.' The remark was occasioned by my leaning back on a chair, which a little before I had perceived to be broken, and pleading forgetfulness as an excuse. 'Sir, (said he,) its being broken was certainly in your mind.'

When I observed that a housebreaker was in general very timorous; JOHNSON. 'No wonder, Sir; he is afraid of being shot getting *into* a house, or hanged when he has got *out* of it.'

He told us, that he had in one day written six sheets of a translation from the French, adding, 'I should be glad to see it now. I wish that I had copies of all the pamphlets written against me, as it is said Pope had. Had I known that I should make so much noise in the world, I should have been at pains to collect them. I believe there is hardly a day in which there is not something about me in the newspapers.'

On Monday, June 4, we all went to Luton-Hoe, to see Lord Bute's magnificent seat, for which I had obtained a ticket. As we entered the park, I talked in a high style of my old friendship with Lord Mountstuart, and said, 'I shall probably be much at this place.' The Sage, aware of human vicissitudes, gently checked me: 'Don't you be too sure of that.' He made two or three peculiar observations; as when shewn the botanical garden, 'Is not *every* garden a botanical garden?' When told that there was a shrubbery to the extent of several miles: 'That is making a very foolish use of the ground; a little of it is very well.' When it was proposed that we should walk on the pleasure-ground; 'Don't let us fatigue ourselves. Why should we walk there? Here's a fine tree, let's get to the top of it.' But upon the whole, he was very much pleased. He said, 'This is one of the places I do not regret having come to see. It is a very stately place, indeed; in the house magnificence is not sacrificed to convenience, nor convenience to magnificence. The library is very splendid: the dignity of the rooms is very great; and the quantity of pictures is beyond expectation, beyond hope.'

It happened without any previous concert, that we visited the seat of Lord Bute upon the King's birth-day; we dined and drank his Majesty's health at an inn, in the village of Luton.

In the evening I put him in mind of his promise to favour me with a copy of his celebrated Letter to the Earl of Chesterfield, and he was at last pleased to comply with this earnest request, by dictating it to me from his memory; for he believed that he himself had no copy. There was an animated glow in his countenance while he thus recalled his high-minded indignation.

He laughed heartily at a ludicrous action in the Court of Session, in which I was Counsel. The Society of *Procurators*, or Attornies, entitled to practise in the inferiour courts at Edinburgh, had obtained a royal charter, in which they had taken care to have their ancient designation of *Procurators* changed into that of *Solicitors*, from a notion, as they supposed, that it was more *genteel*; and this new title they displayed by a publick advertisement for a *General Meeting* at their Hall.

It has been said, that the Scottish nation is not distinguished for humour; and, indeed, what happened on this occasion may in some degree justify the remark: for although this society had contrived to make themselves a very prominent object for the ridicule of such as might stoop to it, the only joke to which it gave rise, was the following paragraph, sent to the newspaper called *The Caledonian Mercury*:—

'A correspondent informs us, that the Worshipful Society of *Chaldeans, Cadies*, or *Running Stationers* of this city are resolved, in imitation, and encouraged by the singular success of their brethren, of an *equally respectable* Society, to apply for a Charter of their Privileges, particularly of the sole privilege of PROCUR-ING, in the most extensive sense of the word, exclusive of chair-men, porters, penny-post men, and other *inferiour* ranks; their brethren the R—y—l S—ll—rs, *alias* P—c—rs, *before the* INFERIOUR Courts of this City, always excepted.

'Should the Worshipful Society be successful, they are farther resolved not to be *puffed up* thereby, but to demean themselves with more equanimity and decency than their *R-y-l, learned*, and *very modest* brethren above mentioned have done, upon their late dignification and exaltation.'

A majority of the members of the Society prosecuted Mr. Robertson, the publisher of the paper, for damages; and the first judgement of the whole Court very wisely dismissed the action: *Solventur risu tabulæ, tu missus abibis*.[1] But a new trial or review was granted upon a petition, according to the forms in Scotland. This petition I was engaged to answer, and Dr. Johnson with great alacrity furnished me this evening with what follows:—

'All injury is either of the person, the fortune, or the fame. Now it is a certain thing, it is proverbially known, that *a jest breaks no bones*. They never have gained half-a-crown less in the whole profession since this mischievous paragraph has appeared; and, as to their reputation, What is their reputation but an instrument of getting money? If, therefore, they have lost no money, the question upon reputation may be answered by a very old position,—*De minimis non curat Prætor*.[2]

'Whether there was, or was not, an *animus injuriandi*,[3] is not worth inquiring, if no *injuria* can be proved. But the truth is, there was no *animus injuriandi*. It was only an *animus irritandi*,[4] which, happening to be exercised upon a *genus irritabile*,[5] produced unexpected violence of resentment. Their irritability arose only from an opinion of their own importance, and their delight in their new exaltation. What might have been borne by a *Procurator* could not be borne by a *Solicitor*. Your Lordships well know, that *honores mutant mores*.[6] Titles and dignities play strongly upon the fancy. As a madman is apt to think himself grown suddenly great, so he that grows suddenly great is apt to borrow a little from the madman. To co-operate with their resentment would be to promote their phrenzy; nor is it possible

[1] ['In a tempest of laughter the tables will go to pieces. You will leave the court without a stain on your character.' Horace, *Satires* II. i. 86. (Wickham.)]

[2] [*De minimis non curat lex*, 'the law does not trouble itself about trifles.']

[3] [an intention to injure.]

[4] [an intention to annoy.] Mr. Robertson altered this word to *jocandi*, he having found in Blackstone that to *irritate* is actionable.

[5] [*genus irritabile vatum*, 'the sensitive race of poets.' Horace, *Epistles* II. ii. 102.]

[6] ['Honours change manners.']

to guess to what they might proceed, if to the new title of Solicitor, should be added the elation of victory and triumph.

'We consider your Lordships as the protectors of our rights, and the guardians of our virtues; but believe it not included in your high office, that you should flatter our vices, or solace our vanity: and, as vanity only dictates this prosecution, it is humbly hoped your Lordships will dismiss it.

'If every attempt, however light or ludicrous, to lessen another's reputation, is to be punished by a judicial sentence, what punishment can be sufficiently severe for him who attempts to diminish the reputation of the Supreme Court of Justice, by reclaiming upon a cause already determined, without any change in the state of the question? Does it not imply hopes that the Judges will change their opinion? Is not uncertainty and inconstancy in the highest degree disreputable to a Court? Does it not suppose, that the former judgement was temerarious or negligent? Does it not lessen the confidence of the publick? Will it not be said, that *jus est aut incognitum aut vagum?* and will not the consequence be drawn, *misera est servitus?*[1] Will not the rules of action be obscure? Will not he who knows himself wrong to-day, hope that the Courts of Justice will think him right to-morrow? Surely, my Lords, these are attempts of dangerous tendency, which the Solicitors, as men versed in the law, should have foreseen and avoided. It was natural for an ignorant printer to appeal from the Lord Ordinary; but from lawyers, the descendants of lawyers, who have practised for three hundred years, and have now raised themselves to a higher denomination, it might be expected, that they should know the reverence due to a judicial determination; and, having been once dismissed, should sit down in silence.'

I am ashamed to mention, that the Court, by a plurality of voices, without having a single additional circumstance before them, reversed their own judgement, made a serious matter of this dull and foolish joke, and adjudged Mr. Robertson to pay to the Society five pounds (sterling money) and costs of suit. The decision will seem strange to English lawyers.

[1] [See note on p. 497.]

On Tuesday, June 5, Johnson was to return to London. He was very pleasant at breakfast; I mentioned a friend of mine[1] having resolved never to marry a pretty woman. JOHNSON. 'Sir, it is a very foolish resolution to resolve not to marry a pretty woman. Beauty is of itself very estimable. No, Sir, I would prefer a pretty woman, unless there are objections to her. A pretty woman may be foolish; a pretty woman may be wicked; a pretty woman may not like me. But there is no such danger in marrying a pretty woman as is apprehended: she will not be persecuted if she does not invite persecution. A pretty woman, if she has a mind to be wicked, can find a readier way than another; and that is all.'

I accompanied him in Mr. Dilly's chaise to Shefford, where talking of Lord Bute's never going to Scotland, he said, 'As an Englishman, I should wish all the Scotch gentlemen to be educated in England; Scotland would become a province; they would spend all their rents in England.' This is a subject of much consequence, and much delicacy. The advantage of an English education is unquestionably very great to Scotch gentlemen of talents and ambition; and regular visits to Scotland, and perhaps other means, might be effectually used to prevent them from being totally estranged from their native country, any more than a Cumberland or Northumberland gentleman who has been educated in the South of England. I own, indeed, that it is no small misfortune for Scotch gentlemen, who have neither talents nor ambition, to be educated in England, where they may be perhaps distinguished only by a nick-name, lavish their fortune in giving expensive entertainments to those who laugh at them, and saunter about as mere idle insignificant hangers on even upon the foolish great; when if they had been judiciously brought up at home, they might have been comfortable and creditable members of society.

At Shefford, I had another affectionate parting from my revered friend, who was taken up by the Bedford coach and carried to the metropolis. I went with Messieurs Dilly, to see some friends at Bedford; dined with the officers of the militia of the county, and next day proceeded on my journey.

[1] [Charles Dilly. *Boswell Papers*, xiv. 245.]

'*To* BENNET LANGTON, ESQ.

'DEAR SIR,—How welcome your account of yourself and your invitation to your new house was to me, I need not tell you, who consider our friendship not only as formed by choice, but as matured by time. We have been now long enough acquainted to have many images in common; and, therefore, to have a source of conversation which neither the learning nor the wit of a new companion can supply.

'My *Lives* are now published; and if you will tell me whither I shall send them, that they may come to you, I will take care that you shall not be without them.

'You will, perhaps, be glad to hear, that Mrs. Thrale is disencumbered of [from] her brewhouse; and that it seemed to the purchaser so far from an evil, that he was content to give for it an hundred and thirty-five thousand pounds. Is the nation ruined?

'Please to make my respectful compliments to Lady Rothes, and keep me in the memory of all the little dear family, particularly pretty Mrs. Jane. I am, Sir, your affectionate humble servant,

'Bolt-Court, June 16, 1781.'   'SAM. JOHNSON.'

Johnson's charity to the poor was uniform and extensive, both from inclination and principle. He not only bestowed liberally out of his own purse, but what is more difficult as well as rare, would beg from others, when he had proper objects in view. This he did judiciously as well as humanely. Mr. Philip Metcalfe tells me, that when he has asked him for some money for persons in distress, and Mr. Metcalfe has offered what Johnson thought too much, he insisted on taking less, saying, 'No, no, Sir; we must not *pamper* them.'

I am indebted to Mr. Malone, one of Sir Joshua Reynolds's executors, for the following note, which was found among his papers after his death, and which, we may presume, his unaffected modesty prevented him from communicating to me with the other letters from Dr. Johnson with which he was pleased to furnish me. However slight in itself, as it does honour to that illustrious painter, and most amiable man, I am happy to introduce it.

'*To* SIR JOSHUA REYNOLDS

'DEAR SIR,—It was not before yesterday that I received your splendid benefaction. To a hand so liberal in distributing, I hope nobody will envy the power of acquiring. I am, dear Sir, your obliged and most humble servant,

'June 23, 1781.'   'SAM. JOHNSON.'

'*To* THOMAS ASTLE, ESQ.

'SIR,—I am ashamed that you have been forced to call so often for your books, but it has been by no fault on either side. They have never been out of my hands, nor have I ever been at home without seeing you; for to see a man so skilful in the antiquities of my country, is an opportunity of improvement not willingly to be missed.

'Your notes on Alfred[1] appear to me very judicious and accurate, but they are too few. Many things familiar to you, are unknown to me, and to most others; and you must not think too favourably of your readers: by supposing them knowing, you will leave them ignorant. Measure of land, and value of money, it is of great importance to state with care. Had the Saxons any gold coin?

'I have much curiosity after the manners and transactions of the middle ages, but have wanted either diligence or opportunity, or both. You, Sir, have great opportunities, and I wish you both diligence and success. I am, Sir, &c.,

'July 17, 1781.'   'SAM. JOHNSON.'

The following curious anecdote I insert in Dr. Burney's own words:—

'Dr. Burney related to Dr. Johnson the partiality which his writings had excited in a friend of Dr. Burney's, the late Mr. Bewley, well known in Norfolk by the name of the *Philosopher of Massingham*: who, from the *Ramblers* and Plan of his *Dictionary*, and long before the authour's fame was established by the

[1] The will of King Alfred, alluded to in this letter, from the original Saxon, in the library of Mr. Astle, has been printed at the expence of the University of Oxford.

Dictionary itself, or any other work, had conceived such a reverence for him, that he urgently begged Dr. Burney to give him the cover of the first letter he had received from him, as a relick of so estimable a writer. This was in 1755. In 1760, when Dr. Burney visited Dr. Johnson at the Temple in London, where he had then chambers, he happened to arrive there before he was up; and being shewn into the room where he was to breakfast, finding himself alone, he examined the contents of the apartment, to try whether he could undiscovered steal anything to send to his friend Bewley, as another relick of the admirable Dr. Johnson. But finding nothing better to his purpose, he cut some bristles off his hearth-broom, and enclosed them in a letter to his country enthusiast, who received them with due reverence. The Doctor was so sensible of the honour done him by a man of genius and science, to whom he was an utter stranger, that he said to Dr. Burney, "Sir, there is no man possessed of the smallest portion of modesty, but must be flattered with the admiration of such a man. I'll give him a set of my *Lives*, if he will do me the honour to accept of them." In this he kept his word; and Dr. Burney had not only the pleasure of gratifying his friend with a present more worthy of his acceptance than the segment from the hearth-broom, but soon after of introducing him to Dr. Johnson himself in Bolt-court, with whom he had the satisfaction of conversing a considerable time, not a fortnight before his death; which happened in St. Martin's-street, during his visit to Dr. Burney, in the house where the great Sir Isaac Newton had lived and died before.'

In one of his little memorandum-books is the following minute:—

'August 9, 3 P.M. ætat. 72, in the summer-house at Streatham.

'After innumerable resolutions formed and neglected, I have retired hither, to plan a life of greater diligence, in hope that I may yet be useful, and be daily better prepared to appear before my Creator and my Judge, from whose infinite mercy I humbly call for assistance and support.

'My purpose is,

'To pass eight hours every day in some serious employment.
[1]'Having prayed, I purpose to employ the next six weeks upon
the Italian language, for my settled study.'

How venerably pious does he appear in these moments of
solitude, and how spirited are his resolutions for the improvement of his mind, even in elegant literature, at a very advanced
period of life, and when afflicted with many complaints.

In autumn he went to Oxford, Birmingham, Lichfield, and
Ashbourne, for which very good reasons might be given in the
conjectural yet positive manner of writers, who are proud to
account for every event which they relate. He himself, however,
says, 'The motives of my journey I hardly know; I omitted it
last year, and am not willing to miss it again.'[2]

But some good considerations arise, amongst which is the
kindly recollection of Mr. Hector, surgeon, at Birmingham.
'Hector is likewise an old friend, the only companion of my
childhood that passed through the school with me. We have
always loved one another; perhaps we may be made better by
some serious conversation, of which however I have no distinct
hope.' He says too, 'At Lichfield, my native place, I hope to
shew a good example by frequent attendance on publick worship.'

My correspondence with him during the rest of this year was,
I know not why, very scanty, and all on my side. I wrote him
one letter to introduce Mr. Sinclair (now Sir John), the member
for Caithness, to his acquaintance; and informed him in another
that my wife had again been affected with alarming symptoms
of illness.

1782: ÆTAT. 73.]—IN 1782, his complaints increased, and the
history of his life this year, is little more than a mournful recital
of the variations of his illness, in the midst of which, however, it
will appear from his letters, that the powers of his mind were
in no degree impaired.

'*To* JAMES BOSWELL, ESQ.

'DEAR SIR,—I sit down to answer your letter on the same day
in which I received it, and am pleased that my first letter of the

------

[1] [MS: 11[th Aug.]]   [2] *Pr. and Med.* p. 201.

year is to you. No man ought to be at ease while he knows himself in the wrong; and I have not satisfied myself with my long silence. The letter relating to Mr. Sinclair, however, was, I believe, never brought.

'My health has been tottering this last year; and I can give no very laudable account of my time. I am always hoping to do better than I have ever hitherto done.

'My journey to Ashbourne and Staffordshire was not pleasant; for what enjoyment has a sick man visiting the sick?—Shall we ever have another frolick like our journey to the Hebrides?

'I hope that dear Mrs. Boswell will surmount her complaints; in losing her you would lose your anchor, and be tost, without stability, by the waves of life.[1] I wish both her and you very many years, and very happy.

'For some months past I have been so withdrawn from the world, that I can send you nothing particular. All your friends, however, are well, and will be glad of your return to London. I am, dear Sir, yours most affectionately,

'January 5, 1782.'   'SAM. JOHNSON.'

At a time when he was less able than he had once been to sustain a shock, he was suddenly deprived of Mr. Levett, which event he thus communicated to Dr. Lawrence:—

'SIR,—Our old friend, Mr. Levett, who was last night eminently cheerful, died this morning. The man who lay in the same room, hearing an uncommon noise, got up and tried to make him speak, but without effect. He then called Mr. Holder, the apothecary, who, though when he came he thought him dead, opened a vein, but could draw no blood. So has ended the long life of a very useful and very blameless man. I am, Sir, your most humble servant,

'Jan. 17, 1782.'   'SAM. JOHNSON.'

In one of his memorandum-books in my possession, is the following entry:—'January 20, Sunday. Robert Levett was

---

[1] The truth of this has been proved by sad experience. [Mrs. Boswell died June 4, 1789—M.]

buried in the church-yard of Bridewell, between one and two in the afternoon. He died on Thursday 17, about seven in the morning, by an instantaneous death. He was an old and faithful friend; I have known him from about 46. *Commendavi.*[1] May GOD have mercy on him. May he have mercy on me.'

Such was Johnson's affectionate regard for Levett,[2] that he honoured his memory with the following pathetick verses:--

'CONDEMN'D to Hope's delusive mine,
  As on we toil from day to day,
By sudden blast or slow decline
  Our social comforts drop away.

Well try'd through many a varying year,
  See LEVETT to the grave descend;
Officious, innocent, sincere,
  Of every friendless name the friend.

Yet still he fills Affection's eye,
  Obscurely wise, and coarsely kind;
Nor, letter'd arrogance,[3] deny
  Thy praise to merit unrefin'd.

When fainting Nature call'd for aid,
  And hov'ring Death prepar'd the blow,
His vigorous remedy display'd
  The power of art without the show.

In Misery's darkest caverns known,
  His ready help was ever nigh,
Where hopeless Anguish pour'd his groan,
  And lonely Want retir'd to die.[4]

No summons mock'd by chill delay,
  No petty gains disdain'd by pride;
The modest wants of every day
  The toil of every day supply'd.

[1] ['I commended' (his soul to heaven).]
[2] See an account of him in the *Gent. Mag.* Feb. 1785.
[3] In both editions of Sir John Hawkins's *Life of Dr. Johnson*, 'letter'd *ignorance*' is printed.
[4] Johnson repeated this line to me thus:—
        'And Labour steals an hour to die.'
But he afterwards altered it to the present reading.

His virtues walk'd their narrow round,
Nor made a pause, nor left a void;
And sure th'Eternal Master found
His single talent well employ'd.

The busy day, the peaceful night,
Unfelt, uncounted, glided by;
His frame was firm, his powers were bright,
Though now his eightieth year was nigh.

Then, with no throbs of fiery pain,
No cold gradations of decay,
Death broke at once the vital chain,
And freed his soul the nearest way.'

In one of Johnson's registers of this year, there occurs the following curious passage:—'Jan. 20. The Ministry is dissolved. I prayed with Francis and gave thanks.'[1]

It has been the subject of discussion, whether there are two distinct particulars mentioned here? or that we are to understand the giving of thanks to be in consequence of the dissolution of the Ministry? In support of the last of these conjectures may be urged his mean opinion of that Ministry, which has frequently appeared in the course of this work; and it is strongly confirmed by what he said on the subject to Mr. Seward:—'I am glad the Ministry is removed. Such a bunch of imbecility never disgraced a country. If they sent a messenger into the City to take up a printer, the messenger was taken up instead of the printer, and committed by the sitting Alderman. If they sent one army to the relief of another, the first army was defeated and taken before the second arrived. I will not say that what they did was always wrong; but it was always done at a wrong time.'

'*To* MRS. STRAHAN

'DEAR MADAM,—Mrs. Williams shewed me your kind letter. This little habitation is now but a melancholy place, clouded with the gloom of disease and death. Of the four inmates, one has been suddenly snatched away; two are oppressed by very

[1] *Pr. and Med.* p. 209 [207].

afflictive and dangerous illness; and I tried yesterday to gain some relief by a third bleeding, from a disorder which has for some time distressed me, and I think myself to-day much better.

'I am glad, dear Madam, to hear that you are so far recovered as to go to Bath. Let me once more entreat you to stay till your health is not only obtained, but confirmed. Your fortune is such as that no moderate expence deserves your care; and you have a husband, who, I believe, does not regard it. Stay, therefore, till you are quite well. I am, for my part, very much deserted;[1] but complaint is useless. I hope GOD will bless you, and I desire you to form the same wish for me. I am, dear Madam, your most humble servant,

    'Feb. 4, 1782.'   'SAM. JOHNSON.'

'*To* EDMOND MALONE, ESQ.

'SIR,—I have for many weeks been so much out of order, that I have gone out only in a coach to Mrs. Thrale's, where I can use all the freedom that sickness requires. Do not, therefore, take it amiss, that I am not with you and Dr. Farmer. I hope hereafter to see you often. I am, Sir, your most humble servant,

    'Feb. 27, 1782.'   'SAM. JOHNSON.'

'*To* THE SAME

'DEAR SIR,—I hope I grow better, and shall soon be able to enjoy the kindness of my friends. I think this wild adherence to Chatterton[2] more unaccountable than the obstinate defence of Ossian. In Ossian there is a national pride, which may be forgiven, though it cannot be applauded. In Chatterton there is nothing but the resolution to say again what has once been said. I am, Sir, your humble servant,

    'March 7, 1782.'   'SAM. JOHNSON.'

---

[1] [Johnson wrote *dejected*.]

[2] This Note was in answer to one which accompanied one of the earliest pamphlets on the subject of Chatterton's forgery, entitled *Cursory Observations on the Poems attributed to Thomas Rowley*, &c. Mr. Thomas Warton's very able *Inquiry* appeared about three months afterwards; and Mr. Tyrwhitt's admirable *Vindication of his Appendix* in the summer of the same year, left the believers in this daring imposture nothing but 'the resolution to say again what had been said before.' [M.]

These short letters shew the regard which Dr. Johnson entertained for Mr. Malone, who the more he is known is the more highly valued. It is much to be regretted that Johnson was prevented from sharing the elegant hospitality of that gentleman's table, at which he would in every respect have been fully gratified. Mr. Malone, who has so ably succeeded him as an Editor of Shakspeare, has, in his Preface, done great and just honour to Johnson's memory.

'*To* Mrs. Lucy Porter, *in Lichfield*

'Dear Madam,—I went away from Lichfield ill, and have had a troublesome time with my breath; for some weeks I have been disordered by a cold, of which I could not get the violence abated, till I had been let blood three times. I have not, however, been so bad but that I could have written, and I am sorry that I neglected it.

'My dwelling is but melancholy; both Williams, and Desmoulins, and myself, are very sickly; Frank is not well; and poor Levett died in his bed the other day, by a sudden stroke; I suppose not one minute passed between health and death; so uncertain are human things.

'Such is the appearance of the world about me; I hope your scenes are more cheerful. But whatever befalls us, though it is wise to be serious, it is useless and foolish, and perhaps sinful, to be gloomy. Let us, therefore, keep ourselves as easy as we can; though the loss of friends will be felt, and poor Levett had been a faithful adherent for thirty years.

'Forgive me, my dear love, the omission of writing; I hope to mend that and my other faults. Let me have your prayers.

'Make my compliments to Mrs. Cobb, and Miss Adey, and Mr. Pearson, and the whole company of my friends. I am, my dear, your most humble servant,

'London, March 2, 1782.'   'Sam. Johnson.'

To The Same

'Dear Madam,—My last was but a dull letter, and I know not

that this will be much more cheerful; I am, however, willing to write, because you are desirous to hear from me.

'My disorder has now begun its ninth week, for it is not yet over. I was last Thursday blooded for the fourth time, and have since found myself much relieved, but I am very tender and easily hurt; so that since we parted I have had but little comfort, but I hope that the spring will recover me; and that in the summer I shall see Lichfield again, for I will not delay my visit another year to the end of autumn.

'I have, by advertising, found poor Mr. Levett's brothers in Yorkshire, who will take the little that he has left: it is but little, yet it will be welcome, for I believe they are of very low condition.

'To be sick, and to see nothing but sickness and death, is but a gloomy state; but I hope better times, even in this world, will come, and whatever this world may with-hold or give, we shall be happy in a better state. Pray for me, my dear Lucy.

'Make my compliments to Mrs. Cobb, and Miss Adey, and my old friend Hetty Baily, and to all the Lichfield ladies. I am, dear Madam, yours, affectionately,

'Bolt-court, Fleet-street,   'SAM. JOHNSON.'
  March 19, 1782.'

On the day on which this letter was written, he thus feelingly mentions his respected friend and physician, Dr. Lawrence:—
'Poor Lawrence has almost lost the sense of hearing; and I have lost the conversation of a learned, intelligent, and communicative companion, and a friend whom long familiarity has much endeared. Lawrence is one of the best men whom I have known.— *Nostrum omnium miserere Deus.*[1]

It was Dr. Johnson's custom when he wrote to Dr. Lawrence concerning his own health, to use the Latin language. I have been favoured by Miss Lawrence with one of these letters as a specimen:—

[1] ['God have mercy on us all.'] *Pr. and Med.* p. 207.

'T. Lawrencio, *Medico*, S.[1]

'Novum *frigus, nova tussis, nova spirandi difficultas, novam sanguinis*[2] *missionem suadent, quam tamen te inconsulto nolim fieri. Ad te venire vix possum, nec est cur ad me venias. Licere vel non licere uno verbo dicendum est; cætera mihi et Holdero*[3] *reliqueris. Si per te licet, imperatur*[4] *nuncio Holderum ad me deducere.*

'*Maiis Calendis,* 1782.

'*Postquàm tu discesseris, quò me vertam?*'[5]

---

[1] ['To Dr. Lawrence. A fresh chill, a fresh cough, and a fresh difficulty in breathing call for a fresh letting of blood. Without your advice, however, I would not submit to the operation. I cannot well come to you, nor need you come to me. Say yes or no in one word, and leave the rest to Holder and to me. If you say yes, let the messenger be bidden to bring Holder to me. May 1, 1782. When *you* have left, whither shall I turn?"]

[2] (orig. *sanguinosi*.)

[3] Mr. Holder, in the Strand, Dr. Johnson's apothecary.

[4] [Johnson wrote *imperetur*: 'tell the messenger to send Holder.' This closes an ancient controversy.]

[5] Soon after the above letter, Dr. Lawrence left London, but not before the palsy had made so great a progress as to render him unable to write for himself. The following are extracts from letters addressed by Dr. Johnson to one of his daughters:—

'You will easily believe with what gladness I read that you had heard once again that voice to which we have all so often delighted to attend. May you often hear it. If we had his mind, and his tongue, we could spare the rest.

'I am not vigorous, but much better than when dear Dr. Lawrence held my pulse the last time. Be so kind as to let me know, from one little interval to another, the state of his body. I am pleased that he remembers me, and hope that it never can be possible for me to forget him. July 22, 1782.'

'I am much delighted even with the small advances which dear Dr. Lawrence makes towards recovery. If we could have again but his mind, and his tongue in his mind, and his right hand, we should not much lament the rest. I should not despair of helping the swelled hand by electricity, if it were frequently and diligently supplied.

'Let me know from time to time whatever happens; and I hope I need not tell you, how much I am interested in every change. Aug. 26, 1782.'

'Though the account with which you favoured me in your last letter could not give me the pleasure that I wished, yet I was glad to receive it; for my affection to my dear friend makes me desirous of knowing his state, whatever it be. I beg, therefore, that you continue to let me know, from time to time, all that you observe.

'Many fits of severe illness have, for about three months past, forced my kind physician often upon my mind. I am now better; and hope gratitude, as well as distress, can be a motive to remembrance. Bolt-court, Fleet-street, Feb. 4, 1783.'

'*To* CAPTAIN LANGTON,[1] *in Rochester*

'DEAR SIR,—It is now long since we saw one another; and whatever has been the reason neither you have written to me, nor I to you. To let friendship die away by negligence and silence, is certainly not wise. It is voluntarily to throw away one of the greatest comforts of this weary pilgrimage, of which when it is, as it must be, taken finally away, he that travels on alone, will wonder how his esteem could be so little. Do not forget me; you see that I do not forget you. It is pleasing in the silence of solitude to think, that there is one at least, however distant, of whose benevolence there is little doubt, and whom there is yet hope of seeing again.

'Of my life, from the time we parted, the history is mournful. The spring of last year deprived me of Thrale, a man whose eye for fifteen years had scarcely been turned upon me but with respect or tenderness; for such another friend, the general course of human things will not suffer man to hope. I passed the summer at Streatham, but there was no Thrale; and having idled away the summer with a weakly body and neglected mind, I made a journey to Staffordshire on the edge of winter. The season was dreary, I was sickly, and found the friends sickly whom I went to see. After a sorrowful sojourn, I returned to a habitation possessed for the present by two sick women, where my dear old friend, Mr. Levett, to whom as he used to tell me, I owe your acquaintance, died a few weeks ago, suddenly in his bed; there passed not, I believe, a minute between health and death. At night, as at Mrs. Thrale's I was musing in my chamber, I thought with uncommon earnestness, that however I might alter my mode of life, or whithersoever I might remove, I would endeavour to retain Levett about me; in the morning my servant brought me word that Levett was called to another state, a state for which, I think, he was not unprepared, for he was very useful to the poor. How much soever I valued him, I now wish that I had valued him more.

'I have myself been ill more than eight weeks of a disorder,

[1] Mr. Langton being at this time on duty at Rochester, he is addressed by his military title.

from which at the expence of about fifty ounces of blood, I hope I am now recovering.

'You, dear Sir, have, I hope, a more cheerful scene; you see George fond of his book, and the pretty misses airy and lively, with my own little Jenny equal to the best: and in whatever can contribute to your quiet or pleasure, you have Lady Rothes ready to concur. May whatever you enjoy of good be encreased, and whatever you suffer of evil be diminished. I am, dear Sir, your humble servant,   'SAM. JOHNSON.'

'Bolt-court, Fleet-street, March 20, 1782.'

'To MR. HECTOR, *in Birmingham*[1]

'DEAR SIR,—I hope I do not very grossly flatter myself to imagine that you and dear Mrs. Careless[2] will be glad to hear some account of me. I performed the journey to London with very little inconvenience, and came safe to my habitation, where I found nothing but ill health, and, of consequence, very little cheerfulness. I then went to visit a little way into the country, where I got a complaint by a cold which has hung eight weeks upon me, and from which I am, at the expence of fifty ounces of blood, not yet free. I am afraid I must once more owe my recovery to warm weather, which seems to make no advances towards us.

'Such is my health, which will, I hope, soon grow better. In other respects I have no reason to complain. I know not that I have written anything more generally commended than the *Lives of the Poets*; and have found the world willing enough to caress me, if my health had invited me to be in much company; but this season I have been almost wholly employed in nursing myself.

'When summer comes I hope to see you again, and will not put off my visit to the end of the year. I have lived so long in London, that I did not remember the difference of seasons.

---

[1] A part of this letter having been torn off, I have, from the evident meaning, supplied a few words and half-words at the ends and beginnings of lines.
[2] See p. 704.

'Your health, when I saw you, was much improved. You will be prudent enough not to put it in danger. I hope, when we meet again, we shall all congratulate each other upon fair prospects of longer life; though what are the pleasures of the longest life, when placed in comparison with a happy death? I am, dear Sir, yours most affectionately,

'London, March 21, 1782.   'SAM. JOHNSON.'

To THE SAME

'DEAR SIR,

[Without a date, but supposed to be about this time.][1]

'That you and dear Mrs. Careless should have care or curiosity about my health, gives me that pleasure which every man feels from finding himself not forgotten. In age we feel again that love of our native place and our early friends, which in the bustle or amusements of middle life were overborne and suspended. You and I should now naturally cling to one another: we have outlived most of those who could pretend to rival us in each other's kindness. In our walk through life we have dropped our companions, and are now to pick up such as chance may offer us, or to travel on alone. You, indeed, have a sister, with whom you can divide the day: I have no natural friend left; but Providence has been pleased to preserve me from neglect; I have not wanted such alleviations of life as friendship could supply. My health has been, from my twentieth year, such as has seldom afforded me a single day of ease; but it is at least not worse: and I sometimes make myself believe that it is better. My disorders are, however, still sufficiently oppressive.

'I think of seeing Staffordshire again this autumn, and intend to find my way through Birmingham, where I hope to see you and dear Mrs. Careless well. I am, Sir, your affectionate friend,

'SAM. JOHNSON.'

I wrote to him at different dates; regretted that I could not come to London this spring, but hoped we should meet some-

---

[1] [Boswell overlooked the postmark, 28 August. The letter must belong to an earlier year.]

where in the summer; mentioned the state of my affairs, and suggested hopes of some preferment; informed him, that as *The Beauties of Johnson* had been published in London, some obscure scribbler[1] had published at Edinburgh what he called *The deformities of Johnson*.

'*To* James Boswell, Esq.

'Dear Sir,—The pleasure which we used to receive from each other on Good-Friday and Easter-day, we must be this year content to miss. Let us, however, pray for each other, and hope to see one another yet from time to time with mutual delight. My disorder has been a cold, which impeded the organs of respiration, and kept me many weeks in a state of great uneasiness; but by repeated phlebotomy it is now relieved; and next to the recovery of Mrs. Boswell, I flatter myself, that you will rejoice at mine.

'What we shall do in the summer it is yet too early to consider. You want to know what you shall do now; I do not think this time of bustle and confusion likely to produce any advantage to you. Every man has those to reward and gratify who have contributed to his advancement. To come hither with such expectations at the expence of borrowed money, which, I find, you know not where to borrow, can hardly be considered as prudent. I am sorry to find, what your solicitation seems to imply, that you have already gone the whole length of your credit. This is to set the quiet of your whole life at hazard. If you anticipate your inheritance, you can at last inherit nothing; all that you receive must pay for the past. You must get a place, or pine in penury, with the empty name of a great estate. Poverty, my dear friend, is so great an evil, and pregnant with so much temptation, and so much misery, that I cannot but earnestly enjoin you to avoid it. Live on what you have; live if you can on less; do not borrow either for vanity or pleasure; the vanity will end in shame, and the pleasure in regret: stay therefore at home, till you have saved money for your journey hither.

'*The Beauties of Johnson* are said to have got money to the

---

[1] [J. Thomson Callender.]

collector; if the *Deformities* have the same success, I shall be still a more extensive benefactor.

'Make my compliments to Mrs. Boswell, who is, I hope, reconciled to me; and to the young people, whom I never have offended.

'You never told me the success of your plea against the Solicitors. I am, dear Sir, your most affectionate,

'London, March 28, 1782.'　　　　　　'SAM. JOHNSON.'

Notwithstanding his afflicted state of body and mind this year, the following correspondence affords a proof not only of his benevolence and conscientious readiness to relieve a good man from errour, but by his cloathing one of the sentiments in his *Rambler* in different language, not inferiour to that of the original, shews his extraordinary command of clear and forcible expression.

A clergyman at Bath wrote to him, that in *The Morning Chronicle*, a passage in *The Beauties of Johnson*, article DEATH, had been pointed out as supposed by some readers to recommend suicide, the words being, 'To die is the fate of man; but to die with lingering anguish is generally his folly;' and respectfully suggesting to him, that such an erroneous notion of any sentence in the writings of an acknowledged friend of religion and virtue, should not pass uncontradicted.

Johnson thus answered the clergyman's letter:—

To THE REVEREND MR. ————,[1] *at Bath*

'SIR,—Being now in the country in a state of recovery, as I hope, from a very oppressive disorder, I cannot neglect the acknowledgement of your Christian letter. The book called *The Beauties of Johnson* is the production of I know not whom: I never saw it but by casual inspection, and considered myself as utterly disengaged from its consequences. Of the passage you mention, I remember some notice in some paper; but, knowing that it must be misrepresented, I thought of it no more, nor do I know[2]

---

[1] [Johnson's correspondent was Lancelot St. Albyn.]
[2] [Johnson wrote *now know*.]

where to find it in my own books. I am accustomed to think little of newspapers; but an opinion so weighty and serious as yours has determined me to do, what I should, without your seasonable admonition, have omitted; and I will direct my thought to be shewn in its true state.[1] If I could find the passage, I would direct you to it. I suppose the tenour is this:—"Acute diseases are the immediate and inevitable strokes of Heaven; but of them the pain is short, and the conclusion speedy: chronical disorders, by which we are suspended in tedious torture between life and death, are commonly the effect of our own misconduct and intemperance. To die, &c."—This, Sir, you see, is all true and all blameless. I hope, some time in the next week, to have all rectified. My health has been lately much shaken; if you favour this with any answer, it will be a comfort to me to know that I have your prayers. I am, &c.,

'May 15, 1782.'   'SAM. JOHNSON.'

This letter, as might be expected, had its full effect, and the clergyman acknowledged it in grateful and pious terms.[2]

The following letters require no extracts from mine to introduce them:—

'*To* JAMES BOSWELL, ESQ.

'DEAR SIR,—The earnestness and tenderness of your letter is such, that I cannot think myself shewing it more respect than it claims by sitting down to answer it the day on which I received it.

'This year has afflicted me with a very irksome and severe

[1] What follows appeared in the *Morning Chronicle* of May 29, 1782:— 'A correspondent having mentioned, in the *Morning Chronicle* of December 12, the last clause of the following paragraph, as seeming to favour suicide; we are requested to print the whole passage, that its true meaning may appear, which is not to recommend suicide but exercise.

'Exercise cannot secure us from that dissolution to which we are decreed; but while the soul and body continue united, it can make the association pleasing, and give probable hopes that they shall be disjoined by an easy separation. It was a principle among the ancients, that acute diseases are from Heaven, and chronical from ourselves; the dart of death, indeed, falls from Heaven, but we poison it by our own misconduct: to die is the fate of man; but to die with lingering anguish is generally his folly.' [*Rambler*, 85.]

[2] The Correspondence may be seen at length in the *Gent. Mag.* Feb. 1786.

disorder. My respiration has been much impeded, and much blood has been taken away. I am now harrassed by a catarrhous cough, from which my purpose is to seek relief by change of air; and I am, therefore, preparing to go to Oxford.

'Whether I did right in dissuading you from coming to London this spring, I will not determine. You have not lost much by missing my company; I have scarcely been well for a single week. I might have received comfort from your kindness; but you would have seen me afflicted, and, perhaps, found me peevish. Whatever might have been your pleasure or mine, I know not how I could have honestly advised you to come hither with borrowed money. Do not accustom yourself to consider debt only as an inconvenience; you will find it a calamity. Poverty takes away so many means of doing good, and produces so much inability to resist evil, both natural and moral, that it is by all virtuous means to be avoided. Consider a man whose fortune is very narrow; whatever be his rank by birth, or whatever his reputation by intellectual excellence, what good can he do? or what evil can he prevent? That he cannot help the needy is evident; he has nothing to spare. But, perhaps, his advice or admonition may be useful. His poverty will destroy his influence: many more can find that he is poor, than that he is wise; and few will reverence the understanding that is of so little advantage to its owner. I say nothing of the personal wretchedness of a debtor, which, however, has passed into a proverb. Of riches, it is not necessary to write the praise. Let it, however, be remembered, that he who has money to spare, has it always in his power to benefit others; and of such power a good man must always be desirous.

'I am pleased with your account of Easter.[1] We shall meet, I hope, in Autumn, both well and both cheerful; and part each the better for the other's company.

'Make my compliments to Mrs. Boswell, and to the young charmers. I am, &c.

'London, June 3, 1782.'   'SAM. JOHNSON.'

[1] Which I celebrated in the Church of England chapel at Edinburgh, founded by Lord Chief Baron Smith, of respectable and pious memory.

'*To* Mr. Perkins

'Dear Sir,—I am much pleased that you are going a very long journey, which may by proper conduct restore your health and prolong your life.

'Observe these rules:

'1. Turn all care out of your head as soon as you mount the chaise.

'2. Do not think about frugality; your health is worth more than it can cost.

'3. Do not continue any day's journey to fatigue.

'4. Take now and then a day's rest.

'5. Get a smart sea-sickness, if you can.

'6. Cast away all anxiety, and keep your mind easy.

'This last direction is the principal; with an unquiet mind, neither exercise, nor diet, nor physick, can be of much use.

'I wish you, dear Sir, a prosperous journey, and a happy recovery.[1] I am, dear Sir, your most affectionate, humble servant,

'July 28, 1782.'   'Sam. Johnson.'

'*To* James Boswell, Esq.

'Dear Sir,—Being uncertain whether I should have any call this autumn into the country, I did not immediately answer your kind letter. I have no call; but if you desire to meet me at Ashbourne, I believe I can come thither; if you had rather come to London, I can stay at Streatham; take your choice.

'This year has been very heavy. From the middle of January to the middle of June I was battered by one disorder after another; I am now very much recovered, and hope still to be better. What happiness it is that Mrs. Boswell has escaped.

'My *Lives* are reprinting, and I have forgotten the authour of Gray's character:[2] write immediately, and it may be perhaps yet inserted.

'Of London or Ashbourne you have your free choice; at any place I shall be glad to see you. I am, dear Sir, yours, &c.

'Aug. 24, 1782.'   'Sam. Johnson.'

[1] [Johnson wrote *recovery, for.*]
[2] The Reverend Mr. Temple, Vicar of St. Gluvias, Cornwall.

On the 30th of August, I informed him that my honoured father had died that morning; a complaint under which he had long laboured having suddenly come to a crisis, while I was upon a visit at the seat of Sir Charles Preston, from whence I had hastened the day before, upon receiving a letter by express.

'*To* JAMES BOSWELL, ESQ.

'DEAR SIR,—I have struggled through this year with so much infirmity of body, and such strong impressions of the fragility of life, that death, wherever it appears, fills me with melancholy; and I cannot hear without emotion, of the removal of any one, whom I have known, into another state.

'Your father's death had every circumstance that could enable you to bear it; it was at a mature age, and it was expected; and as his general life had been pious, his thoughts had doubtless for many years past been turned upon eternity. That you did not find him sensible must doubtless grieve you; his disposition towards you was undoubtedly that of a kind, though not of a fond father. Kindness, at least actual, is in our power, but fondness is not; and if by negligence or imprudence you had extinguished his fondness, he could not at will rekindle it. Nothing then remained between you but mutual forgiveness of each other's faults, and mutual desire of each other's happiness.

'I shall long to know his final disposition of his fortune.

'You, dear Sir, have now a new station, and have therefore new cares, and new employments. Life, as Cowley seems to say, ought to resemble a well-ordered poem; of which one rule generally received is, that the exordium should be simple, and should promise little. Begin your new course of life with the least show, and the least expence possible; you may at pleasure encrease both, but you cannot easily diminish them. Do not think your estate your own, while any man can call upon you for money which you cannot pay; therefore, begin with timorous parsimony. Let it be your first care not to be in any man's debt.

'When the thoughts are extended to a future state, the present life seems hardly worthy of all those principles of conduct, and maxims of prudence, which one generation of men has transmitted to another; but upon a closer view, when it is perceived how much evil is produced, and how much good is impeded by embarrassment and distress, and how little room the expedients of poverty leave for the exercise of virtue, it grows manifest that the boundless importance of the next life enforces some attention to, the interests of this.

'Be kind to the old servants, and secure the kindness of the agents and factors; do not disgust them by asperity, or unwelcome gaiety, or apparent suspicion. From them you must learn the real state of your affairs, the characters of your tenants, and the value of your lands.

'Make my compliments to Mrs. Boswell; I think her expectations from air and exercise are the best that she can form. I hope she will live long and happily.

'I forget whether I told you that Rasay has been here; we dined cheerfully together. I entertained lately a young gentleman from Corrichatachin.

'I received your letters only this morning. I am, dear Sir, yours, &c.

'London, Sept. 7, 1782.'   'SAM. JOHNSON.'

In answer to my next letter, I received one from him, dissuading me from hastening to him as I had proposed; what is proper for publication is the following paragraph, equally just and tender:—'One expence, however, I would not have you to spare: let nothing be omitted that can preserve Mrs. Boswell, though it should be necessary to transplant her for a time into a softer climate. She is the prop and stay of your life. How much must your children suffer by losing her.'

My wife was now so much convinced of his sincere friendship for me, and regard for her, that, without any suggestion on my part, she wrote him a very polite and grateful letter:—

'DR. JOHNSON *to* MRS. BOSWELL

'DEAR LADY,—I have not often received so much pleasure as from your invitation to Auchinleck. The journey thither and back is, indeed, too great for the latter part of the year; but if my health were fully recovered, I would suffer no little heat and cold, nor a wet or a rough road to keep me from you. I am, indeed, not without hope of seeing Auchinleck again; but to make it a pleasant place I must see its lady well, and brisk, and airy. For my sake, therefore, among many greater reasons, take care, dear Madam, of your health, spare no expence, and want no attendance that can procure ease, or preserve it. Be very careful to keep your mind quiet; and do not think it too much to give an account of your recovery to, Madam, your, &c.

'London, Sept. 7, 1782.'[1] 'Sam. Johnson.'

'*To* James Boswell, Esq.

'Dear Sir,—Having passed almost this whole year in a succession of disorders, I went in October to Brighthelmston, whither I came in a state of so much weakness, that I rested four times in walking between the inn and the lodging. By physick and abstinence I grew better, and am now reasonably easy, though at a great distance from health. I am afraid, however, that health begins, after seventy, and often long before, to have a meaning different from that which it had at thirty. But it is culpable to murmur at the established order of the creation, as it is vain to oppose it. He that lives must grow old; and he that would rather grow old than die, has God to thank for the infirmities of old age.

'At your long silence I am rather angry. You do not, since now you are the head of your house, think it worth your while to try whether you or your friend can live longer without writing, nor suspect that after so many years of friendship, that when I do not write to you, I forget you. Put all such useless jealousies out of your head, and disdain to regulate your own practice by the practice of another, or by any other principle than the desire of doing right.

'Your œconomy, I suppose, begins now to be settled; your expences are adjusted to your revenue, and all your people in their proper places. Resolve not to be poor: whatever you have, spend less. Poverty is a great enemy to human happiness; it

[1] [The letter is misdated by Johnson.]

certainly destroys liberty, and it makes some virtues impracticable, and others extremely difficult.

'Let me know the history of your life, since your accession to
your estate. How many houses, how many cows, how much land
in your own hand, and what bargains you make with your
tenants. . . .

'Of my *Lives of the Poets,* they have printed a new edition in
octavo, I hear, of three thousand. Did I give a set to Lord
Hailes? If I did not, I will do it out of these. What did you make
of all your copy?

'Mrs. Thrale and the three Misses are now for the winter in
Argyll-street. Sir Joshua Reynolds has been out of order, but is
well again; and I am, dear Sir, your affectionate humble servant,

'London, Dec. 7, 1782.'   'SAM. JOHNSON.'

'*To* DR. SAMUEL JOHNSON.

'DEAR SIR,   'Edinburgh, Dec. 20, 1782.
    'I was made happy by your kind letter, which gave us the
agreeable hopes of seeing you in Scotland again.

'I am much flattered by the concern you are pleased to take in
my recovery. I am better, and hope to have it in my power to
convince you by my attention of how much consequence I
esteem your health to the world and to myself. I remain, Sir,
with grateful respect, your obliged and obedient servant,

'MARGARET BOSWELL.'

The death of Mr. Thrale had made a very material alteration
with respect to Johnson's reception in that family. The manly
authority of the husband no longer curbed the lively exuberance
of the lady; and as her vanity had been fully gratified, by having
the Colossus of Literature attached to her for many years, she
gradually became less assiduous to please him. Whether her
attachment to him was already divided by another object, I am
unable to ascertain; but it is plain that Johnson's penetration was
alive to her neglect or forced attention; for on the 6th of October
this year, we find him making a 'parting use of the library' at

Streatham, and pronouncing a prayer, which he composed on leaving Mr. Thrale's family.[1]

'Almighty God, Father of all mercy, help me by thy grace, that I may, with humble and sincere thankfulness, remember the comforts and conveniences which I have enjoyed at this place; and that I may resign them with holy submission, equally trusting in thy protection when Thou givest, and when Thou takest away. Have mercy upon me, O Lord, have mercy upon me. 'To thy fatherly protection, O Lord, I commend this family. Bless, guide, and defend them, that they may so pass through this world, as finally to enjoy in thy presence everlasting happiness, for Jesus Christ's sake. Amen.'

One cannot read this prayer, without some emotions not very favourable to the lady whose conduct occasioned it.

In one of his memorandum-books I find, 'Sunday, went to church at Streatham. *Templo valedixi cum osculo.*'[2]

He met Mr. Philip Metcalfe often at Sir Joshua Reynolds's, and other places, and was a good deal with him at Brighthelmston this autumn, being pleased at once with his excellent table and animated conversation. Mr. Metcalfe shewed him great respect, and sent him a note that he might have the use of his carriage whenever he pleased. Johnson (3rd October, 1782) returned this polite answer:—'Mr. Johnson is very much obliged by the kind offer of the carriage; but he has no desire of using Mr. Metcalfe's carriage, except when he can have the pleasure of Mr. Metcalfe's company.' Mr. Metcalfe could not but be highly pleased that his company was thus valued by Johnson, and he frequently attended him in airings. They also went together to Chichester, and they visited Petworth, and Cowdry, the venerable seat of the Lords Montacute. 'Sir, (said Johnson,) I should like to stay here four-and-twenty hours. We see here how our ancestors lived.'

That his curiosity was still unabated, appears from two letters to Mr. John Nichols, of the 10th and 20th of October this year. In one he says, 'I have looked into your *Anecdotes*, and you will

[1] *Pr. and Med.* p. 214.
[2] ['I bade good-bye to the church with a kiss.']

hardly thank a lover of literary history for telling you, that he has been much informed and gratified. I wish you would add your own discoveries and intelligence to those of Dr. Rawlinson, and undertake the Supplement to Wood. Think of it.' In the other, 'I wish, Sir, you could obtain some fuller information of Jortin, Markland, and Thirlby. They were three contemporaries of great eminence.'

'*To* Sir Joshua Reynolds

'Dear Sir,—I heard yesterday of your late disorder, and should think ill of myself if I had heard of it without alarm. I heard likewise of your recovery, which I sincerely wish to be complete and permanent. Your country has been in danger of losing one of its brightest ornaments, and I of losing one of my oldest and kindest friends: but I hope you will still live long, for the honour of the nation: and that more enjoyment of your elegance, your intelligence, and your benevolence, is still reserved for, dear Sir, your most affectionate, &c.

'Brighthelmston, Nov. 14, 1782.'   'Sam. Johnson.'

The Reverend Mr. Wilson having dedicated to him his *Archæological Dictionary*, that mark of respect was thus acknowledged:—

'*To* The Reverend Mr. Wilson, *Clitheroe, Lancashire*

'Reverend Sir,—That I have long omitted to return you thanks for the honour conferred upon me by your Dedication, I intreat you with great earnestness not to consider as more faulty than it is. A very importunate and oppressive disorder has for some time debarred me from the pleasures, and obstructed me in the duties of life. The esteem and kindness of wise and good men is one of the last pleasures which I can be content to lose; and gratitude to those from whom this pleasure is received, is a duty of which I hope never to be reproached with the final neglect. I therefore now return you thanks for the notice which I have received from you, and which I consider as giving to my name not only more bulk, but more weight; not only as extending its superficies, but as increasing its value. Your book was evidently wanted, and will, I hope, find its way into the school,[1] to which, however, I do not mean to confine it; for no man has so much skill in ancient rites and practices as not to want it. As I suppose myself to owe part of your kindness to my excellent friend, Dr. Patten, he has likewise a just claim to my acknowledgements, which I hope you, Sir, will transmit. There will soon appear a new edition of my Poetical Biography; if you will accept of a copy to keep me in your mind, be pleased to let me know how it may be conveniently conveyed to you. The present is small, but it is given with good will by, Reverend Sir, your most, &c.

'December 31, 1782.'   'SAM. JOHNSON.'

1783: ÆTAT. 74.]—IN 1783, he was more severely afflicted than ever, as will appear in the course of his correspondence; but still the same ardour for literature, the same constant piety, the same kindness for his friends, and the same vivacity both in conversation and writing, distinguished him.

Having given Dr. Johnson a full account of what I was doing at Auchinleck, and particularly mentioned what I knew would please him,—my having brought an old man[2] of eighty-eight from a lonely cottage to a comfortable habitation within my enclosures, where he had good neighbours near to him,—I received an answer in February, of which I extract what follows:—

'I am delighted with your account of your activity at Auchinleck, and wish the old gentleman, whom you have so kindly removed, may live long to promote your prosperity by his prayers. You have now a new character and new duties; think on them and practise them.

'Make an impartial estimate of your revenue, and whatever it is, live upon less. Resolve never to be poor. Frugality is not only the basis of quiet, but of beneficence. No man can help others that wants help himself; we must have enough before we have to spare.

---

[1] [Johnson probably wrote *schools*.]
[2] [John Colvil. *Boswell Papers*, xv. 144.]

'I am glad to find that Mrs. Boswell grows well; and hope that to keep her well, no care nor caution will be omitted. May you long live happily together.

'When you come hither, pray bring with you Baxter's *Anacreon.* I cannot get that edition in London.'

On Friday, March 21, having arrived in London the night before, I was glad to find him at Mrs. Thrale's house, in Argyll-street, appearances of friendship between them being still kept up. I was shewn into his room, and after the first salutation he said, 'I am glad you are come. I am very ill.' He looked pale, and was distressed with a difficulty of breathing; but after the common inquiries he assumed his usual strong animated style of conversation. Seeing me now for the first time as a *Laird,* or proprietor of land, he began thus: 'Sir, the superiority of a country-gentleman over the people upon his estate is very agreeable; and he who says he does not feel it to be agreeable, lies; for it must be agreeable to have a casual superiority over those who are by nature equal with us.' BOSWELL. 'Yet, Sir, we see great proprietors of land who prefer living in London.' JOHNSON. 'Why, Sir, the pleasure of living in London, the intellectual superiority that is enjoyed there, may counterbalance the other. Besides, Sir, a man may prefer the state of the country-gentleman upon the whole, and yet there may never be a moment when he is willing to make the change to quit London for it.' He said, 'It is better to have five *per cent.* out of land than out of money, because it is more secure; but the readiness of transfer, and promptness of interest, make many people rather choose the funds. Nay, there is another disadvantage belonging to land, compared with money. A man is not so much afraid of being a hard creditor, as of being a hard landlord.' BOSWELL. 'Because there is a sort of kindly connection between a landlord and his tenants.' JOHNSON. 'No, Sir; many landlords with us never see their tenants. It is because if a landlord drives away his tenants, he may not get others; whereas the demand for money is so great, it may always be lent.'

He talked with regret and indignation of the factious opposition to Government at this time, and imputed it, in a great measure, to the Revolution. 'Sir, (said he, in a low voice, having come nearer to me, while his old prejudices seemed to be fermenting in his mind,) this Hanoverian family is *isolée* here. They have no friends. Now the Stuarts had friends who stuck by them so late as 1745. When the right of the King is not reverenced, there will not be reverence for those appointed by the King.'

His observation that the present royal family has no friends, has been too much justified by the very ungrateful behaviour of many who were under great obligations to his Majesty; at the same time there are honourable exceptions; and the very next year after this conversation, and ever since, the King has had as extensive and generous support as ever was given to any monarch, and has had the satisfaction of knowing that he was more and more endeared to his people.

He repeated to me his verses on Mr. Levett, with an emotion which gave them full effect; and then he was pleased to say, 'You must be as much with me as you can. You have done me good. You cannot think how much better I am since you came in.'

He sent a message to acquaint Mrs. Thrale that I was arrived. I had not seen her since her husband's death. She soon appeared, and favoured me with an invitation to stay to dinner, which I accepted. There was no other company but herself and three of her daughters, Dr. Johnson, and I. She too said, she was very glad I was come, for she was going to Bath, and should have been sorry to leave Dr. Johnson before I came. This seemed to be attentive and kind; and I who had not been informed of any change, imagined all to be as well as formerly. He was little inclined to talk at dinner, and went to sleep after it; but when he joined us in the drawing-room, he seemed revived, and was again himself.

Talking of conversation, he said, 'There must, in the first place, be knowledge, there must be materials; in the second place, there must be a command of words; in the third place, there must be imagination, to place things in such views as they are not commonly seen in; and in the fourth place, there must be presence of mind, and a resolution that is not to be overcome by failures: this last is an essential requisite; for want of it many people do not excel in conversation. Now *I* want it: I throw up the game upon losing a trick.' I wondered to hear him talk thus of himself, and said, 'I don't know, Sir, how this may be; but I am sure you beat other people's cards out of their hands.' I doubt whether he heard this remark. While he went on talking triumphantly, I was fixed in admiration, and said to Mrs. Thrale, 'O, for short-hand to take this down!' 'You'll carry it all in your head, (said she;) a long head is as good as short-hand.'

It has been observed and wondered at, that Mr. Charles Fox never talked with any freedom in the presence of Dr. Johnson, though it is well known, and I myself can witness, that his conversation is various, fluent, and exceedingly agreeable. Johnson's own experience, however, of that gentleman's reserve was a sufficient reason for his going on thus: 'Fox never talks in private company; not from any determination not to talk, but because he has not the first motion. A man who is used to the applause of the House of Commons, has no wish for that of a private company. A man accustomed to throw for a thousand pounds, if set down to throw for sixpence, would not be at the pains to count his dice. Burke's talk is the ebullition of his mind; he does not talk from a desire of distinction, but because his mind is full.'

He thus curiously characterised one of our old acquaintance:[1] '********* is a good man, Sir; but he is a vain man and a liar. He, however, only tells lies of vanity; of victories, for instance, in conversation, which never happened.' This alluded to a story which I had repeated from that gentleman, to entertain Johnson with its wild bravado: 'This Johnson, Sir, (said he,) whom you are all afraid of, will shrink if you come close to him in argument, and roar as loud as he. He once maintained the paradox, that there is no beauty but in utility. "Sir, (said I,) what say you to the peacock's tail, which is one of the most beautiful objects in nature, but would have as much utility if its feathers were all of one colour." He *felt* what I thus produced, and had recourse to his usual expedient, ridicule; exclaiming, "A peacock has a tail, and a fox has a tail;" and then he burst out into a laugh. "Well,

[1] [Old Mr. Sheridan. *Boswell Papers*, xv. 175.]

Sir, (said I, with a strong voice, looking him full in the face,) you have unkennelled your fox; pursue him if you dare." He had not a word to say, Sir.' Johnson told me, that this was a fiction from beginning to end.[1]

After musing for some time, he said, 'I wonder how I should have any enemies; for I do harm to nobody.'[2] BOSWELL. 'In the first place, Sir, you will be pleased to recollect, that you set out with attacking the Scotch; so you got a whole nation for your enemies.' JOHNSON. 'Why, I own, that by my definition of *oats* I meant to vex them.' BOSWELL. 'Pray, Sir, can you trace the cause of your antipathy to the Scotch?' JOHNSON. 'I cannot, Sir.' BOSWELL. 'Old Mr. Sheridan says, it was because they sold Charles the First.' JOHNSON. 'Then, Sir, old Mr. Sheridan has found out a very good reason.'

Surely the most obstinate and sulky nationality, the most determined aversion to this great and good man, must be cured, when he is seen thus playing with one of his prejudices, of which he candidly admitted that he could not tell the reason. It was, however, probably owing to his having had in his view the worst part of the Scottish nation, the needy adventurers, many of whom he thought were advanced above their merits by means which he did not approve. Had he in his early life been in Scotland, and seen the worthy, sensible, independent gentlemen, who live rationally and hospitably at home, he never could have

[1] Were I to insert all the stories which have been told of contests boldly maintained with him, imaginary victories obtained over him, of reducing him to silence, and of making him own that his antagonist had the better of him in argument, my volumes would swell to an immoderate size. One instance, I find, has circulated both in conversation and in print; that when he would not allow the Scotch writers to have merit, the late Dr. Rose, of Chiswick, asserted, that he could name one Scotch writer, whom Dr. Johnson himself would allow to have written better than any man of the age; and upon Johnson's asking who it was, answered, 'Lord Bute, when he signed the warrant for your pension.' Upon which Johnson, struck with the repartee, acknowledged that this *was* true. When I mentioned it to Johnson, 'Sir, (said he,) if Rose said this, I never heard it.'

[2] This reflection was very natural in a man of a good heart, who was not conscious of any ill-will to mankind, though the sharp sayings which were sometimes produced by his discrimination and vivacity, and which he perhaps did not recollect, were, I am afraid, too often remembered with resentment.

entertained such unfavourable and unjust notions of his fellow-subjects. And accordingly we find, that when he did visit Scotland, in the latter period of his life, he was fully sensible of all that it deserved, as I have already pointed out, when speaking of his *Journey to the Western Islands*.

Next day, Saturday, March 22, I found him still at Mrs. Thrale's, but he told me that he was to go to his own house in the afternoon. He was better, but I perceived he was but an unruly patient, for Sir Lucas Pepys, who visited him, while I was with him said, 'If you were *tractable*, Sir, I should prescribe for you.'

I related to him a remark which a respectable friend[1] had made to me, upon the then state of Government, when those who had been long in opposition had attained to power, as it was supposed, against the inclination of the Sovereign. 'You need not be uneasy (said this gentleman,) about the King. He laughs at them all; he plays them one against another.' JOHNSON. 'Don't think so, Sir. The King is as much oppressed as a man can be. If he plays them one against another, he *wins* nothing.'

I had paid a visit to General Oglethorpe in the morning, and was told by him that Dr. Johnson saw company on Saturday evenings, and he would meet me at Johnson's, that night. When I mentioned this to Johnson, not doubting that it would please him, as he had a great value for Oglethorpe, the fretfulness of his disease unexpectedly shewed itself; his anger suddenly kindled, and he said, with vehemence, 'Did not you tell him not to come? Am I to be *hunted* in this manner?' I satisfied him that I could not divine that the visit would not be convenient, and that I certainly could not take it upon me of my own accord to forbid the General.

I found Dr. Johnson in the evening in Mrs. Williams's room, at tea and coffee with her and Mrs. Desmoulins, who were also both ill; it was a sad scene, and he was not in a very good humour. He said of a performance[2] that had lately come out, 'Sir, if you should search all the mad-houses in England, you would not find ten men who would write so, and think it sense.'

[1] [General Paoli. *Boswell Papers*, xv. 176.]   [2] Elphinstone's *Martial*.

I was glad when General Oglethorpe's arrival was announced, and we left the ladies. Dr. Johnson attended him in the parlour, and was as courteous as ever. The General said he was busy reading the writers of the middle age. Johnson said they were very curious. OGLETHORPE. 'The House of Commons has usurped the power of the nation's money, and used it tyrannically. Government is now carried on by corrupt influence, instead of the inherent right in the King.' JOHNSON. 'Sir, the want of inherent right in the King occasions all this disturbance. What we did at the Revolution was necessary: but it broke our constitution.'[1] OGLETHORPE. 'My father did not think it necessary.'

On Sunday, March 23, I breakfasted with Dr. Johnson, who seemed much relieved, having taken opium the night before. He however protested against it, as a remedy that should be given with the utmost reluctance, and only in extreme necessity. I mentioned how commonly it was used in Turkey, and that therefore it could not be so pernicious as he apprehended. He grew warm and said, 'Turks take opium, and Christians take opium; but Russel, in his account of Aleppo, tells us, that it is as disgraceful in Turkey to take too much opium, as it is with us to get drunk. Sir, it is amazing how things are exaggerated. A gentleman was lately telling in a company where I was present, that in France, as soon as a man of fashion marries, he takes an opera girl into keeping; and this he mentioned as a general custom. "Pray, Sir, (said I,) how many opera girls may there be?" He answered, "About fourscore." "Well then, Sir, (said I,) you see there can be no more than fourscore men of fashion who can do this." '

Mrs. Desmoulins made tea; and she and I talked before him upon a topick which he had once borne patiently from me when we were by ourselves,—his not complaining of the world, be-

---

[1] I have, in my *Journal of a Tour to the Hebrides*, fully expressed my sentiments upon this subject. The Revolution was *necessary*, but not a subject for *glory*; because it for a long time blasted the generous feelings of *Loyalty*. And now, when by the benignant effect of time the present Royal Family are established in our *affections*, how unwise it is to revive by celebrations the memory of a shock, which it would surely have been better that our constitution had not required.

cause he was not called to some great office, nor had attained to great wealth. He flew into a violent passion, I confess with some justice, and commanded us to have done. 'Nobody, (said he,) has a right to talk in this manner, to bring before a man his own character, and the events of his life, when he does not choose it should be done. I never have sought the world; the world was not to seek me. It is rather wonderful that so much has been done for me. All the complaints which are made of the world are unjust. I never knew a man of merit neglected: it was generally by his own fault that he failed of success. A man may hide his head in a hole: he may go into the country, and publish a book now and then, which nobody reads, and then complain he is neglected. There is no reason why any person should exert himself for a man who has written a good book: he has not written it for any individual. I may as well make a present to the postman who brings me a letter. When patronage was limited, an authour expected to find a Mæcenas, and complained if he did not find one. Why should he complain? This Mæcenas has others as good as he, or others who have got the start of him.' BOSWELL. 'But surely, Sir, you will allow that there are men of merit at the bar who never get practice.' JOHNSON. 'Sir, you are sure that practice is got from an opinion that the person employed deserves it best; so that if a man of merit at the bar does not get practice, it is from errour, not from injustice. He is not neglected. A horse that is brought to market may not be bought, though he is a very good horse: but that is from ignorance, not from intention.'

There was in this discourse much novelty, ingenuity, and discrimination, such as is seldom to be found. Yet I cannot help thinking that men of merit, who have no success in life, may be forgiven for *lamenting*, if they are not allowed to *complain*. They may consider it as *hard* that their merit should not have its suitable distinction. Though there is no intentional injustice towards them on the part of the world, their merit not having been perceived, they may yet repine against *fortune*, or *fate*, or by whatever name they choose to call the supposed mythological power of *Destiny*. It has, however, occurred to me, as a consolatory thought, that men of merit should consider thus:—How much harder would it be if the same persons had both all the merit and all the prosperity. Would not this be a miserable distribution for the poor dunces? Would men of merit exchange their intellectual superiority, and the enjoyments arising from it, for external distinction and the pleasures of wealth? If they would not, let them not envy others, who are poor where they are rich, a compensation which is made to them. Let them look inwards and be satisfied; recollecting with conscious pride what Virgil finely says of the *Corycius Senex*, and which I have, in another place,[1] with truth and sincerity applied to Mr. Burke:—

'*Regum æquabat opes animis.*'[2]

On the subject of the right employment of wealth, Johnson observed, 'A man cannot make a bad use of his money, so far as regards Society, if he does not hoard it; for if he either spends it or lends it out, Society has the benefit. It is in general better to spend money than to give it away; for industry is more promoted by spending money than by giving it away. A man who spends his money is sure he is doing good with it: he is not so sure when he gives it away. A man who spends ten thousand a year will do more good than a man who spends two thousand and gives away eight.'

In the evening I came to him again. He was somewhat fretful from his illness. A gentleman[3] asked him, whether he had been abroad to-day. 'Don't talk so childishly, (said he.) You may as well ask if I hanged myself to-day.' I mentioned politicks. JOHNSON. 'Sir, I'd as soon have a man to break my bones as talk to me of publick affairs, internal or external. I have lived to see things all as bad as they can be.'

Having mentioned his friend the second Lord Southwell, he said, 'Lord Southwell was the highest-bred man without insolence that I ever was in company with; the most *qualitied* I ever

[1] Letter to the People of Scotland against the attempt to diminish the number of the Lords of Session, 1785.
[2] ['He matched in contentment the riches of kings.' Virgil, *Georgics* iv. 132. (Jackson.)]
[3] [Boswell. *Boswell Papers*, xv. 180.]

saw. Lord Orrery was not dignified: Lord Chesterfield was, but he was insolent. Lord *********[1] is a man of coarse manners, but a man of abilities and information. I don't say he is a man I would set at the head of a nation, though perhaps he may be as good as the next Prime Minister that comes; but he is a man to be at the head of a Club; I don't say *our* CLUB; for there's no such Club.' BOSWELL. 'But, Sir, was he not once a factious man?' JOHNSON. 'O yes, Sir; as factious a fellow as could be found: one who was for sinking us all into the mob.' BOSWELL. 'How then, Sir, did he get into favour with the King?' JOHNSON. 'Because, Sir, I suppose he promised the King to do whatever the King pleased.'

He said, 'Goldsmith's blundering speech to Lord Shelburne, which has been so often mentioned, and which he really did make to him, was only a blunder in emphasis: "I wonder they should call your Lordship *Malagrida*, for Malagrida was a very good man;" meant, I wonder they should use *Malagrida* as a term of reproach.'

Soon after this time I had an opportunity of seeing, by means of one of his friends,[2] a proof that his talents, as well as his obliging service to authours, were ready as ever. He had revised *The Village*, an admirable poem, by the Reverend Mr. Crabbe. Its sentiments as to the false notions of rustick happiness and rustick virtue were quite congenial with his own; and he had taken the trouble not only to suggest slight corrections and variations, but to furnish some lines, when he thought he could give the writer's meaning better than in the words of the manuscript.[3]

On Sunday, March 30, I found him at home in the evening,

[1] [Lord Shelburne. *Boswell Papers*, xv. 181.]
[2] [Reynolds. *Ib.* 184.]
[3] I shall give an instance, marking the original by Roman, and Johnson's substitution in Italick characters:—

> 'In fairer scenes, where peaceful pleasures spring,
> Tityrus, the pride of Mantuan swains, might sing:
> But charmed by him, or smitten with his views,
> Shall modern poets court the Mantuan muse?
> From Truth and Nature shall we widely stray,
> Where Fancy leads, or Virgil led the way?'

and had the pleasure to meet with Dr. Brocklesby, whose reading, and knowledge of life, and good spirits, supply him with a
never-failing source of conversation. He mentioned a respectable
gentleman,[1] who became extremely penurious near the close of
his life. Johnson said there must have been a degree of madness
about him. 'Not at all, Sir, (said Dr. Brocklesby,) his judgement
was entire.' Unluckily, however, he mentioned that although he
had a fortune of twenty-seven thousand pounds, he denied himself many comforts, from an apprehension that he could not
afford them. 'Nay, Sir, (cried Johnson,) when the judgement is
so disturbed that a man cannot count, that is pretty well.'

I shall here insert a few of Johnson's sayings, without the
formality of dates, as they have no reference to any particular
time or place.

'The more a man extends and varies his acquaintance the
better.' This, however, was meant with a just restriction; for, he
on another occasion said to me, 'Sir, a man may be so much of
every thing, that he is nothing of any thing.'

'Raising the wages of day-labourers is wrong; for it does not
make them live better, but only makes them idler, and idleness
is a very bad thing for human nature.'

'It is a very good custom to keep a journal for a man's own
use; he may write upon a card a day all that is necessary to be
written, after he has had experience of life. At first there is a
great deal to be written, because there is a great deal of novelty;
but when once a man has settled his opinions, there is seldom
much to be set down.'

'There is nothing wonderful in the journal which we see

> *On Mincio's banks, in Cæsar's bounteous reign,*
> *If Tityrus found the golden age again,*
> *Must sleepy bards the flattering dream prolong,*
> *Mechanick echoes of the Mantuan song?*
> From Truth and Nature shall we widely stray,
> *Where Virgil, not where Fancy, leads the way?'*

Here we find Johnson's poetical and critical powers undiminished. I must,
however, observe, that the aids he gave to this poem, as to *The Traveller*
and *Deserted Village* of Goldsmith, were so small as by no means to impair
the distinguished merit of the authour.

[1] [Sir John Pringle. *Boswell Papers*, xv. 188.]

Swift kept in London, for it contains slight topicks, and it might soon be written.'

I praised the accuracy of an account-book of a lady[1] whom I mentioned. JOHNSON. 'Keeping accounts, Sir, is of no use when a man is spending his own money, and has nobody to whom he is to account. You won't eat less beef to-day, because you have written down what it cost yesterday.' I mentioned another lady[2] who thought as he did, so that her husband could not get her to keep an account of the expence of the family, as she thought it enough that she never exceeded the sum allowed her. JOHNSON. 'Sir, it is fit she should keep an account, because her husband wishes it; but I do not see its use.' I maintained that keeping an account has this advantage, that it satisfies a man that his money has not been lost or stolen, which he might sometimes be apt to imagine, were there no written state of his expence; and besides, a calculation of œconomy so as not to exceed one's income, cannot be made without a view of the different articles in figures, that one may see how to retrench in some particulars less necessary than others. This he did not attempt to answer.

Talking of an acquaintance of ours,[3] whose narratives, which abounded in curious and interesting topicks, were unhappily found to be very fabulous; I mentioned Lord Mansfield's having said to me, 'Suppose we believe one *half* of what he tells.' JOHNSON. 'Ay; but we don't know *which* half to believe. By his lying we lose not only our reverence for him, but all comfort in his conversation.' BOSWELL. 'May we not take it as amusing fiction?' JOHNSON. 'Sir, the misfortune is, that you will insensibly believe as much of it as you incline to believe.'

It is remarkable, that notwithstanding their congeniality in politicks, he never was acquainted with a late eminent noble judge,[4] whom I have heard speak of him as a writer, with great respect. Johnson, I know not upon what degree of investigation, entertained no exalted opinion of his Lordship's intellectual character. Talking of him to me one day, he said, 'It is wonderful,

---

[1] [The Hon. Mrs. Stuart. *Boswell Papers*, xv. 191.]
[2] [Mrs. Boswell. *Ib.*]
[3] [George Steevens. *Croker*[3]. Cf. *Ib.* xiv. 178.]
[4] [Perhaps Lord Mansfield. *Croker*.[1]]

Sir, with how little real superiority of mind men can make an
eminent figure in publick life.' He expressed himself to the same
purpose concerning another law-Lord,[1] who, it seems, once took
a fancy to associate with the wits of London; but with so little
success, that Foote said, 'What can he mean by coming among
us? He is not only dull himself, but the cause of dullness in
others.' Trying him by the test of his colloquial powers, Johnson
had found him very defective. He once said to Sir Joshua Reynolds, 'This man now has been ten years about town, and has
made nothing of it;' meaning as a companion.[2] He said to me,
'I never heard any thing from him in company that was at all
striking; and depend upon it, Sir, it is when you come close to
a man in conversation, that you discover what his real abilities
are; to make a speech in a publick assembly is a knack. Now I
honour Thurlow, Sir; Thurlow is a fine fellow; he fairly puts
his mind to yours.'

After repeating to him some of his pointed, lively sayings, I
said, 'It is a pity, Sir, you don't always remember your own
good things, that you may have a laugh when you will.' JOHN-
SON. 'Nay, Sir, it is better that I forget them, that I may be
reminded of them, and have a laugh on their being brought to
my recollection.'

When I recalled to him his having said as we sailed upon
Loch-lomond, 'That if he wore any thing fine, it should be *very*
fine;' I observed that all his thoughts were upon a great scale.
JOHNSON. 'Depend upon it, Sir, every man will have as fine a
thing as he can get; as a large diamond for his ring.' BOSWELL.
'Pardon me, Sir: a man of a narrow mind will not think of it, a
slight trinket will satisfy him:

"*Nec sufferre queat majoris pondera gemmæ.*" '[3]

---

[1] [Wedderburn. *Mrs. Piozzi, Croker*[1].]

[2] Knowing as well as I do what precision and elegance of oratory his
Lordship can display, I cannot but suspect that his unfavourable appearance
in a social circle, which drew such animadversions upon him, must be owing
to a cold affectation of consequence, from being reserved and stiff. If it be so,
and he might be an agreeable man if he would, we cannot be sorry that he
misses his aim.

[3] ['Unable to support a gem of weight.' Juvenal, *Satires* i. 29. (Dryden.)]

I told him I should send him some *Essays*[1] which I had written, which I hoped he would be so good as to read, and pick out the good ones. JOHNSON. 'Nay, Sir, send me only the good ones; don't make *me* pick them.'

I heard him once say, 'Though the proverb *Nullum numen abest, si sit prudentia,*[2] does not always prove true, we may be certain of the converse of it, *Nullum numen adest, si sit imprudentia.*'[3]

Once, when Mr. Seward was going to Bath, and asked his commands, he said, 'Tell Dr. Harrington that I wish he would publish another volume of the *Nugæ antiquæ*;[4] it is a very pretty book.' Mr. Seward seconded this wish, and recommended to Dr. Harrington to dedicate it to Johnson, and take for his motto, what Catullus says to Cornelius Nepos:—

> '———— *namque tu solebas,*
> *Meas esse aliquid putare* NUGAS.'[5]

As a small proof of his kindliness and delicacy of feeling, the following circumstance may be mentioned: One evening when we were in the street together, and I told him I was going to sup at Mr. Beauclerk's, he said, 'I'll go with you.' After having walked part of the way, seeming to recollect something, he suddenly stopped and said, 'I cannot go,—but *I do not love Beauclerk the less.*'

On the frame of his portrait, Mr. Beauclerk had inscribed,—

> '———— *Ingenium ingens*
> *Inculto latet hoc sub corpore.*'[6]

After Mr. Beauclerk's death, when it became Mr. Langton's property, he made the inscription be defaced. Johnson said complacently, 'It was kind in you to take it off;' and then after a short pause, added, 'and not unkind in him to put it on.'

[1] [*The Hypochondriack.*]
[2] ['Heaven's help is not refused, if wisdom be present.' Juvenal, *Satires* x. 365].
[3] ['Heaven's help is not given, if unwisdom be present.']
[4] ['Ancient Trifles.'] It has since appeared.
[5] ['For though they are but trifles, thou Some value didst to them allow.' Catullus I. (Sir T. Martin.)]
[6] ['Under that uncouth outside are hidden vast gifts of mind.' Horace, *Satires* I. iii. 33. (Wickham.)]

He said, 'How few of his friends' houses would a man choose to be at when he is sick.' He mentioned one or two. I recollect only Thrale's.

He observed, 'There is a wicked inclination in most people to suppose an old man decayed in his intellects. If a young or middle-aged man, when leaving a company, does not recollect where he laid his hat, it is nothing; but if the same inattention is discovered in an old man, people will shrug up their shoulders, and say, "His memory is going."'

When I once talked to him of some of the sayings which every body repeats, but nobody knows where to find, such as *Quos* DEUS *vult perdere, prius dementat*;[1] he told me that he was once offered ten guineas to point out from whence *Semel insanivimus omnes*[2] was taken. He could not do it; but many years afterwards met with it by chance in *Johannes Baptista Mantuanus.*

I am very sorry that I did not take a note of an eloquent argument in which he maintained that the situation of Prince of Wales was the happiest of any person's in the kingdom, even beyond that of the Sovereign. I recollect only—the enjoyment of hope,—the high superiority of rank, without the anxious cares of government,—and a great degree of power, both from natural influence wisely used, and from the sanguine expectations of those who look forward to the chance of future favour.

Sir Joshua Reynolds communicated to me the following particulars:—

Johnson thought the poems published as translations from Ossian had so little merit, that he said, 'Sir, a man might write such stuff for ever, if he would *abandon* his mind to it.'

He said, 'A man should pass a part of his time with *the laughers*, by which means any thing ridiculous or particular about him might be presented to his view, and corrected.' I observed, he must have been a bold laugher who would have ventured to tell Dr. Johnson of any of his particularities.[3]

[1] ['Those whom God would destroy he first makes mad.']
[2] ['We have all been mad once.' *Eclogue* i. 117–18.]
[3] I am happy, however, to mention a pleasing instance of his enduring with great gentleness to hear one of his most striking particularities pointed

Having observed the vain ostentatious importance of many people in quoting the authority of Dukes and Lords, as having been in their company, he said, he went to the other extreme, and did not mention his authority when he should have done it, had it not been that of a Duke or a Lord.

Dr. Goldsmith said once to Dr. Johnson, that he wished for some additional members to the LITERARY CLUB, to give it an agreeable variety; for (said he,) there can now be nothing new among us: we have travelled over one another's minds. Johnson seemed a little angry, and said, 'Sir, you have not travelled over *my* mind, I promise you.' Sir Joshua, however, thought Goldsmith right; observing, that 'when people have lived a great deal together, they know what each of them will say on every subject. A new understanding, therefore, is desirable; because though it may only furnish the same sense upon a question which would have been furnished by those with whom we are accustomed to live, yet this sense will have a different colouring; and colouring is of much effect in every thing else as well as in painting.'

Johnson used to say that he made it a constant rule to talk as well as he could both as to sentiment and expression, by which means, what had been originally effort became familiar and easy. The consequence of this, Sir Joshua observed, was, that his common conversation in all companies was such as to secure him universal attention, as something above the usual colloquial style was expected.

Yet, though Johnson had this habit in company, when another mode was necessary, in order to investigate truth, he could descend to a language intelligible to the meanest capacity. An instance of this was witnessed by Sir Joshua Reynolds, when they were present at an examination of a little blackguard boy, by Mr. Saunders Welch, the late Westminster Justice. Welch, who imagined that he was exalting himself in Dr. Johnson's

out:—Miss Hunter, a niece of his friend Christopher Smart, when a very young girl, struck by his extraordinary motions, said to him, 'Pray, Dr. Johnson, why do you make such strange gestures?' 'From bad habit,' (he replied). 'Do you, my dear, take care to guard against bad habits.' This I was told by the young lady's brother at Margate.

eyes by using big words, spoke in a manner that was utterly unintelligible to the boy; Dr. Johnson perceiving it, addressed himself to the boy, and changed the pompous phraseology into colloquial language. Sir Joshua Reynolds, who was much amused by this procedure, which seemed a kind of reversing of what might have been expected from the two men, took notice of it to Dr. Johnson, as they walked away by themselves. Johnson said, that it was continually the case; and that he was always obliged to *translate* the Justice's swelling diction, (smiling,) so as that his meaning might be understood by the vulgar, from whom information was to be obtained.

Sir Joshua once observed to him, that he had talked above the capacity of some people with whom they had been in company together. 'No matter, Sir, (said Johnson;) they consider it as a compliment to be talked to, as if they were wiser than they are. So true is this, Sir, that Baxter made it a rule in every sermon that he preached, to say something that was above the capacity of his audience.'[1]

Johnson's dexterity in retort, when he seemed to be driven to an extremity by his adversary, was very remarkable. Of his power in this respect, our common friend, Mr. Windham, of Norfolk, has been pleased to furnish me with an eminent instance. However unfavourable to Scotland, he uniformly gave liberal praise to George Buchanan, as a writer. In a conversation concerning the literary merits of the two countries, in which Buchanan was introduced, a Scotchman, imagining that on this ground he should have an undoubted triumph over him, exclaimed, 'Ah, Dr. Johnson, what would you have said of Buchanan, had he been an Englishman?' 'Why, Sir, (said Johnson, after a little pause,) I should *not* have said of Buchanan, had he been an *Englishman*, what I will now say of him as a *Scotchman*, —that he was the only man of genius his country ever produced.'

And this brings to my recollection another instance of the

[1] The justness of this remark is confirmed by the following story, for which I am indebted to Lord Eliot:—A country parson, who was remarkable for quoting scraps of Latin in his sermons, having died, one of his parishioners was asked how he liked his successor: 'He is a very good preacher,' (was his answer,) 'but no *latiner*.'

same nature. I once reminded him that when Dr. Adam Smith was expatiating on the beauty of Glasgow, he had cut him short by saying, 'Pray, Sir, have you ever seen Brentford?' and I took the liberty to add, 'My dear Sir, surely that was *shocking*.' 'Why, then, Sir, (he replied,) you have never seen Brentford.'

Though his usual phrase for conversation was *talk*, yet he made a distinction; for when he once told me that he dined the day before at a friend's house, with 'a very pretty company;' and I asked him if there was good conversation, he answered, 'No, Sir; we had *talk* enough, but no *conversation*; there was nothing *discussed*.'

Talking of the success of the Scotch in London, he imputed it in a considerable degree to their spirit of nationality. 'You know, Sir, (said he,) that no Scotchman publishes a book, or has a play brought upon the stage, but there are five hundred people ready to applaud him.'

He gave much praise to his friend Dr. Burney's elegant and entertaining travels, and told Mr. Seward that he had them in his eye, when writing his *Journey to the Western Islands of Scotland*.

Such was his sensibility, and so much was he affected by pathetick poetry, that, when he was reading Dr. Beattie's *Hermit* in my presence, it brought tears into his eyes.

He disapproved much of mingling real facts with fiction. On this account he censured a book entitled *Love and Madness*.

Mr. Hoole told him, he was born in Moorfields, and had received part of his early instruction in Grub-street. 'Sir, (said Johnson, smiling,) you have been *regularly* educated.' Having asked who was his instructor, and Mr. Hoole having answered, 'My uncle, Sir, who was a taylor;' Johnson, recollecting himself, said, 'Sir, I knew him; we called him the *metaphysical taylor*. He was of a club in Old-street, with me and George Psalmanazar, and some others: but pray, Sir, was he a good taylor?' Mr. Hoole having answered that he believed he was too mathematical, and used to draw squares and triangles on his shop-board, so that he did not excel in the cut of a coat;—'I am sorry for it (said Johnson,) for I would have every man to be master of his own business.'

In pleasant reference to himself and Mr. Hoole, as brother authours, he often said, 'Let you and I, Sir, go together, and eat a beef-steak in Grub-street.'

Sir William Chambers, that great Architect,[1] whose works shew a sublimity of genius, and who is esteemed by all who know him for his social, hospitable, and generous qualities, submitted the manuscript of his *Chinese Architecture* to Dr. Johnson's perusal. Johnson was much pleased with it, and said, 'It wants no addition nor correction, but a few lines of introduction;' which he furnished, and Sir William adopted.[2]

He said to Sir William Scott, 'The age is running mad after innovation; all the business of the world is to be done in a new way; men are to be hanged in a new way; Tyburn itself is not safe from the fury of innovation.' It having been argued that this was an improvement,—'No, Sir, (said he, eagerly,) it is *not* an improvement: they object that the old method drew together a number of spectators. Sir, executions are intended to draw spectators. If they do not draw spectators they don't answer their purpose. The old method was most satisfactory to all parties; the publick was gratified by a procession; the criminal was supported by it. Why is all this to be swept away?' I perfectly agree with Dr. Johnson upon this head, and am persuaded that executions now, the solemn procession being discontinued, have not nearly the effect which they formerly had.

[1] The Honourable Horace Walpole, late Earl of Orford, thus bears testimony to this gentleman's merit as a writer:—'Mr. Chambers's *Treatise on Civil Architecture*, is the most sensible book, and the most exempt from prejudices, that ever was written on that science.'—Preface to *Anecdotes of Painting in England*.

[2] The introductory lines are these:—'It is difficult to avoid praising too little or too much. The boundless panegyricks which have been lavished upon the Chinese learning, policy, and arts, shew with what power novelty attracts regard, and how naturally esteem swells into admiration. I am far from desiring to be numbered among the exaggerators of Chinese excellence. I consider them as great, or wise, only in comparison with the nations that surround them; and have no intention to place them in competition either with the antients or with the moderns of this part of the world; yet they must be allowed to claim our notice as a distinct and very singular race of men: as the inhabitants of a region divided by its situation from all civilized countries, who have formed their own manners, and invented their own arts, without the assistance of example.'

Magistrates both in London, and elsewhere, have, I am afraid, in this, had too much regard to their own ease.

Of Dr. Hurd, Bishop of Worcester, Johnson said to a friend, 'Hurd, Sir, is one of a set of men who account for every thing systematically; for instance, it has been a fashion to wear scarlet breeches; these men would tell you, that according to causes and effects, no other wear could at that time have been chosen.' He, however, said of him at another time to the same gentleman, 'Hurd, Sir, is a man whose acquaintance is a valuable acquisition.'

That learned and ingenious Prelate, it is well known, published at one period of his life *Moral and Political Dialogues*, with a woefully whiggish cast. Afterwards, his Lordship having thought better, came to see his errour, and republished the work with a more constitutional spirit. Johnson, however, was unwilling to allow him full credit for his political conversion. I remember when his Lordship declined the honour of being Archbishop of Canterbury, Johnson said, 'I am glad he did not go to Lambeth; for, after all, I fear he is a Whig in his heart.'

Johnson's attention to precision and clearness in expression was very remarkable. He disapproved of parentheses; and I believe in all his voluminous writings, not half a dozen of them will be found. He never used the phrases *the former* and *the latter*, having observed, that they often occasioned obscurity; he therefore contrived to construct his sentences so as not to have occasion for them, and would even rather repeat the same words, in order to avoid them. Nothing is more common than to mistake surnames when we hear them carelessly uttered for the first time. To prevent this, he used not only to pronounce them slowly and distinctly, but to take the trouble of spelling them; a practice which I have often followed; and which I wish were general.

Such was the heat and irritability of his blood, that not only did he pare his nails to the quick; but scraped the joints of his fingers with a pen-knife, till they seemed quite red and raw.

The heterogeneous composition of human nature was remarkably exemplified in Johnson. His liberality in giving his money to persons in distress was extraordinary. Yet there lurked about him a propensity to paltry saving. One day I owned to him that

'I was occasionally troubled with a fit of *narrowness*.' 'Why, Sir, (said he,) so am I. *But I do not tell it.*' He has now and then borrowed a shilling of me; and when I asked for it again, seemed to be rather out of humour. A droll little circumstance once occurred: as if he meant to reprimand my minute exactness as a creditor, he thus addressed me;—'Boswell, *lend* me sixpence— *not to be repaid.*'

This great man's attention to small things was very remarkable. As an instance of it, he one day said to me, 'Sir, when you get silver in change for a guinea, look carefully at it; you may find some curious piece of coin.'

Though a stern *true-born Englishman*, and fully prejudiced against all other nations, he had discernment enough to see, and candour enough to censure, the cold reserve too common among Englishmen towards strangers: 'Sir, (said he,) two men of any other nation who are shewn into a room together, at a house where they are both visitors, will immediately find some conversation. But two Englishmen will probably go each to a different window, and remain in obstinate silence. Sir, we as yet do not enough understand the common rights of humanity.'

Johnson was at a certain period of his life a good deal with the Earl of Shelburne, now Marquis of Lansdown, as he doubtless could not but have a due value for that nobleman's activity of mind, and uncommon acquisitions of important knowledge, however much he might disapprove of other parts of his Lordship's character, which were widely different from his own.

Maurice Morgann, Esq. authour of the very ingenious *Essay on the character of Falstaff*,[1] being a particular friend of his Lordship, had once an opportunity of entertaining Johnson for a day or two at Wickham,[2] when its Lord was absent, and by him I have been favoured with two anecdotes.

One is not a little to the credit of Johnson's candour. Mr. Morgann and he had a dispute pretty late at night, in which

[1] Johnson being asked his opinion of this *Essay*, answered, 'Why, Sir, we shall have the man come forth again; and as he has proved Falstaff to be no coward, he may prove Iago to be a very good character.'

[2] [Wycombe, Bucks.]

Johnson would not give up, though he had the wrong side, and in short, both kept the field. Next morning, when they met in the breakfasting-room, Dr. Johnson accosted Mr. Morgann thus:—'Sir, I have been thinking on our dispute last night—*You were in the right.*'

The other was as follows:—Johnson, for sport perhaps, or from the spirit of contradiction, eagerly maintained that Derrick had merit as a writer. Mr. Morgann argued with him directly, in vain. At length he had recourse to this device. 'Pray, Sir, (said he,) whether do you reckon Derrick or Smart the best poet?' Johnson at once felt himself rouzed; and answered, 'Sir, there is no settling the point of precedency between a louse and a flea.'

Once, when checking my boasting too frequently of myself in company, he said to me, 'Boswell, you often vaunt so much as to provoke ridicule. You put me in mind of a man who was standing in the kitchen of an inn with his back to the fire, and thus accosted the person next him, "Do you know, Sir, who I am?" "No, Sir, (said the other,) I have not that advantage." "Sir, (said he,) I am the *great* TWALMLEY, who invented the New Flood-gate Iron."'[1] The Bishop of Killaloe, on my repeating the story to him, defended Twalmley, by observing, that he was entitled to the epithet of *great*; for Virgil in his groupe of worthies in the Elysian fields—

> *Hic manus ob patriam pugnando vulnera passi;* &c.[2]

mentions

> *Inventas aut qui vitam excoluere per artes.*[3]

He was pleased to say to me one morning when we were left alone in his study, 'Boswell, I think I am easier with you than with almost any body.'

He would not allow Mr. David Hume any credit for his

---

[1] What the *great* TWALMLEY was so proud of having invented, was neither more nor less than a kind of box-iron for smoothing linen.

[2] ['Here was the company of those who battled and bled for their fatherland.' *Aeneid* vi. 660. (Jackson.)]

[3] ['Those who ennobled life by the arts they discovered.' *Ib.*]

political principles, though similar to his own; saying of him, 'Sir, he was a Tory by chance.'

His acute observation of human life made him remark, 'Sir, there is nothing by which a man exasperates most people more, than by displaying a superiour ability or brilliancy in conversation. They seem pleased at the time; but their envy makes them curse him in their hearts.'

My readers will probably be surprised to hear that the great Dr. Johnson could amuse himself with so slight and playful a species of composition as a *Charade*. I have recovered one which he made on Dr. *Barnard*, now Lord Bishop of Killaloe; who has been pleased for many years to treat me with so much intimacy and social ease, that I may presume to call him not only my Right Reverend, but my very dear Friend. I therefore with peculiar pleasure give to the world a just and elegant compliment thus paid to his Lordship by Johnson.

CHARADE.

'My *first*[1] shuts out thieves from your house or your room,
My *second*[2] expresses a Syrian perfume.
My *whole*[3] is a man in whose converse is shar'd,
The strength of a Bar and the sweetness of Nard.'

Johnson asked Richard Owen Cambridge, Esq. if he had read the Spanish translation of *Sallust*, said to be written by a Prince of Spain[4], with the assistance of his tutor[5], who is professedly the authour of a treatise annexed, on the Phœnician language.

Mr. Cambridge commended the work particularly, as he thought the Translator understood his authour better than is commonly the case with Translators: but said, he was disappointed in the purpose for which he borrowed the book; to see whether a Spaniard could be better furnished with inscriptions from monuments, coins, or other antiquities which he might more probably find on a coast, so immediately opposite to Carthage, than the Antiquaries of any other countries. JOHNSON. 'I am very sorry you was not gratified in your expectations.' CAMBRIDGE. 'The language would have been of little use, as

---

[1] Bar.   [2] Nard.   [3] Barnard.
[4] and [5] [Don Gabriel Antonio and F. Pérez Bayer. *Powell.*]

there is no history existing in that tongue to balance the partial accounts which the Roman writers have left us.' JOHNSON. 'No, Sir. They have not been *partial,* they have told their own story, without shame or regard to equitable treatment of their injured enemy; they had no compunction, no feeling for a Carthaginian. Why, Sir, they would never have borne Virgil's description of Æneas's treatment of Dido, if she had not been a Carthaginian.'

I gratefully acknowledge this and other communications from Mr. Cambridge, whom, if a beautiful villa on the banks of the Thames, a few miles distant from London, a numerous and excellent library, which he accurately knows and reads, a choice collection of pictures, which he understands and relishes, an easy fortune, an amiable family, an extensive circle of friends and acquaintance, distinguished by rank, fashion and genius, a literary fame, various, elegant and still increasing, colloquial talents rarely to be found, and with all these means of happiness, enjoying, when well advanced in years, health and vigour of body, serenity and animation of mind, do not entitle to be addressed *fortunate senex!*[1] I know not to whom, in any age, that expression could with propriety have been used. Long may he live to hear and to feel it!

Johnson's love of little children, which he discovered upon all occasions, calling them 'pretty dears,' and giving them sweet-meats, was an undoubted proof of the real humanity and gentleness of his disposition.

His uncommon kindness to his servants, and serious concern, not only for their comfort in this world, but their happiness in the next, was another unquestionable evidence of what all, who were intimately acquainted with him, knew to be true.

Nor would it be just, under this head, to omit the fondness which he shewed for animals which he had taken under his protection. I never shall forget the indulgence with which he treated Hodge, his cat: for whom he himself used to go out and buy oysters, lest the servants having that trouble should take a dislike to the poor creature. I am, unluckily, one of those who have an antipathy to a cat, so that I am uneasy when in the

[1] ['happy old man.']

room with one; and I own, I frequently suffered a good deal from the presence of this same Hodge. I recollect him one day scrambling up Dr. Johnson's breast, apparently with much satisfaction, while my friend smiling and half-whistling, rubbed down his back, and pulled him by the tail; and when I observed he was a fine cat, saying, 'why yes, Sir, but I have had cats whom I liked better than this;' and then as if perceiving Hodge to be out of countenance, adding, 'but he is a very fine cat, a very fine cat indeed.'

This reminds me of the ludicrous account which he gave Mr. Langton, of the despicable state of a young Gentleman of good family. 'Sir, when I heard of him last, he was running about town shooting cats.' And then in a sort of kindly reverie, he bethought himself of his own favourite cat, and said, 'But Hodge shan't be shot; no, no, Hodge shall not be shot.'

He thought Mr. Beauclerk made a shrewd and judicious remark to Mr. Langton, who, after having been for the first time in company with a well known wit about town, was warmly admiring and praising him, 'See him again,' said Beauclerk.

His respect for the Hierarchy, and particularly the Dignitaries of the Church, has been more than once exhibited in the course of this work. Mr. Seward saw him presented to the Archbishop of York, and described his *Bow to an* ARCH-BISHOP, as such a studied elaboration of homage, such an extension of limb, such a flexion of body, as have seldom or ever been equalled.

I cannot help mentioning with much regret, that by my own negligence I lost an opportunity of having the history of my family from its founder Thomas Boswell, in 1504, recorded and illustrated by Johnson's pen. Such was his goodness to me, that when I presumed to solicit him for so great a favour, he was pleased to say, 'Let me have all the materials you can collect, and I will do it both in Latin and English; then let it be printed and copies of it be deposited in various places for security and preservation.' I can now only do the best I can to make up for this loss, keeping my great Master steadily in view. Family histories, like the *imagines majorum*[1] of the Ancients, excite to

[1] ['statues of our ancestors.']

virtue; and I wish that they who really have blood, would be more careful to trace and ascertain its course. Some have affected to laugh at the history of the house of Yvery:[1] it would be well if many others would transmit their pedigrees to posterity, with the same accuracy and generous zeal with which the Noble Lord, who compiled that work has honoured and perpetuated his ancestry.

On Thursday, April 10, I introduced to him, at his house in Bolt-court, the Honourable and Reverend William Stuart, son of the Earl of Bute; a gentleman truly worthy of being known to Johnson; being, with all the advantages of high birth, learning, travel, and elegant manners, an exemplary parish priest in every respect.

After some compliments on both sides, the tour which Johnson and I had made to the Hebrides was mentioned. JOHNSON. 'I got an acquisition of more ideas by it than by any thing that I remember. I saw quite a different system of life.' BOSWELL. 'You would not like to make the same journey again?' JOHNSON. 'Why no, Sir; not the same: it is a tale told. Gravina, an Italian critick, observes, that every man desires to see that of which he has read; but no man desires to read an account of what he has seen: so much does description fall short of reality. Description only excites curiosity: seeing satisfies it. Other people may go and see the Hebrides.' BOSWELL. 'I should wish to go and see some country totally different from what I have been used to; such as Turkey, where religion and every thing else are different.' JOHNSON. 'Yes, Sir; there are two objects of curiosity,—the Christian world, and the Mahometan world. All the rest may be considered as barbarous.' BOSWELL. 'Pray, Sir, is the *Turkish Spy* a genuine book?' JOHNSON. 'No, Sir. Mrs. Manley, in her *Life*, says that her father wrote the first two volumes: and in another book, *Dunton's Life and Errours*, we find that the rest was written by one *Sault*, at two guineas a sheet, under the direction of Dr. Midgeley.'[2]

[1] Written by John, Earl of Egmont. [M.]
[2] The real authour . . . was I. P. Marana, a Genoese, who died at Paris in 1693. John Dunton in his *Life* says, that Mr. *William Bradshaw* received from Dr. Midgeley forty shillings a sheet for writing part of the *Turkish*

BOSWELL. 'This has been a very factious reign, owing to the too great indulgence of Government.' JOHNSON. '*I* think so, Sir. What at first was lenity, grew timidity. Yet this is reasoning *à posteriori*,[1] and may not be just. Supposing a few had at first been punished, I believe faction would have been crushed; but it might have been said, that it was a sanguinary reign. A man cannot tell *à priori*[2] what will be best for Government to do. This reign has been very unfortunate. We have had an unsuccessful war; but that does not prove that we have been ill governed. One side or other must prevail in war, as one or other must win at play. When we beat Louis, we were not better governed; nor were the French better governed when Louis beat us.'

On Saturday, April 12, I visited him, in company with Mr. Windham, of Norfolk, whom, though a Whig, he highly valued. One of the best things he ever said was to this gentleman; who, before he set out for Ireland as Secretary to Lord Northington, when Lord Lieutenant, expressed to the Sage some modest and virtuous doubts, whether he could bring himself to practise those arts which it is supposed a person in that situation has occasion to employ. 'Don't be afraid, Sir, (said Johnson, with a pleasant smile,) you will soon make a very pretty rascal.'

He talked to-day a good deal of the wonderful extent and variety of London, and observed, that men of curious enquiry might see in it such modes of life as very few could even imagine. He in particular recommended to us to *explore Wapping*, which we resolved to do.[3]

Mr. Lowe, the painter, who was with him, was very much distressed that a large picture which he had painted was refused to be received into the Exhibition of the Royal Academy. Mrs. Thrale knew Johnson's character so superficially, as to represent him as unwilling to do small acts of benevolence; and mentions

---

Spy; but I do not find that he any where mentions *Sault* as engaged in that work. [M.]

[1] ['from effect to cause.']   [2] ['from cause to effect.']

[3] We accordingly carried our scheme into execution, in October, 1792; but whether from that uniformity which has in modern times, in a great degree, spread through every part of the Metropolis, or from our want of sufficient exertion, we were disappointed.

in particular, that he would hardly take the trouble to write a letter in favour of his friends. The truth, however, is, that he was remarkable, in an extraordinary degree, for what she denies to him; and, above all, for this very sort of kindness, writing letters for those to whom his solicitations might be of service. He now gave Mr. Lowe the following, of which I was diligent enough, with his permission, to take copies at the next coffee-house, while Mr. Windham was so good as to stay by me.

'*To* SIR JOSHUA REYNOLDS

'SIR,—Mr. Lowe considers himself as cut off from all credit and all hope, by the rejection of his picture from the Exhibition. Upon this work he has exhausted all his powers, and suspended all his expectations: and, certainly, to be refused an opportunity of taking the opinion of the publick, is in itself a very great hardship. It is to be condemned without a trial.

'If you could procure the revocation of this incapacitating edict, you would deliver an unhappy man from great affliction. The Council has sometimes reversed its own determination; and I hope, that by your interposition this luckless picture may be got[1] admitted. I am, &c.

'April 12, 1783.'   'SAM. JOHNSON.'

'*To* MR. BARRY

'SIR,—Mr. Lowe's exclusion from the exhibition gives him more trouble than you and the other gentlemen of the Council could imagine or intend. He considers disgrace and ruin as the inevitable consequence of your determination.

'He says, that some pictures have been received after rejection; and if there be any such precedent, I earnestly intreat that you will use your interest in his favour. Of his work I can say nothing; I pretend not to judge of painting; and this picture I never saw: but I conceive it extremely hard to shut out any man from the possibility of success; and therefore I repeat my request that you will propose the re-consideration of Mr. Lowe's case; and if there be any among the Council with whom my name can

[1] [Johnson probably wrote *yet.*]

have any weight, be pleased to communicate to them the desire of, Sir, your most humble servant,

    'April 12, 1783.'   'Sam. Johnson.'

Such intercession was too powerful to be resisted; and Mr. Lowe's performance was admitted at Somerset Place. The subject, as I recollect, was the Deluge, at that point of time when the water was verging to the top of the last uncovered mountain. Near to the spot was seen the last of the antediluvian race, exclusive of those who were saved in the ark of Noah. This was one of those giants, then the inhabitants of the earth, who had still strength to swim, and with one of his hands held aloft his infant child. Upon the small remaining dry spot appeared a famished lion, ready to spring at the child and devour it. Mr. Lowe told me that Johnson said to him, 'Sir, your picture is noble and probable.' 'A compliment, indeed, (said Mr. Lowe,) from a man who cannot lie, and cannot be mistaken.'

About this time he wrote to Mrs. Lucy Porter, mentioning his bad health, and that he intended a visit to Lichfield. 'It is, (says he,) with no great expectation of amendment that I make every year a journey into the country; but it is pleasant to visit those whose kindness has been often experienced.'

On April 18, (being Good-Friday,) I found him at breakfast, in his usual manner upon that day, drinking tea without milk, and eating a cross-bun to prevent faintness; we went to St. Clement's church, as formerly. When we came home from church, he placed himself on one of the stone-seats at his garden-door, and I took the other, and thus in the open air and in a placid frame of mind, he talked away very easily. JOHNSON. 'Were I a country gentleman, I should not be very hospitable, I should not have crowds in my house.' BOSWELL. 'Sir Alexander Dick tells me, that he remembers having a thousand people in a year to dine at his house: that is, reckoning each person as one, each time that he dined there.' JOHNSON. 'That, Sir, is about three a day.' BOSWELL. 'How your statement lessens the idea.' JOHNSON. 'That, Sir, is the good of counting. It brings every thing to a certainty, which before floated in the mind

indefinitely.' B O S W E L L. 'But *Omne ignotum pro magnifico est*:[1]
one is sorry to have this diminished.' J O H N S O N. 'Sir, you should
not allow yourself to be delighted with errour.' B O S W E L L.
'Three a day seem but few.' J O H N S O N. 'Nay, Sir, he who
entertains three a day, does very liberally. And if there is a
large family, the poor entertain those three, for they eat what
the poor would get: there must be superfluous meat; it must
be given to the poor, or thrown out.' B O S W E L L. 'I observe in
London, that the poor go about and gather bones, which I
understand are manufactured.' J O H N S O N. 'Yes, Sir; they boil
them, and extract a grease from them for greasing wheels and
other purposes. Of the best pieces they make a mock ivory,
which is used for hafts to knives, and various other things; the
coarser pieces they burn and pound, and sell the ashes.' B O S -
W E L L. 'For what purpose, Sir?' J O H N S O N. 'Why, Sir, for
making a furnace for the chymists for melting iron. A paste
made of burnt bones will stand a stronger heat than any thing
else. Consider, Sir; if you are to melt iron, you cannot line your
pot with brass, because it is softer than iron, and would melt
sooner; nor with iron, for though malleable iron is harder than
cast iron, yet it would not do; but a paste of burnt-bones will
not melt.' B O S W E L L. 'Do you know, Sir, I have discovered a
manufacture to a great extent, of what you only piddle at,—
scraping and drying the peel of oranges.[2] At a place in Newgate-
street, there is a prodigious quantity prepared, which they sell
to the distillers.' J O H N S O N. 'Sir, I believe they make a higher
thing out of them than a spirit; they make what is called
orange-butter, the oil of the orange inspissated, which they mix
perhaps with common pomatum, and make it fragrant. The oil
does not fly off in the drying.'

B O S W E L L. 'I wish to have a good walled garden.' J O H N S O N.
'I don't think it would be worth the expence to you. We com-

---

[1] ['The unknown always passes for something grand.' Tacitus, *Agricola*,
ch. xxx.]

[2] It is suggested to me by an anonymous Annotator on my Work, that
the reason why Dr. Johnson collected the peels of squeezed oranges may be
found in the 558th [358th] Letter in Mrs. Piozzi's *Collection*, where it appears
that he recommended 'dried orange-peel, finely powdered,' as a medicine.

pute in England, a park wall at a thousand pounds a mile; now a garden-wall must cost at least as much. You intend your trees should grow higher than a deer will leap. Now let us see; for a hundred pounds you could only have forty-four square yards,[1] which is very little; for two hundred pounds, you may have eighty-four square yards,[2] which is very well. But when will you get the value of two hundred pounds of walls, in fruit, in your climate? No, Sir, such contention with Nature is not worth while. I would plant an orchard, and have plenty of such fruit as ripen well in your country. My friend, Dr. Madden, of Ireland, said, that "in an orchard there should be enough to eat, enough to lay up, enough to be stolen, and enough to rot upon the ground." Cherries are an early fruit, you may have them; and you may have the early apples and pears.' BOSWELL. 'We cannot have nonpareils.' JOHNSON. 'Sir, you can no more have nonpareils than you can have grapes.' BOSWELL. 'We have them, Sir; but they are very bad.' JOHNSON. 'Nay, Sir, never try to have a thing merely to shew that you *cannot* have it. From ground that would let for forty shillings you may have a large orchard; and you see it costs you only forty shillings. Nay, you may graze the ground when the trees are grown up; you cannot while they are young.' BOSWELL. 'Is not a good garden a very common thing in England, Sir?' JOHNSON. 'Not so common, Sir, as you imagine. In Lincolnshire there is hardly an orchard; in Staffordshire very little fruit.' BOSWELL. 'Has Langton no orchard?' JOHNSON. 'No, Sir.' BOSWELL. 'How so, Sir?' JOHNSON. 'Why, Sir, from the general negligence of the county. He has it not, because nobody else has it.' BOSWELL. 'A hot-house is a certain thing; I may have that.' JOHNSON. 'A hot-house is pretty certain; but you must first build it, then you must keep fires in it, and you must have a gardener to take care of it.' BOSWELL. 'But if I have a gardener at any rate?—' JOHNSON. 'Why, yes.' BOSWELL. I'd have it near my house; there is no need to have it in the orchard.' JOHNSON. 'Yes, I'd have it near my house. I would plant a great many currants; the fruit is good, and they make a pretty sweetmeat.'

I record this minute detail, which some may think trifling, in

---

[1] [He means 'yards square'.]   [2] [88 yards square.]

order to shew clearly how this great man, whose mind could grasp such large and extensive subjects, as he has shewn in his literary labours, was yet well-informed in the common affairs of life, and loved to illustrate them.

Mr. Walker, the celebrated master of elocution, came in, and then we went up stairs into the study. I asked him if he had taught many clergymen. JOHNSON. 'I hope not.' WALKER. 'I have taught only one, and he is the best reader I ever heard, not by my teaching, but by his own natural talents.' JOHNSON. 'Were he the best reader in the world, I would not have it told that he was taught.' Here was one of his peculiar prejudices. Could it be any disadvantage to the clergyman to have it known that he was taught an easy and graceful delivery? BOSWELL. 'Will you not allow, Sir, that a man may be taught to read well?' JOHNSON. 'Why, Sir, so far as to read better than he might do without being taught, yes. Formerly it was supposed that there was no difference in reading, but that one read as well as another.' BOSWELL. 'It is wonderful to see old Sheridan as enthusiastick about oratory as ever.' WALKER. 'His enthusiasm as to what oratory will do, may be too great: but he reads well.' JOHNSON. 'He reads well, but he reads low; and you know it is much easier to read low than to read high; for when you read high, you are much more limited, your loudest note can be but one, and so the variety is less in proportion to the loudness. Now some people have occasion to speak to an extensive audience, and must speak loud to be heard.' WALKER. 'The art is to read strong, though low.'

Talking of the origin of language; JOHNSON. 'It must have come by inspiration. A thousand, nay, a million of children could not invent a language. While the organs are pliable, there is not understanding enough to form a language; by the time that there is understanding enough, the organs are become stiff. We know that after a certain age we cannot learn to pronounce a new language. No foreigner, who comes to England when advanced in life, ever pronounces English tolerably well; at least such instances are very rare. When I maintain that language must have come by inspiration, I do not mean that inspiration is required for rhetorick, and all the beauties of language; for when once man has language, we can conceive that he may gradually form modifications of it. I mean only, that inspiration seems to me to be necessary to give man the faculty of speech; to inform him that he may have speech; which I think he could no more find out without inspiration, than cows or hogs would think of such a faculty.' WALKER. 'Do you think, Sir, that there are any perfect synonimes in any language?' JOHNSON. 'Originally there were not; but by using words negligently, or in poetry, one word comes to be confounded with another.'

He talked of Dr. Dodd. 'A friend of mine, (said he,) came to me and told me, that a lady wished to have Dr. Dodd's picture in a bracelet, and asked me for a motto. I said, I could think of no better than *Currat Lex*.[1] I was very willing to have him pardoned, that is, to have the sentence changed to transportation: but, when he was once hanged, I did not wish he should be made a saint.'

Mrs. Burney, wife of his friend Dr. Burney, came in, and he seemed to be entertained with her conversation.

Garrick's funeral was talked of as extravagantly expensive. Johnson, from his dislike to exaggeration, would not allow that it was distinguished by any extraordinary pomp. 'Were there not six horses to each coach?' said Mrs. Burney. JOHNSON. 'Madam, there were no more six horses than six phœnixes.'

Mrs. Burney wondered that some very beautiful new buildings should be erected in Moorfields, in so shocking a situation as between Bedlam and St. Luke's Hospital; and said she could not live there. JOHNSON. 'Nay, Madam, you see nothing there to hurt you. You no more think of madness by having windows that look to Bedlam, than you think of death by having windows that look to a church-yard.' MRS. BURNEY. 'We may look to a church-yard, Sir; for it is right that we should be kept in mind of death.' JOHNSON. 'Nay, Madam, if you go to that, it is right that we should be kept in mind of madness, which is occasioned by too much indulgence of imagination. I think a very moral use may be made of these new buildings: I would have those who

[1] ['Let the law take its course.']

have heated imaginations live there, and take warning.' Mrs. Burney. 'But, Sir, many of the poor people that are mad, have become so from disease, or from distressing events. It is, therefore, not their fault, but their misfortune; and, therefore, to think of them is a melancholy consideration.'

Time passed on in conversation till it was too late for the service of the church at three o'clock. I took a walk, and left him alone for some time; then returned, and we had coffee and conversation again by ourselves.

I stated the character of a noble friend[1] of mine, as a curious case for his opinion:—'He is the most inexplicable man to me that I ever knew. Can you explain him, Sir? He is, I really believe, noble-minded, generous, and princely. But his most intimate friends may be separated from him for years, without his ever asking a question concerning them. He will meet them with a formality, a coldness, a stately indifference; but when they come close to him, and fairly engage him in conversation, they find him as easy, pleasant, and kind, as they could wish. One then supposes that what is so agreeable will soon be renewed; but stay away from him for half a year, and he will neither call on you, nor send to inquire about you.' Johnson. 'Why, Sir, I cannot ascertain his character exactly, as I do not know him; but I should not like to have such a man for my friend. He may love study, and wish not to be interrupted by his friends; *Amici fures temporis.*[2] He may be a frivolous man, and be so much occupied with petty pursuits, that he may not want friends. Or he may have a notion that there is a dignity in appearing indifferent, while he in fact may not be more indifferent at his heart than another.'

We went to evening prayers at St. Clement's, at seven, and then parted.

On Sunday, April 20, being Easter-day, after attending solemn service at St. Paul's, I came to Dr. Johnson, and found Mr. Lowe, the painter, sitting with him. Mr. Lowe mentioned the great number of new buildings of late in London, yet that Dr. Johnson

---

[1] [Lord Mountstuart. *Boswell Papers*, xv. 205.]
[2] ['Friends are the thieves of time.' Bacon, *Advancement of Learning*, bk. ii.]

had observed, that the number of inhabitants was not increased. JOHNSON. 'Why, Sir, the bills of mortality prove that no more people die now than formerly; so it is plain no more live. The register of births proves nothing, for not one tenth of the people of London are born there.' BOSWELL. 'I believe, Sir, a great many of the children born in London die early.' JOHNSON. 'Why, yes, Sir.' BOSWELL. 'But those who do live, are as stout and strong people as any: Dr. Price says, they must be naturally stronger to get through.' JOHNSON. 'That is system, Sir. A great traveller observes, that it is said there are no weak or deformed people among the Indians; but he with much sagacity assigns the reason of this, which is, that the hardship of their life as hunters and fishers does not allow weak or diseased children to grow up. Now had I been an Indian, I must have died early; my eyes would not have served me to get food. I indeed now could fish, give me English tackle; but had I been an Indian I must have starved, or they would have knocked me on the head, when they saw I could do nothing.' BOSWELL. 'Perhaps they would have taken care of you: we are told they are fond of oratory, you would have talked to them.' JOHNSON. 'Nay, Sir, I should not have lived long enough to be fit to talk; I should have been dead before I was ten years old. Depend upon it, Sir, a savage, when he is hungry, will not carry about with him a looby of nine years old, who cannot help himself. They have no affection, Sir.' BOSWELL. 'I believe natural affection, of which we hear so much, is very small.' JOHNSON. 'Sir, natural affection is nothing: but affection from principle and established duty is sometimes wonderfully strong.' LOWE. 'A hen, Sir, will feed her chickens in preference to herself.' JOHNSON. 'But we don't know that the hen is hungry; let the hen be fairly hungry, and I'll warrant she'll peck the corn herself. A cock, I believe, will feed hens instead of himself; but we don't know that the cock is hungry.' BOSWELL. 'And that, Sir, is not from affection but gallantry. But some of the Indians have affection.' JOHNSON. 'Sir, that they help some of their children is plain; for some of them live, which they could not do without being helped.'

I dined with him; the company were, Mrs. Williams, Mrs.

Desmoulins, and Mr. Lowe. He seemed not to be well, talked little, grew drowsy soon after dinner, and retired, upon which I went away.

Having next day gone to Mr. Burke's seat in the country, from whence I was recalled by an express, that a near relation[1] of mine had killed his antagonist in a duel, and was himself dangerously wounded, I saw little of Dr. Johnson till Monday, April 28, when I spent a considerable part of the day with him, and introduced the subject, which then chiefly occupied my mind. JOHNSON. 'I do not see, Sir, that fighting is absolutely forbidden in Scripture; I see revenge forbidden, but not self-defence.' BOSWELL. 'The Quakers say it is; "Unto him that smiteth thee on one cheek, offer also the other."' JOHNSON. 'But stay, Sir; the text is meant only to have the effect of moderating passion; it is plain that we are not to take it in a literal sense. We see this from the context, where there are other recommendations, which I warrant you the Quaker will not take literally; as, for instance, "From him that would borrow of thee, turn thou not away." Let a man whose credit is bad, come to a Quaker, and say, "Well, Sir, lend me a hundred pounds;" he'll find him as unwilling as any other man. No, Sir, a man may shoot the man who invades his character, as he may shoot him who attempts to break into his house.[2] So in 1745, my friend,

[1] [Lieut. David Cuninghame, who killed Mr. Riddell. *Boswell Papers*, xv. 203.]

[2] I think it necessary to caution my readers against concluding that in this or any other conversation of Dr. Johnson, they have his serious and deliberate opinion on the subject of duelling. In my *Journal of a Tour to the Hebrides*, 3rd edit. p. 386 [p. 366, Oct. 24], it appears that he made this frank confession:— 'Nobody at times, talks more laxly than I do;' and, *ib.*, p. 231 [Sept. 19, 1773], 'He fairly owned he could not explain the rationality of duelling.' We may, therefore, infer, that he could not think that justifiable, which seems so inconsistent with the spirit of the Gospel. At the same time it must be confessed, that from the prevalent notions of honour, a gentleman who receives a challenge is reduced to a dreadful alternative. A remarkable instance of this is furnished by a clause in the will of the late Colonel Thomas, of the Guards, written the night before he fell in a duel, Sept. 3, 1783:—'In the first place, I commit my soul to Almighty GOD, in hopes of his mercy and pardon for the irreligious step I now (in compliance with the unwarrantable customs of this wicked world) put myself under the necessity of taking.'

Tom Cumming, the Quaker, said, he would not fight, but he would drive an ammunition cart; and we know that the Quakers have sent flannel waistcoats to our soldiers, to enable them to fight better.' BOSWELL. 'When a man is the aggressor, and by ill-usage forces on a duel in which he is killed, have we not little ground to hope that he is gone into a state of happiness?' JOHNSON. 'Sir, we are not to judge determinately of the state in which a man leaves this life. He may in a moment have repented effectually, and it is possible may have been accepted by GOD. There is in *Camden's Remains*, an epitaph upon a very wicked man, who was killed by a fall from his horse, in which he is supposed to say,

> "Between the stirrup and the ground,
> I mercy ask'd, I mercy found." '

BOSWELL. 'Is not the expression in the Burial-service, "in the *sure* and *certain* hope of a blessed resurrection," too strong to be used indiscriminately, and, indeed, sometimes when those over whose bodies it is said, have been notoriously profane?' JOHNSON. 'It is sure and certain *hope*, Sir; not *belief*.' I did not insist further; but cannot help thinking that less positive words would be more proper.[1]

Talking of a man who was grown very fat, so as to be incommoded with corpulency; he said, 'He eats too much, Sir.' BOSWELL. 'I don't know, Sir, you will see one man fat who eats moderately, and another lean who eats a great deal.' JOHNSON. 'Nay, Sir, whatever may be the quantity that a man eats,

---

[1] Upon this objection the Reverend Mr. Ralph Churton, Fellow of Brazen-nose College, Oxford, has favoured me with the following satisfactory observation:—'The passage in the Burial-service does not mean the resurrection of the person interred, but the general resurrection; it is in sure and certain hope of *the* resurrection; not *his* resurrection. Where the deceased is really spoken of, the expression is very different, "as our hope is this our brother doth" [rest in Christ]; a mode of speech consistent with every thing but absolute certainty that the person departed doth *not* rest in Christ, which no one can be assured of, without immediate revelation from Heaven. In the first of these places also, "eternal life" does not necessarily mean eternity of bliss, but merely the eternity of the state, whether in happiness or in misery, to ensue upon the resurrection; which is probably the sense of "the life everlasting," in the Apostles' Creed. See *Wheatly and Bennet on the Common Prayer*.'

it is plain that if he is too fat, he has eaten more than he should have done. One man may have a digestion that consumes food better than common; but it is certain that solidity is encreased by putting something to it.' BOSWELL. 'But may not solids swell and be distended?' JOHNSON. 'Yes, Sir, they may swell and be distended; but that is not fat.'

We talked of the accusation against a gentleman[1] for supposed delinquencies in India. JOHNSON. What foundation there is for accusation I know not, but they will not get at him. Where bad actions are committed at so great a distance, a delinquent can obscure the evidence till the scent becomes cold; there is a cloud between, which cannot be penetrated: therefore all distant power is bad. I am clear that the best plan for the government of India is a despotick governour; for if he be a good man, it is evidently the best government; and supposing him to be a bad man, it is better to have one plunderer than many. A governour whose power is checked, lets others plunder, that he himself may be allowed to plunder; but if despotick, he sees that the more he lets others plunder, the less there will be for himself, so he restrains them; and though he himself plunders, the country is a gainer, compared with being plundered by numbers.'

I mentioned the very liberal payment which had been received for reviewing; and, as evidence of this, that it had been proved in a trial, that Dr. Shebbeare had received six guineas a sheet for that kind of literary labour. JOHNSON. 'Sir, he might get six guineas for a particular sheet, but not *communibus sheetibus.*'[2] BOSWELL. 'Pray, Sir, by a sheet of review is it meant that it shall be all of the writer's own composition, or are extracts, made from the book reviewed, deducted?' JOHNSON. 'No, Sir: it is a sheet, no matter of what.' BOSWELL. 'I think that it is not reasonable.' JOHNSON. 'Yes, Sir, it is. A man will more easily write a sheet all his own, than read an octavo volume to get extracts.' To one of Johnson's wonderful fertility of mind I believe writing was really easier than reading and extracting; but with ordinary men the case is very different. A great deal,

---

[1] [Sir Thomas Rumbold. *Boswell Papers,* xv. 203.]
[2] ['for average sheets.']

indeed, will depend upon the care and judgement with which the extracts are made. I can suppose the operation to be tedious and difficult: but in many instances we must observe crude morsels cut out of books as if at random; and when a large extract is made from one place, it surely may be done with very little trouble. One, however, I must acknowledge, might be led, from the practice of reviewers, to suppose that they take a pleasure in original writing; for we often find that, instead of giving an accurate account of what has been done by the authour whose work they are reviewing, which is surely the proper business of a literary journal, they produce some plausible and ingenious conceits of their own, upon the topicks which have been discussed.

Upon being told that old Mr. Sheridan, indignant at the neglect of his oratorical plans, had threatened to go to America; JOHNSON. 'I hope he will go to America.' BOSWELL. 'The Americans don't want oratory.' JOHNSON. 'But we can want Sheridan.'

On Monday, April 29,[1] I found him at home in the forenoon, and Mr. Seward with him. Horace having been mentioned; BOSWELL. 'There is a great deal of thinking in his works. One finds there almost every thing but religion.' SEWARD. 'He speaks of his returning to it, in his Ode *Parcus Deorum cultor et infrequens.*'[2] JOHNSON. 'Sir, he was not in earnest: this was merely poetical.' BOSWELL. 'There are, I am afraid, many people who have no religion at all.' SEWARD. 'And sensible people too.' JOHNSON. 'Why, Sir, not sensible in that respect. There must be either a natural or a moral stupidity, if one lives in a total neglect of so very important a concern.' SEWARD. 'I wonder that there should be people without religion.' JOHNSON. 'Sir, you need not wonder at this, when you consider how large a proportion of almost every man's life is passed without thinking of it. I myself was for some years totally regardless of religion. It had dropped out of my mind. It was at an early part of my life. Sickness brought it back, and I hope I have never lost it

[1] [Actually Wednesday, April 30.]
[2] ['A grudging and infrequent worshipper of the gods.' *Odes* i. 34. (Wickham.)]

since.' BOSWELL. 'My dear Sir, what a man must you have been without religion! Why you must have gone on drinking, and swearing, and—' JOHNSON. (with a smile,) 'I drank enough and swore enough, to be sure.' SEWARD. 'One should think that sickness, and the view of death, would make more men religious.' JOHNSON. 'Sir, they do not know how to go about it: they have not the first notion. A man who has never had religion before, no more grows religious when he is sick, than a man who has never learnt figures can count when he has need of calculation.'

I mentioned a worthy friend[1] of ours whom we valued much, but observed that he was too ready to introduce religious discourse upon all occasions. JOHNSON. 'Why, yes, Sir, he will introduce religious discourse without seeing whether it will end in instruction and improvement, or produce some profane jest. He would introduce it in the company of Wilkes, and twenty more such.'

I mentioned Dr. Johnson's excellent distinction between liberty of conscience and liberty of teaching. JOHNSON. 'Consider, Sir; if you have children whom you wish to educate in the principles of the Church of England, and there comes a Quaker who tries to pervert them to his principles, you would drive away the Quaker. You would not trust to the predomination of right, which you believe is in your opinions; you would keep wrong out of their heads. Now the vulgar are the children of the State. If any one attempts to teach them doctrines contrary to what the State approves, the magistrate may and ought to restrain him.' SEWARD. 'Would you restrain private conversation, Sir?' JOHNSON. 'Why, Sir, it is difficult to say where private conversation begins, and where it ends. If we three should discuss even the great question concerning the existence of a Supreme Being by ourselves, we should not be restrained; for that would be to put an end to all improvement. But if we should discuss it in the presence of ten boarding-school girls, and as many boys, I think the magistrate would do well to put us in the stocks, to finish the debate there.'

[1] [Langton. *Boswell Papers,* xv. 207.]

Lord Hailes had sent him a present of a curious little printed poem, on repairing the University of Aberdeen, by David *Malloch*, which he thought would please Johnson, as affording clear evidence that Mallet had appeared even as a literary character by the name of *Malloch*; his changing which to one of softer sound, had given Johnson occasion to introduce him into his *Dictionary*, under the article *Alias*.[1] This piece was, I suppose, one of Mallet's first essays. It is preserved in his works, with several variations. Johnson having read aloud, from the beginning of it, where there were some common-place assertions as to the superiority of ancient times;—'How false (said he,) is all this, to say that in ancient times learning was not a disgrace to a Peer as it is now. In ancient times a Peer was as ignorant as any one else. He would have been angry to have it thought he could write his name. Men in ancient times dared to stand forth with a degree of ignorance with which nobody would dare now to stand forth. I am always angry when I hear ancient times praised at the expence of modern times. There is now a great deal more learning in the world than there was formerly; for it is universally diffused. You have, perhaps, no man who knows as much Greek and Latin as Bentley; no man who knows as much mathematicks as Newton: but you have many more men who know Greek and Latin, and who know mathematicks.'

On Thursday, May 1, I visited him in the evening along with young Mr. Burke. He said, 'It is strange that there should be so little reading in the world, and so much writing. People in general do not willingly read, if they can have any thing else to amuse them. There must be an external impulse; emulation, or vanity, or avarice. The progress which the understanding makes through a book, has more pain than pleasure in it. Language is scanty, and inadequate to express the nice gradations and mixtures of our feelings. No man reads a book of science from pure inclination. The books that we do read with pleasure are light compositions, which contain a quick succession of events. How-

---

[1] Malloch continued to write his name thus, *after he came to London*. His verses prefixed to the second edition of Thomson's *Winter* are so subscribed. [M.]

ever, I have this year read all Virgil through. I read a book of
the *Æneid* every night, so it was done in twelve nights, and I
had great delight in it. The *Georgicks* did not give me so much
pleasure, except the fourth book. The *Eclogues* I have almost all
by heart. I do not think the story of the *Æneid* interesting. I like
the story of the *Odyssey* much better; and this not on account of
the wonderful things which it contains; for there are wonderful
things enough in the *Æneid*;—the ships of the Trojans turned
to sea-nymphs,—the tree at Polydorus's tomb dropping blood.
The story of the *Odyssey* is interesting, as a great part of it is
domestick. It has been said, there is pleasure in writing, particularly in writing verses. I allow you may have pleasure from
writing, after it is over, if you have written well; but you don't
go willingly to it again. I know when I have been writing
verses, I have run my finger down the margin, to see how many
I had made, and how few I had to make.'

He seemed to be in a very placid humour, and although I have
no note of the particulars of young Mr. Burke's conversation, it
is but justice to mention in general, that it was such that Dr.
Johnson said to me afterwards, 'He did very well indeed; I have
a mind to tell his father.'

'*To* Sir Joshua Reynolds

'Dear Sir,—The gentleman who waits on you with this, is
Mr. Cruikshanks, who wishes to succeed his friend Dr. Hunter
as Professor of Anatomy in the Royal Academy. His qualifications are very generally known, and it adds dignity to the
institution that such men[1] are candidates. I am, Sir, your most
humble servant,

'May 2, 1783.'   'Sam. Johnson.'

I have no minute of any interview with Johnson till Thursday,
May 15, when I find what follows:—Boswell. 'I wish much
to be in Parliament, Sir.' Johnson. 'Why, Sir, unless you come
resolved to support any administration, you would be the worse

---

[1] Let it be remembered by those who accuse Dr. Johnson of illiberality
that both were *Scotchmen*.

for being in Parliament, because you would be obliged to live more expensively.' BOSWELL. 'Perhaps, Sir, I should be the less happy for being in Parliament. I never would sell my vote, and I should be vexed if things went wrong.' JOHNSON. 'That's cant, Sir. It would not vex you more in the house, than in the gallery: publick affairs vex no man.' BOSWELL. 'Have not they vexed yourself a little, Sir? Have not you been vexed by all the turbulence of this reign, and by that absurd vote of the House of Commons, "That the influence of the Crown has increased, is increasing, and ought to be diminished?"' JOHNSON. 'Sir, I have never slept an hour less, nor eat an ounce less meat. I would have knocked the factious dogs on the head, to be sure; but I was not *vexed*.' BOSWELL. 'I declare, Sir, upon my honour, I did imagine I was vexed, and took a pride in it; but it *was*, perhaps, cant; for I own I neither ate less, nor slept less.' JOHNSON. 'My dear friend, clear your *mind* of cant. You may *talk* as other people do: you may say to a man, "Sir, I am your most humble servant." You are *not* his most humble servant. You may say, "These are sad times; it is a melancholy thing to be reserved to such times." You don't mind the times. You tell a man, "I am sorry you had such bad weather the last day of your journey, and were so much wet." You don't care six-pence whether he was wet or dry. You may *talk* in this manner; it is a mode of talking in Society: but don't *think* foolishly.'

I talked of living in the country. JOHNSON. 'Don't set up for what is called hospitality; it is a waste of time, and a waste of money; you are eaten up, and not the more respected for your liberality. If your house be like an inn, nobody cares for you. A man who stays a week with another, makes him a slave for a week.' BOSWELL. 'But there are people, Sir, who make their houses a home to their guests, and are themselves quite easy.' JOHNSON. 'Then, Sir, home must be the same to the guests, and they need not come.'

Here he discovered a notion common enough in persons not much accustomed to entertain company; that there must be a degree of elaborate attention, otherwise company will think themselves neglected; and such attention is no doubt very fatiguing. He proceeded: 'I would not, however, be a stranger in my own county; I would visit my neighbours, and receive their visits; but I would not be in haste to return visits. If a gentleman comes to see me, I tell him he does me a great deal of honour. I do not go to see him perhaps for ten weeks; then we are very complaisant to each other. No, Sir, you will have much more influence by giving or lending money where it is wanted, than by hospitality.'

On Saturday, May 17, I saw him for a short time. Having mentioned that I had that morning been with old Mr. Sheridan, he remembered their former intimacy with a cordial warmth, and said to me, 'Tell Mr. Sheridan, I shall be glad to see him, and shake hands with him.' BOSWELL. 'It is to me very wonderful that resentment should be kept up so long.' JOHNSON. 'Why, Sir, it is not altogether resentment that he does not visit me; it is partly falling out of the habit,—partly disgust, as one has at a drug that has made him sick. Besides, he knows that I laugh at his oratory.'

Another day I spoke of one of our friends,[1] of whom he, as well as I, had a very high opinion. He expatiated in his praise; but added, 'Sir, he is a cursed Whig, a *bottomless* Whig, as they all are now.'

I mentioned my expectations from the interest of an eminent person[2] then in power; adding, 'but I have no claim but the claim of friendship; however, some people will go a great way from that motive.' JOHNSON. 'Sir, they will go all the way from that motive.' A gentleman[3] talked of retiring. 'Never think of that,' said Johnson. The gentleman urged, 'I should then do no ill.' JOHNSON. 'Nor no good either, Sir, it would be a civil suicide.'

On Monday, May 26, I found him at tea, and the celebrated Miss Burney, the authour of *Evelina* and *Cecilia*, with him. I asked if there would be any speakers in Parliament, if there were no places to be obtained. JOHNSON. 'Yes, Sir. Why do you speak here? Either to instruct and entertain, which is a benevolent

---

[1] [Burke. *Croker*[1].]   [2] [Probably Burke. *Powell*.]
[3] [*Hill suggests* Burke.]

motive; or for distinction, which is a selfish motive.' I mentioned *Cecilia*. JOHNSON. (with an air of animated satisfaction,) 'Sir, if you talk of *Cecilia*, talk on.'

We talked of Mr. Barry's exhibition of his pictures. JOHNSON. 'Whatever the hand may have done, the mind has done its part. There is a grasp of mind there which you find nowhere else.'[1]

I asked whether a man naturally virtuous, or one who has overcome wicked inclinations, is the best. JOHNSON. 'Sir, to *you*, the man who has overcome wicked inclinations is not the best. He has more merit to *himself*. I would rather trust my money to a man who has no hands, and so a physical impossibility to steal, than to a man of the most honest principles. There is a witty satirical story of Foote. He had a small bust of Garrick placed upon his bureau. "You may be surprized (said he,) that I allow him to be so near my gold;—but you will observe he has no hands." '

On Friday,[2] May 29, being to set out for Scotland next morning, I passed a part of the day with him in more than usual earnestness; as his health was in a more precarious state than at any time when I had parted from him. He, however, was quick and lively, and critical as usual. I mentioned one who was a very learned man.[3] JOHNSON. 'Yes, Sir, he has a great deal of learning; but it never lies straight. There is never one idea by the side of another; 'tis all entangled: and then he drives it so aukwardly upon conversation.'

I stated to him an anxious thought, by which a sincere Christian might be disturbed, even when conscious of having lived a good life, so far as is consistent with human infirmity; he might fear that he should afterwards fall away, and be guilty of such crimes as would render all his former religion vain. Could there be, upon this aweful subject, such a thing as balancing of accounts? Suppose a man who has led a good life for seven years,

---

[1] In Mr. Barry's printed analysis, or description of these pictures, he speaks of Johnson's character in the highest terms.

[2] [Actually Thursday.]

[3] [Langton. *Boswell Papers*, xv. 232.]

commits an act of wickedness, and instantly dies; will his former good life have any effect in his favour? JOHNSON. 'Sir, if a man has led a good life for seven years, and then is hurried by passion to do what is wrong, and is suddenly carried off, depend upon it he will have the reward of his seven years' good life; GOD will not take a catch of him. Upon this principle Richard Baxter believes that a Suicide may be saved. "If, (says he,) it should be objected that what I maintain may encourage suicide, I answer, I am not to tell a lie to prevent it." ' BOSWELL. 'But does not the text say, "As the tree falls, so it must lie"?' JOHNSON. 'Yes, Sir; as the tree falls: but,—(after a little pause) —that is meant as to the general state of the tree, not what is the effect of a sudden blast.' In short, he interpreted the expression as referring to condition, not to position. The common notion, therefore, seems to be erroneous; and Shenstone's witty remark on Divines trying to give the tree a jerk upon a death-bed, to make it lie favourably, is not well founded.

I asked him what works of Richard Baxter's I should read. He said, 'Read any of them; they are all good.'

He said, 'Get as much force of mind as you can. Live within your income. Always have something saved at the end of the year. Let your imports be more than your exports, and you'll never go far wrong.'

I assured him, that in the extensive and various range of his acquaintance there never had been any one who had a more sincere respect and affection for him than I had. He said, 'I believe it, Sir. Were I in distress, there is no man to whom I should sooner come than to you. I should like to come and have a cottage in your park, toddle about, live mostly on milk, and be taken care of by Mrs. Boswell. She and I are good friends now; are we not?'

Talking of devotion, he said, 'Though it be true that "GOD dwelleth not in temples made with hands," yet in this state of being, our minds are more piously affected in places appropriated to divine worship, than in others. Some people have a particular room in their house, where they say their prayers; of which I do not disapprove, as it may animate their devotion.'

He embraced me, and gave me his blessing, as usual when I was leaving him for any length of time. I walked from his door to-day, with a fearful apprehension of what might happen before I returned.

'*To* THE RIGHT HONOURABLE WILLIAM WINDHAM

'SIR,—The bringer of this letter is the father of Miss Philips,[1] a singer, who comes to try her voice on the stage at Dublin.

'Mr. Philips is one of my old friends; and as I am of opinion that neither he nor his daughter will do any thing that can disgrace their benefactors, I take the liberty of entreating you to countenance and protect them so far as may be suitable to your station[2] and character; and shall consider myself as obliged by any favourable notice which they shall have the honour of receiving from you. I am, Sir, your most humble servant,

'London, May 31, 1783.'   'SAM. JOHNSON.'

The following is another instance of his active benevolence:—

'*To* SIR JOSHUA REYNOLDS

'DEAR SIR,—I have sent you some of my god-son's[3] performances, of which I do not pretend to form any opinion. When I took the liberty of mentioning him to you, I did not know what I have since been told, that Mr. Moser had admitted him among the Students of the Academy. What more can be done for him I earnestly entreat you to consider; for I am very desirous that he should derive some advantage from my connection with him. If you are inclined to see him, I will bring him to wait on you, at any time that you shall be pleased to appoint. I am, Sir, your most humble servant,

'June 2, 1783.'   'SAM. JOHNSON.'

My anxious apprehensions at parting with him this year proved to be but too well founded; for not long afterwards he

---

[1] Now the celebrated Mrs. Crouch.
[2] Mr. Windham was at this time in Dublin, Secretary to the Earl of Northington, then Lord Lieutenant of Ireland.
[3] Son of Mr. Samuel Paterson.

had a dreadful stroke of the palsy, of which there are very full and accurate accounts in letters written by himself, which shew with what composure of mind, and resignation to the Divine Will, his steady piety enabled him to behave.

'*To* MR. EDMUND ALLEN

'DEAR SIR,—It has pleased GOD, this morning, to deprive me of the powers of speech; and as I do not know but that it may be his further good pleasure to deprive me soon of my senses, I request you will on the receipt of this note, come to me, and act for me, as the exigencies of my case may require. I am, sincerely yours,

'June 17, 1783.'   'SAM. JOHNSON.'

'*To* THE REVEREND DR. JOHN TAYLOR

'DEAR SIR,—It has pleased GOD, by a paralytick stroke in the night, to deprive me of speech.

'I am very desirous of Dr. Heberden's assistance, as I think my case is not past remedy. Let me see you as soon as it is possible. Bring Dr. Heberden with you, if you can; but come yourself at all events. I am glad you are so well, when I am so dreadfully attacked.

'I think that by a speedy application of stimulants much may be done. I question if a vomit, vigorous and rough, would not rouse the organs of speech to action. As it is too early to send, I will try to recollect what I can, that can be suspected to have brought on this dreadful distress.

'I have been accustomed to bleed frequently for an asthmatick complaint; but have forborne for some time by Dr. Pepys's persuasion, who perceived my legs beginning to swell. I sometimes alleviate a painful, or more properly an oppressive, constriction of my chest, by opiates; and have lately taken opium frequently, but the last, or two last times, in smaller quantities. My largest dose is three grains, and last night I took but two. You will suggest these things (and they are all that I can call to mind) to Dr. Heberden. I am, &c.

'June 17, 1783.'   'SAM. JOHNSON.'

Two days after he wrote thus to Mrs. Thrale:—[1]

'On Monday, the 16th, I sat for my picture, and walked a considerable way with little inconvenience. In the afternoon and evening I felt myself light and easy, and began to plan schemes of life. Thus I went to bed, and in a short time waked and sat up, as has been long my custom, when I felt a confusion and indistinctness in my head, which lasted, I suppose, about half a minute. I was alarmed, and prayed God, that however he might afflict my body, he would spare my understanding. This prayer, that I might try the integrity of my faculties, I made in Latin verse. The lines were not very good, but I knew them not to be very good: I made them easily, and concluded myself to be unimpaired in my faculties.

'Soon after I perceived that I had suffered a paralytick stroke, and that my speech was taken from me. I had no pain, and so little dejection in this dreadful state, that I wondered at my own apathy, and considered that perhaps death itself, when it should come, would excite less horrour than seems now to attend it.

'In order to rouse the vocal organs, I took two drams. Wine has been celebrated for the production of eloquence. I put myself into violent motion, and I think repeated it; but all was vain. I then went to bed, and, strange as it may seem, I think, slept. When I saw light, it was time to contrive what I should do. Though God stopped my speech, he left me my hand; I enjoyed a mercy which was not granted to my dear friend Lawrence, who now perhaps overlooks me as I am writing, and rejoices that I have what he wanted. My first note was necessarily to my servant, who came in talking, and could not immediately comprehend why he should read what I put into his hands.

'I then wrote a card to Mr. Allen, that I might have a discreet friend at hand, to act as occasion should require. In penning this note, I had some difficulty; my hand, I knew not how nor why, made wrong letters. I then wrote to Dr. Taylor to come to me, and bring Dr. Heberden; and I sent to Dr. Brocklesby, who is my neighbour. My physicians are very friendly, and give me great hopes; but you may imagine my situation. I have so far

[1] Vol. ii. p. 268, of Mrs. Thrale's Collection.

recovered my vocal powers, as to repeat the Lord's Prayer with no very imperfect articulation. My memory, I hope, yet remains as it was; but such an attack produces solicitude for the safety of every faculty.'

'*To* Mr. Thomas Davies

'Dear Sir,—I have had, indeed, a very heavy blow; but God, who yet spares my life, I humbly hope will spare my understanding, and restore my speech. As I am not at all helpless, I want no particular assistance, but am strongly affected by Mrs. Davies's tenderness; and when I think she can do me good, shall be very glad to call upon her. I had ordered friends to be shut out; but one or two have found the way in; and if you come you shall be admitted: for I know not whom I can see, that will bring more amusement on his tongue, or more kindness in his heart. I am, &c.

'June 18, 1783.'   'Sam. Johnson.'

It gives me great pleasure to preserve such a memorial of Johnson's regard for Mr. Davies, to whom I was indebted for my introduction to him.[1] He indeed loved Davies cordially, of which I shall give the following little evidence. One day, when he had treated him with too much asperity, Tom, who was not without pride and spirit, went off in a passion; but he had hardly reached home when Frank, who had been sent after him, delivered this note:—'Come, come, dear Davies, I am always sorry when we quarrel; send me word that we are friends.'

'*To* James Boswell, Esq.

'Dear Sir,—Your anxiety about my health is very friendly, and very agreeable with your general kindness. I have, indeed, had a very frightful blow. On the 17th of last month, about three in the morning, as near as I can guess, I perceived myself almost totally deprived of speech. I had no pain. My organs were so obstructed, that I could say *no*, but could scarcely say *yes*. I wrote

---

[1] Poor Derrick, however, though he did not himself introduce me to Dr. Johnson as he promised, had the merit of introducing me to Davies, the immediate introductor.

the necessary directions, for it pleased GOD to spare my hand, and sent for Dr. Heberden and Dr. Brocklesby. Between the time in which I discovered my own disorder, and that in which I sent for the doctors, I had, I believe, in spite of my surprize and solicitude, a little sleep, and Nature began to renew its operations. They came, and gave the directions which the disease required, and from that time I have been continually improving in articulation. I can now speak, but the nerves are weak, and I cannot continue discourse long; but strength, I hope, will return. The physicians consider me as cured. I was last Sunday at church. On Tuesday I took an airing to Hampstead, and dined with THE CLUB, where Lord Palmerston was proposed, and, against my opinion, was rejected.[1] I design to go next week with Mr. Langton to Rochester, where I purpose to stay about ten days, and then try some other air. I have many kind invitations. Your brother has very frequently enquired after me. Most of my friends have, indeed, been very attentive. Thank dear Lord Hailes for his present.

'I hope you found at your return every thing gay and prosperous, and your lady, in particular, quite recovered and confirmed. Pay her my respects. I am, dear Sir, your most humble servant,

'London, July 3, 1783.'   'SAM. JOHNSON.'

To MRS. LUCY PORTER, *in Lichfield*

'DEAR MADAM,—The account which you give of your health is but melancholy. May it please GOD to restore you. My disease affected my speech, and still continues, in some degree, to obstruct my utterance; my voice is distinct enough for a while; but the organs being still weak are quickly weary: but in other respects I am, I think, rather better than I have lately been; and can let you know my state without the help of any other hand.

'In the opinion of my friends, and in my own, I am gradually mending. The physicians consider me as cured; and I had leave, four days ago, to wash the cantharides from my head. Last Tuesday I dined at THE CLUB.

[1] His Lordship was soon after chosen, and is now a member of THE CLUB.

'I am going next week into Kent, and purpose to change the air frequently this summer; whether I shall wander so far as Staffordshire I cannot tell. I should be glad to come. Return my thanks to Mrs. Cobb, and Mr. Pearson, and all that have shewn attention to me.

'Let us, my dear, pray for one another, and consider our sufferings as notices mercifully given us to prepare ourselves for another state.

'I live now but in a melancholy way. My old friend Mr. Levett is dead, who lived with me in the house, and was useful and companionable; Mrs. Desmoulins is gone away; and Mrs. Williams is so much decayed, that she can add little to another's gratifications. The world passes away, and we are passing with it; but there is, doubtless, another world, which will endure for ever. Let us all fit ourselves for it. I am, &c.,

'London, July 5, 1783.'   'SAM. JOHNSON.'

Such was the general vigour of his constitution, that he recovered from this alarming and severe attack with wonderful quickness; so that in July he was able to make a visit to Mr. Langton at Rochester, where he passed about a fortnight, and made little excursions as easily as at any time of his life. In August he went as far as the neighbourhood of Salisbury, to Heale, the seat of William Bowles, Esq. a gentleman whom I have heard him praise for exemplary religious order in his family. In his diary I find a short but honourable mention of this visit:—'August 28, I came to Heale without fatigue. 30. I am entertained quite to my mind.'

'*To* DR. BROCKLESBY

'DEAR SIR,   'Heale, near Salisbury, Aug. 29, 1783.

'Without appearing to want a just sense of your kind attention, I cannot omit to give an account of the day which seemed to appear in some sort perilous. I rose at five and went out at six, and having reached Salisbury about nine, went forward a few miles in my friend's chariot. I was no more wearied with the journey, though it was a high-hung, rough coach, than

I should have been forty years ago. We shall now see what air
will do. The country is all a plain; and the house in which I am,
so far as I can judge from my window, for I write before I have
left my chamber, is sufficiently pleasant.

'Be so kind as to continue your attention to Mrs. Williams;
it is great consolation to the well, and still greater to the sick,
that they find themselves not neglected; and I know that you
will be desirous of giving comfort even where you have no
great hope of giving help.

'Since I wrote the former part of the letter, I find that by the
course of the post I cannot send it before the thirty-first. I am, &c.
                                          'SAM. JOHNSON.'

While he was here he had a letter from Dr. Brocklesby,
acquainting him of the death of Mrs. Williams, which affected
him a good deal. Though for several years her temper had not
been complacent, she had valuable qualities, and her departure
left a blank in his house. Upon this occasion he, according to his
habitual course of piety, composed a prayer.[1]

I shall here insert a few particulars concerning him, with
which I have been favoured by one of his friends.[2]

'He had once conceived the design of writing the Life of
Oliver Cromwell, saying, that he thought it must be highly
curious to trace his extraordinary rise to the supreme power,
from so obscure a beginning. He at length laid aside his scheme,
on discovering that all that can be told of him is already in
print; and that it is impracticable to procure any authentick
information in addition to what the world is already possessed
of.'[3]

'He had likewise projected; but at what part of his life is not
known, a work to shew how small a quantity of REAL FICTION

---

[1] *Pr. and Med.* p. 226.   [2] [William Bowles.]
[3] Mr. Malone observes, 'This, however, was certainly a mistake, as
appears from the *Memoirs* published by Mr. Noble. Had Johnson been
furnished with the materials which the industry of that gentleman has
procured, and with others which, it is believed, are yet preserved in manuscript, he would, without doubt, have produced a most valuable and curious
history of Cromwell's life.'

there is in the world; and that the same images, with very little variation, have served all the authours who have ever written.'

'His thoughts in the latter part of his life were frequently employed on his deceased friends. He often muttered these, or such like sentences: "Poor man! and then he died." '

'Speaking of a certain literary friend,[1] "He is a very pompous puzzling fellow, (said he); he lent me a letter once that somebody had written to him, no matter what it was about; but he wanted to have the letter back, and expressed a mighty value for it; he hoped it was to be met with again, he would not lose it for a thousand pounds. I layed my hand upon it soon afterwards, and gave it him. I believe I said, I was very glad to have met with it. O, then he did not know that it signified any thing. So you see, when the letter was lost it was worth a thousand pounds, and when it was found it was not worth a farthing." '

'The style and character of his conversation is pretty generally known; it was certainly conducted in conformity with a precept of Lord Bacon, but it is not clear, I apprehend, that this conformity was either perceived or intended by Johnson. The precept alluded to is as follows: "In all kinds of speech, either pleasant, grave, severe, or ordinary, it is convenient to speak leisurely, and rather drawingly than hastily: because hasty speech confounds the memory, and oftentimes, besides the unseemliness, drives the man either to stammering, a non-plus, or harping on that which should follow; whereas a slow speech confirmeth the memory, addeth a conceit of wisdom to the hearers, besides a seemliness of speech and countenance." Dr. Johnson's method of conversation was certainly calculated to excite attention, and to amuse or instruct, (as it happened,) without wearying or confusing his company. He was always most perfectly clear and perspicuous; and his language was so accurate, and his sentences so neatly constructed, that his conversation might have been all printed without any correction. At the same time, it was easy and natural; the accuracy of it had no appearance of labour, constraint, or stiffness; he seemed more

[1] [Probably Joseph Warton. *Powell.*]

correct than others, by the force of habit, and the customary exercises of his powerful mind.'

'He spoke often in praise of French literature. "The French are excellent in this, (he would say,) they have a book on every subject." From what he had seen of them he denied them the praise of superior politeness, and mentioned, with very visible disgust, the custom they have of spitting on the floors of their apartments. "This, (said the Doctor,) is as gross a thing as can well be done; and one wonders how any man, or set of men, can persist in so offensive a practice for a whole day together; one should expect that the first effort toward civilization would remove it even amongst savages."'

'Baxter's *Reasons of the Christian Religion*, he thought contained the best collection of the evidences of the divinity of the Christian system.'

'Chymistry was always an interesting pursuit with Dr. Johnson. Whilst he was in Wiltshire, he attended some experiments that were made by a physician at Salisbury, on the new kinds of air. In the course of the experiments frequent mention being made of Dr. Priestley, Dr. Johnson knit his brows, and in a stern manner inquired, "Why do we hear so much of Dr. Priestley?"[1] He was very properly answered, "Sir, because we

---

[1] I do not wonder at Johnson's displeasure when the name of Dr. Priestley was mentioned; for I know no writer who has been suffered to publish more pernicious doctrines. I shall instance only three. First, *Materialism*; by which *mind* is denied to human nature; which, if believed, must deprive us of every elevated principle. Secondly, *Necessity*; or the doctrine that every action, whether good or bad, is included in an unchangeable and unavoidable system; a notion utterly subversive of moral government. Thirdly, that we have no reason to think that the *future* world, (which, as he is pleased to *inform* us, will be adapted to our *merely improved* nature,) will be materially different from *this*; which, if believed, would sink wretched mortals into despair, as they could no longer hope for the 'rest that remaineth for the people of GOD' [*Hebrews*, iv. 9], or for that happiness which is revealed to us as something beyond our present conceptions; but would feel themselves doomed to a continuation of the uneasy state under which they now groan. I say nothing of the petulant intemperance with which he dares to insult the venerable establishments of his country.

As a specimen of his writings, I shall quote the following passage, which appears to me equally absurd and impious, and which might have been retorted upon him by the men who were prosecuted for burning his house. 'I cannot, (says he,) as a *necessarian*, [meaning *necessitarian*,] hate *any man*;

are indebted to him for these important discoveries." On this, Dr. Johnson appeared well content; and replied, "Well, well, I believe we are; and let every man have the honour he has merited." '

'A friend was one day, about two years before his death, struck with some instance of Dr. Johnson's great candour. "Well, Sir, (said he,) I will always say that you are a very candid man." "Will you, (replied the Doctor,) I doubt then you will be very singular. But, indeed, Sir, (continued he,) I look upon myself to be a man very much misunderstood. I am not an uncandid, nor am I a severe man. I sometimes say more than I mean, in jest; and people are apt to believe me serious: however, I am more candid than I was when I was younger. As I know more of mankind I expect less of them, and am ready now to call a man *a good man*, upon easier terms than I was formerly." '

On his return from Heale he wrote to Dr. Burney:—

'I came home on the 18th at noon to a very disconsolate[1] house. You and I have lost our friends; but you have more friends at home. My domestick companion is taken from me. She is much missed, for her acquisitions were many, and her curiosity universal; so that she partook of every conversation. I am not well enough to go much out; and to sit, and eat, or

because I consider him as *being*, in all respects, just what GOD has *made him to be*; and also as *doing with respect to me*, nothing but what he was *expressly designed* and *appointed* to do; GOD being the *only cause*, and men nothing more than the *instruments* in his hands to *execute all his pleasure*.'—*Illustrations of Philosophical Necessity*, p. 111.

The Reverend Dr. Parr, in a late tract, appears to suppose that *Dr. Johnson not only endured, but almost solicited, an interview with Dr. Priestley.* In justice to Dr. Johnson, I declare my firm belief that he never did. My illustrious friend was particularly resolute in not giving countenance to men whose writings he considered as pernicious to society. I was present at Oxford when Dr. Price, even before he had rendered himself so generally obnoxious by his zeal for the French Revolution, came into a company where Johnson was, who instantly left the room. Much more would he have reprobated Dr. Priestley.

Whoever wishes to see a perfect delineation of this *Literary Jack of all Trades*, may find it in an ingenious tract, entitled, 'A SMALL WHOLE-LENGTH OF DR. PRIESTLEY,' printed for Rivingtons, in St. Paul's Church-Yard.

[1] [Johnson wrote *desolate*.]

fast alone, is very wearisome. I always mean to send my compliments to all the ladies.'

His fortitude and patience met with severe trials during this
year. The stroke of the palsy has been related circumstantially;
but he was also afflicted with the gout, and was besides troubled
with a complaint which not only was attended with immediate
inconvenience, but threatened him with a painful chirurgical
operation, from which most men would shrink. The complaint
was a *sarcocele*, which Johnson bore with uncommon firmness,
and was not at all frightened while he looked forward to amputation. He was attended by Mr. Pott and Mr. Cruikshank. I have
before me a letter of the 30th of July this year, to Mr. Cruikshank, in which he says, 'I am going to put myself into your
hands;' and another, accompanying a set of his *Lives of the Poets*,
in which he says, 'I beg your acceptance of these volumes, as an
acknowledgement of the great favours which you have bestowed
on, Sir, your most obliged and most humble servant.' I have in
my possession several more letters from him to Mr. Cruikshank,
and also to Dr. Mudge at Plymouth, which it would be improper
to insert, as they are filled with unpleasing technical details. I
shall, however, extract from his letters to Dr. Mudge such
passages as shew either a felicity of expression, or the undaunted
state of his mind.

'My conviction of your skill, and my belief of your friendship,
determine me to intreat your opinion and advice.'—'In this state
I with great earnestness desire you to tell me what is to be done.
Excision is doubtless necessary to the cure, and I know not any
means of palliation. The operation is doubtless painful; but is it
dangerous? The pain I hope to endure with decency; but I am
loth to put life into much hazard.'—'By representing the gout as
an antagonist to the palsy, you have said enough to make it
welcome. This is not strictly the first fit, but I hope it is as good
as the first; for it is the second that ever confined me; and
the first was ten years ago, much less fierce and fiery than
this.'—'Write, dear Sir, what you can, to inform or encourage
me. The operation is not delayed by any fears or objections of
mine.'

'*To* BENNET LANGTON, ESQ.

'DEAR SIR,—You may very reasonably charge me with insensibility of your kindness, and that of Lady Rothes, since I have suffered so much time to pass without paying any acknowledgement. I now, at last, return my thanks; and why I did it not sooner I ought to tell you. I went into Wiltshire as soon as I well could, and was there much employed in palliating my own malady. Disease produces much selfishness. A man in pain is looking after ease; and lets most other things go as chance shall dispose of them. In the meantime I have lost a companion,[1] to whom I have had recourse for domestick amusement for thirty years, and whose variety of knowledge never was exhausted; and now return to a habitation vacant and desolate. I carry about a very troublesome and dangerous complaint, which admits no cure but by the chirurgical knife. Let me have your prayers. I am, &c.

'London, Sept. 20, 1783.'   'SAM. JOHNSON.'

Happily the complaint abated without his being put to the torture of amputation. But we must surely admire the manly resolution which he discovered while it hung over him.

In a letter to the same gentleman he writes, 'The gout has within these four days come upon me with a violence which I never experienced before. It made me helpless as an infant.' And in another, having mentioned Mrs. Williams, he says,— 'whose death following that of Levett, has now made my house a solitude. She left her little substance to a charity-school. She is, I hope, where there is neither darkness, nor want, nor sorrow.'

I wrote to him, begging to know the state of his health, and mentioned that Baxter's *Anacreon*, 'which is in the library at Auchinleck, was, I find, collated by my father in 1727, with the MS. belonging to the University of Leyden, and he has made a number of Notes upon it. Would you advise me to publish a new edition of it?'

His answer was dated September 30:—

'You should not make your letters such rarities, when you know, or might know, the uniform state of my health. It is very

[1] Mrs. Anna Williams.

long since I heard from you; and that I have not answered is a very insufficient reason for the silence of a friend. Your *Anacreon* is a very uncommon book; neither London nor Cambridge can supply a copy of that edition. Whether it should be reprinted, you cannot do better than consult Lord Hailes.—Besides my constant and radical disease, I have been for these ten days much harrassed with the gout; but that has now remitted. I hope GOD will yet grant me a little longer life, and make me less unfit to appear before him.'

He this autumn received a visit from the celebrated Mrs. Siddons. He gives this account of it in one of his letters to Mrs. Thrale:—

'Mrs. Siddons, in her visit to me, behaved with great modesty and propriety, and left nothing behind her to be censured or despised. Neither praise nor money, the two powerful corrupters of mankind, seem to have depraved her. I shall be glad to see her again. Her brother Kemble calls on me, and pleases me very well. Mrs. Siddons and I talked of plays; and she told me her intention of exhibiting this winter the characters of Constance, Catharine, and Isabella, in Shakspeare.'

Mr. Kemble has favoured me with the following minute of what passed at this visit:—

'When Mrs. Siddons came into the room, there happened to be no chair ready for her, which he observing, said with a smile, "Madam, you who so often occasion a want of seats to other people, will the more easily excuse the want of one yourself."

'Having placed himself by her, he with great good humour entered upon a consideration of the English drama; and, among other inquiries, particularly asked her which of Shakspeare's characters she was most pleased with. Upon her answering that she thought the character of Queen Catharine, in *Henry the Eighth*, the most natural:—"I think so too, Madam, (said he;) and whenever you perform it, I will once more hobble out to the theatre myself." Mrs. Siddons promised she would do herself the honour of acting his favourite part for him; but many circumstances happened to prevent the representation of *King Henry the Eighth* during the Doctor's life.

'In the course of the evening he thus gave his opinion upon the merits of some of the principal performers whom he remembered to have seen upon the stage. "Mrs. Porter in the vehemence of rage, and Mrs. Clive in the sprightliness of humour, I have never seen equalled. What Clive did best, she did better than Garrick; but could not do half so many things well; she was a better romp than any I ever saw in nature. Pritchard, in common life, was a vulgar ideot; she would talk of her *gownd*: but, when she appeared upon the stage, seemed to be inspired by gentility and understanding. I once talked with Colley Cibber, and thought him ignorant of the principles of his art. Garrick, Madam, was no declaimer; there was not one of his own scene-shifters who could not have spoken *To be, or not to be*, better than he did; yet he was the only actor I ever saw whom I could call a master both in tragedy and comedy; though I liked him best in comedy. A true conception of character, and natural expression of it, were his distinguishing excellencies." Having expatiated, with his usual force and eloquence, on Mr. Garrick's extraordinary eminence as an actor, he concluded with this compliment to his social talents: "And after all, Madam, I thought him less to be envied on the stage than at the head of a table." '

Johnson, indeed, had thought more upon the subject of acting than might be generally supposed. Talking of it one day to Mr. Kemble, he said, 'Are you, Sir, one of those enthusiasts who believe yourself transformed into the very character you represent?' Upon Mr. Kemble's answering that he had never felt so strong a persuasion himself; 'To be sure not, Sir, (said Johnson;) the thing is impossible. And if Garrick really believed himself to be that monster, Richard the Third, he deserved to be hanged every time he performed it.'[1]

---

[1] My worthy friend, Mr. John Nichols, was present when Mr. Henderson, the actor, paid a visit to Dr. Johnson; and was received in a very courteous manner. See *Gent. Mag.* June, 1791.

I found among Dr. Johnson's papers, the following letter to him, from the celebrated Mrs. Bellamy:—

'To Dr. Johnson.

'Sir,—The flattering remembrance of the partiality you honoured me

A pleasing instance of the generous attention of one of his friends has been discovered by the publication of Mrs. Thrale's collection of *Letters*. In a letter to one of the Miss Thrales,[1] he writes,—'A friend, whose name I will tell when your mamma has tried to guess it, sent to my physician to enquire whether this long train of illness had brought me into difficulties for want of money, with an invitation to send to him for what occasion required. I shall write this night to thank him, having no need to borrow.' And afterwards, in a letter to Mrs. Thrale,—'Since you cannot guess, I will tell you, that the generous man was Gerard Hamilton. I returned him a very thankful and respectful letter.'[2]

I applied to Mr. Hamilton, by a common friend,[3] and he has been so obliging as to let me have Johnson's letter to him upon this occasion, to adorn my collection.

'*To* The Right Honourable William Gerard Hamilton

'Dear Sir,—Your kind enquiries after my affairs, and your generous offers, have been communicated to me by Dr. Brocklesby. I return thanks with great sincerity, having lived long enough to know what gratitude is due to such friendship; and entreat

with, some years ago, as well as the humanity you are known to possess, has encouraged me to solicit your patronage at my Benefit.

'By a long Chancery suit, and a complicated train of unfortunate events, I am reduced to the greatest distress; which obliges me, once more, to request the indulgence of the publick.

'Give me leave to solicit the honour of your company, and to assure you, if you grant my request, the gratification I shall feel, from being patronized by Dr. Johnson, will be infinitely superiour to any advantage that may arise from the Benefit; as I am, with the profoundest respect, Sir, your most obedient, humble servant, G. A. Bellamy.

'No. 10 Duke-street, St. James's, May 11, 1783.

I am happy in recording these particulars, which prove that my illustrious friend lived to think much more favourably of Players than he appears to have done in the early part of his life.

[1] *Piozzi Letters,* vol. ii. p. 328.
[2] *Ib.,* p. 342.
[3] [Probably Malone. *Powell.*]

that my refusal may not be imputed to sullenness or pride. I am, indeed, in no want. Sickness is, by the generosity of my physicians, of little expence to me. But if any unexpected exigence should press me, you shall see, dear Sir, how cheerfully I can be obliged to so much liberality. I am, Sir, your most obedient and most humble servant,

'November 19, 1783.'   'SAM. JOHNSON.'

I find in this, as in former years, notices of his kind attention to Mrs. Gardiner, who, though in the humble station of a tallow-chandler upon Snow-hill, was a woman of excellent good sense, pious, and charitable. She told me, she had been introduced to him by Mrs. Masters, the poetess, whose volumes he revised, and, it is said, illuminated here and there with a ray of his own genius. Mrs. Gardiner was very zealous for the support of the Ladies' charity-school, in the parish of St. Sepulchre. It is confined to females; and, I am told, it afforded a hint for the story of *Betty Broom* in *The Idler*. Johnson this year, I find, obtained for it a sermon from the late Bishop of St. Asaph, Dr. Shipley, whom he, in one of his letters to Mrs. Thrale, characterises as 'knowing and conversible'; and whom all who knew his Lordship, even those who differed from him in politicks, remember with much respect.

The Earl of Carlisle having written a tragedy, entitled *The Father's Revenge*, some of his Lordship's friends applied to Mrs. Chapone, to prevail on Dr. Johnson to read and give his opinion of it, which he accordingly did, in a letter to that lady. Sir Joshua Reynolds having informed me that this letter was in Lord Carlisle's possession, though I was not fortunate enough to have the honour of being known to his Lordship, trusting to the general courtesy of literature, I wrote to him, requesting the favour of a copy of it, and to be permitted to insert it in my life of Dr. Johnson. His Lordship was so good as to comply with my request, and has thus enabled me to enrich my work with a very fine piece of writing, which displays both the critical skill and politeness of my illustrious friend; and perhaps the curiosity which it will excite, may induce the noble and elegant Authour to gratify the world by the publication[1] of a performance, of which Dr. Johnson has spoken in such terms.

'To Mrs. Chapone

'Madam,—By sending the tragedy to me a second time,[2] I think that a very honourable distinction has been shewn me, and I did not delay the perusal, of which I am now to tell the effect.

'The construction of the play is not completely regular; the stage is too often vacant, and the scenes are not sufficiently connected. This, however, would be called by Dryden only a mechanical defect; which takes away little from the power of the poem, and which is seen rather than felt.

'A rigid examiner of the diction might, perhaps, wish some words changed, and some lines more vigorously terminated. But from such petty imperfections what writer was ever free?

'The general form and force of the dialogue is of more importance. It seems to want that quickness of reciprocation which characterises the English drama, and is not always sufficiently fervid or animated.

'Of the sentiments I remember not one that I wished omitted. In the imagery I cannot forbear to distinguish the comparison of joy succeeding grief to light rushing on the eye accustomed to darkness. It seems to have all that can be desired to make it please. It is new, just, and delightful.[3]

'With the characters, either as conceived or preserved, I have no fault to find; but was much inclined to congratulate a writer, who, in defiance of prejudice and fashion, made the Archbishop a good man, and scorned all thoughtless applause, which a vicious churchman would have brought him.

'The catastrophe is affecting. The Father and Daughter both

[1] A few copies only of this tragedy have been printed, and given to the authour's friends.
[2] Dr. Johnson having been very ill when the tragedy was first sent to him, had declined the consideration of it.
[3] 'I could have borne my woes; that stranger Joy
    Wounds while it smiles:—The long imprison'd wretch,
    Emerging from the night of his damp cell,
    Shrinks from the sun's bright beams; and that which flings
    Gladness o'er all, to him is agony.'

culpable, both wretched, and both penitent, divide between them our pity and our sorrow.

'Thus, Madam, I have performed what I did not willingly undertake, and could not decently refuse. The noble writer will be pleased to remember, that sincere criticism ought to raise no resentment, because judgement is not under the controul of will; but involuntary criticism, as it has still less of choice, ought to be more remote from possibility of offence. I am, &c.

'November 28, 1783.'   'SAM. JOHNSON.'

I consulted him on two questions of a very different nature: one, whether the unconstitutional influence exercised by the Peers of Scotland in the election of the representatives of the Commons, by means of fictitious qualifications, ought not to be resisted;—the other, What, in propriety and humanity, should be done with old horses unable to labour. I gave him some account of my life at Auchinleck: and expressed my satisfaction that the gentlemen of the county had, at two publick meetings, elected me their *Præses* or Chairman.

'*To* JAMES BOSWELL, ESQ.

'DEAR SIR,—Like all other men who have great friends, you begin to feel the pangs of neglected merit; and all the comfort that I can give you is, by telling you that you have probably more pangs to feel, and more neglect to suffer. You have, indeed, begun to complain too soon; and I hope I am the only confidant of your discontent. Your friends have not yet had leisure to gratify personal kindness; they have hitherto been busy in strengthening their ministerial interest. If a vacancy happens in Scotland, give them early intelligence; and as you can serve Government as powerfully as any of your probable competitors, you may make in some sort a warrantable claim.

'Of the exaltations and depressions of your mind you delight to talk, and I hate to hear. Drive all such fancies from you.

'On the day when I received your letter, I think, the foregoing page was written; to which, one disease or another has hindered me from making any additions. I am now a little better. But sickness and solitude press me very heavily. I could bear sickness better, if I were relieved from solitude.

'The present dreadful confusion of the publick ought to make you wrap yourself up in your hereditary possessions, which, though less than you may wish, are more than you can want; and in an hour of religious retirement return thanks to GOD, who has exempted you from any strong temptation to faction, treachery, plunder, and disloyalty.

'As your neighbours distinguish you by such honours as they can bestow, content yourself with your station, without neglecting your profession. Your estate and the Courts will find you full employment; and your mind, well occupied, will be quiet.

'The usurpation of the nobility, for they apparently usurp all the influence they gain by fraud and misrepresentation, I think it certainly lawful, perhaps your duty, to resist. What is not their own they have only by robbery.

'Your question about the horses gives me more perplexity. I know not well what advice to give you. I can only recommend a rule which you do not want;—give as little pain as you can. I suppose that we have a right to their service while their strength lasts; what we can do with them afterwards I cannot so easily determine. But let us consider. Nobody denies that man has a right first to milk the cow, and to sheer the sheep, and then to kill them for his table. May he not, by parity of reason, first work a horse, and then kill him the easiest way, that he may have the means of another horse, or food for cows and sheep? Man is influenced in both cases by different motives of self-interest. He that rejects the one must reject the other. I am, &c.

'London, Dec. 24, 1783.'   'SAM. JOHNSON.'

'A happy and pious Christmas; and many happy years to you, your lady, and children.'

The late ingenious Mr. Mickle, some time before his death, wrote me a letter concerning Dr. Johnson, in which he mentions, —'I was upwards of twelve years acquainted with him, was frequently in his company, always talked with ease to him, and can truly say, that I never received from him one rough word.'

In this letter he relates his having, while engaged in translating the *Lusiad*, had a dispute of considerable length with Johnson, who, as usual, declaimed upon the misery and corruption of a sea life, and used this expression:—'It had been happy for the world, Sir, if your hero Gama, Prince Henry of Portugal, and Columbus, had never been born, or that their schemes had never gone farther than their own imaginations.'

'This sentiment, (says Mr. Mickle,) which is to be found in his *Introduction to the World displayed*, I, in my Dissertation prefixed to the *Lusiad*, have controverted; and though authours are said to be bad judges of their own works, I am not ashamed to own to a friend, that that dissertation is my favourite above all that I ever attempted in prose. Next year, when the *Lusiad* was published, I waited on Dr. Johnson, who addressed me with one of his good-humoured smiles:—"Well, you have remembered our dispute about Prince Henry, and have cited me too. You have done your part very well indeed: you have made the best of your argument; but I am not convinced yet."

'Before publishing the *Lusiad*, I sent Mr. Hoole a proof of that part of the introduction, in which I make mention of Dr. Johnson, yourself, and other well-wishers to the work, begging it might be shewn to Dr. Johnson. This was accordingly done; and in place of the simple mention of him which I had made, he dictated to Mr. Hoole the sentence as it now stands.

'Dr. Johnson told me in 1772, that, about twenty years before that time, he himself had a design to translate the *Lusiad*, of the merit of which he spoke highly, but had been prevented by a number of other engagements.'

Mr. Mickle reminds me in this letter of a conversation, at dinner one day at Mr. Hoole's with Dr. Johnson, when Mr. Nicol the King's bookseller and I attempted to controvert the maxim, 'better that ten guilty should escape, than one innocent person suffer;' and were answered by Dr. Johnson with great power of reasoning and eloquence. I am very sorry that I have no record of that day: but I well recollect my illustrious friend's having ably shewn, that unless civil institutions insure protection to the innocent, all the confidence which mankind should have in them would be lost.

I shall here mention what, in strict chronological arrangement, should have appeared in my account of last year; but may more properly be introduced here, the controversy having not been closed till this. The Reverend Mr. Shaw, a native of one of the Hebrides, having entertained doubts of the authenticity of the poems ascribed to Ossian, divested himself of national bigotry; and having travelled in the Highlands and Islands of Scotland, and also in Ireland, in order to furnish himself with materials for a *Gaelick Dictionary*, which he afterwards compiled, was so fully satisfied that Dr. Johnson was in the right upon the question, that he candidly published a pamphlet, stating his conviction and the proofs and reasons on which it was founded. A person at Edinburgh, of the name of Clark, answered this pamphlet with much zeal, and much abuse of its authour. Johnson took Mr. Shaw under his protection, and gave him his assistance, in writing a reply, which has been admired by the best judges, and by many been considered as conclusive. A few paragraphs, which sufficiently mark their great Authour, shall be selected:—

'My assertions are, for the most part, purely negative: I deny the existence of Fingal, because in a long and curious peregrination through the Gaelick regions I have never been able to find it. What I could not see myself I suspect to be equally invisible to others; and I suspect with the more reason, as among all those who have seen it no man can shew it.

'Mr. Clark compares the obstinacy of those who disbelieve the genuineness of Ossian to a blind man, who should dispute the reality of colours, and deny that the British troops are cloathed in red. The blind man's doubt would be rational, if he did not know by experience that others have a power which he himself wants: but what perspicacity has Mr. Clark which Nature has with-held from me or the rest of mankind?

'The true state of the parallel must be this. Suppose a man, with eyes like his neighbours, was told by a boasting corporal, that the troops, indeed, wore red clothes for their ordinary dress,

but that every soldier had likewise a suit of black velvet, which
he put on when the King reviews them. This he thinks strange,
and desires to see the fine clothes, but finds nobody in forty
thousand men that can produce either coat or waistcoat. One,
indeed, has left them in his chest at Port Mahon; another has
always heard that he ought to have velvet clothes somewhere;
and a third has heard somebody say, that soldiers ought to wear
velvet. Can the enquirer be blamed if he goes away believing
that a soldier's red coat is all that he has?

'But the most obdurate incredulity may be shamed or silenced
by acts. To overpower contradictions, let the soldier shew his
velvet-coat, and the Fingalist the original of Ossian.

'The difference between us and the blind man is this:—the
blind man is unconvinced, because he cannot see; and we,
because though we can see, we find that nothing can be shown.'

Notwithstanding the complication of disorders under which
Johnson now laboured, he did not resign himself to despondency
and discontent, but with wisdom and spirit endeavoured to console and amuse his mind with as many innocent enjoyments as
he could procure. Sir John Hawkins has mentioned the cordiality
with which he insisted that such of the members of the old club
in Ivy-lane as survived, should meet again and dine together,
which they did, twice at a tavern and once at his house: and in
order to insure himself society in the evening for three days in
the week, he instituted a club at the Essex Head, in Essex-street,
then kept by Samuel Greaves, an old servant of Mr. Thrale's.

'*To* SIR JOSHUA REYNOLDS

'DEAR SIR,—It is inconvenient to me to come out, I should
else have waited on you with an account of a little evening Club
which we are establishing in Essex-street, in the Strand, and of
which you may be sure that you are desired to be one. It will
be held at the Essex Head, now kept by an old servant of
Thrale's. The company is numerous, and, as you will see by
the list, miscellaneous. The terms are lax, and the expences
light. Mr. Barry was adopted by Dr. Brocklesby, who joined
with me in forming the plan. We meet thrice a week, and he
who misses forfeits two-pence.

'If you are willing to become a member, draw a line under your name. Return the list. We meet for the first time on Monday at eight. I am, &c.

'Dec. 4, 1783.'   'SAM. JOHNSON.'

It did not suit Sir Joshua to be one of this Club. But when I mention only Mr. Daines Barrington, Dr. Brocklesby, Mr. Murphy, Mr. John Nichols, Mr. Cooke, Mr. Joddrel, Mr. Paradise, Dr. Horsley, Mr. Windham,[1] I shall sufficiently obviate the misrepresentation of it by Sir John Hawkins, as if it had been a low ale-house association, by which Johnson was degraded. Johnson himself, like his name-sake Old Ben, composed the Rules of his Club.[2]

[1] I was in Scotland when this Club was founded, during all the winter. Johnson, however, declared I should be a member, and invented a word upon the occasion: 'Boswell (said he) is a very *clubable* man.' When I came to town I was proposed by Mr. Barrington, and chosen. I believe there are few societies where there is better conversation or more decorum. Several of us resolved to continue it after our great founder was removed by death. Other members were added; and now, above eight years since that loss, we go on happily.

[2]   RULES.
'To-day deep thoughts with me resolve to drench
    In mirth, which after no repenting draws.'—MILTON.
'The club shall consist of four-and-twenty.
'The meetings shall be on the Monday, Thursday, and Saturday of every week; but in the week before Easter there shall be no meeting.
'Every member is at liberty to introduce a friend once a week, but not oftener.
'Two members shall oblige themselves to attend in their turn every night from eight to ten, or to procure two to attend in their room.
'Every member present at the Club shall spend at least sixpence; and every member who stays away shall forfeit three-pence.
'The master of the house shall keep an account of the absent members; and deliver to the President of the night a list of the forfeits incurred.
'When any member returns after absence, he shall immediately lay down his forfeits; which if he omits to do, the President shall require.
'There shall be no general reckoning, but every man shall adjust his own expences.
'The night of indispensable attendance will come to every member once a month. Whoever shall for three months together omit to attend himself, or by substitution, nor shall make any apology in the fourth month, shall be considered as having abdicated the Club.
'When a vacancy is to be filled, the name of the candidate, and of the member recommending him, shall stand in the Club-room three nights. On

In the end of this year he was seized with a spasmodick asthma of such violence, that he was confined to the house in great pain, being sometimes obliged to sit all night in his chair, a recumbent posture being so hurtful to his respiration, that he could not endure lying in bed; and there came upon him at the same time that oppressive and fatal disease, a dropsy. It was a very severe winter, which probably aggravated his complaints; and the solitude in which Mr. Levett and Mrs. Williams had left him, rendered his life very gloomy. Mrs. Desmoulins, who still lived, was herself so very ill, that she could contribute very little to his relief. He, however, had none of that unsocial shyness which we commonly see in people afflicted with sickness. He did not hide his head from the world, in solitary abstraction; he did not deny himself to the visits of his friends and acquaintances; but at all times, when he was not overcome by sleep, was ready for conversation as in his best days.

'To Mrs. Lucy Porter, *in Lichfield*

'Dear Madam,—You may perhaps think me negligent that I have not written to you again upon the loss of your brother; but condolences and consolations are such common and such useless things, that the omission of them is no great crime: and my own diseases occupy my mind, and engage my care. My nights are miserably restless, and my days, therefore, are heavy. I try, however, to hold up my head as high as I can.

'I am sorry that your health[1] is impaired; perhaps the spring and the summer may, in some degree, restore it: but if not, we must submit to the inconveniencies of time, as to the other dis-

the fourth he may be chosen by ballot; six members at least being present, and two-thirds of the ballot being in his favour; or the majority, should the numbers not be divisible by three.

'The master of the house shall give notice, six days before, to each of those members whose turn of necessary attendance is come.

'The notice may be in these words:—"Sir, On —— the —— of —— will be your turn of presiding at the Essex-Head. Your company is therefore earnestly requested."

'One penny shall be left by each member for the waiter.'

Johnson's definition of a Club in this sense, in his *Dictionary*, is, 'An assembly of good fellows, meeting under certain conditions.'

[1] [Johnson wrote *hearing*.]

pensations of Eternal Goodness. Pray for me, and write to me, or let Mr. Pearson write for you. I am, &c.

'London, Nov. 29, 1783.'   'SAM. JOHNSON.'

1784: ÆTAT. 75.]—AND now I am arrived at the last year of the life of SAMUEL JOHNSON, a year in which, although passed in severe indisposition, he nevertheless gave many evidences of the continuance of those wondrous powers of mind, which raised him so high in the intellectual world. His conversation and his letters of this year were in no respect inferiour to those of former years.

The following is a remarkable proof of his being alive to the most minute curiosities of literature.

'*To* MR. DILLY, *Bookseller, in the Poultry*

'SIR,—There is in the world a set of books which used to be sold by the booksellers on the bridge, and which I must entreat you to procure me. They are called *Burton's Books*; the title of one is *Admirable Curiosities, Rarities, and Wonders in England*. I believe there are about five or six of them; they seem very proper to allure backward readers; be so kind as to get them for me, and send me them with the best printed edition of *Baxter's Call to the Unconverted*. I am, &c.

'Jan. 6, 1784.'   'SAM. JOHNSON.'

'*To* MR. PERKINS

'DEAR SIR,—I was very sorry not to see you when you were so kind as to call on me; but to disappoint friends, and if they are not very good-natured, to disoblige them, is one of the evils of sickness. If you will please to let me know which of the afternoons in this week I shall be favoured with another visit by you and Mrs. Perkins, and the young people,[1] I will take all the measures that I can to be pretty well at that time. I am, dear Sir, your most humble servant,

'Jan. 21, 1784.'   'SAM. JOHNSON.'

[1] [Johnson wrote *pretty young people*.]

His attention to the Essex-Head Club appears from the following letter to Mr. Alderman Clark, a gentleman for whom he deservedly entertained a great regard.

'*To* RICHARD CLARK, ESQ.

'DEAR SIR,—You will receive a requisition, according to the rules of the Club, to be at the house as President of the night. This turn comes once a month, and the member is obliged to attend, or send another in his place. You were enrolled in the Club by my invitation, and I ought to introduce you; but as I am hindered by sickness, Mr. Hoole will very properly supply my place as introductor, or yours as President. I hope in milder weather to be a very constant attendant. I am, Sir, &c.

'Jan. 27, 1784.'   'SAM JOHNSON.'

'You ought to be informed that the forfeits began with the year, and that every night of non-attendance incurs the mulct of three-pence, that is, nine-pence a week.'

On the 8th of January I wrote to him, anxiously inquiring as to his health, and enclosing my *Letter to the People of Scotland, on the present state of the nation.*

'I trust, (said I,) that you will be liberal enough to make allowance for my differing from you on two points, (the Middlesex Election, and the American War,) when my general principles of government are according to your own heart, and when, at a crisis of doubtful event, I stand forth with honest zeal as an ancient and faithful Baron. My reason for introducing those two points was, that as my opinions with regard to them had been declared at the periods when they were least favourable, I might have the credit of a man who is not a worshipper of ministerial power.'

'*To* JAMES BOSWELL, ESQ.

'DEAR SIR,—I hear of many enquiries which your kindness has disposed you to make after me. I have long intended you a long letter, which perhaps the imagination of its length hindered me from beginning. I will, therefore, content myself with a shorter.

'Having promoted the institution of a new Club in the neighbourhood, at the house of an old servant of Thrale's, I went thither to meet the company, and was seized with a spasmodick asthma so violent, that with difficulty I got to my own house, in which I have been confined eight or nine weeks, and from which I know not when I shall be able to go even to church. The asthma, however, is not the worst. A dropsy gains ground upon me; my legs and thighs are very much swollen with water, which I should be content if I could keep there, but I am afraid that it will soon be higher. My nights are very sleepless and very tedious. And yet I am extremely afraid of dying.

'My physicians try to make me hope, that much of my malady is the effect of cold, and that some degree at least of recovery is to be expected from vernal breezes and summer suns. If my life is prolonged to autumn, I should be glad to try a warmer climate; though how to travel with a diseased body, without a companion to conduct me, and with very little money, I do not well see. Ramsay has recovered his limbs in Italy; and Fielding was sent to Lisbon, where, indeed, he died; but he was, I believe, past hope when he went. Think for me what I can do.

'I received your pamphlet, and when I write again may perhaps tell you some opinion about it; but you will forgive a man struggling with disease his neglect of disputes, politicks, and pamphlets. Let me have your prayers. My compliments to your lady, and young ones. Ask your physicians about my case: and desire Sir Alexander Dick to write me his opinion. I am, dear Sir, &c.

'Feb. 11, 1784.'   'SAM. JOHNSON.'

'*To* MRS. LUCY PORTER, *in Lichfield*

'MY DEAREST LOVE,—I have been extremely ill of an asthma and dropsy, but received, by the mercy of GOD, sudden and unexpected relief last Thursday, by the discharge of twenty pints of water. Whether I shall continue free, or shall fill again, cannot be told. Pray for me.

'Death, my dear, is very dreadful; let us think nothing worth our care but how to prepare for it: what we know amiss in ourselves let us make haste to amend, and put our trust in the mercy of GOD, and the intercession of our Saviour. I am, dear Madam, your most humble servant,

    'Feb. 23, 1784.'   'SAM. JOHNSON.'

'*To* JAMES BOSWELL, ESQ.

'DEAR SIR,—I have just advanced so far towards recovery as to read a pamphlet; and you may reasonably suppose that the first pamphlet which I read was yours. I am very much of your opinion, and, like you, feel great indignation at the indecency with which the King is every day treated. Your paper contains very considerable knowledge of history and of the constitution, very properly produced and applied. It will certainly raise your character,[1] though perhaps it may not make you a Minister of State. . . .

'I desire you to see Mrs. Stewart once again, and tell her, that in the letter-case was a letter relating to me, for which I will give her, if she is willing to give it me, another guinea. The letter is of consequence only to me. I am, dear Sir, &c.

    'London, Feb. 27, 1784.'   'SAM. JOHNSON.'

In consequence of Johnson's request that I should ask our physicians about his case, and desire Sir Alexander Dick to send his opinion, I transmitted him a letter from that very amiable Baronet, then in his eighty-first year, with his faculties as entire as ever; and mentioned his expressions to me in the note accompanying it: 'With my most affectionate wishes for Dr.

---

[1] I sent it to Mr. Pitt, with a letter, in which I thus expressed myself: —'My principles may appear to you too monarchical: but I know and am persuaded, they are not inconsistent with the true principles of liberty. Be this as it may, you, Sir, are now the Prime Minister, called by the Sovereign to maintain the rights of the Crown, as well as those of the people, against a violent faction. As such, you are entitled to the warmest support of every good subject in every department.' He answered:—'I am extremely obliged to you for the sentiments you do me the honour to express, and have observed with great pleasure the *zealous and able support* given to the CAUSE OF THE PUBLICK in the work you were so good to transmit to me.'

Johnson's recovery, in which his friends, his country, and all mankind have so deep a stake:' and at the same time a full opinion upon his case by Dr. Gillespie, who, like Dr. Cullen, had the advantage of having passed through the gradations of surgery and pharmacy, and by study and practice had attained to such skill, that my father settled on him two hundred pounds a year for five years, and fifty pounds a year during his life, as an *honorarium* to secure his particular attendance. The opinion was conveyed in a letter to me, beginning, 'I am sincerely sorry for the bad state of health your very learned and illustrious friend, Dr. Johnson, labours under at present.'

'*To* James Boswell, Esq.

'Dear Sir,—Presently after I had sent away my last letter, I received your kind medical packet. I am very much obliged both to you and your physicians for your kind attention to my disease. Dr. Gillespie has sent me an excellent *consilium medicum*,[1] all solid practical experimental knowledge. I am at present, in the opinion of my physicians, (Dr. Heberden and Dr. Brocklesby,) as well as my own, going on very hopefully. I have just begun to take vinegar of squills. The powder hurt my stomach so much, that it could not be continued.

'Return Sir Alexander Dick my sincere thanks for his kind letter; and bring with you the rhubarb[2] which he so tenderly offers me.

'I hope dear Mrs. Boswell is now quite well, and that no evil, either real or imaginary, now disturbs you. I am, &c.

'London, March 2, 1784.'   'Sam. Johnson.'

I also applied to three of the eminent physicians who had chairs in our celebrated school of medicine at Edinburgh, Doctors Cullen, Hope, and Monro, to each of whom I sent the following letter:—

'Dear Sir,—Dr. Johnson has been very ill for some time;

[1] ['medical advice.']
[2] From his garden at Prestonfield, where he cultivated that plant with such success, that he was presented with a gold medal by the Society of London for the Encouragement of Arts, Manufactures, and Commerce.

and in a letter of anxious apprehension he writes to me, "Ask your physicians about my case."

'This, you see, is not authority for a regular consultation: but I have no doubt of your readiness to give your advice to a man so eminent, and who, in his *Life of Garth*, has paid your profession a just and elegant compliment: "I believe every man has found in physicians great liberality and dignity of sentiment, very prompt effusions of beneficence, and willingness to exert a lucrative art, where there is no hope of lucre."

'Dr. Johnson is aged seventy-four. Last summer he had a stroke of the palsy, from which he recovered almost entirely. He had, before that, been troubled with a catarrhous cough. This winter he was seized with a spasmodick asthma, by which he has been confined to his house for about three months. Dr. Brocklesby writes to me, that upon the least admission of cold, there is such a constriction upon his breast, that he cannot lie down in his bed, but is obliged to sit up all night, and gets rest and sometimes sleep, only by means of laudanum and syrup of poppies; and that there are œdematous tumours on his legs and thighs. Dr. Brocklesby trusts a good deal to the return of mild weather. Dr. Johnson says, that a dropsy gains ground upon him; and he seems to think that a warmer climate would do him good. I understand he is now rather better, and is using vinegar of squills. I am, with great esteem, dear Sir, your most obedient humble servant,

'March 7, 1784.'   'JAMES BOSWELL.'

All of them paid the most polite attention to my letter, and its venerable object. Dr. Cullen's words concerning him were, 'It would give me the greatest pleasure to be of any service to a man whom the publick properly esteem, and whom I esteem and respect as much as I do Dr. Johnson.' Dr. Hope's, 'Few people have a better claim on me than your friend, as hardly a day passes that I do not ask his opinion about this or that word.' Dr. Monro's, 'I most sincerely join you in sympathizing with that very worthy and ingenious character, from whom his country has derived much instruction and entertainment.'

Dr. Hope corresponded with his friend Dr. Brocklesby. Doctors Cullen and Monro wrote their opinions and prescriptions to me, which I afterwards carried with me to London, and, so far as they were encouraging, communicated to Johnson. The liberality on one hand, and grateful sense of it on the other, I have great satisfaction in recording.

'*To* JAMES BOSWELL, ESQ.

'DEAR SIR,—I am too much pleased with the attention which you and your dear lady[1] show to my welfare, not to be diligent in letting you know the progress which I make towards health. The dropsy, by GOD's blessing, has now run almost totally away by natural evacuation; and the asthma, if not irritated by cold, gives me little trouble. While I am writing this, I have not any sensation of debility or disease. But I do not yet venture out, having been confined to the house from the thirteenth of December, now a quarter of a year.

'When it will be fit for me to travel as far as Auchinleck, I am not able to guess; but such a letter as Mrs. Boswell's might draw any man, not wholly motionless, a great way. Pray tell the dear lady how much her civility and kindness have touched and gratified me.

'Our parliamentary tumults have now begun to subside, and the King's authority is in some measure re-established. Mr. Pitt will have great power: but you must remember, that what he has to give must, at least for some time, be given to those who gave, and those who preserve, his power. A new minister can sacrifice little to esteem or friendship; he must, till he is settled, think only of extending his interest. . . .

'If you come hither through Edinburgh, send for Mrs. Stewart, and give from me another guinea for the letter in the old case, to which I shall not be satisfied with my claim, till she gives it me.

'Please to bring with you Baxter's *Anacreon*; and if you procure heads of *Hector Boece*, the historian, and *Arthur Johnston*,

---

[1] Who had written him a very kind letter.

the poet, I will put them in my room; or any other of the fathers of Scottish literature.

'I wish you an easy and happy journey, and hope I need not tell you that you will be welcome to, dear Sir, your most affectionate, humble servant,

'London, March 18, 1784.'   'SAM. JOHNSON.'

I wrote to him, March 28, from York, informing him that I had a high gratification in the triumph of monarchical principles over aristocratical influence, in that great county, in an address to the King; that I was thus far on my way to him, but that news of the dissolution of Parliament having arrived, I was to hasten back to my own county, where I had carried an Address to his Majesty by a great majority, and had some intention of being a candidate to represent the county in Parliament.

'To JAMES BOSWELL, ESQ.

'DEAR SIR,—You could do nothing so proper as to haste back when you found the Parliament dissolved. With the influence which your Address must have gained you, it may reasonably be expected that your presence will be of importance, and your activity of effect.

'Your solicitude for me gives me that pleasure which every man feels from the kindness of such a friend: and it is with delight I relieve it by telling, that Dr. Brocklesby's account is true, and that I am, by the blessing of GOD, wonderfully relieved.

'You are entering upon a transaction which requires much prudence. You must endeavour to oppose without exasperating; to practise temporary hostility, without producing enemies for life. This is, perhaps, hard to be done; yet it has been done by many, and seems most likely to be effected by opposing merely upon general principles, without descending to personal or particular censures or objections. One thing I must enjoin you, which is seldom observed in the conduct of elections;—I must entreat you to be scrupulous in the use of strong liquors. One night's drunkenness may defeat the labours of forty days well employed. Be firm, but not clamorous; be active, but not malicious; and you may form such an interest, as may not only exalt yourself, but dignify your family.

'We are, as you may suppose, all busy here. Mr. Fox resolutely stands for Westminster, and his friends say will carry the election. However that be, he will certainly have a seat. Mr. Hoole has just told me, that the city leans towards the King.

'Let me hear, from time to time, how you are employed, and what progress you make.

'Make dear Mrs. Boswell, and all the young Boswells, the sincere compliments of, Sir, your affectionate humble servant,

'London, March 30, 1784.'   'SAM. JOHNSON.'

To Mr. Langton he wrote with that cordiality which was suitable to the long friendship which had subsisted between him and that gentleman.

March 27. 'Since you left me, I have continued in my own opinion, and in Dr. Brocklesby's, to grow better with respect to all my formidable and dangerous distempers; though to a body battered and shaken as mine has lately been, it is to be feared that weak attacks may be sometimes mischievous. I have, indeed, by standing carelessly at an open window, got a very troublesome cough, which it has been necessary to appease by opium, in larger quantities than I like to take, and I have not found it give way so readily as I expected; its obstinacy, however, seems at last disposed to submit to the remedy, and I know not whether I should then have a right to complain of any morbid sensation. My asthma is, I am afraid, constitutional and incurable; but it is only occasional, and unless it be excited by labour or by cold, gives me no molestation, nor does it lay very close siege to life; for Sir John Floyer, whom the physical race consider as authour of one of the best books upon it, panted on to ninety, as was supposed; and why were we content with supposing a fact so interesting, of a man so conspicuous, because he corrupted, at perhaps seventy or eighty, the register, that he might pass for younger than he was? He was not much less than eighty; when to a man of rank who modestly asked him his age, he answered,

"Go look;" though he was in general a man of civility and elegance.

'The ladies, I find, are at your house all well, except Miss Langton, who will probably soon recover her health by light suppers. Let her eat at dinner as she will, but not take a full stomach to bed. Pay my sincere respects to the two principal ladies in your house; and when you write to dear Miss Langton in Lincolnshire, let her know that I mean not to break our league of friendship, and that I have a set of *Lives* for her, when I have the means of sending it.'

April 8. 'I am still disturbed by my cough; but what thanks have I not to pay, when my cough is the most painful sensation that I feel? and from that I expect hardly to be released, while winter continues to gripe us with so much pertinacity. The year has now advanced eighteen days beyond the equinox, and still there is very little remission of the cold. When warm weather comes, which surely must come at last, I hope it will help both me and your young lady.

'The man so busy about addresses is neither more nor less than our own Boswell, who had come as far as York towards London, but turned back on the dissolution, and is said now to stand for some place. Whether to wish him success, his best friends hesitate.

'Let me have your prayers for the completion of my recovery: I am now better than I ever expected to have been. May GOD add to his mercies the grace that may enable me to use them according to his will. My compliments to all.'

April 13. 'I had this evening a note from Lord Portmore,[1] desiring that I would give you an account of my health. You might have had it with less circumduction. I am, by GOD's blessing, I believe, free from all morbid sensations, except a cough, which is only troublesome. But I am still weak, and can

[1] To which Johnson returned this answer:—

'TO THE RIGHT HONOURABLE EARL OF PORTMORE.

'DR. JOHNSON acknowledges with great respect the honour of Lord Portmore's notice. He is better than he was; and will, as his Lordship directs, write to Mr. Langton.

'Bolt-court, Fleet-street, April 13, 1784.'

have no great hope of strength till the weather shall be softer. The summer, if it be kindly, will, I hope, enable me to support the winter. GOD, who has so wonderfully restored me, can preserve me in all seasons.

'Let me enquire in my turn after the state of your family, great and little. I hope Lady Rothes and Miss Langton are both well. That is a good basis of content. Then how goes George on with his studies? How does Miss Mary? And how does my own Jenny? I think I owe Jenny a letter, which I will take care to pay. In the mean time tell her that I acknowledge the debt.

'Be pleased to make my compliments to the ladies. If Mrs. Langton comes to London, she will favour me with a visit, for I am not well enough to go out.'

'To OZIAS HUMPHRY,[1] ESQ.

'SIR,—Mr. Hoole has told me with what benevolence you listened to a request which I was almost afraid to make, of leave to a young painter[2] to attend you from time to time in your painting-room, to see your operations, and receive your instructions.

'The young man has perhaps good parts, but has been without a[3] regular education. He is my god-son, and therefore I interest myself in his progress and success, and shall think myself much favoured if I receive from you a permission to send him.

'My health is, by GOD's blessing, much restored, but I am

---

[1] The eminent painter, representative of the ancient family of Homfrey (now Humphry) in the west of England; who, as appears from their arms which they have invariably used, have been, (as I have seen authenticated by the best authority,) one of those among the Knights and Esquires of honour who are represented by Holinshed as having issued from the Tower of London on coursers apparelled for the justes, accompanied by ladies of honour, leading every one a Knight, with a chain of gold, passing through the streets of London into Smithfield, on Sunday, at three o'clock in the afternoon, being the first Sunday after Michaelmas, in the fourteenth year of King Richard the Second. This family once enjoyed large possessions, but, like others, have lost them in the progress of ages. Their blood, however, remains to them well ascertained; and they may hope, in the revolution of events, to recover that rank in society for which, in modern times, fortune seems to be an indispensable requisite.

[2] Son of Mr. Samuel Paterson. [See *ante*, pp. 785, 1239.]   [3] [MS *any*.]

not yet allowed by my[1] physicians to go abroad; nor, indeed, do I think myself yet able to endure the weather. I am, Sir, your most humble servant,

　　'April 5, 1784.'　　　　　　　　　　　　'SAM. JOHNSON.'

To THE SAME

'SIR,—The bearer is my god-son, whom I take the liberty of recommending to your kindness; which I hope he will deserve by his respect to your excellence, and his gratitude for your favours. I am, Sir, your most humble servant,

　　'April 10,[2] 1784.'　　　　　　　　　　　'SAM. JOHNSON.'

To THE SAME

'SIR,—I am very much obliged by your civilities to my god-son, but must beg of you to add to them the favour of permitting him to see you paint, that he may know how a picture is begun, advanced and completed.

'If he may attend you in a few of your operations, I hope he will show that the benefit has been properly conferred, both by his proficiency and his gratitude. At least I shall consider you as enlarging your kindness to, Sir, your humble servant,

　　'May 31, 1784.'　　　　　　　　　　　　'SAM. JOHNSON.'

'To THE REVEREND DR. TAYLOR, *Ashbourne, Derbyshire*

'DEAR SIR,—What can be the reason that I hear nothing from you? I hope nothing disables you from writing. What I have seen, and what I have felt, gives me reason to fear every thing. Do not omit giving me the comfort of knowing, that after all my losses I have yet a friend left.

'I want every comfort. My life is very solitary and very cheerless. Though it has pleased GOD wonderfully to deliver me from the dropsy, I am yet very weak, and have not passed the door since the 13th of December. I hope for some help from warm weather, which will surely come in time.

'I could not have the consent of the physicians to go to church yesterday; I therefore received the holy sacrament at home, in the room where I communicated with dear Mrs. Williams, a

　　　　　　　　[1] [MS *the*.]　　　　　　　[2] [MS 13.]

little before her death. O! my friend, the approach of death is very dreadful. I am afraid to think on that which I know I cannot avoid. It is vain to look round and round for that help which cannot be had. Yet we hope and hope, and fancy that he who has lived to-day may live to-morrow. But let us learn to derive our hope only from GOD.

'In the mean time, let us be kind to one another. I have no friend now living but you and Mr. Hector, that was the friend of my youth. Do not neglect, dear Sir, yours affectionately,

'London, Easter-Monday,   'SAM. JOHNSON.'
'April 12, 1784.'

What follows is a beautiful specimen of his gentleness and complacency to a young lady his god-child, one of the daughters of his friend Mr. Langton, then I think in her seventh year. He took the trouble to write it in a large round hand, nearly resembling printed characters, that she might have the satisfaction of reading it herself. The original lies before me, but shall be faithfully restored to her; and I dare say will be preserved by her as a jewel as long as she lives.

'*To* MISS JANE LANGTON, *in Rochester, Kent*

'MY DEAREST MISS JENNY,—I am sorry that your pretty letter has been so long without being answered; but, when I am not pretty well, I do not always write plain enough for young ladies. I am glad, my dear, to see that you write so well, and hope that you mind your pen, your book, and your needle, for they are all necessary. Your books will give you knowledge, and make you respected; and your needle will find you useful employment when you do not care to read. When you are a little older, I hope you will be very diligent in learning arithmetick, and, above all, that through your whole life you will carefully say your prayers, and read your Bible. I am, my dear, your most humble servant,

'May 10, 1784.'   'SAM. JOHNSON.'

On Wednesday, May 5, I arrived in London, and next morning

had the pleasure to find Dr. Johnson greatly recovered. I but just saw him; for a coach was waiting to carry him to Islington, to the house of his friend the Reverend Mr. Strahan, where he went sometimes for the benefit of good air, which, notwithstanding his having formerly laughed at the general opinion upon the subject, he now acknowledged was conducive to health.

One morning afterwards, when I found him alone, he communicated to me, with solemn earnestness, a very remarkable circumstance which had happened in the course of his illness, when he was much distressed by the dropsy. He had shut himself up, and employed a day in particular exercises of religion,— fasting, humiliation, and prayer. On a sudden he obtained extraordinary relief, for which he looked up to Heaven with grateful devotion. He made no direct inference from this fact; but from his manner of telling it, I could perceive that it appeared to him as something more than an incident in the common course of events. For my own part, I have no difficulty to avow that cast of thinking, which by many modern pretenders to wisdom is called *superstitious*. But here I think even men of dry rationality may believe, that there was an intermediate interposition of Divine Providence, and that 'the fervent prayer of this righteous man' availed.[1]

On Sunday, May 9, I found Colonel Vallancy, the celebrated antiquarian and engineer of Ireland, with him. On Monday, the 10th, I dined with him at Mr. Paradise's, where was a large

---

[1] Upon this subject there is a very fair and judicious remark in the life of Dr. Abernethy, in the first edition of the *Biographia Britannica*, which I should have been glad to see in his Life which has been written for the second edition of that valuable work. 'To deny the exercise of a particular providence in the Deity's government of the world is certainly impious: yet nothing serves the cause of the scorner more than an incautious forward zeal in determining the particular instances of it.'

In confirmation of my sentiments, I am also happy to quote that sensible and elegant writer Mr. *Melmoth*, in Letter VIII [XLVIII] of his collection, published under the name *Fitzosborne*. 'We may safely assert, that the belief of a particular Providence is founded upon such probable reasons as may well justify our assent. It would scarce, therefore, be wise to renounce an opinion which affords so firm a support to the soul, in those seasons wherein she stands in the most need [most in need] of assistance, merely because it is not possible, in questions of this kind, to solve every difficulty which attends them.'

company; Mr. Bryant, Mr. Joddrel, Mr. Hawkins Browne, &c. On Thursday, the 13th, I dined with him at Mr. Joddrel's, with another large company; the Bishop of Exeter, Lord Monboddo,[1] Mr. Murphy, &c.

On Saturday, May 15, I dined with him at Dr. Brocklesby's, where were Colonel Vallancy, Mr. Murphy, and that ever-cheerful companion Mr. Devaynes, apothecary to his Majesty. Of these days, and others on which I saw him, I have no memorials, except the general recollection of his being able and animated in conversation, and appearing to relish society as much as the youngest man. I find only these three small particulars:— One, when a person was mentioned, who said, 'I have lived fifty-one years in this world without having had ten minutes of uneasiness;' he exclaimed, 'The man who says so, lies: he attempts to impose on human credulity.' The Bishop of Exeter in vain observed, that men were very different. His Lordship's manner was not impressive, and I learnt afterwards that Johnson did not find out that the person who talked to him was a Prelate; if he had, I doubt not that he would have treated him with more respect; for once talking of George Psalmanazar, whom he reverenced for his piety, he said, 'I should as soon think of contradicting a BISHOP.' One of the company[2] provoked him greatly by doing what he could least of all bear, which was quoting something of his own writing, against what he then maintained. 'What, Sir, (cried the gentleman,) do you say to

"The busy day, the peaceful night,
    Unfelt, uncounted, glided by?" '[3]

Johnson finding himself thus presented as giving an instance of

---

[1] I was sorry to observe Lord Monboddo avoid any communication with Dr. Johnson. I flattered myself that I had made them very good friends (see *Journal of a Tour to the Hebrides*, 3rd edit., p. 67), but unhappily his Lordship had resumed and cherished a violent prejudice against my illustrious friend, to whom I must do the justice to say, there was on his part not the least anger, but a good-humoured sportiveness. Nay, though he knew of his Lordship's indisposition towards him, he was even kindly; as appeared from his inquiring of me after him, by an abbreviation of his name, 'Well, how does *Monny*?'

[2] [Boswell. *Croker*[1].]

[3] Verses on the death of Mr. Levett.

a man who had lived without uneasiness, was much offended, for he looked upon such quotation as unfair. His anger burst out in an unjustifiable retort, insinuating that the gentleman's remark was a sally of ebriety; 'Sir, there is one passion I would advise you to command: when you have drunk out that glass, don't drink another.' Here was exemplified what Goldsmith said of him, with the aid of a very witty image from one of Cibber's Comedies: 'There is no arguing with Johnson; for if his pistol misses fire, he knocks you down with the butt end of it.' Another was this: when a gentleman of eminence[1] in the literary world was violently censured for attacking people by anonymous paragraphs in newspapers; he, from the spirit of contradiction as I thought, took up his defence, and said, 'Come, come, this is not so terrible a crime; he means only to vex them a little. I do not say that I should do it; but there is a great difference between him and me; what is fit for Hephæstion is not fit for Alexander.' Another, when I told him that a young and handsome Countess had said to me, 'I should think that to be praised by Dr. Johnson would make one a fool all one's life;' and that I answered, 'Madam, I shall make him a fool to-day, by repeating this to him,' he said, 'I am too old to be made a fool; but if you say I am made a fool, I shall not deny it. I am much pleased with a compliment, especially from a pretty woman.'

On the evening of Saturday, May 15, he was in fine spirits, at our Essex-Head Club. He told us, 'I dined yesterday at Mrs. Garrick's, with Mrs. Carter, Miss Hannah More, and Miss Fanny Burney. Three such women are not to be found: I know not where I could find a fourth, except Mrs. Lennox, who is superiour to them all.' BOSWELL. 'What! had you them all to yourself, Sir?' JOHNSON. 'I had them all as much as they were had; but it might have been better had there been more company there.' BOSWELL. 'Might not Mrs. Montagu have been a fourth?' JOHNSON. 'Sir, Mrs. Montagu does not make a trade of her wit; but Mrs. Montagu is a very extraordinary woman; she has a constant stream of conversation, and it is always impregnated; it has always meaning.' BOSWELL. 'Mr. Burke

[1] [George Steevens. *Croker*[1]. Cf. *ante*, p. 939, and *Boswell Papers*, x. 217.]

has a constant stream of conversation.' JOHNSON. 'Yes, Sir; if a man were to go by chance at the same time with Burke under a shed, to shun a shower, he would say—"this is an extraordinary man." If Burke should go into a stable to see his horse drest, the ostler would say—"we have had an extraordinary man here." ' BOSWELL. 'Foote was a man who never failed in conversation. If he had gone into a stable—' JOHNSON. 'Sir, if he had gone into a stable, the ostler would have said, "here has been a comical fellow"; but he would not have respected him.' BOSWELL. 'And, Sir, the ostler would have answered him, would have given him as good as he brought, as the common saying is.' JOHNSON. 'Yes, Sir; and Foote would have answered the ostler.—When Burke does not descend to be merry, his conversation is very superiour indeed. There is no proportion between the powers which he shews in serious talk and in jocularity. When he lets himself down to that, he is in the kennel.' I have in another place[1] opposed, and I hope with success, Dr. Johnson's very singular and erroneous notion as to Mr. Burke's pleasantry. Mr. Windham now said low to me, that he differed from our great friend in this observation; for that Mr. Burke was often very happy in his merriment. It would not have been right for either of us to have contradicted Johnson at this time, in a Society all of whom did not know and value Mr. Burke as much as we did. It might have occasioned something more rough, and at any rate would probably have checked the flow of Johnson's good-humour. He called to us with a sudden air of exultation, as the thought started into his mind, 'O! Gentlemen, I must tell you a very great thing. The Empress of Russia has ordered the *Rambler* to be translated into the Russian language:[2] so I shall be read on the banks of the Wolga. Horace boasts that his fame would extend as far as the banks of the Rhone; now the Wolga is farther from me than the Rhone was from Horace.' BOSWELL. 'You must certainly be pleased with this, Sir.'

---

[1] *Journal of a Tour to the Hebrides*, 3rd edit., p. 20 [Aug. 15].
[2] I have since heard that the report was not well-founded; but the elation discovered by Johnson in the belief that it was true, shewed a noble ardour for literary fame.

JOHNSON. 'I am pleased, Sir, to be sure. A man is pleased to find he has succeeded in that which he has endeavoured to do.'

One of the company mentioned his having seen a noble person driving in his carriage, and looking exceedingly well, notwithstanding his great age. JOHNSON. 'Ah, Sir; that is nothing. Bacon observes, that a stout healthy old man is like a tower undermined.'

On Sunday, May 16, I found him alone; he talked of Mrs. Thrale with much concern, saying, 'Sir, she has done every thing wrong, since Thrale's bridle was off her neck;' and was proceeding to mention some circumstances which have since been the subject of publick discussion, when he was interrupted by the arrival of Dr. Douglas, now Bishop of Salisbury.

Dr. Douglas, upon this occasion, refuted a mistaken notion which is very common in Scotland, that the ecclesiastical discipline of the Church of England, though duly enforced, is insufficient to preserve the morals of the clergy, inasmuch as all delinquents may be screened by appealing to the Convocation, which being never authorized by the King to sit for the dispatch of business, the appeal never can be heard. Dr. Douglas observed, that this was founded upon ignorance; for that the Bishops have sufficient power to maintain discipline, and that the sitting of the Convocation was wholly immaterial in this respect, it being not a Court of judicature, but like a parliament, to make Canons and regulations as times may require.

Johnson, talking of the fear of death, said, 'Some people are not afraid, because they look upon salvation as the effect of an absolute decree, and think they feel in themselves the marks of sanctification. Others, and those the most rational in my opinion, look upon salvation as conditional; and as they never can be sure that they have complied with the conditions, they are afraid.'

In one of his little manuscript diaries, about this time, I find a short notice, which marks his amiable disposition more certainly than a thousand studied declarations.—'Afternoon spent cheerfully and elegantly, I hope without offence to GOD or man; though in no holy duty, yet in the general exercise and cultivation of benevolence.'

On Monday, May 17, I dined with him at Mr. Dilly's, where were Colonel Vallancy, the Reverend Dr. Gibbons, and Mr. Capel Lofft, who, though a most zealous Whig, has a mind so full of learning and knowledge, and so much exercised in various departments, and withal so much liberality, that the stupendous powers of the literary Goliath, though they did not frighten this little David of popular spirit, could not but excite his admiration. There was also Mr. Braithwaite of the Post-office, that amiable and friendly man, who, with modest and unassuming manners, has associated with many of the wits of the age. Johnson was very quiescent to-day. Perhaps too I was indolent. I find nothing more of him in my notes, but that when I mentioned that I had seen in the King's library sixty-three editions of my favourite *Thomas à Kempis*, amongst which it was in eight languages, Latin, German, French, Italian, Spanish, English, Arabick, and Armenian, he said, he thought it unnecessary to collect many editions of a book, which were all the same, except as to the paper and print; he would have the original, and all the translations, and all the editions which had any variations in the text. He approved of the famous collection of editions of *Horace* by Douglas, mentioned by Pope, who is said to have had a closet filled with them; and he added, 'every man should try to collect one book in that manner, and present it to a publick library.'

On Tuesday, May 18, I saw him for a short time in the morning. I told him that the mob had called out, as the King passed, 'No Fox—No Fox,' which I did not like. He said, 'They were right, Sir.' I said, I thought not; for it seemed to be making Mr. Fox the King's competitor. There being no audience, so that there could be no triumph in a victory, he fairly agreed with me. I said it might do very well, if explained thus:—'Let us have no Fox;' understanding it as a prayer to his Majesty not to appoint that gentleman minister.

On Wednesday, May 19, I sat a part of the evening with him, by ourselves. I observed, that the death of our friends might be a consolation against the fear of our own dissolution, because we might have more friends in the other world than in this. He perhaps felt this as a reflection upon his apprehension as to death; and said, with heat, 'How can a man know *where* his departed friends are, or whether they will be his friends in the other world? How many friendships have you known formed upon principles of virtue? Most friendships are formed by caprice or by chance, mere confederacies in vice or leagues in folly.'

We talked of our worthy friend Mr. Langton. He said, 'I know not who will go to Heaven if Langton does not. Sir, I could almost say, *Sit anima mea cum Langtono.*[1] I mentioned a very eminent friend[2] as a virtuous man. JOHNSON. 'Yes, Sir; but ————— has not the evangelical virtue of Langton. —————, I am afraid, would not scruple to pick up a wench.'

He however charged Mr. Langton with what he thought want of judgement upon an interesting occasion. 'When I was ill, (said he) I desired he would tell me sincerely in what he thought my life was faulty. Sir, he brought me a sheet of paper, on which he had written down several texts of Scripture, recommending christian charity. And when I questioned him what occasion I had given for such an animadversion, all that he could say amounted to this,—that I sometimes contradicted people in conversation. Now what harm does it do to any man to be contradicted?' BOSWELL. 'I suppose he meant the *manner* of doing it; roughly,—and harshly.' JOHNSON. 'And who is the worse for that?' BOSWELL. 'It hurts people of weak nerves.' JOHNSON. 'I know no such weak-nerved people.' Mr. Burke, to whom I related this conference, said, 'It is well, if when a man comes to die, he has nothing heavier upon his conscience than having been a little rough in conversation.'

Johnson, at the time when the paper was presented to him, though at first pleased with the attention of his friend, whom he thanked in an earnest manner, soon exclaimed, in a loud and angry tone, 'What is your drift, Sir?' Sir Joshua Reynolds pleasantly observed, that it was a scene for a comedy, to see a penitent get into a violent passion and belabour his confessor.[3]

---

[1] ['May my soul be with Langton.']   [2] [*Hill suggests* Burke.]
[3] After all, I cannot but be of opinion, that as Mr. Langton was seriously requested by Dr. Johnson to mention what appeared to him erroneous in the

I have preserved no more of his conversation at the times when I saw him during the rest of this month, till Sunday, the 30th of May, when I met him in the evening at Mr. Hoole's, where there was a large company both of ladies and gentlemen; Sir James Johnston happened to say, that he paid no regard to the arguments of counsel at the bar of the House of Commons, because they were paid for speaking. JOHNSON. 'Nay, Sir, argument is argument. You cannot help paying regard to their arguments, if they are good. If it were testimony, you might disregard it, if you knew that it were purchased. There is a beautiful image in Bacon upon this subject: testimony is like an arrow shot from a long bow; the force of it depends on the strength of the hand that draws it. Argument is like an arrow from a crossbow, which has equal force though shot by a child.'

He had dined that day at Mr. Hoole's, and Miss Helen Maria Williams being expected in the evening, Mr. Hoole put into his hands her beautiful *Ode on the Peace*:[1] Johnson read it over, and when this elegant and accomplished young lady[2] was

character of his friend, he was bound, as an honest man, to intimate what he really thought, which he certainly did in the most delicate manner; so that Johnson himself, when in a quiet frame of mind, was pleased with it. The texts suggested are now before me, and I shall quote a few of them. 'Blessed are the meek, for they shall inherit the earth.' *Matt.* v. 5.—'I therefore, the prisoner of the LORD, beseech you, that ye walk worthy of the vocation wherewith ye are called; with all lowliness and meekness, with longsuffering, forbearing one another in love.' *Ephes.* v. [iv.] 1, 2.—'And above all these things put on charity, which is the bond of perfectness.' *Col.* iii. 14. —'Charity suffereth long and is kind; charity envieth not, charity vaunteth not itself, is not puffed up: doth not behave itself unseemly, is not easily provoked.' 1 *Cor.* xiii. 4, 5.

[1] The Peace made by that very able statesman, the Earl of Shelburne, now Marquis of Lansdown, which may fairly be considered as the foundation of all the prosperity of Great Britain since that time.

[2] In the first edition of my Work, the epithet *amiable* was given. I was sorry to be obliged to strike it out; but I could not in justice suffer it to remain, after this young lady had not only written in favour of the savage Anarchy with which France has been visited, but had (as I have been informed by good authority), walked, without horrour, over the ground at the Thuillieries, when it was strewed with the naked bodies of the faithful Swiss Guards, who were barbarously massacred for having bravely defended, against a crew of ruffians, the Monarch whom they had taken an oath to defend. From Dr. Johnson she could now expect not endearment but repulsion.

presented to him, he took her by the hand in the most courteous manner, and repeated the finest stanza of her poem; this was the most delicate and pleasing compliment he could pay. Her respectable friend, Dr. Kippis, from whom I had this anecdote, was standing by, and was not a little gratified.

Miss Williams told me, that the only other time she was fortunate enough to be in Dr. Johnson's company, he asked her to sit down by him, which she did, and upon her enquiring how he was, he answered, 'I am very ill indeeed, Madam. I am very ill even when you are near me; what should I be were you at a distance.'

He had now a great desire to go to Oxford, as his first jaunt after his illness; we talked of it for some days, and I had promised to accompany him. He was impatient and fretful to-night, because I did not at once agree to go with him on Thursday. When I considered how ill he had been, and what allowance should be made for the influence of sickness upon his temper, I resolved to indulge him, though with some inconvenience to myself, as I wished to attend the musical meeting in honour of Handel, in Westminster-Abbey, on the following Saturday.

In the midst of his own diseases and pains, he was ever compassionate to the distresses of others, and actively earnest in procuring them aid, as appears from a note to Sir Joshua Reynolds, of June 1, in these words:—'I am ashamed to ask for some relief for a poor man, to whom, I hope, I have given what I can be expected to spare. The man importunes me, and the blow goes round. I am going to try another air on Thursday.'

On Thursday, June 3, the Oxford post-coach took us up in the morning at Bolt-court. The other two passengers were Mrs. Beresford and her daughter, two very agreeable ladies from America; they were going to Worcestershire, where they then resided. Frank had been sent by his master the day before to take places for us; and I found, from the way-bill, that Dr. Johnson had made our names be put down. Mrs. Beresford, who had read it, whispered me, 'Is this the great Dr. Johnson?' I told her it was; so she was then prepared to listen. As she soon happened to mention in a voice so low that Johnson did not hear it, that her husband had been a member of the American Congress, I cautioned her to beware of introducing that subject, as she must know how very violent Johnson was against the people of that country. He talked a great deal, but I am sorry I have preserved little of the conversation. Miss Beresford was so much charmed, that she said to me aside, 'How he does talk! Every sentence is an essay.' She amused herself in the coach with knotting; he would scarcely allow this species of employment any merit. 'Next to mere idleness (said he,) I think knotting is to be reckoned in the scale of insignificance; though I once attempted to learn knotting. Dempster's sister (looking to me,) endeavoured to teach me it; but I made no progress.'

I was surprised at his talking without reserve in the publick post-coach of the state of his affairs; 'I have (said he,) about the world I think above a thousand pounds, which I intend shall afford Frank an annuity of seventy pounds a year.' Indeed his openness with people at a first interview was remarkable. He said once to Mr. Langton, 'I think I am like Squire Richard in *The Journey to London,* "*I'm never strange in a strange place.*" ' He was truly *social.* He strongly censured what is much too common in England among persons of condition,—maintaining an absolute silence, when unknown to each other; as for instance, when occasionally brought together in a room before the master or mistress of the house has appeared. 'Sir, that is being so uncivilised as not to understand the common rights of humanity.'

At the inn where we stopped he was exceedingly dissatisfied with some roast mutton which we had for dinner. The ladies I saw wondered to see the great philosopher, whose wisdom and wit they had been admiring all the way, get into ill-humour from such a cause. He scolded the waiter, saying, 'It is as bad as bad can be: it is ill-fed, ill-killed, ill-kept, and ill-drest.'

He bore the journey very well, and seemed to feel himself elevated as he approached Oxford, that magnificent and venerable seat of Learning, Orthodoxy, and Toryism. Frank came in the heavy coach, in readiness to attend him; and we were received with the most polite hospitality at the house of his old friend Dr. Adams, Master of Pembroke College, who had given

us a kind invitation. Before we were set down, I communicated
to Johnson my having engaged to return to London directly, for
the reason I have mentioned, but that I would hasten back to
him again. He was pleased that I had made this journey merely
to keep him company. He was easy and placid, with Dr. Adams,
Mrs. and Miss Adams, and Mrs. Kennicot, widow of the learned
Hebræan, who was here on a visit. He soon dispatched the
inquiries which were made about his illness and recovery, by a
short and distinct narrative; and then assuming a gay air,
repeated from Swift,—

> 'Nor think on our approaching ills,
> And talk of spectacles and pills.'

Dr. Newton, the Bishop of Bristol, having been mentioned,
Johnson, recollecting the manner in which he had been censured
by that Prelate,[1] thus retaliated:—'Tom knew he should be
dead before what he has said of me would appear. He durst not
have printed it while he was alive.' DR. ADAMS. 'I believe his
Dissertations on the Prophecies is his great work.' JOHNSON.

---

[1] Dr. Newton in his *Account of his own Life*, after animadverting upon
Mr. Gibbon's *History*, says, 'Dr. Johnson's *Lives of the Poets* afforded more
amusement; but candour was much hurt and offended at the malevolence
that predominates in every part. Some passages, it must be allowed, are
judicious and well written, but make not sufficient compensation for so
much spleen and ill humour. Never was any biographer more sparing of
his praise, or more abundant in his censures. He seemingly delights more in
exposing blemishes, than in recommending beauties; slightly passes over
excellencies, enlarges upon imperfections, and not content with his own
severe reflections, revives old scandal, and produces large quotations from
the forgotten works of former criticks. His reputation was so high in the
republick of letters, that it wanted not to be raised upon the ruins of others.
But these *Essays*, instead of raising a higher idea than was before entertained
of his understanding, have certainly given the world a worse opinion of his
temper.—The Bishop was therefore the more surprized and concerned for
his townsman, for *he respected him not only for his genius and learning, but
valued him much more for the more amiable part of his character, his humanity
and charity, his morality and religion.*' The last sentence we may consider as
the general and permanent opinion of Bishop Newton; the remarks which
precede it must, by all who have read Johnson's admirable work, be imputed
to the disgust and peevishness of old age. I wish they had not appeared, and
that Dr. Johnson had not been provoked by them to express himself, not in
respectful terms, of a Prelate, whose labours were certainly of considerable
advantage both to literature and religion.

'Why, Sir, it is *Tom's* great work; but how far it is great, or how much of it is Tom's, are other questions. I fancy a considerable part of it was borrowed.' DR. ADAMS. 'He was a very successful man.' JOHNSON. 'I don't think so, Sir. He did not get very high. He was late in getting what he did get; and he did not get it by the best means. I believe he was a gross flatterer.'

I fulfilled my intention by going to London, and returned to Oxford on Wednesday the 9th of June, when I was happy to find myself again in the same agreeable circle at Pembroke College, with the comfortable prospect of making some stay. Johnson welcomed my return with more than ordinary glee.

He talked with great regard of the Honourable Archibald Campbell, whose character he had given at the Duke of Argyll's table, when we were at Inverary;[1] and at this time wrote out for me, in his own hand, a fuller account of that learned and venerable writer, which I have published in its proper place. Johnson made a remark this evening which struck me a good deal. 'I never (said he,) knew a nonjuror who could reason.'[2] Surely he did not mean to deny that faculty to many of their writers; to Hickes, Brett, and other eminent divines of that persuasion; and did not recollect that the seven Bishops, so justly celebrated for their magnanimous resistance of arbitrary power, were yet Nonjurors to the new Government. The nonjuring clergy of Scotland, indeed, who, excepting a few, have lately, by a sudden stroke, cut off all ties of allegiance to the house of Stuart, and resolved to pray for our present lawful Sovereign by name, may be thought to have confirmed this remark; as it may be said, that the divine indefeasible hereditary right which they professed

---

[1] *Journal of a Tour to the Hebrides*, 3rd edit. p. 371 [Oct. 25].

[2] The Rev. Mr. Agutter has favoured me with a note of a dialogue between Mr. John Henderson and Dr. Johnson on this topick, as related by Mr. Henderson, and it is evidently so authentick that I shall here insert it:— HENDERSON. 'What do you think, Sir, of William Law?' JOHNSON. 'William Law, Sir, wrote the best piece of Parenetick Divinity; but William Law was no reasoner.' HENDERSON. 'Jeremy Collier, Sir?' JOHNSON. 'Jeremy Collier fought without a rival, and therefore could not claim the victory.' Mr. Henderson mentioned Kenn and Kettlewell; but some objections were made; at last he said, 'But, Sir, what do you think of Lesley?' JOHNSON. 'Charles Lesley I had forgotten. Lesley *was* a reasoner, and a *reasoner who was not to be reasoned against.*'

to believe, if ever true, must be equally true still. Many of my readers will be surprized when I mention, that Johnson assured me he had never in his life been in a nonjuring meeting-house.

Next morning at breakfast, he pointed out a passage in Savage's *Wanderer*, saying, 'These are fine verses.' 'If (said he) I had written with hostility of Warburton in my *Shakspeare*, I should have quoted this couplet:—

> "Here Learning, blinded first and then beguil'd,
> Looks dark as Ignorance, as Fancy wild."

You see they'd have fitted him to a *T*,' (smiling.) Dr. Adams. 'But you did not write against Warburton.' Johnson. 'No, Sir, I treated him with great respect both in my Preface and in my Notes.'

Mrs. Kennicot spoke of her brother, the Reverend Mr. Chamberlayne, who had given up great prospects in the Church of England on his conversion to the Roman Catholick faith. Johnson, who warmly admired every man who acted from a conscientious regard to principle, erroneous or not, exclaimed fervently, 'God bless him.'

Mrs. Kennicot, in confirmation of Dr. Johnson's opinion, that the present was not worse than former ages, mentioned that her brother assured her, there was now less infidelity on the Continent than there had been; Voltaire and Rousseau were less read. I asserted, from good authority, that Hume's infidelity was certainly less read. Johnson. 'All infidel writers drop into oblivion, when personal connections and the floridness of novelty are gone; though now and then a foolish fellow, who thinks he can be witty upon them, may bring them again into notice. There will sometimes start up a College joker, who does not consider that what is a joke in a College will not do in the world. To such defenders of Religion I would apply a stanza of a poem which I remember to have seen in some old collection:—

> "Henceforth be quiet and agree,
> Each kiss his empty brother;
> Religion scorns a foe like thee,
> But dreads a friend like t'other."

The point is well, though the expression is not correct; *one*, and not *thee*, should be opposed to *t'other*.'[1]

On the Roman Catholick religion he said, 'If you join the Papists externally, they will not interrogate you strictly as to your belief in their tenets. No reasoning Papist believes every article of their faith. There is one side on which a good man might be persuaded to embrace it. A good man, of a timorous disposition, in great doubt of his acceptance with GOD, and pretty credulous, might be glad to be of a church where there are so many helps to get to Heaven. I would be a Papist if I could. I have fear enough; but an obstinate rationality prevents me. I shall never be a Papist, unless on the near approach of death, of which I have a very great terrour. I wonder that women are not all Papists.' BOSWELL. 'They are not more afraid of death than men are.' JOHNSON. 'Because they are less wicked.' DR. ADAMS. 'They are more pious.' JOHNSON. 'No, hang 'em, they are not more pious. A wicked fellow is the most pious when he takes to it. He'll beat you all at piety.'

He argued in defence of some of the peculiar tenets of the Church of Rome. As to the giving the bread only to the laity, he said, 'They may think, that in what is merely ritual, deviations from the primitive mode may be admitted on the ground of convenience, and I think they are as well warranted to make this alteration, as we are to substitute sprinkling in the room of the ancient baptism.' As to the invocation of saints, he said, 'Though I do not think it authorised, it appears to me, that "the communion of saints" in the Creed means the communion with the saints in Heaven, as connected with "The holy catholick

---

[1] I have inserted the stanza as Johnson repeated it from memory; but I have since found the poem itself, in *The Foundling Hospital for Wit*, printed at London, 1749. It is as follows:—

'EPIGRAM, *occasioned by a religious dispute at Bath.*

'On Reason, Faith, and Mystery high,
    Two wits harangue the table;
B————y believes he knows not why.
N———— swears 'tis all a fable.

Peace, coxcombs, peace, and both agree,
N————, kiss thy empty brother;
Religion laughs at foes like thee,
    And dreads a friend like t'other.'

church."' [1] He admitted the influence of evil spirits upon our minds, and said, 'Nobody who believes the New Testament can deny it.'

I brought a volume of Dr. Hurd the Bishop of Worcester's *Sermons,* and read to the company some passages from one of them, upon this text, *'Resist the Devil, and he will fly from you.'* *James,* iv. 7. I was happy to produce so judicious and elegant a supporter[2] of a doctrine, which, I know not why, should, in this

[1] Waller, in his *Divine Poesie,* Canto first, has the same thought finely expressed:—

'The Church triumphant, and the Church below,
In songs of praise their present union show;
Their joys are full; our expectation long,
In life we differ, but we join in song;
Angels and we assisted by this art,
May sing together, though we dwell apart.'

[2] The Sermon thus opens:—'That there are angels and spirits good and bad; that at the head of these last there is ONE more considerable and malignant than the rest, who, in the form, or under the name of a *serpent,* was deeply concerned in the fall of man, and whose *head,* as the prophetick language is, the son of man was one day to *bruise;* that this evil spirit, though that prophecy be in part completed, has not yet received his death's wound, but is still permitted, for ends unsearchable to us, and in ways which we cannot particularly explain, to have a certain degree of power in this world hostile to its virtue and happiness, and sometimes exerted with too much success; all this is so clear from Scripture, that no believer, unless he be first of all *spoiled by philosophy and vain deceit* [*Colossians,* ii. 8], can possibly entertain a doubt of it.'

Having treated of *possessions,* his Lordship says, 'As I have no authority to affirm that there *are* now any such, so neither may I presume to say with confidence, that there are *not* any.'

'But then with regard to the influence of evil spirits at this day upon the SOULS of men, I shall take leave to be a great deal more peremptory.—(Then, having stated the various proofs, he adds,) All this, I say, is so manifest to every one who reads the Scriptures, that if we respect their authority, the question concerning the reality of the demonick influence upon the minds of men is clearly determined.'

Let it be remembered, that these are not the words of an antiquated or obscure enthusiast, but of a learned and polite Prelate now alive; and were spoken, not to a vulgar congregation, but to the Honourable Society of Lincoln's-Inn. His Lordship in this sermon explains the words, 'deliver us from evil,' in the Lord's Prayer, as signifying a request to be protected from 'the evil one,' that is the Devil. This is well illustrated in a short but excellent Commentary by my late worthy friend, the Reverend Dr. Lort, of whom it may truly be said, *Multis ille bonis flebilis occidit* ['He died mourned by many good men']. It is remarkable that Waller, in his *Reflections on the several Petitions,* in that sacred form of devotion, has understood this in the same sense:— 'Guard us from all temptations of the Foe.'

world of imperfect knowledge, and, therefore, of wonder and mystery in a thousand instances, be contested by some with an unthinking assurance and flippancy.

After dinner, when one of us talked of there being a great enmity between Whig and Tory;—JOHNSON. 'Why not so much, I think, unless when they come into competition with each other. There is none when they are only common acquaintance, none when they are of different sexes. A Tory will marry into a Whig family, and a Whig into a Tory family, without any reluctance. But indeed in a matter of much more concern than political tenets, and that is religion, men and women do not concern themselves much about difference of opinion: and ladies set no value on the moral character of men who pay their addresses to them; the greatest profligate will be as well received as the man of the greatest virtue, and this by a very good woman, by a woman who says her prayers three times a day.' Our ladies endeavoured to defend their sex from this charge; but he roared them down! 'No, no; a lady will take Jonathan Wild as readily as St. Austin, if he has three-pence more; and, what is worse, her parents will give her to him. Women have a perpetual envy of our vices; they are less vicious than we, not from choice, but because we restrict them; they are the slaves of order and fashion; their virtue is of more consequence to us than our own, so far as concerns this world.'

Miss Adams mentioned a gentleman of licentious character, and said, 'Suppose I had a mind to marry that gentleman, would my parents consent?' JOHNSON. 'Yes, they'd consent, and you'd go. You'd go though they did not consent.' MISS ADAMS. 'Perhaps their opposing might make me go.' JOHNSON. 'O, very well; you'd take one whom you think a bad man, to have the pleasure of vexing your parents. You put me in mind of Dr. Barrowby, the physician, who was very fond of swine's flesh. One day, when he was eating it, he said, 'I wish I was a Jew.' 'Why so? (said somebody);' the Jews are not allowed to eat your favourite meat.' 'Because, (said he,) I should then have the gust of eating it, with the pleasure of sinning.' Johnson then proceeded in his declamation.

Miss Adams soon afterwards made an observation that I do not recollect, which pleased him much: he said with a good-humoured smile, 'That there should be so much excellence united with so much *depravity*, is strange.'

Indeed, this lady's good qualities, merit, and accomplishments, and her constant attention to Dr. Johnson, were not lost upon him. She happened to tell him that a little coffee-pot, in which she had made his coffee, was the only thing she could call her own. He turned to her with a complacent gallantry, 'Don't say so, my dear; I hope you don't reckon my heart as nothing.'

I asked him if it was true as reported, that he had said lately, 'I am for the King against Fox; but I am for Fox against Pitt.' JOHNSON. 'Yes, Sir; the King is my master; but I do not know Pitt; and Fox is my friend.'

'Fox, (added he,) is a most extraordinary man; here is a man (describing him in strong terms of objection in some respects according as he apprehended, but which exalted his abilities the more) who has divided the Kingdom with Cæsar; so that it was a doubt whether the nation should be ruled by the sceptre of George the Third, or the tongue of Fox.'

Dr. Wall, physician at Oxford, drank tea with us. Johnson had in general a peculiar pleasure in the company of physicians, which was certainly not abated by the conversation of this learned, ingenious, and pleasing gentleman. Johnson said, 'It is wonderful how little good Radcliffe's travelling fellowships have done. I know nothing that has been imported by them; yet many additions to our medical knowledge might be got in foreign countries. Inoculation, for instance, has saved more lives than war destroys: and the cures performed by the Peruvian-bark are innumerable. But it is in vain to send our travelling physicians to France, and Italy, and Germany, for all that is known there is known here; I'd send them out of Christendom; I'd send them among barbarous nations.'

On Friday, June 11, we talked at breakfast, of forms of prayer. JOHNSON. 'I know of no good prayers but those in the *Book of Common Prayer*.' DR. ADAMS. (in a very earnest manner) 'I wish, Sir, you would compose some family prayers.' JOHNSON.

'I will not compose prayers for you, Sir, because you can do it for yourself. But I have thought of getting together all the books of prayers which I could, selecting those which should appear to me the best, putting out some, inserting others, adding some prayers of my own, and prefixing a discourse on prayer.' We all now gathered about him, and two or three of us at a time joined in pressing him to execute this plan. He seemed to be a little displeased at the manner of our importunity, and in great agitation called out, 'Do not talk thus of what is so aweful. I know not what time GOD will allow me in this world. There are many things which I wish to do.' Some of us persisted, and Dr. Adams said, 'I never was more serious about any thing in my life.' JOHNSON. 'Let me alone, let me alone; I am over-powered.' And then he put his hands before his face, and reclined for some time upon the table.

I mentioned Jeremy Taylor's using, in his forms of prayer, 'I am the chief of sinners,' and other such self-condemning expressions. 'Now, (said I) this cannot be said with truth by every man, and therefore is improper for a general printed form. I myself cannot say that I am the worst of men; I *will* not say so.' JOHNSON. 'A man may know, that physically, that is, in the real state of things, he is not the worst man; but that morally he may be so. Law observes, that "Every man knows something worse of himself, than he is sure of in others." You may not have committed such crimes as some men have done; but you do not know against what degree of light they have sinned. Besides, Sir, "the chief of sinners" is a mode of expression for "I am a great sinner." So St. Paul, speaking of our SAVIOUR'S having died to save sinners, says, "of whom I am the chief;" yet he certainly did not think himself so bad as Judas Iscariot.' BOSWELL. 'But, Sir, Taylor means it literally, for he founds a conceit upon it. When praying for the conversion of sinners, and of himself in particular, he says, "LORD, thou wilt not leave thy *chief* work undone.' JOHNSON. 'I do not approve of figurative expressions in addressing the Supreme Being; and I never use them. Taylor gives a very good advice: "Never lie in your prayers; never confess more than you really believe; never promise more than you mean to perform." I recollected this precept in his *Golden Grove*; but his *example* for prayer contradicts his *precept.*'

Dr. Johnson and I went in Dr. Adams's coach to dine with Dr. Nowell, Principal of St. Mary Hall, at his beautiful villa at Iffley, on the banks of the Isis, about two miles from Oxford. While we were upon the road, I had the resolution to ask Johnson whether he thought that the roughness of his manner had been an advantage or not, and if he would not have done more good if he had been more gentle. I proceeded to answer myself thus: 'Perhaps it has been of advantage, as it has given weight to what you said: you could not, perhaps, have talked with such authority without it.' JOHNSON. 'No, Sir; I have done more good as I am. Obscenity and Impiety have always been repressed in my company.' BOSWELL. 'True, Sir; and that is more than can be said of every Bishop. Greater liberties have been taken in the presence of a Bishop, though a very good man, from his being milder, and therefore not commanding such awe. Yet, Sir, many people who might have been benefited by your conversation, have been frightened away. A worthy friend of ours has told me, that he has often been afraid to talk to you.' JOHNSON. 'Sir, he need not have been afraid, if he had any thing rational to say. If he had not, it was better he did not talk.'

Dr. Nowell is celebrated for having preached a sermon before the House of Commons, on the 30th of January, 1772, full of high Tory sentiments, for which he was thanked as usual, and printed it at their request; but, in the midst of that turbulence and faction which disgraced a part of the present reign, the thanks were afterwards ordered to be expunged. This strange conduct sufficiently exposes itself; and Dr. Nowell will ever have the honour which is due to a lofty friend of our monarchical constitution. Dr. Johnson said to me, 'Sir, the Court will be very much to blame, if he is not promoted.' I told this to Dr. Nowell, and asserting my humbler, though not less zealous exertions in the same cause, I suggested that whatever return we might receive, we should still have the consolation of being like Butler's steady and generous Royalist,

> 'True as the dial to the sun,
> Although it be not shone upon.'

We were well entertained and very happy at Dr. Nowell's, where was a very agreeable company, and we drank 'Church and King' after dinner, with true Tory cordiality.

We talked of a certain clergyman[1] of extraordinary character, who by exerting his talents in writing on temporary topicks, and displaying uncommon intrepidity, had raised himself to affluence. I maintained that we ought not to be indignant at his success; for merit of every sort was entitled to reward. JOHNSON. 'Sir, I will not allow this man to have merit. No, Sir; what he has is rather the contrary; I will, indeed, allow him courage, and on this account we so far give him credit. We have more respect for a man who robs boldly on the highway, than for a fellow who jumps out of a ditch, and knocks you down behind your back. Courage is a quality so necessary for maintaining virtue, that it is always respected, even when it is associated with vice.'

I censured the coarse invectives which were become fashionable in the House of Commons, and said that if members of parliament must attack each other personally in the heat of debate, it should be done more genteely. JOHNSON. 'No, Sir; that would be much worse. Abuse is not so dangerous when there is no vehicle of wit or delicacy, no subtle conveyance. The difference between coarse and refined abuse is as the difference between being bruised by a club, and wounded by a poisoned arrow.' I have since observed his position elegantly expressed by Dr. Young:—

> 'As the soft plume gives swiftness to the dart,
> Good breeding sends the satire to the heart.'

On Saturday, June 12, there drank tea with us at Dr. Adams's, Mr. John Henderson, student of Pembroke College, celebrated for his wonderful acquirements in Alchymy, Judicial Astrology, and other abstruse and curious learning;[2] and the Reverend Herbert Croft, who, I am afraid, was somewhat mortified by

---

[1] [The Rev. (Sir) Henry Bate (Dudley). *Croker*[1].]
[2] See an account of him, in a sermon by the Reverend Mr. Agutter.

Dr. Johnson's not being highly pleased with some *Family Dis-*
courses, which he had printed; they were in too familiar a style
to be approved of by so manly a mind. I have no note of this
evening's conversation, except a single fragment. When I mentioned Thomas Lord Lyttelton's vision, the prediction of the
time of his death, and its exact fulfilment;—JOHNSON. 'It is the
most extraordinary thing that has happened in my day. I heard
it with my own ears, from his uncle, Lord Westcote. I am so
glad to have every evidence of the spiritual world, that I am
willing to believe it.' DR. ADAMS. 'You have evidence enough;
good evidence, which needs not such support.' JOHNSON. 'I like
to have more.'

Mr. Henderson, with whom I had sauntered in the venerable
walks of Merton-College, and found him a very learned and
pious man, supt with us. Dr. Johnson surprised him not a
little, by acknowledging with a look of horrour, that he was
much oppressed by the fear of death. The amiable Dr. Adams
suggested that GOD was infinitely good. JOHNSON. 'That he is
infinitely good, as far as the perfection of his nature will allow,
I certainly believe; but it is necessary for good upon the whole,
that individuals should be punished. As to an *individual*, therefore, he is not infinitely good; and as I cannot be *sure* that I have
fulfilled the conditions on which salvation is granted, I am afraid
I may be one of those who shall be damned.' (looking dismally.)
DR. ADAMS. 'What do you mean by damned?' JOHNSON.
(passionately and loudly) 'Sent to Hell, Sir, and punished ever-
lastingly.' DR. ADAMS. 'I don't believe that doctrine.' JOHN-
SON. 'Hold, Sir; do you believe that some will be punished at
all?' DR. ADAMS. 'Being excluded from Heaven will be a
punishment; yet there may be no great positive suffering.'
JOHNSON. 'Well, Sir; but, if you admit any degree of punishment, there is an end of your argument for infinite goodness
simply considered; for, infinite goodness would inflict no punishment whatever. There is not infinite goodness physically considered; morally there is.' BOSWELL. 'But may not a man attain
to such a degree of hope as not to be uneasy from the fear of
death?' JOHNSON. 'A man may have such a degree of hope as

to keep him quiet. You see I am not quiet, from the vehemence with which I talk; but I do not despair.' MRS. ADAMS. 'You seem, Sir, to forget the merits of our Redeemer.' JOHNSON. 'Madam, I do not forget the merits of my Redeemer; but my Redeemer has said that he will set some on his right hand and some on his left.' He was in gloomy agitation, and said, 'I'll have no more on't.' If what has now been stated should be urged by the enemies of Christianity, as if its influence on the mind were not benignant, let it be remembered, that Johnson's temperament was melancholy, of which such direful apprehensions of futurity are often a common effect. We shall presently see that when he approached nearer to his aweful change, his mind became tranquil, and he exhibited as much fortitude as becomes a thinking man in that situation.

From the subject of death we passed to discourse of life, whether it was upon the whole more happy or miserable. Johnson was decidedly for the balance of misery:[1] in confirmation of

---

[1] The Reverend Mr. Ralph Churton, Fellow of Brazen-Nose College, Oxford, has favoured me with the following remarks on my Work, which he is pleased to say, 'I have hitherto extolled, and cordially approve.'

'The chief part of what I have to observe is contained in the following transcript from a letter to a friend, which, with his concurrence, I copied for this purpose; and, whatever may be the merit or justness of the remarks, you may be sure that being written to a most intimate friend, without any intention that they ever should go further, they are the genuine and undisguised sentiments of the writer:—

'Jan. 6, 1792.

'Last week, I was reading the second volume of Boswell's *Johnson*, with increasing esteem for the worthy authour, and increasing veneration of the wonderful and excellent man who is the subject of it. The writer throws in, now and then, very properly some serious religious reflections; but there is one remark, in my mind an obvious and just one, which I think he has not made, that Johnson's "morbid melancholy," and constitutional infirmities, were intended by Providence, like St. Paul's thorn in the flesh, to check intellectual conceit and arrogance; which the consciousness of his extraordinary talents, awake as he was to the voice of praise, might otherwise have generated in a very culpable degree. Another observation strikes me, that in consequence of the same natural indisposition, and habitual sickliness, (for he says he scarcely passed one day without pain after his twentieth year,) he considered and represented human life, as a scene of much greater misery than is generally experienced. There may be persons bowed down with affliction all their days; and there are those, no doubt, whose iniquities rob them of rest; but neither calamities nor crimes, I hope and believe, do so much and so generally abound, as to justify the dark picture of life which

which I maintained, that no man would choose to lead over
again the life which he had experienced. Johnson acceded to
that opinion in the strongest terms. This is an inquiry often
made; and its being a subject of disquisition is a proof that

Johnson's imagination designed, and his strong pencil delineated. This I
am sure, the colouring is far too gloomy for what I have experienced, though
as far as I can remember, I have had more sickness (I do not say more
severe, but only more in quantity,) than falls to the lot of most people. But
then daily debility and occasional sickness were far overbalanced by intervenient days, and, perhaps, weeks, void of pain, and overflowing with comfort. So that in short, to return to the subject, human life, as far as I can
perceive from experience or observation, is not that state of constant
wretchedness which Johnson always insisted it was; which misrepresentation,
(for such it surely is,) his Biographer has not corrected, I suppose, because,
unhappily, he has himself a large portion of melancholy in his constitution,
and fancied the portrait a faithful copy of life.'

The learned writer then proceeds thus in his letter to me:—

'I have conversed with some sensible men on this subject, who all seem
to entertain the same sentiments respecting life with those which are expressed or implied in the foregoing paragraph. It might be added that as
the representation here spoken of, appears not consistent with fact and
experience, so neither does it seem to be countenanced by Scripture. There
is, perhaps, no part of the sacred volume which at first sight promises so
much to lend its sanction to these dark and desponding notions as the book
of *Ecclesiastes,* which so often, and so emphatically, proclaims the vanity of
things sublunary. But the design of this whole book, (as it has been justly
observed,) is not to put us out of conceit with life, but to cure our vain
expectations of a compleat and perfect happiness in this world; to convince
us, that there is no such thing to be found in mere external enjoyments;—
and to teach us to seek for happiness in the practice of virtue, in the knowledge and love of God, and in the hopes of a better life. For this is the
application of all; *Let us hear,* &c. xii. 13. Not only his duty, but his happiness
too; *For* GOD, &c. ver. 14.—See *Sherlock on Providence,* p. 299.

'The New Testament tells us, indeed, and most truly, that "sufficient
unto the day is the evil thereof;" and, therefore, wisely forbids us to increase
our burden by forebodings of sorrows; but I think it no where says that
even our ordinary afflictions are not consistent with a very considerable
degree of positive comfort and satisfaction. And, accordingly, one whose
sufferings as well as merits were conspicuous, assures us, that in proportion
"as the sufferings of Christ abounded in them, so their consolation also
abounded by Christ." 2 *Cor.* i. 5. It is needless to cite, as indeed it would be
endless even to refer to, the multitude of passages in both Testaments
holding out, in the strongest language, promises of blessings, even in this
world, to the faithful servants of GOD. I will only refer to *St. Luke,* xviii.
29, 30, and 1 *Tim.* iv. 8.

'Upon the whole, setting aside instances of great and lasting bodily pain,
of minds peculiarly oppressed by melancholy, and of severe temporal
calamities, from which extraordinary cases we surely should not form our

much misery presses upon human feelings; for those who are
conscious of a felicity of existence, would never hesitate to
accept of a repetition of it. I have met with very few who would.
I have heard Mr. Burke make use of a very ingenious and

estimate of the general tenour and complexion of life; excluding these from
the account, I am convinced that as well the gracious constitution of things
which Providence has ordained, as the declarations of Scripture and the
actual experience of individuals, authourize the sincere Christian to hope
that his humble and constant endeavours to perform his duty, checquered as
the best life is with many failings, will be crowned with a greater degree of
present peace, serenity, and comfort, than he could reasonably permit himself to expect, if he measured his views and judged of life from the opinion
of Dr. Johnson, often and energetically expressed in the Memoirs of him,
without any animadversion or censure by his ingenious Biographer. If He
himself, upon reviewing the subject, shall see the matter in this light, he
will, in an octavo edition, which is eagerly expected, make such additional
remarks or correction as he shall judge fit; lest the impressions which these
discouraging passages may leave on the reader's mind, should in any degree
hinder what otherwise the whole spirit and energy of the work tends, and,
I hope, successfully, to promote,—pure morality and true religion.'

Though I have, in some degree, obviated any reflections against my
illustrious friend's dark views of life, when considering, in the course of this
Work, his *Rambler* [*ante,* p. 152] and his *Rasselas* [*ante,* p. 242], I am obliged
to Mr. Churton for complying with my request of his permission to insert
his Remarks, being conscious of the weight of what he judiciously suggests
as to the melancholy in my own constitution. His more pleasing views of
life, I hope, are just. *Valeant quantum valere possunt* ['May they have all the
weight they can'].

Mr. Churton concludes his letter to me in these words:—'Once, and only
once, I had the satisfaction of seeing your illustrious friend; and as I feel a
particular regard for all whom he distinguished with his esteem and friendship, so I derive much pleasure from reflecting that I once beheld, though
but transiently near our College gate, one whose works will for ever delight
and improve the world, who was a sincere and zealous son of the Church of
England, an honour to his country, and an ornament to human nature.'

His letter was accompanied with a present from himself of his *Sermons
at the Bampton Lecture,* and from his friend, Dr. Townson, the venerable
Rector of Malpas, in Cheshire, of his *Discourses on the Gospels,* together with
the following extract of a letter from that excellent person, who is now gone
to receive the reward of his labours:—'Mr. Boswell is not only very entertaining in his works, but they are so replete with moral and religious
sentiments, without an instance, as far as I know, of a contrary tendency,
that I cannot help having a great esteem for him; and if you think such a
trifle as a copy of the *Discourses, ex dono authoris* ['the gift of the
author'], would be acceptable to him, I should be happy to give him this
small testimony of my regard.'

Such spontaneous testimonies of approbation from such men, without any
personal acquaintance with me, are truly valuable and encouraging.

plausible argument on this subject;—'Every man (said he,) would lead his life over again; for, every man is willing to go on and take an addition to his life, which, as he grows older, he has no reason to think will be better, or even so good as what has preceded.' I imagine, however, the truth is, that there is a deceitful hope that the next part of life will be free from the pains, and anxieties, and sorrows, which we have already felt. We are for wise purposes 'Condemn'd to Hope's delusive mine;' as Johnson finely says; and I may also quote the celebrated lines of Dryden, equally philosophical and poetical:—

> 'When I consider life, 'tis all a cheat,
> Yet fool'd with hope, men favour the deceit:
> Trust on, and think to-morrow will repay;
> To-morrow's falser than the former day;
> Lies worse; and while it says we shall be blest
> With some new joys, cuts off what we possess.
> Strange cozenage! none would live past years again;
> Yet all hope pleasure in what yet remain;
> And from the dregs of life think to receive,
> What the first sprightly running could not give.'[1]

It was observed to Dr. Johnson, that it seemed strange that he, who has so often delighted his company by his lively and brilliant conversation, should say he was miserable. JOHNSON. 'Alas! it is all outside; I may be cracking my joke, and cursing the sun. *Sun, how I hate thy beams!*' I knew not well what to think of this declaration; whether to hold it as a genuine picture of his mind,[2] or as the effect of his persuading himself contrary to fact, that the position which he had assumed as to human unhappiness, was true. We may apply to him a sentence in Mr. Greville's *Maxims, Characters, and Reflections*;[3] a book which is entitled to much more praise than it has received: 'ARISTARCHUS is charming: how full of knowledge, of sense, of sentiment. You get him with difficulty to your supper; and after having delighted every

---

[1] *Aurungzebe* [act iv. sc. 1].

[2] Yet there is no doubt that a man may appear very gay in company who is sad at heart. His merriment is like the sound of drums and trumpets in a battle, to drown the groans of the wounded and dying.

[3] Page 139.

body and himself for a few hours, he is obliged to return home;—he is finishing his treatise, to prove that unhappiness is the portion of man.'

On Sunday, June 13, our philosopher was calm at breakfast. There was something exceedingly pleasing in our leading a College life, without restraint, and with superiour elegance, in consequence of our living in the Master's house, and having the company of ladies. Mrs. Kennicot related, in his presence, a lively saying of Dr. Johnson to Miss Hannah More, who had expressed a wonder that the poet who had written *Paradise Lost* should write such poor Sonnets:—'Milton, Madam, was a genius that could cut a Colossus from a rock; but could not carve heads upon cherry-stones.'

We talked of the casuistical question, Whether it was allowable at any time to depart from *Truth?* JOHNSON. 'The general rule is, that Truth should never be violated, because it is of the utmost importance to the comfort of life, that we should have a full security by mutual faith; and occasional inconveniencies should be willingly suffered that we may preserve it. There must, however, be some exceptions. If, for instance, a murderer should ask you which way a man is gone, you may tell him what is not true, because you are under a previous obligation not to betray a man to a murderer.' BOSWELL. 'Supposing the person who wrote *Junius* were asked whether he was the authour, might he deny it?' JOHNSON. 'I don't know what to say to this. If you were *sure* that he wrote *Junius*, would you, if he denied it, think as well of him afterwards? Yet it may be urged, that what a man has no right to ask, you may refuse to communicate; and there is no other effectual mode of preserving a secret, and an important secret, the discovery of which may be very hurtful to you, but a flat denial; for if you are silent, or hesitate, or evade, it will be held equivalent to a confession. But stay, Sir; here is another case. Supposing the authour had told me confidentially that he had written *Junius*, and I were asked if he had, I should hold myself at liberty to deny it, as being under a previous promise, express or implied, to conceal it. Now what I ought to do for the authour, may I not do for myself? But I deny the lawfulness of telling a lie to a sick man for fear of alarming him. You have no business with consequences; you are to tell the truth. Besides, you are not sure what effect your telling him that he is in danger may have. It may bring his distemper to a crisis, and that may cure him. Of all lying, I have the greatest abhorrence of this, because I believe it has been frequently practised on myself.'

I cannot help thinking that there is much weight in the opinion of those who have held, that Truth, as an eternal and immutable principle, ought, upon no account whatever, to be violated, from supposed previous or superiour obligations, of which every man being to judge for himself, there is great danger that we may too often, from partial motives, persuade ourselves that they exist; and probably whatever extraordinary instances may sometimes occur, where some evil may be prevented by violating this noble principle, it would be found that human happiness would, upon the whole, be more perfect were Truth universally preserved.

In the notes to the *Dunciad*, we find the following verses, addressed to Pope:—[1]

> 'While malice, Pope, denies thy page
>   Its own celestial fire;
> While criticks, and while bards in rage
>   Admiring, won't admire:
>
> While wayward pens thy worth assail,
>   And envious tongues decry;
> These times, though many a friend bewail,
>   These times bewail not I.
>
> But when the world's loud praise is thine,
>   And spleen no more shall blame;
> When with thy Homer thou shalt shine
>   In one establish'd fame!
>
> When none shall rail, and every lay
>   Devote a wreath to thee:
> That day (for come it will) that day
>   Shall I lament to see.'

[1] The annotator calls them 'amiable verses.'

It is surely not a little remarkable, that they should appear without a name. Miss Seward, knowing Dr. Johnson's almost universal and minute literary information, signified a desire that I should ask him who was the authour. He was prompt with his answer: 'Why, Sir, they were written by one Lewis, who was either under-master or an usher of Westminster-school, and published a Miscellany, in which *Grongar Hill* first came out.'[1] Johnson praised them highly, and repeated them with a noble animation. In the twelfth line, instead of 'one establish'd fame,' he repeated 'one unclouded flame,' which he thought was the reading in former editions: but I believe was a flash of his own genius. It is much more poetical than the other.

On Monday, June 14, and Tuesday, 15, Dr. Johnson and I dined, on one of them, I forget which, with Mr. Mickle, translator of the *Lusiad*, at Wheatley, a very pretty country place a few miles from Oxford; and on the other with Dr. Wetherell, Master of University College. From Dr. Wetherell's he went to visit Mr. Sackville Parker, the bookseller; and when he returned to us, gave the following account of his visit, saying, 'I have been to see my old friend, Sack. Parker; I find he has married his maid; he has done right. She had lived with him many years in great confidence, and they had mingled minds: I do not think he could have found any wife that would have made him so happy. The woman was very attentive and civil to me; she pressed me to fix a day for dining with them, and to say what I liked, and she would be sure to get it for me. Poor Sack! He is very ill, indeed. We parted as never to meet again. It has quite broke me down.' This pathetic narrative was strangely diversified with the grave and earnest defence of a man's having married his maid. I could not but feel it as in some degree ludicrous.

In the morning of Tuesday, June 15, while we sat at Dr.

---

[1] Lewis's Verses addressed to Pope were first published in a Collection of Pieces on occasion of *The Dunciad*, 8vo., 1732. They do not appear in Lewis's own *Miscellany*, printed in 1726.—*Grongar Hill* was first printed in Savage's *Miscellanies* as an Ode, and was *reprinted* in the same year in Lewis's *Miscellany*, in the form it now bears.

In his *Miscellanies*, 1726, the beautiful poem,—'Away, let nought to love displeasing,'—reprinted in Percy's *Reliques*, vol. i. book iii. No. 13, first appeared. [M.]

Adams's, we talked of a printed letter from the Reverend Herbert Croft, to a young gentleman who had been his pupil, in which he advised him to read to the end of whatever books he should begin to read. JOHNSON. 'This is surely a strange advice; you may as well resolve that whatever men you happen to get acquainted with, you are to keep to them for life. A book may be good for nothing; or there may be only one thing in it worth knowing; are we to read it all through? These Voyages, (pointing to the three large volumes of *Voyages to the South Sea*, which were just come out) *who* will read them through? A man had better work his way before the mast, than read them through; they will be eaten by rats and mice, before they are read through. There can be little entertainment in such books; one set of Savages is like another.' BOSWELL. 'I do not think the people of Otaheité can be reckoned Savages.' JOHNSON. 'Don't cant in defence of Savages.' BOSWELL. 'They have the art of navigation.' JOHNSON. 'A dog or a cat can swim.' BOSWELL. 'They carve very ingeniously.' JOHNSON. 'A cat can scratch, and a child with a nail can scratch.' I perceived this was none of the *mollia tempora fandi*;[1] so desisted.

Upon his mentioning that when he came to College he wrote his first exercise twice over; but never did so afterwards; MISS ADAMS. 'I suppose, Sir, you could not make them better?' JOHNSON. 'Yes, Madam, to be sure, I could make them better. Thought is better than no thought.' MISS ADAMS. 'Do you think, Sir, you could make your *Ramblers* better?' JOHNSON. 'Certainly I could.' BOSWELL. 'I'll lay a bet, Sir, you cannot.' JOHNSON. 'But I will, Sir, if I choose. I shall make the best of them you shall pick out, better.' BOSWELL. 'But you may add to them. I will not allow of that.' JOHNSON. 'Nay, Sir, there are three ways of making them better;—putting out,—adding,—or correcting.'

During our visit at Oxford, the following conversation passed between him and me on the subject of my trying my fortune at the English bar: Having asked whether a very extensive acquaintance in London, which was very valuable, and of great advan-

[1] ['the most propitious time to address him.' *Aeneid* iv. 293.]

tage to a man at large, might not be prejudicial to a lawyer, by preventing him from giving sufficient attention to his business;— JOHNSON. 'Sir, you will attend to business, as business lays hold of you. When not actually employed, you may see your friends as much as you do now. You may dine at a Club every day, and sup with one of the members every night; and you may be as much at publick places as one who has seen them all would wish to be. But you must take care to attend constantly in West-minster-Hall; both to mind your business, as it is almost all learnt there, (for nobody reads now;) and to shew that you want to have business. And you must not be too often seen at publick places, that competitors may not have it to say, 'He is always at the Playhouse or at Ranelagh, and never to be found at his chambers.' And, Sir, there must be a kind of solemnity in the manner of a professional man. I have nothing particular to say to you on the subject. All this I should say to any one; I should have said it to Lord Thurlow twenty years ago.'

THE PROFESSION may probably think this representation of what is required in a Barrister who would hope for success, to be by much too indulgent; but certain it is, that as

'The wits of Charles found easier ways to fame,'

some of the lawyers of this age who have risen high, have by no means thought it absolutely necessary to submit to that long and painful course of study which a Plowden, a Coke, and a Hale considered as requisite. My respected friend, Mr. Langton, has shewn me in the hand-writing of his grandfather, a curious account of a conversation which he had with Lord Chief Justice Hale, in which that great man tells him, 'That for two years after he came to the inn of court, he studied sixteen hours a day; however (his Lordship added) that by this intense application he almost brought himself to his grave, though he were of a very strong constitution, and after reduced himself to eight hours; but that he would not advise any body to so much; that he thought six hours a day, with attention and constancy, was sufficient; that a man must use his body as he would his horse, and his stomach; not tire him at once, but rise with an appetite.'

On Wednesday, June 19,[1] Dr. Johnson and I returned to London; he was not well to-day, and said very little, employing himself chiefly in reading Euripides. He expressed some displeasure at me, for not observing sufficiently the various objects upon the road. 'If I had your eyes, Sir, (said he,) I should count the passengers.' It was wonderful how accurate his observation of visual objects was, notwithstanding his imperfect eyesight, owing to a habit of attention. That he was much satisfied with the respect paid to him at Dr. Adams's, is thus attested by himself: 'I returned last night from Oxford, after a fortnight's abode with Dr. Adams, who treated me as well as I could expect or wish; and he that contents a sick man, a man whom it is impossible to please, has surely done his part well.'[2]

After his return to London from this excursion, I saw him frequently, but have few memorandums: I shall therefore here insert some particulars which I collected at various times.

The Reverend Mr. Astle, of Ashbourne, in Derbyshire, brother to the learned and ingenious Thomas Astle, Esq., was from his early years known to Dr. Johnson, who obligingly advised him as to his studies, and recommended to him the following books, of which a list which he has been pleased to communicate, lies before me in Johnson's own hand-writing:—

Universal History (ancient.)—Rollin's Ancient History.—Puffendorf's Introduction to History.—Vertot's History of Knights of Malta.—Vertot's Revolution[s] of Portugal.—Vertot's Revolutions of Sweden.—Carte's History of England.—Present State of England.—Geographical Grammar.—Prideaux's Connection.—Nelson's Feasts and Fasts.—Duty of Man.—Gentleman's Religion.—Clarendon's History.—Watt's Improvement of the Mind.—Watts's Logick.—Nature Displayed.—Lowth's English Grammar.—Blackwall on the Classicks.—Sherlock's Sermons.—Burnet's Life of Hale.—Dupin's History of the Church.—Shuckford's Connections.—Law's Serious Call.—Walton's Complete Angler.—Sandys's Travels.—Sprat's History of the Royal Society.—England's Gazetteer.—Goldsmith's Roman History.—Some Commentaries on the Bible.

---

[1] [Wednesday was the 16th.]
[2] *Letters to Mrs. Thrale,* vol. ii. p. 372.

It having been mentioned to Dr. Johnson that a gentleman who had a son whom he imagined to have an extreme degree of timidity, resolved to send him to a publick school, that he might acquire confidence;—'Sir, (said Johnson,) this is a preposterous expedient for removing his infirmity; such a disposition should be cultivated in the shade. Placing him at a publick school is forcing an owl upon day.'

Speaking of a gentleman[1] whose house was much frequented by low company; 'Rags, Sir, (said he,) will always make their appearance where they have a right to do it.'

Of the same gentleman's mode of living, he said, 'Sir, the servants, instead of doing what they are bid, stand round the table in idle clusters, gaping upon the guests; and seem as unfit to attend a company, as to steer a man of war.'

A dull country magistrate[2] gave Johnson a long tedious account of his exercising his criminal jurisdiction, the result of which was his having sentenced four convicts to transportation. Johnson, in an agony of impatience to get rid of such a companion, exclaimed, 'I heartily wish, Sir, that I were a fifth.'

Johnson was present when a tragedy was read, in which there occurred this line:—

'Who rules o'er freemen should himself be free.'

The company having admired it much, 'I cannot agree with you (said Johnson). It might as well be said,—

'Who drives fat oxen should himself be fat.'

He was pleased with the kindness of Mr. Cator, who was joined with him in Mr. Thrale's important trust, and thus describes him[3]:—'There is much good in his character, and much usefulness in his knowledge.' He found a cordial solace at that gentleman's seat at Beckenham, in Kent, which is indeed one of the finest places at which I ever was a guest; and where I find more and more a hospitable welcome.

Johnson seldom encouraged general censure of any profession;

---

[1] [Dr. John Taylor.]
[2] [The Mayor of Windsor. *Boswelliana*, p. 211.]
[3] *Letters to Mrs. Thrale*, vol. ii. p. 284.

but he was willing to allow a due share of merit to the various departments necessary in civilised life. In a splenetick, sarcastical, or jocular frame, however, he would sometimes utter a pointed saying of that nature. One instance has been mentioned,[1] where he gave a sudden satirical stroke to the character of an *attorney*. The too indiscriminate admission to that employment, which requires both abilities and integrity, has given rise to injurious reflections, which are totally inapplicable to many very respectable men who exercise it with reputation and honour.

Johnson having argued for some time with a pertinacious gentleman; his opponent, who had talked in a very puzzling manner, happened to say, 'I don't understand you, Sir:' upon which Johnson observed, 'Sir, I have found you an argument; but I am not obliged to find you an understanding.'

Talking to me of Horry Walpole, (as Horace late Earl of Orford was often called,) Johnson allowed that he got together a great many curious little things, and told them in an elegant manner. Mr. Walpole thought Johnson a more amiable character after reading his *Letters to Mrs. Thrale*: but never was one of the true admirers of that great man. We may suppose a prejudice conceived, if he ever heard Johnson's account to Sir George Staunton, that when he made the speeches in parliament for the *Gentleman's Magazine*, 'he always took care to put Sir Robert Walpole in the wrong, and to say every thing he could against the electorate of Hanover.' The celebrated *Heroick Epistle*, in which Johnson is satyrically introduced, has been ascribed both to Mr. Walpole and Mr. Mason. One day at Mr. Courtenay's, when a gentleman[2] expressed his opinion that there was more energy in that poem than could be expected from Mr. Walpole; Mr. Warton, the late Laureat, observed, 'It may have been written by Walpole, and *buckram'd* by Mason.'

He disapproved of Lord Hailes, for having modernised the language of the ever-memorable John Hales of Eton, in an edition which his Lordship published of that writer's works. 'An authour's language, Sir, (said he,) is a characteristical part of

[1] See p. 443.   [2] [Possibly Boswell. *Powell.*]

his composition, and is also characteristical of the age in which he writes. Besides, Sir, when the language is changed we are not sure that the sense is the same. No, Sir; I am sorry Lord Hailes has done this.'

Here it may be observed, that his frequent use of the expression, *No, Sir*, was not always to intimate contradiction; for he would say so, when he was about to enforce an affirmative proposition which had not been denied, as in the instance last mentioned. I used to consider it as a kind of flag of defiance; as if he had said, 'Any argument you may offer against this, is not just. No, Sir, it is not.' It was like Falstaff's 'I deny your Major.'

Sir Joshua Reynolds having said that he took the altitude of a man's taste by his stories and his wit, and of his understanding by the remarks which he repeated; being always sure that he must be a weak man who quotes common things with an emphasis as if they were oracles; Johnson agreed with him; and Sir Joshua having also observed that the real character of a man was found out by his amusements,—Johnson added, 'Yes, Sir; no man is a hypocrite in his pleasures.'

I have mentioned Johnson's general aversion to a pun. He once, however, endured one of mine. When we were talking of a numerous company in which he had distinguished himself highly, I said, 'Sir, you were a COD surrounded by smelts. Is not this enough for you? at a time too when you were not *fishing* for a compliment?' He laughed at this with a complacent approbation. Old Mr. Sheridan observed, upon my mentioning it to him, 'He liked your compliment so well, he was willing to take it with *pun sauce*.' For my own part, I think no innocent species of wit or pleasantry should be suppressed; and that a good pun may be admitted among the smaller excellencies of lively conversation.

Had Johnson treated at large *De Claris Oratoribus*,[1] he might have given us an admirable work. When the Duke of Bedford attacked the ministry as vehemently as he could, for having taken upon them to extend the time for the importation of corn, Lord Chatham, in his first speech in the House of Lords, boldly

---

[1] ['Of famous orators.']

avowed himself to be an adviser of that measure. 'My colleagues, (said he,) as I was confined by indisposition, did me the signal honour of coming to the bedside of a sick man, to ask his opinion. But, had they not thus condescended, I should have *taken up my bed and walked*, in order to have delivered that opinion at the Council-Board.' Mr. Langton, who was present, mentioned this to Johnson, who observed, 'Now, Sir, we see that he took these words as he found them; without considering, that though the expression in Scripture, *take up thy bed and walk*, strictly suited the instance of the sick man restored to health and strength, who would of course be supposed to carry his bed with him, it could not be proper in the case of a man who was lying in a state of feebleness, and who certainly would not add to the difficulty of moving at all, that of carrying his bed.'

When I pointed out to him in the newspaper one of Mr. Grattan's animated and glowing speeches, in favour of the freedom of Ireland, in which this expression occurred (I know not if accurately taken): 'We will persevere, till there is not one link of the English chain left to clank upon the rags of the meanest beggar in Ireland;' 'Nay, Sir, (said Johnson,) don't you perceive that *one* link cannot clank?'

Mrs. Thrale has published,[1] as Johnson's, a kind of parody or counterpart of a fine poetical passage in one of Mr. Burke's speeches on American Taxation. It is vigorously but somewhat coarsely executed; and I am inclined to suppose, is not quite correctly exhibited. I hope he did not use the words *'vile agents'* for the Americans in the House of Parliament; and if he did so, in an extempore effusion, I wish the lady had not committed it to writing.

Mr. Burke uniformly shewed Johnson the greatest respect; and when Mr. Townshend, now Lord Sydney, at a period when he was conspicuous in opposition, threw out some reflection in parliament upon the grant of a pension to a man of such political principles as Johnson; Mr. Burke, though then of the same party with Mr. Townshend, stood warmly forth in defence of his friend, to whom, he justly observed, the pension was granted

[1] *Anecdotes*, p. 43.

solely on account of his eminent literary merit. I am well assured, that Mr. Townshend's attack upon Johnson was the occasion of his 'hitching in a rhyme;' for, that in the original copy of Goldsmith's character of Mr. Burke, in his *Retaliation*, another person's name stood in the couplet where Mr. Townshend is now introduced:—

'Though fraught with all learning kept straining his throat,
To persuade *Tommy Townshend* to lend him a vote.'

It may be worth remarking, among the *minutiæ* of my collection, that Johnson was once drawn to serve in the militia, the Trained Bands of the City of London, and that Mr. Rackstrow, of the Museum in Fleet-street, was his Colonel. It may be believed he did not serve in person; but the idea, with all its circumstances, is certainly laughable. He upon that occasion provided himself with a musket, and with a sword and belt, which I have seen hanging in his closet.

He was very constant to those whom he once employed, if they gave him no reason to be displeased. When somebody talked of being imposed on in the purchase of tea and sugar, and such articles: 'That will not be the case, (said he,) if you go to a *stately shop*, as I always do. In such a shop it is not worth their while to take a petty advantage.'

An authour of most anxious and restless vanity[1] being mentioned, 'Sir, (said he,) there is not a young sapling upon Parnassus more severely blown about by every wind of criticism than that poor fellow.'

The difference, he observed, between a well-bred and an ill-bred man is this: 'One immediately attracts your liking, the other your aversion. You love the one till you find reason to hate him; you hate the other till you find reason to love him.'

The wife[2] of one of his acquaintance had fraudulently made a purse for herself out of her husband's fortune. Feeling a proper compunction in her last moments, she confessed how much she had secreted; but before she could tell where it was placed, she was seized with a convulsive fit and expired. Her husband said,

[1] [Perhaps Richard Cumberland. *Powell.*]
[2] [Mrs. Cave. *Cooke's Life of Johnson*, p. 47.]

he was more hurt by her want of confidence in him, than by the loss of his money. 'I told him, (said Johnson,) that he should console himself: for *perhaps* the money might be *found*, and he was *sure* that his wife was *gone.*'

A foppish physician[1] once reminded Johnson of his having been in company with him on a former occasion. 'I do not remember it, Sir.' The physician still insisted; adding that he that day wore so fine a coat that it must have attracted his notice. 'Sir, (said Johnson,) had you been dipt in Pactolus, I should not have noticed you.'

He seemed to take a pleasure in speaking in his own style; for when he had carelessly missed it, he would repeat the thought translated into it. Talking of the Comedy of *The Rehearsal*, he said, 'It has not wit enough to keep it sweet.' This was easy; he therefore caught himself, and pronounced a more rounded sentence; 'It has not vitality enough to preserve it from putrefaction.'

He censured a writer[2] of entertaining Travels for assuming a feigned character, saying, (in his sense of the word,) 'He carries out one lye; we know not how many he brings back.' At another time, talking of the same person, he observed, 'Sir, your assent to a man whom you have never known to falsify, is a debt: but after you have known a man to falsify, your assent to him then is a favour.'

Though he had no taste for painting, he admired much the manner in which Sir Joshua Reynolds treated of his art, in his *Discourses to the Royal Academy*. He observed one day of a passage in them, 'I think I might as well have said this myself:' and once when Mr. Langton was sitting by him, he read one of them very eagerly, and expressed himself thus:—'Very well, Master Reynolds; very well, indeed. But it will not be understood.'

When I observed to him that Painting was so far inferiour to Poetry, that the story or even emblem which it communicates

---

[1] [Perhaps Sir Lucas Pepys. *Powell.*]
[2] [Dr. John Moore.]

must be previously known, and mentioned as a natural and laughable instance of this, that a little Miss[1] on seeing a picture of Justice with the scales, had exclaimed to me, 'See, there's a woman selling sweetmeats;' he said, 'Painting, Sir, can illustrate, but cannot inform.'

No man was more ready to make an apology when he had censured unjustly, than Johnson. When a proof-sheet of one of his works was brought to him, he found fault with the mode in which a part of it was arranged, refused to read it, and in a passion desired that the compositor[2] might be sent to him. The compositor was Mr. Manning, a decent sensible man, who had composed about one half of his *Dictionary*, when in Mr. Strahan's printing-house; and a great part of his *Lives of the Poets*, when in that of Mr. Nichols; and who (in his seventy-seventh year), when in Mr. Baldwin's printing-house, composed a part of the first edition of this work concerning him. By producing the manuscript, he at once satisfied Dr. Johnson that he was not to blame. Upon which Johnson candidly and earnestly said to him, 'Mr. Compositor, I ask your pardon. Mr. Compositor, I ask your pardon, again and again.'

His generous humanity to the miserable was almost beyond example. The following instance is well attested:—Coming home late one night, he found a poor woman lying in the street, so much exhausted that she could not walk; he took her upon his back, and carried her to his house, where he discovered that she was one of those wretched females who had fallen into the lowest state of vice, poverty, and disease. Instead of harshly upbraiding her, he had her taken care of with all tenderness for a long time, at considerable expence, till she was restored to health, and endeavoured to put her into a virtuous way of living.[3]

He thought Mr. Caleb Whitefoord singularly happy in hitting

[1] [Jeanie Campbell, Mrs. Boswell's sister's step-daughter. *Boswell Papers*, ix. 29.]

[2] Compositor in the Printing-house means, the person who adjusts the types in the order in which they are to stand for printing; and arranges what is called the *form*, from which an impression is taken.

[3] This circumstance therefore alluded to in Mr. Courtenay's *Poetical Character* of him is strictly true. My informer was Mrs. Desmoulins, who lived many years in Dr. Johnson's house.

on the signature of *Papyrius Cursor*, to his ingenious and diverting cross-readings of the newspapers; it being a real name of
an ancient Roman, and clearly expressive of the thing done in
this lively conceit.

He once in his life was known to have uttered what is called
a *bull*: Sir Joshua Reynolds, when they were riding together in
Devonshire, complained that he had a very bad horse, for that
even when going down hill he moved slowly step by step. 'Ay
(said Johnson,) and when he *goes* up hill, he *stands still.*'

He had a great aversion to gesticulating in company. He
called once to a gentleman[1] who offended him in that point,
'Don't *attitudenise.*' And when another gentleman[2] thought he
was giving additional force to what he uttered, by expressive
movements of his hands, Johnson fairly seized them, and held
them down.

An authour of considerable eminence[3] having engrossed a good
share of the conversation in the company of Johnson, and having
said nothing but what was very trifling and insignificant; Johnson when he was gone, observed to us, 'It is wonderful what a
difference there sometimes is between a man's powers of writing
and of talking. ******* writes with great spirit, but is a poor
talker; had he held his tongue we might have supposed him to
have been restrained by modesty; but he has spoken a great
deal to-day; and you have heard what stuff it was.'

A gentleman having said that a *congé d'élire* has not, perhaps,
the force of a command, but may be considered only as a strong
recommendation; 'Sir, (replied Johnson, who overheard him,)
it is such a recommendation, as if I should throw you out of a
two-pair-of-stairs window, and recommend to you to fall soft.'[4]

Mr. Steevens, who passed many a social hour with him during
their long acquaintance, which commenced when they both lived

---

[1] [Sir Richard Musgrave. *Croker*[1].]
[2] [*Hill suggests* Dr. Joseph Warton.]
[3] [Perhaps Beattie. *Hill-Powell.*]
[4] This has been printed in other publications, 'fall *to the ground.*' But
Johnson himself gave me the true expression which he had used as above;
meaning that the recommendation left as little choice in the one case as the
other.

in the Temple, has preserved a good number of particulars concerning him, most of which are to be found in the department of
Apothegms, &c. in the Collection of *Johnson's Works*. But he
has been pleased to favour me with the following, which are
original:—

'One evening, previous to the trial of Baretti, a consultation
of his friends was held at the house of Mr. Cox, the Solicitor, in
Southampton-buildings, Chancery-lane. Among others present
were, Mr. Burke and Dr. Johnson, who differed in sentiments
concerning the tendency of some part of the defence the prisoner
was to make. When the meeting was over, Mr. Steevens
observed, that the question between him and his friend had been
agitated with rather too much warmth. "It may be so, Sir,
(replied the Doctor,) for Burke and I should have been of one
opinion, if we had had no audience."

'Dr. Johnson once assumed a character in which perhaps even
Mr. Boswell never saw him. His curiosity having been excited
by the praises bestowed on the celebrated Torré's fireworks at
Marybone-Gardens, he desired Mr. Steevens to accompany him
thither. The evening had proved showery; and soon after the
few people present were assembled, publick notice was given,
that the conductors to the wheels, suns, stars, &c., were so
thoroughly water-soaked, that it was impossible any part of the
exhibition should be made. "This is a mere excuse, (says the
Doctor,) to save their crackers for a more profitable company.
Let us but hold up our sticks, and threaten to break those
coloured lamps that surround the Orchestra, and we shall soon
have our wishes gratified. The core of the fireworks cannot be
injured; let the different pieces be touched in their respective
centers, and they will do their offices as well as ever." Some
young men who overheard him, immediately began the violence
he had recommended, and an attempt was speedily made to fire
some of the wheels which appeared to have received the smallest
damage; but to little purpose were they lighted, for most of
them completely failed. The authour of *The Rambler*, however,
may be considered, on this occasion, as the ringleader of a successful riot, though not as a skilful pyrotechnist.'

'It has been supposed that Dr. Johnson, so far as fashion was concerned, was careless of his appearance in publick. But this is not altogether true, as the following slight instance may show:— Goldsmith's last Comedy was to be represented during some court-mourning; and Mr. Steevens appointed to call on Dr. Johnson, and carry him to the tavern where he was to dine with others of the Poet's friends. The Doctor was ready dressed, but in coloured cloaths; yet being told that he would find every one else in black, received the intelligence with a profusion of thanks, hastened to change his attire, all the while repeating his gratitude for the information that had saved him from an appearance so improper in the front row of a front box. "I would not (added he,) for ten pounds, have seemed so retrograde to any general observance."

'He would sometimes found his dislikes on very slender circumstances. Happening one day to mention Mr. Flexman, a Dissenting Minister, with some compliment to his exact memory in chronological matters; the Doctor replied, "Let me hear no more of him, Sir. That is the fellow who made the Index to my *Ramblers*, and set down the name of Milton thus: Milton, *Mr.* John." '

Mr. Steevens adds this testimony:—

'It is unfortunate, however, for Johnson, that his particularities and frailties can be more distinctly traced than his good and amiable exertions. Could the many bounties he studiously concealed, the many acts of humanity he performed in private, be displayed with equal circumstantiality, his defects would be so far lost in the blaze of his virtues, that the latter only would be regarded.'

Though from my very high admiration of Johnson, I have wondered that he was not courted by all the great and all the eminent persons of his time, it ought fairly to be considered, that no man of humble birth, who lived entirely by literature, in short no authour by profession, ever rose in this country into that personal notice which he did. In the course of this work a numerous variety of names has been mentioned, to which many might be added. I cannot omit Lord and Lady Lucan, at whose

house he often enjoyed all that an elegant table and the best
company can contribute to happiness; he found hospitality united
with extraordinary accomplishments, and embellished with
charms of which no man could be insensible.

On Tuesday, June 22, I dined with him at THE LITERARY
CLUB, the last time of his being in that respectable society. The
other members present were the Bishop of St. Asaph, Lord Eliot,
Lord Palmerston, Dr. Fordyce, and Mr. Malone. He looked ill;
but had such a manly fortitude, that he did not trouble the
company with melancholy complaints. They all shewed evident
marks of kind concern about him, with which he was much
pleased, and he exerted himself to be as entertaining as his
indisposition allowed him.

The anxiety of his friends to preserve so estimable a life, as
long as human means might be supposed to have influence, made
them plan for him a retreat from the severity of a British winter,
to the mild climate of Italy. This scheme was at last brought to
a serious resolution at General Paoli's, where I had often talked
of it. One essential matter, however, I understood was necessary
to be previously settled, which was obtaining such an addition
to his income, as would be sufficient to enable him to defray the
expence in a manner becoming the first literary character of a
great nation, and, independent of all his other merits, the
Authour of THE DICTIONARY OF THE ENGLISH LANGUAGE. The
person to whom I above all others thought I should apply to
negociate this business, was the Lord Chancellor,[1] because I
knew that he highly valued Johnson, and that Johnson highly
valued his Lordship; so that it was no degradation of my illustrious friend to solicit for him the favour of such a man. I have
mentioned what Johnson said of him to me when he was at the
bar; and after his Lordship was advanced to the seals, he said
of him, 'I would prepare myself for no man in England but Lord
Thurlow. When I am to meet with him I should wish to know
a day before.' How he would have prepared himself I cannot
conjecture. Would he have selected certain topicks, and considered them in every view so as to be in readiness to argue them

[1] Edward Lord Thurlow.

at all points? and what may we suppose those topicks to have been? I once started the curious enquiry to the great man who was the subject of this compliment: he smiled, but did not pursue it.

I first consulted with Sir Joshua Reynolds, who perfectly coincided in opinion with me; and I therefore, though personally very little known to his Lordship, wrote to him,[1] stating the case, and requesting his good offices for Dr. Johnson. I mentioned that I was obliged to set out for Scotland early in the following week, so that if his Lordship should have any commands for me as to this pious negociation, he would be pleased to send them before that time; otherwise Sir Joshua Reynolds would give all attention to it.

This application was made not only without any suggestion on the part of Johnson himself, but was utterly unknown to him, nor had he the smallest suspicion of it. Any insinuations, therefore, which since his death have been thrown out, as if he had stooped to ask what was superfluous, are without any foundation. But, had he asked it, it would not have been superfluous; for though the money he had saved proved to be more than his friends imagined, or than I believe he himself, in his carelessness concerning worldly matters, knew it to be, had he travelled upon the Continent, an augmentation of his income would by no means have been unnecessary.

On Wednesday, June 23, I visited him in the morning, after having been present at the shocking sight of fifteen men executed before Newgate. I said to him, I was sure that human life was not machinery, that is to say, a chain of fatality planned and directed by the Supreme Being, as it had in it so much wickedness and misery, so many instances of both, as that by which my mind was now clouded. Were it machinery it would be better than it is in these respects, though less noble, as not being a system of moral government. He agreed with me now, as he always did, upon the great question of the liberty of the

[1] It is strange that Sir John Hawkins should have related that the application was made by Sir Joshua Reynolds, when he could so easily have been informed of the truth by inquiring of Sir Joshua. Sir John's carelessness to ascertain facts is very remarkable.

human will, which has been in all ages perplexed with so much sophistry. 'But, Sir, as to the doctrine of Necessity, no man believes it. If a man should give me arguments that I do not see, though I could not answer them, should I believe that I do not see?' It will be observed, that Johnson at all times made the just distinction between doctrines *contrary* to reason, and doctrines *above* reason.

Talking of the religious discipline proper for unhappy convicts, he said, 'Sir, one of our regular clergy will probably not impress their minds sufficiently: they should be attended by a Methodist preacher,[1] or a Popish priest.' Let me however observe, in justice to the Reverend Mr. Vilette, who has been Ordinary of Newgate for no less than eighteen years, in the course of which he has attended many hundreds of wretched criminals, that his earnest and humane exhortations have been very effectual. His extraordinary diligence is highly praiseworthy, and merits a distinguished reward.[2]

On Thursday, June 24, I dined with him at Mr. Dilly's, where were the Rev. Mr. (now Dr.) Knox, master of Tunbridge-school, Mr. Smith, Vicar of Southill, Dr. Beattie, Mr. Pinkerton, authour of various literary performances, and the Rev. Dr. Mayo. At my desire old Mr. Sheridan was invited, as I was earnest to have Johnson and him brought together again by chance, that a reconciliation might be effected. Mr. Sheridan happened to come early, and having learned that Dr. Johnson was to be there, went away; so I found, with sincere regret, that my friendly intentions were hopeless. I recollect nothing that passed this day, except Johnson's quickness, who, when Dr. Beattie observed, as something remarkable which had happened to him, that he had chanced to see both No. 1, and No. 1000, of the hackney-coaches, the first and the last; 'Why, Sir,

[1] A friend of mine happened to be passing by a *field congregation* in the environs of London, when a Methodist preacher quoted this passage with triumph.

[2] I trust that THE CITY OF LONDON, now happily in unison with THE COURT, will have the justice and generosity to obtain preferment for this Reverend Gentleman, now a worthy old servant of that magnificent Corporation.

(said Johnson,) there is an equal chance for one's seeing those
two numbers as any other two.' He was clearly right; yet the
seeing of the two extremes, each of which is in some degree
more conspicuous than the rest, could not but strike one in a
stronger manner than the sight of any other two numbers.
Though I have neglected to preserve his conversation, it was
perhaps at this interview that Dr. Knox formed the notion of it
which he has exhibited in his *Winter Evenings*.

On Friday, June 25, I dined with him at General Paoli's,
where, he says in one of his letters to Mrs. Thrale, 'I love to
dine.' There was a variety of dishes much to his taste, of all
which he seemed to me to eat so much, that I was afraid he
might be hurt by it; and I whispered to the General my fear,
and begged he might not press him. 'Alas! (said the General,)
see how very ill he looks; he can live but a very short time.
Would you refuse any slight gratifications to a man under sentence of death? There is a humane custom in Italy, by which
persons in that melancholy situation are indulged with having
whatever they like best to eat and drink, even with expensive
delicacies.'

I shewed him some verses on Lichfield by Miss Seward,
which I had that day received from her, and had the pleasure to
hear him approve of them. He confirmed to me the truth of a
high compliment which I had been told he had paid to that lady,
when she mentioned to him *The Colombiade*, an epick poem, by
Madame du Boccage:—'Madam, there is not in it any thing
equal to your description of the sea round the North Pole, in
your Ode on the death of Captain Cook.'

On Sunday, June 27, I found him rather better. I mentioned
to him a young man[1] who was going to Jamaica with his wife
and children, in expectation of being provided for by two of her
brothers settled in that island, one a clergyman, and the other a
physician. JOHNSON. 'It is a wild scheme, Sir, unless he has a
positive and deliberate invitation. There was a poor girl, who
used to come about me, who had a cousin in Barbadoes, that, in

[1] [John Lawrie. J. B.'s former clerk. Boswell's Letter Book *teste* F. A.
Pottle.]

a letter to her, expressed a wish she should come out to that Island, and expatiated on the comforts and happiness of her situation. The poor girl went out: her cousin was much surprised, and asked her how she could think of coming. "Because, (said she,) you invited me." "Not I," answered the cousin. The letter was then produced. "I see it is true, (said she,) that I did invite you: but I did not think you would come." They lodged her in an out-house, where she passed her time miserably; and as soon as she had an opportunity she returned to England. Always tell this, when you hear of people going abroad to relations, upon a notion of being well received. In the case which you mention, it is probable the clergyman spends all he gets, and the physician does not know how much he is to get.'

We this day dined at Sir Joshua Reynolds's, with General Paoli, Lord Eliot, (formerly Mr. Eliot, of Port Eliot,) Dr. Beattie, and some other company. Talking of Lord Chesterfield; —JOHNSON. 'His manner was exquisitely elegant, and he had more knowledge than I expected.' BOSWELL. 'Did you find, Sir, his conversation to be of a superiour style?' JOHNSON. 'Sir, in the conversation which I had with him I had the best right to superiority, for it was upon philology and literature.' Lord Eliot, who had travelled at the same time with Mr. Stanhope, Lord Chesterfield's natural son, justly observed, that it was strange that a man who shewed he had so much affection for his son as Lord Chesterfield did, by writing so many long and anxious letters to him, almost all of them when he was Secretary of State, which certainly was a proof of great goodness of disposition, should endeavour to make his son a rascal. His Lordship told us, that Foote had intended to bring on the stage a father who had thus tutored his son, and to shew the son an honest man to every one else, but practising his father's maxims upon him, and cheating him. JOHNSON. 'I am much pleased with this design; but I think there was no occasion to make the son honest at all. No; he should be a consummate rogue: the contrast between honesty and knavery would be the stronger. It should be contrived so that the father should be the only sufferer by the son's villainy, and thus there would be poetical justice.'

He put Lord Eliot in mind of Dr. Walter Harte. 'I know (said he,) Harte was your Lordship's tutor, and he was also tutor to the Peterborough family. Pray, my Lord, do you recollect any particulars that he told you of Lord Peterborough? He is a favourite of mine, and is not enough known; his character has been only ventilated in party pamphlets.' Lord Eliot said, if Dr. Johnson would be so good as to ask him any questions, he would tell what he could recollect. Accordingly some things were mentioned. 'But, (said his Lordship,) the best account of Lord Peterborough that I have happened to meet with, is in *Captain Carleton's Memoirs*. Carleton was descended of an ancestor who had distinguished himself at the siege of Derry. He was an officer; and, what was rare at that time, had some knowledge of engineering.' Johnson said, he had never heard of the book. Lord Eliot had it at Port Eliot; but, after a good deal of enquiry, procured a copy in London, and sent it to Johnson, who told Sir Joshua Reynolds that he was going to bed when it came, but was so much pleased with it, that he sat up till he had read it through, and found in it such an air of truth, that he could not doubt of its authenticity; adding, with a smile, (in allusion to Lord Eliot's having recently been raised to the peerage,) 'I did not think a *young Lord* could have mentioned to me a book in the English history that was not known to me.'

An addition to our company came after we went up to the drawing-room; Dr. Johnson seemed to rise in spirits as his audience increased. He said, 'He wished Lord Orford's pictures, and Sir Ashton Lever's Museum, might be purchased by the publick, because both the money, and the pictures, and the curiosities, would remain in the country; whereas, if they were sold into another kingdom, the nation would indeed get some money, but would lose the pictures and curiosities, which it would be desirable we should have, for improvement in taste and natural history. The only question was, as the nation was much in want of money, whether it would not be better to take a large price from a foreign State?'

He entered upon a curious discussion of the difference between intuition and sagacity; one being immediate in its effect, the other requiring a circuitous process; one he observed was the *eye* of the mind, the other the *nose* of the mind.

A young gentleman[1] present took up the argument against him, and maintained that no man ever thinks of the *nose of the mind*, not adverting that though that figurative sense seems strange to us, as very unusual, it is truly not more forced than Hamlet's 'In my *mind's eye*, Horatio.' He persisted much too long, and appeared to Johnson as putting himself forward as his antagonist with too much presumption; upon which he called to him in a loud tone, 'What is it you are contending for, if you *be* contending?' And afterwards imagining that the gentleman retorted upon him with a kind of smart drollery, he said, 'Mr. *****, it does not become you to talk so to me. Besides, ridicule is not your talent; you have *there* neither intuition nor sagacity.' The gentleman protested that he had intended no improper freedom, but had the greatest respect for Dr. Johnson. After a short pause, during which we were somewhat uneasy,—JOHNSON. 'Give me your hand, Sir. You were too tedious, and I was too short.' MR. *****. 'Sir, I am honoured by your attention in any way.' JOHNSON. 'Come, Sir, let's have no more of it. We offended one another by our contention; let us not offend the company by our compliments.'

He now said, 'He wished much to go to Italy, and that he dreaded passing the winter in England.' I said nothing; but enjoyed a secret satisfaction in thinking that I had taken the most effectual measures to make such a scheme practicable.

On Monday, June 28, I had the honour to receive from the Lord Chancellor the following letter:—

'*To* JAMES BOSWELL, ESQ.

'SIR,—I should have answered your letter immediately; if, (being much engaged when I received it) I had not put it in my pocket, and forgot to open it till this morning.

'I am much obliged to you for the suggestion; and I will adopt and press it as far as I can. The best argument, I am sure, and I hope it is not likely to fail, is Dr. Johnson's merit. But it

---

[1] [Burke's son, Richard. *Croker*[1].]

will be necessary, if I should be so unfortunate as to miss seeing you, to converse with Sir Joshua on the sum it will be proper to ask,—in short, upon the means of setting him out. It would be a reflection on us all, if such a man should perish for want of the means to take care of his health. Yours, &c.   'THURLOW.'

This letter gave me a very high satisfaction; I next day went and shewed it to Sir Joshua Reynolds, who was exceedingly pleased with it. He thought that I should now communicate the negociation to Dr. Johnson, who might afterwards complain if the attention with which he had been honoured, should be too long concealed from him. I intended to set out for Scotland next morning; but Sir Joshua cordially insisted that I should stay another day, that Johnson and I might dine with him, that we three might talk of his Italian Tour, and, as Sir Joshua expressed himself, 'have it all out.' I hastened to Johnson, and was told by him that he was rather better to-day. BOSWELL. 'I am very anxious about you, Sir, and particularly that you should go to Italy for the winter, which I believe is your own wish.' JOHN-SON. 'It is, Sir.' BOSWELL. 'You have no objection, I presume, but the money it would require.' JOHNSON. 'Why, no, Sir.' Upon which I gave him a particular account of what had been done, and read to him the Lord Chancellor's letter. He listened with much attention; then warmly said, 'This is taking pro-digious pains about a man.' 'O! Sir, (said I, with most sincere affection,) your friends would do every thing for you.' He paused, grew more and more agitated, till tears started into his eyes, and he exclaimed with fervent emotion, 'GOD bless you all.' I was so affected that I also shed tears. After a short silence, he renewed and extended his grateful benediction, 'GOD bless you all, for JESUS CHRIST's sake.' We both remained for some time unable to speak. He rose suddenly and quitted the room, quite melted in tenderness. He staid but a short time, till he had recovered his firmness; soon after he returned I left him, having first engaged him to dine at Sir Joshua Reynolds's, next day. I never was again under that roof which I had so long reverenced.

On Wednesday, June 30, the friendly confidential dinner with

Sir Joshua Reynolds took place, no other company being present. Had I known that this was the last time that I should enjoy in this world, the conversation of a friend whom I so much respected, and from whom I derived so much instruction and entertainment, I should have been deeply affected. When I now look back to it, I am vexed that a single word should have been forgotten.

Both Sir Joshua and I were so sanguine in our expectations, that we expatiated with confidence on the liberal provision which we were sure would be made for him, conjecturing whether munificence would be displayed in one large donation, or in an ample increase of his pension. He himself catched so much of our enthusiasm, as to allow himself to suppose it not impossible that our hopes might in one way or other be realised. He said that he would rather have his pension doubled than a grant of a thousand pounds; 'For, (said he,) though probably I may not live to receive as much as a thousand pounds, a man would have the consciousness that he should pass the remainder of his life in splendour, how long soever it might be.' Considering what a moderate proportion an income of six hundred pounds a year bears to innumerable fortunes in this country, it is worthy of remark, that a man so truly great should think it splendour.

As an instance of extraordinary liberality of friendship, he told us, that Dr. Brocklesby had upon this occasion offered him a hundred a year for his life. A grateful tear started into his eye, as he spoke this in a faultering tone.

Sir Joshua and I endeavoured to flatter his imagination with agreeable prospects of happiness in Italy. 'Nay, (said he,) I must not expect much of that; when a man goes to Italy merely to feel how he breathes the air, he can enjoy very little.'

Our conversation turned upon living in the country, which Johnson, whose melancholy mind required the dissipation of quick successive variety, had habituated himself to consider as a kind of mental imprisonment. 'Yet, Sir, (said I,) there are many people who are content to live in the country.' JOHNSON. 'Sir, it is in the intellectual world as in the physical world; we are told by natural philosophers that a body is at rest in the place that is fit for it; they who are content to live in the country, are *fit* for the country.'

Talking of various enjoyments, I argued that a refinement of taste was a disadvantage, as they who have attained to it must be seldomer pleased than those who have no nice discrimination, and are therefore satisfied with every thing that comes in their way. JOHNSON. 'Nay, Sir; that is a paltry notion. Endeavour to be as perfect as you can in every respect.'

I accompanied him in Sir Joshua Reynolds's coach, to the entry of Bolt-court. He asked me whether I would not go with him to his house; I declined it, from an apprehension that my spirits would sink. We bade adieu to each other affectionately in the carriage. When he had got down upon the foot-pavement, he called out, 'Fare you well;' and without looking back, sprung away with a kind of pathetick briskness, if I may use that expression, which seemed to indicate a struggle to conceal uneasiness, and impressed me with a foreboding of our long, long separation.

I remained one day more in town, to have the chance of talking over my negociation with the Lord Chancellor; but the multiplicity of his Lordship's important engagements did not allow of it; so I left the management of the business in the hands of Sir Joshua Reynolds.

Soon after this time Dr. Johnson had the mortification of being informed by Mrs. Thrale, that, 'what she supposed he never believed,'[1] was true; namely, that she was actually going to marry Signor Piozzi, an Italian musick-master. He endeavoured to prevent it; but in vain. If she would publish the whole of the correspondence that passed between Dr. Johnson and her on the subject, we should have a full view of his real sentiments. As it is, our judgement must be biassed by that characteristick specimen which Sir John Hawkins has given us: 'Poor Thrale! I thought that either her virtue or her vice would have restrained her from such a marriage. She is now become a subject for her enemies to exult over; and for her friends, if she has any left, to forget, or pity.'[2]

---

[1] *Letters to Mrs. Thrale,* vol. ii. p. 375.
[2] Dr. Johnson's letter to Sir John Hawkins, *Life,* p. 570.

It must be admitted that Johnson derived a considerable portion of happiness from the comforts and elegancies which he
enjoyed in Mr. Thrale's family; but Mrs. Thrale assures us he
was indebted for these to her husband alone, who certainly
respected him sincerely. Her words are,—'*Veneration for his
virtue, reverence for his talents,* delight *in his conversation, and*
habitual endurance of a yoke my husband first put upon me, *and
of which he contentedly bore his share for sixteen or seventeen years,
made me go on so long with* Mr. Johnson; *but the perpetual confinement I will own to have been* terrifying *in the first years of our
friendship, and* irksome *in the last; nor could I pretend to* support
it without help, when my coadjutor was no more.'[1]

Alas! how different is this from the declarations which I have
heard Mrs. Thrale make in his life-time, without a single murmur against any peculiarities, or against any one circumstance
which attended their intimacy.

As a sincere friend of the great man whose *Life* I am writing,
I think it necessary to guard my readers against the mistaken
notion of Dr. Johnson's character, which this lady's *Anecdotes*
of him suggest; for from the very nature and form of her book,
'it lends deception lighter wings to fly.'

'Let it be remembered, (says an eminent critick,)[2] that she
has comprised in a small volume all that she could recollect of
Dr. Johnson in *twenty years*, during which period, doubtless,
some severe things were said by him; and they who read the
book in *two hours*, naturally enough suppose that his whole
conversation was of this complexion. But the fact is, I have been
often in his company, and never *once* heard him say a severe
thing to any one; and many others can attest the same. When
he did say a severe thing, it was generally extorted by ignorance
pretending to knowledge, or by extreme vanity or affectation.

'Two instances of inaccuracy, (adds he,) are peculiarly worthy
of notice:

'It is said,[3] "*That natural roughness of his manner so often*

---

[1] *Anec.* p. 293.
[2] [Malone. *Croker*[1].] Who has been pleased to furnish me with his
remarks.   [3] *Anec.* p. 183.

mentioned, would, notwithstanding the regularity of his notions, burst through them all from time to time; and he once bade a very celebrated lady, who praised him with too much zeal perhaps, or perhaps too strong an emphasis, (which always offended him,) consider what her flattery was worth, before she choaked him *with it."*

'Now let the genuine anecdote be contrasted with this. The person thus represented as being harshly treated, though a very celebrated lady,[1] was *then* just come to London from an obscure situation in the country. At Sir Joshua Reynolds's one evening, she met Dr. Johnson. She very soon began to pay her court to him in the most fulsome strain. "Spare me, I beseech you, dear Madam," was his reply. She still *laid it on.* "Pray, Madam, let us have no more of this;" he rejoined. Not paying any attention to these warnings, she continued still her eulogy. At length, provoked by this indelicate and *vain* obtrusion of compliment, he exclaimed, "Dearest lady, consider with yourself what your flattery is worth, before you bestow it so freely."

'How different does this story appear, when accompanied with all these circumstances which really belong to it, but which Mrs. Thrale either did not know, or has suppressed.

'She says, in another place,[2] *"One gentleman, however, who dined at a nobleman's house in his company, and that of* Mr. Thrale, *to whom I was obliged for the anecdote, was willing to enter the lists in defence of* King William's *character; and having opposed and contradicted* Johnson *two or three times, petulantly enough, the master of the house began to feel uneasy, and expect disagreeable consequences; to avoid which, he said, loud enough for the Doctor to hear,—'Our friend here has no meaning now in all this, except just to relate at club to-morrow how he teized* Johnson *at dinner to-day; this is all to do himself* honour.' *No, upon my word, (replied the other,) I see no* honour *in it, whatever you may do. Well, Sir, (returned* Mr. Johnson, *sternly,) if you do not see the honour, I am sure I* feel *the disgrace."*

'This is all sophisticated. Mr. Thrale was *not* in the company, though he might have related the story to Mrs. Thrale. A friend, from whom I had the story, was present; and it was *not*

[1] [Hannah More. *Mrs. Piozzi; Croker.*]   [2] *Anec.* p. 202.

at the house of a nobleman. On the observation being made by the master of the house[1] on a gentleman's[2] contradicting Johnson, that he had talked for the honour, &c., the gentleman muttered, in a low voice, "I see no honour in it;" and Dr. Johnson said nothing: so all the rest, (though *bien trouvée*) is mere garnish.'

I have had occasion several times, in the course of this work, to point out the incorrectness of Mrs. Thrale, as to particulars which consisted with my own knowledge. But indeed she has, in flippant terms enough, expressed her disapprobation of that anxious desire of authenticity which prompts a person who is to record conversations, to write them down *at the moment*.[3] Unquestionably, if they are to be recorded at all, the sooner it is done the better. This lady herself says,[4]—'*To recollect, however, and to repeat the sayings of* Dr. Johnson, *is almost all that can be done by the writers of his Life; as his life, at least since my acquaintance with him, consisted in little else than talking, when he was not* [absolutely] *employed in some serious piece of work.*'

She boasts of her having kept a common-place book; and we find she noted, at one time or other, in a very lively manner, specimens of the conversation of Dr. Johnson, and of those who talked with him; but had she done it recently, they probably would have been less erroneous; and we should have been relieved from those disagreeable doubts of their authenticity, with which we must now peruse them.

She says of him,[5]—'*He was the most charitable of mortals, without being what we call an* active friend. *Admirable at giving counsel; no man saw his way so clearly; but he* would not stir a finger *for the assistance of those to whom he was willing enough to give advice.*' And again on the same page, '*If you wanted a* slight favour, *you must apply to people of other dispositions; for* not a step would Johnson move *to obtain a man a vote in a society, to repay a compliment which might be useful or pleasing, to write a letter of request, &c., or to obtain a hundred pounds a year more for a friend*

---

[1] [Pottinger. *Mrs. Piozzi*; *Malone.*]
[2] [Hon. Thomas Fitzmaurice. *Ib.*]
[3] *Anec.* p. 44.   [4] *Ib.* p. 23.   [5] *Ib.* p. 51 [192].

who, perhaps, had already two or three. No force could urge him to diligence, no importunity could conquer his resolution to stand still.'

It is amazing that one who had such opportunities of knowing Dr. Johnson, should appear so little acquainted with his real character. I am sorry this lady does not advert, that she herself contradicts the assertion of his being obstinately defective in the *petites morales*, in the little endearing charities of social life, in conferring smaller favours; for she says,[1]—'Dr. Johnson *was liberal enough in granting literary assistance to others, I think; and innumerable are the Prefaces, Sermons, Lectures, and Dedications which he used to make for people who begged of him.'*

I am certain that a *more active friend* has rarely been found in any age. This work, which I fondly hope will rescue his memory from obloquy, contains a thousand instances of his benevolent exertions in almost every way that can be conceived; and particularly in employing his pen with a generous readiness for those to whom its aid could be useful. Indeed his obliging activity in doing little offices of kindness, both by letters and personal application, was one of the most remarkable features in his character; and for the truth of this I can appeal to a number of his respectable friends: Sir Joshua Reynolds, Mr. Langton, Mr. Hamilton, Mr. Burke, Mr. Windham, Mr. Malone, the Bishop of Dromore, Sir William Scott, Sir Robert Chambers. And can Mrs. Thrale forget the advertisements which he wrote for her husband at the time of his election contest; the epitaphs on him and her mother; the playful and even trifling verses, for the amusement of her and her daughters; his corresponding with her children, and entering into their minute concerns, which shews him in the most amiable light?

She relates,[2]—'That Mr. Ch—lm—ley unexpectedly rode up to Mr. Thrale's carriage, in which Mr. Thrale and she, and Dr. Johnson were travelling; that he paid them all his proper compliments, but observing that Dr. Johnson, who was reading, did not see him, *tapt him gently on the shoulder.* "'Tis Mr. Ch—lm—ley;" *says my husband.* "Well, Sir—and what if it is Mr. Ch—lm—ley;" *says the other, sternly, just lifting his eyes a*

[1] *Anec.* p. 193 [51].   [2] *Ib.* p. 258.

moment from his book, and returning to it again, with renewed avidity.'

This surely conveys a notion of Johnson, as if he had been grossly rude to Mr. Cholmondeley,[1] a gentleman whom he always loved and esteemed. If, therefore, there was an absolute necessity for mentioning the story at all, it might have been thought that her tenderness for Dr. Johnson's character would have disposed her to state any thing that could soften it. Why then is there a total silence as to what Mr. Cholmondeley told her?—that Johnson, who had known him from his earliest years, having been made sensible of what had doubtless a strange appearance, took occasion, when he afterwards met him, to make a very courteous and kind apology. There is another little circumstance which I cannot but remark. Her book was published in 1785, she had then in her possession a letter from Dr. Johnson, dated in 1777,[2] which begins thus:—'Cholmondeley's story shocks me, if it be true, which I can hardly think, for I am utterly unconscious of it: I am very sorry, and very much ashamed.' Why then publish the anecdote? Or if she did, why not add the circumstances, with which she was well acquainted?

In his social intercourse she thus describes him[3]:—*'Ever musing till he was called out to converse, and conversing till the fatigue of his friends, or the promptitude of his own temper to take offence, consigned him back again to silent meditation.'*

Yet, in the same book,[4] she tells us,—*'He was, however, seldom inclined to be silent, when any moral or literary question was started; and it was on such occasions that, like the Sage in "Rasselas," he spoke, and attention watched his lips; he reasoned, and conviction closed his periods.'*

His conversation, indeed, was so far from ever *fatiguing* his friends, that they regretted when it was interrupted, or ceased, and could exclaim in Milton's language,—

'With thee conversing, I forget all time.'

[1] George James Cholmondeley, Esq., grandson of George, third Earl of Cholmondeley, and one of the Commissioners of Excise; a gentleman respected for his abilities, and elegance of manners.

[2] *Letters to Mrs. Thrale*, vol. ii. p. 12.

[3] *Anec.* p. 23.   [4] *Ib.* p. 302.

I certainly, then, do not claim too much in behalf of my illustrious friend in saying, that however smart and entertaining Mrs. Thrale's *Anecdotes* are, they must not be held as good evidence against him; for wherever an instance of harshness and severity is told, I beg leave to doubt its perfect authenticity; for though there may have been *some* foundation for it, yet, like that of his reproof to the 'very celebrated lady,' it may be so exhibited in the narration as to be very unlike the real fact.

The evident tendency of the following anecdote[1] is to represent Dr. Johnson as extremely deficient in affection, tenderness, or even common civility:—'*When I one day lamented the loss of a first cousin killed in* America,—"*Prithee, my dear,* (*said he,*) *have done with canting; how would the world be the worse for it, I may ask, if all your relations were at once spitted like larks, and roasted for* Presto's *supper?*"—Presto *was the dog that lay under the table while we talked.*' I suspect this too of exaggeration and distortion. I allow that he made her an angry speech; but let the circumstances fairly appear, as told by Mr. Baretti, who was present:—

'Mrs. Thrale, while supping very heartily upon larks, laid down her knife and fork, and abruptly exclaimed, "O, my dear Mr. Johnson, do you know what has happened? The last letters from abroad have brought us an account that our poor cousin's head was taken off by a cannon-ball." Johnson, who was shocked both at the fact, and her light unfeeling manner of mentioning it, replied, "Madam, it would give *you* very little concern if all your relations were spitted like those larks, and drest for Presto's supper." '[2]

[1] *Anec.* p. 63.

[2] Upon mentioning this to my friend Mr. Wilkes, he, with his usual readiness, pleasantly matched it with the following *sentimental anecdote*. He was invited by a young man of fashion at Paris, to sup with him and a lady, who had been for some time his mistress, but with whom he was going to part. He said to Mr. Wilkes that he really felt very much for her, she was in such distress; and that he meant to make her a present of two hundred louis-d'ors. Mr. Wilkes observed the behaviour of Mademoiselle, who sighed indeed very piteously, and assumed every pathetick air of grief; but eat no less than three French pigeons, which are as large as English partridges, besides other things. Mr. Wilkes whispered the gentleman, 'We often say in England, *Excessive sorrow is exceeding dry*, but I never heard

It is with concern that I find myself obliged to animadvert on the inaccuracies of Mrs. Piozzi's *Anecdotes*, and perhaps I may be thought to have dwelt too long upon her little collection. But as from Johnson's long residence under Mr. Thrale's roof, and his intimacy with her, the account which she has given of him may have made an unfavourable and unjust impression, my duty, as a faithful biographer, has obliged me reluctantly to perform this unpleasing task.

Having left the *pious negociation*, as I called it, in the best hands, I shall here insert what relates to it. Johnson wrote to Sir Joshua Reynolds on July 6 [8], as follows:—

'I am going, I hope, in a few days, to try the air of Derbyshire, but hope to see you before I go. Let me, however, mention to you what I have much at heart. If the Chancellor should continue his attention to Mr. Boswell's request, and confer with you on the means of relieving my languid state, I am very desirous to avoid the appearance of asking money upon false pretences. I desire you to represent to his Lordship, what, as soon as it is suggested, he will perceive to be reasonable,—That, if I grow much worse, I shall be afraid to leave my physicians, to suffer the inconveniences of travel, and pine in the solitude of a foreign country; That, if I grow much better, of which indeed there is now little appearance, I shall not wish to leave my friends and my domestick comforts; for I do not travel for pleasure or curiosity; yet if I should recover, curiosity would revive. In my present state, I am desirous to make a struggle for a little longer life, and hope to obtain some help from a softer climate. Do for me what you can.'

He wrote to me July 26:—'I wish your affairs could have permitted a longer and continued exertion of your zeal and kindness. They that have your kindness may want your ardour. In the mean time I am very feeble and very dejected.'

By a letter from Sir Joshua Reynolds I was informed, that the Lord Chancellor had called on him, and acquainted him that the application had not been successful; but that his Lordship, after

Excessive sorrow is exceeding hungry. Perhaps *one* hundred will do.' The gentleman took the hint.

speaking highly in praise of Johnson, as a man who was an
honour to his country, desired Sir Joshua to let him know, that
on granting a mortgage of his pension, he should draw on his
Lordship to the amount of five or six hundred pounds; and that
his Lordship explained the meaning of the mortgage to be,
that he wished the business to be conducted in such a manner,
that Dr. Johnson should appear to be under the least possible
obligation. Sir Joshua mentioned, that he had by the same post
communicated all this to Dr. Johnson.

How Johnson was affected upon the occasion will appear from
what he wrote to Sir Joshua Reynolds:—

'Ashbourne, Sept. 9. Many words I hope are not necessary
between you and me, to convince you what gratitude is excited
in my heart by the Chancellor's liberality, and your kind
offices. . . .

'I have enclosed a letter to the Chancellor, which, when you
have read it, you will be pleased to seal with a head, or any other
general seal, and convey it to him: had I sent it directly to him,
I should have seemed to overlook the favour of your intervention.'

'*To* THE LORD HIGH CHANCELLOR[1]

'MY LORD,—After a long and not inattentive observation of
mankind, the generosity of your Lordship's .offer raises in me
not less wonder than gratitude. Bounty, so liberally bestowed,
I should gladly receive, if my condition made it necessary; for,
to such a mind, who would not be proud to own his obligations?
But it has pleased GOD to restore me to so great a measure of
health, that if I should now appropriate so much of a fortune
destined to do good, I could not escape from myself the charge
of advancing a false claim. My journey to the continent, though
I once thought it necessary, was never much encouraged by my

[1] Sir Joshua Reynolds, on account of the excellence both of the sentiment
and expression of this letter, took a copy of it which he shewed to some of
his friends; one of whom [perhaps Lady Lucan. *Powell.*], who admired it,
being allowed to peruse it leisurely at home, a copy was made, and found
its way into the newspapers and magazines. It was transcribed with some
inaccuracies. I print it from the original draft in Johnson's own hand-writing.

physicians; and I was very desirous that your Lordship should be told of it by Sir Joshua Reynolds, as an event very uncertain; for if I grew much better, I should not be willing, if much worse, not able, to migrate. Your Lordship was first solicited without my knowledge; but, when I was told, that you were pleased to honour me with your patronage, I did not expect to hear of a refusal; yet, as I have had no long time to brood hope, and have not rioted in imaginary opulence, this cold reception has been scarce a disappointment; and, from your Lordship's kindness, I have received a benefit, which only men like you are able to bestow. I shall now live *mihi carior*,[1] with a higher opinion of my own merit. I am, my Lord, your Lordship's most obliged, most grateful, and most humble servant,

'September, 1784.'   'SAM. JOHNSON.'

Upon this unexpected failure I abstain from presuming to make any remarks, or to offer any conjectures.

Having after repeated reasonings, brought Dr. Johnson to agree to my removing to London, and even to furnish me with arguments in favour of what he had opposed; I wrote to him requesting he would write them for me; he was so good as to comply, and I shall extract that part of his letter to me of June 11, as a proof how well he could exhibit a cautious yet encouraging view of it:—

'I remember, and intreat you to remember, that *virtus est vitium fugere*;[2] the first approach to riches is security from poverty. The condition on which you have my consent to settle in London is, that your expence never exceeds your annual income. Fixing this basis of security, you cannot be hurt, and you may be very much advanced. The loss of your Scottish business, which is all that you can lose, is not to be reckoned as any equivalent to the hopes and possibilities that open here upon you. If you succeed, the question of prudence is at an end; every body will think that done right which ends happily; and though

---

[1] ['more dear to myself.']
[2] ['To flee vice is the beginning of virtue.' Horace, *Epistles* I. i. 41. (Wickham.)]

your expectations, of which I would not advise you to talk too much, should not be totally answered, you can hardly fail to get friends who will do for you all that your present situation allows you to hope; and if, after a few years, you should return to Scotland, you will return with a mind supplied by various conversation, and many opportunities of enquiry, with much knowledge, and materials for reflection and instruction.'

Let us now contemplate Johnson thirty years after the death of his wife, still retaining for her all the tenderness of affection.

'*To* THE REVEREND MR. BAGSHAW, *at Bromley*[1]

'SIR,—Perhaps you may remember, that in the year 1753,[2] you committed to the ground my dear wife. I now entreat your permission to lay a stone upon her; and have sent the inscription, that, if you find it proper, you may signify your allowance.

'You will do me a great favour by showing the place where she lies, that the stone may protect her remains.

'Mr. Ryland will wait on you for the inscription,[3] and procure it to be engraved. You will easily believe that I shrink from this mournful office. When it is done, if I have strength remaining, I will visit Bromley once again, and pay you part of the respect to which you have a right from, Reverend Sir, your most humble servant,

'July 12, 1784.'   'SAM. JOHNSON.'

On the same day he wrote to Mr. Langton:—

'I cannot but think that in my languid and anxious state, I have some reason to complain that I receive from you neither enquiry nor consolation. You know how much I value your friendship, and with what confidence I expect your kindness, if I wanted any act of tenderness that you could perform; at least, if you do not know it, I think your ignorance is your own fault. Yet how long is it that I have lived almost in your neighbourhood without the least notice. I do not, however, consider this neglect as particularly shown to me; I hear two of your most

---

[1] See p. 546.   [2] A mistake for 1752.
[3] Printed in his *Works* [i. 150].

valuable friends make the same complaint. But why are all thus overlooked? You are not oppressed by sickness, you are not distracted by business; if you are sick, you are sick of leisure:— And allow yourself to be told, that no disease is more to be dreaded or avoided. Rather to do nothing than to do good, is the lowest state of a degraded mind. Boileau says to his pupil,

> '*Que les vers ne soient pas votre éternel emploi,*
>   *Cultivez vos amis.*'——

That voluntary debility, which modern language is content to term indolence, will, if it is not countcracted by resolution, render in time the strongest faculties lifeless, and turn the flame to the smoke of virtue. I do not expect nor desire to see you, because I am much pleased to find that your mother stays so long with you, and I should think you neither elegant nor grateful, if you did not study her gratification. You will pay my respects to both the ladies, and to all the young people. I am going Northward for a while, to try what help the country can give me; but, if you will write the letter will come after me.'

Next day he set out on a jaunt to Staffordshire and Derbyshire, flattering himself that he might be in some degree relieved.

During his absence from London he kept up a correspondence with several of his friends, from which I shall select what appears to me proper for publication, without attending nicely to chronological order.

To DR. BROCKLESBY, he writes, Ashbourne, July 20:—

'The kind attention which you have so long shewn to my health and happiness, makes it as much a debt of gratitude as a call of interest, to give you an account of what befals me, when accident recovers[1] me from your immediate care. The journey of the first day was performed with very little sense of fatigue; the second day brought me to Lichfield, without much lassitude; but I am afraid that I could not have borne such violent agitation for many days together. Tell Dr. Heberden, that in the coach I read *Ciceronianus* which I concluded as I entered Lichfield. My

---

[1] Johnson wrote *removes*.

affection and understanding went along with Erasmus, except
that once or twice he somewhat unskilfully entangles Cicero's
civil or moral, with his rhetorical, character. I staid five days at
Lichfield, but, being unable to walk, had no great pleasure, and
yesterday (19th) I came hither, where I am to try what air and
attention can perform. Of any improvement in my health I cannot
yet please myself with the perception. . . . The asthma has no
abatement. Opiates stop the fit, so as that I can sit and sometimes
lie easy, but they do not now procure me the power of motion;
and I am afraid that my general strength of body does not
encrease. The weather indeed is not benign; but how low is he
sunk whose strength depends upon the weather! I am now looking into Floyer who lived with his asthma to almost his ninetieth
year. His book by want of order is obscure, and his asthma, I
think, not of the same kind with mine. Something however I
may perhaps learn. My appetite still continues keen enough;
and what I consider as a symptom of radical health, I have a
voracious delight in raw summer fruit, of which I was less eager
a few years ago. You will be pleased to communicate this account
to Dr. Heberden, and if any thing is to be done, let me have
your joint opinion. Now—*abite curæ*[1];—let me inquire after the
Club.'[2]

JULY 31. 'Not recollecting that Dr. Heberden might be at
Windsor, I thought your letter long in coming. But, you know,
nocitura petuntur[3], the letter which I so much desired, tells me
that I have lost one of my best and tenderest friends.[4] My comfort is, that he appeared to live like a man that had always
before his eyes the fragility of our present existence, and was
therefore, I hope, not unprepared to meet his judge. Your attention, dear Sir, and that of Dr. Heberden, to my health, is
extremely kind. I am loth to think that I grow worse; and
cannot fairly prove even to my own partiality, that I grow much
better.'

AUGUST 5. 'I return you thanks, dear Sir, for your unwearied

---

[1] ['Hence, worries.'].   [2] At the Essex Head, Essex-street.
[3] [Juvenal, *Satires* x. 8: 'We ask things hurtful.']
[4] Mr. Allen, the printer.

attention, both medicinal and friendly, and hope to prove the effect of your care by living to acknowledge it.'

August 12. 'Pray be so kind as to have me in your thoughts, and mention my case to others as you have opportunity. I seem to myself neither to gain nor lose strength. I have lately tried milk, but have yet found no advantage, and am afraid of it merely as a liquid. My appetite is still good, which I know is dear Dr. Heberden's criterion of the *vis vitæ*[1]. As we cannot now see each other, do not omit to write, for you cannot think with what warmth of expectation I reckon the hours of a post-day.'

August 14. 'I have hitherto sent you only melancholy letters, you will be glad to hear some better account. Yesterday the asthma remitted, perceptibly remitted, and I moved with more ease than I have enjoyed for many weeks. May God continue his mercy. This account I would not delay, because I am not a lover of complaints, or complainers, and yet I have since we parted uttered nothing till now but terrour and sorrow. Write to me, dear Sir.'

August 16. 'Better I hope, and better. My respiration gets more and more ease and liberty. I went to church yesterday, after a very liberal dinner, without any inconvenience; it is indeed no long walk, but I never walked it without difficulty, since I came, before. ****** the intention was only to over-power the seeming *vis inertiæ*[2] of the pectoral and pulmonary muscles. I am favoured with a degree of ease that very much delights me, and do not despair of another race upon the stairs of the Academy. If I were, however, of a humour to see, or to show the state of my body, on the dark side, I might say,

"Quid te exempta juvat spinis de pluribus una?"[3]

The nights are still sleepless, and the water rises, though it does not rise very fast. Let us, however, rejoice in all the good that we have. The remission of one disease will enable nature to combat the rest. The squills I have not neglected; for I have taken more than a hundred drops a day, and one day took two

[1] ['living force']   [2] ['power of inertia']
[3] ['How does it relieve you to pluck out one thorn out of many?' Horace, *Epistles* II. ii. 212. (Wickham.)]

hundred and fifty, which, according to the popular equivalence of a drop to a grain, is more than half an ounce. I thank you, dear Sir, for your attention in ordering the medicines; your attention to me has never failed. If the virtue of medicines could be enforced by the benevolence of the prescriber, how soon should I be well.'

August 19. 'The relaxation of the asthma still continues, yet I do not trust it wholly to itself, but soothe it now and then with an opiate. I not only perform the perpetual act of respiration with less labour, but I can walk with fewer intervals of rest, and with greater freedom of motion. I never thought well of Dr. James's compounded medicines; his ingredients appeared to me sometimes inefficacious and trifling, and sometimes heterogeneous and destructive of each other. This prescription exhibits a composition of about three hundred and thirty grains, in which there are four grains of emetick tartar, and six drops [of] thebaick tincture. He that writes thus, surely writes for show. The basis of his medicine is the gum ammoniacum, which dear Dr. Lawrence used to give, but of which I never saw any effect. We will, if you please, let this medicine alone. The squills have every suffrage, and in the squills we will rest for the present.'

August 21. 'The kindness which you shew by having me in your thoughts upon all occasions, will, I hope, always fill my heart with gratitude. Be pleased to return my thanks to Sir George Baker, for the consideration which he has bestowed upon me. Is this the balloon that has been so long expected, this balloon to which I subscribed, but without payment? It is pity that philosophers have been disappointed, and shame that they have been cheated; but I know not well how to prevent either. Of this experiment I have read nothing; where was it exhibited? and who was the man that ran away with so much money? Continue, dear Sir, to write often and more at a time; for none of your prescriptions operate to their proper uses more certainly than your letters operate as cordials.'

August 26. 'I suffered you to escape last post without a letter, but you are not to expect such indulgence very often; for I write not so much because I have any thing to say, as because

I hope for an answer; and the vacancy of my life here makes a letter of great value. I have here little company and little amusement, and thus abandoned to the contemplation of my own miseries, I am sometimes gloomy and depressed; this too I resist as I can, and find opium, I think, useful, but I seldom take more than one grain. Is not this strange weather? Winter absorbed the spring, and now autumn is come before we have had summer. But let not our kindness for each other imitate the inconstancy of the seasons.'

Sept. 2. 'Mr. Windham has been here to see me; he came, I think, forty miles out of his way, and staid about a day and a half, perhaps I make the time shorter than it was. Such conversation I shall not have again till I come back to the regions of literature; and there Windham is, *inter stellas Luna minores.*'[1] He then mentions the effects of certain medicines, as taken, that 'Nature is recovering its original powers, and the functions returning to their proper state. God continue his mercies, and grant me to use them rightly.'

Sept. 9. 'Do you know the Duke and Duchess of Devonshire? And have you ever seen Chatsworth? I was at Chatsworth on Monday: I had indeed seen it before, but never when its owners were at home; I was very kindly received, and honestly pressed to stay: but I told them that a sick man is not a fit inmate of a great house. But I hope to go again some time.'

Sept. 11. 'I think nothing grows worse, but all rather better, except sleep, and that of late has been at its old pranks. Last evening, I felt what I had not known for a long time, an inclination to walk for amusement; I took a short walk, and came back again neither breathless nor fatigued. This has been a gloomy, frigid, ungenial summer, but of late it seems to mend; I hear the heat sometimes mentioned, but I do not feel it:

"*Præterea minimus gelido jam in corpore sanguis*
Febre calet solâ.————"[2]

[1] ['the Moon among the lesser fires.' Horace, *Odes* i. xii. 46.] It is remarkable that so good a Latin scholar as Johnson should have been so inattentive to the metre, as by mistake to have written *stellas* instead of *ignes*.

[2] ['The little blood that creeps within his veins, Is but just warmed in a hot fever's pains.' Juvenal, *Satires* x. 217. (Dryden.)]

I hope, however, with good help, to find means of supporting a winter at home, and to hear and tell at the Club what is doing, and what ought to be doing in the world. I have no company here, and shall naturally come home hungry for conversation. To wish you, dear Sir, more leisure, would not be kind; but what leisure you have, you must bestow upon me.'

SEPT. 16. 'I have now let you alone for a long time, having indeed little to say. You charge me somewhat unjustly with luxury. At Chatsworth, you should remember, that I have eaten but once; and the Doctor, with whom I live, follows a milk diet. I grow no fatter, though my stomach, if it be not disturbed by physick, never fails me. I now grow weary of solitude, and think of removing next week to Lichfield, a place of more society, but otherwise of less convenience. When I am settled, I shall write again. Of the hot weather that you mention, we have [not] had in Derbyshire very much, and for myself I seldom feel heat, and suppose that my frigidity is the effect of my distemper; a supposition which naturally leads me to hope that a hotter climate may be useful. But I hope to stand another English winter.'

LICHFIELD, SEPT. 29. 'On one day I had three letters about the air-balloon: yours was far the best, and has enabled me to impart to my friends in the country an idea of this species of amusement. In amusement, mere amusement, I am afraid it must end, for I do not find that its course can be directed so as that it should serve any purposes of communication; and it can give no new intelligence of the state of the air at different heights, till they have ascended above the height of mountains, which they seem never likely to do. I came hither on the 27th. How long I shall stay, I have not determined. My dropsy is gone, and my asthma much remitted, but I have felt myself a little declining these two days, or at least to-day; but such vicissitudes must be expected. One day may be worse than another; but this last month is far better than the former; if the next should be as much better than this, I shall run about the town on my own legs.'

OCTOBER 6. 'The fate of the balloon I do not much lament: to make new balloons, is to repeat the jest again. We now know a method of mounting into the air, and, I think, are not likely to know more. The vehicles can serve no use till we can guide them; and they can gratify no curiosity till we mount with them to greater heights than we can reach without; till we rise above the tops of the highest mountains, which we have yet not done. We know the state of the air in all its regions, to the top of Teneriffe, and therefore, learn nothing from those who navigate a balloon below the clouds. The first experiment, however, was bold, and deserved applause and reward. But since it has been performed, and its event is known, I had rather now find a medicine that can ease an asthma.'

OCTOBER 25. 'You write to me with a zeal that animates, and a tenderness that melts me. I am not afraid either of a journey to London, or a residence in it. I came down with little fatigue, and am now not weaker. In the smoky atmosphere I was delivered from the dropsy, which I consider as the original and radical disease. The town is my element;[1] there are my friends, there are my books, to which I have not yet bidden farewell, and there are my amusements. Sir Joshua told me long ago, that my vocation was to publick life, and I hope still to keep my station, till GOD shall bid me *Go in peace*.'

To MR. HOOLE:—

ASHBOURNE, AUG. 7. 'Since I was here I have two little letters from you, and have not had the gratitude to write. But every man is most free with his best friends, because he does not suppose that they can suspect him of intentional incivility. One reason for my omission is, that being in a place to which you are wholly a stranger, I have no topicks of correspondence. If you had any knowledge of Ashbourne, I could tell you of two

---

[1] His love of London continually appears. In a letter from him to Mrs. Smart, wife of his friend the Poet, which is published in a well-written life of him, prefixed to an edition of his Poems, in 1791, there is the following sentence:—'To one that has passed so many years in the pleasures and opulence of London, there are few places that can give much delight.'

Once, upon reading that line in the curious epitaph quoted in *The Spectator*,
    'Born in New-England, did in London die;'
he laughed and said, 'I do not wonder at this. It would have been strange, if born in London, he had died in New-England.'

Ashbourne men, who, being last week condemned at Derby to be hanged for a robbery, went and hanged themselves in their cell. But this, however it may supply us with talk, is nothing to you. Your kindness, I know, would make you glad to hear some good of me, but I have not much good to tell; if I grow not worse, it is all that I can say. I hope Mrs. Hoole receives more help from her migration. Make her my compliments, and write again to, dear Sir, your affectionate servant.'

Aug. 13. 'I thank you for your affectionate letter. I hope we shall both be the better for each other's friendship, and I hope we shall not very quickly be parted. Tell Mr. Nichols that I shall be glad of his correspondence, when his business allows him a little remission; though to wish him less business, that I may have more pleasure, would be too selfish. To pay for seats at the balloon is not very necessary, because in less than a minute, they who gaze at a mile's distance will see all that can be seen. About the wings, I am of your mind; they cannot at all assist it, nor I think regulate its motion. I am now grown somewhat easier in my body, but my mind is sometimes depressed. About the Club, I am in no great pain. The forfeitures go on, and the house, I hear, is improved for our future meetings. I hope we shall meet often, and sit long.'

Sept. 4. 'Your letter was, indeed, long in coming, but it was very welcome. Our acquaintance has now subsisted long, and our recollection of each other involves a great space, and many little occurrences, which melt the thoughts to tenderness. Write to me, therefore, as frequently as you can. I hear from Dr. Brocklesby and Mr. Ryland, that the Club is not crouded. I hope we shall enliven it when winter brings us together.'

To Dr. Burney:—

August 2. 'The weather, you know, has not been balmy; I am now reduced to think, and am at last content to talk of the weather. Pride must have a fall. I have lost dear Mr. Allen, and wherever I turn, the dead or the dying meet my notice, and force my attention upon misery and mortality. Mrs. Burney's escape from so much danger, and her ease after so much pain, throws, however, some radiance of hope upon the gloomy prospect. May her recovery be perfect, and her continuance long. I struggle hard for life. I take physick, and take air; my friend's chariot is always ready. We have run this morning twenty-four miles, and could run forty-eight more. *But who can run the race with death?*'

SEPT. 4. [Concerning a private transaction, in which his opinion was asked, and after giving it he makes the following reflections, which are applicable on other occasions.] 'Nothing deserves more compassion than wrong conduct with good meaning; than loss or obloquy suffered by one who, as he is conscious only of good intentions, wonders why he loses that kindness which he wishes to preserve; and not knowing his own fault, if, as may sometimes happen, nobody will tell him, goes on to offend by his endeavours to please. I am delighted by finding that our opinions are the same.[1] You will do me a real kindness by continuing to write. A post-day has now been long a day of recreation.'

Nov. 1. 'Our correspondence paused for want of topicks. I had said what I had to say on the matter proposed to my consideration; and nothing remained but to tell you, that I waked or slept; that I was more or less sick. I drew my thoughts in upon myself, and supposed yours employed upon your book. That your book has been delayed I am glad, since you have gained an opportunity of being more exact. Of the caution necessary in adjusting narratives there is no end. Some tell what they do not know, that they may not seem ignorant, and others from mere indifference about truth. All truth is not, indeed, of equal importance; but, if little violations are allowed, every violation will in time be thought little; and a writer should keep himself vigilantly on his guard against the first temptations to negligence or supineness. I had ceased to write, because respecting you I had no more to say, and respecting myself

---

[1] [Johnson wrote *that you like so well what I have done*. The text had to be faked, because Burney could not let Boswell reveal Johnson's authorship of the dedication, to the King, of his *Account of the Musical Performances in Commemoration of Handel* (1785).]

could say little good. I cannot boast of advancement, and in cases of convalescence it may be said, with few exceptions, *non progredi, est regredi.*[1] I hope I may be excepted. My great difficulty was with my sweet Fanny,[2] who, by her artifice of inserting her letter in yours, had given me a precept of frugality which I was not at liberty to neglect; and I know not who were in town under whose cover I could send my letter. I rejoice to hear that you are all so well, and have a delight particularly sympathetick in the recovery of Mrs. Burney.'

To MR. LANGTON:—

AUG. 25 [26]. 'The kindness of your last letter, and my omission to answer it, begins to give you, even in my opinion, a right to recriminate, and to charge me with forgetfulness of the absent. I will, therefore, delay no longer to give an account of myself, and wish I could relate what would please either myself or my friend. —On July 13, I left London, partly in hope of help from new air and change of place, and partly excited by the sick man's impatience of the present. I got to Lichfield in a stage vehicle, with very little fatigue, in two days, and had the consolation to find, that since my last visit my three old acquaintances are all dead. July 20, I went to Ashbourne, where I have been till now; the house in which we live is repairing. I live in too much solitude, and am often deeply dejected: I wish we were nearer, and rejoice in your removal to London. A friend, at once cheerful and serious, is a great acquisition. Let us not neglect one another for the little time which Providence allows us to hope. Of my health I cannot tell you, what my wishes persuaded me to expect, that it is much improved by the season or by remedies. I am sleepless; my legs grow weary with a very few steps, and the water breaks its boundaries in some degree. The asthma, however, has remitted; my breath is still much obstructed, but is more free than it was. Nights of watchfulness produce torpid days; I read very little, though I am alone; for I am tempted to supply in the day what I lost in bed. This is my history; like all

---

[1] ['Not to make progress is to go back.']
[2] The celebrated Miss Fanny Burney.

other histories, a narrative of misery. Yet am I so much better than in the beginning of the year, that I ought to be ashamed of complaining. I now sit and write with very little sensibility of pain or weakness; but when I rise, I shall find my legs betraying me. Of the money which you mentioned, I have no immediate need; keep it, however, for me, unless some exigence requires it. Your papers I will shew you certainly when you would see them, but I am a little angry at you for not keeping minutes of your own *acceptum et expensum*,[1] and think a little time might be spared from Aristophanes, for the *res familiares*.[2] Forgive me for I mean well. I hope, dear Sir, that you and Lady Rothes, and all the young people, too many to enumerate, are well and happy. God bless you all.'

To Mr. Windham:—

August. 'The tenderness with which you have been pleased to treat me, through my long illness, neither health nor sickness can, I hope, make me forget; and you are not to suppose, that after we parted you were no longer in my mind. But what can a sick man say, but that he is sick? His thoughts are necessarily concentered in himself; he neither receives nor can give delight; his inquiries are after alleviations of pain, and his efforts are to catch some momentary comfort. Though I am now in the neighbourhood of the Peak, you must expect no account of its wonders, of its hills, its waters, its caverns, or its mines; but I will tell you, dear Sir, what I hope you will not hear with less satisfaction, that, for about a week past, my asthma has been less afflictive.'

Lichfield. October 2. 'I believe you have been long enough acquainted with the *phænomena* of sickness, not to be surprised that a sick man wishes to be where he is not, and where it appears to every body but himself that he might easily be, without having the resolution to remove. I thought Ashbourne a solitary place, but did not come hither till last Monday. I have here more company, but my health has for this last week not advanced; and in the languor of disease how little can be done? Whither or when I shall make my next remove, I cannot tell;

[1] ['income and expense'.]   [2] ['domestic economies'.]

but I entreat you, dear Sir, to let me know, from time to time, where you may be found, for your residence is a very powerful attractive to, Sir, your most humble servant.'

'*To* MR. PERKINS

'DEAR SIR,—I cannot but flatter myself that your kindness for me will make you glad to know where I am, and in what state.

'I have been struggling very hard with my diseases. My breath has been very much obstructed, and the water has attempted to encroach upon me again. I past the first part of the summer at Oxford, afterwards I went to Lichfield, thence to Ashbourne, in Derbyshire, and a week ago I returned to Lichfield.

'My breath is now much easier, and the water is in a great measure run away, so that I hope to see you again before winter.

'Please to make my compliments to Mrs. Perkins, and to Mr. and Mrs. Barclay. I am, dear Sir, your most humble servant,

'Lichfield, Oct. 4, 1784.'   'SAM. JOHNSON.'

'*To* THE RIGHT HON. WILLIAM GERARD HAMILTON

'DEAR SIR,—Considering what reason you gave me in the spring to conclude that you took part in whatever good or evil might befal me, I ought not to have omitted so long the account which I am now about to give you. My diseases are an asthma and a dropsy, and, what is less curable, seventy-five. Of the dropsy, in the beginning of the summer, or in the spring, I recovered to a degree which struck with wonder both me and my physicians: the asthma now is[1] likewise, for a time, very much relieved. I went to Oxford, where the asthma was very tyrannical, and the dropsy began again to threaten me; but seasonable physick stopped the inundation: I then returned to London, and in July took a resolution to visit Staffordshire and Derbyshire, where I am yet struggling with my diseases. The dropsy made another attack, and was not easily ejected, but at last gave way. The asthma suddenly remitted in bed, on the

---

[1] Johnson wrote *was*, not *now is*.

13th of August, and, though now very oppressive, is, I think, still something gentler than it was before the remission. My limbs are miserably debilitated, and my nights are sleepless and tedious. When you read this, dear Sir, you are not sorry that I wrote no sooner. I will not prolong my complaints. I hope still to see you *in a happier hour*, to talk over what we have often talked, and perhaps to find new topicks of merriment, or new incitements to curiosity. I am, dear Sir, &c.

'Lichfield, Oct. 20, 1784.'   'SAM. JOHNSON.'

'To JOHN PARADISE, ESQ.[1]

'DEAR SIR,—Though in all my summer's excursion I have given you no account of myself, I hope you think better of me than to imagine it possible for me to forget you, whose kindness to me has been too great and too constant not to have made its impression on a harder breast than mine. Silence is not very culpable when nothing pleasing is suppressed. It would have alleviated none of your complaints to have read my vicissitudes of evil. I have struggled hard with very formidable and obstinate maladies; and though I cannot talk of health, think all praise due to my Creator and Preserver for the continuance of my life. The dropsy has made two attacks, and has given way to medicine; the asthma is very oppressive, but that has likewise once remitted. I am very weak, and very sleepless; but it is time to conclude the tale of misery. I hope, dear Sir, that you grow better, for you have likewise your share of human evil, and that your lady and the young charmers are well. I am, dear Sir, &c.

'Lichfield, Oct. 20, 1784.'   'SAM. JOHNSON.'

'To MR. GEORGE NICOL[2]

'DEAR SIR,—Since we parted, I have been much oppressed by my asthma, but it has lately been less laborious. When I sit I

---

[1] Son of the late Peter Paradise, Esq., his Britannick Majesty's Consul at Salonica, in Macedonia, by his lady, a native of that country. He studied at Oxford, and has been honoured by that University with the degree of LL.D. He is distinguished not only by his learning and talents, but by an amiable disposition, gentleness of manners, and a very general acquaintance with well-informed and accomplished persons of almost all nations.

[2] Bookseller to his Majesty.

am almost at ease, and I can walk, though yet very little, with less difficulty for this week past than before. I hope I shall again enjoy my friends, and that you and I shall have a little more literary conversation. Where I now am, every thing is very liberally provided for me but conversation. My friend is sick himself, and the reciprocation of complaints and groans affords not much of either pleasure or instruction. What we have not at home this town does not supply, and I shall be glad of a little imported intelligence, and hope that you will bestow, now and then, a little time on the relief and entertainment of, Sir, yours, &c.

'Ashbourne, Aug. 19, 1784.'   'SAM. JOHNSON.'

'*To* MR. CRUIKSHANK

'DEAR SIR,—Do not suppose that I forget you; I hope I shall never be accused of forgetting my benefactors. I had, till lately, nothing to write but complaints upon complaints, of miseries upon miseries; but within this fortnight I have received great relief. Have your Lectures any vacation? If you are released from the necessity of daily study, you may find time for a letter to me. [In this letter he states the particulars of his case.] In return for this account of my health, let me have a good account of yours, and of your prosperity in all your undertakings. I am, dear Sir, yours, &c.

'Ashbourne, Sept. 4, 1784.'   'SAM. JOHNSON.'

To MR. THOMAS DAVIES:—

AUGUST 14. 'The tenderness with which you always treat me, makes me culpable in my own eyes for having omitted to write in so long a separation; I had, indeed, nothing to say that you could wish to hear. All has been hitherto misery accumulated upon misery, disease corroborating disease, till yesterday my asthma was perceptibly and unexpectedly mitigated. I am much comforted with this short relief, and am willing to flatter myself that it may continue and improve. I have at present, such a degree of ease, as not only may admit the comforts, but the duties of life. Make my compliments to Mrs. Davies. Poor dear Allen, he was a good man.'

To Sir Joshua Reynolds:—

Ashbourne, July 21. 'The tenderness with which I am treated by my friends, makes it reasonable to suppose that they are desirous to know the state of my health, and a desire so benevolent ought to be gratified. I came to Lichfield in two days without any painful fatigue, and on Monday came hither, where I purpose to stay and try what air and regularity will effect. I cannot yet persuade myself that I have made much progress in recovery. My sleep is little, my breath is very much encumbered, and my legs are very weak. The water has encreased a little, but has again run off. The most distressing symptom is want of sleep.'

August 19. 'Having had since our separation, little to say that[1] could please you or myself by saying, I have not been lavish of useless letters; but I flatter myself that you will partake of the pleasure with which I can now tell you that about a week ago, I felt suddenly a sensible remission of my asthma, and consequently a greater lightness of action and motion. Of this grateful alleviation I know not the cause, nor dare depend upon its continuance, but while it lasts I endeavour to enjoy it, and am desirous of communicating, while it lasts, my pleasure to my friends. Hitherto, dear Sir, I had written before the post, which stays in this town but a little while, brought me your letter. Mr. Davies seems to have represented my little tendency to recovery in terms too splendid. I am still restless, still weak, still watery, but the asthma is less oppressive. Poor Ramsay![2] On which side soever I turn, mortality presents its formidable frown. I left three old friends at Lichfield when I was last there, and now found them all dead. I no sooner lose sight of dear Allen, than I am told that I shall see him no more. That we must all die, we always knew; I wish I had sooner remembered it.

[1] [Johnson wrote *that I*.]
[2] Allan Ramsay, Esq., painter to his Majesty, who died Aug. 10, 1784, in the 71st year of his age, much regretted by his friends.

Do not think me intrusive or importunate, if I now call, dear Sir, on you to remember it.'

SEPT. 2. 'I am glad that a little favour from the court has intercepted your furious purposes. I could not in any case have approved such publick violence of resentment, and should have considered any who encouraged it, as rather seeking sport for themselves, than honour for you. Resentment gratifies him who intended an injury, and pains him unjustly who did not intend it. But all this is now superfluous. I still continue, by GOD's mercy, to mend. My breath is easier, my nights are quieter, and my legs are less in bulk, and stronger in use. I have, however, yet a great deal to overcome, before I can yet attain even an old man's health. Write, do write to me now and then; we are now old acquaintance, and perhaps few people have lived so much and so long together, with less cause of complaint on either side. The retrospection of this is very pleasant, and I hope we shall never think on each other with less kindness.'

SEPT. 9. 'I could not answer your letter before this day, because I went on the sixth to Chatsworth, and did not come back till the post was gone. Many words, I hope, are not necessary between you and me, to convince you what gratitude is excited in my heart, by the Chancellor's liberality and your kind offices. I did not indeed expect that what was asked by the Chancellor would have been refused, but since it has, we will not tell that any thing has been asked. I have enclosed a letter to the Chancellor, which, when you have read it, you will be pleased to seal with a head, or other general seal, and convey it to him; had I sent it directly to him, I should have seemed to overlook the favour of your intervention. My last letter told you of my advance in health, which, I think, in the whole still continues. Of the hydropick tumour there is now very little appearance; the asthma is much less troublesome, and seems to remit something day after day. I do not despair of supporting an English winter. At Chatsworth, I met young Mr. Burke, who led me very commodiously into conversation with the Duke and Duchess. We had a very good morning. The dinner was publick.'

SEPT. 18. 'I flattered myself that this week would have given me a letter from you, but none has come. Write to me now and then, but direct your next to Lichfield. I think, and I hope, am sure, that I still grow better; I have sometimes good nights; but am still in my legs weak, but so much mended, that I go to Lichfield in hope of being able to pay my visits on foot, for there are no coaches. I have three letters this day, all about the balloon, I could have been content with one. Do not write about the balloon, whatever else you may think proper to say.'

OCTOBER 2. 'I am always proud of your approbation, and therefore was much pleased that you liked my letter. When you copied it, you invaded the Chancellor's right rather than mine. The refusal I did not expect, but I had never thought much about it, for I doubted whether the Chancellor had so much tenderness for me as to ask. He, being keeper of the King's conscience, ought not to be supposed capable of an improper petition. All is not gold that glitters, as we have often been told; and the adage is verified in your place and my favour; but if what happens does not make us richer, we must bid it welcome, if it makes us wiser. I do not at present grow better, nor much worse; my hopes, however, are somewhat abated, and a very great loss is the loss of hope, but I struggle on as I can.'

To MR. JOHN NICHOLS:—

LICHFIELD, OCT. 20. 'When you were here, you were pleased, as I am told, to think my absence an inconvenience. I should certainly have been very glad to give so skilful a lover of antiquities any information about my native place, of which, however, I know not much, and have reason to believe that not much is known. Though I have not given you any amusement, I have received amusement from you. At Ashbourne, where I had very little company, I had the luck to borrow *Mr. Bowyer's Life*; a book so full of contemporary history, that a literary man must find some of his old friends. I thought that I could, now and then, have told you some hints worth your notice; and perhaps we may talk a life over. I hope we shall be much together; you must now be to me what you were before, and what dear Mr. Allen was, besides. He was taken unexpectedly away, but

I think he was a very good man. I have made little progress in recovery. I am very weak, and very sleepless; but I live on and hope.'

This various mass of correspondence, which I have thus brought together, is valuable, both as an addition to the store which the publick already has of Johnson's writings, and as exhibiting a genuine and noble specimen of vigour and vivacity of mind, which neither age nor sickness could impair or diminish.

It may be observed, that his writing in every way, whether for the publick, or privately to his friends, was by fits and starts; for we see frequently, that many letters are written on the same day. When he had once overcome his aversion to begin, he was, I suppose, desirous to go on, in order to relieve his mind from the uneasy reflection of delaying what he ought to do.

While in the country, notwithstanding the accumulation of illness which he endured, his mind did not lose its powers. He translated an Ode of Horace, which is printed in his *Works*, and composed several prayers. I shall insert one of them, which is so wise and energetick, so philosophical and so pious, that I doubt not of its affording consolation to many a sincere Christian, when in a state of mind to which I believe the best are sometimes liable.[1]

And here I am enabled fully to refute a very unjust reflection, by Sir John Hawkins, both against Dr. Johnson, and his faithful

---

[1] *Against inquisitive and perplexing thoughts.* 'O LORD, my Maker and Protector, who hast graciously sent me into this world to work out my salvation, enable me to drive from me all such unquiet and perplexing thoughts as may mislead or hinder me in the practice of those duties which Thou hast required. When I behold the works of thy hands, and consider the course of thy providence, give me grace always to remember that thy thoughts are not my thoughts, nor thy ways my ways. And while it shall please Thee to continue me in this world, where much is to be done, and little to be known, teach me by thy Holy Spirit, to withdraw my mind from unprofitable and dangerous inquiries, from difficulties vainly curious, and doubts impossible to be solved. Let me rejoice in the light which Thou hast imparted, let me serve Thee with active zeal and humble confidence, and wait with patient expectation for the time in which the soul which Thou receivest shall be satisfied with knowledge. Grant this, O LORD, for JESUS CHRIST's sake. Amen.'

servant, Mr. Francis Barber; as if both of them had been guilty of culpable neglect towards a person of the name of Heely, whom Sir John chooses to call a *relation* of Dr. Johnson's. The fact is, that Mr. Heely was not his relation; he had indeed been married to one of his cousins, but she had died without having children, and he had married another woman; so that even the slight connection which there once had been by *alliance* was dissolved. Dr. Johnson, who had shewn very great liberality to this man while his first wife was alive, as has appeared in a former part of this work,[1] was humane and charitable enough to continue his bounty to him occasionally; but surely there was no strong call of duty upon him or upon his legatee, to do more. The following letter, obligingly communicated to me by Mr. Andrew Strahan, will confirm what I have stated:—

'*To* MR. HEELY, *No. 5, in Pye-street, Westminster*

'SIR,—As necessity obliges you to call so soon again upon me, you should at least have told the smallest sum that will supply your present want; you cannot suppose that I have much to spare. Two guineas is as much as you ought to be behind with your creditor. If you wait on Mr. Strahan, in New-street, Fetter-lane, or in his absence, on Mr. Andrew Strahan, shew this, by which they are entreated to advance you two guineas, and to keep this as a voucher. I am, Sir, your humble servant,

'Ashbourne, Aug. 12, 1784.'   'SAM. JOHNSON.'

Indeed it is very necessary to keep in mind that Sir John Hawkins has unaccountably viewed Johnson's character and conduct in almost every particular, with an unhappy prejudice.[2]

---

[1] P. 377.

[2] I shall add one instance only to those which I have thought it incumbent on me to point out. Talking of Mr Garrick's having signified his willingness to let Johnson have the loan of any of his books to assist him in his edition of Shakspeare [p. 493]; Sir John says (p. 444), 'Mr. Garrick knew not what risque he ran by this offer. Johnson had so strange a forgetfulness of obligations of this sort, that few who lent him books ever saw them again.' This surely conveys a most unfavourable insinuation, and has been so understood. Sir John mentions the single case of a curious edition of Politian [*ante*, p. 65], which he tells us, 'appeared to belong to Pembroke College, and which,

We now behold Johnson for the last time, in his native city, for which he ever retained a warm affection, and which, by a sudden apostrophe, under the word *Lich*, he introduces with reverence, into his immortal Work, THE ENGLISH DICTIONARY: *Salve magna parens!*[1] While here, he felt a revival of all the tenderness of filial affection, an instance of which appeared in his ordering the grave-stone and inscription over Elizabeth Blaney[2] to be substantially and carefully renewed.

To Mr. Henry White, a young clergyman, with whom he now formed an intimacy, so as to talk to him with great freedom,

probably, had been considered by Johnson as his own, for upwards of fifty years.' Would it not be fairer to consider this as an inadvertence, and draw no general inference? The truth is, that Johnson was so attentive, that in one of his manuscripts in my possession, he has marked in two columns, books borrowed, and books lent.

In Sir John Hawkins's compilation, there are, however, some passages concerning Johnson which have unquestionable merit. One of them I shall transcribe, in justice to a writer whom I have had too much occasion to censure, and to shew my fairness as the biographer of my illustrious friend: 'There was wanting in his conduct and behaviour, that dignity which results from a regular and orderly course of action, and by an irresistible power commands esteem. He could not be said to be a stayed man, nor so to have adjusted in his mind the balance of reason and passion, as to give occasion to say what may be observed of some men, that all they do is just, fit, and right.' [Hawkins's *Johnson*, p. 409.] Yet a judicious friend [probably Malone. *Powell*.] well suggests, 'It might, however, have been added, that such men are often merely just, and rigidly correct, while their hearts are cold and unfeeling; and that Johnson's virtues were of a much higher tone than those of the *stayed, orderly man*, here described.'

[1] ['Hail, great Mother!' Virgil, *Georgics* ii. 173.] The following circumstance, mutually to the honour of Johnson, and the corporation of his native city, has been communicated to me by the Reverend Dr. Vyse, from the Town-Clerk:—'Mr. Simpson has now before him, a record of the respect and veneration which the Corporation of Lichfield, in the year 1767, had for the merits and learning of Dr. Johnson. His father built the corner-house in the Market-place, the two fronts of which, towards Market and Broad- [Bread-] market-street, stood upon waste land of the Corporation, under a forty years' lease, which was then expired. On the 15th of August, 1767, at a common-hall of the bailiffs and citizens, it was ordered (and that without any solicitation,) that a lease should be granted to Samuel Johnson, Doctor of Laws, of the encroachments at his house, for the term of ninety-nine years, at the old rent, which was five shillings. Of which, as Town-Clerk, Mr. Simpson had the honour and pleasure of informing him, and that he was desired to accept it, without paying any fine on the occasion, which lease was afterwards granted, and the Doctor died possessed of this property.'

[2] See p. 28.

he mentioned that he could not in general accuse himself of having been an undutiful son. 'Once, indeed, (said he,) I was disobedient; I refused to attend my father to Uttoxeter-market. Pride was the source of that refusal, and the remembrance of it was painful. A few years ago, I desired to atone for this fault; I went to Uttoxeter in very bad weather, and stood for a considerable time bareheaded in the rain, on the spot where my father's stall used to stand. In contrition I stood, and I hope the penance was expiatory.'

'I told him (says Miss Seward) in one of my latest visits to him, of a wonderful learned pig, which I had seen at Nottingham; and which did all that we have observed exhibited by dogs and horses. The subject amused him.' 'Then, (said he,) the pigs are a race unjustly calumniated. *Pig* has, it seems, not been wanting to *man*, but *man* to *pig*. We do not allow *time* for his education, we kill him at a year old.' Mr. Henry White, who was present, observed that if this instance had happened in or before Pope's time, he would not have been justified in instancing the swine as the lowest degree of groveling instinct. Dr. Johnson seemed pleased with the observation, while the person who made it proceeded to remark, that great torture must have been employed, ere the indocility of the animal could have been subdued. 'Certainly, (said the Doctor;) but, (turning to me,) how old is your pig?' I told him, three years old. 'Then, (said he,) the pig has no cause to complain; he would have been killed the first year if he had not been *educated*, and protracted existence is a good recompence for very considerable degrees of torture.'

As Johnson had now very faint hopes of recovery, and as Mrs. Thrale was no longer devoted to him, it might have been supposed that he would naturally have chosen to remain in the comfortable house of his beloved wife's daughter, and end his life where he began it. But there was in him an animated and lofty spirit, and however complicated diseases might depress ordinary mortals, all who saw him, beheld and acknowledged the *invictum animum Catonis*.[1] Such was his intellectual ardour

[1] [*atrocem animum Catonis*. 'Cato's stubborn soul'; or, with *invictum*, 'unsubdued soul'. Horace, *Odes* II. i. 24.] Mr. Burke suggested to me as

even at this time, that he said to one friend, 'Sir, I look upon every day to be lost, in which I do not make a new acquaintance;' and to another, when talking of his illness, 'I will be conquered; I will not capitulate.' And such was his love of London, so high a relish had he of its magnificent extent, and variety of intellectual entertainment, that he languished when absent from it, his mind having become quite luxurious from the long habit of enjoying the metropolis; and, therefore, although at Lichfield, surrounded with friends, who loved and revered him, and for whom he had a very sincere affection, he still found that such conversation as London affords, could be found no where else. These feelings, joined, probably, to some flattering hopes of aid from the eminent physicians and surgeons in London, who kindly and generously attended him without accepting of fees, made him resolve to return to the capital.

From Lichfield he came to Birmingham, where he passed a few days with his worthy old schoolfellow, Mr. Hector, who thus writes to me:—'He was very solicitous with me to recollect some of our most early transactions, and transmit them to him, for I perceive nothing gave him greater pleasure than calling to mind those days of our innocence. I complied with his request, and he only received them a few days before his death. I have transcribed for your inspection, exactly the minutes I wrote to him.' This paper having been found in his repositories after his death, Sir John Hawkins has inserted it entire, and I have made occasional use of it, and other communications from Mr. Hector,[1]

applicable to Johnson, what Cicero, in his *Cato Major*, says of Appius: 'Intentum enim animum tanquam arcum habebat, nec languescens succumbebat senectuti' [His mind was always resilient as a strung bow, and he was never affected by the slackening of old age]; repeating at the same time, the following noble words in the same passage: 'Ita enim senectus honesta est, si se ipsa defendit, si jus suum retinet, si nemini emancipata est, si usque ad extremum vitæ spiritum vindicet jus suum' [A truly admirable old age is one in which a man still defends his opinions, still claims justice for himself, is beholden to no-one, and sticks up for his just rights to his last breath].

[1] It is a most agreeable circumstance attending the publication of this Work, that Mr. Hector has survived his illustrious schoolfellow so many years; that he still retains his health and spirits; and has gratified me with

in the course of this Work. I have both visited and corresponded with him since Dr. Johnson's death, and by my inquiries concerning a great variety of particulars have obtained additional information. I followed the same mode with the Reverend Dr. Taylor, in whose presence I wrote down a good deal of what he could tell; and he, at my request, signed his name, to give it authenticity. It is very rare to find any person who is able to give a distinct account of the life even of one whom he has known intimately, without questions being put to them. My friend, Dr. Kippis, has told me, that on this account it is a practice with him to draw out a biographical catechism.

Johnson then proceeded to Oxford, where he was again kindly received by Dr. Adams, who was pleased to give me the following account in one of his letters (Feb. 17th, 1785):—

'His last visit was, I believe, to my house, which he left after a stay of four or five days. We had much serious talk together, for which I ought to be the better as long as I live. You will remember some discourse which we had in the summer upon the subject of prayer, and the difficulty of this sort of composition. He reminded me of this, and of my having wished him to try his hand, and to give us a specimen of the style and manner that he approved. He added, that he was now in a right frame of mind, and as he could not possibly employ his time better, he would in earnest set about it. But I find upon enquiry, that no papers of this sort were left behind him, except a few short ejaculatory forms suitable to his present situation.'

Dr. Adams had not then received accurate information on this subject; for it has since appeared that various prayers had been composed by him at different periods, which, intermingled with pious resolutions, and some short notes of his life, were entitled by him *Prayers and Meditations*, and have, in pursuance of his earnest requisition, in the hopes of doing good, been published,

the following acknowledgement: 'I thank you, most sincerely thank you, for the great and long continued entertainment your *Life of Dr. Johnson* has afforded me, and others, of my particular friends.' Mr. Hector, besides setting me right as to the verses on a sprig of Myrtle (see p. 67 note), has favoured me with two English odes, written by Dr. Johnson, at an early period of his life, which will appear in my edition of his Poems.

with a judicious well-written Preface, by the Reverend Mr. Strahan, to whom he delivered them. This admirable collection, to which I have frequently referred in the course of this Work, evinces, beyond all his compositions for the publick, and all the eulogies of his friends and admirers, the sincere virtue and piety of Johnson. It proves with unquestionable authenticity, that amidst all his constitutional infirmities, his earnestness to conform his practice to the precepts of Christianity was unceasing, and that he habitually endeavoured to refer every transaction of his life to the will of the Supreme Being.

He arrived in London on the 16th of November, and next day sent to Dr. Burney the following note, which I insert as the last token of his remembrance of that ingenious and amiable man, and as another of the many proofs of the tenderness and benignity of his heart:—

'MR. JOHNSON, who came home last night, sends his respects to dear Dr. Burney, and all the dear Burneys, little and great.'

To MR. HECTOR, *in Birmingham*

'DEAR SIR,—I did not reach Oxford until Friday morning, and then I sent Francis to see the balloon fly, but could not go myself. I staid at Oxford till Tuesday, and then came in the common vehicle easily to London. I am as I was, and having seen Dr. Brocklesby, am to ply the squills; but, whatever be their efficacy, this world must soon pass away. Let us think seriously on our duty. I send my kindest respects to dear Mrs. Careless: let me have the prayers of both. We have all lived long, and must soon part. GOD have mercy on us, for the sake of our Lord JESUS CHRIST. Amen. I am, &c.

'London, Nov. 17, 1784.'   'SAM. JOHNSON.'

His correspondence with me, after his letter on the subject of my settling in London, shall now, so far as is proper, be produced in one series:—

July 26, he wrote to me from Ashbourne:—

'On the 14th I came to Lichfield, and found every body glad enough to see me. On the 20th, I came hither, and found a house half-built, of very uncomfortable appearance; but my own room has not been altered. That a man worn with diseases, in his seventy-second or third year, should condemn part of his remaining life to pass among ruins and rubbish, and that no inconsiderable part, appears to me very strange. I know that your kindness makes you impatient to know the state of my health, in which I cannot boast of much improvement. I came through the journey without much inconvenience, but when I attempt self-motion I find my legs weak, and my breath very short; this day I have been much disordered. I have no company; the Doctor[1] is busy in his fields, and goes to bed at nine, and his whole system is so different from mine, that we seem formed for different elements; I have, therefore, all my amusement to seek within myself.'

Having written to him, in bad spirits, a letter filled with dejection and fretfulness, and at the same time expressing anxious apprehensions concerning him, on account of a dream which had disturbed me; his answer was chiefly in terms of reproach, for a supposed charge of 'affecting discontent, and indulging the vanity of complaint.' It, however, proceeded,—

'Write to me often, and write like a man. I consider your fidelity and tenderness as a great part of the comforts which are yet left me, and sincerely wish we could be nearer to each other. . . . My dear friend, life is very short and very uncertain; let us spend it as well as we can. My worthy neighbour, Allen, is dead. Love me as well as you can. Pay my respects to dear Mrs. Boswell. Nothing ailed me at that time; let your superstition at last have an end.'

Feeling very soon, that the manner in which he had written might hurt me, he two days afterwards, July 28,[2] wrote to me again, giving me an account of his sufferings; after which, he thus proceeds:—

'Before this letter, you will have had one which I hope you

---

[1] The Rev. Dr. Taylor.

[2] [This date can hardly be right; Johnson probably wrote on or about 7 August. Boswell's mistake came from adding two days to his last date, 26 July; he overlooked the intervening letter, to which he had not given a date.]

will not take amiss; for it contains only truth, and that truth kindly intended. . . . *Spartam quam nactus es orna*;[1] make the most and best of your lot, and compare yourself not with the few that are above you, but with the multitudes which are below you. . . . Go steadily forward with lawful business or honest diversions. *Be* (as Temple says of the Dutchmen) *well when you are not ill, and pleased when you are not angry*. . . . This may seem but an ill return for your tenderness; but I mean it well, for I love you with great ardour and sincerity. Pay my respects to dear Mrs. Boswell, and teach the young ones to love me.'

I unfortunately was so much indisposed during a considerable part of the year, that it was not, or at least I thought it was not, in my power to write to my illustrious friend as formerly, or without expressing such complaints as offended him. Having conjured him not to do me the injustice of charging me with affectation, I was with much regret long silent. His last letter to me then came, and affected me very tenderly:—

'To JAMES BOSWELL, ESQ.

'DEAR SIR,—I have this summer sometimes amended, and sometimes relapsed, but, upon the whole, have lost ground, very much. My legs are extremely weak, and my breath very short, and the water is now encreasing upon me. In this uncomfortable state your letters used to relieve; what is the reason that I have them no longer? Are you sick, or are you sullen? Whatever be the reason, if it be less than necessity, drive it away; and of the short life that we have, make the best use for yourself and for your friends. . . . I am sometimes afraid that your omission to write has some real cause, and shall be glad to know that you are not sick, and that nothing ill has befallen dear Mrs. Boswell, or any of your family. I am, Sir, your, &c.

'Lichfield, Nov. 3, 1784.'   'SAM. JOHNSON.'

Yet it was not a little painful to me to find, that in a paragraph of this letter, which I have omitted, he still persevered in arraign-

---

[1] ['Sparta is your country, make the most of it.' Erasmus, *Chiliades* II. i (1559), p. 485.]

ing me as before, which was strange in him who had so much experience of what I suffered. I, however, wrote to him two as kind letters as I could; the last of which came too late to be read by him, for his illness encreased more rapidly upon him than I had apprehended; but I had the consolation of being informed that he spoke of me on his death-bed, with affection, and I look forward with humble hope of renewing our friendship in a better world.

I now relieve the readers of this Work from any farther personal notice of its authour, who if he should be thought to have obtruded himself too much upon their attention, requests them to consider the peculiar plan of his biographical undertaking.

Soon after Johnson's return to the metropolis, both the asthma and dropsy became more violent and distressful. He had for some time kept a journal in Latin of the state of his illness, and the remedies which he used, under the title of *Ægri Ephemeris*,[1] which he began on the 6th of July, but continued it no longer than the 8th of November; finding, I suppose, that it was a mournful and unavailing register. It is in my possession; and is written with great care and accuracy.

Still his love of literature[2] did not fail. A very few days before

---

[1] ['A sick man's journal.']

[2] It is truly wonderful to consider the extent and constancy of Johnson's literary ardour, notwithstanding the melancholy which clouded and embittered his existence. Besides the numerous and various works which he executed, he had, at different times, formed schemes of a great many more, of which the following catalogue was given by him to Mr. Langton, and by that gentleman presented to his Majesty:

'DIVINITY.

'A small book of precepts and directions for piety; the hint taken from the directions in Morton's exercise.

'PHILOSOPHY, HISTORY, and LITERATURE in general.

'*History of Criticism*, as it relates to judging of authours, from Aristotle to the present age. An account of the rise and improvements of that art; of the different opinions of authours, ancient and modern.

'Translation of the *History of Herodian*.

'New edition of Fairfax's Translation of *Tasso*, with notes, glossary, &c.

'Chaucer, a new edition of him, from manuscripts and old editions, with various readings, conjectures, remarks on his language, and the changes it

his death he transmitted to his friend Mr. John Nichols, a list
of the authours of the *Universal History*, mentioning their several

had undergone from the earliest times to his age, and from his to the present:
with notes explanatory of customs, &c., and references to Boccace, and other
authours from whom he has borrowed, with an account of the liberties he
has taken in telling the stories; his life, and an exact etymological glossary.

'Aristotle's *Rhetorick*, a translation of it into English.

'A Collection of Letters, translated from the modern writers, with some
account of the several authours.

'Oldham's Poems, with notes, historical and critical.

'Roscommon's Poems, with notes.

'Lives of the Philosophers, written with a polite air, in such a manner as
may divert as well as instruct.

'History of the Heathen Mythology, with an explication of the fables,
both allegorical and historical; with references to the poets.

'History of the State of Venice, in a compendious manner.

'Aristotle's *Ethicks*, an English translation of them, with notes.

'Geographical Dictionary, from the French.

'Hierocles upon Pythagoras, translated into English, perhaps with notes.
This is done by Norris.

'A book of Letters, upon all kinds of subjects.

'Claudian, a new edition of his works, *cum notis variorum*, in the manner of
Burman.

'Tully's Tusculan Questions, a translation of them.

'Tully's De Naturâ Deorum, a translation of those books.

'Benzo's New History of the New World, to be translated.

'Machiavel's History of Florence, to be translated.

'History of the Revival of Learning in Europe, containing an account of
whatever contributed to the restoration of literature; such as controversies,
printing, the destruction of the Greek empire, the encouragement of great
men, with the lives of the most eminent patrons and most eminent early
professors of all kinds of learning in different countries.

'A Body of Chronology, in verse, with historical notes.

'A Table of the Spectators, Tatlers, and Guardians, distinguished by
figures into six degrees of value, with notes, giving the reasons of preference or degradation.

'A Collection of Letters from English authours, with a preface giving
some account of the writers; with reasons for selection, and criticism upon
styles; remarks on each letter, if needful.

'A Collection of Proverbs from various languages. Jan. 6,—53.

'A Dictionary to the Common Prayer, in imitation of Calmet's *Dictionary
of the Bible*. March,—52.

'A Collection of Stories and Examples, like those of Valerius Maximus.
Jan. 10,—53.

'From Ælian, a volume of select Stories, perhaps from others. Jan. 28,
—53.

'Collection of Travels, Voyages, Adventures, and Descriptions of
Countries.

'Dictionary of Ancient History and Mythology.

shares in that work. It has, according to his direction, been deposited in the British Museum, and is printed in the *Gentleman's Magazine* for December, 1784.

'Treatise on the Study of Polite Literature, containing the history of learning, directions for editions, commentaries, &c.

'Maxims, Characters, and Sentiments, after the manner of Bruyère, collected out of ancient authours, particularly the Greek, with Apophthegms.

'Classical Miscellanies, Select Translations from ancient Greek and Latin authours.

'Lives of Illustrious Persons, as well of the active as the learned, in imitation of Plutarch.

'Judgement of the learned upon English authours.

'Poetical Dictionary of the English tongue.

'Considerations upon the present state of London.

'Collection of Epigrams, with notes and observations.

'Observations on the English language, relating to words, phrases, and modes of Speech.

'Minutiæ Literariæ, Miscellaneous reflections, criticisms, emendations, notes.

'History of the Constitution.

'Comparison of Philosophical and Christian Morality, by sentences collected from the moralists and fathers.

'Plutarch's Lives, in English, with notes.

           'POETRY and works of IMAGINATION.

'Hymn to Ignorance.

'The Palace of Sloth,—a vision.

'Coluthus, to be translated.

'Prejudice,—a poetical essay.

'The Palace of Nonsense,—a vision.'

Johnson's extraordinary facility of composition, when he shook off his constitutional indolence, and resolutely sat down to write, is admirably described by Mr. Courtenay, in his *Poetical Review*, which I have several times quoted:

> 'While through life's maze he sent a piercing view,
> His mind expansive to the object grew.
> With various stores of erudition fraught,
> The lively image, the deep-searching thought,
> Slept in repose;—but when the moment press'd,
> The bright ideas stood at once confess'd;
> Instant his genius sped its vigorous rays,
> And o'er the letter'd world diffus'd a blaze:
> As womb'd with fire the cloud electrick flies,
> And calmly o'er th' horizon seems to rise;
> Touch'd by the pointed steel, the lightning flows,
> And all th' expanse with rich effulgence glows.'

We shall in vain endeavour to know with exact precision every production of Johnson's pen. He owned to me, that he had written about forty sermons; but as I understood that he had given or sold them to different persons, who were to preach them as their own, he did not consider himself at liberty to

During his sleepless nights he amused himself by translating
into Latin verse, from the Greek, many of the epigrams in the

acknowledge them. Would those who were thus aided by him, who are still
alive, and the friends of those who are dead, fairly inform the world, it
would be obligingly gratifying a reasonable curiosity, to which there should,
I think, now be no objection. Two volumes of them, published since his
death, are sufficiently ascertained; see p. 861. I have before me, in
his hand-writing, a fragment of twenty quarto leaves, of a translation into
English of Sallust, *De Bello Catilinario.* When it was done I have no notion;
but it seems to have no very superior merit to mark it as his. Beside the
publications heretofore mentioned, I am satisfied, from internal evidence, to
admit also as genuine the following, which, notwithstanding all my chronological care, escaped me in the course of this work:

'Considerations on the Case of Dr. Trapp's Sermons,'† published in
1739, in the *Gentleman's Magazine.* It is a very ingenious defence of the
right of *abridging* an authour's work, without being held as infringing his
property. This is one of the nicest questions in the *Law of Literature*; and I
cannot help thinking, that the indulgence of abridging is often exceedingly
injurious to authours and booksellers, and should in very few cases be
permitted. At any rate, to prevent difficult and uncertain discussion, and
give an absolute security to authours in the property of their labours, no
abridgement whatever should be permitted, till after the expiration of such
a number of years as the Legislature may be pleased to fix.

But, though it has been confidently ascribed to him, I cannot allow that
he wrote a Dedication to both Houses of Parliament of a book entitled *The
Evangelical History Harmonized.* He was no *croaker*; no declaimer against
the times. He would not have written, 'That we are fallen upon an age in
which corruption is not barely universal, is universally confessed.' Nor
'Rapine preys on the publick without opposition, and perjury betrays it
without inquiry.' Nor would he, to excite a speedy reformation, have conjured up such phantoms of terrour as these: 'A few years longer, and perhaps
all endeavours will be in vain. We may be swallowed by an earthquake: we
may be delivered to our enemies.' This is not Johnsonian.

There are, indeed, in this Dedication, several sentences constructed upon
the model of those of Johnson. But the imitation of the form, without the
spirit of his style, has been so general, that this of itself is not sufficient
evidence. Even our newspaper writers aspire to it. In an account of the
funeral of Edwin, the comedian, in *The Diary* of Nov. 9, 1790, that son of
drollery is thus described: 'A man who had so often cheered the sullenness
of vacancy, and suspended the approaches of sorrow.' And in *The Dublin
Evening Post*, August 16, 1791, there is the following paragraph: 'It is a
singular circumstance, that, in a city like this, containing 200,000 people,
there are three months in the year during which no place of publick amusement is open. Long vacation is here a vacation from pleasure, as well as
business; nor is there any mode of passing the listless evenings of declining
summer, but in the riots of a tavern, or the stupidity of a coffee-house.'

I have not thought it necessary to specify every copy of verses written
by Johnson, it being my intention to publish an authentick edition of all his
Poetry, with notes.

Anthologia. These translations, with some other poems by him in Latin, he gave to his friend Mr. Langton, who, having added a few notes, sold them to the booksellers for a small sum, to be given to some of Johnson's relations, which was accordingly done; and they are printed in the collection of his works.

A very erroneous notion has circulated as to Johnson's deficiency in the knowledge of the Greek language, partly owing to the modesty with which, from knowing how much there was to be learnt, he used to mention his own comparative acquisitions. When Mr. Cumberland[1] talked to him of the Greek fragments which are so well illustrated in *The Observer*, and of the Greek dramatists in general, he candidly acknowledged his insufficiency in that particular branch of Greek literature. Yet it may be said, that though not a great, he was a good Greek scholar. Dr. Charles Burney, the younger, who is universally acknowledged by the best judges to be one of the few men of this age who are very eminent for their skill in that noble language, has assured me, that Johnson could give a Greek word for almost every English one; and that although not sufficiently conversant in the niceties of the language, he upon some occasions discovered, even in these, a considerable degree of critical acumen. Mr. Dalzel, Professor of Greek at Edinburgh, whose skill in it is unquestionable, mentioned to me, in very liberal terms, the impression which was made upon him by Johnson, in a conversation which they had in London concerning that language. As Johnson, therefore, was undoubtedly one of the first Latin scholars in modern times, let us not deny to his fame some additional splendour from Greek.

I shall now fulfil my promise of exhibiting specimens of various sorts of imitation of Johnson's style.

In the *Transactions of the Royal Irish Academy*, 1787, there is an 'Essay on the Style of Dr. Samuel Johnson,' by the Reverend

---

[1] Mr. Cumberland assures me, that he was always treated with great courtesy by Dr. Johnson, who, in his *Letters to Mrs. Thrale*, vol. ii. p. 68, thus speaks of that learned, ingenious, and accomplished gentleman: 'The want of company is an inconvenience: but Mr. Cumberland is a million.'

Robert Burrowes, whose respect for the great object of his criticism[1] is thus evinced in the concluding paragraph:—

'I have singled him out from the whole body of English writers, because his universally-acknowledged beauties would be most apt to induce imitation; and I have treated rather on his faults than his perfections, because an essay might comprize all the observations I could make upon his faults, while volumes would not be sufficient for a treatise on his perfections.'

Mr. Burrowes has analysed the composition of Johnson, and pointed out its peculiarities with much acuteness; and I would recommend a careful perusal of his Essay to those, who being captivated by the union of perspicuity and splendour which the writings of Johnson contain, without having a sufficient portion of his vigour of mind, may be in danger of becoming bad copyists of his manner. I, however, cannot but observe, and I observe it to his credit, that this learned gentleman has himself caught no mean degree of the expansion and harmony, which, independent of all other circumstances, characterise the sentences of Johnson. Thus, in the Preface to the volume in which his Essay appears, we find:—

'If it be said that in societies of this sort, too much attention is frequently bestowed on subjects barren and speculative, it may be answered, that no one science is so little connected with the rest, as not to afford many principles whose use may extend considerably beyond the science to which they primarily belong; and that no proposition is so purely theoretical as to be totally incapable of being applied to practical purposes. There is no apparent connection between duration and the cycloidal arch, the properties of which duly attended to, have furnished us with our best regulated methods of measuring time: and he who has made himself master of the nature and affections of the logarithmick curve, is not aware that he has advanced considerably towards ascertaining the proportionable density of the air at its various distances from the surface of the earth.'

---

[1] We must smile at a little inaccuracy of metaphor in the Preface to the *Transactions*, which is written by Mr. Burrowes. The *critick of the style of* Johnson having, with a just zeal for literature, observed, that the whole nation are called on to exert themselves, afterwards says: 'They are *called on* by every *tye* which can have a laudable influence on the heart of man.'

The ludicrous imitators of Johnson's style are innumerable. Their general method is to accumulate hard words, without considering, that, although he was fond of introducing them occasionally, there is not a single sentence in all his writings where they are crowded together, as in the first verse of the following imaginary Ode by him to Mrs. Thrale, which appeared in the newspapers:—

> '*Cervisial coctor's viduate* dame,
> *Opin'st* thou this gigantick frame,
> *Procumbing* at thy shrine:
> Shall, *catenated* by thy charms,
> A captive in thy *ambient* arms,
> *Perennially* be thine?'

This, and a thousand other such attempts, are totally unlike the original, which the writers imagined they were turning into ridicule. There is not similarity enough for burlesque, or even for caricature.

Mr. COLMAN, in his *Prose on several occasions*, has *A Letter from* LEXIPHANES; *containing Proposals for a Glossary or Vocabulary of the Vulgar Tongue: intended as a Supplement to a larger* DICTIONARY. It is evidently meant as a sportive sally of ridicule on Johnson, whose style is thus imitated, without being grossly overcharged:—

'It is easy to foresee, that the idle and illiterate will complain that I have increased their labours by endeavouring to diminish them; and that I have explained what is more easy by what is more difficult—*ignotum per ignotius*.[1] I expect, on the other hand, the liberal acknowledgements of the learned. He who is buried in scholastick retirement, secluded from the assemblies of the gay, and remote from the circles of the polite, will at once comprehend the definitions, and be grateful for such a seasonable and necessary elucidation of his mother-tongue.

'Annexed to this letter is a short specimen of the work, thrown together in a vague and desultory manner, not even adhering to alphabetical concatenation.'[2]

---

[1] ['The unknown by the less well-known.']

[2] '*Higgledy piggledy*,—Conglomeration and confusion.
'*Hodge-podge*,—A culinary mixture of heterogeneous ingredients: applied metaphorically to all discordant combinations.

The serious imitators of Johnson's style, whether intentionally or by the imperceptible effect of its strength and animation, are, as I have had already occasion to observe, so many, that I might introduce quotations from a numerous body of writers in our language, since he appeared in the literary world. I shall point out only the following:—

William Robertson, D.D.

'In other parts of the globe, man, in his rudest state, appears as lord of the creation, giving law to various tribes of animals which he has tamed and reduced to subjection. The Tartar follows his prey on the horse which he has reared, or tends his numerous herds, which furnish him both with food and clothing; the Arab has rendered the camel docile, and avails himself of its persevering strength; the Laplander has formed the rein-deer to be subservient to his will; and even the people of Kamschatka have trained their dogs to labour. This command over the inferiour creatures is one of the noblest prerogatives of man, and among the greatest efforts of his wisdom and power. Without this, his dominion is incomplete. He is a monarch who has no subjects; a master without servants; and must perform every operation by the strength of his own arm.'[1]

Edward Gibbon, Esq.

'Of all our passions and appetites, the love of power is of the most imperious and unsociable nature, since the pride of one man requires the submission of the multitude. In the tumult of civil discord the laws of society lose their force, and their place is seldom supplied by those of humanity. The ardour of contention, the pride of victory, the despair of success, the memory of

'*Tit for Tat*,—Adequate retaliation.
'*Shilly Shally*,—Hesitation and irresolution.
'*Fee! fau! fum!*—Gigantick intonations.
'*Rigmarole*,—Discourse, incoherent and rhapsodical.
'*Crincum-crancum*,—Lines of irregularity and involution.
'*Dingdong*,—Tintinabulary chimes, used metaphorically to signify dispatch and vehemence.'
[1] *History of America*, vol. i. quarto, p. 332.

past injuries, and the fear of future dangers, all contribute to inflame the mind, and to silence the voice of pity.'[1]

Miss Burney

'My family, mistaking ambition for honour, and rank for dignity, have long planned a splendid connection for me, to which, though my invariable repugnance has stopped any advances, their wishes and their views immovably adhere. I am but too certain they will now listen to no other. I dread, therefore, to make a trial where I despair of success; I know not how to risk a prayer with those who may silence me by a command.'[2]

Reverend Mr. Nares[3]

'In an enlightened and improving age, much perhaps is not to be apprehended from the inroads of mere caprice; at such a period it will generally be perceived, that needless irregularity is the worst of all deformities, and that nothing is so truly elegant in language as the simplicity of unviolated analogy. Rules will, therefore, be observed, so far as they are known and acknowledged: but, at the same time, the desire of improvement having been once excited will not remain inactive; and its efforts, unless assisted by knowledge, as much as they are prompted by zeal, will not unfrequently be found pernicious; so that the very persons whose intention it is to perfect the instrument of reason, will deprave and disorder it unknowingly. At such a time, then, it becomes peculiarly necessary that the analogy of language should be fully examined and understood; that its rules should be carefully laid down; and that it should be clearly known [shown] how much it contains, which being already right should be defended from change and violation: how much it has

---

[1] *Decline and Fall of the Roman Empire*, vol. i. chap. iv.

[2] *Cecilia*, Book vii. chap. i. [v.]

[3] The passage which I quote is taken from that gentleman's *Elements of Orthoepy*; containing a distinct View of the whole Analogy of the English Language, so far as relates to *Pronunciation, Accent, and Quantity*, London, 1784. I beg leave to offer my particular acknowledgements to the authour of a work of uncommon merit and great utility. I know no book which contains, in the same compass, more learning, polite literature, sound sense, accuracy of arrangement, and perspicuity of expression.

that demands amendment; and how much that, for fear of greater inconveniences, must, perhaps, be left unaltered, though irregular.'

A distinguished authour[1] in *The Mirror*,[2] a periodical paper, published at Edinburgh, has imitated Johnson very closely. Thus, in No. 16:—'The effects of the return of spring have been frequently remarked as well in relation to the human mind as to the animal and vegetable world. The reviving power of this season has been traced from the fields to the herds that inhabit them, and from the lower classes of beings up to man. Gladness and joy are described as prevailing through universal Nature, animating the low of the cattle, the carol of the birds, and the pipe of the shepherd.'

The Reverend Dr. KNOX, master of Tunbridge school, appears to have the *imitari aveo*[3] of Johnson's style perpetually in his mind; and to his assiduous, though not servile, study of it, we may partly ascribe the extensive popularity of his writings.[4]

In his *Essays, Moral and Literary*, No. 3, we find the following passage:—'The polish of external grace may indeed be deferred till the approach of manhood. When solidity is obtained by

[1] ⌐Henry Mackenzie. *Hill-Powell.*⌐

[2] That collection was presented to Dr. Johnson, I believe by its authours; and I heard him speak very well of it.

[3] ⌐'eager emulation.' Lucretius, iii. 6.⌐

[4] It were to be wished, that he had imitated that great man in every respect, and had not followed the example of Dr. Adam Smith in ungraciously attacking his venerable *Alma Mater* Oxford. It must, however, be observed, that he is much less to blame than Smith: he only objects to certain particulars; Smith to the whole institution; though indebted for much of his learning to an exhibition which he enjoyed for many years at Balliol College. Neither of them, however, will do any hurt to the noblest university in the world. While I animadvert on what appears to me exceptionable in some of the works of Dr. Knox, I cannot refuse due praise to others of his productions: particularly his sermons, and to the spirit with which he maintains, against presumptuous hereticks, the consolatory doctrines peculiar to the Christian Revelation. This he has done in a manner equally strenuous and conciliating. Neither ought I to omit mentioning a remarkable instance of his candour. Notwithstanding the wide difference of our opinions, upon the important subject of University education, in a letter to me concerning this Work, he thus expresses himself: 'I thank you for the very great entertainment your *Life of Johnson* gives me. It is a most valuable work. Yours is a new species of biography. Happy for Johnson, that he had so able a recorder of his wit and wisdom.'

pursuing the modes prescribed by our forefathers, then may the file be used. The firm substance will bear attrition, and the lustre then acquired will be durable.'

There is, however, one in No. 11, which is blown up into such tumidity, as to be truly ludicrous. The writer means to tell us, that Members of Parliament, who have run in debt by extravagance, will sell their votes to avoid an arrest,[1] which he thus expresses: —'They who build houses and collect costly pictures and furniture with the money of an honest artisan or mechanick, will be very glad of emancipation from the hands of a bailiff, by a sale of their senatorial suffrage.'

But I think the most perfect imitation of Johnson is a professed one, entitled *A Criticism on Gray's Elegy in a Country Church-Yard*, said to be written by Mr. Young, Professor of Greek, at Glasgow, and of which let him have the credit, unless a better title can be shewn. It has not only the peculiarities of Johnson's style, but that very species of literary discussion and illustration for which he was eminent. Having already quoted so much from others, I shall refer the curious to this performance, with an assurance of much entertainment.

Yet whatever merit there may be in any imitations of Johnson's style, every good judge must see that they are obviously different from the original; for all of them are either deficient in its force, or overloaded with its peculiarities; and the powerful sentiment to which it is suited is not to be found.

Johnson's affection for his departed relations seemed to grow warmer as he approached nearer to the time when he might hope to see them again. It probably appeared to him that he should upbraid himself with unkind inattention, were he to leave the world without having paid a tribute of respect to their memory.

'*To* Mr. Green, Apothecary, *at Lichfield*

'Dear Sir,—I have enclosed the Epitaph for my Father, Mother, and Brother, to be all engraved on the large size, and

[1] Dr. Knox, in his *Moral and Literary* abstraction, may be excused for not knowing the political regulations of his country. No senator can be in the hands of a bailiff.

laid in the middle aisle in St. Michael's church, which I request
the clergyman and church-wardens to permit.

'The first care must be to find the exact place of interment,
that the stone may protect the bodies. Then let the stone be
deep, massy, and hard; and do not let the difference of ten
pounds, or more, defeat our purpose.

'I have enclosed ten pounds, and Mrs. Porter will pay you
ten more, which I gave her for the same purpose. What more is
wanted shall be sent; and I beg that all possible haste may be
made, for I wish to have it done while I am yet alive. Let me
know, dear Sir, that you receive this. I am, Sir, your most
humble servant,

'Dec. 2, 1784.'   'SAM. JOHNSON.'

'*To* MRS. LUCY PORTER, *in Lichfield*

'DEAR MADAM,—I am very ill, and desire your prayers. I
have sent Mr. Green the Epitaph, and a power to call on you for
ten pounds.

'I laid this summer a stone over Tetty, in the chapel of
Bromley, in Kent. The inscription is in Latin, of which this is
the English. [Here a translation.]

'That this is done, I thought it fit that you should know. What
care will be taken of us, who can tell? May GOD pardon and
bless us, for JESUS CHRIST's sake. I am, &c.

'Dec. 2, 1784.'   'SAM. JOHNSON.'

My readers are now, at last, to behold SAMUEL JOHNSON preparing himself for that doom, from which the most exalted
powers afford no exemption to man. Death had always been to
him an object of terrour; so that, though by no means happy, he
still clung to life with an eagerness at which many have wondered. At any time when he was ill, he was very much pleased
to be told that he looked better. An ingenious member[1] of the
Eumelian Club,[2] informs me, that upon one occasion when he

[1] [William Seward. *Mrs. Piozzi.*]

[2] A Club in London, founded by the learned and ingenious physician,
Dr. Ash, in honour of whose name it was called *Eumelian*, from the Greek
Εὐμέλιας; though it was warmly contended, and even put to a vote, that it
should have the more obvious appellation of *Fraxinean*, from the Latin.

said to him that he saw health returning to his cheek, Johnson seized him by the hand and exclaimed, 'Sir, you are one of the kindest friends I ever had.'

His own state of his views of futurity will appear truly rational; and may, perhaps, impress the unthinking with seriousness.

'You know, (says he,)[1] I never thought confidence with respect to futurity, any part of the character of a brave, a wise, or a good man. Bravery has no place where it can avail nothing; wisdom impresses strongly the consciousness of those faults, of which it is, perhaps, itself an aggravation; and goodness, always wishing to be better, and imputing every deficience to criminal negligence, and every fault to voluntary corruption, never dares to suppose the condition of forgiveness fulfilled, nor what is wanting in the crime supplied by penitence.

'This is the state of the best; but what must be the condition of him whose heart will not suffer him to rank himself among the best, or among the good? Such must be his dread of the approaching trial, as will leave him little attention to the opinion of those whom he is leaving for ever; and the serenity that is not felt, it can be no virtue to feign.'

His great fear of death, and the strange dark manner in which Sir John Hawkins imparts the uneasiness which he expressed on account of offences with which he charged himself, may give occasion to injurious suspicions, as if there had been something of more than ordinary criminality weighing upon his conscience. On that account, therefore, as well as from the regard to truth which he inculcated,[2] I am to mention, (with all possible respect and delicacy, however,) that his conduct, after he came to London, and had associated with Savage and others, was not so strictly virtuous, in one respect, as when he was a younger man. It was well known, that his amorous inclinations were uncommonly strong and impetuous. He owned to many of his friends, that he used to take women of the town to taverns, and hear them relate their history. In short, it must not be concealed, that, like many other good and pious men, among whom we

[1] Mrs. Thrale's Collection [of *Letters*], March 10, 1784. Vol. ii. p. 350.
[2] See what he said to Mr. Malone, p. 1105 of this volume.

may place the Apostle Paul upon his own authority, Johnson was not free from propensities which were ever 'warring against the law of his mind,'—and that in his combats with them, he was sometimes overcome.

Here let the profane and licentious pause; let them not thoughtlessly say that Johnson was an *hypocrite*, or that his *principles* were not firm, because his *practice* was not uniformly conformable to what he professed.

Let the question be considered independent of moral and religious association; and no man will deny that thousands, in many instances, act against conviction. Is a prodigal, for example, an *hypocrite*, when he owns he is satisfied that his extravagance will bring him to ruin and misery? We are *sure* he *believes* it; but immediate inclination, strengthened by indulgence, prevails over that belief in influencing his conduct. Why then shall credit be refused to the *sincerity* of those who acknowledge their persuasion of moral and religious duty, yet sometimes fail of living as it requires? I heard Dr. Johnson once observe, 'There is something noble in publishing truth, though it condemns one's self.'[1] And one who said in his presence, 'he had no notion of people being in earnest in their good professions, whose practice was not suitable to them,' was thus reprimanded by him:—'Sir, are you so grossly ignorant of human nature as not to know that a man may be very sincere in good principles, without having good practice?'[2]

But let no man encourage or soothe himself in 'presumptuous sin,' from knowing that Johnson was sometimes hurried into indulgences which he thought criminal. I have exhibited this circumstance as a shade in so great a character, both from my sacred love of truth, and to shew that he was not so weakly scrupulous as he has been represented by those who imagine

---

[1] *Journal of a Tour to the Hebrides*, 3rd ed. p. 209. [Sept. 14.] On the same subject, in his Letter to Mrs. Thrale, dated Nov. 29, 1783, he makes the following just observation:—'Life, to be worthy of a rational being, must be always in progression; we must always purpose to do more or better than in time past. The mind is enlarged and elevated by mere purposes, though they end as they began [in the original, *begin*], by airy contemplation. We compare and judge, though we do not practise.'

[2] *Journal of a Tour to the Hebrides*, p. 374. [Oct. 25.]

that the sins, of which a deep sense was upon his mind, were merely such little venial trifles as pouring milk into his tea on Good-Friday. His understanding will be defended by my statement, if his consistency of conduct be in some degree impaired. But what wise man would, for momentary gratifications, deliberately subject himself to suffer such uneasiness as we find was experienced by Johnson in reviewing his conduct as compared with his notion of the ethicks of the gospel? Let the following passages be kept in remembrance:—

'O, GOD, giver and preserver of all life, by whose power I was created, and by whose providence I am sustained, look down upon me with tenderness and mercy; grant that I may not have been created to be finally destroyed; that I may not be preserved to add wickedness to wickedness.'[1] 'O, LORD, let me not sink into total depravity; look down upon me, and rescue me at last from the captivity of sin.'[2] 'Almighty and most merciful Father, who hast continued my life from year to year, grant that by longer life I may become less desirous of sinful pleasures, and more careful of eternal happiness.'[3] 'Let not my years be multiplied to increase my guilt; but as my age advances, let me become more pure in my thoughts, more regular in my desires, and more obedient to thy laws.'[4] 'Forgive, O merciful LORD, whatever I have done contrary to thy laws. Give me such a sense of my wickedness as may produce true contrition and effectual repentance; so that when I shall be called into another state, I may be received among the sinners to whom sorrow and reformation have obtained pardon, for JESUS CHRIST's sake. Amen.'[5]

Such was the distress of mind, such the penitence of Johnson, in his hours of privacy, and in his devout approaches to his Maker. His *sincerity*, therefore, must appear to every candid mind unquestionable.

It is of essential consequence to keep in view, that there was in this excellent man's conduct no false principle of *commutation*, no *deliberate* indulgence in sin, in consideration of a counter-

[1] *Pr. and Med.* p. 47.   [2] *Ib.* p. 68.
[3] *Ib.* p. 84.   [4] *Ib.* p. 120.   [5] *Ib.* p. 130.

balance of duty. His offending, and his repenting, were distinct and separate:[1] and when we consider his almost unexampled attention to truth, his inflexible integrity, his constant piety, who will dare to 'cast a stone' at him? Besides, let it never be forgotten, that he cannot be charged with any offence indicating badness of *heart*, any thing dishonest, base, or malignant; but that, on the contrary, he was charitable in an extraordinary degree: so that even in one of his own rigid judgements of himself, (Easter-eve, 1781,) while he says, 'I have corrected no external habits;' he is obliged to own, 'I hope that since my last communion I have advanced, by pious reflections, in my submission to GOD, and my benevolence to man.'[2]

I am conscious that this is the most difficult and dangerous part of my biographical work, and I cannot but be very anxious concerning it. I trust that I have got through it, preserving at once my regard to truth,—to my friend,—and to the interests of virtue and religion. Nor can I apprehend that more harm can ensue from the knowledge of the irregularity of Johnson, guarded as I have stated it, than from knowing that Addison and Parnell were intemperate in the use of wine; which he himself, in his *Lives* of those celebrated writers and pious men, has not forborne to record.

It is not my intention to give a very minute detail of the particulars of Johnson's remaining days, of whom it was now evident, that the crisis was fast approaching, when he must '*die like men, and fall like one of the Princes.*' Yet it will be instructive, as well as gratifying to the curiosity of my readers, to record a few circumstances, on the authenticity of which they may perfectly rely, as I have been at the utmost pains to obtain an accurate account of his last illness, from the best authority.

Dr. Heberden, Dr. Brocklesby, Dr. Warren, and Dr. Butter, physicians, generously attended him, without accepting of any fees, as did Mr. Cruikshank, surgeon; and all that could be done

---

[1] Dr. Johnson related, with very earnest approbation, a story of a gentleman, who, in an impulse of passion, overcame the virtue of a young woman. When she said to him, 'I am afraid we have done wrong!' he answered, 'Yes, we have done wrong;—for I would not *debauch her mind*.'

[2] *Pr. and Med.*, p. 192.

from professional skill and ability, was tried, to prolong a life
so truly valuable. He himself, indeed, having, on account of his
very bad constitution, been perpetually applying himself to medical inquiries, united his own efforts with those of the gentlemen
who attended him; and imagining that the dropsical collection
of water which oppressed him might be drawn off by making
incisions in his body, he, with his usual resolute defiance of pain,
cut deep, when he thought that his surgeon had done it too
tenderly.[1]

About eight or ten days before his death, when Dr. Brocklesby
paid him his morning visit, he seemed very low and desponding,
and said, 'I have been as a dying man all night.' He then emphatically broke out, in the words of Shakspeare:—

> 'Can'st thou not minister to a mind diseas'd;
> Pluck from the memory a rooted sorrow;
> Raze out the written troubles of the brain;
> And, with some sweet oblivious antidote,
> Cleanse the stuff'd bosom of that perilous stuff,
> Which weighs upon the heart?'

To which Dr. Brocklesby readily answered, from the same great
poet:—

> '——————— therein the patient
> Must minister to himself.'

Johnson expressed himself much satisfied with the application.

On another day after this, when talking on the subject of
prayer, Dr. Brocklesby repeated from Juvenal,—

> '*Orandum est, ut sit mens sana in corpore sano,*'[2]

and so on to the end of the tenth satire; but in running it quickly
over, he happened, in the line,

> '*Qui spatium vitæ extremum inter munera ponat,*'[3]

[1] This bold experiment, Sir John Hawkins has related in such a manner as
to suggest a charge against Johnson of intentionally hastening his end; a
charge so very inconsistent with his character in every respect, that it is
injurious even to refute it, as Sir John has thought it necessary to do. It is
evident, that what Johnson did in hopes of relief, indicated an extraordinary
eagerness to retard his dissolution.

[2] ['We should pray for a sound mind in a sound body.' Juvenal, x. 356.]

[3] ['Who reckons long life the least of [Nature's] gifts.' *Ib.* x. 358.]

to pronounce *supremum* for *extremum*; at which Johnson's critical ear instantly took offence, and discoursing vehemently on the unmetrical effect of such a lapse, he shewed himself as full as ever of the spirit of the grammarian.

Having no near relations, it had been for some time Johnson's intention to make a liberal provision for his faithful servant, Mr. Francis Barber, whom he looked upon as particularly under his protection, and whom he had all along treated truly as an humble friend. Having asked Dr. Brocklesby what would be a proper annuity to bequeath to a favourite servant, and being answered that it must depend on the circumstances of the master; and, that in the case of a nobleman, fifty pounds a year was considered as an adequate reward for many years' faithful service; 'Then, (said Johnson,) shall I be *nobilissimus*,[1] for I mean to leave Frank seventy pounds a year, and I desire you to tell him so.' It is strange, however, to think, that Johnson was not free from that general weakness of being averse to execute a will, so that he delayed it from time to time; and had it not been for Sir John Hawkins's repeatedly urging it, I think it is probable that his kind resolution would not have been fulfilled. After making one, which, as Sir John Hawkins informs us, extended no further than the promised annuity, Johnson's final disposition of his property was established by a Will and Codicil, of which copies are subjoined.[2]

---

[1] ['most noble.']
[2] 'IN THE NAME OF GOD. AMEN. I, SAMUEL JOHNSON, being in full possession of my faculties, but fearing this night may put an end to my life, do ordain this my last Will and Testament. I bequeath to GOD, a soul polluted with many sins, but I hope purified by JESUS CHRIST. I leave seven hundred and fifty pounds in the hands of Bennet Langton, Esq.: three hundred pounds in the hands of Mr. Barclay and Mr. Perkins, brewers; one hundred and fifty pounds in the hands of Dr. Percy, Bishop of Dromore; one thousand pounds, three *per cent.* annuities, in the publick funds; and one hundred pounds now lying by me in ready money: all these before-mentioned sums and property I leave, I say, to Sir Joshua Reynolds, Sir John Hawkins, and Dr. William Scott, of Doctors Commons, in trust, for the following uses:— That is to say, to pay to the representatives of the late William Innys, bookseller, in St. Paul's Church-yard, the sum of two hundred pounds; to Mrs. White, my female servant, one hundred pounds stock in the three *per cent.* annuities aforesaid. The rest of the aforesaid sums of money and property, together with my books, plate, and household furniture, I leave

The consideration of the numerous papers of which he was possessed, seems to have struck Johnson's mind with a sudden

to the before-mentioned Sir Joshua Reynolds, Sir John Hawkins, and Dr. William Scott, also in trust, to be applied, after paying my debts, to the use of Francis Barber, my man-servant, a negro, in such a manner as they shall judge most fit and available to his benefit. And I appoint the aforesaid Sir Joshua Reynolds, Sir John Hawkins, and Dr. William Scott, sole executors of this my last will and testament, hereby revoking all former wills and testaments whatever. In witness whereof I hereunto subscribe my name, and affix my seal, this eighth day of December, 1784.

　　　　　　　　　　　　　　　　　　'SAM. JOHNSON, (L. S.)

'Signed, sealed, published, declared, and delivered, by the said testator as his last will and testament, in the presence of us, the word *two* being first inserted in the opposite page.
　　　　　　　　　　　　　　　　　　'GEORGE STRAHAN.
　　　　　　　　　　　　　　　　　　'JOHN DESMOULINS.'

'By way of Codicil to my last Will and Testament, I, SAMUEL JOHNSON, give, devise, and bequeath, my messuage or tenement situate at Lichfield, in the county of Stafford, with the appurtenances, in the tenure or occupation of Mrs. Bond, of Lichfield aforesaid, or of Mr. Hinchman, her under-tenant, to my executors, in trust, to sell and dispose of the same; and the money arising from such sale I give and bequeath as follows, viz. to Thomas and Benjamin, the sons of Fisher Johnson, late of Leicester, and —— Whiting, daughter of Thomas Johnson, late of Coventry, and the grand-daughter of the said Thomas Johnson, one full and equal fourth part each; but in case there shall be more grand-daughters than one of the said Thomas Johnson, living at the time of my decease, I give and bequeath the part or share of that one to and equally between such grand-daughters. I give and bequeath to the Rev. Mr. Rogers, of Berkley, near Froom, in the county of Somerset, the sum of one hundred pounds, requesting him to apply the same towards the maintenance of Elizabeth Herne, a lunatick. I also give and bequeath to my god-children, the son and daughter of Mauritius Lowe, painter, each of them, one hundred pounds of my stock in the three *per. cent.* consolidated annuities, to be applied and disposed of by and at the discretion of my Executors, in the education or settlement in the world of them my said legatees. Also I give and bequeath to Sir John Hawkins, one of my Executors, the Annales Ecclesiastici of Baronius, and Holinshed's and Stowe's Chronicles, and also an octavo Common Prayer-Book. To Bennet Langton, Esq. I give and bequeath my Polyglot Bible. To Sir Joshua Reynolds, my great French Dictionary, by Martiniere, and my own copy of my folio English Dictionary, of the last revision. To Dr. William Scott, one of my Executors, the Dictionnaire de Commerce, and Lectius's edition of the Greek poets. To Mr. Windham, Poetæ Græci Heroici per Henricum Stephanum. To the Rev. Mr. Strahan, vicar of Islington, in Middlesex, Mill's Greek Testament, Beza's Greek Testament, by Stephens, all my Latin Bibles, and my Greek Bible, by Wechelius. To Dr. Heberden, Dr. Brocklesby, Dr. Butter, and Mr. Cruikshank, the surgeon who attended me, Mr. Holder, my apothecary, Gerard Hamilton, Esq., Mrs. Gardiner, of Snowhill, Mrs. Frances Reynolds, Mr. Hoole, and the Reverend Mr. Hoole, his son, each a book at their election, to keep as a token of remembrance. I also anxiety, and as they were in great confusion, it is much to be lamented that he had not entrusted some faithful and discreet

give and bequeath to Mr. John Desmoulins, two hundred pounds consolidated three *per cent.* annuities: and to Mr. Sastres, the Italian master, the sum of five pounds, to be laid out in books of piety for his own use. And whereas the said Bennet Langton hath agreed, in consideration of the sum of seven hundred and fifty pounds, mentioned in my Will to be in his hands, to grant and secure an annuity of seventy pounds payable during the life of me and my servant, Francis Barber, and the life of the survivor of us, to Mr. George Stubbs, in trust for us; my mind and will is, that in case of my decease before the said agreement shall be perfected, the said sum of seven hundred and fifty pounds, and the bond for securing the said sum, shall go to the said Francis Barber; and I hereby give and bequeath to him the same, in lieu of the bequest in his favour, contained in my said Will. And I hereby empower my Executors to deduct and retain all expences that shall or may be incurred in the execution of my said Will, or of this Codicil thereto, out of such estate and effects as I shall die possessed of. All the rest, residue, and remainder, of my estate and effects, I give and bequeath to my said Executors, in trust for the said Francis Barber, his Executors and Administrators. Witness my hand and seal, this ninth day of December, 1784.

'SAM. JOHNSON, (L. S.)

'Signed, sealed, published, declared, and delivered, by the said Samuel Johnson, as, and for a Codicil to his last Will and Testament, in the presence of us, who, in his presence, and at his request, and also in the presence of each other, have hereto subscribed our names as witnesses.

'JOHN COPLEY.

'WILLIAM GIBSON.

'HENRY COLE.'

Upon these testamentary deeds it is proper to make a few observations.

His express declaration with his dying breath of his faith as a Christian, as it had been often practised in such solemn writings, was of real consequence from this great man; for the conviction of a mind equally acute and strong, might well overbalance the doubts of others, who were his contemporaries. The expression *polluted*, may, to some, convey an impression of more than ordinary contamination; but that is not warranted by its genuine meaning, as appears from *The Rambler*, No. 42. The same word is used in the will of Dr. Sanderson, Bishop of Lincoln, who was piety itself.

His legacy of two hundred pounds to the representatives of Mr. Innys, bookseller, in St. Paul's Church-yard, proceeded from a very worthy motive. He told Sir John Hawkins, that his father having become a bankrupt, Mr. Innys had assisted him with money or credit to continue his business. 'This, (said he,) I consider as an obligation on me to be grateful to his descendants.'

The amount of his property proved to be considerably more than he had supposed it to be. Sir John Hawkins estimates the bequest to Francis Barber at a sum little short of fifteen hundred pounds, including an annuity of seventy pounds to be paid to him by Mr. Langton, in consideration of seven hundred and fifty pounds, which Johnson had lent to that gentleman. Sir John seems not a little angry at this bequest, and mutters 'a caveat person with the care and selection of them; instead of which, he, in a precipitate manner, burnt large masses of them, with little regard, as I apprehend, to discrimination. Not that I suppose we have thus been deprived of any compositions which he had ever intended for the publick eye; but, from what escaped the flames, I judge that many curious circumstances relating both to himself and other literary characters have perished.

Two very valuable articles, I am sure, we have lost, which were two quarto volumes, containing a full, fair, and most

against ostentatious bounty and favour to negroes.' But surely when a man has money entirely of his own acquisition, especially when he has no near relations, he may, without blame, dispose of it as he pleases, and with great propriety to a faithful servant. Mr. Barber, by the recommendation of his master, retired to Lichfield, where he might pass the rest of his days in comfort.

It has been objected that Johnson has omitted many of his best friends, when leaving books to several as tokens of his last remembrance. The names of Dr. Adams, Dr. Taylor, Dr. Burney, Mr. Hector, Mr. Murphy, the Authour of this Work, and others who were intimate with him, are not to be found in his Will. This may be accounted for by considering, that as he was very near his dissolution at the time, he probably mentioned such as happened to occur to him; and that he may have recollected, that he had formerly shewn others such proofs of his regard, that it was not necessary to crowd his Will with their names. Mrs. Lucy Porter was much displeased that nothing was left to her; but besides what I have now stated, she should have considered, that she had left nothing to Johnson by her Will, which was made during his life-time, as appeared at her decease.

His enumerating several persons in one group, and leaving them 'each a book at their election,' might possibly have given occasion to a curious question as to the order of choice, had they not luckily fixed on different books. His library, though by no means handsome in its appearance, was sold by Mr. Christie, for two hundred and forty-seven pounds, nine shillings; many people being desirous to have a book which had belonged to Dr. Johnson. In many of them he had written little notes: sometimes tender memorials of his departed wife; as, 'This was dear Tetty's book:' sometimes occasional remarks of different sorts. Mr. Lysons, of Clifford's Inn, has favoured me with the two following:

In *Holy Rules and Helps to Devotion*, by Bryan Duppa, Lord Bishop of Winton, '*Preces quidam* (? *quidem*) *videtur diligenter tractasse; spero non inauditus* (? *inauditas*)' ['He seems to have been careful in his prayers; I hope they were heard.']

In *The Rosicrucian infallible Axiomata*, by John Heydon, Gent., prefixed to which are some verses addressed to the authour, signed Ambr. Waters, A.M. Coll. Ex. Oxon. '*These Latin verses were written to Hobbes by Bathurst, upon his Treatise on Human Nature, and have no relation to the* [*this*] *book. ———An odd fraud.*'

particular account of his own life, from his earliest recollection.
I owned to him, that having accidentally seen them, I had read a
great deal in them; and apologizing for the liberty I had taken,
asked him if I could help it. He placidly answered, 'Why, Sir,
I do not think you could have helped it.' I said that I had, for
once in my life, felt half an inclination to commit theft. It had
come into my mind to carry off those two volumes, and never
see him more. Upon my inquiring how this would have affected
him, 'Sir, (said he,) I believe I should have gone mad.'[1]

During his last illness, Johnson experienced the steady and
kind attachment of his numerous friends. Mr. Hoole has drawn
up a narrative of what passed in the visits which he paid him
during that time, from the 10th of November to the 13th of
December, the day of his death, inclusive, and has favoured me
with a perusal of it, with permission to make extracts, which I
have done. Nobody was more attentive to him than Mr. Langton,
to whom he tenderly said, *Te teneam moriens deficiente manu.*[2]
And I think it highly to the honour of Mr. Windham, that his
important occupations as an active statesman did not prevent
him from paying assiduous respect to the dying Sage, whom he
revered. Mr. Langton informs me, that, 'one day he found Mr.
Burke and four or five more friends sitting with Johnson. Mr.

---

[1] One of these volumes, Sir John Hawkins informs us, he put into his
pocket; for which the excuse he states is, that he meant to preserve it from
falling into the hands of a person [George Steevens. *Croker*[1]] whom he
describes so as to make it sufficiently clear who is meant; 'having strong
reasons (said he,) to suspect that this man might find and make an ill use
of the book.' Why Sir John should suppose that the gentleman alluded to
would act in this manner, he has not thought fit to explain. But what he
did was not approved of by Johnson; who, upon being acquainted of it
without delay by a friend, expressed great indignation, and warmly insisted
on the book being delivered up; and, afterwards, in the supposition of his
missing it, without knowing by whom it had been taken, he said, 'Sir, I
should have gone out of the world distrusting half mankind.' Sir John next
day wrote a letter to Johnson, assigning reasons for his conduct; upon which
Johnson observed to Mr. Langton, 'Bishop Sanderson could not have dictated a better letter. I could almost say, *Melius est sic penituisse quam non
errâsse.*' ['Better so to have repented than not to have sinned.'] The
agitation into which Johnson was thrown by this incident, probably made
him hastily burn those precious records which must ever be regretted.

[2] ['When dying may I hold you with my failing hand?' Tibullus i. i. 60
(Johnson, in *Adventurer*, No. 58.)]

Burke said to him, "I am afraid, Sir, such a number of us may be oppressive to you." "No, Sir, (said Johnson,) it is not so; and I must be in a wretched state, indeed, when your company would not be a delight to me." Mr. Burke, in a tremulous voice, expressive of being very tenderly affected, replied, "My dear Sir, you have always been too good to me." Immediately afterwards he went away. This was the last circumstance in the acquaintance of these two eminent men.'

The following particulars of his conversation, within a few days of his death, I give on the authority of Mr. John Nichols:—[1]

[1] On the same undoubted authority, I give a few articles, which should have been inserted in chronological order; but which, now that they are before me, I should be sorry to omit:—

'In 1736, Dr. Johnson had a particular inclination to have been engaged as an assistant to the Reverend Mr. Budworth, then head master of the Grammar-school, at Brewood, in Staffordshire, "an excellent person, who possessed every talent of a perfect instructor of youth, in a degree which, (to use the words of one of the brightest ornaments of literature, the Reverend Dr. Hurd, Bishop of Worcester,) has been rarely found in any of that profession since the days of Quintilian." Mr. Budworth, "who was less known in his life-time, from that obscure situation to which the caprice of fortune oft condemns the most accomplished characters, than his highest merit deserved," had been bred under Mr. Blackwell [Blackwall], at Market Bosworth, where Johnson was some time an usher [*ante*, 60]; which might naturally lead to the application. Mr. Budworth was certainly no stranger to the learning or abilities of Johnson; as he more than once lamented his having been under the necessity of declining the engagement, from an apprehension that the paralytick affection, under which our great Philologist laboured through life, might become the object of imitation or of ridicule, among his pupils.' Captain Budworth, his grandson, has confirmed to me this anecdote.

'Among the early associates of Johnson, at St. John's Gate, was Samuel Boyse, well known by his ingenious productions; and not less noted for his imprudence. It was not unusual for Boyse to be a customer to the pawnbroker. On one of these occasions, Dr. Johnson collected a sum of money to redeem his friend's clothes, which in two days after were pawned again. "The sum, (said Johnson,) was collected by sixpences, at a time when to me sixpence was a serious consideration."

'Speaking one day of a person for whom he had a real friendship, but in whom vanity was somewhat too predominant, he observed, that "Kelly was so fond of displaying on his sideboard the plate which he possessed, that he added to it his spurs. For my part, (said he,) I never was master of a pair of spurs, but once; and they are now at the bottom of the ocean. By the carelessness of Boswell's servant, they were dropped from the end of the boat, on our return from the Isle of Sky." '

The late Reverend Mr. Samuel Badcock, having been introduced to Dr.

'He said, that the Parliamentary Debates were the only part of his writings which then gave him any compunction: but that at the time he wrote them, he had no conception he was imposing upon the world, though they were frequently written from very slender materials, and often from none at all,—the mere coinage of his own imagination. He never wrote any part of his works with equal velocity. Three columns of the *Magazine*, in an hour, was no uncommon effort, which was faster than most persons could have transcribed that quantity.

'Of his friend Cave, he always spoke with great affection. "Yet (said he,) Cave, (who never looked out of his window, but with a view to the *Gentleman's Magazine*,) was a penurious paymaster; he would contract for lines by the hundred, and expect the long hundred; but he was a good man, and always delighted to have his friends at his table."

'When talking of a regular edition of his own works, he said, "that he had power, [from the booksellers,] to print such an edition, if his health admitted it; but had no power to assign over any edition, unless he could add notes, and so alter them as to make them new works; which his state of health forbade him to think of. I may possibly live, (said he,) or rather breath, three days, or perhaps three weeks; but find myself daily and gradually weaker."

'He said at another time, three or four days only before his death, speaking of the little fear he had of undergoing a chirurgical operation, "I would give one of these legs for a year more of

Johnson, by Mr. Nichols, some years before his death, thus expressed himself in a letter to that gentleman:—

'How much I am obliged to you for the favour you did me in introducing me to Dr. Johnson! *Tantùm vidi Virgilium.* ["I had but a glimpse of Virgil." Ovid, *Tristia* IV. x. 5.] But to have seen him, and to have received a testimony of respect from him, was enough. I recollect all the conversation, and shall never forget one of his expressions. Speaking of Dr. P******** [Priestley], (whose writings, I saw, he estimated at a low rate,) he said, "You have proved him as deficient in *probity* as he is in learning." I called him an "*Index-scholar*;" but he was not willing to allow him a claim even to that merit. He said, that "he borrowed from those who had been borrowers themselves, and did not know that the mistakes he adopted had been answered by others." I often think of our short, but precious, visit to this great man. I shall consider it as a kind of an *æra* in my life.'

life, I mean of comfortable life, not such as that which I now suffer;"—and lamented much his inability to read during his hours of restlessness. "I used formerly, (he added,) when sleepless in bed, *to read like a Turk."*

'Whilst confined by his last illness, it was his regular practice to have the church-service read to him, by some attentive and friendly Divine. The Rev. Mr. Hoole performed this kind office in my presence for the last time, when, by his own desire, no more than the Litany was read; in which his responses were in the deep and sonorous voice which Mr. Boswell has occasionally noticed, and with the most profound devotion that can be imagined. His hearing not being quite perfect, he more than once interrupted Mr. Hoole, with "Louder, my dear Sir, louder, I entreat you, or you pray in vain!"—and, when the service was ended, he, with great earnestness, turned round to an excellent lady[1] who was present, saying, "I thank you, Madam, very heartily, for your kindness in joining me in this solemn exercise. Live well, I conjure you; and you will not feel the compunction at the last, which I now feel." So truly humble were the thoughts which this great and good man entertained of his own approaches to religious perfection.

'He was earnestly invited to publish a volume of *Devotional Exercises;* but this, (though he listened to the proposal with much complacency, and a large sum of money was offered for it,) he declined, from motives of the sincerest modesty.

'He seriously entertained the thought of translating *Thuanus.* He often talked to me on the subject; and once, in particular, when I was rather wishing that he would favour the world, and gratify his sovereign, by a Life of Spenser, (which he said that he would readily have done, had he been able to obtain any new materials for the purpose,) he added, "I have been thinking again, Sir, of *Thuanus:* it would not be the laborious task which you have supposed it. I should have no trouble but that of dictation, which would be performed as speedily as an amanuensis could write."'

It is to the mutual credit of Johnson and Divines of different

[1] [Mrs. John Hoole. Narrative of John Hoole in *Johnson. Misc.* ii. 157.]

communions, that although he was a steady Church-of-England man, there was, nevertheless, much agreeable intercourse between him and them. Let me particularly name the late Mr. La Trobe, and Mr. Hutton, of the Moravian profession. His intimacy with the English Benedictines, at Paris, has been mentioned; and as an additional proof of the charity in which he lived with good men of the Romish Church, I am happy in this opportunity of recording his friendship with the Reverend Thomas Hussey, D.D., His Catholick Majesty's Chaplain of Embassy at the Court of London, that very respectable man, eminent not only for his powerful eloquence as a preacher, but for his various abilities and acquisitions. Nay, though Johnson loved a Presbyterian the least of all, this did not prevent his having a long and uninterrupted social connection with the Reverend Dr. James Fordyce, who, since his death, hath gratefully celebrated him in a warm strain of devotional composition.

Amidst the melancholy clouds which hung over the dying Johnson, his characteristical manner shewed itself on different occasions.

When Dr. Warren, in the usual style, hoped that he was better; his answer was, 'No, Sir; you cannot conceive with what acceleration I advance towards death.'

A man whom he had never seen before was employed one night to sit up with him. Being asked next morning how he liked his attendant, his answer was, 'Not at all, Sir: the fellow's an ideot; he is as aukward as a turn-spit when first put into the wheel, and as sleepy as a dormouse.'

Mr. Windham having placed a pillow conveniently to support him, he thanked him for his kindness, and said, 'That will do,—all that a pillow can do.'

He repeated with great spirit a poem, consisting of several stanzas, in four lines, in alternate rhyme, which he said he had composed some years before, on occasion of a rich, extravagant young gentleman's[1] coming of age; saying he had never repeated it but once since he composed it, and had given but one copy of it. That copy was given to Mrs. Thrale, now Piozzi, who has

[1] [Sir John Lade. *Hill-Powell.*]

published it in a Book which she entitles *British Synonimy*, but
which is truly a collection of entertaining remarks and stories,
no matter whether accurate or not. Being a piece of exquisite
satire, conveyed in a strain of pointed vivacity and humour, and
in a manner of which no other instance is to be found in Johnson's
writings, I shall here insert it:—

> Long-expected one-and-twenty,
>   Ling'ring year, at length is flown;
> Pride and pleasure, pomp and plenty,
>   Great*** ****,[1] are now your own.
>
> Loosen'd from the Minor's tether,
>   Free to mortgage or to sell,
> Wild as wind, and light as feather,
>   Bid the sons of thrift farewell.
>
> Call the Betseys, Kates, and Jennies,
>   All the names that banish care;
> Lavish of your grandsire's guineas,
>   Shew the spirit of an heir.
>
> All that prey on vice or folly
>   Joy to see their quarry fly;
> There the gamester, light and jolly,
>   There the lender, grave and sly.
>
> Wealth, my lad, was made to wander,
>   Let it wander as it will;
> Call the jockey, call the pander,
>   Bid them come and take their fill.
>
> When the bonny blade carouses,
>   Pockets full, and spirits high—
> What are acres? what are houses?
>   Only dirt, or wet or dry.
>
> Should the guardian friend or mother
>   Tell the woes of wilful waste;
> Scorn their counsel, scorn their pother,—
>   You can hang or drown at last.

[1] [Sir John.]

As he opened a note which his servant brought to him, he said, 'An odd thought strikes me: we shall receive no letters in the grave.'

He requested three things of Sir Joshua Reynolds:—To forgive him thirty pounds which he had borrowed of him; to read the Bible; and never to use his pencil on a Sunday. Sir Joshua readily acquiesced.

Indeed he shewed the greatest anxiety for the religious improvement of his friends, to whom he discoursed of its infinite consequence. He begged of Mr. Hoole to think of what he had said, and to commit it to writing: and, upon being afterwards assured that this was done, pressed his hands, and in an earnest tone thanked him. Dr. Brocklesby having attended him with the utmost assiduity and kindness as his physician and friend, he was peculiarly desirous that this gentleman should not entertain any loose speculative notions, but be confirmed in the truths of Christianity, and insisted on his writing down in his presence, as nearly as he could collect it, the import of what passed on the subject: and Dr. Brocklesby having complied with the request, he made him sign the paper, and urged him to keep it in his own custody as long as he lived.

Johnson, with that native fortitude, which, amidst all his bodily distress and mental sufferings, never forsook him, asked Dr. Brocklesby, as a man in whom he had confidence, to tell him plainly whether he could recover. 'Give me (said he,) a direct answer.' The Doctor having first asked him if he could bear the whole truth, which way soever it might lead, and being answered that he could, declared that, in his opinion, he could not recover without a miracle. 'Then, (said Johnson,) I will take no more physick, not even my opiates; for I have prayed that I may render up my soul to God unclouded.' In this resolution he persevered, and, at the same time, used only the weakest kinds of sustenance. Being pressed by Mr. Windham to take somewhat more generous nourishment, lest too low a diet should have the very effect which he dreaded, by debilitating his mind, he said, 'I will take any thing but inebriating sustenance.'

The Reverend Mr. Strahan, who was the son of his friend,

and had been always one of his great favourites, had, during his last illness, the satisfaction of contributing to soothe and comfort him. That gentleman's house, at Islington, of which he is Vicar, afforded Johnson, occasionally and easily, an agreeable change of place and fresh air; and he attended also upon him in town in the discharge of the sacred offices of his profession.

Mr. Strahan has given me the agreeable assurance, that, after being in much agitation, Johnson became quite composed, and continued so till his death.

Dr. Brocklesby, who will not be suspected of fanaticism, obliged me with the following accounts:—

'For some time before his death, all his fears were calmed and absorbed by the prevalence of his faith, and his trust in the merits and *propitiation* of JESUS CHRIST.

'He talked often to me about the necessity of faith in the *sacrifice* of Jesus, as necessary beyond all good works whatever, for the salvation of mankind.

'He pressed me to study Dr. Clarke and to read his Sermons. I asked him why he pressed Dr. Clarke, an Arian.[1] "Because, (said he,) he is fullest on the *propitiatory sacrifice*." '

Johnson having thus in his mind the true Christian scheme, at once rational and consolatory, uniting justice and mercy in the DIVINITY, with the improvement of human nature, previous to his receiving the Holy Sacrament in his apartment, composed and fervently uttered this prayer:—[2]

'Almighty and most merciful Father, I am now, as to human

[1] The change of his sentiments with regard to Dr. Clarke, is thus mentioned to me in a letter from the late Dr. Adams, Master of Pembroke College, Oxford:—'The Doctor's prejudices were the strongest, and certainly in another sense the weakest, that ever possessed a sensible man. You know his extreme zeal for orthodoxy. But did you ever hear what he told me himself? That he had made it a rule not to admit Dr. Clarke's name in his *Dictionary*. This, however, wore off. At some distance of time he advised with me what books he should read in defence of the Christian Religion. I recommended Clarke's *Evidences of Natural and Revealed Religion*, as the best of the kind; and I find in what is called his *Prayers and Meditations*, that he was frequently employed in the latter part of his time in reading Clarke's *Sermons*.'

[2] The Reverend Mr. Strahan took care to have it preserved, and has inserted it in *Prayers and Meditations*, p. 216.

eyes, it seems, about to commemorate, for the last time, the death of thy Son JESUS CHRIST, our Saviour and Redeemer. Grant, O LORD, that my whole hope and confidence may be in his merits, and thy mercy; enforce and accept my imperfect repentance; make this commemoration available to the confirmation of my faith, the establishment of my hope, and the enlargement of my charity; and make the death of thy Son JESUS CHRIST effectual to my redemption. Have mercy upon me, and pardon the multitude of my offences. Bless my friends; have mercy upon all men. Support me, by thy Holy Spirit, in the days of weakness, and at the hour of death; and receive me, at my death, to everlasting happiness, for the sake of JESUS CHRIST. Amen.'

Having, as has been already mentioned, made his will on the 8th and 9th of December, and settled all his worldly affairs, he languished till Monday, the 13th of that month, when he expired, about seven o'clock in the evening, with so little apparent pain that his attendants hardly perceived when his dissolution took place.

Of his last moments, my brother, Thomas David, has furnished me with the following particulars:—

'The Doctor, from the time that he was certain his death was near, appeared to be perfectly resigned, was seldom or never fretful or out of temper, and often said to his faithful servant, who gave me this account, "Attend, Francis, to the salvation of your soul, which is the object of greatest importance:" he also explained to him passages in the scripture, and seemed to have pleasure in talking upon religious subjects.

'On Monday, the 13th of December, the day on which he died, a Miss Morris, daughter to a particular friend of his, called, and said to Francis, that she begged to be permitted to see the Doctor, that she might earnestly request him to give her his blessing. Francis went into his room, followed by the young lady, and delivered the message. The Doctor turned himself in the bed, and said, "GOD bless you, my dear!" These were the last words he spoke. His difficulty of breathing increased till about seven o'clock in the evening, when Mr. Barber and Mrs.

Desmoulins, who were sitting in the room, observing that the noise he made in breathing had ceased, went to the bed, and found he was dead.'

About two days after his death, the following very agreeable account was communicated to Mr. Malone, in a letter by the Honourable John Byng, to whom I am much obliged for granting me permission to introduce it in my work.

'DEAR SIR,—Since I saw you, I have had a long conversation with Cawston,[1] who sat up with Dr. Johnson, from nine o'clock, on Sunday evening, till ten o'clock, on Monday morning. And, from what I can gather from him, it should seem, that Dr. Johnson was perfectly composed, steady in hope, and resigned to death. At the interval of each hour, they assisted him to sit up in his bed, and move his legs, which were in much pain; when he regularly addressed himself to fervent prayer; and though, sometimes, his voice failed him, his senses never did, during that time. The only sustenance he received, was cyder and water. He said his mind was prepared, and the time to his dissolution seemed long. At six in the morning, he enquired the hour, and, on being informed, said that all went on regularly, and he felt he had but a few hours to live.

'At ten o'clock in the morning, he parted from Cawston, saying, "You should not detain Mr. Windham's servant:—I thank you; bear my remembrance to your master." Cawston says, that no man could appear more collected, more devout, or less terrified at the thoughts of the approaching minute.

'This account, which is so much more agreeable than, and somewhat different from, yours, has given us the satisfaction of thinking that that great man died as he lived, full of resignation, strengthened in faith, and joyful in hope.'

A few days before his death, he had asked Sir John Hawkins, as one of his executors, where he should be buried; and on being answered, 'Doubtless, in Westminster-Abbey,' seemed to feel a satisfaction, very natural to a Poet; and indeed, in my opinion,

[1] Servant to the Right Honourable William Windham.

very natural to every man of any imagination, who has no
family sepulchre in which he can be laid with his fathers.
Accordingly, upon Monday, December 20, his remains were
deposited in that noble and renowned edifice; and over his grave
was placed a large blue flag-stone, with this inscription:—

> 'Samuel Johnson, LL.D.
> *Obiit* xiii *die Decembris,*
> *Anno Domini*
> m.dcc.lxxxiv.
> *Ætatis suæ* lxxv.'

His funeral was attended by a respectable number of his
friends, particularly such of the members of the Literary Club
as were then in town; and was also honoured with the presence
of several of the Reverend Chapter of Westminster. Mr. Burke,
Sir Joseph Banks, Mr. Windham, Mr. Langton, Sir Charles
Bunbury, and Mr. Colman, bore his pall. His school-fellow,
Dr. Taylor, performed the mournful office of reading the burial
service.

I trust, I shall not be accused of affectation, when I declare,
that I find myself unable to express all that I felt upon the loss
of such a 'Guide, Philosopher, and Friend.'[1] I shall, therefore,
not say one word of my own, but adopt those of an eminent
friend,[2] which he uttered with an abrupt felicity, superior to all
studied compositions:—'He has made a chasm, which not only

[1] On the subject of Johnson I may adopt the words of Sir John Harrington,
concerning his venerable Tutor and Diocesan, Dr. John Still, Bishop of
Bath and Wells; 'who hath given me some helps, more hopes, all encouragements in my best studies: to whom I never came but I grew more religious;
from whom I never went, but I parted better instructed. Of him therefore,
my acquaintance, my friend, my instructor, if I speak much, it were not to
be marvelled; if I speak frankly, it is not to be blamed; and though I speak
partially, it were to be pardoned.' *Nugæ Antiquæ*, vol. i. p. 136. There is
one circumstance in Sir John's character of Bishop Still, which is peculiarly
applicable to Johnson: 'He became so famous a disputer, that the learnedest
were even afraid to dispute with him; and he finding his own strength,
could not stick to warn them in their arguments to take heed to their
answers, like a perfect fencer that will tell aforehand in which button he will
give the venew, or like a cunning chess-player that will appoint aforehand
with which pawn and in what place he will give the mate.'
[2] The late Right Hon. William Gerard Hamilton. [M.]

nothing can fill up, but which nothing has a tendency to fill up. Johnson is dead. Let us go to the next best:—there is nobody; no man can be said to put you in mind of Johnson.'

As Johnson had abundant homage paid to him during his life,[1]

[1] Beside the Dedications to him by Dr. Goldsmith, the Reverend Dr. Franklin, and the Reverend Mr. Wilson, which I have mentioned according to their dates, there was one by a lady [Anne Penny. *Powell*], of a versification of *Aningait and Ajut*, and one by the ingenious Mr. Walker of his *Rhetorical Grammar*. I have introduced into this work several compliments paid to him in the writings of his contemporaries; but the number of them is so great, that we may fairly say that there was almost a general tribute.

Let me not be forgetful of the honour done to him by Colonel Myddleton, of Gwaynynog, near Denbigh; who, on the banks of a rivulet in his park, where Johnson delighted to stand and repeat verses, erected an urn with the following inscription:

'This spot was often dignified by the presence of
SAMUEL JOHNSON, LL.D.
Whose moral writings, exactly conformable to the precepts of
Christianity,
Give ardour to Virtue and confidence to Truth.'

As no inconsiderable circumstance of his fame, we must reckon the extraordinary zeal of the artists to extend and perpetuate his image. I can enumerate a bust by Mr. Nollekens, and the many casts which are made from it; several pictures by Sir Joshua Reynolds, from one of which, in the possession of the Duke of Dorset, Mr. Humphry executed a beautiful miniature in enamel; one by Mrs. Frances Reynolds, Sir Joshua's sister; one by Mr. Zoffani; and one by Mr. Opie; and the following engravings of his portrait: 1. One by Cooke, from Sir Joshua, for the Proprietors' edition of his folio *Dictionary*.—2. One from ditto, by ditto, for their quarto edition.— 3. One from Opie, by Heath, for Harrison's edition of his *Dictionary*.—4. One from Nollekens' bust of him, by Bartolozzi, for Fielding's quarto edition of his *Dictionary*.—5. One small, from Harding, by Trotter, for his *Beauties*.—6. One small, from Sir Joshua, by Trotter, for his *Lives of the Poets*.—7. One small, from Sir Joshua, by Hall, for *The Rambler*.—8. One small, from an original drawing, in the possession of Mr. John Simco, etched by Trotter, for another edition of his *Lives of the Poets*.—9. One small, no painter's name, etched by Taylor, for his *Johnsoniana*.—10. One folio whole-length, with his oak-stick, as described in Boswell's *Tour*, drawn and etched by Trotter.—11. One large mezzotinto, from Sir Joshua, by Doughty. —12. One large Roman head, from Sir Joshua, by Marchi.—13. One octavo, holding a book to his eye, from Sir Joshua, by Hall, for his *Works*.—14. One small, from a drawing from the life, and engraved by Trotter, for his *Life* published by Kearsley.—15. One large, from Opie, by Mr. Townley, (brother of Mr. Townley, of the Commons,) an ingenious artist, who resided some time at Berlin, and has the honour of being engraver to his Majesty the King of Prussia. This is one of the finest mezzotintos that ever was executed; and what renders it of extraordinary value, the plate was so no writer in this nation ever had such an accumulation of literary honours after his death. A sermon upon that event was preached in St. Mary's Church, Oxford, before the University, by the Reverend Mr. Agutter, of Magdalen College.[1] The *Lives*, the *Memoirs*, the *Essays*, both in prose and verse, which have been published concerning him, would make many volumes. The numerous attacks too upon him, I consider as part of his consequence, upon the principle which he himself so well knew and asserted. Many who trembled at his presence, were forward in assault, when they no longer apprehended danger. When one of his little pragmatical foes was invidiously snarling at his fame, at Sir Joshua Reynolds's table, the Reverend Dr. Parr exclaimed, with his usual bold animation, 'Ay, now that the old lion is dead, every ass thinks he may kick at him.'

A monument for him, in Westminster-Abbey, was resolved upon soon after his death, and was supported by a most respectable contribution; but the Dean and Chapter of St. Paul's having come to a resolution of admitting monuments there, upon a liberal and magnificent plan, that Cathedral was afterwards fixed on, as the place in which a cenotaph should be erected to his memory: and in the cathedral of his native city of Lichfield, a smaller one is to be erected. To compose his epitaph, could not

destroyed after four or five impressions only were taken off. One of them is in the possession of Sir William Scott. Mr. Townley has lately been prevailed with to execute and publish another of the same, that it may be more generally circulated among the admirers of Dr. Johnson.—16. One large, from Sir Joshua's first picture of him, by Heath, for this work, in quarto.—17. One octavo, by Baker, for the octavo edition.—18. And one for Lavater's *Essay on Physiognomy*, in which Johnson's countenance is analysed upon the principles of that fanciful writer.—There are also several seals with his head cut on them, particularly a very fine one by that eminent artist, Edward Burch, Esq. R.A., in the possession of the younger Dr. Charles Burney.

Let me add, as a proof of the popularity of his character, that there are copper pieces struck at Birmingham, with his head impressed on them, which pass current as half-pence there, and in the neighbouring parts of the country.

[1] It is not yet published.—In a letter to me, Mr. Agutter says, 'My sermon before the University was more engaged with Dr. Johnson's *moral* than his *intellectual* character. It particularly examined his fear of death, and suggested several reasons for the apprehension of the good, and the indifference of the infidel in their last hours; this was illustrated by contrasting the death of Dr. Johnson and Mr. Hume: the text was Job xxi. 22–26.'

but excite the warmest competition of genius.[1] If *laudari à laudato viro*[2] be praise which is highly estimable, I should not forgive myself were I to omit the following sepulchral verses on the authour of THE ENGLISH DICTIONARY, written by the Right Honourable Henry Flood:—[3]

> 'No need of Latin or of Greek to grace
> Our JOHNSON's memory, or inscribe his grave;
> His native language claims this mournful space,
> To pay the Immortality he gave.'

[1] The Reverend Dr. Parr, on being requested to undertake it, thus expressed himself in a letter to William Seward, Esq.:

'I leave this mighty task to some hardier and some abler writer. The variety and splendour of Johnson's attainments, the peculiarities of his character, his private virtues, and his literary publications, fill me with confusion and dismay, when I reflect upon the confined and difficult species of composition, in which alone they can be expressed, with propriety, upon his monument.'

But I understand that this great scholar, and warm admirer of Johnson, has yielded to repeated solicitations, and executed the very difficult undertaking. [Dr. Johnson's Monument, consisting of a colossal figure leaning against a column, has since the death of our authour been placed in St. Paul's Cathedral. The Epitaph was written by the Rev. Dr. Parr, and is as follows:

A ✶ Ω
SAMVELI · IOHNSON
GRAMMATICO · ET · CRITICO
SCRIPTORVM · ANGLICORVM · LITTERATE · PERITO
POETAE · LVMINIBVS · SENTENTIARVM
ET · PONDERIBVS · VERBORVM · ADMIRABILI
MAGISTRO · VIRTVTIS · GRAVISSIMO
HOMINI · OPTIMO · ET · SINGVLARIS · EXEMPLI
QVI · VIXIT · ANN · L̅x̅x̅v · MENS · II · DIEB · xiiiI
DECESSIT · IDIB · DECEMBR · ANN · CHRIST · cIↄ · Iↄcc · LxxxiiiI
SEPVLT · IN · AED · SANCT · PETR · WESTMONASTERIENS ·
xiiI · KAL · IANVAR · ANN · CHRIST · cIↄ · Iↄcc · Lxxxv
AMICI · ET · SODALES · LITTERARII
PECVNIA · CONLATA
H · M · FACIVND · CVRAVER.

On a scroll in his hand are the following words:
ΕΝΜΑΚΑΡΕΣΣΙΠΟΝΩΝΑΝΤΑΞΙΟΣΕΙΗΑΜΟΙΒΗ.

On one side of the Monument—FACIEBAT JOHANNES BACON SCVLPTOR ANN. CHRIST. M.DCC.LXXXXV. [For a translation see p. xxiv.]

The Subscription for this monument, which cost eleven hundred guineas, was begun by the LITERARY CLUB and completed by the aid of Dr. Johnson's other friends and admirers.—M.]

[2] ['to be praised by one whom all men praise.']

[3] To prevent any misconception on this subject, Mr. Malone, by whom

The character of SAMUEL JOHNSON has, I trust, been so developed in the course of this work, that they who have honoured it with a perusal, may be considered as well acquainted with him. As, however, it may be expected that I should collect into one view the capital and distinguishing features of this extraordinary man, I shall endeavour to acquit myself of that part of my biographical undertaking,[1] however difficult it may be to do that which many of my readers will do better for themselves.

His figure was large and well formed, and his countenance of the cast of an ancient statue; yet his appearance was rendered strange and somewhat uncouth, by convulsive cramps, by the scars of that distemper which it was once imagined the royal touch could cure, and by a slovenly mode of dress. He had the use only of one eye; yet so much does mind govern and even supply the deficiency of organs, that his visual perceptions, as far as they extended, were uncommonly quick and accurate. So morbid was his temperament, that he never knew the natural joy of a free and vigorous use of his limbs: when he walked, it was like the struggling gait of one in fetters; when he rode, he had no command or direction of his horse, but was carried as if in a balloon. That with his constitution and habits of life he

these lines were obligingly communicated, requests me to add the following remark:—

'In justice to the late Mr. Flood, now himself wanting, and highly meriting, an epitaph from his country, to which his transcendent talents did the highest honour, as well as the most important service; it should be observed that these lines were by no means intended as a regular monumental inscription for Dr. Johnson. Had he undertaken to write an appropriated and discriminative epitaph for that excellent and extraordinary man, those who knew Mr. Flood's vigour of mind, will have no doubt that he would have produced one worthy of his illustrious subject. But the fact was merely this: In Dec. 1789, after a large subscription had been made for Dr. Johnson's monument, to which Mr. Flood liberally contributed, Mr. Malone happened to call on him at his house, in Berners-street, and the conversation turning on the proposed monument, Mr. Malone maintained that the epitaph, by whomsoever it should be written, ought to be in Latin. Mr. Flood thought differently. The next morning, in the postscript to a note on another subject, he mentioned that he continued of the same opinion as on the preceding day, and subjoined the lines above given.'

[1] As I do not see any reason to give a different character of my illustrious friend now, from what I formerly gave, the greatest part of the sketch of him in my *Journal of a Tour to the Hebrides*, is here adopted.

should have lived seventy-five years, is a proof that an inherent *vivida vis*[1] is a powerful preservative of the human frame.

Man is, in general, made up of contradictory qualities; and these will ever shew themselves in strange succession, where a consistency in appearance at least, if not in reality, has not been attained by long habits of philosophical discipline. In proportion to the native vigour of the mind, the contradictory qualities will be the more prominent, and more difficult to be adjusted; and, therefore, we are not to wonder, that Johnson exhibited an eminent example of this remark which I have made upon human nature. At different times, he seemed a different man, in some respects; not, however, in any great or essential article, upon which he had fully employed his mind, and settled certain principles of duty, but only in his manners, and in the display of argument and fancy in his talk. He was prone to superstition, but not to credulity. Though his imagination might incline him to a belief of the marvellous and the mysterious, his vigorous reason examined the evidence with jealousy. He was a sincere and zealous Christian, of high Church-of-England and monarchical principles, which he would not tamely suffer to be questioned; and had, perhaps, at an early period, narrowed his mind somewhat too much, both as to religion and politicks. His being impressed with the danger of extreme latitude in either, though he was of a very independent spirit, occasioned his appearing somewhat unfavourable to the prevalence of that noble freedom of sentiment which is the best possession of man. Nor can it be denied, that he had many prejudices; which, however, frequently suggested many of his pointed sayings, that rather shew a playfulness of fancy than any settled malignity. He was steady and inflexible in maintaining the obligations of religion and morality; both from a regard for the order of society, and from a veneration for the GREAT SOURCE of all order; correct, nay stern in his taste; hard to please, and easily offended; impetuous and irritable in his temper, but of a most humane and benevolent heart,[2] which shewed itself not only in a most liberal charity, as

---

[1] ['lively force.']

[2] In the *Olla Podrida*, a collection of Essays published at Oxford, there is

far as his circumstances would allow, but in a thousand instances of active benevolence. He was afflicted with a bodily disease, which made him often restless and fretful; and with a constitutional melancholy, the clouds of which darkened the brightness of his fancy, and gave a gloomy cast to his whole course of thinking: we, therefore, ought not to wonder at his sallies of impatience and passion at any time; especially when provoked by obtrusive ignorance, or presuming petulance; and allowance must be made for his uttering hasty and satirical sallies, even against his best friends. And, surely, when it is considered, that, 'amidst sickness and sorrow,' he exerted his faculties in so many works for the benefit of mankind, and particularly that he atchieved the great and admirable DICTIONARY of our language, we must be astonished at his resolution. The solemn text, 'of him to whom much is given, much will be required,' seems to have been ever present to his mind, in a rigorous sense, and to have made him dissatisfied with his labours and acts of goodness, however comparatively great; so that the unavoidable consciousness of his superiority was, in that respect, a cause of disquiet. He suffered so much from this, and from the gloom which perpetually haunted him, and made solitude frightful, that it may be said of him, 'If in this life only he had hope, he was of all men most miserable.' He loved praise, when it was brought to him; but was too proud to seek for it. He was somewhat susceptible of flattery. As he was general and unconfined in his studies, he cannot be considered as master of any one particular science; but he had accumulated a vast and various collection of learning and knowledge, which was so arranged in his mind, as to be ever in readiness to be brought forth. But his superiority over other learned men consisted chiefly in what may be called the art of thinking, the art of using his mind; a certain continual power of seizing the useful substance of all that he knew, and

an admirable paper upon the character of Johnson, written by the Reverend Dr. Horne, the late excellent Bishop of Norwich. The following passage is eminently happy: 'To reject wisdom, because the person of him who communicates it is uncouth, and his manners are inelegant;—what is it, but to throw away a pine-apple, and assign for a reason the roughness of its coat?'

exhibiting it in a clear and forcible manner; so that knowledge, which we often see to be no better than lumber in men of dull understanding, was, in him, true, evident, and actual wisdom. His moral precepts are practical; for they are drawn from an intimate acquaintance with human nature. His maxims carry conviction; for they are founded on the basis of common sense, and a very attentive and minute survey of real life. His mind was so full of imagery, that he might have been perpetually a poet; yet it is remarkable, that, however rich his prose is in this respect, his poetical pieces, in general, have not much of that splendour, but are rather distinguished by strong sentiment and acute observation, conveyed in harmonious and energetick verse, particularly in heroick couplets. Though usually grave, and even aweful, in his deportment, he possessed uncommon and peculiar powers of wit and humour; he frequently indulged himself in colloquial pleasantry; and the heartiest merriment was often enjoyed in his company; with this great advantage, that as it was entirely free from any poisonous tincture of vice or impiety, it was salutary to those who shared in it. He had accustomed himself to such accuracy in his common conversation,[1] that he at

[1] Though a perfect resemblance of Johnson is not to be found in any age, parts of his character are admirably expressed by Clarendon in drawing that of Lord Falkland, whom the noble and masterly historian describes at his seat near Oxford:—'Such an immenseness of wit, such a solidity of judgement, so infinite a fancy, bound in by a most logical ratiocination.—His acquaintance was cultivated by the most polite and accurate men, so that his house was an University in less volume, whither they came, not so much for repose as study, and to examine and refine those grosser propositions, which laziness and consent made current in conversation.'

Bayle's account of Menage may also be quoted as exceedingly applicable to the great subject of this work:—'His illustrious friends erected a very glorious monument to him in the collection entitled *Menagiana*. Those who judge of things aright, will confess that this collection is very proper to shew the extent of genius and learning which was the character of Menage. And I may be bold to say, that *the excellent works he published will not distinguish him from other learned men so advantageously as this*. To publish books of great learning, to make Greek and Latin verses exceedingly well turned, is not a common talent, I own; neither is it extremely rare. It is incomparably more difficult to find men who can furnish discourse about an infinite number of things, and who can diversify them an hundred ways. How many authours are there, who are admired for their works, on account of the vast learning that is displayed in them, who are not able to sustain a conversation. Those who know Menage only by his books, might think he resembled all times expressed his thoughts with great force, and an elegant choice of language, the effect of which was aided by his having a loud voice, and a slow deliberate utterance. In him were united a most logical head with a most fertile imagination, which gave him an extraordinary advantage in arguing: for he could reason close or wide, as he saw best for the moment. Exulting in his intellectual strength and dexterity, he could, when he pleased, be the greatest sophist that ever contended in the lists of declamation; and, from a spirit of contradiction and a delight in shewing his powers, he would often maintain the wrong side with equal warmth and ingenuity; so that, when there was an audience, his real opinions could seldom be gathered from his talk; though when he was in company with a single friend, he would discuss a subject with genuine fairness: but he was too conscientious to make errour permanent and pernicious, by deliberately writing it; and, in all his numerous works, he earnestly inculcated what appeared to him to be the truth; his piety being constant, and the ruling principle of all his conduct.

Such was SAMUEL JOHNSON, a man whose talents, acquirements, and virtues, were so extraordinary, that the more his character is considered, the more he will be regarded by the present age, and by posterity, with admiration and reverence.

those learned men: but if you shew the MENAGIANA, you distinguish him from them, and make him known by a talent which is given to very few learned men. There it appears that he was a man who spoke off-hand a thousand good things. His memory extended to what was ancient and modern; to the court and to the city; to the dead and to the living languages; to things serious and things jocose; in a word, to a thousand sorts of subjects. That which appeared a trifle to some readers of the *Menagiana*, who did not consider circumstances, caused admiration in other readers, who minded the difference between what a man speaks without preparation, and that which he prepares for the press. And, therefore, we cannot sufficiently commend the care which his illustrious friends took to erect a monument so capable of giving him immortal glory. They were not obliged to rectify what they had heard him say; for, in so doing, they had not been faithful historians of his conversations.'

INDEX

This index is based upon Dr. L. F. Powell's admirably complete index to the six-volume Hill-Powell edition, though of course omitting the subject-matter of the footnotes peculiar to that edition, and of Johnson's and Boswell's Scotch tours (vol. v in that edition). To keep the present index within reasonable limits, the following devices have been adopted: (1) the most common Christian names are usually represented by their initials only, thus C. = Charles, E. = Edward, G. = George, H. = Henry, J. = John, R. = Robert, T. = Thomas, W. = William; (2) in the analysed entries the usual conjunctions, prepositions, verbs, &c., showing the relation of each item to the main entry are omitted, and it is left to the text to show what this relation is; (3) the reference to footnotes is by page-number only, not followed by *n*.

man, 318; Windham, 810; Prof. J. Young, 1373.

Glasse, Hannah (*fl.* 1747), 942.

'Gloomy, perhaps sinful to be', 1176.

Glover, R. (1712–85), 272.

Glow-worm, S.J.'s Latin poem on, 393, 524.

Goa, 56.

Goat, Sir Joseph Banks's, 457.

Gobelins, 647.

God, 984, 1296.

Goldsmith, Rev. H. (*d.* 1768), 486, 792.

Goldsmith, Dr. Isaac (*d.* 1769), 293.

Goldsmith, Oliver (1730–74).

  I. *Life, character, opinions, &c.* S.J. on him, 289; absurdities, 292, 530, 917, 1074; Addison, 544; Aleppo, 1081; arguing alone, 527; beaten, 508; birth, 779; bloom-coloured coat, 411; boastfulness, 293; his books, 918; J.B., 489,545,547,930; Bluebeard, 485; Burke, 291, 849; Lord Camden, 962; Lord Clare, 450, 962; The Club, 339, 363, 530, 558, 1074, 1208; Colman, 969; not an agreeable companion,912; his company liked, 527; consequential at times, 545; conversation, 292–3, 300, 489, 495, 523, 527, 542, 545, 912, 917, 1087; Courtenay's *Moral . . . Character of S.J.*, 159; death, 562–3, 847; debts, 563–4; at Dilly's, 537; disputes his passage, 292; 'Doctor Major', 793; Dodsley, 743; dog-butchers, 525; Dryden, 518; duelling, 483; Edgware Road, 485; Edinburgh University, 291, 301; envy, 293, 384, 545, 547, 930; epitaph in Greek, 781; — in Latin, 777–81; Evans, 507; excellence, 918; fable of the fishes, 524; his fame, 845, 849, 912, 1087; Fantoccini, 293; flowered late, 849, 917; to France, 293; friendship, 485; Garrick, 292, 411, 526, 969; *The Gentleman*, 485; a ghost, 486; Gibbon, 558; 'Goldy', 545, 793; 'happy

revolutions', 518; James Harris, 519; as historian, 527; horses' blood, 525; ignorance, 495, 511, 527, 1081; improvidence, 294; 'inspired idiot', 292; irritable, 545; Jacobitism, 518; **S.J.**, admiration, 289, 495, 512, 527, 564; — *The Good-natured Man*, 384, 387; — style, 159; — a tetrastick, 564; — the Scottish tour, 547; — 'a bear only in the skin', 400; — 'the big man', 361; — claim for more writings, 361; — Burke, 547; competition with him, 295, 512, 545; — copies his manner, 292; — not his style, 512; *Heroic Epistle*, 1151; — interview with the King, 384; —jealous of him, 545; — of his accommodation, 1085; — at his levee, 437, 1085; — takes liberties with him, 1151; — on his literary reputation, 525; his pension, 1152; quarrel and reconciliation, 542–4; respect for him, 295; theatre-going, 361; witty contests, 524; on Kames's *Elements*, 414; Kenrick, 351; Mrs. Lennox's play, 1071–2; 'loose in his principles', 289; luxury, 513; bottle of Madeira, 294; Malagrida, 1202; Mallet, 525; Martinelli, 516; martyrdom, 539; mathematics, 291; medical studies, 291; merit late to be acknowledged, 917; migration of birds, 538; mind: 'at no pains to fill his', 918; — 'never exchanged mind', 743; — not at ease, 847; Moser, 545; musical performers, 519; nidification, 538; *Nihil quod tetigit*, 292, 778; *Nil te quaesiveris extra*, 1085; craving for notice, 489; 'an odd character', 485; Paoli, 515; paradox, 295; partiality of his friends, 917; 'pleasure of being liked', 292; 'poor Poll', 292, 1087; Pope on Addison, 412; 'a privileged man', 298; the public, 917; religion, 511; Reynolds, 292; Professor of

537, 686, 899, 900, 1375; un-chastity, 1357; uncle, 36; no unsocial shyness, 688, 1262, 1285; deliberate utterance, 599, 1402; no valetudinarian, 716; his vine, 1029; Virgil, 445, 571, 1234; vocation to public life, 1343; voice, 367–8, 384, 542, 836, 1387; vows, 367–8, 371, 998: *see* WALES; the Temple, 328; warrants against him, 103; watch, 395; a watchman, 686; water-drinking, 958; a waterfall, 868: *see* WEATHER; Westminster Police Court, 888; his wife, 68, 71, 166–71, 185, 196, 213, 336, 407, 650, 957, 1046, 1336, 1374: *see also* JOHNSON, Elizabeth; wig, 280, 973; his will, 1380; wine, 284, 291, 341, 574, 687, 747, 911, 915, 958, 974, 981, 1016, 1022, 1036, 1121, 1390; wit, 523, 777; women of the town, 1313, 1375; words, *see* Section IV; 'workmanlike', 762; the world, 154, 302, 731, 1153, 1199, 1200; young people, 315.

II. *Letters*: General: 17, 60, 169, 334, 396, 559, 562, 882, 935, 1004, 1143–4, 1220. Particular: to Allen, 1240; Astle, 1169; Bagshaw, 546, 1336; Banks, 457; Barber, 397, 434; Baretti, 256, 262, 269; Sir F. A. Barnard, 379; James Barry, 1220; Beattie, 1058; Beauclerk, 171; Birch, 117, 162; Bond, 506; Miss Boothby, 1108; Boswell, from 334 *passim*; Mrs. Boswell, 781, 818, 1188; Mme de Boufflers, 660; Dr. Brocklesby, 1244, 1337–43; Dr. Burney, 204, 229, 232, 352; Lord Bute, 266, 269; Edward Cave, 65, 77, 88–90, 98–101, 112–14; Sir R. Chambers, 193; Mrs. Chapone, 1255; Lord Chesterfield, 183–4; R. Clark, 1264; clergyman at Bath, 1183; a young clergyman, 1060; Dr. Cruikshank, 1249, 1350;

Tom Davies, 1242, 1350; C. Dilly, 1026, 1263; E. Dilly (actually W. Sharp), 815; Dr. Dodd, 832–4; W. Drummond, 373–7; Dr. Edwards, 1006; J. Elphinston, 150–1; Dr. Farmer, 432, 1052; S. Ford, 71; Dr. Fothergill, 605; R. Green, 1373; W. G. Hamilton, 1253, 1348; Warren Hastings, 1117–20; E. Hector, 60, 1180–1, 1360; Heely, 1355; J. Hoole, 571, 1343; Dr. Huddesford, 201; O. Humphry, 1273; J. Hussey, 1008; C. Jenkinson (Lord Liverpool), 832; Kearsley, 153; a Lady, 261; B. Langton, 206, 230, 238–9, 252, 362–6, 386, 450, 455, 459, 564, 625, 687, 814, 1004, 1168, 1179, 1250, 1271, 1336, 1346; Jane Langton, 1275; C. Lawrence, 1060; Dr. T. Lawrence, 577, 1046, 1172, 1177–8; Miss Lawrence, 1178; R. Levett, 565, 641, 786; T. Levett, 117; J. Macpherson, 579; Malone, 1175; Metcalfe, 1191; Mudge, 927, 1249; J. Nichols, 1091, 1109, 1191, 1353; G. Nicol, 1349; C. O'Conor, 227, 803; J. Paradise, 1349; J. Perkins, 568, 1155, 1186, 1263, 1348; Lucy Porter, 644–5, 1025, 1134, 1176, 1221, 1243, 1262, 1265, 1374; Lord Portmore, 1272; Reynolds, 344, 454, 457, 778, 785, 1131, 1220, 1234, 1239, 1260, 1284, 1334, 1351–3; W. Sharp, 815; J. Simpson, 245; Mrs. Smart, 1343; Dr. Staunton, 260; G. Steevens, 557, 792; W. Strahan, 790, 1004; Mrs. Strahan, 1142, 1174; Dr. Taylor, 169, 1240, 1274; Mrs. Thrale, 1050, 1053, 1241, 1251–3; Susannah Thrale, 1253; Thurlow, 1334. Dr. Vyse, 814; J. Warton, 178, 433; T. Warton, 190, 195–8, 201–2, 207–8, 228, 237, 401, 433; S. Welch, 889; J. Wesley, 1026; Wetherell, 677; Dr. Wheeler, 1005; Rev. W. White, 506;

THE WORLD'S CLASSICS

ARISTOTLE: The Nicomachean Ethics
Translated and with an introduction by W. D. Ross

JANE AUSTEN: Emma
Edited by James Kinsley and David Lodge

Pride and Prejudice
Edited by James Kinsley and Frank Bradbrook

Sense and Sensibility
Edited by James Kinsley and Claire Lamont

MAX BEERBOHM: Seven Men and Two Others
With an introduction by Lord David Cecil

JAMES BOSWELL: Life of Johnson
The Chapman edition, revised by David Fleeman
With a new introduction by Pat Rogers

CHARLOTTE BRONTË: Jane Eyre
Edited by Margaret Smith

WILKIE COLLINS: The Woman in White
Edited by H. P. Sucksmith

ARTHUR CONAN DOYLE: Sherlock Holmes: Selected Stories
With an introduction by S. C. Roberts

Eirik the Red and Other Icelandic Sagas
Translated and with an introduction by Gwyn Jones

ELIZABETH GASKELL: Cranford
Edited by Elizabeth Porges Watson

ALEXANDER HERZEN: Childhood, Youth and Exile
With an introduction by Isaiah Berlin

HENRY JAMES: What Maisie Knew
Edited by Douglas Jefferson

RICHARD JEFFERIES: After London *or* Wild England
With a new introduction by John Fowles

THE WORLD'S CLASSICS

THE WORLD'S CLASSICS

Jane Austen

EMMA

Edited by James Kinsley and David Lodge

The moral and emotional education of Emma Woodhouse is perhaps Jane Austen's most perfect and representative work, happily combining the qualities for which she has been most admired: irony, wit, realism, vivid characterization, moral seriousness and faultless control of tone and narrative method.

PRIDE AND PREJUDICE

Edited by James Kinsley and F. W. Bradbrook

Of all Jane Austen's novels, *Pride and Prejudice* has earned a special place in the hearts of the reading public as her best-loved and most intimately known novel. With its combination of wit and humour and wise percipience into the follies of humankind, the story of Elizabeth and Darcy has delighted readers since its first appearance in 1813.

SENSE AND SENSIBILITY

Edited by James Kinsley and Claire Lamont

The first of Jane Austen's novels to be published, in 1811, *Sense and Sensibility* tells the story of two sisters whose contrasting temperaments are examined, amid a wealth of engaging minor characters and incidents, as they undergo comparable experiences in the loss of the men they love.

Forthcoming

PERSUASION

MANSFIELD PARK

NORTHANGER ABBEY, LADY SUSAN, SANDITON, AND THE WATSONS

THE WORLD'S CLASSICS

Anthony Trollope

THE CHRONICLES OF BARSETSHIRE

These six novels offer an unsurpassed portrait of the landed and professional classes of Victorian England. They brought Trollope fame and financial success, and in their perennial popularity have outstripped even his *Palliser* novels. The cathedral town of Barchester (modelled on Salisbury) is the setting for these stories of ambition and love. Like any other community, it is all too prone to corruption, hypocrisy, snobbery, and domination by the ruthless. Trollope's characters, endowed with the usual mixture of virtues and vices, are judged by their behaviour within this social framework. Trollope skilfully portrays the struggle between society and the individual which generates the excitement, suspense, and emotional involvement that distinguish most great fiction.

Introductions and unobtrusive notes are provided by outstanding Trollope scholars of today. Wherever available, the text of the Oxford Illustrated Edition of Trollope's novels by Michael Sadleir has been used.

THE WARDEN
Introduction and notes by David Skilton

BARCHESTER TOWERS
Introduction by James Kincaid

DOCTOR THORNE
Introduction and notes by David Skilton

FRAMLEY PARSONAGE
Introduction and notes by P. D. Edwards

THE SMALL HOUSE AT ALLINGTON
Introduction and notes by James Kincaid

THE LAST CHRONICLE OF BARSET
Introduction and notes by Stephen Gill

THE WORLD'S CLASSICS

ANTHONY TROLLOPE: An Autobiography

Edited by Michael Sadleir and Frederick Page; new Introduction and notes by P. D. Edwards

Although he is best known for his Palliser and Barsetshire novels, Anthony Trollope is also the author of one of the most fascinating autobiographies of the nineteenth century. In it he writes of his hated schooldays, his stormy career in the General Post Office, his addiction to hunting, his opinion of contemporary writers like Dickens and George Eliot, and the rigidly disciplined writing habits which brought him money and fame.

MARY WOLLSTONECRAFT: Mary and The Wrongs of Woman

Edited with an introduction by Gary Kelly

Mary Wollstonecraft's life has tended to overshadow her writing. Not only was her life romantically short and dramatically ended, but it was crammed with varied and often melodramatic incident. Her powerful and original imagination shaped her experience and hard-won knowledge into the ardent radical philosophy which lay behind all her writing. Both the pre-revolutionary *Mary* (1788) and *The Wrongs of Woman* (1798) are autobiographical.

THE WORLD'S CLASSICS

Leo Tolstoy: Anna Karenina

This is probably the greatest novel ever written. It is certainly a work of incomparable richness and power, and remarkable for its truth-telling. The tragic story of the impossible and destructive triangle linking Anna, her husband Karenin, and her lover Vronsky runs in parallel with the more hopeful account of the courtship and marriage of Kitty and Levin. Levin is of special interest as a partial self-portrait of Tolstoy himself.

Wilkie Collins: The Woman in White

Edited with an introduction by Harvey Sucksmith

Millais told the story of how he was walking with Collins and his brother one evening in North London when they heard a scream come from a garden, and a young and beautiful woman dressed in flowing white robes ran towards them and paused in an attitude of supplication and terror. Collins followed her and did not come back that evening. Whether or not Millais embellished the story, Collins's real-life meeting with Caroline Graves, with whom he subsequently set up house, is recalled in the dramatic opening scene of *The Woman in White*. Thereafter Collins maintains the suspense throughout this great mystery story, told in turn in the words of the various characters, including the famous flamboyant villain Count Fosco.

THE WORLD'S CLASSICS

MARY SHELLEY: Frankenstein

Edited with an introduction by M. K. Joseph

Mary Shelley wrote *Frankenstein* while spending a wet summer with Byron and Shelley in Switzerland, when she was eighteen years old. The story concerns a student of natural philosophy who learns the secret of imparting life to a creature constructed from bones he has collected from charnel-houses. It shows how man can pervert his own destiny through the use of science, and this makes it a profoundly disturbing book.

EDGAR ALLAN POE: Selected Tales

Edited by Julian Symons

There was undoubtedly something psychopathic in Poe's personality which found expression in his tales of intense but indefinable terror like 'The Fall of the House of Usher' and 'The Masque of the Red Death'. It is for these stories, as well as his brilliant detective pieces, that he is best remembered. But in this new selection Julian Symons, critic and author of crime fiction himself, also includes stories that reveal Poe in the less familiar roles of social commentator and savagely comic writer.

FORTHCOMING WORLD'S CLASSICS